Business Ethics

Contemporary Environment

Contemporary Business and Online Commerce Law

Legal, Internet, Ethical, and Global Environments,

Fifth Edition

Henry R. Cheeseman

Clinical Professor of Business Law
Director of the Legal Studies Program
Marshall School of Business
University of Southern California

PEARSON

Prentice Hall

Upper Saddle River, New Jersey 07458

Library of Congress Cataloging-in-Publication Data
Cheeseman, Henry R.
    Contemporary Business and Online Commerce Law / Henry R. Cheeseman.—5th ed.
        p. cm.
    Includes bibliographical references and index.
    ISBN 0-13-149660-3
        1. Business law—United States. 2. Electronic commerce—Law and legislation—United
States. I. Title.
KF889.C4332 2005
346.7307—dc22   2004060022

Editorial Director: Jeff Shelstad
Acquisitions Editor: Bill Larkin
Senior Managing Editor (Editorial): Alana Bradley
Assistant Editor: Sam Goffinet
Senior Editorial Assistant: Jane Avery
Media Project Manager: Caroline Kasterine
Executive Marketing Manager: Beth Toland
Marketing Assistant: Tina Panagiotou
Managing Editor (Production): Cynthia Regan
Production Editor: Michael Reynolds
Permissions Coordinator: Charles Morris
Manufacturing Buyer: Diane Pierano
Design Manager: Maria Lange
Art Director: Kevin Kall
Interior Design: Jill Little
Cover Design: Karen Quigley
Cover Illustration/Photo: Henry R. Cheeseman
Illustrator (Interior): GGS Book Services, Atlantic Highlands
Director, Image Resource Center: Melinda Reo
Manager, Rights and Permissions: Zina Arabia
Manager: Visual Research: Beth Brenzel
Manager, Cover Visual Research & Permissions: Karen Sanatar
Image Permission Coordinator: Fran Toepfer
Manager, Print Production: Christy Mahon
Print Production Liaison: Suzanne Duda
Composition/Full-Service Project Management: GGS Book Services, Atlantic Highlands
Printer/Binder: Courier/Kendalville
Typeface: 10.75/13 Caslon

Credits and acknowledgments borrowed from other sources and reproduced, with permission, in this textbook appear on appropriate page within text. The cover and all interior photos are © Henry R. Cheeseman.

Pearson Education LTD.
Pearson Education Singapore, Pte. Ltd
Pearson Education, Canada, Ltd
Pearson Education–Japan

Pearson Education Australia PTY, Limited
Pearson Education North Asia Ltd
Pearson Educación de Mexico, S.A. de C.V.
Pearson Education Malaysia, Pte. Ltd

10 9 8 7 6 5 4
ISBN 0-13-149660-3

Autumn breezes toss
    Magnolia fragances
through my bedroom window.

What right do they
    have to enter
when you are not here.

About the Author

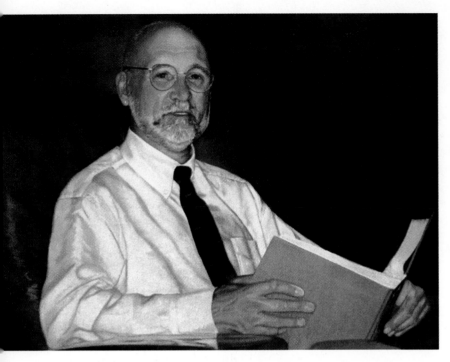

Henry R. Cheeseman is Clinical Professor of Business Law and Director of the Legal Studies Program at the Marshall School of Business of the University of Southern California (USC), Los Angeles, California.

Professor Cheeseman earned a Bachelor's degree in Finance from Marquette University, Masters of Business Administration (MBA) and Masters of Tax degrees from the University of Southern California, a Juris Doctor (J.D.) degree from the University of California at Los Angeles (UCLA) School of Law, a Masters of Business Administration with emphasis on Law and Economics from the University of Chicago, and a Masters in Law (L.L.M.) degree from Boston University.

Professor Cheeseman earned the "Golden Apple" Teaching Award on many occasions by having been voted the best professor at the Marshall School of Business of the University of Southern California. He has been named a Faculty Fellow at the Center for Excellence in Teaching at USC by the Dean of the Marshall School of Business. USC's Torch and Tassel Chapter of the Mortar Board has named Professor Cheeseman Faculty of the Month of USC.

Professor Cheeseman writes leading business law and legal environment textbooks that are published by Prentice Hall Publishing Company. These include: *Business Law: Legal, E-Commerce, Ethical and International Environments; Contemporary Business and Online Commerce; The Legal Environment of Business and Online Commerce; Essentials of Contemporary Business Law;* and *Introduction to Law: Its Dynamic Nature.*

Professor Cheeseman is an avid traveller and amateur photographer. The cover and all interior photos for this book have been taken by Professor Cheeseman.

Contents in Brief

Contents

Preface

To the Students

Each semester, as I stand up in front of a new group of business majors in my business law class I am struck by the thought that, cases and statutes aside, I know two very important things that they have yet to learn. The first is that I draw as much from them as they do from me. Their youth, enthusiasm, questions, and even the doubts a few of them hold about the relevance of law to their futures, fuel my teaching. They don't know that every time they open their minds to look at a point from a new perspective or critically question something they have taken for granted, I get a wonderful reward for the work that I do.

The other thing I know is that both teaching and learning the legal and ethical environment are all about stories. The stories I tell provide the framework on which students will hang everything they learn about the law in my class. It is my hope that long after the specific language of cases or statutes have faded, they will retain that framework. Several years from now, "unintentional torts" may draw only a glimmer of recognition with business managers who learn about them as students in my class this year. However, they will likely recall the story of the woman who sued McDonalds for serving her coffee that was too hot and caused her injuries. The story sticks and gives students the hook on which to hang the concepts.

I remind myself of these two facts every time I sit down to work on writing and revising *Contemporary Business and Online Commerce Law* as well. My goal is to present law and ethics in a way that will spur students to ask questions, to go beyond rote memorization. Business law is an evolving outgrowth of its environment, and that environment keeps changing. In addition to the social, ethical, and international contexts I have incorporated in previous editions of *Contemporary Business and Online Commerce Law*, this fifth edition emphasizes coverage of e-commerce and the Internet as two vital catalysts to the law and a key part of its environment.

It is my wish that my commitment to these goals shines through in this labor of love, and I hope you have as much pleasure in using it as I have had in creating it for you.

Henry Cheeseman

Making the Most of the Fifth Edition

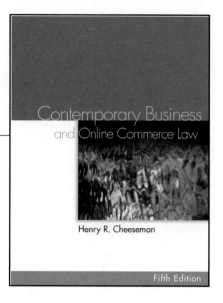

Contemporary Business and Online Commerce Law

Henry R. Cheeseman

Fifth Edition

These cases and boxes focus on the legal and ethical issues businesses, managers, and entrepreneurs face as they start businesses, operate existing enterprises, launch new Internet ventures, and incorporate on-line technologies into their current businesses.

Cases

Cases—Over *75 new cases* have been added to the Fifth Edition. Each chapter includes 3 to 6 interesting and lively cases presented in an edited format. The format of each case: Background and Facts, Issue, Language of the Court, Decision and Remedy. Three questions follow each case to promote active learning.

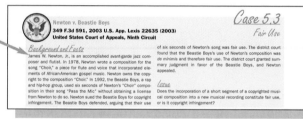

Newton v. Beastie Boys
349 F.3d 591, 2003 U.S. App. Lexis 22635 (2003)
United States Court of Appeals, Ninth Circuit

Case 5.3
Fair Use

Background and Facts
James W. Newton, Jr., is an accomplished avant-garde jazz composer and flutist. In 1978, Newton wrote a composition for the song "Choir," a piece for flute and voice that incorporated elements of African-American gospel music. Newton owns the copyright to the composition "Choir." In 1992, the Beastie Boys, a rap and hip-hop group, used six seconds of Newton's "Choir" composition in their song "Pass the Mic" without obtaining a license from Newton to do so. Newton sued the Beastie Boys for copyright infringement. The Beastie Boys defended, arguing that their use

of six seconds of Newton's song was fair use. The district court found that the Beastie Boys's use of Newton's composition was de minimis and therefore fair use. The district court granted summary judgment in favor of the Beastie Boys, and Newton appealed.

Issue
Does the incorporation of a short segment of a copyrighted musical composition into a new musical recording constitute fair use, or is it copyright infringement?

U.S. SUPREME COURT CASE
Grutter v. Bollinger and the University of Michigan Law School
539 U.S. 306, 123 S.Ct. 2325, 2003 U.S. Lexis 4800 (2003)
Supreme Court of the United States

Case 1.2
Affirmative Action

Background and Facts
Barbara Grutter, a Caucasian resident of the state of Michigan, applied to the Law School of the University of Michigan, a state government-supported institution, in 1996 with a 3.8 undergraduate grade point average and a 161 LSAT score. The Law School received 3,500 applications for a class of 350 students. The Law School used race as one of the factors in considering applicants for admission to law school. The race of minority applicants, defined as blacks, Hispanics, and Native Americans, was considered as a "plus factor" in considering their applications to law school. Caucasians and Asians were not given such a plus factor. Evidence showed that the Law School accepted approximately 35 percent of minority applicants, but that if race was not considered in admissions, only 10 percent of those applicants would have been admitted.

When the Law School rejected Grutter's application, she brought a class action lawsuit against the Law School of the University of Michigan, alleging that its use of a minority's race as a plus factor in admissions violated the Equal Protection Clause of the Fourteenth Amendment to the U.S. Constitution. The district court held in favor of plaintiff Grutter, finding that the Law School's use of race as a factor in admissions violated the Equal Protection Clause. The court of appeals reversed. The U.S. Supreme Court granted certiorari to hear the appeal.

Issue
Does the University of Michigan Law School's use of race as a plus factor in accepting minority applicants for admission to the Law School violate the Equal Protection Clause of the Fourteenth Amendment to the U.S. Constitution?

Court's Reasoning
The Equal Protection Clause of the Fourteenth Amendment states "no State shall . . . deny to any person within its jurisdiction the equal protection of the laws." The Supreme Court applies a strict scrutiny test whenever the government treats a person differently because of his or her race. To withstand such scrutiny, the government must prove a compelling state interest for such different

treatment of persons based on race. The Supreme Court held that having a diverse student body at an educational institution was a compelling state interest sufficient to justify using a minority applicant's race as a plus factor in selecting a student body.

The Supreme Court held that once a state has demonstrated a compelling state interest for treating persons differently because of their race, the state's action must be narrowly tailored to accomplish this state interest. The Supreme Court stated, "A university may consider race or ethnicity only as a 'plus' in a particular student's file. . . . Here, the Law School engages in a highly individualized, holistic review of each applicant's file, giving serious consideration to all ways an applicant might contribute to a diverse educational environment. The Law School affords this individualized consideration to applicants of all races. . . . The Law School's race conscious admissions policy does not unduly harm nonminority applicants. We expect that 25 years from now, the use of racial preferences will no longer be necessary to further the interest approved today."

Decision and Remedy
The U.S. Supreme Court held that the University of Michigan Law School's policy of using race as a plus factor in admitting minority applicants furthers a compelling state interest and is narrowly tailored to accomplish that interest. The Supreme Court affirmed the decision of the court of appeals that held that the Law School's race-conscious admissions policy does not violate the Equal Protection Clause of the Fourteenth Amendment to the U.S. Constitution.

Case Questions
Critical Legal Thinking What is the difference between the U.S. Supreme Court's decision in this case and it's decision in the Gratz v. Bollinger and the Regents of the University of Michigan case? Explain.

Business Ethics Is it socially responsible for the University of Michigan Law School to consider a minority applicant's race as a plus factor in its admissions decisions?

Contemporary Business Is anyone hurt by the University of Michigan Law School's race-conscious admissions policy? Explain.

United States Supreme Court Cases—Over 70 cases of the United States Supreme Court are presented throughout the book. These are the most important and modern cases affecting business that have been decided by the Supreme Court.

The *ethical environment* of business is covered in many ways in the Fifth Edition. **Chapter 7 "Ethics and Social Responsibility of Business,"** is just the beginning of the ethics coverage in the fifth edition.

Ethics and Social Responsibility of Business

"Ethical considerations can no more be excluded from the administration of justice, which is the end and purpose of all civil laws, than one can exclude the vital air from his room and live."

—John F. Dillon
Laws and Jurisprudence of England and America Lecture I (1894)

Chapter Objectives

After studying this chapter, you should be able to:

1. Describe how law and ethics intertwine.

Business Ethics

Sarbanes-Oxley Act Prompts Public Companies to Adopt Code of Ethics

In the late 1990s and early 2000s, many large corporations in the United States were found to have engaged in massive financial frauds. Many of these frauds were perpetrated by the chief executive officer's and other senior officers of the companies. Financial officers, such as chief financial officers and controllers, were also found to have been instrumental in creating these frauds. In response, Congress enacted the **Sarbanes-Oxley Act of 2002**, which makes certain conduct illegal and establishes criminal penalties for violations.

In addition, the Sarbanes-Oxley Act prompts companies to encourage senior officers of public companies to act ethically in their dealings with shareholders, employees, and other constituents. **Section 406** of the Sarbanes-Oxley Act requires a public company to disclose whether it has adopted a **code of ethics** for senior financial officers, including its principal financial officer and principal accounting officer. In response, public companies have adopted codes of ethics for their senior financial officers. Many public companies have included all officers and employees in the coverage of their codes of ethics.

A typical code of ethics follows.

Big Cheese Corporation
Code of Ethics

Big Cheese Corporation's mission includes the promotion of professional conduct in the practice of general management worldwide. Big Cheese's Chief Executive Officer (CEO), Chief Financial Officer (CFO), corporate Controller, and other employees of the finance organization and other employees of the corporation hold an important and elevated role in the corporate governance of the corporation. They are empowered and uniquely capable to ensure that all constituents' interests are appropriately balanced, protected, and preserved.

This Code of Ethics embodies principles to which we are expected to adhere and advocate. The CEO, CFO, finance organization employees, and other employees of the corporation are expected to abide by this Code of Ethics and all business conduct standards of the corporation relating to areas covered by this Code of Ethics. Any violation of the Code of Ethics may result in disciplinary action, up to and including termination of employment. All employees will:

- Act with honesty and integrity, avoiding actual or apparent conflicts of interest in their personal and professional relations.
- Provide stakeholders with information that is accurate, fair, complete, timely, objective, relevant, and understandable, including in our filings with and other submissions to the U.S. Securities and Exchange Commission.
- Comply with rules and regulations of federal, state, provincial, and local governments and other appropriate private and public regulatory agencies.

More than 35 **"Business Ethics" boxes** use issues from real companies to highlight the importance of ethics in making business decisions.

---

the photographs. JPI produced a line of children's clothes for Wal-Mart that copied the designs, colors, and patterns of Samara's clothing. Wal-Mart then sold this line of children's clothing in its stores, making a gross profit of over $1.15 million on these clothes sales during the 1996 selling season.

Samara discovered that Wal-Mart was selling the knock-off clothes at a price that was lower than Samara's retailers were paying Samara for its clothes. After sending unsuccessful cease-and-desist letters to Wal-Mart, Samara sued Wal-Mart, alleging that Wal-Mart stole Samara's trade dress (i.e., look and feel) in violation of Section 43(a) of the Lanham Act. Although not finding that Samara's clothes had acquired a secondary meaning in the minds of the public, the district court held in favor of Samara and awarded damages. The court of appeals affirmed. Wal-Mart appealed to the U.S. Supreme Court.

Issue

Must a product's design have acquired a *secondary meaning* before it is protected as trade dress?

Decision and Remedy

The U.S. Supreme Court held that a product's design has to have acquired a secondary meaning in the public's eye before it is protected as trade dress under Section 43(a) of the Lanham Act. The Supreme Court reversed the decision of the court of appeals.

Case Questions

Critical Legal Thinking What is trade dress? Should it have been protected in this case?

Business Ethics Even though Wal-Mart's conduct was ruled legal, was it ethical?

Contemporary Business Before reading this case, had you heard or read about Samara's childrens' clothing?

Every case in the text ends with an *ethics question* for discussion.

Business Ethics Cases

7.1 Business Ethics The Warner-Lambert Company has manufactured and distributed Listerine antiseptic mouthwash since 1879. Its formula has never changed. Ever since Listerine's introduction, the company has represented it as being beneficial in preventing and curing colds and sore throats. Direct advertising of these claims to consumers began in 1921. In 1971, Warner-Lambert spent $10 million advertising these claims in print media and in television commercials.

In 1972, the Federal Trade Commission (FTC) filed a complaint against Warner-Lambert, alleging that the company engaged in false advertising in violation of federal law. Four months of hearings were held before an administrative law judge that produced an evidentiary record of more than 4,000 pages of documents from 46 witnesses. In 1975, after examining the evidence, the FTC issued an opinion which held that the company's representations that Listerine prevented and cured colds and sore throats were false. The U.S. court of appeals affirmed.

Did Warner-Lambert act ethically in making its claims for Listerine? What remedy should the court impose on the company? Would making Warner-Lambert cease such advertising be sufficient? [*Warner-Lambert Company v. Federal Trade Commission*, 562 F.2d 749, 1977 U.S. App. Lexis 11599 (D.C. Cir. 1977)]

7.2 Business Ethics Stanford University is one of the premiere research universities in the country. Stanford has an operating budget of approximately $400 million a year and receives about $175 million a year in direct research funding from the federal government. In addition, the government reimburses the university for certain overhead and indirect costs associated with the research. This amounts to about $85 million a year.

In 1990, a navy accountant took a close look at Stanford's books and alleged that the university may have overstated overhead and indirect costs associated with research by as much as $200 million during the 1980s. The university provided a house for its president, Donald Kennedy. Some of the expenses charged against overhead for research were (a) $3,000 for a cedar-lined closet at the president's home, (b) $4,000 for the president's 1987 wedding reception, (c) $7,000 in bed sheets and table linens, and (d) $184,000 in depreciation on a yacht donated to Stanford's sailing program. Did the administration of Stanford act ethically in charging these expenditures as overhead against research? What penalty should be assessed?

7.3 Business Ethics The Johns-Manville Corporation was a profitable company that made a variety of building and other products. It was a major producer of asbestos, which was used for

---

Each chapter ends with additional business ethics case questions.

Two chapters dedicated to coverage of Intellectual Property, the Internet and E-Commerce Law.

- **Chapter 5 "Intellectual Property and Internet Law"**

- **Chapter 17 "E-Commerce, Domain Names, and Internet Law"**

Over 45 **"Online Commerce & Internet Law" boxes** focus on the legal issues businesses face as they either launch new Internet ventures or rise to the challenge of incorporating on-line technologies into their existing business models.

Online Commerce & Internet Law
Electronic Signatures Recognized by Federal Law

In the past, signatures have been hand-applied by the person signing the document. No more. In the electronic commerce world, it is now "What is your mother's maiden name?" "Slide your smart card in the sensor," or "Look into the iris scanner." But are electronic signatures sufficient to form an enforceable contract? In 2000, the federal government stepped into the breach and enacted the **Electronic Signature in Global and National Commerce Act**.

One of the main features of this federal law is that it recognizes an electronic signature, or e-signature. The act gives an e-signature the same force and effect as a pen-inscribed signature on paper. The act is technology neutral, however, in that the law does not define or decide which technologies should be used to create a legally binding signature in cyberspace. Loosely defined, a *digital signature* is some electronic method that identifies an individual. The challenge is to makes sure that someone who uses a digital signature is the person he or she claims to be. The act provides that a digital signature can basically be verified in one of three ways:

1. By something the signatory knows, such as a secret password, pet's name, and so forth.
2. By something a person has, such as a smart card, which looks like a credit card and stores personal information.
3. By biometrics, which uses a device that digitally recognizes fingerprints or the retina or iris of the eye.

The verification of electronic signatures is creating a need for the use of scanners and methods for verifying personal information. ∎

The 45-plus **"Contemporary Environment" boxes** recognize that not all of the modern challenges facing businesses are Internet-related. These boxes explore other types of legal issues currently confronting businesses.

Contemporary Environment
Department of Homeland Security

On September 11, 2001, the World Trade Center buildings in New York City were destroyed and the Pentagon in Washington, D.C., was damaged by terrorist attacks. After the attacks, President George W. Bush issued an executive order creating the Office of Homeland Security. The president called for the office to be made into a Cabinet-level agency. Congress responded by enacting the **Homeland Security Act of 2002**, which created the Cabinet-level **Department of Homeland Security (DHS)**. The creation of the DHS is the largest government reorganization in over 50 years.

The act placed 22 existing federal agencies with more than 180,000 employees under the umbrella of the DHS. The DHS is the second largest government agency, after the Department of Defense. The DHS contains the Bureau of Customs and Border Protection, the Bureau of Citizenship and Immigration Services, the U.S. Secret Service, the Federal Emergency Management Agency, the Federal Computer Incident Response Center, the National Domestic Preparedness Office, the U.S. Coast Guard,

and portions of the Federal Bureau of Investigation, Treasury Department, Commerce Department, Justice Department, and other federal government agencies.

The mission of the DHS is to prevent domestic terror attacks, reduce vulnerability to terror attacks, minimize the harm caused by such attacks, and assist in the recovery if a terrorist attack occurs. The DHS provides services in the following critical areas: (1) border and transportation security, including protecting airports, seaports, and borders, and providing immigration and visa processing; (2) chemical, biological, radiological, and nuclear countermeasures, including metering the air for biological agents and developing vaccines and treatments for biological agents; (3) information analysis and infrastructure protection, including protection of communications systems, power grids, transportation networks, telecommunications, and cyber systems; and (4) emergency preparedness and response to terrorist incidents, including training first responders and coordinating government disaster relief. ■

Chapter 39 "International and Comparative Law," is devoted exclusively to coverage of international laws, courts, organizations, dispute resolution, and regional trade agreements.

UNIT IX / The Global Environment

International and Comparative Law

39

" International law, or the law that governs between nations, has at times, been like the common law within states, a twilight existence during which it is hardly distinguishable form morality or justice, till at length the imprimatur of a court attests its jural quality. "

—Justice Cardozo
New Jersey v. Delaware, 291 U.S. 361, 54 S.Ct. 407, 1934 U.S. Lexis 973 (1934)

Chapter Objectives

After studying this chapter, you should be able to:

1. Describe the federal government's power under the Foreign Commerce and Treaty Clauses of the U.S. Constitution.

2. List and describe the sources of international law.

3. Describe the functions and governance of the United Nations.

International Law
China Joins the WTO

For the past 50 years, China and the United States have pursued divergent paths. China became the world's largest communist country and the United States the leading democracy. China maintained its agricultural base, while the United States pursued industrialization. Most of China's businesses were state owned, while those in the United States were privately owned under a capitalist system. For over a decade, these two countries engaged in on-again, off-again trade negotiations. Then in November 1999 they formed a landmark trade pact. In exchange for being granted the right to import most goods and services into the United States, China, which had substantially restricted imports into its country, agreed to open its markets to foreign goods and services.

The China-U.S. trade agreement was a prelude to China's trade agreements with other countries. These trade agreements supported China's application to join the WTO. In 2002, China became a member of the WTO. China's entry into the WTO makes it a full partner in the world's trading system.

China's entry into the WTO is not without critics. In the United States, labor unions complain that U.S. manufacturing jobs will be lost to China, while environmentalists complain that little is being done to protect the environment from an industrialized economy the size of China's. In China, workers at state-owned enterprises might lose their jobs to foreign capitalist companies that can produce goods and services more efficiently, and China's already impoverished farmers may be harmed by cheap farm products imported from other countries. ■

More than 40 **"International Law" boxes** provide students the opportunity to draw comparisons between the American system of justice and various other systems abroad.

Landmark Case

Landmark Case—"Landmark Case" boxes highlight the most important cases and statutes that have shaped the law in the United States.

Landmark Case
Brown v. Board of Education

When the original 13 states ratified the Constitution of the United States of America in 1788, it created a democratic form of government and granted certain rights to its people. But all persons were not treated equally, as many people, including drafters of the Constitution such as Thomas Jefferson, owned African American slaves. It was more than 75 years before the Civil War was fought between the northern states and the southern Confederate states over the preservation of the Union and slavery. Slavery was abolished by the **Thirteenth Amendment** to the Constitution in 1865. In addition, the **Fourteenth Amendment** of 1868 provided that no state shall "deny to any person within its jurisdiction the equal protection of the laws." The original intent of this amendment was to guarantee equality to freed African Americans.

But equality was denied to African Americans for years to come. This included discrimination in housing, transportation, education, jobs, service at restaurants, and other activities. In

1896, the U.S. Supreme Court decided the case of *Plessy v. Ferguson*. In that case, the state of Louisiana had a law that provided for separate but equal accommodations for African American and white railway passengers. An African American passenger challenged the state law. The Supreme Court held that the "separate but equal" state law did not violate the Equal Protection Clause of the Fourteenth Amendment. The "separate but equal" doctrine was then applied to all areas of life, including public education. Thus, African American and white children attended separate schools, often with unequal facilities.

It was not until 1954 that the U.S. Supreme Court decided a case that challenged the separate but equal doctrine as it applied to public elementary and high schools. In *Brown v. Board of Education*, a consolidated case that challenged the separate school systems of four states—Kansas, South Carolina, Virginia, and Delaware—the Supreme Court decided to revisit the separate but equal doctrine announced by its forbearers in another

Text

The text of the fifth edition covers comprehensive legal concepts for a business law and legal environment course. The text is written in clear, understandable language for university and college students.

The World Trade Organization (WTO)

In 1995, the **World Trade Organization (WTO)** was created as part of the Uruguay Round of trade negotiations on the *General Agreement on Tariffs and Trade (GATT)*. GATT is a multilateral treaty that establishes trade agreements and limits tariffs and trade restrictions among its more than 130 member nations.

The WTO is an international organization whose headquarters is located in Geneva, Switzerland. WTO members have entered into many trade agreements among themselves, including international agreements on investments, sale of goods, provision of services, intellectual property, licensing, tariffs, subsidies, and the removal of trade barriers.

The WTO, which has been referred to as the "Supreme Court of Trade," has become the world's most important trade organization. The WTO has jurisdiction to enforce the most important and comprehensive trade agreements in the world among its more than 130 member nations. Many herald the WTO as a much-needed world court that can peaceably solve trade disputes among nations.

Additional Features

Exhibits help clarify legal formats and documents that may be foreign to students.

Concept Summaries appear periodically within each chapter to give students a chance to pause and be sure they have mastered the preceding material.

Working the Web Internet Exercises— at the end of each chapter, these exercises require students to work through interactive web-based activities.

Critical Legal Thinking Cases at the end of each chapter encourage the application of students' analytical skills.

Briefing the Case Writing Assignments at the end of each chapter give students experience in briefing cases.

Chapter Summaries appear at the end of each chapter. These summaries help students reinforce the concepts covered in each chapter.

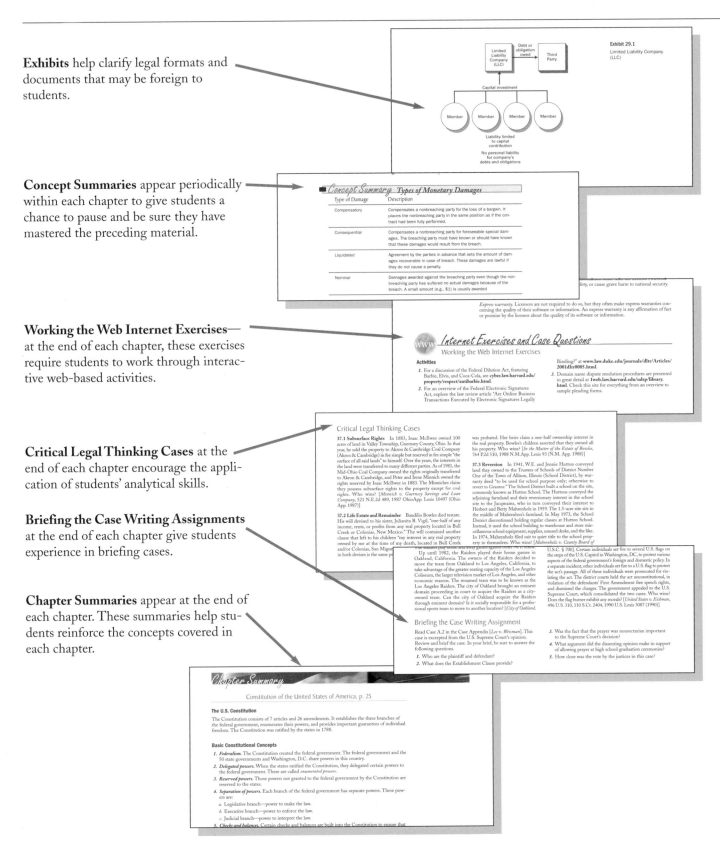

An Integrated Supplements Package

To ensure consistency of style, approach, and coverage among the key *print* and *online supplements*, these critical pieces were created by an author team working in conjunction with Henry Cheeseman. The supplements include:

Companion Web site Access at **www.prenhall.com/cheeseman**. This Web site will contain an Online Study Guide, including true/false and multiple choice questions, as well as PowerPoint presentations for each chapter. Also available is the **Business Law Case Library**, featuring regularly updated cases covering the key topics in most business law courses, including consumer protection, cyberlaw, and securities. Cases include actual legal decisions as well as hypothetical legal situations with questions for students. Answers to the hypothetical cases are provided. In addition, the business law timeline places all of the significant legal decisions, legislation, and other legal events on an easy-to-use interface.

Instructor's Manual A comprehensive outline of each text chapter. Also included are terms with definitions, chapter objectives, a key questions checklist, and sample syllabi.

Test Item File A bank of questions specially designed to aid in the preparation of tests. Each question includes a corresponding difficulty level, enabling the easy creation of tailor-made testing material.

TestGen Test management software containing all the material from the Test Item File. This software is completely user-friendly and allows instructors to view, edit, and add test questions with a few clicks of the mouse.

PowerPoints A ready-to-use PowerPoint slideshow, designed for classroom presentation. Use "as-is," or edit content to fit your individual class needs.

Study Guide A student aid designed to facilitate learning by enforcing key concepts. Each chapter contains a chapter overview, a list of objectives, and an explanation of the practical applications of each chapter. Also included is a "helpful hints" section and a sample quiz in addition to several exercises.

Instructor's Resource Center on CD A compilation of instructor's tools, including the Instructor's Manual, PowerPoints, Test Item File, and TestGen.

Enron Case Study This brief case explores the Enron debacle and the legal implications that are surrounding the case. It can be packaged with the text at no additional cost.

Acknowledgments

When I first began writing this book, I was a solitary figure researching cases and statutes in the law library and online, and writing text at my desk. As time passed, others entered upon the scene—editors, research assistants, reviewers, production personnel—and touched the project and made it better. Although my name appears on the cover of this book, it is no longer mine alone. I humbly thank the following persons for their contributions to this project.

The Professionals at Prentice Hall

For this fifth edition of *Contemporary Business and Online Commerce Law* a special group of people from Prentice Hall have come together: Alana Bradley and Bill Larkin, acquisitions editors, who brought wonderful new ideas to revision who was the guiding light during the entire production, and whose imprint is everywhere in the new edition; Sandra Krausman, production coordinator, who was a joy to work with through the patient task of shepherding the manuscript from first manuscript pages to the final bound book; Beth Toland, executive marketing manager, who conducted marketing surveys to assure the fifth edition served the needs of its users and helped implement those suggestions; and Jerome Grant, president of Prentice Hall Business Publishing, who authorized all the resources necessary to make this fifth edition possible.

The Supplements Team

Sam Goffinet, supplements editor, is in charge of producing the extensive supplements that support this fifth edition of *Contemporary Business and Online Commerce Law*. The supplements have been produced by a remarkable team of authors: Vonda Laughlin, Carson–Newman College; Romona Atkins, Hancock College; Les Wiletzky, Wiletzky & Associates. I have worked closely with this team in producing the *Instructor's Manual*, *Study Guide*, *Test Item File*, *PowerPoint slides*, and *web support* for this edition.

The Prentice Hall "family" has come together and produced a book and supplement package that I believe is the best available. My success is theirs, and theirs' mine. They are my friends.

Personal Acknowledgments

My family: My parents—Henry B. and Florence, deceased; my twin brother Gregory and his wife Lana; my sister Marcia; my nephew Gregory and niece Nikki, and my great nieces Lauren and Addison.

The students at the Marshall School of Business at the University of Southern California. Their spirit, energy, and joy is contagious, and I love teaching them (and as important, they teaching me).

While writing this Preface and Acknowledgment, I have thought about the thousands of hours I have spent researching, writing, and preparing this manuscript. I loved every minute, and the knowledge gained has been sufficient reward for the endeavor.

I hope this book and its supplementary materials will serve you as well as they have served me.

With joy and sadness,
emptiness and fullness,
honor and humility,
I surrender the fruits of this labor

Henry R. Cheeseman

Choose from any of the following outstanding titles by Henry R. Cheeseman:

Business Law, 5/e

Essentials of Business and Online Commerce Law

Contemporary Business and Online Commerce Law, 5/e

The Legal Environment of Business and Online Commerce, 4/e

Introduction to Law: Its Dynamic Nature

***Paralegal Professional: Essentials* Cheeseman / Goldman**

Legal Heritage and Critical Legal Thinking

1

" Where there is no law, there is no freedom. "

—John Locke
Second Treatise of Government. Sec. 57

Chapter Objectives

After studying this chapter, you should be able to:

1. Define law and describe the functions of law.

2. Explain the development of the U.S. legal system.

3. List and describe the sources of law in the United States.

4. Describe the international civil law legal system used in some other countries.

5. Apply critical legal thinking in analyzing judicial decisions.

Chapter Contents

■ What Is Law?

■ Schools of Jurisprudential Thought

■ History of American Law

■ Sources of Law in the United States

■ Critical Legal Thinking

Let every American, every lover of liberty, every well-wisher to his posterity, swear by the blood of the Revolution never to violate in the least particular the laws of the country, and never to tolerate their violation by others.

Abraham Lincoln Speech
January 27, 1837

Every society makes and enforces laws that govern the conduct of the individuals, businesses, and other organizations that function within it. In the words of Judge Learned Hand, "Without law we cannot live; only with it can we insure the future which by right is ours. The best of men's hopes are enmeshed in its success."[1]

Although the law of the United States is primarily based on English common law, other legal systems, such as Spanish and French civil law, also influenced it. The sources of law in this country are the U.S. Constitution, state constitutions, federal and state statutes, ordinances, administrative agency rules and regulations, executive orders, and judicial decisions by federal and state courts.

Businesses that are organized in the United States are subject to its laws. They are also subject to the laws of other countries in which they operate. Businesses organized in other countries must obey the laws of the United States when doing business here. In addition, businesspeople owe a duty to act ethically in the conduct of their affairs, and businesses owe a responsibility not to harm society.

This chapter discusses the nature and definition of law, the history and sources of law, and critical legal thinking, as applied by the U.S. Supreme Court in deciding actual cases.

What Is Law?

A lawyer without history or literature is a mechanic, a mere working mason: if he possesses some knowledge of these, he may venture to call himself an architect.

Sir Walter Scott
Guy Mannering, Ch. 37 (1815)

The law consists of rules that regulate the conduct of individuals, businesses, and other organizations within society. It is intended to protect persons and their property against unwanted interference from others. In other words, the law forbids persons from engaging in certain undesirable activities.

Consider the following passage:

Hardly anyone living in a civilized society has not at some time been told to do something or to refrain from doing something, because there is a law requiring it, or because it is against the law. What do we mean when we say such things? Most generally, how are we to understand statements of the form "x is law"? This is an ancient question. In his Memorabilia (I, ii), Xenophon reports a statement of the young Alcibiades, companion of Socrates, who in conversation with the great Pericles remarked that "no one can really deserve praise unless he knows what a law is."

Statue of Liberty, New York City, New York. The United States is the world's leading democracy. Peoples from around the world immigrate to the United States to seek the protection of its Constitution and laws.

At the end of the 18th century, Immanuel Kant wrote of the question "What is law?" that it "may be said to be about as embarrassing to the jurist as the well-known question 'What is truth?' is to the logician."[2]

Online Commerce & Internet Law
Students Plug In to the Internet and the Law

Every year millions of students arrive on college campuses and unpack an array of items—clothes, books, furniture, decorations, and their computers. College students used to be judged by the size of their stereo speakers; today it is their computers and their Internet savvy. Ninety percent of college students now own personal computers.

The Internet has revolutionized campus life. Computer kiosks abound around college campuses, occupying more space in libraries, dorm rooms, and hallways of athletic departments. Traditional libraries have become obsolete for many students as they conduct almost all of their research online. More than 80 percent of college students check out the Web daily, while others communicate through e-mail, pick up course assignments, download course notes, and socialize online. Current university and college students use modern technology and are leading their parents, employers, and sometimes even their professors into the new world of high technology. Today's college students are the leaders of the technology generation.

Universities and colleges are now rated on not only how well they are connected with alumni but also on how well they are connected to computer technology. Some universities have installed software that allows their students to sit anywhere on campus with their laptops and "plug" in to the school's computers. The computer is no longer just a study tool; it has become totally integrated into the lives of college students. Students of the new generation study online, shop online, and even date online.

To help the student understand his or her legal rights and duties, this business law book fully integrates online commerce and Internet law. Through this total integration of online commerce and Internet law, a student will learn traditional business law topics and will also be well versed in his or her legal rights while using the Internet. ■

Definition of Law

The concept of **law** is broad. Although it is difficult to state a precise definition, *Black's Law Dictionary* gives one that is sufficient for this text:

> Law, in its generic sense, is a body of rules of action or conduct prescribed by controlling authority, and having binding legal force. That which must be obeyed and followed by citizens subject to sanctions or legal consequences is a law.[3]

Functions of the Law

The law is often described by the function it serves within a society. The primary *functions* served by the law in this country are:

1. Keeping the peace, which includes making certain activities crimes.
2. Shaping moral standards (e.g., enacting laws that discourage drug and alcohol abuse).
3. Promoting social justice (e.g., enacting statutes that prohibit discrimination in employment).
4. Maintaining the status quo (e.g., passing laws preventing the forceful overthrow of the government).
5. Facilitating orderly change (e.g., passing statutes only after considerable study, debate, and public input).
6. Facilitating planning (e.g., well-designed commercial laws allow businesses to plan their activities, allocate their productive resources, and assess the risks they take).
7. Providing a basis for compromise (approximately 90 percent of all lawsuits are settled prior to trial).

> Commercial law lies within a narrow compass, and is far purer and freer from defects than any other part of the system.
>
> Henry Peter Brougham
> *House of Commons,*
> *February 7, 1828*

8. Maximizing individual freedom (e.g., the rights of freedom of speech, religion, and association granted by the First Amendment to the U.S. Constitution).

Fairness of the Law

On the whole, the American legal system is one of the most comprehensive, fair, and democratic systems of law ever developed and enforced. Nevertheless, some misuses and oversights of our legal system—including abuses of discretion and mistakes by judges and juries, unequal applications of the law, and procedural mishaps—allow some guilty parties to go unpunished.

In *Standefer v. United States*[4] the Supreme Court *affirmed* (let stand) the criminal conviction of a Gulf Oil Corporation executive for aiding and abetting the bribery of an Internal Revenue Service agent. The agent had been acquitted in a separate trial. In writing the opinion of the Court, Chief Justice Warren Burger stated, "This case does no more than manifest the simple, if discomforting, reality that different juries may reach different results under any criminal statute. That is one of the consequences we accept under our jury system."

Flexibility of the Law

Business Brief

Laws cannot be written in advance to anticipate every dispute that could arise in the future. Therefore, general principles are developed to be applied by courts and juries to individual disputes. This flexibility in the law leads to some uncertainty in predicting the results of lawsuits.

U.S. law evolves and changes along with the norms of society, technology, and the growth and expansion of commerce in the United States and the world. The following quote by Judge Jerome Frank discusses the value of the adaptability of law:

> The law always has been, is now, and will ever continue to be, largely vague and variable. And how could this be otherwise? The law deals with human relations in their most complicated aspects. The whole confused, shifting helter-skelter of life parades before it—more confused than ever, in our kaleidoscopic age.
>
> Men have never been able to construct a comprehensive, eternalized set of rules anticipating all possible legal disputes and formulating in advance the rules which would apply to them. Situations are bound to occur which were never contemplated when the original rules were made. How much less is such a frozen legal system possible in modern times?
>
> The constant development of unprecedented problems requires a legal system capable of fluidity and pliancy. Our society would be straightjacketed were not the courts, with the able assistance of the lawyers, constantly overhauling the law and adapting it to the realities of ever-changing social, industrial, and political conditions; although changes cannot be made lightly, yet rules of law must be more or less impermanent, experimental and therefore not nicely calculable.
>
> Much of the uncertainty of law is not an unfortunate accident; it is of immense social value.[5]

Landmark Case
Brown v. Board of Education

When the original 13 states ratified the Constitution of the United States of America in 1788, it created a democratic form of government and granted certain rights to its people. But all persons were not treated equally, as many people, including drafters of the Constitution such as Thomas Jefferson, owned African American slaves. It was more than 75 years before the Civil War was fought between the northern states and the southern Confederate states over the preservation of the Union and slavery. Slavery was abolished by the **Thirteenth Amendment** to the Constitution in 1865. In addition, the **Fourteenth Amendment** of 1868 provided that no state shall "deny to any person within its jurisdiction the equal protection of the laws."

The original intent of this amendment was to guarantee equality to freed African Americans.

But equality was denied to African Americans for years to come. This included discrimination in housing, transportation, education, jobs, service at restaurants, and other activities. In 1896, the U.S. Supreme Court decided the case of ***Plessy v. Ferguson***. In that case, the state of Louisiana had a law that provided for separate but equal accommodations for African American and white railway passengers. An African American passenger challenged the state law. The Supreme Court held that the "separate but equal" state law did not violate the Equal Protection Clause of the Fourteenth Amendment. The "separate but equal" doctrine was then applied to all areas of life, including public education. Thus, African American and white children attended separate schools, often with unequal facilities.

It was not until 1954 that the U.S. Supreme Court decided a case that challenged the separate but equal doctrine as it applied to public elementary and high schools. In ***Brown v. Board of Education***, a consolidated case that challenged the separate school systems of four states—Kansas, South Carolina, Virginia, and Delaware—the Supreme Court decided to revisit the separate but equal doctrine announced by its forbearers in another century. This time a unanimous Supreme Court, in an opinion written by Chief Justice Earl Warren, reversed prior precedent and held that the separate but equal doctrine violated the Equal Protection Clause of the Fourteenth Amendment to the Constitution. In its opinion, the Court stated:

> We cannot turn the clock back to 1868 when the Amendment was adopted, or even to 1896 when *Plessy v. Ferguson* was written. Today, education is perhaps the most important function of state and local governments.
>
> We conclude that in the field of public education the doctrine of "separate but equal" has no place. Separate educational facilities are inherently unequal. Therefore, we hold that the plaintiffs and others similarly situated for whom actions have been brought are, by reason of the segregation complained of, deprived of the equal protection of the laws guaranteed by the Fourteenth Amendment.

After *Brown v. Board of Education* was decided, it took court orders as well as federal army enforcement to integrate many of the public schools in this country. The *Brown v. Board of Education* case demonstrates that one Supreme Court case can overrule prior Supreme Court cases to promote justice. [*Brown v. Board of Education of Topeka*, 347 U.S. 483, 74 S.Ct. 686, 1954 U.S. Lexis 2094 (1954)] ■

Contemporary Environment
Feminist Legal Theory

In the past the law treated men and women unequally. For example, women were denied the right to vote, could not own property if they were married, were unable to have legal abortions, and could not hold the same jobs as men. The interpretation of constitutional provisions by the courts and the enactment of statutes have changed all these things. The Nineteenth Amendment to the U.S. Constitution in 1920 gave women the right to vote. States have repealed constraints on the ability of women to own property. The famous U.S. Supreme Court decision in *Roe v. Wade*, 410 U.S. 959 (1973), gave women the constitutional right to an abortion.

Title VII of the Civil Rights Act of 1964 prohibits employment discrimination based on sex. In addition, the Equal Protection Clause of the U.S. Constitution and state constitutions provides that women cannot be treated differently than men (and vice versa) by the government unless some imperative reason warrants different treatment.

But is it enough for women to be treated like men? Should the female perspective be taken into account when legislators and judges develop, interpret, and apply the law? A body of scholarship known as **feminist legal theory** or **feminist jurisprudence** has been created around just such a theory.

The "battered woman's syndrome" illustrates how this type of theory works. It has been introduced into evidence to prove self-defense in homicide cases where a woman is accused of killing her husband or another male. This defense asserts that sustained domestic violence against a woman may justify such a murder. Although many courts have rejected this defense, some courts have recognized battered woman's syndrome as a justifiable defense.

Some other areas of the law where a woman's perspective might differ from a man's include rights to privacy, family law, child custody, surrogate motherhood, job security for pregnant women, rape, sexual assault, abortion, and sexual harassment. Even the traditional "reasonable man standard," so prevalent in American law, is attacked as being gender biased. ■

Schools of Jurisprudential Thought

The philosophy or science of the law is referred to as **jurisprudence**. There are several different philosophies about how the law developed, ranging from the classical natural theory to modern theories of law and economics and critical legal studies. Legal philosophies can generally be grouped into the major categories discussed in the paragraphs that follow.

The Natural Law School The **Natural Law School** of jurisprudence postulates that the law is based on what is "correct." Natural law philosophers emphasize a **moral theory of law**—that is, law should be based on morality and ethics. Natural law is "discovered" by humans through the use of reason and choosing between good and evil. Documents such as the U.S. Constitution, the Magna Carta, and the United Nations Charter reflect this theory.

> Human beings do not ever make laws; it is the accidents and catastrophes of all kinds happening in every conceivable way that make law for us.
>
> Plato, Laws IV. 709

The Historical School The **Historical School** of jurisprudence believes that the law is an aggregate of social traditions and customs that have developed over the centuries. It believes that changes in the norms of society will gradually be reflected in the law. To these legal philosophers, the law is an evolutionary process. Thus, historical legal scholars look to past legal decisions (precedent) to solve contemporary problems.

> Law must be stable and yet it cannot stand still
>
> Roscoe Pound
> *Interpretations of Legal History (1923)*

The Analytical School The **Analytical School** of jurisprudence maintains that the law is shaped by logic. Analytical philosophers believe that results are reached by applying principles of logic to the specific facts of the case. The emphasis is on the logic of the result rather than on how the result is reached.

The Sociological School The **Sociological School** of jurisprudence asserts that the law is a means of achieving and advancing certain sociological goals. The followers of this philosophy, known as *realists*, believe that the purpose of law is to shape social behavior. Sociological philosophers are unlikely to adhere to past law as precedent.

The Command School The philosophers of the **Command School** of jurisprudence believe that the law is a set of rules developed, communicated, and enforced by the ruling party rather than a reflection of the society's morality, history, logic, or sociology. This school maintains that the law changes when the ruling class changes.

> The law is not a series of calculating machines where definitions and answers come tumbling out when the right levers are pushed.
>
> William O. Douglas
> *The Dissent, A Safeguard of Democracy (1948)*

The Critical Legal Studies School The **Critical Legal Studies School** proposes that legal rules are unnecessary and are used as an obstacle by the powerful to maintain the status quo. Critical legal theorists (the "*Crits*") argue that legal disputes should be solved by applying arbitrary rules that are based on broad notions of what is "fair" in each circumstance. Under this theory, subjective decision making by judgers would be permitted.

Contemporary Environment
The Law and Economics School of Jurisprudential Thought

Should free market principles, like the supply-and-demand and cost–benefit theories, determine the outcome of lawsuits and legislation? A growing number of judges and legal theorists think so. These people are members of the **Law and Economics School** (or the "Chicago School") of jurisprudence, which began at the University of Chicago. According to the Law and Economics School, promoting market efficiency should be the central goal of legal decision making.

For example, proponents of law and economics theory suggest that the practice of appointing counsel, free of charge, to prisoners who bring civil rights cases should be abolished. If a prisoner cannot find a lawyer who will take the case on a contingency-fee basis or *pro bono* (free of charge), it probably means that the case is not worth bringing. Naysayers warn that the morality of certain rights and liberties must be safe-guarded even if it is unpopular or costly from an economic point of view. ■

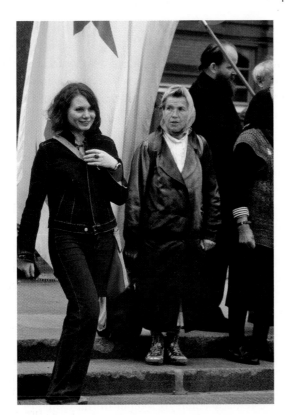

Moscow, Russia. After the fall of communism in 1989, Russia adopted capitalism. New laws have been enacted to allow for the private ownership of property, to provide for the enforcement of contracts, and to otherwise support trade and commerce.

Concept Summary Schools of Jurisprudential Thought

School	Philosophy
Natural Law	Postulates that law is based on what is "correct." It emphasizes a moral theory of law—that is, law should be based on morality and ethics.
Historical	Believes that law is an aggregate of social traditions and customs.
Analytical	Maintains that law is shaped by logic.
Sociological	Asserts that the law is a means of achieving and advancing certain sociological goals.
Command	Believes that the law is a set of rules developed, communicated, and enforced by the ruling party.
Critical Legal Studies	Maintains that legal rules are unnecessary and that legal disputes should be solved by applying arbitrary rules based on fairness.
Law of Economics	Believes that promoting market efficiency should be the central concern of legal decision making.

History of American Law

When the American colonies were first settled, the English system of law was generally adopted as the system of jurisprudence. This was the foundation from which American judges developed a common law in America.

English Common Law

English **common law** was law developed by judges who issued their opinions when deciding cases. The principles announced in these cases became *precedent* for later judges deciding similar cases. The English common law can be divided into cases decided by the law courts, equity courts, and merchant courts.

Law Courts Prior to the Norman Conquest of England in 1066, each locality in England was subject to local laws as established by the lord or chieftain in control of the local area. There was no countrywide system of law. After 1066, William the Conqueror and his successors to the throne of England began to replace the various local laws with one uniform system of law. To accomplish this, the king or queen appointed loyal followers as judges in all local areas. These judges were charged with administering the law in a uniform manner in courts that were called **law courts**. Law at that time tended to emphasize the form (legal procedure) over the substance (merit) of a case. The only relief available at law courts was a monetary award for damages.

Chancery (Equity) Courts Because of the unfair results and the limited remedy available in the law courts, a second set of courts—the **Court of Chancery** (or **equity court**)—was established. These courts were under the authority of the Lord Chancellor. Persons who believed that the decision of the law court was unfair or believed that the law court could not grant an appropriate remedy could seek relief in the Court of Chancery. Rather than emphasize legal procedure, the Chancery Court inquired into the merits of the case. The Chancellor's remedies were called *equitable remedies* because they were shaped to fit each situation. Equitable order and remedies of the Court of Chancery took precedence over the legal decisions and remedies of the law courts.

Merchant Courts As trade developed in the Middle Ages, the merchants who traveled about England and Europe developed certain rules to solve their commercial disputes. These rules, known as the "law of merchants" or the **Law Merchant**, were based upon common trade practices and usage. Eventually, a separate set of courts was established to administer these rules. This court was called the **Merchant Court**. In the early 1900s, the Merchant Court was absorbed into the regular law court system of England.

International Law

Adoption of English Common Law in America

All the states of the United States of America (except Louisiana) base their legal systems primarily on the English *common law*. In the United States, the law, equity, and merchant courts have been merged. Thus, most U.S. courts permit the aggrieved party to seek both law and equitable orders and remedies.

The importance of common law to the American legal system is described in the following excerpt from Justice Douglas's opinion in the 1841 case of *Penny v. Little* [4 Ill. 301 (IL 1841)]:

The common law is a beautiful system, containing the wisdom and experiences of ages. Like the people it ruled and protected, it was simple and crude in its infancy and became enlarged, improved, and polished as the nation advanced in civilization, virtue, and intelligence. Adapting itself to the conditions and circumstances of the people and relying upon them for its administration, it necessarily improved as the condition of the people was elevated. The inhabitants of this country always claimed the common law as their birthright, and at an early period established it as the basis of their jurisprudence. ■

Sources of Law in the United States

In the more than 200 years since the founding of the United States and adoption of the English common law, the lawmakers of this country have developed a substantial body of law. The *sources of modern law* in the United States are discussed in the paragraphs that follow.

Constitutions

The **Constitution of the United States of America** is the *supreme law of the land*. This means that any law—whether federal, state, or local—that conflicts with the U.S. Constitution is unconstitutional and, therefore, unenforceable.

The principles enumerated in the Constitution are extremely broad because the founding fathers intended them to be applied to evolving social, technological, and economic conditions. The U.S. Constitution is often referred to as a "living document" because it is so adaptable.

The U.S. Constitution established the structure of the federal government. It created the following three branches of government and gave them the following powers:

- *Legislative (Congress):* Power to make (enact) the law.
- *Executive (president):* Power to enforce the law.
- *Judicial (courts):* Power to interpret and determine the validity of the law.

Powers not given to the federal government by the Constitution are reserved for the states. States also have their own constitutions. These are often patterned after the U.S. Constitution, although many are more detailed. State constitutions establish the legislative, executive, and judicial branches of state government and establish the powers of each branch. Provisions of state constitutions are valid unless they conflict with the U.S. Constitution or any valid federal law.

> The Constitution of the United States is not a mere lawyers' document: it is a vehicle of life, and its spirit is always the spirit of age.
>
> Woodrow Wilson
> *Constitutional Government in the United States (1927)*

Treaties

The U.S. Constitution provides that the president, with the advice and consent of two-thirds of the Senate, may enter into **treaties** with foreign governments. Treaties become part of the supreme law of the land. With increasing international economic relations among nations, treaties will become an even more important source of law that will affect business in the future.

Codified Law

Statutes are written laws that establish certain courses of conduct that must be adhered to by covered parties. The U.S. Congress is empowered by the Commerce Clause and other provisions of the U.S. Constitution to enact *federal statutes* to regulate foreign and interstate commerce. Federal statutes include antitrust laws, securities laws, bankruptcy laws, labor laws, equal employment opportunity laws, environmental protection laws, consumer protection laws, and such. State legislatures enact *state statutes*. State statutes include corporation laws, partnership laws, workers' compensation laws, the Uniform Commercial Code, and the like. The statutes enacted by the legislative branches of the federal and state governments are organized by topic into code books. This is often called *codified law*.

State legislatures often delegate lawmaking authority to local government bodies, including cities and municipalities, countries, school districts, water districts, and such. These governmental units are empowered to adopt **ordinances**. Examples of ordinances are traffic laws, local building codes, and zoning laws. Ordinances are also codified.

The Great Wall, China. The United States has entered into treaties with other countries of the world.

Executive Orders

The executive branch of government, which includes the president of the United States and state governors, is empowered to issue **executive orders**. This power is derived from express delegation from the legislative branch and is implied from the U.S. Constitution and state constitutions. For example, on October 8, 2001, President George W. Bush, by executive order established within the Executive Office of the President an Office of Homeland Security to be headed by the assistant to the president for homeland security.

Regulations and Order of Administrative Agencies

The legislative and executive branches of federal and state governments are empowered to establish **administrative agencies** to enforce and interpret statutes enacted by Congress and state legislatures. Many of these agencies regulate business. For example, Congress

U.S. Congress, Washington, DC. The U.S. Congress, which is a bicameral system made up of the U.S. Senate and the U.S. House of Representatives, creates federal law by enacting statutes. Each state has two senators and is allocated a certain number of representatives based on population.

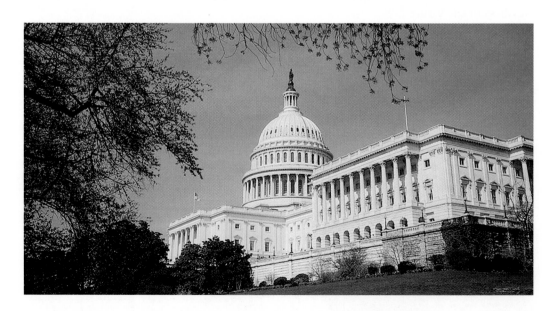

has created the Securities and Exchange Commission (SEC) and the Federal Trade Commission (FTC), among others.

Congress or the state legislatures usually empower these agencies to adopt **administrative rules and regulations** to interpret the statutes that the agency is authorized to enforce. These rules and regulations have the force of law. Administrative agencies usually have the power to hear and decide disputes. Their decisions are called *orders*. Because of their power, administrative agencies are often informally referred to as the "fourth branch of government."

Contemporary Environment
Department of Homeland Security

On September 11, 2001, the World Trade Center buildings in New York City were destroyed and the Pentagon in Washington, D.C., was damaged by terrorist attacks. After the attacks, President George W. Bush issued an executive order creating the Office of Homeland Security. The president called for the office to be made into a Cabinet-level agency. Congress responded by enacting the **Homeland Security Act of 2002**, which created the Cabinet-level **Department of Homeland Security (DHS)**. The creation of the DHS is the largest government reorganization in over 50 years.

The act placed 22 existing federal agencies with more than 180,000 employees under the umbrella of the DHS. The DHS is the second largest government agency, after the Department of Defense. The DHS contains the Bureau of Customs and Border Protection, the Bureau of Citizenship and Immigration Services, the U.S. Secret Service, the Federal Emergency Management Agency, the Federal Computer Incident Response Center, the National Domestic Preparedness Office, the U.S. Coast Guard,

and portions of the Federal Bureau of Investigation, Treasury Department, Commerce Department, Justice Department, and other federal government agencies.

The mission of the DHS is to prevent domestic terror attacks, reduce vulnerability to terror attacks, minimize the harm caused by such attacks, and assist in the recovery if a terrorist attack occurs. The DHS provides services in the following critical areas: (1) border and transportation security, including protecting airports, seaports, and borders, and providing immigration and visa processing; (2) chemical, biological, radiological, and nuclear countermeasures, including metering the air for biological agents and developing vaccines and treatments for biological agents; (3) information analysis and infrastructure protection, including protection of communications systems, power grids, transportation networks, telecommunications, and cyber systems; and (4) emergency preparedness and response to terrorist incidents, including training first responders and coordinating government disaster relief. ■

Judicial Decisions

When deciding individual lawsuits, federal and state courts issue **judicial decisions**. In these written opinions, the judge or justice usually explains the legal reasoning used to decide the case. These opinions often include interpretations of statutes, ordinances, administrative regulations, and the announcement of legal principles used to decide the case. Many court decisions are printed (reported) in books that are available in law libraries.

Doctrine of Stare Decisis Based on the common law tradition, past court decisions become **precedent** for deciding future cases. Lower courts must follow the precedent established by higher courts. That is why all federal and state courts in the United States must follow the precedents established by U.S. Supreme Court decisions.

The courts of one jurisdiction are not bound by the precedent established by the courts of another jurisdiction, although they may look to each other for guidance. For example, state courts of one state are not required to follow the legal precedent established by the courts of another state.

Adherence to precedent is called **stare decisis** ("to stand by the decision"). The doctrine of *stare decisis* promotes uniformity of law within a jurisdiction, makes the court system more efficient, and makes the law more predictable for individuals and businesses. A court may later change or reverse its legal reasoning if a new case is presented to it and change is warranted. The doctrine of *stare decisis* is discussed in the following excerpt from Justice Musmanno's decision in *Flagiello v. Pennsylvania*[6]:

> Without stare decisis, there would be no stability in our system of jurisprudence. Stare decisis channels the law. It erects lighthouses and flies the signal of safety. The ships of jurisprudence must follow that well-defined channel which, over the years, has been proved to be secure and worthy.

The following are two judicial decisions of the Supreme Court of the United States that address the issue of affirmative action in university admissions.

U.S. SUPREME COURT CASE

Gratz v. Bollinger and the Regents of the University of Michigan

539 U.S. 244, 123 S.Ct. 2411, 2003 U.S. Lexis 4801 (2003)
Supreme Court of the United States

Case 1.1

Affirmative Action

Background and Facts

Jennifer Gratz, a Caucasian resident of the state of Michigan, applied for admission to the College of Literature, Sciences, and the Arts at the University of Michigan, a state government–supported university. In its review of applicants, the University of Michigan considered high school grade point average; standardized test scores (i.e., SAT, ACT); high school quality, curriculum strength, geography, and alumni relationships; and leadership. Each item was assigned a certain number of points for each applicant. If an applicant received 100 points, he or she would be guaranteed admission to the university. Minority applicants, defined as blacks, Hispanics, and Native Americans, were automatically given 20 points, or one-fifth of the points needed to guarantee admission. Gratz was originally placed in a postponed decision category but was ultimately rejected for admission. A minority applicant with Gratz's score, with the extra 20 points, would have been admitted.

Gratz brought a class action lawsuit against the University of Michigan, alleging that the university violated the Equal Protection Clause of the Fourteenth Amendment to the U.S. Constitution. Plaintiff Gratz sought damages for past violations and an injunction prohibiting the university from continuing to discriminate on the basis of race in violation of the Fourteenth Amendment. The district court granted the university's motion for summary judgment and upheld the university's policy of adding 20 points to minority applicants' applications for admission. The U.S. Supreme Court granted certiorari to hear the appeal of this issue.

Issue

Does the University of Michigan's automatic award of 20 points to minority applicants for admission to the university's undergraduate College of Literature, Sciences, and the Arts violate the Equal Protection Clause of the Fourteenth Amendment to the U.S. Constitution?

Court's Reasoning

The Equal Protection Clause of the Fourteenth Amendment states that "no State shall . . . deny to any person within its jurisdiction the equal protection of the laws." The U.S. Supreme Court has held that the government can treat persons differently if there is a compelling state interest for doing so and the law is narrowly tailored to accomplish the state's interest. The Supreme Court held that all racial qualifications reviewable under the Equal Protection Clause must be analyzed using the strict scrutiny test.

The Supreme Court has held that having diversity in a university student body is a compelling state interest. The Court held, however, that the University of Michigan's admissions program that automatically added 20 points to a minority applicant's score in applying to the university was not narrowly tailored to accomplish this compelling state interest.

The Supreme Court found that the University of Michigan's policy that automatically added 20 points to every minority applicant had the effect of making the fact of race decisive for virtually every minimally qualified minority applicant. The Supreme Court held that the university did not pass the strict scrutiny test for justifying this 20-point minority applicant admissions program. The Court noted that the university should consider each applicant on an individual basis and that an applicant's race should be just one factor of many factors used in deciding whether to admit an applicant. The Supreme Court rejected the university's contention that it was not possible to individually examine each of the thousands of applications it received each year.

Decision and Remedy

The U.S. Supreme Court held that the University of Michigan's undergraduate admission policy that automatically assigned 20 points, or one-fifth of the points needed to guarantee admission, to minority applicants did not pass the strict scrutiny test and was not narrowly tailored to accomplish the compelling state interest of obtaining a diverse student population. The Supreme Court held that the University of Michigan had violated the Equal Protection Clause of the Fourteenth Amendment. The Supreme Court reversed the decision of the district court and remanded the case for further proceedings.

Case Questions

Critical Legal Thinking   What does the Equal Protection Clause provide? Should the government ever be allowed to treat persons differently because of their race? Explain.

Business Ethics   Did the University of Michigan act socially responsibly by using the plus 20-point program for minority applicants?

Contemporary Business   After this decision, can race still be used in university admissions decisions? Explain.

U.S. SUPREME COURT CASE
Grutter v. Bollinger and the University of Michigan Law School
539 U.S. 306, 123 S.Ct. 2325, 2003 U.S. Lexis 4800 (2003)
Supreme Court of the United States

Case 1.2
Affirmative Action

Background and Facts

Barbara Grutter, a Caucasian resident of the state of Michigan, applied to the Law School of the University of Michigan, a state government–supported institution, in 1996 with a 3.8 undergraduate grade point average and a 161 LSAT score. The Law School received 3,500 applications for a class of 350 students. The Law School used race as one of the factors in considering applicants for admission to law school. The race of minority applicants, defined as blacks, Hispanics, and Native Americans, was considered as a "plus factor" in considering their applications to law school. Caucasians and Asians were not given such a plus factor. Evidence showed that the Law School accepted approximately 35 percent of minority applicants, but that if race was not considered in admissions, only 10 percent of those applicants would have been admitted.

When the Law School rejected Grutter's application, she brought a class action lawsuit against the Law School of the University of Michigan, alleging that its use of a minority's race as a plus factor in admissions violated the Equal Protection Clause of the Fourteenth Amendment to the U.S. Constitution. The district court held in favor of plaintiff Grutter, finding that the Law School's use of race as a factor in admissions violated the Equal Protection Clause. The court of appeals reversed. The U.S. Supreme Court granted certiorari to hear the appeal.

Issue

Does the University of Michigan Law School's use of race as a plus factor in accepting minority applicants for admission to the Law School violate the Equal Protection Clause of the Fourteenth Amendment to the U.S. Constitution?

Court's Reasoning

The Equal Protection Clause of the Fourteenth Amendment states "no State shall . . . deny to any person within its jurisdiction the equal protection of the laws." The Supreme Court applies a strict scrutiny test whenever the government treats a person differently because of his or her race. To withstand such scrutiny, the government must prove a compelling state interest for such different treatment of persons based on race. The Supreme Court held that having a diverse student body at an educational institution was a compelling state interest sufficient to justify using a minority applicant's race as a plus factor in selecting a student body.

The Supreme Court held that once a state has demonstrated a compelling state interest for treating persons differently because of their race, the state's action must be narrowly tailored to accomplish this state interest. The Supreme Court stated, "A university may consider race or ethnicity only as a 'plus' in a particular student's file. . . . Here, the Law School engages in a highly individualized, holistic review of each applicant's file, giving serious consideration to all ways an applicant might contribute to a diverse educational environment. The Law School affords this individualized consideration to applicants of all races. . . . The Law School's race conscious admissions policy does not unduly harm nonminority applicants. We expect that 25 years from now, the use of racial preferences will no longer be necessary to further the interest approved today."

Decision and Remedy

The U.S. Supreme Court held that the University of Michigan Law School's policy of using race as a plus factor in admitting minority applicants furthers a compelling state interest and is narrowly tailored to accomplish that interest. The Supreme Court affirmed the decision of the court of appeals that held that the Law School's race-conscious admissions policy does not violate the Equal Protection Clause of the Fourteenth Amendment to the U.S. Constitution.

Case Questions

Critical Legal Thinking   What is the difference between the U.S. Supreme Court's decision in this case and it's decision in the *Gratz v. Bollinger and the Regents of the University of Michigan* case? Explain.

Business Ethics   Is it socially responsible for the University of Michigan Law School to consider a minority applicant's race as a plus factor in its admissions decisions?

Contemporary Business   Is anyone hurt by the University of Michigan Law School's race-conscious admissions policy? Explain.

Priority of Law in the United States

As mentioned previously, the U.S. Constitution and treaties take precedence over all other laws in the United States. Federal statutes take precedence over federal regulations. Valid federal law takes precedence over any conflicting state or local law. State constitutions rank as the highest state law. State statutes take precedence over state regulations. Valid state law takes precedence over local laws.

Concept Summary *Sources of Law in the United States*

Source of Law	Description
Constitutions	The U.S. Constitution establishes the federal government and enumerates its powers. Powers not given to the federal government are reserved to the states. State constitutions establish state governments and enumerate their powers.
Treaties	The president, with the advice and consent of the Senate, may enter into treaties with foreign countries.
Codified law: statutes and ordinances	Statutes are enacted by Congress and state legislatures. Ordinances are enacted by municipalities and local government agencies. They establish courses of conduct that covered parties must follow.
Administrative agency rules and regulations	Administrative agencies are created by the legislative and executive branches of government. They may adopt rules and regulations that regulate the conduct of covered parties.
Executive orders	Issued by the president and governors of states, executive orders regulate the conduct of covered parties.
Judicial decisions	Courts decide controversies. In doing so, a court issues decisions that state the holding of the case and the rationale the court used in reaching that decision.

International Law

The Civil Law System

One of the major legal systems that has developed in the world in addition to the Anglo-American common law system is the **Romano-Germanic civil law system**. This legal system, which is commonly called the **civil law**, dates to 450 B.C., when Rome adopted the Twelve Tables, a code of laws applicable to the Romans. A compilation of Roman law, called the *Corpus Juris Civilis* (the Body of Civil Law), was completed in A.D. 534. Later, two national codes—the French Civil Code of 1804 (the Napoleonic Code) and the German Civil Code of 1896—became models for countries that adopted civil codes.

Eiffel Tower, Paris, France. France follows the civil law. The French Civil Code, also called the Napoleonic Code, was adopted in 1804. In a civil law country, the adjudication of a case consists of the application of the code or statutes to a particular set of facts.

In contrast to the Anglo-American common law, where laws are created by the judicial system as well as by congressional legislation, the civil code and the parliamentary statutes that expand and interpret it are the sole sources of the law in most civil law countries. Thus, the adjudication of a case is simply the application of the code or the statutes to a particular set of facts. In some civil law countries, court decisions do not have the force of law.

Today, Austria, Belgium, Greece, Indonesia, Japan, Latin America, the Netherlands, Poland, Portugal, South Korea, Spain, Sub-Saharan Africa, Switzerland, and Turkey follow the civil law. Because of its French heritage, the state of Louisiana bases its law on the *civil law*. Based on their Spanish heritage, California and Texas, as well as other southwestern states, are also some what rooted in civil law. ■

Critical Legal Thinking

Judges apply *legal reasoning* in reaching a decision in a case. That is, the judge must specify the issue presented by the case, identify the key facts in the case and the applicable law, and then apply the law to the facts to come to a conclusion that answers the issue presented. This process is called **critical legal thinking**. Skills of analysis and interpretation are important in deciding legal cases.

Key Terms

Before you embark upon the study of law, you should know the following key legal terms:

- *Plaintiff.* The party who originally brought the lawsuit.
- *Defendant.* The party against whom the lawsuit has been brought.
- *Petitioner* **or** *appellant.* The party who has appealed the decision of the trial court or lower court. The petitioner may be either the plaintiff or the defendant, depending on who lost the case at the trial court or lower court level.
- *Respondent* **or** *appellee.* The party who must answer the petitioner's appeal. The respondent may be either the plaintiff or the defendant, depending on which party is the petitioner. In some cases, both the plaintiff *and* the defendant may disagree with the trial court's or lower court's decision, and both parties may appeal the decision.

Briefing a Case

It is often helpful for a student to "brief" a case to clarify the legal issues involved and to gain a better understanding of the case.

The procedure for briefing a case is as follows. The student must summarize, or brief, the court's decision in no more than 400 words (some professors may shorten or lengthen this limit). The assignment's format is highly structured, consisting of five parts, each of which is numbered and labeled:

Part	Maximum Words
1. The case name, citation, and court	25
2. A summary of the key facts in the case	125
3. The *issue* presented by the case, stated as a one-sentence question answerable only by *yes* or *no*	25
4. The court's resolution of the issue (the "holding")	25
5. A summary of the court's reasoning justifying the holding	200
Total words	400

Briefing a case consists of making a summary of each of the following items of the case:

1. ***Case name, citation and court.*** The name of the case should be placed at the beginning of each briefed case. The case name usually contains the names of the parties to the lawsuit (for example, *Grutter v. Bolinger and the University of Michigan Law School*). Where there are multiple plaintiffs or defendants, however, some of the names of the parties may be omitted from the case name. Abbreviations are often used in case names as well.

   The case citation, which consists of a number plus the year in which the case was decided, such as "539 U.S. 306, 123 S.Ct. 2325, 2003 U.S. Lexis 4800," is set forth below the case name. The case citation identifies the book in the law library or the Internet site where the case may be found. For example, the case in the above citation may be found in volume 539 of the *United States Reports*, page 306, in volume 123 of the *Supreme Court Reporter*, page 2325, and on the Lexis Web site at 2003 U.S. Lexis 4800. The name of the court that decided the case should be set forth below the case name for the case.

2. ***Summary of the key facts in the case.*** The important facts of a case should be stated briefly. Extraneous facts and facts of minor importance should be omitted from the brief. The facts of the case can usually be found at the beginning of the case, but not necessarily. Important facts may be found throughout the case.

3. ***Issue presented by the case.*** In the briefing of a case, it is crucial to identify the issue presented to the court to decide. The issue on appeal is most often a legal question, although questions of fact are sometimes the subject of an appeal. The issue presented in each case is usually quite specific and should be asked in a one-sentence question that is answerable only by *yes* or *no*. For example, the issue statement "Is Mary liable?" is too broad. A more proper statement of the issue would be "Is Mary liable to Joe for breach of the contract made between them based on her refusal to make the payment due on September 30?"

4. ***Holding.*** The *holding* is the decision reached by the present court. It should be *yes* or *no*. The holding should also state which party won.

5. ***Summary of the court's reasoning.*** When an appellate court or a supreme court issues a decision, which is often called an *opinion*, the court will normally state the reasoning it used in reaching its decision. The rationale for the decision may be based on the specific facts of the case, public policy, prior law, or other matters. In stating the reasoning of the court, the student should reword the court's language into his or her own language. This summary of the court's reasoning should pick out the meat of the opinions and weed out the nonessentials.

Briefing the Case Writing Assignment

The following is an excerpted decision by the Supreme Court of the United States. The case is presented in the language of the Supreme Court. Following the case is a *brief of the case* using the model previously described.

Case name, Citation, and Court	**PGA TOUR, Inc. v. Martin, 532 U.S. 661, 121 S.Ct. 1879, 2001 U.S. Lexis 4115 (2001) U.S. Supreme Court**
Opinion of the Court	***OPINION, STEVENS, JUSTICE*** *This case raises two questions concerning the application of the Americans with Disabilites Act of 1990 [42 U.S.C. § 12101 et seq.] to a gifted athlete: first, whether*
Issue	*the Act protects access to professional golf tournaments by a qualified entrant with a disability; and*

second, whether a disabled contestant may be denied the use of a golf cart because it would "fundamentally alter the nature" of the tournaments to allow him to ride when all other contestants must walk.

Facts

Petitioner PGA TOUR, Inc., a nonprofit entity formed in 1968, sponsors and cosponsors professional golf tournaments conducted on three annual tours. About 200 golfers participate in the PGA TOUR; about 170 in the NIKE TOUR; and about 100 in the SENIOR PGA TOUR. PGA TOUR and NIKE TOUR tournaments typically are four-day events, played on courses leased and

Petitioner: PGA TOUR Inc.

operated by petitioner. The revenues generated by television, admissions, concessions, and contributions from cosponsors amount to about $300 million a year, much of which is distributed in prize money. The "Conditions of Competition and Local Rules," often described as the "hard card," apply specifically to petitioner's professional tours. The hard cards for the PGA TOUR and NIKE TOUR required players to walk the golf course during tournaments, but not during open qualifying rounds. On the SENIOR PGA TOUR, which is limited to golfers age 50 and older, the contestants may use golf carts. Most seniors, however, prefer to walk.

Respondent: Casey Martin

Casey Martin is a talented golfer. As an amateur, he won 17 Oregon Golf Association junior events before he was 15, and he won the state championship as a high school senior. He played on the Stanford University golf team that won the 1994 National Collegiate Athletic Association (NCAA) championship. As a professional, Martin qualified for the NIKE TOUR in 1998 and 1999, and based on his 1999 performance, qualified for the PGA TOUR in 2000. In the 1999 season, he entered 24 events, made the cut 13 times, and had six top-10 finishes, coming in second twice and third once.

Martin is also an individual with a disability, as defined in the Americans with Disabilities Act of 1990 (ADA or Act). Since birth he has been afflicted with Klippel-Trenaunay-Weber Syndrome, a degenerative circulatory disorder that obstructs the flow of blood from his right leg back to his heart. The disease is progressive; it causes severe pain and has atrophied his right leg. During the latter part of his college career, because of the progress of the disease, Martin could no longer walk an 18-hole golf course. Walking not only caused him pain, fatigue, and anxiety, but also created a significant risk of hemorrhaging, developing blood clots, and fracturing his tibia so badly that an amputation might be required.

When Martin turned pro and entered petitioner's Qualifying-School, the hard card permitted him to use a cart during his successful progress through the first two stages. He made a request, supported by detailed medical records, for permission to use a golf cart during the third stage. Petitioner refused to review those records or to waive its walking rule for the third stage. Martin therefore filed this action.

District Court's Decision 994 F. Supp. 1242, 1998 U.S Dist. Lexis 1980 [District: Oregon (1998)]

At trial, petitioner PGA TOUR did not contest the conclusion that Martin has a disability covered by the ADA, or the fact that his disability prevents him from walking the course during a round of golf. Rather, petitioner asserted that the condition of walking is a substantive rule of competition and that waiving it as to any individual for any reason would fundamentally alter the nature of the competition. Petitioner's evidence included the testimony of a number of experts, among them some of the greatest golfers in history. Arnold Palmer, Jack Nicklaus, and Ken Venturi explained that fatigue can be a critical factor in a tournament, particularly on the last day, when psychological pressure is at a maximum. Their testimony makes it clear that, in their view, permission to use a cart might well give some players a competitive advantage over other players who must walk.

The judge found that the purpose of the rule was to inject fatigue into the skill of shot-making, but that the fatigue injected "by walking the course cannot be deemed significant under normal circumstances." Furthermore, Martin presented evidence, and the judge found, that even with the use of a cart, Martin must walk over a mile during an 18-hole round, and that the fatigue he suffers from coping with his disability is "undeniably greater" than the fatigue his able-bodied competitors endure from walking the course. As a result, the judge concluded that it would "not fundamentally alter the nature of the PGA Tour's game to accommodate him with a cart." The judge accordingly entered a permanent injunction requiring petitioner to permit Martin to use a cart in tour and qualifying events.

Court of Appeals Decision 204 F.3d 994, 2000 U.S. App. Lexis 3376 [9th Circuit (2000)]

The Court of Appeals concluded that golf courses remain places of public accommodation during PGA tournaments. On the merits, because there was no serious dispute about the fact that permitting Martin to use a golf cart was both a reasonable and a necessary solution to the problem of providing him access to the tournaments, the Court of Appeals regarded the central dispute as whether such permission would "fundamentally alter" the nature of the PGA TOUR or NIKE TOUR. Like the District Court, the Court of Appeals viewed the issue not as "whether use of carts generally would fundamentally alter the competition, but whether the use of a cart by Martin would do so." That issue turned on "an intensively fact-based inquiry," and, the court concluded, had been correctly resolved by the trial judge. In its words, "all that the cart does is permit Martin access to a type of competition in which he otherwise could not engage because of his disability."

Federal Statute Being Interpreted

Congress enacted the ADA in 1990 to remedy widespread discrimination against disabled individuals. To effectuate its sweeping purpose, the ADA forbids discrimination against disabled individuals in major areas of public life, among them employment (Title I of the Act), public services (Title II), and public accommodations (Title III). At issue now is the applicability of Title III to petitioner's golf tours and qualifying rounds, in particular to petitioner's treatment of a qualified disabled golfer wishing to compete in those events.

U.S. Supreme Court's Reasoning

It seems apparent, from both the general rule and the comprehensive definition of "public accommodation," that petitioner's golf tours and their qualifying rounds fit comfortably within the coverage of Title III, and Martin within its protection. The events occur on "golf courses," a type of place specifically identified by the Act as a public accommodation [Section 12181(7)(L)]. In this case, the narrow dispute is whether allowing Martin to use a golf cart, despite the walking requirement that applies to the PGA TOUR, the NIKE TOUR, and the third stage of the Qualifying-School, is a modification that would "fundamentally alter the nature" of those events.

As an initial matter, we observe that the use of carts is not itself inconsistent with the fundamental character of the game of golf. From early on, the essence of the game has been shot-making—using clubs to cause a ball to progress from the teeing ground to a hole some distance away with as few strokes as possible. Golf carts started appearing with increasing regularity on American golf courses in the 1950s. Today they are everywhere. And they are encouraged. For one thing, they often speed up play, and for another, they are great revenue producers. There is nothing in the rules of golf that either forbids the use of carts or penalizes a player for using a cart.

Petitioner, however, distinguishes the game of golf as it is generally played from the game that it sponsors in the PGA TOUR, NIKE TOUR, and the last stage of the Qualifying-School—golf at the "highest level." According to petitioner, "the goal of the highest-level competitive athletics is to assess and compare the performance of different competitors, a task that is meaningful only if the competitors are subject to identical substantive rules." The waiver of any possibly "outcome-affecting" rule for a contestant would violate this principle and therefore, in petitioner's view, fundamentally alter the nature of the highest-level athletic event. The walking rule is one such rule, petitioner submits, because its purpose is "to inject the element of fatigue into the skill of shot-making," and thus its effect may be the critical loss of a stroke. As a consequence, the reasonable modification Martin seeks would fundamentally alter the nature of petitioner's highest-level tournaments.

The force of petitioner's argument is, first of all, mitigated by the fact that golf is a game in which it is impossible to guarantee that all competitors will play under exactly the same conditions or that an individual's ability will be the sole determinant of the outcome. For example, changes in the weather may produce harder greens and more head winds for the tournament leader than for his closest pursuers. A lucky bounce may save a shot or two. Whether such happenstance events are more or less probable than the likelihood that a golfer afflicted with Klippel-Trenaunay-Weber Syndrome would one day qualify for the NIKE TOUR and PGA TOUR, they at least demonstrate that pure chance may have a greater impact on the outcome of elite golf tournaments than the fatigue resulting from the enforcement of the walking rule.

Further, the factual basis of petitioner's argument is undermined by the District Court's finding that the fatigue from walking during one of petitioner's 4-day tournaments cannot be deemed significant. The District Court credited the testimony of a professor in physiology and expert on fatigue, who calculated the calories expended in walking a golf course (about five miles) to be approximately 500 calories—"nutritionally less than a Big Mac." What is more, that energy is expended over a 5-hour period, during which golfers have numerous intervals for rest and refreshment. In fact, the expert concluded, because golf is a low-intensity activity, fatigue from the game is primarily a psychological phenomenon in which stress and motivation are the key ingredients. And even under conditions of severe heat and humidity, the critical factor in fatigue is fluid loss rather than exercise from walking. Moreover, when given the option of using a cart, the majority of golfers in petitioner's tournaments have chosen to walk, often to relieve stress or for other strategic reasons. As NIKE TOUR member Eric Johnson testified, walking allows him to keep in rhythm, stay warmer when it is chilly, and develop a better sense of the elements and the course than riding a cart. As we have demonstrated, the walking rule is at best peripheral to the nature of petitioner's athletic events, and thus it might be waived in individual cases without working a fundamental alteration.

Holding and Remedy

Under the ADA's basic requirement that the need of a disabled person be evaluated on an individual basis, we have no doubt that allowing Martin to use a golf cart would not fundamentally alter the nature of petitioner's tournaments. As we have discussed, the purpose of the walking rule is to subject players to fatigue, which in turn may influence the outcome of tournaments. Even if the rule does serve that purpose, it is an uncontested finding of the District Court that Martin "easily endures greater fatigue even with a cart than his able-bodied competitors do by walking." The purpose of the walking rule is therefore not compromised in the slightest by allowing Martin to use a cart. A modification that provides an exception to a peripheral tournament rule without impairing its purpose cannot be said to "fundamentally alter" the tournament. What it can be said to do, on the other hand, is to allow Martin the chance to qualify for and compete in the athletic events petitioner offers to those members of the public who have the skill and desire to enter. That is exactly what the ADA requires. As a result, Martin's request for a waiver of the walking rule should have been granted.

Dissenting Opinion

The judgment of the Court of Appeals is affirmed. It is so ordered.

DISSENTING OPINION, SCALIA, JUSTICE *In my view today's opinion exercises a benevolent compassion that the law does not place it within our power to impose. The judgment distorts the text of Title III, the structure of the ADA, and common sense. I respectfully dissent.*

The Court, for its part, assumes that conclusion for the sake of argument, but pronounces respondent to be a "customer" of the PGA TOUR or of the golf courses on which it is played. That seems to me quite incredible. The PGA TOUR is a professional sporting event, staged for the entertainment of a live and TV audience. The professional golfers on the tour are no more "enjoying" (the statutory term) the entertainment that the tour provides, or the facilities of the golf courses on which it is held, than professional baseball players "enjoy" the baseball games in which they play or the facilities of Yankee Stadium. To be sure, professional ballplayers participate in the games, and use the ball fields, but no one in his right mind would think that they are customers of the American League or of Yankee Stadium. They are themselves the entertainment that the customers pay to watch. And professional golfers are no different. A professional golfer's practicing his profession is not comparable to John Q. Public's frequenting "a 232-acre amusement area with swimming, boating, sunbathing, picnicking, miniature golf, dancing facilities, and a snack bar."

Having erroneously held that Title III applies to the "customers" of professional golf who consist of its practitioners, the Court then erroneously answers—or to be accurate simply ignores—a second question. The ADA requires covered businesses to make such reasonable modifications of "policies, practices, or procedures" as are necessary to "afford" goods, services, and privileges to individuals with disabilities; but it explicitly does not require "modifications that would fundamentally alter the nature" of the goods, services, and privileges [Section 12182(b)(2)(A)(ii)]. In other words, disabled individuals must be given access to the same goods, services, and privileges that others enjoy.

A camera store may not refuse to sell cameras to a disabled person, but it is not required to stock cameras specially designed for such persons. It is hardly a feasible judicial function to decide whether shoe stores should sell single shoes to one-legged persons and if so at what price, or how many braille books the Borders or Barnes and Noble bookstore chains should stock in each of their stores. Eighteen-hole golf courses, 10-foot-high basketball hoops, 90-foot baselines, 100-yard football fields—all are arbitrary and none is essential. The only support for any of them is tradition and (in more modern times) insistence by what has come to be regarded as the ruling body of the sport—both of which factors support the PGA TOUR's position in the present case. One can envision the parents of a Little League player with attention deficit disorder trying to convince a judge that their son's disability makes it at least 25 percent more difficult to hit a pitched ball. (If they are successful, the only thing that could prevent a court order giving the kid four strikes would be a judicial determination that, in baseball, three strikes are metaphysically necessary, which is quite absurd.)

Agility, strength, speed, balance, quickness of mind, steadiness of nerves, intensity of concentration —these talents are not evenly distributed. No wild-eyed dreamer has ever suggested that the managing bodies of the competitive sports that test precisely these qualities should try to take account of the uneven distribution of God-given gifts when writing and enforcing the rules of competition. And I have no doubt Congress did not authorize misty-eyed judicial supervision of such a revolution. The year was 2001, and "everybody was finally equal." K. Vonnegut, Harrison Bergeron, in Animal Farm and Related Readings *129 (1997).*

Brief of Case: PGA Tour, Inc. v. Martin

1. Case Name, Citation, and Court
PGA TOUR, Inc. v Martin
532 U.S. 661, 121 S.Ct. 1879, 2001 Lexis 4115 (2001)
U.S. Supreme Court

2. Key Facts
A. PGA TOUR, Inc., is a nonprofit organization that sponsors professional golf tournaments.
B. The PGA establishes rules for its golf tournaments. A PGA rule requires golfers to walk the golf course and not use golf carts.
C. Casey Martin is a professional golfer who suffers from Klippel-Trenaunay-Weber Syndrome, a degenerative circulatory disorder that atrophied Martin's right leg and causes him pain, fatigue, and anxiety when walking.
D. When Martin petitioned the PGA to use a golf cart during golf tournaments, the PGA refused.
E. Martin sued the PGA, alleging discrimination against a disabled individual in violation of the Americans with Disabilities Act of 1990, a federal statute.

3. Issue
Does the Americans with Disabilities Act require the PGA to accommodate Martin by permitting him to use a golf cart while playing in PGA tournaments?

4. Holding
Yes. The Supreme Court held that the PGA must allow Martin to use a golf cart when competing in PGA golf tournaments. Affirmed.

5. Court's Reasoning
The Supreme Court held that:
A. Martin was disabled and covered by the act.
B. Golf courses are "public accommodations" covered by the act.
C. The use of golf carts is not a fundamental character of the game of golf.
D. Other than the PGA rule, there is no rule of golf that forbids the use of golf carts.
E. It is impossible to guarantee that all players in golf will play under exactly the same conditions, so allowing Martin to use a golf cart gives him no advantage over other golfers.
F. Martin, because of his disease, will probably suffer more fatigue playing golf using a golf cart than other golfers will suffer without using a cart.
G. The PGA's "walking rule" is only peripheral to the game of golf and not a fundamental part of golf.
H. Allowing Martin to use a golf cart will not fundamentally alter the PGA's highest-level professional golf tournaments.

Golden Pavilon, Kyoto, Japan. Each country has developed its own laws. A company conducting business in a foreign country is subject to that country's laws.

Chapter Summary

What Is Law?, p. 2

Law

Law is a body of rules of action or conduct that has binding legal force. Laws must be obeyed by citizens subject to sanction or legal consequences.

Functions of the Law

1. Keep the peace
2. Shape moral standards
3. Promote social justice
4. Maintain the status quo
5. Facilitate orderly change
6. Facilitate planning
7. Provide a basis for compromise
8. Maximize individual freedom

Flexibility and Fairness of the Law

1. *Flexibility.* The law must be flexible to meet social, technological, and economic changes in the United States and the world.
2. *Fairness.* Although the U.S. legal system is one of the fairest and most democratic systems of law, abuses of process and mistakes in the application of the law do occur.

Schools of Jurisprudential Thought, p. 5

Schools of Jurisprudential Thought

1. *Natural Law School.* Postulates that law is based on what is "correct." It emphasizes a moral theory of law—that is, law should be based on morality and ethics.
2. *Historical School.* Believes that law is an aggregate of social traditions and customs.
3. *Analytical School.* Maintains that law is shaped by logic.
4. *Sociological School.* Asserts that law is a means of achieving and advancing certain sociological goals.
5. *Command School.* Believes that law is a set of rules developed, communicated, and enforced by the ruling party.
6. *Critical Legal Studies School.* Maintains that legal rules are unnecessary and that legal disputes should be solved by applying arbitrary rules based on fairness.
7. *Law and Economics School.* Believes that promoting market efficiency should be the central concern of legal decision making.

History of American Law, p. 7

Foundation of American Law

The English common law (judge-made law) forms the basis of the legal systems of most states in the United States. Louisiana bases its law on the French civil code.

Sources of Law in the United States, p. 9

Sources of Law in the United States

1. *Constitutions.* The U.S. Constitution establishes the federal government and enumerates its powers. Powers not given to the federal government are reserved to the states. State constitutions establish state governments and enumerate their powers.

2. ***Treaties.*** The president, with the advice and consent of the Senate, may enter into treaties with foreign countries.

3. ***Codified Law.*** Statutes are enacted by the federal Congress and state legislatures. Ordinances are passed by municipalities and local government bodies. They establish courses of conduct that must be followed by covered parties.

4. ***Administrative agency regulations and orders.*** Administrative agencies are created by the legislative and executive branches of government. They may adopt administrative regulations and issue orders.

5. ***Executive orders.*** Issued by the president and governors of states, executive orders regulate the conduct of covered parties.

6. ***Judicial decisions.*** Federal and state courts decide controversies. In doing so, they issue decisions that state the holding of each case and the reasoning used by the court in reaching its decision.

Doctrine of *Stare Decisis*

Stare decisis. This doctrine provides for the adherence to precedent. *Stare decisis* means "to stand by the decision."

Critical Legal Thinking, p. 15

Briefing a Case

1. Case name, citation, and court.
2. Summary of the key facts in the case.
3. Issue presented by the case.
4. Holding.
5. Summary of the court's reasoning.

Internet Exercises and Case Questions
Working the Web Internet Exercises

Activities

Visit the Web sites listed below for more information about the topics covered in this chapter:

1. For a broad overview of legal history visit **jurist.law.pitt. edu/sg_hist.htm**.

2. To better understand the conceptual differences between law and equity see **www.law.cornell.edu/topics/equity.html**.

3. For a working definition of basic legal categories, visit *The Columbia Encyclopedia*, Sixth Edition, 2001, at **www.bartleby.com/65/co/commonla.html**.

4. The Law, Commerce & Technology Center, University of Washington Law, provides online information about Internet issues, biotechnology, electronic commerce, and technology news in the northwest. Visit **www.law. washington.edu/lct**.

5. Check out the latest developments at the Business Law— Committee on Cyberspace Law home page, **www.abanet. org/buslaw/cyber/home.html**.

Critical Legal Thinking Cases

1.1 Fairness of the Law In 1909, the state legislature of Illinois enacted a statute called the "Woman's 10-Hour Law." The law prohibited women who were employed in factories and other manufacturing facilities from working more than 10 hours per day. The law did not apply to men. W. C. Ritchie & Co., an employer, brought a lawsuit that challenged the statute as being unconstitutional in violation of the Equal Protection Clause of

the Illinois constitution. In upholding the statute, the Illinois supreme court stated,

> *It is known to all men (and what we know as men we cannot profess to be ignorant of as judges) that woman's physical structure and the performance of maternal functions place her at a great disadvantage in the battle of life; that while a man can work for more than 10 hours a day without injury to himself, a woman, especially when the burdens of motherhood are upon*

her, cannot; that while a man can work standing upon his feet for more than 10 hours a day, day after day, without injury to himself, a woman cannot; and that to require a woman to stand upon her feet for more than 10 hours in any one day and perform severe manual labor while thus standing, day after day, has the effect to impair her health, and that as weakly and sickly women cannot be mothers of vigorous children.

We think the general consensus of opinion, not only in this country but in the civilized countries of Europe, is, that a working day of not more than 10 hours for women is justified for the following reasons: (1) the physical organization of women, (2) her maternal function, (3) the rearing and educa-tion of children, (4) the maintenance of the home; and these conditions are, so far, matters of general knowledge that the courts will take judicial cognizance of their existence.

Surrounded as women are by changing conditions of society, and the evolution of employment which environs them, we agree fully with what is said by the Supreme Court of Washington in the Buchanan case; "law is, or ought to be, a progressive science."

Is the statute fair? Would the statute be lawful today? Should the law be a "progressive science"? [*W. C. Ritchie & Co. v. Wayman, Attorney for Cook County, Illinois*, 91 N.E. 695, 1910 Ill. Lexis 1958 (IL 1910)]

Business Ethics Cases

1.2 Business Ethics   In 1975, after the war in Vietnam, the U.S. government discontinued draft registration for men in this country. In 1980, after the Soviet Union invaded Afghanistan, President Jimmy Carter asked Congress for funds to reactivate draft registration. President Carter suggested that both males and females be required to register. Congress allocated funds only for the registration of males. Several men who were subject to draft registration brought a lawsuit that challenged the law as being unconstitutional in violation of the Equal Protection Clause of the U.S. Constitution. The U.S. Supreme Court upheld the con-stitutionality of the draft registration law, reasoning as follows:

The question of registering women for the draft not only received considerable national attention and was the subject of wide-ranging public debate, but also was extensively consid-ered by Congress in hearings, floor debate, and in committee. The foregoing clearly establishes that the decision to exempt women from registration was not the "accidental by-product of a traditional way of thinking about women."

This is not a case of Congress arbitrarily choosing to burden one of two similarly situated groups, such as would be the case with an all-black or all-white, or an all-Catholic or all-Lutheran, or an all-Republican or all-Democratic registra-tion. Men and women are simply not similarly situated for purposes of a draft or registration for a draft.

Justice Marshall dissented, stating that "The Court today places its imprimatur on one of the most potent remaining public expressions of 'ancient canards about the proper role of women.' It upholds a statute that requires males but not females to register for the draft, and which thereby categori-cally excludes women from a fundamental civil obligation. I dissent."

Was the decision fair? Has the law been a "progressive sci-ence" in this case? Is it ethical for males, but not females, to have to register for the draft? [*Rostker, Director of the Selective Service v. Goldberg*, 453 U.S. 57, 101 S.Ct. 2646, 1981 U.S. Lexis 126 (1981)]

Briefing the Case Writing Assignment

Read Case A.1 in the Case Appendix [*Anheuser-Busch Incorporated v. Schmoke, Mayor of Baltimore City*]. This case is excerpted from the court of appeals opinion. Review and brief the case. In your brief, be sure to answer the following questions.

1. What law was at issue in this case and what was the source of the law?

2. Who challenged the law? On what grounds did the plain-tiff challenge the law?

3. Do you think the challenged law was fair? Explain.

4. How did the court of appeals decide the case? Was this an easy case for the court to decide?

Endnotes

1. *The Spirit of Liberty*, 3rd ed. (New York: Alfred A. Knopf, 1960).
2. "Introduction," *The Nature of Law: Readings in Legal Philosophy*, ed. M. P. Golding (New York: Random House, 1966).

3. *Black's Law Dictionary*, 5th ed. (St. Paul, MN: West, 1979).
4. 447 U.S. 10, 100 S.Ct. 1999, 1980 U.S. Lexis 127 (1980).
5. *Law and the Modern Mind* (New York: Brentano's, 1930).
6. 208 A.2d 193, 1965 Pa. Lexis 442 (PA 1965).

Constitutional Law for Business and Online Commerce

2

"We the People of the United States, in Order to form a more perfect Union, establish Justice, insure domestic Tranquility, provide for the common defense, promote the general Welfare, and secure the Blessings of Liberty to ourselves and our Posterity, do ordain and establish this Constitution for the United States of America."

—Preamble to the Constitution of the United States of America

Chapter Objectives

After studying this chapter, you should be able to:

1. Describe the concept of federalism and the doctrine of separation of powers.
2. Define and apply the Supremacy Clause of the U.S. Constitution.
3. Explain the federal government's authority to regulate foreign commerce and interstate commerce.
4. Explain how speech is protected by the First Amendment.
5. Explain the doctrines of equal protection and due process.

Chapter Contents

- Constitution of the United States of America
- Supremacy Clause
- Commerce Clause
- Bill of Rights
- Other Constitutional Clauses

Prior to the American Revolution, each of the 13 original colonies operated as a separate sovereignty under the rule of England. In September 1774, representatives of the colonies met as a Continental Congress. In 1776, the colonies declared independence from England, and the American Revolution ensued.

This chapter examines the major provisions of the U.S. Constitution and the amendments that have been adopted to the Constitution. Of particular importance, this chapter discusses how these provisions affect the operations of business in this country. The Constitution, with amendments, is set forth as Appendix B to this book.

> The Constitution of the United States is not a mere lawyers' document: It is a vehicle of life, and its spirit is always the spirit of the age.
>
> Woodrow Wilson
> *Constitutional Government in the United States 69 (1927)*

Constitution of the United States of America

In 1778, the Continental Congress formed a *federal government* and adopted the **Articles of Confederation**. The Articles of Confederation created a federal Congress composed of representatives of the 13 new states. The Articles of Confederation was a particularly weak document that gave limited power to the newly created federal government. For example, it did not provide Congress with the power to levy and collect taxes, to regulate commerce with foreign countries, or to regulate interstate commerce among the states.

The **Constitutional Convention** was convened in Philadelphia in May 1787. The primary purpose of the Convention was to strengthen the federal government. After substantial debate, the delegates agreed to a new **U.S. Constitution**. The constitution was reported to Congress in September 1787. State ratification of the Constitution was completed in 1788. Many amendments, including the **Bill of Rights**, have been added to the Constitution since that time.

The U.S. Constitution serves two major functions:

1. It creates the three branches of the federal government (i.e., the executive, legislative, and judicial branches) and allocates powers to these branches.
2. It protects individual rights by limiting the government's ability to restrict those rights.

The Constitution itself provides that it may be amended to address social and economic changes. Some important constitutional concepts are discussed in the following paragraphs.

New York, New York. The Constitution of the United States of America establishes the structure of the federal government, delegates powers to the federal government, and guarantees certain fundamental rights.

Federalism and Delegated Powers

Our country's form of government is referred to as **federalism**. That means that the federal government and the 50 state governments share powers.

When the states ratified the Constitution, they *delegated* certain powers to the federal government. They are called **enumerated powers**. The federal government is authorized to deal with national and international affairs. Any powers that are not specifically delegated to the federal government by the Constitution are reserved to the state governments. State governments are empowered to deal with local affairs.

Doctrine of Separation of Powers

As mentioned previously, the federal government is divided into three branches:

1. Article I of the Constitution established the **legislative branch** of government. This branch is bicameral; that is, it consists of the Senate and the House of Representatives. Collectively, they are referred to as *Congress*.[1] Each state has two senators. The number of representatives to the House of Representatives is determined according to the population of each state. The current number of representatives is determined from the 2000 census.
2. Article II of the Constitution establishes the **executive branch** of government by providing for the election of the president and vice president. The president is not elected by popular vote but instead is selected by the *electoral college*, whose representatives are appointed by state delegations.[2]
3. Article III establishes the **judicial branch** of the government by establishing the Supreme Court and providing for the creation of other federal courts by Congress.[3]

Checks and Balances

Business Brief

Checks and balances is the way the U.S. Constitution prevents any one of the three branches of the government from becoming too powerful.

Certain **checks and balances** are built into the Constitution to ensure that no one branch of the federal government becomes too powerful. Some of the checks and balances in our system of government are as follows:

1. The judicial branch has authority to examine the acts of the other two branches of government and determine whether those acts are constitutional.[4]

United States Post Office, Alhambra, California. The United States is the world's leading democracy. The country, however, has had many blemishes on its citizens' constitutional rights. For example, during World War II Japanese Americans were involuntarily placed in camps. During the McCarthy hearings of the 1950s, citizens who were communists or associated with communists were "blackballed" from their occupations, most notably in the film industry. It was not until the mid-1960s that equal opportunity laws outlawed discrimination in the workplace based on race and sex.

2. The executive branch can enter into treaties with foreign governments only with the advice and consent of the Senate.

3. The legislative branch is authorized to create federal courts and determine their jurisdiction and to enact statutes that change judicially made law.

Supremacy Clause

The **Supremacy Clause** establishes that the federal Constitution, treaties, federal laws, and federal regulations are the supreme law of the land.[5] State and local laws that conflict with valid federal law are unconstitutional. The concept of federal law taking precedence over state or local law is commonly called the **preemption doctrine**.

Congress may expressly provide that a particular federal statute *exclusively* regulates a specific area or activity. No state or local law regulating the area or activity is valid if there is such a statute. More often, though, federal statutes do not expressly provide for exclusive jurisdiction. In these instances, state and local governments have *concurrent jurisdiction* to regulate the area or activity. However, any state or local law that "directly and substantially" conflicts with valid federal law is preempted under the Supremacy Clause.

The following case applies the Supremacy Clause.

U.S. SUPREME COURT CASE

Geier v. American Honda Motor Company, Inc.

529 U.S. 861, 120 S.Ct. 1913, 2000 U.S. Lexis 3425 (2000)
Supreme Court of the United States

Case 2.1
Supremacy Clause

Background and Facts

In 1987, the U.S. Department of Transportation, a federal administrative agency, adopted the Federal Motor Vehicle Safety Standard, which required automobile manufacturers to equip 10 percent of their 1987 vehicles with passive restraints, including automatic seat belts or air bags. In 1992, Alexis Geier, driving a 1987 Honda Accord automobile in the District of Columbia, collided with a tree and was seriously injured. The car was equipped with manual shoulder and lap belts that were buckled up at the time of the accident; the car was not equipped with air bags, however. Geier sued the car's manufacturer, the American Honda Motor Company, Inc., to recover damages under the District of Columbia's tort law, alleging that American Honda had negligently and defectively designed the car because it lacked a driver's side air bag. The trial court dismissed Geier's lawsuit, finding that the District of Columbia's tort law conflicted with the federal passive restraint safety standard and was therefore preempted under the Supremacy Clause of the U.S. Constitution. The court of appeals affirmed. Geier appealed to the U.S. Supreme Court.

Issue

Does the federal passive restraint safety standard preempt the District of Columbia's common law tort law?

Court's Reasoning

Petitioner Geier's tort action depends upon his claim that the manufacturer had a duty to install an air bag when it manufactured his 1987 Honda Accord. The petitioner's position would

have required all manufacturers to have installed air bags in the entire District of Columbia–related portion of their 1987 new car fleet. The federal safety standard at that time required that only 10 percent of a manufacturer's nationwide fleet be equipped with any passive restraint device at all. The Supreme Court stated that the language of the federal passive restraint standard was clear enough: The federal standard sought a gradually developing mix of passive restraint devices for safety–related reasons. Thus, the rule of state tort law for which petitioner Geier argues would stand as an "obstacle" to the accomplishment of the federal objective. Hence the tort action was preempted.

Decision and Remedy

The U.S. Supreme Court held that the federal passive restraint safety standard preempted the District of Columbia's tort law under which petitioner Geier sued. The U.S. Supreme Court affirmed the dismissal of Geier's lawsuit against American Honda.

Case Questions

Critical Legal Thinking   What would be the consequences if there were no Supremacy Clause? Explain.

Business Ethics   Do you think American Honda owed a duty to equip all of its 1987 vehicles with air bags, even though federal law did not require this?

Contemporary Business   Do laws ever protect—rather than harm—businesses? Do you think defendant American Honda would say "there are too many laws" in this case?

Kracow, Poland. Following the United States of America, Poland was the second country to adopt a constitution.

Commerce Clause

The **Commerce Clause** of the U.S. Constitution grants Congress the power "to regulate commerce with foreign nations, and among the several states, and with Indian tribes."[6] Because this clause authorizes the federal government to regulate commerce, it has a greater impact on business than any other provision in the Constitution. Among other things, this clause is intended to foster the development of a national market and free trade among the states.

Federal Regulation of Interstate Commerce

The Commerce Clause also gives the federal government the authority to regulate **interstate commerce**. Originally, the courts interpreted this clause to mean that the federal government could only regulate commerce that moved *in* interstate commerce. The modern rule, however, allows the federal government to regulate activities that *affect* interstate commerce.

Under the **effects on interstate commerce test**, the regulated activity does not itself have to be in interstate commerce. Thus, any local (*intrastate*) activity that has an effect on interstate commerce is subject to federal regulation. Theoretically, this test subjects a substantial amount of business activity in the United States to federal regulation.

For example, in the famous case *Wickard, Secretary of Agriculture v. Filburn*,[7] a federal statute limited the amount of wheat that a farmer could plant and harvest for home consumption. Filburn, a farmer, violated the law. The U.S. Supreme Court upheld the statute on the grounds that it prevented nationwide surpluses and shortages of wheat. The Court reasoned that wheat grown for home consumption would affect the supply of wheat available in interstate commerce.

In several recent cases, the U.S. Supreme Court held that the federal government had enacted statutes beyond its Interstate Commerce Clause powers. For example, in *United States v. Lopez*, the Supreme Court invalidated the Gun-Free School Zone Act, a federal statute that made it a crime to knowingly possess a firearm in a school zone.[8] The Court found that there was no commercial activity that was being regulated.

Business Brief

The federal government may regulate:

1. *Interstate* commerce that crosses state borders.
2. *Intrastate* commerce that affects interstate commerce.

The American Constitution is, so far as I can see, the most wonderful work ever struck off at a given time by the brain and purpose of man.

W. E. Glastone
Kin Beyond Sea (1878)

The federal government's authority to enact federal statutes pursuant to the Interstate Commerce Clause was at issue in the following case.

U.S. SUPREME COURT CASE

Reno, Attorney General of the United States v. Condon, Attorney General of South Carolina

528 U.S. 141, 120 S.Ct. 666, 2000 U.S. Lexis 503 (2000)
Supreme Court of the United States

Case 2.2

Interstate Commerce Clause

Background and Facts

State departments of motor vehicles (DMVs) register automobiles and issue driver's licenses. State DMVs require automobile owners and drivers to provide personal information, which includes a person's name, address, telephone number, vehicle description, Social Security number, medical Information, and a photograph, as a condition for registering an automobile or obtaining a driver's license. Many states DMVs sold this personal information to individuals, advertisers, and businesses. These sales generated significant revenues for the states.

After receiving thousands of complaints from individuals whose personal information had been sold, the Congress of the United States enacted the Driver's Privacy Protection Act of 1994 (DPPA) [18 U.S.C. §§ 2721–2775]. This federal statute prohibits a state from selling the personal information of a person unless the state obtains that person's affirmative consent to do so. South Carolina sued the United States, alleging that the Commerce Clause was violated by the federal government by adopting the DPPA. The district court and the court of appeals held for South Carolina. The U.S. Supreme Court granted review.

Issue

Was the Driver's Privacy Protection Act properly enacted pursuant to the Interstate Commerce Clause power granted to the federal government by the U.S. Constitution?

Court's Reasoning

The Supreme Court reasoned that the motor vehicle information which the states have historically sold is used by insurers, manufacturers, direct marketers, and others engaged in interstate commerce to contact drivers with customized solicitations. The information is also used in the stream of interstate commerce by various public and private entities for matters related to interstate motoring. The Supreme Court held that because drivers' information is an article of commerce, its sale or release into the interstate stream of business is sufficient to support congressional regulation, and therefore the Driver's Privacy Protection Act is a proper exercise of Congress's authority to regulate interstate commerce under the Commerce Clause.

Decision and Remedy

The U.S. Supreme Court held that Congress had the authority under the Commerce Clause to enact the federal Driver's Privacy Protection Act. The Supreme Court reversed the decisions of the district court and court of appeals that held in favor of South Carolina.

Case Questions

Critical Legal Thinking   How often do you think one government (the federal government) saves people from the intrusiveness of another government (state or local government)?

Business Ethics   Was it ethical for the states to sell the personal information of automobile owners and drivers?

Contemporary Business   Who were the winners from this decision? Who were the losers?

State and Local Government Regulation of Business— State "Police Power"

The states did not delegate all power to regulate business to the federal government. They retained the power to regulate *intrastate* and much interstate business activity that occurs within their borders. This is commonly referred to as states' **police power**.

Police power permits states (and, by delegation, local governments) to enact laws to protect or promote the *public health, safety, morals, and general welfare*. This includes the authority to enact laws that regulate the conduct of business. Zoning ordinances, state environmental laws, corporation and partnership laws, and property laws are enacted under this power.

Business Brief

States may enact laws that protect or promote the public health, safety, morals, and general welfare, as long as the law does not unduly burden interstate commerce.

State and local laws cannot **unduly burden interstate commerce**. If they do, they are unconstitutional because they violate the Commerce Clause. For example, if the federal government has chosen not to regulate an area that it has the power to regulate (*dormant Commerce Clause*), but the state does regulate it, the state law cannot unduly burden interstate commerce.

Consider This Example Each state has enacted a Corporations Code that regulates the establishment and operations of corporations in that state. Assume that one state's corporation's code permits only corporations from that state, but from no other state, to conduct business in that state. This state law would unduly burden interstate commerce and would be unconstitutional.

International Law

Foreign Commerce Clause

The Commerce Clause of the U.S. Constitution gives the federal government the *exclusive power* to regulate commerce with foreign nations. Direct and indirect regulation of **foreign commerce** by state or local governments that discriminates against foreign commerce violates the Foreign Commerce Clause and is therefore unconstitutional.

Consider the Following Examples The state of Michigan is the home of General Motors Corporation, Ford Motor Company, and Chrysler Corporation, the three largest automobile manufacturers in the United States. Suppose the Michigan state legislature enacts a law that imposes a 100 percent tax on any automobile imported from a foreign country that is sold in Michigan but does not impose the same tax on domestic automobiles sold in Michigan. The Michigan tax violates the Foreign Commerce Clause and is therefore unconstitutional and void. If, on the other hand, Michigan enacts a law that imposes a 100 percent tax on all automobiles sold in Michigan, domestic and foreign, the law does not discriminate against foreign commerce and therefore does not violate the Foreign Commerce Clause. The federal government could enact a 100 percent tax on all foreign automobiles but not domestic automobiles sold in the United States, and that law would be valid, however. ∎

Bill of Rights

The U.S. Constitution provides that it may be amended. In 1791, the 10 amendments that are commonly referred to as the **Bill of Rights** were approved by the states and became part of the U.S. Constitution. The Bill of Rights guarantees certain fundamental rights to natural persons and protects these rights from intrusive government action. Most of these rights have also been found applicable to so called artificial persons (i.e., corporations).

In addition to the Bill of Rights, 17 other **amendments** have been added to the Constitution. These amendments cover a variety of things. For instance, they have abolished slavery, prohibited discrimination, authorized the federal income tax, given women the right to vote, and specifically recognized that persons 18 years of age and older have the right to vote.

Originally, the Bill of Rights limited intrusive action by the *federal government* only. Intrusive actions by state and local governments were not limited until the **Due Process Clause of the Fourteenth Amendment** was added to the Constitution in 1868. The Supreme Court has applied the **incorporation doctrine** and held that most of the fundamental guarantees contained in the Bill of Rights are applicable to state and local government action. The amendments to the Constitution that are most applicable to business are discussed in the paragraphs that follow.

Freedom of Speech

One of the most honored freedoms guaranteed by the Bill of Rights is the **freedom of speech** of the First Amendment. Many other constitutional freedoms would be meaningless without it. The First Amendment's Freedom of Speech Clause protects speech only, not conduct. The U.S. Supreme Court places speech into three categories: (1) *fully protected*, (2) *limited protected*, and (3) *unprotected speech*.

Fully Protected Speech

Fully protected speech is speech that the government cannot prohibit or regulate. Political speech is an example of such speech. For example, the government could not enact a law that forbids citizens from criticizing the current administration. The First Amendment protects oral, written, and symbolic speech.

> I disapprove of what you say, but I will defend to the death your right to say it.
>
> Voltaire

Limited Protected Speech

The Supreme Court has held that certain types of speech have only *limited protection* under the First Amendment. The government cannot forbid this type of speech, but it can subject this speech to **time, place**, and **manner restrictions**. The following types of speech are accorded limited protection:

1. *Offensive speech.* **Offensive speech** is a speech that offends many members of society. (It is not the same as obscene speech, however.) The Supreme Court has held that offensive speech may be restricted by the government under time, place, and manner restrictions. For example, the Federal Communications Commission (FCC) can regulate the use of offensive language on television by limiting such language to time periods when children would be unlikely to be watching (e.g., late at night).

2. *Commercial speech.* **Commercial speech**, such as advertising, was once considered unprotected by the First Amendment. The Supreme Court's landmark decision in *Virginia State Board of Pharmacy v. Virginia Citizens Consumer Council, Inc.*[9] changed

Protest, Los Angeles. The Freedom of Speech Clause of the First Amendment to the U.S. Constitution protects the right to engage in political speech.

this rule. In that case, the Supreme Court held that a state statute prohibiting a pharmacist from advertising the price of prescription drugs was unconstitutional because it violated the Freedom of Speech Clause. However, the Supreme Court held that commercial speech is subject to proper time, place, and manner restrictions. For example, a city can prohibit billboards along its highways for safety and aesthetic reasons as long as other forms of advertising (e.g., print media) are available.

In the following case, the court upheld the U.S. government's regulation of commercial speech.

Fax.com, Inc. v. United States of America

323 F.3d 649, 2003 U.S. App. Lexis 5469 (2003)
United States Court of Appeals, Eighth Circuit

Case 2.3

Commercial Speech

Background and Facts

The use of fax machines has made the conduct of business and individuals' transactions more efficient. However, faxes have also spurned a growth industry that sends unsolicited advertising "junk faxes" to fax machines all over the country. The recipients of these junk faxes complained to the government that these faxes tied up their fax machines and cost them money to receive and process. In order to regulate this practice, Congress enacted a provision in the Telephone Consumer Protection Act of 1991 (TCPA) that outlaws junk faxes. Fax.com, Inc., which provides promotional services to clients, continued to transmit unsolicited advertisements to fax machines of potential customers after the TCPA was enacted. In response to numerous consumer complaints, the U.S. government sued Fax.com for violating the TCPA. Fax.com argued in defense that the TCPA's regulation of unsolicited faxes violated its free speech rights under the First Amendment to the U.S. Constitution. The U.S. government argued that junk faxes were commercial speech that it could regulate in this manner. The U.S. district court held that the TCPA violated Fax.com's free speech rights and dismissed the government's lawsuit. The U.S. government appealed.

Issue

Is the federal government's prohibition against unsolicited commercial advertising faxes a constitutionally permitted regulation of commercial speech?

Court's Reasoning

The court of appeals held that unsolicited advertising faxes—junk faxes—was commercial speech. The court cited legislative history of the passage of the TCPA as well as evidence from the district court which proved that unsolicited junk faxes caused recipients of these faxes substantial costs and time loss. The court of appeals held that the federal government's enactment of the TCPA, which prohibits junk faxes, was a constitutional "time, place, and manner" regulation of commercial speech and did not violate Fax.com's free speech rights. The court stated, "There is a substantial governmental interest in protecting the public from the cost shifting and interference caused by unwanted fax advertisements."

Decision and Remedy

The court of appeals held that the TCPA's prohibition against unsolicited advertising faxes was a lawful constitutional regulation of commercial speech. The court of appeals reversed the district court's judgment, dismissing the government's lawsuit, and remanded the case for further proceedings.

Case Questions

Critical Legal Thinking What is "commercial speech"? How can commercial speech be regulated by the government? Explain.

Business Ethics Did Fax.com act ethically in sending unsolicited junk faxes to unsuspecting parties?

Contemporary Business Was Fax.com making profits from its endeavors? Did it shift costs to the recipients of its junk faxes? What will be the effect of the ruling of the court of appeals?

Unprotected Speech

The Supreme Court has held that the following types of speech are **unprotected speech**; they are not protected by the First Amendment and may be totally forbidden by the government:

1. Dangerous speech (including such things as yelling "fire" in a crowded theater when there is no fire)
2. Fighting words that are likely to provoke a hostile or violent response from an average person[10]

3. Speech that incites the violent or revolutionary overthrow of the government; the mere abstract teaching of the morality and consequences of such action is protected[11]
4. Defamatory language[12]
5. Child pornography[13]
6. Obscene speech[14]

The definition of **obscene speech** is quite subjective. One Supreme Court justice stated, "I know it when I see it."[15] In *Miller v. California*, the Supreme Court determined that speech is obscene when

1. The average person, applying contemporary community standards, would find that the work, taken as a whole, appeals to the prurient interest.
2. The work depicts or describes, in a patently offensive way, sexual conduct specifically defined by the applicable state law.
3. The work, taken as a whole, lacks serious literary, artistic, political, or scientific value.[16]

States are free to define what constitutes obscene speech. Movie theaters, magazine publishers, and so on are often subject to challenges that the materials they display or sell are obscene and therefore not protected by the First Amendment.

The following case demonstrates the application of the Freedom of Speech Clause.

> The nation's armour of defence against the passions of men is the Constitution. Take that away, and the nation goes down into the field of its conflicts like a warrior without armour.
>
> Henry Ward Beecher
> *Proverbs from Plymouth Pulpit,*
> *1887*

U.S. SUPREME COURT CASE

United States v. Playboy Entertainment Group, Inc.

529 U.S. 803, 120 S.Ct. 1878, 2000 U.S. Lexis 3427 (2000)
Supreme Court of the United States

Case 2.4
Free Speech

Background and Facts

Many entertainment companies, including Playboy Entertainment Group, Inc., produce and distribute sexually explicit adult entertainment features for transmission over cable television stations. These shows are usually offered on a pay-per-view subscription service basis. Cable operators provide viewers with a converter box that attaches to the television set and scrambles these sexually explicit materials so they can only be viewed by subscribers who pay the subscription fee. However, with analog television sets, there often occurs "signal bleed" of either a blurred visual image or muted audio transmission of these materials. Digital television eliminates the signal bleed problem.

To address the signal bleed problem, Congress enacted Section 505 of the Telecommunications Act of 1996, which requires cable operators not to transmit sexually explicit materials during the hours from 6:00 A.M. to 10:00 P.M. if the signal bleed problem can occur.

Playboy Entertainment Group, Inc., a cable operator of Playboy Television and Spice, two adult entertainment cable television networks, sued the federal government, alleging that Section 505 violated its free speech rights guaranteed by the U.S. Constitution. The district court declared Section 505 unconstitutional. The court found it feasible to allow cable operators to block individual cable boxes in the home, and therefore Section 505 was an overly broad restriction on content-based speech. The U.S. Supreme Court agreed to hear the case on direct appeal.

Issue

Is Section 505 an overly broad restriction on content-based speech that violates the free speech rights of Playboy Entertainment Group, Inc.?

Court's Reasoning

The U.S. Supreme Court noted that the programming in this case is not alleged to be obscene and that adults have a constitutional right to view it. The Supreme Court stated that the only reasonable way for a substantial number of cable operators to comply with the letter of Section 505 is to "time channel," which silences the protected speech for two-thirds of the day in every home in a cable service area, regardless of the presence or likely presence of children or of the wishes of the viewers. Thirty to 50 percent of all adult programming is viewed by households prior to 10 P.M., when the safeharbor period begins. The Supreme Court stated, "To prohibit this much speech is a significant restriction of communication between speakers and willing adult listeners, communication which enjoys First Amendment protection." The Court cited the fact that cable systems have the capacity to block unwanted channels on a household-by-household basis.

Decision and Remedy

The U.S. Supreme Court held that Section 505 was an overly broad restriction on legal content-based speech and was therefore an unconstitutional violation of free speech rights. The Supreme Court affirmed the judgment of the district court.

United States v. Playboy Entertainment Group, Inc.

529 U.S. 803, 120 S.Ct. 1878, 2000 U.S. Lexis 3427 (2000)
Supreme Court of the United States
(continued)

Case Questions

Critical Legal Thinking   Do you think that Section 505 was an overly broad restriction on free speech rights? Why or why not?

Business Ethics   Why do you think Congress enacted Section 505 rather than require each home to choose to individually block the challenged programming?

Contemporary Business   What economic consequences did the Supreme Court's ruling have for Playboy Entertainment and other adult entertainment cable companies?

Online Commerce & Internet Law
Broad Free Speech Rights Granted in Cyberspace

Once or twice a century, a new medium comes along that presents new problems for applying freedom of speech rights. This time it is the Internet. In 1996 Congress enacted the **Computer Decency Act**, which made it a felony to knowingly make "indecent" or "patently offensive" materials available on computer systems, including the Internet, to persons under 18 years of age. Immediately, more than 50 cyberspace providers and users filed a lawsuit challenging the act as a violation of their free speech rights, granted under the First Amendment to the Constitution. The U.S. district court agreed with the plaintiffs and declared the act an unconstitutional violation of the Freedom of Speech Clause.

On appeal, the U.S. Supreme Court agreed and held that the act was an unconstitutional violation of free speech rights. The Supreme Court concluded that the Internet allows an individual to reach an audience of millions at almost no cost, setting it apart from TV, radio, and print media, which are prohibitively expensive to use. The Court stated, "As the most participatory form of mass speech yet developed, the Internet deserves the highest protection from government intrusion." The Court declared emphatically that the Internet must be given the highest possible level of First Amendment free speech protection.

Proponents of the act argued that it was necessary to protect children from indecent materials. The Supreme Court reasoned that limiting the content on the Internet to what is suitable for a child resulted in unconstitutionally limiting adult speech. The Court noted that children are far less likely to trip over indecent material on the Internet than on TV or radio because the information must be actively sought out on the Internet. The Court noted that less obtrusive means for protecting children are available, such as requiring parents to regulate their children's access to materials on the Internet and placing filtering and blocking software on computers to control what their children see on the Internet. [*Reno v. American Civil Liberties Union*, 521 U.S. 844, 117 S.Ct. 2329, 1997 U.S. Lexis 4037 (1997)] [*Note*: It still remains a crime under existing laws to transmit *obscene* materials over the Internet.] ∎

Mackinac Island, Michigan/ Freedom of Religion. The **Establishment Clause** prohibits the government from establishing a state religion or promoting one religion over another; the **Free Exercise Clause** prohibits the government from interfering with the free exercise of religion.

Freedom of Religion

The U.S. Constitution requires federal, state, and local governments to be neutral toward religion. The First Amendment actually contains two separate religion clauses. They are:

1. **The Establishment Clause.** The **Establishment Clause** prohibits the government from either establishing a state religion or promoting one religion over another. Thus, it guarantees that there will be no state-sponsored religion. The Supreme Court used this clause as its reason for ruling that an Alabama statute that authorized a one-minute period of silence in school for "meditation or voluntary prayer" was invalid.[17] The Court held that the statute endorsed religion.

2. **The Free Exercise Clause.** The **Free Exercise Clause** prohibits the government from interfering with the free exercise of religion in the United States. Generally, this clause prevents the government from enacting laws that either prohibit or inhibit individuals from participating in or practicing their chosen religion. For example, in *Church of Lukumi Babalu Aye, Inc. v. City of Hialeah, Florida*,[18] the U.S. Supreme Court held that a city ordinance that prohibited ritual sacrifices of animals (chickens) during church services violated the Free Exercise Clause and that such sacrifices should be allowed. Of course, this right to be free from government intervention in the practice of religion is not absolute. For example, human sacrifices are unlawful and are not protected by the First Amendment.

Concept Summary *Freedom of Religion*

Clause	Description
Establishment Clause	Prohibits the government from either establishing a government-sponsored religion or promoting one religion over other religions.
Free Exercise Clause	Prohibits the government from enacting laws that either prohibit or inhibit individuals from participating in or practicing their chosen religions.

Beijing, China. People throughout the world seek freedom to practice their chosen religion.

Other Constitutional Clauses

The **Fourteenth Amendment** was added to the U.S. Constitution in 1868. Its original purpose was to guarantee equal rights to all persons after the Civil War. The provisions of the Fourteenth Amendment prohibit discriminatory and unfair action by the government. Several of these provisions—namely, the *Equal Protection Clause*, the *Due Process Clause*, and the *Privileges and Immunities Clause*—have important implications for business.

The Equal Protection Clause

The **Equal Protection Clause** provides that a state cannot "deny to any person within its jurisdiction the equal protection of the laws." Although this clause expressly applies to state and local government action, the Supreme Court has held that it also applies to federal government action.

This clause prohibits state, local, and federal governments from enacting laws that classify and treat "similarly situated" persons differently. Artificial persons, such as corporations, are also protected. Note that this clause is designed to prohibit invidious discrimination: It does not make the classification of individuals unlawful per se.

The Supreme Court has adopted three different standards for reviewing equal protection cases. They are:

1. ***Strict scrutiny test.*** Any government activity or regulation that classifies persons based on a *suspect class* (i.e., **race**) is reviewed for lawfulness using a **strict scrutiny test**. Under this standard, most government classifications of persons based on race are found to be unconstitutional. For example, a government rule that permitted persons of one race, but not of another race, to receive government benefits such as Medicaid, would violate this test. However, affirmative action programs that give racial minorities a "plus factor" when considered for public university admission is lawful, as long as it does not constitute a quota system.

2. ***Intermediate scrutiny test.*** The lawfulness of government classifications based on *protected classes* other than race (such as **sex** or **age**) are examined using an **intermediate scrutiny test**. Under this standard, the courts determine whether the government classification is "reasonably related" to a legitimate government purpose. For example, a rule prohibiting persons over a certain age from military combat would be lawful, but a rule prohibiting persons over a certain age from acting as government engineers would not be. With regard to a person's gender, the U.S. Supreme Court has held that the federal government can require males, but not females, to register with the military for a possible draft.

3. ***Rational basis test.*** The lawfulness of all government classifications that do not involve suspect or protected classes is examined using a **rational basis test**. Under this test, the courts will uphold government regulation as long as there is a justifiable reason for the law. This standard permits much of the government regulation of business. For example, providing government subsidies to farmers but not to those in other occupations is permissible.

Due Process Clause

The Fifth and Fourteenth Amendments to the U.S. Constitution both contain **Due Process Clauses**. These clauses provide that no person shall be deprived of "life, liberty, or property" without due process of the law. The Due Process Clause of the Fifth Amendment applies to federal government action; that of the Fourteenth Amendment applies to state and local government action. It is important to understand that the government is not prohibited from taking a person's life, liberty, or property. However, the government must follow due process to do so. There are two categories of due process: *substantive* and *procedural*.

Substantive Due Process The **substantive due process** category of due process requires that government statutes, ordinances, regulations, or other laws be clear on their face and not overly broad in scope. The test of whether substantive due process is met is whether a "reasonable person" could understand the law to be able to comply with it. Laws that do not meet this test are declared *void for vagueness*. Suppose, for example, that a city ordinance made it illegal for persons to wear "clothes of the opposite sex." Such an ordinance would be held unconstitutional as void for vagueness because a reasonable person could not clearly determine whether his or her conduct violates the law.

Procedural Due Process The **procedural due process** form of due process requires that the government give a person proper *notice* and *hearing* of legal action before that person is deprived of his or her life, liberty, or property. For example, if the federal government or a state government brings a criminal lawsuit against a defendant, the government must notify the person of its intent (by charging the defendant with a crime) and provide the defendant with a proper hearing (a trial). If the government wants to take a person's home by **eminent domain** to build a highway, the government must (1) give the homeowner sufficient notice of its intention and (2) provide a hearing. Under the **Just Compensation Clause** of the Fifth Amendment, the government must pay the owner just compensation for taking the property. Often times, a lawsuit is brought for a court to determine just compensation.

Concept Summary   Due Process

Type of Due Process	Description
Substantive due process	Requires government laws to be clear and not overly broad. The test is whether a reasonable person could understand the law.
Procedural due process	Requires the government to give a person proper notice and hearing before depriving that person of his or her life, liberty, or property.

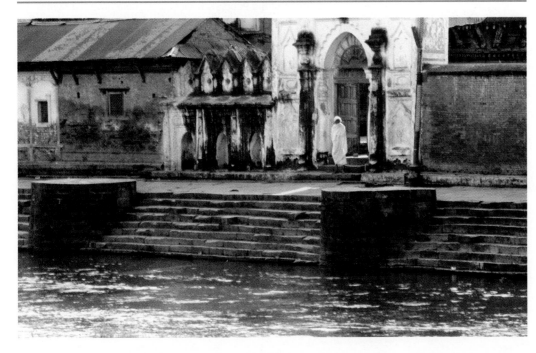

Nepal. Many countries of the world are not democracies like the United States. The Kingdom of Nepal, for example, is a monarchy.

The Privileges and Immunities Clause

The purpose of the U.S. Constitution is to promote nationalism. If the states were permitted to enact laws that favored their residents over out-of-state residents, the concept of nationalism would be defeated. Both Article IV of the Constitution and the Fourteenth Amendment contain **Privileges and Immunities Clause** that prohibit states from enacting laws that unduly discriminate in favor of their residents. For example, a state cannot enact a law that prevents residents of other states from owning property or businesses in that state. Only invidious discrimination is prohibited. Thus, state universities are permitted to charge out-of-state residents higher tuition than in-state residents. Note that this clause applies only to citizens; it does not protect corporations.

International Law

Constitution of the People's Republic of China

The Fundamental Rights and Duties of Citizens

Article 33

All citizens of the People's Republic of China are equal before the law.

Article 34

All citizens of the People's Republic of China who have reached the age of 18 have the right to vote and stand for election, regardless of ethnic status, race, sex, occupation, family background, religious belief, education, property status or length of residence, except persons deprived of political rights according to law.

Article 35

Citizens of the People's Republic of China enjoy freedom of speech, of the press, of assembly, of association, of procession and of demonstration.

Article 36

Citizens of the People's Republic of China enjoy freedom of religious belief. No state organ, public organization or individual may compel citizens to believe in, or not to believe in, any religion; nor may they discriminate against citizens who believe in, or do not believe in, any religion.

Article 41

Citizens of the People's Republic of China have the right to criticize and make suggestions regarding any state organ or functionary.

Article 48

Women in the People's Republic of China enjoy equal rights with men in all spheres of life, in political, economic, cultural, social and family life. ■

Chapter Summary

Constitution of the United States of America, p. 25

The U.S. Constitution

The Constitution consists of 7 articles and 26 amendments. It establishes the three branches of the federal government, enumerates their powers, and provides important guarantees of individual freedom. The Constitution was ratified by the states in 1788.

Basic Constitutional Concepts

1. ***Federalism.*** The Constitution created the federal government. The federal government and the 50 state governments and Washington, D.C. share powers in this country.

2. ***Delegated powers.*** When the states ratified the Constitution, they delegated certain powers to the federal government. These are called *enumerated powers.*

3. ***Reserved powers.*** Those powers not granted to the federal government by the Constitution are reserved to the states.

4. ***Separation of powers.*** Each branch of the federal government has separate powers. These powers are:

   a. Legislative branch—power to make the law.

   b. Executive branch—power to enforce the law.

   c. Judicial branch—power to interpret the law.

5. ***Checks and balances.*** Certain checks and balances are built into the Constitution to ensure that no one branch of the federal government becomes too powerful.

Supremacy Clause, p. 27

Supremacy Clause

This clause stipulates that the U.S. Constitution, treaties, and federal law (statutes and regulations) are the *supreme law of the land.* State or local laws that conflict with valid federal law are unconstitutional. This is called the *preemption doctrine.*

Commerce Clause, p. 28

Commerce Clause

1. ***Commerce Clause.*** This clause authorizes the federal government to regulate commerce with foreign nations, among the states, and with Indian tribes.

2. ***Interstate commerce.*** Under the broad *effects test*, the federal government may regulate any activity (even intrastate commerce) that *affects* interstate commerce.

3. ***Undue burden on interstate commerce.*** Any state or local law that causes an undue burden on interstate commerce is unconstitutional as a violation of the Commerce Clause.

Bill of Rights, p. 30

The Bill of Rights

The Bill of Rights consists of the first 10 amendments to the Constitution, which establish basic individual rights. The Bill of Rights was ratified in 1791.

Freedom of Speech

1. ***Freedom of Speech Clause.*** A clause of the First Amendment which guarantees that the government shall not infringe on a person's right to speak. Protects oral, written, and symbolic speech. This right is not absolute—that is, some speech is not protected and other speech is granted only limited protection.

2. ***Fully protected speech.*** Speech that cannot be prohibited or regulated by the government.

3. ***Limited protected speech.*** Types of speech that are granted only limited protection under the Freedom of Speech Clause—that is, they are subject to governmental *time, place, and manner restrictions*:

   a. Offensive speech

   b. Commercial speech

4. ***Unprotected speech.*** Speech that is not protected by the Freedom of Speech Clause:

   a. Dangerous speech

    b. Fighting words

    c. Speech that advocates the violent overthrow of the government

    d. Defamatory language

    e. Child pornography

    f. Obscene speech

Freedom of Religion

There are two religion clauses in the First Amendment. They are:

1. *Establishment Clause.* Prohibits the government from establishing a state religion or promoting religion.

2. *Free Exercise Clause.* Prohibits the government from interfering with the free exercise of religion. This right is not absolute: for example, human sacrifices are forbidden.

Other Constitutional Clauses, p. 36

Equal Protection Clause

Equal Protection Clause. Prohibits the government from enacting laws that classify and treat "similarly situated" persons differently. This standard is not absolute and the government can treat persons differently in certain situations. The U.S. Supreme Court has applied the following tests to determine if the Equal Protection Clause has been violated:

1. *Strict scrutiny test.* Applies to *suspect classes* (e.g., race, national origin).

2. *Intermediate scrutiny test.* Applies to other *protected classes* (e.g., sex, age).

3. *Rational basis test.* Applies to government classifications that do not involve a suspect or protected class.

Due Process Clause

Due Process Clause. This clause provides that no person shall be deprived of "life, liberty, or property" without due process. There are two categories of due process:

1. *Substantive due process.* Requires that laws be clear on their face and not overly broad in scope. Laws that do not meet this test are *void for vagueness*.

2. *Procedural due process.* Requires that the government give a person proper *notice* and *hearing* before that person is deprived of his or her life, liberty, or property. An owner must be paid *just compensation* if the government takes his or her property.

Privileges and Immunities Clause

This clause prohibits states from enacting laws that unduly discriminate in favor of their residents over residents of other states.

Internet Exercises and Case Questions
Working the Web Internet Exercises

Activities

Visit **www.infoctr.edu/fwl**, the Web site for the Federal Law Locator. Try the following:

1. Check on the product safety record for selected products at the U.S. Consumer Product Safety Commission site. For example, "CPSC, Burger King Corporation Announce Voluntary Recall of Pokemon Ball."

2. Find and compare the U.S. Constitution to the Washington State Constitution, at **www.access.wa.gov**. How are they similar? How are they different?

3. Locate the Municipal Code for your city. Find the law on loitering in public places. Is it constitutional?

4. Find and review the USA Patriot Act of 2001. Is it constitutional?

Critical Legal Thinking Cases

2.1 Separation of Powers   In 1951, a dispute arose between steel companies and their employees about the terms and conditions that should be included in a new labor contract. At the time, the United States was engaged in a military conflict in Korea that required substantial steel resources from which to make weapons and other military goods. On April 4, 1952, the steelworkers' union gave notice of a nationwide strike called to begin at 12:01 A.M. on April 9. The indispensability of steel as a component in weapons and other war materials led President Dwight D. Eisenhower to believe that the proposed strike would jeopardize the national defense and that governmental seizure of the steel mills was necessary in order to ensure the continued availability of steel. Therefore, a few hours before the strike was to begin, the president issued Executive Order 10340, which directed the secretary of commerce to take possession of most of the steel mills and keep them running. The steel companies obeyed the order under protest and brought proceedings against the president. Was the seizure of the steel mills constitutional? [*Youngstown Co. v. Sawyer, Secretary of Commerce*, 343 U.S. 579, 72 S.Ct. 863, 1952 U.S. Lexis 2625 (1952)]

2.2 Commerce Clause   The Heart of Atlanta Motel, located in the state of Georgia, has 216 rooms available to guests. The motel is readily accessible to interstate highways 75 and 85 and to state highways 23 and 41. The motel solicits patronage from outside the state of Georgia through various national advertising media, including magazines of national circulation, and it maintains more than 50 billboards and highway signs within the state. Approximately 75 percent of the motel's registered guests are from out of state. Congress enacted the Civil Rights Act of 1964, which made it illegal for public accommodations to discriminate against guests based on their race. Prior to that, the Heart of Atlanta Motel had refused to rent rooms to blacks. After the act was passed, it alleged that it intended to continue not to rent rooms to blacks. The owner of the motel brought an action to have the Civil Rights Act of 1964 declared unconstitutional, alleging that Congress, in passing the act, had exceeded its powers to regulate commerce under the Commerce Clause of the U.S. Constitution. Who wins? [*Heart of Atlanta Motel v. United States*, 379 U.S. 241, 85 S.Ct. 348, 1964 U.S. Lexis 2187 (1964)]

2.3 Commerce and Supremacy Clauses   In 1972, Congress enacted a federal statute, called the Ports and Waterways Safety Act, that established uniform standards for the operation of boats on inland waterways in the United States. The act coordinated its provisions with those of foreign countries so that there was a uniform body of international rules that applied to vessels that traveled between countries. Pursuant to the act, a federal rule was adopted that regulated the design, length, and size of oil tankers, some of which traveled the waters of the Puget Sound area in the state of Washington. Oil tankers from various places entered Puget Sound to bring crude oil to refineries located in Washington. In 1975, the state of Washington enacted a statute that established different designs, smaller lengths, and smaller sizes for oil tankers serving Puget Sound than allowed by the federal law. Oil tankers used by the Atlantic Richfield Company (ARCO) to bring oil into Puget Sound met the federal standards but not the state standards. ARCO sued to have the state statute declared unconstitutional. Who wins? [*Ray, Governor of Washington v. Atlantic Richfield Co.*, 435 U.S. 151, 98 S.Ct. 988, 1978 U.S. Lexis 18 (1978)]

2.4 Undue Burden on Interstate Commerce   Most trucking firms, including Consolidated Freightways Corporation, use 65-foot-long "double" trailer trucks to ship commodities on the highway system across the United States. Almost all states permit these vehicles on their highways. The federal government does not regulate the length of trucks that can use the nation's highways. The state of Iowa enacted a statute that restricts the length of trucks that can use highways in the state to 55 feet. This means that if Consolidated wants to move goods through Iowa it must either use smaller trucks or detach the double trailers and shuttle them through the state separately. Its only other alternative is to divert its 65-foot doubles around Iowa. Consolidated filed suit against Iowa, alleging that the state statute is unconstitutional. Is it? [*Kassel v. Consolidated Freightways Corporation*, 450 U.S. 662, 101 S.Ct. 1309, 1981 U.S. Lexis 17 (1981)]

2.5 Privileges and Immunities Clause   During the 1970s, a period of a booming economy in Alaska, many residents of other states moved there in search of work. Construction work on the Trans-Alaska Pipeline was a major source of employment. In 1972, the Alaska legislature enacted an act titled the "Local Hire" Statute. This act required employers to hire Alaska residents in preference to nonresidents. Is this statute constitutional? [*Hicklin v. Orbeck, Commissioner of the Department of Labor of Alaska*, 437 U.S. 518, 98 S.Ct. 2482, 1978 U.S. Lexis 36 (1978)]

2.6 Commercial Speech   The city of San Diego, California, enacted a city zoning ordinance that prohibited outdoor advertising display signs—including billboards. On-site signs at a business location were exempted from this rule. The city based the restriction on traffic safety and aesthetics. Metromedia, Inc., a company that is in the business of leasing commercial billboards to advertisers, sued the city of San Diego, alleging that the zoning ordinance is unconstitutional. Is it? [*Metromedia, Inc. v. City of San Diego*, 453 U.S. 490, 101 S.Ct. 2882, 1981 U.S. Lexis 50 (1981)]

2.7 Substantive Due Process   On February 20, 1978, the village of Hoffman Estates, Illinois, enacted an ordinance regulating drug paraphernalia. The ordinance made it unlawful for any person "to sell any items, effect, paraphernalia, accessory or thing which is designed or marketed for use with illegal cannabis or drugs as defined by Illinois Revised Statutes, without obtaining a license therefore." The license fee was $150. A violation was subject to a fine of not more than $500. The Flipside, a retail store located in the village, sold a variety of merchandise, including smoking accessories, clamps, roach clips, scales, water pipes, vials, cigarette rolling papers, and other items. On May 30, 1978, instead of applying for a license, Flipside filed a lawsuit against the village, alleging that the ordinance was unconstitutional as a violation of substantive due process because it was overly broad and vague. Who wins? [*Village of Hoffman Estates v. Flipside, Hoffman Estates, Inc.*, 455 U.S. 489, 102 S.Ct. 1186, 1982 U.S. Lexis 78 (1982)]

2.8 Equal Protection Clause The state of Alabama enacted a statute that imposed a tax on premiums earned by insurance companies. The statute imposed a 1 percent tax on domestic insurance companies (i.e., insurance companies that were incorporated in Alabama and had their principal office in the state). The statute imposed a 4 percent tax on the premiums earned by out-of-state insurance companies that sold insurance in Alabama. Out-of-state insurance companies could reduce the premium tax by 1 percent by investing at least 10 percent of their assets in Alabama. Domestic insurance companies did not have to invest any of their assets in Alabama. Metropolitan Life Insurance Company, an out-of-state insurance company, sued the state of Alabama, alleging that the Alabama statute violated the Equal Protection Clause of the U.S. Constitution. Who wins? [*Metropolitan Life Insurance Co. v. Ward, Commissioner of Insurance of Alabama*, 470 U.S. 869, 105 S.Ct. 1676, 1985 U.S. Lexis 80 (1985)]

Business Ethics Cases

2.9 Business Ethics The Raiders are a professional football team and a National Football League (NFL) franchise. Each NFL franchise is independently owned. Al Davis was an owner and the managing general partner of the Raiders. The NFL establishes schedules, negotiates television contracts, and otherwise promotes NFL football, including conducting the Super Bowl each year. The Raiders play home and away games against other NFL teams.

Up until 1982, the Raiders played their home games in Oakland, California. The owners of the Raiders decided to move the team from Oakland to Los Angeles, California, to take advantage of the greater seating capacity of the Los Angeles Coliseum, the larger television market of Los Angeles, and other economic reasons. The renamed team was to be known as the Los Angeles Raiders. The city of Oakland brought an eminent domain proceeding in court to acquire the Raiders as a city-owned team. Can the city of Oakland acquire the Raiders through eminent domain? Is it socially responsible for a professional sports team to move to another location? [*City of Oakland,*

California v. Oakland Raiders, 174 C.A.3d 414, 220 Cal. Rptr. 153, 1985 Cal. App. Lexis 2751 (Cal. App. 1985)]

2.10 Business Ethics In 1989, Congress enacted the Flag Protection Act, which made it a crime to knowingly mutilate, deface, physically defile, burn, or trample the U.S. flag. The law provided for fines and up to one year in prison upon conviction [18 U.S.C. § 700]. Certain individuals set fire to several U.S. flags on the steps of the U.S. Capitol in Washington, DC, to protest various aspects of the federal government's foreign and domestic policy. In a separate incident, other individuals set fire to a U.S. flag to protest the act's passage. All of these individuals were prosecuted for violating the act. The district courts held the act unconstitutional, in violation of the defendants' First Amendment free speech rights, and dismissed the charges. The government appealed to the U.S. Supreme Court, which consolidated the two cases. Who wins? Does the flag burner exhibit any morals? [*United States v. Eichman*, 496 U.S. 310, 110 S.Ct. 2404, 1990 U.S. Lexis 3087 (1990)]

Briefing the Case Writing Assignment

Read Case A.2 in the Case Appendix [*Lee v. Weisman*]. This case is excerpted from the U.S. Supreme Court's opinion. Review and brief the case. In your brief, be sure to answer the following questions.

1. Who are the plaintiff and defendant?

2. What does the Establishment Clause provide?

3. Was the fact that the prayer was nonsectarian important to the Supreme Court's decision?

4. What argument did the dissenting opinion make in support of allowing prayer at high school graduation ceremonies?

5. How close was the vote by the justices in this case?

Endnotes

1. To be elected to Congress, an individual must be a U.S. citizen, either naturally born or granted citizenship. To serve in the Senate, a person must be 30 years of age or older. To serve in the House of Representatives, a person must be 25 years of age or older.

2. To be president, a person must be 35 years of age or older and a natural citizen of the United States. By amendment to the Constitution (Amendment XXII), a person can serve only two full terms as president.

3. Federal court judges and justices are appointed by the president with the consent of the Senate.

4. The principle that the U.S. Supreme Court is the final arbiter of the U.S. Constitution evolved from *Marbury v. Madison*, 1 Cranch 137 (1803). In that case, the Supreme Court held that a judiciary statute enacted by Congress was unconstitutional.

5. Article VI, Section 2.

6. Article I, Section 8, clause 3.

7. 317 U.S. III., 63 S.Ct. 82, 1942 U.S. Lexis 1046 (1942).

8. 514 U.S. 549, 115 S.Ct. 1624, 1995 U.S. Lexis 3039 (1995).

9. 425 U.S. 748, 96 S.Ct. 1817, 1976 U.S. Lexis 55 (1976).

10. *Chaplinsky v. New Hampshire*, 315 U.S. 568, 62 S.Ct. 766, 1942 U.S. Lexis 851 (1942).

11. *Brandenburg v. Ohio*, 395 U.S. 444, 89 S.Ct. 1827, 1969 U.S. Lexis 1367 (1969).

12. *Beauharnais v. Illinois*, 343 U.S. 250, 72 S.Ct. 725, 1952 U.S. Lexis 2799 (1952).

13. *New York v. Ferber*, 458 U.S. 747, 102 S.Ct. 3348, 1982 U.S. Lexis 12 (1982).

14. *Roth v. United States*, 354 U.S. 476, 77 S.Ct. 1304, 1957 U.S. Lexis 587 (1957).

15. Justice Stewart in *Jacobellis v. Ohio*, 378 U.S. 184, 84 S.Ct. 1676, 1964 U.S. Lexis 822 (1963).

16. 413 U.S. 15, 93 S.Ct. 2607, 1973 U.S. Lexis 149 (1973).

17. *Wallace v. Jaffree*, 472 U.S. 38, 105 S.Ct. 2479, 1985 U.S. Lexis 91 (1985).

18. 508 U.S. 520, 113 S.Ct. 2217, 1993 U.S. Lexis 4022 (1993).

Traditional, Alternative, and E-Commerce Dispute Resolution

> " I was never ruined but twice; once when I lost a lawsuit, and once when I won one. "
>
> —Voltaire

Chapter Objectives

After studying this chapter, you should be able to:

1. Describe and compare the state court systems and the federal court system.
2. Explain subject matter jurisdiction and venue of federal and state courts.
3. Describe the pretrial litigation process.
4. Describe how a case proceeds through trial and how a trial court decision is appealed.
5. Explain the use of arbitration and other nonjudicial methods of alternative dispute resolution.

Chapter Contents

- The State Court Systems
- The Federal Court System
- The Jurisdiction and Venue of Courts
- The Pretrial Litigation Process
- The Trial
- The Appeal
- Alternative Dispute Resolution

There are two major court systems in the United States: (1) the federal court system and (2) the court systems of the 50 states and the District of Columbia. Each of these systems has jurisdiction to hear different types of lawsuits. The process of bringing, maintaining, and defending a lawsuit is called **litigation**. Litigation is a difficult, time-consuming, and costly process that must comply with complex procedural rules. Although it is not required, most parties employ a lawyer to represent them when they are involved in a lawsuit.

Several forms of *nonjudicial* dispute resolution have developed in response to the expense and difficulty of bringing a lawsuit. These methods, collectively called **alternative dispute resolution**, are being used more and more often to resolve commercial and e-commerce disputes.

This chapter discusses the various court systems, the jurisdiction of courts to hear and decide cases, the litigation process, and alternative dispute resolution.

The State Court Systems

Each state and the District of Columbia has a separate court system. Most state court systems include the following: *limited-jurisdiction trial courts, general-jurisdiction trial courts, intermediate appellate courts*, and a *supreme court*.

Limited-Jurisdiction Trial Courts

State **limited-jurisdiction trial courts**, which are sometimes referred to as **inferior trial courts**, hear matters of a specialized or limited nature. In many states, traffic courts, juvenile courts, justice-of-the-peace courts, probate courts, family law courts, and courts that hear misdemeanor criminal law cases and civil cases involving lawsuits under a certain dollar amount are examples of such courts. Because these courts are trial courts, evidence can be introduced and testimony given. Most limited-jurisdiction courts keep records of their proceedings. Their decisions can usually be appealed to a general-jurisdiction court or an appellate court.

Many states have also created **small claims courts** to hear civil cases involving small dollar amounts (e.g., $5,000 or less). Generally, the parties must appear individually and cannot have lawyers represent them. The decisions of small claims courts are often appealable to general-jurisdiction trial courts or appellate courts.

General-Jurisdiction Trial Courts

Every state has a **general-jurisdiction trial court**. These courts are often referred to as **courts of record** because the testimony and evidence at trial are recorded and stored for future reference. They hear cases that are not within the jurisdiction of limited-jurisdiction trial courts, such as felonies, civil cases over a certain dollar amount, and so on. Some states divide their general-jurisdiction courts into two divisions, one for criminal cases and another for civil cases. Evidence and testimony are given at general-jurisdiction trial courts. The decision handed down by these courts are appealable to an intermediate appellate court or the state supreme court, depending on the circumstances.

Intermediate Appellate Courts

In many states, **intermediate appellate courts** (also called **appellate courts** or **courts of appeal**) hear appeals from trial courts. They review the trial court record to determine if there have been any errors at trial that would require reversal or modification of the trial court's decision. Thus, the appellate court reviews either pertinent parts or the whole trial court record from the lower court. No new evidence or testimony is permitted. The parties usually file legal *briefs* with the appellate court, stating the law and facts that support their positions. Appellate courts usually grant a brief oral hearing to the parties. Appellate court decisions are appealable to the state's highest court. In sparsely populated states that do not have an intermediate appellate court, trial court decisions can be appealed directly to the state's highest court.

Highest State Court

Each state has a highest court in its court system. Most states call this highest court the **supreme court**. The function of a state supreme court is to hear appeals from intermediate state courts and certain trial courts. No new evidence or testimony is heard. The parties usually submit pertinent parts of or the entire lower court record for review. The parties also submit legal briefs to the court and are usually granted a brief oral hearing. Decisions of state supreme courts are final, unless a question of law is involved that is appealable to the U.S. Supreme Court.

Exhibit 3.1 portrays a typical state court system.

Exhibit 3.1

A Typical State Court System

Contemporary Environment
Cost–Benefit Analysis of a Lawsuit

In most civil lawsuits, each party is responsible for paying its own attorneys' fees, whether the party wins or loses. This is called the "American rule." The court can award lawyers' fees to the winning party if a statute so provides, the parties have so agreed (e.g., in a contract), or the losing party has acted maliciously or pursued a frivolous case.

An attorney in a civil or criminal lawsuit can represent him or her client on an hourly or project fee basis. Hourly fees usually range from $100 to $500 per hour, depending on the type of case, the expertise of the lawyer, and the locality of the lawsuit. In a civil lawsuit, plaintiffs' lawyers often work under a *contingency fee arrangement* where the lawyer receives a percentage of the amount recovered for the plaintiff upon winning or settling the case. Contingency fees normally range from 20 to 50 percent of the award or settlement, with the average being about 35 percent. Lawyers for defendants in civil lawsuits are normally paid on an hourly basis.

The choice of whether to bring or defend a lawsuit should be analyzed like any other business decision. This includes perform-

ing a **cost–benefit analysis** of the lawsuit. For the plaintiff, it may be wise not to sue. For the defendant, it may be wise to settle. The following factors should be considered in deciding whether to bring or settle a lawsuit:

- The probability of winning or losing.
- The amount of money to be won or lost.
- Lawyers' fees and other costs of litigation.
- Loss of time by managers and other personnel.
- The long-term effects on the relationship and reputation of the parties.
- The amount of prejudgment interest provided by law.
- The aggravation and psychological costs associated with a lawsuit.
- The unpredictability of the legal system and the possibility of error.
- Other factors peculiar to the parties and lawsuit. ■

The Federal Court System

Pieces of evidence, each by itself insufficient, may together constitute a significant whole and justify by their combined effect a conclusion.

Lord Wright
Grant V. Australian Knitting Mills, Ltd.
(1936)

Article III of the U.S. Constitution provides that the federal government's judicial power is vested in one "Supreme Court." This court is the **U.S. Supreme Court**. The Constitution also authorized Congress to establish "inferior" federal courts. Pursuant to this power, Congress has established special federal courts, the U.S. district courts, and the U.S. courts of appeal. Federal judges are appointed for life by the president, with the advice and consent of the Senate (except bankruptcy court judges, who are appointed for 14-year terms).

Supreme Court of the United States. The highest court in the land is the Supreme Court of the United States, located in Washington, D.C. The Supreme Court's decisions are precedent for all the other courts in the country. In *Bush v. Gore* 531 U.S. 98 (2000) the Supreme Court decided that George W. Bush had been elected President of the United States.

Special Federal Courts

The **special federal courts** established by Congress have limited jurisdiction. They include the following:

- **U.S. tax court.** Hears cases involving federal tax laws.
- **U.S. claims court.** Hears cases brought against the United States.
- **U.S. Court of International Trade.** Hears cases involving tariffs and international commercial disputes.
- **U.S. bankruptcy court.** Hears cases involving federal bankruptcy laws.

U.S. District Courts

The **U.S. district courts** are the federal court system's trail courts of general jurisdiction. There is at least one federal district court in each state and the District of Columbia, although heavily populated states have more than one district court. The geographical area served by each court is referred to as a *district*. There are presently 96 federal district courts. The federal district courts are empowered to impanel juries, receive evidence, hear testimony, and decide cases. Most federal cases originate in federal district courts.

U.S. Courts of Appeals

The **U.S. courts of appeals** are the federal court system's intermediate appellate courts. There are 13 circuits in the federal court system. The first 12 are geographical. Eleven are designated by a number, such as the "First Circuit," "Second Circuit," and so on. The geographical area served by each court is referred to as a *circuit*. The 12th circuit court is located in Washington, DC, and is called the "District of Columbia Circuit."

As an appellate court, each of these courts hears appeals from the district courts located in its circuit as well as from certain special courts and federal administrative agencies. The court reviews the record of the lower court or administrative agency proceedings to determine if there has been any error that would warrant reversal or modification of the lower court decision. No new evidence or testimony is heard. The parties file legal briefs with the court and are given a short oral hearing. Appeals are usually heard by a three-judge panel. After a decision is rendered by the three-judge panel, a petitioner can request a review *en banc* by the full court.

The 13th court of appeals was created by Congress in 1982. It is called the **Court of Appeals for the Federal Circuit** and is located in Washington, DC.[1] This court has special appellate jurisdiction to review the decision of the Claims Court, the Patent and Trademark Office, and the Court of International Trade. This court was created to provide uniformity in the application of federal law in certain areas, particularly patent law.

Exhibit 3.2 shows the 13 federal circuit courts of appeals.

The U.S. Supreme Court

The highest court in the land is the **Supreme Court of the United States**, located in Washington, DC. The Court is composed of nine justices who are nominated by the president and confirmed by the Senate. The president appoints one justice as *chief justice*, who is responsible for the administration of the Supreme Court. The other eight justices are *associate justices*.

Exhibit 3.2

The 13 Federal Judicial Circuits

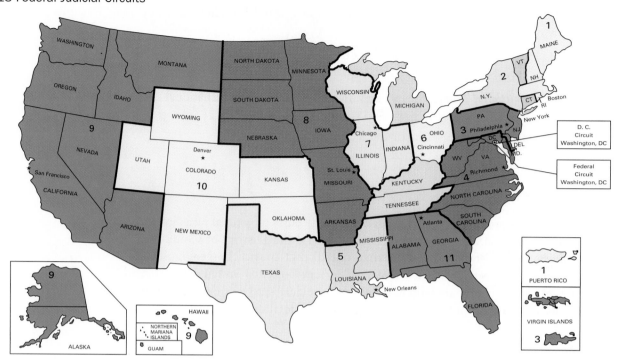

The Supreme Court, which is an appellate court, hears appeals from federal circuit courts of appeals and, under certain circumstances, from federal district courts, special federal courts, and the highest state courts. No new evidence or testimony is heard. As with other appellate courts, the lower court record is reviewed to determine whether there has been an error that warrants a reversal or modification of the decision. Legal briefs are filed, and the parties are granted a brief oral hearing. The Supreme Court's decision is final.

The federal court system is illustrated in Exhibit 3.3.

Decisions by the U.S. Supreme Court

The U.S. Constitution gives Congress the authority to establish rules for the appellate review of cases by the Supreme Court, except in the rare case where mandatory review is required. Congress has given the Supreme Court discretion to decide what cases it will hear.[2]

A petitioner must file a **petition for certiorari** asking the Supreme Court to hear the case. If the Court decides to review a case, it will issue a **writ of certiorari**. Because the Court issues only about 100 opinions each year, writs are granted only in cases involving constitutional and other important issues.

Each justice of the Supreme Court, including the chief justice, has an equal vote. The Supreme Court can issue the following types of decisions:

- **Unanimous decision.** If all of the justices voting agree as to the outcome and reasoning used to decide a case, it is a unanimous opinion. Unanimous decisions are precedent for later cases. For example, suppose all nine justices hear a case and all nine agree to the outcome (the petitioner wins) and the reason why (the Equal Protection Clause of the U.S. Constitution had been violated); this is a unanimous decision. This unanimous decision becomes precedent for later cases.

Exhibit 3.3

The Federal Court System

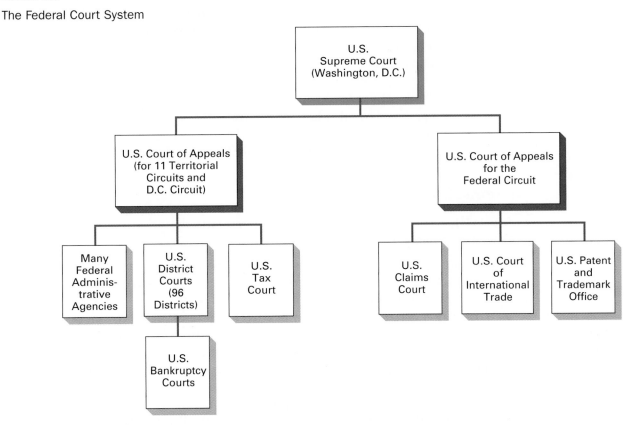

- *Majority decision.* If a majority of the justices agree as to the outcome and reasoning used to decide a case, it is a majority opinion. Majority decisions are precedent for later cases. For example, if all nine justices hear a case, and five of them agree as to the outcome (the petitioner wins) and all of these five justices agree to the same reason why (The Equal Protection Clause of the U.S. Constitution has been violated), it is a majority opinion. The majority opinion becomes precedent for later cases and has the same force of law as a unanimous decision. The remaining four justices' vote for the respondent has no legal effect whatsoever. Remember: A majority decision occurs if five, six, seven, or eight justices vote for the same outcome for the same reason.

- *Plurality decision.* If a majority of the justices agree as to the outcome of a case, but not as to the reasoning for reaching the outcome, it is a plurality opinion. A plurality decision settles the case but is not precedent for later cases. For example, if all nine justices hear a case, and five of them agree as to the outcome (the petitioner wins), but not all of these five agree to the reason why—let's suppose three base their vote on a violation of the Equal Protection Clause and two base their vote on a violation of the Freedom of Speech Clause of the U.S. Constitution—this is a plurality decision. Five justices have agreed to the same outcome, but those five have not agreed to the same reason. The petitioner wins his or her case, but the decision is not precedent for later cases. The remaining four justices' vote for the respondent has no legal effect whatsoever.

- *Tie decision.* Sometimes the Supreme Court sits without all nine justices being present. This could happen because of illness, conflict of interest, or a justice not having been confirmed to fill a vacant seat on the Court. If there is a tie vote, the lower court decision is affirmed. Such votes are not precedent for later cases. For example,

Sancho: But if this is hell, why do we see no lawyers?

Clarindo: They won't receive them, lest they bring lawsuits here.

Sancho: If there are no lawsuits here, hell's not so bad.

Lope de Vega
The Star of Seville, Act 3, Scene 2

suppose a petitioner won her case at the court of appeals. At the U.S. Supreme Court, only eight justices hear the case. Suppose four justices vote for the petitioner and four justices vote for the respondent. This is a tie vote. The petitioner remains the winner because she won at the court of appeals. The decision of the Supreme Court sets no precedent for later cases.

Concurring and Dissenting Opinions A justice who agrees with the outcome of a case, but not the reason proffered by other justices, can issue a *concurring opinion* that sets forth his or her reasons for deciding the case. A justice who does not agree with a decision can file a *dissenting opinion* that sets forth the reasons for his or her dissent.

Jurisdiction of Federal Courts

Article III, Section 2 of the U.S. Constitution sets forth the jurisdiction of federal courts. Federal courts have *limited jurisdiction* to hear cases involving:

1. *Federal questions.* **Federal cases** are cases arising under the U.S. Constitution, treaties, and federal statutes and regulations. There is no dollar-amount limit on federal question cases that can be brought in federal court.[3]
2. *Diversity of citizenship.* **Diversity of citizenship** cases occur between (a) citizens of different states, and (b) a citizen of a state and a citizen or subject of a foreign country. A corporation is considered to be a citizen of the state in which it is incorporated and in which it has its principal place of business. The reason for providing diversity of citizenship jurisdiction was to prevent state court bias against nonresidents. The federal court must apply the appropriate state's law in deciding the case. The dollar amount of the controversy must exceed $75,000.[4] If this requirement is not met, action must be brought in the appropriate state court.

Federal courts have **exclusive jurisdiction** to hear cases involving federal crimes, antitrust, bankruptcy, patent and copyright cases, suits against the United States, and most admiralty cases. State courts cannot hear these cases.

State and federal courts have **concurrent jurisdiction** to hear cases involving diversity of citizenship and federal questions over which federal courts do not have exclusive juris-

Courthouse, St. Louis Missouri.
State Courts hear and decide the majority of cases in this country.

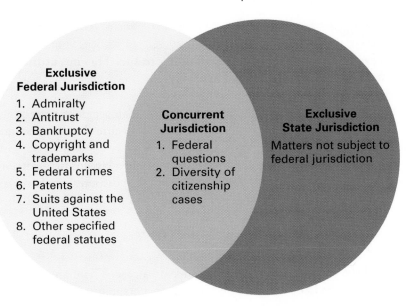

Exhibit 3.4
Jurisdiction of Federal and State Courts

Exclusive Federal Jurisdiction

1. Admiralty
2. Antitrust
3. Bankruptcy
4. Copyright and trademarks
5. Federal crimes
6. Patents
7. Suits against the United States
8. Other specified federal statutes

Concurrent Jurisdiction

1. Federal questions
2. Diversity of citizenship cases

Exclusive State Jurisdiction

Matters not subject to federal jurisdiction

diction (e.g., cases involving federal securities laws). If a case involving concurrent jurisdiction is brought by a plaintiff in state court, the defendant can remove the case to federal court. If a case does not qualify to be brought in federal court, it must be brought in the appropriate state court.

Exhibit 3.4 illustrates the jurisdiction of federal and state courts.

Contemporary Environment

I'll Take You to the U.S. Supreme Court!–Not!

In reality, the chance of ever having your case heard by the highest court is slim to none. Each year, more than 7,000 petitioners ask the Supreme Court to hear their cases. These petitioners usually pay big law firms from $30,000 to $100,000 or more to write the appeal petition. In recent years, the Supreme Court has accepted only fewer than 100 of these cases for full review each term.

Each of the nine Supreme Court justices has three law clerks—recent law school graduates usually chosen from the elite law schools across the country—who assist them. The justices rarely read the appellate petitions but instead delegate this task to their law clerks. A clerk then writes a short memorandum, discussing the key issues raised by the appeal, and recommends to the justices whether they should grant or deny a review. The justices meet once a week to discuss what cases merit review. The votes of four justices are necessary to grant an appeal and schedule an oral argument before the Court ("rule of four"). Written opinions by the justices are usually issued many months later.

So what does it take to win a review by the Supreme Court? The U.S. Supreme Court usually decides to hear cases involving major constitutional questions such as freedom of speech, freedom of religion, equal protection, and due process. The Court, therefore, rarely decides day-to-day legal issues such as breach of contract, tort liability, or corporations law unless they involve more important constitutional or federal law questions. So the next time you hear someone say, "I'll take you to the U.S. Supreme Court!" just say, "Not!" ∎

The Jurisdiction and Venue of Courts

Not every court has the authority to hear all types of cases. First, to bring a lawsuit in a court, the plaintiff must have *standing to sue*. In addition, the court must have *jurisdiction* to hear the case, and the case must be brought in the proper *venue*. These topics are discussed in the following paragraphs.

Standing to Sue

To bring a lawsuit, a plaintiff must have **standing to sue**. This means the plaintiff must have some stake in the outcome of the lawsuit.

Consider This Example   Linda's friend Jon is injured in an accident caused by Emily. Jon refuses to sue. Linda cannot sue Emily on Jon's behalf because she does not have an interest in the result of the case.

A few states now permit investors to invest money in a lawsuit for a percentage return of any award of judgment. Courts hear and decide actual disputes involving specific controversies. Hypothetical questions will not be heard, and trivial lawsuits will be dismissed.

Jurisdiction

A court must have **jurisdiction** to hear and decide a case. There are two types of jurisdiction: (1) subject matter jurisdiction and (2) in personam, in rem, or quasi in rem jurisdiction.

1. ***Subject matter jurisdiction.*** To hear and decide a case, a court must have **subject matter jurisdiction** over the subject matter of the case. Some courts have only limited jurisdiction. For example, federal courts have jurisdiction to hear only certain types of cases (as discussed later in this chapter). Certain state courts, such as probate courts and small claims courts, can hear only designated types of cases. If a court does not have subject matter jurisdiction, it cannot hear the case.
2. ***In personam, in rem, and quasi in rem jurisdiction.*** Jurisdiction over the person is called **in personam jurisdiction**, or **personal jurisdiction**. A *plaintiff*, by filing a lawsuit with a court, gives the court in personam jurisdiction over himself or herself. The court must also have in personam jurisdiction over the *defendant*, which is usually obtained by having a summons served to that person within the territorial boundaries of the state (i.e., **service of process**). Service of process is usually accomplished by personal service of the summons and complaint on the defendant. If this is not possible, alternative forms of notice, such as mailing of the summons or publication of a notice in a newspaper, may be permitted. A corporation is subject to personal jurisdiction in the state in which it is incorporated, has its principal office, and is doing business. A party who disputes the jurisdiction of a court can make a *special appearance* in that court to argue against imposition of jurisdiction. Service of process is not permitted during such an appearance.

A court may have jurisdiction to hear and decide a case because it has jurisdiction over the property of the lawsuit. This is called **in rem jurisdiction** ("jurisdiction over the thing"). For example, a state court would have jurisdiction to hear a dispute over the ownership of a piece of real estate located within the state. This is so even if one or more of the disputing parties live in another state or states.

Sometimes a plaintiff who obtains a judgment against a defendant in one state will try to collect the judgment by attaching property of the defendant that is located in another state. This is permitted under **quasi in rem**, or **attachment, jurisdiction**.[5]

Long-Arm Statutes In most states, a state court can obtain jurisdiction over persons and businesses located in another state or country through the state's **long-arm statute**. These statutes extend a state's jurisdiction to nonresidents who were not served a summons within the state. The nonresident must have had some *minimum contact* with the state.[6] In addition, the maintenance of the suit must uphold the traditional notions of fair play and substantial justice.

The exercise of long-arm jurisdiction is generally permitted over nonresidents who have (1) committed torts within the state (e.g., caused an automobile accident in the state), (2) entered into a contract either in the state or that affects the state (and allegedly breached the contract), or (3) transacted other business in the state that allegedly caused injury to another person.

Parties to a contract may include a **forum-selection clause** that designates a certain court to hear any dispute concerning nonperformance of the contract.

The following case illustrates the application of a forum-selection clause.

U.S. SUPREME COURT CASE

Carnival Cruise Lines, Inc. v. Shute

499 U.S. 585, 111 S.Ct. 1522, 1991 U.S. Lexis 2221 (1991)
Supreme Court of the United States

Case 3.1
Forum-Selection Clause

Background and Facts

Mr. and Mrs. Shute, residents of the state of Washington, purchased passage for a seven-day cruise on the *Tropicale*, a cruise ship operated by Carnival Cruise Lines, Inc. (Carnival). They paid the fare to the travel agent, who forwarded the payment to Carnival's headquarters in Miami, Florida. Carnival prepared the tickets and sent them to the Shutes. Each ticket consisted of five pages, including contract terms. The ticket contained a forum-selection clause that designated the state of Florida as the forum for any lawsuits arising under or in connection with the ticket and cruise. The Shutes boarded the *Tropicale* in Los Angeles, which set sail for Puerto Vallarta, Mexico. While the ship was on its return voyage and in international waters off the Mexican coast, Mrs. Shute was injured when she slipped on a deck mat during a guided tour of the ship's galley. Upon return to Washington, she filed a negligence lawsuit against Carnival in U.S. district court in Washington seeking damages. Carnival filed a motion for summary judgment, contending that the lawsuit could be brought only in a court located in the state of Florida. The district court granted Carnival's motion. The court of appeals reversed, holding that Mrs. Shute could sue Carnival in Washington. Carnival appealed to the U.S. Supreme Court.

Issue

Is the forum-selection clause in the Carnival Cruise Lines ticket enforceable?

Court's Reasoning

The Supreme Court stated that as an initial matter, it did not adopt the determination of the court of appeals that a nonnegotiated forum-selection clause in a form ticket contract is never enforceable simply because it is not the subject of bargaining.

The Supreme Court held that including a reasonable forum clause in a form contract of this kind is permissible for several reasons: (1) A cruise line has a special interest in limiting the forums in which it potentially could be subject to suit. Because a cruise ship typically carries passengers from many locales, it is not unlikely that a mishap on a cruise could subject the cruise line to litigation in several different forums. (2) A clause establishing the forum for dispute resolution has the salutary effect of dispelling any confusion where suits arising from the contract must be brought and defended, sparing litigants the time and expense of pretrial motions to determine the correct forum, and conserving judicial resources that otherwise would be devoted to deciding those motions. (3) That passengers who purchase tickets containing a forum clause like that at issue in this case benefit in the form of reduced fares, reflecting the savings that the cruise line enjoys by limiting the fora in which it may be sued.

Decision and Remedy

The U.S. Supreme Court held that the forum-selection clause in Carnival's ticket is fair and reasonable and therefore enforceable against Mrs. Shute. If she wishes to sue Carnival, she must do so in a court in the state of Florida, not in a court in the state of Washington. The U.S. Supreme Court reversed the decision of the court of appeals.

Case Questions

Critical Legal Thinking Should forum-selection clauses be enforced? Why or why not?

Business Ethics Did Carnival Cruise Lines act ethically by placing the forum-selection clause in its tickets?

Contemporary Business Do forum-selection clauses serve any legitimate business purpose? Explain.

Venue

Venue requires lawsuits to be heard by the court with jurisdiction nearest the location in which the incident occurred or where the parties reside.

Samarkan, Uzbekistan. Each
country has its own national
courts that hear and decide
legal disputes in that country.

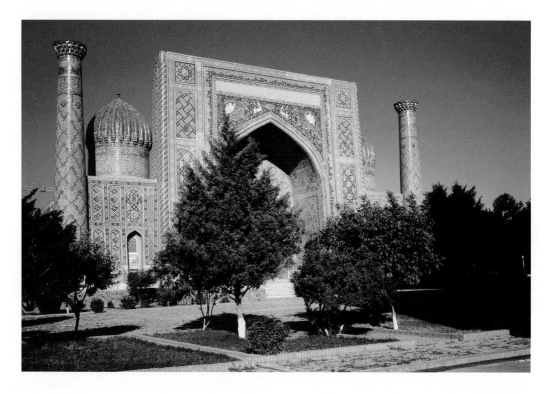

Consider This Example Harry, a Georgia resident, commits a felony crime in Los Angeles County, California. The California Superior Court located in Los Angeles is the proper venue because the crime was committed there, the witnesses are probably from the area, and so on.

Occasionally, pretrial publicity may prejudice jurors located in the proper venue. In such cases, a *change of venue* may be requested so that a more impartial jury can be found. The courts generally frown upon *forum shopping* (i.e., looking for a favorable court without a valid reason).

The Pretrial Litigation Process

The bringing, maintaining, and defense of a lawsuit are generally referred to as the *litigation process*, or **litigation**. The pretrial litigation process can be divided into the following major phases: *pleadings, discovery, dismissals and pretrial judgments*, and *settlement conference*. Each of these phases is discussed in the paragraphs that follow.

The Pleadings

The paperwork that is filed with the court to initiate and respond to a lawsuit is referred to as the **pleadings**. The major pleadings are the *complaint*, the *answer*, the *cross-complaint*, and the *reply*.

Complaint and Summons To initiate a lawsuit, the party who is suing (the **plaintiff**) must file a **complaint** with the proper court. The complaint must name the parties to the lawsuit, allege the ultimate facts and law violated, and contain a "prayer for relief" for a remedy to be awarded by the court. The complaint can be as long as necessary, depending on the case's complexity. A sample complaint appears in Exhibit 3.5.

Exhibit 3.5

A Sample Complaint

In the United States District Court for the District of Idaho

John Doe   Civil No. 2-1005   Plaintiff

      v.   COMPLAINT

Jane Roe

      Defendant

The plaintiff, by and through his attorney, alleges:

1. The plaintiff is a resident of the State of Idaho, the defendant is a resident of the State of Washington, and there is diversity of citizenship between the parties.
2. The amount in controversy exceeds the sum of $75,000, exclusive of interest and costs.
3. On January 10, 2005, plaintiff was exercising reasonable care while walking across the intersection of Sun Valley Road and Main Street, Ketchum, Idaho, when defendant negligently drove her car through a red light at the intersection and struck plaintiff.
4. As a result of the defendant's negligence, plaintiff has incurred medical expenses of $104,000 and suffered severe physical injury and mental distress.

WHEREFORE, plaintiff claims judgment in the amount of $1,000,000, interest at the maximum legal rate, and costs of this action.

By _____
Edward Lawson
Attorney for Plaintiff
100 Main Street
Ketchum, Idaho

Once a complaint has been filed with the court, the court issues a **summons**. A summons is a court order directing the defendant to appear in court and answer the complaint. The complaint and summons are served on the defendant by a sheriff, another government official, or a private process server.

Answer   The defendant must file an **answer** to the plaintiff's complaint. The defendant's answer is filed with the court and served on the plaintiff. In the answer, the defendant admits or denies the allegations contained in the plaintiff's complaint. A judgment will be entered against a defendant who admits all of the allegations in the complaint. The case will proceed if the defendant denies all or some of the allegations. If the defendant does not answer the complaint, a *default judgment* is entered against him or her. A default judgment establishes the defendant's liability. The plaintiff then has only to prove damages.

In addition to answering the complaint, a defendant's answer can assert *affirmative defenses*. For example, if a complaint alleges that the plaintiff was personally injured by the defendant, the defendant's answer could state that he or she acted in self-defense. Another affirmative defense would be an assertion that the plaintiff's lawsuit is barred because the *statute of limitations* (time within which to bring the lawsuit) has expired.

Business Brief

Some complaints in complicated cases exceed 100 pages.

Cross-Complaint and Reply   A defendant who believes that he or she has been injured by the plaintiff can file a **cross-complaint** against the plaintiff in addition to an answer. In the cross-complaint, the defendant (now the *cross-complainant*) sues the plaintiff (now the *cross-defendant*) for damages or some other remedy. The original plaintiff must file a **reply** (answer) to the cross-complaint. The reply, which can include affirmative defenses, must be filed with the court and served on the original defendant.

Intervention and Consolidation If other persons have an interest in a lawsuit, they may **intervene** and become parties to the lawsuit. For instance, a bank that has made a secured loan on a piece of real estate can intervene in a lawsuit between parties who are litigating ownership of the property.

If several plaintiffs have filed separate lawsuits stemming from the same fact situation against the same defendant, the court can **consolidate** the cases into one case if it would not cause undue prejudice to the parties. Suppose, for example, that a commercial airplane crashes, killing and injuring many people. The court could consolidate all of the lawsuits against the defendant airplane company.

Statute of Limitations

A **statute of limitations** establishes the period during which a plaintiff must bring a lawsuit against a defendant. If a lawsuit is not filed within this time period, the plaintiff loses his or her right to sue. A statute of limitations begins to "run" at the time the plaintiff first has the right to sue the defendant (e.g., when the accident happens, when the breach of contract occurs).

Federal and state governments have established statutes of limitations for each type of lawsuit. Most are from one to four years, depending on the type of lawsuit. For example, a one-year statute of limitations is common for ordinary negligence actions. Thus, if on July 1, 2005, Otis negligently causes an automobile accident in which Cha-Yen is injured, Cha-Yen has until July 1, 2006, to bring a negligence lawsuit against Otis. If she waits longer than that, she loses her right to sue him.

In the following case, the court held that the statute of limitations barred the plaintiff's lawsuit.

Norgart v. The Upjohn Company

21 Cal.4th 383, 87 Cal.Rpt. 2nd 453, 1999 Cal. Lexis 5308 (1999)

Supreme Court of California

Case 3.2

Statute of Limitations

Facts and Background

Kristi Norgart McBride lived with her husband in Santa Rosa, California. Kristi suffered from manic-depressive mental illness (now called bipolar disorder). In this disease, the person cycles between manic (ultrahappy, expansive, extroverted) episodes to depressive episodes. The disease is often treated with prescription drugs. In April 1984, Kristi attempted suicide. A psychiatrist prescribed an antianxiety drug. In May 1985, Kristi attempted suicide again by overdosing on drugs. The doctor prescribed Halcion, a hypnotic drug, and added Darvocet-N, a mild narcotic analgesic. On October 16, 1985, after descending into a severe depression, Kristi committed suicide by overdosing on Halcion and Darvocet-N. On October 16, 1991, exactly six years after Kristi's death, Leo and Phyllis Norgart, Kristi's parents, filed a lawsuit against the Upjohn Company, the maker of Halcion, for

wrongful death based on Upjohn's alleged failure to warn of the unreasonable dangers of taking Halcion. The trial court granted Upjohn's motion for summary judgment based on the fact that the one-year statute of limitations for wrongful death actions had run. The court of appeals reversed, and Upjohn appealed to the supreme court of California.

Issue

Is the plaintiff's action for wrongful death barred by the one-year statute of limitations?

Court's Reasoning

The court noted that the statute of limitations has a purpose to protect defendants from the stale claims of dilatory plaintiffs. It has as a related purpose to stimulate plaintiffs to assert fresh claims against defendants in a diligent fashion. The court stated that under the statute of limitations, a plaintiff must bring a cause of action from wrongful death within one year of accrual—that means that the date of accrual of a cause of action for wrongful death is the date of death. The Norgarts had to bring the cause of action for wrongful death within one year of accrual. The court stated, "They did not do so. Pursuant to this rule, the Norgarts were too late, exactly five years too late."

Decision and Remedy

The supreme court of California held that the defendant, the Upjohn Company, was entitled to judgment as a matter of law based on the fact that the one-year statute of limitations for wrong-

ful death actions had run out, thus barring the plaintiff's lawsuit. The supreme court reversed the decision of the court of appeals.

Case Questions

Critical Legal Thinking   What is the public policy behind having statutes of limitations? What is the public policy against having such statutes? Which policy should dominate and why?

Business Ethics   Was it ethical for the Upjohn Company to avoid facing the merits of the lawsuit by asserting the one-year statute of limitations?

Contemporary Business   What are the business implications for having statutes of limitations?

Discovery

The legal process provides for a detailed pretrial procedure called **discovery**. During discovery, both parties engage in various activities to discover facts of the case from the other party and witnesses prior to trial. Discovery serves several functions, including preventing surprise, allowing parties to thoroughly prepare for trial, preserving evidence, saving court time, and promoting the settlement of cases. The major forms of discovery are as follows:

1. *Depositions.* A **deposition** is the oral testimony given by a party or witness prior to trial. The person giving the deposition is called the **deponent**. The *parties* to the lawsuit must give their depositions, if called upon by the other party to do so. The deposition of a *witness* can be given voluntarily or pursuant to a subpoena (court order). The deponent can be required to bring documents to the deposition. Most depositions are taken at the office of one of the attorneys. The deponent is placed under oath and then asked oral questions by one or both of the attorneys. The questions and answers are recorded in written form by a court reporter. Depositions can also be videotaped. The deponent is given an opportunity to correct his or her answers prior to signing the deposition. Depositions are used to preserve evidence (e.g., if the deponent is deceased, ill, or not otherwise available at trial) and impeach testimony given by witnesses at trial.

2. *Interrogatories.* **Interrogatories** are written questions submitted by one party to a lawsuit to another party. The questions can be very detailed. In addition, it might be necessary to attach certain documents to the answers. A party is required to answer the interrogatories in writing within a specified time period (e.g., 60 to 90 days). An attorney usually helps with the preparation of the answers. The answers are signed under oath.

3. *Production of documents.* Often, particularly in complex business cases, a substantial portion of the lawsuit may be based on information contained in documents (e.g., memorandums, correspondence, company records, and such). One party to a lawsuit may request that the other party produce all documents that are relevant to the case prior to trial. This is called **production of documents**. If the documents sought are too voluminous to be moved or are in permanent storage, or if their movement would disrupt the ongoing business of the party who is to produce them, the requesting party may be required to examine the documents at the other party's premises.

4. *Physical and mental examination.* In cases that concern the physical or mental condition of a party, a court can order the party to submit to certain **physical or mental examinations** to determine the extent of the alleged injuries. This would occur, for example, where the plaintiff has been injured in an accident and is seeking damages for physical injury and mental distress.

Online Commerce & Internet Law
E-Filings in Court

When litigation ensues, the clients, lawyers, and judges involved in the case are usually buried in papers. These papers include pleadings, interrogatories, documents, motions to the court, briefs, and memorandums; the list goes on and on. By the time a case is over, reams of paper are stored in dozens, if not hundreds, of boxes. In addition, court appearances, for no matter how small the matter, must be made in person. For example, lawyers often wait hours for a 10-minute scheduling or other conference with the judge. The time it takes to drive to and from court also has to be taken into account, which in an urban area may amount to hours.

Some forward-thinking judges and lawyers envision a day when the paperwork and hassle are reduced or eliminated in a virtual courthouse. Technology allows for the electronic filing—**e-filing**—of pleadings, briefs, and other documents related to a lawsuit. E-filing includes using CD-ROMs for briefs, scanning evidence and documents into a computer for storage and retrieval, and e-mailing correspondence and documents to the court and the opposing counsel. Scheduling and other conferences with the judge or opposing counsel are held via telephone conferences and e-mail.

Many courts have instituted e-filing. In some courts, e-filing is now mandatory. Companies such as Microsoft and LexisNexis have developed systems to manage e-filings of court documents. ■

Dismissals and Pretrial Judgments

There are several **pretrial motions** that parties to a lawsuit can make to try to dispose of all or part of a lawsuit prior to trial. The two major pretrial motions are:

1. *Motion for judgment on the pleadings.* A **motion for judgment on the pleadings** can be made by either party once the pleadings are complete. This motion alleges that if all of the facts presented in the pleadings are true, the party making the motion would win the lawsuit when the proper law is applied to these facts. In deciding this motion, the judge cannot consider any facts outside the pleadings.

2. *Motion for summary judgment.* The trier of fact (i.e., the jury or, if there is no jury, the judge) determines factual issues. A **motion for summary judgment** asserts that there are no factual disputes to be decided by the jury and that the judge should apply the relevant law to the undisputed facts to decide the case. Motions for summary judgment, which can be made by either party, are supported by evidence outside the pleadings. Affidavits from the parties and witnesses, documents (e.g., a written contract between the parties), depositions, and such are common forms of evidence. If, after examining the evidence, the court finds no factual dispute, it can decide the issue or issues raised in the summary judgment motion. This may dispense with the entire case or with part of the case. If the judge finds that a factual dispute exists, the motion will be denied, and the case will go to trial.

Settlement Conference

Federal court rules and most state court rules permit the court to direct the attorneys or parties to appear before the court for a **pretrial hearing**, or **settlement conference**. One of the major purposes of such hearings is to facilitate the settlement of the case. Pretrial conferences are often held informally in the judge's chambers. If no settlement is reached, the pretrial hearing is used to identify the major trial issues and other relevant factors. More than 90 percent of all cases are settled before they go to trial.

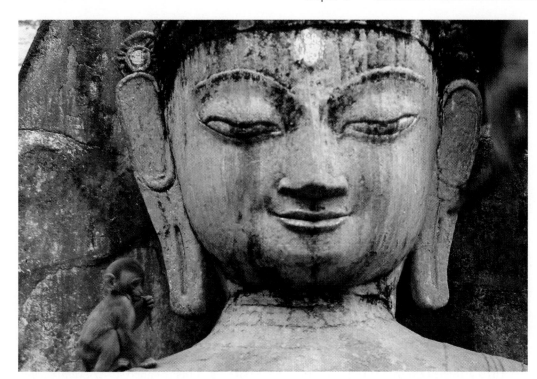

Nepal. Each country has developed its own laws. A company conducting business in a foreign country is subject to that country's laws.

Business Ethics

Ford Settles SUV Rollover Lawsuit

On June 23, 1992, Nabil Boury was driving a 1992 Ford Explorer SUV on the Elsenhower Expressway in Chicago, with five passengers in the vehicle. When another car clipped the Explorer on the driver's-side rear wheel well, the Explorer immediately rolled over. By the time it came to rest, the Explorer had rolled over three times, ejecting several of the passengers. Boury's sister and another teenager were killed, Boury's cousin lost vision in one eye, and another passenger was rendered a quadriplegic; Boury and his mother suffered minor injuries.

After the accident, the injured persons and the estates of the two deceased teenagers sued Ford Motor Company in a product liability lawsuit, alleging that there was a defect in the design of the Explorer SUV that caused it to roll over. The plaintiffs sued Packey Webb Ford, the car dealer that sold the Explorer, for putting Michelin tires on the SUV in a size and type specifically contrary to the warnings in the Ford owner's manual. The plaintiffs also sued Cassidy Tire Company, the distributor of the Michelin tires.

Several months before the case was to proceed to trial in the fall of 2001, the parties reached settlement. Ford agreed to pay $8 million, Packey Webb $10.5 million, Cassidy Tire $3 million, and Michelin Tire $500,000. The plaintiffs reached a separate agreement as to how to divide the settlement proceeds. This is just one example of the hundreds of thousands of lawsuits that are settled every year. [*Boury v. Ford Motor Company*, Cook County Circuit Court, Illinois (2001)]

1. Why do parties settle? Explain.
2. Do you think settlements lead to fair results? Explain. ▪

The Trial

Pursuant to the Seventh Amendment to the U.S. Constitution, a party to an action at law is guaranteed the right to a *jury trial* in a case in federal court.[7] Most state constitutions contain a similar guarantee for state court actions. If either party requests a jury, the trial will be by jury. If both parties waive their right to a jury, the trial will occur without a jury. The judge sits as the **trier of fact** in nonjury trials. At the time of trial, each party usually submits to the judge a **trial brief** that contains legal support for its side of the case.

Phases of a Trial

A trial can last for less than one day to many months, depending on the type and complexity of the case. A typical trial is divided into the following stages.

1. *Jury selection.* The pool of the potential jurors is usually selected from voter or automobile registration lists. Individuals are selected to hear specific cases through the process called **voir dire** ("to speak the truth"). Lawyers for each party and the judge can ask prospective jurors questions to determine if they would be biased in their decisions. Biased jurors can be prevented from sitting on a particular case. Once the appropriate number of jurors is selected (usually 6 to 12 jurors), they are *impaneled* to hear the case and are sworn in. The trial is ready to begin. A jury can be *sequestered* (i.e., separated from family, etc.) in important cases. Jurors are paid minimum fees for the service.

2. *Opening statements.* Each party's attorney is allowed to make an **opening statement** to the jury. In opening statements, an attorney usually summarizes the main factual and legal issues of the case and describes why he or she believes the client's position is valid. The information given in this statement is not considered as evidence.

3. *The plaintiff's case.* A plaintiff bears the **burden of proof** to persuade the trier of fact of the merits of his or her case. This is called the **plaintiff's case.** The plaintiff's attorney will call witnesses to give testimony. After a witness has been sworn in, the plaintiff's attorney examines (i.e., questions) the witness. This is called *direct examination.* Documents and other evidence can be introduced through each witness. After the plaintiff's attorney has completed his or her questions, the defendant's attorney can question the witness. This is called *cross-examination.* The defendant's attorney can ask questions only about the subjects that were brought up during the direct examination. After the defendant's attorney completes his or her questions, the plaintiff's attorney can ask questions of the witness. This is called *redirect examination.*

4. *The defendant's case.* The **defendant's case** proceeds after the plaintiff has concluded his or her case. The defendant's case must (1) rebut the plaintiff's evidence, (2) prove any affirmative defenses asserted by the defendant, and (3) prove any allegations contained in the defendant's cross-complaint. The defendant's witnesses are examined in much the same way as the plaintiff's attorney cross-examines each witness. This is followed by redirect and recross-examination.

5. *Rebuttal and rejoinder.* After the defendant's attorney has completed calling witnesses, the plaintiff's attorney can call witnesses and put forth evidence to rebut the defendant's case. This is called a *rebuttal.* The defendant's attorney can call additional witnesses and introduce other evidence to counter the rebuttal. This is called the *rejoinder.*

6. *Closing arguments.* At the conclusion of the presentation of the evidence, each party's attorney is allowed to make a **closing argument** to the jury. Both attorneys try to convince the jury to render a verdict for their clients by pointing out the strengths in the client's case and the weaknesses in the other side's case. Information given by the attorneys in their closing statements is not evidence.

7. *Jury instructions.* Once the closing arguments are completed, the judge reads **jury instructions** (or **charges**) to the jury. These instructions inform the jury about what law to apply when they decide the case. For example, in a criminal trial, the judge will read the jury the statutory definition of the crime charged. In an accident case, the judge will read the jury the legal definition of *negligence.*

8. *Jury deliberation.* The jury then retires to the jury room to deliberate its findings. This can take from a few minutes to many weeks. After deliberation, the jury assesses penalties in criminal cases.

9. *Entry of judgment.* After the jury has returned its **verdict**, in most cases the judge will enter **judgment** to the successful party based on the verdict. This is the official decision of the court. The court may, however, overturn the verdict if it finds bias or

jury misconduct. This is called a **judgment notwithstanding the verdict** or **judgment n.o.v.** or **j.n.o.v.**. In a civil case, the judge may reduce the amount of monetary damages awarded by the jury if he or she finds the jury to have been biased, emotional, or inflamed. This is called *remittitur*. The trial court usually issues a *written memorandum* setting forth the reasons for the judgment. This memorandum, together with the trial transcript and evidence introduced at trial, constitutes the permanent *record* of the trial court proceeding.

In the following case, the court was asked to grant a judgment notwithstanding the verdict.

Ferlito v. Johnson & Johnson Products, Inc.
771 F.Supp. 196, 1991 U.S. Dist. Lexis 11747 (1991)
United States District Court, Eastern District, Michigan

Case 3.3
Judgment Notwithstanding the Verdict

Background and Facts

Susan and Frank Ferlito were invited to a Halloween party. They decided to attend as "Little Bo Peep" (Mrs. Ferlito) and her little sheep (Mr. Ferlito). Mrs. Ferlito constructed a lamb costume for her husband by gluing cotton batting manufactured by Johnson & Johnson Products, Inc., to a suit of long underwear. She used the same cotton batting to fashion a headpiece, complete with ears. The costume covered Mr. Ferlito from his head to his ankles, except for his face and hands, which were blackened with paint. At the party, Mr. Ferlito attempted to light a cigarette with a butane lighter. The flame passed close to his left arm, and the cotton batting ignited. He suffered burns over one-third of his body. The Ferlitos sued Johnson & Johnson to recover damages, alleging that Johnson & Johnson failed to warn them of the ignitability of cotton batting. The jury returned a verdict for Mr. Ferlito in the amount of $555,000 and for Mrs. Ferlito in the amount of $70,000. Johnson & Johnson filed a motion for judgment notwithstanding the verdict (j.n.o.v.).

Issue

Should defendant Johnson & Johnson's motion for j.n.o.v. be granted?

Court's Reasoning

The court noted that if, after reviewing the evidence, the court is of the opinion that reasonable minds could not come to the result reached by the jury, then the motion for j.n.o.v. should be granted.

At trial, both plaintiffs testified that they knew that cotton batting burns when exposed to flame. The court stated, "Because both plaintiffs were already aware of the danger, a warning by Johnson & Johnson would have been superfluous." Mrs. Ferlito testified that the idea for the costume was hers alone. As described on the product's package, its intended uses are for cleansing, applying medications, and infant care. The court concluded that the plaintiffs failed to demonstrate the foreseeability of an adult male encapsulating himself from head to toe in cotton batting and then lighting up a cigarette.

Decision and Remedy

The trial court granted defendant Johnson & Johnson's motion for j.n.o.v. By doing so, the court vacated the verdict entered by the jury in favor of Mr. and Mrs. Ferlito. The court of appeals affirmed the grant of j.n.o.v.

Case Questions

Critical Legal Thinking Should trial courts have the authority to enter a j.n.o.v., or should jury verdicts always be allowed to stand? Explain your answer.

Business Ethics Did the Ferlitos act ethically in suing Johnson & Johnson in this case? Were they responsible for their own injuries?

Contemporary Business What would have been the business implications had Johnson & Johnson been found liable?

The Appeal

In a civil case, either party can **appeal** the trial court's decision once a *final judgment* is entered. Only the defendant can appeal in a criminal case. The appeal is made to the appropriate appellate court. A *notice of appeal* must be filed within a prescribed time after judgment

Japan. Multinational corporations have grown to immense size and power in recent years. For example, the Mitsubishi Group of Japan operates subsidiary corporations in many nations of the world.

is entered (usually within 60 or 90 days). The appealing party is called the **appellant,** or **petitioner.** The responding party is called the **appellee,** or the **respondent.** The appellant is often required to post a bond (e.g., one-and-one-half times the judgment) on appeal.

The parties may designate all or relevant portions of the trial record to be submitted to the appellate court for review. The appellant's attorney may file an *opening brief* with the court that sets forth legal research and other information to support his or her contentions on appeal. The appellee can file a *responding brief,* answering the appellant's contentions. Appellate courts usually permit a brief oral argument at which each party's attorney is heard.

An appellate court will reverse a lower court decision if it finds an *error of law* in the record. An error of law occurs if the jury was improperly instructed by the trial court judge, prejudicial evidence was admitted at trial when it should have been excluded, prejudicial evidence was obtained through an unconstitutional search and seizure, and the like. An appellate court will not reverse a *finding of fact* unless such finding is unsupported by the evidence or is contradicted by the evidence.

Business Brief

Trial court decisions are overturned on appeal only if there has been an error of law or the decision is not supported by the evidence.

Alternative Dispute Resolution

The use of the court system to resolve business and other disputes can take years and cost thousands, if not millions, of dollars in legal fees and expenses. In commercial litigation, the normal business operations of the parties are often disrupted. To avoid or lessen these problems, businesses are increasingly turning to methods of **alternative dispute resolution (ADR)** and other aids to resolving disputes. The most common form of ADR is *arbitration.* Other forms of ADR are *mediation, conciliation, minitrial, fact-finding,* and using a *judicial referee.*

Arbitration

In **arbitration,** the parties choose an impartial third party to hear and decide the dispute. This neutral party is called the *arbitrator.* Arbitrators are usually selected from members of the American Arbitration Association (AAA) or another arbitration association. Labor union agreements, franchise agreements, leases, and other commercial contracts often contain **arbitration clauses** that require disputes arising out of the contract to be submitted to arbitration. If there is no arbitration clause, the parties can enter into a *submission agreement* whereby they agree to submit a dispute to arbitration after the dispute arises.

Evidence and testimony are presented to the arbitrator at a hearing held for this purpose. Less formal evidentiary rules are usually applied in arbitration hearings than at court. After the hearing, the arbitrator reaches a decision and enters an *award*. The parties often agree in advance to be bound by the arbitrator's decision and award. If the parties have not so agreed, the arbitrator's award can be appealed to court. The court gives great deference to the arbitrator's decision.

Congress enacted the **Federal Arbitration Act** to promote the arbitration of disputes.[8] About half of the states have adopted the **Uniform Arbitration Act**. This act promotes the arbitration of disputes at the state level. Many federal and state courts have instituted programs to refer legal disputes to arbitration or another form of ADR.

Business Brief

Litigation is expensive and time-consuming. Businesses should consider using ADR to solve their disputes.

The Federal Arbitration Act

The **Federal Arbitration Act (FAA)** was originally enacted in 1925 to reverse the long-standing judicial hostility to arbitration agreements that had existed as English common law and had been adopted by American courts. The act provides that arbitration agreements involving commerce are valid, irrevocable, and enforceable contracts, unless some grounds exist at law or equity (e.g., fraud, duress) to revoke them. The FAA permits one party to obtain a court order to compel arbitration if the other party has failed, neglected, or refused to comply with an arbitration agreement.

Since the FAA's enactment, the courts have wrestled with the problem of which types of disputes should be arbitrated. Breach of contract cases, tort claims, and such are clearly candidates for arbitration if there is a valid arbitration agreement. In addition, the U.S. Supreme Court has enforced arbitration agreements that call for the resolution of disputes arising under federal statutes. The Supreme Court has stated, "By agreeing to arbitrate a statutory claim, a party does not forgo the substantive rights afforded by the statute, it only submits to their resolution in an arbitral, rather than a judicial, forum." [*Gilmer v. Interstate/Johnson Lane Corporation*, 500 U.S. 20, 111 S.Ct. 1647, 1991 U.S. Lexis 2529 (1991).]

Because the U.S. Supreme Court has placed its imprimatur on the use of arbitration to solve employment disputes, it is likely that such clauses will appear in more contracts. In the following case, the U.S. Supreme Court addressed the issue of arbitration clauses in employment contracts.

Case 3.4
Arbitration

U.S. SUPREME COURT CASE

Circuit City Stores, Inc. v. Adams

532 U.S. 105, 121 S.Ct. 1302, 2001 U.S. Lexis 2459 (2001)
Supreme Court of the United States

Background and Facts

In October 1995, Saint Clair Adams was hired as a sales counselor by Circuit City Stores, Inc., a national retailer of consumer electronics. Adams signed an employment contract that included the following arbitration clause:

I agree that I will settle any and all previously unasserted claims, disputes or controversies arising out of or relating to my application or candidacy for employment, employment and/or cessation of employment with Circuit City, exclusively

by final and binding arbitration before a neutral Arbitrator. By way of example only, such claims include claims under federal, state, and local statutory or common law, such as the Age Discrimination in Employment Act. Title VII of the Civil Rights Act of 1964, the Americans with Disabilities Act, the law of contract and the law of tort.

Two years later Adams filed an employment discrimination lawsuit against Circuit City in court. Circuit City sought to enjoin the court proceeding and to compel arbitration, pursuant to the FAA.

Circuit City Stores, Inc. v. Adams

532 U.S. 105, 121 S.Ct. 1302, 2001 U.S. Lexis 2459 (2001)
Supreme Court of the United States
(continued)

The district court granted Circuit City's request. The court of appeals reversed, holding that employment contracts are not subject to arbitration. The U.S. Supreme Court granted certiorari to hear the appeal.

Issue

Are employment contracts subject to arbitration if a valid arbitration agreement has been entered into between the parties?

Court's Reasoning

Congress enacted the Federal Arbitration Act (FAA) in 1925. The FAA was a response to hostility of American courts to the enforcement of arbitration agreements. To give effect to this purpose, the FAA compels judicial enforcement of a wide range of written arbitration agreements. The FAA's coverage provision, Section 2, provides that "a written provision in any contract evidencing a transaction involving commerce to settle by arbitration a controversy thereafter arising out of such contract or transaction, or the refusal to perform the whole or any part thereof, shall be valid, irrevocable, and enforceable, save upon such grounds as exist at law or in equity for the revocation of any contract."

Decision and Remedy

The U.S. Supreme Court held that employment contracts, including the one in this case between Circuit City and Adams, are subject to arbitration if a valid arbitration agreement has been executed. The Supreme Court reversed the decision of the court of appeals and remanded the case.

Case Questions

Critical Legal Thinking   How do you think transportation workers became exempted from arbitration under the Federal Arbitration Act?

Business Ethics   Is it ethical for employers to include arbitration clauses in employment contracts?

Contemporary Business   Who do you think benefits most from arbitration clauses in employment contracts: employers or employees? Why?

Mediation and Conciliation

In **mediation**, the parties choose a neutral third party to act as the mediator of the dispute. Unlike an arbitrator, a mediator does not make a decision or an award. Instead, the mediator acts as a conveyor of information between the parties and assists them in trying to reach a settlement of the dispute. A mediator often meets separately with each of the parties. A settlement agreement is reached if the mediator is successful. If not, the case proceeds to trial. In a **conciliation**, the parties choose an interested third party, the *conciliator*, to act as the mediator.

Minitrial

A *minitrial* is a session, usually lasting a day or less, in which the lawyers for each side present their cases to representatives of each party who have authority to settle the dispute. In many cases, the parties hire a neutral person (e.g., a retired judge) to preside over the minitrial. Following the presentations, the parties meet to try to negotiate a settlement.

Fact-Finding

Fact-finding is a process whereby the parties hire a neutral person to investigate the dispute. The *fact-finder* reports his or her findings to the adversaries and may recommend a basis for settlement.

Judicial Referee

If the parties agree, the court may appoint a *judicial referee* to conduct a private trial and render a judgment. Referees, who are often retired judges, have most of the powers of a trial judge, and their decisions stand as judgments of the court. The parties usually reserve their right to appeal.

International Law

Comparison of the Japanese and American Legal Systems

Businesses often complain that there are too many lawyers and there is too much litigation in the United States. There are currently more than 900,000 lawyers and more than 20 million lawsuits per year in this country. On the other hand, in Japan, a country with about half the population of the United states, there are only 20,000 lawyers and there is little litigation. Why the difference?

Much of the difference is cultural: Japan nurtures the attitude that confrontation should be avoided. Litigious persons in Japan are looked down upon. Thus, companies rarely do battle in court. Instead, they opt for private arbitration of most of their disputes. Other differences are built into the legal system itself. For example, there is only one place to go to become a *bengoshi*, or lawyer, in Japan—the government-operated National Institute for

Legal Training. Only 2 percent of 35,000 applicants are accepted annually, and only 400 new *bengoshi* are admitted to Japan's exclusive legal club per year.

There are other obstacles, too. For example, no class actions or contingency fee arrangements are allowed. Plaintiffs must pay their lawyers a front fee of up to 8 percent of the damages sought, plus a nonrefundable filing fee to the court of one-half of 1 percent of the damages. To make matters even more difficult, no discovery is permitted, and plaintiffs are denied access before trial to an opponent's potential evidence. Even if the plaintiff wins the lawsuit, damage awards are low.

The Japanese bias against courtroom solutions remains strong. The current system is designed to save time and money and to preserve long-term relationships. ■

Chapter Summary

The State Court Systems, p. 44

State Court Systems

1. ***Limited-jurisdiction trial courts.*** State courts that hear matters of a specialized or limited nature (e.g., misdemeanor criminal matters, traffic tickets, civil matters under a certain dollar amount). Many states have created small claims courts that hear small-dollar-amount civil cases (e.g., under $5,000) where the parties cannot be represented by lawyers.

2. ***General-jurisdiction trial courts.*** State courts that hear cases of a general nature that are not within the jurisdiction of limited-jurisdiction trial courts.

3. ***Intermediate appellate courts.*** State courts that hear appeals from state trial courts. The appellate court reviews the trial court record in making its decision. No new evidence is introduced at this level.

4. ***Highest state court.*** Each state has a highest court in its court system. This court hears appeals from appellate courts, and where appropriate, trial courts. This court reviews the record in making its decision. No new evidence is introduced at this level. Most states call this court the *supreme court*.

The Federal Court System, p. 46

Federal Court System

1. ***Special federal courts.*** Federal courts that have specialized or limited jurisdiction. They include:

   a. *U.S. tax court.* Hears cases involving federal tax laws.

   b. *U.S. claims court.* Hears cases brought against the United States.

   c. *U.S. Court of International Trade.* Hears cases involving tariffs and international commercial disputes.

   d. *U.S. bankruptcy courts.* Hear cases involving federal bankruptcy law.

2. ***U.S. districts courts.*** Federal trial courts of general jurisdiction that hear cases not within the jurisdiction of specialized courts. There is at least one U.S. district court per state: More populated states have several district courts. The area served by one of these courts is called a *district*.

3. **U.S. courts of appeals.** Intermediate federal appellate courts that hear appeals from district courts located in their circuit, and in certain instances from special federal courts and federal administrative agencies. There are 12 geographical circuits in the United States. Eleven serve areas that comprise several states, while another is located in Washington, DC. A 13th circuit court—the *Court of Appeals for the Federal circuit*—is located in Washington, DC, and it reviews patent, trademark, and international trade cases.

4. **U.S. Supreme Court.** This is the highest court of the federal court system. It hears appeals from the circuit courts and, in some instances, from special courts and U.S. district courts. The Court, which is located in Washington, DC, is composed of nine justices, one of whom is named chief justice.

5. **Decisions by the U.S. Supreme Court:**
   a. *Writ or certiorari.* To have a case heard by the U.S. Supreme Court, a petitioner must file a *petition for certiorari* with the Court. If the Court decides to hear the case, it will issue a *writ of certiorari.*
   b. Voting by the U.S. Supreme Court:
      i. *Unanimous decision.* All of the justices agree as to the outcome and reasoning used to decide the case. The decision becomes precedent.
      ii. *Majority decision.* A majority of the justices agrees as to the outcome and reasoning used to decide the case. The decision becomes precedent.
      iii. *Plurality decision.* A majority of the justices agrees to the outcome but not the reasoning. The decision is not precedent.
      iv. *Tie decision.* If there is a tie vote, the lower court's decision stands. The decision is not precedent.
      v. *Concurring opinion.* A justice who agrees as to the outcome of the case but not the reasoning used by other justices may write a concurring opinion setting forth his or her reasoning.
      vi. *Dissenting opinion.* A justice who disagrees with the outcome of a case may write a dissenting opinion setting forth his or her reasoning for dissenting.

Jurisdiction of Federal and State Courts

1. **Jurisdiction of federal courts.** Federal courts may hear the following cases:
   a. *Federal question.* Cases arising under the U.S. Constitution, treaties, and federal statutes and regulations. There is no dollar-amount limit in federal question cases.
   b. *Diversity of citizenship.* Cases between (i) citizens of different states and (ii) a citizen of a state and a citizen or subject of a foreign country. Federal courts must apply the appropriate state law in such cases. The controversy must exceed $75,000 for the federal court to hear the case.

2. **Jurisdiction of state courts.** State courts hear some cases that may be heard by federal courts.
   a. *Exclusive jurisdiction.* Federal courts have exclusive jurisdiction to hear cases involving federal crimes, antitrust and bankruptcy, patent and copyright cases, suits against the United States, and most admiralty cases. State courts may not hear these matters.
   b. *Concurrent jurisdiction.* State courts have concurrent jurisdiction to hear cases involving diversity of citizenship cases and federal question cases over which the federal courts do not have exclusive jurisdiction. The defendant may have the case removed to federal court.

The Jurisdiction and Venue of Courts, p. 51

Standing to Sue, Jurisdiction and Venue

1. **Standing to sue.** To bring a lawsuit, the plaintiff must have some stake in the outcome of the lawsuit.

2. **Subject matter jurisdiction.** The court must have jurisdiction over the subject matter of the lawsuit. Each court has limited jurisdiction to hear only certain types of cases.

3. **In personam jurisdiction (or personal jurisdiction).** The court must have jurisdiction over the parties to a lawsuit. The plaintiff submits to the jurisdiction of the court by filing the lawsuit there. Personal jurisdiction is obtained over the defendant through *service of process* to that person.

4. *In rem jurisdiction.* A court may have jurisdiction to hear and decide a case because it has jurisdiction over the property at issue in the lawsuit (e.g., real property located in the state).

5. *Quasi in rem jurisdiction* (**or** *attachment jurisdiction*). A plaintiff who obtains a judgment against a defendant in one state may utilize the court system of another state to attach property of the defendant's that is located in the second state.

6. *Long-arm statutes.* These statutes permit a state to obtain personal jurisdiction over an out-of-state defendant as long as the defendant had the requisite minimum contact with the state. The out-of-state defendant may be served process outside the state in which the lawsuit has been brought.

7. *Venue.* A case must be heard by the court that has jurisdiction nearest to where the incident at issue occurred or where the parties reside. A *change of venue* will be granted if prejudice would occur because of pretrial publicity or another reason.

8. *Forum-selection clause.* A clause in a contract that designates the court that will hear any dispute that arises out of the contract.

The Pretrial Litigation Process, p. 54

Pleadings

Pleadings are paperwork that initiates and responds to a lawsuit. Pleadings include:

1. *Complaint.* The complaint is filed by the plaintiff with the court and served with a *summons* on the defendant. It sets forth the basis of the lawsuit.

2. *Answer.* The answer is filed by the defendant with the court and served on the plaintiff. It usually denies most allegations of the complaint.

3. *Cross-complaint.* The cross-complaint is filed and served by the defendant if he or she countersues the plaintiff. The defendant is the *cross-complainant* and the plaintiff is the *cross-defendant*. The cross-defendant must file and serve a *reply* (answer).

4. *Intervention.* A person who has an interest in a lawsuit may intervene and become a party to the lawsuit.

5. *Consolidation.* Separate cases against the same defendant arising from the same incident may be consolidated by the court into one case if doing so would not cause prejudice to the parties.

Discovery

Discovery is the pretrial litigation process for discovering facts of the case from the other party and witnesses. Discovery consists of:

1. *Depositions.* Depositions are oral testimony given by a *deponent*, either a party or witness. Depositions are transcribed.

2. *Interrogatories.* These written questions are submitted by one party to the other party. They must be answered within a specified period of time.

3. *Production of documents.* A party to a lawsuit may obtain copies of all relevant documents from the other party.

4. *Physical and mental examination.* These examinations of a party are permitted upon order of the court where injuries are alleged that could be verified or disputed by such examination.

Dismissals and Pretrial Judgments

1. *Motion for summary judgment on the pleadings.* This motion alleges that if all facts as pleaded are true, the moving party would win the lawsuit. No facts outside the pleadings may be considered.

2. *Motion for summary judgment.* This motion alleges that there are no factual disputes, so the judge may apply the law and decide the case without a jury. Evidence outside the pleadings may be considered (e.g., affidavits, documents, depositions).

Settlement Conference

This conference occurs prior to trial between the parties in front of the judge to facilitate the settlement of the case. Also called the *pretrial hearing*. If a settlement is not reached, the case proceeds to trial.

The Trial, p. 59

Phases of a Trial

1. *Jury selection.* Jury selection occurs through a process called *voir dire*. Biased jurors are dismissed and replaced.

2. *Opening statements.* The parties' lawyers make opening statements, which are not evidence.

3. *The plaintiff's case.* The plaintiff bears the burden of proof. The plaintiff calls witnesses and introduces evidence to try to prove his or her case.

4. *The defendant's case.* The defendant calls witnesses and introduces evidence to rebut the plaintiff's case and to prove affirmative defenses and cross-complaints.

5. *Rebuttal and rejoinder.* The plaintiff and defendant may call additional witnesses and introduce additional evidence.

6. *Closing arguments.* The parties' lawyers make closing arguments, which are not evidence.

7. *Jury instructions.* The judge reads instructions to the jury as to what law they are to apply to the case.

8. *Jury deliberation.* The jury retires to the jury room and deliberates until it reaches a *verdict*.

9. *Entry of judgment.* The judge may:

   a. Enter the verdict reached by the jury as the court's *judgment*.

   b. Grant a motion for *judgment n.o.v.* if the judge finds that the jury was biased. This means that the jury's verdict does not stand.

   c. Order *remittitur* (reduction) of any damages awarded if the judge finds the jury to have been biased or emotional.

The Appeal, p. 61

Appeal

Both parties in a civil suit and the defendant in a criminal trial may appeal the decision of the trial court. *Notice of appeal* must be filed within a specified period of time. The appeal must be made to the appropriate appellate court.

Alternative Dispute Resolution, p. 62

Alternative Dispute Resolution (ADR)

ADR is a *nonjudicial* means of solving legal disputes. ADR usually saves time and money compared to litigation.

Types of ADR

1. *Arbitration.* An impartial third party, called the arbitrator, hears and decides the dispute. The arbitrator makes an award. The award is appealable to a court if the parties have not given up this right. Arbitration is designated by the parties pursuant to:

   a. *Arbitration clause.* Agreement contained in a contract stipulating that any dispute arising out of the contract will be arbitrated.

   b. *Submission agreement.* Agreement to submit a dispute to arbitration after the dispute arises.

2. *Mediation.* A neutral third party, called a *mediator*, assists the parties in trying to reach a settlement of their dispute. The mediator does not make an award.

3. *Conciliation.* An interested third party, called a *conciliator*, assists the parties in trying to reach a settlement of their dispute. The conciliator does not make an award.

4. *Minitrial.* A minitrial is a short session in which the lawyers for each side present their cases to representatives of each party who have the authority to settle the dispute.

5. *Fact-finding.* The parties may hire a neutral third person, called a *fact-finder*, to investigate the dispute and report his or her findings to the adversaries.

6. *Judicial referee.* With consent of the parties, the court may appoint a judicial referee (usually a retired judge or lawyer) to conduct a private trial and render a judgment. The judg-

ment stands as the judgment of the court and may be appealed to the appropriate appellate court.

Internet Exercises and Case Questions

Working the Web Internet Exercises

Activities

1. At the International Chamber of Commerce (ICC) Web site, **www.iccwbo.org/court/english/news_archives/2001/adr.asp,** you will find information about rules and procedures for settlement of international commercial disputes. Under what circumstances would you advise a client to elect ICC arbitration rules as compared with AAA rules?

2. Go to the U.S. Supreme Court site, **www.supremecourtus.gov.** Find a case from your state that recently has been

appealed to the Court. Outline the procedural steps involved in the process of appealing a case to the Supreme Court.

3. The site **guide.lp.findlaw.com/10fedgov/judicial/appeals_courts.html** contains links to each of the federal judicial circuits. Find your jurisdiction and review the cases available there. What is the oldest case you can find? the most recent? Compare your search results with the same two questions, looking at state court cases available in your state.

Critical Legal Thinking Cases

3.1 Federal Question   Nutrilab, Inc., manufactures and markets a product known as "Starch Blockers." The purpose of the product is to block the human body's digestion of starch as an aid in controlling weight. On July 1, 1982, the U.S. FDA classified Starch Blockers as a drug and requested that it be removed from the market until the FDA approved of its use. The FDA claimed that it had the right to classify new products as drugs and prevent their distribution until their safety is determined. Nutrilab disputed the FDA's decision and wanted to bring suit to halt the FDA's actions. Do the federal courts have jurisdiction to hear this case? [*Nutrilab, Inc. v. Schweiker*, 713 F.2d 335, 1983 U.S. App. Lexis 25121 (7th Cir. 1983)]

3.2 In Personam Jurisdiction   Saul and Elaine Kozuck borrowed money from the Peoples Trust Company of Bergen County, New Jersey, and consigned a promissory note promising to repay the money. When Peoples Trust contacted the Kozucks about payment, they denied liability on the ground that the bank improperly filled in the due date on the note. Peoples Trust filed suit against the Kozucks in a New Jersey state court. A process server went to the Kozucks' home in New Jersey to serve the summons. The process server rang the bell at the home, and a woman appeared at the upstairs window. The process server asked her if she was Mrs. Kozuck, and the woman replied in the affirmative. When the process server identified himself, the woman denied that she was Mrs. Kozuck and refused to come out of the house. The process server told the woman that he would leave the papers in the mailbox if she refused to open the door. When the woman did not reappear, the process server placed the summons in the mailbox and left. Is the service of process good? [*Peoples Trust Co. v. Kozuck*, 236 A.2d 630, 1967 N.J.Super. Lexis 389 (N.J.Super. 1967)]

3.3 Long-Arm Statute   Sean O'Grady, a professional boxer, was managed by his father, Pat. Sean was a contender for the world featherweight title. On January 30, 1978, Pat entered into a contract with Magna Verde Corporation, a Los Angeles–based business, to copromote a fight between Sean and the current featherweight champion. The fight was scheduled to take place on February 5, 1978, in Oklahoma City, Oklahoma. To promote

the fight, Pat O'Grady scheduled a press conference for January 30, 1978. At the conference, Pat was involved in a confrontation with a sportswriter named Brooks. He allegedly struck Brooks in the face. Brooks brought suit against Pat O'Grady and Magna Verde Corporation in an Oklahoma state court. Court records showed that the only contact Magna Verde had with Oklahoma was that a few of its employees had taken several trips to Oklahoma in January 1978 to plan the title fight. The fight was never held. Oklahoma has a long-arm statute. Magna Verde was served by mail and made a special appearance in Oklahoma state court to argue that Oklahoma does not have personal jurisdiction over it. Does Oklahoma have jurisdiction over Magna Verde Corporation? [*Brooks v. Magna Verde Corp.*, 619 P.2d 1271, 1980 Okla. Civ. App. Lexis 118 (Okla. App. 1980)]

3.4 Minimum Contacts   The National Enquirer, Inc., is a Florida corporation with its principal place of business in Florida. It publishes the *National Enquirer*, a national weekly newspaper with a total circulation of more than 5 million copies. About 600,000 copies, almost twice the level in the next highest state, are sold in California. On October 9, 1979, the *Enquirer* published an article about Shirley Jones, an entertainer. Jones, a California resident, filed a lawsuit in California state court against the *Enquirer* and its president, who was a resident of Florida. The suit sought damages for alleged defamation, invasion of privacy, and intentional infliction of emotional distress. Are the defendants subject to suit in California? [*Calder v. Jones*, 465 U.S. 783, 104 S.Ct. 1482, 1984 U.S. Lexis 41 (1984)]

3.5 Physical Examination   Robert Schlagenhauf worked as a bus driver for the Greyhound Corporation. One night the bus he was driving rear-ended a tractor-trailer. Seven passengers on the bus who were injured sued Schlagenhauf and Greyhound for damages. The complaint alleged that Greyhound was negligent for allowing Schlagenhauf to drive a bus when it knew that his eyes and vision "were impaired and deficient." The plaintiffs petitioned the court to order Schlagenhauf to be medically examined concerning these allegations. Schlagenhauf objected to the examination. Who wins? [*Schlagenhauf v. Holder*, 379 U.S. 104, 85 S.Ct. 234, 1964 U.S. Lexis 152 (1964)]

3.6 Interrogatories Cine Forty-Second Street Theatre Corporation operates a movie theater in New York City's Times Square area. Cine filed a lawsuit against Allied Artists Pictures Corporation, alleging that Allied Artists and local theater owners illegally attempted to prevent Cine from opening its theater in violation of federal antitrust law. The suit also alleged that once Cine opened the theater, the defendants conspired with motion picture distributors to prevent Cine from exhibiting first-run, quality films. Attorneys for Allied Artists served a set of written questions concerning the lawsuit on Cine. Does Cine have to answer these questions? [*Cine Forty-Second Street Theatre Corp. v. Allied Artists Pictures Corp.*, 602 F.2d 1062, 1979 U.S. App. Lexis 13586 (2d Cir. 1979)]

3.7 Judgment n.o.v. On November 9, 1964, Mr. Simblest was driving a car that collided with a fire engine at an intersection in Burlington, Vermont. The accident occurred on a night on which a power blackout left most of the state without lights. Mr. Simblest, who was injured in the accident, sued the driver of the fire truck for damages. During the trial, Simblest testified that when he entered the intersection, the traffic light was green in his favor. All of the other witnesses testified that the traffic light had gone dark at least 10 minutes before the accident. Simblest testified that the accident was caused by the fire truck's failure to use any warning lights or sirens. Simblest's testimony was contradicted by four witnesses, who testified that the fire truck had used both its lights and sirens. The jury found that the driver of the fire truck had been negligent and rendered a verdict for Simblest. The defense made a motion for judgment n.o.v. Who wins? [*Simblest v. Maynard*, 427 F.2d 1, 1970 U.S. App. Lexis 9265 (2d Cir. 1970)]

3.8 Arbitration AMF Incorporated and Brunswick Corporation both manufacture electric and automatic bowling center equipment. In 1983 the two companies became involved in a dispute over whether Brunswick had advertised certain automatic scoring devices in a false and deceptive manner. The two parties settled the dispute by signing an agreement that any future problems between them involving advertising claims would be submitted to the National Advertising Council for arbitration. In March 1985, Brunswick advertised a new product, Armor Plate 3000, a synthetic laminated material used to make bowling lanes. Armor Plate 3000 competed with wooden lanes produced by AMF. Brunswick's advertisements claimed that bowling centers could save up to $500 per lane per year in maintenance and repair costs if they switched to Armor Plate 3000 from wooden lanes. AMF disputed this claim and requested arbitration. Is the arbitration agreement enforceable? [*AMF Incorporated v. Brunswick Corp.*, 621 F.Supp. 456, 1985 U.S. Dist. Lexis 14205 (E.D.N.Y. 1985)]

Business Ethics Cases

3.9 Business Ethics One day Joshua Gnaizda, a three-year-old, received what he (or his mother) thought was a tantalizing offer in the mail from Time, Inc. The front of the envelope contained a see-through window that revealed the following statement: "Joshua Gnaizda, I'll give you this versatile new calculator watch free just for opening this envelope before Feb. 15, 1985." Beneath the offer was a picture of the calculator watch itself. When Joshua's mother opened the envelope, she realized that the see-through window had not revealed the full text of Time's offer. Not viewable through the see-through window were the following words: "And mailing this Certificate today." The certificate required Joshua to purchase a subscription to *Fortune* magazine in order to receive the free calculator watch. Joshua (through his father, a lawyer) sued Time in a class action, seeking compensatory damages in an amount equal to the value of the calculator watch and $15 million in punitive damages. The trial court dismissed the lawsuit as being too trivial for the court to hear. Joshua appealed. Should Joshua be permitted to maintain his lawsuit against Time, Inc.? Did Time act ethically? Should Joshua's father have sued for $15 million? [*Harris v. Time, Inc.*, 191 C.A.3d 449, 237 Cal. Rptr. 584, 1987 Cal. App. Lexis 1617 (Cal. App. 1987)]

3.10 Business Ethics Dennis and Francis Burnham were married in 1976 in West Virginia. In 1977, the couple moved to New Jersey, where their two children were born. In July 1987, the Burnhams decided to separate. Mrs. Burnham, who intended to move to California, was to have custody of the children. Mr. Burnham agreed to file for divorce on grounds of "irreconcilable differences." In October 1987, Mr. Burnham threatened to file for divorce in New Jersey on grounds of "desertion." After unsuccessfully demanding that Mr. Burnham adhere to the prior agreement, Mrs. Burnham brought suit for divorce in California state court in early January 1988. In late January, Mr. Burnham visited California on a business trip. He then visited his children in the San Francisco Bay area, where his wife resided. He took the older child to San Francisco for the weekend. Upon returning the child to Mrs. Burnham's home, he was served with a California court summons and a copy of Mrs. Burnham's divorce petition. He then returned to New Jersey. Mr. Burnham made a special appearance in the California court and moved to quash the service of process. Did Mr. Burnham act ethically in trying to quash the service of process? Did Mrs. Burnham act ethically in having Mr. Burnham served on his visit to California? Is the service of process good? [*Burnham v. Superior Court of California*, 495 U.S. 604, 110 S.Ct. 2105, 1990 U.S. Lexis 2700 (1990)]

Briefing the Case Writing Assignment

Read Case A.3 in the Case Appendix [*Gnazzo v. G.D. Searle & Co.*]. This case is excerpted from the court of appeals opinion. Review and brief the case. In your brief, be sure to answer the following questions.

1. What is a statute of limitations? What purposes are served by such a statute?

2. What was the Connecticut statute of limitations for the injury alleged by the plaintiff?

3. What is summary judgment? When will it be granted?

4. What was the decision of the trial court? of the court of appeals?

5. Was the decision fair? Should the plaintiff have been granted her day in court against the defendant?

Endnotes

1. Federal Courts Improvement Act of 1982. Public Law 97–164, 96 Stat. 25, 28 U.S.C. § 1292 and § 1295.
2. Effective September 25, 1988, mandatory appeals were all but eliminated, except for reapportionment cases and cases brought under the Civil Rights and Voting Rights Acts, antitrust laws, and the Presidential Election Campaign Fund Act.
3. Prior to 1980, there was a minimum dollar amount controversy requirement of $10,000 to bring a federal question action in federal court. This minimum amount was eliminated by the Federal Question Jurisdictional Amendment Act of 1980, Public Law 96–486.
4. The amount was raised from $50,000 to $75,000 by the 1996 Federal Courts Improvement Act.
5. Under the Full Faith and Credit Clause of the U.S. Constitution, a judgment of a court in one state must be given "full faith and credit" by the courts of another state. (Article IV, Section 1.)
6. *International Shoe Co. v. Washington*, 326 U.S. 310, 66 S.Ct. 154, 1945 U.S. Lexis 1447 (1945).
7. There is no right to a jury trial for actions in equity (e.g., injunctions, specific performance).
8. 9 U.S.C. §§ 1 et seq.

Torts and Privacy

4

"Negligence is not actionable unless it involves the invasion of a legally protected interest, the violation of a right. Proof of negligence in the air, so to speak, will not do."

—C.J. Cardozo

Palsgraf v. Long Island Railroad Co., 248 N.Y. 339, 162 N.E. 99, 1928 N.Y. Lexis 1269 (1928)

Chapter Objectives

After studying this chapter, you should be able to:

1. List and describe intentional torts against persons and against property.
2. List and explain the elements necessary to prove negligence.
3. Describe the business torts of unfair competition, disparagement, and fraud.
4. Describe and apply the doctrine of strict liability.
5. Describe cyber torts conducted on the Internet.

Chapter Contents

- ■ Intentional Torts Against Persons
- ■ Intentional Torts Against Property
- ■ Unintentional Torts (Negligence)
- ■ Special Negligence Doctrines
- ■ Defenses Against Negligence
- ■ Special Business Torts
- ■ Strict Liability

Tort is the French word for a "wrong." Tort law protects a variety of injuries and provides remedies for them. Under tort law, an injured party can bring a *civil lawsuit* to seek compensation for a wrong done to the party or to the party's property. Many torts have their origin in common law. The courts and legislatures have extended tort law to reflect changes in modern society.

Tort damages are monetary damages that are sought from the offending party. They are intended to compensate the injured party for the injury suffered. Such injury may consist of past and future medical expenses, loss of wages, pain and suffering, mental distress, and other damages caused by the defendant's tortious conduct. If the victim of a tort dies, his or her beneficiaries can bring a *wrongful death action* to recover damages from the defendant. *Punitive damages*, which are awarded to punish the defendant, may be recovered in intentional tort and strict liability cases. Other remedies, such as injunctions, may be available, too.

This chapter discusses various tort laws, including intentional torts, negligence, strict liability, and cyber torts.

Intentional Torts Against Persons

The law protects a person from unauthorized touching, restraint, or other contact. In addition, the law protects a person's reputation and privacy. Violations of these rights are actionable as torts. **Intentional torts** against persons are discussed in the paragraphs that follow.

Assault

Assault is (1) the threat of immediate harm or offensive contact or (2) any action that arouses reasonable apprehension of imminent harm. Actual physical contact is unnecessary. Threats of future harm are not actionable. For example, suppose a 6-foot-5-inch, 250-pound male makes a first and threatens to punch a 5-foot, 100-pound woman. If the woman is afraid that the man will physically harm her, she can sue him for assault. If she is a black-belt karate champion and laughs at the threat, there is no assault because the threat does not cause any apprehension.

Battery

Battery is unauthorized and harmful or offensive physical contact with another person. Basically, the interest protected here is each person's reasonable sense of dignity and safety. For example, intentionally hitting someone is considered battery because it is harmful. Note that there does not have to be direct physical contact between the victim and the perpetrator. If an injury results, throwing a rock, shooting an arrow or a bullet, knocking off a hat, pulling a chair out from under someone, and poisoning a drink are all instances of actionable battery. The victim need not be aware of the harmful or offensive contact (e.g., it may take place while the victim is asleep). Assault and battery often occur together, although they do not have to (e.g., the perpetrator hits the victim on the back of the head without any warning).

Transferred Intent Doctrine   Sometimes a person acts with the intent to injure one person but actually injures another. The *doctrine of transferred intent* applies to such situations. Under this doctrine, the law transfers the perpetrator's intent from the target to the actual victim of the act. The victim can then sue the defendant.

Business Brief

Tort law imposes a duty on persons and business agents not to intentionally or negligently injure others in society.

Thoughts much too deep for tears subdue the Court When I assumpsit bring, and godlike waive a tort.

J. L. Adolphus
The Circuiteers (1885)

Business Brief

Civil lawsuits allow injured victims to recover dollar damages from the responsible parties.

False Imprisonment

The intentional confinement or restraint of another person without authority or justification and without that person's consent constitutes **false imprisonment**. The victim may be restrained or confined by physical force, barriers, threats of physical harm, or the perpetrator's false assertion of legal authority (i.e., *false arrest*). A threat of future harm or moral pressure is not considered false imprisonment. The false imprisonment must be complete. For example, merely locking one door to a building when other exits are not locked is not false imprisonment. In such a case, a person is not obliged to risk danger or an affront to his or her dignity by attempting to escape.

Business Brief

Merchant protection statutes allow merchants to stop, detain, and investigate suspected shoplifters without being held liable for false imprisonment if (1) there are reasonable grounds for the suspicion, (2) suspects are detained for only a reasonable time, and (3) investigations are conducted in a reasonable manner.

Merchant Protection Statutes Shoplifting causes substantial losses to merchants each year. Almost all states have enacted **merchant protection statutes**, also known as the **shopkeeper's privilege**. These statutes allow merchants to stop, detain, and investigate suspected shoplifters without being held liable for false imprisonment if

1. There are reasonable grounds for the suspicion.
2. Suspects are detained for only a reasonable time.
3. Investigations are conducted in a reasonable manner.

Contemporary Environment
Wal-Mart Shopper Wins

On Christmas Eve 1995, LaShawna Goodman went to a local Wal-Mart store in Opelika, Alabama, to do some last-minute holiday shopping. She brought along her two young daughters and a telephone she had purchased earlier at Wal-Mart to exchange. She presented the telephone and receipt to a Wal-Mart employee, who took the telephone. Unable to find another telephone she wanted, Goodman retrieved the previously purchased telephone from the employee, bought another item, and left. Outside, Ms. Goodman was stopped by Wal-Mart security personnel and was accused of stealing the phone. Goodman offered to show the Wal-Mart employees the original receipt, but the Wal-Mart employees detained her and called the police. Ms. Goodman was handcuffed in front of her children. Wal-Mart filed criminal charges against Ms. Goodman.

At the criminal trial, Ms. Goodman was acquitted of all charges. Now it was Ms. Goodman's turn: She filed a civil lawsuit against Wal-Mart Stores, Inc., to recover damages for falsely accusing her

of stealing the telephone. Ms. Goodman presented her evidence. Wal-Mart asserted the defense that it was within its rights to have detained Ms. Goodman as it did and to have prosecuted Ms. Goodman based on its investigation. Wal-Mart asserted that the merchant protection statute protected its actions in this case.

The jury did not accept Wal-Mart's plea that it had acted reasonably. The jury rejected Wal-Mart's defenses, including the shopkeeper's privilege and its allegations that it had not maliciously prosecuted her. The jury determined that Ms. Goodman should be awarded $200,000 in compensatory damages for her suffering. The jury then decided that Wal-Mart had acted so badly in this case that it tacked on punitive damages to its award to Ms. Goodman just to teach Wal-Mart a lesson.

The Supreme Court of Alabama upheld liability, the award of $200,000 in compensatory damages, and an award of $600,000 in punitive damages [*Wal-Mart Stores, Inc. v. Goodman*, 789 So.2d 166, 2000 Ala. Lexis 548 (2000)] ■

Misappropriation of the Right to Publicity

Each person has the exclusive legal right to control and profit from the commercial use of his or her name and personality during his or her lifetime. This is a valuable right, particularly to well-known persons such as sports figures and movie stars. Any attempt by another person to appropriate a living person's name or identify for commercial purposes is actionable. The wrongdoer is liable for the **tort of misappropriation of the right to publicity** (also called the **tort of appropriation**). In such cases, the plaintiff can (1) recover the unauthorized profits made by the offending party and (2) obtain an injunction against further unauthorized use of his or her name or identity. Many states provide that the right to publicity survives a person's death and may be enforced by the deceased's heirs.

Consider This Example   Brad Pitt is a famous movie star. If an advertising agency places Brad Pitt's likeness (e.g., photo) on a billboard advertising a product without Brad Pitt's permission, it has engaged in the tort of misappropriation of the right to publicity. Brad Pitt could sue and recover the profits made by the offending party as well as an injunction to prevent unauthorized use of his likeness by the offending party.

Invasion of the Right to Privacy

The law recognizes each person's right to live his or her life without being subjected to unwarranted and undesired publicity. A violation of this right constitutes the tort of **invasion of the right to privacy**. Examples of this tort include reading someone else's mail, wiretapping, and such. In contrast to defamation, with invasion of the right to privacy, the fact does not have to be untrue. Therefore, truth is not a defense to a charge of invasion of privacy. If the fact is public information, there is no claim to privacy. However, a fact that was once public (e.g., commission of a crime) may become private after the passage of time.

Placing someone in a "false light" constitutes an invasion of privacy. For example, sending an objectionable telegram to a third party and signing another's name would place the purported sender in a false light in the eyes of the receiver. Falsely attributing beliefs or acts to another can also form the basis of a lawsuit.

In the following case, the court found invasion of privacy.

Lewis, Dennis, and Shemanski v. LeGrow
670 N.W.2d 175, 2003 Mich.App. Lexis 1957 (2003)
Court of Appeals of Michigan

Case 4.1
Invasion of Privacy

Background and Facts

James Francis LeGrow had sexual relations in his bedroom at different times with three different women. On each occasion, LeGrow secretly videotaped his sexual relations with them. One day, one of the women found a videotape on her side door that contained an unlabeled videotape which showed each of the women having sex with LeGrow. She called one of the other women, who obtained the tape and brought it to the police. When LeGrow was contacted by the police, he stated that he thought his girlfriend stole the videotape. The three women who were taped sued LeGrow in a civil action to obtain damages for invasion of privacy. The jury found LeGrow liable for the tort of invasion of privacy and awarded two of the women $100,000 and the third women $155,000. LeGrow appealed.

Issue

Did defendant LeGrow commit the tort of invasion of privacy?

Court's Reasoning

The court of appeals held that LeGrow's bedroom was a private place and that the women would have a reasonable expectation of privacy while having consensual sexual relations with the

defendant there. The court found that none of the women had expressly or impliedly consented to the videotaping of their activities. The court of appeals upheld the trial court's finding of invasion of privacy and the award of damages to each of the women.

Decision and Remedy

The court of appeals held that the defendant had committed the tort of invasion of privacy. The court of appeals affirmed the judgment of the trial court.

Case Questions

Critical Legal Thinking   Describe the tort of invasion of privacy. What elements are necessary to prove this tort?

Business Ethics   Do you think many invasions of privacy like the ones here are not reported and prosecuted?

Contemporary Business   Does the Internet increase the probability that more invasions of privacy will occur than before?

Defamation of Character

A person's reputation is a valuable asset. Therefore, every person is protected from false statements made by others during his or her lifetime. This protection ends upon a person's death. The tort of **defamation of character** requires a plaintiff to prove that (1) the defendant made an *untrue statement of fact* about the plaintiff and (2) the statement was intentionally or accidentally *published* to a third party. In this context, *publication* simply means that a third person heard or saw the untrue statement. It does not just mean appearance in newspapers, magazines, or books.

The name for an oral defamatory statement is **slander**. A false statement that appears in a letter, newspaper, magazine, book, photograph, movie, video, and the like is called **libel**. Most courts hold that defamatory statements in radio and television broadcasts are considered libel because of the permanency of the media.

The publication of an untrue statement of fact is not the same as the publication of an opinion. the publication of opinions is usually not actionable. For example, the statement "My lawyer is lousy" is an opinion. Because defamation is defined as an untrue statement of fact, truth is an absolute defense to a charge of defamation.

Landmark Law

In *New York Times v. Sullivan*, the U.S. Supreme Court held that public officials cannot recover for defamation unless they can prove that the defendant acted with *actual malice*.

Public Figures as Plaintiffs In *New York Times Co. v. Sullivan*,[1] the U.S. Supreme Court held that *public officials* cannot recover for defamation unless they can prove that the defendant acted with "actual malice." Actual malice means that the defendant made the false statement knowingly or with reckless disregard of its falsity. This requirement has since been extended to *public figure* plaintiffs such as movie stars, sports personalities, and other celebrities.

Contemporary Environment

Eminem Not Liable for Slander

Eminem is a famous white rapper who has won a Grammy award for his music in the movie *8-Mile* in which he starred. Eminem's lyrics often contain references to his personal experiences. In the song "Brain Damage," a song from his 1999 CD *The Slim Shady LP*, Eminem sang lyrics he had written, which read in part:

I was harassed daily by this fat kid named DeAngelo Bailey,
He banged my head against the urinal till he broke my nose.
Soaked my clothes in blood.
Grabbed me and choked my throat.

DeAngelo Bailey sued Eminem for $1 million, alleging that the lyrics were untrue and slanderous. Eminem's mother publicly defended her son's account of the bullying by Bailey. After hearing all the evidence, Judge Deborah Servitto wrote:

Mr. Bailey complains that his rap is trash
So he's seeking compensation in the form of cash.
Bailey thinks he's entitled to some money gain
Because Eminem used his name in vain.
The lyrics are stories no one would take as fact
They're an exaggeration of a childish act.
It is therefore this court's ultimate position
That Eminem is entitled to summary disposition.

Judge Servitto ruled in favor of Eminem. [*Bailey v. Eminem*, Michigan Trial Court, 2003] ■

Intentional Infliction of Emotional Distress

In some situations, a victim may suffer mental or emotional distress without first being physically harmed. *Restatement (Second) of Torts* provides that a person whose *extreme and outrageous* conduct intentionally or recklessly causes severe emotional distress to another is liable for that emotional distress.[2] This is called the tort of **intentional infliction of emotional distress**, or the **tort of outrage**. The plaintiff must prove that the defendant's conduct was "so outrageous in character and so extreme in degree as to go beyond all possible bounds of decency, and to be regarded as atrocious and utterly intolerable in a civilized society."[3] An indignity, an annoyance, rough language, or an occasional inconsiderate or unkind act does not constitute outrageous behavior. However, repeated annoyances or harassment coupled with threats are considered outrageous.

The tort does not require any publication to a third party or physical contact between the plaintiff and defendant. For example, a credit collection agency making harassing telephone calls to a debtor every morning between 1:00 and 5:00 A.M. is outrageous conduct.

The mental distress suffered by the plaintiff must be severe. Many states require that this mental distress be manifested by some form of physical injury, discomfort, or illness, such as nausea, ulcers, headaches, or miscarriage. This requirement is intended to prevent false claims. Some states have abandoned this requirement. The courts have held that shame, humiliation, embarrassment, anger, fear, and worry constitute severe mental distress.

The tort of intentional infliction of emotional distress was asserted in the following case.

Roach v. Stern

675 N.Y.S.2d 133, (1998) 1998 N.Y.App. Div. Lexis 7998 (7998)
Supreme Court, Appellate Division, New York

Case 4.2
Intentional Infliction of Emotional Distress

Background and Facts

Howard Stern is a famous television talk-show host who emcees an irreverent daily show on the radio. The show is syndicated by Infinity Broadcasting, Inc. (Infinity), and is listened to by millions of people across the country. Deborah Roach, a self-described topless dancer and cable-access television host, was a perennial guest on the Howard Stern radio show. She was famous for her stories about encounters with aliens. Roach died of a drug overdose at the age of 27. Roach's sister, Melissa Driscoll, had Roach's body cremated and gave a portion of the remains to Roach's close friend Chaunce Hayden. Driscoll said she did so with the understanding that Hayden would "preserve and honor said remains in an appropriate and private manner."

On July 18, 1995, Hayden brought a box containing Roach's cremated remains to Stern's radio show. Hayden said she did so as a memorial to Roach because "the only happiness Debbie had was the Howard Stern show." Thereafter, Stern, Hayden, and other participants in the broadcast played with Roach's ashes and made crude comments about the remains. The radio show was videotaped and later broadcast on a national cable television station. Roach's sister and brother sued Stern, Infinity, and Hayden to recover damages for intentional infliction of emotional distress. The trial court dismissed the complaint. The plaintiffs appealed.

Issue

Did the plaintiffs sufficiently plead a cause of action to recover damages for the intentional infliction of emotional distress?

Court's Reasoning

The court stated that to impose liability for intentional infliction of emotional distress, "the conduct complained of must be so outrageous in character, and so extreme in degree, as to be beyond all

possible bounds of decency, and to be regarded as atrocious, and utterly intolerable in a civilized community." The court noted that the element of outrageous conduct is rigorous and difficult to satisfy and that its purpose is to filter out trivial complaints and ensure that the claim of severe emotional distress is genuine. The court decided that a jury could reasonably conclude that the manner in which Roach's remains were handled for entertainment purposes went beyond the bounds of decent behavior. The court reinstated the plaintiffs' complaint.

Decision and Remedy

The court held that the complaint and the facts of the case as pleaded sufficiently stated a cause of action to recover damages for intentional infliction of emotional distress. The supreme court reversed the judgment of the trial court and reinstated the case against Stern and Infinity.

Case Questions

Critical Legal Thinking   Should the tort of intentional infliction of emotional distress be recognized by the law? What difficulties arise in trying to apply this tort?

Business Ethics   Was Stern's and the other participants' conduct on the radio show tasteless? Did it amount to "outrageous conduct" for which legal damages should be awarded?

Contemporary Business   If Stern and Infinity are found liable, will a chilling effect on future broadcasts result?

Malicious Prosecution

Businesses and individuals often believe they have a reason to sue someone to recover damages or other remedies. If the plaintiff has a legitimate reason to bring the lawsuit and does so, but the plaintiff does not win the lawsuit, he or she does not have to worry about being sued by the person whom he or she sued. But a losing plaintiff does have to worry about being sued by the defendant in a second lawsuit for **malicious prosecution** if certain elements are met. In a lawsuit for malicious prosecution, the original defendant sues the original plaintiff. In this second lawsuit, which is a *civil* action for damages, the original defendant is the plaintiff and the original plaintiff is the defendant. To succeed in a malicious prosecution lawsuit, the courts require the plaintiff to prove all of the following:

- The plaintiff in the original lawsuit (now the defendant) instituted or was responsible for instituting the original lawsuit.
- There was no *probable cause* for the first lawsuit; that is, it was a frivolous lawsuit.
- The plaintiff in the original action brought it with *malice*. [Caution: This is a very difficult element to prove.]
- The original lawsuit was terminated in favor of the original defendant (now the plaintiff).
- The current plaintiff suffered injury as a result of the original lawsuit.

The courts do not look favorably on malicious prosecution lawsuits because they feel such lawsuits inhibit the original plaintiff's incentive to sue.

Intentional Torts Against Property

There are two general categories of property: real property and personal property. *Real property* consists of land and anything permanently attached to that land. *Personal property* consists of things that are movable, such as automobiles, books, clothes, pets, and such. The law recognizes certain torts against real and personal property. These torts are discussed in the paragraphs that follow.

Trespass to Land

Interference with an owner's right to exclusive possession of land constitutes the tort of **trespass to land**. There does not have to be any interference with the owner's use or enjoyment of the land; the ownership itself is what counts. Thus, unauthorized use of another person's land is trespass even if the owner is not using it. Actual harm to the property is not necessary.

Examples of trespass to land include entering another person's land without permission, remaining on the land of another after permission to do so has expired (e.g., a guest refuses to leave), or causing something or someone to enter another's land (e.g., one person builds a dam that causes another person's land to flood). A person who is pushed onto another's land or enters that land with good reason is not liable for trespass. For example, a person may enter onto another person's land to save a child or a pet from harm.

Trespass to and Conversion of Personal Property

The tort of **trespass to personal property** occurs whenever one person injures another person's personal property or interferes with that person's enjoyment of his or her personal property. The injured party can sue for damages. For example, breaking another's car window is trespass to personal property.

Depriving a true owner of the use and enjoyment of his or her personal property by taking over such property and exercising ownership rights over it constitutes the tort of **conversion of personal property**. Conversion also occurs when someone who originally is given possession of personal property fails to return it (e.g., fails to return a borrowed car). The rightful owner can sue to recover the property. If the property was lost or destroyed, the owner can sue to recover its value.

Unintentional Torts (Negligence)

Under the doctrine of **unintentional tort**, commonly referred to as **negligence**, a person is liable for harm that is the *foreseeable consequence* of his or her actions. *Negligence* is defined as "the omission to do something which a reasonable man would do, or doing something which a prudent and reasonable man would not do."[4]

Consider This Example   A driver who causes an automobile accident because he or she fell asleep at the wheel is liable for any resulting injuries caused by his or her negligence.

Elements of Negligence

To be successful in a negligence lawsuit, the plaintiff must prove that (1) the defendant owed a *duty of care* to the plaintiff, (2) the defendant *breached* this duty of care, (3) the plaintiff suffered *injury*, and (4) the defendant's negligent act *caused* the plaintiff's injury. Each of these elements is discussed in the paragraphs that follow.

> Negligence is the omission to do something which a reasonable man would do, or doing something which a prudent and reasonable man would not do.
>
> B. Alderson Blyth v. Brimingham Waterworks Co. *(1856)*

Duty of Care   To determine whether a defendant is liable for negligence, it must first be ascertained whether the defendant owed a **duty of care** to the plaintiff. Duty of care refers to the obligation people owe each other—that is, the duty not to cause any unreasonable harm or risk of harm. For example, each person owes a duty to drive his or her car carefully, not to push or shove on escalators, not to leave skateboards on the sidewalk, and the like. Businesses owe a duty to make safe products, not to cause accidents, and so on.

Exposition Boulevard, Los Angeles, California. Few of us can pass one of these familiar roadside memorials without thinking about the pain and suffering of the occupants of the vehicle and their surviving loved ones.

The courts decide whether a duty of care is owed in specific cases by applying a *reasonable person standard*. Under this test, the courts attempt to determine how an *objective, careful, and conscientious person would have acted in the same circumstances* and then measure the defendant's conduct against that standard. The defendant's subjective intent ("I did not mean to do it") is immaterial in assessing liability. Certain impairments do not affect the reasonable person standard. For example, there is no reasonable alcoholic standard.

Defendants with a particular expertise or competence are measured against a *reasonable professional standard*. This standard is applied in much the same way as the reasonable person standard. For example, a brain surgeon is measured against a reasonable brain surgeon standard rather than a lower reasonable doctor standard. Children are generally required to act as a *reasonable child* of similar age and experience would act.

Breach of Duty

Once a court finds that the defendant actually owed the plaintiff a duty of care, it must determine whether the defendant breached that duty. A **breach of the duty of care** is the failure to exercise care. In other words, it is the failure to act as a reasonable person would act. A breach of this duty may consist of either an action (e.g., throwing a lit match on the ground in the forest and causing a fire) or a failure to act when there is a duty to act (e.g., a firefighter refusing to put out a fire). Generally, passersby are not expected to rescue others gratuitously to save them from harm.

In the first case that follows, the court found the defendants liable for negligence. In the second case that follows, the court held that the defendants were not liable for negligence.

Wilhelm v. Flores

133 S.W.3d 726, 2003 Tex.App. Lexis 9335 (2003)
Court of Appeals of Texas

Case 4.3

Negligence

Background and Facts

Curtis R. Wilhelm owned beehives and kept the hives on property he owned. John Black, who operated a honeybee business, contracted to purchase some beehives from Wilhelm. Black employed Santos Flores, Sr., to help him pick up the beehives from Wilhelm. Black provided Flores with a protective suit to wear while picking up the beehives. Neither Wilhelm nor Black informed Flores of the danger of working with bees. After picking up beehives from Wilhelm's home, Black and Flores drove to remote property owned by Wilhelm to pick up other beehives. Flores opened the veil on his protective suit. After loading one beehive onto the truck, Flores started staggering and yelling for help. Flores sustained several bee stings, suffered anaphylactic shock reaction, and died before an ambulance could reach him. Flores's wife and children sued Wilhelm and Black for negligence for failing to warn Flores of the dangers of working with beehives and the possibility of dying of anaphylactic shock if stung by a bee. The jury found Wilhelm and Black each 50 percent liable and awarded $1,591,000 to the plaintiffs. Wilhelm appealed.

Issue

Did Wilhelm act negligently by failing to warn Flores of the dangers of working with beehives?

Court's Reasoning

The court of appeals held that the owner of bees owes a duty to warn others of the dangers of working around bees, including the possibility of dying from anaphylactic shock if stung by a bee. The court found that Wilhelm had a college degree in entomology, had owned beehives for about five years, and knew people could die from bee stings. The evidence showed that Wilhelm did not provide any warning to Flores concerning the dangers associated with bee stings. The court held that Wilhelm was negligent in failing to warn Flores of the dangers of working with bees.

Decision and Remedy

The court of appeals held that Wilhelm owed a duty of care to warn Flores of the dangers of working with beehives and was negligent in not doing so. The court of appeals affirmed the award of damages to Flores's estate.

Case Questions

Critical Legal Thinking Should failure to warn be a basis for a negligence lawsuit? Explain.

Business Ethics Do you think Wilhelm should have been held liable? Explain.

Contemporary Business Should businesses carry liability insurance to protect against lawsuit judgments? Explain.

James v. Meow Media, Inc.

300 F.3d 683, 2002 U.S.App. Lexis 16185 (2002)
United States Court of Appeals, Sixth Circuit

Case 4.4
No Duty of Care

Background and Facts

Michael Carneal was a 14-year-old freshman student at Heath High School in Paducah, Kentucky. Carneal regularly played the violent interactive video and computer games "Doom," "Quake," "Castle Wolfenstein," "Rampage," "Nightmare Creatures," "Mech Warrior," "Resident Evil," and "Final Fantasy." These games involved the player shooting virtual opponents with computer guns and other weapons. Carneal also watched videotaped movies, including one called *The Basketball Diaries*, in which a high-school-student protagonist dreams of killing his teacher and several of his fellow classmates. On December 1, 1997, Carneal took a .22-caliber pistol and five shotguns into the lobby of Heath High School and shot several of his fellow students, killing three and wounding many others. The three students killed were Jessica James, Kayce Steger, and Nicole Hadley.

The parents of the three dead children ("James") sued the producers and distributors of the violent video games and movies that Carneal had watched previous to the shooting. The parents sued to recover damages for wrongful death, alleging that the defendants were negligent in producing and distributing such games and movies to Carneal. The U.S. district court applied Kentucky law and held that the defendants did not owe or breach a duty to the plaintiffs and therefore were not liable for negligence. The plaintiffs appealed.

Issue

Did the defendant video and movie producers and distributors owe a duty of care to the plaintiffs by selling and licensing violent video games and movies to Carneal, who killed the three children?

Court's Reasoning

The court of appeals stated that the existence of a duty of care is determined by the "foreseeability" test and that this is a policy decision to be determined by the court. The court also stated that the court must act as a filter and dismiss cases lacking a duty of care. The court of appeals first noted, "Individuals are generally entitled to assume that third parties will not commit intentional criminal acts." The court then noted, however, "Carneal's reaction was not a normal reaction. Indeed, Carneal is not a normal person, but it is not utter craziness to predict that someone like Carneal is out there." The court applied its policy analysis as to foreseeability and held that the defendants did not owe a duty of care to the plaintiffs. The court of appeals stated, "It appears simply impossible to predict that these games, movie, and Internet sites (alone, or in what combinations) would incite a young person to violence. Carneal's reaction to the games and movies at issue here, assuming that his violent actions were such a reaction, was simply too idiosyncratic to expect the defendants to have anticipated it. We find that it is simply too far a leap from shooting characters on a video screen (an activity undertaken by millions) to shooting people in a classroom (an activity undertaken by a handful, at most) for Carneal's actions to have been reasonably foreseeable to the manufacturers of the media that Carneal played and viewed."

Decision and Remedy

The court of appeals held that the defendant video game and movie producers and distributors did not owe a duty of care to the plaintiffs by selling and licensing violent video games and movies to Carneal, who murdered the three children.

Case Questions

Critical Legal Thinking   How does the court define *foreseeability*? Did the court use a narrow, middle, or broad interpretation of foreseeability in deciding this case? Explain.

Business Ethics   Do producers and distributors of video games and movies owe a duty of care to society not to produce and distribute violent games and movies?

Contemporary Business   What would have been the consequences for the video game and movie industries if the court had held in favor of the plaintiffs? Explain.

Injury to Plaintiff   Even though a defendant's act may have breached a duty of care owed to the plaintiff, this breach is not actionable unless the plaintiff suffers **injury**. For example, a business's negligence causes an explosion and fire to occur at its factory at night. No one is injured and there is no damage to the neighbors' property. The negligence is not actionable.

The damages recoverable depend on the effect of the injury on the plaintiff's life or profession. Suppose two men injure their hands when a train door malfunctions. The first man is a professional basketball player. The second is a college professor. The first man can recover greater damages than the second.

In the following case, the court awarded damages for the plaintiffs' injuries caused by the defendant's negligence.

Wal-Mart Stores, Inc. v. Frierson
818 So.2d 1135, 2002 Miss. Lexis 191 (2002)
Supreme Court of Mississippi

Case 4.5
Slip-and-Fall

Background and Facts

Turner Frierson and his wife, Pinkie Mae Frierson, went to a Wal-Mart store in Indianola, Mississippi. As the Friersons were leaving the store, Mr. Frierson slipped and fell in the vestibule of the store. Evidence showed that it had rained that afternoon and that Wal-Mart employees had left open an outside door that led to the vestibule so that Wal-Mart employees could return shopping carts to the inside of the store. Rain blew through the open door and into the vestibule, and water dripped off the shopping carts, making the tile floor slippery. Mr. Frierson sued Wal-Mart Stores, Inc., for negligence to recover injuries he suffered from the slip and fall. Mrs. Frierson sued Wal-Mart for loss of consortium caused to her because of Mr. Frierson's injuries. The jury returned a verdict awarding $100,000 to Mr. Frierson and $25,000 to Mrs. Frierson, and the court entered judgment. Wal-Mart Stores appealed, alleging that the jury's verdict was based on bias, passion, and prejudice.

Issue

Was the jury verdict in favor of the Friersons the result of the jury's bias, passion, or prejudice?

Court's Reasoning

The supreme court of Mississippi noted that the law requires a verdict to be set aside if it is so contrary to the overwhelming weight of the evidence that to allow it to stand would be unconscionable. The supreme court upheld the decision that Wal-Mart was liable for negligence. The supreme court found that Mr. Frierson was credible when he testified that he was in pain most of the time, takes medicine daily for the pain, and cannot do the things he used to do. The supreme court held that the jury's award of $100,000 to Turner Frierson, which was more than six times the $16,574 medical costs he suffered (paid by Medicaid/Medicare), was not contrary to the weight of the evidence. The supreme court also held that the award of $25,000 to Mrs. Pinkie Mae Frierson was reasonable because evidence showed that Mr. Frierson was irritable because of his injuries, took it out on Mrs. Frierson, and was unable to perform conjugal duties. The court stated, "A married woman shall have a cause of action for loss of consortium through negligent injury to her husband."

Decision and Remedy

The supreme court of Mississippi found no jury bias, passion, or prejudice in reaching its verdicts. The supreme court affirmed the trial court's judgment and upheld the monetary awards to both Mr. and Mrs. Frierson.

Case Questions

Critical Legal Thinking   What are the elements of negligence? Were they found in this case? Explain.

Business Ethics   Did Wal-Mart act ethically in alleging that the jury had acted with bias, passion, or prejudice?

Contemporary Business   Do you think retail stores face many faked slip-and-fall cases? Is faking such a case easy to do?

Causation   A person who commits a negligent act is not liable unless this act was the cause of the plaintiff's injuries. Courts have divided **causation** into two categories—*causation in fact* and *proximate cause*—and require each to be shown before the plaintiff may recover damages:

1. *Causation in fact.* The defendant's negligent act must be the **causation in fact**, or **actual cause**, of the plaintiff's injuries. For example, suppose a corporation negligently pollutes the plaintiff's drinking water. The plaintiff dies of a heart attack unrelated to the polluted water. Although the corporation has acted negligently, it is not liable for the plaintiff's death. There were a negligent act and an injury, but there was no cause-and-effect relationship between them. If, instead, the plaintiff had died from the pollution, there would have been causation in fact, and the polluting corporation would have been liable. If two (or more) persons are liable for negligently causing the plaintiff's injuries, both (or all) can be held liable to the plaintiff if each of their acts is a substantial factor in causing the plaintiff's injuries.

2. *Proximate cause.* Under the law, a negligent party is not necessarily liable for all damages set in motion by his or her negligent act. Based on public policy, the law establishes a point along the damage chain after which the negligent party is no longer responsible for the consequences of his or her actions. This limitation on liability is referred to as **proximate cause** or **legal cause**. The general test of proximate cause is *forseeability*. A negligent party who is found to be the actual cause—but not the prox-

imate cause—of the plaintiff's injuries is not liable to the plaintiff. Situations are examined on a case-by-case basis.

The classical articulation of the doctrine of proximate cause appears in the famous Palsgraf case that follows.

Landmark Case
Palsgraf v. The Long Island Railroad Company

The landmark case establishing the doctrine of proximate cause is *Palsgraf v. Long Island Railroad Company*, a New York case decided in 1928. Helen Palsgraf was standing on a platform waiting for a passenger train. The Long Island Railroad Company owned and operated the trains and employed the station guards. As a man carrying a package wrapped in a newspaper tried to board the moving train, railroad guards tried to help him. In doing so, the package was dislodged from the man's arm, fell to the railroad tracks, and exploded. The package contained hidden fireworks. The explosion shook the railroad platform, causing a scale located on the platform to fall on Helen Palsgraf, injuring her. She sued the railroad for negligence. Justice Cardoza eloquently addressed the issue of proximate cause:

The conduct of the defendant's guard, if a wrong in its relation to the holder of the package, was not a wrong in its relation to the plaintiff, standing far away. Relatively to her it was not negligence at all. Nothing in the situation gave notice that the falling package had in it the potency of peril to persons thus removed. Negligence is not actionable unless it involves the invasion of a legally protected interest, the violation of a right. Proof of negligence in the air, so to speak, will not do. In every instance, before negligence can be predicated of a given act, back of the act must be sought and found a duty to the individual complaining, the observance of which would have averted or avoided the injury.

The argument for the plaintiff is built upon the shifting meanings of such words as "wrong" and "wrongful," and shares their instability. What the plaintiff must show is "a wrong" to herself, *i.e.*, a violation of her own right, and not merely a wrong to some one else, nor conduct "wrongful" because unsocial. The risk reasonably to be perceived defines the duty to be obeyed, and risk imports relation; it is risk to another or to others within the range of apprehension. Here, by concession, there was nothing in the situation to suggest to the most cautious mind that the parcel wrapped in newspaper would spread wreckage through the station. If the guard had thrown it down knowingly and willfully, he would not have threatened the plaintiff's safety, so far as appearances could warn him. His conduct would not have involved, even then, an unreasonable probability of invasion of her bodily security. Liability can be no greater where the act is inadvertent.

Negligence, like risk, is thus a term of relation. Negligence in the abstract, apart from things related, is surely not a tort, if indeed it is understandable at all. One who seeks redress at law does not make out a cause of action by showing without more that there has been damage to his person. If the harm was not willful, he must show that the act as to him had possibilities of danger so many and apparent as to entitle him to be protected against the doing of it though the harm was unintended.

Justice Cardoza denied Palsgraf's recovery, finding that the railroad was not the proximate cause of her injuries. [*Palsgraf v. The Long Island Railroad Company*, 248 N.Y. 339, 162 N.E. 99, 1928 N.Y. Lexis 1269 (N.Y. 1928)] ■

Pier, Santa Monica, California.
Who would be liable if the roller-coaster broke, causing injury to a rider?

Professional Malpractice

Professionals, such as doctors, lawyers, architects, accountants, and others, owe a duty of ordinary care in providing their services. This duty is known as the *reasonable professional standard*. A professional who breaches this duty of care is liable for the injury his or her negligence causes. This liability is commonly referred to as **professional malpractice**. For example, a doctor who amputates a wrong leg is liable for *medical malpractice*. A lawyer who fails to file a document with the court on time, causing the client's case to be dismissed, is liable for *legal malpractice*. An accountant who fails to use reasonable care, knowledge, skill, and judgment when providing auditing and other accounting services to a client is liable for *accounting malpractice*.

Professionals who breach this duty are liable to their patients or clients. They may also be liable to some third parties.

Business Ethics

Ouch! The Coffee's Too Hot!

Studies have shown that people care less about how good their coffee tastes than whether it is hot. So restaurants, coffee shops, and other sellers make their coffee hot. McDonald's, however, discovered that it was in hot water for making its coffee too hot. Consider this case.

Stella Liebeck, and 81-year-old resident of Albuquerque, New Mexico, visited a drive-through window of a McDonald's restaurant with her grandson. Her grandson, the driver of the vehicle, placed the order. When it came, he handed a hot cup of coffee to Liebeck. As her grandson drove away from the drive-through window, Liebeck took the lid off the coffee cup she held in her lap. The coffee spilled all over Liebeck, who suffered third-degree burns on her legs, groin, and buttocks. She required medical treatment, was hospitalized, and suffered permanent scars from the incident.

Liebeck sued McDonald's for selling coffee that was too hot and for failing to warn her of the danger of the hot coffee it served. McDonald's rejected Liebeck's pretrial offer to settle the case for $300,000 and went to trial.

At trial, McDonald's denied that it had been negligent and asserted that Liebeck's own negligence—opening a hot coffee cup on her lap—caused her injuries. The jury heard evidence that McDonald's enforces a quality-control rule requiring its restaurants and franchises to serve coffee at 180 to 190 degrees Fahrenheit. Evidence showed that this was 10 to 30 degrees hotter than coffee served by competing restaurant chains, and approximately 40 to 50 degrees hotter than normal house-brewed coffee.

Based on this evidence, the jury concluded that McDonald's acted recklessly and awarded Liebeck $200,000 compensatory damages (reduced by $40,000 for her own negligence) and $2.7 million punitive damages. After the trial court judge reduced the amount of punitive damages to $480,000, the parties reached an out-of-court settlement for an undisclosed amount. Because of this case, McDonald's and other purveyors of coffee have reduced the temperature at which they sell coffee and have placed warnings on their coffee cups.

1. Do you think McDonald's acted recklessly?
2. Was an award of punitive damages warranted? Explain. ■

Special Negligence Doctrines

The courts have developed many *special negligence doctrines*. The most important of these are discussed in the paragraphs that follow.

Negligent Infliction of Emotional Distress

Some jurisdictions have extended the tort of emotional distress to include the **negligent infliction of emotional distress**. The most common examples of this involve bystanders who witness the injury or death of a loved one that is caused by another's negligent conduct. The bystander, even though not personally physically injured, can sue the negligent party for his or her own mental suffering under this tort.

Generally, to be successful in this type of case, the plaintiff must prove that (1) a relative was killed or injured by the defendant, (2) the plaintiff suffered severe emotional distress, and (3) the plaintiff's mental distress resulted from a sensory and contemporaneous observance of the accident. Some states require that the plaintiff's mental distress be manifested by some physical injury; other states have eliminated this requirement.

Consider This Example   A father is driving his young daughter to school in his automobile when another driver negligently runs a red light and hits their automobile. Suppose that the young daughter dies from her injuries, and the father is uninjured. The father suffers severe emotional distress because of the loss of his daughter and manifests this distress by suffering physically. In this case, the father can sue the driver for negligence (1) to recover for his daughter's death and (2) for negligent infliction of emotional distress to recover damages for the severe distress he suffers.

Negligence Per Se

Statutes often establish duties owed by one person to another. The violation of a statute that proximately causes an injury is **negligence per se**. The plaintiff in such an action must prove that (1) a statute existed, (2) the statute was enacted to prevent the type of injury suffered, and (3) the plaintiff was within a class of persons meant to be protected by the statute.

Consider This Example   Most cities have an ordinance that places the responsibility for fixing public sidewalks in residential areas on the homeowners whose homes front the sidewalks. A homeowners is liable if he or she fails to repair a damaged sidewalk in front of his or her home and a pedestrian trips and is injured because of the damage. The injured party does not have to prove that the homeowner owed the duty because the statute establishes that.

Res Ipsa Loquitur

If a defendant is in control of a situation in which a plaintiff has been injured and has superior knowledge of the circumstances surrounding the injury, the plaintiff might have difficulty proving the defendant's negligence. In such a situation, the law applies the doctrine of **res ipsa loquitur** (Latin for "the thing speaks for itself"). This doctrine raises a presumption of negligence and switches the burden to the defendant to prove that he or she was not negligent. *Res ipsa loquitur* applies in cases where the following elements are met:

1. The defendant had exclusive control of the instrumentality or situation that caused the plaintiff's injury.
2. The injury would not have ordinarily occurred but for someone's negligence.

Consider These Examples   Haeran goes in for major surgery and is given anesthesia to put her to sleep during the operation. Sometime after the operation, it is discovered that a surgical instrument had been left in Haeran during the operation. She suffers severe injury because of the left-in instrument. Haeran would be hard-pressed to identify which doctor or nurse had been careless and left the instrument in her body. In this case, the court can apply the doctrine of *res ipsa loquitur* and place the presumption of negligence on the defendants. Any defendant who can prove he or she did not leave the instrument in Haeran escapes liability; any defendant who does not disprove his or her negligence is liable. Other typical *res ipsa loquitur* cases involve commercial airplane crashes, falling elevators, and the like.

Good Samaritan Laws

In the past, liability exposure made many doctors, nurses, and other medical professionals reluctant to stop and render aid to victims in emergency situations, such as highway accidents. Almost all states have enacted **Good Samaritan laws** that relieve medical

> No court has ever given, nor do we think ever can give, a definition of what constitutes a reasonable or an average man.
>
> Lord Goddard C.J.R. v. McCarthy
> *(1954)*

professionals from liability for injury caused by their ordinary negligence in such circumstances. Good Samaritan laws protect medical professionals only from liability for their *ordinary negligence*, not for injuries caused by their gross negligence or reckless or intentional conduct. Most Good Samaritan laws protect licensed doctors and nurses and laypersons who have been certified in CPR. Laypersons not trained in CPR are not generally protected by Good Samaritan statutes—that is, they are liable for injuries caused by their ordinary negligence in rendering aid.

Consider This Example   Sam is injured in an automobile accident and is unconscious in his automobile alongside the road. Doctor Pamela Heathcoat, who is driving by the scene of the accident, stops, pulls Sam from the burning wreckage, and administers first aid. In doing so, Pamela negligently breaks Sam's shoulder. If Pamela's negligence is ordinary negligence, she is not liable to Sam because the Good Samaritan law protects her from liability; if Pamela was grossly negligent or reckless in administering aid to Sam, she is liable to him for the injuries she caused. It is a question of fact for the jury to decide whether a doctor's conduct was ordinary negligence or gross negligence or recklessness. If Cathy, a layperson not trained in CPR, had rendered aid to Sam and caused Sam injury because of her ordinary negligence, the Good Samaritan law would not protect her and she would be liable to Sam.

Dram Shop Acts

Many states have enacted **dram shop acts** that make a tavern and bartender civilly liable for injuries caused to or by patrons who are served too much alcohol. The alcohol must be either served in sufficient quantity to make the patron intoxicated or served to an already intoxicated person. Both the tavern and the bartender are liable to third persons injured by the patron and for injuries suffered by the patron. They are also liable for injuries caused by or to minors served by the tavern, regardless of whether the minors are intoxicated.

Guest Statutes

Many states have enacted **guest statutes** which provide that if a driver voluntarily and without compensation gives a ride in a vehicle to another person (e.g., a hitchhiker), the driver is not liable to the passenger for injuries caused by the driver's ordinary negligence. However, if the passenger pays compensation to the driver, the driver owes a duty of ordinary care to the passenger and will be held liable. The driver is always liable to the passenger for wanton and gross negligence—for example, injuries caused because of excessive speed.

Fireman's Rule

Under the **fireman's rule**, a firefighter who is injured while putting out a fire may not sue the party whose negligence caused the fire. This rule has been extended to police officers and other government workers. The bases for this rule are (1) people might not call for help if they could be held liable; (2) firefighters, police officers and other such workers receive special training for their jobs; and (3) these workers have special medical and retirement programs that are paid for by the public.

"Danger Invites Rescue" Doctrine

The law recognizes a **"danger invites rescue" doctrine**. Under this doctrine, a rescuer who is injured while going to someone's rescue can sue the person who caused the dangerous situation. For example, a passerby who is injured while trying to rescue children from a fire set by an arsonist can bring a civil suit against the arsonist.

Social Host Liability

Several states have adopted the **social host liability** rule. This rule provides that a social host is liable for injuries caused by guests who are served alcohol at a social function (e.g., birthday party, wedding reception) and later cause injury because they are intoxicated. The injury may be to a third person or to the guest himself or herself. The alcohol served at the social function must be the cause of the injury. A few states have adopted statutes that relieve social hosts from such liability.[5]

Liability of Landowners

Owners and renters of real property owe certain duties to protect visitors from injury while on the property. A landowner's and tenant's liability generally depends on the status of the visitor. Visitors fall into the following categories:

1. ***Invites and licensees.*** An *invitee* is a person who has been expressly or impliedly invited onto the owner's premises for the *mutual benefit* of both parties (e.g., guests invited for dinner, the mail carrier, and customers of a business). A licensee is a person who, *for his or her own benefit*, enters onto the premises with the express or implied consent of the owner (e.g., an Avon representative, salespersons, Jehovah's Witnesses). An owner owes a **duty of ordinary care** to invitees and licensees. An owner is liable if he or she negligently causes injury to an invitee or licensee. For example, a homeowner is liable if she leaves a garden hose across the walkway on which an invitee or a licensee trips and is injured.

2. ***Trespassers.*** A *trespasser* is a person who has no invitation, permission, or right to be on another's property. Burglars are a common type of trespasser. Generally, an owner does not owe a duty of ordinary care to a trespasser. For example, if a trespasser trips and injures himself on a bicycle the owner negligently left out, the owner is not liable. An owner does owe a **duty not to willfully or wantonly injure a trespasser**. Thus, an owner cannot set traps to injure trespassers.

Grand Hotel, Mackinac Island, Michigan. An innkeeper owes a duty of utmost care to his or her guests.

A few states have eliminated the invitee-licensee-trespasser distinction. These states hold that owners and renters owe a duty of ordinary care to all persons who enter upon the property.

Liability of Common Carriers and Innkeepers

The common law holds common carriers and innkeepers to a higher standard of care than it does most other businesses. Common carriers and innkeepers owe a **duty of utmost care**— rather than a duty of ordinary care—to their passengers and guests. For example, innkeepers must provide security for their guests. The concept of utmost care is applied on a case-by-case basis. Obviously, a large hotel must provide greater security to guests than a "mom-and-pop" motel. Some states and cities have adopted specific statutes and ordinances relating to this duty.

In the following case, the court found that a landowner had engaged in *willful and wanton conduct*, and it awarded punitive damages.

Matthias v. Accor Economy Lodging, Inc. and Motel 6 Operating L.P.

347 F.3d 672, 2003 U.S.App. Lexis 21299 (2003)
United States Court of Appeals, Seventh Circuit

Case 4.6
Willful and Wanton Conduct

Background and Facts

The defendants, Accor Economy Lodging, Inc., and Motel 6 Operating L.P. (hereinafter referred to as Motel 6) operate the Motel 6 nationwide chain of motels and hotels. One of these hotels is in downtown Chicago. In 1998, EcoLab, an extermination service that the motel used, discovered bedbugs in several rooms in the motel and recommended that it be hired to spray every room, for which EcoLab would charge the motel $500 total, but the motel refused. The next year, bedbugs were again discovered in a room, but EcoLab was hired to spray just that room. By the spring of 2000, the motel had given refunds to several guests bitten by bedbugs in their rooms. The motel manager looked at several rooms and found bedbugs. Further incidents of guests being bitten by bedbugs led the motel's manager to recommend that the motel be closed while every room was sprayed, but Motel 6 refused. The infestation continued, and several of the rooms were placed on "Do not rent, bugs in room" status.

In November 2000, Burl Matthias and Desiree Matthias, brother and sister, checked in to the Motel 6 in downtown Chicago. They were given Room 514, even though it was on the "Do not rent, bugs in room" list. That night, 190 of the motel's 191 rooms were rented. That night the Matthiases were severely bitten by bedbugs. The Matthiases sued Motel 6 to recover damages, alleging that it had engaged in willful and wanton conduct. The jury agreed and awarded each plaintiff $5,000 in compensatory damages and $186,000 in punitive damages. Motel 6 appealed.

Issue

Was Motel 6 liable for willful and wanton conduct that supported the award of punitive damages of $186,000 to each plaintiff?

Court's Reasoning

The court of appeals held that Motel 6's failure to control the bedbug infestation constituted willful and wanton conduct that warranted the imposition of punitive damages. The court of appeals rejected the defendants' claim that punitive damages should be limited to a maximum amount of $20,000. The court of appeals held that the 37.2-to-1 ratio of punitive damages to compensatory damages in this case did not violate due process of the U.S. Supreme Court's suggestion that punitive damages should usually not exceed a 4-to-1 ratio. The court of appeals held that Motel 6's willful and wanton conduct in this case justified the award of $186,000 of punitive damages to each plaintiff.

Decision and Remedy

The court of appeals held that Motel 6's willful and wanton conduct warranted the trial court's award of $186,000 in punitive damages to each defendant. The court of appeals affirmed the judgment of the district court.

Case Questions

Critical Legal Thinking   Define *punitive damages*. Why are they awarded?

Business Ethics   Did Motel 6 act ethically in this case? Explain.

Contemporary Business   Does the possibility of an award of punitive damages make businesses act more responsibly?

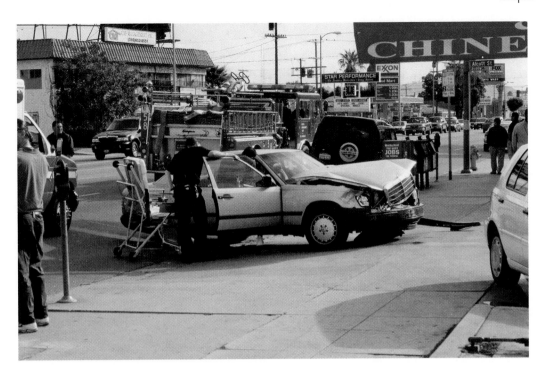

Defenses Against Negligence

A defendant in a negligence lawsuit may raise several defenses to the imposition of liability. These defenses are discussed in the following paragraphs.

Superseding or Intervening Event

Under negligence, a person is liable only for foreseeable events. Therefore, an original negligent party can raise a **superseding**, or **intervening event** as a defense to liability. For example, assume that an avid golfer negligently hits a spectator with a golf ball, knocking the spectator unconscious. While lying on the ground waiting for an ambulance to come, the spectator is struck by a bolt of lightning and killed. The golfer is liable for the injuries caused by the golf ball. He is not liable for the death of the spectator, however, because the lightning bolt was an unforeseen intervening event.

Assumption of the Risk

If a plaintiff knows of and voluntarily enters into or participates in a risky activity that results in injury, the law recognizes that the plaintiff assumed, or took on, the risk involved. Thus, the defendant can raise the defense of **assumption of the risk** against the plaintiff. This defense assumes that the plaintiff (1) had knowledge of the specific risk and (2) voluntarily assumed that risk. For example, under this theory, a race-car driver assumes the risk of being injured or killed in a crash.

In the following case, the court had to decide whether the plaintiff had assumed the risk.

Lilya v. The Greater Gulf State Fair, Inc.
855 So.2d 1049, 2003 Ala. Lexis 57 (2003)
Supreme Court of Alabama

Case 4.7

Assumption of the Risk

Background and Facts

The Greater Gulf State Fair, Inc., operated the Gulf State Fair in Mobile County, Alabama. One of the events at the fair was a mechanical bull ride for which participants paid money to ride the mechanical bull. A mechanical bull is a ride where the rider sits on a motorized device shaped like a real bull, and the ride simulates a real bull ride as the mechanical bull turns, twists, and bucks. The challenge is to stay on the bull and not be thrown off the bull. A large banner above the ride read "Rolling Thunder."

John Lilya and a friend watched as a rider was thrown from the mechanical bull. Lilya also watched as his friend paid and rode the bull but also was thrown off. Lilya then paid the $5 admission charge and signed a release agreement that stated: "I acknowledge that riding a mechanical bull entails known and unanticipated risks which could result in physical or emotional injury, paralysis, death, or damage to my self, to property, or to third parties. I expressly agree and promise to accept and assume all of the risks existing in this activity. My participation in this activity is purely voluntary, and I elect to participate in spite of the risks."

Lilya boarded the mechanical bull and was immediately thrown off onto a soft pad underneath the bull. Lilya reboarded the bull for a second ride. The bull ride began again and became progressively faster, spinning and bucking to the left and right until Lilya fell off the bull. On the fall, Lilya landed on his head and shoulders, and he suffered a fractured neck. Lilya sued Gulf State Fair to recover damages for his severe injuries. The trial court granted summary judgment to Gulf State Fair, finding that Lilya had voluntarily assumed an open and obvious danger. Lilya appealed.

Issue

Was riding a mechanical bull an open and obvious danger for which Lilya had voluntarily assumed the risk when he rode the mechanical bull?

Court's Reasoning

The supreme court of Alabama stated that a landowner owes a duty of reasonable care to an invitee but has no duty to warn the invitee of open and obvious danger on the premises. The court held that the evidence of riding a mechanical bull is an open and obvious danger. Lilya had watched two other men be thrown from the bull during their rides, and Lilya himself had been thrown once before boarding the bull the second time, when he was thrown and injured. The court applied the legal maxim *Volenti non fit injuria*, which means that a person who knowingly and voluntarily risks danger cannot recover for any resulting injury.

Decision and Remedy

The supreme court of Alabama held that riding a mechanical bull and being thrown and injured by the bull is an open and obvious danger, and that Lilya had voluntarily assumed the risk when he rode the bull and was thrown and injured. The supreme court affirmed the trial court's grant of summary judgment in favor of Gulf State Fair.

Case Questions

Critical Legal Thinking   Do you think the doctrine of assumption of the risk should be recognized by the law? Explain.

Business Ethics   Did Gulf State Fair act ethically by making money from such a dangerous activity as mechanical bull riding?

Contemporary Business   Give several examples of sports or activities that rely on the doctrine of assumption of the risk.

Contributory Negligence

Under the common law doctrine of **contributory negligence**, a plaintiff who is partially at fault for his or her own injury cannot recover against the negligent defendant. For example, suppose a driver who is driving over the speed limit negligently hits and injures a pedestrian who is jaywalking. Suppose the jury finds that the driver is 80 percent responsible for the accident and the jaywalker is 20 percent responsible. The pedestrian suffered $100,000 in injuries. Under the doctrine of contributory negligence, the pedestrian cannot recover any damages from the driver.

There is one major exception to the doctrine of contributory negligence: The defendant has a duty under the law to avoid the accident if at all possible. This rule is known as the *last clear chance rule*. For example, a driver who sees a pedestrian walking across the street against a "Don't Walk" sign must avoid hitting him or her if possible. When deciding cases involving this rule, the courts consider the attentiveness of the parties and the amount of time each had to respond to the situation.

Comparative Negligence

The application of the doctrine of contributory negligence could reach an unfair result where a party only slightly at fault for his or her injuries could not recover from an otherwise negligent defendant. Many states have replaced the doctrine of contributory negligence with the doctrine of **comparative negligence**. Under this doctrine, damages are apportioned according to fault.

When the comparative negligence rule is applied to the previous example, the result is much fairer. The plaintiff-pedestrian can recover 80 percent of his damages (or $80,000) from the defendant-driver. This is an example of *pure comparative negligence*. Several states have adopted *partial comparative negligence*, which provides that a plaintiff must be less than 50 percent responsible for causing his or her own injuries to recover under comparative negligence; otherwise, contributory negligence applies.

Concept Summary Contributory and Comparative Negligence Compared

Situation	Doctrine	Liability of the Defendant
Defendant liable for causing injury to plaintiff, but plaintiff partially at fault for causing his own injuries.	Contributory negligence	Defendant not liable exception: Last clear chance rule
	Comparative negligence 1. Pure comparative negligence	Defendant liable for plaintiff's injuries according to fault
	2. Partial comparative negligence a. Plaintiff less than 50 percent responsible b. Plaintiff 50 percent or more responsible	Defendant liable for plaintiff's injuries according to fault Defendant not liable

Special Business Torts

Many of the torts previously discussed are committed by or against businesses. Certain other torts commonly involve businesses. Several of these torts are discussed in the following paragraphs.

Entering Certain Businesses and Professions Without a License

There are government restrictions and prohibitions on the freedom of entry into certain businesses and professions. These restrictions are intended to protect the public from unqualified practitioners and to promote the efficient operation of the economy.

For example, a person cannot simply erect a television or radio transmitter and start broadcasting: The Federal Communications Commission grants television and radio station licenses for assigned frequencies. In addition, many occupations, such as lawyers, physicians, dentists, real estate brokers, hairdressers, and the like, require state licenses. In some states, even palm readers and astrologers must be licensed. To obtain the necessary license, an applicant must (1) meet certain educational requirements and (2) demonstrate a certain level of proficiency in the subject matter through examination, experience, or both. Entry into these industries or professions without permission subjects the violator to

He that's cheated twice by the same man, is an accomplice with the Cheater.

Thomas Fuller
Gnomologia (1732)

Business Brief

A license must be obtained from the government to enter certain industries, such as banking and broadcasting, and to practice certain professions, such as law and medicine.

various civil and criminal penalties. In many states, a licensed professional can bring an action to prevent an unlicensed person from practicing.

Unfair Competition

In most situations, competitors are free to compete vigorously, even if it means that someone is driven out of business or sustains severe losses. However, competitors may not engage in illegal **unfair competition** or **predatory practices**.

The common law tort of **palming off** is one of the oldest forms of unfair competition. This tort usually occurs when one company tries to "palm off" its products as those of a rival. For example, if a company implied that it was affiliated with International Business Machines (IBM) by selling computers under the IBM label, it would be liable for the business tort of palming off.

To prove the tort of palming off, the plaintiff must prove that (1) the defendant used the plaintiff's logo, symbol, mark, and so on and (2) there is a likelihood of confusion as to the source of the product. Actual consumer confusion need not be shown. The key element is whether consumers are likely to be confused as to the origin of the copied product.

Disparagement

Business firms rely on their reputation and the quality of their products and services to attract and keep customers. That is why state unfair-competition laws protect businesses from disparaging statements made by competitors or others. A disparaging statement is an untrue statement made by one person or business about the products, services, property, or reputation of another business.

To prove **disparagement**, which is also called **product disparagement, trade libel**, or **slander of title**, the plaintiff must show that the defendant (1) made an untrue statement about the plaintiff's products, services, property, or business reputation; (2) published that untrue statement to a third party; (3) knew the statement was not true; and (4) made the statement maliciously (i.e., with intent to injure the plaintiff).

False Advertising

Companies often engage in comparative advertising in which they compare the qualities of their products to those of competitors. Truthful comparative advertising is lawful. However, untruthful comparative advertising constitutes disparagement of product and false and misleading advertising in violation of **Section 43(a) of the Lanham Act**,[6] a federal statute.

Section 43(a) prohibits false and misleading advertising. Under the Lanham Act, private parties may obtain injunctions and recover damages from competitors who make disparaging or false or misleading statements about the plaintiff's products.

Intentional Misrepresentation (Fraud)

One of the most pervasive business torts is **intentional misrepresentation**. This tort is also known as **fraud** or **deceit**. It occurs when a wrongdoer deceives another person out of money, property, or something else of value. A person who has been injured by an intentional misrepresentation can recover damages from the wrongdoer. The elements required to find fraud are

1. The wrongdoer made a false representation of material fact.
2. The wrongdoer had knowledge that the representation was false and intended to deceive the innocent party.
3. The innocent party justifiably relied on the misrepresentation.
4. The innocent party was injured.

Vietnam. The tort laws of countries differ.

Item 2, which is called **scienter**, includes situations in which the wrongdoer recklessly disregards the truth in making a representation that is false. Intent or recklessness can be inferred from the circumstances.

Strict Liability

Strict liability is another category of torts. Strict liability is *liability without fault*. That is, a participant in a covered activity will be held liable for any injuries caused by the activity, even if he or she was not negligent. This doctrine holds that (1) there are certain activities that can place the public at risk of injury even if reasonable care is taken and (2) the public should have some means of compensation if such injury occurs.

Strict liability was first imposed for *abnormally dangerous activities*, such as crop dusting, blasting, fumigation, burning fields, storage of explosives, and the keeping of wild animals as pets.

In the following case, the court imposed strict liability.

> **Business Brief**
>
> Whereas intentional torts and negligence require the defendant to have been at fault, strict liability imposes liability without the defendant's having been at fault.

Cook v. Whitsell-Sherman
796 N.E.2d 271, 2003 Ind. Lexis 793 (2003)
Supreme Court of Indiana

Case 4.8
Strict Liability

Background and Facts

Tamara Cook owned a 100-pound Rottweiler dog named Maggie. Maggie had never demonstrated any aggressive or violent tendencies. Cook went out of town and left Maggie in the care of Marva and Joseph Hart. When Kenneth Whitsell-Sherman was delivering mail as a letter carrier for the U.S. Postal Service to the Harts' home, the Harts were on the sidewalk outside their yard, and their eight-year-old daughter was several feet away, holding Maggie on a leash. Maggie broke free and bit Whitsell-Sherman on the left hand, causing injuries. Whitsell-Sherman sued Cook to recover damages based on an Indiana statute that made dog owners strictly liable for pets who injured postal carriers. The trial court found Cook strictly liable and awarded Whitsell-Sherman $87,000 in damages. The court of appeals reversed, and Whitsell-Sherman appealed.

Cook vs. Whitsell-Sherman

796 N.E.2d 271, 2003 Ind. Lexis 793 (2003)
Supreme Court of Indiana
(continued)

Issue

Is the owner of a dog strictly liable for injuries caused by the dog biting a postal carrier?

Court's Reasoning

The supreme court of Indiana noted that the common law previously made owners of dogs liable for injuries caused by their dogs' biting other people if the owners failed to use reasonable care under the circumstances. Using this negligence doctrine, some courts did not impose liability on a dog owner for his or her dog's bites unless the dog had a prior propensity toward aggressiveness. Thus developed the famous common law "one free bite" rule. The Indiana supreme court found, however, that the Indiana statute changed common law and imposed strict liability on a dog owner whose dog's bite caused injury to a postal carrier. The court held that even though Cook was not there the day Maggie bit Whitsell-Sherman, she was still strictly liable for the injuries Maggie's bite caused to Whitsell-Sherman.

Decision and Remedy

The Indiana supreme court held that Indiana law made a dog owner strictly liable to mail carriers for injuries caused by their dog biting a mail carrier and upheld the liability of Maggie's owner. The supreme court held that the damages were incorrectly calculated by the trial court and remanded the case for a proper determination of damages.

Case Questions

Critical Legal Thinking   Describe the doctrine of strict liability. How does it differ from the doctrine of negligence? Explain.

Business Ethics   Did Cook act ethically by trying to avoid liability in this case?

Contemporary Business   Does household liability insurance cover injuries caused by the homeowner's pets?

International Law

Israeli Tort Law

David Ben Gurion proclaimed the establishment of the State of Israel on May 14, 1948. Historically, the Jewish people have been governed by biblical law. With the advent of a national state, secular laws were developed, and they now coexist with religious law. One of the laws developed by the State of Israel was *tort* law. Israeli tort law is based on the theory that monetary compensation is awarded to promote justice and to ensure fair compensation when a tort occurs.

Under Israeli tort law, there is no right to trial by jury. Instead, all actions are tried by a panel of three judges or three laypeople who decide questions of both fact and law. In essence, they are closer to arbitrators than to judges.

Also, under Israeli tort law, all damages awarded must be assessed under one of these categories of damages:

1. Medical expenses (ripui)
2. Loss of earnings (shevet)
3. Loss of income (nezek)
4. Pain and suffering (tza'ar)
5. Embarrassment (boshet)

Israeli law limits the assessment of noneconomic damages (categories 4 and 5) to cases of willful, intentional, or grossly negligent infliction of harm. Jewish law excuses doctors from liability for their negligence in most situations. ■

Chapter Summary

Intentional Torts Against Persons, p. 73

Intentional Torts Against Persons

1. ***Assault.*** Threat of immediate harm or offensive contact, or any action that arouses reasonable apprehension of imminent harm.

2. ***Battery.*** Unauthorized and harmful or offensive physical contact with another person.

   a. *Transferred intent doctrine.* If a person intends to injure one person but actually harms another person, the law transfers the perpetrator's intent from the target to the actual victim.

3. **False imprisonment.** Intentional confinement or restraint of another person without authority or justification and without that person's consent.

    a. Merchant protection statutes. These statutes permit businesses to stop, detain, and investigate suspected shoplifters (and not be held liable for false imprisonment) if the following requirements are met:

        i. There are reasonable grounds for the suspicion.

        ii. Suspects are detained for only a reasonable time.

        iii. Investigations are conducted in a reasonable manner.

4. **Defamation of character.** The defendant makes an untrue statement of fact about the plaintiff that is published to a third party. Truth is an absolute defense.

    a. Types of defamation:

        i. *Slander.* Oral defamation is called slander.

        ii. *Libel.* Written defamation is called libel.

    b. Public figure plaintiffs. These plaintiffs must prove the additional element of *malice*.

5. **Misappropriation of the right to publicity.** This refers to appropriating another person's name or identity for commercial purposes without that person's consent. Also called the tort of appropriation.

6. **Invasion of privacy.** Invasion of privacy is the unwarranted and undesired publicity of a private fact about a person. The fact does not have to be untrue. Truth is not a defense.

7. **Intentional infliction of emotional distress.** This tort involves extreme and outrageous conduct intentionally or recklessly done that causes severe emotional distress. Some states require that the mental distress be manifested by physical injury. Also known as the *tort of outrage*.

8. **Malicious prosecution.** A successful defendant in a prior lawsuit can sue the plaintiff if the first lawsuit was frivolous.

Intentional Torts Against Property, p. 78

Intentional Torts Against Property

1. **Trespass to land.** Trespass to land involves interference with a landowner's right to exclusive possession of his or her land.

2. **Trespass to personal property.** Trespass to personal property occurs when a person injures another person's personal property or interferes with that person's enjoyment of his or her property.

3. **Conversion of personal property.** This tort involves taking over another person's personal property and depriving him or her of the use and enjoyment of the property.

Unintentional Torts (Negligence), p. 79

Negligence

"The omission to do something which a reasonable man would do, or doing something which a prudent and reasonable man would not do."

Elements of Negligence

To establish negligence, the plaintiff must prove:

1. The defendant owed a *duty of care* to the plaintiff.

2. The defendant *breached this duty*.

3. The plaintiff suffered *injury*.

4. The defendant's negligent act *caused* the plaintiff's injury. Two types of causation must be shown:

    a. Causation in fact (or actual cause). The defendant's negligent act was the actual cause of the plaintiff's injury.

    b. Proximate cause (or legal cause). The defendant is liable only for the *foreseeable* consequences of his or her negligent act.

Professional Malpractice

Doctors, lawyers, architects, accountants, and other professionals owe a duty of ordinary care in providing their services. They are judged by a *reasonable professional standard*. Professionals who breach this duty are liable to clients and some third parties for *professional malpractice*.

Special Negligence Doctrines, p. 84

Special Negligence Doctrines

1. ***Negligent infliction of emotional distress.*** A person who witnesses a close relative's injury or death may sue the negligent party who caused the accident to recover damages for any emotional distress suffered by the bystander. To recover for *negligent infliction of emotional distress*, the plaintiff must prove:

   a. A relative was killed or injured by the defendant.

   b. The plaintiff suffered severe emotional distress.

   c. The plaintiff's mental distress resulted from a sensory and contemporaneous observance of the accident.

   Some states require that the mental distress be manifested by physical injury.

2. ***Negligence per se.*** A statute or an ordinance establishes the duty of care. A violation of the statute or ordinance constitutes a breach of this duty of care.

3. ***Res ipsa loquitur.*** A presumption of negligence is established if the defendant had exclusive control of the instrumentality or situation that caused the plaintiff's injury and the injury would not have ordinarily occured but for someone's negligence. The defendant may rebut this presumption.

4. ***Good Samaritan laws.*** These laws relieve doctors and other medical professionals from liability for ordinary negligence when rendering medical aid in emergency situations.

5. ***Dram shop acts.*** These state statutes make taverns and bartenders liable for injuries caused to or by patrons who are served too much alcohol and cause injury to themselves or others.

6. ***Guest statutes.*** These statutes provide that a driver of a vehicle is not liable for ordinary negligence to passengers he or she gratuitously transports. The driver is liable for gross negligence.

7. ***Fireman's rule.*** Firefighters, police officers, and other government employees who are injured in the performance of their duties cannot sue the person who negligently caused the dangerous situation that caused the injury.

8. ***"Danger invites rescue" doctrine.*** A person who is injured while going to someone's rescue may sue the person who caused the dangerous situation.

9. ***Social host liability.*** Some states make social hosts liable for injuries caused by guests who are served alcohol at a social function and later cause injury because they are intoxicated.

10. ***Liability of landowners.*** Landowners (and tenants) owe the following duties to persons who come upon their property:

    a. Invitees—Duty of ordinary care

    b. Licensees—Duty of ordinary care

    c. Trespassers—Duty not to willfully and wantonly injure trespassers.

11. ***Liability of common carriers and innkeepers.*** Common carriers and innkeepers give a *duty of utmost care*, rather than the duty of ordinary care, to protect their passengers and patrons from injury.

Defenses Against Negligence, p. 89

Defenses Against Negligence

1. ***Superseding event.*** A superseding event is an intervening event caused by another person that caused the plaintiff's injuries that relieves the defendant from liability.

2. ***Assumption of the risk.*** A defendant is not liable for the plaintiff's injuries if the plaintiff had knowledge of a specific risk and voluntarily assumed that risk.

3. *Plaintiff partially at fault.* States have adopted one of the following two rules that affect a defendant's liability if the plaintiff had been partially at fault for causing his or her own injuries:

    a. Contributory negligence. A plaintiff cannot recover anything from the defendant.

    b. Comparative negligence. Damages are apportioned according to the parties' fault. Also called *comparative fault.*

Special Business Torts, p. 91

Business Torts

1. *Entering business without a license.* The law requires that persons obtain licenses from the government prior to entering certain businesses or professions.

2. *Palming off.* A company passes off its products or services as those of another company.

3. *Disparagement.* Disparagement is an untrue statement about the products, services, property, or reputation of a business. Also called *product disparagement, trade libel,* or *slander of title.*

4. *False advertising.* Section 43(a) of the Lanham Act, a federal law, prohibits false and misleading advertising. State laws also prohibit false and misleading advertising.

5. *International misrepresentation.* When this tort occurs, a wrongdoer defrauds another person out of money, property, or something else of value. Also known as *fraud* or *deceit.* The following elements must be shown:

    a. The wrongdoer made a false representation of material fact.

    b. The wrongdoer had knowledge that the representation was false and intended to deceive the innocent party.

    c. The innocent party justifiably relied on the misrepresentation.

    d. The innocent party was injured

6. *Intentional interference with contractual relations.* With this tort, a third party intentionally interferes with another party's contract and induces the other party to that contract to breach it, causing the nonbreaching party injury.

7. *Breach of the implied covenant of good faith and fair dealing.* With this tort, a party to a contract does not act in good faith or fails to deal fairly in achieving the object of the contract. This duty is implied in only certain contracts (e.g., insurance contracts). Also called the *tort of bad faith.*

Tort Damages

1. *Actual damages.* Actual damages include compensation for personal injury, pain and suffering, emotional distress, and other injuries caused by the defendant's tortious conduct.

2. *Punitive damages.* Punitive damages are recoverable against a defendant for intentional or egregious conduct. They are awarded to punish the defendant, to deter the defendant from similar conduct in the future, and to set an example for others. The plaintiff may keep these damages.

Strict Liability, p. 93

Strict Liability

With strict liability, liability is assessed on defendants without regard to fault. This tort applies to *abnormally dangerous activities* and certain products.

Internet Exercises and Case Questions

Working the Web Internet Exercises

Activities

1. Find a state court case opinion that relates to intentional torts. See, for example, a state-based plaintiffs' trial lawyers association site: **www.wstla.org**, or, at the national level, The Association of Trial Lawyers of America: **www.atla.org**, or the ABA Tort and Insurance Practice Section: **www.abanet.org/tips/thebrief.html**.

2. Find a medical malpractice case. For the viewpoint of the defense, see **www.dri.org**. For the insurance industry's view, see **www.ircweb.org**.

Check the following site as a starting point for the questions below:

www.law.cornell.edu/topics/torts.html

3. Find a state court case that establishes the rule in your jurisdiction on social host liability.

Critical Legal Thinking Cases

4.1 Intentional Tort On September 16, 1975, the Baltimore Orioles professional baseball team was at Boston's Fenway Park to play the Boston Red Sox. Ross Grimsley was a pitcher for the visiting Baltimore club. During one period of the game, Grimsley was warming up in the bullpen, throwing pitches to a catcher. During this warmup, Boston spectators in the stands heckled Grimsley. After Grimsley had completed warming up and the catcher had left from behind the plate in the bullpen, Grimsley wound up as if he were going to throw the ball in his hand at the plate, then turned and threw the ball at one of the hecklers in the stand. The ball traveled at about 80 miles an hour, passed through a wire fence protecting the spectators, missed the heckler that Grimsley was aiming at, and hit another spectator, David Manning, Jr., causing injury. Manning sued Grimsley and the Baltimore Orioles. Are the defendants liable? [*Manning v. Grimsley*, 643 F.2d 20, 1981 U.S. App. Lexis 19782 (1st Cir. 1981)]

4.2 Merchant Protection Statute At about 7:30 P.M. on September 8, 1976, Deborah A. Johnson entered a Kmart store located in Madison, Wisconsin, to purchase some diapers and several cans of motor oil. She took her small child along to enable her to purchase the correct size diapers, carrying the child in an infant seat that she had purchased at Kmart two or three weeks previously. A large Kmart price tag was still attached to the infant seat. Johnson purchased the diapers and oil and some children's clothes. She was in a hurry to leave because it was 8:00 P.M., her child's feeding time, and she hurried through the checkout lane. She paid for the diapers, the oil, and the clothing. Just after leaving the store she heard someone ask her to stop. She turned around and saw a Kmart security officer. He showed her a badge and asked her to come back into the store, which she did. The man stated, "I have reason to believe that you have stolen this car seat." Johnson explained that she had purchased the seat previously. She demanded to see the manager, who was called to the scene. When Johnson pointed out that the seat had cat hairs, food crumbs, and milk stains on it, the man said, "I'm really sorry, there's been a terrible mistake. You can go." Johnson looked at the clock, which read 8:20 P.M., when she left. Johnson sued Kmart for false imprisonment. Is Kmart liable? [*Johnson v. Kmart Enterprises, Inc.*, 297 N.W.2d 74, 1980 Wisc.App. Lexis 3197 (Wis. App. 1980)]

4.3 Trespass A. C. Wade operated a liquor store in Cordele, Georgia. Because the store had been burglarized on several occasions and money had been stolen from a cigarette vending machine, Wade booby-trapped the machine with dynamite, with the intent to scare away thieves when they tried to steal money from the vending machine. Robert McKinsey, a 16-year-old, was killed when the dynamite attached to the vending machine exploded while McKinsey was burglarizing the liquor store. Mrs. Ella McKinsey, Robert's mother, although admitting her son was committing a crime at the time he was killed, brought action for damages against Wade for the wrongful death of her son. Who wins? [*McKinsey v. Wade*, 220 SE.2d 30, 1975 Ga.App. Lexis 1264 (Ga. 1975)]

4. Find the statute in your jurisdiction that contains the Good Samaritan rule.

5. Find the statute in your jurisdiction that contains the innkeepers' liability law.

4.4 Negligence In January 1984, George Yanase was a paying guest at the Royal Lodge-Downtown Motel in San Diego, California. Yanase was a member of the Automobile Club of Southern California. The Auto Club publishes a "Tourbook" in which it lists hotels and motels and rates the quality of their services, including the cleanliness of rooms, quality of the restaurant, level of personal service, and the like. Yanase had selected the Royal from the Tourbook. On the night of his stay at the Royal, Yanase was shot in the parking lot adjacent to the motel and died as a result of his injuries. Yanase's widow sued the Auto Club for negligence. Is the Auto Club liable? [*Yanase v. Automobile Club of Southern California*, 212 Cal.App.3d 468, 260 Cal.Rptr. 513, 1989 Cal.App. Lexis 746 (Cal. App. 1989)]

4.5 Causation In February 1973, W. L. Brown purchased a new large Chevrolet truck from Days Chevrolet. The truck had been manufactured by General Motors Corporation. On March 1, 1973, an employee of Brown's was operating the truck when it ceased to function in rush-hour traffic on Interstate Highway 75 in the Atlanta suburbs. A defect within the alternator caused a complete failure of the truck's electrical system. The defect was caused by General Motors's negligence in manufacturing the truck. When the alternator failed to operate, the truck came to rest in the right-hand lane of two north-bound lanes of freeway traffic. Because of the electrical failure, no blinking lights could be used to warn traffic of the danger. The driver, however, tried to motion traffic around the truck. Some time later, when the freeway traffic had returned to normal, the large Chevrolet truck was still motionless on the freeway. At approximately 6:00 P.M. a panel truck approached the stalled truck in the right-hand lane of traffic at freeway speed. Immediately behind the panel truck, Mr. Davis, driving a Volkswagen fastback, was unable to see the stalled truck. At the last moment the driver of the panel truck saw the stalled truck and swerved into another lane to avoid it. Mr. Davis drove his Volkswagen into the stalled truck at freeway speed, causing his death. Mr. Davis's wife brought a wrongful death action based on negligence against General Motors. Was there causation linking the negligence of the defendant to the fatal accident? [*General Motors Corporation v. Davis*, 233 S.E.2d 825, 1977 Ga.App. Lexis 1961 (Ga. App. 1977)]

4.6 Negligence Per Se On March 21, 1980, Julius Ebanks set out from his home in East Elmhurst, Queens, New York, en route to his employment in the downtown district of Manhattan. When Ebanks reached the Bowling Green subway station, he boarded an escalator owned and operated by the New York City Transit Authority. While the escalator was ascending, Ebanks's left foot became caught in a two-inch gap between the escalator step on which he was standing and the side wall of the escalator. Ebanks was unable to free himself. When he reached the top of the escalator he was thrown to the ground, fracturing his hip and causing other serious injuries. The two-inch gap exceeded the three-eighths-inch standard required by the city's building code. Ebanks sued the Transit Authority to recover damages for his injuries. Who wins? [*Ebanks v. New York City Transit Authority*, 70 N.Y.2d 621, 518 N.Y.S.2d 776, 1987 N.Y. Lexis 17294 (N.Y. App. 1986)]

4.7 Liability of Landowners   George and Beverly Wagner owned a 1.6-acre parcel of land on which they operated "Bowag Kennels," which catered to training, boarding, and caring for show dogs. The property was entirely surrounded by land owned by Reuben Shiling and W. Dale Hess. In August 1964, Shiling and Hess granted the Wagners an easement right-of-way over their land that connected the kennel to Singer Road, a public road. Singer Road was a rural, unlit two-lane road running through a wooded area. The right-of-way was an unpaved, unlit, narrow road that crossed an uninhabited wooded area leading to Bowag Kennels. On numerous occasions, unauthorized motorcyclists drove on the right-of-way. On several occasions, the bikers had loud parties along the right-of-way. In September 1982, the Wagners stretched a large metal chain between two poles at the entrance of the right-of-way. The Wagners testified that they marked the chain with reflectors and signs. Just before midnight on October 2, 1982, William E. Doehring, Jr., and his passenger, Kelvin Henderson, drove their motorcycle off Singer Road and turned on to the right- of-way. The motorcycle they were riding was not equipped with a headlight, and the riders were not wearing helmets. Doehring and Henderson had not been granted permission by the Wagners or Shiling or Hess to use the right-of-way. The motorcycle struck the chain, and the riders were thrown off. Doehring died several hours later at a hospital. Doehring's father filed a wrongful death and survival action against the Wagners. Who wins? [*Wagner v. Doehring*, 553 A.2d 684, 1989 Md. Lexis 29 (Md.App. 1089)]

4.8 Liability of Common Carrier   The Southern California Rapid Transit District (RTD) is a public common carrier that operates public buses throughout the Los Angeles area. Carmen and Carla Lopez were fare-paying passengers on an RTD bus when a group of juveniles began harassing them and other passengers. When the bus driver was notified of this problem, he failed to take any precautionary measures and continued to operate the bus. The juveniles eventually physically assaulted Carmen and Carla, who were injured. The RTD was aware of a history of violent attacks on its bus line. Carmen and Carla sued the RTD to recover damages for their injuries. Who wins? [*Lopez v. Southern California Rapid Transit District*, 40 Cal.3d 780, 221 Cal.Rptr. 840, 1985 Cal. Lexis 434 (Cal. 1985)]

4.9 Emotional Distress   On August 10, 1983, Gregory and Demetria James, brother and sister, were riding their bicycles north on 50th Street in Omaha, Nebraska. Spaulding Street intersects 50th Street. A garbage truck owned by Watts Trucking Service, Inc., and driven by its employee, John Milton Lieb, was backing up into the intersection of 50th and Spaulding streets. The truck backed into the intersection, through a stop sign, and hit and ran over Demetria, killing her. Gregory helplessly watched the entire accident but was not in danger himself. As a result of watching his sister's peril, Gregory suffered severe emotional distress. Gregory sued Watts and Lieb to recover damages for his emotional distress. Who wins? [*James v. Watts Trucking Service, Inc.*, 375 N.W.2d 109, 1985 Neb. Lexis 1209 (Neb. 1985)]

4.10 Defense   On the night of June 13, 1975, the New York Yankees professional baseball team played the Chicago White Sox at Shea Stadium, New York. Elliot Maddox played center field for the Yankees that night. It had rained the day before, and the previous night's game had been canceled because of bad weather. On the evening of June 13 the playing field was still wet, and Maddox commented on this fact several times to the club's manager but continued to play. In the ninth inning, when Maddox was attempting to field a ball in center field, he slipped on a wet spot, fell, and injured his right knee. Maddox sued the City of New York, which owned Shea Stadium; the Metropolitan Baseball Club, Inc., as lessee; the architect; the consulting engineer; and the American League. Maddox alleged that the parties were negligent in causing the field to be wet and that the injury ended his professional career. Who wins? [*Maddox v. City of New York*, 496 N.Y.S.2d 726, 1985 N.Y. Lexis 17254 (N.Y.App. 1985)]

Business Ethics Cases

4.11 Business Ethics   Radio station KHJ was a successful Los Angeles broadcaster of rock music that commanded a 48 percent market share of the teenage audience in the Los Angeles area. KHJ was owned and operated by RKO General, Inc. In July 1973, KHJ inaugurated a promotion titled "The Super Summer Spectacular." As part of this promotion, KHJ had a disc jockey known as "The Real Don Steele" ride around the Los Angeles area in a conspicuous red automobile. Periodically KHJ would announce to its radio audience Steele's location. The first listener to thereafter locate Steele and answer a question received a cash prize and participated in a brief interview on the air with Steele. On July 16, 1973, one KHJ broadcast identified Steele's next destination as Canoga Park. Robert Sentner, 17 years old, heard the broadcast and immediately drove to Canoga Park. Marsha Baime, 19 years old, also heard the broadcast and drove to Canoga Park. By the time Sentner and Baime located Steele, someone else had already claimed the prize. Without the knowledge of the other, Sentner and Baime each decided to follow Steele to the next destination and to be first to "find" him.

Steele proceeded onto the freeway. For the next few miles Sentner and Baime tried to jockey for position closest to the Steele vehicle, reaching speeds of up to 80 miles per hour. There is no evidence that the Steele vehicle exceeded the speed limit. When Steele left the freeway at the Westlake off ramp, Sentner and Baime tried to follow. In their attempts to do so, they knocked another vehicle, driven by Mr. Weirum, into the center divider of the freeway, where it overturned. Mr. Weirum died in the accident. Baime stopped to report the accident. Sentner, after pausing momentarily to relate the tragedy to a passing police officer, got back into his car, pursued and successfully located Steele, and collected the cash prize. The wife and children of Mr. Weirum brought a wrongful death negligence action against Sentner, Baime, and RKO General. Who wins? Did RKO General, Inc., act responsibly in this case? [*Weirum v. RKO General, Inc.*, 15 Cal.3d 40, 123 Cal.Rptr. 468, 175 Cal. Lexis 220 (Cal. 1975)]

4.12 Business Ethics Guy Portee, a seven-year-old, resided with his mother in an apartment building in Newark, New Jersey. Edith and Nathan Jaffee owned and operated the building. On the afternoon of May 22, 1976, Guy became trapped in the building's elevator, between its outer door and the wall of the elevator shaft. When someone activated the elevator, the boy was dragged up to the third floor. Another child who saw the accident ran to seek help. Soon afterward, Renee Portee, the boy's mother, and officers at the Newark Police Department arrived. The officers worked for 4 1/2 hours, trying to release the boy, during which time the mother watched as her son moaned, cried out, and flailed his arms. The police contacted the Atlantic Elevator Company, which was responsible for the installation and maintenance of the elevator, and requested that the company send a mechanic to assist in the effort to free the boy. Apparently no one came. The boy suffered multiple bone fractures and massive internal hemorrhaging. He died while still trapped, his mother a helpless observer.

After her son's death, Renee became severely distressed and seriously self-destructive. On March 24, 1979, she attempted to take her own life. She survived, and the wound was repaired by surgery, but she has since required considerable physical therapy. She had received extensive counseling and psychotherapy to help overcome the mental and emotional problems associated with her son's death. Renee sued the Jaffees and Atlantic to recover damages for her emotional distress. Who wins? Did either of the defendants act unethically in this case? [*Portee v. Jaffee*, 417 A.2d 521, 1980 N.J. Lexis 1387 (N.J. 1980)]

Briefing the Case Writing Assignment

Read Case A.4 in the Case Appendix [*Braun v. Soldier of Fortune Magazine, Inc.*]. This case is excerpted from the court of appeals opinion. Review and brief the case. In your brief, be sure to answer the following questions.

1. Who are the plaintiffs? What are they suing for?

2. When does a magazine owe a duty to refrain from publishing an advertisement?

3. Was the advertisement the proximate cause of the plaintiff's injuries?

4. Should the award of punitive damages have been reduced?

Endnotes

1. 376 U.S. 254, 84 S. Ct. 710, 1964 U.S. Lexis 1655 (1964).
2. *Restatement (Second) of Torts*, Section 46.
3. *Restatement (Second) of Torts*, Section 46, comment d.
4. Justice B. Anderson, *Blyth a Birmingham Waterworks Co.*, 11 Exch. 781, 784 (1856).
5. For example, see Cal. Civil Code, Section 1714(c).
6. 15 U.S.C.§ 1125 (a).

Intellectual Property and Internet Law

5

> " The Congress shall have the power . . . to promote the Progress of Science and useful Arts, by securing for limited Times to Authors and Inventors the exclusive Right to their respective Writings and Discoveries. "
>
> —Article I, Section 8, clause 8 of the U.S. Constitution

Chapter Objectives

After studying this chapter, you should be able to:

1. Describe the business tort of misappropriating a trade secret.

2. Describe how an invention can be patented under federal patent laws and the penalties for patent infringement.

3. List the writings that can be copyrighted and describe the penalties of copyright infringement.

4. Define trademarks and service marks, and describe the penalties for trademark infringement.

5. Describe international protection of intellectual property rights.

Chapter Contents

- Trade Secrets and Information Technology
- Traditional and Cyber Patents
- Copyrights and Internet Law
- Trademarks and Online Commerce

The U.S. economy is based on the freedom of ownership of property. In addition to real estate and personal property, **intellectual property rights** have value to both business and individuals. This is particularly the case in the modern era of the Information Age, computers, and the Internet.

Trade secrets form the basis of many successful businesses, and they are protected from misappropriation. Federal law provides protections for intellectual property rights, such as patents, copyrights, and trademarks. In addition, businesses and individuals may register domain names to use on the Internet. Anyone who infringes on these rights may be stopped from doing so and is liable for damages.

This chapter discusses the protection of trade secrets, patents, copyrights, trademarks, and information technology.

Trade Secrets and Information Technology

Many businesses are successful because their **trade secrets** set them apart from their competitors. Trade secrets may be product formulas, patterns, designs, compilations of data, customer lists, or other business secrets. Many trade secrets either do not qualify to be—or simply are not—patented, copyrighted, or trademarked. Many states have adopted the **Uniform Trade Secrets Act** to give statutory protection to trade secrets.

State unfair competition laws allow the owner of a trade secret to bring a lawsuit for *misappropriation* against anyone who steals a trade secret. For the lawsuit to be actionable, the defendant (often an employee of the owner or a competitor) must have obtained the trade secret through unlawful means such as theft, bribery, or industrial espionage. No tort has occurred if there is no misappropriation. For example, a competitor can lawfully discover a trade secret by performing reverse engineering (i.e., taking apart and examining a rival's product).

The owner of a trade secret is obliged to take all reasonable precautions to prevent that secret from being discovered by others. Such precautions include fencing in buildings, placing locks on doors, hiring security guards, and the like. If the owner fails to take such actions, the secret is no longer subject to protection under state unfair competition laws.

Ethics Brief

Businesses must take all necessary precautions to protect their trade secrets from unwanted discovery.

Generally, a successful plaintiff in a trade secret action can (1) recover the profits made by the offender from the use of the trade secret, (2) recover for damages, and (3) obtain an injunction prohibiting the offender from divulging or using the trade secret.

Online Commerce & Internet Law
The Economic Espionage Act

Stealing of trade secrets exposes the offender to a civil lawsuit by the injured party to recover economic damages. In addition, the enactment by Congress of the federal **Economic Espionage Act of 1996** [18 U.S.C. §§ 1831–1839] makes it a federal crime to steal another's trade secrets. Under the Espionage Act, it is a federal crime for any person to convert a trade secret to his or her benefit or for the benefit of others, knowing or intending that the act would cause injury to the owner of the trade secret. The definition of *trade secret* under the Espionage Act is very broad and parallels the definition used under the civil laws of misappropriating a trade secret.

One of the major reasons for the passage of the Espionage Act was to address the ease of stealing trade secrets through computer espionage and using the Internet. For example, hundreds of pages of confidential information can be downloaded onto a small computer disk, placed in a pocket, and taken from the legal owner. In addition, computer hackers can crack into a company's computers and steal customer lists, databases, formulas, and other trade secrets. The Espionage Act is a very important weapon in addressing and penalizing computer and Internet espionage.

The Espionage Act provides for severe criminal penalties. An organization can be fined up to $5 million per criminal act and $10 million if the criminal act was committed to benefit a foreign government. The act imposes prison terms on individuals of up to 15 years per criminal violation, which can be increased to 25 years per violation if the criminal act was done with the intent to benefit a foreign government. ∎

Traditional and Cyber Patents

When drafting the Constitution of the United States of America, the founders of the United States provided for protection of the work of inventors and writers. Article I, Section 8 of the constitution provides, "The Congress shall have Power . . . To promote the Progress of Science and useful Arts, by securing for limited Times to Authors and Inventors the exclusive Right to their respective Writings and Discoveries."

> The patent system added the fuel of interest to the fire of genius.
>
> Abraham Lincoln
> *Lectures on Discoveries, Inventions, and Improvements (1859)*

Federal Patent Statute of 1952

Pursuant to the express authority granted in the U.S. Constitution, Congress enacted the **Federal Patent Statute of 1952**.[1] This law is intended to provide an incentive for inventors to invent and make their inventions public and to protect patented inventions from infringement. Federal patent law is exclusive; there are no state patent laws. Applications for patents must be filed with the **United States Patent and Trademark Office (PTO)** in Washington, DC. The U.S. Court of Appeals for the Federal Circuit in Washington, DC, was created in 1982 to hear patent appeals. The court was established to promote uniformity in patent law.

In 1995, in order to bring the U.S. patent system into harmony with the systems of the majority of other developed nations, Congress made the following important changes in U.S. patent law:

1. Patents for inventions are valid for *20 years* (instead of the previous term of 17 years). Design patents are valid for 14 years.
2. The patent term begins to run from the date the patent application is *filed* (instead of when the patent is issued, as was previously the case).

Business Brief

In the United States, patents are valid for 20 years from the date the patent application is filed.

After the patent period runs out, the invention or design enters the *public domain*, which means that anyone can produce and sell the invention without paying the prior patent holder.

The United States still follows the *first-to-invent rule* rather than the *first-to-file rule* followed by some other countries. Thus, in the United States the first person to invent an item or process is given patent protection over another party who was first to file a patent application.

Patenting an Invention

To be patented, an invention must be *novel, useful,* and *nonobvious.* In addition, only certain subject matters can be patented. Patentable subject matters include (1) machines; (2) processes; (3) compositions of matter; (4) improvements to existing machines, processes, or compositions of matter; (5) designs for an article of manufacture; (6) asexually reproduced plants; and (7) living material invented by a person. Abstractions and scientific principles cannot be patented unless they are part of the tangible environment. For example, Einstein's Theory of Relativity ($E = mc^2$) cannot be patented.

A *patent application* must contain a written description of the invention and be filed with the PTO in Washington, DC. If a patent is granted, the invention is assigned a patent number. Patent holders usually affix the word *patent* or *pat.* and the patent number to the patented article. If a patent application is filed but a patent has not yet been issued, the applicant usually places the words *patent pending* on the article. Any party can challenge either the issuance of a patent or the validity of an existing patent.

In the following case, the U.S. Supreme Court had to decide whether the subject matter was patentable.

Business Brief

Patent applications are complicated. An inventor should hire a patent attorney to assist in obtaining a patent for an invention.

U.S. SUPREME COURT CASE
J.E.M. Ag Supply, Inc., d.b.a. Farm Advantage, Inc. v. Pioneer Hi-Bred International, Inc.

Case 5.1
Patent

534 U.S. 124, 122 S.Ct. 593, 2001 U.S. Lexis 10949 (2001)
Supreme Court of the United States

Background and Facts

Pioneer Hi-Bred International, Inc. (Pioneer) holds patents that cover the company's inbred and hybrid corn and corn seed products. A hybrid plant patent protects the plant, its seeds, variants, mutants, and modifications of the hybrid. Pioneer sells its patented hybrid seeds under a limited label license that provides: "License is granted solely to produce grain and/or forage." The license states that it "does not extend to the use of seed from such crop or the progeny thereof for propagation or seed multiplication."

J.E.M. Ag Supply, Inc., doing business as Farm Advantage, Inc., purchased patented hybrid seeds from Pioneer in bags bearing this license agreement. Farm Advantage created seed from the hybrid corn products it grew from Pioneer's patented hybrid seed. Pioneer sued Farm Advantage, alleging that Farm Advantage had infringed its patent. Farm Advantage filed a counterclaim of patent invalidity, arguing that Pioneer hybrid plant seed patents are not patentable subject matter. The U.S. district court granted summary judgment to Pioneer, and the court of appeals affirmed. The U.S. Supreme Court agreed to hear Farm Advantage's appeal.

Issue

Are sexually reproducing hybrid plants patentable subject matter?

Court's Reasoning

The Supreme Court recognized over 20 years ago in *Diamond v. Chakrabarty*, 447 U.S. 303, 100 S.Ct. 2204, 1980 U.S. Lexis 112 (1980) that living things are patentable. Several years after *Chakrabarty*, the PTO held that plants are patentable subject matter. It has been the unbroken practice of the PTO since that time to confer utility patents for plants. To obtain utility patent protection, a plant breeder must show that the plant he has developed is new, useful, and non-obvious. The Supreme Court stated, "Petitioner Farm Advantage essentially asks us to deny utility patent protection for sexually reproduced plants because it was unforeseen in 1930 that such plants could receive patent protection. Denying patent protection simply because such coverage was thought technologically infeasible in 1930, however, would be inconsistent with the forward-looking perspective of the utility patent statute."

Decision and Remedy

The U.S. Supreme Court held that sexually reproducing hybrid plants are patentable subject matter. The Supreme Court affirmed the judgment of the court of appeals.

Case Questions

Critical Legal Thinking   Do you think sexually reproducing hybrid plants should be patentable subject matter? Why or why not?

Business Ethics   Did Farm Advantage act ethically in this case? Explain.

Contemporary Business   What are the economic implications of the U.S. Supreme Court's decision in this case?

Patent Infringement

Patent holders own exclusive rights to use and exploit their patents. **Patent infringement** occurs when someone makes unauthorized use of another's patent. In a suit for patent infringement, a successful plaintiff can recover (1) money damages equal to a reasonable royalty rate on the sale of the infringed articles, (2) other damages caused by the infringement (such as loss of customers), (3) an order requiring the destruction of the infringing article, an (4) an injunction preventing the infringer from such action in the future. The court has the discretion to award up to treble damages if the infringement was intentional.

Business Ethics

Inventor Wipes Ford's and Chrysler's Windshields Clean

In 1967, Robert Kearns, a professor at Wayne State University in Detroit, Michigan patented his design for the electronic intermittent-speed windshield wiper for automobiles and other vehicles. He peddled his invention around to many automobile manufacturers but never reached a licensing deal with any of them. In 1969, automobile manufacturers began producing cars using Kearns's intermittent-speed windshield wiper invention. Virtually all cars sold in the United States today now have these wipers as standard equipment. Kearns filed patent infringement lawsuits against virtually all automobile manufacturers.

The Ford case went to trial first. Ford alleged that Kearns's patents were not valid because of obviousness and prior art. The jury disagreed with Ford, decided that Kearns's patents were valid, and ordered Ford to pay $5.2 million, plus interest, for patent infringement. In 1990, Ford settled by paying Kearns $10.2 million and agreeing to drop all appeals. This represented 50¢ per Ford vehicle that used the wiper system.

In the Chrysler case, Kearns fired his lawyers and represented himself. Kearns won a second victory: In 1991, the jury found that Chrysler had infringed Kearns's patents and awarded him $11.3 million. Kearns received over $21 million from Chrysler, which amounted to 90¢ for every vehicle sold by Chrysler with the wiper system.

In 1993 and 1994 courts dismissed Kearns's lawsuits against 23 other automobile manufacturers, including General Motors, Porsche, Nissan, Toyota, and Honda because Kearns failed to comply with court orders to disclose documents. Thus ended Kearns's legal battle with the automobile industry.

1. Do you think that intermittent-speed windshield wipers were obvious when Kearns invented them?
2. Did the automobile manufacturers that used Kearns' invention without paying him act ethically? Explain. ▪

Online Commerce & Internet Law

Cyber Business Plans Are Patentable

Federal patent law recognizes four categories of innovation: (1) machines, (2) articles of manufacture, (3) compositions, and (4) processes. For centuries most patents involved tangible inventions, such as the telephone and the light bulb. Next, chemical, polymer, and biotechnology patents were granted. Now, the computer and the Internet have added to what can be patented.

Signature Financial Group, Inc. (Signature), filed for and was granted a patent for a computerized accounting system that

Online Commerce & Internet Law
(continued)

determines share prices through a series of mathematical calculations and is then used to manage mutual funds [U.S. Patent No. 5,193,056]. State Street Bank, another financial institution that wanted to offer a similar mutual fund investment program to clients, sued to have Signature's patent declared invalid. Signature defended, arguing that its intangible financial business model was a "process" that was protected under federal patent law. The U.S. Court of Appeals, Federal Circuit, upheld the patent as a "practical application of a mathematical, algorithm, formula, or calculation, because it produces a useful, concrete and tangible result."

Taking the lead from the *State Street* case, many persons and businesses have filed for and received patents for business and financial models that are used over the Internet. Critics contend that Congress did not intend to grant patents for intangible processes when it enacted federal patent law. Business plan patent holders counter that the trend reflects a necessary evolution in patent law and claim that business plan patterns are to the Internet Age what machine patents were to the Industrial Age. [*State Street Bank & Trust Co. v. Signature Financial Group, Inc.*, 149 F3d 1368, 1998 U.S. App. Lexis 16869 (Fed. Cir. 1998)]. ∎

One-Year "On Sale" Doctrine

Under the **one-year "on sale" doctrine**, also called the **public use doctrine**, a patent may not be granted if the invention was used by the public for more than one year prior to the filing of the patent application. This doctrine forces inventors to file their patent applications at the proper time.

Consider This Example   Suppose Cindy Parsons invents a new invention on January 1. She allows the public to use this invention and does not file a patent application until February of the following year. The inventor has lost the right to patent her invention.

The American Inventors Protection Act

In 1999, Congress enacted the **American Inventors Protection Act**. This statute does the following:

- Permits an inventor to file a **provisional application** with the PTO, pending the preparation and filing of a final and complete patent application. This part of the law grants "provisional rights" to an inventor for three months, pending the filing of a final application.

- Requires the PTO to issue a patent within three years after the filing of a patent application unless the applicant engages in dilatory activities.

- Provides that non–patent holders may challenge a patent as being overly broad by requesting a contested reexamination of the patent application by the PTO. This provides that the reexamination will be within the confines of the PTO; the decision of the PTO can be appealed to the U.S. Court of Appeals for the Federal Circuit in Washington, DC.

Online Commerce & Internet Law
Amazon.com Loses Its 1-Click Patent

Amazon.com, Inc., enables customers to find and purchase books, music, videos, consumer electronics, games, toys, gifts, and other items over the Internet by using its Web site, **www.amazon.com**. As an early entrant into this market,

Amazon.com became a leader in electronic commerce. Amazon.com devised a method that enabled online customers to purchase selected items with a single click of a computer mouse button. Customers who had previously registered their name, address, and credit card number with Amazon.com could complete purchases by clicking an instant "buy" button. This ordering system was implemented by Amazon.com in September 1997. On September 21, 1997, Amazon.com applied for a patent for its one-click ordering system, and on September 28, 1998, the U.S. PTO granted Patent No. 5,960,411 (411 patent) to Amazon.com. This was designated the 1-click® ordering system by Amazon.com.

While Amazon.com's patent application was pending, other online retailers began offering similar one-click ordering systems. One was Barnesandnoble.com, which operates a Web site that sells books, software, music, videos, and other items. Barnesandnoble.com called its one-click ordering system "Express Lane." On October 21, 1999, Amazon.com sued Barnesandnoble.com, alleging patent infringement, and sought an injunction against Barnesandnoble.com from using its one-click ordering system. Barnesandnoble.com defended, asserting

that a one-click ordering system was clearly obvious and, therefore, did not meet the required "nonobvious" test of federal patent law for an invention to qualify for a patent.

After examining the evidence, the U.S. district court decided that Amazon.com's one-click system was nonobvious when it was invented in 1997 and upheld Amazon.com's patent. Barnesandnoble.com appealed to the U.S. Court of Appeals, arguing that Amazon.com's one-click ordering system was not novel or nonobvious as required by patent law. Barnesandnoble.com cited evidence that one-click ordering systems existed in the *prior art*, before Amazon.com filed for its patent. The U.S. Federal Court of Appeals relied on these prior art references and reversed the trial court's decision. The court of appeals allowed Barnesandnoble.com to use its Express Lane one-click ordering system. [*Amazon.com, Inc. v. Barnesandnoble.com, Inc.*, 239 F.3d 1343, 2001 U.S. App. Lexis 2163 (Fed. Cir. 2001)]. ■

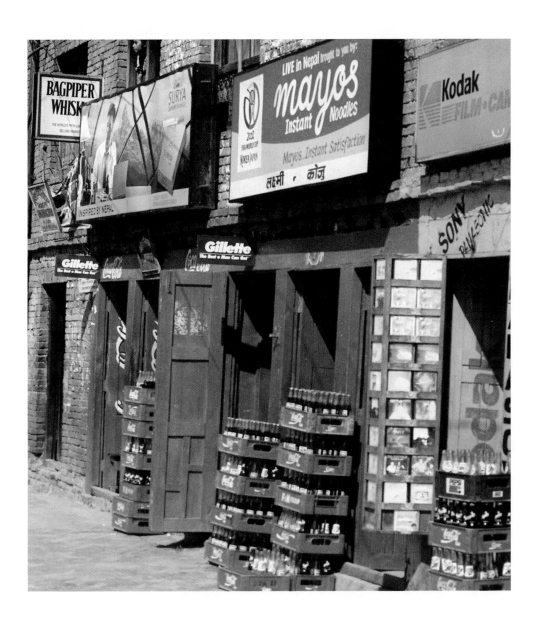

Nepal. Certain U.S. companies' brand names have worldwide name recognition.

Copyrights and Internet Law

Article I, Section 8 of the Constitution of the United States of America authorizes Congress to enact statutes to protect the works of writers for limited times.

Pursuant to this authority, Congress has enacted copyright laws. The **Copyright Revision Act of 1976** currently governs copyright law.[2] The act establishes the requirements for obtaining a copyright and protects copyrighted works from infringement. Federal copyright law is exclusive; there are no state copyright laws. Federal copyright law protects the work of authors and other creative persons from the unauthorized use of their copyrighted materials and provides a financial incentive for authors to write, thereby increasing the number of creative works available in society.

Only *tangible writings*—writings that can be physically seen—are subject to copyright registration and protection. The term *writing* has been broadly defined to include books, periodicals, and newspapers; lectures, sermons, addresses; and poems (see Exhibit 5.1); musical compositions; plays, motion pictures, and radio and television productions; maps; works of art, including paintings, drawings, sculpture, jewelry, glassware, tapestry, and lithographs; architectural drawings and models; photographs, including prints, slides, and filmstrips; greeting cards and picture postcards; photoplays, including feature films, cartoons, newsreels, travelogues, and training films; and sound recordings published in the form of tapes, cassettes, and compact discs.

Business Brief

The expression of an idea is copyrightable. The idea itself is not.

The law in respect to literature ought to remain upon the same footing as that which regards the profits of mechanical inventions and chemical discoveries.

William Wordsworth
Letter (1838)

Registration of Copyrights

To be protected under federal copyright law, a work must be the original work of the author. A copyright is created when an author produces his or her work. For example, when a student writes a term paper for her class, she owns a copyright to her work.

Published and unpublished works may be registered with the **United States Copyright Office** in Washington, DC. Registration is permissive and voluntary and can be effected at any time during the term of the copyright.

In 1989, the United States signed the **Berne Convention**, an international copyright treaty. This law eliminated the need to place the symbol © or the word "copyright" or "copr." on a copyrighted work.

The **Sonny Bono Copyright Term Extension Act of 1998** granted individuals copyright protection for their life plus 70 years. For example, if an author writes a novel at age 25 and she dies when she is 85, the copyright on her novel applies for the remaining 60 years of her life, and her heirs have copyright protection for an additional 70 years beyond the author's life. Copyrights owned by businesses are protected for 95 years from the year of first publication or for 120 years from the year of creation, whichever is shorter. After the copyright period runs out, the work enters the *public domain*, which means that anyone can publish the work without paying the prior copyright holder.

Business Brief

The symbol © or the word "copyright" or "copr." are no longer needed to be placed on a copyrighted work.

Business Brief

Copyrights are valid for the life of the creator plus 70 years; copyrights owned by businesses are valid for 95 years from the year of first publication or 120 years from the year of creation, whichever is shorter.

Exhibit 5.1

Poems Qualify for Copyright Protection

Tangible writings, such as this poem, qualify for copyright protection:

Like oceans, we have spent
this time together before.
In galley slave pits you fed me
water and removed my slivers.
Riding Ch'u dynasty chariots
we perished on Mongol swords.
We toiled rocks in chains
and built Stonehenge,
drank with King Arthur
and danced with Black Elk.

We fled, hand-in-hand, dodging
Hitler's bullets, and
I carried you over the border
to have our baby in freedom.
During past full moons, the sun set
the seas in orbit
and as driftwood we tumbled
onto the shores of Los Angeles.
Another life together, my love?

Henry Cheeseman

Reflecting Pool, Los Angeles County Museum of Art.
Photographs such as this one titled Colorful Dream, no longer need the © to be placed on it to be copyrighted.

Copyrighting Software

In 1980, Congress enacted the **Computer Software Copyright Act**,[3] which amended the Copyright Act of 1976. The 1980 amendments included computer programs in the list of tangible items protected by copyright law. The creator of a copyrightable software program obtains automatic copyright protection. The Registrar of Copyright is authorized to accept and record any document pertaining to computer software and to issue a *certificate of recordation* to the recorder.

Congress passed the **Semiconductor Chip Protection Act of 1984** to provide greater protection of the hardware components of a computer.[4] This law protects masks that are used to create computer chips. A *mask* is an original layout of software programs that is used to create a semiconductor chip. This act is sometimes referred to as the "Mask Work Act." Notice on the work is optional, but when used must contain the words *mask work* or the symbol *M* or (M) and the name of the owner.

Business Brief
Federal statutes grant copyright protection to computer software and computer chips.

Copyright Infringement

Copyright infringement occurs when a party copies a substantial and material part of the plaintiff's copyrighted work without permission. The copying does not have to be either word for word or the entire work. A successful plaintiff can recover (1) the profit made by the infringer from the copyright infringement, (2) damages suffered by the plaintiff, (3) an order requiring the impoundment and destruction of the infringing works, and (4) an injunction preventing the infringer from doing so in the future. The court, in its discretion, can award statutory damages up to $150,000 for willful infringement in lieu of actual damages.

The Fair Use Doctrine

The copyright holder's rights in the work are not absolute. The law permits certain limited unauthorized use of copyrighted materials under the **fair use doctrine**. The following uses are protected under this doctrine: (1) quotation of the copyrighted work for review or criticism or in a scholarly or technical work, (2) use in a parody or satire, (3) brief quotation in a news report, (4) reproduction by teacher or student of a small part of the work to illustrate a lesson, (5) incidental reproduction of a work in a newsreel or broadcast of an event being reported, and (6) reproduction of a work in a legislative or judicial proceeding. The copyright holder cannot recover for copyright infringement where fair use is found.

In the following two cases, the court had to decide whether there was copyright infringement or fair use.

Elvis Presley Enterprises, Inc. v. Passport Video
349 F.3d 622, 2003 U.S. App. Lexis 22775 (2003)
United States Court of Appeals, Ninth Circuit

Background and Facts

Elvis Presley became a musical icon during a career that spanned more than 20 years, until he died on August 16, 1977. Many companies and individuals own copyrights to Presley's songs, lyrics, photographs, movies, and appearances on TV shows. Millions of dollars of these copyrighted materials are sold or licensed annually. Passport Video produced a video documentary titled *The Definitive Elvis*, comprising 16 one-hour episodes. The producers interviewed more than 200 people regarding virtually all aspects of Elvis's life. Passport sold the videos commercially for a profit. Approximately 5 to 10 percent of the videos were composed of copyrighted music and appearances of Presley on TV and in movies owned by copyright holders other than Passport. Passport did not obtain permission to use those copyrighted works. Elvis Presley Enterprises, Inc., and other companies and individuals that owned copyrights to the Presley works used by Passport sued Passport for copyright infringement. Passport defended, arguing that its use of the copyrighted materials was fair use. The U.S. District Court held in favor of the plaintiff copyright holders and enjoined Passport from further distribution of its documentary videos. Passport appealed.

Issue

Did Passport's use of the copyrighted Elvis Presley materials constitute fair use, or was it copyright infringement?

Court's Reasoning

The court of appeals stated, "The King is dead. His legacy, and those who wish to profit from it, remain very much alive." The court of appeals held that Passport's use of others' copyrighted materials was for commercial use rather than for a nonprofit purpose. The court rejected Passport's claim that the videos consisted of scholarly research that would be protected as fair use. The court found that Passport's use of the copyrighted material caused market harm to the copyright holders because it would act as a substitute for the original copyrights and thus deny the copyright holders of the value of their copyrights. The court of appeals denied Passport's claim of fair use.

Decision and Remedy

The U.S. Court of Appeals held that Passport's use of the copyrighted Elvis Presley materials was not fair use but instead constituted copyright infringement. The Court of Appeals affirmed the district court's judgment that enjoined Passport from distributing its videos containing these copyrighted materials.

Case Questions

Critical Legal Thinking   Define *fair use*. What is the effect on the parties if fair use is found?

Business Ethics   Did Passport Video act ethically in this case? Do you think Passport Video knew it was engaging in copyright infringement?

Contemporary Business   How valuable do you think the copyrights to Elvis Presley songs, movies, and TV appearances are?

Newton v. Beastie Boys
349 F.3d 591, 2003 U.S. App. Lexis 22635 (2003)
United States Court of Appeals, Ninth Circuit

Background and Facts

James W. Newton, Jr., is an accomplished avant-garde jazz composer and flutist. In 1978, Newton wrote a composition for the song "Choir," a piece for flute and voice that incorporated elements of African-American gospel music. Newton owns the copyright to the composition "Choir." In 1992, the Beastie Boys, a rap and hip-hop group, used six seconds of Newton's "Choir" composition in their song "Pass the Mic" without obtaining a license from Newton to do so. Newton sued the Beastie Boys for copyright infringement. The Beastie Boys defended, arguing that their use of six seconds of Newton's song was fair use. The district court found that the Beastie Boys's use of Newton's composition was *de minimis* and therefore fair use. The district court granted summary judgment in favor of the Beastie Boys, and Newton appealed.

Issue

Does the incorporation of a short segment of a copyrighted musical composition into a new musical recording constitute fair use, or is it copyright infringement?

Court's Reasoning

The U.S. Court of Appeals noted that the dispute between Newton and the Beastie Boys centers around the copyright implications of "sampling," a practice now common to many types of popular music. Sampling entails the incorporation of short segments of prior sound recordings into new recordings. The Court of Appeals held that the unauthorized use of a copyrighted work is actionable if there is substantial copying. The court noted that *de minimis* copying is not actionable, but constitutes fair use. The Court of Appeals found that the sampled portion of Newton's composition comprised a six-second three-note sequence from his four-and-a-half minute "Choir." The Court of Appeals held that the Beastie Boys's use of this small segment in their "Pass the Mic" song was *de minimis* and therefore constituted fair use and not copyright infringement.

Decision and Remedy

The Court of Appeals held that the Beastie Boys's *de minimis* sampling of Newton's "Choir" composition constituted fair use and not copyright infringement. The Court of Appeals affirmed the district court's grant of summary judgment in favor of the Beastie Boys.

Case Questions

Critical Legal Thinking   Should sampling be allowed as fair use? Why or why not?

Business Ethics   Did the Beastie Boys act ethically when they used part of Newton's "Choir" composition in their song?

Contemporary Business   Has the use of sampling become a big part of today's music recordings? Why do you think recording artists engage in sampling?

Online Commerce & Internet Law
The NET Act: Criminal Copyright Infringement

In 1997, Congress enacted the **No Electronic Theft Act (NET Act)**, which criminalizes certain copyright infringement. The NET Act prohibits any person from willfully infringing a copyright for the purpose of either commercial advantage or financial gain, or by reproduction or distribution, even without commercial advantage or financial gain, including by electronic means, where the retail value of the copyrighted work exceeds $1,000. Criminal penalties for violating the act include Imprisonment for up to one year and fines of up to $100,000.

The NET Act adds a new law for the federal government to criminally attack copyright infringement and curb digital piracy. ■

Medina, Fez, Morocco. One of the most important markets for the expansion of valuable intellectual property rights by U.S. companies is international markets.

Online Commerce & Internet Law
The Digital Millennium Copyright Act

The Internet makes it easier than ever before for people to illegally copy and distribute copyrighted works. To combat this, software and entertainment companies have developed "wrappers" and encryption technology to protect their copyrighted works from unauthorized access. Not to be outdone, software pirates and other Internet users have devised ways to crack these wrappers and protection devices. Software and entertainment companies have lobbied Congress to enact legislation to make the cracking of their wrappers and selling of technology to do so illegal. In response, Congress has enacted the **Digital Millennium Copyright Act (DMCA)** [17 U.S.C. 1201], which does the following:

- Prohibits unauthorized access to copyrighted *digital* works by circumventing the wrapper or encryption technology that protects the intellectual property. This "black box" protection prohibits simply accessing the protected information and does not require that the accessed information be misused.
- Prohibits the manufacture and distribution of technologies, products, or services primarily designed for the purpose of circumventing wrappers or encryption technology protecting *digital* works. However, multipurpose devices that can be used in ways other than for cracking wrappers or encryption technology can be manufactured and sold without violating the DMCA.

Thus, for digital protected works, the DMCA makes it illegal to merely access the copyrighted material by breaking through the digital wrapper or encryption technology that protects the work.

Congress granted exceptions to DMCA liability to (1) software developers to achieve compatibility of their software with the protected work; (2) federal, state, and local law enforcement agencies conducting criminal investigations; (3) parents who are protecting children from pornography or other harmful materials available on the Internet; (4) Internet users who are identifying and disabling cookies and other identification devices that invade their personal privacy rights; and (5) nonprofit libraries, educational institutions, and archives that access a protected work to determine whether to acquire the work.

The DMCA imposes civil and criminal penalties. A successful plaintiff in a civil action can recover actual damages from first-time offenders and treble damages from repeat offenders, costs and attorneys' fees, an order for the destruction of illegal products and devices, and an injunction against future violations by the offender. As an alternative to actual damages, a plaintiff can recover statutory damages of not less than $2,500 and up to $25,000 per act of circumvention. The following criminal penalties can be accessed for willful violations committed for "commercial advantage" or "private financial gain": First-time violators can be fined up to $500,000 and imprisoned for up to 5 years; subsequent violators can be fined up to $1 million and imprisoned for up to 10 years. ■

Trademarks and Online Commerce

Businesses often develop company names, as well as advertising slogans and commercial logos, to promote the sale of their goods and services. Companies, such as Nike, Microsoft, Louis Vuitton, and McDonald's, spend millions of dollars annually to gain market recognition from consumers. The U.S. Congress has enacted trademark laws to provide legal protection for these names, slogans, and logos.

Federal Lanham Trademark Act

In 1946, Congress enacted the **Lanham Act**[5] to provide federal protection to trademarks, service marks, and other marks. This act, as amended, is intended to (1) protect the owner's investment and goodwill in a **mark** and (2) prevent consumers from being confused as to the origin of goods and services.

Trademarks are registered with the **United States** PTO in Washington, DC. The original registration of a mark is valid for 10 years and can be renewed for an unlimited number of 10 year periods. The registration of a trademark, which is given nationwide effect, serves as constructive notice that the mark is the registrant's personal property. The registrant is entitled to use the registered trademark symbol ® in connection with a registered trademark or service mark. Use of the symbol is not mandatory. Note that the frequently used notations "TM" and "SM" have no legal significance.

Business Brief

A trademark can be registered for 10 years and can be renewed for an unlimited number of 10-year periods.

An applicant can register a mark if it has been used in commerce (e.g., actually used in the sale of goods or services). An applicant can also register a mark six months prior to its proposed use in commerce, but if the mark is not used within this period, the applicant loses the mark. A party other than the registrant can submit an opposition to a proposed registration of a mark or the cancellation of a previously registered mark.

Business Brief

An applicant can register a mark six months prior to its proposed use in commerce. If the mark is not used within this period, the applicant loses the mark.

Marks That Can Be Trademarked

The word **mark** collectively refers to *trademarks, service marks, certification marks*, and *collective marks*. The following types of marks can be trademarked:

- **Trademarks.** A **trademark** is a distinctive mark, symbol, name, word, motto, or device that identifies the *goods* of a particular business. For example, the words *Chevrolet, Coca-Cola*, and *IBM* are trademarks.

- **Service marks.** A **service mark** is used to distinguish the *services* of the holder from those of its competitors. The trade names *United Airlines, Marriott Hotels*, and *Weight Watchers* are examples of service marks.

- **Certification marks.** A **certification mark** is a mark that is used to certify that goods and services are of a certain quality or originate from particular geographical areas (for example, wines from the *Napa Valley* of California or *Florida* oranges). The owner of the mark is usually a nonprofit corporation that licenses producers that meet certain standards or conditions to use the mark.

- **Collective marks.** A **collective mark** is a mark used by cooperatives, associations, and fraternal organizations. *Boy Scouts of America* is an example of a collective mark.

Certain marks cannot be registered. They include (1) the flag or coat of arms of the United States, any state, municipality, or foreign nation; (2) marks that are immoral or

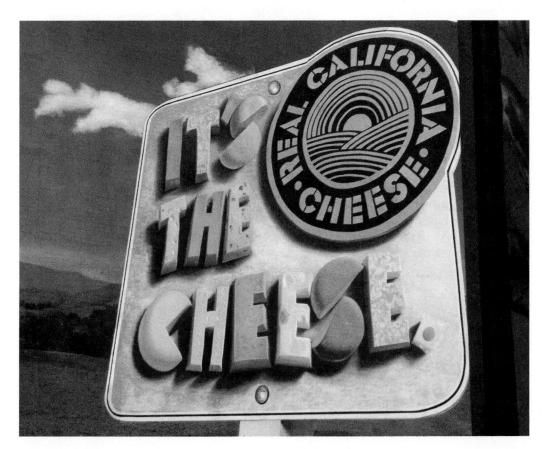

Napa Valley, California. This certification mark designates California cheese manufacturers.

scandalous; (3) geographical names standing alone (e.g., "South"); (4) surnames standing alone (note that a surname can be registered if it is accompanied by a picture or fanciful name, such as *Smith Brothers' Cough Drops*); and (5) any mark that resembles a mark already registered with the federal PTO.

Distinctiveness of a Mark

To qualify for federal protection, a mark must be **distinctive** or have acquired a "**secondary meaning**." For example, marks such as *Xerox* and *Acura* are *distinctive*. A term such as *English Leather*, which literally means leather processed in England, has taken on a **secondary meaning** as a trademark for an aftershave lotion. For example, Nike, Inc. has trademarked its name *Nike*, its *swoosh* symbol, and its *Just Do It* slogan. Words that are *descriptive* but have no secondary meaning cannot be trademarked. For example, the word *cola* alone could not be trademarked.

Trademark Infringement

The owner of a mark can sue a third party for the unauthorized use of a mark. To succeed in a **trademark infringement** case, the owner must prove that (1) the defendant infringed the plaintiff's mark by using it in an unauthorized manner and (2) such use is likely to cause

Beijing, China. Now that China has joined the World Trade Organization (WTO), the country is expected to increase the enforcement of intellectual property rights.

confusion, mistake, or deception of the public as to the origin of the goods or services. A successful plaintiff can recover (1) the profits made by the infringer through the unauthorized use of the mark, (2) damages caused to the plaintiff's business and reputation, (3) an order requiring the defendant to destroy all goods containing the unauthorized mark, and (4) an injunction preventing the defendant from such infringement in the future. The court has discretion to award up to *treble* damages where intentional infringement is found.

Trade Dress

Section 43(a) of the Lanham Act protects certain forms of **trade dress**. This consists of the "look and feel" of a product, a product's packaging, or a service establishment. The area of trade dress protection is an evolving area of the law.

In the following case, the U.S. Supreme Court found infringing copying of trade dress.

U.S. SUPREME COURT CASE
Two Pesos, Inc. v. Taco Cabana, Inc.
505 U.S. 763, 112 S.Ct. 2753, 1992 U.S. Lexis 4533 (1992)
Supreme Court of the United States

Case 5.4
Trade Dress

Background and Facts

Since 1975, Taco Cabana, Inc. (Taco Cabana), had operated a chain of fast-food Mexican restaurants in Texas. Its restaurants provided a festive eating atmosphere of interior dining and patio areas decorated with artifacts, bright colors, paintings, and murals. The exterior of its buildings had a vivid color scheme, using top border paint and neon stripes. Bright awnings and umbrellas continued the theme. Beginning in 1985, Two Pesos, Inc. (Two Pesos), opened a chain of competing Mexican fast-food restaurants in Texas. When Two Pesos adopted a motif similar to Taco Cabana's, Taco Cabana sued Two Pesos, alleging trade dress infringement in violation of Section 43(a) of the Lanham Act. Two Pesos argued that Taco Cabana's trade dress should not be protected because it had not yet acquired a secondary meaning. The U.S. district court found that Taco Cabana's trade dress was protected. The court of appeals affirmed. Two Pesos appealed to the U.S. Supreme Court.

Issue

Does a restaurant's design have to have acquired a secondary meaning before it is protected as trade dress under Section 43(a) of the Lanham Act?

Court's Reasoning

The Supreme Court noted that trade dress is the total image of a business. Taco Cabana's trade dress may include the shape and general appearance of the exterior restaurant, the identifying sign, the interior kitchen floor plan, the decor, the menu, the equipment used to serve food, the servers' uniforms, and other features reflecting on the total image of the restaurant. The Supreme Court

stated, "The trade dress of a product is essentially its total image and overall appearance."

The Supreme Court held that there was no basis for requiring secondary meaning for inherently distinctive trade dress protection. The Supreme Court stated, "Adding a secondary meaning requirement could have anticompetitive effects, creating particular burdens on the start-up of small companies. It would present special difficulties for a business, such as Taco Cabana, that seeks to start a new product in a limited area and then expand into new markets." The Supreme Court concluded that denying protection for inherently distinctive trade dress until after secondary meaning has been established would allow a competitor that has not adopted a distinctive trade dress of its own to appropriate the originator's dress in other markets and to deter the originator from expanding into and competing in those areas.

Decision and Remedy

The Supreme Court held that distinctive trade dress is protectable under the Lanham Act without proof that it has acquired a secondary meaning. The Supreme Court affirmed the decision of the court of appeals.

Case Questions

Critical Legal Thinking   Should trade dress be protected under the Lanham Act? Why or why not?

Business Ethics   Did Two Pesos act ethically in copying Taco Cabana's trade dress?

Contemporary Business   Does the Supreme Court decision in this case have a pro- or anticompetitive effect on business? Explain.

Generic Names

Most companies promote their trademarks and service marks to increase the public's awareness of the availability and quality of their products and services. At some point in time, however, the public may begin to treat the mark as a common name to denote the type of product or service being sold, rather than as the trademark or trade name of an individual seller. A trademark that becomes a common term for a product line or type of service is called a **generic name**. Once a trademark becomes a generic name, the term loses its protection under federal trademark law because it has become *descriptive* rather than *distinctive* (see Exhibit 5.2).

Exhibit 5.2

Reprinted with permission of Xerox Corporation

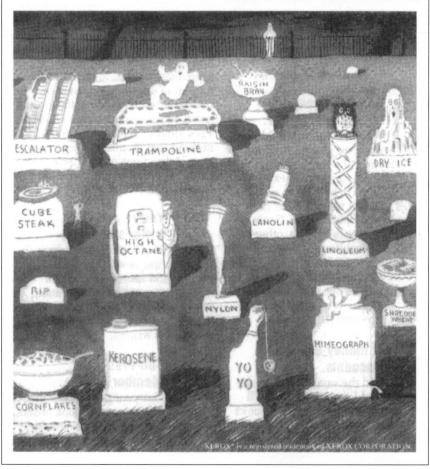

Concept Summary Types of Intellectual Property Protected by Federal Law

Type	Subject Matter	Term
Patent	Inventions (e.g., machines; processes compositions of matter; designs for articles of manufacture; and improvements to existing machines, processes). Invention must be 1. Novel 2. Useful 3. Nonobvious *Public use doctrine*: Patent will not be granted if the invention was used in public for more than one year prior to the filing of the patent application.	Patents on articles of manufacture; and processes: 20 years; design patents: 14 years.
Copyright	Tangible writing (e.g., books, magazines, newspapers, lectures, operas, plays, screenplays, musical compositions, maps, works of art, lithographs, photographs, postcards, greeting cards, motion pictures, newsreels, sound recordings, computer programs, and mask works fixed to semiconductor chips). Writing must be the original work of the author. *Fair use doctrine*: It permits use of copyrighted material without consent for limited uses (e.g., scholarly work, parody or satire, and brief quotation in news reports).	Author (individual registrant): life of author plus 70 years. Work for hire (business registrant) for the shorter of either 120 years from the date of creation or 95 years from the date of first publication.
Trademark	Marks (e.g., name, symbol, word, logo, or device). Marks include trademarks, service marks, certification marks, and collective marks. Mark must be distinctive or have acquired a secondary meaning. *Generic name*: A mark that becomes a common term for a product line or type of service loses its protection under federal trademark law.	Original registration: 10 years. Renewal registration: unlimited number of renewals for 10-year terms.

Federal Dilution Act of 1995

Companies owning trademarks often spend millions of dollars each year advertising and promoting the quality of the goods and services sold under their names. Many of these become household names that are recognized by millions of consumers, such as Coca-Cola, McDonald's, Microsoft, and Nike.

Traditional trademark law protected these marks where an infringer used the mark and confused consumers as to the source of the goods or services. For example, if a knock-off company sold athletic shoes and apparel under the name "Nike," there would be trademark infringement.

Arch de Triumphe Paris, France.
International agreements, such as the Paris Convention, Berne Convention, Phonogram Treaty, and other treaties provide international protection of patents, copyrights, trademarks, domain names, and other intellectual property rights.

Often, however, a party would use a name similar to, but not exactly identical to, a holder's trademark. Congress enacted the **Federal Dilution Act of 1995** to protect *famous marks* from *dilution*. The Federal Dilution Act provides that owners of marks have a valuable property right in their marks that should not be *eroded, blurred, tarnished,* or *diluted* in any way by another. The Federal Dilution Act has three fundamental requirements:

1. The mark must be famous.
2. The use by the other party must be commercial.
3. The use must cause dilution of the distinctive quality of the mark.

Dilution is broadly defined as the lessening of the capacity of a famous mark to identify and distinguish its holder's goods and services, regardless of the presence or absence of competition between the owner of the mark and the other party. For example, if someone other than Nike had a Web site entitled **www.nikeathletes.com,** it would be unlawful dilution.

Business Brief

Dilution is broadly defined as the lessening of the capacity of a famous mark to identify and distinguish goods and services. Dilution does not require the owner of one mark and the other party to be in competition with each other.

International Law

International Protection of Intellectual Property Rights

For centuries, national patent, copyright, and trademark laws defined the rights of inventors, authors, and businesses. These laws offered protection within a country's borders but not in other countries. Beginning in the late 1800s, countries began entering into treaties and conventions with other countries that provided international protection of intellectual property rights. Several of these treaties are:

1. **Patents.** The major convention that provides international protection to patents is the **1883 Convention of the Union of Paris (Paris Convention)**. The convention's major purpose

is to allow the nationals of each member country to file for patents in all other member nations. The convention does not, however, eliminate the need to file separate patent applications in each member nation in which the applicant desires protection. The convention gives an applicant who has filed for a patent in one member country 12 months to submit applications in other member countries.

2. **Trademarks.** The Paris Convention also allows nationals of each member nation to file for trademarks and service marks in all other member nations on an individual, nondiscriminatory basis, even if the applicant does not own the

mark in the country of origin. The applicant has six months after his or her original registration to submit application to other member countries.

3. **Copyright.** The major copyright treaty is the **Berne Convention of 1886**, as revised. This convention provides for the recognition of a copyright in all member nations. The convention establishes a minimum copyright term of the life of the author plus 70 years and eliminates the requirement to put a © on copyrighted works.

4. **Internet.** In 1997, the World Intellectual Property Organization (WIPO), an agency of the United Nations, pro-

mulgated two new "Internet treaties." These treaties recognized the importance of new digital technologies and the Internet. The first treaty, the **WIPO Copyright Treaty**, extends copyright protection to computer programs and data compilations and grants copyright holders the exclusive right to make their works available on the Internet as well as by any other wire or wireless means. The second treaty, the **WIPO Phonogram Treaty**, gives performers and producers the exclusive right to broadcast, reproduce, and distribute copies of their performances by any means, including video recording, digital sound, or encryption signal. ■

Chapter Summary

Trade Secrets and Information Technology, p. 102

Trade Secrets

1. **Trade secret.** A *trade secret* is a product formula, pattern, design, compilation of data, customer list, or other business secret that makes a business successful. The owner of a trade secret must take reasonable precautions to prevent its trade secret from being discovered by others.

2. **Misappropriation of a trade secret.** Obtaining another's trade secret through unlawful means such as theft, bribery, or espionage is a tort. A successful plaintiff can recover profits, damages, and an injunction against the offender.

3. **The Economic Espionage Act.** This act is a federal statute that makes it a crime for any person to convert a trade secret for his or her own or another's benefit, knowing or intending to cause injury to the owners of the trade secret.

Traditional and Cyber Patents, p. 103

Patents

Patent law is exclusively federal law; there are no state patent laws.

1. **Patent.** Patentable subject matter includes inventions such as machines; processes; compositions of matter; improvements to existing machines, processes, or compositions of matter; designs for articles of manufacture; asexually reproduced plants; and living matter invented by man.

   To be patented, an invention must be:

   a. Novel

   b. Useful

   c. Nonobvious

2. **Business plans.** In *State Street Bank & Trust Co. v. Signature Financial Group, Inc.*, the U.S. Court of Appeals held that business plans are patentable.

3. **Patent application.** An application containing a written description of the invention must be filed with the *U.S. Patent and Trademark Office* in Washington, DC.

4. **Term.** Patents are valid for 20 years.

5. **Public use doctrine.** A patent may not be granted if the invention was used by the public for more than one year prior to the filing of the patent application.

6. **Patent infringement.** The unauthorized use of an author's patent constitutes patent infringement. The patent holder may recover damages and other remedies against the infringer.

7. **The American Inventors Protection Act.** This federal statute does the following:

   a. Permits an inventor to file a *provisional application* with the U.S. Patent and Trademark Office (PTO) three months before the filing of a final patent application.

   b. Requires the PTO to issue a patent within three years after the filing of a patent application.

8. **Patent appeals.** These appeals are heard by the *U.S. Court of Appeals for the Federal Circuit* in Washington, DC.

Copyrights

Copyright law is exclusively federal law; there are no state copyright laws.

1. *Copyright.* Only tangible writings can be copyrighted. These include books, newspapers, addresses, musical compositions, motion pictures, works of art, architectural plans, greeting cards, photographs, sound recordings, computer programs, and mask works fixed in semiconductor chips.

2. *Requirements for copyright.* The writing must be the original work of the author.

3. *Copyright registration.* Copyright registration is permissive and voluntary. Published and unpublished works may be registered with the *U.S. Copyright Office* in Washington, DC. Registration itself does not create the copyright.

4. *Term.* Copyrights are for the following terms:

   a. *Individual holder.* Life of the author plus 70 years.

   b. *Corporate holder.* Either (1) 120 years from the date of creation or (2) 95 years from the date of publication, whichever is shorter.

5. *Copyright infringement.* Copyright infringement is the copying of a substantial and material part of a copyrighted work without the holder's permission. The copyright holder may recover damages and other remedies against the infringer.

6. *Fair use doctrine.* This doctrine permits use of copyrighted material without the consent of the copyright holder for limited uses (e.g., scholarly work, parody or satire, and brief quotation in news reports).

7. *No Electronic Theft Act (NET Act).* This federal statute makes it a crime for a person to willfully infringe a copyright work exceeding $1,000 in retail value.

8. *Digital Millennium Copyright Act (DMCA).* This federal statute, enacted in 1998, provides civil and criminal penalties that

   a. Prohibit the manufacture and distribution of technologies, products, or services primarily designed for the purpose of circumventing wrappers or encryption protection.

   b. Prohibit unauthorized *access* to copyrighted digital works by circumventing the wrapper or encryption technology that protects the intellectual property.

Trademarks and Service Marks

1. *Mark.* A mark is a trade name, symbol, word, logo, design, or device that distinguishes the owner's goods or services. Marks are often referred to collectively as trademarks. Types of marks are:

   a. *Trademark.* Identifies goods of a particular business.

   b. *Service mark.* Identifies services of a particular business.

   c. *Certification mark.* Certifies that goods or services are of a certain quality or origin.

   d. *Collective mark.* Used by cooperatives, associations, and fraternal organizations.

2. *Requirements for a trademark.* The mark must either (a) be *distinctive* or (b) have acquired a *secondary meaning.* The mark must have been used in commerce or the holder must intend to use the mark in commerce and actually do so within six months after registering the mark.

3. *Trademark registration.* Marks are registered with the *U.S. Patent and Trademark Office* in Washington, DC.

4. *Term.* The original registration of a mark is valid for 10 years and can be renewed for an unlimited number of 10-year periods.

5. *Trademark infringement.* The unauthorized use of another's registered mark is called trademark infringement. The mark holder may recover damages and other remedies from the infringer.

6. *Trade dress.* Trade dress involves the protection of the "look and feel" of a product, a product's packaging, or a service establishment.

7. *Generic name.* A mark that becomes a common term for a product line or type of service loses its protection under federal trademark law.

8. *Federal Dilution Act of 1995.* This federal statute protects famous marks from dilution. A violation of the act requires that the mark be famous, the use by the other party be commercial, and the use cause dilution of the distinctive quality of the mark.

Internal Protection of Intellectual Property Rights

1. *Paris Convention.* This international treaty protects patents and trademarks.

2. *Berne Convention.* This international treaty protects copyrights.

3. *WIPO Copyright Treaty.* This international treaty protects copyrights to computer programs and data compilations.

4. *WIPO Phonogram Treaty.* This international treaty gives performers and producers the exclusive right to broadcast, reproduce, and distribute copies of their performances.

 Internet Exercises and Case Questions
Working the Web Internet Exercises

Activities

1. Research the Web to determine whether your state has adopted the Uniform Trade Secrets Act. Visit the Trade Secrets home page, at **www.execpc.com/~mhallign**.

2. The site **www.uspto.gov** contains information about the federal copyright registration system. Does the most recent copyright law require authors to use the copyright notice on printed material in order to protect it from infringement?

3. What is the current duration of a U.S. patent? What was the duration of a U.S. patent under previous law, and why was it changed? See **www.uspto.gov**.

4. Visit **www.wipo.int** and outline the process for international registration of a patent.

Critical Legal Thinking Cases

5.1 Trade Secret   CRA-MAR Video Center, Inc., sells electronic equipment and videocassettes, as does its competitor, Koach's Sales Corporation. Both CRA-MAR and Koach's purchased computers from Radio Shack. CRA-MAR used the computer to store customer lists, movie lists, personnel files, and financial records. Because the computer was new to CRA-MAR, Randall Youts, Radio Shack's salesman and programmer, agreed to modify CRA-MAR's programs when needed, including the customer list program. At one point, CRA-MAR decided to send a mailing to everyone on its customer list. The computer was unable to perform the function, so Youts took the disks containing the customer lists to the Radio Shack store to work on the program. Somehow Koach's came into possession of CRA-MAR's customer lists and sent advertising mailings to the parties on the lists. When CRA-MAR discovered this fact, it sued Koach's, seeking an injunction against any further use of its customer lists. Is a customer list a trade secret that can be protected from misappropriation? [*Koachs Sales Corp. v. CRA-MAR Video Center, Inc.*, 478 N.E.2d 110, 1985 Ind. App. Lexis 2432 (Ind. App. 1985)]

5.2 Patent   In 1968, Patent No. 3,397,928 (928) was issued to Edward M. Galle, an executive of Hughes Tool Company. Galle assigned the patent, and other related patents, to Hughes. The patent was for an O-ring rubber seal that was used to seal bearings in the cone of a rock bit that rotated to drill holes in rocks. Rock bits were used to drill oil wells. Hughes did not license its 928 patent, which was a substantial commercial success. Smith International, Inc., was Hughes's major competitor in this industry. Between 1971 and 1984, Smith made more than 460,000 rock bits (reaping sales of about $1.3 billion) that contained rubber seals that infringed on Hughes's patents. Hughes sued Smith for patent infringement and requested $1.2 billion in lost royalties and interest. Smith offered $20 million to $60 million in settlement. The case went to trial, and the court found Smith liable for patent infringement. How much should Hughes be awarded in damages? [*Smith Internat'l, Inc. v. Hughes Tool Co.*, 229 U.S.P.Q. 81, 1986 U.S. Dist. Lexis 2847 (Fed. Cir. 1986)]

5.3 Copyright   When Spiro Agnew resigned as vice president of the United States, President Richard M. Nixon appointed Gerald R. Ford as vice president. In 1974, amid growing controversy surrounding the Watergate scandal, President Nixon resigned, and Vice President Ford acceded to the presidency. As president, Ford pardoned Nixon for any wrongdoing regarding the Watergate affair and related matters. Ford served as president until he was defeated by Jimmy Carter in the 1976 presidential election. In 1973, Ford entered into a contract with Harper & Row, Publishers, Inc., to publish his memoirs in book form. The memoirs were to contain significant unpublished materials concerning the Watergate affair and Ford's personal reflections on that time in history. The publisher instituted security measures to protect the confidentiality of the manuscript. Several weeks before the book was to be released, an unidentified person secretly brought a copy of the manuscript to Victor Navasky, editor of *The Nation*, a weekly political commentary magazine. Navasky, knowing that his possession of the purloined manuscript was not authorized, produced a 2,250-word piece titled "The Ford Memoirs" and published it in the April 3, 1979, issue of *The Nation*. Verbatim quotes of between 300 and

400 words from Ford's manuscript, including some of the most important parts, appeared in the article. Harper & Row sued the publishers of *The Nation* for copyright infringement. Who wins? [*Harper & Row, Publishers, Inc. v. Nation Enterprises*, 471 U.S. 539, 105 S.Ct. 2218, 1985 U.S. Lexis 17 (1985)]

5.4 Copyright   The Sony Corporation of America manufactures videocassette recorders (VCRs) that can be used to videotape programs and films that are shown on television and cable stations. VCRs are used by consumers and others to videotape both copyrighted and uncopyrighted works. The primary use for VCRs is by consumers for "time-shifting"—that is, taping a television program for viewing at a more convenient time. Universal City Studios, Inc., and Walt Disney Productions hold copyrights on a substantial number of motion-picture and audiovisual works that are shown on television and cable stations, which pay them a fee to do so. Some of Universal's and Disney's copyrighted works have been copied by consumers using Sony's VCRs. Universal and Disney sued Sony, seeking an injunction against the sale of VCRs by Sony. Is Sony liable for contributory copyright infringement? [*Sony Corp. of America v. Universal City Studios, Inc.*, 464 U.S. 417, 104 S.Ct. 774, 1984 U.S. Lexis 19 (1984)]

5.5 Fair Use Doctrine   In the dark days of 1977, when the City of New York teetered on the brink of bankruptcy, on the television screens of America there appeared an image of a top-hatted Broadway showgirl, backed by an advancing phalanx of dancers, chanting: "I-I-I-I-I-I Love New Yo-o-o-o-o-o-o-rk." As an ad campaign for an ailing city, it was an unparalleled success. Crucial to the campaign was a brief but exhilarating musical theme written by Steve Karmin called "I Love New York." Elsmere Music, Inc., owned the copyright to the music. The success of the campaign did not go unnoticed. On May 20, 1978, the popular weekly variety program *Saturday Night Live* (*SNL*) performed a comedy sketch over National Broadcasting Company's network (NBC). In the sketch, the cast of *SNL*, portraying the mayor and members of the chamber of commerce of the biblical city of Sodom, were seen discussing Sodom's poor public image with out-of-towners and its effect on the tourist trade. In an attempt to recast Sodom's image in a more positive light, a new advertising campaign was revealed, with the highlight of the campaign being a song "I Love Sodom" sung a cappella by a chorus line of *SNL* regulars to the tune of "I Love New York." Elsmere Music did not see the humor of the sketch and sued NBC for copyright infringement. Who wins? [*Elsmere Music, Inc. v. National Broadcasting Co., Inc.*, 623 F.2d 252, 1980 U.S. App. Lexis 16820 (2d Cir. 1980)]

5.6 Trademark   Clairol Incorporated manufactures and distributes hair tinting, dyeing, and coloring preparations. In 1956,

Clairol embarked on an extensive advertising campaign to promote the sale of its "Miss Clairol" hair-color preparations that included advertisements in national magazines, on outdoor billboards, on radio and television, in mailing pieces, and on point-of-sale display materials to be used by retailers and beauty salons. The advertisements prominently displayed the slogans "Hair Color So Natural Only Her Hairdresser Knows for Sure" and "Does She or Doesn't She?" Clairol registered these slogans as trademarks. During the next decade Clairol spent more than $22 million for advertising materials, resulting in more than a billion separate audio and visual impressions using the slogans. Roux Laboratories, Inc., a manufacturer of hair-coloring products and a competitor of Clairol's, filed an opposition to Clairol's registration of the slogans as trademarks. Do the slogans qualify for trademark protection? [*Roux Laboratories, Inc. v. Clairol Inc.*, 427 F.2d 823, 1970 CCPA Lexis 344 (Cust.Pat.App. 1979)]

5.7 Trademark   Since 1972, Mead Data Central, Inc., has provided computer-assisted legal research services to lawyers and others under the trademark "Lexis." Lexis is based on *lex*, the Latin word for law, and *IS*, for information systems. Through extensive sales and advertising, Mead has made Lexis a strong mark in the computerized legal research field, particularly among lawyers. However, Lexis is recognized by only 1 percent of the general population, with almost half of this 1 percent being attorneys. Toyota Motor Corporation has for many years manufactured automobiles, which it markets in the United States through its subsidiary Toyota Motor Sales, U.S.A., Inc. On August 24, 1987, Toyota announced a new line of luxury automobiles to be called Lexus. Toyota planned on spending almost $20 million for marketing and advertising Lexus during the first nine months of 1989. Mead filed suit against Toyota, alleging that Toyota's use of the name Lexus violated New York's antidilution statute and would cause injury to the business reputation of Mead and a dilution of the distinctive quality of the Lexis mark. Who wins? [*Mead Data Central, Inc. v. Toyota Motor Sales, U.S.A., Inc.*, 875 F.2d 1026, 1989 U.S. App. Lexis 6644 (2d Cir. 1989)]

5.8 Generic Name   The Miller Brewing Company, a national brewer, produces a reduced-calorie beer called Miller Lite. Miller began selling beer under this name in the 1970s and has spent millions of dollars promoting the Miller Lite brand name on television, in print, and via other forms of advertising. Since July 11, 1980, Falstaff Brewing Corporation has been brewing and distributing a reduced-calorie beer called "Falstaff Life." Miller brought suit under the Lanham Act, seeking an injunction to prevent Falstaff from using the term *Lite*. Is the term *Lite* a generic name that does not qualify for trademark protection? [*Miller Brewing Co. v. Falstaff Brewing Corp.*, 655 F.2d 5, 1981 U.S. App. Lexis 11345 (1st Cir. 1981)]

Business Ethics Cases

5.9 Business Ethics   Integrated Cash Management Services, Inc. (ICM), designs and develops computer software programs and systems for banks and corporate financial departments. ICM's computer programs and systems are not copyrighted, but they are secret. After Alfred Sims Newlin and Behrouz Vafa completed graduate school, they were employed by ICM as computer programmers. They worked at ICM for several years, writing computer programs. In March 1987, they left ICM to

work for Digital Transactions, Inc. (DTI). Before leaving ICM, however, they copied certain ICM files onto computer disks. Within two weeks of starting to work at DTI, they created prototype computer programs that operated in substantially the same manner as comparable ICM programs and were designed to compete directly with ICM's programs. ICM sued Newlin, Vafa, and DTI for misappropriation of trade secrets. Are the defendants liable? Did the defendants act ethically in this case?

[*Integrated Cash Management Services, Inc. v. Digital Transactions, Inc.*, 920 F.2d 171, 1990 U.S. App. Lexis 20985 (2nd Cir. 1990)]

5.10 Business Ethics   John W. Carson was the host and star of *The Tonight Show*, a well-known nightly television talk show broadcast by the National Broadcasting Company (NBC) until he retired in 1992. Carson also appeared as an entertainer in theaters and night clubs around the country. From the time that he began hosting *The Tonight Show* in 1962, he had been introduced on the show each night with the phrase "Here's Johnny." The phrase "Here's Johnny" was generally associated with Carson by a substantial segment of the television viewing public. Carson had licensed the use of the phrase to a chain of restaurants, a line of toiletries, and other business ventures. Johnny Carson Apparel, Inc., founded in 1970, manufactured and marketed men's clothing to retail stores. Carson, president of Apparel and owner of 20 percent of its stock, had licensed Apparel to use the phrase "Here's Johnny" on labels for clothing and in advertising campaigns. The phrase had never been registered by Carson or Apparel as a trademark or service mark.

Earl Broxton was the owner and president of Here's Johnny Portable Toilets, Inc., a Michigan corporation that engages in the business of renting and selling "Here's Johnny" portable toilets. Broxton was aware when he formed the corporation that the phrase "Here's Johnny" was the introductory slogan for Carson on *The Tonight Show*. Broxton indicated that he coupled the phrase "Here's Johnny" with a second one, "The World's Foremost Commodian," to make a good play on the phrase. Shortly after Toilets went into business in 1976, Carson and Apparel sued Toilets, seeking an injunction prohibiting the further use of the phrase "Here's Johnny" as a corporate name for or in connection with the sale or rental of its portable toilets. Who wins? Did Broxton act ethically by appropriating the phrase "Here's Johnny" to promote the sale and rental of portable toilets? [*Carson v. Here's Johnny Portable Toilets, Inc.*, 698 F.2d 831, 1983 U.S. App. Lexis 30866 (6th Cir. 1983)]

Briefing the Case Writing Assignment

Read Case A.5 in the Case Appendix [*Feist Publications, Inc. v. Rural Telephone Service Company, Inc.*]. This case is excerpted from the U.S. Supreme Court opinion. Review and brief the case. In your brief, be sure to answer the following questions.

1. Who was the plaintiff? Who was the defendant?

2. What had the defendant done that caused the plaintiff to sue?

3. What is the issue in this case?

4. What was the decision of the U.S. Supreme Court?

Endnotes

1. 35 U.S.C. §§ 10 et seq.
2. 17 U.S.C. §§ 101 et seq.
3. 17 U.S.C. § 101.
4. 17 U.S.C. §§ 901–14.
5. 15 U.S.C. §§ 1114 et seq.

6

Business and Cyber Crimes

"In our complex society the accountant's certificate and the lawyer's opinion can be instruments for inflicting pecuniary loss more potent than the chisel or the crowbar."

—Justice Blackmun, Dissenting Opinion.
Ernest & Ernst v. Hochfelder, 425 U.S. 185 (1976)

Chapter Objectives

After studying this chapter, you should be able to:

1. Define and list the essential elements of a crime.

2. Describe criminal procedure, including arrest, indictment, arraignment, and the criminal trial.

3. Define major white-collar crimes, such as embezzlement, bribery, and criminal fraud.

4. Explain the constitutional safeguards provided by the Fourth, Fifth, Sixth, and Eighth Amendments to the U.S. Constitution.

5. List and describe laws involving computer and Internet crimes.

Chapter Contents

- Definition of Crime
- Criminal Procedure
- Common Crimes
- White-Collar Crimes
- Constitutional Safeguards

For members of society to peacefully coexist and commerce to flourish, people and their property must be protected from injury by other members of society. Federal, state, and local governments' **criminal laws** are intended to accomplish this by providing an incentive for persons to act reasonably in society and imposing penalties on persons who violate them.

The United States has one of the most advanced and humane criminal law systems in the world. It differs from any other criminal law systems in several respects. A person charged with a crime in the United States is *presumed innocent until proven guilty*. The *burden of proof* is on the government to prove that the accused is guilty of the crime charged. Further, the accused must be found guilty "beyond a reasonable doubt." Conviction requires unanimous jury vote. Under many other legal systems, a person accused of a crime is presumed guilty unless the person can prove he or she is not. A person charged with a crime in the United States is also provided with substantial constitutional safeguards during the criminal justice process.

This chapter discusses crime, criminal procedure, crimes affecting business, white-collar crime, computer and Internet crime, inchoate crime, international crime, criminal penalties, and constitutional safeguards afforded criminal defendants.

Business Brief

In the United States, a person accused of a crime is *presumed innocent until proven guilty*. The government has the burden of proving that the accused is guilty of the crime charged.

Definition of Crime

A **crime** is defined as any act done by an individual in violation of those duties that he or she owes to society and for the breach of which the law provides that the wrongdoer shall make amends to the public. Many activities have been considered crimes through the ages, whereas other crimes are of recent origin.

Penal Codes and Regulatory Statutes

Statutes are the primary source of criminal law. Most states have adopted comprehensive **penal codes** that define in detail the activities considered to be crimes within their jurisdictions and the penalties that will be imposed for their commission. A comprehensive federal criminal code defines federal crimes.[1] In addition, state and federal **regulatory statutes** often provide for criminal violations and penalties. The state and federal legislatures are continually adding to the list of crimes.

London, England. Most industrialized countries and many other countries have well-developed criminal laws and legal systems to enforce these laws.

The penalty for committing a crime may consist of the imposition of a fine, imprisonment, both, or some other form of punishment (e.g., probation). Generally, imprisonment is imposed to (1) incapacitate the criminal so he or she will not harm others in society, (2) provide a means to rehabilitate the criminal, (3) deter others from similar conduct, and (4) inhibit personal retribution by the victim.

Parties to a Criminal Action

In a criminal lawsuit, the government (not a private party) is the **plaintiff**. The government is represented by a lawyer called the *prosecutor*. The accused, which is usually an individual or a business, is the **defendant**. The accused is represented by a *defense attorney*. If the accused cannot afford a defense lawyer, the government will provide one free of charge.

Classification of Crimes

All crimes can be classified in one of the following categories.

Felonies   **Felonies** are the most serious kinds of crimes. Felonies include crimes that are *mala in se*—that is, inherently evil. Most crimes against persons (e.g., murder, rape) and certain business-related crimes (e.g., embezzlement, bribery) are felonies in most jurisdictions. Felonies are usually punishable by imprisonment. In some jurisdictions, certain felonies (e.g., first-degree murder) are punishable by death. Federal law[2] and some state laws require mandatory sentencing for specified crimes. Many statutes define different degrees of crimes (e.g., first-, second-, and third-degree murder). Each degree earns different penalties. Serious violations of regulatory statutes are also felonies.

Misdemeanors   **Misdemeanors** are less serious than felonies. They are crimes *mala prohibita*; that is, they are not inherently evil but are prohibited by society. Many crimes against property, such as robbery, burglary, and less serious violations of regulatory statutes, are included in this category. Misdemeanors carry lesser penalties than felonies. They are usually punishable by fines and/or imprisonment for one year or less.

Violations   Crimes such as traffic violations, jaywalking and such are neither felonies nor misdemeanors. These crimes, which are called **violations**, are generally punishable by fines. Occasionally, a few days of imprisonment are imposed.

Essential Elements of a Crime

The following two elements must be proven for a person to be found guilty of most crimes:

1. *Criminal act.* The defendant must have actually performed the prohibited act. The actual performance of the criminal act is called the **actus reus** (guilty act). Killing someone without legal jurisdiction is an example of *actus reus*. Sometimes, the omission of an act constitutes the requisite *actus reus*. For example, a crime has been committed if a taxpayer who is under a legal duty to file a tax return fails to do so. However, merely thinking about committing a crime is not a crime because no action has been taken.

2. *Criminal intent.* To be found guilty of a crime, the accused must be found to have possessed the requisite state of mind (i.e., specific or general intent) when the act was performed. This is called the **mens rea** (evil intent). *Specific intent* is found where the accused purposefully, intentionally, or with knowledge commits a prohibited act. *General intent* is found where there is a showing of recklessness or a lesser degree of mental culpability. The individual criminal statutes state whether the crime requires a

showing of specific or general intent. Juries may infer an accused's intent from the facts and circumstances of the case. There is no crime if the requisite *mens rea* cannot be proven. Thus, no crime is committed if one person accidentally injures another person.

Some statutes impose criminal liability based on **strict**, or **absolute, liability**. That is, a finding of *mens rea* is not required. Criminal liability is imposed if the prohibited act is committed. Absolute liability is often imposed by regulatory statutes, such as environmental laws.

Criminal Acts as the Basis for Tort Actions

An injured party may bring a *civil tort action* against a wrongdoer who has caused the party injury during the commission of a criminal act. Civil lawsuits are separate from the government's criminal action against the wrongdoer. In many cases, a person injured by a criminal act will not sue the criminal to recover civil damages. This is because the criminal is often *judgment proof*—that is, the criminal does not have the money to pay a civil judgment.

Business Brief

The same act may be the basis for both a criminal lawsuit and a civil lawsuit.

Concept Summary   Civil and Criminal Law Compared

Issue	Civil Law	Criminal Law
Party who brings the action	The plaintiff	The government
Trial by jury	Yes, except actions for equity	Yes
Burden of proof	Preponderance of the evidence	Beyond a reasonable doubt
Jury vote	Judgment for plaintiff requires specific jury vote (e.g., 9 of 12 jurors)	Conviction requires unanimous jury vote
Sanctions and penalties	Monetary damages and equitable remedies (e.g., injunction, specific performance)	Imprisonment, capital punishment, fine, probation

Cambodia. Different countries and cultures have different criminal laws. Some acts that are considered criminal in one country may not be thought so in other countries.

Business Ethics

Martha Stewart Guilty

Martha Stewart is an icon of fine living. Through her company, Martha Stewart Living Omnimedia Inc. (Omnimedia), Stewart built a business conglomerate involved in publishing magazines and cookbooks, selling clothing and home-based merchandise, and producing a syndicated television program. She and her business became so successful that when the company went public in 1999, Stewart became an instant billionaire.

In 2003, Stewart's friend Sam Waksal, the primary owner of ImClone Systems Inc. (ImClone), received news that the U.S. Food and Drug Administration (FDA) had not given approval for ImClone to market a cancer-fighting drug. Waksal received this information one day before the news would be made public. Waksal and a number of his family members tried to sell their ImClone stock through a securities broker named Peter E. Bacanovic. Bacanovic was also Martha Stewart's stockbroker, and Stewart was a shareholder of ImClone. Bacanovic had his assistant, Douglas Faneuil, notify Stewart of Waksal's activities. Stewart sold her ImClone stock at $58 per share. When the FDA's negative decision regarding the anticancer drug was released, ImClone stock fell in value. Stewart saved $45,000 by selling her ImClone stock early.

When the U.S. government investigated the substantial selling activity in ImClone stock prior to the public announcement of the FDA's adverse ruling, they netted the Waksal family *and* Martha Stewart. Sam Waksal pleaded guilty to insider trading

and was sent to jail. When the federal government questioned Stewart about her sale of ImClone stock, she said that she had a prior $60 "sell order" (to sell the stock if it ever dropped to $60). Although both Bacanovic and Faneuil first collaborated this story, eventually Faneuil reached a plea-bargain with the government and became a witness: He then told the government that the $60 sell order story was a lie and cover-up.

The U.S. government brought criminal charges against Stewart for criminal conspiracy, lying to the federal government, and obstruction of justice. Stewart pleaded the Fifth Amendment and did not testify at trial. The government called many witnesses, including Faneuil and several of Stewart's friends to whom she had talked to about the ImClone stock sale. One witness testified that Stewart told her that Stewart knew of Waksal's trading before she sold her ImClone stock and then stated, "Isn't it nice to have brokers who tell you these things?" The jury returned a verdict of guilty on all charges. On the day the judgment was announced, Stewart's Omnimedia stock plummeted, and Stewart lost about $100 million in one day. Stewart was sentenced to five months in jail. [*United States v. Stewart* (2004)]

1. Did Stewart act ethically in this case?
2. Why do you think Stewart sold her ImClone stock to save only $45,000?

Criminal Procedure

No! No! Sentence first—verdict afterward.

Lewis Carroll
Alice in Wonderland, Ch. 12

The procedure for initiating and maintaining a criminal action is quite detailed. It includes both pretrial procedures and the actual trial.

Pretrial Criminal Procedure

Pretrial criminal procedure consists of several distinct stages, including *arrest, indictment* or *information, arraignment*, and *plea bargaining*.

Arrest Before the police can arrest a person for the commission of a crime, they usually must obtain an **arrest warrant** based on a showing of probable cause. *Probable cause* is defined as the substantial likelihood that the person either committed or is about to commit a crime. If there is no time for the police to obtain a warrant (e.g., if the police arrive during the commission of a crime, when a person is fleeing from the scene of a crime, or when it is likely that evidence will be destroyed), the police may still arrest the suspect. *Warrantless arrests* are also judged by the probable cause standard.

After a person is arrested, he or she is taken to the police station to be booked. *Booking* is the administrative procedure for recording the arrest, fingerprinting, and so on.

Indictment or Information Accused persons must be formally charged with a crime before they can be brought to trial. This is usually done by the issuance of a *grand jury indictment* or a *magistrate's information statement*.

Evidence of serious crimes, such as murder, is usually presented to a *grand jury*. Most grand juries comprise between 6 and 24 citizens who are charged with evaluating the evidence presented by the government. Grand jurors sit for a fixed period of time, such as one year. If the grand jury determines that there is sufficient evidence to hold the accused for trial, it issues an **indictment**. Note that the grand jury does not determine guilt. If an indictment is issued, the accused will be held for later trial.

For lesser crimes (e.g., burglary, shoplifting), the accused will be brought before a *magistrate* (judge). A magistrate who finds that there is enough evidence to hold the accused for trial will issue an **information**.

The case against the accused is dismissed if neither an indictment nor an information is issued.

Arraignment If an indictment or information is issued, the accused is brought before a court for an **arraignment** proceeding, during which the accused is (1) informed of the charges against him or her and (2) asked to enter a **plea**. The accused may plead *guilty, not guilty*, or *nolo contendere*. A plea of *nolo contendere* means that the accused agrees to the imposition of a penalty but does not admit guilt. A *nolo contendere* plea cannot be used as evidence of liability against the accused at a subsequent civil trial. Corporate defendants often enter this plea. The government has the option of accepting a *nolo contendere* plea or requiring the defendant to plead guilty or not guilty.

In the following case, the U.S. Supreme Court held that a police officer may make a warrantless arrest pursuant to a minor criminal offense.

U.S. SUPREME COURT CASE
Atwater v. Lago Vista, Texas

532 U.S. 318, 121 S.Ct. 1536, 2001 U.S. Lexis 3366 (2001)
Supreme Court of the United States

Case 6.1
Arrest

Background and Facts

Texas law requires that front-seat drivers and passengers wear seat belts and that a driver secure any small child riding in front. In March 1997, Gail Atwater was driving her pickup truck in Lago Vista, Texas, with her three-year-old son and five-year-old daughter in the front seat. None of them were wearing seat belts. Bart Turek, a Lago Vista police officer, observed the seat-belt violation and pulled Atwater over. A friend of Atwater's arrived at the scene and took charge of the children. Turek handcuffed Atwater, placed her in his squad car, and drove her to the police station. Atwater was booked, her mug shot was taken, and she was placed in a jail cell for about one hour until she was released on $310 bond. Atwater ultimately pleaded no contest to the misdemeanor seat-belt offenses and paid a $50 fine. Atwater sued the City of Lago Vista and the police officer for compensatory and punitive damages for allegedly violating her Fourth Amendment right to be free from unreasonable seizure. The district court ruled against

Atwater, and the court of appeals affirmed. The U.S. Supreme Court granted certiorari to hear the appeal.

Issue

Does the Fourth Amendment permit police to make a warrantless arrest pursuant to a minor criminal offense?

Court's Reasoning

The U.S. Supreme Court stated that there was no support for Atwater's position. The Court noted that both the legislative tradition of granting warrantless misdemeanor arrest authority and the judicial tradition of sustaining such statutes against constitutional attack have for more than a century uniformly recognized the constitutionality of extending warrantless arrest power to misdemeanors without limitation to breaches of the peace. The Court held that if an officer has probable cause to believe that an individual has committed even a very minor criminal offense in his

Atwater v. Lago Vista, Texas

532 U.S. 318, 121 S.Ct. 1536, 2001 U.S. Lexis 3366 (2001)
Supreme Court of the United States
(continued)

presence, he may, without violating the Fourth Amendment, arrest the offender.

Decision and Remedy

The U.S. Supreme Court held that the Fourth Amendment permits police officers to make a warrantless arrest pursuant to a minor criminal offense. The Supreme Court affirmed the judgments of the district court and the court of appeals.

Case Questions

Critical Legal Thinking   Do you agree with the U.S. Supreme Court's decision in this case? Why or why not?

Business Ethics   Did the police officer act ethically in this case? Should he have used more discretion?

Contemporary Business   What would be the consequences if the Supreme Court had held in favor of Atwater?

Plea Bargaining   Sometimes the accused and the government enter into a **plea bargaining agreement**. The government engages in plea bargaining to save costs, avoid the risks of a trial, and prevent further overcrowding of the prisons. This type of arrangement allows the accused to admit to a lesser crime than charged. In return, the government agrees to impose a lesser penalty or sentence than might have been obtained had the case gone to trial.

The Criminal Trial

> The magnitude of a crime is proportionate to the magnitude of the injustice which prompts it. Hence, the smallest crimes may be actually the greatest.
>
> Aristotle
> *The Rhetoric, BK. 1, Ch. XIV*

At a criminal trial, all jurors must *unanimously* agree before the accused is found *guilty* of the crime charged. If even one juror disagrees (i.e., has reasonable doubt) about the guilt of the accused, the accused cannot be found guilty of the crime charged. If all the jurors agree that the accused did not commit the crime, the accused is found *not guilty* of the crime charged. After trial, the following rules apply:

- If the defendant is found guilty, he or she may appeal.
- If the defendant is found not guilty, the government cannot appeal.
- If the jury cannot come to a unanimous decision about the defendant's guilt one way or the other, the jury is considered a **hung jury**. The government may choose to retry the case before a new judge and jury.

Tibet. Religious beliefs are often reflected in the criminal laws of a country.

Contemporary Environment
Federal Sentencing Guidelines

In the past, different persons convicted of the same federal crime might have been sentenced to substantially different criminal penalties. To remedy this situation, Congress enacted the **Sentencing Reform Act of 1984** [18 U.S.C. § 3551 et. seq.]. This act created the **United States Sentencing Commission**, which was empowered to, and did, adopt **Sentencing Guidelines** for federal crimes. These guidelines establish a range of sentences for each federal crime.

Generally, a judge must impose on a convicted defendant a sentence that falls within the specific range of sentences provided for the crime involved. The court considers the seriousness of the crime, the defendant's past record, and other relevant factors. A judge may depart from the Sentencing Guidelines based

on the evidence produced at trial, information provided by the prosecuting attorney and defense attorney, and a pretrial services officer that reviews the case.

In 1991, the Sentencing Commission adopted special sentencing guidelines for white-collar crimes committed by corporate and business employees. These guidelines increased the penalties for such white-collar crimes as bribery, money laundering, and wire fraud and mail fraud, and criminal violations of antitrust, employment, and securities laws. A judge may impose sentences from the range provided based on the seriousness of the violation, the company's past history of violations, and the cooperation of management in the investigation of the wrongdoing. ■

Common Crimes

Many crimes are committed against business property. These crimes often involve the theft, misappropriation, or fraudulent taking of property. Many of the most important crimes against business property are discussed in the following paragraphs.

Robbery

In common law, **robbery** is defined as the taking of personal property from another person or business by the use of fear or force. For example, if a robber threatens to physically harm a storekeeper unless that victim surrenders the contents of the cash register, it is robbery. If a criminal pickpockets somebody's wallet, it is not robbery because there has been no use of force or fear. Robbery with a deadly weapon is generally considered aggravated robbery (or armed robbery) and carries a harsher penalty.

Burglary

In common law, **burglary** is defined as "breaking and entering a dwelling at night" with the intent to commit a felony. Modern penal codes have broadened this definition to include daytime thefts from offices and commercial and other buildings. In addition, the "breaking-in" element has been abandoned by most modern definitions of burglary. Thus, unauthorized entering of a building through an unlocked door is sufficient. Aggravated burglary (or armed burglary) carries stiffer penalties.

Larceny

In common law, **larceny** is defined as the wrongful and fraudulent taking of another person's personal property. Most personal property—including tangible property, trade secrets, computer programs, and other business property—is subject to larceny. The stealing of automobiles and car stereos, pickpocketing, and such are larceny. Neither the use of force nor the entry of a building is required. Some states distinguish between grand larceny and petit larceny. This distinction depends of the value of the property taken.

Theft

Some states have dropped the distinction among the crimes of robbery, burglary, and larceny. Instead, these states group these crimes under the general crime of **theft**. Most of these states distinguish between grand theft and petit theft. The distinction depends on the value of the property taken.

Receiving Stolen Property

It is a crime for a person to (1) knowingly **receive stolen property** and (2) intend to deprive the rightful owner of that property. Knowledge and intent can be inferred from the circumstances. The stolen property can be any tangible property (e.g., personal property, money, negotiable instruments, stock certificates).

Arson

In common law, **arson** is defined as the malicious or willful burning of the dwelling of another person. Modern penal codes have expanded this definition to include the burning of all types of private, commercial, and public buildings. Thus, in most states, an owner who burns his or her own building to collect insurance proceeds can be found liable for arson. If arson is found, the insurance company does not have to pay proceeds of any insurance policy on the burned property.

Extortion

The crime of **extortion** involves the obtaining of property from another, with his or her consent, induced by wrongful use of actual or threatened force, violence, or fear. For example, extortion occurs when a person threatens to expose something about another person unless that other person gives money or property. The truth or falsity of the information is immaterial. Extortion of private persons is commonly referred to as **blackmail**. Extortion of public officials is called **extortion "under color of official right."**

Online Commerce & Internet Law
The Information Infrastructure Protection (IIP) Act

The Internet and Information Age ushered in a whole new world for education, business, and consumer transactions. But with it followed a new rash of digital crimes. Prosecutors and courts wrestled over how to apply existing laws written in a nondigital age to new Internet-related abuses.

In 1996, Congress responded by enacting the **Information Infrastructure Protection Act (IIP Act)**. In this federal law, Congress addressed computer-related crimes as distinct offenses. The IIP Act provides protection for any computer attached to the Internet.

The IIP Act makes it a federal crime for anyone to intentionally access and obtain information from a protected computer without authorization. The IIP Act does not require that the defendant accessed a protected computer for commercial benefit. Thus, persons who transmit a computer virus over the Internet or hackers who trespass into Internet-connected computers may be criminally prosecuted under the IIP Act. Even merely observing data on a protected computer without authorization is sufficient to meet the requirement that the defendant has accessed a protected computer. Criminal penalties for violating the IIP Act include imprisonment for up to 10 years and fines.

The IIP Act gives the federal government a much-needed weapon for directly prosecuting cyber-crooks, hackers, and others who enter, steal, destroy, or look at others' computer data without authorization. ∎

Finland. Multinational corporations have to obey the criminal laws of all the countries in which they conduct business.

White-Collar Crimes

Certain types of crime are prone to being committed by businesspersons. These crimes are often referred to as **white-collar crimes**. These crimes usually involve cunning and deceit rather than physical force. Many of the most important white-collar crimes are discussed in the paragraphs that follow.

Forgery

The crime of **forgery** occurs if a written document is fraudulently made or altered and that change affects the legal liability of another person. Counterfeiting, falsifying public records, and materially altering legal documents are examples of forgery. One of the most common forms of forgery is signing another person's signature to a check or changing the amount of a check. Note that signing another person's signature without intent to defraud is not forgery. For example, forgery has not been committed if one spouse signs the other spouse's payroll check for deposit in a joint checking or savings account at the bank.

Embezzlement

Unknown in common law, the crime of **embezzlement** is not a statutory crime. Embezzlement is the fraudulent conversion of property by a person to whom that property was entrusted. Typically, embezzlement is committed by an employer's employees, agents, or representatives (e.g., accountants, lawyers, trust officers, treasurers). Embezzlers often try to cover their tracks by preparing false books, records, or entries.

The key element here is that the stolen property was *entrusted* to the embezzler. This differs from robbery, burglary, and larceny, where property is taken by someone not entrusted with the property. For example, embezzlement has been committed if a bank teller absconds with money that was deposited by depositors. The employer (the bank) entrusted the teller to take deposits from its customers.

Bribery

Bribery is one of the most prevalent forms of white-collar crime. A bribe can be money, property, favors, or anything else of value. The crime of commercial bribery prohibits the payment of bribes to private persons and businesses. This type of bribe is often referred to as a **kickback** or **payoff**. Intent is a necessary element of this crime. The offeror of a bribe commits the crime of bribery when the bribe is tendered. The offeree is guilty of the crime of bribery when he or she accepts the bribe. The offeror can be found liable for the crime of bribery even if the person to whom the bribe is offered rejects the bribe.

Business Brief

Bribery is probably the most prevalent form of business crime.

Fraud includes the pretense of knowledge when knowledge there is none.

C. J. Cardozo,
Ultramares Corp. v. Touche (1931)

Consider This Example   Harriet Landers is the purchasing agent for the ABC Corporation and is in charge of purchasing equipment to be used by the corporation. Neal Brown, the sales representative of a company that make equipment that can be used by the ABC Corporation, offers to pay her a 10 percent kickback if she buys equipment from him. She accepts the bribe and orders the equipment. Both parties are guilty of bribery.

In common law, the crime of bribery is defined as the giving or receiving of anything of value in corrupt payment for an "official act" by a public official. Public officials include legislators, judges, jurors, witnesses at trial, administrative agency personnel, and other government officials. Modern penal codes also make it a crime to bribe public officials. For example, a developer who is constructing an apartment building cannot pay the building inspector to overlook a building code violation.

International Law

The Foreign Corrupt Practices Act

It is well known that the payment of bribes is pervasive in conducting international business. To prevent U.S. companies from engaging in this type of conduct, the U.S. Congress enacted the **Foreign Corrupt Practices Act of 1977 (FCPA)** [15 U.S.C. § 78m]. The FCPA makes it illegal for U.S. companies, or their officers, directors, agents, or employees, to bribe a foreign official, a foreign political party official, or a candidate for foreign political office. A bribe is illegal only where it is meant to influence the awarding of new business or the retention of a continuing business activity.

The FCPA imposes criminal liability where a person pays the illegal bribe himself or herself, or supplies a payment to a third party or an agent, knowing that it will be used as a bribe. A firm can be fined up to $2 million, and an individual can be fined up to $100,000 and imprisoned for up to five years for violations of the FCPA.

The 1988 amendments to the FCPA created two defenses. One excuses a firm or person charged with bribery under the FCPA if the firm or person can show that the payment was lawful under the written laws of that country. The other allows a defendant to show that a payment was a reasonable and bona fide expenditure related to the furtherance or execution of a contract. This latter exemption is difficult to interpret.

Some people argue that U.S. companies are placed at a disadvantage in international markets where commercial bribery is commonplace and firms from other countries are not hindered by laws similar to the FCPA. ■

Criminal Fraud

Obtaining title to property through deception or trickery constitutes the crime of **false pretenses**. This crime is commonly referred to as **criminal fraud** or **deceit**.

Consider This Example   Bob Anderson, a stockbroker, promises Mary Greenberg, a prospective investor, that he will use any money she invests to purchase interests in oil wells. Based on this promise, Ms. Greenberg decides to make the investment. Mr. Anderson never intended to invest the money. Instead, he used the money for his personal needs. This is criminal fraud.

Mail and Wire Fraud   Federal law prohibits the use of mails or wires (e.g., telegraphs, telephone, Internet) to defraud another person. These crimes are called **mail fraud**[3] and **wire fraud**[4], respectively. The government often prosecutes a suspect under these statutes if there is insufficient evidence to prove the real crime that the criminal was attempting to commit or did commit. The maximum penalty for mail, wire, and Internet fraud is 20 years in prison.

Money Laundering

When criminals make money from illegal activities, they are often faced with the problem of having large sums of money and no record of how this money was earned. This could easily tip the government off to their illegal activities. In order to "wash" the money and make it look as though it was earned legitimately, many criminals purchase legitimate businesses and run the money through that business to clean it before the criminal receives the money. The legitimate business has "cooked" books showing faked expenditures and receipts, in which the illegal money is buried. Restaurants, motels, and other cash businesses make excellent money laundries.

To address this problem the federal government enacted the **Money Laundering Control Act** [18 U.S.C. § 1957]. This act makes it a crime to

- Knowingly engage in a *monetary transaction* through a financial institution involving property worth more than $10,000. For example, this would include making deposits, withdrawals, transactions between accounts, or obtaining monetary instruments such as cashiers' checks, money orders, and travelers' checks from a bank or other financial institution.

- Knowingly engage in a *financial transaction* involving the proceeds of an illegal activity. For example, this would include buying real estate, automobiles, personal property, intangible assets, or anything of value with money obtained from illegal activities.

Thus, money laundering itself is now a federal crime. The money that is washed could have been made from illegal gambling operations, drug dealing, fraud, and other crimes, including white-collar crimes. Persons convicted of money laundering can be fined up to $500,000 or twice the value of the property involved, whichever is greater, and sentenced to up to 20 years in federal prison. In addition, violation of the act subjects any property involved in or traceable to the offense to forfeiture to the government.

Online Commerce & Internet Law
Cyber Crime—Identity Fraud

For centuries, some people—for various purposes, mostly financial in nature—have attempted to take the identities of other persons. Today, taking on the identity of another can be extremely lucrative, earning the spoils of another's credit cards, bank accounts, Social Security benefits, and such. The use of new technology—computers and the Internet—has made such "identity fraud" even easier. But the victim of such fraud is left with funds stolen, a dismantled credit history, and thousands of dollars in costs trying to straighten out the mess. Identity fraud is the fastest-growing financial fraud in America.

To combat such fraud, Congress passed the Identity **Theft and Assumption Deterrence Act of 1998**. This act criminalizes identity fraud, making it a federal felony punishable with prison sentences ranging from 3 to 25 years. The act also appoints a federal administrative agency, the Federal Trade Commission (FTC), to help victims restore their credit and erase the impact of the imposter. Law enforcement officials suggest the following steps to protect against identity fraud: Never put your Social Security number on any document unless it is legally required, obtain and review copies of your credit report at least twice each year, and use safe passwords (e.g., other than family names and birthdays) on bank accounts and other accounts that require personal identification numbers (PINs). ■

Racketeer Influenced and Corrupt Organizations Act (RICO)

Organized crime has a pervasive influence on many parts of the American economy. In 1980, Congress enacted the Organized Crime Control Act. The **Racketeer Influenced and Corrupt Organizations Act (RICO)** is part of this act.[5] Originally, RICO was intended to apply only to organized crime. However, the broad language of the RICO statute has been used against non–organized crime defendants as well. RICO, which provides for both criminal and civil penalties, is one of the most important laws affecting business today.

Criminal Rico RICO makes it a federal crime to acquire or maintain an interest in, use income from, or conduct or participate in the affairs of an enterprise through a pattern of racketeering activity. An *enterprise* is defined as a corporation, a partnership, a sole proprietorship, another business or organization, or the government. *Racketeering activity* consists of a number of specifically enumerated federal and state crimes, including such activities as gambling, arson, robbery, counterfeiting, and dealing in narcotics. Business-related crimes, such as bribery, embezzlement, mail fraud, and wire fraud, are also considered racketeering. To prove a *pattern of racketeering*, at least two of these acts must be committed by the defendant within a 10-year period. For example, committing two different frauds would be considered a pattern.

Individual defendants found criminally liable for RICO violations can be fined up to $25,000 per violation, imprisoned for up to 20 years, or both. In addition, RICO provides for the *forfeiture* of any property or business interests (even interests in a legitimate business) that were gained because of RICO violations. This provision allows the government to recover investments made with monies derived from racketeering activities. The government may also seek civil penalties for RICO violations. These include injunctions, orders of dissolution, reorganization of business, and the divestiture of the defendant's interest in an enterprise.

Civil RICO Persons injured by a RICO violation can bring a private *civil* action against the violator to recover injury to business or property. A successful plaintiff may recover *treble damages* (three times actual loss), plus attorneys' fees.

The Bahamas. Certain countries provide bank secrecy laws that protect the identity of depositors from disclosure. The Bahamas has such a law, and many of its chartered "banks" are no more than lawyers' offices in office buildings. Who do you think uses these bank accounts?

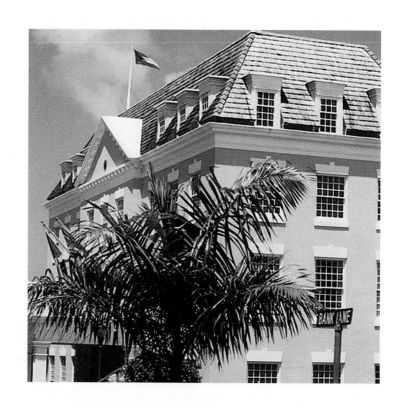

Corporate Criminal Liability

A *corporation* is a fictitious legal person that is granted legal existence by the state only after certain requirements are met. A corporation cannot act on its own behalf. Instead, it must act through *agents*, such as managers, representatives, and employees.

The question of whether a corporation can be held criminally liable has intrigued legal scholars for some time. Originally, under the common law, it was generally held that corporations lacked the criminal mind (*mens rea*) to be held criminally liable. Modern courts, however, are more pragmatic. These courts have held that corporations are criminally liable for the acts of their managers, agents, and employees. In any event, because corporations cannot be put in prison, they are usually sanctioned with fines, loss of a license or franchise, and the like.

Corporate directors, officers, and employees are individually liable for crimes that they personally commit, whether for personal benefit or on behalf of the corporation. In addition, under certain circumstances a corporate manager can be held criminally liable for the criminal activities of his or her subordinates. To be held criminally liable, the manager must have failed to supervise the subordinate appropriately. This is an evolving area of the law.

Business Brief

Corporations may be held criminally liable for actions of their officers, employees, or agents.

Business Brief

Corporate directors, officers, and employees are personally liable for the crimes they commit while acting on behalf of the corporation.

Business Ethics

Whistle-Blowers Sing for Millions

The federal government is the largest purchaser of goods and services in the country. As such, it is also the target of substantial fraud by the firms it deals with. If caught, a government contractor that defrauds the government is subject to criminal prosecution. In addition, the federal government relies on a revamped law that elicits employees of government contractors and others to become modern-day bounty hunters and report anyone who defrauds the government. The law is the **Civil False Claims Act**, commonly known as the **whistle-blower statute**. This act was originally enacted in 1863 to protect the federal government from corrupt government contractors after the Civil War. It was strengthened in 1986 to provide a penalty of *treble damages* plus up to $10,000 per false claim against the defendant and allows the court to award between 15 and 25 percent of the recovery to the whistle-blower, who is now politely called a "relator." These lawsuits are called ***qui tam*** cases (from the Latin phrase "he who sues as much for the king as for himself").

The procedure for bringing a *qui tam* lawsuit is simple: The relator files the lawsuit, notifies the federal government, and then waits to see if the federal government chooses to intervene in the lawsuit. If the federal government intervenes, it pursues the lawsuit; if not, the relator must pursue the lawsuit alone, which is very costly. The federal government intervenes in only 20 percent of the *qui tam* cases filed, and 95 percent of the recoveries are from these cases. Many cases in which the federal government does not intervene are dropped. There is a strong incentive for a defendant to settle *qui tam* cases that are pursued by the federal government, however. If the defendant loses, it faces the possibility of treble damages, plus a penalty of up to $10,000 per false claim and a ban on ever doing business with the federal government again.

1. Do you think there is much fraud in government contracting? Does the Civil False Claims Act make government contractors more honest?
2. Do employees face an ethical dilemma when filing a *qui tam* action against their employer? If so, how do you think most employees solve this dilemma? ▪

Constitutional Safeguards

When our forefathers drafted the U.S. Constitution, they included provisions that protect persons from unreasonable government intrusion and provide safeguards for those accused of crimes. Although these safeguards originally applied only to federal cases, the Fourteenth Amendment's Due Process Clause made them applicable to state criminal law cases as well. The most important of these constitutional safeguards are discussed in the following paragraphs.

The criminal is to go free because the constable has blundered.
C. J. Cardozo
People v. Defore (1926)

Fourth Amendment Protection Against Unreasonable Search and Seizure

The *Fourth Amendment* to the U.S. Constitution protects persons and corporations from overzealous investigative activities by the government. It protects the rights of the people from **unreasonable search and seizure** by the government. It permits people to be secure in their persons, houses, papers, and effects.

"Reasonable" search and seizure by the government is lawful. **Search warrants** based on probable cause are necessary in most cases. Such a warrant specifically states the place and scope of the authorized search. General searches beyond the specified area are forbidden. *Warrantless searches* are permitted only (1) incident to arrest, (2) where evidence is in "plain view," or (3) where it is likely that evidence will be destroyed. Warrantless searches are also judged by the probable cause standard.

Evidence obtained from an unreasonable search and seizure is considered tainted evidence ("fruit of a tainted tree"). Under the **exclusionary rule**, such evidence can generally be prohibited from introduction at a trial or an administrative proceeding against the person searched. However, this evidence is freely admissible against other persons. The U.S. Supreme Court created a *good faith exception* to the exclusionary rule.[6] This exception allows evidence otherwise obtained illegally to be introduced as evidence against the accused if the police officers who conducted the unreasonable search reasonably believed that they were acting pursuant to a lawful search warrant.

The following U.S. Supreme Court cases examine the reach of the Fourth Amendment's protection against unreasonable search and seizure.

U.S. SUPREME COURT CASE

Kyllo v. United States

533 U.S. 27, 121 S.Ct. 2038, 2001 U.S. Lexis 4487 (2001)
Supreme Court of the United States

Case 6.2
Search

Background and Facts

In 1992, government agents suspected that marijuana was being grown in the home of Danny Kyllo, which was part of a triplex building in Florence, Oregon. Indoor marijuana growth typically requires high-intensity lamps. In order to determine whether an amount of heat was emanating from Kyllo's home consistent with the use of such lamps, federal agents used a thermal imager to scan the triplex. Thermal imagers detect infrared radiation and produce images of the radiation. The scan of Kyllo's home, which was performed from an automobile on the street, showed that the roof over the garage and a side wall of Kyllo's home were "hot." The agents used this scanning evidence to obtain a search warrant authorizing a search of Kyllo's home. During the search, the agents found an indoor growing operation involving more than 100 marijuana plants.

Kyllo was indicted for manufacturing marijuana, a violation of federal criminal law. Kyllo moved to suppress the imaging evidence and the evidence it led to, arguing that it was an unreasonable search that violated the Fourth Amendment to the U.S. Constitution. The trial court disagreed with Kyllo and let the evidence be introduced and considered at trial. Kyllo then entered a conditional guilty plea and appealed the trial court's failure to suppress the challenged evidence. The court of appeals affirmed the trial court's decision admitting the evidence. The U.S. Supreme Court granted certiorari to hear the appeal.

Issue

Is the use of a thermal-imaging device aimed at a private home from a public street to detect relative amounts of heat within the home a "search" within the meaning of the Fourth Amendment?

Court's Reasoning

The U.S. Supreme Court stated, "At the very core of the Fourth Amendment stands the right of a man to retreat into his own home and there be free from unreasonable government intrusion." With few exceptions, a warrantless search of a home is unconstitutional. The Court noted, however, that the visual observation of a house is no "search" at all. The present case involves officers on a public street engaged in more than naked-eye surveillance of a home. The Supreme Court held, "We think that obtaining by sense-enhancing technology any information regarding the interior of the home that could not otherwise have been obtained without physical intrusion into a constitutionally protected area constitutes a search." On the basis of this criterion, the information obtained by the thermal imager in this case was the product of a search.

Decision and Remedy

The U.S. Supreme Court held that the use of a thermal-imaging device aimed at a private home from a public street to detect relative amounts of heat within the home is a "search" within the meaning of the Fourth Amendment. The Supreme Court reversed the decision of the court of appeals and remanded the case for further proceedings.

Case Questions

Critical Legal Thinking   Is the Fourth Amendment's prohibition against unreasonable search and seizure an easy standard to apply? Explain.

Business Ethics   Did the police act ethically in obtaining the evidence in this case? Did Kyllo act ethically in trying to suppress the evidence?

Contemporary Business   How can the government catch entrepreneurs such as Kyllo? Explain.

U.S. SUPREME COURT CASE
City of Indianapolis v. Edmond
531 U.S. 32, 121 S.Ct. 447, 2000 U.S. Lexis 8084 (2000)
Supreme Court of the United States

Case 6.3
Search and Seizure

Background and Facts

In August 1998, the police of the city of Indianapolis, Indiana, began to operate vehicle roadblock checkpoints on Indianapolis roads in an effort to interdict unlawful drugs. Once a car had been stopped, police questioned the driver and passengers and conducted an open-view examination of the vehicle from the outside. A narcotics-detection dog walked around outside each vehicle. The police conducted a search and seizure of the occupants and vehicle only if particular suspicion developed from the initial investigation. The overall "hit rate" of the program was approximately 9 percent.

James Edmond and Joel Palmer, each attorneys who had been stopped at one of Indianapolis's checkpoints, filed a lawsuit on behalf of themselves and the class of all motorists who had been stopped or were subject to being stopped at such checkpoints. They claimed that the roadblocks violated the Fourth Amendment to the Constitution. The district court found for Indianapolis, but the court of appeals reversed. The U.S. Supreme Court granted certiorari to hear the appeal.

Issue

Does Indianapolis's highway checkpoint program, whereby police, without individualized suspicion, stop vehicles for the primary purpose of discovering and interdicting illegal narcotics, violate the Fourth Amendment to the U.S. Constitution?

Court's Reasoning

A search or seizure is ordinarily unreasonable in the absence of individualized suspicion of wrongdoing. We have recognized only limited circumstances in which the usual rule does not apply. The U.S. Supreme Court has upheld brief, suspicionless seizures of motorists at a fixed border patrol checkpoint designed to intercept

illegal aliens, *United States v. Martinez-Fuerte*, 428 U.S. 543, 96 S.Ct. 3074, 1976 U.S. Lexis 87 (1976), and a sobriety checkpoint aimed at removing drunk drivers from the road, *Michigan Dept. of State Police v. Sitz*, 496 U.S. 444, 110 S.Ct. 2481, 1990 U.S. Lexis 3144 (1990). The Supreme Court held, however, that because the primary purpose of the Indianapolis narcotics checkpoint program was to uncover evidence of ordinary criminal wrongdoing, the program contravened the Fourth Amendment. On the other hand, the Court noted that the Fourth Amendment would almost certainly permit an appropriately tailored roadblock set up to thwart an imminent terrorist attack or to catch a dangerous criminal who is likely to flee by way of a particular route.

Decision and Remedy

The U.S. Supreme Court held that Indianapolis's general highway checkpoint, whereby police, without individualized suspicion, stopped vehicles for the primary purpose of discovering and interdicting narcotics, was an unreasonable search and seizure in violation of the Fourth Amendment. The Supreme Court affirmed the decision of the court of appeals.

Case Questions

Critical Legal Thinking   How did the Supreme Court reconcile its decision in this case with its prior decisions in *Martinez-Fuerte* and *Sitz*? Explain.

Business Ethics   Should the 9 percent of criminals who were caught by the roadblock get off because of the Fourth Amendment?

Contemporary Business   How big of a business is illegal narcotics sales in this country? Should that industry be legalized and taxed? Why or why not?

Searches of Business Premises

Generally, the government does not have the right to search business premises without a search warrant.[7] Certain hazardous and regulated industries—such as sellers of firearms and liquor, coal mines, and the like—are subject to warrantless searches if proper statutory procedures are met.

Fifth Amendment Privilege Against Self-Incrimination

The *Fifth Amendment* to the U.S. Constitution provides that no person "shall be compelled in any criminal case to be a witness against himself." Thus, a person cannot be compelled to give testimony against him or herself, although nontestimonial evidence (e.g., fingerprints, body fluids) may be required. A person who asserts this right is described as having "taken the Fifth." This protection applies to federal cases and is extended to state and local criminal cases through the Due Process Clause of the Fourteenth Amendment.

Business Brief
It is improper for a jury to infer guilt from the defendant's exercise of his or her constitutional right to remain silent.

The protection against **self-incrimination** applies only to natural persons who are accused of crimes. Therefore, artificial persons (such as corporations and partnerships) cannot raise this protection against incriminating testimony.[8] Thus, business records of corporations and partnerships are not generally protected from disclosure, even if they incriminate individuals who work for the business. However, certain "private papers" of businesspersons (such as personal diaries) are protected from disclosure.

Miranda **Rights** Most people have not read and memorized the provisions of the U.S. Constitution. The U.S. Supreme Court recognized this fact when it decided the landmark case *Miranda v. Arizona* in 1966 [384 U.S. 436, 86, S.Ct. 1603, 1996 U.S. Lexis 2817 (1966)] In that case, the Supreme Court held that the Fifth Amendment privilege against self-incrimination is not useful unless a criminal suspect has knowledge of this right. Therefore, the Supreme Court required that the following warning—colloquially called the ***Miranda* rights**—be read to a criminal suspect before he or she is interrogated by the police or other government officials:

- You have the right to remain silent.
- Anything you say can and will be used against you.
- You have the right to consult a lawyer and to have a lawyer present with you during Interrogation.
- If you cannot afford a lawyer, a lawyer will be appointed free of charge to represent you.

Any statements or confessions obtained from a suspect prior to being read his or her *Miranda* rights can be excluded from evidence at trial. In 2000, the U.S. Supreme Court upheld *Miranda* in *Dickerson v. United States*.[9] The Supreme Court stated, "We do not think there is justification for overruling *Miranda*. *Miranda* has become embedded in routine police practice to the point where the warnings have become part of our national culture."

The Attorney–Client Privilege and Other Privileges To obtain a proper defense, the accused person must be able to tell his or her attorney facts about the case without fear that the attorney will be called as a witness against the accused. The **attorney–client privilege** is protected by the Fifth Amendment. Either the client or the attorney can raise this privilege. For the privilege to apply, the information must be told to the attorney in his or her capacity as an attorney, and not as a friend or neighbor or such.

The following privileges have also been recognized under the Fifth Amendment: (1) *psychiatrist/psychologist–patient privilege*, (2) *priest/minister/rabbi–penitent privilege*, (3) *spouse–spouse privilege*, and (4) *parent–child privilege*. There are some exceptions. For example, a spouse or child who is beaten by a spouse or parent may testify against the accused.

The U.S. Supreme Court has held that there is no accountant–client privilege under federal law.[10] Thus, an accountant could be called as a witness in cases involving federal securities laws, federal mail or wire fraud, or other federal crimes. Nevertheless, approximately 20 states have enacted special statutes that create an **accountant–client privilege**. An accountant cannot be called as a witness against a client in a court action in a state where these statutes are in effect. Federal courts do not recognize these laws, however.

Immunity from Prosecution   On occasion, the government may want to obtain information from a suspect who has asserted his or her Fifth Amendment privilege against self-incrimination. The government can often achieve this by offering the suspect **immunity from prosecution**. Immunity from prosecution means that the government agrees not to use against a person granted immunity any evidence given by that person. Once immunity is granted, the suspect loses the right to assert his or her Fifth Amendment privilege. Grants of immunity are often given when the government wants the suspect to give information that will lead to the prosecution of other, more important, criminal suspects. Partial grants of immunity are also available. For example, a suspect may be granted immunity from prosecution for a serious crime, but not a lesser crime, in exchange for information. The suspect must agree to a partial grant of immunity.

Fifth Amendment Protection Against Double Jeopardy

The **Double Jeopardy Clause** of the Fifth Amendment protects persons from being tried twice for the same crime. For example, if the state tries a suspect for the crime of murder, and the suspect is found not guilty, the state cannot bring another trial against the accused for the same crime. However, if the same criminal act involves several different crimes, the accused may be tried for each of the crimes without violating the Double Jeopardy Clause. Suppose the accused kills two people during a robbery. The accused may be tried for two murders and the robbery.

If the same act violates the laws of two or more jurisdictions, each jurisdiction may try the accused. For example, if an accused kidnaps a person in one state and brings the victim across a state border into another state, the act violates the laws of two states and the federal government. Thus, three jurisdictions can prosecute the accused without violating the Double Jeopardy Clause.

Sixth Amendment Right to a Public Jury Trial

The *Sixth Amendment* guarantees certain rights to criminal defendants. These rights are (1) to be tried by an impartial jury of the state or district in which the alleged crime was committed, (2) to confront (cross-examine) the witnesses against the accused, (3) to have the assistance of a lawyer, and (4) to have a speedy trial.[11]

Eighth Amendment Protection Against Cruel and Unusual Punishment

The *Eighth Amendment* protects criminal defendants from **cruel and unusual punishment**. For example, it prohibits the torture of criminals. However, this clause does not prohibit capital punishment.[12]

Business Brief

There is no accountant-client privilege under federal law. Some states have enacted statutes that create an accountant-client privilege for state law criminal matters.

Business Brief

Some persons who are granted immunity are placed in witness protection programs. They are usually given new identities, relocated, and found jobs.

At the present time in this country there is more danger that criminals will escape justice than that they will be subjected to tyranny.

J. Holmes Dissenting
Kepner v. United States (1904)

There can be no equal justice where the kind of trial a man gets depends on the amount of money he has.

J. Black
Griffin v. Illinois (1956)

Moral Theory. Should the death penalty be permitted?

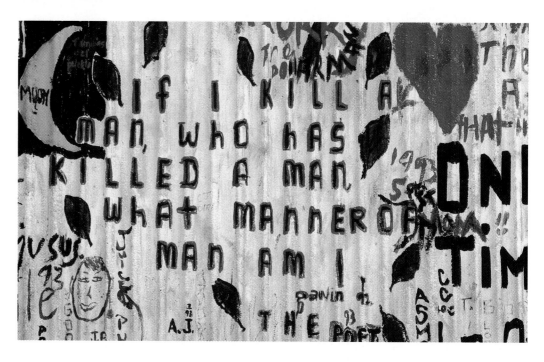

International Law
Federal Antiterrorism Act of 2001

The devastating terrorist attacks on the World Trade Center in New York and the Pentagon in Washington, DC, on September 11, 2001, shocked the nation. The attacks were organized and orchestrated by terrorists who crossed nations' borders easily, secretly planned and prepared for the attacks undetected, and financed the attacks using money located in banks in the United States, Great Britain, and other countries. In response, Congress enacted a federal Antiterrorism Act that assists the government in detecting, investigating, and prosecuting terrorists. The bill was signed into law on October 26, 2001. The act contains the following main features:

- **Special Intelligence Court.** The act authorizes the Special Intelligence Court to issue expanded wiretap orders and subpoenas to obtain evidence of suspected terrorism.
- **Nationwide search warrant.** The act creates a nationwide search warrant to obtain evidence of terrorist activities.
- **Roving wiretaps.** The act permits "roving wiretaps" on a person suspected of involvement in terrorism so that any telephone or electronic device used by the person may be monitored.
- **Sharing of information.** The act permits evidence obtained by government law enforcement and intelligence agencies to be shared among the agencies.

- **Detention of noncitizens.** The act gives the federal government authority to detain a nonresident in the United States for up to seven days without filing charges against that person. Nonresidents who are certified by a court as a threat to national security may be held for up to six months without a trial.
- **Bioterrorism provision.** The act makes it illegal for people or groups to possess substances that can be used as biological or chemical weapons for any purpose besides a "peaceful" one.
- **Anti–money laundering provisions.** The act requires U.S. banks to determine sources of large overseas private bank accounts and to disclose information about such accounts to U.S. investigators. The U.S. Treasury Department may cut off all dealings in the United States of foreign banking institutions located in nations with bank secrecy laws that refuse to disclose information about bank accounts to U.S. investigators.

Proponents argue that the federal Antiterrorism Act is needed to detect and prevent terrorist activities and to investigate and prosecute terrorists. Critics of the act argue that constitutional freedoms are trampled on by the provisions of the act. ■

Chapter Summary

Specifics of a Criminal Trial

1. The accused is *presumed innocent until proven guilty*.
2. The plaintiff (the government) bears the *burden of proof*.
3. The government must prove *beyond a reasonable doubt* that the accused is guilty of the crime charged.
4. The accused does not have to testify against him- or herself.

Definition of a Crime

1. *Crime.* A crime is any act done by a person in violation of those duties that he or she owes to society and for the breach of which the law provides a penalty.
2. *Penal codes.* State and federal statutes define many crimes. Criminal conduct is also defined in many *regulatory statutes*.
3. Parties to a criminal lawsuit are:
   a. *Plaintiff.* The government, which is represented by the *prosecuting attorney* (or *prosecutor*).
   b. *Defendant.* The person or business accused of the crime, who is represented by a *defense attorney*.

Classification of Crimes

1. *Felonies.* The most serious kinds of crimes are felonies. They are *mala in se* (inherently evil), and they are usually punishable by imprisonment.
2. *Misdemeanors.* Misdemeanors are less serious crimes than felonies. They are *mala prohibita* (prohibited by society), and they are usually punishable by fine and/or imprisonment for less than one year.
3. *Violations.* A violation is neither a felony nor a misdemeanor. Violations are generally punishable by a fine.

Elements of a Crime

Most crimes require that the following two elements be proven:

1. *Actus reus.* Guilty act.
2. *Mens rea.* Evil intent.

Pretrial Criminal Procedure

1. *Arrest.* An arrest is made pursuant to an *arrest warrant*, based on a showing of "probable cause," or, where permitted, by a *warrantless* arrest.
2. *Indictment or information.* Grand juries issue *indictments*, magistrates (judges) issue *informations*. These formally charge the accused with specific crimes.
3. *Arraignment.* The accused is informed of the charges against him or her and enters a *plea* in court. The plea may be *not guilty, guilty,* or *nola contendere*.
4. *Plea bargaining.* In a plea bargain, the government and the accused may negotiate a settlement agreement wherein the accused agrees to admit to a lesser crime than charged.

Criminal Trial and Appeal

1. A criminal trial may involve the following:
   a. *Guilty.* Requires unanimous vote of the jury.
   b. *Not guilty.* Requires unanimous vote of the jury.
   c. *Hung jury.* Nonunanimous vote of the jury. The government may prosecute the case again.

2. An appeal involves the following:
   a. *Defendant.* May appeal his or her conviction.
   b. *Plaintiff (government).* May not appeal a verdict of innocent.

Common Crimes, p. 131

Crimes Affecting Business

1. *Robbery.* Robbery is the taking of personal property from another by fear or force.
2. *Burglary.* Burglary is the unauthorized entering of a building to commit a felony.
3. *Larceny.* Larceny is the wrongful taking of another's property other than from his person or building.
4. *Theft.* Theft is the wrongful taking of another's property, whether by robbery, burglary, or larceny.
5. *Receiving stolen property.* A person may knowingly receive stolen property with the intent to deprive the rightful owner of that property.
6. *Arson.* Arson is the malicious and willful burning into a building.
7. *Extortion.* Extortion involves a threat to expose something about another person unless that person gives up money or property.

White-Collar Crimes, p. 133

White-Collar Crimes

White-collar crimes. These crimes are prone to be committed by businesspersons that involve cunning and trickery rather than physical force.

1. *Forgery.* Forgery involves fraudulently making or altering a written document that affects the legal liability of another person.
2. *Embezzlement.* Embezzlement is the fraudulent conversion of property by a person to whom the property was *entrusted.*
3. *Criminal fraud.* Criminal fraud involves obtaining title to another's property through deception or trickery. Also called *false pretenses* or *deceit.*
4. *Mail fraud.* Mail fraud is the use of mail to defraud another person.
5. *Wire fraud.* Wire fraud is the use of wire (telephone or telegraph) to defraud another person.
6. *Bribery.* Bribery is the offer of payment of money or property or something else of value in return for an unwarranted favor. The payor of a bribe and the recipient are both guilty of the crime of bribery.
   a. *Commercial bribery* is the offer of a payment of a bribe to private persons and business. This is often referred to as a kickback or *payoff.*
   b. Bribery of public officials for an "official act" is a crime.
7. *Money Laundering Control Act.* This federal statute makes it a crime to:
   a. Knowingly engage in a *money transaction* through a financial institution involving property worth more than $10,000.
   b. Knowingly engage in a *financial transaction* involving the proceeds of an illegal activity.
8. *Racketeer Influenced and Corrupt Organizations Act (RICO).* RICO makes it a federal crime to acquire or maintain an interest in, use income from, or conduct or participate in the affairs of an enterprise through a pattern of racketeering activity. Criminal penalties include the *forfeiture* of any property or business interests gained through a RICO violation.

Corporate Criminal Liability

1. Corporate directors, officers, and employees are criminally liable for crimes they commit for personal benefit or on behalf of the corporation.
2. A corporation is criminally liable for crimes committed by directors, officers, and employees while acting on behalf of the corporation.

Constitutional Safeguards, p. 137

Fourth Amendment Protection Against Unreasonable Search and Seizures

This amendment protects persons and corporations from *unreasonable search and seizures*.

1. *Reasonable search and seizure* based on *probable cause* is lawful.
   a. *Search warrant.* Stipulates the place and scope of the search.
   b. *Warrantless search.* Permitted only:
      i. Incident to an arrest.
      ii. Where evidence is in plain view.
      iii. Where it is likely that evidence will be destroyed.
2. *Exclusionary rule.* Evidence obtained from an unreasonable search and seizure is *tainted evidence* that may not be introduced at a government proceeding against the person searched.
3. *Business premises.* Business premises are protected by the Fourth Amendment, except that certain *regulated industries* may be subject to warrantless searches authorized by statute.

Fifth Amendment Privilege Against Self-Incrimination

Privilege against self-incrimination. This amendment provides that no person "shall be compelled in any criminal case to be a witness against himself." A person asserting this privilege is said to have taken the Fifth.

1. *Nontestimonial evidence.* This evidence (e.g., fingerprints, body fluids) is not protected.
2. *Businesses.* The privilege applies only to natural persons; businesses cannot assert the privilege.
3. *Miranda rights.* A criminal suspect must be informed of his or her Fifth Amendment rights before the suspect can be interrogated by the police or government officials.
4. *Immunity from prosecution.* Immunity is granted by the government to obtain otherwise privileged evidence. The government agrees not to use the evidence given against the person who gave it.
5. *Attorney-client privilege.* An accused's lawyer cannot be called as a witness against the accused.
6. *Other privileges.* The following privileges have been recognized, with some limitations:
   a. Psychiatrist/psychologist–patient
   b. Priest/minister/rabbi–penitent
   c. Spouse–spouse
   d. Parent–child
7. *Accountant–client privilege.* Such privilege is not recognized at the federal level. Some states recognize this privilege in state law actions.

Fifth Amendment Protection Against Double Jeopardy Sixth Amendment Right to a Public Jury Trial

This amendment protects persons from being tried twice by the same jurisdiction for the same crime. If the act violates the law of two or more jurisdictions, each jurisdiction may try the accused. The Fifth Amendment guarantees criminal defendants the following rights:

1. To be tried by an impartial jury.
2. To confront the witness.
3. To have the assistance of a lawyer.
4. To have a speedy trial.

Eighth Amendment Protection Against Cruel and Unusual Punishment

The Eighth Amendment protects criminal defendants from cruel and unusual punishment. Capital punishment is permitted by this amendment.

Internet Exercises and Case Questions

Working the Web Internet Exercises

Activities

1. Check on the U.S. Department of Justice Web site for information about computer-related crimes: **www.usdoj.gov/criminal**.

2. See **www.hg.org/crime.html** for a comprehensive list of criminal law resources. Find the listing for your jurisdiction and research state laws relating to white-collar crime.

Critical Legal Thinking Cases

6.1 Criminal Liability of Corporations   Representatives of hotels, restaurants, hotel and restaurant supply companies, and other businesses located in Portland, Oregon, organized an association to attract conventions to their city. Members were asked to make contributions equal to 1 percent of their sales to finance the association. To aid collections, hotel members, including Hilton Hotels Corporation, agreed to give preferential treatment to suppliers who paid their assessments and to curtail purchases from those who did not. This agreement violated federal antitrust laws. The United States sued the members of the association, including Hilton Hotels, for the crime of violating federal antitrust laws. Can a corporation be held criminally liable for the acts of its representatives? If so, what criminal penalties can be assessed against the corporation? [*United States v. Hilton Hotels Corp.*, 467 F.2d 1000, 1972 U.S. App. Lexis 7414 (9th Cir. 1973)]

6.2 Forgery   Evidence showed that there was a burglary in which a checkbook belonging to Mary J. Harris, doing business as The Report Department, and a check encoder machine were stolen. Two of the checks from that checkbook were cashed at the Citizens & Southern National Bank branch office in Riverdale, Georgia, by Joseph Leon Foster, who was accompanied by a woman identified as Angela Foxworth. The bank teller who cashed the checks testified that the same man and woman cashed the checks on two different occasions at her drive-up window at the bank and that on both occasions they were in the same car. Each time the teller wrote the license tag number of the car on the back of the check. The teller testified that both times the checks and the driver's license used to identify the woman were passed to her by the man driving and that the man received the money from her. What crime has been committed? [*Foster v. State of Georgia*, 387 S.E.2d 637, 1989 Ga.App. Lexis 1456 (Ga. App. 1989)]

6.3 Extortion   On February 3, 1987, the victim (Mr. X) went to the premises at 42 Taylor Terrace in New Milford, Connecticut, where his daughter and her husband lived. Lisa Percoco, who was Gregory Erhardt's girlfriend, was at the residence. Mr. X and Percoco were in the bedroom, partially dressed, engaging in sexual activity, when Erhardt entered the room and photographed them. He then informed Mr. X that unless he procured $5,000 and placed it in a mailbox at a designated address by 8 P.M. that night, Erhardt would show the photographs to Mr. X's wife. Mr. X proceeded to make telephone arrangements for the procurement and placement of the money according to Erhardt's instructions. If the money were paid,

what crime would have been committed? [*State of Connecticut v. Erhardt*, 553 A.2d 188, 1989 Conn.App. Lexis 21 (Conn. App. 1989)]

6.4 Criminal Fraud   In 1978, Miriam Marlowe's husband purchased a life insurance policy on his own life, naming his wife as the beneficiary. After Marlowe's husband died in a swimming accident in July 1981, she received payment on the policy. Marlowe later met John Walton, a friend of a friend. He convinced her and her representative that he had a friend who worked for the State Department and had access to gold in Brazil, and that the gold could be purchased in Brazil for $100 an ounce and sold in the United States for $300 an ounce. Walton convinced Miriam to invest $25,000. Instead of investing the money in gold in Brazil, Walton opened an account at Tracy Collins Bank in the name of Jeffrey McIntyre Roberts and deposited Miriam's money in the account. He later withdrew the money in cash. What crime is Walton guilty of? [*State of Utah v. Roberts*, 711 P.2d 235, 1985 Utah Lexis 872 (Utah 1985)]

6.5 Bribery   In 1979, the city of Peoria, Illinois, received federal funds from the Department of Housing and Urban Development (HUD) to be used for housing rehabilitation assistance. The city of Peoria designated United Neighborhoods, Inc. (UNI), a corporation, to administer the funds. Arthur Dixon was UNI's executive director, and James Lee Hinton was its housing rehabilitation coordinator. In these capacities, they were responsible for contracting with suppliers and tradespeople to provide the necessary goods and services to rehabilitate the houses. Evidence showed that Dixon and Hinton used their positions to extract 10 percent payments back on all contracts they awarded. What crime have they committed? [*Dixon and Hinton v. United States*, 465 U.S. 482, 104 S.Ct. 1172, 1984 U.S. Lexis 35 (1984)]

6.6 Administrative Search   Lee Stuart Paulson owned the liquor license for My House, a bar in San Francisco. The California Department of Alcoholic Beverage Control is the administrative agency that regulates bars in that state. The California Business and Professions Code, which the department administers, prohibits "any kind of illegal activity on licensed premises." On February 11, 1988, an anonymous informer tipped the department that narcotics sales were occurring on the premises of My House and that the narcotics were kept in a safe behind the bar on the premises. A special department investigator entered the bar during its hours of operation, identified himself, and informed Paulson that he was conducting an inspection. The investigator, who did not have a search warrant, opened the safe without seeking Paulson's consent. Twenty-two bundles of cocaine, totaling 5.5 grams, were found in the safe. Paulson was arrested. At his criminal trial, Paulson challenged the lawfulness of the search. Was the warrantless search of the safe a lawful search? [*People v. Paulson*, 216 Cal.App.3d 1480, 265 Cal.Rptr. 579, 1990 Cal.App. Lexis 10 (Cal. App. 1990)]

6.7 Search Warrant   The Center Art Galleries–Hawaii sells artwork. Approximately 20 percent of its business involves art by Salvador Dalí. The federal government, which suspected the center of fraudulently selling forged Dalí artwork, obtained identical search warrants for six locations controlled by the center. The warrants commanded the executing officer to seize items that were "evidence of violations of federal criminal law." The warrants did not describe the specific crimes suspected and did not stipulate that only items pertaining to the sale of Dalí's work could be seized. There was no evidence of any criminal activity unrelated to that artist. Is the search warrant valid? [*Center Art Galleries–Hawaii, Inc. v. United States*, 875 F.2d 747, 1989 U.S. App. Lexis 6983 (9th Cir. 1989)]

6.8 Fifth Amendment's Privilege Against Self-Incrimination
John Doe is the owner of several sole-proprietorship businesses. In 1980, during the course of an investigation of corruption in awarding county and municipal contracts, a federal grand jury served several subpoenas on John Doe, demanding the production of certain business records. The subpoenas demanded the production of the following record: (1) general ledgers and journals, (2) invoices, (3) bank statements and canceled checks, (4) financial statements, (5) telephone-company records, (6) safe-deposit box records, and (7) copies of tax returns. John Doe filed a motion in federal court, seeking to quash the subpoenas, alleging that producing these business records would violate his Fifth Amendment privilege of not testifying against himself. Do the records have to be disclosed? [*United States v. John Doe*, 465 U.S. 605, 104 S.Ct. 1237, 1984 U.S. Lexis 169 (1984)]

6.9 Business Ethics   In 1979, Leo Shaw, an attorney, entered into a partnership agreement with three other persons to build and operate an office building. From the outset, it was agreed that Shaw's role was to manage the operation of the building. Management of the property was Shaw's contribution to the partnership; the other three partners contributed the necessary capital. In January 1989, the other partners discovered that the loan on the building was in default and that foreclosure proceedings were imminent. Upon investigation, they discovered that Shaw had taken approximately $80,000 from the partnership's checking account. After heated discussions, Shaw repaid $13,000. In May 1989, when no further payment was forthcoming, a partner filed a civil suit against Shaw and notified the

police. The state filed a criminal complaint against Shaw on March 15, 1990. On April 3, 1990, Shaw repaid the remaining funds as part of a civil settlement. At his criminal trial in November 1990, Shaw argued that the repayment of the money was a defense to the crime of embezzlement. Did Shaw act ethically in this case? Would your answer be different if he had really only "borrowed" the money and had intended to return it? [*People v. Shaw*, 10 Cal. App.4th 969, 12 Cal.Rptr.2d 665, 1992 Cal.App. Lexis 1256 (Cal. App. 1992)]

6.10 Business Ethics   In 1980, Ronald V. Cloud purchased the Cal-Neva Lodge, a hotel and casino complex located in the Lake Tahoe area near the California–Nevada border, for $10 million. Cloud was a sophisticated 68-year-old entrepreneur who was experienced in buying and selling real estate and had real estate holdings valued at more than $65 million. He also had experience in banking and finance, having been the founder and chairman of Continental National Bank of Fresno. After two years of mounting operation losses, Cloud closed the Cal-Neva Lodge and actively began seeking a new buyer. In December 1984, Cloud met with Jon Perroton and orally agreed to transfer the lodge to Perroton for approximately $17 million. On January 2, 1985, Perroton met with an executive of Hibernia Bank (Hibernia) to discuss a possible loan to finance the purchase of the lodge. Perroton made multiple false representations and presented false documents to obtain a $20 million loan from Hibernia. In particular, Perroton misrepresented the sale price for the lodge ($27.5 million) and stated that $7.5 million had already been paid to Cloud. An escrow account was opened with Transamerica Title Company (Transamerica).

On January 15, 1985, Cloud and his attorney and Perroton met at Transamerica to sign mutual escrow instructions. Cloud reviewed the instructions and noticed that the sale price and down payment figures were incorrectly stated at $27.5 million and $7.5 million, respectively, and that the Hibernia loan was for $20 million, almost $3 million above what he knew to be the true sale price. Cloud signed the escrow instructions. Later, Cloud signed a settlement statement containing the same false figures and signed a grant deed to the property. The sale closed on January 23, 1985, with Hibernia making the $20 million loan to Perroton. Subsequently, when the loan went into default, Continental Insurance Company (Continental) paid Hibernia its loss of $7.5 million on the bank's blanket bond insurance policy. The United States sued Cloud for aiding and abetting a bank fraud in violation of federal law (18 U.S.C. §§ 2 and 1344). The jury convicted Cloud of the crime and ordered him to make restitution of $7.5 million to Continental. Cloud appealed. Did cloud act ethically in this case? Explain. Is Cloud guilty of aiding and abetting a bank fraud? [*United States v. Cloud* 872 F.2d 846, 1989 U.S. App. Lexis 4534 (9th Cir. 1989)]

Briefing the Case Writing Assignment

Read Case A.6 in the Case Appendix [*Schalk v. Texas*]. This case is excerpted from the appellate court opinion. Review and brief the case. In your brief, be sure to answer the following questions.

1. What activities had the defendants engaged in?

2. What crime were the defendants accused of?

3. What was the decision of the appellate court?

Endnotes

1. Title 18 of the U.S. Code contains the federal criminal code.
2. Sentencing Reform Act of 1984, 18 U.S.C. § 3551 et. seq.
3. 18 U.S.C. § 1341.
4. 18 U.S.C. § 1343.
5. 18 U.S.C. §§ 1961–1968.
6. *United States v. Leon*, 468 U.S. 897, 104 S.Ct. 3405, 82 1984 U.S. Lexis 153 (1984).
7. *Marshall v. Barlow's Inc.*, 436 U.S. 307, 98 S.Ct. 1816, 1978 U.S. Lexis 26 (1978).
8. *Bellis v. United States*, 417 U.S. 85, 94 S.Ct. 2179, 1974 U.S. Lexis 58 (1974).
9. 530 U.S. 428, 120 S.Ct. 2326, 2000 U.S. Lexis 4305 (2000).
10. 409 U.S. 322, 93 S.Ct. 611, 1973 U.S. Lexis 23 (1973).
11. The Speedy Trial Act requires that a criminal defendant be brought to trial within 70 days after indictment [18 U.S.C. § 316(c)(1)]. Continuances may be granted by the court to serve the "ends of justice."
12. *Baldwin v. Alabama*, 472 U.S. 372, 105 S.Ct. 2727, 1985 U.S. Lexis 106 (1985).

Ethics and Social Responsibility of Business

"Ethical considerations can no more be excluded from the administration of justice, which is the end and purpose of all civil laws, than one can exclude the vital air from his room and live."

—John F. Dillon
Laws and Jurisprudence of England and America Lecture I (1894)

Chapter Objectives

After studying this chapter, you should be able to:

1. Describe how law and ethics intertwine.

2. Describe the moral theories of business ethics.

3. Describe the theories of the social responsibility of business.

4. Describe corporate social audits.

5. Examine how international ethical standards differ from country to country.

Chapter Contents

■ Ethics

■ Moral Theories and Business Ethics

■ Social Responsibility of Business

Ethics precede laws as man precedes society.

Jason Alexander
Philosophy for Investors (1979)

Businesses organized in the United States are subject to its laws. They are also subject to the laws of other countries in which they operate. In addition, businesspersons owe a duty to act ethically in the conduct of their affairs, and businesses owe a social responsibility not to harm society.

Although much of the law is based on ethical standards, not all ethical standards have been enacted as law. The law establishes a minimum degree of conduct expected by persons and businesses in society. Ethics demands more. This chapter discusses business ethics and the social responsibility of business.

Ethics

Sometimes the rule of law and the golden rule of **ethics** demand the same response by the person confronted with a problem. For example, federal and state laws make bribery unlawful. A person violates the law if he or she bribes a judge for a favorable decision in a case. Ethics would also prohibit this conduct.

The law may permit something that would be ethically wrong.

Business Brief

What is lawful conduct is not always ethical conduct

Consider This Example   Occupational safety laws set standards for emissions of dust from toxic chemicals in the workplace. Suppose a company can reduce the emissions below the legal standard by spending additional money. The only benefit from the expenditure would be better employee health. Ethics would require the extra expenditure; the law would not.

Another alternative occurs where the law demands certain conduct but a person's ethical standards are contrary.

Business Brief

Corruption by government officials and the influence of criminal mafias are the largest impediments to the growth of the economies of several countries. Can such corruption be contained?

Consider This Example   Federal law prohibits employees from hiring certain illegal alien workers. Suppose an employer advertises the availability of a job and receives no response except from a person who cannot prove he or she is a citizen of this country or does not possess a required visa. The worker and his or her family are destitute. Should the employer hire him or her? The law says no, but ethics says yes (see Exhibit 7.1).

Myanmar (Burma). Some companies refuse to do business with Myanmar because of allegations that its military-led government engages in humanitarian violations.

Ethical Fundamentalism

Under **ethical fundamentalism** a person looks to an *outside source* for ethical rules or commands. This may be a book (e.g., the Bible or the Koran) or a person (e.g., Karl Marx). Critics argue that ethical fundamentalism does not permit people to determine right and wrong for themselves. Taken to an extreme, the result could be considered unethical under most other moral theories. For example, a literal interpretation of the maxim "an eye for an eye" would permit retaliation.

The ethics of a fast-food restaurant chain are raised in the following case.

Bradley v. McDonald's Corporation

2003 U.S.Dist. Lexis 15202 (2003)
United States District Court, Southern District of New York

Case 7.1
Business Ethics

Background and Facts

McDonald's Corporation operates the largest fast-food restaurant chain in the United States and the world. It produces such famous foods as the "Big Mac" hamburger, chicken "McNuggets," the egg "McMuffin," French fries, shakes, and other foods. A McDonald's survey showed that 22% of its customers are "Super Heavy Users," meaning that they eat at McDonald's at least 10 times or more a month. Super Heavy Users make up approximately 75% of McDonald's sales. The survey also found that 72% of McDonald's customers were "Heavy Users," meaning they ate at McDonald's at least once a week.

Jazlym Bradley consumed McDonald's foods her entire life during school lunch breaks and before and after school, approximately five times per week, ordering two meals per day. When Bradley was 19 years old she sued McDonald's Corporation for causing her obesity and health problems associated with obesity.

Plaintiff Bradley sued McDonald's in U.S. district court for violating the New York Consumer Protection Act, which prohibits deceptive and unfair acts and practices. She alleged that McDonald's misled her, through its advertising campaigns and other publicity, that its food products were nutritious, of a beneficial nutritional nature, and easily part of a healthy lifestyle if consumed on a daily basis. The plaintiff sued on behalf of herself and a class of minors residing in New York State who purchased and consumed McDonald's products. McDonald's filed a motion with the district court to dismiss the plaintiff's complaint.

Issue

Did the plaintiff state a case against McDonald's for deceptive and unfair acts and practices in violation of the New York Consumer Protection Act?

Court's Reasoning

The district court held that the plaintiff failed to state a claim that McDonald's advertisements and publicity were deceptive or unfair.

The court stated that the standard for whether an act or a practice is deceptive or misleading is objective, requiring a showing that a reasonable consumer would have been misled by the defendant's conduct. The court found that the plaintiff had a reasonable opportunity to discover the facts about transactions with McDonald's beforehand by using ordinary intelligence.

The district court also held that the plaintiff failed to allege that her consumption of McDonald's food caused her injuries. The court stated that other pertinent, but unanswered, questions include: What else did the plaintiff eat? How much did she exercise? Is there a family history of the diseases that are alleged to have been caused by McDonald's foods? The district court stated that the plaintiff failed to "show that a McDiet is a substantial factor" of the plaintiff's obesity.

Decision and Remedy

The district court granted defendant McDonald's motion to dismiss the plaintiff's complaint.

Note: Because of this case and other threatened obesity-related litigation, fast-food franchisors introduced salads, low-fat fare, and low-carb offerings to their menus.

Case Questions

Critical Legal Thinking   What is the purpose of consumer protection laws?

Business Ethics   Do you think McDonald's has a duty to warn consumers of the dangers of eating its fast food? Do parents owe a duty to their children not to let them eat fast food too often?

Contemporary Business   What would have been the effect on McDonald's and other fast-food companies if the plaintiff had won her lawsuit against McDonald's? Explain.

Utilitarianism

Utilitarianism is a moral theory with origins in the works of Jeremy Bentham (1748–1832) and John Stuart Mill (1806–1873). This moral theory dictates that people must choose the actions or follow the rule that provides the *greatest good to society*. This does not mean the greatest good for the greatest number of people. For instance, if one action would increase the good of 25 people 1 unit each, and an alternative action would increase the good of 1 person 26 units, the latter action should be taken.

Utilitarianism has been criticized because it is difficult to estimate the "good" that will result from different actions, it is hard to apply in an imperfect world, and it treats morality as if it were an impersonal mathematical calculation.

> The ultimate justification of the law is to be found, and can only be found, in moral considerations.
>
> Lord MacMillian
> *Law and Other Things (1937)*

Consider This Example A company is trying to determine whether it should close an unprofitable plant located in a small community. Utilitarianism would require that the benefits to shareholders from closing the plant be compared to the benefits to employees, their families, and others in the community in keeping it open.

Business Ethics

Used-Car Dealer Punished for Fraud

On December 11, 1992, Charles Forshey did what millions of people in this country have done—bought a used vehicle from a used-car dealership. Forshey brought two older vehicles he owned, traded them in for a value of $3,100, added some cash, and purchased a used 1983 three-quarter-ton Chevrolet Suburban truck for $5,995 from Carr Chevrolet, Inc., in Oregon. Forshey bought the vehicle "as-is," which means that the dealership disclaimed any warranties as to quality.

Shortly after the purchase, Forshey noticed that the Suburban was missing all of its emission control equipment. He learned later that the 1983 Suburban had a 1981 engine. He also noticed that the vehicle identification number (VIN) was not on the door, transmission, or glove box. Forshey took the vehicle to an environmental agency and was told that it did not have the required smog control equipment and that the vehicle could not be brought into compliance because of the difference in age between the vehicle and the engine. Forshey conducted his own title search and found that the truck had been stolen at some previous time in California and stripped of its parts.

After discovering this information, Forshey tried to return the truck to the dealer and recover his two vehicles and the cash he paid. The dealer told Forshey that he had purchased the Suburban "as-is" and it was his problem. Forshey sued the dealership for fraud.

At trial, evidence proved that the vehicle had had a rear-wheel alignment; the driver's door was misaligned, was a different color, and had been replaced; the dash-board came from a different vehicle; the VIN had been cut out of the glove box and the door; the VIN had been ground off the transmission; the engine was not the original; the odometer had been tampered with; and the truck had been heavily reconditioned. The dealership denied any knowledge of these facts, however. The trial court disagreed. The jury returned a verdict in favor of Forshey.

On appeal, the dealership argued that the "as-is" clause saved it from liability. The court of appeals rejected this argument, stating that an "as-is" clause saves a seller from being liable for normal features—for example, the engine fails because of honestly disclosed miles—but does not save a seller who concealed facts from the buyer and who has engaged in fraud. The court of appeals awarded Forshey $11,486 in compensatory damages, $55,468 to cover his attorney's fees, and $300,000 in punitive damages. The court stated that this award would "accomplish the legitimate state interest in punishing the defendant and deterring its future misconduct." [*Forshey v. Carr Chevrolet, Inc.*, 965 P.2d 440, 1998 Ore.App. Lexis 1560 (OR 1998)]

1. How reprehensible was the dealership's conduct? Was this conduct ethical?
2. Should an "as-is" clause shield the seller from liability? Why or why not?
3. Was the award of punitive damages sufficient in this case?

Kantian Ethics

Immanuel Kant (1724–1804) is the best-known proponent of **duty ethics**, or **deontology** (from the Greek word *deon*, meaning duty). Kant believed that people owe moral duties that are based on *universal* rules. For example, keeping a promise to abide by a contract is a moral duty even if that contract turns out to be detrimental to the obligated party. Kant's philosophy is based on the premise that people can use reasoning to reach ethical decisions. His ethical theory would have people behave according to the *categorical imperative* "Do unto others as you would have them do unto you."

Deontology's universal rules are based on two important principles: (1) consistency—that is, all cases are treated alike with no exceptions—and (2) reversibility—that is, the actor must abide by the rule he or she uses to judge the morality of someone else's conduct. Thus, if you are going to make an exception for yourself, that exception becomes a universal rule that applies to all others. For example, if you rationalize that it is all right for you to engage in deceptive practices, it is all right for competitors to do so also. A criticism of Kantian ethics is that it is hard to reach a consensus as to what the universal rules should be.

In the following case, a company alleged that a competitor had engaged in false advertising.

Pizza Hut, Inc. v. Papa John's International, Inc.
227 F.3d 489, 2000 U.S.App. Lexis 23444 (2000)
United States Court of Appeals, Fifth Circuit

Case 7.2
Comparative Advertising

Background and Facts

Papa John's International, Inc., is the third largest pizza chain in the United States, with more than 2,050 locations. In May 1995, Papa John's adopted a new slogan— "Better Ingredients. Better Pizza."—and applied for and received a federal trademark for this slogan. Papa John's spent over $300 million building customer recognition and goodwill for this slogan. The slogan has appeared on millions of signs, shirts, menus, pizza boxes, napkins, and other items, and it has regularly appeared as the tag line at the end of Papa John's radio and television advertisements.

Pizza Hut, Inc., is the largest pizza chain in the United States, with more than 7,000 restaurants. On May 1, 1997, Pizza Hut launched a new advertising campaign in which it declared "war" on poor-quality pizza. The advertisements touted the "better taste" of Pizza Hut's pizza and "dared" anyone to find a better pizza. A few weeks later Papa John's launched a comparative advertising campaign that touted the superiority of Papa John's pizza over Pizza Hut's pizza. Papa John's claimed it had superior sauce and dough to Pizza Hut. Many of these advertisements were accompanied by Papa John's slogan "Better Ingredients. Better Pizza."

In 1998, Pizza Hut filed a civil action in federal district court, charging Papa John's with false advertising in violation of Section 43(a) of the federal Lanham Act. The district court found that Papa John's slogan "Better Ingredients. Better Pizza." standing alone, was mere puffery and did not constitute false advertising. The district court found, however, that Papa John's claims of superior sauce and dough were misleading and that Papa John's slogan "Better Ingredients. Better Pizza." became tainted because it was associated with these misleading statements. The district court enjoined Papa John's from using the slogan "Better Ingredients. Better Pizza." Papa John's appealed.

Issue

Is Papa John's slogan, "Better Ingredients. Better Pizza." false advertising?

Court's Reasoning

The court of appeals noted that statements of general opinion—referred to as "puffery"—are not actionable under Section 43(a) of the Lanham Act. The court stated that *puffery* is defined as "an exaggerated, blustering, and boasting statement which no reasonable buyer would be justified in relying on" or "a general claim of superiority over comparative products that is so vague that it can be understood as nothing more than a mere expression of opinion." The court of appeals found that Papa John's slogan "Better Ingredients. Better Pizza." is a statement of opinion and is not a statement of fact on which consumers would be justified in relying. The court also held that Papa John's claims of superior sauce and dough compared to Pizza Hut's was not material because Pizza Hut had failed to show that these statements would influence the purchasing decisions of consumers.

Decision and Remedy

The court of appeals held that Papa John's trademarked slogan "Better Ingredients. Better Pizza." was mere puffery and a statement of opinion that was not false advertising and did not violate Section 43(a) of the Lanham Act. The court of appeals reversed the judgment of the district court and remanded the case to the district court for entry of judgment for Papa John's.

Case Questions

Critial Legal Thinking   What is false advertising? What is puffery? How do they differ?

Business Ethics   Do businesses sometimes make exaggerated claims about their products? Are consumers smart enough to see through companies' puffery?

Contemporary Business   If the court of appeals had found in favor of Pizza Hut, what would have been the effect on advertising in this country? Explain.

Rawls's Social Justice Theory

John Locke (1632–1704) and Jean-Jacques Rousseau (1712–1778) proposed a **social contract** theory of morality. Under this theory, each person is presumed to have entered into a social contract with all others in society to obey moral rules that are necessary for people to live in peace and harmony. This implied contract states, "I will keep the rules if everyone else does." These moral rules are then used to solve conflicting interests in society.

The leading proponent of the modern social justice theory is John Rawls, a contemporary philosopher at Harvard University. Under **Rawls's** *social justice theory*, fairness is considered the essence of justice. The principles of justice should be chosen by persons who do not yet know their station in society—thus, their "veil of ignorance" would permit the fairest possible principles to be selected. For example, the principle of equal opportunity would be promulgated by people who would not yet know if they were in a favored class. As a caveat, Rawls also proposes that the least advantaged in society must receive special assistance to allow them to realize their potential.

Rawls's theory of social justice is criticized for two reasons. First, establishing the blind "original position" for choosing moral principles is impossible in the real world. Second, many persons in society would choose not to maximize the benefit to the least advantaged persons in society.

In the following case, the court found that a company had engaged in unfair competition.

U.S. SUPREME COURT CASE

Cooper Industries, Inc. v. Leatherman Tool Group, Inc.

532 U.S. 424, 121 S.Ct. 1678, 2001 U.S. Lexis 3520 (2001)
Supreme Court of the United States

Case 7.3
Unfair Competition

Background and Facts

Leatherman Tool Group, Inc., manufactures and sells a multifunctional tool called the PST that improves upon the classic Swiss Army knife. Leatherman dominates the market for multifunctional pocket tools. In 1995, Cooper Industries, Inc., decided to design and sell a competing multifunctional tool under the name "ToolZall." Cooper introduced the ToolZall in August 1996 at the National Hardware Show in Chicago. At that show, Cooper used photographs in its posters, packaging, and advertising materials that purported to be a ToolZall but were actually of a modified PST. When those materials were prepared, the first of the ToolZalls had not yet been manufactured. A Cooper employee created a ToolZall "mock-up" by grinding the Leatherman trademark from a PST and substituting the unique fastenings that were to be used on the ToolZall. At least one of the photographs was retouched to remove a curved indention where the Leatherman trademark had been. The photographs were used not only at the trade show, but also in marketing materials and catalogs used by Cooper's sales force throughout the United States.

Shortly after the trade show, Leatherman sued Cooper in district court for unfair competition. The district court jury found that Cooper had engaged in unfair competition and awarded Leatherman $50,000 in compensatory damages and $4.5 million in punitive damages. Cooper appealed the award of punitive dam-

ages, but the court of appeals refused to reduce the award. Cooper appealed to the U.S. Supreme Court.

Issue

Should the appellate court analyze the lawfulness of an award of punitive damages using a *de novo* independent standard of review?

Court's Reasoning

The Supreme Court noted that although compensatory damages and punitive damages are typically awarded at the same time by the same decision maker, they serve distinct purposes. The former are intended to redress the concrete loss that the plaintiff has suffered by reason of the defendant's wrongful conduct. The latter, which have been described as "quasi-criminal," operates as private fines intended to punish the defendant and to deter future wrongdoing. A jury's assessment of the extent of a plaintiff's injury is essentially a factual determination, whereas its imposition of punitive damages is an expression of its moral condemnation. The Supreme Court held that the question of whether a fine is constitutionally excessive calls for the application of a constitutional standard to the facts of a particular case, and in this context, the court determined that *de novo* review of that question was appropriate.

Decision and Remedy

The U.S. Supreme Court held that an appellate court should engage in a *de novo* independent review of the trial court's decision in awarding punitive damages. Since the court of appeals used the abuse of discretion standard, rather than the *de novo* standard, in reviewing the size of the punitive damage award in this case, the Supreme Court reversed and remanded the case for a determination of whether the award of $4.5 million of punitive damages against defendant Cooper Industries was lawful.

Case Questions

Critical Legal Thinking   What is the purpose of punitive damages? Explain.

Business Ethics   Do you think a jury's ability to award punitive damages makes businesses act more ethically?

Contemporary Business   Do you think an award of $4.5 million in punitive damages was warranted in this case? How much would you award?

Business Ethics

Enron Corporation Plunges into Bankruptcy

By the year 2000, the Enron Corporation, a Houston-based energy company, had become the sixth-largest corporation in America. Its rise to this status was meteoric, and the company's stock was trading at over $90 per share. The company's main business was brokering energy between buyers and sellers. It also engaged in building huge energy projects worldwide, as well as speculating in oil and gas futures on the world's commodities markets. Enron spread its money around by making large political campaign donations to presidential candidates and members of the U.S. Congress.

But all was not well with the corporation. Enron had created hundreds of partnerships, many located in off-shore tax havens. These partnerships were used to borrow money from banks and other creditors and to engage in speculative business dealings. Enron booked its investments and money from these partnerships as assets, but the debts of these partnerships and much of the self-dealing with and among them were not reported on Enron's consolidated financial statements. Enron executives purposefully created this maze of entities to perpetrate accounting fraud. Thus, the company looked profitable when in fact it was not. Enron was able to run this charade for years before the bubble finally burst.

In 2002, reporters and securities analysts began investigating Enron's financial empire. As rumors of Enron's "creative accounting" reached the public, the price of its stock began to fall. Many of its top executives sold their Enron shares before the stock price plummeted. Investors who did not have inside information were not so lucky; they lost their investments as the price of Enron stock tumbled to less than 50 cents per share.

The Securities and Exchange Commission (SEC), a federal government agency, announced that it was investigating the Enron affair. Officers and employees at Enron began to shred thousands of documents relevant to the investigation. Andersen LLP, one of the "Big Five" accounting firms in the United States, had been Enron's auditor for years. Andersen was making between $2 million and $4 million per month providing auditing and other services to Enron. Andersen's malpractice or fraud contributed to Enron's being able to conceal its fraud from the investing public. Several of Andersen's partners in the Houston office who were responsible for auditing Enron also shredded thousands of documents pertaining to the Enron audits. Once alerted, the court issued an injunction prohibiting the destruction of any more documents by Enron or Andersen.

In late 2002, Enron Corporation filed for Chapter 11 bankruptcy. By that time, billions of dollars of shareholder wealth had been wiped out. Enron's employees, who had their pension funds invested in Enron stock, saw their dreams of a comfortable retirement evaporate. And bond-holders, banks, suppliers, and other creditors lost billions of dollars in unpaid debts. Enron was the largest company in America ever to file for bankruptcy. Some parts of it were sold to other energy companies, but the majority of its businesses were worthless. Andersen LLP unraveled, was sued criminally by the U.S. government, and eventually went out of business.

The Enron debacle is one of the grossest examples of corporate greed and fraud in America.

1. Did the Enron executives act ethically by using off-shore, "off balance sheet" partnerships to hide Enron's liabilities?
2. Did the Enron executives and Andersen partners act ethically in shredding documents? ▪

Ethical Relativism

Ethical relativism holds that individuals must decide what is ethical based on their own feelings as to what is right or wrong. Under this moral theory, if a person meets his or her own moral standard in making a decision, no one can criticize him or her for it. Thus, there are no universal ethical rules to guide a person's conduct. This theory has been criticized because action that is usually thought to be unethical (e.g., committing fraud) would not be unethical if the perpetrator thought it was in fact ethical. Few philosophers advocate ethical relativism as an acceptable moral theory.

Hue, Vietnam. Companies such as Nike have instituted inspection programs to prevent labor and employment abuses by subcontractors in foreign countries.

Concept Summary *Theories of Ethics*

Theory	Description
Ethical fundamentalism	Persons look to an outside source (e.g., Bible or Koran) or central figure for ethical guidelines.
Utilitarianism	Persons choose the alternative that would provide the greatest good to society.
Kantian ethics	A set of universal rules establishes ethical duties. The rules are based on reasoning and require (1) consistency in application and (2) reversibility.
Rawls's social justice theory	Moral duties are based on an implied social contract. Fairness is justice. The rules are established from an original position of a "veil of ignorance."
Ethical relativism	Individuals decide what is ethical based on their own feelings as to what is right or wrong.

Business Ethics

Sarbanes-Oxley Act Prompts Public Companies to Adopt Code of Ethics

In the late 1990s and early 2000s, many large corporations in the United States were found to have engaged in massive financial frauds. Many of these frauds were perpetrated by the chief executive officer's and other senior officers of the companies. Financial officers, such as chief financial officers and controllers, were also found to have been instrumental in creating these frauds. In response, Congress enacted the **Sarbanes-Oxley Act of 2002**, which makes certain conduct illegal and establishes criminal penalties for violations.

In addition, the Sarbanes-Oxley Act prompts companies to encourage senior officers of public companies to act ethically in their dealings with shareholders, employees, and other constituents. **Section 406** of the Sarbanes-Oxley Act requires a public company to disclose whether it has adopted a **code of ethics** for senior financial officers, including its principal financial officer and principal accounting officer. In response, public companies have adopted codes of ethics for their senior financial officers. Many public companies have included all officers and employees in the coverage of their codes of ethics.

A typical code of ethics follows.

Big Cheese Corporation
Code of Ethics

Big Cheese Corporation's mission includes the promotion of professional conduct in the practice of general management worldwide. Big Cheese's Chief Executive Officer (CEO), Chief Financial Officer (CFO), corporate Controller, and other employees of the finance organization and other employees of the corporation hold an important and elevated role in the corporate governance of the corporation. They are empowered and uniquely capable to ensure that all constituents' interests are appropriately balanced, protected, and preserved.

This Code of Ethics embodies principles to which we are expected to adhere and advocate. The CEO, CFO, finance organization employees, and other employees of the corporation are expected to abide by this Code of Ethics and all business conduct standards of the corporation relating to areas covered by this Code of Ethics. Any violatioin of the Code of Ethics may result in disciplinary action, up to and including termination of employment. All employees will:

- Act with honesty and integrity, avoiding actual or apparent conflicts of interest in their personal and professional relations.
- Provide stakeholders with information that is accurate, fair, complete, timely, objective, relevant, and understandable, including in our filings with and other submissions to the U.S. Securities and Exchange Commission.
- Comply with rules and regulations of federal, state, provincial, and local governments and other appropriate private and public regulatory agencies.
- Act in good faith, responsibly, with due care, competence, and diligence, without misrepresent-ing materials facts or allowing one's independent judgment to be subordinated.
- Respect the confidentiality of information acquired in the course of one's work, except when authorized or otherwise legally obligated to disclose. Confidential information acquired in the course of one's work will not be used for personal advantage.
- Share knowledge and maintain professional skills important and relevant to stakeholders' needs.
- Proactively promote and be an example of ethical behavior as a responsible partner among peers, in the work environment and the community.
- Achieve responsible use, control, and stewardship over all Big Cheese's assets and resources that are employed or entrusted to us.
- Not unduly or fraudulently influence, coerce, manipulate, or mislead any authorized audit or interfere with any auditor engaged in the performance of an internal or independent audit of Big Cheese's financial statements or accounting books and records.

If you are aware of any suspected or known violations of this Code of Ethics or other Big Cheese policies or guidelines, you have a duty to promptly report such concerns either to your manager, another responsible member of management, a Human Resources representative, or the Director of Compliance or the 24-hour Business Conduct Line.

If you have a concern about a questionable accounting or auditing matter and wish to submit the concern confidentially or anonymously, you may do so by sending an e-mail to (bc.codeofethics@bigcheese.cc) or calling the Business Conduct Line 24-hour number at 1-888-666-BIGC (2442).

Big Cheese will handle all inquiries discretely and make every effort to maintain, within the limits allowed by law, the confidentiality of anyone requesting guidance or reporting questionable behavior and/or a compliance concern.

It is Big Cheese's intention that this Code of Ethics to be its written code of ethics under Section 406 of the Sarbanes-Oxley Act of 2002 complying with the standards set forth in Securities and Ex-change Commission Regulation S-K Item 406.

---

1. Do you think the Sarbanes-Oxley Act will be effective in promoting ethical conduct by officers and directors? Explain.

2. Can ethics be mandated? In other words, will crooks still be crooks? ■

International Law

United Nations Code of Conduct for Transnational Corporations

Respect for National Sovereignty

Transnational corporations shall respect the national sovereignty of the countries in which they operate and the right of each state to exercise its permanent sovereignty over its natural wealth and resources.

Transnational corporations should carry out their activities in conformity with the development policies, objectives and priorities set out by the governments of the countries in which they operate and work seriously toward making a positive contribution to the achievement of such goals at the national and, as appropriate, the regional level, within the framework of regional integration programs.

Transnational corporations should cooperate with the governments of the countries in which they operate with a view to contributing to the development process and should be responsive to requests for consultation in this respect, thereby establishing mutually beneficial relations with these countries.

International Law
(continued)

Adherence to Sociocultural Objectives and Values

Transnational corporations should respect the social and cultural objectives, values, and traditions of the countries in which they operate. While economic and technological development is normally accompanied by social change, transnational corporations should avoid practices, products or services which cause detrimental effects on cultural patterns and socio-cultural objectives as determined by governments. For this purpose, transnational corporations should respond positively to requests for consultations from governments concerned.

Respect for Human Rights and Fundamental Freedoms

Transnational corporations shall respect human rights and fundamental freedoms in the countries in which they oper-ate. In their social and industrial relations, transnational corporations shall not discriminate on the basis of race, color, sex, religion, language, social, national and ethnic origin or political or other opinion. Transnational corporations shall conform to government policies designed to extend quality of opportunity and treatment.

Abstention from Corrupt Practices

Transnational corporations shall refrain, in their transactions, from the offering, promising or giving of any payment, gift or other advantage to or for the benefit of a public official as consideration for performing or refraining from the performance of his duties in connection with those transactions. ■

Social Responsibility of Business

Business Brief

Corporations that conduct social audits will be more apt to prevent unethical and illegal conduct by managers, employees, and agents.

Businesses do not operate in a vacuum. Decisions made by businesses have far-reaching effects on society. In the past, many business decisions were based solely on a cost–benefit analysis and how they affected the "bottom line." Such decisions, however, may cause negative externalities for others. For example, the dumping of hazardous wastes from a manufacturing plant into a river affects the homeowners, farmers, and others who use the river's waters. Thus, corporations are considered to owe some degree of **social responsibility** for their actions. Four theories of the social responsibility of business are discussed in the following paragraphs.

Maximizing Profits

Public policy: That principle of the law which holds that no subject can lawfully do that which has a tendency to be injurious to the public or against the public good.

Lord Truro
Egerton v. Brownlow (1853)

The traditional view of the social responsibility of business is that business should **maximize profits** for shareholders. This view, which dominated business and the law during the nineteenth century, holds that the interests of other constituencies (e.g., employees, suppliers, residents of the communities in which businesses are located) are not important in and of themselves.

In the famous case *Dodge v. Ford Motor Company*,[1] a shareholder sued the car company when Henry Ford introduced a plan to reduce the price of cars so that more people would be put to work and more people could own cars. The shareholders alleged that such a plan would not increase dividends. Mr. Ford testified, "My ambition is to employ still more men, to spread the benefits of this industrial system to the greatest number, to help them build up their lives and their homes." The court sided with the shareholders and stated that

> [Mr. Ford's] testimony creates the impression that he thinks the Ford Motor company has made too much money, has had too large profits and that, although large profits might still be earned, a sharing of them with the public, by reducing the price of the output of the company, ought to be undertaken.

There should be no confusion of the duties which Mr. Ford conceives that he and the stockholders owe to the general public and the duties which in law he and his codirectors owe to protesting, minority stockholders. A business corporation is organized and carried on primarily for the profit of the stockholders. The powers of the directors are to be employed for that end. The discretion of directors is to be exercised in the choice of means to attain that end and does not extend to a change in the end itself, to the reduction of profits, or to the nondistribution of profits among stockholders in order to devote them to other purposes.

Milton Friedman, who won the Nobel Prize in economics when he taught at the University of Chicago, advocated this theory. Friedman asserted that in a free society, "there is one and only one social responsibility of business—to use its resources and engage in activities designed to increase its profits as long as it stays within the rules of the game, which is to say, engages in open and free competition without deception and fraud."[2]

In the following case, one company is accused of knocking off another company's product design.

U.S. SUPREME COURT CASE
Wal-Mart Stores, Inc. v. Samara Brothers, Inc.
529 U.S. 205, 123 S.Ct. 1339, 2000 U.S. Lexis 2197 (2000)
Supreme Court of the United States

Case 7.4
Knock-Offs

Background and Facts

Samara Brothers, Inc. (Samara), is a designer and manufacturer of children's clothing. The core of Samara's business is its annual new line of spring and summer children's garments. Samara sold its clothing to retailers, who in turn sold the clothes to consumers. Wal-Mart Stores, Inc. (Wal-Mart), operates a large chain of budget warehouse stores that sell thousands of items at very low prices. In 1995, Wal-Mart contacted one of its suppliers, Judy-Philippine, Inc. (JPI), about the possibility of making a line of children's clothes just like Samara's successful line. Wal-Mart sent photographs of Samara's children's clothes to JPI (the name "Samara" was readily discernible on the labels of the garments) and directed JPI to produce children's clothes exactly like those in the photographs. JPI produced a line of children's clothes for Wal-Mart that copied the designs, colors, and patterns of Samara's clothing. Wal-Mart then sold this line of children's clothing in its stores, making a gross profit of over $1.15 million on these clothes sales during the 1996 selling season.

Samara discovered that Wal-Mart was selling the knock-off clothes at a price that was lower than Samara's retailers were paying Samara for its clothes. After sending unsuccessful cease-and-desist letters to Wal-Mart, Samara sued Wal-Mart, alleging that Wal-Mart stole Samara's trade dress (i.e., look and feel) in violation of Section 43(a) of the Lanham Act. Although not finding that Samara's clothes had acquired a *secondary meaning* in the minds of the public, the district court held in favor of Samara and awarded damages. The court of appeals affirmed. Wal-Mart appealed to the U.S. Supreme Court.

Issue

Must a product's design have acquired a *secondary meaning* before it is protected as trade dress?

Court's Reasoning

Section 43(a) of the Lanham Act gives a producer a cause of action for the use by any person of "any word, term, name, symbol, or device, or any combination thereof which is likely to cause confusion as to the origin, sponsorship, or approval of his or her goods." The text of Section 43(a) provides little guidance as to the circumstances under which unregistered trade dress may be protected. It does require that a producer show that the allegedly infringing feature is likely to cause confusion with the product for which protection is sought. The Supreme Court held that in an action for infringement of unregistered trade dress a product's design is protectible only upon a showing of secondary meaning.

Decision and Remedy

The U.S. Supreme Court held that a product's design has to have acquired a secondary meaning in the public's eye before it is protected as trade dress under Section 43(a) of the Lanham Act. The Supreme Court reversed the decision of the court of appeals.

Case Questions

Critical Legal Thinking What is trade dress? Should it have been protected in this case?

Business Ethics Even though Wal-Mart's conduct was ruled legal, was it ethical?

Contemporary Business Before reading this case, had you heard or read about Samara's childrens' clothing?

Kathmandu, Nepal. Religious principles often help shape the moral beliefs of the residents of a country.

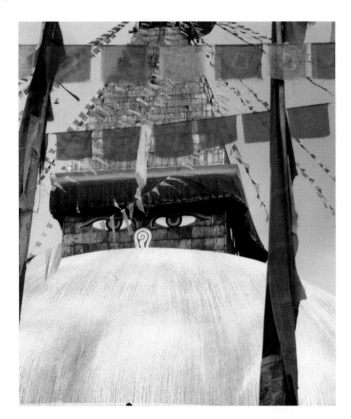

Moral Minimum

Some proponents of corporate social responsibility argue that a corporation's duty is to *make a profit while avoiding causing harm to others*. This theory of social responsibility is called the **moral minimum**. Under this theory, as long as business avoids or corrects the social injury it causes, it has met its duty of social responsibility. For instance, a corporation that pollutes the waters and then compensates those whom it injures has met its moral minimum duty of social responsibility.

The legislative and judicial branches of government have established laws that enforce the moral minimum of social responsibility on corporations. For example, occupational safety laws establish minimum safety standards for protecting employees from injuries in the workplace. Consumer protection laws establish safety requirements for products and make manufactures and sellers liable for injuries caused by defective products. Other laws establish similar minimum standards for conduct for business in other areas.

Ethics Brief

Many people do not buy tuna because the tuna nets also catch dolphins. Is this socially responsible behavior? Should someone care about the dolphins?

International Law
Nike Just Did It In Vietnam

Nike produces basketball, running, and other athletic shoes that it sells in the United States and worldwide. Nike has over 40 percent of the athletic shoe market in the United States. The majority of Nike's shoes are produced by subcontractors located in some of the poorest countries of the world including Vietnam. In the late 1900s Nike faced a public relations and ethical nightmare: It was being charged with selling shoes made by slave and child laborers who worked in horrid conditions.

In Vietnam, where Nike has 12 percent of its shoes manufactured, subcontractors worked employees eight hours per day, six days per week, and paid them as little as $40 per month in wages. These workers, who were mostly women in their 20s, worked under terrible conditions. They were subjected to hot and noisy working environments, exposed to toxic chemicals and fumes, and mistreated by the managers. These conditions were brought to light not by Nike but by humanitarian organizations. After first vehemently denying the allegations, Nike backed down and agreed to improve the working conditions at its subcontractors in Vietnam.

Nike took the following steps:

- Required many managers of the subcontractors to be fired for their abusive conduct.
- Reduced toxic petroleum-based compounds used in making Nike shoes.
- Banned its subcontractors from paying below Vietnam's minimum wage of $45 per month.

- Installed Nike managers in the subcontractors' plants to monitor working conditions.

Nike states that it has taken the necessary steps to prohibit and prevent abuses by its subcontractors in Vietnam. Critics contend that Nike is outsourcing the production of its shoes to workers in poor countries that do not have the same worker protections as provided in the United States. ■

Stakeholder Interest

Businesses have relationship with all sorts of people other than their stockholders, including employees, suppliers, customers, creditors, and the local community. Under the **stakeholder interest** theory of social responsibility, a corporation must consider the effects its actions have on these *other stakeholders*. For example, a corporation would violate the stakeholder interest theory if it viewed employees solely as a means of maximizing stockholder wealth.

This theory is criticized because it is difficult to harmonize the conflicting interests of stakeholders. For example, in closing a plant, certain stakeholders may benefit (e.g., stockholders and creditors) while other stakeholders may not (e.g., current employees and the local community).

In the following case, the U.S. Supreme Court examined an award of punitive damages.

U.S. SUPREME COURT CASE

State Farm Mutual Automobile Insurance Company v. Campbell

538 U.S. 408, 123 S.Ct. 1513, 2003 U.S. Lexis 2713 (2003)
Supreme Court of the United States

Case 7.5
Punitive Damages

Background and Facts

In 1981, Curtis Campbell was driving with his wife in Utah when he decided to pass six vans traveling ahead of him on a two-lane highway. Todd Ospital, who was driving on the opposite side of the road toward Campbell, swerved to avoid a collision with Campbell and collided with an automobile driven by Robert Slusher. Ospital was killed; Slusher was rendered permanently disabled; the Campbells escaped unscathed. Early investigations determined that Campbell made an unsafe pass and had caused the crash. Ospital's heirs and Slusher sued Campbell for wrongful death and injuries, respectively. Campbell's insurance company, State Farm Mutual Automobile Insurance Company (State Farm) declined offers by Ospital's estate and Slusher to settle their claims for the insurance policy limit of $50,000 and took the case to trial. The jury determined that Campbell was 100 percent at fault and returned a judgment for $185,000.

Campbell reached a settlement with Ospital's and Slusher's attorneys whereby Campbell agreed to pursue a bad faith tort action against State Farm, and Ospital's estate and Slusher would

receive 90 percent of any verdict against State Farm. One and one-half years after the initial judgment, State Farm paid all of the $185,000 judgment against Campbell, even though it exceeded the $50,000 policy limit. The bad faith tort case went to trial against State Farm in a Utah trial court. At trial, evidence was introduced that State Farm had a policy to take many cases to trial even though they could be settled within the insurance policy limits. The jury held against State Farm and awarded Campbell $2.6 million in compensatory damages and $145 million in punitive damages. The trial court judge reduced compensatory damages to $1 million and punitive damages to $25 million. The Utah Supreme Court reinstated the $145 million punitive damage award. State Farm appealed to the U.S. Supreme Court.

Issue

Is an award of $145 million in punitive damages, where compensatory damages are $1 million, excessive and a violation of the Due Process Clause of the Fourteenth Amendment to the Constitution of the United States?

State Farm Mutual Automobile Insurance Company v. Campbell

538 U.S. 408, 123 S.Ct. 1513, 2003 U.S. Lexis 2713 (2003)
Supreme Court of the United States
(continued)

Court's Reasoning

The U.S. Supreme Court noted that while states possess discretion over the imposition of punitive damages, it is well established that there are procedural and substantive constitutional limitations on these awards. The Due Process Clause of the Fourteenth Amendment prohibits the imposition of grossly excessive or arbitrary punishments on a tortfeasor. This case is neither close nor difficult. It was an error to reinstate the jury's $145 million punitive damages award.

The Supreme Court stated that this case was used as a platform to expose, and punish, the perceived deficiencies of State Farm's operations throughout the country. The Utah supreme court's opinion makes explicit that State Farm was being condemned for its nationwide policies rather than for the conduct directed toward the Campbells. The Utah court awarded punitive damages to punish and deter conduct that bore no relation to the Campbells' harm. A defendant's dissimilar acts, independent from the acts on which liability was premised, may not serve as the basis for punitive damages. A defendant should be punished for the conduct that harmed the plaintiff, not for being an unsavory individual or business. The Court concluded that due process does not permit courts, in the calculation of punitive damages, to adjudicate the merits of other parties' hypothetical claims against a defendant, under the guise of the reprehensibility analysis.

The Supreme Court stated that few awards exceeding a single-digit ratio between punitive and compensatory damages, to a significant degree, will satisfy due process. In a previous case, the Supreme Court concluded that an award of more than four times the amount of compensatory damages might be close to the line of constitutional impropriety. [*BMW of North America, Inc.*

v. Gore, 517 U.S. 559, 116 S.Ct. 1589, 1996 U.S. Lexis 3390 (1996)] While these ratios are not binding, they are instructive. Single-digit multipliers are more likely to comport with due process, while still achieving the state's goals of deterrence and retribution, than awards with ratios in the range of 500 to 1, or, in this case, of 145 to 1.

The Court concluded that because there are no rigid benchmarks that a punitive damages award may not surpass, ratios greater than those previously upheld by the Court may comport with due process where a particularly egregious act has resulted in only a small amount of economic damages.

Decision and Remedy

The U.S. Supreme Court held that an award of $145 million in punitive damages where compensatory damages were $1 million was excessive and violated the Due Process Clause of the Fourteenth Amendment to the U.S. Constitution. The U.S. Supreme Court reversed the decision of the Utah supreme court and remanded the case for proceedings consistent with the U.S. Supreme Court's opinion.

Case Questions

Critical Legal Thinking What is the purpose of punitive damages? What is the protection afforded by the Due Process Clause? Explain.

Business Ethics Did Campbell act ethically in this case? Did State Farm act ethically in this case?

Contemporary Business How important is this case for businesses? Explain.

Corporate Citizenship

The **corporate citizenship** theory of social responsibility argues that business has a responsibility to do good. That is, business is responsible for helping to solve social problems that it did little, if anything, to cause. For example, under this theory, corporations owe a duty to subsidize schools and help educate children.

This theory contends that corporations owe a duty to promote the same social goals as do individual members of society. Proponents of the "do good" theory argue that corporations owe a debt to society to make it a better place and that this duty arises because of the social power bestowed on them. That is, this social power is a gift from society and should be used to good ends.

A major criticism of this theory is that the duty of a corporation to do good cannot be expanded beyond certain limits. There is always some social problem that needs to be addressed, and corporate funds are limited. Further, if this theory were taken to its maximum limit, potential shareholders might be reluctant to invest in corporations.

> The notion that a business is clothed with a public interest and has been devoted to the public use is little more than a fiction intended to beautify what is disagreeable to the sufferers.
>
> Justice Holmes
> *Tyson & Bro-United Theatre Ticket Officers v. Banton (1927)*

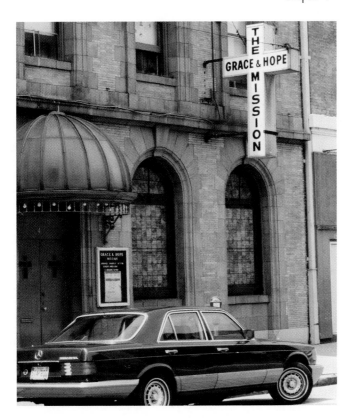

St. Louis, Missouri. The corporate citizenship theory of social responsibility states that businesses have the responsibility to do good for society.

Business Ethics
The Corporate Social Audit

It has been suggested that corporate audits should be extended to include not only audits of the financial health of a corporation but also of its moral health. Corporations that conduct social audits will be more apt to prevent unethical and illegal conduct by managers, employees, and agents. The audit would examine how well employees have adhered to the company's code of ethics and how well the corporation has met its duty of social responsibility. Such audits would focus on the corporation's efforts to promote employment opportunities for members of protected classes, worker safety, environmental protection, consumer protection, and the like. Social audits are not easy. First, it may be hard to conceptualize just what is being audited. Second, it may be difficult to measure results. Despite these factors, more companies are expected to undertake social audits.

Companies should institute the following procedures when conducting a social audit:

■ An independent outside firm should be hired to conduct the audit. This will ensure autonomy and objectivity in conducting the audit.

■ The company's personnel should cooperate fully with the auditing firm while the audit is being conducted.
■ The auditing firm should report its findings directly to the company's board of directors.
■ The results of the audit should be reviewed by the board of directors.
■ The board of directors should determine how the company can better meet its duty of social responsibility and can use the audit to implement a program to correct any deficiencies it finds.

1. What are the purposes of conducting a social audit of a business? Explain.
2. Do you think that conducting social audits of businesses will increase ethical behavior of these businesses? ■

■ *Concept Summary* *Theories of Social Responsibility*

Theory	Social Responsibility
Maximizing profits	To maximize profits for stockholders.
Moral minimum	To avoid causing harm and to compensate for harm caused.
Stakeholder interest	To consider the interests of all stakeholders, including stockholders, employees, customers, suppliers, creditors, and the local community.
Corporate citizenship	To do good and solve social problems.

International Law

Holocaust Victims' Asset Litigation Settled

During World War II, the German Nazi regime engaged in years of persecution of Jews, including genocide, slave labor, and a wholesale and systematic looting of personal and business property of the Jewish victims. World War II ended in 1945 when the Allies defeated Germany and its Axis collaborators. During World War II, the European country of Switzerland remained neutral.

Switzerland has been a financial center to Europe for centuries. It is famous for its bank secrecy laws; that is, Swiss law protects the names of depositors and other information. Before and during the war, many Swiss banks held money and other property of Jews throughout Europe. But during the war, the Swiss banks obtained new clients—the Nazis, who stole their Jewish victims' property and placed it with the Swiss banks for safekeeping.

Over 50 years later, beginning in 1996, a series of class action lawsuits were filed in U.S. district courts by the survivors of the Holocaust and their heirs against Union Bank of Switzerland and many other Swiss banks. The plaintiffs alleged that during World War II the Swiss banks knowingly retained, concealed, and laundered the money and assets of Holocaust vic-

tims stolen by the Nazis. The lawsuits also alleged that Swiss banks did not pay money back to the Jewish survivors or to the heirs of the deceased victims that was on deposit at the banks once World War II was over.

After substantial negotiations, the plaintiffs reached a settlement with the defendant Swiss banks. The defendants dropped their defense that the claims were time-barred and agreed to pay $1.25 billion into a settlement fund. In exchange, the plaintiffs agreed to release all further claims against the banks. The district court judge approved the settlement agreement. Ernest Lobet, a survivor of the Holocaust, commented about the settlement: "I have no quarrel with the settlement. I do not say it is fair, because fairness is a relative term. No amount of money can possibly be fair under those circumstances."

A procedure was established for the plaintiffs to make claims against the settlement fund. Were the Swiss banks neutral during and after World War II? Should the offending Swiss banks have been punished in any way? Explain. [*In re Holocaust Victim Asset Litigation*, 105 F.Supp.2d 139, 2000 U.S. Dist. Lexis 10721 (E.D.N.Y. 2000)] ■

Chapter Summary

Ethics, p. 150

Ethics

Ethics is a set of moral principles or values that governs the conduct of an individual or a group.

Moral Theories and Business Ethics, p. 152

Moral Theories

1. *Ethical fundamentalism.* Persons look to an outside source (e.g., Bible or Koran) or central figure to set ethical guidelines.

2. *Utilitarianism.* Persons choose the alternative that would provide the greatest good to society.

3. *Kantian ethics.* A set of universal rules establishes ethical duties. The rules are based on reasoning and require (1) consistency in application and (2) reversibility.

4. *Rawls's social justice theory.* Moral duties are based on an implied social contract. Fairness is justice. The rules are established from an original position of a "veil of ignorance."

5. *Ethical relativism.* Individuals decide what is ethical based on their own feelings of what is right or wrong.

Social Responsibility of Business, p. 160

Theories of Social Responsibility

1. *Maximizing profits.* The goal of this theory is to maximize profits for shareholders.

2. *Moral minimum.* The goal of this theory is to make a profit and avoid harm and to compensate for harm caused.

3. *Stakeholder interests.* The goal of this theory is to consider the interests of stakeholders other than stockholders, such as employees, suppliers, customers, creditors, and the local community.

4. *Corporate citizenship.* The goal of this theory is to do good and help solve social problems.

Corporate Social Audit

A Corporate Social audit is an audit of a corporation by independent auditors that examines how well employees have adhered to the company's code of ethics and how well the company has met its duty of social responsibility.

Internet Exercises and Case Questions

Working the Web Internet Exercises

Activities

1. Find the list titled "Baby Boomer Sports Injuries" at **www.cpsc.gov**. What is the ethical duty of the companies who sell sports equipment to consumers in this age bracket?

2. Locate the Drudge Report at **www.drudgereport.com**. What is the ethical basis for the press to report on topics such as consumer fraud, arrests and trials of notorious criminals, questionable tax policies, and so on?

3. Locate and review the story on the use of torture and drugs to interrogate captured suspected terrorists at **www.alchemind.org/news/narcointerrogation1.html**. Is it constitutional? Is it ethical?

Business Ethics Cases

7.1 Business Ethics The Warner-Lambert Company has manufactured and distributed Listerine antiseptic mouthwash since 1879. Its formula has never changed. Ever since Listerine's introduction, the company has represented it as being beneficial in preventing and curing colds and sore throats. Direct advertising of these claims to consumers began in 1921. In 1971, Warner-Lambert spent $10 million advertising these claims in print media and in television commercials.

In 1972, the Federal Trade Commission (FTC) filed a complaint against Warner-Lambert, alleging that the company engaged in false advertising in violation of federal law. Four months of hearings were held before an administrative law judge that produced an evidentiary record of more than 4,000 pages of documents from 46 witnesses. In 1975, after examining the evidence, the FTC issued an opinion which held that the company's representations that Listerine prevented and cured colds and sore throats were false. The U.S. court of appeals affirmed.

Did Warner-Lambert act ethically in making its claims for Listerine? What remedy should the court impose on the company? Would making Warner-Lambert cease such advertising be sufficient? [*Warner-Lambert Company v. Federal Trade Commission*, 562 F.2d 749, 1977 U.S. App. Lexis 11599 (D.C. Cir. 1977)]

7.2 Business Ethics Stanford University is one of the premiere research universities in the country. Stanford has an operating budget of approximately $400 million a year and receives about $175 million a year in direct research funding from the federal government. In addition, the government reimburses the university for certain overhead and indirect costs associated with the research. This amounts to about $85 million a year.

In 1990, a navy accountant took a close look at Stanford's books and alleged that the university may have overstated overhead and indirect costs associated with research by as much as

$200 million during the 1980s. The university provided a house for its president, Donald Kennedy. Some of the expenses charged against overhead for research were (a) $3,000 for a cedar-lined closet at the president's home, (b) $4,000 for the president's 1987 wedding reception, (c) $7,000 in bed sheets and table linens, and (d) $184,000 in depreciation on a yacht donated to Stanford's sailing program. Did the administration of Stanford act ethically in charging these expenditures as overhead against research? What penalty should be assessed?

7.3 Business Ethics The Johns-Manville Corporation was a profitable company that made a variety of building and other products. It was a major producer of asbestos, which was used for insulation in buildings and for a variety of other uses. It has been medically proven that excessive exposure to asbestos causes asbestosis, a fatal lung disease. Thousands of employees of the company and consumers who were exposed to asbestos and contracted this fatal disease sued the company for damages. In 1983, the lawsuits were being filed at a rate of more than 400 per week.

As a response, the company filed for reorganization bankruptcy. It argued that if it did not, an otherwise viable company that provided thousands of jobs and served a useful purpose in this country would be destroyed, and that without the declaration of bankruptcy, a few of the plaintiffs who first filed their lawsuits would win awards of hundreds of million of dollars, leaving nothing for the remainder of the plaintiffs. Under the bankruptcy court's protection, the company was restructured to survive. As part of the release from bankruptcy, the company contributed money to a fund to pay current and future claimants. The fund is not large enough to pay all injured persons the full amount of their claims.

Was it ethical for Johns-Manville to declare bankruptcy? Did it meet its duty of social responsibility in this case? If you were a member of the board of directors of the company, would you have voted to place the company in bankruptcy? Why or why not? [*In re Johns-Manville Corporation*, 36 B.R. 727, 1984 Bankr. Lexis 6384 (B.C. S.D.N.Y. 1984)]

7.4 Business Ethics In 1977, Reverend Leon H. Sullivan, a Baptist minister from Philadelphia who was also a member of the board of directors of General Motors Corporation, proposed a set of rules to guide American-owned companies doing business in the Republic of South Africa. The **Sullivan Principles**, as they became known, call for the nonsegregation of races in South Africa. They call for employers to (a) provide equal and fair employment practices for all employees and (b) improve the quality of employees' lives outside the work environment in such areas as housing, schooling, transportation, recreation, and health facilities. The principles also require signatory companies to report regularly and be graded on their conduct in South Africa.

Eventually, the Sullivan Principles were subscribed to by several hundred U.S. corporations with affiliates doing business in South Africa. Concerning the companies that have subscribed to the Sullivan Principles, which of the following theories of social responsibility are they following?

1. Maximizing profits
2. Moral minimum
3. Stakeholder interest
4. Corporate citizenship

To put additional pressure on the government of the Republic of South Africa to end apartheid, in 1987 Reverend Sullivan called for the complete withdrawal of all U.S. companies from doing business in or with South Africa. Very few companies agreed to do so. Do companies owe a social duty to withdraw from South Africa? Should universities divest themselves of investments in companies that do not withdraw from South Africa?

7.5 Business Ethics In 1974, Kaiser Aluminum & Chemical Corporation covered into a collective bargaining agreement with the United Steelworkers of America, a union that represented employees at Kaiser's plants. The agreement contained an affirmative-action program to increase the representation of minorities in craft jobs. To enable plants to meet these goals, on-the-job training programs were established to teach unskilled production workers the skills necessary to become craft workers. Assignment to the training program was based on seniority, except that the plan reserved 50 percent of the openings for black employees.

In 1974, 13 craft trainees were selected from Kaiser's Gramercy plant for the training program. Of these, 7 were black and 6 white. The most senior black selected had less seniority than several white production workers who had applied for the positions but were rejected. Brian Webster, one of the white rejected employees, instituted a class action lawsuit alleging that the affirmative action plan violated Title VII of the Civil Rights Act of 1964, which made it "unlawful to discriminate because of race" in hiring and selecting apprentices for training programs. The U.S. Supreme Court upheld the affirmative-action plan in this case. The decision stated,

> We therefore hold that Title VII's prohibition against racial discrimination does not condemn all private, voluntary, race-conscious affirmative action plans. At the same time, the plan does not unnecessarily trammel the interests of the white employees. Moreover, the plan is a temporary measure; it is not intended to maintain racial balance, but simply to eliminate a manifest racial imbalance.

Do companies owe a duty of social responsibility to provide affirmative-action programs? [*Steelworkers v. Weber*, 443 U.S. 193, 99 S.Ct. 2721, 1979 U.S. Lexis 40 (1979)]

7.6 Business Ethics Iroquois Brands, Ltd., is a Delaware corporation that had $78 million in assets, $141 million in sales, and $6 million in profits in 1984. As part of its business, Iroquois importsed pâté de foie gras (goose pâté) from France and sold it in the United States. Iroquois derived only $79,000 in revenues from sales of such pâté. The French producer force-fed the geese from which the pâté was made. Peter C. Lovenheim, who owned 200 shares of Iroquois common stock, proposed to include a shareholder proposal in Iroquois's annual proxy materials to be sent to shareholders. His proposal criticized the company because the force-feeding caused "undue stress, pain and suffering" to the geese and requested that shareholders vote to have Iroquois discontinue importing and selling pâté produced by this method.

Iroquois refused to allow the information to be included in its proxy materials. Iroquois asserted that its refusal was based on the fact that Lovenheim's proposal was "not economically significant" and had only "ethical and social" significance. The company reasoned that because corporations are economic entities, only an economic test applied to its activities, and it was not subject to an ethical or a social responsibility test. Is the company correct; that is, should only an economic test be applied in judging the activities of a corporation? Or should a corporation also be subject to an ethical or a social responsibility test? [*Lovenheim v. Iroquois Brands, Ltd.*, 618 F.Supp. 554, 1985 U.S. Dist. Lexis 21259 (D.C. 1985)]

Briefing the Case Writing Assignment

Read Case A. 7 in the Case Appendix [*Ramirez v. Plough, Inc.*]. This case is excerpted from the court of appeals opinion. Review and brief the case. In your brief, be sure to answer the following questions.

1. Did Plough, Inc., act ethically in participating in efforts to influence the government to reject mandatory warning labels?

2. Did the company act ethically in voluntarily providing the warning labels? How "voluntary" was its decision?

3. Does a company owe a duty of social responsibility to provide warning labels in foreign languages? If so, under what circumstances?

4. If a causal connection is shown between the use of aspirin and Reye's syndrome, would you find Plough liable for the death of the child? If so, what amount of damages would you award?

Endnotes

1. 170 N.W. 668, 1919 Mich. Lexis 720 (MI 1919).
2. Milton Friedman, "The Social Responsibility of Business Is to Increase Its Profits," *New York Times Magazine*, September 13, 1970.

Nature of Traditional and Online Contracts

8

"The movement of the progressive societies has hitherto been a movement from status to contract."

—Sir Henry Maine
Ancient Law, Ch. 5

Chapter Objectives

After studying this chapter, you should be able to:

1. Define contract.

2. List the elements necessary to form a valid contract.

3. Distinguish between bilateral and unilateral contracts.

4. Describe and distinguish between express and implied-in-fact contracts.

5. Describe and distinguish among valid, void, voidable, and unenforceable contracts.

Chapter Contents

- Definition of Contract
- Sources of Contract Law
- Classifications of Contracts
- Equity

Contracts are the basis of many of our daily activities. They provide the means for individuals and businesses to sell and otherwise transfer property, services, and other rights. The purchase of goods, such as books and automobiles, is based on sales contracts; the hiring of employees is based on service contracts; the lease of an apartment is based on a rental contract; the sale of goods and services over the Internet is based on electronic contracts. The list is almost endless. Without enforceable contracts, commerce would collapse.

Contracts are voluntarily entered into by parties. The terms of a contract become *private law* between the parties. One court has stated that "The contract between parties is the law between them and the courts are obliged to give legal effect to such contracts according to the true interests of the parties."[1]

Nevertheless, most contracts are performed without the aid of the court system. This is usually because the parties feel a moral duty to perform as promised. Although some contracts, such as illegal contracts, are not enforceable, most are **legally enforceable**.[2] This means that if a party fails to perform a contract, the other party may call upon the courts to enforce the contract.

This chapter introduces you to the study of traditional and Internet contract law. Such topics as the definition of *contract*, requirements for forming a contract, sources of contract law, and the various classifications of contracts are discussed.

> Contracts must not be the sports of an idle hour, mere matters of pleasantry and badinage, never intended by the parties to have any serious effect whatever.
>
> Lord Stowell
> *Dalrymple v. Dalrymple (1811)*

Definition of Contract

A *contract* is an agreement that is enforceable by a court of law or equity. A simple and widely recognized definition of *contract* is provided by the *Restatement (Second) of Contracts*: "A contract is a promise or a set of promises for the breach of which the law gives a remedy or the performance of which the law in some way recognizes a duty."[3]

Courthouse, Santa Barbara, California. Courts are often called upon to enforce contracts between contracting parties.

Exhibit 8.1

Parties to a Contract

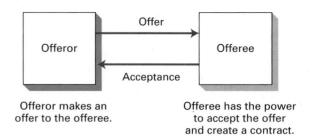

Offeror makes an
offer to the offeree.

Offeree has the power
to accept the offer
and create a contract.

Parties to a Contract

Every contract involves at least two parties. The **offeror** is the party who makes an offer to enter into a contract. The **offeree** is the party to whom the offer is made (see Exhibit 8.1). In making an offer, the offeror promises to do—or to refrain from doing—something. The offeree then has the power to create a contract by accepting the offeror's offer. A contract is created if the offer is accepted. No contract is created if the offer is not accepted.

Elements of a Contract

To be an enforceable contract, the following four basic requirements must be met:

1. *Agreement.* To have an enforceable contract, there must be an agreement between the parties. This requires an *offer* by the offeror and an *acceptance* of the offer by the offeree. There must be mutual assent by the parties (Chapter 9).
2. *Consideration.* The promise must be supported by a bargained-for consideration that is legally sufficient. Gift promises and moral obligations are not considered supported by valid consideration (Chapter 9).
3. *Contractual capacity.* The parties to a contract must have contractual capacity. Certain parties, such as persons adjudged insane, do not have contractual capacity (Chapter 10).
4. *Lawful object.* The object of the contract must be lawful. Contracts to accomplish illegal objects or contracts that are against public policy are void (Chapter 10).

Defenses to the Enforcement of a Contract

There are two *defenses* that may be raised to the enforcement of contracts. These defenses are as follows:

1. *Genuineness of assent.* The consent of the parties to create a contract must be genuine. If the consent is obtained by duress, undue influence, or fraud, there is no real consent (Chapter 11).
2. *Writing and form.* The law requires that certain contracts be in writing or in a certain form. Failure of these contracts to be in writing or to be in proper form may be raised against the enforcement of the contract (Chapter 11).

> Justice is the end of government. It is the end of civil society. It ever has been, and ever will be pursued, until it be obtained, or until liberty be lost in the pursuit.
>
> James Madison
> *The Federalist No. 51 (1788)*

Contemporary Environment

The Evolution of the Modern Law of Contracts

The use of contracts originally developed in ancient times. The common law of contracts developed in England around the fifteenth century. American contract law evolved from the English common law.

At first, the United States adopted a *laissez-faire* approach to the law of contracts. The central theme of this theory was

freedom of contract. The parties (such as consumers, shopkeepers, farmers, and traders) generally dealt with one another face-to-face, had equal knowledge and bargaining power, and had the opportunity to inspect the goods prior to sale. Contract terms were openly negotiated. There was little, if any, government regulation of the right to contract. This "pure," or **classical, law of contracts** produced objective rules, which, in turn, produced certainty and predictability in the enforcement of contracts. It made sense until the Industrial Revolution.

The Industrial Revolution changed many of the underlying assumptions of pure contract law. For example, as large corporations developed and gained control of crucial resources, the traditional balance of parties' bargaining power shifted: Large corporations now had the most power. The chain of distribution for goods also changed because (1) buyers did not have to deal face-to-face with sellers and (2) there was not always an opportunity to inspect the goods prior to sale.

Eventually, sellers began using *form contracts* that offered their goods to buyers on a take-it-or-leave-it basis. The majority of contracts in this country today are form contracts. Automobile contracts, mortgage contracts, sales contracts for consumer goods, and such are examples of form contracts.

Both federal and state governments have enacted statutes intended to protect consumers, debtors and others from unfair contracts. In addition, the courts have developed certain common law legal theories that allow some oppressive or otherwise unjust contracts to be avoided. Today, under this **modern law of contracts**, there is substantial government regulation of the right to contract. ■

Sources of Contract Law

There are several sources of contract law in the United States, including the *common law of contracts*, the *Uniform Commercial Code*, and the *Restatement (Second) of Contracts*. The following paragraphs explain these sources in more detail.

The Common Law of Contracts

A major source of contract law is the **common law of contracts**. The common law of contracts developed from early court decisions that became precedent for later decisions. There is a limited federal common law of contracts that applies to contracts made by the federal government. The larger and more prevalent body of common law has been developed from state court decisions. Thus, although the general principles remain the same throughout the country, there is some variation from state to state.

The Uniform Commercial Code (UCC)

Another major source of contract law is the **Uniform Commercial Code (UCC)** . The UCC, which was first drafted by the National Conference of Commissioners on Uniform State Law in 1952, has been amended several times. Its goal is to create a uniform system of commercial law among the 50 states. The provisions of the UCC normally take precedence over the common law of contracts (Chapters 14–17).

The UCC is divided into nine main articles. Every state has adopted at least part of the UCC. In the area of contract law, two of the major provisions of the UCC are:

- **Article 2 (Sales)**, which prescribes a set of uniform rules for the creation and enforcement of contracts for the sale of goods. These contracts are often referred to as **sales contracts**. For example, the sale of equipment is a sales contract subject to Article 2 of the UCC.
- **Article 2A (Leases)**, which prescribes a set of uniform rules for the creation and enforcement of contracts for the lease of goods. These contracts are referred to as **lease contracts**. For example, the lease of an automobile is a lease subject to Article 2A of the UCC.

The Restatement of the Law of Contracts

In 1932, the American Law Institute completed the **Restatement of the Law of Contracts**. The *Restatement* is a compilation of contract law principles as agreed upon by the drafters. The *Restatement*, which is currently in its second edition, is cited in this book as ***Restatement (Second) of Contracts***. Note that the *Restatement* is not law. However, lawyers and judges often refer to it for guidance in contract disputes because of its stature.

Objective Theory of Contracts

The **objective theory of contracts** holds that the intent to enter into an express or implied-in-fact contract is judged by the **reasonable person standard**. Would a hypothetical reasonable person conclude that the parties intended to create a contract after considering (1) the words and conduct of the parties and (2) the surrounding circumstances? For example, no valid contract results from offers that are made in jest, anger, or undue excitement.

Under the objective theory of contracts, the subjective intent of a party to enter into a contract is irrelevant.

The following case illustrates the application of the objective theory of contracts.

City of Everett, Washington v. Mitchell
631 P.2d 366, 1981 Wash. Lexis 1139 (1981)
Supreme Court of Washington

Case 8.1
Objective Theory of Contracts

Background and Facts

Al and Rosemary Mitchell owned a small secondhand store. On August 12, 1978, the Mitchells attended Alexander's Auction, where they frequently shopped to obtain merchandise for their business. While at the auction, they purchased a used safe for $50. They were told by the auctioneer that the inside compartment of the safe was locked and that no key could be found to unlock it. The safe was part of the Sumstad Estate. Several days after the auction, the Mitchells took the safe to a locksmith to have the locked compartment opened. When the locksmith opened the compartment, he found $32,207 in cash. The locksmith called the City of Everett Police, who impounded the money. The City of Everett commenced an interpleader action against the Sumstad Estate and the Mitchells. The trial court entered summary judgment in favor of Sumstad Estate. The court of appeals affirmed. The Mitchells appealed.

Issue

Was a contract formed between the seller and the buyer of the safe?

Court's Reasoning

The objective theory of contracts stresses the outward manifestation of assent made by the parties. In this case, evidence showed that the rule of the auction was that all sales were final.

Furthermore, the auctioneer made no statement reserving the rights to any contents of the safe. Under these circumstances, the court held that reasonable persons would conclude that the auctioneer manifested an objective intent to sell the safe and its contents, including the contents of the locked compartment. The subjective intention of the parties is irrelevant. The court stated: "If, however, it were proved by twenty bishops that either party, when he used the words, intended something else than the usual meaning which the law imposes upon them, he would still be held."

Decision and Remedy

The state supreme court held that under the objective theory of contracts, a contract was formed between the seller and the buyer of the safe. The court reversed the appelate court's grant of summary judgment to the Sumstad Estate and remanded the case to the trial court for entry of judgment in favor of the Mitchells.

Case Questions

Critical Legal Thinking   Does the objective theory of contracts work? Is it easy to define a "reasonable person"?

Business Ethics   Did the seller of the safe act ethically in alleging that no contract had been made with the Mitchells?

Contemporary Business   What do you think the economic consequences to business would be if the courts recognized a subjective theory of contracts?

Online Commerce & Internet Law
Uniform Electronic Commerce Act Adopted

As we entered the twenty-first century, a new economic shift brought the United States and the rest of the world into the Information Age. Computer technology and the use of the Internet increased dramatically. A new form of commerce—**electronic commerce**, or **e-commerce**—is flourishing. All sorts of goods and services are now sold over the Internet. You can purchase automobiles and children's toys, participate in auctions, purchase airline tickets, make hotel reservations, and purchase other goods and services over the Internet.

Much of the new cyberspace economy is based on electronic contracts and the licensing of computer information. E-commerce created problems for forming contracts over the Internet, enforcing e-commerce contracts, and providing consumer protection. To address these problems, the National Conference of

Commissioners on Uniform State Laws (a group of lawyers, judges, and legal scholars) drafted the **Uniform Computer Information Transactions Act (UCITA)**.

The UCITA establishes uniform legal rules for the formation and enforcement of electronic contracts and licenses. The UCITA addresses most of the legal issues that are encountered while conducting e-commerce over the Internet. The UCITA is a model act that does not become law until a state legislature adopts it as a statute for the state. Since its promulgation in July 1999, the UCITA has been adopted in whole or in part by many states. Because of the need for uniformity of e-commerce rules, the UCITA is becoming the basis for the creation and enforcement of cyberspace contracts and licenses. The UCITA is discussed in detail in Chapter 17. ■

Classifications of Contracts

There are several types of contracts. Each differs somewhat in formation, enforcement, performance, and discharge. The different types of contracts are discussed in the following paragraphs.

Bilateral and Unilateral Contracts

Contracts are either *bilateral* or *unilateral*, depending on what the offeree must do to accept the offeror's offer. A contract is **bilateral** if the offeror's promise is answered with the offeree's promise of acceptance. In other words, a bilateral contract is a "promise for a promise." This exchange of promises creates an enforceable contract. No act of performance is necessary to create a bilateral contract.

A contract is **unilateral** if the offeror's offer can be accepted only by the performance of an act by the offeree. There is no contract until the offeree performs the requested act. An offer to create a unilateral contract cannot be accepted by a promise to perform. It is a "promise for an act."

The language of the offeror's promise must be carefully scrutinized to determine whether it is an offer to create a bilateral or a unilateral contract. If there is any ambiguity as to which it is, it is presumed to be a bilateral contract.

Consider This Example   Suppose Mary Douglas, the owner of the Chic Dress Shop, says to Peter Jones, a painter, "If you promise to paint my store by July 1, I will pay you $3,000." Peter promises to do so. A bilateral contract was created at the moment Peter promised to paint the dress shop (a promise for a promise). If Peter fails to paint the store, he can be sued for whatever damages result from his breach of contract. Similarly, Peter can sue Mary if she refuses to pay him after he has performed as promised.

Business Brief

Bilateral and unilateral contracts are distinguished from one another according to the number of promises involved. Bilateral is "promise for promise." Unilateral is "promise for act."

However, if Mary had said, "If you paint my shop by July 1, I will pay you $3,000," the offer would have created a unilateral contract. The offer can be accepted only by the painter's performance of the requested act. If Peter does not paint the shop by July 1, there has been no acceptance and the painter cannot be sued for damages.

Incomplete or Partial Performance Problems can arise if the offeror in a unilateral contract attempts to revoke an offer after the offeree has begun performance. Generally, an offer to create a unilateral contract can be revoked by the offeror any time prior to the offeree's performance of the requested act. However, the offer cannot be revoked if the offeree has begun or has substantially completed performance. For example, suppose Alan Matthews tells Sherry Levine that he will pay her $5,000 if she finishes the Boston Marathon. Alan cannot revoke the offer once Sherry starts running the marathon.

Express and Implied-in-Fact Contracts

An *actual contract* (as distinguished from a quasi-contract, which is discussed later in this chapter) may be either *express* or *implied-in-fact*.

Express contracts are stated in oral or written words. Examples of such contracts include an oral agreement to purchase a neighbor's bicycle and a written agreement to buy an automobile from a dealership.

Implied-in-fact contracts are implied from the conduct of the parties. Implied-in-fact contracts leave more room for questions. The following elements must be established to create an implied-in-fact contract:

1. The plaintiff provided property or services to the defendant.
2. The plaintiff expected to be paid by the defendant for the property or services and did not provide the property or services gratuitously.
3. The defendant was given an opportunity to reject the property or services provided by the plaintiff but failed to do so.

In the following case, the court had to decide whether the plaintiffs could sue a defendant for breach of an implied-in-fact contract.

Wrench LLC v. Taco Bell Corporation
256 F.3d 446, 2001 U.S.App. Lexis 15097 (2003)
United States Court of Appeals, Sixth Circuit

Case 8.2

Implied-in-Fact Contract

Background and Facts

Thomas Rinks and Joseph Shields created the "Psycho Chihuahua" cartoon character, which they promote, market, and license through their company, Wrench LLC. The Psycho Chihuahua is a clever, feisty, cartoon character dog with an attitude; a self-confident, edgy, cool dog who knows what he wants and will not back down. In June 1996, Rinks and Shields attended a licensing trade show in New York City, where they were approached by two Taco Bell employees, Rudy Pollak, a vice president, and Ed Alfaro, a creative services manager. Taco Bell owns and operates a nationwide chain of fast-food Mexican restaurants. Pollak and Alfaro expressed interest in the Psycho Chihuahua character for Taco Bell advertisements because they thought his character would appeal to Taco Bell's core consumers, males aged 18 to 24. Pollak and Alfaro obtained some Psycho Chihuahua materials to take back with them to Taco Bell's headquarters.

Later, Alfaro contacted Rinks and asked him to create art boards combining Psycho Chihuahua with the Taco Bell name and image. Rinks and Shields prepared art boards and sent them to Alfaro, along with Psycho Chihuahua T-shirts, hats, and stickers. Alfaro showed these materials to Taco Bell's vice president of brand management as well as to Taco Bell's outside advertising agency. Alfaro tested the Psycho Chihuahua marketing concept with focus groups. Rinks suggested to Alfaro that instead of using the cartoon version of Psycho Chihuahua in its advertisements, Taco Bell should use a live Chihuahua dog manipulated by computer graphic imaging, who had the personality of Psycho Chihuahua and a love for Taco Bell food. In early March 1997, Rinks and Shields gave a formal presentation of this concept to Taco Bell's marketing department. One idea presented by Rinks and Shields was a commercial in which a male Chihuahua dog passed by a female Chihuahua dog in order to get to Taco Bell food. Taco Bell did not enter into an express contract with Wrench LLC, Rinks, or Shields.

On March 18, 1997, Taco Bell hired a new outside advertising agency, Chiat/Day. Taco Bell gave Chiat/Day materials received from Rinks and Shields regarding the Psycho Chihuahua. On June 2, 1997, Chiat/Day proposed using a Chihuahua in Taco Bell commercials. One commercial had a male Chihuahua passing up a female Chihuahua to get to a person seated on a bench eating Taco Bell food. Chiat/Day says that it conceived these ideas by itself. In July 1997, Taco Bell aired its first Chihuahua commercial in the United States, and it became an instant success and the basis of its advertising. Taco Bell paid nothing to Wrench LLC or to Rinks and Shields. Plaintiffs Wrench LLC, Rinks, and Shields sued defendant Taco Bell to recover damages for breach of an implied-in-fact contract. The district court granted summary judgment in favor of Taco Bell. Wrench LLC, Rinks, and Shields appealed.

Issue

Do the plaintiffs Wrench LLC, Rinks, and Shields state a cause of action for the breach of an implied-in-fact contract?

Court's Reasoning

The U.S. Court of Appeals held that although no specific dollar numbers were ever mentioned, Taco Bell understood that if it used the Psycho Chihuahua concept, it would have to pay the plaintiffs for doing so. The court noted that the plaintiffs' state law implied-in-fact contract claim is for Taco Bell's breach of this promise to pay for the plaintiffs' creative work and ideas. The Court of Appeals stated that there was strong circumstantial evidence proving that Taco Bell used the plaintiffs' Psycho Chihuahua concept.

Decision and Remedy

The U.S. Court of Appeals held that the plaintiffs had stated a proper cause of action against defendant Taco Bell for breach of an implied-in-fact contract. The Court of Appeals reversed the judgment of the district court and remanded the case for trial.

Case Questions

Critical Legal Thinking   What does the doctrine of implied-in-fact contract provide? Explain.

Business Ethics   Did Taco Bell act ethically in this case? Did Chiat/Day act ethically in this case?

Contemporary Business   Do you think there was an implied-in-fact contract in this case? If so, what damages should be awarded to the plaintiffs?

Quasi-Contracts (Implied-in-Law Contracts)   The equitable doctrine of **quasi-contract**, also called **implied-in-law contract**, allows a court to award monetary damages to a plaintiff for providing work or services to a defendant even though no actual contract existed between the parties. Recovery is generally based on the reasonable value of the services received by the defendant.

The doctrine is intended to prevent *unjust enrichment* and *unjust detriment*. It does not apply where there is an enforceable contract between the parties. A quasi-contract is imposed where (1) one person confers a benefit on another who retains the benefit and (2) it would be unjust not to require that person to pay for the benefit received.

Consider This Example   Heather is driving her automobile when she is involved in a serious automobile accident in which she is knocked unconscious. She is rushed to Metropolitan Hospital, where the doctors and other staff perform the necessary medical procedures to save her life. Heather comes out of her coma, and after recovering is released from the hospital. Subsequently, Metropolitan Hospital sends Heather a bill for its services. The charges are reasonable. Under the doctrine of quasi-contract, Heather is responsible for any charges that are not covered by her insurance coverage.

Formal and Informal Contracts

Contracts may be classified as either *formal* or *informal*. **Formal contracts** are contracts that require a special form or method of creation. The *Restatement (Second) of Contracts* identifies the following types of formal contracts[4]:

- *Negotiable instruments.* Negotiable instruments, which include checks, drafts, notes, and certificates of deposit, are special forms of contracts recognized by the UCC. They require a special form and language for their creation and must meet certain requirements for their transfer.
- *Letters of credit.* A letter of credit is an agreement by the issuer of the letter to pay a sum of money upon the receipt of an invoice and other documents. Letters of credit are governed by the UCC.
- *Recognizances.* In a recognizance, a party acknowledges in court that he or she will pay a specified sum of money if a certain event occurs. A bail bond is an example of a recognizance.
- *Contracts under seal.* This type of contract is one to which a seal (usually a wax seal) is attached. Although no state currently requires contracts to be under seal, a few states provide that no consideration is necessary if a contract is made under seal.

All contracts that do not qualify as formal contracts are called **informal contracts** (or **simple contracts**). The term is a misnomer. Valid informal contracts (e.g., leases, sales contracts, service contracts) are fully enforceable and may be sued upon if breached. They are called informal contracts only because no special form or method is required for their creation.

Valid, Void, Voidable, and Unenforceable Contracts

Contract law places contracts in the following categories:

1. *Valid contract.* A **valid contract** meets all the essential elements to establish a contract. In other words, it must (1) consist of an agreement between the parties, (2) be supported by legally sufficient consideration, (3) be between parties with contractual capacity, and (4) accomplish a lawful object. Valid contracts are enforceable by at least one of the parties.
2. *Void contract.* A **void contract** has no legal effect. It is as if no contract had ever been created. For example, a contract to commit a crime is void. If a contract is void, neither party is obligated to perform and neither party can enforce the contract.
3. *Voidable contract.* A **voidable contract** is one where at least one party has the *option* to avoid his or her contractual obligations. If the contract is avoided, both parties are released from their obligations under the contract. If the party with the option chooses to ratify the contract, both parties must fully perform their obligations. With certain exceptions, contracts may be voided by minors; insane persons;

intoxicated persons; persons acting under duress, undue influence or fraud; and cases involving mutual mistake.

4. *Unenforceable contract.* With an **unenforceable contract**, there is some legal defense to the enforcement of the contract. For example, if a contract is required to be in writing under the Statute of Frauds but is not, the contract is unenforceable. The parties may voluntarily perform a contract that is unenforceable.

Executed and Executory Contracts

A completed contract—that is, one that has been fully performed on both sides—is called an **executed contract**. A contract that has not been performed by both sides is called an **executory contract**. Contracts that have been fully performed by one side but not by the other are classified as executory contracts.

Consider These Examples (1) Suppose Elizabeth Andrews signs a contract to purchase a new Jaguar automobile from Ace Motors. She has not yet paid for the car and Ace Motors has not yet delivered it. This is an executory contract. (2) Assume that the car was paid for, but Ace Motors has not yet delivered the car. Here, the contract is executed by Elizabeth but is executory as to Ace Motors. This is an executory contract. (3) Assume that Ace Motors now delivers the car to Elizabeth. The contract has been fully performed by both parties. It is an executed contract.

◼ Concept Summary _Classifications of Contracts_

Formation	1. **Bilateral contract.** A promise for a promise.
	2. **Unilateral contract.** A promise for an act.
	3. **Express contract.** A contract expressed in oral or written words.
	4. **Implied-in-fact contract.** A contract inferred from the conduct of the parties.
	5. **Quasi-contract.** A contract implied by law to prevent unjust enrichment.
	6. **Formal-contract.** A contract that requires a special form or method of creation.
	7. **Informal-contract.** A contract that requires no special form or method of creation.
Enforceability	1. **Valid contract.** A contract that meets all the essential elements of establishing a contract.
	2. **Void contract.** No contract exists.
	3. **Voidable contract.** A contract for which a party has the option of voiding or enforcing the contract.
	4. **Unenforceable contract.** A contract that cannot be enforced because of a legal defense.
Performance	1. **Executed contract.** A contract that is fully performed on both sides.
	2. **Executory contract.** A contract that is not fully performed by one or both parties.

Equity

Recall that two separate courts developed in England: the courts of law and the Chancery Courts (or courts of equity). The equity courts developed a set of maxims based on fairness, equality, moral rights, and natural law that were applied in settling disputes. **Equity** was resorted to when (1) an award of money damages "at law" would not be the proper remedy or (2) fairness required the application of equitable principles. Today, in most states of the United States, the courts of law and equity have been merged into one court. In an action "in equity," the judge decides the equitable issue; there is no right to a jury trial in an equitable action. The doctrine of equity is sometimes applied in contract cases.

Business Ethics

Equity Saves Contracting Party

The courts usually interpret a valid contract as a solemn promise to perform. This view of the sanctity of a contract can cause an ethical conflict. Consider the following case.

In 1975, a landlord leased a motel he owned to lessees for a 10-year period. The lessees had an option to extend the lease for an additional 10 years, commencing on March 1, 1985. To do so, they had to give written notice to the landlord on or before December 1, 1984. The lease provided for forfeiture of all furniture, fixtures, and equipment installed by the lessees, free of any liens, upon termination of the lease.

From 1975 to 1985, the lessees devoted most of their assets and a great deal of their energy building up the business. During this time, they transformed a disheveled, unrated motel into a AAA three-star operation. With the landlord's knowledge, the lessees made extensive long-term improvements that greatly increased the value of both the property and the business. The landlord knew that the lessees had obtained long-term financing for the improvements that would extend well beyond the first 10-year term of the lease. The landlord also knew that the only source of income the lessees had to pay for these improvements was the income generated from the motel business. The lessees told the landlord in a conversation that they intended to extend the lease.

The lessees had instructed their accountant to exercise the option by December 1, 1984. Despite reminders from the lessees, the accountant failed to give the written notice by December 1, 1984. On December 13, 1984, as soon as they discovered the mistake, the lessees personally delivered written notice of renewal of the option to the landlord, who rejected it as late and instituted a lawsuit for unlawful detainer to evict the lessees.

The trial and appellate courts held in favor of the lessees. They rejected the landlord's argument for the strict adherence to the deadline for giving written notice of renewal of the lease. Instead, the courts granted **equitable relief** and permitted the late renewal notice. The court reasoned that "there is only minimal delay in giving notice, the harm to the lessor is slight, and the hardship to the lessee is severe." [*Romasanta v. Mitton*, 234 Cal. Rptr. 729, 1987 Cal. App. Lexis 1428 (Cal. App. 1987)]

1. Did the landlord act ethically in this case?
2. Should the court have applied equity and saved the lessees from their mistake? Or should they have been held to the terms of the lease? ■

International Law

The United Nations Convention on Contracts for the International Sale of Goods

The United Nations Convention on Contracts for the International Sale of Goods (CISG) came into effect on January 1, 1988, climaxing more than 50 years of negotiations. The CISG is the work of more than 60 countries and several international organizations. Many of its provisions are remarkably similar to those of the American Uniform Commercial Code, for example. It incorporates rules from all the major legal systems. It has, accordingly, received widespread support from developed, developing, and Communist countries. Because the United States has ratified the CISG, Americans engaged in sales overseas need to be aware of the CISG.

The CISG applies to contracts for the international sale of goods. That is, the buyer and seller must have their places of business in different countries. In addition, either (1) both of the nations must be parties to the convention or (2) the contract must specify that the CISG controls. The contracting parties may agree to exclude (i.e., opt out of) or modify its application. ■

Singapore. The United Nations CISG provides rules for the enforcement of contracts for the international sale of goods if (1) the nations of the contracting parties recognize the CISG and (2) the international contract specifies that the CISG has control.

Chapter Summary

Definition of Contract, p. 171

Definition of *Contract*

A contract is "a promise or a set of promises for the breach of which the law gives a remedy or the performance of which the law in some way recognizes a duty."

Parties to a Contract

1. *Offeror.* The party who makes an offer to enter into a contract is the offeror.
2. *Offeree.* The party to whom the offer is made is the offeree.

Elements of a Contract

1. Agreement
2. Consideration
3. Contractual capacity
4. Lawful object

Defenses to the Enforcement of a Contract

1. Genuineness of assent
2. Writing and form

Sources of Contract Law, p. 173

Sources of Contract Law

1. Common law of contracts (law)
2. Uniform Commercial Code (law)
3. *Restatement (Second) of Contracts* (advisory only, not law)

Theories of Contract Law

1. *Classical law of contracts.* According to this theory; parties were free to negotiate contract terms without government interference.
2. *Modern law of contracts.* According to this theory; parties may negotiate contract terms subject to government regulations.

Classifications of Contracts, p. 175

Formation

1. **Bilateral contract.** This is a promise for a promise.

2. **Unilateral contract.** This is a promise for an act.

3. **Express contract.** This is a contract expressed in oral or written words.

4. **Implied-in-fact contract.** This is a contract implied from the conduct of the parties.

5. **Quasi-contract.** This is a contract implied by law to prevent unjust enrichment and unjust detriment.

6. **Formal contract.** This is a contract that requires a special form or method for creation.

7. **Informal contract.** This is a contract that requires no special form or method for creation.

Enforceability

1. **Valid contract.** A valid contract meets all the essential elements to establish a contract.

2. **Void contract.** No contract exists.

3. **Voidable contract.** A voidable contract is one where one or both parties have the option of avoiding or enforcing the contract.

4. **Unenforceable contract.** An unenforceable contract is a contract that cannot be enforced because of a legal defense.

Performance

1. **Executed contract.** A contract that is fully performed on both sides is called an executed contract.

2. **Executory contract.** A contract that is not fully performed by one or both parties is called an executory contract.

Equity, p. 180

Equity

Equity is a doctrine that permits judges to make decisions based on fairness, equality, moral rights, and natural law.

Internet Exercises and Case Questions

Working the Web Internet Exercises

Activities

1. Go to **www.findlaw.com** and review the extensive material on contracts. Determine the statute of limitations on written contracts in your jurisdiction.

2. Review **www.perkinscoie.com** as an example of one law firm's Web site. Examine the materials collected there on contract law by using the search feature for "contracts." How many different kinds can you find?

3. For international sales contracts, compare the CISG and the UCC by visiting the Web site **www.cisg.law.pace.edu**. It contains the entire text of the CISG and related information.

4. What is the rule regarding contractual capacity of minors in your jurisdiction? Use FindLaw again to locate the statute. Hint: Using FindLaw, narrow your search by selecting your state first. Then enter your search terms.

Critical Legal Thinking Cases

8.1 Objective Theory of Contracts   On January 23, 1974, G. S. Adams, Jr., vice president of the Washington Bank & Trust Co., met with Bruce Bickham. An agreement was reached whereby Bickham agreed to do his personal and corporate banking business with the bank and the bank agreed to loan Bickham money at 7 1/2 percent interest per annum. Bickham would have 10 years to repay the loans. From January 1974 to September 1976, the bank made several loans to Bickham at 7 1/2 percent interest. In September 1976, Adams resigned from the bank. The bank then notified Bickham that general economic changes made it necessary to charge a higher rate of interest on both outstanding and new loans. Bickham sued the bank for breach of contract. Was the contract a bilateral or a unilateral contract? Does Bickham win? [*Bickham v. Washington Bank & Trust Company*, 515 So.2d 457, 1987 La. App. Lexis 10442 (La. App. 1987)]

8.2 Implied-in-Fact Contract   From October 1964 through May 1970, Lee Marvin, an actor, lived with Michelle Marvin. They were not married. In May 1970, Lee Marvin compelled Michelle Marvin to leave his household. He continued to support her until November 1971 but thereafter refused to provide further support. During their time together, Lee Marvin earned substantial income and acquired property, including motion-picture rights worth over $1 million. Michelle Marvin brought an action against Lee Marvin, alleging that an implied-in-fact contract existed between them and that she was entitled to half of the property that they had acquired while living together. She claimed that she had given up a lucrative career as an entertainer and singer to be a full-time companion, homemaker, house-keeper, and cook. Can an implied-in-fact contract result from the conduct of unmarried persons who live together? [*Marvin v. Marvin, 557* P.2d 106, 134 Cal.Rptr. 815, 1976 Cal. Lexis 377 (Cal. 1976)]

Business Ethics Cases

8.3 Business Ethics   On Sunday, October 6, 1974, the Lewiston Lodge of Elks sponsored a golf tournament at the Fairlawn Country Club in Poland, Maine. For promotional pur-poses, Marcel Motors, an automobile dealership, agreed to give any golfer who shot a hole-in-one a new 1974 Dodge Colt. Fliers advertising the tournament were posted in the Elks Club and sent to potential participants. On the day of the tourna-ment, the 1974 Dodge Colt was parked near the clubhouse with one of the posters conspicuously displayed on the vehicle. Alphee Chenard, Jr., who had seen the promotional literature regarding the hole-in-one offer, registered for the tournament and paid the requisite entrance fee. While playing the thirteenth hole of the golf course, in the presence of the other members of his foursome, Chenard shot a hole-in-one. When Marcel Motors refused to tender the automobile, Chenard sued for breach of contract. Was the contract a bilateral or a unilateral contract? Does Chenard win? Was it ethical for Marcel Motors to refuse to give the automobile to Chenard? [*Chenard v. Marcel Motors*, 387 A.2d 596, 1978 Me. Lexis 911 (Maine 1978)]

8.4 Business Ethics   Loren Vranich, a doctor practicing under the corporate name Family Health Care, P.C., entered into a written employment contract to hire Dennis Winkel. The con-tract provided for an annual salary, insurance benefits, and other employment benefits. Another doctor, Dr. Quan, also practiced with Dr. Vranich. About nine months later, when Dr. Quan left the practice, Vranich and Winkel entered into an oral modifica-tion of their written contract whereby Winkel was to receive a higher salary and a profit-sharing bonus. During the next year Winkel received the increased salary. However, a disagreement arose, and Winkel sued to recover the profit-sharing bonus. Under Montana law, a written contract can be altered only in writing or by an executed oral agreement. Dr. Vranich argued that the contract could not be enforced because it was not in writing. Does Winkel receive the profit-sharing bonus? Did Dr. Vranich act ethically in raising the defense that the contract was not in writing? [*Winkel v. Family Health Care, P.C.*, 668 P.2d 208, 1983 Mont. Lexis 785 (Mont. 1983)]

Briefing the Case Writing Assignment

Read Case A.8 in the Case Appendix [*Mark Realty, Inc. v. Rogness*]. This case is excerpted from the appellate court's opinion. Review and brief the case. In your brief, be sure to answer the following questions.

1. Who is the plaintiff? Who is the defendant?

2. Why did it make a difference if the court found the con-tract to be unilateral or bilateral? Who would win in each situation?

3. Which party did the appellate court find in favor of? What evidence did the court cite in reaching its conclusion?

4. How might an owner of property protect him- or herself from paying a broker's commission if the owner sold the property him- or herself?

Endnotes

1. *Rebstock v. Birthright Oil & Gas Co.*, 406 So.2d 636, 1981 La.App. Lexis 5242 (La.App. 1981).
2. *Restatement (Second) of Contracts*, § 1.
3. *Restatement (Second) of Contracts*, § 1.
4. *Restatement (Second) of Contracts*, § 6.

Agreement and Consideration

9

"When I use a word," Humpty Dumpty said, in rather a scornful tone, "it means just what I choose it to mean—neither more nor less."

"The question is," said Alice, "whether you can make words mean so many different things."

"The question is," said Humpty Dumpty, "which is to be master—that's all."

—Lewis Carroll
Alice's Adventures in Wonderland (1865)

Chapter Objectives

After studying this chapter, you should be able to:

1. Define offer and acceptance.
2. Describe how offers are terminated by actions of the parties.
3. Define counteroffer and describe the effects of counteroffers.
4. Define consideration.
5. Analyze whether contracts are lacking in consideration.

Chapter Contents

- Agreement
- Offer
- Acceptance
- Consideration

Contracts are voluntary agreements between the parties. One party makes an offer, and the other accepts it. Without mutual assent, there is no contract. Assent may be expressly evidenced by the words of the parties or implied from their conduct.

To be enforceable, a contract must be supported by "consideration," which is broadly defined as something of legal value. It can consist of money, property, the provision of services, the forbearance of a right, or anything else of value. Most contracts that are not supported by consideration are not enforceable. The parties may voluntarily perform a contract that is lacking in consideration, however.

This chapter discusses the primary elements of a contract: agreement (i.e., offer and acceptance) and consideration.

> A contract is a mutual promise.
>
> William Paley
> *The Principles of Moral and Political Philosophy (1784)*

Agreement

Agreement is the manifestation by two or more persons of the substance of a contract. It requires an *offer* and an *acceptance*. The process of reaching an agreement usually proceeds as follows. Prior to entering into a contract, the parties may engage in preliminary negotiations about price, time of performance, and such. At some point during these negotiations, one party makes an **offer**. The person who makes the offer is called the **offeror**, and the person to whom the offer is made is called the **offeree**. The offer sets forth the terms under which the offeree is willing to enter into the contract. The offeree has the power to create an agreement by accepting the offer.

Offer

Section 24 of the *Restatement (Second) of Contracts* defines an **offer** as "the manifestation of willingness to enter into a bargain, so made as to justify another person in understanding that his assent to that bargain is invited and will conclude it." The following three elements are required for an offer to be effective:

1. The offeror must *objectively intend* to be bound by the offer.
2. The terms of the offer must be definite or reasonably *certain*.
3. The offer must be *communicated* to the offeree.

Objective Intent

The intent to enter a contract is determined using the **objective theory of contracts**, that is, whether a reasonable person viewing the circumstances would conclude that the parties intended to be legally bound.

The statement, "I will buy your building for $2 million" is a valid offer because it indicates the offeror's present intent to contract. A question such as "Are you interested in selling your building for $2 million?" is not an offer. It is an invitation to make an offer or an invitation to negotiate.

Offers that are made in jest, anger, or undue excitement do not include the necessary objective intent. For example, suppose the owner of Company A has lunch with the owner of Company B. In the course of their conversation, Company A's owner exclaims in frustration, "For $2 I'd sell the whole computer division!" An offer such as that cannot result in a valid contract.

> There is grim irony in speaking of freedom of contract of those who, because of their economic necessities, give their service for less than is needful to keep body and soul together.
>
> Harlan Fiske Stone
> *Morehead v. N.Y. ex rel. Tipaldo (1936)*

Definiteness of Terms

The terms of an offer must be clear enough for the offeree to be able to decide whether to accept or reject the terms of the offer. If the terms are indefinite, the courts cannot enforce the contract or determine an appropriate remedy for its breach.

To be considered definite, an offer (and contract) generally must contain the following terms (1) identification of the parties, (2) identification of the subject matter and quantity, (3) consideration to be paid, and (4) time of performance. Complex contracts usually state additional terms.

Implied Terms

The common law of contracts required an exact specification of contract terms. If one essential term was omitted, the courts would hold that no contract had been made. This rule was inflexible.

The modern law of contracts is more lenient. The *Restatement (Second) of Contracts* merely requires that the terms of the offer be "reasonably certain."[1] Accordingly, the court can supply a missing term if a reasonable term can be implied.[2] The definition of *reasonable* depends on the circumstances. Terms that are supplied in this way are called **implied terms**.

Generally, time of performance can be implied. Price can be implied if there is a market or source from which to determine the price of the item or service—for example, the "blue book" for an automobile price, the New York Stock Exchange for a stock price. The parties or subject matter of the contract usually cannot be implied if an item or a service is unique or personal, such as the construction of a house or the performance of a professional sports contract.

Business Ethics

Owner of Mighty Morphin Power Rangers Battles Logo Designer

Mighty Morphin Power Rangers was a phenomenal success as a television series. The Power Rangers battled to save the universe from all sorts of diabolical plots and bad guys. They were also featured in a profitable line of toys and garments bearing the Power Rangers' logo. The Power Rangers' name and logo are known to millions of children and their parents worldwide. The claim of ownership of the logo for the Power Rangers ended up in a battle in a courtroom.

David Dees is a designer who works as d.b.a. David Dees Illustration. Saban Entertainment, Inc. (Saban), which owns the copyright and trademark to Power Rangers figures and the name "Power Ranger," hired Dees as an independent contractor to design a logo for the Power Rangers. The contract signed by the parties was titled "Work-for-Hire/Independent Contractor Agreement." The contract was drafted by Saban with the help of its attorneys; Dees signed the agreement without the representation of legal counsel.

Dees designed the logo currently used for the Power Rangers and was paid $250 to transfer his copyright ownership in the logo. Subsequently, Dees sued Saban to recover damages for copyright and trademark infringement. Saban defended, arguing that Dees was bound by the agreement he had signed.

The trial court agreed with Saban, finding that the "Work-for-Hire/Independent Contractor Agreement" was an enforceable contract between the parties and that Dees had transferred his ownership interests in the logo to Saban. Dees appealed. The court of appeals affirmed the judgment for Saban, stating, "The disputed agreement transferred plaintiff's copyright in the Mighty Morphin Power Rangers' logo with as much specificity as the law requires." The court found that a contract is a contract is a contract, at least in this case. Dees's appeal to the U.S. Supreme Court was denied. [*Dees, d/b/a David Dees Illustration v. Saban Entertainment, Inc.*, 131 F.3d 146, 1997 U.S. App. Lexis 39173 (1997)]

1. Did Dees act ethically by suing for more money?
2. Should contracts be enforced as written, even though it is later discovered that one party benefited substantially more than the other party to the contract? ■

Communication

An offer cannot be accepted if it is not communicated to the offeree by the offeror or a representative or an agent of the offeror. For example, suppose Mr. Jones, the CEO of Ace Corporation, wants to sell a manufacturing division to Baker Corporation. He puts the offer in writing, but he does not send it. Assume that Mr. Griswald, the CEO of Baker Corporation, visits Mr. Jones and sees the written offer lying on Jones's desk. Griswald tells his CEO about the offer. Because Mr. Jones never communicated the offer to the CEO of Baker Corporation, there is no offer to be accepted.

Advertisements

Advertisements for the sale of goods, even at specific prices, generally are treated as *invitations to make an offer*. For example, catalogs, price lists, quotation sheets, offering circulars, and other sales materials are viewed in the same way. This rule is intended to protect advertiser-sellers from the unwarranted breach of contract suits for nonperformance that would otherwise arise if the seller ran out of the advertised goods.

There is one exception to this rule: An advertisement is considered an offer if it is so definite or specific that it is apparent that the advertiser has the present intent to bind himself or herself to the terms of the advertisement. For example, an automobile dealer's advertisement to sell a "previously owned maroon 2000 Lexus 400 SC, serial no. 3210674, $25,000" is an offer. Because the advertisement identifies the exact automobile for sale, the first person to accept the offer owns the automobile.

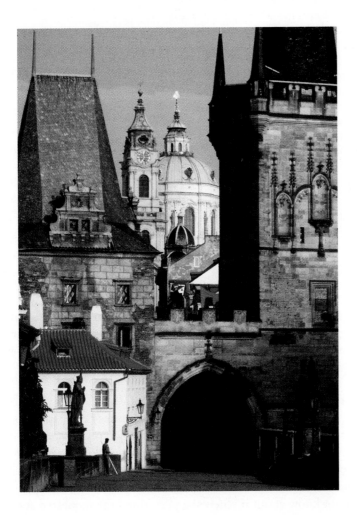

Prague, Czech Republic.
International trade is often governed by contracts between businesses or parties from different nations.

In the following case, the court had to decide whether an advertisement was a solicitation of an offer or an offer.

Mesaros v. United States
845 F.2d 1576, 1988 U.S. App. Lexis 6055 (1988)
United States Court of Appeals, Federal Circuit

Case 9.1
Solicitation to Make an Offer

Background and Facts

In July 1985, the U.S. Congress directed the Secretary of the Treasury to mint and sell a stated number of specially minted commemorative coins to raise funds to restore and renovate the Statue of Liberty. In November and December 1985, the U.S. Mint mailed advertising materials to persons, including Mary and Anthony C. Mesaros, husband and wife, that described the various types of coins that were to be issued. Payment could be made by check, money order, or credit card. The materials included an order form. Directly above the space provided on this form for the customer's signature was the following: "YES, Please accept my order for the U.S. Liberty Coins I have indicated." On November 26, 1985, Mary Mesaros forwarded to the mint a credit-card order of $1,675 for certain coins, including the $5 gold coin. All credit-card orders were forwarded by the Mint to Mellon Bank in Pittsburgh, Pennsylvania, for verification, which took a period of time. Meanwhile, cash orders were filled immediately, and orders by check were filled as the checks cleared. The issuance of 500,000 gold coins was exhausted before Mesaros's credit-card order could be filled. The Mint sent a letter to the Mesaroses notifying them of this fact. The gold coin increased in value by 200 percent within the first few months of 1986. On May 23, 1986, Mary and Anthony C. Mesaros filed a class action lawsuit against the United States, seeking in the alternative either damages for breach of contract or a decree of mandamus ordering the Mint to deliver the gold coins to the plaintiffs. The district court held for the Mint. The Mesaroses appealed.

Issue

Was the United States Mint's advertisement a solicitation of an offer or an offer?

Court's Reasoning

It is well established that materials such as those mailed to prospective customers by the Mint are no more than advertisements or invitations to deal. They are mere solicitations for offers that create no power of acceptance in the recipient. The court stated:

Generally, it is considered unreasonable for a person to believe that advertisements and solicitations are offers that bind the advertiser. Otherwise, the advertiser could be bound by an excessive number of contracts requiring delivery of goods far in excess of amounts available. That is particularly true in the instant case where the gold coins were limited to 500,000 by the Act of Congress. We conclude that a thorough reading, construction, and interpretation of the materials sent to the plaintiffs by the Mint makes clear that the contention of the plaintiffs that they reasonably believed the materials were intended as an offer is unreasonable as a matter of law.

Decision and Remedy

The court of appeals held that the advertising materials sent out by the U.S. Mint were a solicitation to make an offer and not an offer. Therefore, the Mint wins.

Case Questions

Critical Legal Thinking Should an advertisement be treated as an offer instead of as an invitation to make an offer? Why or why not?

Business Ethics Do you think the Mesaroses acted ethically by suing the Mint?

Contemporary Business Would it cause any problems for businesses if advertisements were considered offers? Explain.

Rewards

An offer to pay a **reward** (e.g., for the return of lost property or the capture of a criminal) is an offer to form a unilateral contract. To be entitled to collect the reward, the offeree must (1) have knowledge of the reward offer prior to completing the requested act and (2) perform the requested act.

Consider This Example John Anderson accidentally leaves a briefcase containing $500,000 in negotiable bonds on a subway train. He places newspaper ads stating "$5,000 reward for return of briefcase left on a train in Manhattan on January 10, 2002, at approximately 10 A.M. Call 212-555-6789." Helen Smith, who is unaware of the offer, finds the briefcase. She reads the luggage tag containing Anderson's name, address, and telephone number, and she returns the briefcase to him. She is not entitled to the reward money because she did not know about it when she performed the requested act.

Auctions

At an auction, the seller offers goods for sale through an auctioneer. Unless otherwise expressly stated, an auction is considered an **auction with reserve**, that is, it is an invitation to make an offer. The seller retains the right to refuse the highest bid and withdraw the goods from sale. A contract is formed only when the auctioneer strikes the gavel down or indicates acceptance by some other means. The bidder may withdraw his or her bid prior to that time.

If an auction is expressly announced to be an **auction without reserve**, the participants reverse the roles: The seller is the offeror, and the bidders are the offerees. The seller must accept the highest bid and cannot withdraw the goods from sale. A seller who sets a minimum bid has to sell the item only if the highest bid is equal to or greater than the minimum bid.

In the following case, the court addressed the issue of an auction.

Lin v. The.TV Corporation International

99 Cal.App.4th 684, 121 Cal.Rptr.2d 323, 2002 Cal.App. Lexis 4315 (2002)
Supreme Court of California

Case 9.2
Auction

Background and Facts

The island nation of Tuvalu was awarded the top-level domain name "tv." Thus, Tuvalu controlled who could use domain names with the suffix "tv" on the Internet. For example, if a person named Jones acquired the suffix tv, her domain name on the Internet would be "jones.tv." Tuvalu hired The.TV Corporation International, a California corporation doing business under the name dotTV, to sell Internet names bearing the top-level domain name "tv." In April 2000, dotTV posted the name "golf.tv" for sale on its Web site, to be sold to the highest bidder. Je Ho Lim, a resident of South Korea, submitted the highest bid of $1,010 and authorized dotTV to charge his credit card for the amount of the bid. dotTV sent the following e-mail to Lim confirming the sale:

DotTV—The New Frontier on the Internet
E-Mail Invoice for Domain Registration
NAME: Je Ho Lim
Congratulations!
You have won the auction for the following domain name:
    DOMAIN NAME: — —golf
SUBSCRIPTION LENGTH: 2 years, starts from activation date
Amount (US$): $1,010 (first year registration fee)
Please remember that the annual registration fee increases by 5 annually.
You have the guaranteed right to renew the registration indefinitely.
DotTV expects to charge your card and activate the registered domain name By May 15, 2000.
See ya on the new frontier of the Internet!
Lou Kerner CEO, dotTV Corporation www.TV

Shortly thereafter, dotTV sent another e-mail to Lim that stated "we have decided to release you from your bid" and that Lim should disregard the prior e-mail because of "an e-mail error that occurred." Later, dotTV publicly offered the domain name "golf.tv" with a beginning bid of $1 million. DotTV claimed that its original

e-mail to Lim concerned a different domain name "— —golf" instead of "golf." Lim countered that characters such as two dashes ("— —") are not recognized on the Internet and therefore the name "— —golf" is an invalid domain name. When dotTV refused to transfer the domain name "golf.tv" to Lim, Lim sued dotTV for breach of contract. The trial court dismissed Lim's case against dotTV. Lim appealed.

Issue

Did Lim properly state a cause of action for breach of contract against dotTV?

Court's Reasoning

The court of appeals noted that there is a presumption that auctions are with reserve unless there is a contrary manifestation. The court stated that if dotTV's Web site announcement of the auction was an invitation to make an offer, then plaintiff Lim's bid was an offer, and that this offer was accepted by dotTV when it sent its confirmation e-mail to Lim. The court rejected dotTV's argument that Lim had purchased the domain name "— —golf" and not "golf" because the name "— —golf" was not a valid Internet domain name.

Decision and Remedy

The court of appeals held that plaintiff Lim had properly pleaded a cause of action against defendant dotTV for breach of contract and reinstated Lim's case against dotTV.

Case Questions

Critical Legal Thinking   Explain the difference between an auction with reserve and an auction without reserve. Which is presumed if there is no other statement to the contrary?

Business Ethics   Did dotTV act ethically in this case? Why do you think that dotTV reneged on its e-mail confirmation to Lim?

Contemporary Business   Are Internet domain names valuable? How do you register an Internet domain name?

Concept Summary   *Types of Auctions*

Type	Offer
Auction with reserve	No. It is an invitation to make an offer. Because the bidder is the offeror, the seller (the offeree) may refuse to sell the goods. An auction is with reserve unless otherwise stated.
Auction without reserve	Yes. The seller is the offeror and must sell the goods to the highest bidder (the offeree). An auction is without reserve only if it is stipulated as such.

Revocation of an Offer by the Offeror

Business Brief

Generally, an offeror can revoke an offer at any time prior to its acceptance by the offeree.

Under the common law, an offeror may **revoke** (i.e., withdraw) an offer any time prior to its acceptance by the offeree. Generally, an offer can be so revoked even if the offeror promised to keep the offer open for a longer time. The revocation may be communicated to the offeree by the offeror or by a third party and made by (1) the offeror's express statement (e.g., "I hereby withdraw my offer") or (2) an act of the offeror that is inconsistent with the offer (e.g., selling the goods to another party). Most states provide that the revocation is not effective until it is actually received by the offeree or the offeree's agent.

Offers made to the public may be revoked by communicating the revocation by the same means used to make the offer. For example, if a reward offer for a lost watch was published in two local newspapers each week for four weeks, notice of revocation must be published in the same newspapers for the same length of time. The revocation is effective against all offerees, even those who saw the reward offer but not the notice of revocation.

Rejection of an Offer by the Offeree

An offer is terminated if the offeree **rejects** it. Any subsequent attempt by the offeree to accept the offer is ineffective and is construed as a new offer that the original offeror (now the offeree) is free to accept or reject. A rejection may be evidenced by the offeree's express words (oral or written) or conduct. Generally, a rejection is not effective until it is actually received by the offeror.

Consider This Example   Harriet Jackson, sales manager of IBM Corporation, offers to sell 1,000 computers to Ted Green, purchasing manager of General Motors Corporation, for $250,000. The offer is made on August 1. Green telephones Jackson to say that he is not interested. This rejection terminates the offer. If Green later decides that he wants to purchase the computers, an entirely new contract must be formed.

Counteroffer by the Offeree

A **counteroffer** by the offeree simultaneously terminates the offeror's offer and creates a new offer. For example, suppose that in the prior example Green says, "I think $250,000 is too high for the computers. I will pay you $200,000." He has made a counteroffer. The original offer is terminated, and the counteroffer is a new offer that Jackson is free to accept or reject.

Destruction of the Subject Matter

An offer terminates if the subject matter of the offer is destroyed through no fault of either party prior to the offer's acceptance. For example, if a fire destroys an office building that has been listed for sale, the offer automatically terminates.

Business Brief

Destruction of the subject matter terminates an offer; it does not terminate the contract if the offer has already been accepted, however.

Death or Incompetency of the Offeror or Offeree

The death or incompetancy of either the offeror or the offeree terminates an offer. Notice of the other party's death or incompetence is not a requirement. For example, suppose on June 1 Shari Hunter offers to sell her house to Damian Coe for $100,000, provided that he decides on or before June 15. Hunter dies on June 7, before Coe has made up his mind. Because there is no contract prior to her death, the offer automatically terminates on June 7.

Supervening Illegality

If the object of an offer is made illegal prior to the acceptance of the offer, the offer terminates. This situation, which usually occurs when a statute is enacted or a court case is announced that makes the object of the offer illegal, is called a **supervening illegality**. For example, suppose City Bank offers to loan ABC Corporation $5 million at an 18 percent interest rate. Prior to ABC's acceptance of the offer, the state legislature enacts a statute that sets a usury interest rate of 12 percent. City Bank's offer to ABC Corporation is automatically terminated when the usury statute became effective.

Lapse of Time

An offer expires at the **lapse of time** of an offer. An offer may state that it is effective only until a certain date. Unless otherwise stated, the time period begins to run when the offer is actually received by the offeree and terminates when the stated time period expires. Statements such as "This offer is good for 10 days" or "This offer must be accepted by January 1, 2002" are examples of such notices. If no time is stated in the offer, the offer terminates after a "reasonable time" dictated by the circumstances. A reasonable time to accept an offer to purchase stock traded on a national stock exchange may be a few moments, but a reasonable time to accept an offer to purchase a house may be a few days. Unless otherwise stated, an offer made face-to-face or during a telephone call usually expires when the conversation ends.

Contemporary Environment

Option Contracts

An offeree can prevent the offeror from revoking his or her offer by paying the offeror compensation to keep the offer open for an agreed-upon period of time. This payment is called an **option contract**. In other words, the offeror agrees not to sell the property to anyone but the offeree during the option period. The death or incompetency of either party does not terminate an option contract unless the contract is for the performance of a personal service.

Consider This Example Anne Mason offers to sell a piece of real estate to Harold Greenberg for $1 million. Greenberg wants time to make a decision, so he pays Mason $20,000 to keep her offer open to him for six months. At any time during the option period, Greenberg may exercise his option and pay Mason the $1 million purchase price. If Greenberg lets the option expire, however, Mason may keep the $20,000 and sell the property to someone else. ■

Acceptance

Acceptance is a manifestation of assent by the offeree to the terms of the offer in a manner invited or required by the offer as measured by the objective theory of contracts.[3] Recall that generally (1) unilateral contracts can be accepted only by the offeree's performance of the required act and (2) a bilateral contract can be accepted by an offeree who promises to perform (or, where permitted, by performance of) the requested act.

Who Can Accept an Offer?

Only the offeree has the legal power to accept an offer and create a contract. Third persons usually do not have the power to accept an offer. If an offer is made individually to two or more persons, each has the power to accept the offer. Once one of the offerees accepts the offer, it terminates as to the other offerees. An offer that is made to two or more persons jointly must be accepted jointly.

Unequivocal Acceptance

The law has outgrown its primitive stage of formalism when the precise word was the sovereign talisman, and every slip was fatal. It takes a broader view today. A promise may be lacking, and yet the whole writing may be "instinct with an obligation," imperfectly expressed.

J. Cardozo
Wood v. Duff-Gordon (1917)

The offeree's acceptance must be **unequivocal**. The **mirror image rule** requires an offeree to accept the offeror's terms. Generally, a "grumbling acceptance" is a legal acceptance. For example, a response such as "Okay, I'll take the car, but I sure wish you would make me a better deal" creates an enforceable contract. An acceptance is equivocal if certain conditions are added to the acceptance. For example, suppose the offeree had responded, "I accept, but only if you repaint the car red." There is no acceptance in this case.

Silence as Acceptance

Silence usually is not considered acceptance, even if the offeror states that it is. This rule is intended to protect offerees from being legally bound to offers because they failed to respond. Nevertheless, silence *does* constitute acceptance in the following situations:

1. The offeree has indicated that silence means assent. (For example, "If you do not hear from me by Friday, ship the order.")
2. The offeree signed an agreement indicating continuing acceptance of delivery until further notification. Book-of-the-month and CD-of-the-month club memberships are examples of such acceptances.
3. Prior dealings between the parties indicate that silence means acceptance. For example, a fish wholesaler who delivers 30 pounds of fish to a restaurant each Friday for several years and is paid for the fish can continue the deliveries with expectation of payment until notified otherwise by the restaurant.
4. The offeree takes the benefit of goods or services provided by the offeror even though he or she (a) has an opportunity to reject the goods or services but fails to do so and (b) knows the offeror expects to be compensated. For example, a homeowner who stands idly by and watches a painter whom she has not hired mistakenly paint her house owes the painter for the work.

Time and Mode of Acceptance

Under the common law of contracts, acceptance of a bilateral contract occurs when the offeree *dispatches* the acceptance by an authorized means of communication. This rule is called the **acceptance-upon-dispatch rule** or, more commonly, the **mailbox rule**. Under this rule, the acceptance is effective when it is dispatched, even if it is lost in transmission. If an offeree first dispatches a rejection and then sends an acceptance, the mailbox rule does not apply to the acceptance.[4]

The problem of lost acceptances can be minimized by expressly altering the mailbox rule. The offeror can do this by stating in the offer that acceptance is effective only upon actual receipt of the acceptance.

The acceptance must be **properly dispatched**. The acceptance must be properly addressed, packaged in an appropriate envelope or container, and have prepaid postage or delivery charges. Under common law, if an acceptance is not properly dispatched, it is not effective until it is actually received by the offeror.

Generally, an offeree must accept an offer by an *authorized* means of communication. The offer can stipulate that acceptance must be by a specified means of communication (e.g., registered mail, telegram). Such stipulation is called **express authorization**. If the offeree uses an unauthorized means of communication to transmit the acceptance, the acceptance is not effective, even if it is received by the offeror within the allowed time period because the means of communication was a condition of acceptance.

Most offers do not expressly specify the means of communication required for acceptance. The common law recognizes certain implied means of communication. **Implied authorization** may be inferred from what is customary in similar transactions, usage of trade, or prior dealings between the parties. Section 30 of the *Restatement (Second) of Contracts* permits implied authorization "by any medium reasonable in the circumstances."

Mailbox Rule. The mailbox rule provides that an acceptance is effective when it is dispatched.

◼ Concept Summary *Offer and Acceptance*

Communication by Offeror	Effective When
Offer	Received by offeree
Revocation of offer	Received by offeree

Communication by Offeree	Effective When
Rejection of offer	Received by offeror
Counteroffer	Received by offeror
Acceptance of offer	Sent by offeree
Acceptance after previous rejection of offer	Received by offeror

Online Commerce & Internet Law
Nondisclosure Agreements

A nondisclosure agreement—or NDA, as they are called— swears the signatory to secrecy about confidential ideas, trade secrets, and other nonpublic information revealed by the party proffering the NDA.

NDAs have traditionally been used among lawyers, investment bankers, and others involved in secret takeovers and other large corporate deals. But today many entrepreneurs, particularly those in high-tech industries, are also using NDAs. An NDA serves a purpose in that it protects a person who has a great idea (or so he or she thinks) and wants to share it with a potential partner, investor, lawyer, or investment banker, but wants an assurance that the recipient of the information will not steal or reveal the information to anyone else.

An NDA is an enforceable contract, so if someone violates it, the disclosing party can sue the breaching party for damages. Bill Gates of Microsoft requires plumbers and other persons who work on his house to sign NDAs. Sabeer Bhatia, founder of Hotmail, collected more then 400 NDAs in two years before selling his company to Microsoft for $400 million.

Although it may not be hard to get some people to sign NDAs, others balk. Some friends and relatives refuse to sign NDAs thrust on them because they present an aura of distrust. Industry big-wigs—venture capitalists, securities analysts, and successful technology companies—routinely refuse to sign NDAs because they see too many similar ideas and do not want their tongues tied by any single one. NDAs will continue to increase in use, though. ◼

Consideration

Consideration must be given before a contract can exist. **Consideration** is defined as something of legal value given in exchange for a promise. Consideration can come in many forms. The most common types consist of either a tangible payment (e.g., money, property) or the performance of an act (e.g., providing legal services). Less usual forms of consideration include the forbearance of a legal right (e.g., accepting an out-of-court settlement in exchange for dropping a lawsuit) and noneconomic forms of consideration (e.g., refraining from "drinking, using tobacco, swearing, or playing cards or billiards for money"[5] for a specified time period).

Written contracts are presumed to be supported by consideration. This rebuttable presumption, however, may be overcome by sufficient evidence. A few states provide that contracts made under seal cannot be challenged for lack of consideration.

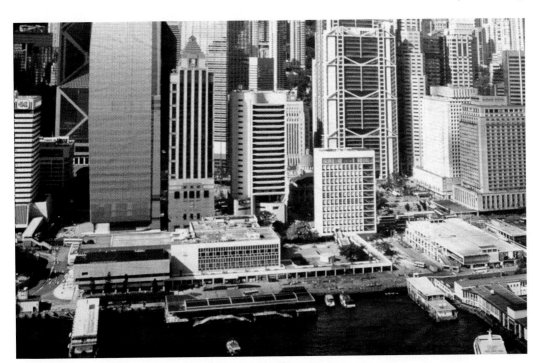

Hong Kong. Consideration must support a commercial or private contract.

Requirements of Consideration

Consideration consists of two elements: (1) Something of legal value must be given (e.g., either a legal benefit must be received or legal detriment must be suffered) and (2) there must be a bargained-for exchange. Each of these is discussed in the paragraphs that follow:

1. *Legal value.* Under the modern law of contracts, a contract is considered supported by **legal value** if (1) the promisee suffers a *legal detriment* or (2) the promisor receives a *legal benefit*. For example, suppose the Dallas Cowboys contract with a tailor to have the tailor make uniforms for the team. The tailor completes the uniforms, but the team manager thinks the color is wrong and refuses to allow the team to wear them. The tailor has suffered a legal detriment (time spent making the uniforms). Under the modern rule of contracts, there is sufficiency of consideration and the contract is enforceable.

2. *Bargained-for exchange.* To be enforceable, a contract must arise from a **bargained-for exchange**. In most business contracts, the parties engage in such exchanges. The commercial setting in which business contracts are formed leads to this conclusion.

   Gift promises, also called **gratuitous promises**, are unenforceable because they lack consideration. To change a gift promise into an enforceable promise, the promisee must offer to do something in exchange—that is, consideration—for the promise. For example, suppose Mrs. Colby promised to give her son $10,000 and then rescinded the promise. The son would have no recourse because it was a gift promise that lacked consideration. If, however, Mrs. Colby promised her son $10,000 for getting an "A" in his business law course and the son performed as required, the contract would be enforceable.

A completed gift promise cannot be rescinded for lack of consideration. For example, on May 1 Mr. Smith promises to give his granddaughter $10,000 on June 1. If on June 1 Mr. Smith actually gives the $10,000 to his granddaughter, it is a completed gift promise. Mr. Smith cannot thereafter recover the money from his granddaughter, even if the original promise lacked consideration.

Business Brief

The more formal approach to finding consideration has been replaced by a modern definition that considers a contract supported by consideration if either (1) the promisee suffers a legal detriment or (2) the promisor receives a legal benefit.

The first case that follows involves an uncompleted gift promise. The second case that follows involves completed gifts.

Alden v. Presley
637 S.W. 2d 862, 1982 Tenn. Lexis 340 (1982)
Supreme Court of Tennessee

Case 9.3
Gift Promise

Background and Facts

Elvis Presley, a singer of great renown and a man of substantial wealth, became engaged to Ginger Alden. He was generous with the Alden family, paying for landscaping the lawn, installing a swimming pool, and making other gifts. When his fiancée's mother, Jo Laverne Alden, sought to divorce her husband, Presley promised to pay off the remaining mortgage indebtedness on the Alden home, which Mrs. Alden was to receive in the divorce settlement. On August 16, 1977, Presley died suddenly, leaving the mortgage unpaid. When the legal representative of Presley's estate refused to pay the $39,587 mortgage, Mrs. Alden brought an action to enforce Presley's promise. The trial court denied recovery. Mrs. Alden appealed.

Issue

Was Presley's promise to pay the mortgage enforceable?

Court's Reasoning

Under contract law, gift promises are unenforceable because they lack consideration. The court found that plaintiff Alden had not given any consideration in exchange for Presley's promise. The court also found that the gift promise had not been completed by Presley. Therefore, the unexpected gift promise could not be enforced against Presley's estate.

Decision and Remedy

The supreme court held that Presley's promise was a gratuitous executory promise that was not supported by consideration. As such, it was unenforceable against Presley's estate. The court dismissed the case and assessed costs against the plaintiff.

Case Questions

Critical Legal Thinking   Should gratuitous promises be enforced? Why or why not?

Business Ethics   Was it unethical for the representative of Presley's estate to refuse to complete the gift? Did he have any other choice?

Contemporary Business   Does it make a difference if a gift promise is executed or executory? Explain.

Cooper v. Smith
800 N.E.2d 372, 2003 Ohio App. Lexis 5446 (2003)
Court of Appeals of Ohio

Case 9.4
Completed Gifts

Background and Facts

In May 2001, Lester Cooper suffered serious injuries that caused him to be hospitalized for an extended period of time. While he was hospitalized, Julie Smith, whom Cooper had met the year before, and Janet Smith, Julie's mother, made numerous trips to visit him. Although Julie was married to another man at the time, a romantic relationship developed between Cooper and Julie. While in the hospital, Cooper proposed marriage to Julie, and she accepted. Julie obtained a divorce from her husband in October 2001. Cooper ultimately received an $180,000 settlement for his injuries.

After being released from the hospital, Cooper moved into Janet's house and lived with Janet and Julie. Over the next couple months, Cooper purchased a number of items for Julie, including a diamond engagement ring, a car, a computer, a tanning bed, and horses. On Julie's request, Cooper paid off Janet's car. Cooper also paid for various improvements to Janet's house, such as having a new furnace installed and having wood flooring laid in the kitchen. By December 2001, the settlement money had run out, and Julie had not yet married Cooper. In the summer of 2002, Julie and Cooper had a disagreement, and Cooper moved out of the house. Julie returned the engagement ring to Cooper. Cooper sued Julie and Janet to recover the gifts or the value of the gifts he gave them. The magistrate who heard the case dismissed Cooper's case, and the trial court affirmed the dismissal of the case. Cooper appealed.

Issue

Can Cooper recover the gifts or the value of the gifts he gave to Julie and Janet Smith?

Court's Reasoning

The court of appeals stated that unless the parties agreed otherwise, a donor is entitled to recover the engagement ring (or its value) if the marriage does not occur, regardless of who ended the engagement. Here, Julie had returned the engagement ring to Cooper, so that is not an issue. The court refused, however, to extend this rule to other gifts made during an engagement period. The court stated that the best approach is to treat other gifts exchanged during an engagement period as absolute and irrevocable gifts unless the donor has expressed intent that the gifts be conditioned on the subsequent marriage. The court held that Cooper had not made the gifts to Julie or Janet conditioned on future marriage to Julie, so therefore the gifts were completed, irrevocable gifts that Julie and Janet could keep.

Decision and Remedy

The court of appeals held that the gifts made by Cooper to Julie (other than the engagement ring) and to Janet were irrevocable gifts that he could not recover simply because his engagement with Julie ended. The court of appeals affirmed the judgment of the trial court allowing Julie and Janet Smith to keep these gifts.

Case Questions

Critical Legal Thinking   Should the return of an engagement ring and other gifts made during the engagement period be treated differently when the engagement is broken off? Explain.

Business Ethics   Did Julie and Janet Smith act ethically in keeping the gifts Cooper had given them? Did Cooper act ethically in trying to get the gifts back?

Contemporary Business   Does the no-fault rule regarding the return of engagement rings upon the termination of an engagement save court expenses? Explain.

Contracts Lacking Consideration

Some contracts seem as though they are supported by consideration even though they are not. The following types of contracts fall into this category:

- *Illegal consideration.* A contract cannot be supported by a promise to refrain from doing an illegal act because that is **illegal consideration**. Contracts based on illegal consideration are void. For example, statements such as, "I will burn your house down unless you agree to pay me $10,000" cannot become enforceable contracts. Even if the threatened party agrees to make the payment, the contract is unenforceable and void because it is supported by illegal consideration (arson is unlawful).

- *Illusory promises.* If the parties enter into a contract but one or both of the parties can choose not to perform their contractual obligations, the contract lacks consideration. Such promises, which are known as **illusory promises** (or **illusory contracts**), are unenforceable. For example, a contract that provides that one of the parties has to perform only if he or she chooses to do so is an illusory contract.

- *Moral obligations.* Promises made out of a sense of **moral obligation** or honor are generally not enforceable on the ground that they lack consideration. In other words, moral consideration is not treated as legal consideration. Contracts based on love and affection and deathbed promises are examples of such promises. A minority of states hold that moral obligations are enforceable.

- *Preexisting duty.* A promise lacks consideration if a person promises to perform an act or do something he or she is already under an obligation to do. This is called a **preexisting duty**. The promise is unenforceable because no new consideration has been given. For example, many states have adopted statutes that prohibit police officers from accepting rewards for apprehending criminals.

    In the private sector, the preexisting duty rule often arises when one of the parties to an existing contract seeks to change the terms of the contract during the course of its performance. Such midstream changes are unenforceable: The parties have a preexisting duty to perform according to the original terms of the contract. Sometimes a party to a contract runs into substantial **unforeseen difficulties** while performing his or her contractual duties. If the parties modify their contract to accommodate these unforeseen difficulties, the modification will be enforced even though it is not supported by new consideration.

    For example, suppose a landowner enters into a contract with a contractor who agrees to excavate the hole for the foundation of a major office building. When the excavation is partially completed, toxic wastes are unexpectedly found at the site. Removal of toxic wastes is highly regulated by law and would substantially increase

Business Brief

If a party runs into substantial unforeseen difficulties while performing his or her contractual duties, the contract can be modified without new consideration being given.

the cost of the excavation. If the landowner agrees to pay the contractor increased compensation to remove the toxic wastes, this modification of the contract is enforceable, even though it is unsupported by new consideration.

■ *Past consideration.* A promise that is based on a party's **past consideration** (i.e., prior act or performance) lacks consideration. Such contracts are unenforceable unless some new consideration is given to support the contract. For example, say that a friend says to another friend, "I promise to give you $50,000 for all the help you have been to me over the years." If the friend who made this promise later refuses to perform, the other friend cannot recover the money because she gave no consideration.

Contemporary Environment
Best-Efforts Contracts

A business contract may contain a clause that requires one or both of the parties to use their *best efforts* to achieve the objective of the contract. For example, real estate listing contracts often require a real estate broker to use his or her best efforts to find a buyer for the listed real estate. Contracts often require underwriters to use their best efforts to sell securities on behalf of their corporate clients. The courts generally have held that the imposition of the best-efforts duty provides sufficient consideration to make a contract enforceable. ■

Concept Summary   *Promises Lacking Consideration*

Type of Consideration	Description of Promise
Illegal consideration	Promise to refrain from doing an illegal act.
Illusory promise	Promise where one or both parties can choose not to perform their obligation.
Moral obligation	Promise made out of a sense of moral obligation, honor, love, or affection. Some states enforce these types of contracts.
Preexisting duty	Promise based on the preexisting duty of the promisee to perform. The promise is enforceable if (1) the parties rescind the contract and enter into a new contract or (2) there are unforeseen difficulties.
Past consideration	Promise based on the past performance of the promisee.

Settlement of Claims

The law promotes the voluntary settlement of disputed claims. Settlement saves judicial resources and serves the interests of the parties entering into the settlement.

In some situations, one of the parties to a contract believes that he or she did not receive what he or she was due. This party may attempt to reach a compromise with the other party (e.g., by paying less consideration than was provided for in the contract). The compromise agreement is called an **accord**. If the accord is performed, it is called a **satisfaction**. This type of settlement is called an **accord and satisfaction** or a **compromise**. If the accord is not satisfied, the other party can sue to enforce either the accord or the original contract.

Business Brief

Businesses should consider settling potential legal disputes. The law promotes the settlement of disputes because it saves judicial time and resources.

Consider This Example   Suppose that a contract stipulated that the cost of a computer system that keeps track of inventory, accounts receivable, and so on is $100,000. After it is installed, the computer system does not perform as promised. To settle the dispute, the parties agree that $70,000 is to be paid as full and final payment for the computer. This accord is enforceable even though no new consideration is given because reasonable persons would disagree as to the worth of the computer system that was actually installed.

Promissory Estoppel

The courts have developed the doctrine of **promissory estoppel** or (**detrimental reliance**) to avoid injustice. This doctrine is a broad policy-based doctrine. It is used to provide a remedy to a person who has relied on another person's promise, but that person withdraws his or her promise and is not subject to a breach of contract action because one of the two elements discussed in this chapter (i.e., agreement or consideration) is lacking. The doctrine of promissory estoppel *estops* (prevents) the promisor from revoking his or her promise. Therefore, the person who has detrimentally relied on the promise for performance may sue the promisor for performance or other remedy the court feels is fair to award in the circumstances.

For the doctrine of promissory estoppel to be applied, the following elements must be shown:

1. The promisor made a promise.
2. The promisor should have reasonably expected to induce the promisee to rely on the promise.
3. The promisee actually relied on the promise and engaged in an action or forbearance of a right of a definite and substantial nature.
4. Injustice would be caused if the promise were not enforced.

Consider This Example   XYZ Construction Company, a general contractor, requests bids from subcontractors for work to be done on a hospital building that XYZ plans to submit a bid to build. Bert Plumbing Company submits the lowest bid for the plumbing work, and XYZ incorporates Bert's low bid in its own bid for the general contract. In this example, the doctrine of promissory estoppel prevents Bert from withdrawing its bid. If XYZ is awarded the contract to build the hospital, it could enforce Bert's promise to perform.

> Now equity is no part of the law, but a moral virtue, which qualifies, moderates, and reforms the rigor, hardness, and edge of the law, and is a universal truth.
>
> Lord Cowper
> *Dudley v. Dudley (1705)*

Advertisement, China. China opened its markets and has become a full member of the international economic community.

Chapter Summary

Agreement, p. 185

Offer

1. **Offer.** An offer is a manifestation by one party of a willingness to enter into a contract.
2. **Offeror.** The offeror is the party who makes an offer.
3. **Offeree.** The offeree is the party to whom an offer is made. This party has the power to create an agreement by accepting the terms of the offer.

Offer, p. 185

Requirements of an Offer

1. **Objective intent.** The intent to enter into a contract is determined by the *objective theory of contract*—that is, whether a reasonable person viewing the circumstances would conclude that the parties intended to be legally bound.
2. **Definite terms.** The terms of an offer must be definite so that the agreement between the parties can be determined. Reasonable terms (e.g., price, time for performance) may be *implied*.
3. **Communication.** The offer must be communicated to the offeree by the offeror.

Special Offer Situations

1. *Advertisement.*
   a. *General rule.* Generally, an advertisement is an invitation to make an offer.
   b. *Exception.* An advertisement is an offer if it is so definite and specific as to show that the advertiser's intent to be bound to the terms of the advertisement.
2. *Reward.* A reward is an offer to create a unilateral contract.
3. *Auction:*
   a. *Action with reserve.* An action with reserve is an invitation to make an offer. The seller retains the right to refuse the highest bid and withdraw the good from sale.
   b. *Auction without reserve.* An action without reserve is an offer. The seller must accept the highest bid (above the minimum bid). This type of auction must be stipulated.

Termination of an Offer by Action of the Parties

1. **Revocation.** The offeror may *revoke* (withdraw) an offer any time prior to its acceptance by the offeree.
2. **Rejection.** An offer is terminated if the offeree rejects the offer by his or her words or conduct.
3. **Counteroffer.** A counteroffer by the offeree terminates the offeror's offer (and creates a new offer).

Termination of an Offer by Operation of Law

1. **Destruction of the subject matter.** An offer terminates if the subject matter of the offer is destroyed prior to acceptance through no fault of either party.
2. **Death or incompetency.** The death or incompetency of either the offeror or the offeree prior to acceptance terminates the offer.
3. **Supervening illegality.** If prior to the acceptance of an offer the object of the offer is made illegal by statute, regulation, court decision, or other law, the offer terminates.
4. **Lapse of time.** An offer terminates upon the expiration of a stated time in the offer. If no time is stated, the offer terminates after a "reasonable time."

Option Contract

If an offeree pays the offeror compensation to keep an offer open for an agreed upon period of time, an *option contract* is created. The offeror cannot sell the property to anyone else during the option period.

Acceptance, p. 192

Acceptance

Acceptance is manifestation of assent by the offeree to the terms of the offer. Acceptance of the offer by the offeree creates a contract.

Rules for Acceptance

1. *Mirror image rule.* Under the common law of contracts, an offeree must accept the terms offered by the offeror to create a contract. Any change in terms by the offeree constitutes a counteroffer, not an acceptance.
2. *Acceptance-upon-dispatch rule.* Unless otherwise provided in the offer, acceptance is effective when it is dispatched by the offeree. This rule is often called the *mailbox rule.*
3. *Proper dispatch rule.* An acceptance must be properly addressed, packaged, and have prepaid postage or delivery charges to be effective when dispatched. Generally, improperly dispatched acceptances are not effective until actually received by the offeror.
4. *Mode of acceptance.* Acceptance must be by the express means of communication stipulated in the offer, or, if no means is stipulated, then by reasonable means in the circumstances.

Consideration, p. 194

Consideration

Consideration involves a thing of value being given in exchange for a promise. It may be tangible or intangible property, performance of a service, forbearance of a legal right, or another thing of value.

Requirements of Consideration

1. *Legal value.* Something of legal value must be given as consideration. Either (a) the promisee suffers a *legal detriment* or (b) the promisor receives a *legal benefit.*
2. *Bargained-for-exchange.* A contract must arise from a bargained-for-exchange. *Gift promises* (or *gratuitous promises*) are unenforceable because they lack consideration.

Special Contracts

1. *Requirements contracts.* Contracts where the buyer agrees to purchase all the requirements for an item from a single seller are enforceable if the parties act in good faith.
2. *Output contracts.* Contracts where the seller agrees to sell all its production to a single buyer are enforceable if the parties act in good faith.
3. *Best efforts contracts.* Contracts that require a party to use its best efforts to accomplish the objective of the contract are enforceable.

Contracts Lacking Consideration

The following contracts are unenforceable because they lack consideration:

1. *Illegal consideration.* Promise to retrain from doing an illegal act.
2. *Illusory promise.* If one or both parties to a contract can choose not to perform their contractual duties.
3. *Moral obligation.* Promise made out of a sense of moral obligation, honor, love, or affection.
4. *Preexisting duty.* Promise to perform an act or do something that a person is already under an obligation to do.
5. *Past consideration.* Promise based on a party's past consideration.

Settlement of Claims

Accord and satisfaction. This is a compromise agreement where the parties agree to settle a contract dispute and do so.

1. **Unliquidated debt.** This is a debt in which reasonable persons would disagree as to the amount owed. It can be compromised without the payment of new consideration.

2. **Liquidated debt.** This is a debt that is due and certain. It cannot be compromised unless new consideration is paid.

Promissory Estoppel

Promissory estoppel is a policy-based equitable doctrine that prevents a promisor from revoking his or her promise even though the promise lacks consideration. The requirements are:

1. The promisor made a promise.
2. The promisor should have reasonably expected to induce the promisee to rely on the promise.
3. The promisee actually relied on the promise and engaged in an action or forbearance of a right of a definite and substantial nature.
4. Injustice would be caused if the promise were not enforced.

Internet Exercises and Case Questions
Working the Web Internet Exercises

Activities

1. Visit **cori.missouri.edu**. Use this site to aid in drafting specific types of contracts and/or clauses. Test your ability by visiting the site and searching for employment agreements that have non-competition clauses.

2. To review the basic elements of a contract, visit **www.freeadvice.com/law/518us.htm**.

3. For some tips on entering into contracts, see **www.itslegal.com/infonet/consumer/contracts.html**.

4. Professor Smith outlines the law of consideration at **www.west.net/~smith/contracts.htm**.

5. For a simplified explanation of the concept of consideration, see **www.nolo.com** and visit the encyclopedia section. Type in "consideration."

6. Check out the summary of consideration available at **www4.law.cornell.edu**.

Critical Legal Thinking Cases

9.1 Essential Terms Ben Hunt and others operated a farm under the name S. B. H. Farms. Hunt went to McIlroy Bank and Trust and requested a loan to build hog houses, buy livestock, and expand farming operations. The bank agreed to loan S. B. H. Farms $175,000, for which short-term promissory notes were signed by Hunt and the other owners of S. B. H. Farms. At that time, oral discussions were held with the bank officer regarding long-term financing of S. B. H.'s farming operations: No dollar amount, interest rate, or repayment terms were discussed. When the owners of S. B. H. Farms defaulted on the promissory notes, the bank filed for foreclosure on the farm and other collateral. S. B. H. Farms counterclaimed for $750,000 in damages, alleging that the bank breached its oral contract to provide long-term financing. Was there an oral contract for long-term financing? [*Hunt v. McIlroy Bank and Trust*, 616 S.W.2d 759, 1981 Ark.App. Lexis 716 (Ark. App. 1981)]

9.2 Implied Terms MacDonald Group, Ltd. (MacDonald) is the managing general partner of "Fresno Fashion Square," a regional shopping mall in Fresno, California. The mall has several major anchor tenants and numerous smaller stores and shops, including Edmond's of Fresno, a jeweler. In 1969,

Edmond's signed a lease with MacDonald that provided that "there shall not be more than two jewelry stores" located in the mall. In 1978, MacDonald sent Edmond's notice that it intended to expand the mall and lease space to other jewelers. The lease was silent as to the coverage of additional mall space. Edmond's sued MacDonald, arguing that the lease applied to mall additions. Who wins? [*Edmond's of Fresno v. MacDonald Group, Ltd.*, 171 Cal.App.3d 598, 217 Cal.Rptr. 375, 1985 Cal.App. Lexis 2436 (Cal. App. 1985)]

9.3 Counteroffer Glende Motor Company (Glende), an automobile dealer that sold new cars, leased premises from certain landlords. In October 1979, fire destroyed part of the leased premises, and Glende restored the leasehold premises. The landlords received payment of insurance proceeds for the fire. Glende sued the landlords to recover the insurance proceeds. On May 7, 1982, 10 days before the trial was to begin, the defendants jointly served on Glende a document titled "Offer to Compromise Before Trial," which was a settlement of $190,000. On May 16, Glende agreed to the amount of the settlement but made it contingent upon the execution of a new lease. On May 17, the defendants notified Glende that they were revoking the settlement offer. Glende thereafter tried to accept the original settlement offer. Has there been a settlement of the lawsuit? [*Glende Motor Company v. Superior Court*, 159 Cal.App.3d 389, 205 Cal.Rptr. 682, 1984 Cal.App. Lexis 2435 (Cal. App. 1984)]

9.4 Silence   Peter Andrus owned an apartment building that he had insured under a fire insurance policy sold by J. C. Durick Insurance (Durick). Two months prior to the expiration of the policy, Durick notified Andrus that the building should be insured for $48,000 (or 80 percent of the building's value), as required by the insurance company. Andrus replied that (1) he wanted insurance to match the amount of the outstanding mortgage on the building (i.e., $24,000) and (2) if Durick could not sell this insurance, he would go elsewhere. Durick sent a new insurance policy in the face amount of $48,000, with the notation that the policy was automatically accepted unless Andrus notified him to the contrary. Andrus did not reply. He did not, however, pay the premiums on the policy. Durick sued Andrus to recover these premiums. Who wins? [*J. C. Durick Insurance v. Andrus*, 424 A.2d 249, 1980 Vt. Lexis 1490 (Vt. 1980)]

9.5 Time for Acceptance   Economic Research Properties (ERP), a partnership, owned a tract of land in Florida. Donald R. Sullivan, who became interested in purchasing the property, mailed a written offer and deposit to Dwayne R. Klein, the managing partner of ERP, to purchase the property. The offer stated that it must be accepted by ERP by February 4, 1980, after which time the deposit was to be returned to Sullivan. ERP made several changes to the offer, including changing the time for acceptance from February 4 to February 14 so as to allow sufficient time for its counteroffer to reach Sullivan, and signed it.

Sullivan received the counteroffer several days before February 14. On February 18, 1980, Sullivan signed the counteroffer and mailed it to ERP. On February 19, Klein, having neither received the contract nor been notified of its acceptance, telephoned Sullivan and advised him that the negotiations were terminated. ERP later sold the property to another buyer. Sullivan sued ERP for breach of contract. Was a contract formed between ERP and Sullivan? [*Sullivan v. Economic Research Properties*, 455 So.2d 630, 1984 Fla.App. Lexis 14966 (Fla. App. 1984)]

9.6 The Mailbox Rule   William Jenkins and Nathalie Monk owned a building in Sacramento, California. In 1979, they leased the building to Tuneup Masters for five years. The lease provided that Tuneup Masters could extend the lease for an additional five years if it gave written notice of its intention to do so by certified or registered mail at least six months prior to the expiration of the term of the lease, or August 1, 1983.

On July 29, 1983, Larry Selditz, vice president of Tuneup Masters, prepared a letter exercising the option, prepared and sealed an envelope with the letter in it, prepared U.S. Postal Service Form 3800, affixed the certified mail sticker on the envelope, and had his secretary deliver the envelope to the Postal Service annex located on the ground floor of the office building. Postal personnel occupied the annex only between the hours of 9 A.M. and 10 A.M. At the end of each day, between 5 P.M. and 5:15 P.M., a postal employee picked up outgoing mail. The letter to the landlords was lost in the mail. The landlords thereafter refused to renew the lease and brought an unlawful detainer action against Tuneup Masters. Was the notice renewing the option effective? [*Jenkins v. Tuneup Masters*, 190 Cal.App.3d 1, 235 Cal.Rptr. 214, 1987 Cal.App. Lexis 1475 (Cal. App. 1987)]

9.7 Consideration   Clyde and Betty Penley were married in 1949. In late 1967, Clyde operated an automotive tire business, and Betty owned an interest in a Kentucky Fried Chicken (KFC) franchise. That year, when Betty became ill, she requested that Clyde begin spending additional time at the KFC franchise to ensure its continued operation. Subsequently, Betty agreed that if Clyde would devote full time to the KFC franchise, they would operate the business as a joint enterprise, share equally in the ownership of its assets, and divide its returns equally. Pursuant to this agreement, Clyde terminated his tire business and devoted himself full time to the KFC franchise. On December 31, 1979, Betty abandoned Clyde and denied him any rights in the KFC franchise. Clyde sued to enforce the agreement with Betty. Is the agreement enforceable? [*Penley v. Penley*, 332 S.E.2d 51, 1985 N.C. Lexis 1706 (N.C. 1985)]

9.8 Past Consideration   A. J. Whitmire and R. Lee Whitmire were brothers. From 1923 to 1929, A. J. lived with his brother and his brother's wife, Lillie Mae. During this period, A. J. performed various services for his brother and sister-in-law. In 1925, R. Lee and Lillie Mae purchased some land. In 1944, in the presence of Lillie Mae, R. Lee told A. J., "When we're gone, this land is yours." A. J. had not done any work for R. Lee or Lillie Mae since 1929, and none was expected or provided in the future. On May 26, 1977, after both R. Lee and Lillie Mae had died, A. J. filed a claim with the estate of Lillie Mae, seeking specific performance of the 1944 promise. Does A. J. get the property? [*Whitmire v. Watkins*, 267 So.2d 6, 1980 Ga. Lexis 908 (Ga. 1980)]

9.9 Preexisting Duty   Robert Chuckrow Construction Company (Chuckrow) was employed as the general contractor to build a Kinney Shoe Store. Chuckrow employed Ralph Gough to perform the carpentry work on the store. The contract with Gough stipulated that he was to provide all labor, materials, tools, equipment, scaffolding, and other items necessary to complete the carpentry work. On May 15, 1965, Gough's employees erected 38 trusses at the job site. The next day, 32 of the trusses fell off the building. The reason for the trusses' falling was unexplained, and evidence showed that it was not due to Chuckrow's fault or a deficiency in the building plans. Chuckrow told Gough that he would pay him to reerect the trusses and continue work. When the job was complete, Chuckrow paid Gough the original contract price but refused to pay him for the additional cost of reerecting the trusses. Gough sued Chuckrow for this expense. Can Gough recover? [*Robert Chuckrow Construction Company v. Gough*, 159 S.E.2d 469, 1968 Ga.App. Lexis 1007 (Ga. App. 1968)]

9.10 Promissory Estoppel   Nalley's, Inc. (Nalley's), was a major food distribution, with its home office in the state of Washington. In 1964, Jacob Aronowicz and Samuel Duncan approached Nalley's about the possibility of their manufacturing a line of sliced meat products to be distributed by Nalley's. When Nalley's showed considerable interest, Aronowicz and Duncan incorporated as Major Food Products, Inc. (Major). Meetings to discuss the proposal continued at length with Charles Gardiner, a vice president and general manager of the Los Angeles division of Nalley's. On February 5, 1965, Gardiner delivered a letter to Major, agreeing to become the exclusive Los Angeles and Orange County distributor for Major's products, but stated in the letter "that should we determine your product line is not representative or is not compatible with our operation we are free to terminate our agreement within 30 days." Nalley's was to distribute the full production of products produced by Major.

Based on Gardiner's assurances, Major leased a plant, built out the plant to its specifications, purchased and installed equipment, signed contracts to obtain meat to be processed, and hired personnel. Both Aronowicz and Duncan resigned from their positions at other meat processing companies to devote themselves full time to the project. Financing was completed when Aronowicz and Duncan used their personal fortunes to purchase the stock of Major. Gardiner and other representatives of Nalley's visited Major's plant and expressed satisfaction with the premises. Major obtained the necessary government approvals regarding health standards on June 15, 1965, and immediately achieved full production. Because Nalley's was to pick up the finished products at Major's plant, Nalley's drivers visited Major's plant to acquaint themselves with its operations.

Gardiner sent the final proposal regarding the Nalley's–Major relationship to Nalley's home office for final approval. On June 22, 1965, Nalley's home office in Washington made a decision not to distribute Major's products. Nalley's refused to give any reason to Major for its decision. No final agreement was ever executed between the parties. Immediate efforts by Major to secure other distribution for its products proved unsuccessful. Further, because Major owned no trucks itself and had no sales organization, it could not distribute the products itself. In less than six months, Major had failed, and Aronowicz's and Duncan's stock in Major was worthless. Major, Aronowicz, and Duncan sued Nalley's for damages under the doctrine of promissory estoppel. Do they win? [*Aronowicz v. Nalley's Inc.*, 30 C.A.3d 27, 106 Cal.Rptr. 424, 1972 Cal.App. Lexis 667 (Cal. App. 1972)]

Business Ethics Cases

9.11 Business Ethics Kortney Dempsey took a cruise on a ship operated by Norwegian Cruise Line (Norwegian). In general, suits for personal injuries arising out of maritime torts are subject to a three-year statute of limitations. Congress permits this period to be reduced to one year by contract, however. The Norwegian passenger ticket limited the period to one year. Evidence showed that the cruise line ticket contained the notation "Important Notice" in a bright red box at the bottom-right corner of each of the first four pages of the ticket. The information in the box stated that certain pages of the ticket contain information that "affect[s] important legal rights." In addition, at the top of page 6 of the ticket, where the terms and conditions began, it was stated in bold letters: "Passengers are advised to read the terms and conditions of the Passenger Ticket Contract set forth below." The clause at issue, which appears on page 8, clearly provides that suits must be brought within one year of injury.

More than one year after Dempsey had taken the cruise (but within three years), she filed suit against Norwegian, seeking damages for an alleged injury suffered while on the cruise. Dempsey asserted that the one-year limitations period had not been reasonably communicated to her. Did Dempsey act ethically in suing when she did? Did Norwegian act ethically in reducing the limitations period to one year? Who wins the lawsuit? [*Dempsey v. Norwegian Cruise Line*, 972 F.2d 998, 1992 U.S. App. Lexis 10939 (9th Cir. 1992)]

9.12 Business Ethics Ocean Dunes of Hutchinson Island Development Corporation (Ocean Dunes) was a developer of condominium units. Prior to the construction, Albert and Helen Colangelo entered into a purchase agreement to buy one of the units and paid a deposit to Ocean Dunes. A provision in the purchase agreement provided that

If Developer shall default in the performance of its obligations pursuant to this agreement. Purchaser's only remedy shall be to terminate this agreement, whereupon the Deposit shall be refunded to Purchaser and all rights and obligations thereunder shall thereupon become null and void.

The purchase agreement provided that if the buyer defaulted, the developer could retain the buyer's deposit or sue the buyer for damages and any other legal or equitable remedy. When Ocean Dunes refused to sell the unit to the Colangelos, they sued, seeking a decree of specific performance to require Ocean Dunes to sell the unit to them. Ocean Dunes alleged that the above-quoted provision prevented the plaintiffs from seeking any legal or equitable remedy. Was the defendant's duty under the contract illusory? Was it ethical for Ocean Dunes to place the provision at issue in the contract? [*Ocean Dunes of Hutchinson Island Development Corporation v. Colangelo*, 463 So.2d 437, 1985 Fla.App. Lexis 12298 (Fla. App. 1985)]

Briefing the Case Writing Assignment

Read Case A.9 in the Case Appendix [*Traco, Inc. v. Arrow Glass Co., Inc.*]. This case is excerpted from the appellate court opinion. Review and brief the case. In your brief, be sure to answer the following questions.

1. Who was the plaintiff? Who was the defendant?

2. Was there an express agreement between the parties?

3. What does the doctrine of promissory estoppel provide? Explain.

4. Did the court apply the doctrine of promissory estoppel in this case?

Endnotes

1. *Restatement (Second) of Contracts*, § 33 (1).
2. *Restatement (Second) of Contracts*, § 204.
3. *Restatement (Second) of Contracts*, § 50(1).
4. *Restatement (Second) of Contracts*, § 40.
5. *Hamer v. Sidwa*, 27 N.Y. 538, 27 N.E. 256, 1891 N.Y. Lexis 1396 (NY 1891).

Capacity and Legality

"An unconscionable contract is one which no man in his senses, not under delusion, would make, on the one hand, and which no fair and honest man would accept on the other."

—Hume v. United States,
132 U.S. 406, 10 S.Ct. 134, 1889 U.S. Lexis 1888 (1889)

Chapter Objectives

After studying this chapter, you should be able to:

1. Define and describe the infancy doctrine.

2. Define legal insanity and intoxication and explain how they affect contractual capacity.

3. Identify illegal contracts that are contrary to statutes and those that violate public policy.

4. Describe covenants not to compete and exculpatory clauses and identify when they are lawful.

5. Define unconscionable contracts and determine when they are unlawful.

Chapter Contents

- Minors
- Mentally Incompetent Persons
- Intoxicated Persons
- Illegality
- Unconscionable Contracts

The right of a minor to disaffirm his contract is based upon sound public policy to protect the minor from his own improvidence and the overreaching of adults.

Justice Sullivan
Star Chevrolet v. Green (1985)

Generally, the law presumes that the parties to a contract have the requisite **contractual capacity** to enter into the contract. Certain persons do not have this capacity, however, including minors, insane persons, and intoxicated persons. The common law of contracts and many state statutes protect persons who lack contractual capacity from having contracts enforced against them. The party asserting incapacity, his or her guardian, conservator, or other legal representative bears the burden of proof.

An essential element for the formation of a contract is that the object of the contract be lawful. A contract to perform an illegal act is called an **illegal contract**. Illegal contracts are void. That is, they cannot be enforced by either party to the contract. The term *illegal contract* is a misnomer, however, since no contract exists if the object of the contract is illegal. In addition, courts hold that **unconscionable contracts** are unenforceable. An unconscionable contract is one that is so oppressive or manifestly unfair that it would be unjust to enforce it.

Capacity to contract and the lawfulness of contracts are discussed in this chapter.

Minors

Minors do not always have the maturity, experience, or sophistication needed to enter into contracts with adults. Common law defines minors as females under the age of 18 and males under the age of 21. In addition, many states have enacted statutes that specify the *age of majority*. The most prevalent age of majority is 18 years of age for both males and females. Any age below the statutory age of majority is called the *period of minority*.

The Infancy Doctrine

To protect minors, the law recognizes the **infancy doctrine**, which gives minors the right to *disaffirm* (or *cancel*) most contracts they have entered into with adults. This right is based on public policy which reasons that minors should be protected from the unscrupulous behavior of adults. In most states, the infancy doctrine is an objective standard. If a person's age is below the age of majority, the court will not inquire into his or her knowledge, experience, or sophistication. Generally, contracts for the necessaries of life, which we discuss later in this chapter, are exempted from the scope of this doctrine.

The Cheeseman Twins. The infancy doctrine protects minors by permitting them to disavow (void) certain contracts. These contracts are voidable because only the minor, and not the adult on the other side of the contract, may disavow the contract.

Under the infancy doctrine, a minor has the option of choosing whether to enforce a contract (i.e., the contract is *voidable* by a minor). The adult party is bound to the minor's decision. If both parties to a contract are minors, both parties have the right to disaffirm the contract.

If performance of the contract favors the minor, the minor will probably enforce the contract. Otherwise, he or she will probably disaffirm the contract. A minor may not affirm one part of a contract and disaffirm another part.

Disaffirmance

A minor can expressly **disaffirm** a contract orally, in writing, or through his or her conduct. No special formalities are required. The contract may be disaffirmed at any time prior to the person's reaching the age of majority plus a "reasonable time." The designation of a reasonable time is determined on a case-by-case basis.

Duties of Restoration and Restitution

If a minor's contract is executory and neither party has performed, the minor can simply disaffirm the contract: There is nothing to recover since neither party has given the other party anything of value. If the parties have exchanged consideration and partially or fully performed the contract by the time the minor disaffirms the contract, however, the issue becomes one of what consideration or restitution must be made. The following rules apply:

- ■ *Competent party's duty of restitution.* If the minor has transferred consideration—money, property, or other valuables—to the competent party before disaffirming the contract, that party must place the minor in status quo. That is, the minor must be restored to the same position he or she was in before the minor entered into the contract. This restoration is usually done by returning the consideration to the minor. If the consideration has been sold or has depreciated in value, the competent party must pay the minor the cash equivalent. This action is called the **competent party's duty of restitution**.

- ■ *Minor's duty of restoration.* Generally, a minor is obligated only to return the goods or property he or she has received from the adult in the condition it is in at the time of disaffirmance (subject to several exceptions, discussed later in this chapter), even if the item has been consumed, lost, or destroyed or has depreciated in value by the time of disaffirmance. This rule is called the **minor's duty of restoration**. It is based on the rationale that if a minor had to place the adult in status quo upon disaffirmance of a contract, there would be no incentive for an adult not to deal with a minor.

- ■ *Minor's duty of restitution.* Most states provide that the minor must put the adult in status quo upon disaffirmance of the contract if the minor's intentional or grossly negligent conduct caused the loss of value to the adult's property. A few states have enacted statutes that require the minor to make restitution of the reasonable value of the item when disaffirming any contract. This rule is called the **minor's duty of restitution**.

Misrepresentation of Age

On occasion, minors might misrepresent their age to an adult when entering into a contract. Under the common law, such a minor would still have the right to disaffirm the contract. Most states, however, have changed this rule in recognition of its unfairness to adults. The revised rule provides that minors who misrepresent their age must place the adult in status quo if they disaffirm the contract. In other words, a minor who has misrepresented his or her age when entering into a contract owes the duties of restoration and restitution when disaffirming it.

Consider This Example Sherry McNamara, a minor, misrepresents that she is an adult and enters into a contract to purchase an automobile costing $20,000 from Bruce Ruffino, a competent adult. Ruffino delivers the automobile after he receives payments in full. The automobile later sustains $7,000 worth of damage in an accident that is not McNamara's fault. To disaffirm the contract, McNamara must return the damaged automobile plus $13,000 to Ruffino.

Ratification

If a minor does not disaffirm a contract either during the period of minority or within a reasonable time after reaching the age of majority, the contract is considered ratified (accepted). Hence, the minor (who is now an adult) is bound by the contract: The right to disaffirm the contract is lost. Note that any attempt by a minor to ratify a contract while still a minor can be disaffirmed just as the original contract can be disaffirmed.

The **ratification**, which relates back to the inception of the contract, can be by express oral or written words or implied from the minor's conduct (e.g., after reaching the age of majority the minor remains silent regarding the contract).

The following case presents the issue of whether a minor had ratified a contract when he reached the age of majority.

Jones v. Free Flight Sport Aviation, Inc.
623 P.2d 370, 1981 Colo. Lexis 571 (1981)
Supreme Court of Colorado

Case 10.1
Ratification

Background and Facts

On November 17, 1973, William Michael Jones, a 17-year-old minor, signed a contract with Free Flight Sport Aviation, Inc. (Free Flight), for the use of recreational sky-diving facilities. A covenant not to sue and an exculpatory clause exempting Free Flight from liability were included in the contract. On December 28, 1973, Jones attained the age of majority (18 years of age). Ten months later, while on a Free Flight skydiving operation, the airplane crashed shortly after takeoff from Littleton Airport, causing severe personal injuries to Jones. Jones filed suit against Free Flight, alleging negligence and willful and wanton misconduct. The trial court granted summary judgment in favor of Free Flight. The Colorado court of appeals affirmed, Jones appealed.

Issue

Did Jones ratify the contract?

Court's Reasoning

A minor may disaffirm a contract made during his or her minority within a reasonable time after attaining the age of majority or he or she may, after becoming of legal age, by acts recognizing the contract, ratify it. The Colorado supreme court stated: "Affirmance is not merely a matter of intent. It may be deter-

mined by the actions of a minor who accepts the benefits of a contract after reaching the age of majority, or who is silent or acquiesces in the contract for a considerable length of time. We conclude that the trial court properly determined that Jones ratified the contract, as a matter of law, by accepting the benefits of the contract when he used Free Flight's facilities on October 19, 1974."

Decision and Remedy

The supreme court held that Jones had ratified his contract with Free Flight by continuing, for 10 months after reaching the age of majority, to perform under the contract. Therefore, the covenant not to sue and the exculpatory clause exempting Free Flight from liability to Jones were enforceable.

Case Questions

Critical Legal Thinking Should a person be allowed to disaffirm his or her minor's contract after reaching the age of majority? What is a reasonable length of time after reaching the age of majority to permit disaffirmance?

Business Ethics Did Jones act ethically by suing Free Flight Sport Aviation in this case?

Contemporary Business Should the covenant not to sue have been enforced here even though Jones was an adult?

Necessaries of Life

Minors are obligated to pay for the **necessaries of life** that they contract for. Otherwise, many adults would refuse to sell these items to them. There is no standard definition of what is a *necessary of life*, but items such as food, clothing, shelter, and medical services are generally understood to fit this category. Goods and services such as automobiles, tools of trade, education, and vocational training have also been found to be necessaries of life in some situations. The minor's age, lifestyle, and status in life influence what is considered necessary. For example, necessaries for a married minor are greater than those for an unmarried minor.

The seller's recovery is based on the equitable doctrine of **quasi-contract** rather than on the contract itself. Under this theory, the minor is obligated only to pay the reasonable value of the goods or services received. Reasonable value is determined on a case-by-case basis.

Contemporary Environment

Statutes That Make Minors Liable for Special Types of Contracts

The infancy doctrine of the common law of contracts allows minors to disaffirm many contracts they have entered into with adults. Based on public policy, many states have enacted statutes that make certain specified contracts enforceable against minors—that is, minors cannot assert the infancy doctrine against enforcement for these contracts. These usually include contracts for

- Medical, surgical, and pregnancy care
- Psychological counseling
- Health insurance

- Life insurance
- The performance of duties relating to stock and bond transfers, bank accounts, and the like
- Educational loan agreements
- Contracts to support children
- Contracts to enlist in the military
- Artistic, sports, and entertainment contracts that have been entered into with the approval of the court (many of these statutes require that a certain portion of the wages and fees earned by the minor be put in trust until the minor reaches the age of majority) ■

Parent's Liability for Their Children's Contracts

Generally, parents owe a legal duty to provide food, clothing, shelter, and other necessaries of life for their minor children. Parents are liable for their children's contracts for necessaries of life if they have not adequately provided such items.

The parental duty of support terminates if a minor becomes *emancipated*. **Emancipation** occurs when a minor voluntarily leaves home and lives apart from his or her parents. The courts consider factors such as getting married, setting up a separate household, or joining the military service in determining whether a minor is emancipated. Each situation is examined on its merits.

Mentally Incompetent Persons

Mental incapacity may arise because of mental illness, brain damage, mental retardation, senility, and the like. The law protects people suffering from substantial mental incapacity from enforcement of contracts against them because such persons may not understand the consequences of their actions in entering into a contract.

> Insanity vitiates all acts.
> Sir John Nicholl
> *Countess of Portsmouth v. Earl of Portsmouth (1828)*

To be relieved of his or her duties under a contract, the law requires a person to have been legally insane at the time of entering into the contract. This state is called **legal insanity**. Most states use the *objective cognitive "understanding" test* to determine legal insanity. Under this test, the person's mental incapacity must render that person incapable of understanding or comprehending the nature of the transaction. Mere weakness of intellect, slight psychological or emotional problems, or delusions do not constitute legal insanity. The law has developed the following two standards concerning contracts of mentally incompetent persons:

1. *Adjudged insane.* In certain cases, a relative, a loved one, or another interested party may institute a legal action to have someone declared legally (i.e., adjudged) insane. If after hearing the evidence at a formal judicial or administrative hearing the person is **adjudged insane,** the court will make that person a ward of the court and appoint a guardian to act on that person's behalf. Any contract entered into by a person who has been adjudged insane is *void.* That is, no contract exists. The court-appointed guardian is the only one who has the legal authority to enter into contracts on behalf of the person.

2. *Insane, but not adjudged insane.* If no formal ruling has been made—that is, if a person is **insane, but not adjudged insane**—any contracts entered into by a person who suffers from a mental impairment that makes him or her legally insane are voidable by the insane person. Unless the other party does not have contractual capacity, he or she does not have the option to avoid the contract.

Some people have alternating periods of sanity and insanity. Any contracts made by such persons during a lucid interval are enforceable. Contracts made while the person was not legally sane can be disaffirmed.

A person who has dealt with an insane person must place that insane person in status quo if the contract is either void or voided by the insane person. Most states hold that a party who did not know he or she was dealing with an insane person must be placed in status quo upon avoidance of the contract. Insane persons are liable in *quasi-contract* to pay the reasonable value for the necessaries of life they receive.

Concept Summary Disaffirmance of Contracts Based on Legal Insanity

Type of Legal Insanity	Disaffirmance Rule
Adjudged insane	Contract is void. Neither party can enforce the contract.
Insane, but not adjudged insane	Contract is voidable by the insane person; the competent party cannot void the contract.

Intoxicated Persons

Most states provide that contracts entered into by certain **intoxicated persons** are voidable by those persons. The intoxication may occur because of alcohol or drugs. The contract is not voidable by the other party if that party had contractual capacity.

Under the majority rule, the contract is voidable only if the person was so intoxicated when the contract was entered into that he or she was incapable of understanding or comprehending the nature of the transaction. In most states, this rule holds even if the intoxication was self-induced. Some states allow the person to disaffirm the contract only if the person was forced to become intoxicated or did so unknowingly.

The amount of alcohol or drugs that is necessary to be consumed for a person to be considered legally intoxicated to disaffirm contracts varies from case to case. The factors

Men intoxicated are sometimes stunned into sobriety.

Lord Mansfield
R. v. Wilkes (1770)

that are considered include the user's physical characteristics and his or her ability to "hold" intoxicants.

A person who disaffirms a contract based on intoxication generally must be returned to the status quo. In turn, the intoxicated person generally must return the consideration received under the contract to the other party and make restitution that returns the other party to status quo. After becoming sober, an intoxicated person can ratify the contracts he or she entered into while intoxicated. Intoxicated persons are liable in *quasi-contract* to pay the reasonable value for necessaries they receive.

Illegality

One requirement to have an enforceable contract is that the object of the contract must be lawful. Contracts with an illegal object are *void* and therefore unenforceable. The following paragraphs discuss various illegal contracts.

Contracts Contrary to Statutes

Both federal and state legislatures have enacted statutes that prohibit certain types of conduct. For example, penal codes make certain activities crimes, antitrust statutes prohibit certain types of agreements between competitors, and so on. Contracts to perform an activity that is prohibited by statute are illegal contracts.

Usury Laws

State **usury laws** set an upper limit on the annual interest rate that can be charged on certain types of loans. The limits vary from state to state. Lenders who charge a higher rate than the state limit are guilty of usury. These laws are intended to protect unsophisticated borrowers from loan sharks and others who charge exorbitant rates of interest.

Most states provide criminal and civil penalties for making usurious loans. Some states require lenders to remit the difference between the interest rate charged on the loan and the usury rate to the borrower. Other states prohibit lenders from collecting any interest on the loan. Still other states provide that a usurious loan is a void contract, permitting the borrower not to have to pay the interest or the principal of the loan to the lender.

Most usury laws exempt certain types of lenders and loan transactions involving legitimate business transactions from the reach of the law. Often, these exemptions include loans made by banks and other financial institutions, loans above a certain dollar amount, and loans made to corporations and other businesses.

Gambling Statutes

All states either prohibit or regulate gambling, wagering, lotteries, and games of chance via **gambling statutes**. States provide various criminal and civil penalties for illegal gambling. There is a distinction between lawful risk-shifting contracts and gambling contracts. For example, if property insurance is purchased on one's own car and the car is destroyed in an accident, the insurance company must pay the claim. This agreement is a lawful risk-shifting contract because the purchaser had an "insurable interest" in the car. Insurance purchased on a neighbor's car would be considered to be gambling, however. The purchaser does not have an insurable interest in the car and is betting only on its destruction.

There are many exceptions to wagering laws. For example, many states have enacted statutes that permit games of chance under a certain dollar amount, bingo games, lotteries conducted by religious and charitable organizations, and the like. Many states also permit and regulate horse racing, harness racing, dog racing, and state-operated lotteries.

Business Brief

The federal government authorizes Native American Indians to legally operate gambling casinos on Indian reservation property if state law permits such gambling.

Lawful. Federal law permits lawful gambling on American Indian reservation land if the state permits such gambling.

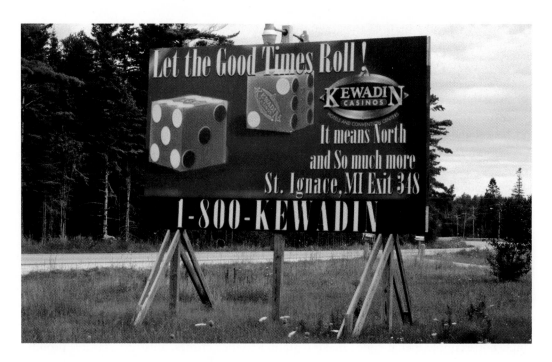

Sabbath Laws

Certain states have enacted laws—called **Sabbath laws**, **Sunday laws**, or **blue laws**—that prohibit or limit the carrying on of certain secular activities on Sundays. Except for contracts for the necessaries of life, charitable donations, and such, these laws generally prohibit or invalidate executory contracts that are entered into on Sunday. Many states do not actively enforce these laws. In some states, they have even been found to be unconstitutional.

Contracts to Commit a Crime

As mentioned previously, contracts to commit criminal acts are void. If the object of a contract became illegal after the contract was entered into because the government enacted a statute that made it unlawful, the parties are discharged from the contract. The contract is not an illegal contract unless the parties agree to go forward and complete it.

Licensing Statutes

All states have **licensing statutes** that require members of certain professions and occupations to be licensed by the state in which they practice. Lawyers, doctors, real estate agents, insurance agents, certified public accountants, teachers, contractors, hairdressers, and such are among them. In most instances, a license is granted to a person who demonstrates that he or she has the proper schooling, experience, and moral character required by the relevant statute. Sometimes, a written examination is also required.

Problems arise if an unlicensed person tries to collect payment for services provided to another under a contract. Some statutes expressly provide that unlicensed persons cannot enforce contracts to provide these services. If the statute is silent on the point, enforcement depends on whether it is a *regulatory statute* or a *revenue-raising statute*:

- ■ *Regulatory statutes.* Licensing statutes enacted to protect the public are called **regulatory statutes**. Generally, unlicensed persons cannot recover payment for services that a regulatory statute requires a licensed person to provide. For example, state law provides that legal services can be provided only by lawyers who have graduated from law school and passed the appropriate bar exam. Nevertheless, suppose Marie Sweiger, a first-year law student, agrees to draft a will for Randy McCabe for a $150 fee. Since Sweiger is not licensed to provide legal services, she has violated a regulatory statute. She cannot enforce the contract and recover payment from McCabe.

■ ***Revenue-raising statutes.*** Licensing statutes enacted to raise money for the government are called **revenue-raising statutes**. A person who provides services pursuant to a contract without the appropriate license required by such a statute can enforce the contract and recover payment for services rendered. For example, suppose a state licensing statute requires licensed attorneys to pay an annual $200 license fee without requiring continuing education or other new qualifications. A licensed attorney who forgets to pay the fee can enforce contracts and recover payment for the legal services he or she renders. The statute merely gathers revenue; protection of the public is not a factor.

Business Ethics
An Unlicensed Contractor Gets Dunked

Hydrotech Systems, Ltd. (Hydrotech), was a New York corporation that manufactured and installed patented equipment to simulate ocean waves. Oasis Waterpark (Oasis) was a California corporation that owned and operated a water-oriented amusement park in Palm Springs, California. Wessman Construction Company, Inc. (Wessman), is Oasis's general contractor at the park.

In July 1985, Wessman contracted with Hydrotech to design and construct a 29,000-square-foot "surfing pool" at the park, using Hydrotech's wave equipment. The total contract price was $850,000. Hydrotech was aware of a California law that requires a contractor to have a California contractor's license to provide construction services in California. The statute stipulates that an unlicensed contractor cannot sue in a California court to recover compensation for work requiring a California contractor's license. [California Business and Professional Code § 7031]

Because it was concerned with the licensing problem, Hydrotech wished only to sell and deliver the equipment and to avoid involvement in the design and construction of the pool. However, Oasis insisted that Hydrotech's unique expertise in design and construction was essential. Oasis induced Hydrotech to provide these services by promising to pay Hydrotech even if the law provided otherwise.

In reliance on these promises, Hydrotech furnished equipment and services in full compliance with the contract. Hydrotech had been paid $740,000 during the course of the contract. When it billed Oasis for the remaining $110,000, Oasis refused to pay. Hydrotech sued Oasis and Wessman for damages in California court for breach of contract and fraud. The defendants moved the court to dismiss the action because Hydrotech did not possess a California contractor's license as required by law.

The California supreme court agreed with the defendants and ordered Hydrotech's complaint dismissed. The court found that Hydrotech had violated the licensing statute. The supreme court stated: "The obvious statutory intent is to discourage persons who have failed to comply with the licensing law from offering or providing their unlicensed services for pay. Because of the strength and clarity of this policy, it is well settled that Section 7031 applies despite injustice to the unlicensed contractor." [*Hydrotech Systems, Ltd. v. Oasis Waterpark*, 52 Cal.3d 988, 277 Cal.Rptr. 517, 1991 Cal. Lexis 139 (CA 1991)]

1. Did Oasis act unethically by not paying Hydrotech? Explain.
2. Did Hydrotech act unethically by providing services in California without the proper license? Explain. ■

Contracts Contrary to Public Policy

Certain contracts are illegal because they are **contrary to public policy**. Such contracts are void. Although *public policy* eludes a precise definition, the courts have held contracts to be contrary to public policy if they have a negative impact on society or interfere with the public's safety and welfare.

Immoral contracts—that is, contracts whose objective is the commission of an act that is considered immoral by society—may be found to be against public policy. For example, a contract that is based on sexual favors has been held to be an immoral contract void as against public policy. Judges are not free to define morality based on their individual views. Instead, they must look to the practices and beliefs of society when defining immoral conduct.

The following case raises the issue of whether a contract violated public policy and was therefore illegal.

Flood v. Fidelity & Guaranty Life Insurance Co.
394 So.2d 1311, 1981 La.App. Lexis 3538 (1981)
Court of Appeals of Louisiana

Case 10.2
Contract Contrary to Public Policy

Background and Facts

Ellen and Richard Alvin Flood, who were married in 1965, lived in a mobile home in Louisiana. Richard worked as a maintenance man, and Ellen was employed at an insurance agency. Evidence at trial showed that Ellen was unhappy with her marriage. Ellen took out a life insurance policy on the life of her husband and named herself as beneficiary. The policy was issued by Fidelity & Guaranty Life Insurance Company (Fidelity). In June 1972, Richard became unexpectedly ill. He was taken to the hospital, where his condition improved. After a visit at the hospital from his wife, however, Richard died. Ellen was criminally charged with the murder of her husband by poisoning. Evidence showed that six medicine bottles at the couple's home, including Tylenol and paregoric bottles, contained arsenic. The court found that Ellen had fed Richard ice cubes laced with arsenic at the hospital. Ellen was tried and convicted of the murder of her husband. Ellen, as beneficiary of Richard's life insurance policy, requested Fidelity to pay her the benefits. Fidelity refused to pay the benefits and returned all premiums paid on the policy. This suit followed. The district court held in favor of Ellen Flood and awarded her the benefits of the life insurance policy. Fidelity appealed.

Issue

Was the life insurance policy an illegal contract that is void?

Court's Reasoning

Louisiana follows the majority rule that holds, as a matter of public policy, that a beneficiary named in a life insurance policy is not entitled to the proceeds of the insurance if the beneficiary feloniously kills the insured. Applying this rule, the appellate court held that Ellen Flood could not recover the life insurance benefits from the policy she had taken out on her husband's life. The court stated: "Life insurance policies are procured because life is, indeed, precarious and uncertain. Our law does not and cannot sanction any scheme which has as its purpose the certain infliction of death for, inter alia, financial gain through receipt of the proceeds of life insurance. To sanction this policy in any way would surely shackle the spirit of the letter and life of our laws."

Decision and Remedy

The appellate court held that the life insurance policy that Ellen Flood had taken out on the life of her husband was void based on public policy. The appellate court reversed the decision of the district court.

Case Questions

Critical Legal Thinking   Should Ellen Flood have been allowed to retain the insurance proceeds in this case?

Business Ethics   Did Ellen Flood act unethically in this case? Did she act illegally?

Contemporary Business   What would be the economic consequences if persons could recover insurance proceeds for losses caused by their illegal activities (e.g., murder, arson)?

Contracts in Restraint of Trade

The general economic policy of this country favors competition. At common law, **contracts in restraint of trade**—that is, contracts that unreasonably restrain trade—are held to be unlawful. For example, it would be an illegal restraint of trade if all the bakers in a neighborhood agreed to fix the prices of the bread they sold. The bakers' contract would be void.

Exculpatory Clauses

An **exculpatory clause** is a contractual provision that relieves one (or both) parties to the contract from tort liability. Exculpatory clauses can relieve a party of liability for ordinary negligence. They cannot be used in situations involving willful conduct, intentional torts, fraud, recklessness, or gross negligence. Exculpatory clauses are often found in leases, sales contracts, ticket stubs to sporting events, parking lot tickets, service contracts, and the like. Such clauses do not have to be reciprocal (i.e., one party may be relieved of tort liability, whereas the other party is not).

Generally, the courts do not favor exculpatory clauses unless both parties have equal bargaining power. The courts are willing to permit competent parties of equal bargaining power to establish which of them bears the risk.

Consider This Example   Jim Jackson voluntarily enrolled in a parachute jump course and signed a contract containing an exculpatory clause that relieved the parachute center of liability. After receiving proper instruction, he jumped from an airplane. Unfortunately, Jim was injured when he could not steer his parachute toward the target area. He sued the parachute center for damages, but the court enforced the exculpatory clause, reasoning that parachute jumping did not involve an essential service and that there was no decisive advantage in bargaining power between the parties.

Exculpatory clauses that either affect the public interest or result from superior bargaining power are usually found to be void as against public policy. Although the outcome varies with the circumstances of the case, the greater the degree to which the party serves the general public, the greater the chance that the exculpatory clause will be struck down as illegal. The courts will consider such factors as the type of activity involved, the relative bargaining power, knowledge, experience, and sophistication of the parties as well as other relevant factors.

In the following case, the court had to decide the legality of an exculpatory clause.

Business Brief

Exculpatory clauses are void as against public policy if they either (1) affect the public interest or (2) result from the superior bargaining power of the party asserting the clause.

Zivich v. Mentor Soccer Club, Inc.
696 N.E.2d 201, 1998 Ohio Lexis 1832 (1998)
Supreme Court of Ohio

Case 10.3
Exculpatory Clause

Background and Facts

In May 1993, Pamela Zivich registered her seven-year-old son, Bryan, to play soccer with the Mentor Soccer Club, Inc. (Club), for the 1993–1994 season. The Club is a nonprofit organization composed primarily of volunteers in the Mentor, Ohio, area who provide children with the opportunity to learn and play soccer. The Club's registration form, which Mrs. Zivich signed, contained the following language:

Recognizing the possibility of physical injury associated with soccer and for the Mentor Soccer Club, and the USYSA [United States Youth Soccer Association] accepting the registrant for its soccer programs and activities, I hereby release, discharge and/or otherwise indemnify the Mentor Soccer Club and the USYSA, its affiliated organizations and sponsors, their employees, and associated personnel, including the owners of the fields and facilities utilized by the Soccer Club, against any claim by or on behalf of the registrant as a result of the registrant's participation in the Soccer Club.

On October 7, 1993, Bryan attended soccer practice with his father, Philip Zivich. During practice, the team participated in an intrasquad scrimmage. After the scrimmage, Bryan jumped onto the soccer goal and was swinging back and forth on it, but the goal was not anchored down. It tipped backward, and Bryan fell. The goal came down on his chest, breaking three of his ribs and his collarbone and severely bruising his lungs. Bryan's parents sued the Club for negligence to recover damages for injuries suffered by Bryan and the loss of consortium for themselves. The Club moved for summary judgment, asserting that the exculpatory agreement signed by Bryan's mother barred the claims. The trial court agreed and granted the Club's summary judgment motion. The court of appeals affirmed. The plaintiffs appealed to the supreme court of Ohio.

Issue

Did the exculpatory agreement signed by Mrs. Zivich on behalf of her son release the Club from liability for the child's claims and the parents' claims?

Court's Reasoning

The Ohio supreme court commented that without the work of their volunteers, nonprofit organizations could not exist, and scores of children would be without the benefit and enjoyment of organized sports. Yet the threat of liability strongly deters many individuals from volunteering for nonprofit organizations. Therefore, faced with the very real threat of a lawsuit, and the potential for substantial damage awards, nonprofit organizations and their volunteers could very well decide that the risks are not worth the effort. Hence, invalidation of exculpatory agreements would reduce the number of activities made possible through the uncompensated services of volunteers and their sponsoring organizations.

The court concluded that although Bryan, like many children before him, gave up his right to sue for the negligent acts of others, the public as a whole received the benefit of the exculpatory agreement. The court stated, "Because of this agreement, the Club was able to offer affordable recreation and to continue to do so without the risks and overwhelming costs of litigation. Bryan's parents agreed to shoulder the risk. Public

Zivich v. Mentor Soccer Club, Inc.

696 N.E.2d 201 1998 Ohio Lexis 1832 (1998)
Supreme Court of Ohio
(continued)

policy does not forbid such an agreement. In fact, public policy supports it."

Decision and Remedy

A parent's signature on an exculpatory agreement on behalf of his or her child releases the other party from liability to the child, the parent who signed the agreement, and the other parent. The supreme court affirmed the decisions of the trial court and court of appeals.

Case Questions

Critical Legal Thinking Do exculpatory agreements serve any valid purpose? Should exculpatory agreements be enforceable?

Business Ethics Was it ethical for Mrs. Zivich to sign the exculpatory agreement and then bring this lawsuit?

Contemporary Business What would have been the consequences if the court had found the exculpatory agreement to be invalid in this case?

Contemporary Environment
Covenant Not to Compete

Entrepreneurs and others often buy and sell businesses. The sale of a business includes its "goodwill" or reputation. To protect this goodwill after the sale, the seller often enters into an agreement with the buyer not to engage in a similar business or occupation within a specified geographic area for a specified period of time following the sale. This agreement is called a **covenant not to compete**, or a **noncompete clause**.

Covenants not to compete that are *ancillary* to a legitimate sale of a business or employment contract are lawful if they are reasonable in three aspects: (1) the line of business protected, (2) the geographic area protected, and (3) the duration of the restriction. A covenant that is found to be unreasonable is not enforceable as written. The reasonableness of covenants not to compete is examined on a case-by-case basis. If a covenant not to compete is unreasonable, the courts may either refuse to enforce it or change it so that it is reasonable. Usually, the courts choose the first option.

Consider This Example Suppose Stacy Rogers is a certified public accountant (CPA) with a lucrative practice in San Diego, California. Her business includes a substantial amount of goodwill. When she sells her practice, she agrees not to open another accounting practice in the state of California for a 20-year period. This covenant not to compete is reasonable in the line of business protected but is unreasonable in geographic scope and duration. It will not be enforced by the courts as written. The covenant not to compete would be reasonable and enforceable if it prohibited Ms. Rogers only from practicing as a CPA in the city of San Diego for 3 years.

Employment contracts often contain noncompete clauses that prohibit an employee from competing with his or her employer for a certain time period after leaving the employment. These covenants not to compete are also judged using the reasonableness standard. ■

Effect of Illegality

Business Brief

As a general rule, the courts will refuse to enforce or rescind an illegal contract and will leave the parties where it finds them.

Because illegal contracts are void, the parties cannot sue for nonperformance. Further, if an illegal contract is executed, the court will generally leave the parties where it finds them.

Exceptions to the General Rule Certain situations are exempt from the general rule of the effect of finding an illegal contract. If an exception applies, the innocent party may use the court system to sue for damages or to recover consideration paid under the illegal contract. Persons who can assert an exception are:

1. Innocent persons who were justifiably ignorant of the law or fact that made the contract illegal. For example, a person who purchases insurance from an unlicensed insurance company may recover insurance benefits from the unlicensed company.

2. Persons who were induced to enter into an illegal contract by fraud, duress, or undue influence. For example, a shop owner who pays $5,000 "protection money" to a mobster so that his store will not be burned down by the mobster can recover the $5,000.

3. Persons who entered into an illegal contract withdrawn before the illegal act is performed. For example, if the president of New Toy Corporation pays $10,000 to an employee of Old Toy Corporation to steal a trade secret from his employer but reconsiders and tells the employee not to do it before he has done it, the New Toy Corporation may recover the $10,000.

4. Persons who were less at fault than the other party for entering into the illegal contract. At common law, parties to an illegal contract were considered **in pari delicto** (in equal fault). Some states have changed this rule and permit less-at-fault parties to recover restitution of the consideration they paid under an illegal contract from the more-at-fault party.

In the following case, the court had to decide the lawfullness of a contract.

Ryno v. Tyra
752 S.W.2d 148, 1988 Tex.App. Lexis 1646 (1988)
Court of Appeals of Texas

Case 10.4
Lawfullness of a Contract

Background and Facts

R. D. Ryno, Jr., owned Bavarian Motors, an automobile dealership in Fort Worth, Texas. On March 5, 1981, Lee Tyra discussed purchasing a 1980 BMW M-1 from Ryno for $125,000. Ryno then suggested a double or nothing coin flip, to which Tyra agreed. If the seller Ryno won the coin flip, Tyra would have to pay $250,000 for the car; if the buyer Tyra won the coin flip, he would get the car for free. When Tyra won the coin flip, Ryno said, "It's yours," and handed Tyra the keys and German title to the car. Tyra drove away in the car. This suit ensued as to the ownership of the car. The trial court held in favor of Tyra. Ryno appealed.

Issue

Was there an illegal contract? Who owns the car?

Court's Reasoning

Ryno argued that the trial court erred in granting Tyra judgment because the judgment enforced a gambling contract. However, the court of appeals held that there was sufficient evidence to sustain the jury finding that Ryno intended to transfer to Tyra his ownership interest in the BMW at the time he delivered the docu-ments, keys, and possession of the automobile to Tyra. The court of appeals agreed with Ryno that his wager with Tyra was unenforceable, and that the trial court could not have compelled Ryno to honor his wager by delivering the BMW to Tyra. However, Ryno did deliver the BMW to Tyra, and the facts incident to that delivery are sufficient to establish a transfer by gift of the BMW from Ryno to Tyra.

Decision and Remedy

Tyra, the patron at the car dealership who won the coin toss, owns the car. The appellate court found that there was an illegal contract and left the parties where it found them—that is, with Tyra in possession of the car. The court of appeals affirmed the trial court's judgment in favor of Tyra.

Case Questions

Critical Legal Thinking   Should the court have lent its resources to help Ryno recover the car?

Business Ethics   Did Ryno act ethically in this case?

Contemporary Business   What is the moral of this story if you ever win anything in an illegal gambling contract?

Unconscionable Contracts

The general rule of freedom of contract holds that if (1) the object of a contract is lawful and (2) the other elements for the formation of a contract are met, the courts will enforce a contract according to its terms. Although it is generally presumed that parties are capable of protecting their own interests when contracting, it is a fact of life that dominant parties sometimes take advantage of weaker parties. As a result, some otherwise lawful contracts are so oppressive or manifestly unfair that they are unjust. To

Morocco. In many parts of the world, the parties usually engage in negotiations that involve substantial posturing prior to agreeing on a final price.

prevent the enforcement of such contracts, the courts developed the equitable **doctrine of unconscionability**, which is based on public policy. A contract found to be unconscionable under this doctrine is called an **unconscionable contract**, or a **contract of adhesion**.

The courts are given substantial discretion in determining whether a contract or contract clause is unconscionable. There is no single definition of *unconscionability*. The doctrine may not be used merely to save a contracting party from a bad bargain.

Elements of Unconscionability

The following elements must be shown to prove that a contract or clause in a contract is unconscionable:

1. The parties possessed severely unequal bargaining power.
2. The dominant party unreasonably used its unequal bargaining power to obtain oppressive or manifestly unfair contract terms.
3. The adhering party had no reasonable alternative.

Unconscionable contracts are sometimes found where there is a consumer contract that takes advantage of uneducated, poor, or elderly people who have been persuaded to enter into an unfair contract. This often involves door-to-door sales and sales over the telephone. For example, suppose a door-to-door salesperson sells a poor family a freezer full of meat and other foods for $3,000, with monthly payments for 60 months at 20 percent interest. If the actual cost of the freezer and the food is $1,000, this contract could be found to be unconscionable.

If the court finds that a contract or contract clause is unconscionable, it may (1) refuse to enforce the contract, (2) refuse to enforce the unconscionable clause but enforce the remainder of the contract, or (3) limit the applicability of any unconscionable clause so as to avoid any unconscionable result. The appropriate remedy depends on the facts and circumstances of each case. Note that because unconscionability is a matter of law, the judge may opt to decide the case without a jury trial.

Chapter Summary

Minors, p. 206

Minors

1. ***Infancy doctrine.*** Minors under the age of majority may *disaffirm* (cancel) most contracts they have entered into with adults. Such a contract is *voidable* by the minor but not by the adult.

2. ***Disaffirmance.*** Disaffirmance must occur before or within a reasonable time after the minor reaches the age of majority.

3. ***Competent party's duty of restitution.*** If a minor disaffirms a contract, the adult must place the minor in status quo by returning the value of the consideration that the minor paid.

4. ***Minor's duty upon disaffirmance:***

   a. *Minor's duty of restoration.* Generally, upon disaffirmance of a contract, a minor owes a duty to return the consideration to the adult in whatever condition it is in at the time of disaffirmance.

   b. *Minor's duty of restitution.* A minor's duty is to place the adult in status quo by returning the value of the consideration paid by the adult at the time of contracting if the minor (1) misrepresented his or her age or (2) intentionally or with gross negligence caused the loss to the adult's property.

5. ***Ratification.*** If a minor does not disaffirm a contract during the period of minority or within a reasonable time after reaching the age of majority, the contract is *ratified* (accepted).

6. ***Necessaries of life.*** Minors are obligated to pay the reasonable value for the necessaries of life (e.g., food, clothing, shelter).

7. ***Special contracts.*** Many states have enacted statutes that make minors liable on certain types of contracts, such as for medical care, health and life insurance, educational loan agreements, and the like.

8. ***Emancipation.*** Emancipation occurs when a minor voluntarily leaves home and lives apart from his or her parents. The parents' duty to support the minor terminates upon emancipation.

Mentally Incompetent Persons, p. 209

Mentally Incompetent Persons

1. ***Adjudged insane.*** Contracts by persons who have been adjudged insane are *void.* That is, such a contract cannot be enforced by either the same or insane party.

2. ***Insane, but not adjudged insane.*** Contracts by persons who are insane but have not been adjudged insane are *voidable* by the insane person but not by the competent party to the contract.

3. ***Duty of restitution.*** A person who has dealt with an insane person must place the insane person in status quo by returning the value of the consideration paid by the insane person at the time of contracting. Most states place the same duty on insane persons when they void a contract.

4. ***Necessaries of life.*** Insane persons are obligated to pay the reasonable value for the necessaries of life.

Intoxicated Persons, p. 210

Intoxicated Persons

1. ***Intoxicated persons.*** Contracts by intoxicated persons are *voidable* by the intoxicated person but not by the competent party to the contract.

2. ***Duty of restitution.*** Both parties owe a duty to place the other party in status quo by returning the value of the consideration paid by the other party at the time of contracting.

3. ***Necessaries of life.*** Intoxicated persons are obliged to pay the reasonable value for the necessaries of life.

Contracts Contrary to Statutes

Contracts that violate statutes are illegal, void, and unenforceable.

1. *Usury laws.* These set the upper limit on the annual interest rate that can be charged on certain types of loans by certain lenders.
2. *Gambling statutes.* These make certain types of gambling illegal.
3. *Sabbath laws.* These prohibit or limit the carrying on of certain secular activities on Sundays. They are also called *Sunday laws* or *blue laws*.
4. *Criminal statutes.* Contracts to commit crimes are illegal.
5. *Licensing statutes:*
   a. *Regulatory statutes.* These are licensing statutes enacted to protect the public. Unlicensed persons cannot recover payment for providing services that a licensed person is required to provide.
   b. *Revenue-raising statutes.* These are licensing statutes enacted to raise money for the government. Unlicensed persons can enforce contracts and recover for rendering services.

Contracts Contrary to Public Policy

Contracts that violate public policy are illegal, void, and unenforceable.

1. *Immoral contracts.* A contract whose objective is the commission of an act that is considered immoral by society is illegal.
2. *Contracts in restraint of trade.* Contracts that unreasonably restrain trade are illegal contracts.
3. *Exculpatory clauses.* Contract clauses that relieve one or both of the parties to the contract from tort liability for ordinary negligence are called exculpatory clauses. Exculpatory clauses that affect public interests, that result from superior bargaining power, or that attempt to relieve one of liability for intentional torts, fraud, recklessness, or gross negligence are illegal. Reasonable exculpatory clauses between parties of equal bargaining power are legal.
4. *Covenants not to compete.* These are contracts that provide that a seller of a business or an employee will not engage in a similar business or occupation within a specified geographical area for a specified time following the sale of the business or termination of employment. Also called *noncompete clauses.* They are illegal if they are *unreasonable* in line of business, geographic area, or time. Reasonable noncompete clauses are legal and enforceable.

Effect of Illegality

1. *General rule.* An illegal contract is *void.* Therefore, the parties cannot sue for nonperformance. If the contract has been executed, the court will *leave the parties where it finds them.*
2. *Exceptions to the general rule.* An innocent party can use the courts to recover consideration paid or damages under an illegal contract where the person
   a. Was justifiably ignorant of the law or fact that made the contract illegal.
   b. Was induced to enter into the illegal contract by fraud, duress, or undue influence.
   c. Withdrew from the illegal contract before it was performed.
   d. Was less at fault than the other party to the illegal contract.

Unconscionable Contracts

Contracts that are oppressively unfair or unjust are called *unconscionable contracts*, or *contracts of adhesion*.

1. *Elements of unconscionable contracts:*
   a. The parties possessed severely unequal bargaining power.
   b. The dominant party unreasonably used its power to obtain oppressive or manifestly unfair contract terms.
   c. The adhering party had no reasonable alternative.

2. *Remedies for unconscionability:* Where a contract or contract clause is found to be unconscionable, the court may do one of the following:

   a. Refuse to enforce the contract.

   b. Refuse to enforce the unconscionable clause but enforce the remainder of the contract.

   c. Limit the applicability of any unconscionable clause so as to avoid any unconscionable result.

Internet Exercises and Case Questions

Working the Web Internet Exercises

Activities

Note: To search for statutory law of the 50 U.S. states, try **www.hg.org/usstates.html**. A good summary of the rules relating to capacity can be found at **consumer.pub.findlaw. com/newcontent/consumerlaw/chp2_a.html**. Capacity as it relates to other areas of the law is summarized at **cobrands.consumer.findlaw.com/newcontent/flg/ch15/st7/ mc1.html**.

1. Review the laws of your jurisdiction regarding minors and purchases of alcohol and tobacco, purchases of motor vehicles, and renting of an apartment.

2. Find the Web site for your state that explains the requisite level of intoxication for a driving-while-impaired traffic citation. Would that minimum amount be sufficient to provide a lack of capacity defense to a contract claim?

3. Find your state statutes relating to usury. What is the maximum allowable interest rate?

4. An extensive overview of contract law can be found at Contracts Home Page (Craig Smith, Santa Barbara College of Law), **www.west.net/~smith/contracts.htm**. Review the "Policing the Bargain" page. Note that *capacity* is listed with other problem areas.

Critical Legal Thinking Cases

10.1 Infancy Doctrine   James Halbman, Jr., a minor, entered into a contract to purchase a 1968 Oldsmobile automobile from Michael Lemke. Halbman paid $1,000 cash and agreed to pay $25 per week until the full purchase price was paid. Five weeks later, a connecting rod on the vehicle's engine broke, and Halbman took the car to a garage, where it was repaired at a cost of $637.40. Halbman refused to pay for the repairs, disaffirmed the contract with Lemke, and notified Lemke where the car was located. When Lemke refused to pick up the car and pay the repair bill, the garage legally satisfied its garageman's lien by removing the vehicle's engine. It then towed the car to Halbman's residence. Halbman notified Lemke to remove the car, but Lemke refused to do so. The car was subsequently vandalized, making it worthless and unsalvageable. Halbman sued to disaffirm the contract and recover the consideration from Lemke. Lemke argued that Halbman must make full restitution. Who is correct? [*Halbman v. Lemke*, 298 N.W.2d 562, 1980 Wisc. Lexis 2825 (Wis. 1980)]

10.2 Ratification of a Minor's Contract   Charles Edwards Smith, a minor, purchased an automobile from Bobby Floars Toyota (Toyota) on August 15, 1973. Smith executed a security agreement to finance part of the balance due on the purchase price, agreeing to pay off the balance in 30 monthly installments. On September 25, 1973, Smith turned 18, which was the age of majority in his state. Smith made 10 monthly payments after turning 18. He then decided to disaffirm the contract and stopped making the payments. Smith claims that he may disaffirm the contract entered into when he was a minor. Toyota argues that Smith had ratified the contract since attaining the age of majority. Who is correct? [*Bobby Floars Toyota, Inc. v. Smith*, 269 S.E. 320, 1980 N.C.App. Lexis 3263 (N.C. App. 1980)]

10.3 Emancipation   Dwaine Ebsen, an 18-year-old minor, lived with his widowed mother, Violet. After numerous arguments with his mother regarding the people he associated with, Dwaine and his mother agreed that he should move out and support himself. Dwaine took his personal belongings and moved to Orchard, Nebraska. After moving out, Dwaine received no further support from his mother. While living in Orchard, Dwaine was shot and taken to a hospital for treatment. He remained in the hospital for two weeks. Thereafter, the hospital sought payment from Violet. When she refused to pay, the hospital turned the matter over to Accent Service Company, a collection agency, which brought this action against Violet. Is Violet liable for her son's medical expenses? [*Accent Service Company v. Ebsen*, 306 N.W.2d 575, 1981 Neb. Lexis 878 (NE 1981)]

10.4 Adjudicated Insane   Manzelle Johnson, who had been adjudicated insane, executed a quitclaim and warranty deed conveying real estate she owned to her guardian, Obbie Neal. Neal subsequently conveyed the real estate to James R. Beavers by warranty deed. Charles L. Weatherly, Johnson's present guardian, brought this action seeking a decree of the court that title to the real estate be restored to Johnson because of her inability to contract. Should Johnson be allowed to void the contract? [*Beavers v. Weatherly*, 299 S.E.2d 730, 1983 Ga. Lexis 581 (GA 1983)]

10.5 Intoxication   Betty Galloway, an alcoholic, signed a settlement agreement upon her divorce from her husband, Henry Galloway. Henry, in Betty's absence in court, stated that she had lucid intervals from her alcoholism, had been sober for two months, and was lucid when she signed the settlement agreement on September 22, 1978. Betty moved only to vacate the settlement agreement on September 27, 1978, after she had retained present legal counsel. On January 23, 1979, Betty was declared incompetent to handle her person and her affairs, and a guardian and conservator was appointed. Betty, through her guardian, sued to have the settlement agreement voided. Who wins? [*Galloway v. Galloway*, 281 N.W.2d 804, 1979 N.D. Lexis 279 (N.D. 1979)]

10.6 Licensing or Revenue-Raising Statute   The state of Hawaii requires a person who wants to practice architecture to meet certain educational requirements and to pass a written examination before that person is granted a license to practice. After receiving the license, an architect must pay an annual license fee of $15. In 1967, Ben Lee Wilson satisfied the initial requirements and was granted an architecture license. He renewed his license by paying the annual fee up until April 1971, when he failed to pay the annual fee. In February 1972, Wilson contracted with Kealakekua Ranch, Ltd., and Gentry Hawaii (defendants) to provide architectural services for the Kealakekua Ranch Center project. During the period February 1972 through May 1972, Wilson provided $33,994 of architectural services to the defendants. The defendants refused to pay this fee because Wilson did not have an architectural license. Wilson sued to collect his fees. Who wins? [*Wilson v. Kealakekua Ranch, Ltd., and Gentry Hawaii*, 551 P.2d 525, 1976 Harv. Lexis 119 (HI 1976)]

10.7 Covenant Not to Compete   Gerry Morris owned a silk screening and lettering shop in Tucson, Arizona. On April 11, 1974, Morris entered into a contract to sell the business to Alfred and Connie Gann. The contract contained the following covenant not to compete: "Seller agrees not to enter into silk screening or lettering shop business within Tucson and a 100-mile radius of Tucson, for a period of ten (10) years from the date of this agreement and will not compete in any manner whatsoever with buyers, and seller further agrees that he will refer all business contracts to buyers." Morris opened a silk screening and lettering business in competition with the Ganns and in violation of the noncompetition clause. The Ganns brought this action against Morris for breach of contract and to enforce the covenant not to compete. Is the covenant not to compete valid and enforceable in this case? [*Gann v. Morris*, 596 P.2d 43, 1979 Ariz.App. Lexis 487 (Ariz. App. 1979)]

10.8 Exculpatory Clause   Grady Perkins owned the Raleigh Institute of Cosmetology (Institute), and Ray Monk and Rovetta Allen were employed as instructors there. The school trained students to do hair styling and coloring, cosmetology, and other beauty services. The students received practical training by providing services to members of the public under the supervision of the instructors. On March 28, 1985, Francis I. Alston went to the Institute to have her hair colored and styled by a student who was under the supervision of Monk and Allen. Before receiving any services, Alston signed a written release form that released the Institute and its employees from liability for their negligence. While coloring Alston's hair, the student negligently used a chemical that caused Alston's hair to fall out. Alston sued the Institute, Perkins, Monk, and Allen for damages. The defendants asserted that the release form signed by Alston barred her suit. Is the exculpatory clause valid? [*Alston v. Monk*, 373 S.E.2d 463, 1988 N.C. App. Lexis 987 (N.C. App. 1988)]

10.9 Exculpatory Clause   Wilbur Spaulding owned and operated the Jacksonville racetrack at the Morgan County Fairgrounds, where automobile races were held. Lawrence P. Koch was a flagman at the raceway. On May 28, 1982, when Koch arrived at the pit shack at the raceway, he was handed a clipboard upon which was a track release and waiver of liability form that released the racetrack from liability for negligence. Koch signed the form and took up his position as flagman. During the first race, the last car on the track lost control and slid off the end of the track, striking Koch. Koch suffered a broken leg and other injuries and was unable to work for 14 months. Koch sued Spaulding for damages for negligence. Spaulding asserted that the release form signed by Koch barred his suit. Is the exculpatory clause valid against Koch? [*Koch v. Spaulding*, 529 N.E.2d 19, 1988 Ill.App. Lexis 1427 (Ill. App. 1988)]

10.10 Unconscionable Contract   Bill Graham, an experienced promoter and producer of musical concerts, entered into a contract with Leon Russell, a rock singer who did business under the corporate name Scissor-Tail, Inc., whereby Graham would promote several concerts for Russell. Russell belonged to the American Federation of Musicians (AFM), a union that represented most big-name musicians. The contract between Graham and Russell was on a standard, preprinted form required to be used by all AFM members. The contract contained an arbitration clause that required any disputes regarding the contract to be heard and decided by the executive board of the AFM. When a monetary dispute arose between Graham and Russell regarding the division of proceeds from the concerts, Graham sued Russell in court. Russell filed a motion to compel arbitration. Graham asserted that the arbitration clause in the AFM contract was unconscionable. Is it? [*Graham v. Scissor-Tail, Inc.*, 28 Cal.App. 3d 807, 171 Cal.Rptr. 604, 1981 Cal. Lexis 115 (Cal. App. 1981)]

Business Ethics Cases

10.11 Business Ethics   Joe Plumlee owned and operated an ambulance company. He alleged that the law firm of Paddock, Loveless & Roach agreed to pay him an up-front fee and a percentage of the law firm's fees generated from personal injury case referrals. When the law firm did not pay Plumlee, he sued to recover damages for breach of contract. Texas law prohibits lawyers from sharing fees with laypersons. [Tex. Penal Code § 38.12; supreme court of Texas] A disciplinary rule also forbids such activity. [State Bar Rules Art. X, § 9] The law firm asserted that the contract could not be enforced because it would be an illegal contract. Who wins? Did Plumlee act ethically in this case? If the contract existed, did the lawyers act ethically? [*Plumlee v. Paddock, Loveless, and Roach*, 832 S.W.2d 757, 1992 Tex.App. Lexis 1544 (Tex. App. 1992)]

10.12 Business Ethics   Richard Zientara was friends with Chester and Bernice Kaszuba. All three were residents of Indiana. Bernice, who was employed in an Illinois tavern where Illinois state lottery tickets were sold, had previously obtained lottery tickets for Zientara because Indiana did not have a state lottery. In early April 1984, Zientara requested that Kaszuba purchase an Illinois lottery ticket for him. He gave Kaszuba the money for the ticket and the numbers 6–15–16–23–24–37. Kaszuba purchased the ticket, but when it turned out to be the winning combination worth $1,696,800 she refused to give the ticket to Zientara and unsuccessfully tried to collect the money. Zientara filed suit against Kaszuba in Indiana, claiming the ticket and proceeds thereof. Was the contract legal? Did the Kaszubas act ethically in this case? [*Kaszuba v. Zientara*, 506 N.E.2d 1, 1987 Ind. Lexis 874 (Ind. 1987)]

Briefing the Case Writing Assignment

Read Case A.10 in the Case Appendix [*Carnival Leisure Industries, Ltd. v. Aubin*]. This case is excerpted from the court of appeals opinion. Review and brief the case. In your brief, be sure to answer the following questions:

1. What were the plaintiff's contentions on appeal?

2. What law was applied by the court in this case, Bahamian law or Texas law? Why was that law applied?

3. What is the consequence of finding an illegal contract? Apply this rule to the facts of this case.

4. Did Aubin act ethically in avoiding an obligation that he knowingly made? Do you think he would have given back the money if he had won at gambling?

Reality of Consent and Writing

> " A verbal contract isn't worth the paper it's written on. "
>
> —Samuel Goldwyn

Chapter Objectives

After studying this chapter, you should be able to:

1. Explain genuineness of assent.
2. Distinguish between unilateral and mutual mistakes of fact.
3. Describe fraudulent misrepresentation, undue influence, and duress.
4. List and describe the contracts that must be in writing under the Statute of Frauds.
5. Apply the parol evidence rule.

Chapter Contents

- Mistakes
- Fraudulent Misrepresentation
- Undue Influence
- Duress
- Statute of Frauds
- Sufficiency of the Writing

A contract may not be enforced even if all the required elements of a legal contract are met. This situation happens when the party against whom enforcement is sought raises certain defenses against its enforcement.

There are two primary defenses to the enforcement of a contract. The first is that the assent of one or both of the parties to the contract was not genuine or real. **Genuine assent** may be missing because a party entered into a contract based on mistake, fraudulent misrepresentation, duress, or undue influence. The second defense is that the contract did not meet the requirements of the Statute of Frauds. The Statute of Frauds requires certain contracts to be in writing or in a stipulated form.

Problems concerning genuineness of assent and writing are discussed in this chapter.

> Most of the disputes in the world arise from words.
>
> Lord Mansfield, C. J.
> *Morgan v. Jones* (1773)

Mistakes

A **mistake** occurs where one or both of the parties has an erroneous belief about the subject matter, value, or some other aspect of a contract. Mistakes may be either *unilateral* or *mutual*. The law permits **rescission** of some contracts made in mistake.

Unilateral Mistakes

Unilateral mistakes occur when only one party is mistaken about a material fact regarding the subject matter of the contract. There are three types of situations in which a contract may not be enforced due to such a mistake:

1. One party makes a unilateral mistake of fact and the other party knew (or should have known) that a mistake was made.
2. A unilateral mistake occurs because of a clerical or mathematical error that is not the result of gross negligence.
3. The mistake is so serious that enforcing the contract would be unconscionable.[1]

In most cases, however, the mistaken party will not be permitted to rescind the contract. The contract will be enforced on its terms.

Consider This Example   Suppose Trent Anderson wants to purchase a car from the showroom floor. He looks at several models. Although he decides to purchase a car with a sunroof, he does not tell the salesperson about this preference. The model named in the contract he signs does not have this feature, although he believes it does. Anderson's unilateral mistake will not relieve him of his contractual obligation to purchase the car.

In the following case, the court had to decide whether to allow a party out of a contract because of the party's unilateral mistake.

> Words are chameleons, which reflect the color of their environment.
>
> Justice L. Hand
> *Commissioner v. National Carbide Co.* (1948)

Wells Fargo Credit Corp. v. Martin

650 So.2d 531, 1992 Fla.App. Lexis 9927 (1992)
District Court of Appeals of Florida

Case 11.1
Unilateral Mistake

Background and Facts

Wells Fargo Credit Corporation (Wells Fargo) obtained a judgment of foreclosure on a house owned by Mr. and Mrs. Clevenger. The total indebtedness stated in the judgment was $207,141. The foreclosure sale was scheduled for 11:00 A.M. on July 12, 1991, at the west front door of the Hillsborough County Courthouse.

Wells Fargo was represented by a paralegal, who had attended more than 1,000 similar sales. Wells Fargo's handwritten instruction sheet informed the paralegal to make one bid at $115,000, the tax-appraised value of the property. Because the first "1" in the number was close to the "$," the paralegal misread the bid instruction as $15,000 and opened the bidding at that amount.

Wells Fargo Credit Corp. v. Martin

650 So.2d 531, 1992 Fla.App. Lexis 9927 (1992)
District Court of Appeals of Florida
(continued)

Harley Martin, who was attending his first judicial sale, bid $20,000. The county clerk gave ample time for another bid and then announced, "$20,000 going once, $20,000 going twice, sold to Harley..." The paralegal screamed, "Stop, I'm sorry, I made a mistake!" The certificate of sale was issued to Martin. Wells Fargo filed suit to set aside the judicial sale based on its unilateral mistake. The trail court held for Martin. Wells Fargo appealed.

Issue

Does Wells Fargo's unilateral mistake constitute grounds for setting aside the judicial sale?

Court's Reasoning

The appellate court held that Martin's right to purchase the property vested at the moment the county clerk announced "sold." Generally, a unilateral mistake will not permit the mistaken party

to rescind a contract. The appellate court held that the trial court had the discretion to place the risk of the mistake on Wells Fargo.

Decision and Remedy

The appellate court held that Wells Fargo's unilateral mistake did not entitle it to relief from the judicial sale.

Case Questions

Critical Legal Thinking Should contracts be allowed to be rescinded because of unilateral mistakes? Why or why not?

Business Ethics Did Wells Fargo act ethically in trying to set aside the judicial sale?

Contemporary Business Do you think mistakes such as that made by Wells Fargo happen very often in business?

Mutual Mistakes

Either party may rescind a contract if there has been a **mutual mistake of a past or existing material fact**.[2] A *material fact* is a fact that is important to the subject matter of a contract. An ambiguity in a contract may constitute a mutual mistake of a material fact. An ambiguity occurs where a word or term in the contract is susceptible to more than one logical interpretation. If there has been a mutual mistake, the contract may be rescinded on the ground that no contract has been formed because there has been no "meeting of the minds" between the parties.

Landmark Law

In *Raffles v. Wichelhaus*, the court held that a mutual mistake of fact excused performance of the contract.

In the celebrated case *Raffles v. Wichelhaus*,[3] which has become better known as the case of the good ship *Peerless*, the parties agreed on a sale of cotton that was to be delivered from Bombay by the ship. There were two ships named *Peerless*, however, and each party, in agreeing to the sale, was referring to a different ship. Because the sailing time of the two ships was materially different, neither party was willing to agree to shipment by the other *Peerless*. The court ruled that there was no binding contract because each party had a different ship in mind when the contract was entered into.

The courts must distinguish between *mutual mistakes of fact* and *mutual mistakes of value*. A **mutual mistake of value** exists if both parties know the object of the contract but are mistaken as to its value. Here, the contract remains enforceable by either party because the identity of the subject matter of the contract is not at issue. If the rule were different, almost all contracts could later be rescinded by the party who got the "worst" of the deal.

The meaning of words varies according to the circumstances of and concerning which they are used.

Justice Blackburn
Allgood v. Blake (1873)

Consider This Example   Suppose Eileen Ney cleans her attic and finds a painting of tomato soup cans. She has no use for it, so she offers to sell it to Fred Lee for $100. Fred, who likes the painting, accepts the offer and pays Eileen $100. It is later discovered that the painting is worth $200,000 because it was painted by Andy Warhol. Neither party knew this at the time of contracting. It is a mistake of value. Eileen cannot recover the painting.

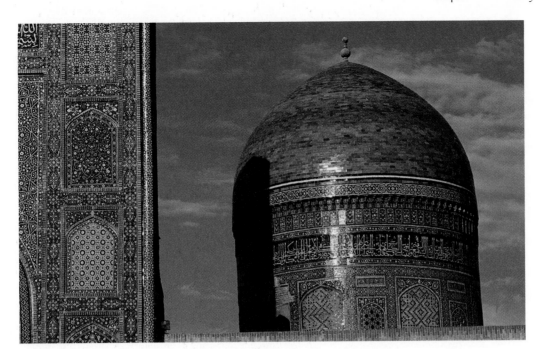

Fraudulent Misrepresentation

A misrepresentation occurs when an assertion is made that is not in accord with the facts.[4] An **intentional misrepresentation** occurs when one person consciously decides to induce another person to rely and act on a misrepresentation. Intentional misrepresentation is commonly referred to as **fraudulent misrepresentation**, or **fraud**. When fraudulent misrepresentation is used to induce another to enter into a contract, the innocent party's assent to the contract is not genuine and the contract is voidable by the innocent party.[5] The innocent party can either rescind the contract and obtain restitution or enforce the contract and sue for contract damages.

> Fraud includes the pretense of knowledge when knowledge there is none.
>
> Chief Justice Cardozo
> *Ultramares Corp. v. Touche (1931)*

Business Ethics
Don't Be Taken by Fraud

Entrepreneurs and other businesspersons must be on guard in their commercial dealings not to be taken by fraud. Basically, if it sounds "too good to be true," it is a signal that the situation might be fraudulent. But some frauds are difficult to detect. To prove fraud, the following elements must be shown:

1. The wrongdoer made a false representation of material fact.
2. The wrongdoer intended to deceive the innocent party.
3. The innocent party justifiably relied on the misrepresentation.
4. The innocent party was injured.

Each of these elements is discussed in the following paragraphs:

- *Material misrepresentation of fact.* A misrepresentation may occur by words (oral or written) or by the conduct of the party. To be actionable as fraud, the misrepresentation must be of a past or existing *material fact*. This means that the misrepresentation must have been a significant factor in inducing the innocent party to enter into the contract. It does not have to have been the sole factor. Statements of opinion or predictions about the future generally do not form the basis for fraud.

- *Intent to deceive.* To prove fraud, the person making the misrepresentation must have either had knowledge that the representation was false or made it without sufficient knowledge of the truth. This is called **scienter** ("guilty mind"). The misrepresentation must have been made with the intent to deceive the innocent party. Intent can be inferred from the circumstances.

Business Ethics

(continued)

■ *Reliance on the misrepresentation.* A misrepresentation is not actionable unless the innocent party to whom the misrepresentation was directed acted upon it. Further, an innocent party who acts in reliance on the misrepresentation must justify his or her reliance.[6] Justifiable reliance is generally found unless the innocent party knew that the misrepresentation was false or was so extravagant as to be obviously false. For example, reliance on a statement such as "This diamond ring is worth $10,000, but I'll sell it to you for $100" would not be justified.

■ *Injury to the innocent party.* To recover damages, the innocent party must prove that the fraud caused economic injury. The measure of damages is the difference between the value of the property as represented and the actual value of the property. This measure of damages gives the innocent party the "benefit of the bargain." In the alternative, the buyer can rescind the contract and recover the purchase price.

1. Are most misrepresentations intended? Explain.
2. What do you think is the probability of being defrauded in life? ■

Types of Fraud

There are various types of fraud. Some of the most common ones follow:

1. *Fraud in the inception.* **Fraud in the inception,** or **fraud in the factum,** occurs if a person is deceived as to the nature of his or her act and does not know what he or she is signing. Such contracts are void rather than just voidable. For example, suppose Heather brings her professor a grade card to sign. The professor signs the front of the grade card. On the back, however, are contract terms that transfer all of the professor's property to Heather. Here there is fraud in the inception. The contract is void.

2. *Fraud in the inducement.* A great many fraud cases concern **fraud in the inducement.** Here, the innocent party knows what he or she is signing but has been fraudulently induced to enter into the contract. Such contracts are voidable by the innocent party. For example, suppose Lyle Green tells Candice Young he is forming a partnership to invest in drilling for oil and invites her to invest in this venture. In reality, though, Green intends to use whatever money he receives for his personal expenses, and he absconds with Young's $30,000 investment. Here, there has been fraud in the inducement. Young can rescind the contract and recover the money from Green, if he can be found.

3. *Fraud by concealment.* **Fraud by concealment** occurs when one party takes specific action to conceal a material fact from another party.[7] For example, suppose that ABC Blouses, Inc. contracts to buy a used sewing machine from Wear-Well Shirts, Inc. Wear-Well did not show ABC the repair invoices from the sewing machine, even though ABC asked to see them. Relying on the knowledge that the machine was in good condition and never had to be repaired, ABC bought the machine. If ABC discovers that a significant repair record has been concealed, it can sue Wear-Well for fraud.

4. *Silence as misrepresentation.* Generally, neither party to a contract owes a duty to disclose all the facts to the other party. Ordinarily, such silence is not a misrepresentation unless (1) nondisclosure would cause bodily injury or death, (2) there is a fiduciary relationship (i.e., a relationship of trust and confidence) between the contracting parties or (3) federal and state statutes require disclosure. The *Restatement (Second) of Contracts* specifies a broader duty of disclosure: Nondisclosure is a misrepresentation if it would constitute a failure to act in "good faith."[8]

5. *Misrepresentation of law.* Usually, a misrepresentation of law is not actionable as fraud. The innocent party cannot generally rescind the contract because each party to a contract is assumed to know the law that applies to the transaction, either through

Business Brief

Although the law permits a victim of fraud to rescind the contract and recover damages from the wrongdoer, often the wrongdoer cannot be found or the money has been spent. Therefore, it is best to be cautious not to become a victim of fraud by questioning deals that are "too good to be true."

A charge of fraud is such a terrible thing to bring against a man that it cannot be maintained in any court unless it is shown that he had a wicked mind.

M. R. Lord Esher
Le Lievre v. Gould (1732)

his or her own investigation or by hiring a lawyer. There is one major exception to this rule: The misrepresentation will be allowed as grounds for rescission of the contract if one party to the contract is a professional who should know what the law is and intentionally misrepresents the law to a less sophisticated contracting party.[9]

In the following case, the court allowed a contract to be rescinded.

Wilson v. Western National Life Insurance Co.
235 Cal.App.3d 981. 1 Cal.Rptr.2d 157, 1991 Cal.App. Lexis. 1249 (1991)
California Court of Appeals

Case 11.2
Fraud

Background and Facts

Daniel and Doris Wilson were husband and wife. On August 13, 1985, Daniel fainted from a narcotics overdose and was rushed, unconscious, to the hospital. Doris accompanied him. Daniel responded to medication used to counteract a narcotics overdose and recovered. The emergency room physician noted that Daniel had probably suffered from a heroin overdose and that Daniel had multiple puncture sites on his arms.

On October 8, 1985, an agent for Western National Life Insurance Company (Western) met with the Wilsons in their home for the purpose of taking their application for life insurance. The agent asked questions and recorded the Wilsons' responses on a written application form. Daniel answered the following questions:

	Yes	No
13. In the past 10 years, have you been treated or joined an organization for alcoholism or drug addiction? If "Yes," explain on the reverse side.		X
17. In the past 5 years, have you consulted or been treated or examined by any physician or practitioner?		X

Both of the Wilsons signed the application form and paid the agent the first month's premium. Under insurance law and the application form, the life insurance policy took effect immediately. Daniel Wilson died from a drug overdose two days later. Western rescinded the policy and rejected Doris Wilson's claim to recover the policy's $50,000 death benefit for Daniel's death, alleging failure to disclose the August 13, 1985, incident. Doris sued to recover the death benefits. The trial court granted summary judgment for Western. Doris appealed.

Issue

Was there a concealment of a material fact that justified Western's rescission of the life insurance policy?

Court's Reasoning

A material misrepresentation or concealment, whether intentional or innocent, entitles the injured party to rescind the contract. The court held that the Wilsons had made such a misrepresentation by concealment, that it was material, and that Western had relied on it and had been injured. The court found that Western would not have issued the life insurance policy to Daniel Wilson if it had been informed of his prior drug overdose.

Decision and Remedy

The appellate court held that there was a concealment by the Wilsons that warranted rescission of the life insurance policy by Western.

Case Questions

Critical Legal Thinking Should a contract be allowed to be rescinded because of an *innocent* misrepresentation? Why or why not?

Business Ethics Do you think the concealment in this case was intentional or innocent?

Contemporary Business Do you think there is very much insurance fraud in this country? Explain.

Innocent Misrepresentation

An **innocent misrepresentation** occurs when a person makes a statement of fact that he or she honestly and reasonably believes to be true, even though it is not. Innocent misrepresentation is not fraud. If an innocent misrepresentation has been made, the aggrieved party may rescind the contract but may not sue for damages. Often, innocent misrepresentation is treated as a mutual mistake.

Concept Summary *Types of Misrepresentation*

Type of Misrepresentation	Legal Consequences—Innocent Party May:	
	Sue for Damages	Rescind Contract
Fraud in the inception	Yes	Yes
Fraud in the inducement	Yes	Yes
Fraud by concealment	Yes	Yes
Silence as a misrepresentation	Yes	Yes
Misrepresentation of law	Usually no	Usually no
Innocent misrepresentation	No	Yes

Undue Influence

The courts may permit the rescission of a contract based on the equitable doctrine of **undue influence**. Undue influence occurs when one person (the dominant party) takes advantage of another person's mental, emotional, or physical weakness and unduly persuades that person (the servient party) to enter into a contract. The persuasion by the wrongdoer must overcome the free will of the innocent party. A contract that is entered into because of undue influence is voidable by the innocent party.[10] Wills are often challenged as having been made under undue influence.

The following elements must be shown to prove undue influence:

1. A fiduciary or confidential relationship must have existed between the parties.
2. The dominant party must have unduly used his or her influence to persuade the servient party to enter into a contract.

If there is a confidential relationship between persons—such as a lawyer and a client, a doctor and a patient, a psychiatrist and a patient—any contract made by the servient party that benefits the dominant party is presumed to be entered into under undue influence. This rebuttable presumption can be overcome through proper evidence.

Consider This Example   Mr. Johnson, 70 years old, has a stroke and is partially paralyzed. He is required to use a wheelchair, and he needs constant nursing care. Prior to his stroke, Mr. Johnson had executed a will, leaving his property upon his death equally to his four grandchildren. Edward, a licensed nurse, is hired to care for Mr. Johnson on a daily basis, and Mr. Johnson relies on Edward's care. Edward works for Mr. Johnson for two years before Mr. Johnson passes away. It is discovered that Mr. Johnson had executed a new will three months before he died, leaving all of his property to Edward. If it is shown that Edward has used his dominant and fiduciary position to unduly influence Mr. Johnson to change his will, then the will is invalid. If no undue influence is shown, the second will is valid, and Edward will receive the property left to him by Mr. Johnson in the will.

Duress

Duress occurs when one party threatens to do some wrongful act unless the other party enters into a contract. If a party to a contract has been forced into making the contract, the assent is not voluntary. Such a contract is not enforceable against the innocent party. For example, if someone threatens to harm another person unless that person signs a contract, this is *physical duress*. This contract cannot be enforced against the duressed party.

The threat to commit physical harm or extortion unless someone enters into a contract constitutes duress. So does a threat to bring (or not drop) a criminal lawsuit. Such threats are duress even if the criminal lawsuit is well founded.[11] A threat to bring (or not drop) a civil lawsuit, however, does not constitute duress unless such a suit is frivolous or brought in bad faith.

Statute of Frauds

In 1677, the English Parliament enacted a statute called "An Act for the Prevention of Frauds and Perjuries." This act required that certain types of contracts had to be in writing and signed by the party against whom enforcement was sought. Today, every U.S. state has enacted a **Statute of Frauds** that requires certain types of contracts to be in *writing*. This statute is intended to ensure that the terms of important contracts are not forgotten, misunderstood, or fabricated.

Writing Requirement

Although the statutes vary slightly from state to state, most states require the following types of contracts to be in writing:[12]

- Contracts involving interests in land
- Contracts that by their own terms cannot possibly be performed within one year
- Collateral contracts in which a person promises to answer for the debt or duty of another
- Promises made in consideration of marriage
- Contracts for the sale of goods for more than $500
- Real estate agents' contracts
- Agents' contracts where the underlying contract must be in writing
- Promises to write a will
- Contracts to pay debts barred by the statute of limitations or discharged in bankruptcy
- Contracts to pay compensation for services rendered in negotiating the purchase of a business
- Finder's fee contracts

> Statute of Frauds: That unfortunate statute, the misguided application of which has been the cause of so many frauds.
>
> Bacon, V.C.
> *Morgan v. Worthington (1878)*

Generally, an *executory contract* that is not in writing even though the Statute of Frauds requires it to be is unenforceable by either party. (If the contract is valid in all other respects, however, it may be voluntarily performed by the parties.) The Statute of Frauds is usually raised by one party as a defense to the enforcement of the contract by the other party. If an oral contract that should have been in writing under the Statute of Frauds is already executed, neither party can seek to rescind the contract on the ground of noncompliance with the Statute of Frauds.

Business Brief

Although only certain contracts must be in writing under the Statute of Frauds, it is good practice to place other contracts in writing so there is no dispute as to the terms of the contract at a later date.

Contracts Involving Interests in Land

Under the Statutes of Frauds, any contract that transfers an ownership interest in **real property** must be in writing to be enforceable. Real property includes the land itself, buildings, trees, soil, minerals, timber, plants, crops, fixtures, and things permanently affixed to the land or buildings. Certain items of personal property that are permanently affixed to the real property—for example, built-in cabinets in a house—are **fixtures** that become part of the real property.

Other contracts that transfer an ownership interest in land must be in writing under the Statute of Frauds. These interests include the following:

- *Mortgages.* Borrowers often give a lender an interest in real property as security for the repayment of a loan. This action must be done through the use of a written **mortgage** or **deed of trust**. For example, suppose ABC Corporation purchases a factory and borrows part of the purchase price from City Bank. City Bank requires that the factory be used as collateral for the loan and takes a mortgage on the factory. Here, the mortgage must be in writing to be enforceable.

- *Leases.* A lease is the transfer of the right to use real property for a specified period of time. Most Statutes of Frauds require leases for a term over one year to be in writing.

- *Life estates.* On some occasions, a person is given a **life estate** in real property. In other words, the person has an interest in the land for the person's lifetime, and the interest will be transferred to another party on that person's death. A life estate is an ownership interest that must be in writing under the Statute of Frauds.

- *Easements.* An **easement** is a given or required right to use another person's land without owning or leasing it. Easements may be either express or implied. Express easements must be in writing to be enforceable, while implied easements need not be written.

Part Performance Exception If an oral contract for the sale of land or transfer of another interest in real property has been partially performed, it may not be possible to return the parties to their *status quo*. To solve this problem, the courts have developed the equitable doctrine of **part performance**. This doctrine allows the court to order such an oral contract to be specifically performed if performance is necessary to avoid injustice. For this performance exception to apply, most courts require that the purchaser either pay part of the purchase price and take possession of the property or make valuable improvements on the land.

The following case applies the doctrine of part performance.

Sutton v. Warner
12 Cal.App.4th 415, 15 Cal.Rptr.2d 632, 1993 Cal.App. Lexis 22 (1993)
California Court of Appeal

Background and Facts

In 1983, Arlene and Donald Warner inherited a one-third interest in a home at 101 Molimo Street in San Francisco. The Warners bought out the other heirs and obtained a $170,000 loan on the property. Donald Warner and Kenneth Sutton were friends. In January 1984, Donald Warner proposed that Sutton and his wife purchase the residence. His proposal included a $15,000 down payment toward the purchase price of $185,000. The Suttons were to pay all the mortgage payments and real estate taxes on the property for five years, and at any time during the five-year period they could purchase the house. All this was agreed to orally. The Suttons paid the down payment and cash payments equal to the monthly mortgage ($1,881) to the Warners. They paid the annual property taxes on the house. The Suttons also made improvements to the property. In July 1988, the Warners reneged on the sales/option agreement. At that time the house had risen in value to between $250,000 and $320,000. The Suttons sued for specific performance of the sales agreement. The Warners defended, alleging that the oral promise to sell real estate had to be in writing under the Statute of Frauds and was therefore unenforceable. The trial court applied the equitable doctrine of part performance and ordered specific performance. The Warners appealed.

Issue

Does the equitable doctrine of part performance make this oral contract for the sale of real property enforceable even though the Statute of Frauds usually requires a contract for the sale of real property to be in writing?

Court's Reasoning

Normally, a contract to purchase real property must be in writing to satisfy the Statute of Frauds. However, in this case the court of appeals held that part performance by the Suttons—making the down payment, paying the monthly mortgage payments and the annual property tax payment, and making improvements to the property—sufficed to remove the bar of the Statute of Frauds. Therefore, the specific performance of the oral contract to sell real estate is equitable.

Decision and Remedy

The appellate court held that the doctrine of part performance applied and that the Statute of Frauds did not prevent the enforcement of the oral contract to sell real estate.

Case Questions

Critical Legal Thinking   What purposes are served by the Statute of Frauds? Explain.

Business Ethics   Did the Warners act ethically in this case? Did the Statute of Frauds give them a justifiable reason not to go through with the deal?

Contemporary Business   Should important business contracts be put in writing? Why or why not?

One-Year Rule

According to the Statute of Frauds, an executory contract that cannot be performed by its own terms within one year of its formation must be in writing.[13] This **one-year rule** is intended to prevent disputes about contract terms that may otherwise occur toward the end of a long-term contract. If the performance of the contract is possible within the one-year period, the contract may be oral.

The extension of an oral contract might cause the contract to violate the Statute of Frauds. For example, suppose the owner of a Burger King franchise hires Eugene Daly as a manager for 6 months. This contract may be oral. Assume that after 3 month, the owner and manager agree to extend the contract for an additional 11 months. At the time of the extension, the contract would be for 14 months (the 3 left on the contract plus 11 added by the extension). The modification would have to be in writing because it exceeds the one-year rule.

Business Brief

Employment contracts are often for periods longer than one year. These contracts must be in writing to be enforceable.

Guaranty Contract

A **guaranty contract** occurs when one person agrees to answer for the debts or duties of another person. Guaranty contracts are required to be in writing under the Statute of Frauds.[14]

Exhibit 11.1

Original and Guaranty Contracts

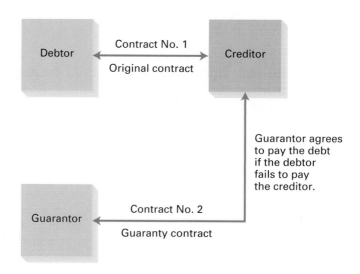

In a guaranty situation, there are at least three parties and two contracts. (See Exhibit 11.1.) The *first contract*, which is known as the **original**, or **primary, contract**, is between the debtor and the creditor. It does not have to be in writing (unless another provision of the Statute of Frauds requires it to be). The *second contract*, called the **guaranty contract**, is between the person who agrees to pay the debt if the primary debtor does not (i.e., the **guarantor**) and the original creditor. The guarantor's liability is secondary because it does not arise unless the party primarily liable fails to perform.

Consider This Example Jay Hoberman, a recent college graduate, offers to purchase a new automobile on credit from a General Motors dealership. Because the purchaser does not have a credit history, the dealer will agree to sell the car only if there is a guarantor. Jay's mother signs the guaranty contract. She becomes responsible for any payments her son fails to make.

The "Main Purpose" Exception If the main purpose of a transaction and an oral collateral contract is to provide pecuniary (i.e., financial) benefit to the guarantor, the collateral contract is treated like an original contract and does not have to be in writing to be enforced.[15] This exception is called the **main purpose**, or **leading object, exception** to the Statute of Frauds. This exception is intended to ensure that the primary benefactor of the original contract (i.e., the guarantor) is answerable for the debt or duty.

Consider This Example Suppose Ethel Brand is president and sole shareholder of Brand Computer Corporation, Inc. Assume that (1) the corporation borrows $100,000 from City Bank for working capital and (2) Ethel orally guarantees to repay the loan if the corporation fails to pay it. City Bank can enforce the oral guaranty contract against Ethel if the corporation does not meet its obligation because the main purpose of the loan was to benefit her as the sole shareholder of the corporation.

Contracts for the Sale of Goods

Section 201 of the **Uniform Commercial Code (UCC)** is the basic Statute of Frauds provision for sales contracts. It requires that contracts for the sale of goods costing *$500 or more* must be in writing to be enforceable.[16] If the contract price of an original sales contract is below $500, it does not have to be in writing under the **UCC Statute or Frauds**, but if a modification of the contract increases the sales price to $500 or more, the **modification** has to be in writing to be enforceable.[17]

Consider This Example   Echo enters into an oral contract to sell James her used car for $10,000, with the delivery date to be May 1. When May 1 comes and James tenders $10,000 to Echo, Echo refuses to sell her car to James. The contract will not be enforced against Echo because it was an oral contract for the sale of goods costing $500 or more, and it should have been in writing.

Agents' Contracts

Many state Statutes of Frauds require that *agents' contracts* to sell real property covered by the Statute of Frauds be in writing to be enforceable. The requirement is often referred to as the **equal dignity rule**.

Consider This Example   Suppose Barney Berkowitz hires Cynthia Lamont, a licensed Century-21 real estate agent, to sell his house. Because a contract to sell real estate must be in writing pursuant to the Statute of Frauds, the equal dignity rule requires the agents' contract to be in writing as well. Some state Statutes of Frauds expressly list the agents' contracts that must be in writing.

Promises Made in Consideration of Marriage

Under the Statute of Frauds, a unilateral promise to pay money or property in consideration for a promise to marry must be in writing. For example, a **prenuptial agreement**, which is a contract entered into by parties prior to marriage that defines their ownership rights in each other's property, must be in writing.

Promissory Estoppel

The doctrine of **promissory estoppel**, or **equitable estoppel**, is another equitable exception to the strict application of the Statute of Frauds. The version of promissory estoppel in the *Restatement (Second) of Contracts* provides that if parties enter into an oral contract that should be in writing under the Statute of Frauds, the oral promise is enforceable against the promisor if these three conditions are met: (1) The promise induces action or forbearance of action by another, (2) the reliance on the oral promise was foreseeable, and (3) injustice can be avoided only by enforcing the oral promise.[18] Where this doctrine applies, the promisor is **estopped** (prevented) from raising the Statute of Frauds as a defense to the enforcement of the oral contract.

> To break an oral agreement which is not legally binding is morally wrong.
>
> Talmud
> *Bava Metzi'a*

Business Ethics

An Oral Contract Isn't Worth the Paper It's Written On

The Statute of Frauds, which requires certain contracts to be in writing before they are enforceable, is designed to prevent fraud. Entrepreneurs and other businesspersons should know the requirements of the state's Statute of Frauds; otherwise, they may find themselves with an unenforceable oral contract. Consider the following case.

Whitman Heffernan Rhein & Co., Inc. (Whitman), is a company that provides financial advice to firms planning mergers and acquisitions. The Griffin Company (Griffin), which is owned primarily by Merv Griffin, was negotiating to purchase Resorts International, Inc., from Donald Trump. Whitman alleged that it entered into an oral contract to provide the Griffin Company with financial and investment advice in connection with the negotiation of the purchase of Resorts International. Once Griffin completed the acquisition of Resorts International from Trump, Whitman requested payment for its services from Griffin. When Griffin did not pay, Whitman sued Griffin to recover payment. Griffin asserted the New York Statute of Frauds in defense, arguing that Whitman's alleged contract to provide services in negotiating the purchase of a business had to be in writing to be enforceable, and because Whitman's complaint alleged that it was an oral contract, it was not enforceable.

Business Ethics

(continued)

The New York court agreed with Griffin and held that the alleged contract was oral and therefore barred by the Statute of Frauds. The court stated:

New York General Obligation Law § 5-701(a)(10) provides that an agreement is void, unless evidenced by a writing signed by the party to be charged, if the agreement is a contract to pay compensation for services rendered in negotiating the purchase of a business. The term "negotiating" includes assisting in the consummation of the transaction.

The moral of the story for agents, entrepreneurs, and other businesspersons is: Get it in writing! [*Whitman Heffernan Rhein & Co., Inc. v. The Griffin Co.*, 557 NY.S.2d 342 1990 N.Y.App.Div. Lexis 8334 (NY 1990)]

1. What is the purpose of the Statute of Frauds? Explain.
2. Does applying the Statute of Frauds ever cause an unfair result? Explain. ■

Sufficiency of the Writing

Business Brief

Written contracts do not have to appear in a formally drafted document. A writing on a napkin, scrap of paper, tie, and so forth is sufficient.

Counsel Randle Jackson: In the book of nature, my lords, it is written—Lord Ellenborough: Will you have the goodness to mention the page, sir, if you please.

Lord Campbell
Lives of the Chief Justices (1857)

Both the common law of contracts and the UCC have adopted several rules regarding the legal sufficiency of written contracts. These rules are discussed in the following paragraphs.

Formality of the Writing

Some written commercial contracts are long, detailed documents that have been negotiated by the parties and drafted and reviewed by their lawyers. Others are preprinted forms with blanks that can be filled in to fit the facts of a particular situation.

A written contract does not, however, have to be either drafted by a lawyer or formally typed to be legally binding. Generally, the law only requires a writing containing the essential terms of the parties' agreement. For example, any writing—including letters, telegrams, invoices, sales receipts, checks, and handwritten agreements written on scraps of paper—can be an enforceable contract under this rule.

Required Signature

Business Brief

Only the signature of the party against whom enforcement is sought needs to be on a written contract.

The Statute of Frauds and the UCC require a written contract, whatever its form, to be signed *by the party against whom enforcement is sought.* The signature of the person who is enforcing the contract is not necessary. Thus, a written contract may be enforceable against one party but not the other party.

Generally, the signature may appear anywhere on the writing. In addition, it does not have to be a person's full legal name. For example, the person's last name, first name, nickname, initials, seal, stamp, engraving, or other symbol or mark (e.g., an *X*) that indicates the person's intent can be binding. The signature may be affixed by an authorized agent.

Integration of Several Writings

Both the common law of contracts and the UCC permit several writings to be **integrated** to form a single written contract. That is, the entire writing does not have to appear in one document to be an enforceable contract.

Integration may be by an *express reference* in one document that refers to and incorporates another document within it. This procedure is called **incorporation by reference**. Thus, what may often look like a simple one-page contract may actually be hundreds of pages long. For example, credit cards often incorporate by express reference such documents as the master agreement between the issuer and cardholders, subsequent amendments to the agreement, and such.

Several documents may be integrated to form a single written contract if they are somehow physically attached to each other to indicate a party's intent to show integration. For example, attaching several documents together with a staple, paper clip, or some other means may indicate integration. Placing several documents in the same container (e.g., an envelope) may also indicate integration. This action is called *implied integration*.

Interpreting Contract Words and Terms

When contracts are at issue in a lawsuit, courts are often called upon to interpret the meaning of certain contract words or terms. The parties to a contract may define the words and terms used in their contract. Many written contracts contain a detailed definition section—usually called a **glossary**—that defines many of the words and terms used in the contract.

If the parties have not defined the words and terms of a contract, the courts apply the following **standards of interpretation**:

- *Ordinary* words are given their usual meaning according to the dictionary.
- *Technical words* are given their technical meaning, unless a different meaning is clearly intended.
- *Specific terms* are presumed to qualify *general terms*. For example, if a provision in a contract refers to the subject matter as "corn," but a later provision refers to the subject matter as "feed corn" for cattle, this specific term qualifies the general term.
- If both parties are members of the same trade or profession, words will be given their meaning as used in the trade (i.e., *usage of trade*). If the parties do not want trade usage to apply, the contract must indicate that.
- Where a preprinted form contract is used, *typed words* in a contract prevail over *preprinted words*. *Handwritten words* prevail over both preprinted and typed words.
- If there is an ambiguity in a contract, the ambiguity will be resolved against the party who drafted the contract.

Bhutan. Oral contracts are used more in many foreign countries than they are in the United States.

The Parol Evidence Rule

By the time a contract is reduced to writing, the parties usually have engaged in prior or contemporaneous discussions and negotiations or exchanged prior writings. Any oral or written words outside the *four corners* of the written contract are called **parol evidence**. *Parol* means "word."

The **parol evidence rule** was originally developed by courts as part of the common law of contracts. The UCC has adopted the parol evidence rule as part of the law of sales contracts.[19] The parol evidence rule states that if a written contract is a complete and final statement of the parties' agreement (i.e., a **complete integration**), any prior or contemporaneous oral or written statements that alter, contradict, or are in addition to the terms of the written contract are inadmissible in any court proceeding concerning the contract.[20] In other words, a completely integrated contract is viewed as the best evidence of the terms of the parties' agreement.

Exceptions to the Parol Evidence Rule

There are several major exceptions to the general rule excluding parol evidence. Parol evidence may be admitted in court if it:

- Shows that a contract is void or voidable (e.g., evidence that the contract was induced by fraud, misrepresentation, duress, undue influence, or mistake).
- Explains ambiguous language.
- Concerns *a prior course of dealing or course of performance* between the parties or a *usage of trade*.[21]
- *Fills in the gaps* in a contract (e.g., if a price term or time of performance term is omitted from a written contract, the court can hear parol evidence to imply the reasonable price or time of performance under the contract).
- Corrects an obvious clerical or typographical error. The court can **reform** the contract to reflect the correction.

Merger, or Integration, Clause

The parties to a written contract may include a clause stipulating that the contract is a complete integration and the exclusive expression of their agreement and that parol evidence may not be introduced to explain, alter, contradict, or add to the terms of the contract. This type of clause, called a **merger**, or **integration, clause**, expressly reiterates the parol evidence rule.

International Law

Japanese *Hankos* and Chinese Chops as Signatures

Americans, Europeans, and many others in the world use their personal hand-applied signatures on legal documents. In Japan, China, and other countries of Asia, however, individuals often do not use their hand-applied signatures to sign legal documents. Instead, they follow the age-old tradition of using a stamp as their signature. The stamp is a character or set of characters carved onto the end of a cylinder-shaped piece held in a person's hand. The characters are carved onto one end of the cylinder. The owner places this end in ink and then applies this end to the document to be signed, leaving an imprint that serves as the owner's signature. In Japan this cylinder is called a *hanko*; in China it is called a *chop*. *Hankos* and *chops* are registered with the government. *Hankos* and *chops* can be made of ivory, jade, agate, gold, animal's horn, wood, or even plastic.

In societies that use personal signatures, if a signature is suspected of being forged, the victim can hire handwriting experts and use modern technology to prove it is not his or her signature. In Japan, China, and other countries where *hankos* and *chops* are used, it is much more difficult to prove forgery since anyone in possession of another's *hanko* or *chop* can apply it. Some people predict the demise of the *hanko* and *chop* because of the possible problem of fraud and the increased use of hand-applied signatures by younger persons in countries used to using the *hanko* and *chop*. Others predict that the rich tradition of using a *hanko* or *chop* will continue. ∎

Chapter Summary

Mistakes, p. 225

Unilateral Mistakes

These mistakes occur when only one party is mistaken about a material fact regarding the subject matter of a contract. The legal consequences are:

1. *General rule.* The mistaken party is not permitted to rescind the contract.
2. *Exceptions.* The mistaken party can rescind the contract if:
   a. The other party knew or should have known of the mistake and took advantage of it.
   b. The mistake occurred because of a clerical or mathematical error that was not the result of gross negligence.
   c. The mistake is so serious that enforcing the contract would be unconscionable.

Mutual Mistakes

1. *Mutual mistake of fact.* If both parties are mistaken about the essence or object of a contract, either party may rescind the contract.
2. *Mutual mistake of value.* If both parties know the object of a contract but are mistaken as to its value, neither party may rescind the contract.

Fraudulent Misrepresentation, p. 227

Elements of Fraud

Fraudulent misrepresentation. Fraudulent misrepresentation occurs when a person intentionally makes an assertion that is not in accord with the facts. Also called *fraud.*

1. *Elements of fraud:*
   a. The wrongdoer made a false representation of material fact.
   b. The wrongdoer intended to deceive the innocent party.
   c. The innocent party justifiably relied on the misrepresentation.
   d. The innocent party was injured.
2. *Legal consequence if fraudulent misrepresentation is found.* The innocent party may:
   a. Rescind the contract and obtain restitution, or
   b. Enforce the contract and sue for damages

Types of Fraud

Common types of fraud:

1. *Fraud in the inception.* With this type of fraud, an innocent person is deceived as to the nature of his or her act. Also called *fraud in the factum.*
2. *Fraud in the inducement.* With this type of fraud, the wrongdoer fraudulently induces another party to enter into a contract.
3. *Fraud by concealment.* With this type of fraud, the wrongdoer takes specific action to conceal a material fact from the other party.
4. *Silence as misrepresentation.* With this type of fraud, the wrongdoer remains silent when he or she is under a legal obligation to disclose a material fact.
5. *Misrepresentation of law.* A professional who should know what the law is may intentionally misrepresent the law to a less sophisticated party.

Innocent Misrepresentation

When a person unintentionally makes an assertion that is not in accord with the facts, the innocent party may rescind the contract but cannot recover damages. Innocent misrepresentation is not fraud.

Undue Influence, p. 230

Undue Influence

Undue influence occurs when one person takes advantage of another person's mental, emotional, or physical weakness and unduly persuades that person to enter into a contract. A contract entered into under undue influence cannot be enforced.

> 1. *Elements of undue influence:*
>   - *a.* A fiduciary or confidential relationship existed between the dominant and servient parties.
>   - *b.* The dominant party unduly used his or her influence to persuade the servient party to enter into a contract.
> 2. *Presumption.* If there is a confidential relationship between person, any contract by the servient party that benefits the dominant party is presumed to have been entered into under undue influence. This position is a *rebuttable presumption.*

Duress, p. 230

Duress

Duress occurs when one party threatens to do some wrongful act unless the other party enters into a contract. A contract entered into under duress cannot be enforced. Types of duress:

1. Physical duress
2. Extortion

Statute of Frauds, p. 231

Writing Requirement

Statute of Frauds. This state statute requires that the following contracts to be in writing:

> 1. *Contracts involving the transfer of interests in real property.* This includes contracts for the sale of land, buildings and items attached to land, mortgages, leases for a term of more than one year, and express easements.
>   - *a. Part performance exception.* This exception permits the specific enforcement of oral contracts for the sale of land when they have been partially performed to avoid injustice.
> 2. *Contracts that cannot be performed within one year of their formation.*
> 3. *Collateral contracts.* These contracts occur where one person promises to answer for the debts or duties of another person. Also called *guaranty contracts.*
>   - *a. Main purpose exception.* This exception permits enforcement of oral collateral promises if the main or leading purpose of the collateral promise is to benefit the guarantor.
> 4. *Promises made in consideration of marriage, such as prenuptial agreements.*
> 5. *Agents' contracts to sell real property.*
> 6. *Contracts for the sale of goods costing $500 or more.* [UCC §201]

Promissory Estoppel

Promissory estoppel is an equitable doctrine that prevents the application of the Statute of Frauds. It permits the enforcement of oral contracts that should otherwise be in writing under the Statute of Frauds to prevent injustice or unjust enrichment.

Sufficiency of the Writing, p. 236

Sufficiency of the Writing

> 1. *Formality of the writing.* A written contract does not have to be formal or drafted by a lawyer to be enforceable. Informal contracts, such as handwritten notes, letters, and invoices, are enforceable contracts.

2. **Required signature.** The party against whom enforcement of the contract is sought must have signed the contract. The signature may be the person's full legal name, last name, first name, nickname, initials, or other symbol or mark.

3. **Integration of several writings.** Several writings may be integrated to form a contract. Integration may be by:

  a. Express reference. In this case, one document expressly incorporates another document.

  b. Implied reference. In this case, documents are physically attached by staple or by paper clip or are placed in the same envelop.

The Parol Evidence Rule

1. **Parol evidence.** Parol evidence consists of any oral or written words that are outside the four corners of a written contract.

2. **Parol evidence rule.** This rule provides that if a written contract is a complete integration, any prior contemporaneous oral or written statements are inadmissible as evidence to alter or contradict the terms of the written contract.

3. **Exceptions to the parol evidence rule.** Parol evidence may be admitted in court to:

  a. Prove mistake, fraud, misrepresentation, undue influence, or duress.

  b. Explain ambiguous language.

  c. Explain a prior course of dealing or course of performance between the parties or a usage of trade.

  d. Fill in the gaps in a contract.

  e. Correct obvious clerical or typographical errors.

Interpretation of Contracts

The courts have developed the following rules for interpreting contracts:

1. *Ordinary words* are given their usual dictionary meaning.

2. *Technical words* are given their technical meaning, unless a different meaning is clearly intended.

3. *Specific terms* are presumed to qualify *general terms*.

4. *Typed words* prevail over *preprinted words; handwritten words* prevail over both preprinted and typed words.

5. Ambiguities in a contract are resolved against the party who drafted the contract.

6. Unless otherwise agreed, words will be given their usual meaning in the trade if both parties are members of the same trade.

 Internet Exercises and Case Questions

Working the Web Internet Exercises

Activities

1. For a practical Q & A on contract basics, see **consumer.pub.findlaw.com/newcontent/flg/ch9/st2/tl.html**.

2. For an interesting case involving genuineness of assent, go to **www.legalwa.org** and type in *Barnes v. Treece, 15 Wn.App. 437.*

3. For an overview of the developing law of e-commerce and digital signatures, see "Are Online Business Transactions Executed by Electronic Signatures Legally Binding?" at **www.law.duke.edu/journals/dltr/ARTICLES/2001dltr 0005.html** and "Protecting the Digital Consumer: The Limits of Cyberspace Utopianism" at **www.law.indiana.edu/ilj/v74/no3/rothchil.pdf**.

4. While common law contract principles have general application, many contracts are regulated on an industry-wide basis, by state statutes. See **www.law.cornell.edu/topics/topic2.html#particular** for examples.

5. For an overview of defenses to contract claims, see **www.west.net/~smith/contracts.htm**.

Critical Legal Thinking Cases

11.1 Unilateral Mistake Mrs. Chaney died in 1985, leaving a house in Annapolis, Maryland. The representative of her estate listed the property for sale with a real estate broker, stating that the property was approximately 15,650 square feet. Drs. Steele and Faust made an offer of $300,000 for the property, which was accepted by the estate. A contract for the sale of the property was signed by all the parties on July 3, 1985. When a subsequent survey done before the deed was transferred showed that the property had an area of 22,047 square feet, the estate requested the buyers to pay more money for the property. When the estate refused to transfer the property to the buyers, they sued for specific performance. Can the estate rescind the contract? [*Steele v. Goettee*, 542 A.2d 847, 1988 Md. Lexis. 91 (Md. App. 1988)]

11.2 Mutual Mistake Ron Boskett, a part-time coin dealer, purchased a dime purportedly minted in 1916 at the Denver Mint for nearly $450. The fact that the *D* on the coin signified Denver mintage made the coin rare and valuable. Boskett sold the coin to Beachcomber Coins, Inc. (Beachcomber), a retail coin dealer, for $500. A principal of Beachcomber examined the coin for 15 to 45 minutes prior to its purchase. Soon thereafter, Beachcomber received an offer of $700 for the coin, subject to certification of its genuineness by the American Numismatic Society. When this organization labeled the coin counterfeit, Beachcomber sued Boskett to rescind the purchase of the coin. Can Beachcomber rescind the contract? [*Beachcomber Coins, Inc. v. Boskett*, 400 A.2d 78, 1979 N.J.Super. Lexis 659 (NJ 1979)]

11.3 Fraud Robert McClure owned a vehicle salvage and rebuilding business. He listed the business for sale and had a brochure printed that described the business and stated that during 1981 the business grossed $581,117 and netted $142,727. Fred H. Campbell saw the brochure and inquired about buying the business. Campbell hired a CPA to review. McClure's business records and tax returns, but the CPA could not reconcile these with the income claimed for the business in the brochure. When Campbell asked McClure about the discrepancy, McClure stated that the business records did and tax returns did not accurately reflect the cash flow or profits of the business because it was such a high-cash operation, with much of the cash not being reported to the Internal Revenue Service on tax returns. McClure signed a warranty which stated that the true income of the business was as represented in the brochure. Campbell bought the business based on these representations. The business, however, although operated in substantially the same manner as when owned by McClure, failed to yield a net income similar to that warranted by McClure. Evidence showed that McClure's representations were substantially overstated. Campbell sued McClure for damages for fraud. Who wins? [*Campbell v. McClure*, 182 Cal.App.3d 806, 227 Cal.Rptr. 450, 1986 Cal.App. Lexis 1751 (Cal. App. 1986)]

11.4 Fraud James L. "Skip" Deupree, a developer, was building a development of town houses called Point South in Destin, Florida. All the town houses in the development were to have individual boat slips. Sam and Louise Butner, husband and wife, bought one of the town houses. The sales contract between Deupree and the Butners provided that a boat slip would be built and included in the price of the town house. The contract stated that permission from the Florida Department of Natural Resources (DNR) had to be obtained to build the boat slips. It is undisputed that a boat slip adds substantially to the value of the property and that the Butners relied on the town house having a boat slip. Prior to the sale of the town house to the Butners, the DNR had informed Deupree that it objected to the plan to build the boat slips and that permission to build them would probably not be forthcoming. Deupree did not tell the Butners this information but instead stated that there would be "no problem" in getting permission from the state to build the boat slips. When the DNR would not approve the building of the boat slips for the Butners' town house, they sued for damages for fraud. Who wins? [*Deupree v. Butner*, 522 So.2d 242, 1988 Ala. Lexis 55 (AL 1988)]

11.5 Undue Influence Conrad Schaneman, Sr., had eight sons and five daughters. He owned four 80-acre farms in the Scottsbluff are of Nebraska. Conrad was born in Russia and could not read or write English. Prior to 1974, all his children had frequent contact with Conrad and helped with his needs. In 1974, his eldest son, Lawrence, advised the other children that he would henceforth manage his father's business affairs. On March 18, 1975, after much urging by Lawrence, Conrad deeded the farm to Lawrence for $23,500. Evidence showed that at the time of the sale, the reasonable fair market value of the farm was between $145,000 and $160,000. At the time of the conveyance, Conrad was over 80 years old; had deteriorated in health; suffered from heart problems, diabetes, high and uncontrollable blood sugar levels; weighed almost 300 pounds; had difficulty breathing; could not walk more than 15 feet; and had to have a jackhoist lift him in and out of the bathtub. He was for all purposes an invalid, relying on Lawrence for most of his personal needs, transportation, banking, and other business matters. After Conrad died, the conservators of the estate brought this action to cancel the deed transferring the farm to Lawrence. Can the conservators cancel the deed? [*Schaneman v. Schaneman*, 291 N.W.2d 412, 1980 Neb. Lexis 823 (NE 1980)]

11.6 Land Contract In 1976, Fritz Hoffman and Fritz Frey contacted the Sun Valley Company (Company) about purchasing a 1.64-acre piece of property known as the "Ruud Mountain Property," located in Sun Valley, Idaho, from the Company. Mr. Conger, a representative of the Company, was authorized to sell the property, subject to the approval of the executive committee of the Company. On January 21, 1977, Conger reached an agreement on the telephone with Hoffman and Frey, whereby they would purchase the property for $90,000, payable at 30 percent down, with the balance to be payable quarterly at an annual interest rate of $9\frac{3}{4}$ percent. The next day Hoffman sent Conger a letter, confirming the conversation. The executive committee of the Company approved the sale. Sun Valley Realty prepared the deed of trust, note, seller's closing statement, and other loan documents. Before the documents were executed by either side, however, the Company sold all its assets, including the Ruud Mountain Property, to another purchaser. When the new owner refused to sell the Ruud Mountain lot to Hoffman and Frey, they brought this action for specific performance of the oral contract. Do they win? [*Hoffman v. Sun Valley Company*, 628 P.2d 218, 1981 Ida. Lexis 320 (ID 1981)]

11.7 Land Contract In 1955, Robert Briggs and his wife purchased a home located at 167 Lower Orchard Drive, Levittown, Pennsylvania. They made a $100 down payment and borrowed the balance of $11,600 on a 30-year mortgage. In late 1961, when the Briggs family was behind on mortgage payments, it entered into an oral contract to sell the house to Winfield and

Emma Sackett if the Sacketts would pay the three months' arrearages on the loan and agree to make future payments on the mortgage. Mrs. Briggs and Mrs. Sackett were sisters. The Sacketts paid the arrearages, moved into the house, and continued to lived there. In 1976, Robert Briggs filed an action to void the oral contract as in violation of the Statute of Frauds and evict the Sacketts from the house. Who wins? [*Briggs v. Sackett*, 418 A.2d 586, 1980 Pa.Super. Lexis 2034 (Pa. App. 1980)]

11.8 One-Year Contract   Robert S. Ohanian was vice president of sales for the West Region of Avis Rent a Car System, Inc. (Avis). Officers of Avis testified that Ohanian's performance in the West Region was excellent and, in a depressed economic period, Ohanian's West Region stood out as the one region that was growing and profitable. In the fall of 1980, when Avis's Northeast Region was doing badly, the president of Avis asked Ohanian to take over that region. Ohanian was reluctant to do so, since he and his family liked living in San Francisco, he had developed a good team in the West Region, he was secure in his position, and he feared he politics of the Northeast Region. Ohanian agreed to the transfer only after the general manager of Avis orally told him, "Unless you screw up badly, there is no way you are going to get fired—you will never get hurt here in this company." Ohanian did a commendable job in the Northeast Region. Approximately one year later, on July 27, 1982, at the age of 47, Ohanian was fired without cause by Avis. Ohanian sued Avis for breach of the oral lifetime contract. Avis asserted the Statute of Frauds against this claim. Who wins? [*Ohanian v. Avis Rent a Car System, Inc.*, 779 F.2d 101, 1985 U.S.App. Lexis 25456 (2nd Cir. 1985)]

11.9 Guaranty Contract   On May 17, 1979, David Brown met with Stan Steele, a loan officer with the Bank of Idaho (later First Interstate Bank) to discuss borrowing $5,000 from the bank to start a new business. After learning that he did not qualify for the loan on the basis of his own financial strength,

Brown told Steele that his former employers, James and Donna West of California, might be willing to guarantee the payment of the loan. On May 18, 1979, Steele talked to Mr. West, who orally stated on the telephone that he would personally guarantee the loan to Brown. Based on this guarantee, the bank loaned Brown $5,000. The bank sent a written guarantee to Mr. and Mrs. West for their signature, but it was never returned to the bank. When Brown defaulted on the loan, the bank filed suit against the Wests to recover on their guarantee contract. Are the Wests liable? [*First Interstate Bank of Idaho, N.A. v. West*, 693 P.2d 1053, 1984 Ida. Lexis 600 (ID 1984)]

11.10 Promissory Estoppel   The Atlantic Wholesale Company (Atlantic), which is located in Florence, South Carolina, is in the business of buying and selling gold and silver for customers' accounts. Gary A. Solondz, a New York resident, became a customer of Atlantic's in 1979 and thereafter made several purchases through Atlantic. On January 23, 1980, Solondz telephoned Atlantic and received a quotation on silver bullion. Solondz then bought 300 ounces of silver for a total price of $12,978. Atlantic immediately contacted United Precious Metals in Minneapolis and purchased the silver for Solondz. The silver was shipped to Atlantic, which paid for it. Atlantic placed the silver in its vault while it awaited payment from Solondz. When Atlantic telephoned Solondz about payment, he told Atlantic to continue to hold the silver in its vault until he decided whether to sell it. Meanwhile, the price of silver had fallen substantially and continued to fall. When Solondz refused to pay for the silver, Atlantic sold it for $4,650, sustaining a loss of $8,328. When Atlantic sued Solondz to recover this loss, Solondz asserted that the Statute of Frauds prevented enforcement of his oral promise to buy the silver. Does the doctrine of promissory estoppel prevent the application of the Statute of Frauds in this case? [*Atlantic Wholesale Co., Inc. v. Solondz*, 320 S.E.2d 720, 1984 S.C.App. Lexis 555 (S.C. App. 1984)]

Business Ethics Cases

11.11 Business Ethics   The First Baptist Church of Moultrie, Georgia, invited bids for the construction of a music, education, and recreation building. The bids, which were to be opened on May 15, 1986, were to be accompanied by a bid bond of 5 percent of the bid amount. Barber Contracting Company (Barber) submitted a bid in the amount of $1,860,000. A bid bond in the amount of 5 percent of the bid—$93,000—was issued by the American Insurance Company. The bids were opened by the church on May 15, 1986, as planned, and Barber's was the lowest bid.

On May 16, 1986, Albert W. Barber, the president of Barber Contracting Company, informed the church that its bid was in error and should have been $143,120 higher. The error was caused in totaling the material costs on Barber's estimate worksheets. The church had not been provided these worksheets. On May 20, 1986, Barber sent a letter to the church, stating that it was withdrawing its bid. The next day the church sent a construction contract to Barber, containing the original bid amount. When Barber refused to sign the contract and refused to do the work for the original contract price, the church signed a contract with the second-lowest bidder, H & H Construction and Supply Company, Inc., to complete the work for $1,919,272. The church sued Barber and the American Insurance Company,

seeking to recover the amount of the bid bond. Who wins? Did Barber act ethically in trying to get out of the contract? Did the church act ethically in trying to enforce Barber's bid? [*First Baptist Church of Moultrie v. Barber Contracting Co.*, 377 S.E.2d 717, 1989 Ga. App. Lexis 25 (Ga. App. 1989)]

11.12 Business Ethics   Adolfo Mozzetti, who owned a construction company, orally promised his son, Remo, that if Remo would manage the family business for their mutual benefit and would take care of him for the rest of his life, he would leave the family home to Remo. Section 2714 of the Delaware Code requires contracts for the transfer of land to be in writing. Section 2715 of the Delaware Code requires testamentary transfers of real property to be in writing. Remo performed as requested: He managed the family business and took care of his father until the father died. When the father died, his will devised the family home to his daughter, Lucia M. Shepard. Remo brought this action to enforce his father's oral promise that the home belonged to him. The daughter argued that the will should be upheld. Who wins? Did the daughter act ethically in trying to defeat the father's promise to leave the property to the son? Did the son act ethically in trying to defeat his father's will? [*Shepard v. Mozzetti*, 545, A.2d 621, 1988 Del. Lexis 217 (DE 1988)]

Briefing the Case Writing Assignment

Read Case A.11 in the Case Appendix [*Continental Airlines, Inc. v. McDonnell Douglas Corporation*]. This case is excerpted from the appellate court opinion. Review and brief the case. In your brief, be sure to answer the following questions.

1. When did the action commence? When was the decision of the appellate court rendered?

2. Were the statements made by McDonnell Douglas opinions (i.e., puffery) or statements of fact?

3. Were the statements made by McDonnell Douglas material? What evidence supports your conclusion?

4. Did Continental rely on the statements of McDonnell Douglas? What evidence supports your conclusion?

5. Do false representations made recklessly and without regard to the truth constitute fraud?

6. What damages were awarded to Continental?

Endnotes

1. *Restatement (Second) of Contracts*, § 153.
2. *Restatement (Second) of Contracts*, § 152.
3. 159 Eng. Rep. 375 (1864).
4. *Restatement (Second) of Contracts*, § 159.
5. *Restatement (Second) of Contracts*, §§ 163 and 164.
6. *Restatement (Second) of Contracts*, § 172.
7. *Restatement (Second) of Contracts*, § 160.
8. *Restatement (Second) of Contracts*, § 161.
9. *Restatement (Second) of Contracts*, § 170.
10. *Restatement (Second) of Contracts*, § 177.
11. *Restatement (Second) of Contracts*, § 176.
12. *Restatement (Second) of Contracts*, § 110.
13. *Restatement (Second) of Contracts*, § 130.
14. *Restatement (Second) of Contracts*, § 112.
15. *Restatement (Second) of Contracts*, § 116.
16. UCC § 2-201(1).
17. UCC § 2-209(3).
18. *Restatement (Second) of Contracts*, § 139.
19. UCC § 2-202.
20. *Restatement (Second) of Contracts*, § 213.
21. UCC §§ 1-205, 2-202, and 2-208.

Third-Party Rights and Discharge

> " An honest man's word is as good as his bond."

—Don Quixote

Chapter Objectives

After studying this chapter, you should be able to:

1. Describe assignment of contracts and what contract rights are assignable.

2. Define an intended beneficiary and describe his or her rights under a contract.

3. Define covenant.

4. Distinguish between conditions precedent, conditions subsequent, and concurrent conditions.

5. Explain when the performance of a contract is excused because of objective impossibility or commercial impracticability.

Chapter Contents

- Assignment of Rights
- Delegation of Duties
- Third-Party Beneficiaries
- Covenants and Conditions
- Discharge of Performance

The parties to a contract are said to be in **privity of contract**. Contracting parties have a legal obligation to perform the duties specified in their contract. A party's duty of performance may be **discharged** by agreement of the parties, excuse of performance, or operation of law. If one party fails to perform as promised, the other party may enforce the contract and sue for breach.

With two exceptions, third parties do not acquire any rights under other people's contracts. The exceptions are (1) **assignees** to whom rights are subsequently transferred and (2) **intended third-party beneficiaries** to whom the contracting parties intended to give rights under the contract at the time of contracting.

This chapter discusses the rights of third parties under a contract, conditions to performance, and ways of discharging the duty of performance.

Assignment of Rights

In many cases, the parties to a contract can transfer their rights under the contract to other parties. The transfer of contractual rights is called an **assignment of rights** or just an **assignment**.

Form of Assignment

The party who owes the duty of performance is called the *obligor*. The party who is owed a right under the contract is called the *obligee*. An obligee who transfers the right to receive performance is called an **assignor**. The party to whom the right has been transferred is called the **assignee**. The assignee can assign the right to yet another person (called a **subsequent assignee**, or **subassignee**). Exhibit 12.1 illustrates these relationships.

Business Brief

The word assignment does not have to be used to create an assignment.

Consider This Example   Suppose a retail clothing store purchases $5,000 worth of goods on credit from a manufacturer. Payment is due in 120 days. Assume that the manufacturer needs cash before the 120-day period expires, so the manufacturer (assignor) sells its right to collect the money to another party (assignee) for $4,000. If the retail store is given proper notice of the assignment, it must pay $5,000 to the assignee.

St. Louis, Arch.   Many contracts, including with an architect, a general contractor, subcontractors, insurance companies, and others were used in order to complete the construction of the St. Louis arch.

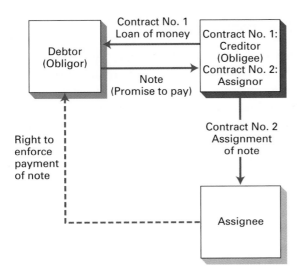

Exhibit 12.1

Assignment of a Right

Generally, no formalities are required for a valid assignment of rights. Although the assignor often uses the word *assign*, other words or terms, such as *sell, transfer, convey*, and *give*, are sufficient to indicate an intent to transfer a contract right.

Rights That Can and Cannot Be Assigned

In the United States, public policy favors a free flow of commerce. Hence, most contract rights are assignable, including sales contracts and contracts for the payment of money.

The types of contracts that present special problems for assignments are discussed in the following paragraph:

1. **Personal service contracts.** Contracts for the provision of personal services are generally not assignable.[1] For example, if an artist contracts to paint someone's portrait, the artist cannot send a different artist to do the painting without the prior approval of the person to be painted. The parties may agree that a personal service contract may be assigned. For example, many professional athletes' contracts contain a clause permitting assignability of the contract.

2. **Assignment of future rights.** Usually, a person cannot assign a currently nonexistent right that he or she expects to have in the future. For example, suppose a multimillion-dollar heiress signs a will, leaving all her property to her grandson. The grandson cannot assign his expected right to receive his inheritance.

3. **Contracts where assignment would materially alter the risk.** A contract cannot be assigned if the assignment would materially alter the risk or duties of the obligor. For example, suppose Laura Peters, who has a safe driving record, purchases automobile insurance from an insurance company. Her rights to be insured cannot be assigned to another driver because the assignment would materially alter the risk and duties of the insurance company.

4. **Assignment of legal action.** Legal actions involving personal rights cannot be assigned. For example, suppose Donald Matthews is severely injured by Alice Hollyfield in an automobile accident caused by her negligence. Matthews can sue Hollyfield to recover damages for his injuries. He may not assign his right to sue her to another person.

A legal right that arises out of a breach of contract may be assigned. For example, suppose Andrea borrows $10,000 from the bank. If she defaults on the loan, the bank may assign the legal rights to collect the money to a collection agency.

Business Brief

Personal service contracts are generally not assignable.

Business Brief

Businesses often sell (assign) their accounts receivable to another party, called a "factor," for collection. Accounts receivable are usually sold at a discount to reflect risk of non-collection of some accounts.

Effect of an Assignment of Rights

Where there has been a valid assignment of rights, the assignee "stands in the shoes of the assignor." That is, the assignor is entitled to performance from the obligor. The unconditional assignment of a contract right extinguishes all the assignor's rights, including the right to sue the obligor directly for nonperformance.[2]

An assignee takes no better rights under the contract than the assignor had. For example, if the assignor has a right to receive $10,000 from a debtor, the right to receive this $10,000 is all that the assignor can assign to the assignee. An obligor can assert any defense he or she had against the assignor or the assignee. For example, an obligor can raise the fraud, duress, undue influence, minority, insanity, illegality of the contract, mutual mistake, or payment by worthless check by the assignor against enforcement of the contract by the assignee. The obligor can also raise any personal defenses (e.g., participation in the assignor's fraudulent scheme) he or she may have directly against the assignee.

In the following case, the court held that an assignment was illegal.

Accrued Financial Services, Incorporated v. Prime Retail, Incorporated

298 F.3d 291, 2002 U.S. App. Lexis 15238 (2002)
United States Court of Appeals, Fourth Circuit

Case 12.1
Assignment

Background and Facts

Accrued Financial Services, Incorporated (AFS), is a corporation engaged in the business of conducting lease audits on behalf of tenants in commercial buildings and factory outlet malls. AFS is paid a percentage—usually 40 to 50 percent—of the discrepancy overcharges that it discovers and collects as a result of its audits. The tenant signs a letter of agreement with AFS and assigns all legal causes of action it may have against the landlord to AFS. The assignment grants AFS the authority to file lawsuits in its name against landlords at its discretion. After AFS conducted an audit of Prime Retail, Incorporated, a landlord, on behalf of tenants that had signed assignment agreements, AFS brought a lawsuit against Prime Retail, asserting various claims of overcharges. The United States district court dismissed the case, finding that the assignment of the tenants' claims to AFS violated public policy and were therefore illegal. AFS appealed.

Issue

Does the assignment by a tenant of its legal claims against a landlord violate public policy and is it therefore illegal?

Court's Reasoning

The U.S. Court of Appeals found that the assignment of legal causes of action by tenants against Prime Retail to AFS was illegal. The court held that the relationships between AFS and the tenants were essentially "law-mining" arrangements under which AFS mined for and prosecuted lawsuits. AFS thus became a promoter of litigation principally for the sake of the fees it would

earn. The court reasoned, "Under these arrangements, even though the tenant might conclude, after reviewing the facts uncovered, that a lawsuit would imprudently damage the landlord–tenant relationship or that pursuing aggressive allegations would do more harm than good, the tenant lost the right to control its destiny." The court continued, "Because we see these broad assignments as nothing more than arrangements through which to intermeddle and stir up litigation for the purpose of making a profit, we conclude that they violate Maryland's strong public policy against stirring up litigation."

Decision and Remedy

The U.S. Court of Appeals held that the tenants' assignment of their legal causes of action against Prime Retail to AFS violated public policy and was therefore illegal and void. The court of appeals affirmed the decision of the district court.

Case Questions

Critical Legal Thinking   Why did the court of appeals find the tenants' assignments of their legal causes of action against Prime Retail to AFS illegal? How can these assignments be distinguished from typical contingency fee arrangements that plaintiffs' lawyers often have with clients?

Business Ethics   Did AFS act ethically in this case?

Contemporary Business   What would be the consequences if a party's legal cause of action could be assigned to another party to pursue? Explain.

Notice of Assignment

When an assignor makes an assignment of a right under a contract, the assignee is under a duty to notify the obligor that (1) the assignment has been made and (2) performance must be rendered to the assignee. If the assignee fails to notify the obligor of the assignment, the obligor may continue to render performance to the assignor, who no longer has a right to it. The assignee cannot sue the obligor to recover payment because the obligor has performed according to the original contract. The assignee's only course of action is to sue the assignor for damages.

The result changes if the obligor is notified of the assignment but continues to render performance to the assignor. In such situations, the assignee can sue the obligor and recover payment. The obligor will then have to pay twice: once wrongfully to the assignor and then rightfully to the assignee. The obligor's only recourse is to sue the assignor for damages.

Business Brief

To protect his or her rights, an assignee should immediately notify the obligor that (1) the assignment has been made and (2) performance must be rendered to the assignee.

Anti-Assignment and Approval Clauses

Some contracts contain **anti-assignment clauses** that prohibit the assignment of rights under the contracts. Such clauses may be used if the obligor does not want to deal with or render performance to an unknown third party. Some contracts contain an **approval clause**. Such clauses require the obligor to approve any assignment. Many states prohibit the obligor from unreasonably withholding approval.

Contemporary Environment

Successive Assignments of the Same Right

An obligee (the party who is owed a performance, money, a right, or another thing of value) has the right to assign a contract right or benefit to another party. If the obligee fraudulently or mistakenly makes successive assignments of the same right to a number of assignees, which assignee has the legal right to the assigned right? To answer this question, the following rules are applied:

- **The American rule** (or **New York rule**) provides that the first assignment *in time* prevails, regardless of notice. Most states follow this rule.
- **The English rule** provides that the first assignee to *give notice* to the obligor (the person who owes the performance, money, duty, or other thing of value) prevails.

- **The possession of tangible token rule** provides that under either the American or English rule, if the assignor makes successive assignments of a contract right that is represented by a tangible token, such as a stock certificate or a savings account passbook, the first assignee who receives delivery of the tangible token prevails over subsequent assignees. However, if the first assignee leaves the tangible token with the assignor, the subsequent assignee prevails. This is because the first assignee could have prevented the problem by having demanded delivery of the tangible token. In other words, physical possession of the tangible token is the pivotal issue. ■

Delegation of Duties

Unless otherwise agreed, the parties to a contract can generally transfer the performance of their duties under the contract to other parties. This transfer is called the **delegation of duties**, or just **delegation**.

An obligor who transfers his or her duty is called a **delegator**. The party to whom the duty is transferred is the **delegatee**. The party to whom the duty is owed is the *obligee*. Generally, no special words or formalities are required to create a delegation of duties. Exhibit 12.2 illustrates the parties to a delegation of a duty.

Exhibit 12.2

Delegation of a Duty

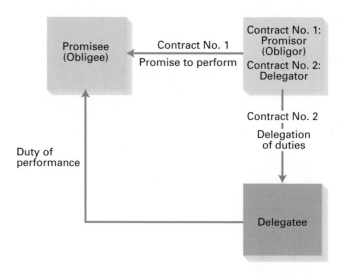

Duties That Can and Cannot Be Delegated

Often, contracts are entered into with companies or firms rather than with individuals. In such cases, a firm may designate any of its qualified employees to perform the contract. For example, if a client retains a firm of lawyers to represent her, the firm can **delegate** the duties under the contract to any qualified member of the firm. If the obligee has a substantial interest in having the obligor perform the acts required by the contract, however, duties may not be transferred.[3] This restriction includes obligations under the following types of contracts:

1. ***Personal service contracts calling for the exercise of personal skills, discretion, or expertise.*** For example, if Dr. Dre is hired to give a concert on campus, the Dixie Chicks cannot appear in his place.
2. ***Contracts whose performance would materially vary if the obligor's duties were delegated.*** For example, if a person hires an experienced surgeon to perform a complex surgery, a recent medical school graduate cannot be substituted in the operating room.

Effect of Delegation of Duties

If a delegation is valid, the delegator remains legally liable for the performance of the contract. If the delegatee does not perform properly, the obligee can sue the obligor–delegator for any resulting damages.

The question of the delegatee's liability to the obligee depends on whether there has been an *assumption of duties* or a *declaration of duties*. Where a delegation of duties contains the term *assumption* or other similar language, there is an **assumption of duties** by the delegatee. The delegatee is liable to the obligee for nonperformance. The obligee can sue either the delegator or the delegatee.

If the delegatee has not assumed the duties under a contract, the delegation of duties is called a **declaration of duties**. Here, the delegatee is not legally liable to the obligee for nonperformance. The obligee's only recourse is to sue the delegator. A delegatee who fails to perform his or her duties is liable to the delegator for damages arising from this failure to perform.

Anti-Delegation Clause

The parties to a contract can include an **anti-delegation clause** indicating that the duties cannot be delegated. Anti-delegation clauses are usually enforced. Some courts, however, have held that duties that are totally impersonal in nature—such as the payment of money—can be delegated despite such clauses.

Assignment and Delegation

An **assignment and delegation** occurs when there is a transfer of both rights and duties under a contract. If the transfer of a contract to a third party contains only language of assignment, the modern view holds that there is corresponding delegation of the duties of the contract.[4]

Third-Party Beneficiaries

Third parties sometimes claim rights under others' contracts. Such third parties are either *intended* or *incidental beneficiaries*. Each of these designations is discussed here.

Intended Beneficiaries

When parties enter into a contract, they can agree that the performance of one of the parties should be rendered to or directly benefit a third party. Under such circumstances, the third party is called an **intended third-party beneficiary**. An intended third-party beneficiary can enforce the contract against the party who promised to render performance.[5]

The beneficiary may be expressly named in the contract from which he or she is to benefit or may be identified by another means. For example, there is sufficient identification if a testator of a will leaves his estate to "all my children, equally."

Intended third-party beneficiaries may be classified as either *donee* or *creditor* beneficiaries. These terms are defined below. The *Restatement (Second) of Contracts* and many state statutes have dropped this distinction, however, and now refer to both collectively as intended beneficiaries.[6]

Donee Beneficiaries When a person enters into a contract with the intent to confer a benefit or gift on an intended third party, the contract is called a **donee beneficiary contract**. A life insurance policy with a named beneficiary is an example of such a contract. The three persons involved in such a contract are:

1. The **promisee** (the contracting party who directs that the benefit be conferred on another)
2. The **promisor** (the contracting party who agrees to confer performance for the benefit of the third person)
3. The **donee beneficiary** (the third person on whom the benefit is to be conferred)

If the promisor fails to perform the contract, the donee beneficiary can sue the promisor directly.

Consider These Examples   Brian Peterson hires a lawyer to draft his will. He directs the lawyer to leave all of his property to his best friend, Jeffrey Silverman. Assume that (1) Peterson dies and (2) the lawyer's negligence in drafting the will causes it to be invalid. Consequently, Peterson's distant relatives receive the property under the state's inheritance statute. Silverman can sue the lawyer for damages because he was the intended donee beneficiary of the will.

Consider another example: A mother, the insured, buys a life insurance policy from a life insurance company, and names her daughter as the beneficiary to be paid the life insurance proceeds if the mother dies. The daughter is the intended beneficiary of the contract between her mother and the life insurance company. Assume that the mother dies. If the life insurance company refuses to pay the life insurance proceeds to the daughter, the daughter can sue the life insurance company and recover the insurance proceeds. (see Exhibit 12.3.)

Exhibit 12.3

Donee Beneficiary
Contract

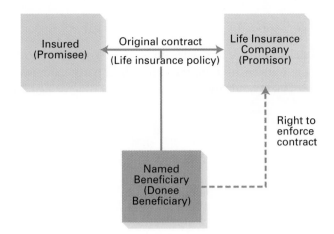

Creditor Beneficiaries   The second type of intended beneficiary is the creditor beneficiary. A **creditor beneficiary contract** usually arises in the following situation:

1. A debtor borrows money from a creditor to purchase some item.
2. The debtor signs an agreement to pay the creditor the amount of the loan plus interest.
3. The debtor sells the item to another party before the loan is paid.
4. The new buyer promises the debtor that he or she will pay the remainder of the loan amount to the creditor.

The creditor is the new intended creditor beneficiary to this second creditor.[7] The parties to the second contract are the original debtor (the promisee), the new party (the promisor), and the original creditor (the **creditor beneficiary**). (See Exhibit 12.4)

If the promisor fails to perform according to the contract, the creditor beneficiary may either (1) enforce the original contract against the debtor-promisee or (2) enforce the new contract against the promisor. However, the creditor can collect only once.

Consider This Example   Suppose Big Hotels obtains a loan from City Bank to refurbish a hotel in Atlanta, Georgia. The parties sign a promissory note requiring the loan to be paid off in equal monthly installments over the next 10 years. Before the loan is paid, Big Hotels sells the hotel to ABC Hotels, another chain of hotels. ABC Hotels agrees with

Exhibit 12.4

Creditor Beneficiary
Contract

with Big Hotels to complete the payments due on the City Bank loan. The bank has two options if ABC Hotels fails to pay: It can sue Big Hotels on the promissory note to recover the unpaid loan amount, or it can use its status as a creditor beneficiary to sue ABC Hotels.

Incidental Beneficiaries

In many instances, the parties to a contract unintentionally benefit a third party when the contract is performed. In such situations, the third party is referred to as an **incidental beneficiary**. An incidental beneficiary has no rights to enforce or sue under other people's contracts. Generally, the public and taxpayers are only incidental beneficiaries to contracts entered into by the government on their behalf. As such, they acquire no rights to enforce government contracts or to sue parties who breach these contracts.

Consider This Example   Suppose Heather owns a house on Residential Street. Her neighbor John owns the house next door. Heather contracts with a painting contractor to paint her house. The painting contractor breaches the contract and does not paint Heather's house. Although John may have benefitted if Heather's house were painted, he is merely an incidental beneficiary and has no cause of action to sue the painting contractor for not painting Heather's house. Heather, of course, can sue the painting contractor for breach of contract.

Often, the courts are asked to decide whether a third party is an intended or an incidental beneficiary, as in the following case.

Bain v. Gillispie
357 N.W.2d 47, 1984 Iowa App. Lexis 1694 (1984)
Court of Appeals of Iowa

Case 12.2
Incidental Beneficiary

Background and Facts

James C. Bain, a college basketball referee, had a contract with the Big 10 Basketball Conference (Big 10) to referee various basketball games. During a game that took place on March 6, 1982, Bain called a foul on a University of Iowa player that permitted free throws by a Purdue University player. That player scored the point that gave Purdue a last-minute victory and eliminated Iowa from the Big 10 championship. Some Iowa fans, including John and Karen Gillispie, asserted that the foul call was clearly in error. The Gillispies operated a novelty store in Iowa City that sold University of Iowa sports memorabilia. They filed a complaint against Bain, alleging that his negligent refereeing constituted a breach of his contract with the Big 10 and destroyed a potential market for their products. The Gillispies sought $175,000 in compensatory damages plus exemplary damages. The trial court granted Bain's motion for summary judgment. The Gillispies appealed.

Issue

Were the Gillispies intended beneficiaries of the contract between Bain and the Big 10 Basketball Conference?

Court's Reasoning

The Gillispies claimed that they were direct donee beneficiaries. The real test is whether the contracting parties intended that a third person should receive a benefit that might be enforced in the courts. The court stated, "The Gillispies can be considered nothing more than incidental beneficiaries and as such are unable to maintain a cause of action."

Decision and Remedy

The appellate court held that the Gillispies were merely incidental beneficiaries of the contract between Bain and the Big 10 Basketball Conference. Therefore, they could not maintain their lawsuit for an alleged breach of that contract. The court of appeals affirmed the judgment of the trial court.

Case Questions

Critical Legal Thinking   Should the law allow incidental beneficiaries to recover damages for the breach of other people's contracts? Why or why not?

Business Ethics   Did the Gillispies have a legitimate lawsuit in this case?

Contemporary Business   Do third parties have rights under many business contracts? Give some examples.

Covenants and Conditions

In contracts, parties make certain promises to each other. These promises may be classified as *covenants* or *conditions*. The difference between these is discussed in the following paragraphs.

Covenants

A **covenant** is an unconditional promise to perform. Nonperformance of a covenant is a breach of contract that gives the other party the right to sue. For example, if Medcliff Corporation borrows $100,000 from a bank and signs a promissory note to repay this amount plus 10 percent interest in one year, this promise is a covenant. That is, it is an unconditional promise to perform.

Conditions of Performance

A conditional promise (or qualified promise) is not as definite as a covenant. The promisor's duty to perform (or not perform) arises only if the **condition** does (or does not) occur.[8] It becomes a covenant if the condition is met, however.

Generally, contractual language such as *if, on condition that, provided that, when, after,* and *as soon as* indicates a condition. A single contract may contain numerous conditions that trigger or excuse performance. There are three types of conditions: *conditions precedent, conditions subsequent,* and *concurrent conditions.*

Conditions Precedent If the contract requires the occurrence (or nonoccurrence) of an event *before* a party is obligated to perform a contractual duty, there is a **condition precedent**. The happening (or nonhappening) of the event triggers the contract or duty of performance. If the event does not occur, no duty to perform arises because there is a failure of condition.

Consider This Example Suppose Company B offers Joan Andrews a job as an industrial engineer upon her graduation from college. If Andrews graduates, the condition has been met. If the employer refuses to hire Andrews at that time, she can sue the employer for breach of contract. If Andrews does not graduate, however, Company B is not obligated to hire her because there has been a failure of condition.

Conditions Precedent Based on Satisfaction

Some contracts reserve the right to a party to pay for services provided by the other only if the services meet the first party's "satisfaction." The courts have developed two tests—the *personal satisfaction test* and the *reasonable person test*—to examine whether this special form of condition precedent has been met:

1. The **personal satisfaction test** is a *subjective* test that applies if the performance involves personal taste and comfort (e.g., contracts for decorating, tailoring, etc.). The only requirement is that the person given the right to reject the contract acts in good faith.

   For example, suppose Gretchen employs an artist to paint her daughter's portrait. Assume that the contract provides that the client does not have to pay for the portrait unless she is satisfied with it. Accordingly, Gretchen may reject the painting if she personally dislikes it, even though a reasonable person would be satisfied with it.

2. The **reasonable person test** is an *objective* test that is used to judge contracts involving mechanical fitness and most commercial contracts. Most contracts that require the work to meet a third person's satisfaction (e.g., engineer, architect) are judged by this standard.

   For example, suppose a large mail-order catalog business, hires someone to install a state-of-the-art computer system that will handle its order entry and record-keeping functions. The system is installed and operates to industry standards. According to the reasonable person test, the company cannot reject the contract as not meeting its satisfaction.

Time of Performance as a Condition Precedent

Generally, there is a breach of contract if the contract is not performed when due. Nevertheless, if the other party is not jeopardized by the delay, most courts treat the delay as a minor breach and give the nonperforming party additional time to perform. Conversely, if the contract expressly provides that *"time is of the essence"* or similar language, performance by the stated time is an express condition. There is a breach of contract if the contracting party does not perform by the stated date.

Business Brief

If "time is of the essence" is stated in a contract, it is an express condition: failure to perform by the stated date is a material breach of contract.

Conditions Subsequent

A **condition subsequent** exists when a contract provides that the occurrence or nonoccurrence of a specific event automatically excuses the performance of an existing duty to perform. For example, many employment contracts include a clause that permits the employer to terminate the contract if the employer fails a drug test.

Note that the *Restatement (Second) of Contracts* eliminates the distinction between conditions precedent and conditions subsequent. Both are referred to as "conditions."[9]

Concurrent Conditions

Concurrent conditions arise when the parties to a contract must render performance simultaneously—that is, when each party's absolute duty to perform is conditioned on the other party's absolute duty to perform.

For example, suppose a contract to purchase goods provides that payment is due upon delivery. In other words, the buyer's duty to pay is conditioned on the seller's duty to deliver the goods, and vice versa. Recovery is available if one party fails to respond to the other party's performance.

Implied Conditions

Any of the previous types of conditions may be further classified as either express or implied conditions. An *express condition* exists if the parties expressly agree on it. An **implied-in-fact condition** is one that can be implied from the circumstances surrounding a contract and the parties' conduct. For example, a contract in which a buyer agrees to purchase grain from a farmer implies that there are proper street access to the delivery site, proper unloading facilities, and the like.

Concept Summary   *Types of Conditions*

Type of Condition	Description
Condition precedent	A specified event must occur (or not occur) before a party is obligated to perform contractual duties.
Condition subsequent	The occurrence (or nonoccurrence) of a specified event excuses the performance of an existing contractual duty to perform.
Concurrent condition	The parties to a contract are obligated to render performance simultaneously. Each party's duty to perform is conditioned on the other party's duty to perform.
Implied condition	An implied-in-fact condition is implied from the circumstances surrounding the contract and the parties' conduct.

Discharge of Performance

A party's duty to perform under a contract may be discharged by *mutual agreement* of the parties, by *impossibility of performance*, or by *operation of law*. These methods of discharge are discussed in the paragraphs that follow.

Discharge by Agreement

In many situations, the parties to a contract mutually decide to discharge their contractual duties. The different types of mutual agreement are discussed in the following paragraphs:

■ *Mutual rescission.* If a contract is wholly or partially executory on both sides, the parties can agree to rescind (i.e., cancel) the contract. **Mutual rescission** requires

Teipei, Taiwan. International contracts contain covenants and conditions of performance as specified or implied by law.

the parties to enter into a second agreement that expressly terminates the first one. Unilateral rescission of the contract by one of the parties without the other party's consent is not effective. Unilateral rescission of a contract constitutes a breach of that contract.

- **Substituted contract.** The parties to a contract may enter into a new contract that revokes and discharges a prior contract. The new contract is called a **substituted contract**. If one of the parties fails to perform his or her duties under a substituted contract, the nonbreaching party can sue to enforce its terms against the breaching party. The prior contract cannot be enforced against the breaching party because it has been discharged.

- **Novation.** A **novation agreement** (commonly called **novation**) substitutes a third party for one of the original contracting parties. The new substituted party is obligated to perform the contract. All three parties must agree to the substitution. In a novation, the existing party is relieved of liability on the contract.

- **Accord and satisfaction.** The parties to a contract may agree to settle a contract dispute by an **accord and satisfaction**. The agreement whereby the parties agree to accept something different in satisfaction of the original contract is called an **accord**.[10] The performance of an accord is called a **satisfaction**.

An accord does not discharge the original contract. It only suspends it until the accord is performed. Satisfaction of the accord discharges both the original contract and the accord. If an accord is not satisfied when it is due, the aggrieved party may enforce either (1) the accord or (2) the original contract.

Discharge by Impossibility

Under certain circumstances, the nonperformance of contractual duties is excused—that is, discharged—because of *impossibility of performance*.

Impossibility of performance (or **objective impossibility**) occurs if the contract becomes impossible to perform.[11] The impossibility must be objective impossibility ("it cannot be done") rather than subjective impossibility ("I cannot do it"). The following types of objective impossibility excuse nonperformance:

1. The death or incapacity of the promisor prior to the performance of a personal service contract.[12] For example, if a professional athlete dies prior to or during a contract period, his or her contract with the team is discharged.
2. The destruction of the subject matter of a contract prior to performance.[13] For example, if a building is destroyed by fire, the lessees are discharged from further performance unless otherwise provided in the lease.
3. A supervening illegality makes performance of the contract illegal.[14] For example, suppose an art dealer contracts to purchase native art found in a foreign country. The contract is discharged if the foreign country enacts a law forbidding native art from being exported from the country before the contract is performed.

Force Majeure Clauses

The parties may agree in a contract that certain events will excuse nonperformance of the contract. These clauses are called **force majeure clauses**.

Usually, force majeure clauses excuse nonperformance caused by natural disasters such as floods, tornadoes, earthquakes, and such. Modern clauses often excuse performance due to labor strikes, shortages of raw materials, and the like.

> If a man will improvidently bind himself up by a voluntary deed, and not reserve a liberty to himself by a power of revocation, this court will not loose the fetters he hath put upon himself, but he must lie down under his own folly.
>
> L. C. Lord Nottingham
> *Villers v. Beaumont (1682)*

In the following case, the court had to decide whether there was impossibility of performance.

Parker v. Arthur Murray, Inc.
295 N.E.2d 487, 1973 Ill.App. Lexis 2760 (1973)
Appellate Court of Illinois

Background and Facts

In November 1959, Ryland S. Parker, a 37-year-old college-educated bachelor, went to the Arthur Murray Studios (Arthur Murray) in Oak Park, Illinois, to redeem a certificate entitling him to three free dancing lessons. At that time he lived alone in a one-room attic apartment. During the free lessons, the instructor told Parker that he had "exceptional potential to be a fine and accomplished dancer." Parker thereupon signed a contract for more lessons. Parker attended lessons regularly and was praised and encouraged by his instructors, despite his lack of progress. Contract extensions and new contracts for additional instructional hours were executed, and Parker prepaid for them. Each written contract contained the bold-type words, "NONCANCELABLE CONTRACT." On September 24, 1961, Parker was severely injured in an automobile accident, rendering him incapable of continuing his dancing lessons. At that time he had contracted for a total of 2,734 hours of dance lessons, for which he had prepaid $24,812. When Arthur Murray refused to refund any of the money, Parker sued to rescind the outstanding contracts. The trial courts held in favor of Parker and ordered Arthur Murray to return the prepaid contract payments. Arthur Murray appealed.

Issue

Does the doctrine of impossibility excuse Parker's performance of the personal service contracts?

Court's Reasoning

In Illinois, impossibility of performance is recognized as a ground for rescission. Arthur Murray contended that the bold-type words "NONCANCELABLE CONTRACT" manifested the parties' mutual intent to waive their respective rights to invoke the doctrine of impossibility. The court replied: "This is a construction that we find unacceptable. We conclude that the plaintiff never contemplated that by signing the contracts he was waiving a remedy expressly recognized by Illinois courts."

Decision and Remedy

The appellate court held that the doctrine of impossibility of performance excused Parker's performance of the personal service contracts. The appellate court affirmed the decision of the trial court in favor of Parker.

Case Questions

Critical Legal Thinking   Should the doctrine of impossibility excuse parties from performance of their contracts? Why or why not?

Business Ethics   Did Arthur Murray act ethically in not returning Parker's money?

Contemporary Business   Why do you think Arthur Murray fought this case?

Commercial Impracticability

Many states recognize the doctrine of **commercial impracticability** as an excuse for nonperformance of contracts. Commercial impracticability excuses performance if an unforeseeable event makes it impractical for the promisor to perform. This doctrine has not yet been fully developed by the courts. It is examined on a case-by-case basis.

Consider This Example   A utility company enters into a contract to purchase uranium for its nuclear-powered generator from a uranium supplier at a fixed price of $1 million per year for five years. Suppose a new uranium cartel is formed worldwide, and the supplier must pay $3 million for uranium to supply the utility with each year's supply. In this case, the court would likely allow the supplier to rescind its contract with the utility, based on commercial impracticability. Note that it is not impossible for the supplier to supply the uranium.

Contemporary Environment
Commercial Impracticability

Sometimes, unforeseen circumstances make the performance of a contract highly impracticable or very expensive. Modern contract law, including the Uniform Commercial Code (UCC), recognizes the doctrine of commercial impracticability as excusing nonperformance in certain situations. Consider the following case.

In July 1980, Alimenta (U.S.A.), Inc. (Alimenta), entered into a contract with Cargill, Incorporated (Cargill), under which Cargill agreed to deliver to Alimenta shelled, edible peanuts. The peanut crop had been planted in the fields at the time the contract was entered into. Cargill, which had contracts with other buyers as well, expected to make $3 million in profit from its peanut sales.

Unfortunately, there was a severe drought that year, and the crop yield was substantially reduced. Thus, Cargill could deliver to Alimenta only about 65 percent of the promised peanuts. Cargill delivered the same percentage to all its customers. Alimenta filed suit against Cargill for breach of contract. Cargill asserted that further performance under the contract was excused by the doctrine of commercial impracticability. At trial the jury rendered a verdict for Cargill. Alimenta appealed.

Both the trial court and the court of appeals held that the drought in this case was unforeseen. The evidence showed that the shortage of peanuts in 1980 was unprecedented. In fact, there had been a surplus of domestic peanuts for the preceding 20 years.

The trial court found that it was not impossible for Cargill to fully perform the contract. Cargill could have gone into the market and purchased the peanuts, which were selling at a much higher price than contracted for, and delivered the peanuts to Alimenta. However, Cargill had already suffered a $47 million loss on its peanut contract, even without taking this step.

The U.S. Court of Appeals affirmed the trial court's ruling in favor of Cargill. The Court held that Cargill was excused from further performance by the doctrine of commercial impracticability. The Court stated that "the focus of impracticability analysis is upon the nature of the agreement and the expectations of the parties" and not on whether it is physically possible for the defendant to perform the contract. [*Alimenta (U.S.A.), Inc. v. Cargill, Incorporated, 861* F.2d 650, 1988 U.S. App. Lexis 16525 (11th Cir. 1988)] ■

Discharge by Operation of Law

Certain legal rules discharge parties from performing contractual duties. These rules are discussed in the following paragraphs:

- ***Statutes of limitations.***   Every state has a **statute of limitations** that applies to contract actions. Although the time periods vary from state to state, the usual period for bringing a lawsuit based on breach of contract is one to five years. The UCC provides that a cause of action based on a breach of sales or lease contract must be brought within four years after the cause of action accrues. [UCC §2-725, UCC §2A-506].

Latvia. The prior countries of the Soviet Union have enacted contract law as they emerged from communism and adopted capitalism.

- **Bankruptcy.** Bankruptcy, which is governed by federal law, is a means of allocating the debtor's nonexempt property to satisfy his or her debts. Debtors may also reorganize in bankruptcy. In most cases, the debtor's assets are insufficient to pay all the creditors' claims. If so, the debtor receives a **discharge** of the unpaid debts. The debtor is then relieved of legal liability to pay the discharged debts.

- **Alteration of the contract.** If a party to a contract intentionally alters the contract materially, the innocent party may opt either to discharge the contract or to enforce it. The contract may be enforced either on its original terms or on the altered terms. A material alteration is a change in price, quantity, or some other important term.

That what is agreed to be done, must be considered as done.

L. C. Lord Hardwicke
Guidot v. Guidot (1745)

Chapter Summary

Assignment of Rights, p. 246

Form of Assignment

1. **Assignment.** Assignment is transfer of contractual rights by a party to a contract to a third person.
2. **Assignor.** An assignor is a contract party who assigns the contractual rights.
3. **Assignee.** An assignee is a third person to whom contract rights are assigned.

Effect of Assignment

The assignee "stands in the shoes of the assignor" and is entitled to performance of the contract by the obligor.

Notice of Assignment

1. **Duty to notify.** The assignee must notify the obligor that (1) the assignment has been made and (2) performance must be rendered to the assignee.
2. **Failure to give notice.** If the assignee fails to give proper notice to the obligor and the obligor renders performance to the assignor, the assignee's only course of action to recover is from the assignor.

Anti-assignment and Approval Clauses

1. **Anti-assignment clause.** This prohibits the assignment of rights under a contract.
2. **Approval clause.** This permits assignment of the contract only upon receipt of the obligor's approval.

Successive Assignments

If the obligee makes successive assignments of the same right, one of the following rules (depending on state law) applies:

1. **American rule.** Under this rule, the first assignment in time prevails, regardless of notice. Also called the *New York rule.*
2. **English rule.** Under this rule, the first assignee to give notice to the obligor prevails.

Delegation of Duties, p. 249

Delegation of Duties

1. **Delegation.** Delegation is transfer of contractual duties by a party to a contract to a third person.
2. **Delegator.** The delegator is the party who transfers his or her contractual duties.
3. **Delegatee.** The delegatee is the third person to whom contractual duties are delegated.

Effect of Delegation

The effect of delegation depends on whether there has been:

1. *Assumption of duties.* The delegatee is liable to the obligee for nonperformance. The obligee may sue either the delegatee or the delegator.

2. *Declaration of duties.* The delegatee is not liable to the obligee for nonperformance. The obligee can sue only the delegator.

The delegatee is liable to the delegator for any damages suffered by the delegator because of the delegatee's nonperformance.

Anti-delegation Clause

This clause prohibits the delegation of duties under a contract.

Third-Party Beneficiaries, p. 251

Intended Beneficiaries

An intended beneficiary is a third person who is owed performance under other parties' contract. There are two types:

1. *Donee beneficiary.* This person is to be rendered performance gratuitously under a contract (for example, a beneficiary of a life insurance policy). A donee beneficiary may sue the promisor for nonperformance.

2. *Creditor beneficiary.* A creditor becomes a beneficiary to a contract between the debtor and a third party who agrees to perform the debtor's obligation. If the debt is not paid, the creditor may sue either (1) the debtor under the original contract or (2) the third party as a creditor beneficiary.

Incidental Beneficiaries

An incidental beneficiary is a third person who incidentally receives some benefit under other parties' contract but who has no rights to enforce it or to sue for its nonperformance.

Covenants and Conditions, p. 254

Covenants

Covenants are unconditional promises to perform. Nonperformance of a covenant is a breach of contract that gives the other party the right to sue.

Conditions of Performance

Condition. A promisor's duty to perform or not perform arises only if the *condition* does or does not occur. Also called a *qualified promise.* There are several types:

1. *Condition precedent.* This requires the occurrence or nonoccurrence of an event before a party is obligated to perform. Conditions precedent based on "satisfaction" are measured by one or two standards:
   a. *Personal satisfaction test.* The subjective intent of the decision maker applies if the performance involves personal taste or comfort.
   b. *Reasonable person test.* The objective intent of a reasonable person in the circumstances applies to contracts involving mechanical fitness or commercial contracts.

2. *Condition subsequent.* This provides that the occurrence or nonoccurrence of a specific event automatically excuses performance under a contract.

3. *Concurrent condition.* This arises when the parties to a contract must render performance simultaneously.

4. *Implied-in-fact condition.* This is a condition that is implied from the circumstances surrounding a contract and the parties' conduct.

Discharge by Agreement

1. **Mutual rescission.** The parties mutually agree to rescind an executory contract.

2. **Substituted contract.** The parties enter into a new contract that revokes a prior contract.

3. **Novation.** The parties agree to the substitution of a third party for one of the original parties. The exiting party is relieved of liability, and the entering party is obligated to perform the contract.

4. **Accord and satisfaction.** The parties agree to settle a contract dispute. The *satisfaction* of the *accord* discharges the original contract.

Discharge by Impossibility

1. **Impossibility of performance.** The contract is objectively impossible to perform because of an event.

2. **Commercial impracticability.** The contract is impractical for the promisor to perform because of an event.

3. **Force majeure clause.** The parties stipulate in the contract what events will excuse performance.

Discharge by Operation of Law

1. **Statute of limitations.** A contract that is not brought within the stipulated limitations period discharges contractual duties.

2. **Bankruptcy.** Discharge in bankruptcy relieves the debtor of legal liability to pay the discharged debts.

3. **Alteration of a contract.** If a party to a contract intentionally alters it materially, the innocent party may opt either to discharge the contract or enforce it on its original or altered terms.

 Internet Exercises and Case Questions

Working the Web Internet Exercises

Activities

1. Which provision of the UCC permits assignment and delegation? An extensive overview of contract law can be found at Contracts Home Page (Craig Smith, Santa Barbara College of Law) at **www.west.net/~smith/contracts.htm**. Review the "Third Party Rights" page.

2. Why does bankruptcy have the effect of discharging contractual obligations? See **www.nolo.com** and search for *bankruptcy*.

3. A good case can be lost because of a statute of limitations. These statutes vary by state and by type of claim. See **www.nolo.com/encyclopedia/articles/cm/timely.html** for a summary of the statutes and find your state law.

Critical Legal Thinking Cases

12.1 Third-Party Beneficiary   Eugene H. Emmick hired L. S. Hamm, an attorney, to draft his will. The will named Robert Lucas and others (Lucas) as beneficiaries. When Emmick died, it was discovered that the will was improperly drafted, violated state law, and was therefore ineffective. Emmick's estate was transferred pursuant to the state's intestate laws. Lucas did not receive the $75,000 he would have otherwise received had the will been valid. Lucas sued Hamm for breach of the Emmick–Hamm contract to recover what he would have received under the will. Who wins? [*Lucas v. Hamm*, 364 P.2d 685, 56 Cal.2d 583, 15 Cal.Rptr. 821, 1961 Cal. Lexis 321 (CA 1961)]

12.2 Third-Party Beneficiary   Abrams and others sponsored a condominium project for a luxury condominium building on Manhattan's East Side. Abrams contracted with Lehrer/McGovern, Inc. (L/M), and other contracting companies to construct the building. After the building was completed and the individual condominium units were sold, certain defects in construction appeared. Monarch Owners Committee, the condominium association, and individual condominium owners sued L/M and other contracting companies for damages for breach of their contracts with Abrams. Can the condominium association and owners sue the contracting companies? [*Monarch Owners Committee v. Abrams*,

454 N.Y.S.2d 4, 1982 N.Y.App.Div. Lexis 17991 (N.Y. Sup. 1982)]

12.3 Third-Party Beneficiary Angelo Boussiacos hired Demetrios Sofias, a general contractor, to build a restaurant for him. Boussiacos entered into a loan agreement with Bank of America (B of A) whereby B of A would provide the construction financing to build the restaurant. As is normal with most construction loans, the loan agreement provided that loan funds would be periodically disbursed by B of A to Boussiacos at different stages of construction, as requested by Boussiacos. Problems arose in the progress of the construction. When Boussiacos did not pay Sofias for certain work that had been done, Sofias sued B of A for breach of contract to collect payment directly from B of A. Can Sofias maintain the lawsuit against B of A? [*Sofias v. Bank of America*, 172 Cal.App.3d. 583, 218 Cal. Rptr 388, 1985 Cal.App. Lexis 2545 (Cal. App. 1985)]

12.4 Assignment William John Cunningham, a professional basketball player, entered into a contract with Southern Sports Corporation, which owned the Carolina Cougars, a professional basketball team. The contract provided that Cunningham was to play basketball for the Cougars for a three-year period, commencing on October 2, 1971. The contract contained a provision that it could not be assigned to any other professional basketball franchise without Cunningham's approval. Subsequently, Southern Sports Corporation sold its assets, including its franchise and Cunningham's contract, to the Munchak Corporation (Munchak). There was no change in the location of the Cougars after the purchase. When Cunningham refused to play for the new owners, Munchak sued to enforce Cunningham's contract. Was Cunningham's contract assignable to the new owner? [*Munchak Corporation v. Cunningham*, 457 F.2d 721, 1972 U.S. App. Lexis 10272 (4th Cir. 1972)]

12.5 Assignment In 1974, Berlinger Foods Corporation (Berlinger), pursuant to an oral contract, became a distributor for Häagen-Dazs ice cream. Over the next decade both parties flourished as the marketing of high-quality, high-priced ice cream took hold. Berlinger successfully promoted the sale of Häagen-Dazs to supermarket chains and other retailers in the Baltimore–Washington, DC, area. In 1983, the Pillsbury Company acquired Häagen-Dazs. Pillsbury adhered to the oral distribution agreement and retained Berlinger as a distributor for Häagen-Dazs ice cream. In December 1985, Berlinger entered into a contract and sold its assets to Dreyers, a manufacturer of premium ice cream that competed with Häagen-Dazs. Dreyers ice cream had previously been sold primarily in the western part of the United States. Dreyers attempted to expand its market to the east by choosing to purchase Berlinger as a means to obtain distribution in the mid-Atlantic region. When Pillsbury learned of the sale, it advised Berlinger that its distributorship for Häagen-Dazs was terminated. Berlinger, which wanted to remain a distributor for Häagen-Dazs, sued Pillsbury for breach of contract, alleging that the oral distribution agreement with Häagen-Dazs and Pillsbury was properly assigned to Dreyers. Who wins? [*Berlinger Foods Corporation v. The Pillsbury Company*, 633 F.Supp. 557, 1986 U.S. Dist. Lexis 26431 (D. Md. 1986)]

12.6 Right of an Assignee John Handy Jones paid Richard Sullivan, the chief of police of the Addison, Texas, Police Department, a $6,400 bribe in exchange for Sullivan's cooperation in allowing Jones and others to bring marijuana by airplane into the Addison airport without police intervention. Sullivan accepted the money, but rather than perform the requested services, he arrested Jones and turned the money over to the Dallas County District Attorney's Office. The $6,400 was introduced as evidence at Jones's criminal trial, where he was convicted. Subsequent to his conviction, Jones assigned his interest in the money to Melvyn Carson Bruder. The City of Addison brought an action, claiming that the money belonged to the city. Bruder intervened in the suit and claimed that he was entitled to the money because of the assignment from Jones. Who wins? [*Bruder v. State of Texas*, 601 S.W.2d 102, 1980 Tex.App. Lexis 3478 (Tex. App. 1980)]

12.7 Anti-assignment Clause In 1976, the city of Vancouver, Washington, contracted with B & B Contracting Corporation (B & B) to construct a well pump at a city-owned water station. The contract contained the following anti-assignment clause: "The contractor shall not assign this contract or any part thereof, or any moneys due or to become due thereunder." The work was not completed on time, and the city withheld $6,510 as liquidated damages from the contract price. B & B assigned the claim to this money to Portland Electric and Plumbing Company (PEPCo). PEPCo, as the assignee, filed suit against the City of Vancouver, alleging that the city breached its contract with B & B by wrongfully refusing to pay $6,510 to B & B. Can PEPCo maintain the lawsuit against the City of Vancouver? [*Portland Electric and Plumbing Company v. City of Vancouver*, 627 P.2d 1350, 1981 Wash.App. Lexis 2295 (Wash. App. 1981)]

12.8 Delegation of Duties C. W. Milford owned a registered quarterhorse named Hired Chico. In March 1969, Milford sold the horse to Norman Stewart. Recognizing that Hired Chico was a good stud, Milford included the following provision in the written contract that was signed by both parties: "I, C. W. Milford, reserve 2 breedings each year on Hired Chico registration # 403692 for the life of this stud horse regardless of whom the horse may be sold to." The agreement was filed with the County Court Clerk of Shelby County, Texas. Stewart later sold Hired Chico to Sam McKinnie. Prior to purchasing the horse, McKinnie read the Milford–Stewart contract and testified that he understood the terms of the contract. When McKinnie refused to grant Milford the stud services of Hired Chico, Milford sued McKinnie for breach of contract. Who wins? [*McKinnie v. Milford*, 597 S.W.2d 953, 1980 Tex.App. Lexis 3345 (TX 1980)]

12.9 Condition Shumann Investments, Inc. (Shumann), hired Pace Construction Corporation (Pace), a general contractor, to build "Outlet World of Pasco County." In turn, Pace hired OBS Company, Inc. (OBS), a subcontractor, to perform the framing, dry wall, insulation, and stucco work on the project. The contract between Pace and OBS stipulated: "Final payment shall not become due unless and until the following conditions precedent to final payment have been satisfied ... (c) receipt of final payment for subcontractor's work by contractor from owner." When Shumann refused to pay Pace, Pace refused to pay OBS. OBS sued Pace to recover payment. Who wins? [*Pace Construction Corporation v. OBS Company, Inc.*, 531 So.2d 737, 1988 Fla.App. Lexis 4020 (Fla. App. 1988)]

12.10 Excuse of Condition In January 1976, Maco, Inc. (Maco), a roofing contractor, hired Brian Barrows as a salesperson. Barrows was assigned a geographical territory and was responsible for securing contracts for Maco within his territory. The employment contract provided that Barrows was to receive a 26 percent commission on the net profits from roofing contracts that he obtained. The contract contained the following provision: "To qualify for payment of the commission, the salesperson must sell and supervise the job; the job must be completed and paid for; and the salesperson must have been in the continuous

employment of Maco, Inc., during the aforementioned period." In July 1977, Barrows obtained a $129,603 contract with the Board of Education of Cook County for Maco to make repairs to the roof of the Hoover School in Evanston, Illinois. During the course of the work, Barrows visited the site more than 60 times. In January 1978, before the work was completed, Maco fired Barrows. Later, Maco refused to pay Barrows the commission when the project was completed and paid for. Barrows sued Maco to recover the commission. Who wins? [*Barrows v. Maco, Inc.*, 419 N.E.2d 634, 1981 Ill.App. Lexis 2371 (Ill. App. 1981)]

Business Ethics Cases

12.11 Business Ethics Pabagold, Inc. (Pabagold), a manufacturer and distributor of suntan lotions, hired Mediasmith, an advertising agency, to develop an advertising campaign for Pabagold's Hawaiian Gold Pabatan suntan lotion. In the contract, Pabagold authorized Mediasmith to enter into agreements with third parties to place Pabagold advertisements for the campaign and to make payments to these third parties for the Pabagold account. Pabagold agreed to pay Mediasmith for its services and to reimburse it for expenses incurred on behalf of Pabagold. The Pabagold–Mediasmith contract provided for arbitration of any dispute arising under the contract.

In April 1981, Medismith entered into a contract with Outdoor Services, Inc. (Outdoor Services), an outdoor advertising company, to place Pabagold ads on billboards owned by Outdoor Services. Outdoor Services provided the agreed-upon work and billed Mediasmith $8,545 for its services. Mediasmith requested payment of this amount from Pabagold so it could pay Outdoor Services. When Pabagold refused to pay, Outdoor Services filed a demand for arbitration as provided in the Pabagold–Mediasmith contract. Pabagold defended, asserting that Outdoor Services could not try to recover the money because it was not in privity of contract with Pabagold.

Did Pabagold act ethically in refusing to pay Outdoor Services? From a moral perspective, does it matter that Outdoor Services and Pabagold were not in privity of contract? Who wins? [*Outdoor Services, Inc. v. Pabagold, Inc.*, 185 Cal.App.3d 676, 230 Cal.Rptr. 73, 1986 Cal.App. Lexis 2030 (Cal. App. 1986)]

12.12 Business Ethics Indiana Tri-City Plaza Bowl (Tri-City) leased a building from Charles H. Glueck for use as a bowling alley. The lease provided that Glueck was to provide adequate paved parking for the building. The lease gave Tri-City the right to approve the plans for the construction and paving of the parking lot. When Glueck submitted paving plans to Tri-City, it rejected the plans, and withheld its approval. Tri-City argued that the plans were required to meet its personal satisfaction before it had to approve them. Evidence showed that the plans were commercially reasonable in the circumstances. A lawsuit was filed between Tri-City and Glueck. Who wins? Was it ethical for Tri-City to reject the plans? [*Indiana Tri-City Plaza Bowl, Inc. v. Estate of Glueck*, 422 N.E.2d 670, 1981 Ind.App. Lexis 1506 (Ind. App. 1981)]

Briefing the Case Writing Assignment

Read Case A.12 in the Case Appendix [*Chase Precast Corp. v. John J. Paonessa Co., Inc.*]. This case is excerpted from the appellate court opinion. Review and brief the case. In your brief, be sure to answer the following questions.

1. Who were the contracting parties, and what did their contract provide?

2. Why did the defendant not complete the contract?

3. What does the doctrine of frustration of purpose provide?

4. Did the doctrine of frustration of purpose excuse the defendant's nonperformance?

Endnotes

1. *Restatement (Second) of Contracts*, §§ 311 and 318.
2. *Restatement (Second) of Contracts*, § 317.
3. *Restatement (Second) of Contracts*, § 318(2).
4. *Restatement (Second) of Contracts*, § 328.
5. *Restatement (Second) of Contracts*, § 302.
6. *Restatement (Second) of Contracts*, § 302(1)(b).
7. *Restatement (Second) of Contracts*, § 302(1)(a).
8. The *Restatement (Second) of Contracts*, § 224, defines a *condition* as "An event, not certain to occur, which must

occur, unless its nonperformance is excused, before performance under a contract is due."
9. *Restatement (Second) of Contracts*, § 224.
10. *Restatement (Second) of Contracts*, § 281.
11. *Restatement (Second) of Contracts*, § 261.
12. *Restatement (Second) of Contracts*, § 262.
13. *Restatement (Second) of Contracts*, § 263.
14. *Restatement (Second) of Contracts*, § 264.

Remedies for Breach of Traditional and Online Contracts

" Contracts must not be sports of an idle hour, mere matters of pleasantry and badinage, never intended by the parties to have any serious effect whatsoever. "

—Lord Stowell
Dalrymple v. Dalrymple, 2 Hag.Con. 54, at 105 (1811)

Chapter Objectives

After studying this chapter, you should be able to:

1. Explain how complete performance discharges contractual duties.

2. Identify inferior performance and the material breach of a contract.

3. Describe compensatory, consequential, and nominal damages.

4. Define the equitable remedies of specific performance, reformation and injunction.

5. Describe torts associated with contracts.

Chapter Contents

- Performance and Breach

- Monetary Damages

- Recission and Restitution

- Equitable Remedies

- Torts Associated with Contracts

There are three levels of performance of a contract: *complete*, *substantial*, and *inferior*. Complete (or strict) performance by a party discharges that party's duties under the contract. Substantial performance constitutes a minor breach of the contract. Inferior performance constitutes a material breach that impairs or destroys the essence of the contract. Various remedies may be obtained by a nonbreaching party if a **breach of contract** occurs—that is, if a contracting party fails to perform an absolute duty owed under a contract.[1]

The most common remedy for a breach of contract is an award of **monetary damages**, often called the "law remedy." If a monetary award does not provide adequate relief, however, the court may order any one of several **equitable remedies**, including specific performance, reformation, and injunction. Equitable remedies are based on the concept of fairness.

This chapter discusses breach of contract and the remedies available to the nonbreaching party.

It is a vain thing to imagine a right without a remedy: for want of right and want of remedy are reciprocal.

C. J. Holt
Ashby v. White (1703)

Performance and Breach

No cause of action arises from a bare promise.

Legal Maxim

If a contractual duty has not been discharged (i.e., terminated) or excused (i.e., relieved of legal liability), the contracting party owes an absolute duty (i.e., covenant) to perform the duty. As mentioned in the chapter introduction, there are three types of performance of a

St. Petersburg, Russia. As capitalism increases around the world, the performance and judicial enforcement of contracts will become more important.

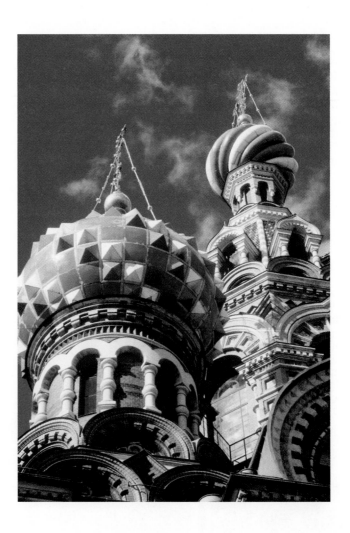

contract: (1) *complete performance*, (2) *substantial performance* (or minor breach), and (3) *inferior performance* (or material breach). These concepts are discussed in the following paragraphs.

Complete Performance

Most contracts are discharged by the **complete**, or **strict**, **performance** of the contracting parties. Complete performance occurs when a party to a contract renders performance exactly as required by the contract. A fully performed contract is called an **executed contract**.

Note that **tender of performance** also discharges a party's contractual obligations. *Tender* is an unconditional and absolute offer by a contracting party to perform his or her obligations under the contract.

Consider This Example   Suppose Ashley's Dress Shops, Inc., contracts to purchase dresses from a manufacturer for $25,000. Ashley's has performed its obligation under the contract once it tenders the $25,000 to the manufacturer. If the manufacturer fails to deliver the dresses, Ashley's can sue it for breach of contract.

Substantial Performance: Minor Breach

Substantial performance occurs when there has been a **minor breach** of contract. In other words, it occurs when a party to a contract renders performance that deviates slightly from complete performance. The nonbreaching party may try to convince the breaching party to elevate his or her performance to complete performance. If the breaching party does not correct the breach, the nonbreaching party can sue to recover *damages* by (1) deducting the cost to repair the defect from the contract price and remitting the balance to the breaching party or (2) suing the breaching party to recover the cost to repair the defect if the breaching party has already been paid (see Exhibit 13.1).

Consider This Example   Suppose Donald Trump contracts with Big Apple Construction Co. to have Big Apple construct an office building for $50 million. The architectural plans call for installation of three-ply windows in the building. Big Apple constructs the building exactly to plan except that it installs two-ply windows. There has been substantial performance. It would cost $300,000 to install the correct windows. If Big Apple agrees to replace the windows, its performance is elevated to complete performance, and Trump must remit the entire contract price. However, if Trump has to hire someone else to replace windows, he may deduct this cost of repair from the contract price and remit the difference to Big Apple.

> The very definition of a good award is that it gives dissatisfaction to both parties.
>
> M. R. Plumer
> *Goodman v. Sayers (1820)*

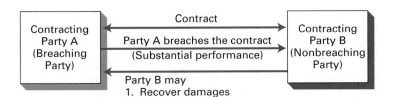

Exhibit 13.1

Remedy Where There Has Been Substantial Performance (Minor Breach)

Exhibit 13.2

Remedies Where There Has Been Incomplete Performance (Material Breach)

Inferior Performance: Material Breach

A **material breach** of a contract occurs when a party renders **inferior performance** of his or her contractual obligations that impairs or destroys the essence of the contract. There is no clear line between a minor breach and a material breach. A determination is made on a case-by-case basis.

Where there has been a material breach of contract, the nonbreaching party may *rescind* the contract and seek restitution of any compensation paid under the contract to the breaching party. The nonbreaching party is discharged from any further performance under the contract.[2] Alternatively, the nonbreaching party may treat the contract as being in effect and sue the breaching party to recover *damages* (see Exhibit 13.2).

> Men keep their agreements when it is an advantage to both parties not to break them.
>
> Solon (c. 600 B.C.)

Consider This Example Suppose a university contracts with a general contractor to build a new three-story building with classroom space for 1,000 students. However, the completed building can support the weight of only 500 students because the contractor used inferior materials. The defect cannot be repaired without rebuilding the entire structure. Because this is a material breach, the university may rescind the contract and require the removal of the building. The university is discharged of any obligations under the contract and is free to employ another contractor to rebuild the building. Alternatively, the university could accept the building and deduct from the contract price damages caused by the defect.

Concept Summary Types of Performance

Type of Performance	Legal Consequence
Complete performance	The contract is discharged.
Substantial performance (minor breach)	The nonbreaching party may recover damages caused by the breach.
Inferior performance (material breach)	The nonbreaching party may either (1) rescind the contract and recover restitution or (2) affirm the contract and recover damages.

Anticipatory Breach

Anticipatory breach (or **anticipatory repudiation**) of contract occurs when the contracting party informs the other party in advance that he or she will not perform his or her contractual duties when due. This type of material breach can be expressly stated or implied from the conduct of the repudiator. Where there is an anticipatory repudiation, the nonbreaching party's obligations under the contract are discharged immediately. The nonbreaching party also has the right to sue the repudiating party when the anticipatory breach occurs; there is no need to wait until performance is due.[3]

In the following case, the court found a breach of contract.

Chodos v. West Publishing Company, Inc.
292 F.3d 992, 2002 U.S. App. Lexis 10823 (2002)
United States Court of Appeals, Ninth Circuit

Case 13.1
Breach of Contract

Background and Facts

Rafael Chodos is a California attorney who specializes in the law of fiduciary duty, which includes a party's obligation to act honestly and with loyalty when performing his or her legal duties to another. In early 1995, Chodos sent a detailed proposal and table of contents to Bancroft-Whitney, the leading publisher of legal texts, to write a treatise on fiduciary duties. The editors at Bancroft-Whitney were enthusiastic about the proposal and sent Chodos a standard form "author agreement" that set forth the terms of the publishing contract. Chodos was to be paid 15 percent of the gross revenues from the sales of the treatise. Chodos and Bancroft-Whitney signed the agreement.

From July 1995 through June 1998, Chodos wrote the manuscript. He significantly limited the time spent on his law practice and spent over 3,600 hours writing the manuscript. During this time, Chodos worked with editors of Bancroft-Whitney in developing and editing the manuscript. In mid-1996, West Publishing Group purchased Bancroft-Whitney, and the two companies merged. The Bancroft-Whitney editors, now employed by West, continued to work with Chodos on editing and developing the manuscript. In June 1998, Chodos submitted the final manuscript to West. During the fall of 1998, West editors suggested changes to the manuscript, which Chodos completed. In December 1998, West sent Chodos a letter apologizing for delays in publication and assuring him publication would take place in the first quarter of 1999.

In February 1999, Chodos received a letter from West's marketing department, stating that West had decided not to publish Chodos's manuscript because it did not "fit with [West's] current product mix" and because of concerns about its "market potential." West admitted, however, that the manuscript was of "high quality" and that its decision was not due to any literary shortcomings of Chodos's work. Chodos filed a lawsuit against West, alleging breach of contract. The U.S. district court granted summary judgment in favor of West. Chodos appealed.

Issue

Did West Publishing breach the author agreement it had with Chodos?

Court's Reasoning

The U.S. Court of Appeals examined the author agreement, which expressly stated that West could legally not publish Chodos's treatise if West found the "form and content" of the manuscript "unacceptable" [paragraphs four and eight of the author agreement]. West argued that pursuant to this language, it had the discretion to reject the manuscript for any good-faith commercial reason. The Court of Appeals rejected West's argument, stating:

> The uncontroverted evidence in this case is that Chodos worked diligently in cooperation with West—indeed with West's encouragement—to produce a work that met the highest professional standard, and that he was successful in that venture. His performance was induced by an agreement that permitted rejection of the completed manuscript only for deficiencies in "form and content." Chodos thus labored to complete a work of high quality with the expectation that, if he did so, it would be published. He devoted thousands of hours of labor to the venture, and passed up substantial professional opportunities, only for West to decide that due to the vagaries of its internal reorganizations and changes in its business strategies or in the national economy or the market for legal treaties, his work, albeit admittedly of high quality, was for naught. It would be inequitable, if not unconscionable, for an author to be forced to bear this considerable burden solely because of his publisher's change of management, its poor planning, or its inadequate financial analyses at the time it entered into the contract, or even because of an unexpected change in the marketplace. Moreover, to allow a publisher to escape its contractual obligations for these reasons would be directly contrary to both the language and the spirit of the standard Author Agreement.

The Court of Appeals concluded, "Because West concedes that the manuscript was of high quality and that it declined to publish it solely for commercial reasons rather than because of any defect in its form and content, we hold as a matter of law that West breached its agreement with Chodos." The Court of Appeals stated that Chodos was entitled to recover restitution for the time and effort he invested in writing the manuscript.

Decision and Remedy

The U.S. Court of Appeals held as a matter of law that West Publishing had breached its contract with Chodos. The Court of Appeals reversed the district court's summary judgment in favor of West, remanded the case to the district court to enter summary judgment as to liability in Chodos's favor, and ordered further proceedings consistent with the opinion of the Court of Appeal.

Case Questions

Critical Legal Thinking   Should a court enforce the terms of a contract literally? Or should the court give contracts a broad interpretation, as requested by West Publishing?

Business Ethics   Did West Publishing act ethically in this case? Should it have read Chodos's treatise on fiduciary duty before terminating its contract with Chodos?

Contemporary Business   If West Publishing wanted to reserve the right to terminate its contract with Chodos based on changes in its own marketing strategy, company reorganization, or changes in the marketplace, how should West have done so? What amount of money should West have paid Chodos?

Monetary Damages

A nonbreaching party may recover **monetary damages** from a breaching party. Monetary damages are available whether the breach was minor or material. Several types of monetary damages may be awarded. These include *compensatory*, *consequential*, *liquidated*, and *nominal damages*.

Compensatory Damages

Compensatory damages are intended to compensate a nonbreaching party for the loss of the bargain. In other words, they place the nonbreaching party in the same position as if the contract had been fully performed by restoring the "benefit of the bargain."

Consider This Example   Suppose Lederle Laboratories enters into a written contract to employ a manager for three years at a salary of $6,000 per month. Before work is to start, the manager is informed that he or she will not be needed. This is a material breach of contract. Assume that the manager finds another job, but it pays only $5,000 a month. The manager may recover $1,000 per month for 36 months (a total of $36,000) from Lederle Laboratories as compensatory damages. These damages place the manager in the same situation as if the contract with Lederle had been performed.

The amount of compensatory damages that will be awarded for breach of contract depends on the type of contract involved and which party breached the contract. The

Chippewa County Courthouse, Sault Ste. Marie, Michigan. State courts hear and decide the majority of breach of contract cases in the United States.

award of compensatory damages in some special types of contracts is discussed in the following paragraphs.

Sale of Goods Compensatory damages for a breach of a sales contract involving goods are governed by the Uniform Commercial Code (UCC). The usual measure of damages for a breach of a sales contract is the difference between the contract price and the market price of the goods at the time and place the goods were to be delivered.[4]

Consider This Example   Suppose (1) Revlon, Inc., contracted to buy a piece of equipment from Greenway Supply Co. for $20,000 and (2) the equipment is not delivered. Revlon then purchases the equipment from another vendor but has to pay $25,000 because the current market price for the equipment has risen. Revlon can recover $5,000—the difference between the market price paid ($25,000) and the contract price ($20,000)—in compensatory damages.

Construction Contracts A construction contract arises when the owner of real property contracts to have a contractor build a structure or do other construction work. The compensatory damages recoverable for a breach of a construction contract vary with the stage of completion the project is in when the breach occurs.

The contractor may recover the profits he or she would have made on the contract if the owner breaches the construction contract before construction begins.

Consider This Example   Suppose RXZ Corporation contracts to have the Ace Construction Co. build a factory for $1.2 million. It will cost Ace $800,000 in materials and labor to build the factory for RXZ. If RXZ Corporation breaches the contract before construction begins, Ace can recover $400,000 in "lost profit."

Assume in the prior example that Ace Construction Co. had spent $300,000 on materials and labor before RXZ breached the contract. Here, Ace can recover $700,000—$400,000 lost profit plus $300,000 expended on materials and labor.

If the builder breaches a construction contract, either before or during construction, the owner can recover the increased cost above the contract price that he or she has to pay to have the work completed by another contractor. For example, suppose that in the previous instance Ace Construction Co., which had contracted to build the factory for RXZ for $1.2 million breached the contract by refusing to build the factory. Assume that RXZ Corporation has to pay $1.5 million to have the same factory built by another contractor. RXZ can recover the increased cost of construction ($300,000) from Ace as compensatory damages.

Employment Contracts

An employee whose employer breaches an employment contract can recover lost wages or salary as compensatory damages. If the employee breaches the contract, the employer can recover the costs to hire a new employee plus any increase in salary paid to the replacement.

Mitigation of Damages

If a contract has been breached, the law places a duty on the innocent nonbreaching party to take reasonable efforts to **mitigate** (i.e., avoid and reduce) the resulting damages. The extent of mitigation required depends on the type of contract involved. For example, if an employer breaches an employment contract, the employee owes a duty to mitigate damages by trying to find substitute employment. The employee is only required to accept *comparable employment*. The courts consider such factors as compensation, rank, status, job description, and geographical location in determining the comparability of jobs.

> Necessitous men are not, truly speaking, free men, but, to answer a present exigency, will submit to any terms that the crafty may impose upon them.
>
> Lord Thomas Henley
> *Vernon v. Bethell (1762)*

> He who derives the advantage ought to sustain the burden.
>
> Legal Maxim

In the following case, the court had to decide whether jobs were comparable.

Parker v. Twentieth Century-Fox Film Corp.
3 Cal.3d 176, 89 Cal.Rptr. 737, 1970 Cal. Lexis 199 (1970)
California Supreme Court

Case 13.2
Mitigation of Damages

Background and Facts

On August 6, 1965, Twentieth Century-Fox Film Corporation (Fox), a major film production studio, entered into an employment contract with Shirley MacLaine Parker (Parker), an actress. Under the contract, Parker was to play the leading female role in a musical production called *Bloomer Girl*, to be filmed in Los Angeles. In the movie, Parker would be able to use her talents as a dancer and as an actress. The contract provided that Parker was to be paid guaranteed compensation of $53,571.42 per week for 14 weeks, commencing on May 23, 1966, for a total of $750,000. On April 4, 1966, Fox sent Parker a letter, notifying her that it was not going to film *Bloomer Girl*. However, the letter offered Parker the leading female role in a film tentatively titled *Big Country*, which was to be a dramatic western to be filmed in Australia. The compensation Fox offered Parker was identical to that offered for *Bloomer Girl*. Fox gave Parker one week to accept. She did not, and the offer expired. Parker sued Fox to recover the guaranteed compensation provided in the *Bloomer Girl* contract. The trial court granted summary judgment to Parker. Fox appealed.

Issue

Was the job that Fox offered Parker in *Big Country* comparable employment that Parker was obligated to accept to mitigate damages?

Court's Reasoning

Before projected earnings from other employment opportunities not sought or accepted by the discharged employee can be applied in mitigation, the employer must show that the other employment was comparable, or substantially similar, to that of which the employee has been deprived. In finding that the offered employment was not comparable, the supreme court stated: "It is clear that the trial court correctly ruled that plaintiff's failure to accept defendant's tendered substitute employment could not be applied in mitigation of damages because the offer of the *Big Country* lead was of employment both different and inferior. The mere circumstances that *Bloomer Girl* was to be a musical review calling upon plaintiff's talents as a dancer as well as an actress, and was to be produced in the City of Los Angeles, whereas *Big Country* was a straight dramatic role in a western-type story taking place in an opal mine in Australia, demonstrates the difference in kind between the two employments: The female lead as a dramatic actress in a western-style motion picture can by no stretch of imagination be considered the equivalent of or substantially similar to the lead in a song-and-dance production."

Decision and Remedy

The supreme court held that the job that Fox offered to Parker in *Big Country* was not comparable employment to the role Fox had contracted Parker to play in *Bloomer Girl*. Therefore, Parker did not fail to mitigate damages by refusing to accept such employment. The supreme court affirmed the trial court's summary judgment.

Case Questions

Critical Legal Thinking Should nonbreaching parties be under a duty to mitigate damages caused by the breaching party? Why or why not?

Business Ethics Did Fox act ethically in this case? Did Parker?

Contemporary Business Who is most likely to be able to mitigate damages when there is a breach of an employment contract: (1) the president of a large corporation, (2) a middle manager, or (3) a bank teller?

Consequential Damages

In addition to compensatory damages, a nonbreaching party sometimes can recover **consequential**, or **special, damages** from the breaching party. Consequential damages are *foreseeable* damages that arise from circumstances outside a contract. To be liable for consequential damages, the breaching party must know or have reason to know that the breach will cause special damages to the other party.

Consider This Example Suppose Soan-Allen Co., a wholesaler, enters into a contract to purchase 1,000 men's suits for $150 each from Fabric Manufacturing Co., a manufacturer. Prior to contracting, the wholesaler tells the manufacturer that the suits will be resold to retailers for $225. The manufacturer breaches the contract by failing to manufacture the suits. The wholesaler cannot get the suits manufactured by anyone else in time to meet his contracts. He or she can recover $75,000 of lost profits on the resale contracts (1,000 suits × $75 profit) as consequential damages from the manufacturer because the manufacturer knew of this special damage to Soan-Allen Co. if it breached the contract.

Liquidated Damages

Under certain circumstances, the parties to a contract may agree in advance to the amount of damages payable upon a breach of contract. These damages are called **liquidated damages**. To be lawful, the actual damages must be difficult or impracticable to determine, and the liquidated amount must be reasonable in the circumstances.[5] An enforceable liquidated damage clause is an exclusive remedy, even if actual damages are later determined to be different.

A liquidated damage clause is considered a **penalty** if actual damages are clearly determinable in advance or if the liquidated damages are excessive or unconscionable. If a liquidated damage clause is found to be a penalty, it is unenforceable. The nonbreaching party may then recover actual damages.

In the following case, the court had to decide whether a liquidated damage clause was a penalty.

Business Brief

Many businesses include liquidated damage clauses in their commercial contracts, which help to provide certainty, avoid lawsuits, and provide an incentive to enter into contracts.

California and Hawaiian Sugar Co. v. Sun Ship, Inc.
794 F.2d 1433, 1986 U.S. App. Lexis 27376 (1986)
United States Court of Appeals, Ninth Circuit

Case 13.3
Liquidated Damages

Background and Facts

The California and Hawaiian Sugar Company (C&H), a California corporation, is an agricultural cooperative owned by 14 sugar plantations in Hawaii. It transports raw sugar to its refinery in Crockett, California. Sugar is a seasonal crop, with about 70 percent of the harvest occurring between April and October. C&H requires reliable seasonal shipping of the raw sugar from Hawaii to California. Sugar stored on the ground or left unharvested suffers a loss of sucrose and goes to waste.

After C&H was notified by its normal shipper that it would be withdrawing its services as of January 1981, C&H commissioned the design of a large hybrid vessel—a tug of a catamaran design consisting of a barge attached to the tug. After substantial negotiation, C&H contracted with Sun Ship, Inc. (Sun Ship), a Pennsylvania corporation, to build the vessel for $25,405,000. The contract, which was signed in the fall of 1979, provided a delivery date of June 30, 1981. The contract also contained a liquidated damage clause calling for a payment of $17,000 per day for each day that the vessel was not delivered to C&H after June 30, 1981. Sun Ship did not complete the vessel until March 16, 1982. The vessel was commissioned in mid-July 1982 and christened the *Moku Pahu*.

During the 1981 season, C&H was able to find other means of shipping the crop from Hawaii to its California refinery. Evidence established that actual damages suffered by C&H because of the nonavailability of the vessel from Sun ship were $368,000. When Sun Ship refused to pay the liquidated damages, C&H filed suit to require payment of $4,413,000 in liquidated damages under the contract. The district court entered judgment in favor of C&H and awarded the corporation $4,413,000 plus interest. Sun Ship appealed.

Issue

Is the liquidated damage clause enforceable, or is it a penalty clause that is not enforceable?

Court's Reasoning

Contracts are contracts because they contain enforceable promises. Absent some overriding public policy, those promises are to be enforced. Parties who agree to pay damages of a fixed amount normally have a good sense of what damages can occur, and the courts are reluctant to override their judgment. In this case, the U.S. Court of Appeals stated: "Proof of this loss is difficult. Whatever the loss, the parties had promised each other that $17,000 per day was a reasonable measure. When sophisticated parties with bargaining parity have agreed what lack of this prize would mean, and it is now difficult to measure what the lack did mean, the court will uphold the parties' bargain."

Decision and Remedy

The Court of Appeals held that the liquidated damage clause was not a penalty and was therefore enforceable. The court of appeals affirmed the judgment of the district court in favor of C&H.

Case Questions

Critical Legal Thinking Should liquidated damage clauses be enforced, or should nonbreaching parties be allowed to recover only actual damages caused by the breaching party?

Business Ethics Did either party act unethically in this case?

Contemporary Business Do you think many businesses use liquidated damage clauses? Can you give some examples?

Nominal Damages

A nonbreaching party can sue a breaching party to a contract for nominal damages even if no financial loss resulted from the breach. **Nominal damages** are usually awarded in a small amount, such as $1. Cases involving nominal damages are usually brought on "principle."

Consider This Example   Suppose Mary enters into an employment contract with Microhard Corporation. It is a three-year contract, and Mary is to be paid $100,000 per year. After Mary works for one year, Microhard Corporation fires Mary. The next day Mary finds a better position at Microsoft Corporation, in the same city, paying $125,000 per year on a two-year contract. Mary has suffered no monetary damages but could bring a civil lawsuit against Microhard Corporation because of its breach and recover nominal damages ($1). Most courts disfavor nominal damage lawsuit because they use valuable court time and resources.

Concept Summary   Types of Monetary Damages

Type of Damage	Description
Compensatory	Compensates a nonbreaching party for the loss of a bargain. It places the nonbreaching party in the same position as if the contract had been fully performed.
Consequential	Compensates a nonbreaching party for foreseeable special damages. The breaching party must have known or should have known that these damages would result from the breach.
Liquidated	Agreement by the parties in advance that sets the amount of damages recoverable in case of breach. These damages are lawful if they do not cause a penalty.
Nominal	Damages awarded against the breaching party even though the nonbreaching party has suffered no actual damages because of the breach. A small amount (e.g., $1) is usually awarded

Enforcement of Remedies

If a nonbreaching party brings a successful lawsuit against a breaching party to a contract, the court will enter a *judgment* in his or her favor. This judgment must then be collected. If the breaching party refuses to pay the judgment, the court may

- *Issue a writ of attachment.* This writ orders the sheriff to seize property in the possession of the breaching party that he or she owns, and to sell the property at auction to satisfy the judgment.
- *Issue a writ of garnishment.* This writ orders that wages, bank accounts, or other property of the breaching party that is in the hands of third parties be paid over to the nonbreaching party to satisfy the judgment. Federal and state laws limit the amount of the breaching party's wages or salary that can be garnished.

Rescission and Restitution

Rescission is an action to undo a contract. It is available where there has been a material breach of contract, fraud, duress, undue influence, or mistake. Generally, to rescind a contract, the parties must make **restitution** of the consideration they received under the contract.[6] Restitution consists of returning the goods, property, money, or other consideration received from the other party. If possible, the actual goods or property must be returned. If the goods or property have been consumed or are otherwise unavailable, restitution must be made by conveying a cash equivalent. The rescinding party must give adequate notice of the rescission to the breaching party. Rescission and restitution restore the parties to the positions they occupied prior to the contract.

Consider This Example   Suppose Filene's Department Store contracts to purchase $100,000 of goods from a sweater manufacturer. The store pays $10,000 as a down payment, and the first $20,000 of goods are delivered. The goods are materially defective, and the defect cannot be cured. This breach is a material breach. Filene's can rescind the contract. The store is entitled to receive its down payment back from the manufacturer, and the manufacturer is entitled to receive the goods back from the store.

Contemporary Environment

Must a Wedding Ring Be Returned if the Engagement Is Broken Off?

When a man and woman are in love, the man often asks the woman to marry him and presents her with an engagement ring. But engagements do not always lead to weddings and are sometimes broken off by one of the parties. The question then is: Who gets the engagement ring? Does the woman get to keep the ring, or can the man recover it? Consider the following case.

In August 1993, Rodger Lindh (Rodger) proposed marriage to Janis Surman (Janis) and presented her with a diamond ring he purchased for $17,400. She accepted his proposal and ring. Discord developed in their relationship, however, and in March 1994 Rodger called off the engagement. He asked Janis to return the engagement ring, but when she refused, Rodger sued her, seeking recovery of the ring. The Pennsylvania trial court and appellate court applied a no-fault rule and held that Janis must return the ring to Rodger. Janis appealed to the Pennsylvania supreme court.

The Pennsylvania supreme court noted that Janis favored the "fault" rule for deciding who gets the ring in a broken engagement case. Under this rule, if "she" breaks off the engagement, "he" gets the ring back; if "he" breaks off the engagement, "she" gets to keep the ring. Although noting that some states still follow this rule, the Pennsylvania supreme court stated that Pennsylvania would not follow the fault rule. The court noted that

the process of determining who is "wrong" and who is "right" is difficult in modern relationships and that this would require parties to aim bitter and unpleasant accusations at each other.

Instead, the Pennsylvania supreme court decided to follow the modern, objective no-fault rule, which holds that an engagement ring must be returned to the donor no matter who breaks off the engagement. The court stated:

> Courts that have applied no-fault principles to engagement ring cases have borrowed from the policies of their respective legislatures that have moved away from the notion of fault in their divorce statutes. We agree with those jurisdictions that have looked toward the development of no-fault divorce law for a principle to decide engagement ring cases, and the inherent weaknesses in any fault-based system lead us to adopt a no-fault approach to resolution of engagement ring disputes. We believe that the benefits from the certainty of our rule outweigh its negatives, and that a strict no-fault approach is less flawed than a fault-based theory.

The Pennsylvania supreme court affirmed the judgment of the lower courts, awarding the engagement ring to Rodger. [*Lindh v. Surman*, 742 A.2d 643, 1999 Pa. Lexis 3498 (PA 1999)] ■

Equitable Remedies

Equitable remedies are available if there has been a breach of contract that cannot be adequately compensated through a legal remedy. They are also available to prevent unjust enrichment. The most common equitable remedies are specific performance, reformation, and injunction.

> Every unjust decision is a reproach to the law or the judge who administers it. If the law should be in danger of doing injustice, then equity should be called in to remedy it. Equity was introduced to mitigate the rigor of the law.
>
> Lord Denning, M. R.
> *Re Vandervell's Trusts* (1974)

Specific Performance

An award of **specific performance** orders the breaching party to perform the acts promised in a contract. The courts have the discretion to award this remedy if the subject matter of the contract is unique.[7] For example, this remedy is available to enforce land contracts because every piece of real property is considered to be unique. Works of art, antiques, items of sentimental value, rare coins, stamps, heirlooms, and such also fit the requirement for uniqueness. Most other personal property does not. Specific performance of personal service contracts is not granted because the courts would find it difficult or impracticable to supervise or monitor performance of such a contract.

Reformation

Reformation is an equitable doctrine that permits the court to rewrite a contract to express the parties' true intentions. For example, suppose a clerical error is made during the typing of a contract, and both parties sign the contract without discovering the error. If a dispute later arises, the court can reform the contract to correct the clerical error to read as the parties originally intended.

Injunction

An **injunction** is a court order that prohibits a person from doing a certain act. To obtain an injunction, the requesting party must show that he or she will suffer irreparable injury if the injunction is not issued.

Consider This Example   Suppose a professional football team enters into a five-year employment contract with a "superstar" quarterback. During this five-year period, the quarterback breaches the contract and enters into a contract to play for a competing team.

Warsaw, Poland. National courts of other countries are often called upon to interpret international contracts and grant remedies if a contract has been breached.

Here, the first team can seek an injunction to prevent the quarterback from playing for the other team.

Concept Summary   Types of Equitable Remedies

Type of Equitable Remedy	Description
Specific performance	A court orders the breaching party to perform the acts promised in the contract. The subject matter of the contract must be unique.
Reformation	A court rewrites a contract to express the parties' true intentions. It is usually used to correct clerical errors.
Injunction	A court prohibits a party from doing a certain act. Injunctions are available in contract actions only in limited circumstances.

Torts Associated with Contracts

The recovery for breach of contract is usually limited to contract damages. A party who can prove a contract-related **tort**, however, may also recover tort damages. Tort damages include compensation for personal injury, pain and suffering, emotional distress, and possibly punitive damages.

Generally, **punitive damages** are not recoverable for breach of contract. They are recoverable, however, for certain tortious conduct that may be associated with the nonperformance of a contract. These actions include fraud, intentional conduct, and other egregious conduct. Punitive damages are in addition to actual damages and may be kept by the plaintiff. Punitive damages are awarded to punish the defendant, to deter the defendant from similar conduct in the future, and to set an example for others.

The major torts associated with contracts are (1) *intentional interference with contractual relations* and (2) *breach of the implied covenant of good faith and fair dealing*.

Intentional Interference with Contractual Relations

A party to a contract may sue any third person who intentionally interferes with the contract and causes that party injury. The third party does not have to have acted with malice or bad faith. This tort, which is known as the tort of **intentional interference with contractual relations**, usually arises when a third party induces a contracting party to breach a contract with another party. The following elements must be shown:

1. A valid, enforceable contract between the contracting parties
2. Third-party knowledge of this contract
3. Third-party inducement to breach the contract

A third party can contract with the breaching party without becoming liable for this tort if a contracting party has already breached the contract because the third party cannot be held to have induced a preexisting breach.

In the following case, the court found interference with a contract and awarded punitive damages.

Business Brief

Many breach of contract actions also involve torts. The merging of these two areas has led some commentators to call this area "contorts."

Brumfield v. Death Row Records, Inc.

No. BC135461 Superior Court of Los Angeles County, California

Case 13.4

Intentional Interference with a Contract

Background and Facts

Ricardo E. Brown, Jr., known as "Kurupt," was an unknown teenage rap singer who lived with his father. In 1989, Lamont Brumfield, a promoter of young rappers, "discovered" Kurupt. Lamont introduced his brother Kenneth Brumfield, who owned a music publishing business, to Kurupt. Beginning in 1990, Lamont produced demos for Kurupt, set up photo shoots, booked him to sing at many clubs, and paid for Kurupt's clothing and personal and living expenses. Kurupt lived with Lamont after Kurupt's father kicked him out of the house. In 1991, Lamont obtained recording work for Kurupt with the rap group SOS. In November 1991, Kurupt signed an exclusive recording agreement with Lamont's company, an exclusive publishing agreement with Kenneth's company, and a management agreement with Kenneth for an initial term of three years, with an additional option term. These contracts gave Kurupt 7 percent royalties on sales. The Brumfields spent at least $65,000 to support and promote Kurupt, often borrowing money from family and friends to do so.

Andre Young, known as Dr. Dre, invited Lamont, Kenneth, and Kurupt to a picnic, where he introduced them to Marion Knight, the owner of Death Row Records, Inc. The Brumfields and Kurupt made it clear to Dr. Dre and Knight that the Brumfields had exclusive contracts with Kurupt. After Kurupt performed at the picnic, Dr. Dre invited Kurupt to his house to record songs for Dr. Dre's album *Chronic*. In December 1992, *Chronic* was released by Death Row Records, Inc., and sold millions of copies. The Brumfields continued to promote Kurupt and to take care of his living expenses. When Dr. Dre invited Kurupt to go on tour to promote the *Chronic* album, Kurupt told the Brumfields that he was going to visit family in Philadelphia but instead went on tour for four weeks. In 1993, Kurupt worked on another Death Row Records album. In May 1994, Kenneth exercised his option and renewed his management agreement with Kurupt. Despite the multimillion-dollar profit of the *Chronic* album, the Brumsfields were paid nothing by Death Row Records. At the end of 1994, Death Row moved Kurupt out of the condominium he shared with Lamont and into a house. While cleaning out the condominium, Lamont found papers showing that Death Row Records had paid Kurupt advances commencing in April 1993.

The Brumfields sued Death Row Records, Inc., in the superior court of Los Angeles County, California, to recover damages for the tort of intentional interference with their contracts with Kurupt. The jury found in favor of the Brumfields and awarded them $14,344,000

in compensatory and punitive damages. The superior court judge reduced the award to $5,519,000, including $1.5 million in punitive damages to Lamont and $1 million in punitive damages to Kenneth.

Issue

Did defendant Death Row Records, Inc., engage in the tort of intentional interference with the contracts that plaintiffs Lamont and Kenneth Brumfield had with rapper Kurupt?

Court's Reasoning

The evidence showed that Kurupt had breached the contracts he had with the Brumfields and had earned approximately $1.5 million in royalties from Death Row records for his work on the *Chronic* album and many other albums. The court held that there was evidence that Death Row Records had caused Kurupt to breach these contracts and was therefore liable for the tort of intentional interference with a contract. The court found that the necessary elements for the tort of intentional interference with a contract had been proven. There were valid contracts between the Brumfields and Kurupt, the defendant had knowledge of these contracts, the defendant intentionally induced Kurupt to breach these contracts, and such breach resulted in damages to the Brumfields.

Decision and Remedy

The court held that defendant Death Row Records, Inc., had committed the tort of intentionally interfering with the contracts that the Brumfields had with rapper Kurupt. The court awarded $5,519,000 to the Brumfields, including $1.5 million in punitive damages to Lamont and $1 million in punitive damages to Kenneth. The judgment of the superior court was upheld by the court of appeals of California in an unpublished opinion, 2003 Cal.App. Unpub. Lexis 7843 (2003).

Case Questions

Critial Legal Thinking   Should there be a tort of intentional interference with a contract? Why or why not? What public policy is served by this tort?

Business Ethics   Did Marion Knight and Dr. Dre act ethically in this case? Did Kurupt act ethically in this case?

Contemporary Business   Does the possibility of the award of punitive damages deter parties from interfering with other parties contracts?

Breach of the Implied Covenant of Good Faith and Fair Dealing

Several states have held that a **covenant of good faith and fair dealing** is implied in certain types of contracts. Under this covenant, the parties to a contract are not only held to the express terms of the contract but are also required to act in "good faith" and deal fairly

Tibet. International trade increases the economic opportunities of peoples and countries worldwide.

in all respects in obtaining the objective of the contract. A breach of this implied covenant is a tort for which tort damages are recoverable. This tort, which is sometimes referred to as the **tort of bad faith**, is an evolving area of the law.

In the following case, the court found a bad faith tort and awarded punitive damages.

O'Neill v. Gallant Insurance Company
769 N.E.2d 100, 2002 Ill.App. Lexis 311 (2002)
Appellate Court of Illinois

Case 13.5
Bad Faith Tort

Background and Facts

On Halloween Day, 1996, Christine Narvaez drove her automobile onto the parking lot of a busy supermarket. Narvaez had her two-year-old grandchild with her. The youngster was riding, unconstrained, in a booster seat. Narvaez saw a friend and decided to stop for a brief chat. She parked the car and exited the car, leaving the keys in the ignition and the motor running. The youngster crawled behind the wheel, slipped the car into gear, and set it in motion. The car struck Marguerite O'Neill, a woman in her eighties, pinned her between the Narvaez car and another car, and slowly crushed the woman's trapped body.

O'Neill was pried loose and airlifted to a hospital trauma center. O'Neill suffered a crushed hip, a broken arm, and four cracked ribs, and she lost more than 40 percent of her blood supply as a result of internal bleeding. She spent one month in the hospital intensive care unit and had to be placed in a nursing home and was deprived of the ability to live independently.

Narvaez carried the $20,000 minimum amount of liability insurance allowed by law. She was insured by Gallant Insurance Company. O'Neill's medical bills totaled $105,000. O'Neill sued

Narvaez and her insurance company, Gallant. O'Neill's attorney demanded the policy limit of $20,000 from Gallant in settlement of O'Neill's claim and offered a complete release from liability for Narvaez. Three Gallant insurance adjusters, its claims manager, and the lawyer of the law firm representing Gallant for the case all stated to John Moss, Gallant's executive vice president, that Gallant should accept the settlement offer. Moss rejected their advice and refused to settle the case.

One year later, on the eve of trial, Moss offered to settle for the $20,000 policy limit, but O'Neill then refused. The case went to trial, and the jury returned a verdict against Narvaez of $731,063. Gallant paid $20,000 of this amount, closed its file, and left Narvaez liable for the $711,063 excess judgment. To settle her debt to O'Neill, Narvaez assigned her claims against Gallant to O'Neill. O'Neill then sued Gallant for a bad faith tort for breaching the covenant of good faith and fair dealing that Gallant owed to Narvaez to settle the case. The jury found Gallant liable for a bad faith tort and awarded O'Neill $710,063 ($1,000 short of the judgment in the first trial) in actual damages and $2.3 million in punitive damages. Gallant appealed.

O'Neill v. Gallant Insurance Company
769 N.E.2d 100, 2002 Ill.App. Lexis 311 (2002)
Appellate Court of Illinois
(continued)

Issue

Was Gallant liable for a bad faith tort?

Court's Reasoning

The appellate court stated, "Where an insurer is pursued for its refusal to settle a claim, bad faith lies in an insurer's failure to give at least equal consideration to the insured's interests when the insurer arrives at a decision to settle the claim." The court found that Gallant had acted in bad faith because it chose its own interests above those of Narvaez in refusing to settle O'Neill's claim. The court cited the fact that in 44 known Illinois cases Gallant had refused to settle claims within the policy limits, causing excess judgments of $10,849,313. The court found bad faith in this case because Moss rejected the recommendations of Gallant's claim adjusters, claims manager, and lawyer to settle O'Neill's claim within the $20,000 policy limit.

Decision and Remedy

The appellate court held that Gallant was liable for a bad faith tort and upheld the trial court's judgment awarding O'Neill $710,063 in actual damages and $2.3 million in punitive damages.

Case Questions

Critical Legal Thinking Define the tort of breach of the implied covenant of good faith and fair dealing. Why is it called the "bad faith" tort?

Business Ethics Did Gallant act ethically in this case?

Contemporary Business Will the implied covenant of good faith and fair dealing make insurance companies act more ethically toward their customers? Explain.

Chapter Summary

Performance and Breach, p. 266

Levels of Performance

1. *Complete performance.* A party in complete performance renders performance exactly as required by the contract. That party's contractual duties are discharged.
2. *Substantial performance.* A party in substantial performance renders performance that deviates only slightly from complete performance. There is a *minor breach*. The nonbreaching party may recover damages caused by the breach.
3. *Inferior performance.* A party in inferior performance fails to perform express or implied contractual duties that impair or destroy the essence of the contract. There is a *material breach*. The nonbreaching party may either (1) rescind the contract and recover restitution or (2) affirm the contract and recover damages.

Anticipatory Breach

In an anticipatory breach, one contracting party informs the other party—by express words or by conduct—that he or she will not perform his or her contractual duties when due. This gives an immediate cause of action to the nonbreaching party to sue for breach of contract. It is also called *anticipatory repudiation.*

Monetary Damages, p. 270

Monetary Damages

1. *Compensatory damages.* These are damages that compensate a nonbreaching party for the loss of a contract. They restore the "benefit of the bargain" to the nonbreaching party as if the contract had been fully performed.

2. ***Consequential damages.*** These are foreseeable damages that arise from circumstances outside the contract and of which the breaching party either knew or had reason to know. They are also called *special damages.*

3. ***Nominal damages.*** These are small damages awarded to a nonbreaching party who has suffered no financial loss because of the defendant's breach of contract. They are usually awarded on principle.

4. ***Liquidated damages.*** These are damages payable upon breach of contract that are agreed on in advance by the contracting parties. Liquidated damages substitute for actual damages. For a liquidated damage clause to be lawful, the following two conditions must be met:

   a. The actual damages must be extremely difficult or impracticable to determine.

   b. The liquidated amount must be a reasonable estimate of the harm that would result from the breach.

   A liquidated damage clause is considered a *penalty* if actual damages are clearly determinable in advance or the liquidated damages are excessive or unconscionable. A penalty is unenforceable and the nonbreaching party may recover actual damages.

Mitigation of Damages

The law places a duty on a nonbreaching party to take reasonable efforts to avoid or reduce the resulting damages from a breach of contract. To mitigate a breach of an employment contract, the nonbreaching party must only accept "comparable" employment.

Rescission and Restitution, p. 274

Rescission and Restitution

Rescission is an action by a nonbreaching party to undo a contract. It is available upon the material breach of a contract. The parties must make restitution of the consideration they have received from the other party. Rescission and restitution restore the parties to the positions they occupied prior to the contract.

Equitable Remedies, p. 275

Equitable Remedies

Equitable remedies are available if a nonbreaching party cannot be adequately compensated by a legal remedy or to prevent unjust enrichment.

1. ***Specific performance.*** This court order requires the breaching party to perform his or her contractual duties. It is available only if the subject matter of the contract is *unique.*

2. ***Reformation.*** Reformation permits the court to rewrite a contract to express the parties' true intention. It is available to correct clerical and mathematical errors.

3. ***Injunction.*** This court order prohibits a person from doing a certain act. The requesting party must show that he or she will suffer irreparable injury if the injunction is not granted.

Torts Associated with Contracts, p. 277

Types of Torts Associated with Contracts

1. ***Intentional interference with contractual relations.*** When this tort is committed, a third party intentionally interferes with another party's contract and induces the other party to that contract to breach it, causing the nonbreaching party injury.

2. ***Breach of the implied covenant of good faith and fair dealing.*** When this tort is committed, a party to a contract does not act in good faith or fails to deal fairly in achieving the object of the contract. This duty is implied in only certain contracts (e.g., insurance contracts). It is also called the *tort of bad faith.*

Tort Damages

1. ***Compensatory damages.*** These include compensation for personal injury, pain and suffering, emotional distress, and other injuries caused by the defendant's tortious conduct.

2. ***Punitive damages.*** These are recoverable against a defendant for intentional or egregious conduct. They are awarded to punish the defendant, to deter the defendant from similar conduct in the future, and to set an example for others.

Internet Exercises and Case Questions
Working the Web Internet Exercises

Activities

1. Review the basic principles of remedies at **consumer.pub. findlaw.com/newcontent/consumerlaw/chp15_b.html**.

2. An outline on several contracts topics, including remedies for breach, is available at **www.law.washington.edu/ courses/ramasastry/A501C/assignments.html**.

Critical Legal Thinking Cases

13.1 Performance Louis Haeuser, who owned several small warehouses, contracted with Wallace C. Drennen, Inc. (Drennen), to construct a road to the warehouses. The contract price was $42,324. After Drennen completed the work, some cracks appeared in the road, causing improper drainage. In addition, "birdbaths" that accumulated water appeared in the road. When Haeuser refused to pay, Drennen sued to recover the full contract price. Haeuser filed a cross complaint to recover the cost of repairing the road. Who wins? [*Wallace C. Drennen, Inc. v. Haeuser*, 402 So.2d 771, 1981 La.App. Lexis 4453 (La. App. 1979)]

13.2 Anticipatory Repudiation In September 1976, Muhammad Ali (Ali) successfully defended his heavyweight boxing championship of the world by defeating Ken Norton. Shortly after the fight, Ali held a press conference and, as he had done on several occasions before, announced his retirement from boxing. At that time Ali had beaten every challenger except Duane Bobick, whom he had not yet fought. In November 1976, Madison Square Garden Boxing, Inc. (MSGB), a fight promoter, offered Ali $2.5 million if he would fight Bobick. Ali agreed, stating, "We are back in business again." MSGB and Ali signed a Fighters' Agreement, and MSGB paid Ali $125,000 advance payment. The fight was to take place in Madison Square Garden on a date in February 1977. On November 30, 1976, Ali told MSGB that he was retiring from boxing and would not fight Bobick in February. Must MSGB wait until the date performance is due to sue Ali for breach of contract? [*Madison Square Garden Boxing, Inc. v. Muhammad Ali*, 430 F.Supp. 679, 1977 U.S.Dist. Lexis 16101 (N.D. Ill. 1977)]

13.3 Damages In 1978, Hawaiian Telephone Company entered into a contract with Microform Data Systems, Inc. (Microform), for Microform to provide a computerized assistance system that would handle 15,000 calls per hour with a one-second response time and with a "nonstop" feature to allow automatic recovery from any component failure. The contract called for installation of the host computer no later than mid-February 1979. Microform was not able to meet the initial installation date, and at that time it was determined that

Microform was at least nine months away from providing a system that met contract specifications. Hawaiian Telephone canceled the contract and sued Microform for damages. Did Microform materially breach the contract to allow recovery of damages? [*Hawaiian Telephone Co. v. Microform Data Systems Inc.*, 829 F.2d 919, 1987 U.S.App. Lexis 13425 (9th Cir. 1987)]

13.4 Damages Raquel Welch was a movie actress who appeared in about 30 films between 1965 and 1980. She was considered a sex symbol, and her only serious dramatic role was as a roller derby queen in *Kansas City Bomber*. In about 1980, Michael Phillips and David Ward developed a film package based on the John Steinbeck novella *Cannery Row*. In early 1981, Metro-Goldwyn-Mayer Film Company (MGM) accepted to produce the project and entered into a contract with Welch to play the leading female character, a prostitute named Suzy. At 40 years old, Welch relished the chance to direct her career toward more serious roles. Welch was to receive $250,000 from MGM, with payment being divided into weekly increments during filming. Filming began on December 1, 1980. On December 22, 1980, MGM fired Welch and replaced her with another actress, Debra Winger. Welch sued MGM to recover the balance of $194,444 that remained unpaid under the contract. Who wins? [*Welch v. Metro-Goldwyn-Mayer Film Co.*, 207 Cal.App.3d 164, 254 Cal.Rptr. 645, 1988 Cal.App. Lexis 1202 (Cal. App. 1989)]

13.5 Damages On August 28, 1979, Ptarmigan Investment Company (Ptarmigan), a partnership, entered into a contract with Gundersons, Inc. (Gundersons), a South Dakota corporation in the business of golf course construction. The contract provided that Gundersons would construct a golf course for Ptarmigan for a contract price of $1,294,129. Gundersons immediately started work and completed about one-third of the work by late November 1979, when bad weather forced cessation of most work. Ptarmigan paid Gundersons for the work to that date. In the spring of 1980, Ptarmigan ran out of funds and was unable to pay for the completion of the golf course. Gundersons sued Ptarmigan and its individual partners to recover the lost profits that it would have made on the remaining two-thirds of the contract. Can Gundersons recover these lost profits as damages? [*Gundersons, Inc. v. Ptarmigan Investment Company*, 678 P.2d 1061, 1983 Colo.App. Lexis 1133 (Colo. App. 1983)]

13.6 Liquidated Damages   In December 1974, H. S. Perlin Company, Inc. (Perlin), and Morse Signal Devices of San Diego (Morse) entered into a contract whereby Morse agreed to provide burglar and fire alarm service to Perlin's coin and stamp store. Perlin paid $50 per month for this service. The contract contained a liquidated damage clause limiting Morse's liability to $250 for any losses incurred by Perlin based on Morse's failure of service. During the evening of August 25, 1980, a burglary occurred at Perlin's store. Before entering the store, the burglars cut a telephone line that ran from the burglar system in Perlin's store to Morse's central location. When the line was cut, a signal indicated the interruption of service at Morse's central station. Inexplicably, Morse took no further steps to investigate the interruption of service at Perlin's store. The burglars stole stamps and coins with a wholesale value of $958,000, and Perlin did not have insurance against this loss. Perlin sued Morse to recover damages. Is the liquidated damage clause enforceable? [*H. S. Perlin Company, Inc. v. Morse Signal Devices of San Diego*, 209 Cal.App.3d 1289, 258 Cal.Rptr. 1, 1989 Cal.App. Lexis 400 (Cal. App. 1989)]

13.7 Liquidated Damages   United Mechanical Contractors, Inc. (UMC), an employer, agreed to provide a pension plan for its unionized workers. UMC was to make monthly payments into a pension fund administered by the Idaho Plumbers and Pipefitters Health and Welfare Fund (Fund). Payments were due by the 15th of each month. The contract between UMC and the Fund contained a liquidated damage clause which provided that if payments due from UMC were received later than the 20th of the month, liquidated damages of 20 percent of the required contribution would be assessed against UMC. In June 1985, the fund received UMC's payment on the 24th. The Fund sued UMC to recover $9,245.23 in liquidated damages. Is the liquidated damage clause enforceable? [*Idaho Plumbers and Pipefitters Health and Welfare Fund v. United Mechanical Contractors, Inc.*, 875 F.2d 212, 1989 U.S.App. Lexis 14528 (9th Cir. 1989)]

13.8 Specific Performance   Liz Claiborne, Inc. (Claiborne), is a large maker of sportswear in the United States and a well-know name in fashion, with sales of over $1 billion per year. Claiborne distributes its products through 9,000 retail outlets in the United States. Avon Products, Inc. (Avon), is a major producer of fragrances, toiletries, and cosmetics, with annual sales of more than $3 billion a year. Claiborne, which desired to promote its well-known name on perfumes and cosmetics, entered into a joint venture with Avon whereby Claiborne would make available its names, trademarks, and marketing experience, and Avon would engage in the procurement and manufacture of the fragrances,

toiletries, and cosmetics. The parties would equally share the financial requirements of the joint venture. In 1986, its first year of operation, the joint venture had sales of more than $16 million. In the second year, sales increased to $26 million, making it one of the fastest-growing fragrance and cosmetic lines in the country. In 1987, Avon sought to "uncouple" the joint venture. Avon thereafter refused to procure and manufacture the line of fragrances and cosmetics for the joint venture. When Claiborne could not obtain the necessary fragrances and cosmetics from any other source for the fall/Christmas season, Claiborne sued Avon for breach of contract, seeking specific performance of the contract by Avon. Is specific performance an appropriate remedy in this case? [*Liz Claiborne, Inc. v. Avon Products, Inc.*, 530 N.Y.S.2d 425, 141 A.D.2d 329, 1988 N.Y.App.Div. Lexis 6423 (N.Y. Sup. App. 1988)]

13.9 Injunction   In 1982, Anita Baker, a then-unknown singer, signed a multiyear recording contract with Beverly Glen Music, Inc. (Beverly Glen). Baker recorded for Beverly Glen a record album that was moderately successful. After having some difficulties with Beverly Glen, Baker was offered a considerably more lucrative contract by Warner Communications, Inc. (Warner). Baker accepted the Warner offer and informed Beverly Glen that she would not complete their contract because she had entered into an agreement with Warner. Beverly Glen sued Baker and Warner, and it sought an injunction to prevent Baker from performing as a singer for Warner. Is an injunction an appropriate remedy in this case? [*Beverly Glen Music, Inc. v. Warner Communications, Inc.*, 178 Cal.App.3d 1142, 224 Cal.Rptr. 260, 1986 Cal.App. Lexis 2729 (Cal. App. 1986)]

13.10 Intentional Interference with Contractual Relations   In 1963, Pacific Gas and Electric Company (PG & E) entered into a contract with Placer County Water Agency (Agency) to purchase hydroelectric power generated by the Agency's Middle Fork American River Project. The contract was not terminable until 2013. As energy prices rose during the 1970s, the contract became extremely valuable to PG & E. The price PG & E paid for energy under the contract was much lower than the cost of energy from other sources. In 1982, Bear Stearns & Company (Bear Stearns), an investment bank and securities underwriting firm, learned of the Agency's power contract with PG & E. Bear Stearns offered to assist the Agency in an effort to terminate the power contract with PG & E in exchange for a share of the Agency's subsequent profits and the right to underwrite any new securities issued by the Agency. Bear Stearns also agreed to pay the legal fees incurred by the Agency in litigation concerning the attempt to get out of the PG & E contract. Who wins and why? [*Pacific Gas and Electric Company v. Bear Stearns & Company*, 50 Cal.3d 1118, 270 Cal.Rptr. 1, 1990 Cal. Lexis 2119 (Cal. App. 1990)]

Business Ethics Cases

13.11 Business Ethics   Walgreen Company has operated a pharmacy in the Southgate Mall in Milwaukee since 1951, when the mall opened. It had a lease, signed in 1971 and carrying a 30-year term, that contained an exclusivity clause in which the landlord, Sara Creek Property Company (Sara Creek), promised not to lease space in the mall to anyone else who wanted to operate a pharmacy

or a store containing a pharmacy. In 1990, after its anchor tenant went broke, Sara Creek informed Walgreen that it intended to lease the anchor tenant space to Phar-Mor Corporation. Phar-Mor, a "deep discount" chain, would occupy 100,000 square feet, of which 12,000 square feet would be occupied by a pharmacy the same size as Walgreen's. The entrances to the two stores would be within a few hundred feet of each other. Walgreen sued Sara Creek for breach of contract and sought a permanent injunction against Sara Creek's leasing the anchor premises to Phar-Mor. Do the facts of this case justify the issuance of a permanent injunction? Did Sara Creek act ethically in not living up to the contract with Walgreen? [*Walgreen Co. v. Sara Creek Property Co.*, 966 F.2d 273, 1992 U.S.App. Lexis 14847 (7th Cir. 1992)]

13.12 Business Ethics   Rosina Crisci owned an apartment building in which Mrs. DiMare was a tenant. One day while DiMare was descending a wooden staircase on the outside of the apartment building, she fell through the staircase and was left hanging 15 feet above the ground until she was saved. Crisci had a $10,000 liability insurance policy on the building from the Security Insurance Company (Security) of New Haven, Connecticut. DiMare sued Crisci and Security for $400,000 for physical injuries and psychosis suffered from the fall. Prior to trial, DiMare agreed to take $10,000 in settlement of the case. Security refused this settlement offer. DiMare reduced her settlement offer to $9,000, of which Crisci offered to pay $2,500. Security again refused to settle the case. The case proceeded to trial, and the jury awarded DiMare and her husband $110,000. Security paid $10,000, pursuant to the insurance contract, and Crisci had to pay the difference. Crisci, a widow of 70 years of age, had to sell her assets, became dependent on her relatives, declined in physical health, and suffered from hysteria and suicide attempts. Crisci sued Security for tort damages for breach of the implied covenant of good faith and fair dealing. Did Security act in bad faith? [*Crisci v. Security Insurance Company of New Haven, Connecticut*, 426 P.2d 173, 66 Cal.App.2d 425, 58 Cal.Rptr. 13, 1967 Cal. Lexis 313 (Cal. App. 1967)]

Briefing the Case Writing Assignment

Read Case A.13 in the Case Appendix [*E. B. Harvey & Company, Inc. v. Protective Systems, Inc.*]. This case is excerpted from the appellate court opinion. Review and brief the case. In your brief, be sure to answer the following questions.

1. What were the duties of Protective Systems under the contract?

2. What amount of damages was Protective Systems liable for under the express terms of the contract?

3. Was Protective Systems negligent in this case?

4. What policy considerations did the court cite in upholding the liquidated damage clause?

Endnotes

1. *Restatement (Second) of Contracts*, § 235(2).
2. *Restatement (Second) of Contracts*, § 241.
3. *Restatement (Second) of Contracts*, § 253; UCC § 2-610.
4. UCC §§ 2-708 and 2-713.
5. *Restatement (Second) of Contracts*, § 356(1).
6. *Restatement (Second) of Contracts*, § 370.
7. *Restatement (Second) of Contracts*, § 359.

Formation of Sales and Lease Contracts

14

"Commercial law lies within a narrow compass, and is far purer and freer from defects than any other part of the system."

—Henry Peter Brougham
House of Commons, February 7, 1828

Chapter Objectives

After studying this chapter, you should be able to:

1. Define sales contracts governed by Article 2 of the UCC.

2. Define lease contracts governed by Article 2A of the UCC.

3. Apply the basic UCC principles of good faith and reasonableness.

4. Describe the formation of sales and lease contracts.

5. Define the UCC's firm offer rule, additional terms rule, and written confirmation rule.

Chapter Contents

- Scope of Article 2 (Sales)

- Scope of Article 2A (Leases)

- Formation of Sales and Lease Contracts

Most tangible items—such as books, clothing, and tools—are considered **goods**. In medieval times, merchants gathered at fairs in Europe to exchange such goods. Over time, certain customs and rules evolved for enforcing contracts and resolving disputes. These customs and rules, which were referred to as the "Law Merchant," were enforced by "fair courts" established by the merchants. Eventually, the customs and rules of the Law Merchant were absorbed into the common law.

Toward the end of the 1800s, England enacted a statute (the Sales of Goods Act) that codified the common law rules of commercial transactions. In the United States, laws governing the sale of goods also developed. In 1906, the **Uniform Sales Act** was promulgated in the United States. This act was enacted in many states. It was quickly outdated, however, as mass production and distribution of goods developed in the twentieth century.

In 1949, the National Conference of Commissioners on Uniform State Laws promulgated a comprehensive statutory scheme called the **Uniform Commercial Code (UCC)**. The UCC covers most aspects of commercial transactions.

Article 2 (Sales) and **Article 2A (Leases)** of the UCC govern personal property leases. These articles are intended to provide clear, easy-to-apply rules that place the risk of loss of the goods on the party most able to either bear the risk or insure against it. The common law of contracts governs if either Article 2 or Article 2A is silent on an issue.

This chapter discusses sales and lease contracts. Other articles of the UCC are discussed in subsequent chapters.

Contemporary Environment
The Uniform Commercial Code (UCC)

One of the major frustrations of businesspersons conducting interstate business is that they are subject to the laws of each state in which they operate. To address this problem, in 1949 the National Conference of Commissioners on Uniform State Laws promulgated the **Uniform Commercial Code (UCC)**. The UCC is a **model act** that contains uniform rules that govern commercial transactions. To create this uniformity, individual states needed to enact the UCC as their commercial law statute. They did, and every state (except Louisiana, which has adopted only parts of the UCC) enacted the UCC as a commercial statute.

The UCC is divided into articles, with each article establishing uniform rules for a particular facet of commerce in this country. The articles of the UCC are:

Article 1	General Provisions
Article 2	Sales
Article 2A	Leases
Article 3	Negotiable Instruments
Article 4	Bank Deposits and Collections
Article 4A	Funds Transfers
Article 5	Letters of Credit
Article 6	Bulk Transfers
Article 7	Documents of Title
Article 8	Investment Securities
Article 9	Secured Transactions
Revised Article 9	

These articles are discussed in the chapters in this section of this book.

The UCC is continually being revised to reflect changes in modern commercial practices and technology. For example, Article 2A was drafted to govern leases of personal property, and Article 4A was added to regulate the use of wire transfers in the banking system. Articles 3 and 4, which cover the creation and transfer of negotiable instruments and the clearing of checks through the banking system, were substantially amended in 1990. Article 2, which establishes rules that govern the sale of goods, and Articles 9, which covers secured transactions in personal property, have also been revised recently. ■

Scope of Article 2 (Sales)

All states except Louisiana have adopted some version of **Article 2 (Sales)** of the UCC. Article 2 is also applied by federal courts to sales contracts governed by federal law. Article 2 has recently been revised. This article, referred to as **Revised Article 2**, has been adopted by some states.

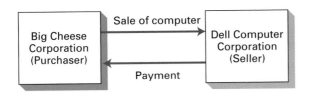

Exhibit 14.1

Sales Transaction

What Is a Sale?

Article 2 of the UCC applies to transactions in goods [UCC 2-102]. All states have held that Article 2 applies to the sale of goods. A **sale** consists of the passing of title from a seller to a buyer for a price [UCC 2-106(1)]. For example, the purchase of a computer is a sale subject to Article 2, whether the computer was paid for by cash, credit card, or other form of consideration (see Exhibit 14.1).

What Are Goods?

Goods are defined as tangible things that are movable at the time of their identification to the contract [UCC 2-105(1)]. Specially manufactured goods and the unborn young of animals are examples of goods. Certain items are not considered goods and are not subject to Article 2. They include:

1. Money and intangible items, such as stocks, bonds, and patents, are not tangible goods.
2. Real estate is not a tangible good because it is not movable [UCC 2-105(1)]. Minerals, structures, growing crops, and other things that are severable from real estate may be classified as goods subject to Article 2, however. For example, the sale and removal of a chandelier in a house is a sale of goods subject to Article 2 because its removal would not materially harm the realty. The sale and removal of the furnace, however, would be a sale of real property because its removal would cause material harm [UCC 2-107(2)].

Goods Versus Services Contracts for the provision of services—including legal services, medical services, and dental services—are not covered by Article 2. Sometimes, however, a sale involves both the provision of a service and a good in the same transaction. This sale is referred to as a **mixed sale**. Article 2 applies to mixed sales only if the goods are the predominant part of the transaction. The UCC provides no guidance for deciding cases based on mixed sales; therefore, the courts decide these issues on a case-by-case basis using the common law of contracts.

In the following case, the court had to decide whether a sale was of a good or a service.

> **Business Brief**
>
> Article 2 of the UCC applies only to transactions in *goods*. Article 2 does not apply to transactions in intangible items, real estate, or services.

Hector v. Cedars-Sinai Medical Center

180 Cal.App. 3d 493, 225 Cal.Rptr. 595, 1986 Cal.App. Lexis 1523 (1986)
California Court of Appeals

Case 14.1
Good Versus Service

Background and Facts

Frances Hector entered Cedars-Sinai Medical Center (Cedars-Sinai), Los Angeles, California, for a surgical operation on her heart. During the operation, a pacemaker was installed in Hector. The pacemaker, which was manufactured by American Technology, Inc., was installed at Cedars-Sinai by Hector's physician, Dr.

Eugene Kompaniez. The pacemaker was defective, causing injury to Hector. Hector sued Cedars-Sinai under Article 2 of the UCC for breach of warranty. The trial court held that the sale was primarily a sale of a service and not of goods; therefore, the UCC did not apply. The trial court granted Cedars-Sinai motion for summary judgment and dismissed Hector's lawsuit. Hector appealed.

Hector v. Cedars-Sinai Medical Center

180 Cal.App. 3d 493, 225 Cal.Rptr. 595, 1986 Cal.App. Lexis 1523 (1986)
California Court of Appeals
(continued)

Issue

Is the installation of a pacemaker by a hospital a sale of a good subject to Article 2 of the UCC?

Court's Reasoning

A hospital is not ordinarily engaged in the business of selling any of the products or equipment it uses in providing services. The essence of the relationship between a hospital and its patients does not relate essentially to any products or pieces of equipment it uses but to the professional services it provides. Testimony in this case indicated that Cedars-Sinai does not routinely stock pacemakers, nor is it in the business of selling, distributing, or testing pacemakers. The treatment provided by Cedars-Sinai in relation to implantation of pacemakers includes pre- and post-operative care, nursing care, a surgical operating room, and technicians. As a provider of services rather than a seller of a product, the hospital is not subject to liability for a defective product provided to the patient during the course of his or her treatment.

Decision and Remedy

The court of appeals held that Cedars-Sinai was a provider of medical services and not a seller of goods. Therefore, Cedars-Sinai was not liable for breach of warranty under the UCC because the UCC did not apply. The court of appeals affirmed the decision of the trial court.

Case Questions

Critical Legal Thinking   Should the UCC be extended to service providers?

Business Ethics   Was it ethical for the hospital to deny liability in this case?

Contemporary Business   Could American Technology, Inc., be held liable to the plaintiff in this case? Why do you think the plaintiff sued Cedars-Sinai in this case?

Who Is a Merchant?

Generally, Article 2 of the UCC applies to all sales contracts, whether they involve merchants or not. However, Article 2 contains several provisions that either apply only to merchants or impose a greater duty on merchants. UCC 2-104(1) defines a **merchant** as (1) a person who deals in the goods of the kind involved in the transaction or (2) a person who by his or her occupation holds himself or herself out as having knowledge or skill peculiar to the goods involved in the transaction. For example, a sporting goods dealer is a merchant with respect to sporting goods, but is not if he sells his lawn mower to a neighbor. The courts disagree as to whether farmers are merchants within this definition.

Rodeo Drive, Beverly Hills.
Businesses offer a variety of goods and services for sale or lease.

Scope of Article 2A (Leases)

Personal property leases are a billion-dollar industry. Consumer leases of automobiles or equipment and commercial leases of such items as aircraft and industrial machinery fall into this category. In the past, these transactions were governed by a combination of common law principles, real estate law, and reference to Article 2. Some of these legal rules and concepts do not quite fit a lease transaction.

Article 2A of the UCC was promulgated in 1987. This article, which is cited as the **Uniform Commercial Code—Leases**, directly addresses personal property leases [UCC 2A-101]. It establishes a comprehensive, uniform law covering the formation, performance, and default of leases in goods [UCC 2A-102, 2A-103(h)].

Article 2A is similar to Article 2. In fact, many Article 2 provisions were changed to reflect leasing terminology and practices that carried over to Article 2A.

Definition of Lease

A **lease** is a transfer of the right to the possession and use of the named goods for a set term in return for certain consideration [UCC 2A-103(1)(i)(x)]. The leased goods can be anything from a hand tool leased to an individual for a few hours to a complex line of industrial equipment leased to a multinational corporation for a number of years.

In an ordinary lease, the **lessor** is the person who transfers the right of possession and use of goods under the lease [UCC 2A-103(1)(p)]. The **lessee** is the person who acquires the right to possession and use of goods under a lease [UCC 2A-103(1)(n)].

Consider This Example Dow Chemical Company decides to lease robotic equipment to manufacture most of its products. Ingersoll-Rand Corporation, which manufactures robotic equipment, enters into a lease contract to lease robotic equipment to Dow Chemical. Ingersoll-Rand is the lessor, and Dow Chemical is the lessee (see Exhibit 14.2).

Finance Lease

A **finance lease** is a three-party transaction consisting of the lessor, the lessee, and the **supplier** (or vendor). The lessor does not select, manufacture, or supply the goods. Instead, the lessor acquires title to the goods or the right to their possession and use in connection with the terms of the lease [UCC 2A-103(1)(g)].

Consider This Example JetBlue Airways, a commercial air carrier, decides to acquire a new airplane. Boeing Company manufactures the airplane JetBlue wants to acquire. To finance the airplane acquisition, JetBlue goes to City Bank, which purchases the airplane from Boeing, and City Bank then leases the airplane to JetBlue. City Bank is the lessor, JetBlue is the lessee, and Boeing is the supplier. City Bank does not take physical delivery of the airplane; the airplane is delivered by Boeing directly to JetBlue. (See Exhibit 14.3.)

Exhibit 14.2

Lease Transaction

Exhibit 14.3

Finance Lease
Transaction

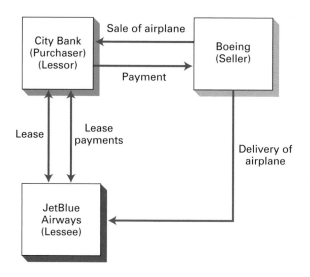

Formation of Sales and Lease Contracts

As with general contracts, the formation of sales and lease contracts requires an offer, an acceptance, consideration, and so on. The UCC-established rules for each of these elements often differ considerably from common law. Any rules established by Articles 2 and 2A of the UCC take precedence over the common law of contracts.

Offer

A contract for the sale or lease of goods may be made in any manner sufficient to show agreement, including conduct by both parties that recognizes the existence of a contract [UCC 2-204,(1), 2A-204(1)]. Under the UCC, an agreement sufficient to constitute a contract for the sale or lease of goods may be found even though the moment of its making is undetermined [UCC 2-204 (2), 2A-204 (2)].

Automobile. Many automobiles are leased. The provisions of Article 2A of the Uniform Commercial Code (UCC) apply to lease contracts.

Open Terms Sometimes the parties to a sale or lease contract leave open a major term in the contract. The UCC is tolerant of open terms. According to UCC 2-204(3) and 2A-204(3), the contract does not fail because of indefiniteness if (1) the parties intended to make a contract and (2) there is a reasonably certain basis for giving an appropriate remedy. In effect, certain **open terms** are permitted to be "read into" a sales or lease contract. This rule is commonly referred to as the **gap-filling rule**.

Some examples of terms that are commonly left open are:

- ***Open price term.*** If a sales contract does not contain a specific price (**open price term**), a "reasonable price" is implied at the time of delivery. The contract may provide that a price is to be fixed by a market rate (e.g., a commodities market), as set or recorded by a third person or agency (e.g., a government agency), or by another standard, either upon delivery or on a set date. If the agreed-upon standard is unavailable when the price is to be set, a reasonable price is implied at the time of delivery of the goods [UCC 2-305(1)].

  A seller or buyer who reserves the right to fix a price must do so in good faith [UCC 2-305(2)]. When one of the parties fails to fix an open price term, the other party may opt either (1) to treat the contract as canceled or (2) to fix a reasonable price for the goods [UCC 2-305(3)].

- ***Open payment term.*** If the parties to a sales contract do not agree on payment terms, payment is due at the time and place at which the buyer is to receive the goods. If delivery is authorized and made by way of document of title, payment is due at the time and place at which the buyer is to receive the document of title, regardless of where the goods are to be received [UCC 2-310].

- ***Open delivery term.*** If the parties to a sales contract do not agree to the time, place, and manner of delivery of the goods, the place for delivery is the seller's place of business. If the seller does not have a place of business, delivery is to be made at the seller's residence. If identified goods are located at some other place, and both parties know of this fact at the time of contracting, that place is the place of delivery [UCC 2-308].

  Where goods are to be shipped but the shipper is not named, the seller is obligated to make the shipping arrangements. Such arrangements must be made in good faith and within limits of commercial reasonableness [UCC 2-311(2)].

- ***Open time term.*** If the parties to a sales contract do not set a specific time of performance for any obligation under the contract, the contract must be performed within a reasonable time. If the sales contract provides for successive performance over an unspecified period of time, the contract is valid for a reasonable time [UCC 2-309].

- ***Open assortment term.*** If the assortment of goods to a sales contract is left open, the buyer is given the option of choosing those goods. For example, suppose Macy's contracts to purchase 1,000 dresses from Liz Claiborne, Inc. The contract is silent as to the assortment of colors of the dresses. The buyer may pick the assortment of colors for the dresses from the seller's stock. The buyer must make the selection in good faith and within limits set by commercial reasonableness [UCC 2-311(2)].

> Law must be stable and yet it cannot stand still.
>
> Roscoe Pound
> *Interpretations of Legal History*
> *(1923)*

Business Brief

In recent years, the leasing of goods has increased dramatically in this country. Lease transactions include consumer leases of automobiles as well as business leasing of equipment such as copying machines, computers, tractors, and the like. In 1987, Article 2A was added to the UCC to address personal property leases. Article 2A establishes uniform rules for the formation and enforcement of personal property leases.

Contemporary Environment
UCC Firm Offer Rule

Recall that the common law of contracts allows the offeror to revoke an offer any time prior to its acceptance. The only exception allowed by the common law is an *option contract* (i.e., where the offeree pays the offeror consideration to keep the offer open).

The UCC recognizes another exception, which is called the **firm offer rule**. This rule states that a merchant who (1) offers to buy, sell, or lease goods and (2) gives a written and signed assurance on a separate form that the offer will be held open cannot revoke the offer for the time stated or, if no time is

Contemporary Environment
(continued)

stated, for a reasonable time. The maximum amount of time permitted under this rule is three months [UCC 2-205, 2A-205].

Consider This Example On June 1, a merchant-seller offers to sell a Mercedes-Benz to a buyer for $50,000. The merchant-seller signs a written assurance to keep that offer open until August 30. On July 1, the merchant-seller sells the car to another buyer. On August 21, the original offeree tenders $50,000 for the car. The merchant-seller is liable to the original offeree for breach of contract. ∎

Acceptance

> The foundation of justice is good faith.
>
> Cicero (106–43 B.C.)
> De Officiis, Bk. I, Ch. VII

Both common law and the UCC provide that a contract is created when the offeree (i.e., the buyer or lessee) sends an acceptance to the offeror, not when the offeror receives the acceptance. For example, a contract is made when the acceptance letter is delivered to the post office. The contract remains valid even if the post office loses the letter.

Unless otherwise unambiguously indicated by language or circumstance, an offer to make a sales or lease contract may be accepted in any manner and by any reasonable medium of acceptance [UCC 2-206(1)(a), 2A-206(1)]. Applications of this rule are discussed in the following paragraphs.

Methods of Acceptance The UCC permits acceptance by any reasonable manner or method of communication.

Business Brief

Under certain circumstances the UCC permits an acceptance to contain terms in addition to or different from those in the offer.

Consider This Example A seller sends a telegram to a proposed buyer, offering to sell the buyer certain goods. The buyer responds by mailing a letter of acceptance to the seller. In most circumstances, mailing the letter of acceptance would be considered reasonable. If the goods were extremely perishable or if the market for the goods were very volatile, however, a faster means of acceptance (such as a telegram) might be warranted.

If an order or other offer to buy goods requires prompt or current shipment, the offer is accepted if the seller (1) promptly promises to ship the goods or (2) promptly ships either conforming or nonconforming goods [UCC 2-206(1)(b)]. The shipment of conforming goods signals acceptance of the buyer's offer.

Acceptance of goods occurs after the buyer or lessee has a reasonable opportunity to inspect them and signifies that (1) the goods are conforming, (2) he or she will take or retain the goods in spite of their nonconformity, or (3) he or she fails to reject the goods within a reasonable time after tender or delivery [UCC 2-513(1), 2A-515(1)].

Contemporary Environment
UCC Permits Additional Terms

Under common law's **mirror image rule**, an offeree's acceptance must be on the same terms as the offer. The inclusion of additional terms in the acceptance is considered a **counteroffer** rather than an acceptance. Thus, the offeror's original offer is extinguished.

UCC 2-207(1) is more liberal than the mirror-image rule. It permits definite and timely expression of acceptance or written confirmation to operate as an acceptance even though they contain terms that are additional to or different from the offered terms, unless the acceptance is expressly conditional on assent to such terms. This rule differs for merchants and nonmerchants, as discussed below.

One or Both Parties Are Nonmerchants

If one or both parties to a sales contract are nonmerchants, any additional terms are considered **proposed additions** to the contract. The proposed additions do not constitute a counteroffer or extinguish the original offer. If the offeree's proposed additions are accepted by the original offeror, they become part of the contract. If they are not accepted, the sales contract is formed on the basis of the terms of the original offer [UCC 2-207(2)].

Consider This Example A salesperson at a Lexus dealership offers to sell a top-of-the-line coupe to a buyer for $47,000. The buyer replies, "I accept your offer, but I would like to have a satellite radio in the car." The satellite radio is a proposed addition to the contract. If the salesperson agrees, the contract between the parties consists of the terms of the original offer plus the additional term regarding the satellite radio. If the salesperson rejects the proposed addition, the sales contract consists of the terms of the original offer because the buyer made a definite expression of acceptance. ∎

Accommodation Shipment

A shipment of nonconforming goods does not constitute an acceptance if the seller reasonably notifies the buyer that the shipment is offered only as an **accommodation** to the buyer [UCC 2-206(1)(b)]. For example, suppose a buyer offers to purchase 500 red candles from a seller. The seller's red candles are temporarily out of stock. The seller sends the buyer 500 green candles and notifies the buyer that these candles are being sent as an accommodation. The seller has not accepted (or breached) the contract. The accommodation is a counteroffer from the seller to the buyer. The buyer is free either to accept or to reject the counteroffer.

Contemporary Environment
The "Battle of the Forms"

When merchants negotiate sales contracts, they often exchange preprinted forms. These "boilerplate" forms usually contain terms that favor the drafter. Thus, an offeror who sends a standard form contract as an offer to the offeree may receive an acceptance drafted on the offeree's own form contract. This scenario—commonly called the **battle of the forms**—raises important questions: Is there a contract? If so, what are its terms? The UCC provides guidance in answering these questions.

Under UCC 2-207(2), if both parties are merchants, any additional terms contained in an acceptance become part of the sales contract unless (1) the offer expressly limits acceptance to the terms of the offer, (2) the additional terms materially alter the terms of the original contract, or (3) the offeror notifies the offeree that he or she objects to the additional terms within a reasonable time after receiving the offeree's modified acceptance.

The most important point in the battle of the forms is that there is no contract if the additional terms so materially alter the terms of the original offer that the parties cannot agree on the contract. This fact-specific determination is made by the courts on a case-by-case basis. ∎

Consideration

The formation of sales and lease contracts requires consideration. However, the UCC changes the common law rule that requires the modification of a contract to be supported by new consideration. An agreement modifying a sales or lease contract needs no consideration to be binding [UCC 2-209(1), 2A-208(1)].

Modification of a sales or lease contract must be made in good faith [UCC 1-203]. As in the common law of contracts, modifications are not binding if they are obtained through fraud, duress, extortion, and such.

Statute of Frauds

The UCC includes **Statute of Frauds** provisions that apply to all sales and lease contracts. All contracts for the sale of goods costing $500 or more and lease contracts involving payments of $1,000 or more must be in writing [UCC 2-201(1), 2A-201(1)]. The writing must be sufficient to indicate that a contract has been made between the parties. Except as discussed in the paragraphs that follow, the writing must be signed by the party against whom enforcement is sought or by his or her authorized agent or broker. If a contract falling within these parameters is not written, it is unenforceable.

Consider This Example   A seller orally agrees to sell her computer to a buyer for $550. When the buyer tenders the purchase price, the seller asserts the Statute of Frauds and refuses to sell the computer to him. The seller is correct. The contract must be in writing to be enforceable because the contract price for the computer exceeds $499.99.

Exceptions to the Statute of Frauds   The three situations in which a sales or lease contract that would otherwise be required to be in writing is enforceable even if it is not in writing are discussed in the following paragraphs [UCC 2-201(3), UCC 2A-201(4)]:

Business Brief

There are three exceptions to the writing requirement of the UCC Statute of Frauds: (1) specially manufactured goods, (2) admissions in pleadings or court, and (3) part acceptance.

1. *Specially manufactured goods.*   Buyers and lessees often order specially manufactured goods. If a contract to purchase or lease such goods is oral, the buyer or lessee may not assert the Statute of Frauds against the enforcement of the contract if (1) the goods are not suitable for sale or lease to others in the ordinary course of the seller's or the lessor's business and (2) the seller or lessor has made either a substantial beginning of the manufacture of the goods or commitments for their procurement.
2. *Admissions in pleadings or court.*   If the party against whom enforcement of an oral sales or lease contract is sought admits in pleadings, testimony, or otherwise in court that a contract for the sale or lease of goods was made, the oral contract is enforceable against that party. However, the contract is only enforceable as to the quantity of goods admitted.
3. *Part acceptance.*   An oral sales or lease contract that should otherwise be in writing is enforceable to the extent to which the goods have been received and accepted by the buyer or lessee.

Business Brief

Note that the written confirmation rule applies to *merchants* only.

Consider This Example   A lessor orally contracts to lease 100 personal computers to a lessee. The lessee accepts the first 20 computers tendered by the lessor. This action is part acceptance. The lessee refuses to take delivery of the remaining 80 computers. Here, the lessee must pay for the 20 computers she originally received and accepted. The lessee does not have to accept or pay for the remaining 80 computers.

Contemporary Environment

UCC Written Confirmation Rule

If both parties to an oral sale or lease contract are merchants, the Statute of Frauds requirement can be satisfied if (1) one of the parties to an oral agreement sends a written confirmation of the sale or lease within a reasonable time after contracting and (2) the other merchant does not give written notice of an objection to the contract within 10 days after receiving the confirmation. This situation is true even though the party receiving the written confirmation has not signed it. The only stipulations are that the confirmation be sufficient and that the party to whom it was sent have reason to know its contents [UCC 2-201(2)].

Consider This Example   A merchant-seller in Chicago orally contracts by telephone to sell goods to a merchant-buyer in Phoenix for $25,000. Within a reasonable time after contracting, the merchant-seller sends a sufficient written confirmation to the buyer. The buyer, who has reason to know the contents of the confirmation, fails to object to the contents of the confirmation in writing within 10 days after receiving it. The Statute of Frauds has been met, and the buyer cannot thereafter raise it against enforcement of the contract. ■

When Written Modification Is Required

Oral modification of a contract is not enforceable if the parties agree that any modification of the sales or lease contract must be signed in writing [UCC 2-209(2), 2A-208(2)]. In the absence of such an agreement, oral modifications to sales and lease contracts are binding if they do not violate the Statute of Frauds.

If the oral modification brings the contract within the Statute of Frauds, it must be in writing to be enforceable.

Consider This Example   A lessor and lessee enter into an oral lease contract for the lease of goods at a rent of $450. Subsequently, the contract is modified by raising the rent to $550. Because the modified contract rent is more than $499.99, the contract comes under the UCC Statute of Frauds, and the modification must be in writing to be enforceable.

Parol Evidence

The **parol evidence rule** states that when a sales or lease contract is evidenced by a writing that is intended to be a final expression of the parties' agreement or a confirmatory memorandum, the terms of the writing may not be contradicted by evidence of (1) a prior oral or written agreement or (2) a contemporaneous oral agreement (i.e., parol evidence) [UCC 2-202, 2A-202]. This rule is intended to ensure certainty in written sales and lease contracts.

Occasionally, the express terms of a written contract are not clear on their face and must be interpreted. In such cases, reference may be made to certain sources outside the contract. These sources are construed together when they are consistent with each other. If that is unreasonable, they are considered in descending order of priority [UCC 2-208(2), 2A-207(2)]:

1. *Course of performance.* The previous conduct of the parties regarding the contract in question.
2. *Course of dealing.* The conduct of the parties in prior transactions and contracts.
3. *Usage of trade.* Any practice or method of dealing that is regularly observed or adhered to in a place, a vocation, a trade, or an industry.

Consider This Example   A cattle rancher contracts to purchase corn from a farmer. The farmer delivers feed corn to the rancher. The rancher rejects this corn and demands delivery of corn that is fit for human consumption. Ordinarily, usage of trade would be the first source of interpretation of the word *corn*. If the parties had prior dealings, though, the usage of the term in their prior dealings would become the primary source of interpretation.

Concept Summary   Comparison of Contract Law and the Law of Sales

Topic	Common Law of Contracts	UCC Law of Sales
Definiteness	Contract must contain all the material terms of the parties' agreement.	The UCC gap-filling rule permits terms to be implied if the parties intended to make a contract [UCC 2-204].
Irrevocable offers	Option contracts.	Option contracts. Firm offers by merchants to keep an offer open are binding up to three months without any consideration [UCC 2-205].
Counteroffers	Acceptance must be a mirror image of the offer. A counteroffer rejects and terminates the offer.	Additional terms of an acceptance become part of the contract if (1) they do not materially alter the terms of the offer and (2) the offeror does not object within a reasonable time after reviewing the acceptance [UCC 2-207].

Concept Summary (continued)

Topic	Common Law of Contracts	UCC Law of Sales
Statute of Frauds	Writing must be signed by the party against whom enforcement is sought.	Writing may be enforced against a party who has not signed it if (1) both parties are merchants, (2) one party sends a written confirmation of oral agreement within a reasonable time after contracting, and (3) the other party does not give written notice of objection within 10 days after receiving the confirmation [UCC 2-201].
Modification	Consideration is required.	Consideration is not required [UCC 2-209].

International Law

Use of Letters of Credit in International Trade

The major risks in any business transaction involving the sale of goods are (1) that the seller will not be paid after delivering the goods and (2) that the buyer will not receive the goods after paying for them. These risks are even more acute in international transactions, where the buyer and seller may not know each other, the parties are dealing at long distance, and the judicial system's of the parties' countries may not have jurisdiction to decide a dispute if one should arise. The irrevocable **letter of credit** has been developed to manage these risks in international sales. The function of a letter of credit is to substitute the credit of a recognized international bank for that of the buyer.

An irrevocable letter of credit works this way. Suppose a buyer in one country and a seller in another country enter into a contract for the sale of goods. The buyer goes to his or her bank and pays the bank a fee to issue a letter of credit in which the bank agrees to pay the amount of the letter (which is the amount of the purchase price of the goods) to the seller's bank if certain conditions are met. These conditions are usually the delivery of documents indicating that the seller has placed the goods in the hands of a shipper. The buyer is called the **account party**, the bank that issues the letter of credit is called the **issuing bank**, and the seller is called the **beneficiary** of the letter of credit.

The issuing bank then forwards the letter of credit to a bank that the seller has designated in his or her country. This bank, which is called the **correspondent** or **confirming bank**, relays the letter of credit to the seller. Now that the seller sees that he or she is guaranteed payment, he or she makes arrangements to ship the goods and receives a **bill of lading** from the carrier proving so. The seller then delivers these documents to the confirming bank. The confirming bank examines the documents and, if it finds them in order, pays the seller and forwards the documents to the issuing bank. By this time, the buyer has usually paid the amount of the purchase price to the issuing bank (unless an extension of credit has been arranged), and the issuing bank then charges the buyer's account. The issuing bank forwards the bill of lading and other necessary documents to the buyer, who then picks up the goods from the shipper when they arrive.

If the documents (e.g., bill of lading, proof of insurance) conform to the conditions specified in the letter of credit, the issuing bank must pay the letter of credit. If the account party does not pay the issuing bank, the issuing bank's only recourse is to sue the account party to recover damages. (See Exhibit 14.4.)

Article 5 (Letters of Credit) of the Uniform Commercial Code governs letters of credit unless otherwise agreed by the parties. The International Chamber of Commerce has promulgated the **Uniform Customs and Practices for Documentary Credits (UCP)**, which contains rules governing the formation and performance of letters of credit. Although the UCP is neither a treaty nor a legislative enactment, most banks incorporate the terms of the UCP in letters of credit they issue. ■

Exhibit 14.4

Letter of Credit

1. Buyer contracts to purchase goods from seller
5. Delivers goods
13. Buyer picks up goods from shipper
6. Delivers bill of lading
12. Delivers bill of lading and documents
11. Pays the issuing bank the sales price*
2. Buyer purchases letter of credit from bank
4. Forwards letter of credit to seller
7. Delivers bill of lading and documents
8. Pays the seller the sales price
3. Forwards letter of credit to confirming bank
9. Forwards documents to issuing bank
10. Pays the confirming bank the sales price

Buyer (Account Party) — Shipper — Seller (Beneficiary) — Buyer's Bank (Issuing Bank) — Seller's Bank (Confirming Bank)

* If the buyer-account party does not pay the issuing bank, the issuing bank's only recourse is to sue the buyer-account party for damages.

Chapter Summary

Scope of Article 2 (Sales), p. 286

Article 2 (Sales)

Article 2 of the UCC applies to transactions in goods [UCC 2-102].

1. ***Goods.*** Goods are tangible things that are movable at the time of their identification in a sales contract [UCC 2-105(1)].
2. ***Scope of Article 2.*** Article 2 applies to all sales contracts, whether they involve merchants or not.

Scope of Article 2A (Leases), p. 289

Article 2A, Leases

Article 2A of the UCC applies to personal property leases of goods [UCC 2A-101].

1. ***Lease.*** A lease is a transfer of the right to the possession and use of the named goods for a set term in return for certain consideration.
2. ***Parties to a lease:***
   a. *Lessor.* A person who transfers the right of possession and use of goods is a lessor [UCC 2A-103(1)(p)].
   b. *Lessee.* A person who acquires the right to possession and use of goods is a lessee [UCC 2A-103(1)(n)].
3. ***Finance lease.*** A finance lease is a three-party transaction of the lessor, the lessee, and the supplier of the leased goods. The parties to a finance lease are:
   a. *Lessor.* The lessor acquires title to the goods from the supplier and leases the goods to the lessee. The lessor is often a bank or another creditor.

b. *Lessee.* The lessee is the person who acquires the right to possession and use of the goods.

c. *Supplier.* The supplier is the third party who supplies the goods. The supplier usually sells the goods to the lessor.

Formation of Sales and Lease Contracts, p. 290

Offer

Open terms. If the parties leave open a major term in a sales or lease contract, the UCC permits the following terms to be read into the contract:

1. Price term
2. Payment term
3. Delivery term
4. Time term
5. Assortment term

This is commonly called the *gap-filling rule* [UCC 2-204(3), 2A-204(3)].

Firm Offer Rule

The firm offer rule is a UCC rule which says that a merchant who (1) makes an offer to buy, sell, or lease goods and (2) assures the other party in a separate writing that the offer will be held open cannot revoke the offer for the time stated, or if no time is stated, for a reasonable time [UCC 2-205, 2A-205].

Acceptance

Accommodation shipment. This is a shipment that is offered to the buyer by the seller as a replacement for the original shipment when the original shipment cannot be filled. The buyer may either accept or reject this shipment [UCC 2-206(1)(b)].

Additional Terms Permitted

The UCC permits an acceptance of a sales contract to contain additional terms and still to act as an acceptance rather than a counteroffer in certain circumstances. The following UCC rules apply [UCC 2-207(2)]:

1. **One or both parties are nonmerchants.** The additional terms are considered proposed additions to the contract. If the offeree's proposed terms are accepted by the offeror, they become part of the contract. If they are not accepted, the sales contract is formed on the basis of the terms of the original offer.

2. **Both parties are merchant.** The additional terms contained in the acceptance become part of the sales contract *unless* (1) the offer expressly limits the acceptance to the terms of the offer, (2) the additional terms materially alter the original contract, or (3) the offerer notifies the offeree that he or she objects to the additional terms within a reasonable time after receiving the offeree's modified acceptance. There is no contract if the additional terms so materially alter the terms of the original offer that the parties cannot agree on the contract.

Statute of Frauds

The UCC Statute of Frauds requires contracts for the sale of goods costing $500 or more and lease contracts involving payments of $1,000 or more to be in writing [UCC 2-201(1), 2A-201(1)].

Exceptions to the Statute of Frauds. The UCC recognizes the following exceptions to the Statute of Frauds where a sales or lease contract that is required to be in writing is enforceable even though it is not in writing:

1. **Specially manufactured goods.** In these contracts, the goods are not suitable for sale or lease to others in the ordinary course of business and the seller or lessor has made either a substantial beginning of manufacture of the goods or commitments for their procurement.

2. **Admissions in pleadings or court.** A party admits in pleadings, testimony, or otherwise in court that he or she has entered into a contract.

3. **Part acceptance.** An oral sales or lease contract is enforceable to the extent to which the goods have been received and accepted by the buyer or lessee.

Written Confirmation Rule

If both parties to an oral sales or lease contract are merchants, the Statute of Frauds requirements are satisfied if (1) one of the parties sends a *written confirmation* of the sale to the other within a reasonable time after contracting and (2) the other merchant does not give written notice of an objection to the contract within 10 days after receiving the confirmation [UCC 2-201(2)].

 Internet Exercises and Case Questions

Working the Web Internet Exercises

Activities

1. Find the major differences in the rules of contract formation under the common law and UCC Article 2. Visit Legal Information Institute (LII) Sales Law Overview at **www.law.cornell.edu/topics/sales.html**.

2. Do the rules change when the parties are both merchants?

3. Although a contract can be created under UCC Article 2 even when several terms are omitted, there is generally one term that must be included in order for the contract to be deemed valid by a court. Which term is it?

Critical Legal Thinking Cases

14.1 Merchant Mark Hemphill was a football player at Southern Illinois State University. As a member of the team, Hemphill was furnished with a uniform and helmet. He was injured while playing football for the school. Hemphill claimed that his helmet was defective and contributed to his injuries. Hemphill's attorneys suggested that he sue the university's athletic director, Sayers, and the head football coach, Shultz. The attorneys told Hemphill that he may be able to recover for his injuries based on several provisions of the Uniform Commercial Code. The attorneys specifically suggested that he use the UCC provisions that impose certain obligations upon merchants. Hemphill brought suit against Sayers and Shultz. Does Article 2 apply to this case? [*Hemphill v. Sayers*, 552 F.Supp. 685, 1982 U.S.Dist. Lexis 16240 (S.D. Ill. 1982)]

14.2 Good or Service Mr. Gulash lived in Shelton, Connecticut. He wanted an above-ground swimming pool installed in his backyard. Gulash contacted Stylarama, Inc. (Stylarama), a company specializing in the sale and construction of pools. The two parties entered into a contract that called for Stylarama to "furnish all labor and materials to construct a Wavecrest brand pool, and furnish and install a pool with vinyl liners." The total cost for materials and labor was $3,690. There was no breakdown in the contract of costs between labor and materials. After the pool was installed, its sides began bowing out, the 2″ × 4″ wooden supports for the pool rotted and misaligned, and the entire pool became tilted. Gulash brought suit, alleging that Stylarama had violated several provisions of Article 2 of the UCC. Is this transaction one involving goods, making it subject to Article 2? [*Gulash v. Stylarama*, 364 A.2d 1221, 1975 Conn.Super. Lexis 209 (CT 1975)]

14.3 Unconscionable Contract Jane Wilson leased a Toyota pickup truck from World Omni Leasing, Inc. (Omni). Wilson had experience in business and had signed contracts before. In the past, Wilson had read the contracts before signing them. When signing the contract for the lease of the truck, however, Wilson did not take the opportunity to read the lease. However, she signed a statement declaring that she had read and understood the lease. The lease contained a provision that made Wilson responsible for payments on the truck even if the truck was destroyed. Several months after leasing the truck, Wilson was involved in a two-vehicle collision. The pickup truck was destroyed. Omni demanded to be paid for the balance of the lease. Wilson refused, claiming that the lease was unconscionable. Is the lease unconscionable? [*Wilson v. World Omni Leasing, Inc.*, 540 So.2d 713, 1989 Ala. Lexis 41 (AL 1989)]

14.4 Statute of Frauds St. Charles Cable TV (St. Charles) was building a new cable television system in Louisiana. It contacted Eagle Comtronics, Inc. (Eagle), by phone and began negotiating to buy descrambler units for its cable system. These units would allow St. Charles's customers to receive the programs they had paid for. Although no written contract was ever signed, St. Charles ordered several thousand descramblers. The descramblers were shipped to St. Charles, along with a sales acknowledgment form. St. Charles made partial payment for the descramblers before discovering that some of the units were defective. Eagle accepted a return of the defective scramblers. St. Charles then attempted to return all the descramblers, asking that they be replaced by a newer model. When Eagle refused to replace all the old descramblers, St. Charles stopped paying Eagle. Eagle sued St. Charles, claiming that no valid contract existed between the parties. Is there a valid sales contract? [*St. Charles Cable TV v. Eagle Comtronics, Inc.*, 687 F.Supp. 820, 1988 U.S.Dist. 4566 (S.D. N.Y. 1988)]

14.5 Firm Offer Gordon Construction Company (Gordon) was a general contractor in the New York City area. Gordon planned on bidding for the job of constructing two buildings for the Port Authority of New York. In anticipation of its own bid, Gordon sought bids from subcontractors. On April 22, 1963, E. A. Coronis Associates (Coronis), a fabricator of structured steel, sent a signed letter to Gordon. The letter quoted a price for work on the Port Authority project and stated that the price could change, based upon the amount of steel used. The letter contained no information other than the price Coronis would charge for the job. On May 27, Gordon was awarded the Port Authority project. On June 1, Coronis sent Gordon a telegram, withdrawing its offer. Gordon replied that it expected Coronis to honor the price quoted in its April 22 letter. When Coronis refused, Gordon sued. Gordon claimed that Coronis was attempting to withdraw a firm offer. Who wins? [*E. A. Coronis Associates v. Gordon Construction Co.*, 216 A.2d 246, 1966 N.J.Super. Lexis 368 (N.J. Super. 1966)]

14.6 Battle of the Forms Dan Miller was a commercial photographer who had taken a series of photographs that had appeared in the *New York Times*. *Newsweek* magazine wanted to use the photographs. When a *Newsweek* employee named Dwyer phoned

Miller, he was told that 72 images were available. Dwyer said that he wanted to inspect the photographs and offered a certain sum of money for each photo *Newsweek* used. The photos were to remain Miller's property. Miller and Dwyer agreed to the price and the date for delivery. *Newsweek* sent a courier to pick up the photographs. Along with the photos, Miller gave the courier a delivery memo that set out various conditions for the use of the photographs. The memo included a clause that required *Newsweek* to pay $1,500 each if any of the photos were lost or destroyed. After *Newsweek* received the package, it decided it no longer needed Miller's work. When Miller called to have the photos returned, he was told that they had all been lost. Miller demanded that *Newsweek* pay him $1,500 for each of the 72 lost photos. Assuming that the court finds Miller and *Newsweek* to be merchants, are the clauses in the delivery memo part of the sales contract? [*Miller v. Newsweek, Inc.*, 660 F.Supp. 852, 1987 U.S.Dist. Lexis 4338 (D. Del. 1987)]

14.7 Open Terms Alvin Cagle was a potato farmer in Alabama who had had several business dealings with the H. C. Schmieding Produce Co. (Schmieding). Several months before harvest, Cagle entered into an oral sales contract with Schmieding. The contract called for Schmieding to pay the market price at harvest time for all the red potatoes that Cagle grew on his 30-acre farm. Schmieding asked that the potatoes be delivered during the normal harvest months. As Cagle began harvesting his red potatoes, he contacted Schmieding to arrange delivery. Schmieding told the farmer that no contract had been formed because the terms of the agreement were too indefinite. Cagle demanded that Schmieding buy his crop. When Schmieding refused, Cagle sued to have the contract enforced. Has a valid sales contract been formed? [*H. C. Schmieding Produce Co. v. Cagle*, 529 So.2d 243, 1988 Ala. Lexis 284 (AL 1988)]

14.8 Statute of Frauds Collins was a sales representative of Donzi Marine Corp. (Donzi), a builder of light speedboats. Collins met Wallach, the owner of a retail boat outlet, at a marine trade show. Collins offered him a Donzi dealership, which would include the right to purchase and then market Donzi speedboats. Wallach tendered a check for $50,000 to Collins. Collins accepted the check, but neither party ever signed a written contract. Wallach ordered several boats. Donzi terminated the dealership because it had found another boat dealer willing to pay more for the franchise. Wallach sued Donzi for breach of contract. Is the contract enforceable under the UCC? [*Wallach Marine Corp. v. Donzi Marine Corp.*, 675 F.Supp. 838, 1987 U.S.Dist. Lexis 11762 (S.D. N.Y. 1987)]

Business Ethics Cases

14.9 Business Ethics Kurt Perschke was a grain dealer in Indiana. In September 1972, he phoned Ken Sebasty, the owner of a large wheat farm, and offered to buy 14,000 bushels of wheat for $1.95 a bushel. Sebasty accepted the offer. Perschke said that he could send a truck for the wheat in March 1973. On the day of the phone call, Perschke's office manager sent a memorandum to Sebasty, stating the price and quantity of wheat that had been contracted for. In February 1973, Perschke called Sebasty to arrange for the loading of the wheat. Sebasty stated that no contract had been made. When Perschke brought suit, Sebasty claimed that the contract was unenforceable because of the Statute of Frauds. Was it ethical for Sebasty to raise the Statute of Frauds as a defense? Assuming that both parties are merchants, who wins the suit? [*Sebasty v. Perschke*, 404 N.E.2d 1200, 1980 Ind.App. Lexis 1489 (Ind. App. 1980)]

14.10 Business Ethics In 1974, Alex Abatti was the sole owner of A&M Produce Company (A&M), a small farming company located in California's Imperial Valley. Although Abatti had never grown tomatoes, he decided to do so. He sought the advice of FMC Corporation (FMC), a large diversified manufacturer of farming and other equipment, as to what kind of equipment he would need to process the tomatoes. An FMC representative recommended a certain type of machine, which A&M purchased from FMC pursuant to a form sales contract provided by FMC. Within the fine print, the contract contained one clause that disclaimed any warranty liability by FMC and a second clause that stated that FMC would not be liable for consequential damages if the machine malfunctioned.

A&M paid $10,680 down toward the $32,041 purchase price, and FMC delivered and installed the machine. A&M immediately began experiencing problems with the machine. It did not process the tomatoes quickly enough. Tomatoes began piling up in front of the belt that separated the tomatoes for weight-sizing. Overflow tomatoes had to be sent through the machine at least twice, causing damage to them. Fungus spread through the damaged crop. Because of these problems, the machine had to be continually started and stopped, which significantly reduced processing speed.

A&M tried on several occasions to get additional equipment from FMC, but on each occasion its request was rejected. Because of the problems with the machine, on June 17, 1974, A&M closed its tomato operation. A&M finally stated, "Let's call the whole thing off," and offered to return the machine if FMC would refund A&M's down payment. When FMC rejected this offer and demanded full payment of the balance due, A&M sued to recover its down payment and damages. It alleged breach of warranty caused by defect in the machine. In defense, FMC pointed to the fine print of the sales contract, stating that the buyer waived any rights to sue it for breach of warranty or to recover consequential damages from it.

Was it ethical for FMC to include waiver of liability and waiver of consequential damage clauses in its form contract? Did A&M act morally in signing the contract and then trying to get out from under its provisions? Legally, are the waiver clauses so unconscionable as to not be enforced? [*A&M Produce Co. v. FMC Corp.*, 135 Cal.App.3d 473, 186 Cal.Rptr. 114, 1982 Cal.App. Lexis 1922 (Cal. App. 1982)]

Briefing the Case Writing Assignment

Read Case A.14 in the Case Appendix [*Cafazzo v. Central Medical Health Services, Inc.*]. This case is excerpted from the opinion of the supreme court of Pennsylvania. Review and brief the case. In your brief, be sure to answer the following questions.

1. What was the plaintiff suing for? Explain.

2. What issue was presented to the court? Why was this issue important? Explain.

3. How did the court decide this case?

15

Performance of Sales and Lease Contracts

> " A lawyer without history or literature is a mechanic, a mere working mason; if he possesses some knowledge of these, he may venture to call himself an architect. "
>
> —Sir Walter Scott
> Guy Mannering, Ch. 37 (1815)

Chapter Objectives

After studying this chapter, you should be able to:

1. Identify when title to goods passes in shipment and destination contracts.

2. Define shipment and delivery terms.

3. Describe who bears the risk of loss when goods are lost or damaged in shipment.

4. Identify who bears the risk of loss when goods are stolen and resold.

5. Define good faith purchaser for value and buyer in the ordinary course of business.

Chapter Contents

- Identification and Passage of Title
- Risk of Loss: No Breach of Sales Contract
- Risk of Loss: Conditional Sales
- Risk of Loss: Breach of Sales Contract
- Risk of Loss: Lease Contracts
- Sales by Nonowners

Under common law, the rights and obligations of the buyer, the seller, and third parties were determined based on who held technical title to the goods. Article 2 of the Uniform Commercial Code (UCC) establishes precise rules for determining the *passage of title* in sales contracts. Other provisions of Article 2 apply, irrespective of title, except as otherwise provided [UCC 2-401].

Common law placed the *risk of loss* to goods on the party who had title to the goods. Article 2 of the UCC rejects this notion and adopts concise rules for risk of loss that are not tied to title. It also gives the parties to the sales contract the right to *insure* the goods against loss if they have an "insurable interest" in the goods. Title, risk of loss, and insurable interest are discussed in this chapter.

Identification and Passage of Title

The identification of goods is rather simple. It means distinguishing the goods named in a contract from the seller's or lessor's other goods. The seller or lessor retains the risk of loss of the goods until he or she identifies them to a sales or lease contract. Further, UCC 2-401(1) and 2-501 prevent title to goods from passing from the seller to the buyer unless the goods are identified to the sales contract. In a lease transaction, title to the leased goods remains with the lessor or a third party. It does not pass to the lessee.

The identification of goods and the passage of title are discussed in the following paragraphs.

Identification of Goods

Identification of goods can be made at any time and in any manner explicitly agreed to by the parties to a contract. In the absence of such an agreement, the UCC mandates when identification occurs [UCC 2-501(1), 2A-217].

Hong Kong. Hong Kong is famous for the variety of goods it offers to local and international shoppers.

Already existing goods are identified when the contract is made and names the specific goods sold or leased. For example, a piece of farm machinery, a car, or a boat is identified when its serial number is listed on the sales or lease contract.

Goods that are part of a larger mass of goods are identified when the specific merchandise is designated. For example, if a food processor contracts to purchase 150 cases of oranges from a farmer who has 1,000 cases of oranges, the buyer's goods are identified when the seller explicitly separates or tags the 150 cases.

Future goods are goods not yet in existence. For example, unborn young animals (such as unborn cattle) are identified when the young are conceived. Crops to be harvested are identified when the crops are planted or otherwise become growing crops. Future goods other than crops and unborn young are identified when the goods are shipped, marked, or otherwise designated by the seller or lessor as the goods to which the contract refers.

Passage of Title

Once the goods that are the subject of a contract exist and have been identified, title to the goods may be transferred from the seller to the buyer. Article 2 of the UCC establishes precise rules for determining the passage of title in sales contracts. (As mentioned earlier, lessees do not acquire title to the goods they lease.)

Under UCC 2-401(1), **title** to goods passes from the seller to the buyer in any manner and on any conditions explicitly agreed upon by the parties. If the parties do not agree to a specific time, title passes to the buyer when and where the seller's performance with reference to the physical delivery is completed. This point in time is determined by applying the rules discussed in the following paragraphs [UCC 2-401(2)].

Shipment and Destination Contracts A **shipment contract** requires the seller to ship the goods to the buyer via a common carrier. The seller is required to (1) make proper shipping arrangements and (2) deliver the goods into the carrier's hands. Title passes to the buyer at the time and place of shipment [UCC 2-401(2)(a)].

A **destination contract** requires the seller to deliver the goods either to the buyer's place of business or to another destination specified in the sales contract. Title passes to the buyer when the seller tenders delivery of the goods at the specified destination [UCC 2-401(2)(b)].

Delivery of Goods Without Moving Them Sometimes a sales contract authorizes goods to be delivered without requiring the seller to move them. In other words, the buyer might be required to pick up goods from the seller. In such situations, the time and place of the passage of title depends on whether the seller is to deliver a **document of title** (i.e., a warehouse receipt or bill of lading) to the buyer. If a document of title is required, title passes when and where the seller delivers the document to the buyer [UCC 2-401(3)(a)]. For example, if the goods named in the sales contract are located at a warehouse, title passes when the seller delivers a warehouse receipt representing the goods to the buyer.

If (1) no document of title is needed and (2) the goods are identified at the time of contracting, title passes at the time and place of contracting [UCC 2-401(3)(b)]. For example, if the buyer signs a sales contract to purchase bricks from the seller, and the contract stipulates that the buyer will pick up the bricks at the seller's place of business, title passes when the contract is signed by both parties. This situation is true even if the bricks are not picked up until a later date.

Contemporary Environment
Bulk Sales Law

Article 6 (Bulk Sales) of the UCC establishes rules that were designed to prevent fraud when there is a bulk transfer of goods. A **bulk transfer** occurs when an owner transfers a major part of a business's material, merchandise, inventory, or equipment not in the ordinary course of business. This usually occurs upon the sale of the assets of a business.

If there is a bulk transfer of assets, Article 6 requires that (1) the seller furnish the buyer with a list of all the creditors of the business and (2) the buyer notify all the listed creditors at least 10 days before taking possession of or paying for the goods, whichever occurs first. The buyer is not responsible for or liable to unlisted creditors [UCC 6-105].

If all the requirements of Article 6 are met, the buyer receives title to the goods free of all claims of the seller's creditors. If the requirements of Article 6 are not met, the goods in the buyer's possession are subject to the claims of the seller's creditors for six months after the date of the possession [UCC 6-111].

In 1988, after much review, the National Conference of Commissioners on Uniform State Laws (NCCUSL) and the American Law Institute (ALI) reported that the regulation of bulk sales was no longer necessary. Consequently, they withdrew their support for Article 6 and encouraged states that had enacted the article to repeal it.

The report criticized the bulk transfer law for adding costs—without corresponding benefits—to business transactions. The report claimed that it was unfair to impose liability on an innocent buyer because a dishonest seller failed to pay its creditors. The committee then stated that changing laws and economics, as well as improved communications, made it more difficult for merchants to sell their merchandise and abscond with the proceeds. Further, the report noted that modern jurisdiction laws make it easier to obtain and enforce judgments against debtors who leave the state.

Recognizing that some state legislatures may wish to continue to regulate bulk transfers, the committee also promulgated a revised version of Article 6. ∎

Risk of Loss: No Breach of Sales Contract

> The law is not a series of calculating machines where definitions and answers come tumbling out when the right levers are pushed.
>
> William O. Douglas
> *The Dissent, A Safeguard of Democracy (1948)*

In the case of sales contracts, common law placed the risk of loss of goods on the party who had title to the goods. Article 2 of the UCC rejects this notion and allows the parties to a sales contract to agree among themselves who will bear the risk of loss if the goods subject to the contract are lost or destroyed. If the parties do not have a specific agreement concerning the assessment of the risk of loss, the UCC mandates who will bear the risk.

Lighthouse, Straits of Mackinac, Michigan. Common carriers, such as freighters and other ships that carry goods for others, are independent contractors. Risk of loss of goods depends on the shipping terms used in the shipping contract.

Carrier Cases: Movement of Goods

Unless otherwise agreed, goods that are shipped via carrier (e.g., railroad, ship, truck) are considered to be sent pursuant to a shipment contract or a destination contract. Absent any indication to the contrary, sales contracts are presumed to be shipment contracts rather than destination contracts.

Shipment Contracts A **shipment contract** requires the seller to ship goods conforming to the contract to a buyer via a carrier. The risk of loss passes to the buyer when the seller delivers the conforming goods to the carrier. The buyer bears the risk of loss of the goods during transportation [UCC 2-509(1)(a)].

Shipment contracts are created in two ways. The first requires the use of the term *shipment contract*. The second requires the use of one of the following delivery terms: F.O.B., F.A.S., C.I.F., or C. & F. (see the following "Contemporary Environment" box).

Destination Contracts A sales contract that requires the seller to deliver conforming goods to a specific destination is a **destination contract**. Such a contract requires the seller to bear the risk of loss of the goods during their transportation. Thus, with the exception of a no-arrival, no-sale contract, the seller is required to replace any goods lost in transit. The buyer does not have to pay for destroyed goods. The risk of loss does not pass until the goods are tendered to the buyer at the specified destination [UCC 2-509(1)(b)].

Unless otherwise agreed, destination contracts are created in two ways. The first method requires the use of the term *destination contract*. The alternative method requires the use of the following delivery terms: F.O.B. *place of destination*, ex-ship, or no-arrival, no-sale contract.

> **Business Brief**
>
> The risk of loss of goods while they are being transported depends on what delivery terms are agreed to in the sales contract.

Contemporary Environment
Shipping Terms

F.O.B. (free on board) point of shipment (e.g., F.O.B. Anchorage, Alaska) requires the seller to arrange to ship goods and put the goods in the carrier's possession. The seller bears the expense and risk of loss until this is done [UCC 2-319(1)(a)].

F.A.S. (free alongside) or F.A.S. (vessel) port of shipment (e.g., *The Gargoyle*, New Orleans) requires the seller to deliver and tender the goods alongside the named vessel or on the dock designated and provided by the buyer. The seller bears the expense and risk of loss until this is done [UCC 2-319(2)(a)].

C.I.F. (cost, insurance, and freight) and C. & F. (cost and freight) are pricing terms that indicate the cost for which the seller is responsible. These terms require the seller to bear the expense and the risk of loss of loading the goods on the carrier [UCC 2-320(1)(3)].

F.O.B. place of destination (e.g., F.O.B. Miami, Florida) requires the seller to bear the expense and risk of loss until the goods are tendered to the buyer at the place of destination [UCC 2-319(1)(b)].

Ex-ship (from the carrying vessel) requires the seller to bear the expense and risk of loss until the goods are unloaded from the ship at its port of destination [UCC 2-322(1)(b)].

No-arrival, no-sale contract requires the seller to bear the expense and risk of loss of the goods during transportation. However, the seller is under no duty to deliver replacement goods to the buyer because there is no contractual stipulation that the goods will arrive at the appointed destination [UCC 2-324(a)(b)]. ∎

Noncarrier Cases: No Movement of Goods

Sometimes a sales contract stipulates that the buyer is to pick up the goods, either at the seller's place of business or another specified location. This type of arrangement raises a question: Who bears the risk of loss if the goods are destroyed or stolen after the contract date and before the buyer picks up the goods from the seller? The UCC provides two different rules for this situation. One applies to merchant-sellers and the other to nonmerchant-sellers [UCC 2-509(3)].

Merchant-Seller If the seller is a merchant, the risk of loss does not pass to the buyer until the goods are received. In other words, a merchant-seller bears the risk of loss between the time of contracting and the time the buyer picks up the goods.

Consider This Example On June 1, Tyus Motors, a merchant, contracts to sell a new automobile to a consumer. Tyus Motors keeps the car for a few days after contracting to prep it. During this period, the car is destroyed by fire. Under the UCC, Tyus Motors bears the risk of loss because of its merchant status.

Nonmerchant-Seller Nonmerchant-sellers pass the risk of loss to the buyer upon "Tender of delivery" of the goods. Tender of delivery occurs when the seller (1) places or holds the goods available for the buyer to take delivery and (2) notifies the buyer of this fact.

Consider This Example On June 1, a nonmerchant contracts to sell his automobile to his next-door neighbor. Delivery of the car is tendered on June 3, and the buyer is notified of this. The buyer tells the seller he will pick up the car "in a few days." The car is destroyed by fire before the buyer picks it up. In this situation, the buyer bears the risk of loss because (1) the seller is a nonmerchant and (2) delivery was tendered on June 3. If the car were destroyed on June 2—that is, before delivery was tendered—the seller would bear the risk of loss.

Goods in the Possession of a Bailee Goods sold by a seller to a buyer are sometimes in the possession of a **bailee** (e.g., a warehouse). If such goods are to be delivered to the buyer without the seller moving them, the risk of loss passes to the buyer when (1) the buyer receives a negotiable document of title (such as a warehouse receipt or bill of lading) covering the goods, (2) the bailee acknowledges the buyer's right to possession of the goods, or (3) the buyer receives a nonnegotiable document of title or other written direction to deliver *and* has a reasonable time to present the document or direction to the bailee and demand the goods. If the bailee refuses to honor the document or direction, the risk of loss remains on the seller [UCC 2-509(2)].

London. Certain shipping terms are used in the international contracts to designate pricing terms, insurance requirements, and who bears the risk of loss to the goods.

Risk of Loss: Conditional Sales

Sellers often entrust possession of goods to buyers on a trial basis. These transactions are classified as *sales on approval, sales or returns,* and *consignment* transactions [UCC 2-326].

Sale on Approval

In a **sale on approval**, there is no sale unless and until the buyer accepts the goods. A sale on approval occurs when a merchant (e.g., a computer store) allows a customer to take the goods (e.g., an Apple computer) home for a specified period of time (e.g., three days) to see if it fits the customer's needs. The prospective buyer may use the goods to try them out during this time.

Acceptance of the goods occurs if the buyer (1) expressly indicates acceptance, (2) fails to notify the seller of rejection of the goods within the agreed-upon trial period (or, if no time is agreed upon, a reasonable time), or (3) uses the goods inconsistently with the purpose of the trial (e.g., the customer resells the computer to another person).

The goods are not subject to the claims of the buyer's creditors until the buyer accepts them. In a sale on approval, the risk of loss and title to the goods remain with seller. They do not pass to the buyer until acceptance [UCC 2-327(1)].

Business Brief

In a *sale on approval* the risk of loss and title remain with the seller.

Sale or Return

In a **sale or return** contract, the seller delivers goods to a buyer with the understanding that the buyer may return them if they are not used or resold within a stated period of time (or within a reasonable time, if no specific time is stated). The sale is considered final if the buyer fails to return the goods within the specified time or reasonable time if no time is specified. The buyer has the option of returning all the goods or any commercial unit of the goods.

Consider This Example   Suppose a fashion designer delivers 10 dresses to a fashion boutique on a sale or return basis. The boutique pays $10,000 ($1,000 per dress). If the boutique does not resell the dresses within three months, it may return the unsold garments to the designer. At the end of three months, the boutique has sold 4 of the dresses. The remaining 6 dresses may be returned to the designer. The boutique can recover the compensation paid for the returned dresses.

In a sale or return contract, the risk of loss and title to the goods pass to the buyer when the buyer takes possession of the goods. In the previous example, if the dresses were destroyed while they were at the boutique, the boutique owner would be responsible for paying the designer for them [UCC 2-327(2)]. Goods sold pursuant to a sale or return contract are subject to the claims of the buyer's creditors while the goods are in the buyer's possession.

Business Brief

In a *sale or return* the risk of loss and title transfer to the buyer when he or she takes possession of the goods.

Consignment

In a **consignment**, a seller (the **consignor**) delivers goods to a buyer (the **consignee**) to sell. The consignee is paid a fee if he or she sells the goods on behalf of the consignor. A consignment is treated as a sale or return under the UCC. Whether the goods are subject to the claims of the buyer's creditors usually depends on whether the seller filed a financing statement as required by Article 9 of the UCC. If the seller files a financing statement, the goods are subject to the claims of the seller's creditors. If the seller fails to file such statement, the goods are subject to the claims of the buyer's creditors [UCC 2-326(3)].

In the following case, the court had to assess risk of loss in a conditioned sale situation.

Prewitt v. Numismatic Funding Corp.
745 F.2d 1175, 1984 U.S.App. Lexis 17926 (1984)
United States Court of Appeals, Eighth Circuit

Case 15.1

Risk of Loss

Background and Facts

Numismatic Funding Corporation (Numismatic), with its principal place of business in New York, sells rare and collector coins by mail throughout the United States. Frederick R. Prewitt, a resident of St. Louis, Missouri, responded to Numismatic's advertisement in the *Wall Street Journal*. Prewitt received several shipments of coins from Numismatic via the mails. These shipments were "on approval" for 14 days. Numismatic gave no instructions as to the method for returning unwanted coins. Prewitt kept and paid for several coins and returned the others to Numismatic, fully insured, via FedEx. On February 10, 1982, Numismatic mailed Prewitt 28 gold and silver coins worth over $60,000 on a 14-day approval. On February 23, 1982, Prewitt returned all the coins via certified mail and insured them for the maximum allowed, $400. Numismatic never received the coins. Prewitt brought this action seeking a declaratory judgment as to his nonliability. Numismatic filed a counterclaim. The district court awarded Prewitt a declaratory judgment of nonliability Numismatic appealed.

Issue

Who bears the risk of loss, Prewitt or Numismatic?

Court's Reasoning

The court determined that the delivery of coins between seller Numismatic and buyer Prewitt constituted a sale "on approval." Under the provisions of the UCC relating to risk of loss for sale on approval contracts, the risk of loss remains with the seller.

Decision and Remedy

The Court of Appeals held that the transaction in question was a sale on approval and that under UCC 2-327(1), Numismatic, the owner of the coins, bore the risk of their loss during the return shipment from Prewitt. The court of appeals affirmed the decision of the district court.

Case Questions

Critical Legal Thinking   Do you agree with how the UCC assesses risk of loss in sale on approval transactions?

Business Ethics   Should Prewitt have fully insured the coins before sending them back to Numismatic?

Contemporary Business   How could Numismatic have protected its interests in this case?

Risk of Loss: Breach of Sales Contract

The risk of loss rules just discussed apply where there is no breach of contract. Separate risk of loss rules apply to situations involving breach of the sales contract [UCC 2-510].

Seller in Breach

A seller breaches a sales contract if he or she tenders or delivers nonconforming goods to the buyer. If the goods are so nonconforming that the buyer has the right to reject them, the risk of loss remains on the seller until (1) the defect or nonconformity is cured or (2) the buyer accepts the nonconforming goods.

Consider This Example   A buyer orders 1,000 talking dolls from a seller. The contract is a shipment contract, which normally places the risk of loss during transportation on the buyer. The seller ships nonconforming dolls that cannot talk. The goods are destroyed in transit. The seller bears the risk of loss because he breached the contract by shipping nonconforming goods.

Buyer in Breach

Laws are not masters but servants, and he rules them who obeys them.

Henry Ward Beecher
Proverbs from Plymouth Pulpit
(1887)

A buyer breaches a sales contract if he or she (1) refuses to take delivery of conforming goods, (2) repudiates the contract, or (3) otherwise breaches the contract. A buyer who breaches a sales contract before the risk of loss would normally pass to him or her bears the risk of loss of any goods identified to the contract. The risk of loss rests on the buyer for only a commercially reasonable time. The buyer is only liable for any loss in excess of insurance recovered by the seller.

Beverly Hills, California, Store Window. The risk of loss to goods subject to a sales contract may depend on which party is in breach of the contract.

Risk of Loss: Lease Contracts

The parties to a lease contract may agree as to who will bear the risk of loss of the goods if they are lost or destroyed. If the parties do not so agree, the UCC supplies the following risk of loss rules:

1. In the case of an ordinary lease, the risk of loss is retained by the lessor. If the lease is a finance lease, the risk of loss passes to the lessee [UCC 2A-219].
2. If a tender of delivery of goods fails to conform to the lease contract, the risk of loss remains with the lessor or supplier until cure or acceptance [UCC 2A-220(1)(a)].

Contemporary Environment
Insuring Against Loss

To protect against financial loss that would occur if goods are damaged, destroyed, lost, or stolen, the parties to sales and lease contracts should purchase insurance against such loss. If the goods are then lost or damaged, the insured party receives reimbursement from the insurance company for the loss.

To purchase insurance, a party must have an *insurable interest* in the goods. A seller has an insurable interest in goods as long as he or she retains title or has a security interest in the goods. A lessor retains an insurable interest in the goods during the term of the lease. A buyer or lessee obtains an insurable interest in the goods when they are identified in the sales or lease contract. Both the buyer and seller, or the lessee and lessor, can have an insurable interest in the goods at the same time [UCC 2-501 and 2A-218].

To obtain and maintain proper insurance coverage on goods, a contacting party should:

- Determine the value of goods subject to the sales or lease contract.
- Purchase insurance from a reputable insurance company to cover the goods subject to the contract.
- Maintain the insurance by paying the premiums when they are due.
- Immediately file the proper claim and supporting documentation with an insurance company if the goods are damaged, destroyed, lost, or stolen. ∎

Sales by Nonowners

Sometimes people sell goods even though they do not hold valid title to them. The UCC anticipated many of the problems this situation could cause and established rules concerning the title, if any, that could be transferred to the purchasers.

Void Title and Lease: Stolen Goods

In a case where a buyer purchases goods or a lessee leases goods from a thief who has stolen them, the purchaser does not acquire title to the goods and the lessee does not acquire any leasehold interest in the goods. The real owner can reclaim the goods from the purchaser or lessee [UCC 2-403(1)]. This is called **void title**.

Consider This Example   Suppose someone steals a truckload of Sony television sets that are owned by Sears. The thief resells the televisions to City-Mart, which does not know that the goods were stolen. If Sears finds out where the televisions are, it can reclaim them. Because the thief had no title in the goods, title was not transferred to City-Mart. City-Mart's only recourse is against the thief, if he or she can be found.

Voidable Title: Sales or Lease of Goods to Good Faith Purchasers for Value

A seller or lessor has **voidable title** to goods if the goods were obtained by fraud, if a check is later dishonored, or if he or she impersonates another person. A person with voidable title to goods can transfer good title to a **good faith purchaser for value** or a **good faith subsequent lessee**. A good faith purchaser or lessee for value is someone who pays sufficient consideration or rent for the goods to the person he or she honestly believes has good title to those goods [UCC 2-201(1), 1-201(44)(d)]. The real owner cannot reclaim goods from such a purchaser [UCC 2-403(1)].

Consider This Example   Suppose a person buys a Rolex watch from his neighbor for nearly fair market value. It is later discovered that the seller obtained the watch from a jewelry store with a "bounced check." The jewelry store cannot reclaim the watch because the second purchaser purchased the watch in good faith and for value.

Assume instead that the purchaser bought the watch from a stranger for far less than fair market value. It is later discovered that the seller obtained the watch from a jewelry store by fraud. The jewelry store can reclaim the watch because the second purchaser was not a good faith purchaser for value.

Entrustment Rule

The rule found in UCC 2-403(2) holds that if an owner **entrusts** the possession of his or her goods to a merchant who deals in goods of that kind, the merchant has the power to transfer all rights (including title) in the goods to a **buyer in the ordinary course of business**. The real owner cannot reclaim the goods from this buyer.

Consider This Example   Kim Jones brings her computer into the Computer Store to be repaired. The Computer Store both sells and services computers. Jones leaves (entrusts) her computer at the store until it is repaired. The Computer Store sells her computer to

Harold Green. Green, a buyer in the ordinary course of business, acquires title to the computer. Jones cannot reclaim the computer from Green. Her only recourse is against the Computer Store.

The entrustment rule also applies to leases. If a lessor entrusts the possession of his or her goods to a lessee who is a merchant who deals in goods of that kind, the merchant-lessee has the power to transfer all the lessor's and lessee's rights in the goods to a buyer or sublessee in the ordinary course of business [UCC 2A-305(2)].

Concept Summary — Passage of Title in Sales by Nonowner Third Parties and Sales of Goods Subject to Security Agreements

Type of Transaction	Title Possessed by Seller	Innocent Purchaser	Purchaser Acquires Title to Goods
Goods acquired by theft are resold.	Void title.	Good faith purchaser for value.	No. Original owner may reclaim the goods.
Goods acquired by fraud or dishonored check are resold.	Voidable title.	Good faith purchaser for value.	Yes. Purchaser takes free of claim of original owner.
Goods entrusted by owner to merchant who deals in that type of good are resold.	No title.	Buyer in ordinary course of business.	Yes. Purchaser takes free of claim of original owner.
Creditor possesses security interest in goods that are sold.	Good title.	Buyer in ordinary course of business.	Yes. Purchaser takes free of creditor's security interest.

Russia. The fall of communism and the adoption of a private property system in Russia means that commercial enterprises may advertise and sell goods and services.

International Law

International Trade Terms

Sales contracts involving transportation customarily contain abbreviated terms describing the time and place where the buyer is to take delivery. These trade terms, such as F.O.B. and C.I.F., may also define other matters, including the time and place of payment, the price, the time the risk of loss shifts from the seller to the buyer, and the costs of freight and insurance.

The same trade abbreviations are widely used in both domestic and international transactions. Unfortunately, they have different meanings, depending on the governing law. In the United States, for example, the UCC defines trade terms for domestic sales. In the United Kingdom, the terms are defined by reference to case law. The United Nations Convention on Contracts for the International Sale of Goods (CISG) also allows parties to incorporate trade terms of their choosing.

The most widely used private trade terms are those published by the International Chamber of Commerce. Called *Incoterms*, they are well known throughout the world. Their use in international sales is encouraged by trade councils, courts, and international lawyers.

Parties who adopt the *Incoterms*, or any other trade terms, should make sure they express their desire clearly. For example, a contract might refer to F.O.B. (*Incoterms 1990*) or C.I.F. (*U.S. UCC*). Otherwise, the courts will apply the definitions used in their own jurisdiction. Finally, the parties should be wary about making additions or varying the meaning of any particular term, except to the extent that it is allowed by the rules they adopt or by judicial decision. The courts are as apt to ignore a variation, or hold that the entire term is ineffective, as they are to apply it. ■

Chapter Summary

Identification and Passage of Title, p. 302

Identification

Identification distinguishes the goods named in the contract from the seller's or lessor's other goods [UCC 2-501(1)].

Passage of Title

1. *Passage of title by agreement.* Title to goods of a sales contract passes from the seller to the buyer in any manner and on any conditions explicitly agreed upon by the parties.

2. *Passage of title where there is no agreement.* If the parties have no agreement as to the passage of title, title passes according to the following UCC rules [UCC 2-401(2)]:

   a. *Shipment contract.* Requires the seller to ship the goods to the buyer via a common carrier. Title passes to the buyer at the time and place of shipment.

   b. *Destination contract.* Requires the seller to deliver the goods to the buyer's place of business or other designated destination. Title passes to the buyer when the seller tenders delivery of the goods at the specified destination.

   c. *Goods that do not move.* If a sales contract authorizes the goods to be delivered without requiring the seller to move them, title passes at the time and place of contracting, unless a document of title is required, in which case title passes when the seller delivers the document of title to the buyer.

3. *Passage of title in lease contracts.* Title to the leased goods remains with the lessor or a third party. Title does not pass to the lessee.

Article 6 (Bulk Sales)

1. *Bulk sales.* These sales occur when an owner/debtor transfers a major part of a business's material, merchandise, inventory, or equipment not in the ordinary course of business.

2. *Article 6 (Bulk Sales).* This article establishes rules that require the buyer to notify the creditors of the seller of the proposed sale of assets. If such notice is given, the buyer receives title to the goods,

Internet Exercises and Case Questions

Working the Web Internet Exercises

Activities

1. Find UCC Article 2 as adopted in your jurisdiction. Review the seller's remedies under UCC 2-703. See **www. hg.org/cgi-bin/redir.cgi?url=www.law.cornell.edu/ uniform/vol7.html**.

2. When may the buyer revoke acceptance? See UCC 2-608 (1).

3. Review UCC 2-712. What is the connection between *cover* and *mitigation of damages*?

Critical Legal Thinking Cases

15.1 Identification of Goods   The Big Knob Volunteer Fire Company (Fire Co.) agreed to purchase a fire truck from Hamerly Custom Productions (Hamerly), which was in the business of assembling various component parts into fire trucks. Fire Co. paid Hamerly $10,000 toward the price two days after signing the contract. Two weeks later, it gave Hamerly $38,000 more toward the total purchase price of $53,000. Hamerly bought an engine chassis for the new fire truck on credit from Lowe and Meyer Garage (Lowe and Meyer). After installing the chassis, Hamerly painted the Big Knob Fire Department's name on the side of the cab. Hamerly never paid for the engine chassis, and the truck was repossessed by Lowe and Meyer. The Fire Co. sought to recover the fire truck from Lowe and Meyer. Although the Fire Co. was the buyer of a fire truck, Lowe and Meyer questioned whether any goods had ever been identified in the contract. Were they? [*Big Knob Volunteer Fire Co. v. Lowe and Meyer Garage*, 487 A.2d 953, 1985 Pa.Super. Lexis 5540 (Pa. Super. 1985)]

15.2 Passage of Title   On October 18, 1980, New England Yacht Sales (Yacht Sales) sold a yacht to Robert Pease. Pease paid for the yacht in full, and Yacht Sales delivered to him a marine bill of sale. The marine bill of sale stated that Yacht Sales was transferring "all of its right, title, and interest" in the yacht to Pease. The yacht never left the Connecticut shipyard that Yacht Sales rented. During the winter of 1980–1981, Yacht Sales did repair work on the yacht. On May 8, 1981, Yacht Sales delivered the yacht to Pease in Rhode Island. At issue in this case was when the sales tax was due to the state of Connecticut—October 18, 1980, or May 8, 1981. When did the title actually pass? [*New England Yacht Sales v. Commissioner of Revenue Services*, 504 A.2d 506, 1986 Conn. Lexis 719 (CT 1986)]

15.3 Stolen Goods   John Torniero was employed by Micheals Jewelers, Inc. (Micheals). During the course of his employment Torniero stole pieces of jewelry, including several diamond rings, a sapphire ring, a gold pendant, and several loose diamonds. Over a period of several months, Torniero sold individual pieces of the stolen jewelry to G&W Watch and Jewelry Corporation (G&W). G&W had no knowledge of how Torniero obtained the jewels. Torniero was arrested when Micheals discovered the thefts. After Torniero admitted that he had sold the stolen jewelry to G&W, Micheals attempted to recover it from G&W. G&W claimed title to the jewelry as a good faith purchaser for value. Micheals challenged G&W's claim to title in court. Who wins? [*United States v. Micheals Jewelers, Inc.*, 42 UCC Rep.Serv. 141, 1985 U.S.Dist. Lexis 15142 (D.C. Conn. 1985)]

15.4 Passage of Title   J. A. Coghill owned a 1979 Rolls Royce Corniche, which he sold in 1984 to a man claiming to be Daniel Bellman. Bellman gave Coghill a cashier's check for $94,500.

When Coghill tried to cash the check, his bank informed him that the check had been forged. Coghill reported the vehicle as stolen. Early in September 1984, Barry Hyken responded to a newspaper ad listing a 1980 Rolls Royce Corniche for sale. Hyken went to meet the seller of the car, the man who claimed to be Bellman, in a parking lot. When Hyken asked why the car was advertised as a 1980 model when it was in fact a 1979, Bellman replied that it was a newspaper mistake. Hyken agreed to pay $62,000 for the car. When Hyken asked to see Bellman's identification, Bellman provided documents with two different addresses. Bellman explained that he was in the process of moving. Although there seemed to be some irregularities in the title documents to the car, Hyken took possession anyway. Three weeks later, the Rolls was seized by the police. Hyken sued to get it back. Who wins? [*Landshire Food Service, Inc. v. Coghill*, 709 S.W.2d 509, 1986 Mo.App. Lexis 3961 (Mo. App. 1986)]

15.5 Passage of Title   On July 19, 1985, Cherry Creek Dodge, Inc. (Cherry Creek), sold a 1985 Dodge Ramcharger to Executive Leasing of Colorado (Executive Leasing). Executive Leasing, which was in the business of buying and selling cars, paid for the Dodge with a draft. Cherry Creek maintained a security interest in the car until the draft cleared. The same day that Executive Leasing bought the Dodge, it sold the car to Bruce and Peggy Carter. The Carters paid in full for the Dodge with a cashier's check, and the vehicle was delivered to them. The Carters had no knowledge of the financial arrangement between Executive Leasing and Cherry Creek. The draft that Executive Leasing gave Cherry Creek was worthless. Cherry Creek attempted to recover the vehicle from the Carters. Who wins? [*Cherry Creek Dodge, Inc. v. Carter*, 733 P.2d 1024, 1987 Wyo. Lexis 408 (WY 1987)]

15.6 Entrustment Rule   Fuqua Homes, Inc. (Fuqua), is a manufacturer of prefabricated houses. MMM was a partnership created by two men named Kirk and Underhill. MMM operated as a dealer of prefabricated homes. On seven occasions before the disputed transactions occurred, MMM had ordered homes from Fuqua. In early 1977, MMM was contacted by Kenneth Ryan. Ryan wanted to purchase a 55-foot modular home. MMM called Fuqua and ordered a prefabricated home that met Ryan's specifications. Fuqua delivered the home to MMM and retained a security interest in it until MMM paid the purchase price. MMM installed the house on Ryan's property and collected full payment from Ryan. Kirk and Underhill then disappeared, taking Ryan's money with them. Fuqua was never paid for the prefabricated home it had manufactured. Ryan had no knowledge of the dealings between MMM and Fuqua. Fuqua claimed title to the house based upon its security interest. Who has title to the home? [*Fuqua Homes, Inc. v. Evanston Bldg. & Loan Co.*, 370 N.E.2d 780, 1977 OhioApp. Lexis 6968 (Ohio App. 1977)]

15.7 Risk of Loss In June 1973, All America Export-Import Corp. (All America) placed an order for several thousand pounds of yarn with A. M. Knitwear (Knitwear). On June 4, All America sent Knitwear a purchase order. The purchase order stated the terms of the sale, including language that stated that the price was F.O.B. the seller's plant. On Friday, June 22, 1973, a truck hired by All America arrived at Knitwear's plant. On Monday, June 24, Knitwear turned the yarn over to the carrier and notified All America that the goods were now on the truck. The truck left Knitwear's plant and proceeded to a local warehouse. Sometime during the night of June 24, the truck was hijacked and all the yarn was stolen. All America had paid for the yarn by check but stopped payment on it when it learned that the goods had been stolen. Knitwear sued All America, claiming that it must pay for the stolen goods because it bore the risk of loss. Who wins? [*A. M. Knitwear v. All America, Etc.*, 390 N.Y.S.2d 832, 41 N.Y.2d 14, 1976 N.Y. Lexis 3201 (N.Y. App. 1976)]

15.8 Risk of Loss Mitsubishi International Corporation (Mitsubishi) entered into a contract with Crown Door Company (Crown) that called for Mitsubishi to sell 12 boxcar loads of plywood to Crown. According to the terms of the contract, Mitsubishi would import the wood from Taiwan and deliver it to Crown's plant in Atlanta. Mitsubishi had the wood shipped from Taiwan to Savannah, Georgia. At Savannah, the plywood was loaded onto trains and hauled to Atlanta. When the plywood arrived in Atlanta, it was discovered that the railroad had been negligent in loading the train. The negligent loading had caused the cargo to shift during the trip, and the shifting had caused extensive damage to the wood. Who bore the risk of loss?

[*Georgia Port Authority v. Mitsubishi International Corporation*, 274 S.E.2d 699, 1980 Ga.App. Lexis 2952 (Ga. App. 1980)]

15.9 Risk of Loss In 1982, Martin Silver ordered two rooms of furniture from Wycombe, Meyer & Co., Inc. (Wycombe), a manufacturer and seller of custom-made furniture. On February 23, 1982, Wycombe sent invoices to Silver, advising him that the furniture was ready for shipment. Silver tendered payment in full for the goods and asked that one room of furniture be shipped immediately and that the other be held for shipment on a later date. Before any instructions were received as to the second room of furniture, it was destroyed in a fire. Silver and his insurance company attempted to recover the money he paid for the destroyed furniture. Wycombe refused to return the payment, claiming that the risk of loss was on Silver. Who wins? [*Silver v. Wycombe, Meyer & Co., Inc.*, 477 N.Y.S.2d 288, 1984 N.Y.Misc. Lexis 3319 (N.Y. City Civ. Ct. 1984)]

15.10 Insurable Interest On February 7, 1967, Donald Hayward signed a sales contract with Dry Land Marina, Inc. (Dry Land). The contract was for the purchase of a 30-foot Revel Craft Playmate Yacht for $10,000. The contract called for Dry Land to install a number of options on Hayward's yacht and then deliver it to him in April 1967. On March 1, 1967, before taking delivery of the yacht, Hayward signed a security agreement in favor of Dry Land and a promissory note. Several weeks later, a fire swept through Dry Land's showroom. Hayward's yacht was among the goods destroyed in the fire. Who had an insurable interest in the yacht? [*Hayward v. Potsma*, 188 N.W.2d 31, 1971 Mich.App. Lexis 2150 (Mich. App. 1971)]

Business Ethics Cases

15.11 Business Ethics In mid-1975, Raceway Auto Auction (Raceway), New York, sold a red two-door 1973 Oldsmobile Toronado automobile to Triangle Auto Sales (Triangle). Triangle paid for the car with a check. Raceway delivered possession of the car to Triangle. Thereafter, Triangle's check bounced because of insufficient funds. In the meantime, Triangle sold the car to Campus Auto Sales (Campus), Rhode Island, which sold it to Charles Motor Co., Inc. (Charles), Rhode Island, which sold it to Lee Oldsmobile-Cadillac, Inc. (Lee Oldsmobile), Maine, which sold it to Stephanie K. LeBlanc of Augusta, Maine. When Triangle's check bounced, Raceway reported the car as stolen. Four months after she purchased the car, Stephanie was stopped by the Maine police, who seized the car. To maintain good relations with its customer, Lee Oldsmobile paid Raceway $2,000 to obtain the certificate of title to the automobile and then sued Charles to recover. Did Triangle Auto Sales act ethically in this case? Did Charles Motor Co. obtain valid title to the automobile? [*Lee Oldsmobile-Cadillac, Inc. v. Labonte*, 30 UCC Rep.Serv. 74, 1980 R.I.Super. Lexis 190 (RI 1980)]

15.12 Business Ethics In the summer and fall of 1982, Executive Financial Services, Inc. (EFS), purchased three tractors from Tri-County Farm Company (Tri-County), a John Deere dealership owned by Gene Mohr and James Loyd. The tractors cost $48,000, $19,000, and $38,000. EFS did not take possession of the tractors but instead left the tractors on Tri-County's lot. EFS leased the tractors to Mohr-Loyd Leasing (Mohr-Loyd), a partnership between Mohr and Loyd, with the understanding and representation by Mohr-Loyd that the tractors would be leased out to farmers. Instead of leasing the tractors, Tri-County sold them to three different farmers. EFS sued and obtained judgment against Tri-County, Mohr-Loyd, and Mohr and Loyd personally for breach of contract. Because that judgment remained unsatisfied, EFS sued the three farmers who bought the tractors to recover the tractors from them. Did Mohr and Loyd act ethically in this case? Who owns the tractors, EFS or the farmers? [*Executive Financial Services, Inc. v. Pagel*, 715 P.2d 381, 1986 Kan. Lexis 290 (KS 1986)]

Briefing the Case Writing Assignment

Read Case A.15 in the Case Appendix [*Burnett v. Purtell*]. This case is excerpted from the court of appeals opinion. Review and brief the case. In your brief, be sure to answer the following questions.

1. Who were the plaintiff and defendant? Were they merchants?

2. Describe the sales transaction.

3. Was there tender of delivery of the goods? Why is this issue important to the outcome of the case?

4. Who bore the risk of loss when the goods were destroyed?

16

Remedies for Breach of Sales and Lease Contracts

" Trade and commerce, if they were not made of Indian rubber, would never manage to bounce over the obstacles which legislators are continually putting in their way. "

—Henry D. Thoreau
Resistance to Civil Government (1849)

Chapter Objectives

After studying this chapter, you should be able to:

1. Describe the performance of sales and lease contracts.

2. List and describe the seller's remedies for the buyer's breach of a sales contract.

3. List and describe the buyer's remedies for the seller's breach of a sales contract.

4. List and describe the lessor's remedies for the lessee's breach of a lease contract.

5. List and describe the lessee's remedies for the lessor's breach of a lease contract.

Chapter Contents

- Seller's and Lessor's Performance

- Buyer's and Lessee's Performance

- Seller's and Lessor's Remedies

- Buyer's and Lessee's Remedies

- Additional Issues Affecting Performance and Breach

Usually, the parties to a sales or lease contract owe a duty to perform the **obligations** specified in their agreement [UCC 2-301, 2A-301]. The seller's or lessor's general obligation is to transfer and deliver the goods to the buyer or lessee. The buyer's or lessee's general obligation is to accept and pay for the goods.

When one party **breaches** a sales or lease contract, the UCC provides the injured party with a variety of prelitigation and litigation remedies. These remedies are designed to place the injured party in as good a position as if the breaching party's contractual obligations were fully performed [UCC 1-106(1), 2A-401(1)]. The best remedy depends on the circumstances of the particular case.

The performance of obligations and remedies available for breach of sales and lease contracts are discussed in this chapter.

Seller's and Lessor's Performance

Tender of delivery, or the transfer and delivery of goods to the buyer or lessee in accordance with a sales or lease contract, is the seller's or lessor's basic obligation [UCC 2-301]. Tender of delivery requires the seller or lessor to (1) put and hold conforming goods at the buyer's or lessee's disposition and (2) give the buyer or lessee any notification reasonably necessary to enable delivery of goods. The parties may agree as to the time, place, and manner of delivery. If there is no special agreement, tender must be made at a reasonable hour, and the goods must be kept available for a reasonable period of time. For example, the seller cannot telephone the buyer at 12:01 A.M. and say that the buyer has 15 minutes to accept delivery [UCC 2-503(1), 2A-508(1)].

> The buyer needs a hundred eyes, the seller not one.
>
> George Herbert
> *Jacula Prudentum (1651).*

Unless otherwise agreed or unless the circumstances permit either party to request delivery in lots, the goods named in the contract must be tendered in a single delivery. Payment of a sales contract is due upon tender of delivery unless an extension of credit between the parties has been arranged. If the goods are rightfully delivered in lots, the payment is apportioned for each lot [UCC 2-307]. Lease payments are due in accordance with the terms of the lease contract.

Place of Delivery

Many sales and lease contracts state where the goods are to be delivered. Often, the contract will say that the buyer or lessee must pick up the goods from the seller or lessor. If the contract does not expressly state where the delivery will take place, the UCC stipulates place of delivery on the basis of whether a carrier is involved.

Noncarrier Cases Unless otherwise agreed, the place of delivery is the seller's or lessor's place of business. If the seller or lessor has no place of business, the place of delivery is the seller's or lessor's residence. If the parties have knowledge at the time of contracting that identified goods are located in some other place, that place is the place of delivery. For example, if the parties contract regarding the sale of wheat that is located in a silo, the silo is the place of delivery [UCC 2-308].

Sometimes the goods are in the possession of a **bailee** (e.g., a warehouse) and are to be delivered without being moved. In such cases, tender of delivery occurs when the seller either (1) tenders to the buyer a negotiable document of title covering the goods, (2) produces acknowledgment from the bailee of the buyer's right to possession of the goods, or (3) tenders a nonnegotiable document of title or a written direction to the bailee to deliver the goods to a buyer. The seller must deliver all such documents in correct from [UCC 2-503(4) and (5)].

Carrier Cases Unless the parties have agreed otherwise, if delivery of goods to a buyer is to be made by carrier, the UCC establishes different rules for shipment contracts and destination contracts. These rules are described below.

Shipment Contracts Sales contracts that require the seller to send the goods to the buyer, but not to a specifically named destination, are called **shipment contracts**. Under such contracts, the seller must do all the following [UCC 2-504]:

1. Put the goods in the carrier's possession and contract for the proper and safe transportation of the goods.
2. Obtain and promptly deliver or tender in correct form any documents (a) necessary to enable the buyer to obtain possession of the goods, (b) required by the sales contract, or (c) required by usage of trade.
3. Promptly notify the buyer of the shipment.

The buyer may reject the goods if a material delay or loss is caused by the seller's failure to make a proper contract for the shipment of goods or properly notify the buyer of the shipment. For example, if a shipment contract involves perishable goods and the seller fails to ship the goods via a refrigerated carrier, the buyer may rightfully reject the goods if they spoil during transit.

Destination Contracts A sales contract that requires the seller to deliver goods to the buyer's place of business or another specified destination is a **destination contract**. Unless otherwise agreed, destination contracts require delivery to be tendered at the buyer's place of business or other location specified in the sales contract. Delivery must be at a reasonable time and in a reasonable manner and with proper notice to the buyer. Appropriate documents of title must be provided by the seller to enable the buyer to obtain the goods from the carrier [UCC 2-503].

Perfect Tender Rule

The seller or lessor is under a duty to deliver conforming goods. If the goods or tender of delivery fails in any respect to conform to the contract, the buyer or lessee may opt either (1) to reject the whole shipment, (2) to accept the whole shipment, or (3) to reject part and accept part of the shipment. This option is referred to as the **perfect tender rule** [UCC 2-601, 2A-509].

Consider This Example A sales contract requires the seller to deliver 100 shirts to a buyer. When the buyer inspects the delivered goods, it is discovered that 99 shirts conform to the contract and 1 shirt does not conform. Pursuant to the perfect tender rule, the buyer may reject the entire shipment. If a buyer accepts nonconforming goods, the buyer may seek remedies against the seller.

Exceptions to the Perfect Tender Rule The UCC alters the perfect tender rule in the following situations:

1. *Agreement of the parties.* The parties to the sales or lease contract may agree to limit the effect of the perfect tender rule. For example, they may decide that (1) only the defective or nonconforming goods may be rejected, (2) the seller or lessor may replace nonconforming goods or repair defects, or (3) the buyer or lessee will accept nonconforming goods with appropriate compensation from the seller or lessor.
2. *Substitution of carriers.* The UCC requires the seller to use a commercially reasonable substitute if (1) the agreed-upon manner of delivery fails or (2) the agreed-upon type of carrier becomes unavailable [UCC 2-614(1)].

Convenience is the basis of mercantile law.

Lord Mansfield
Medcalf v. Hall (1782)

Consider This Example   A sales contract specifies delivery of goods by Mac Trucks, Inc., a common carrier, but a labor strike prevents delivery by this carrier. The seller must use any commercially reasonable substitute (such as another truck line or the rails). The buyer cannot reject the delivery because there is a substitute carrier. Unless otherwise agreed, the seller bears any increased cost of the substitute performance.

Cure The UCC gives a seller or lessor who delivers nonconforming goods an opportunity to **cure** the nonconformity. Although the term *cure* is not defined by the UCC, it generally means an opportunity to repair or replace defective or nonconforming goods [UCC 2-508, 2A-513].

A cure may be attempted if the time for performance has not expired and the seller or lessor notifies the buyer or lessee of his or her intention to make a conforming delivery within the contract time.

Consider This Example   A lessee contracts to lease a BMW 850i automobile from a lessor for delivery July 1. On June 15, the lessor delivers a BMW 740i to the lessee, and the lessee rejects it as nonconforming. The lessor has until July 1 to cure the nonconformity by delivering the BMW 850i specified in the contract.

A cure may also be attempted if the seller or lessor had reasonable grounds to believe the delivery would be accepted. The seller or lessor may have a further reasonable time to substitute a conforming tender.

Consider This Example   A buyer contracts to purchase 100 red dresses from a seller for delivery July 1. On July 1, the seller delivers 100 blue dresses to the buyer. In the past, the buyer has accepted different-colored dresses than those ordered. This time, though, the buyer rejects the blue dresses as nonconforming. The seller has a reasonable time after July 1 to deliver conforming red dresses to the buyer.

In the following case, a seller attempted to cure a defective delivery.

Joc Oil USA, Inc. v. Consolidated Edison Co. of New York, Inc.

443 N.E.2d 932, 457 N.Y.S.2d 458, 1982 N.Y. Lexis 3846 (1982)
Court of Appeals of New York

Case 16.1

Cure

Background and Facts

Joc Oil USA, Inc. (Joc Oil), contracted to purchase low-sulfur fuel oil from an Italian oil refinery. The Italian refinery issued a certificate to Joc Oil, indicating that the sulfur content of the oil was 0.50 percent. Joc Oil entered into a sales contract to sell the oil to Consolidated Edison Company of New York, Inc. (Con Ed). Con Ed agreed to pay $17.875 per barrel for oil not to exceed 0.50 percent sulfur. When the ship delivering the oil arrived, it discharged the oil into three Con Ed storage tanks. On February 20, 1974, a final report issued by Con Ed stated that the sulfur content of the oil was 0.92 percent. At a meeting that day, Joc Oil offered to reduce the price of the oil by $.50 to $.80 per barrel. Con Ed expressed a willingness to accept the oil at $13 per barrel (the market price of oil at that time). Joc Oil then made an offer to cure the defect by substituting a conforming shipment of oil that was already on a ship that was to arrive within two weeks. Con Ed rejected Joc Oil's offer to cure. Joc Oil sued Con Ed for breach of contract. The trial court held that under the circumstances of this case, Joc

Oil had the right to cure the defect in delivery and that Con Ed breached the contract by refusing to permit this cure. The court entered judgment against Con Ed and awarded Joc Oil $1,385,512 in damages plus interest and the costs of this action. The appellate division court affirmed the judgment. Con Ed appealed.

Issue

Did Joc Oil have a right to cure the defect in the delivery?

Court's Reasoning

The UCC statutory right to cure is an exception to the precode "perfect tender rule." The UCC cure provision was conceived to protect a seller from surprise rejection by the buyer. In this case, the court of appeals held that Joc Oil had reasonable grounds to believe that its original shipment would be acceptable to Con Ed. The court found that Joc Oil made its offer to cure by tendering a new conforming shipment that would arrive within two weeks, a reasonable time in the court's view. Under the circumstances, Joc

Oil had the right to—and did—make a reasonable and timely offer to cure. Con Ed's rejection was improper.

Decision and Remedy

The court of appeals held that Joc Oil had made a reasonable and timely offer to cure that was improperly rejected by Con Ed. The court of appeals affirmed the prior courts judgment awarding Joc Oil $1,385,512 in damages plus interest and costs.

Case Questions

Critical Legal Thinking   Should the law recognize the right to cure a defective tender of goods? Why or why not?

Business Ethics   Did Con Ed act ethically in this case? Did Joc Oil?

Contemporary Business   Why do you think Con Ed rejected Joc Oil's offer to cure the defect in delivery? Explain.

Installment Contracts   An **installment contract** is a contract that requires or authorizes goods to be delivered and accepted in separate lots. Such a contract must contain a clause that states "each delivery in a separate contract" or equivalent language. An example of an installment contract is one in which a buyer orders 100 shirts, to be delivered in four equal installments of 25 items.

The UCC alters the perfect tender rule with regard to installment contracts. The buyer or lessee may reject the entire contract only if the nonconformity or default with respect to any installment or installments substantially impairs the value of the entire contract. The buyer or lessee may reject any nonconforming installment if the value of the installment is impaired and the defect cannot be cured. Thus, in each case, the court must determine whether the nonconforming installment impairs the value of the entire contract or only that installment [UCC 2-612, 2A-510].

Destruction of Goods   The UCC provides that if goods identified in a sales or lease contract are totally destroyed without the fault of either party before the risk of loss passes to the buyer or the lessee, the contract is void. Both parties are then excused from performing the contract.

If the goods are only partially destroyed, the buyer or lessee may inspect the goods and then choose either to treat the contract as void or to accept the goods. If the buyer or lessee opts to accept the goods, the purchase price or rent will be reduced in compensation for the damage [UCC 2-613, 2A-221].

Consider This Example   A buyer contracts to purchase a sofa from a seller. The seller agrees to deliver the sofa to the buyer's home. The truck delivering the sofa is hit by an automobile, and the sofa is totally destroyed. Because the risk of loss has not passed to the buyer, the contract is voided, and the buyer does not have to pay for the sofa.

Business Ethics

Good Faith and Reasonableness Govern the Performance of Sales and Lease Contracts

Generally, the common law of contracts only obligates the parties to perform according to the express terms of their contract. There is no breach of contract unless the parties fail to meet these terms.

Recognizing that certain situations may develop that are not expressly provided for in a contract or that strict adherence to the terms of a contract without doing more may not be sufficient to accomplish the contract's objective, the Uniform Commercial Code (UCC) adopts two broad principles that govern the performance of sales and lease contracts: *good faith* and *reasonableness*.

UCC 1-203 states, "Every contract or duty within this Act imposes an obligation of good faith in its performance or enforcement." Although both parties owe a duty of good faith in the performance of a sales or lease contract, merchants are held to a higher standard of good faith than nonmerchants. Nonmerchants are held to the subjective standard of honesty in fact whereas merchants are held to the objective standard of fair dealing in the trade [UCC 2-103(1)(b)].

The words *reasonable* and *reasonably* are used throughout the UCC to establish the duties of performance by the parties to

Business Ethics

(continued)

sales and lease contracts. For example, unless otherwise specified, the parties must act within a "reasonable" time [UCC 1-
204(1)(2)]. As another example, if the seller does not deliver the
goods as contracted, the buyer may make "reasonable" purchases to cover (i.e., obtain substitute performance) [UCC 2-
712(1)]. The term *commercial reasonableness* is used to establish certain duties of merchants under the UCC. Articles 2 and
2A of the UCC do not specifically define the terms *reasonable*
and *commercial reasonableness*. Instead, these terms are
defined by reference to the course of performance or the course
of dealing between the parties, usage of trade, and such.

Note that the concepts of good faith and reasonableness
extend to the "spirit" of the contract as well as the contract
terms. The underlying theory is that the parties are more apt
to perform properly if their conduct is to be judged against
these principles. This is a major advance in the law of
contracts.

1. Do the UCC concepts of *good faith* and *reasonableness*
   enhance ethical conduct?
2. Should the concept of *good faith* be implied in every contract? Why or why not? ■

Buyer's and Lessee's Performance

Once the seller or lessor has properly tendered delivery, the buyer or lessee is obligated to
accept and pay for the goods in accordance with the sales or lease contract. If there is no
agreement, the provisions of the UCC control.

Right of Inspection

Unless otherwise agreed, the buyer or lessee has the right to inspect goods that are tendered, delivered, or identified in the sales contract prior to accepting or paying for them. If
the goods are shipped, the inspection may take place after their arrival. If the inspected
goods do not conform to the contract, the buyer or lessee may reject them without paying
for them [UCC 2-513(1), 2A-515(1)].

The parties may agree as to the time, place, and manner of inspection. If there is no
such agreement, the inspection must occur at a reasonable time and place and in a reasonable manner. Reasonableness depends on the circumstances of the case, common usage of
trade, prior course of dealing between the parties, and such. If the goods conform to the
contract, the buyer pays for the inspection. If the goods are rejected for nonconformance,
the cost of inspection can be recovered from the seller [UCC 2-513(2)].

Buyers who agree to **C.O.D. (cash on delivery)** deliveries are not entitled to inspect
the goods before paying for them. In certain sales contracts (e.g., cost, insurance, and
freight [C.I.F.] contracts), payment is due from the buyer upon receipt of documents of
title, even if the goods have not yet been received. In such a case the buyer is not entitled
to inspect the goods before paying for them [UCC 2-513(3)].

Payment

Goods that are accepted must be paid for [UCC 2-607(1)]. Unless the parties to a contract agree otherwise, payment is due from a buyer when and where the goods are delivered, even if the place of delivery is the same as the place of shipment. Buyers often purchase goods on credit extended by the seller. Unless the parties agree to other terms, the
credit period begins to run from the time the goods are shipped [UCC 2-310]. A lessee
must pay lease payments in accordance with the lease contract [UCC 2A-516(1)].

The goods can be paid for in any manner currently acceptable in the ordinary course
of business (check, credit card, or the like) unless the seller demands payment in cash or

unless the contract names a specific form of payment. If the seller requires cash payment, the buyer must be given an extension of time necessary to procure the cash. If the buyer pays by check, payment is conditional on the check being honored (paid) when it is presented to the bank for payment [UCC 2-511].

Acceptance

Acceptance occurs when the buyer or lessee takes any of the following actions after a reasonable opportunity to inspect the goods: (1) signifies to the seller or lessor in words or by conduct that the goods are conforming or that the buyer or lessee will take or retain the goods despite their nonconformity or (2) fails to effectively reject the goods within a reasonable time after their delivery or tender by the seller or lessor. Acceptance also occurs if a buyer acts inconsistently with the seller's ownership rights in the goods. For example, acceptance occurs if the buyer resells the goods delivered by the seller [UCC 2-606(1), 2A-515(1)].

Buyers and lessees may only accept delivery of a "commercial unit." A commercial unit is a unit of goods that commercial usage deems is a single whole for purpose of sale. Thus, it may be a single article (such as a machine), a set of articles (such as a suite of furniture or an assortment of sizes), a quantity (such as a bale, a gross, or a carload), or any other unit treated in use or in the relevant market as a single whole. Acceptance of a part of any commercial unit is acceptance of the entire unit [UCC 2-606(2), 2A-515(2)].

Revocation of Acceptance

A buyer or lessee who has accepted goods may subsequently **revoke** his or her acceptance if (1) the goods are nonconforming, (2) the nonconformity substantially impairs the value of the goods to the buyer or lessee, and (3) one of the following factors is

Courthouse, Baltimore, Maryland.
Parties may use courts to enforce sales and lease contracts.

shown: (a) the seller's or lessor's promise to timely cure of the nonconformity is not met, (b) the goods were accepted before the nonconformity was discovered and the nonconformity was difficult to discover, or (c) the goods were accepted before the nonconformity was discovered and the seller or lessor assured the buyer or lessee that the goods were conforming.

Revocation is not effective until the seller or lessor is so notified. In addition, the revocation must occur within a reasonable time after the buyer or lessee discovers or should have discovered the grounds for the revocation. The revocation, which must be of a lot or commercial unit, must occur before there is any substantial change in the condition of the goods (e.g., before perishable goods spoil) [UCC 2-608(1), 2A-517(1)].

Seller's and Lessor's Remedies

Various remedies are available to sellers and lessors if a buyer or lessee breaches a contract. These remedies are discussed in the paragraphs that follow.

Right to Withhold Delivery

Delivery of goods may be **withheld** if the seller or lessor is in possession of them when the buyer or lessee breaches the contract. This remedy is available if the buyer or lessee wrongfully rejects or revokes acceptance of the goods, fails to make a payment when due, or repudiates the contract. If part of the goods under the contract have been delivered when the buyer or lessee materially breaches the contract, the seller or lessor may withhold delivery of the remainder of the affected goods [UCC 2-703(a), 2A-523(1)(c)].

A seller or lessor who discovers that the buyer or lessee is insolvent before the goods are delivered may refuse to deliver as promised unless the buyer or lessee pays cash for the goods [UCC 2-702(1), 2A-525(1)]. Under the UCC, a person is insolvent when he or she (1) ceases to pay his or her debts in the ordinary course of business, (2) cannot pay his or her debts as they become due, or (3) is insolvent within the meaning of the federal bankruptcy law [UCC 1-201(23)].

Right to Stop Delivery of Goods in Transit

Often, sellers and lessors employ common carriers and other bailees (e.g., warehouses) to hold and deliver goods to buyers and lessees. The goods are considered to be **in transit** while they are in possession of these carriers or bailees. A seller or lessor that learns of the buyer's or lessee's insolvency while the goods are in transit may **stop delivery of the goods**, irrespective of the size of the shipment.

Essentially, the same remedy is available if the buyer or lessee repudiates the contract, fails to make payment when due, or otherwise gives the seller or lessor some other right to withhold or reclaim the goods. In these circumstances, however, the delivery can be stopped only if it constitutes a carload, a truckload, a planeload, or a larger express or freight shipment [UCC 2-705(1), 2A-526(1)].

The seller or lessor must give sufficient notice to allow the bailee, by reasonable diligence, to prevent delivery of the goods. After receipt of notice, the bailee must hold and deliver the goods according to the directions of the seller or lessor. The seller is responsible for all expenses borne by the bailee in stopping the goods [UCC 2-705(3), 2A-526(3)].

Goods may be stopped in transit until the buyer or lessee obtains possession of the goods or the carrier or other bailee acknowledges that it is holding the goods for the buyer or lessee [UCC 2-705(2), 2A-526(2)].

Right to Reclaim Goods

In certain situations, a seller or lessor may demand the return of the goods it sold or leased that are already in the possession of the buyer or lessee. In a sale transaction, **reclamation** is permitted in two situations. If the goods are delivered in a credit sale and the seller then discovers that the buyer was insolvent, the seller has 10 days within which to demand that the goods be returned [UCC 2-507(2)]. If the buyer misrepresented his or her solvency in writing within three months before delivery [UCC 2-702(2)] or paid for goods in a cash sale with a check that bounces [UCC 2-507(2)], the seller may reclaim the goods at any time.

A lessor may reclaim goods in the possession of the lessee if the lessee is in default of the contract [UCC 2A-525(2)].

To exercise a right of reclamation, the seller or lessor must send the buyer or lessee a written notice demanding return of the goods. The seller or lessor may not use self-help to reclaim the goods if the buyer or lessee refuses to honor his or her demand. Instead, appropriate legal proceedings must be instituted.

Right to Dispose of Goods

If the buyer or lessee breaches or repudiates the seller or lease contract before the seller or lessor has delivered the goods, the seller or lessor may resell or release the goods and recover damages from the buyer or lessee [UCC 2-703(d), 2-706(1), UCC 2A-523(1)(e), 2A-527(1)]. This right also arises if the seller or lessor has reacquired the goods after stopping them in transit.

The **disposition of the goods** by the seller or lessor must be made in good faith and in a commercially reasonable manner. The goods may be disposed of as a unit or in parcels in a public or private transaction. The seller or lessor must give the buyer or lessee reasonable notification of his or her intention to dispose of goods unless the goods threaten to quickly decline in value or are perishable. The party who buys or leases the goods in good faith for value takes the goods, free of any rights of the original buyer or lessee [UCC 2-706(5), 2A-527(4)].

The seller or lessor may recover any damages incurred on the disposition of the goods. In the case of a sales contract, damages are defined as the difference between the disposition price and the original contract price. In the case of a lease contract, damages are the difference between the disposition price and the rent the original lessee would have paid.

The profit does not revert to the original buyer or lessee if the seller or lessor disposes of the goods at a higher price than the buyer or lessee contracted to pay. The seller or lessor may also recover any **incidental damages** (reasonable expenses incurred in stopping delivery, transportation charges, storage charges, sales commission, and the like [UCC 2-710, 2A-530]) incurred on the disposition of the goods [UCC 2-706(1), 2A-527(2)].

Consider This Example   A buyer contracts to purchase a racehorse for $20,000. When the seller tenders delivery, the buyer refuses to accept the horse or pay for it. The seller, in good faith, and in a commercially reasonable manner, resells the horse to a third party for $17,000. Incidental expenses of $500 are incurred on the resale. The seller can recover $3,500 from the original buyer: the $3,000 difference between the resale price and the contract price and $500 for the incidental expenses.

Unfinished Goods Sometimes a sales or lease contract is breached or repudiated before the goods are finished. In such a case the seller or lessor may choose either (1) to cease manufacturing the goods and resell them for scrap or salvage value or (2) to complete the manufacture of the goods and resell, release, or otherwise dispose of them to another party [UCC 2-704(2), 2A-524(2)]. The seller or lessor may recover damages from the breaching buyer or lessee.

Right to Recover the Purchase Price or Rent

In certain circumstances, the UCC provides that a seller or lessor may sue the buyer or lessee to **recover the purchase price or rent** stipulated in the sales or lease contract. This remedy is available in the following situations:

1. The buyer or lessee accepts the goods but fails to pay for them when the price or rent is due.
2. The buyer or lessee breaches the contract after the goods have been identified in the contract and the seller or lessor cannot resell or dispose of them.
3. The goods are damaged or lost after the risk of loss passes to the buyer or lessee [UCC 2-709(1), 2A-529(1)].

To recover the purchase price or rent, the seller or lessor must hold the goods for the buyer or lessee. If resale or other disposition of the goods becomes possible prior to the collection of the judgment, however, the seller or lessor may resell or dispose of them. In such situations, the net proceeds of any disposition must be credited against the judgment [UCC 2-709(2), 2A-529(2) and (3)]. The seller or lessor may also recover incidental damages from the buyer or lessee.

Right to Recover Damages for Breach of Contract

If a buyer or lessee repudiates a sales or lease contract or wrongfully rejects tendered goods, the seller or lessor may sue to **recover the damages** caused by the buyer's or lessee's breach. Generally, the amount of damages is calculated as the difference between the contract price (or rent) and the market price (or rent) of the goods at the time and place the goods were to be delivered to the buyer or lessee plus incidental damages [UCC 2-708(1), 2A-528(1)].

If the preceding measure of damage will not put the seller or lessor in as good a position as performance of the contract would have, the seller or lessor can seek to **recover any lost profits** that would have resulted from the full performance of the contract plus an allowance for reasonable overhead and incidental damages [UCC 2-708(2), 2A-528(2)].

Right to Cancel a Contract

A seller or lessor may cancel a sales or lease contract if the buyer or lessee breaches that contract by rejecting or revoking acceptance of the goods, failing to pay for the goods, or repudiating all or any part of the contract. The **cancellation** may refer only to the affected goods or to the entire contract, if the breach is material [UCC 2-703(f), 2A-523(1)(a)].

A seller or lessor who rightfully cancels a sales or lease contract by notifying the buyer or lessee is discharged of any further obligations under that contract. The buyer's or lessee's duties are not discharged, however. The seller or lessor retains the right to seek damages for the breach [UCC 2-106(4), 2A-523(3)].

Concept Summary   *Seller's and Lessor's Remedies*

Possession of Goods at Time of Buyer's Breach	Seller's or Lessor's Remedies

Goods in the possession of the seller	1. Withhold delivery of the goods [UCC 2-703(a), 2A-523(1)(c)].
	 2. Demand payment in cash if the buyer is insolvent [UCC 2-702(1), 2A-525(1)].
	 3. Resell or re-lease the goods and recover the difference between the contract or lease price and the resale or re-lease price [UCC 2-706, 2A-527].
	 4. Sue for breach of contract and recover as damages either
	   a. The difference between the market price and the contract price [UCC 2-708(1), 2A-528(1)] or
	   b. Lost profits [UCC 2-708(2), 2A-528(2)].
	 5. Cancel the contract [UCC 2-703(f), 2A-523(1)(a)].

Goods in the possession of a carrier or bailee	1. Stop goods in transit [UCC 2-705(1), 2A-526(1)].
	   a. Carload, truckload, planeload, or larger shipment if the buyer is solvent.
	   b. Any size shipment if the buyer is insolvent.

Goods in the possession of the buyer	1. Sue to recover the purchase price or rent [UCC 2-709(1), 2A-529(1)].
	 2. Reclaim the goods [UCC 2-507(2), 2A-525(2)].
	   a. The seller delivers goods in cash sale, and the buyer's check is dishonored.
	   b. The seller delivers goods in a credit sale, and the goods are received by an insolvent buyer.

Contemporary Environment

Lost Volume Seller

Should a seller be permitted to recover the profits it lost on a sale to a defaulting buyer if the seller sold the goods to another buyer? It depends. If the seller had only one item or a limited number of items and could produce no more, the seller cannot recover lost profits from the defaulting buyer. This is because the seller made those profits on the sale of the item to the new buyer. If, however, the seller could have produced more of the item, the seller is a "lost volume seller." In this situation, the seller can make the profit from the sale of the item to the new buyer and sue the defaulting buyer to recover the profit it would have made from this sale. This is because the seller would have realized profits from two sales—the sale to the first buyer who defaulted and the second sale to the new buyer. ■

Buyer's and Lessee's Remedies

The UCC provides a variety of remedies to a buyer or lessee upon the seller's or lessor's breach of a sales or lease contract. These remedies are discussed in the following paragraphs.

Right to Reject Nonconforming Goods or Improperly Tendered Goods

If the goods or the seller's or lessor's tender of delivery fails to conform to a sales or lease contract in any way, the buyer or lessee may (1) **reject** the whole, (2) accept the whole, or (3) accept any commercial unit and reject the rest. If the buyer or lessee chooses to reject the goods, he or she must identify defects that are ascertainable by reasonable inspection. Failure to do so prevents the buyer or lessee from relying on those defects to justify the rejection if the defect could have been cured by a seller or lessor who was notified in a timely manner [UCC 2-601, 2A-509]. Nonconforming or improperly tendered goods must be rejected within a reasonable time after their delivery or tender. The seller or lessor must be notified of the rejection. The buyer or lessee must hold any rightfully rejected goods with reasonable care for a reasonable time [UCC 2-602(2), 2A-512(1)].

If the buyer or lessee is a merchant and the seller or lessor has no agent or place of business at the market where the goods are rejected, the merchant-buyer or merchant-lessee must follow any reasonable instructions received from the seller or lessor with respect to the rejected goods [UCC 2-603, 2A-511]. If the seller or lessor gives no instructions and the rejected goods are perishable or will quickly decline in value, the buyer or lessee may make reasonable efforts to sell them on the seller's or lessor's behalf [UCC 2-604, 2A-512].

Any buyer or lessee who rightfully rejects goods is entitled to reimbursement from the seller or lessor for reasonable expenses incurred in holding, storing, reselling, shipping, and otherwise caring for the rejected goods.

Right to Recover Goods from an Insolvent Seller or Lessor

If a buyer or lessee makes partial or full payment for the goods before they are received and the seller or lessor becomes insolvent within 10 days after receiving the first payment, the buyer or lessee may **recover the goods** from the seller or lessor. To do so, the buyer or lessee must tender the unpaid portion of the purchase price or rent due under the sales or lease contract. Only conforming goods that are identified in the contract may be recovered [UCC 2-502, 2A-522]. This remedy is often referred to as **capture**.

Myanmar (Burma). Many goods sold in the United States are made in foreign countries. Do foreign workers receive the same protection as American workers? Is this "outsourcing" legal?

Right to Obtain Specific Performance

If the goods are unique or the remedy at law is inadequate, a buyer or lessee may obtain **specific performance** of a sales or lease contract. A decree of specific performance orders the seller or lessor to perform the contract. Specific performance is usually used to obtain possession of works of art, antiques, rare coins, and other unique items [UCC 2-716(1), 2A-521(1)].

Consider This Example   A buyer enters into a sales contract to purchase a specific Rembrandt painting from a seller for $10 million. When the buyer tenders payment, the seller refuses to sell the painting to the buyer. The buyer may bring an equity action to obtain a decree of specific performance from the court, ordering the seller to sell the painting to the buyer.

Right to Cover

A buyer or lessee may **cover** by purchasing or renting substitute goods if the seller or lessor fails to make delivery of the goods or repudiates the contract or if the buyer or lessee rightfully rejects the goods or justifiably revokes their acceptance. The buyer's or lessee's cover must be made in good faith and without unreasonable delay. If the exact commodity is not available, the buyer or lessee may purchase or lease any commercially reasonable substitute.

A buyer or lessee who rightfully covers may sue the seller or lessor to recover as damages the difference between the cost of cover and the contract price or rent. The buyer or lessee may also recover incidental and consequential damages, less expenses saved (such as delivery costs) [UCC 2-712, 2A-518]. The UCC does not require a buyer or lessee to cover when a seller or lessor breaches a sales or lease contract. Failure of the buyer or lessee to cover does not bar the buyer from other remedies against the seller.

Right to Replevy Goods

A buyer or lessee may replevy (recover) goods from a seller or lessor who is wrongfully withholding them. The buyer or lessee must show that he or she was unable to cover or that attempts at cover will be unavailing. Thus, the goods must be scarce, but not unique. **Replevin** actions are available only as to goods identified in a sales or lease contract [UCC 2-716(3), 2A-521(3)].

Consider This Example   On January 1, IBM contracts to purchase monitors for computers from a seller for delivery on June 1. IBM intends to attach the monitors to a new computer that will be introduced on June 30. On June 1, the seller refuses to sell the monitors to IBM because it can get a higher price from another buyer. IBM tries to cover but cannot. IBM may successfully replevy the monitors from the seller.

Right to Cancel a Contract

If a seller or lessor fails to deliver conforming goods or repudiates the contract or if the buyer or lessee rightfully rejects the goods or justifiably revokes acceptance of the goods, the buyer or lessee may **cancel** the sales or lease contract. The contract may be canceled with respect to the affected goods or, if there is a material breach, the whole contract may be canceled. A buyer or lessee who rightfully cancels a contract is discharged from any further obligations on the contract and retains his or her rights to other remedies against the seller or lessor [UCC 2-711(1), 2A-508(1)(a)].

Right to Recover Damages for Nondelivery or Repudiation

If a seller or lessor fails to deliver the goods or repudiates the sales or lease contract, the buyer or lessee may recover **damages**. The measure of damages is the difference between the contract price (or original rent) and the market price (or rent) at the time the buyer or lessee learned of the breach. Incidental and consequential damages, less expenses saved, can also be recovered [UCC 2-713, 2A519].

Consider This Example   Fresh Foods Company contracts to purchase 10,000 bushels of soybeans from Sunshine Farms for $5 per bushel. Delivery is to occur on August 1. On August 1 the market price of soybeans is $7 per bushel. Sunshine Farms does not deliver the soybeans. Fresh Foods decides not to cover and to do without the soybeans. Fresh Foods sues Sunshine for market value minus the contract price damages. It can recover $20,000 ($7 market price minus $5 contract price multiplied by 10,000 bushels) plus incidental damages less expenses saved because of Sunshine's breach. Fresh Foods cannot recover consequential damages because it did not attempt to cover.

Right to Recover Damages for Accepted Nonconforming Goods

A buyer or lessee may accept nonconforming goods from a seller or lessor. The acceptance does not prevent the buyer or lessee from suing the seller or lessor to recover the **damages for accepted nonconforming goods** and any loss resulting from the seller's or lessor's breach. Incidental and consequential damages may also be recovered. The buyer or lessee must notify the seller or lessor of the nonconformity within a reasonable time after the breach was or should have been discovered. Failure to do so bars the buyer or lessee from any recovery. If the buyer or lessee accepts nonconforming goods, he or she may deduct all or any part of damages resulting from the breach from any part of the purchase price or rent still due under the contract [UCC 2-714(1), 2A-516(1)].

Consider This Example   A retail clothing store contracts to purchase 100 designer dresses for $100 per dress from a seller. The buyer pays for the dresses prior to delivery. After the dresses are delivered, the buyer discovers that 10 of the dresses have flaws in them. The buyer may accept these nonconforming dresses and sue the seller for reasonable damages resulting from the nonconformity.

Concept Summary   Buyer's and Lessee's Remedies

Situation	Buyer's or Lessee's Remedy
Seller or lessor refuses to deliver the goods or delivers nonconforming goods that the buyer or lessee does not want.	1. Reject nonconforming goods [UCC 2-601, 2A-509]. 2. Revoke acceptance of nonconforming goods [UCC 2-608, 2A-517(1)]. 3. Cover [UCC 2-712, 2A-518]. 4. Sue for breach of contract and recover damages [UCC 2-713, 2A-519]. 5. Cancel the contract [UCC 2-711(1), 2A-508(1)(a)].
Seller or lessor tenders nonconforming goods and buyer or lessee accepts them.	1. Sue for ordinary damages [UCC 2-714(1), 2A-516(1)]. 2. Deduct damages from the unpaid purchase or rent price [UCC 2-714(1), 2A-516(1)].
Seller or lessor refuses to deliver the goods and buyer or lessee wants them.	1. Sue for specific performance [UCC 2-716(1), 2A-521(1)]. 2. Replevy the goods [UCC 2-716(3), 2A-521(3)]. 3. Recover the goods from an insolvent seller or lessor [UCC 2-502, 2A-522].

Japan. Many goods sold in the United States are imported from foreign countries.

Additional Issues Affecting Performance and Breach

UCC Articles 2 (Sales) and 2A (Leases) contain several other provisions that affect the parties' performance of a sales or lease contract. These provisions are discussed in the following paragraphs.

Assurance of Performance

Each party to a sales or lease contract expects that every other party will perform their contractual obligations. If one party to a contract has reasonable grounds to believe that the other party either will not or cannot perform his or her contractual obligations, an **adequate assurance** of due performance may be demanded in writing. If it is commercially reasonable, the party making the demand may suspend his or her performance until adequate assurance of due performance is received from the other party [UCC 2-609, 2A-401].

Consider This Example   A buyer contracts to purchase 1,000 bushels of wheat from a farmer. The contract requires delivery on September 1. In July, the buyer learns that floods have caused substantial crop loss in the area of the seller's farm. The farmer receives the buyer's written demand for adequate assurance on July 15. The farmer fails to give adequate assurance of performance. The buyer may suspend performance and treat the sales contract as having been repudiated.

Anticipatory Repudiation

Occasionally, a party to a sales or lease contract repudiates the contract before his or her performance is due under the contract. If the repudiation impairs the value of the contract to the aggrieved party, it is called **anticipatory repudiation**. Mere wavering on performance does not meet the test for anticipatory repudiation.

If an anticipatory repudiation does occur, the aggrieved party can (1) await performance by the repudiating party for a commercially reasonable time (e.g., until the delivery date or shortly thereafter) or (2) treat the contract as having been breached at the time of the anticipatory repudiation, which gives the aggrieved party an immediate cause of action. In either case, the aggrieved party may suspend performance of his or her obligations under the contract [UCC 2-610, 2A-402].

An anticipatory repudiation may be retracted before the repudiating party's next performance is due if the aggrieved party has not (1) canceled the contract, (2) materially changed his or her position (e.g., purchased goods from another party), or (3) otherwise indicated that the repudiation is considered final. The retraction may be made by any method that clearly indicates the repudiating party's intent to perform the contract [UCC 2-611, 2A-403].

Statute of Limitations

The **UCC statute of limitations** provides that an action for breach of any written or oral sales or lease contract must commence within four years after the cause of the action accrues. The parties may agree to reduce the limitations period to one year, but they cannot extend it beyond four years.

Agreements Affecting Remedies

> A proceeding may be perfectly legal and may yet be opposed to sound commercial principles.
>
> L. J. Lindley
> *Verner v. General and Commercial Trust (1894)*

The parties to a sales or lease contract may agree on remedies in addition to or in substitution for the remedies provided by the UCC. For example, the parties may limit the buyer's or lessee's remedies to repair and replacement of defective goods or parts or to the return of the goods and repayment (refund) of the purchase price or rent. The remedies agreed upon by the parties are in addition to the remedies provided by the UCC unless the parties expressly provide that they are exclusive. If an exclusive remedy fails of its essential purpose (e.g., there is an exclusive remedy of repair but there are no repair parts available), any remedy may be had, as provided in the UCC.

Consequential damages for breach of sales or lease contract may be limited or excluded unless the limitation or exclusion is **unconscionable**. With respect to consumer goods, a limitation of consequential damages for personal injuries is prima facie unconscionable. It is not unconscionable to limit consequential damages for a commercial loss [UCC 2-719, 2A-503].

The UCC permits parties to a sales or lease contract to establish in advance the damages that will be paid upon a breach of the contract. Such preestablished damages, called **liquidated damages**, substitute for actual damages. In a sales or lease contract, liquidated damages are valid if they are reasonable in light of the anticipated or actual harm caused by the breach, the difficulties of proof of loss, and the inconvenience or nonfeasibility of otherwise obtaining an adequate remedy [UCC 2-718(1), 2A-504].

Business Ethics

Unconscionable Contract

UCC Article 2 (Sales) and Article 2A (Leases) have adopted the equity doctrine of **unconscionability**. Under this doctrine, a court may determine as a matter of law that a contract is unconscionable. To prove unconscionability, there must be proof that the parties had substantial unequal bargaining power, that the dominant party misused its power in contracting, and that it would be manifestly unfair or oppressive to enforce the contract. This sometimes happens where a dominant party uses a preprinted form contract and the terms of the contract are unfair or oppressive.

If a court finds that a contract or any clause in a contract is unconscionable, the court may refuse to enforce the contract, or it may enforce the remainder of the contract without the unconscionable clause, or it may so limit the application of any unconscionable clause as to avoid any unconscionable result [UCC 2-302, 2A-108]. Unconscionability is sometimes found in a consumer lease if the consumer has been induced by uncon-

scionable conduct to enter into the lease. The doctrine of unconscionability also applies to Web contracts.

1. Does the doctrine of unconscionability encourage ethical behavior? Explain.
2. Is the doctrine of unconscionability necessary? Explain. ■

Chapter Summary

Seller's and Lessor's Performance, p. 318

Tender of Delivery

Tender of delivery requires the seller or lessor to (1) put and hold *conforming goods* at the buyer's or lessee's disposition and (2) give the buyer or lessee any notification reasonably necessary to enable the buyer or lessee to take delivery of the goods [UCC 2-503(1), 2A-508(1)].

Place of Delivery

1. *Agreement.* The parties may agree in the sales or lease contract as to the place of delivery.
2. *No agreement.* If there is no agreement in the contract as to place of delivery, the following UCC rules apply:
   a. *Noncarrier cases.* The place of delivery is the seller's or lessor's place of business, unless the seller or lessor has no place of business, in which case the place of delivery is the seller's or lessor's residence.
   b. *Carrier cases:*
      i. *Shipment contracts.* The sales contract requires the seller to send goods to the buyer by carrier. Delivery occurs when the seller puts the goods in the carrier's possession [UCC 2-504].
      ii. *Destination contracts.* The sales contract requires the seller to deliver the goods to the buyer's place of business or other destination. Delivery occurs when the goods reach this destination [UCC 2-503].

Perfect Tender Rule

The seller or lessor is under a duty to deliver *conforming goods* to the buyer or lessee. If the goods or tender of delivery fails in any respect to conform to the contract, the buyer or lessee may opt to (1) reject the whole shipment, (2) accept the whole shipment, or (3) reject part and accept part of the shipment [UCC 2-601, 2A-509].

Exceptions to the perfect tender rule:

1. *Agreement of the parties.* The parties may agree to limit the effect of the perfect tender rule.
2. *Substitution of carriers.* A seller must use a commercially reasonable substitute if the agreed-upon manner of deliver fails or the agreed upon type of carrier becomes unavailable [UCC 2-614(1)].
3. *Cure.* A seller or lessor who delivers nonconforming goods has the opportunity to *cure* the nonconformity by repairing or replacing defective or nonconforming goods if the time for performance has not expired and the seller or lessor notifies the buyer or lessee of his or her intention to make a conforming delivery within the contract time [UCC 2-508, 2A-513].
4. *Installment contracts.* The buyer or lessee may reject any nonconforming installment if the value of the installment is impaired and the defect cannot be cured. The buyer or lessee may reject the entire contract upon the tender of a nonconforming installment only if the nonconformity substantially impairs the value of the entire contract [UCC 2-612, 2A-510].
5. *Destruction of goods.* If goods identified in the contract are totally destroyed without fault of either party before the risk of loss passes to the buyer or lessee, the seller or lessor is excused from performance [UCC 2-613].

General Obligations

The UCC has adopted the following broad principles that govern the performance of sales and lease contracts:

1. **Good faith.** Parties to a sales or lease contract must perform their contract obligations in *good faith* [UCC 1-203].
2. **Reasonableness.** Many UCC provisions require parties to take *reasonable* steps or to act *reasonably* in performing contract obligations.
3. **Commercial reasonableness.** Some provisions of the UCC require merchants to use *commercial reasonableness* in the performance of their contract obligations.

Buyer's and Lessee's Performance, p. 322

Right of Inspection

Unless otherwise agreed, the buyer or lessee has the right to inspect goods that are tendered, delivered, or identified in the sales or lease contract prior to accepting or paying for them [UCC 2-513(1), 2A-515(1)].

Payment

Duty to pay. Goods that are accepted by the buyer or lessee must be paid for in accordance with the terms of the sales or lease contract. Unless otherwise agreed, payment or rent is due when and where the goods are delivered [UCC 2-310, 2A-516(1)].

Acceptance

Acceptance occurs when the buyer or lessee takes one of the following actions [UCC 2-606, 2A-515]:

1. Signifies in words or by conduct that the goods are conforming or that the goods will be taken or retained despite their nonconformity.
2. Fails to reject the goods within a reasonable time after their delivery by the seller or lessor.
3. Acts inconsistently with the seller's ownership rights in the goods.

Buyers and lessees may only accept delivery of a *commercial unit.*

Seller's and Lessor's Remedies, p. 324

Right to Withhold Delivery

Delivery of goods may be withheld if the seller or lessor discovers that the buyer or lessee is insolvent before the goods are delivered [UCC 2-703(a), 2A-523(1)(c)].

Demand payment in cash. If the seller or lessor discovers that the buyer or lessee is insolvent, he or she may refuse to deliver the goods unless payment is rendered in cash [UCC 2-702(1), 2A-525(1)].

Right to Stop Delivery of Goods in Transit

If the goods are in transit or in the bailee's possession, the seller or lessor may stop delivery (1) of a carload, a truckload, or a planeload of goods if the buyer or lessee repudiates the contract, fails to make a payment when due, or otherwise breaches the contract or (2) of any size shipment if the buyer or lessee becomes insolvent [UCC 2-705(1), 2A-526(1)].

Right to Reclaim Goods

A seller or lessor may reclaim goods in the possession of the buyer or lessee if:

1. The goods are delivered in a credit sale and the seller then discovers that the buyer was insolvent [UCC 2-000].
2. The buyer misrepresented his or her solvency in writing within three months before delivery or paid for goods in a cash sale with a check that bounces [UCC 2-702(2) and 507(2)].

Right to Dispose of Goods

If a buyer or lessee breaches or repudiates the sales or lease contract before the seller or lessor has delivered the goods, the seller or lessor may resell or release the goods and recover damages from the buyer or lessee. Damages are calculated as the difference between the disposition price or rent and the original contract price or rent [UCC 2-706(1), 2A-527(1)].

Right to Recover the Purchase Price or Rent

If the buyer or lessee accepts the goods but fails to pay for them when the contract price or rent is due, the seller or lessor may sue to recover the contracted-for purchase price or rent from the buyer or lessee [UCC 2-709(1), 2A-529(1)].

Right to Recover Damages for Breach of Contract

If a buyer or lessee repudiates a sales or lease contract, the seller or lessor may sue to recover the damages caused by the breach. Damages are calculated as the difference between the original contract price (or rent) and the market price (or rent) of the goods at the time and place the goods were to be delivered, or lost profits [UCC 2-708(1), 2-708(2), 2A-528(1), 2A-528(2)].

Right to Cancel the Contract

The seller or lessor may cancel the sales or lease contract if the buyer or lessee breaches the contract. The seller or lessor is discharged of any further obligations under the canceled contract [UCC 2-106(4), 2A-523(3)].

Buyer's and Lessee's Remedies, p. 327

Seller or Lessor Refuses to Deliver the Goods or Delivers Nonconforming Goods Lessee Does Not Want

1. *Reject nonconforming goods.* If the goods or the seller's or lessor's tender of delivery fails to conform to a sales or lease contract in any way, the buyer or lessee may (1) reject the whole, (2) accept the whole, or (3) accept any commercial unit and reject the rest [UCC 2-601, 2A-509].

2. *Revoke acceptance of nonconforming goods.* A buyer or lessee who has accepted goods may subsequently revoke his or her acceptance if (1) the goods are nonconforming, (2) the nonconformity substantially impairs the value of the goods to the buyer or lessee, and (3) one of the following factors is shown:

   a. The seller's or lessor's promise to reasonably cure the nonconformity is not met,

   b. The goods were accepted before the nonconformity was discovered and the nonconformity was difficult to discover, or

   c. The goods were accepted before the nonconformity was discovered and the seller or lessor assured the buyer or lessee that the goods were conforming [UCC 2-608(1), 2A-517(1)].

3. *Cover.* If the seller or lessor fails to make delivery of goods or repudiates a sales or lease contract or if the buyer or lessee rightfully rejects the goods or justifiably revokes their acceptance, the buyer or lessee may cover by purchasing or renting substitute goods from another party. The buyer or lessee may recover from the seller or lessor damages calculated as the difference between the cost of cover and the original contract price or rent [UCC 2-712, 2A-518].

4. *Sue for breach of contact and recover damages.* If a seller or lessor fails to deliver the goods or repudiates a sales or lease contract, the buyer or lessee may recover damages from the seller or lessor. Damages are calculated as the difference between the contract price (or original rent) and the market price (or rent) at the time the buyer or lessee learned of the breach [UCC 2-713, 2A-519].

5. *Cancel the contract.* A buyer or lessee may cancel a sales or lease contract if the seller or lessor fails to deliver conforming goods or repudiates the contract or if the buyer or lessee rightfully rejects the goods or justifiably revokes acceptance of the goods. The buyer or lessee is discharged from any further obligations under the canceled contract [UCC 2-711(1), 2A-508(1)(a)].

Seller or Lessor Tenders Nonconforming Goods and Buyer or Lessee Accepts Them

1. *Sue for damages.* If a buyer or lessee accepts nonconforming goods from a seller or lessor, the buyer or lessee may recover as damages any loss resulting from the seller's or lessor's breach [UCC 2-714(1), 2A-516(1)].

2. *Deduct damages from unpaid purchase price or rent.* If a seller or lessor breaches the sales or lease contract and the buyer or lessee accepts nonconforming goods, the buyer or lessee may deduct all or any part of the damages resulting from the breach from any part of the price or rent still due under the sales or lease contract [UCC 2-714(1), 2A-516(1)].

Seller or Lessor Refuses to Deliver the Goods and Buyer or Lessee Wants Them

1. *Specific performance.* If the goods are unique or the remedy at law in inadequate, a buyer or lessee may obtain a decree of specific performance that orders the seller or lessor to perform the sales or lease contract [UCC 2-716(1), 2A-521(1)].

2. *Replevy the goods.* A buyer or lessee may replevy (recover) scarce goods from a seller or lessor who is wrongfully withholding them [UCC 2-716(3), 2A-521(3)].

3. *Recover the goods from an insolvent seller or lessor.* If the buyer or lessee makes partial or full payment for the goods before they are received and the seller or lessor becomes insolvent within 10 days after receiving the first payment, the buyer or lessee may recover the goods from the seller or lessor [UCC 2-502, 2A522].

Unconscionable Sales and Lease Contracts

If a sales or lease contract or any clause in it is *unconscionable*, the court may either refuse to enforce the contract or limit the application of the unconscionable clause [UCC 2-302, 2A-108].

Additional Issues Affecting Performance and Breach, p. 331

Assurance of Performance

If one party to a sales or lease contract has reasonable grounds to believe that the other party either will not or cannot perform his or her contractual obligations, he or she may demand in writing an adequate assurance of performance from the other party. The party making the demand may suspend his or her performance until adequate assurance of performance is received [UCC 2-609, 2A-401].

Anticipatory Repudiation

Anticipatory repudiation occurs when a party to a sales or lease contract repudiates the contract before his or her performance is due. The aggrieved party can (1) await performance when due or (2) treat the contract as having been breached at the time of the anticipatory repudiation [UCC 2-610, 2A-402].

Statute of Limitations

The UCC provides that an action for breach of any written or oral sales or lease contract must commence within four years after the cause of action accrues. The parties may agree to reduce the limitations period to one year, but they cannot extend it beyond four years [UCC 2-725, 2A-506].

Agreements Affecting Remedies

1. *Limitations on remedies.* The parties to a sales or lease contract may agree on remedies in addition to or in substitution for the remedies provided by Article 2 or 2A of the UCC [UCC 2-719(1), 2A-503(1)].

2. *Unconscionable limitations.* Any agreement concerning the limitation or exclusion of damages that is found to be unconscionable is unenforceable. With respect to consumer goods, a limitation of consequential damages for personal injuries is prima facie unconscionable [UCC 2-719(3), 2A-503(3)].

3. *Liquidated damages.* The parties to a sales or lease contract may establish in advance the damages that will be paid upon a breach of the contract [UCC 2-718(1), 2A-504].

Internet Exercises and Case Questions

Working the Web Internet Exercises

Activities

1. Use the Cornell Web site at **www.law.cornell.edu/topics/injunctions.html** to review "U.S. Supreme Court: Recent Injunction Decisions."

2. Visit "LII: Law About…Remedies" at **www.law.cornell.edu/topics/remedies.html** and "Legal Information Institute (LII) Commercial Law Overview" at **www.secure.law.cornell.edu/topics/commercial.html**, which includes information on consumer credit, damages, debtors and creditors, injunctions, and remedies.

Determine whether the following are provided in your jurisdiction. Find a leading case for each:

- Punitive damages
- Implied covenant of good faith and fair dealing
- Intentional interference with contractual relations

Critical Legal Thinking Cases

16.1 Nonconforming Goods The Jacob Hartz Seed Company, Inc. (Hartz), bought soybeans for use as seed from E. R. Coleman. Coleman certified that the seed had an 80 percent germination rate. Hartz paid for the beans and picked them up from a warehouse in Card, Arkansas. After the seed was transported to Georgia, a sample was submitted for testing to the Georgia Department of Agriculture. When the department reported a germination level of only 67 percent, Coleman requested that the seed be retested. The second set of tests reported a germination rate of 65 percent. Hartz canceled the contract after the second test, and Coleman reclaimed the seed. Hartz sought a refund of the money it paid for the seed, claiming that the soybeans were nonconforming goods. Who wins? [*Jacob Hartz Seed Co. v. Coleman*, 612 S.W.2d 91, 1981 Ark. Lexis 1153 (AR 1981)]

16.2 Right to Cure On December 21, 1982, Connie R. Grady purchased a new Chevrolet Chevette from Al Thompson Chevrolet (Thompson). Grady gave Thompson a down payment on the car and financed the remainder of the purchase price through General Motors Acceptance Corporation (GMAC). On December 22, 1982, Grady picked up the Chevette. The next day, the car broke down and had to be towed back to Thompson. Grady picked up the repaired car on December 24. The car's performance was still unsatisfactory in that the engine was hard to start, the transmission slipped, and the brakes had to be pushed to the floor to function. Grady again returned the Chevette for servicing on January 6, 1983. When she picked up the car that evening, the engine started, but the engine and brake warning lights came on. This pattern of malfunction and repair continued until March 3, 1983. On that day, Grady wrote a letter to Thompson, revoking the sale. Thompson repossessed the Chevette. GMAC sued Grady to recover its money. Grady sued Thompson to recover her down payment. Thompson claimed that Grady's suit was barred because the company was not given adequate opportunity to cure. Who wins? [*General Motors Acceptance Corp. v. Grady*, 501 N.E.2d 68, 1985 Ohio App. Lexis 10353 (Ohio App. 1985)]

16.3 Revocation of Acceptance Roy E. Farrar Produce Company (Farrar) was a packer and shipper of tomatoes in Rio Arribon County, New Mexico. Farrar contacted Wilson, an agent and salesman for International Paper Company (International), and ordered 21,500 tomato boxes for $.64 per box. The boxes were to each hold between 20 and 30 pounds of tomatoes for shipping. When the boxes arrived at Farrar's plant, 3,624 of them were immediately used to pack tomatoes. When the boxes were stacked, they began to collapse and crush the tomatoes contained within them. The produce company was forced to repackage the tomatoes and store the unused tomato boxes. Farrar contacted International and informed it that it no longer wanted the boxes because they could not perform as promised. International claimed that Farrar had accepted the packages and must pay for them. Who wins? [*International Paper Co. v. Farrar*, 700 P.2d 642, 1985 N.M. Lexis 2000 (NM 1985)]

16.4 Commercial Impracticability Charles C. Campbell was a farmer who farmed some 600 acres in the vicinity of Hanover, Pennsylvania. In May 1973, Campbell entered into a contract with Hostetter Farms, Inc. (Hostetter), a grain dealer with facilities in Hanover. The sales agreement called for Campbell to sell Hostetter 20,000 bushels of No. 2 yellow corn at $1.70 per bushel. Delivery was made in October 1973. Unfortunately, the summer of 1973 was an unusually rainy one, and Campbell could not plant part of his crop because of the wet ground. After the corn was planted, part of the crop failed due to the excessive rain. As a result, Campbell delivered only 10,417 bushels. Hostetter sued Campbell for breach of contract. Campbell asserted the defense of commercial impracticability. Who wins? [*Campbell v. Hostetter Farms, Inc.*, 380 A.2d 463, 1977 Pa.Super Lexis 2699 (PA 1977)]

16.5 Seller's Right to Reclaim Goods Archer Daniels Midland Company (Archer) sold ethanol for use in gasoline. Between April 11 and April 19, 1984, Archer sold 80,000 gallons of ethanol on credit to Charter International Oil Company (Charter). The ethanol was shipped to Charter's facility in Houston. Charter became insolvent sometime during that period. On April 21, Archer sent a written notice to Charter, demanding the return of the ethanol. At the time Charter received the reclamation demand, it had only 12,000 gallons of ethanol remaining at its Houston facility. When Charter refused to return the unused ethanol, Archer sued to recover the ethanol. Who wins? [*Archer Daniels Midland v. Charter International Oil Company*, 60 B.R. 854, 1986 U.S.Dist. Lexis 25828 (M.D. Fla. 1986)]

16.6 Seller's Right to Resell Goods Meuser Material & Equipment Company (Meuser) was a dealer in construction equipment. On December 13, 1973, Meuser entered into an agreement with Joe McMillan for the sale of a bulldozer to McMillan. The agreement called for Meuser to deliver the bulldozer to McMillan's residence in Greeley, Colorado. McMillan paid Meuser with a check. On December 24, before taking delivery, McMillan stopped payment on the check. Meuser entered into negotiations with McMillan in an attempt to get McMillan to abide by the sales agreement. During this period, Meuser paid for the upkeep of the bulldozer. When it became apparent that further negotiations would be fruitless, Meuser began looking for a new buyer. Fourteen months after the original sale was supposed to have taken place, the bulldozer was resold for less than the original contract price. Meuser sued McMillan to recover the difference between the contract price and the resale price as well as for the cost of upkeep on the bulldozer for 14 months. Who wins? [*McMillan v. Meuser Material & Equipment Company*, 541 S.W.2d 911, 1976 Ark. Lexis 1814 (AR 1976)]

16.7 Seller's Right to Recover the Purchase Price C. R. Daniels, Inc. (Daniels), entered into a contract for the design and sale of grass catcher bags for lawn mowers to Yazoo Manufacturing Company, Inc. (Yazoo). Daniels contracted to design grass catcher bags that would fit the "S" series mower made by Yazoo. Yazoo provided Daniels with a lawn mower to design the bag. After Yazoo approved the design of the bags, it issued a purchase order for 20,000 bags. Daniels began to ship the bags. After accepting 8,000 bags, Yazoo requested that the shipments stop. Officials of Yazoo told Daniels that it would resume accepting shipments in a few months. Despite several attempts, Daniels could not get Yazoo to accept delivery of the remaining 12,000 bags. Daniels sued Yazoo to recover the purchase price of the grass bags still in its inventory. Who wins? [*C. R. Daniels, Inc. v. Yazoo Mfg. Co., Inc.*, 641 F.Supp. 205, 1986 U.S.Dist. Lexis 23550 (S.D. Miss 1986)]

16.8 Seller's Right to Recover Lost Profits Saber Energy, Inc. (Saber), entered into a sales contract with Tri-State Petroleum Corporation (Tri-State). The contract called for Saber to sell Tri-State 110,000 barrels of gasoline per month from July to December 1981. Saber was to deliver the gasoline through the colonial pipeline in Pasadena, Texas. The first 110,000 barrels were delivered on time. On August 1, Saber was informed that Tri-State was canceling the contract. Saber sued Tri-State for breach of contract and sought to recover its lost profits as damages. Tri-State admitted its breach but claimed that lost profits is an inappropriate measure of damages. Who wins? [*Tri-State Petroleum Corporation v. Saber Energy, Inc.* 845 F.2d 575, 1988 U.S.App. Lexis 6819 (5th Cir. 1988)]

16.9 Buyer's Right to Demand Specific Performance Dr. and Mrs. Sedmak (Sedmaks) were collectors of Chevrolet Corvettes. In July 1977, the Sedmaks saw an article in *Vette Vues* magazine concerning a new limited-edition Corvette. The limited edition was designed to commemorate the selection of the Corvette as the official pace car of the Indianapolis 500. Chevrolet was manufacturing only 6,000 of these pace cars. The Sedmaks visited Charlie's Chevrolet, Inc. (Charlie's), a local Chevrolet dealer. Charlie's was to receive only one limited-edition car, which the sales manager agreed to sell to the Sedmaks for the sticker price of $15,000. When the Sedmaks went to pick up and pay for the car, they were told that because of the great demand for the limited edition, it was going to be auctioned to the highest bidder. The Sedmaks sued the dealership for specific performance. Who wins? [*Sedmak v. Charlie's Chevrolet, Inc.*, 622 S.W.2d. 694, 1981 Mo.App. Lexis 2911 (Mo. App. 1981)]

16.10 Buyer's Right to Cover and Recover Damages Kent Nowlin Construction, Inc. (Nowlin), was awarded a contract by the state of New Mexico to pave a number of roads. After Nowlin was awarded the contract, it entered into an agreement with Concrete Sales & Equipment Rental Company, Inc. (C&E). C&E was to supply 20,000 tons of paving material to Nowlin. Nowlin began paving the roads, anticipating C&E's delivery of materials. On the delivery date, however, C&E shipped only 2,099 tons of paving materials. Because Nowlin had a deadline to meet, the company contracted with Gallup Sand and Gravel Company (Gallup) for substitute material. Nowlin sued C&E to recover the difference between the higher price it had to pay Gallup for materials and the contract price C&E had agreed to. C&E claims that it is not responsible for Nowlin's increased costs. Who wins? [*Concrete Sales & Equipment Rental Company, Inc. v. Kent Nowlin Construction, Inc.*, 746 P.2d 645, 1987 N.M. Lexis 3808 (NM 1987)]

Business Ethics Cases

16.11 Business Ethics Ruby and Carmen Ybarra purchased a new double-wide mobile home from Modern Trailer Sales, Inc. (Modern). On March 11, 1974, Modern delivered the mobile home to the Ybarras. A few days after delivery, portions of the floor began to rise and bubble, creating an unsightly and troublesome situation for the Ybarras. The Ybarras complained to Modern about the floor as soon as they discovered the defects. Modern sent repairmen to cure the defective floor on at least three occasions, but each time they were unsuccessful. The Ybarras continued to complain about the defects. The Ybarras continued to rely on Modern's assurances that it was able and willing to repair the floor. After four years of complaints, the Ybarras sued to revoke their acceptance of the sales contract. Did the Ybarras properly revoke their acceptance of the sales contract? Did Modern act ethically in this case? Did the Ybarras? [*Ybarras v. Modern Trailer Sales, Inc.*, 609 P.2d 331, 1980 N.M. Lexis 2676 (NM 1980)]

16.12 Business Ethics Allsopp Sand and Gravel (Allsopp) and Lincoln Sand and Gravel (Lincoln) both were in the business of supplying sand to construction companies. In March 1986, Lincoln's sand dredge became inoperable. To continue in business, Lincoln negotiated a contract with Allsopp to purchase sand over the course of a year. The contract called for the sand to be loaded on Lincoln's trucks during Allsopp's regular operating season (March through November). Loading at other times was to be done by "special arrangement." By November 1986, Lincoln had taken delivery of one-quarter of the sand it had contracted for. At that point, Lincoln requested that several trucks of sand be loaded in December. Allsopp informed Lincoln that it would have to pay extra for this special arrangement. Lincoln refused to pay extra, pointing out that the sand was already stock-piled at Allsopp's facilities. Allsopp also offered to supply an employee to supervise the loading. Negotiations between the parties broke down, and Lincoln informed Allsopp that it did not intend to honor the remainder of the contract. Allsopp sued Lincoln. Was it commercially reasonable for Lincoln to demand delivery of sand during December? Did Lincoln act ethically in this case? [*Allsopp Sand and Gravel v. Lincoln Sand and Gravel*, 525 N.E.2d 1185, 1988 Ill.App. Lexis 939 (Ill. App. 1988)]

Briefing the Case Writing Assignment

Read Case A.16 in the Case Appendix [*LNS-Investment Company, Inc. v. Phillips 66 Company*]. This case is excerpted from the district court opinion. Review and brief the case. In your brief be sure to answer the following questions.

1. What did the sales contract provide?

2. Was the contract performed?

3. What is the issue in this case?

4. In whose favor did the court rule?

17

E-Commerce, Domain Names, and Internet Law

"Through the use of chat rooms, any person with a phone line can become a town crier with a voice that resonates farther than it could from any soapbox. Through the use of Web pages, mail exploders, and newsgroups, the same individual can become a pamphleteer."

—Justice Stevens
Reno v. American Civil Liberties Union, 521 U.S. 844 (1997)

Chapter Objectives

After studying this chapter, you should be able to:

1. Describe the free-speech protection granted the Internet by the U.S. Supreme Court.

2. Describe the process for obtaining Internet domain names and the procedure for arbitrating Internet domain name disputes.

3. Define license and the parties to a licensing agreement.

4. Describe the provisions of the Federal Electronics Signatures Act for e-commerce.

5. Describe the Uniform Computer Information Transactions Act (UCITA).

Chapter Contents

- The Internet
- E-mail and Web Contracts
- Domain Names
- E-Commerce and Licensing

In the late 1990s and early 2000s the use of the Internet and the World Wide Web, and the sale of goods and services through **e-commerce**, exploded. Large and small businesses began selling goods and services over the Internet through Web sites and registered domain names. Consumers and businesses can purchase almost any good or service they want over the Internet, using such sites as Amazon.com, eBay, and others. In addition, software and information may be licensed either by physically purchasing the software or information and installing it on a computer or by merely downloading the software or information directly into the computer.

Many legal scholars and lawyers argued that traditional rules of contract law do not adequately meet the needs of Internet transactions and software and information licensing. These concerns led to an effort to create new contract law for electronic transactions. After much debate, the National Conference of Commissioners on Uniform State Laws developed the **Uniform Computer Information Transactions Act (UCITA)**. This model act provides uniform and comprehensive rules for contracts involving computer information transactions and software and information licenses.

This chapter covers the registration of domain names and the operation of Web businesses and explains how the UCITA and other laws regulate the creation, transfer, and enforcement of e-commerce and informational rights licensing contracts.

The Internet

The **Internet**, or **Net**, is a collection of millions of computers that provide a network of electronic connections between the computers. The Internet began in 1969 when the U.S. Department of Defense created electronic communications for military and national defense purposes. Building on this start, in the 1980s the National Science Foundation, the federal government's main scientific and technical agency, established the Net to facilitate high-speed communications among research centers at academic and research institutions around the world.

Eventually, individuals and businesses began using the Internet for communication of information and data. In 1980 there were fewer than 250 computers hooked to the Internet. Growth was rapid in the late 1990s and into the early 2000s, and today there are several hundred million computers connected to the Internet. The Internet's evolution helped usher in the Information Age of today.

In the following case, the U.S. Supreme Court reviewed an important issue concerning free speech over the Internet.

Business Brief

The use of the Internet and the sale of goods and services through e-commerce has exploded in the United States and worldwide.

Our legal system faces no theoretical dilemma but a single continuous problem: how to apply to ever changing conditions the never changing principles of freedom.

Earl Warren (1995)

E-Commerce. The development of electronic commerce has required courts to apply existing laws to new businesses and spurred the federal Congress and state legislatures to enact new laws to govern modern means of communications and the conduct of electronic business.

U.S. SUPREME COURT CASE

Reno, Attorney General of the United States v. American Civil Liberties Union

521 U.S. 844, 117 S.Ct. 2329, 1997 U.S. Lexis 4037 (1997)
Supreme Court of the United States

Case 17.1
Free Speech and the Internet

Background and Facts

Congress enacted the Telecommunications Act of 1996. Title V of the act, known as the Communications Decency Act of 1996 (CDA), contained two important statutory provisions challenged in this case. The first provision, the "indecent transmission" provision, prohibits the knowing transmission of obscene or indecent messages over the Internet to a recipient under 18 years of age. The second provision, the "patently offensive display" provision, prohibits the knowing sending or displaying of patently offensive messages over the Internet in a manner that is available to a person under 18 years of age. Both provisions provide for criminal penalties, including sentencing to jail. Immediately after the statute was signed into law, 47 plaintiffs, consisting of Internet companies and users, sued the United States, alleging that these provisions violated the Freedom of Speech Clause of the First Amendment to the U.S. Constitution. The district court entered a preliminary injunction against enforcement of the challenged provisions. The U.S. Supreme Court agreed to hear the appeal.

Issue

Do the indecent transmission and the patently offensive display provisions of the CDA violate the Freedom of Speech Clause of the First Amendment to the U.S. Constitution?

Court's Reasoning

The U.S. Supreme Court noted that each medium of expression may present its own problems. The Supreme Court stated that some of its cases have recognized special justifications for regulation of the broadcast media that are not applicable to other speakers. In those cases, the Supreme Court relied on the history of extensive government regulation of the broadcast medium, the scarcity of available frequencies at its inception, and its invasive nature. Those factors are not present in cyberspace. The Internet is not as invasive as radio or television. The district court specifically found that "communications over the Internet do not invade an individual's home or appear on one's computer screen unbidden. Users seldom encounter content by accident." It also found that "almost all sexually explicit images are preceded by warnings as to the content" and cited testimony that "odds are slim that a user would come across a sexually explicit site by accident."

The Supreme Court argued that unlike the conditions that prevailed when Congress first authorized regulation of the broadcast spectrum, the Internet can hardly be considered a "scarce" expressive commodity. It provides relatively unlimited, low-cost capacity for communication of all kinds. The Supreme Court stated, "Through the use of chat rooms, any person with a phone line can become a town crier with a voice that res-

onates farther than it could from any soapbox. Through the use of Web pages, mail exploders, and newsgroups, the same individual can become a pamphleteer. . . . Given the vague contours of the coverage of the statute, it unquestionably silences some speakers whose messages would be entitled to constitutional protection."

The Supreme Court noted that systems have been developed to help parents control the material that may be available on a home computer with Internet access. A system may either limit a computer's access to an approved list of sources that have been identified as containing no adult material, it may block designated inappropriate sites, or it may attempt to block messages containing identifiable objectionable features. Although parental control software currently can screen for certain suggestive words or for known sexually explicit sites, it cannot now screen for sexually explicit images. The Supreme Court stated, "Nevertheless, the evidence indicates that a reasonably effective method by which parents can prevent their children from accessing sexually explicit and other material which parents may believe is inappropriate for their children will soon be available."

The Supreme Court was persuaded that the CDA lacks the precision that the First Amendment requires when a statute regulates the content of speech. The Supreme Court concluded, "In order to deny minors access to potentially harmful speech, the CDA effectively suppresses a large amount of speech that adults have a constitutional right to receive and to address to one another." The Supreme Court continued, "The Government may not reduce the adult population to only what is fit for children. The CDA, casting a far darker shadow over free speech, threatens to torch a large segment of the Internet community."

Decision and Remedy

The U.S. Supreme Court held that the indecent transmission and the patently offensive display provisions of the CDA violated the free speech rights of the plaintiffs. The Supreme Court affirmed the decision of the district court.

Case Questions

Critical Legal Thinking   Should the Internet be treated differently from other types of media, such as radio, cable, and television, when it comes to First Amendment free speech issues? Explain.

Business Ethics   What goals was Congress trying to accomplish by enacting the challenged provisions in this case? Are these laudable goals? Are there any goals of others that are opposed to these goals? Explain.

Contemporary Business   Does the Supreme Court's decision have any important economic consequences? If so, to whom?

The World Wide Web

The **World Wide Web** consists of millions of computers that support a standard set of rules for the exchange of information called Hypertext Transfer Protocol (HTTP). Web-based documents are formatted using common coding languages such as Hypertext Markup Language (HTML) and Java. Businesses and individuals can hook up to the Web by registering with a server such as America Online (AOL) or other servers.

Individuals and businesses can have their own Web sites. A Web site is composed of electronic documents known as Web pages. Web sites and pages are stored on servers throughout the world, which are operated by **Internet service providers (ISPs).** They are viewed by using Web browsing software such as Microsoft Internet Explorer and Netscape Navigator. Each Web site has a unique online address. Web pages can contain a full range of multimedia content, including text, images, video, sound, and animation. Web pages can include references, called *hyperlinks*, or *links*, to other Web pages or sites.

The Web has made it extremely attractive to conduct commercial activities online. Companies such as Amazon.com and eBay are e-commerce powerhouses that sell all sorts of goods and services. Existing brick-and-mortar companies, such as Wal-Mart, Merrill Lynch, and Dell Computers, sell their goods and services online as well. E-commerce over the Web will continue to grow dramatically each year.

In the following case, the court addressed the liability of an ISP.

John Doe v. GTE Corporation

347 F.3d 655, 2003 U.S. App. Lexis 21345 (2003)
United States Court of Appeals, Seventh Circuit

Case 17.2
Internet Service Provider

Background and Facts

Someone secretly took video cameras into the locker room and showers of the Illinois State football team. Visual tapes and audio showing these undressed players were displayed at the Web site univ.youngstuds.com operated by Franco Productions. The Internet name concealed the name of the person responsible. The GTE Corporation, an ISP, provided a high-speed connection and storage space on its server so that the content of the Web site could be assessed. The nude images passed over GTE's network between Franco Productions and its customers. The football players sued Franco Productions and GTE for monetary damages. Franco Productions defaulted when it could not be located. Franco Productions was ordered to pay over $500 million in damages, though there is little hope of collection. The U.S. District Court dismissed the case against GTE. The football players appealed.

Issue

Is GTE Corporation, as the ISP, liable for damages to the plaintiff football players?

Court's Reasoning

The Court of Appeals rested its decision on Section 230(c)(1) of the federal Communications Decency Act of 1996, which provides, "No provider or user of an interactive computer service shall be treated as the publisher or speaker of any information provided by another information content provider." In applying this section, the court of appeals held that GTE was not a "publisher or speaker," and therefore was not liable to the football players harmed by the Franco Productions materials. The Court of Appeals stated, "Just as the telephone company is not liable as an aider and abetter for tapes or narcotics sold by phone, and the Postal Service is not liable for tapes sold (and delivered) by mail, so a web host cannot be classified as an aider and abettor of criminal activities conducted through access to the Internet."

Decision and Remedy

The Court of Appeals held that GTE Corporation, as an ISP, was not liable for the nude videos of the football players transmitted over its system by Franco Productions. The Court of Appeals affirmed the District Court's order, dismissing the plaintiff football players' lawsuit against GTE.

Case Questions

Critical Legal Thinking   Why do you think Congress enacted Section 230(c)(1)? Explain.

Business Ethics   Did the owner of Franco Productions act ethically in this case?

Contemporary Business   Will the taking and posting on the Internet of unconsented to photographs of others escalate? Explain.

Electronic Mail

Electronic mail, or **e-mail**, is one of the most widely used applications for communication over the Internet. Using e-mail, individuals around the world can instantaneously communicate in electronic writing with one another. Each person can have an e-mail address that identifies him or her by a unique address. E-mail will continue to grow in use in the future as it replaces some telephone and paper correspondence and increases new communication between persons.

Online Commerce & Internet Law
Anti-Spam Statute

Americans are being bombarded in their e-mail accounts by "spam"—unsolicited commercial advertising. Spammers try to sell you literally anything. In 2003, spam accounted for over 75 percent of all business e-mail traffic. In addition, many spam messages are fraudulent and deceptive, including misleading headers in their subject lines. It takes time and money to sort through, review, and discard unwanted spam.

In 2003, Congress enacted the federal **Controlling the Assault of Non-Solicited Pornography and Marketing Act**, called the **CAN-SPAM Act**. The act (1) prohibits spammers from using falsified headers in e-mail messages and (2) requires spammers who send sexually oriented e-mail to properly label it as such. The Federal Trade Commission (FTC), a federal administrative agency, is empowered to enforce the CAN-SPAM Act.

In effect, the CAN-SPAM Act does not can spam, but instead approves businesses to spam as long as they do not lie. Spam that is not sexually oriented does not even have to be labeled as spam. The act expressly provides that victims of spam do not have the right to bring civil lawsuits against spammers. The CAN-SPAM Act does not regulate spam sent internationally from other countries. In essence, the CAN-SPAM Act is too weak to help consumers ward off the spam that deluges them on a daily basis.

In 2004, the FTC adopted a rule which requires that sexually explicit spam e-mail contain a warning on the subject line reading "SEXUALLY-EXPLICIT." The FTC rule also prohibits the messages themselves from containing graphic material. The graphic material can only appear after the recipient has opened the e-mail message. ■

E-Mail and Web Contracts

Business Brief

Contracts are now being entered into over the World Wide Web and by e-mail.

E-mail and the Web have exploded as means of personal and business communication. In the business environment, e-mail and the Web are sometimes the methods used to negotiate and agree on contract terms and to send and agree to a final contract. Are e-mail and Web contracts enforceable? Assuming that all the elements to establish a contract are present, an e-mail or Web contract is valid and enforceable. The main problem in a lawsuit seeking to enforce an e-mail or Web contract is evidence, but this problem, which exists in almost all lawsuits, can be overcome by printing out the e-mail or Web contract and its prior e-mail or Web negotiations, if necessary.

Online Commerce & Internet Law
Electronic Contracts Meet Writing Requirement of the Statute of Frauds

In 2000, the federal government enacted the **Electronic Signature in Global and National Commerce Act**. This act is a federal statute enacted by Congress and therefore has national reach. The act is designed to place the world of electronic commerce on a par with the world of paper contracts in the United States.

One of the main features of the act is that it recognizes electronic contracts as meeting the writing requirement of the

Statute of Frauds for most contracts. Statutes of Frauds are state laws that require certain types of contracts to be in writing. The new federal act provides that electronically signed contracts cannot be denied effect because they are in electronic form or delivered electronically. The act also provides that record retention requirements are satisfied if the records are stored electronically.

The federal law was passed with several provisions to protect consumers. First, consumers must consent to receiving electronic records and contracts. Second, to receive electronic records, consumers must be able to demonstrate that they have access to the electronic records. And third, businesses must tell consumers that they have the right to receive hardcopy documents of the transaction. ■

Online Commerce & Internet Law
Electronic Signatures Recognized by Federal Law

In the past, signatures have been hand-applied by the person signing the document. No more. In the electronic commerce world, it is now "What is your mother's maiden name?" "Slide your smart card in the sensor," or "Look into the iris scanner." But are electronic signatures sufficient to form an enforceable contract? In 2000, the federal government stepped into the breach and enacted the **Electronic Signature in Global and National Commerce Act**.

One of the main features of this federal law is that it recognizes an *electronic signature*, or *e-signature*. The act gives an e-signature the same force and effect as a pen-inscribed signature on paper. The act is technology neutral, however, in that the law does not define or decide which technologies should be used to create a legally binding signature in cyberspace. Loosely defined, a *digital signature* is some electronic method that identifies an individual. The challenge is to makes sure that someone who uses a digital signature is the person he or she claims to be. The act provides that a digital signature can basically be verified in one of three ways:

1. By something the signatory knows, such as a secret password, pet's name, and so forth.
2. By something a person has, such as a smart card, which looks like a credit card and stores personal information.
3. By biometrics, which uses a device that digitally recognizes fingerprints or the retina or iris of the eye.

The verification of electronic signatures is creating a need for the use of scanners and methods for verifying personal information. ■

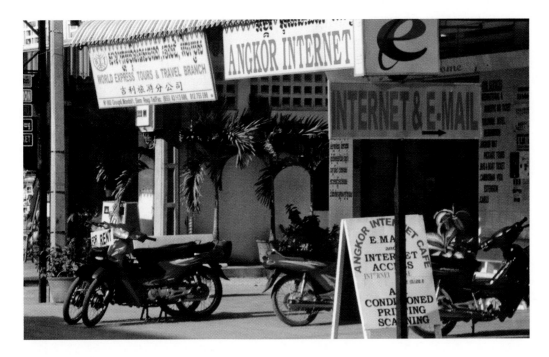

Cambodia. Internet access is available in many countries of the world.

Domain Names

Each Web site is identified by a unique Internet **domain name**. For example, the domain name for the publisher of this book is **www.prenhall.com**. Some of the top-level suffixes for domain names are *.com* for commercial use, *.net* for networks, *.org* for organizations, and *.edu* for educational institutions.

Domain names can be registered. The first step in registering a domain name is to determine whether any other party already owns the name. For this purpose, InterNIC maintains a "Whois" database that contains the domain names that have been registered. The InterNIC Web site is located online at **internic.net**. Domain names can also be registered at Network Solutions, Inc.'s, Web site, which is located at **www.networksolutions.com**, as well as at other sites. An applicant must complete a registration form, which can be done online. It costs less than $50 to register a domain name for one year, and the fee may be paid by credit card online.

The most commonly used top-level extensions for domain names are:

- **.com.** This extension represents the word *commercial* and is the most widely used extension in the world. Most businesses prefer a .com domain name because it is a highly recognized business symbol.

- **.net.** This extension represents the word *network*, and it is most commonly used by ISPs, Web-hosting companies, and other businesses that are directly involved in the infrastructure of the Internet. Some businesses also choose domain names with a .net extension.

- **.org.** This extension represents the word *organization* and is primarily used by non-profit groups and trade associations.

- **.info.** This extension signifies a resource Web site. It is an unrestricted global name that may be used by businesses, individuals, and organizations.

- **.biz.** This extension is used for small-business Web sites.

- **.us.** This extension is for U.S. Web sites. Many businesses choose this extension, which is a relatively new extension.

- **.cc.** This extension was originally the country code for Coco Keeling Islands, but it is now unrestricted and may be registered by anyone from any country. It is often registered by businesses.

- **.bz.** This extension was originally the country code for Belize, but it is now unrestricted and may be registered by anyone from any country. It is commonly used by small businesses.

- **.name.** This new extension is for individuals, who can use it to register personalized domain names.

- **.museum.** This extension enables museums, museum associations, and museum professionals to register Web sites.

- **.coop.** This extension represents the word *cooperative* and may be used by cooperative associations around the world.

- **.aero.** This extension is exclusively reserved for the aviation community. It enables organizations and individuals in that community to reserve Web sites.

- **.pro.** This extension is available to professionals, such as doctors, lawyers, consultants, and other professionals.

- **.edu.** This extension is for educational institutions.

Business Brief

A domain name may be registered by filing the appropriate form with the domain name registration service and paying the appropriate fee.

Online Commerce & Internet Law
Anticybersquatting Act Passed by Congress

In November 1999, the U.S. Congress enacted, and the president signed, the **Anticybersquatting Consumer Protection Act** [15 U.S.C. § 1125(d)]. The act was specifically aimed at cybersquatters who register Internet domain names of famous companies and people and hold them hostage by demanding ransom payments from the famous company or person. In the past, trademark law was of little help in this area, either because the famous person's name was not trademarked or because, even if the name was trademarked, trademark law required distribution of goods or services to find infringement, and most cybersquatters did not distribute goods or services but merely sat on the Internet domain name. The 1999 act has two fundamental requirements: (1) The name must be famous and (2) the domain name must have been registered in bad faith. Thus, the law prohibits the act of cybersquatting itself if it is done in *bad faith*.

The first issue in applying the statute is whether the domain name is someone else's famous name. Trademarked names qualify; nontrademarked names—such as those of famous actors, actresses, singers, sports stars, politicians, and such—are also protected. In determining bad faith, the law provides that courts may consider the extent to which the domain name resembles the holder's name or the famous person's name, whether goods or services are sold under the name, the holder's offer to sell or transfer the name, and whether the holder has acquired multiple Internet domain names of famous companies and persons.

The act provides for the issuance of cease-and-desist orders and injunctions by the court. In addition, the law adds monetary penalties: A plaintiff has the option of seeking statutory damages of between $1,000 and $300,000 in lieu of proving damages. The Anticybersquatting Consumer Protection Act gives owners of trademarks and persons with famous names a new weapon to attack the kidnapping of Internet domain names by cyberpirates.

The following case shows the application of the Anticybersquatting Consumer Protection Act.

For example, the Academy Award–winning actress Julia Roberts won back the domain name *juliaroberts.com* because it had been registered in bad faith by another party. The singer Sting was not so lucky because the word *sting* is generic, allowing someone else to register and keep the domain name sting.com. ∎

E. & J. Gallo Winery v. Spider Webs Ltd.
286 F.3d 270, 2002 U.S. App. Lexis 5928 (2002)
United States Court of Appeals, Fifth Circuit

Case 17.3
Anticybersquatting Consumer Protection Act

Background and Facts

Ernest & Julio Gallo Winery (Gallo) is a famous maker of wines that is located in California. The company registered the trademark "Ernest & Julio Gallo" in 1964 with the United States Patent and Trademark Office. The company has spent over $500 million promoting its brand name and has sold more than four billion bottles of wine. Its name has taken on a secondary meaning as a famous trademark name. In 1999, Steve, Pierce, and Fred Thumann created Spider Webs Ltd., a limited partnership, to register Internet domain names. Spider Webs registered more than 2,000 Internet domain names, including ernestandjuliogallo.com. Spider Webs is in the business of selling domain names. Gallo filed suit against Spider Webs Ltd. and the Thumanns, alleging violation of the federal Anticybersquatting Consumer Protection Act (ACPA). The district court held in favor of Gallo and ordered Spider Webs to transfer the domain name ernestandjuliogallo.com to Gallo. Spider Webs Ltd. appealed.

Issue

Did Spider Webs Ltd. and the Thumanns act in bad faith in registering the Internet domain name ernestandjuliogallo.com?

Court's Reasoning

Spider Webs did not appeal the holdings that Gallo had a valid registration in its trademark, that the mark was famous and distinctive, and that the domain name registered by Spider Webs was identical or confusingly similar to Gallo's mark. However, Spider Webs argued that it did not act with a "bad faith intent to profit," as required by the (ACPA).

The Court of appeals considered the listed bad-faith factors as they applied to this case. The Court found that Spider Webs had no intellectual property rights or trademark in the name "ernestandjuliogallo," aside from its registered domain name. The domain name did not contain the name of Spider Webs or any of the other defendants. Spider Webs had no prior use or

E. & J. Gallo Winery v. Spider Webs Ltd.

286 F.3d 270, 2002 U.S. App. Lexis 5928 (2002)
United States Court of Appeals, Fifth Circuit
(continued)

any current use of the domain name in connection with the bona fide offering of goods or services, and Spider Webs's use was commercial.

In addition, there was uncontradicted evidence that Spider Webs was engaged in commerce in the selling of domain names and that it hoped to sell this domain name some day. The Court stated, "The ACPA was passed to address situations just like this one."

The Court found that Gallo's mark was distinctive and famous. The Court further found that Gallo had registered the mark, which is a family name, 38 years earlier, and "Gallo" had clearly become associated with wine in the United States. The Court stated, "The circumstances of this case all indicate that Spider Webs knew Gallo had a famous mark in which Gallo had built up goodwill, and that they hoped to profit from this by registering **ernestandjuliogallo.com** and waiting for Gallo to contact them so they could assist Gallo."

Decision and Remedy

The Court of Appeals held that the name Ernest and Julio Gallo was a famous trademark name and that Spider Web Ltd. and the Thumanns acted in bad faith when they registered the Internet domain name ernestandjulio.com. The Court of Appeals upheld the district court's decision, ordering the defendants to transfer the domain name to plaintiff E. & J. Gallo Winery.

Case Questions

Critical Legal Thinking   Should Congress have enacted the ACPA? Does it really protect consumers? Explain.

Business Ethics   Did the defendants act ethically in registering so many Internet domain names? What was the motive of the defendants?

Contemporary Business   How valuable is a company's trademark name? Does the ACPA protect that value? Explain.

Online Commerce & Internet Law
Armani Outmaneuvered for Domain Name

G. A. Modefine S. A. is the owner of the famous "Armani" trademark, under which it produces and sells upscale and high-priced apparel. The Armani label is recognized worldwide. But Modefine was surprised when it tried to register for the domain name armani.com and found that it had already been taken. Modefine brought an arbitration action in the World Intellectual Property Organization (WIPO), an international arbitration and mediation center, against the domain name owner to recover the armani.com domain name. To win, Modefine had to prove that the domain name was identical or confusingly similar to its trademark, the owner who registered the name did not have a legitimate interest in the name, and the owner registered the name in bad faith.

The person who owned the domain name, Anand Ramnath Mani, appeared at the proceeding and defended his ownership rights. The arbitrator found that Modefine's trademark and Mr. Mani's domain name were identical but held that Mr. Mani had a legitimate claim to the domain name. The arbitrator wrote that it is "common practice for people to register domain names which are based upon initials and a name, acronyms or otherwise variants of their full names." The court rejected Modefine's claim that Mr. Mani's offer to sell the name for $1,935 constituted bad faith. The arbitrator ruled against Modefine and permitted Mr. Mani to own the domain name armani.com. [*G. A. Modefine S. A. v. A. R. Mani*, WIPO, No. D2001-0537 (2001)] ■

E-Commerce and Licensing

Much of the new cyberspace economy is based on electronic contracts and the licensing of computer information. E-commerce created problems for forming contracts over the Internet, enforcing e-commerce contracts, and providing consumer protection. To address these problems, in 1999 the National Conference of Commissioners on Uniform State Laws (a group of lawyers, judges, and legal scholars) drafted the **Uniform Computer Information Transactions Act (UCITA)**. This is a model act that establishes a uniform and comprehensive set of rules that govern the creation, performance, and enforcement of computer information transactions. A computer information transaction is an agreement to create, transfer, or license computer information or information rights [UCITA § 102(a)(11)].

The UCITA does not become law until a state's legislature enacts it as a state statute. States have adopted the UCITA or laws similar to the UCITA as their law for computer transactions and the licensing of informational rights.

Unless displaced by the UCITA, state law and equity principles, including principal and agent law, fraud, duress, mistake, trade secret law, and other state laws, supplement the UCITA [UCITA § 114]. Any provision of the UCITA that are preempted by federal law are unenforceable to the extent of the preemption [UCITA § 105(a)].

Online Commerce & Internet Law
Counteroffers Ineffectual Against Electronic Agents

In today's e-commerce, many sellers use electronic agents to sell goods and services. An *electronic agent* is any telephonic or computer system that has been established by a seller to accept orders. Voice mail and Web page order systems are examples of electronic agents.

In the past, when humans dealt with each other face-to-face, by telephone, or in writing, their negotiations might have consisted of an exchange of several offers and counteroffers until agreed-upon terms were reached and a contract was formed. Each new counteroffer extinguished the previous offer and became a new viable offer. Most electronic agents do not have the ability to evaluate and accept counteroffers or to make counteroffers. The UCITA recognizes this limitation and provides that a contract is formed if an individual takes action that causes the electronic agent to cause performance or promise benefits to the individual. Thus, counteroffers are not effective against electronic agents [UCITA § 206(a)].

Consider This Example "Birdie" is an electronic ordering system for placing orders for electronic information sold by the Green Company, a producer of computer software and electronic information. Freddie Calloway dials the Green Company's toll-free telephone number and orders new software for $1,000, using the Birdie voice mail electronic ordering system. Freddie enters the product code and description, his mailing address and credit card information, and other data needed to complete the transaction, but at the end of the order states "I will accept this software if, after two weeks of use, I am satisfied with the software." Because Freddie has placed the order with an electronic agent, Freddie has ordered the software, and his counteroffer is ineffectual. ■

Licensing

Intellectual property and information rights are an extremely important asset of many individuals and companies. Patents, trademarks, copyrights, trade secrets, data, software programs, and such constitute valuable intellectual property and information rights.

The owners of intellectual property and information rights often wish to transfer limited rights in the property or information to parties for specified purposes and limited duration. The agreement that is used to transfer such limited rights is called a **license**, which is defined as follows [UCITA § 102(a)(40)]:

> License means a contract that authorizes access to, or use, distribution, performance, modification, or reproduction of, information or informational rights, but expressly limits the access or uses authorized or expressly grants fewer than all rights in the information, whether or not the transferee has title to a licensed copy. The term includes an access contract, a lease of a computer program, and a consignment of a copy.

The parties to a license are the licensor and the licensee. The **licensor** is the party who owns the intellectual property or information rights and obligates him- or herself to transfer rights in the property or information to the licensee. The **licensee** is the party who is granted limited rights in or access to the intellectual property of information rights [UCITA § 102(a)(41), (42)]. A licensing arrangement is illustrated in Exhibit 17.1.

Business Brief

Intellectual property and information rights are valuable assets of individuals and businesses.

Exhibit 17.1

Licensing Arrangement

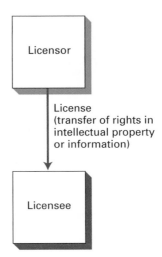

A license grants the contractual rights expressly described in the license and the right to use any information rights within the licensor's control that are necessary to exercise the expressly described rights [UCITA § 307(a)].

Exclusive License

A license can grant the licensee the exclusive rights to use the information. An **exclusive license** means that for the specified duration of the license, the licensor will not grant to any other person rights in the same information [UCITA § 307(f)(2)].

Licensing Agreement

The licensor and licensee usually enter into a written **licensing agreement** that expressly states the terms of their agreement. Licensing agreements tend to be very detailed and comprehensive contracts. This is primarily because of the nature of the subject matter and the limited uses granted in the intellectual property or informational rights.

Beijing, China. The use of the Internet has exploded in China. Chinese is the second-most used language on the Internet after English, and may soon be the first-most used language.

Online Commerce & Internet Law

Consumers Saved from Electronic Errors

The UCITA provides that consumers are not bound by their unilateral electronic errors if the consumer:

1. Promptly upon learning of the error notifies the licensor of the error.
2. Does not use or receive any benefit from the information, or make the information or benefit available to a third party.
3. Delivers all copies of the information to the licensor or destroys all copies of the information, pursuant to reasonable instructions from the licensor.
4. Pays all shipping, reshipping, and processing costs of the licensor. [UCITA § 217]

The UCITA does not relieve a consumer of his or her electronic error if the other party provides a reasonable method to detect and correct or avoid the error. Thus, many sellers establish methods whereby the buyer must verify the information and purchase order a second time before an electronic order is processed. This procedure strips the consumer of the defense of UCITA Section 217. Section 217 of the UCITA applies only to consumers who make electronic errors in contracting. Electronic errors by non-consumers are handled under the common law of contracts or the Uniform Commercial Code (UCC), whichever applies.

Consider This Example Kai, a consumer, intends to order 10 copies of a video game over the Internet from Cybertendo, a video game producer. In fact, Kai makes an error and orders 110 games. The electronic agent maintaining Cybertendo's Web site's ordering process electronically disburses 110 games. The next morning Kai discovers his mistake and immediately e-mails Cybertendo, describing the mistake and offering to return or destroy the copies at his expense. When Kai receives the games, he returns the 110 copies unused. Under the UCITA, Kai has no contract obligation for 110 copies but bears the cost of returning them to Cybertendo or destroying them if Cybertendo instructs him to do so. However, if Cybertendo's Web site's electronic ordering system had asked Kai to confirm his order of 110 copies of the purchase order, and Kai had confirmed the original order of 110 copies, Kai would have had to pay for the 110 copies, even if his confirmation had been in error. ■

Express Warranty

Licensors are not required to do so, but they often make express warranties concerning the quality of their software or information. An **express warranty** is any affirmation of fact or promise by the licensor about the quality of its software or information. An express warranty can result from a description of the information, advertising, samples or models, demonstrations of the final product, and such. An express warranty is not created by the licensor's statements of opinion [UCITA § 402].

Consider This Example   Info, Inc., has developed software for the pricing of securities sold on Nasdaq. Info, Inc., warrants that its software is free from defects and will pay $10,000 liquidated damages and replace the software free of charge if the software does not perform correctly within the first year of use. Here, Info, Inc., has made an express warranty about the quality of its information. Financial Times, Inc., a financial services company, licenses the software from Info, Inc., but after three months of use the software fails. Info, Inc., owes Financial Times, Inc., $10,000 and a free replacement copy of the software [UCITA § 406(a)].

Business Brief

The UCITA does not require a licensor to make an express warranty about the quality of its software or information.

General Disclaimer of Warranties

The UCITA permits a licensor to disclaim all implied warranties by using expressions such as "as is" or "with all faults" or other language that in common understanding calls the licensee's attention to the disclaimer and makes plain that there are no implied warranties [UCITA § 406(c)]. All the implied warranties are also disclaimed with the statement "Except for express warranties stated in this contract, if any, this 'information' [or 'computer program'] is provided with all faults, and the entire risk as to satisfactory quality, performance, accuracy, and effort is with the user" or words of similar import [UCITA § 406(b)(3)]. General disclaimers must be conspicuous.

You must remember that some things that are legally right are not morally right.

Abraham Lincoln (1840)

Online Commerce & Internet Law
Software and Information Access Contracts

Sometimes instead of transferring a copy of information to a licensee, a software license grants the licensee the right to access information in the possession of the licensor. This type of license is called an **access contract**. Access contracts provide for access by the licensee to the information for an agreed-upon time or number of uses. The licensee's access to the information must be available at times and in a manner that complies with the express terms of the license.

The licensee's right of access is to information as periodically modified and updated by the licensor. A change in the content of the information is not a breach of contract unless the change conflicts with express terms in the license. An occasional failure to have access available is not a breach of contract if it is either (1) normal in the business, trade, or industry or (2) caused by scheduling downtime; reasonable periods of failure of equipment, communications, or computer programs; or reasonable needs for maintenance [UCITA § 611]. ■

Breach of License Agreements

> It will be of little avail to the people, that the laws are made by men of their own choice, if the laws be so voluminous that they cannot be read, or so incoherent that they cannot be understood.
>
> Alexander Hamilton
> *The Federalist Papers (1788)*

The parties to a contract for the licensing of information owe a duty to perform the obligations stated in the contract. If a party fails to perform as required, there is a breach of the contract. Breach of contract by one party to a licensing agreement gives the non-breaching party certain rights, including the right to recover damages or other remedies [UCITA § 701].

Licensee's Refusal of Defective Tender If the licensor tenders a copy that is a material breach of the contract, the nonbreaching party to whom tender is made may either (1) refuse the tender, (2) accept the tender, (3) accept any commercially reasonable units and refuse the rest [UCITA § 704].

Licensee's Revocation of Acceptance If a licensee has accepted tender of a copy where the nonconformity is a material breach, the licensee may later revoke his or her acceptance if (1) acceptance was made because discovery was difficult at the time of tender but was then later discovered or (2) the nonconformity was discovered at the time of tender but the licensor agreed to cure the defect, and the defect has not been reasonably cured [UCITA § 707].

Adequate Assurance of Performance Each party to a license agreement expects to receive due performance from the other party. If any reasonable grounds arise prior to the performance date that make one party think that the other party might not deliver performance when due, the aggrieved party may demand adequate assurance of due performance from the other party. Until such assurance is received, the aggrieved party may, if commercially reasonable, suspend performance until assurance is received. Failure to provide assurance within 30 days permits the aggrieved party to repudiate the contract [UCITA § 708].

Remedies

Business Brief
The UCITA provides various remedies that injured parties can obtain against breaching parties.

The UCITA provides certain *remedies* to an aggrieved party upon the breach of a licensing agreement. A party may not recover more than once for the same loss, and his or her remedy (other than liquidated damages) may not exceed the loss caused by the breach [UCITA § 801]. The UCITA provides that a cause of action must be commenced within one year after the breach was or should have been discovered, but not more than five years after the breach actually occurred [UCITA § 805]. Remedies are discussed in the following paragraphs.

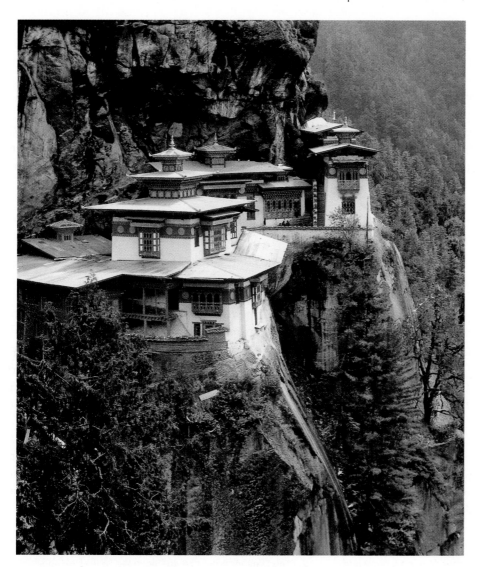

Bhutan. Some countries are behind in developing or permitting Internet access.

Cancellation

If there has been a material breach of a contract that has not been cured or waived, the aggrieved party may cancel the contract. **Cancellation** is effective when the canceling party notifies the breaching party of the cancellation. Upon cancellation, the breaching party in possession or control of copies, information, documentation, or other materials that are the property of the other party must use commercially reasonable efforts to return them or hold them for disposal on instructions from the other party. All obligations that are executory on both sides at the time of cancellation are discharged [UCITA § 802(a) and (b)].

Upon cancellation of a license, the licensor has the right to have all copies of the licensed information returned by the licensee and to prevent the licensee from continuing to use the licensed information.

Licensor's Damages

If a licensee breaches a contract, the licensor may recover **licensor's damages**. The licensor may sue and recover from the licensee monetary damages caused by the breach, plus any consequential and incidental damages [UCITA § 808]. A licensor can recover *lost profits* caused by the licensee's failure to accept or complete performance of the contract. Lost profits is a proper measure of damages in this case because the licensor has effectively unlimited capability to make access available to others so there will be no license to substitute to reduce damages owed by the breaching licensee.

Business Brief

If the contract is a *nonexclusive license*, the licensor can recover lost profits caused by the licensee's failure to accept or complete performance of the contract.

Consider This Example   iSuperSoftware.com licenses a master disk of its software program to Distributors, Inc., to make and distribute 10,000 copies of the software. This is a nonexclusive license, and the license fee is $1 million. It costs iSuperSoftware.com $15 to produce the disk. If Distributors, Inc., refuses the disk and breaches the contract, iSuperSoftware.com can recover $1 million less $15 as damages for the profits lost on the transaction.

Licensor's Right to Cure

Unlike the common law of contracts, the UCITA provides that a licensor has the **right to cure** a breach of a license in certain circumstances. A breach of contract may be cured if (1) the time of performance of the contract has not expired and the licensor makes conforming performance within the time of performance; (2) the time of performance has expired but the licensor had reasonable grounds to believe the performance would be acceptable, in which case the licensor has a reasonable time to make conforming performance; or (3) the licensor makes a conforming performance before the licensee cancels the contract. In all three situations, the licensor must reasonably notify the licensee of the intent to cure [UCITA § 703(a)].

Online Commerce & Internet Law
Electronic Self-Help

Just like normal contracts, electronic licenses can be breached by licensees. If such a breach occurs, the licensor can resort to remedies provided in the UCITA. Sections 815 and 816 of the UCITA provide that a licensor can resort to electronic self-help if a breach occurs—for example, if the licensee fails to pay the license fee. Such electronic self-help can consist of activating disabling bugs and time bombs that have been embedded in the software or information that will prevent the licensee from further using the software or information.

Section 816 provides that a licensor is entitled to use electronic self-help only if the following requirements are met:

1. The licensee must specifically agree to the inclusion in the license of self-help as a remedy. There must be a specific self-help option to which the licensee assents.

2. The licensor must give the licensee at least 15 days' notice prior to the disabling action. The notice period allows the licensee to make lawful adjustments to minimize the effects of the licensor's self-help or to seek a judicial remedy to combat the use of the self-help.

3. The licensor may not use self-help if it would cause a breach of the peace, risk personal injury, cause significant damage or injury to information other than the licensee's information, result in injury to the public health or safety, or cause grave harm to national security.

A licensor who violates these provisions and uses self-help improperly is liable for damages. This liability cannot be disclaimed. ∎

Business Brief

When a licensor breaches a contract, the licensee may sue and recover monetary damages from the licensor.

Licensee's Damages

When a licensor breaches a contract, the licensee may sue and recover monetary damages from the licensor. The amount of the damages depends on the facts of the situation. Upon the licensor's breach, the licensee may either (1) cover by purchasing other electronic information from another source and recover the difference between the value of the promised performance from the licensor and the cost of cover or (2) not cover and recover the value of the performance from the licensor. **Cover** means engaging in a commercially reasonable substitute transaction. The licensee may obtain an award of consequential and incidental damages in either case. A licensee cannot obtain excessive or double recovery [UCITA § 809].

Consider This Example   Auction.com is an Internet company that operates an online auction service. Auction.com enters into a contract with MicroHard, Inc., a software producer, for a site license to use MicroHard, Inc.'s software. Auction.com agrees to pay $500,000 as an initial license fee and $10,000 per month for the license duration of three years. Before Auction.com pays any money under the license, MicroHard, Inc., breaches the contract and does not deliver the software. Auction.com covers by licensing commercially similar software from another software company for the payment of a $600,000 initial licensing fee and $11,000 per month for the license duration of three years. Under the facts of this case, Auction.com can recover $100,000 for the increased initial fee and $36,000 for the increased monthly costs from MicroHard, Inc., for breach of contract.

Licensee Can Obtain Specific Performance

The UCITA provides the remedy of **specific performance** if the parties have agreed to this remedy in their contract or if the agreed-upon performance is unique. The test of uniqueness requires the court to examine the total situation that characterizes the contract [UCITA § 811].

Consider This Example   Nedra enters into a licensing agreement to obtain access to certain informational rights from Info, Inc., for a specified monthly license fee. The data are proprietary to Info, Inc., and are not available from any other vendor. If Info, Inc., breaches the license and refuses to give Nedra access to the information, Nedra can sue and obtain an order of specific performance whereby the court orders Info, Inc., to make the contracted-for information available to Nedra for the duration of the license.

Liquidation of Damages

The parties to a license may provide that damages for breach of contract may be liquidated. **Liquidated damages** are damages that are specified in the contract rather than determined by the court. The amount of liquidated damages must be reasonable in light of the loss anticipated at the time of contracting or the anticipated difficulties of proving loss in the event of breach. The fixing of unreasonably large liquidated damages is void [UCITA § 804].

Limitations of Remedies

The UCITA provides that the parties to an agreement may limit the remedies available for breach of the contract. This is done by including provisions in the contract. Remedies may be restricted to the return of copies and repayment of the licensing fee or limited to the repair or replacement of the nonconforming copies. Limitations of remedies in licenses subject to the UCITA are enforceable unless they are unconscionable [UCITA § 803].

Online Commerce & Internet Law
Electronic Communications Privacy Act

E-mail, computer data, and other electronic communications are sent daily by millions of people using computers and the Internet. Recognizing how the use of computer and electronic communications raise special issues of privacy, the federal government enacted the **Electronic Communications Privacy Act (ECPA)**. The ECPA makes it a crime to intercept an "electronic communication" at the point of transmission, while in transit, when stored by a router or server, or after receipt by the intended recipient. An electronic communication includes any transfer of signals, writings, images, sounds, data, or intelligence of any nature. The ECPA makes it illegal to access stored e-mail as well as e-mail in transmission.

The ECPA provides that stored electronic communications may be accessed without violating the law by the following:

1. The party or entity providing the electronic communication service. The primary example would be an employer who can access stored e-mail communications of employees using the employer's service.
2. Government and law enforcement entities that are investigating suspected illegal activity. Disclosure would be required only pursuant to a validly issued warrant.

The ECPA provides for criminal penalties. In addition, the ECPA provides that an injured party may sue for civil damages for violations of the ECPA. ∎

Chapter Summary

The Internet, p. 341

The Internet and World Wide Web

1. *Internet.* The Internet is a collection of millions of computers that provide a network of electronic connections between computers.
2. *World Wide Web.* The Web is an electronic collection of computers that support a standard set of rules for the exchange of information called Hypertext Transfer Protocol (HTTP).
3. *Electronic mail (e-mail).* E-mail is electronic written communication between individuals using computers connected to the Internet.

E-Mail and Web Contracts, p. 344

E-Mail and Web Contracts

Contracts may be formed electronically over the Internet using e-mail and the World Wide Web.

Electronic Signatures

The Electronic Signature in Global and National Commerce Act (E-Sign Act). This federal statute recognizes and gives electronic signatures—e-signatures—the same force and effect as pen-inscribed signatures on paper. The act is technology neutral in that the law does not define or decide which technologies should be used to create a legally binding signature in cyberspace.

Electronic Privacy

Electronic Communications Privacy Act. This federal statute makes it a crime to intercept an "electronic communication" at the point of transmission, while in transit, when stored by a router or server, or after receipt by the intended recipient.

Domain Names, p. 346

Domain Name

1. ***Domain name.*** A domain name is a unique name that identifies an individual's or a company's Web site.
2. ***Domain name registration.*** Domain names are registered by filing the appropriate form with a domain name registration service and paying the appropriate fee.

Anticybersquatting Act

1. ***Anticybersquatting Consumer Protection Act.*** This federal statute permits a court to issue cease-and-desist orders and injunctions and to award monetary damages against anyone who has registered a domain name (1) of a famous name (2) in bad faith.

E-Commerce and Licensing, p. 348

License

1. ***License.*** A license is a contract that transfers limited rights in intellectual property and informational rights.
2. ***Licensor.*** The owner of intellectual property or informational rights who transfers rights in the property or information to the licensee is called a licensor.
3. ***Licensee.*** The party who is granted limited rights or access to intellectual property or informational rights owned by the licensor is called a licensee.
4. ***Licensing agreement.*** A licensing agreement is a detailed and comprehensive written agreement between the licensor and the licensee that sets forth the express terms of their agreement.
5. ***Access contract.*** An access contract is a type of license that grants the licensee access to the licensed information for an agreed-upon time or number of uses.

The UCITA

1. ***The Uniform Computer Information Transactions Act (UCITA).*** This model act issued by the National Conference of Commissioners on Uniform State Laws establishes a uniform and comprehensive set of rules that govern the creation, performance, and enforcement of computer information transactions.
   a. *Adoption of UCITA by states.* The UCITA does not become law until a state's legislature enacts it as a state statute.

Special Provisions of the UCITA

1. ***Counteroffer rule.*** Counteroffers are not effective against electronic agents. This is because most electronic agents do not have the ability to evaluate and accept counteroffers or make counteroffers.
2. ***Electronic errors.*** The UCITA provides that a *consumer* is not bound by their unilateral electronic errors if the consumer:
   a. Promptly upon learning of the error notifies the other party of the error.
   b. Does not use or receive any benefit from the information, or make the information or benefit available to a third party.
   c. Delivers all copies of the information to the third party or destroys all copies of the information pursuant to reasonable instructions from the other party.
   d. Pays all shipping, reshipping, and processing costs of the other party.
3. ***Electronic self-help.*** If an electronic license has been breached by a licensee, the licensor can resort to electronic self-help such as activating disabling bugs and time bombs that have been embedded in the software or information that will prevent the licensee from further using the software or information. A licensor is entitled to use electronic self-help only if the following requirements are met:

a. The licensee must specifically agree to the inclusion in the license of self-help as a remedy.

b. The licensor must give the licensee at least 15 days' notice prior to the disabling action.

c. The licensor may not use self-help if it would cause a breach of the peace, risk personal injury, cause significant damage or injury to information other than the licensee's information, result in injury to the public health or safety, or cause grave harm to national security.

Warranties

Express warranty. Licensors are not required to do so, but they often make express warranties concerning the quality of their software or information. An express warranty is any affirmation of fact or promise by the licensor about the quality of its software or information.

 Internet Exercises and Case Questions

Working the Web Internet Exercises

Activities

1. For a discussion of the Federal Dilution Act, featuring Barbie, Elvis, and Coca-Cola, see **cyber.law.harvard.edu/ property/respect/antibarbie.html**.

2. For an overview of the Federal Electronic Signatures Act, explore the law review article "Are Online Business Transactions Executed by Electronic Signatures Legally Binding?" at **www.law.duke.edu/journals/dltr/Articles/ 2001dltr0005.html**.

3. Domain name dispute resolution procedures are presented in great detail at **1web.law.harvard.edu/udrp/library. html**. Check this site for everything from an overview to sample pleading forms.

Critical Legal Thinking Cases

17.1 Domain Name   Francis Net, a freshman in college and a computer expert, browses Web sites for hours each day. One day she thinks to herself, "I can make money registering domain names and selling them for a fortune." She has recently seen an advertisement for Classic Coke, a cola drink produced and marketed by the Coca Cola Company. The Coca Cola Company has a famous trademark on the term *Classic Coke* and has spent millions of dollars advertising this brand and making the term famous throughout the United States and the world. Francis goes to the Web site **www.networksolutions.com**, an Internet domain name registration service, to see if the Internet domain name classiccoke.com has been taken. She discovers that it is available, so she immediately registers the Internet domain name classiccoke.com for herself and pays the $70 registration fee with her credit card. Coca Cola Company decides to register the Internet domain name classiccoke.com, but when it checks at Network Solutions, Inc.'s, Web site, it discovers that Francis Net has already registered the Internet domain name. Coca Cola Company contacts Francis, who demands $500,000 for the name. Coca Cola Company sues Francis to prevent Francis from using the Internet domain name classiccoke.com and to recover it from her under the federal ACPA. Who wins?

17.2 E-Mail Contract   The Litle Steel Company is a small steel fabricator that makes steel parts for various metal machine shop clients. When Litle Steel Company receives an order from a client, it must locate and purchase 10 tons of a certain grade of steel to complete the order. The Litle Steel Company sends an e-mail message to West Coast Steel Company, a large steel company, inquiring about the availability of 10 tons of the described grade of steel. The West Coast Steel Company replies by e-mail

that it has available the required 10 tons of steel and quotes $450 per ton. The Litle Steel Company's purchasing agent replies by e-mail that the Litle Steel Company will purchase the 10 tons of described steel at the quoted price of $450 per ton. The e-mails are signed electronically by the Litle Steel Company's purchasing agent and the selling agent of the West Coast Steel Company. When the steel arrives at the Litle Steel Company's plant, the Litle Steel Company rejects the shipment, claiming the defense of the Statute of Frauds. The West Coast Steel Company sues the Litle Steel Company for damages. Who wins?

17.3 Contract   Einstein Financial Analysts, Inc. (EFA), has developed an electronic database that has recorded the number of plastic pails manufactured and sold in the United States since plastic was first invented. Using this data, and a complicated patented software mathematical formula developed by EFA, a user can predict with 100 percent accuracy (historically) how the stock of each of the companies of the Dow Jones Industrial Average will perform on any given day of the year. William Buffet, an astute billionaire investor, wants to increase his wealth, so he enters into an agreement with EFA whereby he is granted the sole right to use the EFA data (updated daily) and its financial model for the next five years. Buffet pays EFA $100 million for the right to the data and mathematical formula. After using the data and software formula for one week, Buffet discovers that EFA has also transferred the right to use the EFA plastic pail database and software formula to his competitor. Buffet sues EFA. What type of arrangement has EFA and Buffet entered into? Who wins?

17.4 License   An Internet firm called Info.com, Inc., licenses computer software and electronic information over the Internet.

Info.com has a Web site, info.com, where users can license Info.com software and electronic information. The Web site is operated by an electronic agent; a potential user enters Info.com's Web site and looks at available software and electronic information that is available from Info.com Mildred Hayward pulls up the Info.com Web site on her computer screen and decides to order a certain type of Info.com software. Hayward enters the appropriate product code and description; her name, mailing address, and credit card information; and other data needed to complete the order for a three-year license at $300 per month; the electronic agent has Hayward verify all the information a second time. When Hayward has completed verifying the information, she types at the end of her order, "I accept this electronic software only if after I have used it for two months I still personally like it." Info.com's electronic agent delivers a copy of the software to Hayward, who downloads the copy of the software onto her computer. Two weeks later Hayward sends the copy of the software back to Info.com, stating, "Read our contract: I personally don't like this software; cancel my license." Info.com sues Hayward to recover the license payments for three years. Who wins?

17.5 Electronic Signature   David Abacus uses the Internet to place an order to license software for his computer from Inet.License, Inc. (Inet), through Inet's electronic Web site ordering system. Inet's Web page order form asks David to type in his name, mailing address, telephone number, e-mail address, credit card information, computer location information, and personal identification number. Inet's electronic agent requests that David verify the information a second time before it accepts the order, which David does. The license duration is two years, at a license fee of $300 per month. Only after receiving the verification of information does Inet's electronic agent place the order and send an electronic copy of the software to David's computer, where he installs the new software program. David later refuses to pay the license fee due Inet because he claims his electronic signature and information were not authentic. Inet sues David to recover the license fee. Is David's electronic signature enforceable against him?

17.6 License   Tiffany Pan, a consumer, intends to order three copies of a financial software program from iSoftware, Inc. Tiffany, using her computer, enters iSoftware's Web site isoftware.com and places an order with the electronic agent taking orders for the Web site. The license provides for a duration of three years at $300 per month for each copy of the software program. Tiffany enters the necessary product code and description; her name, mailing address, and credit card

information; and other data necessary to place the order. When the electronic order form prompts Tiffany to enter the number of copies of the software program she is ordering, Tiffany mistakenly types in "30." Isoftware's electronic agent places the order and ships 30 copies of the software program to Tiffany. When Tiffany receives the 30 copies of the software program, she ships them back to iSoftware with a note stating, "Sorry, there has been a mistake. I only meant to order 3 copies of the software, not 30." When iSoftware bills Tiffany for the license fees for the 30 copies, Tiffany refuses to pay. iSoftware sues Tiffany to recover the license fees for 30 copies. Who wins?

17.7 License   Silvia Miofsky licenses a software program from Accura.com, Inc., to sort information from a database to be used in Silvia's financial planning business. The license is for three years, and the license fee is $500 per month. The new software program from Accura.com will be run in conjunction with other software programs and databases used by Silvia in her business. The licensing agreement between Accura.com and Silvia and the label on the software package state that the copy of the licensed software program has been tested by Accura.com and will run without error. Silvia installs the copy of Accura.com's software, but every fifth or sixth time the program is run, it fails to operate properly and shuts down Silvia's computer and other programs. Silvia sends the software, marked *defective*, back to Accura.com. When Accura.com bills Silvia for the unpaid license fees for the three years of the license, Silvia refuses to pay. Accura.com sues Silvia to recover the license fees under the three-year license. Who wins?

17.8 License   Metatag, Inc., is a developer and distributor of software and electronic information rights over the Internet. Metatag produces a software program called Virtual 4-D Links; a user of the program merely types in the name of a city and address anywhere in the world, and the computer transports the user there and creates a four-dimensional space and a sixth sense unknown to the world before. The software license is nonexclusive, and Metatag licenses its Virtual 4-D Link to millions of users worldwide. Nolan Bates, who has lived alone with his mother too long, licenses the Virtual 4-D Link program for five years for a $350 per month license fee. Bates uses the program for two months before his mother discovers why he has had a smile on his face lately. Bates, upon his mother's urging, returns the Virtual 4-D Link software program to Metatag, stating that he is canceling the license. Metatag sues Bates to recover the unpaid license fees. Who wins?

Business Ethics Cases

17.9 Business Ethics   BluePeace.org is a new environmental group that has decided that expounding its environmental causes over the Internet is the best and most efficient way to spend its time and money to advance its environmental causes. To draw attention to its Web sites, BluePeace.org comes up with catchy Internet domain names. One is macyswearus.org, another is exxonvaldezesseals.org, and another is generalmotorscrashesdummies.org. The macyswearus.org Web site first shows beautiful women dressed in mink fur coats sold by Macy's Department Stores and then goes into graphic photos of minks

being slaughtered and skinned and made into the coats. The exxonvaldezesseals.org Web site first shows a beautiful, pristine bay in Alaska, with the *Exxon Valdez* oil tanker quietly sailing through the waters, and then it shows photos of the ship breaking open and spewing forth oil and then seals who are gooed with oil, suffocating and dying on the shoreline. The Web site generalmotorscrashesdummies.org shows a General Motors automobile involved in normal crash tests with dummies followed by photographs of automobile accident scenes where people and children lay bleeding and dying after an accident involving General Motors automobiles. Macy's Department Stores, the Exxon Oil Company, and the General Motors Corporation sue BluePeace.org for violating the federal ACPA. Who wins? Has BluePeace.org acted unethically in this case?

17.10 Business Ethics Apricot.com is a major software developer that licenses software to be used over the Internet. One of its programs, called Match, is a search engine that searches personal ads on the Internet and provides a match for users for potential dates and possible marriage partners. Nolan Bates subscribes to the Match software program from Apricot.com. The license duration is five years, with a $200 per month license fee. For each subscriber, Apricot.com produces a separate Web page that shows photos of the subscriber and personal data. Bates places a photo of himself with his mother, with the caption, "Male, 30 years old, lives with mother, likes quiet nights at home." Bates licenses the Apricot.com Match software and uses it 12 hours each day, searching for his Internet match. Bates does not pay Apricot.com the required monthly licensing fee for any of the three months he uses the software. After using the Match software but refusing to pay Apricot.com its licensing fee, Apricot.com activates the disabling bug in the software and disables the Match software on Bates's computer. Apricot.com does this with no warning to Bates. It then sends a letter to Bates stating, "Loser, the license is canceled!" Bates sues Apricot.com for disabling the Match software program. Who wins? Did Bates act ethically? Did Apricot.com act ethically?

Briefing the Case Writing Assignment

Read Case A.17 in the Case Appendix [*Toys "R" Us, Inc. v. Abir*]. This case is excerpted from the district court opinion. Review and brief the case. In your brief, be sure to answer the following questions.

1. What law did Toys "R" Us assert had been violated?

2. What elements must be shown to prove that this law has been violated?

3. Did the court find that the law had been violated?

4. Was defendant Abir's conduct ethical?

Warranties and Product Liability

18

"A manufacturer is strictly liable in tort when an article he places on the market, knowing that it is to be used without inspection for defects, proves to have a defect that causes injury to a human being."

—Greenman v. Yuba Power Product, Inc.
59 Cal.2d 57, 27 Cal.Rptr. 697, 1963 Cal. Lexis 140 (1963)

Chapter Objectives

After studying this chapter you should be able to:

1. Identify and describe express warranties.

2. Describe the implied warranties of merchantability and fitness for a particular purpose.

3. Define doctrine of strict liability.

4. Identify defects in manufacture, design, packaging, failure to warn, and failure to provide adequate instructions.

5. List and describe the damages recoverable in warranty and product liability actions.

Chapter Contents

- Warranties of Quality
- Product Liability Based on Fault
- Strict Liability
- The Concept of Defect
- Defenses to Product Liability

The doctrine of *caveat emptor*—let the buyer beware—governed the law of sales and leases for centuries. Finally, the law recognized that consumers and other purchasers and lessees of goods needed greater protection. Article 2 of the Uniform Commercial Code (UCC), which has been adopted in whole or in part by all 50 states, establishes certain **warranties** that apply to the sale of goods. Article 2A of the UCC, which many states have adopted, establishes warranties that apply in lease transactions. Consumers and others can sue to recover damages caused by breach of warranty.

In addition, if a product defect causes injury to purchasers, lessees, users, or bystanders, the injured party may be able to recover for his or her injuries under certain tort theories, including negligence, misrepresentation, and the modern theory of strict liability. The liability of manufacturers, sellers, lessors, and others for injuries caused by defective products is commonly referred to as **products liability**.

The various warranty and tort principles that permit injured parties to recover damages caused by defective products are discussed in this chapter.

Warranties of Quality

Warranties are the buyer's or lessee's assurance that the goods they sell or lease meet certain standards of quality. **Warranties of quality**, which are based on contract law, may be either expressly stated or implied by law. If the goods fail to meet a warranty, the buyer or lessee can sue the seller or lessor for breach of warranty. Warranties are discussed in the following paragraphs.

Express Warranties

Express warranties, which are the oldest form of warranty, are created when a seller or lessor affirms that the goods he or she is selling or leasing meet certain standards of quality, description, performance, or condition [UCC 2-313(1); UCC 2A-210(1)]. Express warranties can be either written, oral, or inferred from the seller's conduct.

It is not necessary to use formal words such as *warrant* or *guarantee* to create an express warranty. Express warranties can be made by mistake because the seller or lessor does not have to specifically intend to make the warranty [UCC 2-313(2); UCC 2A-210(2)].

Sellers and lessors are not required to make such warranties. Generally, they are made to entice consumers and others to buy or lease their products. That is why these warranties are often in the form of advertisements, brochures, catalogs, pictures, illustrations, diagrams, blueprints, and so on.

Express warranties are created when the seller or lessor indicates that the goods will conform to:

1. All *affirmations of fact or promise* made about them (e.g., statements such as "This car will go 100 miles per hour" or "This house paint will last at least five years").
2. Any *description* of them (e.g., terms such as *Idaho potatoes* and *Michigan cherries*).
3. Any *model* or *sample* of them (e.g., a model oil drilling rig or a sample of wheat taken from a silo).

Basis of the Bargain Buyers and lessees can recover for breach of an express warranty if the warranty was a contributing factor—not necessarily the sole factor—that induced the buyer to purchase the product or the lessee to lease the product. This is known as the **basis of the bargain** [UCC 2-313(1); UCC 2A-210(1)]. The UCC does not define the term *basis of the bargain*, so this test is broadly applied by the courts. Generally, all statements by

> When a manufacturer engages in advertising in order to bring his goods and their quality to the attention of the public and thus to create consumer demand, the representations made constitute an express warranty running directly to a buyer who purchases in reliance thereon. The fact that the sale is consummated with an independent dealer does not obviate the warranty.
>
> Justice Francis
> *Henningsen v. Bloomfield Motors, Inc.,* 161 A.2d 69 (NJ 1960)

Ethics Brief

Sellers and lessors of goods do not have to make express warranties concerning the quality of their goods. They often make such warranties to convince people or businesses to purchase or lease goods from them.

the seller or lessor prior to or at the time of contracting are presumed to be part of the basis of the bargain unless good reason is shown to the contrary. Postsale statements that modify the contract are part of the basis of the bargain.

For example, Henry and Michelle go to Metropolitan Jewelers to buy an engagement ring, and the jeweler states that the diamond ring's "four Cs" are 3 carats (the diamond's weight), D color (exceptionally white), VVS clarity (virtually invisible inclusions), and ascher cut. This creates an express warranty. Henry purchases the diamond engagement ring for Michelle, but a later appraisal shows that the actual four Cs of the ring are 1.5 carat, M color (tinted color), P1 clarity (large visible inclusions), and princess cut. Metropolitan jewelers breached the express warranty it made to Henry and Michelle.

Generally, a retailer is liable for the express warranties made by manufacturers of goods it sells. Manufacturers are not liable for express warranties made by wholesalers and retailers unless the manufacturer authorizes or ratifies the warranty.

Statements of Opinion Many express warranties arise during the course of negotiations between a buyer and a seller (or lessor and lessee). The seller's or lessor's **statements of opinion** (i.e., **puffing**) or commendation of the goods do not create an express warranty [UCC 2-313(2)]. For example, a used car salesperson's statement that "This is the best used car available in town" does not create an express warranty. However, a statement such as "This car has been driven only 20,000 miles" is an express warranty. It is often difficult to determine whether the seller's statement is an affirmation of fact (which creates an express warranty) or a statement of opinion (which does not create a warranty).

An affirmation of the *value* of goods does not create an express warranty [UCC 2-313(2)]. For example, statements such as "This painting is worth a fortune" or "Others would gladly pay $20,000 for this car" do not create an express warranty.

Business Brief

Sales "puffing" by salespersons usually does not create a warranty; it is merely a statement of opinion.

Implied Warranty of Merchantability

If the seller or lessor of a good is a merchant with respect to goods of that kind, the sales contract contains an **implied warranty of merchantability** unless it is properly disclaimed [UCC 2-314(1), UCC 2A-212(1)]. This requires the following standards to be met:

- *The goods must be fit for the ordinary purposes for which they are used.* For example, a chair must be able to safely perform the function of a chair. For example, if a normal-sized person sits in a chair that has not been tampered with, and the chair collapses, there has been a breach of the implied warranty of merchantability. If, however, the same person is injured because he or she uses the chair as a ladder and it tips over, there is no breach of implied warranty because serving as a ladder is not the ordinary purpose of a chair.

- *The goods must be adequately contained, packaged, and labeled.* The implied warranty of merchantability applies to the milk bottle as well as to the milk inside the bottle.

- *The goods must be of an even kind, quality, and quantity within each unit.* All the goods in a carton, package, or box must be consistent.

- *The goods must conform to any promise or affirmation of fact made on the container or label.* The goods can be used safely in accordance with the instructions on the package or label.

- *The quality of the goods must pass without objection in the trade.* Other users of the goods should not object to their quality.

- *Fungible goods must meet a fair average or middle range of quality.* To be classified as a certain grade, grain or ore must meet the average range of quality of that grade.

Business Brief

The implied warranty of merchantability does not apply to sales or leases by nonmerchants or casual sales.

Warranties are favored in law, being a part of a man's assurance.

Coke First Institute

Note that the implied warranty of merchantability does not apply to sales or leases by nonmerchants or casual sales. For example, the implied warranty of merchantability applies to the sale of a lawn mower that is sold by a merchant who is in the business of selling lawn mowers. It does not apply when one neighbor sells a lawn mower to another neighbor.

The following case raised the issue of implied warranty of merchantability.

Denny v. Ford Motor Company

639 N.Y.S.2d 250, 87 N.Y.2d 248, 1995 N.Y. Lexis 4445 (1995)
Court of Appeals of New York

Case 18.1
Implied Warranty of Merchantability

Background and Facts

Nancy Denny purchased a Bronco II, a small utility vehicle that was manufactured by Ford Motor Company. Denny testified that she purchased the Bronco for use on paved city and suburban streets, and not for off-road use. On June 9, 1986, when Denny was driving the vehicle on a paved road, she slammed on the brakes in an effort to avoid a deer that had walked directly into her motor vehicle's path. The Bronco II rolled over, and Denny was severely injured. Denny sued Ford Motor Company to recover damages for breach of the implied warranty of merchantability.

Denny alleged that the Bronco II presented a significantly higher risk of occurrence of rollover accidents than did ordinary passenger vehicles. Denny introduced evidence at trial that showed that the Bronco II had a low stability index because of its high center of gravity, narrow tracks, and shorter wheel base, as well as the design of its suspension system. Ford countered that the Bronco II was intended as an off-road vehicle and was not designed to be used as a conventional passenger automobile on paved streets. The trial court found Ford liable and awarded Denny $1.2 million in damages. Ford appealed.

Issue

Did Ford Motor Company breach the implied warranty of merchantability?

Court's Reasoning

The plaintiff introduced a Ford marketing manual that predicted that many buyers would be attracted to the Bronco II because utility vehicles were suitable to "contemporary lifestyles" in some suburban areas. According to this manual, the sales pre-

sentation of the Bronco II should take into account the vehicle's "suitability for commuting and for suburban and city driving." In addition, the vehicle's ability to switch between two-wheel and four-wheel drive would "be particularly appealing to women who may be concerned about driving in snow and ice with their children." The plaintiff also adduced proof that the Bronco II's design characteristics made it unusually susceptible to rollover accidents when used on paved roads. All this evidence was useful in showing that routine highway and street driving was the "ordinary purpose" for which the Bronco II was sold and that it was not "fit"—or safe—for that purpose. The court concluded that under the evidence in this case, a rational fact finder could have concluded that the vehicle was not safe for the "ordinary purpose" of daily driving for which it was marketed and sold.

Decision and Remedy

The court of appeals held that Ford had breached the implied warranty of merchantability and upheld the jury award for the plaintiff.

Case Questions

Critical Legal Thinking Should the law impose an *implied* warranty of merchantability in the sale of goods? What is the public policy underlying this implied warranty?

Business Ethics Did Ford act ethically in defending that the Bronco II was sold only as an off-road vehicle? Was this argument persuasive?

Contemporary Business What are the business implications of this decision? Do you think that utility vehicles such as the Bronco II have a higher rollover danger than normal passenger automobiles?

Implied Warranty of Fitness for Human Consumption The common law implied a special warranty—the **implied warranty of fitness for human consumption**—to food products. The UCC incorporates this warranty, which applies to food and drink consumed on or off the premises, within the implied warranty of merchantability. Restaurants, grocery stores, fast-food outlets, and vending-machine operators are all subject to this warranty. States use one of the following two tests in determining whether there has been a breach of the implied warranty of fitness for human consumption:

- ■ *Foreign substance test.* Under this test, a food product is unmerchantable if a foreign object in that product causes injury to a person. For example, the warranty would be breached if an injury were caused by a nail in a cherry pie. If the same injury were caused by a cherry pit in the pie, the pie would not be unmerchantable.

■ ***Consumer expectation test.*** The majority of states have adopted the modern consumer expectation test to determine the merchantability of food products. For example, under this implied warranty, if a person is injured by a chicken bone while eating fried chicken, the injury is not actionable. However, the warranty would be breached if a person were injured by a chicken bone while eating a chicken salad sandwich. This is because a consumer would expect that the food preparer would have removed all bones from the chicken.

Business Brief

The consumer expectation test is the modern test adopted by the majority of states to determine merchantability based on what the average consumer would expect to find in food products.

Implied Warranty of Fitness for a Particular Purpose

The UCC contains an implied **warranty of fitness for a particular purpose**. This implied warranty is breached if the goods do not meet the buyer's or lessee's expressed needs. The warranty applies to both merchant and nonmerchant sellers and lessors.

The warranty of fitness for a particular purpose is implied at the time of contracting if:

1. The seller or lessor has reason to know the particular purpose for which the buyer is purchasing the goods or the lessee is leasing the goods.
2. The seller or lessor makes a statement that the goods will serve this purpose.
3. The buyer or lessee relies on the seller's or lessor's skill and judgment and purchases or leases the goods [UCC 2-315, UCC 2A-213].

Consider This Example   Susan Logan wants to buy lumber to build a house, so she goes to Winter's lumber yard. Logan describes to Winter the house she intends to build. She also tells Winter that she is relying on him to select the right lumber. Winter selects the lumber, and Logan buys it and builds the house. Unfortunately, the house collapses because the lumber was not strong enough to support it. Logan can sue Winter for breach of the implied warranty of fitness for a particular purpose.

Restaurant, Sault Ste. Marie, Michigan. The majority of states have adopted the modern consumer expectation tests to determine the merchantablity of food products.

Concept Summary   Express and Implied Warranties of Quality

Type of Warranty	How Created	Description
Express warranty	Made by the seller or lessor.	Affirms that the goods meet certain standards of quality, description, performance, or condition [UCC 2-313(1), UCC 2A-210(1)].
Implied warranty of merchantability	Implied by law if the seller or lessor is a merchant.	Implies that the goods: 1. Are fit for the ordinary purposes for which they are used. 2. Are adequately contained, packaged, and labeled. 3. Are of an even kind, quality, and quantity within each unit. 4. Conform to any promise or affirmation of fact made on the container or label. 5. Pass without objection in the trade. 6. Meet a fair, average, or middle range of quality for fungible goods [UCC 2-314(1), UCC 2A-212(1)].
Implied warranty of fitness for a particular purpose	Implied by law.	Implies that the goods are fit for the purpose for which the buyer or lessee acquires the goods if: 1. The seller or lessor has reason to know the particular purpose for which the goods will be used, 2. The seller or lessor makes a statement that the goods will serve that purpose, and 3. The buyer or lessee relies on the statement and buys or leases the goods [UCC 2-315, UCC 2A-213].

Damages Recoverable for Breach of Warranty

Where there has been a breach of warranty, the buyer or lessee may sue the seller or lessor to recover **compensatory damages**. The amount of recoverable compensatory damages is generally equal to the difference between (1) the value of the goods as warranted and (2) the actual value of the goods accepted at the time and place of acceptance [UCC 2-714(2), UCC 2A-508(4)]. A purchaser or lessee can recover for personal injuries that are caused by a breach of warranty.

Consider This Example   Suppose a used car salesperson warrants that a used car has been driven only 20,000 miles. If true, that would make the car worth $10,000. The salesperson gives the buyer a "good deal" and sells the car for $8,000. Unfortunately, the car was worth only $4,000 because it was actually driven 100,000 miles. The buyer discovers the breach of warranty and sues the salesperson for damages. The buyer can recover $6,000 ($10,000 warranted value minus $4,000 actual value). The contract price ($8,000) is irrelevant to this computation.

Consider This Example   Suppose Frances Gordon purchases new tires for her car, and the manufacturer expressly warrants the tires against blowout for 50,000 miles. Suppose one of the tires blows out after being used only 20,000 miles, causing severe injury to Ms. Gordon. She can recover personal injury damages from the manufacturer because of the breach of warranty.

Warranty Disclaimers

Warranties can be **disclaimed** or limited. If an *express warranty* is made, it can be limited only if the **warranty disclaimer** and the warranty can be reasonably construed with each other.

All implied warranties of quality may be disclaimed by expressions such as *as is*, *with all faults*, or other language that makes it clear to the buyer that there are no implied warranties. This type of disclaimer is often included in sales contracts for used products. If the preceding language is not used, disclaimers of the *implied warranty of merchantability* must specifically mention the term *merchantability*. These disclaimers may be oral or written.

The *implied warranty of fitness for a particular purpose* may be disclaimed in general language, without specific use of the term *fitness*. For example, language such as "There are no warranties that extend beyond the description on the fact hereof" is sufficient to disclaim the fitness warranty. The disclaimer must be in writing.

Conspicuous Display of Disclaimer   Written disclaimers must be conspicuously displayed to be valid. The courts construe **conspicuous** as noticeable to a reasonable person [UCC 2-316, UCC 2A-214]. For example, a heading printed in capitals or typeface that is larger or in a different style than the rest of the body of a sales or lease contract will be considered to be conspicuous. Different-color type is also considered conspicuous.

Magnuson–Moss Warranty Act

In 1975, Congress enacted the **Magnuson–Moss Warranty Act**, which covers written warranties relating to *consumer* products.[1] This federal act is administered by the Federal Trade Commission (FTC). Commercial and industrial transactions are not governed by the act.

The act does not require a seller or lessor to make express written warranties. However, persons who do make such warranties are subject to the provisions of the act. If the cost of the good is more than $10 and the warrantor chooses to make an express warranty, the Magnuson–Moss Warranty Act requires that the warranty be labeled as either "full" or "limited."

To qualify as a **full warranty**, the warrantor must guarantee free repair or replacement of the defective product. The warrantor must indicate whether there is a time limit on the full warranty (e.g., "full 36-month warranty"). **In a limited warranty**, the warrantor limits the scope of a full warranty in some way (e.g., a return of the purchase price or replacement or such). The fact that the warranty is full or limited must be conspicuously displayed. The disclosures must be in "understandable language."

A consumer may bring a civil action against a defendant for violating the provisions of the act. A successful plaintiff can recover damages, attorneys' fees, and other costs incurred in bringing the action. The act authorizes warrantors to establish an informal dispute resolution procedure. The procedure must be conspicuously described in the written warranty. Aggrieved consumers must assert their claims through this procedure before they can take legal action.

The act does not create any implied warranties. It does, however, modify the state law of implied warranties in one crucial respect: Sellers or lessors who make express written warranties relating to consumer products are forbidden from disclaiming or modifying the implied warranties of merchantability and fitness for a particular purpose. A seller or lessor may set a time limit on implied warranties, but this time limit must correspond to the duration of any express warranty.

Business Brief
Read all warranty notices carefully to see if any warranties have been disclaimed.

Business Brief
Sellers or lessors who make express written warranties relating to consumer products are forbidden from disclaiming or modifying the implied warranties of merchantability and fitness for a particular purpose.

Online Commerce & Internet Law
Warranty Disclaimers in Software Licenses

Most software companies license their software to users. A software license is a complex contract that contains the terms of the license. Most software licenses contain warranty disclaimer and limitation on liability clauses that limit the licensor's liability if the software malfunctions. Disclaimer of warranty and limitation on liability clauses that are included in a typical software license appear below. ■

SOFTWARE.COM, INC.
LIMITATION AND WAIVERS OF WARRANTIES,
REMEDIES, AND CONSEQUENTIAL DAMAGES

Limited Warranty. Software.com, Inc. warrants that (a) the software will perform substantially in accordance with the accompanying written materials for a period of 90 days from the date of receipt, and (b) any hardware accompanying the software will be free from defects in materials and workmanship under normal use and service for a period of one year from the date of the receipt. Any implied warranties on the software and hardware are limited to 90 days and one (1) year, respectively. Some states do not allow limitations on duration of an implied warranty, so the above limitation may not apply to you.

Customer Remedies. Software.com, Inc.'s entire liability and your exclusive remedy shall be, at Software.com, Inc.'s option, either (a) return of the price paid or (b) repair or replacement of the software or hardware that does not meet Software.com, Inc.'s Limited Warranty and that is returned to Software.com, Inc. with a copy of your receipt. This Limited Warranty is void if failure of the software or hardware has resulted from accident, abuse, or misapplication. Any replacement software will be warranted for the remainder of the original warranty or 30 days, whichever is longer. These remedies are not available outside the United States of America.

No Other Warranties. Software.com, Inc. disclaims all other warranties, either express or implied, including but not limited to implied warranties of merchantability and fitness for a particular purpose, with respect to the software, the accompanying written materials, and any accompanying hardware. This Limited Warranty gives you specific legal rights. You may have others, which vary from state to state.

No Liability for Consequential Damages. In no event shall Software.com, Inc. or its suppliers be liable for any damages whatsoever (including, without limitation, damages for loss of business profits, business interruption, loss of business information, or other pecuniary loss) arising out of the use of or inability to use this Software.com, Inc. product, even if Software.com, Inc. has been advised of the possibility of such damages. Because some states do not allow the exclusion or limitation of liability for consequential or incidental damages, the above limitation may not apply to you.

Product Liability Based on Fault

Depending on the circumstances of the case, persons who are injured by defective products may be able to recover damages under the tort theories of *negligence* and *misrepresentation*. Both theories require the defendant to be *at fault* for causing the plaintiff's injuries. These theories are discussed in the paragraphs that follow.

Misrepresentation

A buyer or lessee who is injured because a seller or lessor fraudulently misrepresented the quality of a product can sue the seller for the tort of **intentional misrepresentation**, or **fraud**. Recovery is limited to persons who were injured because they relied on the misrepresentation.

Intentional misrepresentation occurs where a seller or lessor either (1) affirmatively misrepresents the quality of a product or (2) conceals a defect in it. Because most reputable manufacturers, sellers, and lessors do not intentionally misrepresent the quality of their products, fraud is not often used as the basis for product liability actions.

Negligence

A person injured by a defective product may bring an action for **negligence** against the negligent party. To be successful, the plaintiff must prove that the defendant breached a duty of due care to the plaintiff that caused the plaintiff's injuries. Failure to exercise due care includes failing to assemble the product carefully, negligent product design, negligent inspection or testing of the product, negligent packaging, failure to warn of the dangerous propensities of the product, and such. It is important to note that in a negligence lawsuit, only a party who was actually negligent is liable to the plaintiff.

The plaintiff and the defendant do not have to be in privity of contract.[2] For example, in the landmark case *MacPherson v. Buick Motor Co.*,[3] the court held that an injured consumer could recover damages from the manufacturer of a product even though the consumer was only in privity of the contract with the retailer from whom he had purchased the product. The plaintiff generally bears the difficult burden of proving that the defendant was negligent.

Consider This Example   Assume that the purchaser of a motorcycle is injured in an accident. The accident occurred because a screw was missing from the motorcycle. How does the buyer prove who was negligent? Was it the manufacturer, who left the screw out during the assembly of the motorcycle? Was it the retailer, who negligently failed to discover the missing screw while preparing the motorcycle for sale? Was it the mechanic, who failed to replace the screw after repairing the motorcycle? Negligence remains a viable, yet difficult, theory on which to base a product liability action.

Landmark Law

In *MacPherson v. Buick Motor Co.*, the court held that an injured consumer could recover damages from the manufacturer of a product even though he or she was only in privity of contract with the retailer from whom he or she had purchased the product.

Strict Liability

In the landmark case *Greenmun v. Yuba Power Products, Inc.*,[4] the California supreme court adopted the **doctrine of strict liability in tort** as a basis for product liability actions. Most states have now adopted this doctrine as a basis for product liability actions. The doctrine of strict liability removes many of the difficulties for the plaintiff associated with other theories of product liability. The remainder of this chapter examines the scope of the strict liability doctrine.

Business Brief

In *Greenmun v. Yuba Power Products, Inc.*, the California supreme court adopted the doctrine of strict liability in tort for product liability actions.

Santa Monica, California. The doctrine of strict liability applies to the sale of goods, including food products, in most states in the United States.

All in the Chain of Distribution Are Liable

All parties in the **chain of distribution** of a defective product are **strictly liable** for the injuries caused by that product. Thus, all manufacturers, distributors, wholesalers, retailers, lessors, and subcomponent manufacturers may be sued under the **doctrine of strict liability in tort**. This view is based on public policy. Lawmakers presume that sellers and lessors will insure against the risk of a strict liability lawsuit and spread the cost to their consumers by raising the price of products.

Consider This Example   Suppose a subcomponent manufacturer produces a defective tire and sells it to a truck manufacturer. The truck manufacturer places the defective tire on one of its new-model trucks. The truck is distributed by a distributor to a retail dealer. Ultimately, the retail dealer sells the truck to a buyer. The defective tire causes an accident in which the buyer is injured. All the parties in the tire's chain of distribution can be sued by the injured party; in this case, the liable parties are the subcomponent manufacturer, the truck manufacturer, the distributor, and the retailer.

A defendant who has not been negligent but who is made to pay a strict liability judgment can bring a separate action against the negligent party in the chain of distribution to recover its losses. In the preceding example, for instance, the retailer could sue the manufacturer to recover the strict liability judgment assessed against it.

Exhibit 18.1 compares the doctrines of negligence and strict liability.

Exhibit 18.1

Doctrines of Negligence and Strict Liability Compared

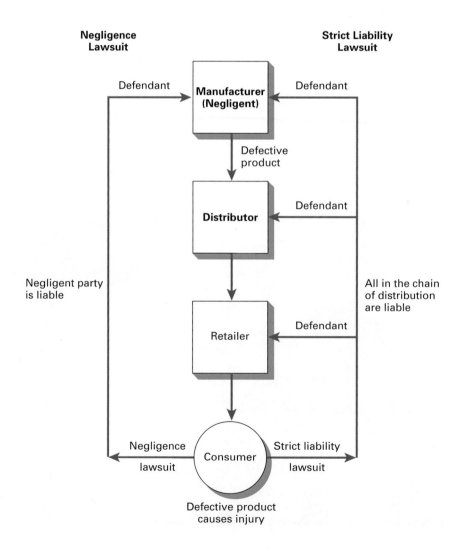

Parties Who Can Recover for Strict Liability

Because strict liability is a tort doctrine, privity of contract between the plaintiff and the defendant is not required. In other words, the doctrine applies even if the injured party had no contractual relations with the defendant. Under strict liability, sellers and lessors are liable to the ultimate user or consumer. Users include the purchaser or lessee, family members, guests, employees, customers, and persons who passively enjoy the benefits of the product (e.g., passengers in automobiles).

Most jurisdictions have judicially or statutorily extended the protection of strict liability to bystanders. The courts have stated that bystanders should be entitled to even greater protection than a consumer or user. This is because consumers and users have the chance to inspect for defects and to limit their purchases to articles manufactured by reputable manufacturers and sold by reputable retailers, whereas bystanders do not have the same opportunity.

Business Brief

Privity of contract is not required for a plaintiff to sue for strict liability.

Business Brief

Strict liability law imposes liability without fault on manufacturers, sellers, and lessors who make and distribute defective products that cause injury to users and others.

Damages Recoverable for Strict Liability

The damages recoverable in a strict liability action vary by jurisdiction. Damages for personal injuries are recoverable in all jurisdictions that have adopted the doctrine of strict liability, although some jurisdictions limit the dollar amount of the award. Property damage is recoverable in most jurisdictions, but economic loss (e.g., lost income) is recoverable in only a few jurisdictions. *Punitive damages* are generally allowed if the plaintiff can prove that the defendant either intentionally injured him or her or acted with reckless disregard for his or her safety.

Business Brief

Punitive damages are often awarded in strict liability lawsuits if the plaintiff proves that the defendant either intentionally injured him or her or acted with reckless disregard for his or her safety.

Contemporary Environment
Strict Liability in Tort

The most widely recognized articulation of the doctrine of strict liability in tort is found in **Section 402A** of the *Restatement (Second) of Torts*, which provides

1. One who sells any product in a defective condition unreasonably dangerous to the user or consumer or to his property is subject to liability for physical harm thereby caused to the ultimate user or consumer, or to his property, if
   a. the seller is engaged in the business of selling such a product, and
   b. it is expected to and does reach the user or consumer without substantial change in the condition in which it is sold.
2. The rule stated in Subsection (1) applies although
   a. the seller has exercised all possible care in the preparation and sale of his product, and
   b. the user or consumer has not bought the product from or entered into any contractual relation with the seller.

In 1997, the American Law Institute (ALI) adopted the *Restatement (Third) of Torts: Product Liability*. This new *Restatement* includes the following definition of defect:

A product is defective when, at the time of sale or distribution, it contains manufacturing defect, is defective in design, or is defective because of inadequate instructions or warnings.

A product:

a. contains a manufacturing defect when the product departs from its intended design even though all possible care was exercised in the preparation and marketing of the product;
b. is defective in design when the foreseeable risks of harm posed by the product could have been reduced or avoided by the adoption of a reasonable alternative design by the seller or other distributor, or a predecessor in the commercial chain of distribution, and the omission of the alternative design renders the product not reasonably safe;
c. is defective because of inadequate instructions or warnings when the foreseeable risks of harm posed by the product could have been reduced or avoided by the provision of reasonable instructions or warnings by the seller or other distributor, or a predecessor in the commercial chain of distribution, and the omission of the instructions or warnings renders the product not reasonably safe. ■

The Concept of Defect

To recover for strict liability, the injured party must first show that the product that caused the injury was somehow **defective**. (Remember that the injured party does not have to prove who caused the product to become defective.) Plaintiffs can allege multiple product defects in one lawsuit. A product can be found to be defective in many ways. The most common types of defects are *defects in manufacture*, *design*, and *packaging* and *failure to warn*. These defects are discussed in the following paragraphs.

Defect in Manufacture

A **defect in manufacture** occurs when the manufacturer fails to (1) properly assemble a product, (2) properly test a product, or (3) adequately check the quality of a product.

The following case is a classic example involving a defect in manufacture.

Shoshone Coca-Cola Bottling Co. v. Dolinski
420 P.2d 855, 1966 Nev. Lexis 260 (1967)
Supreme Court of Nevada

Case 18.2
Defect in Manufacture

Background and Facts

Leo Dolinski purchased a bottle of Squirt, a soft drink, from a vending machine at a Sea and Ski plant, his place of employment. Dolinski opened the bottle and consumed part of its contents. He immediately became ill. Upon examination, it was found that the bottle contained the decomposed body of a mouse, mouse hair, and mouse feces. Dolinski visited a doctor and was given medicine to counteract nausea. Dolinski suffered physical and mental distress from consuming the decomposed mouse and thereafter possessed an aversion to soft drinks. The Shoshone Coca-Cola Bottling Company (Shoshone) had manufactured and distributed the Squirt bottle. Dolinski sued Shoshone, basing his lawsuit on the doctrine of strict liability. The state of Nevada had not previously recognized the doctrine of strict liability. However, the trial court adopted the doctrine of strict liability, and the jury returned a verdict in favor of the plaintiff. Shoshone appealed.

Issue

Should the state of Nevada judicially adopt the doctrine of strict liability? If so, was there a defect in the manufacture of the Squirt bottle that caused the plaintiff's injuries?

Court's Reasoning

In adopting the doctrine of strict liability, the court stated, "Public policy demands that one who places upon the market a bottled beverage in a condition dangerous for use must be held strictly liable to the ultimate user for injuries resulting from such use, although the seller has exercised all reasonable care."

Decision and Remedy

The supreme court of Nevada adopted the doctrine of strict liability and held that the evidence supported the trial court's finding that there was a defect in manufacture. The supreme court affirmed the trial court's decision.

Case Questions

Critical Legal Thinking   Should the courts adopt the theory of strict liability? Why or why not?

Business Ethics   Was it ethical for Shoshone to argue that it was not liable to Dolinski?

Contemporary Business   Should all in the chain of distribution of a defective product—even parties that are not responsible for the defect—be held liable under the doctrine of strict liability? Or should liability be based only on fault?

Defect in Design

A **defect in design** can support a strict liability action. Design defects that have supported strict liability awards include toys that are designed with removable parts that could be swallowed by children, machines and appliances designed without proper safeguards, and trucks and other vehicles designed without a warning device to let people know that the vehicle is backing up.

In evaluating the adequacy of a product's design, the courts apply a risk-utility analysis and consider the gravity of the danger posed by the design, the likelihood that injury will occur, the availability and cost of producing a safer alternative design, the social utility of the product, and other factors.

The following design defect case demonstrates the application of a risk-utility analysis.

Lakin v. Senco Products, Inc.
925 P.2d 107, 1996 One.App. Lexis 1466 (1996)
Court of Appeals of Oregon

Case 18.3
Defect in Design

Background and Facts

Senco Products, Inc. (Senco), manufactures and markets a variety of pneumatic nail guns, including the SN325 nail gun, which discharges 3.25-inch nails. The SN325 uses special nails designed and sold by Senco. The SN325 will discharge a nail only if two trigger mechanisms are activated; that is, the user must both squeeze the nail gun's finger trigger and press the nail gun's muzzle against a surface, activating the bottom trigger, or safety. The SN325 can fire up to nine nails per second if the trigger is continuously depressed and the gun is bounced along the work surface, constantly reactivating the muzzle safety/trigger.

On December 1, 1990, John Lakin was using a Senco SN325 nail gun to help build a new home. When attempting to nail two-by-fours under the eaves of the garage, Lakin stood on tiptoe and raised a two-by-four over his head. As he held the board in position with his left hand and the nail gun in his right hand, he pressed the nose of the SN325 up against the board, depressed the safety, and pulled the finger trigger to fire the nail into the board. The gun fired the first nail and then, in a phenomenon known as "double firing," immediately discharged an unintended second nail that struck the first nail. The gun recoiled violently backward toward Lakin and, with Lakin's finger still on the trigger, came into contact with his check. That contact activated the safety/trigger, causing the nail gun to fire a third nail. This third nail went through Lakin's checkbone and into his brain.

The nail penetrated the frontal lobe of the right hemisphere of Lakin's brain, blocked a major artery, and caused extensive tissue damage. Lakin was unconscious for several days and ultimately underwent multiple surgeries. He suffers permanent brain damage and is unable to perceive information from the left hemisphere of the brain. He also suffers partial paralysis of the left side of his body. Lakin has undergone a radical personality change and is prone to violent outbursts. He is unable to obtain employment. Lakin's previously warm and loving relationship with his wife and four children has been permanently altered. He can no longer live with his family and instead resides in a supervised group home for brain-injured persons. Lakin and his wife sued Senco for strict liability based on design defect. The trial court found Senco liable and awarded $5,323,413 to Lakin, $876,000 to his wife, and $4 million in punitive damages against Senco. Senco appealed.

Issue

Is Senco liable to Lakin for strict liability based on a design defect in the SN325 that allowed it to double fire?

Court's Reasoning

Evidence showed that the SN325 double fired once in every 15 firings. The court found that Senco rushed the SN325's production so as to maintain its position in the market. It modified an existing nail gun to shoot the longer 3.25-inch nails without engaging in additional testing to determine if longer nails in that model would increase the prevalence of double firing which it did. The court found that the SN325 could have been modified with a more restrictive but slower trigger that would have made the nail gun safer. In applying a risk-utility analysis, the court held that the SN325 was defectively designed. The court stated, "Defendant's failure to effectively address the SN325's double firing problem was conscious and was motivated, at least in part, by a profit motive." The court upheld the compensatory and punitive damages awards.

Decision and Remedy

The court of appeals applied a risk-utility analysis and held that the SN325 was defectively designed. The court affirmed the award of damages to Lakin and his wife.

Case Questions

Critical Legal Thinking   Do you think the utility served by the nine-nail-per-second SN325 outweighed its risk of personal injury?

Business Ethics   Did Senco act in a conscious disregard of safety factors when it designed, manufactured, and sold the SN325 nail gun?

Contemporary Business   Do you think the award of punitive damages was warranted in this case?

Crashworthiness Doctrine   Often, when an automobile is involved in an accident, the driver or passengers are not injured by the blow itself. Instead, they are injured when their bodies strike something inside their own automobile (e.g., the dashboard or the steering wheel). This is commonly referred to as the "second collision." The courts have held that automobile manufacturers are under a duty to design automobiles to take into account the possibility of this second collision. This is called the **crashworthiness doctrine**. Failure to design an automobile to protect occupants from foreseeable dangers caused by a second collision subjects the manufacturer and dealer to strict liability.

Business Ethics

General Motors Hit with Billion-Dollar Judgment

On Christmas Eve, Patricia Anderson was driving her Chevrolet Malibu automobile, which was manufactured by the General Motors Corporation (GM), home from church. Her four young children, ages one through nine, and a neighbor, were also in the car. The Chevy Malibu was stopped at a stoplight at 89th Place and Figueroa Street in Los Angeles when a drunken driver plowed his car into the back of the Malibu at 50 to 70 mph. The Malibu burst into flames as its gas tank ruptured and ignited. Although no one died in the crash, the occupants of the Malibu were severely burned. Many required substantial and multiple skin grafts.

The two injured women and four injured children sued GM for product liability. They alleged that the fuel tank of the Chevy Malibu was defectively designed and placed too close to the rear bumper. GM countered that the tragic accident was the fault of the driver who struck the Malibu. The accident victims produced evidence which showed that GM knew that the car's fuel-tank design was unsafe but had not changed the design because of cost. The Chevy Malibu was one of GM's A-Class cars, which also included the Pontiac Grand Am, the Oldsmobile Cutlass, and the Chevrolet Monte Carlo, all of which had similar fuel-tank designs. The plaintiffs produced GM memos that said it would cost GM $8.59 per vehicle to produce and install a safer fuel tank design but that it would cost the company only an estimated $2.40 per car to not fix the cars and pay damages to injured victims.

After a 10-week trial, the jurors returned a verdict of $107 million in compensatory damages to the plaintiffs for injuries, disfigurement, and pain and suffering caused to them by the accident. The jury then tacked on $4.9 billion as punitive damages to punish GM. This was the largest amount ever awarded in a personal-injury lawsuit. GM, the world's largest automobile company,

reported annual earnings of $3 billion in 1998, the year of the verdict. After the trial, one juror stated: "We're just like numbers. Statistics. That's something that is wrong."

GM asked the trial judge to throw out the trial. GM claimed that it was not given a fair trial because the trial court judge refused to allow the jury to hear evidence (1) that the driver of the other car was drunk and went to jail and (2) about crash-test data that showed the safety history of the vehicle. GM also claimed that the jury was prejudiced by repetitive personal attacks on GM as a "soulless company" and its lawyers as "hired guns" who consumed "cappuccinos and designer muffins." GM did not convince the judge that such animosity influenced the jury. GM also alleged that the jury was allowed to hear evidence that it should not have heard, namely, that GM had lobbied Congress in the 1970s to not adopt tougher standards for protecting fuel tanks in crashes.

In its posttrial motions, GM argued that the award of damages, specifically the $4.9 billion in punitive damages, was the result of bias and prejudice of the jury and asked the trial court judge to reduce the award of damages. This the trial court judge did do: He let the compensatory damage award stand but reduced the award of punitive damages to $1 billion. The revised award was equivalent to 2 percent of GM's net worth and 10 times the compensatory damages. GM faced more than 30 other lawsuits involving fuel tank explosions in its A-Class cars.

1. Did GM's "cost–benefit" memos have much bearing on the outcome of the lawsuit? Explain.
2. Do you think GM deserved to be punished with punitive damages? Was the amount of punitive damages awarded appropriate? Explain. ■

Failure to Warn

Certain products are inherently dangerous and cannot be made any safer and still accomplish the task for which they are designed. For example, certain useful drugs cause side effects, allergies, and other injuries to some users. Many machines and appliances include dangerous moving parts that, if removed, would defeat the purpose of the machine or appliance. Manufacturers and sellers of such products are under a *duty to warn* users about such a product's dangerous propensities. A proper and conspicuous warning placed on the product insulates the manufacturer and others in the chain of distribution from strict liability. **Failure to warn** of these dangerous propensities is a defect that will support a strict liability action.

The court found an inadequate warning in the following case.

Nowak v. Faberge USA, Inc.

32 F.3d 755, 1994 U.S.App. Lexis 16580 (1994)
United States Court of Appeals, Third Circuit

Case 18.4
Failure to Warn

Background and Facts

Faberge USA Inc. (Faberge) manufactured Aqua Net, a hair spray that was sold in an aerosol can. In addition to the hair-holding spray, Aqua Net contained a mixture of butane or propane as the aerosol propellant and alcohol as a solvent. Alcohol, butane, and propane all are extremely flammable. Aerosol cans of Aqua Net carried a warning on the back stating, "Do not puncture" and "Do not use near fire or flame."

Alison Nowak, a 14-year-old girl, tried to spray her hair with a newly purchased can of Aqua Net. The spray valve would not work properly, so she cut open the can with a can opener. She thought she could then pour the contents into an empty aerosol bottle and use it. Nowak was standing in the kitchen near a gas stove when she punctured the can. A cloud of hair spray gushed from the can, and the stove's pilot light ignited the spray into a ball of flame. She suffered severe, permanently disfiguring burns over 20 percent of her body. Nowak sued Faberge for damages under strict liability, alleging that Faberge failed to warn her of the dangers of the flammability of Aqua Net. The jury held against Faberge and awarded Nowak $1.5 million. Faberge appealed.

Issue

Did Faberge adequately warn the plaintiff of the flammability of Aqua Net?

Court's Reasoning

A manufacturer owes a duty to adequately warn users of the dangerous propensities of their products. A product is defective if it is distributed without sufficient warnings to notify the ultimate user of the dangers inherent in the product. The trial court properly determined to send the case to the jury for this determination. The jury's verdict that Faberge's warning was inadequate was upheld.

Decision and Remedy

The court of appeals affirmed the district court's judgment that Faberge had failed to warn the plaintiff of the dangers of flammability of its product and was therefore strictly liable.

Case Questions

Critical Legal Thinking Should the law recognize a failure to warn as a basis for imposing strict liability on manufacturers and sellers of products? Why or why not?

Business Ethics Did Faberge violate its duty of social responsibility in this case? Explain.

Contemporary Business Do you think this case was decided properly? What else could Faberge have done to avoid liability?

Defect in Packaging

Manufacturers owe a duty to design and provide safe packages for their products. This duty requires manufacturers to provide packages and containers that are tamperproof or that clearly indicate if they have been tampered with. Certain manufacturers, such as drug manufacturers, owe a duty to place their products in containers that cannot be opened by children. A manufacturer's failure to meet this duty—a **defect in packaging**—subjects the manufacturer and others in the chain of distribution of the product to strict liability.

Other Product Defects

Other product defects can prove the basis for strict liability actions. **Failure to provide adequate instructions** for either the safe assembly or safe use of a product is a defect that subjects the manufacturer and others in the chain of distribution to strict liability.

Other defects include inadequate testing of products, inadequate selection of component parts or materials, and improper certification of the safety of a product. The concept of "defect" is an expanding area of the law.

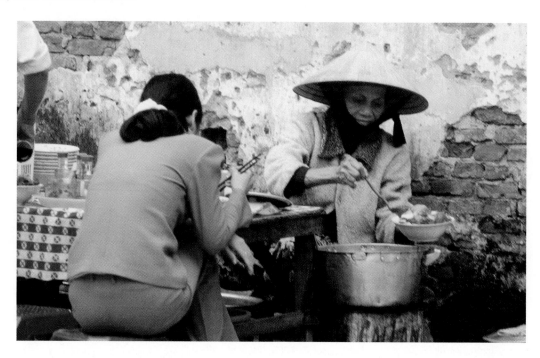

Defenses to Product Liability

Defendants in strict liability or negligence actions may raise several defenses to the imposition of liability. These defenses are discussed in the paragraphs that follow.

Supervening Event

For a seller to be held strictly liable, the product it sells must reach the consumer or user "without substantial change" in its condition.[5] Under the doctrine of **supervening**, or **intervening**, **event**, the original seller is not liable if the product is materially altered or modified after it leaves the seller's possession and the alteration or modification causes an injury. A supervening event absolves all prior sellers in the chain of distribution from strict liability.

Consider This Example   A manufacturer produces a safe piece of equipment. It sells the equipment to a distributor, which removes a safety guard from the equipment. The distributor sells it to a retailer, who sells it to a buyer. The buyer is injured because of the removal of the safety guard. The manufacturer can raise the defense of supervening event against the imposition of liability. However, the distributor and retailer are strictly liable for the buyer's injuries.

Generally Known Dangers

Certain products are inherently dangerous and are known to the general population to be so. Sellers are not strictly liable for failing to warn of **generally known dangers**. For example, it is a known fact that guns shoot bullets. Manufacturers of guns do not have to place a warning on the barrel of a gun warning of this generally known danger.

Government Contractor Defense

Many defense and other contractors manufacture products (e.g., rockets, airplanes, and such) to government specifications. Most jurisdictions recognize a **government contractor defense** to product liability actions. To establish this defense, a government contractor must prove that (1) the precise specifications for the product were provided by the government, (2) the product conformed to those specifications, and (3) the contractor warned the government of any known defects or dangers of the product.

For example, a government contractor manufactures a fighter airplane to specifications provided by the U.S. government. If the airplane proves defective because of its designs, it crashes, and it causes injury, the manufacturer can escape from liability by asserting the government contractor defense if the manufacturer either did not know of the defect or knew of the defect and warned the government of the defect.

Correction of a Product Defect

A manufacturer that produces a defective product and later discovers said defect must (1) notify purchasers and users of the defect and (2) correct the defect. Most manufacturers faced with this situation recall the defective product and either repair the defect or replace the product.

The seller must make reasonable efforts to notify purchasers and users of the defect and the procedure to correct it. Reasonable efforts normally consist of sending letters to known purchasers and users and placing notices in newspapers and magazines of general circulation. If a user ignores the notice and fails to have the defect corrected, the seller may raise this as a defense against further liability with respect to the defect. Many courts have held that reasonable notice is effective even against users who did not see the notice.

Assumption of the Risk

Theoretically, the traditional doctrine of **assumption of the risk** is a defense to a product liability action. For this defense to apply, the defendant must prove that (1) the plaintiff knew and appreciated the risk and (2) the plaintiff voluntarily assumed the risk. In practice, the defense assumption of the risk is narrowly applied by the courts.

Misuse of the Product

Sometimes users are injured when they **misuse** a product. If they bring a product liability action, the defendant-seller may be able to assert the misuse as a defense. Whether the defense is effective depends on whether the misuse was foreseeable. The seller is relieved of product liability if the plaintiff has **abnormally misused** the product—that is, if there has been an *unforeseeable misuse* of the product. However, the seller is liable if there has been a *foreseeable misuse* of the product. This reasoning is intended to provide an incentive for manufacturers to design and manufacture safer products.

Business Ethics

Design Defect in Pool Equipment

On June 1, 2000, Lorenzo Peterson was swimming in a swimming pool with a friend at an apartment complex. Lorenzo watched as his friend swam to the bottom of the pool, slid an unattached drain cover away, and then slid it back. Lorenzo thought his friend had hidden something inside the drain, so he swam to the bottom of the pool. Lorenzo slid the drain cover aside and stuck his arm inside the drain. The 300 to 400 pounds of pull of the drain pump held Lorenzo trapped underwater. At least seven people tried to free Lorenzo to no avail. When the police arrived, they broke down the door to the pool equipment room and turned off the drain pump.

Lorenzo was trapped underwater for 12 minutes, which left him irreversibly brain damaged. Lorenzo, through his relatives, sued Sta-Rite Industries, Inc., the manufacturer of the drain, under the doctrine of strict liability to recover damages for Lorenzo's injuries. The plaintiff alleged that the underwater pool

Business Ethics

(continued)

drain was defectively designed because it did not contain a shut-off mechanism. Evidence at trial showed that Sta-Rite's drain covers are designed to screw down, but often a drain cover becomes loose. Further evidence showed that there had been more than 20 prior suction-entrapment accidents involving Sta-Rite's drain covers and pumps.

Previously, experts had designed a pool drain pump with a mechanism that would automatically shut off a pool drain pump when it detected that it was pulling more than it should. Sta-Rite did not install such safety features on its drain pumps, however. After hearing the evidence, including seeing a video of a typical

day in the life of Lorenzo after the accident, the jury took less than two hours to return a verdict against Sta-Rite. The jury found that a design defect existed in Sta-Rite's pool drain equipment and awarded Lorenzo $32 million for past and future medical expenses and $72 million for pain and suffering. [*Sta-Rite Industries, Inc. v. Peterson*, 837 So.2d 988, 2003 Fla.App. Lexis 1673 (2003)]

1. Do you think Sta-Rite acted unethically in its conduct? Why or why not?
2. Was the award of $104 million warranted? Explain. ◼

Statute of Limitations and Statute of Repose

Most states have **statutes of limitations** that require an injured person to bring an action within a certain number of years from the time that he or she was injured by a defective product. This limitation period varies from state to state. Failure to bring an action within the appropriate time relieves the defendant of liability.

In most jurisdictions, the statute of limitations does not begin to run until the plaintiff suffers an injury. This subjects sellers and lessors to exposure for an unspecified period of time because a defective product may not cause an injury for years, or even decades, after it was sold. Because this may be unfair to the seller, some states have enacted **statutes of repose**. Statues of repose limit the seller's liability to a certain number of years from the date when the product was first sold. The period of repose varies from state to state.

Concept Summary   Comparison of Statutes of Limitation and Statutes of Repose

Statute	Begins to Run
Statute of limitations	When the plaintiff suffers injury
Statute of repose	When the product is first sold

Contributory and Comparative Negligence

Sometimes a person who is injured by a defective product is negligent and contributes to his or her own injuries. The defense of **contributory negligence** bars an injured plaintiff from recovering from the defendant in a negligence action. However, this doctrine generally does not bar recovery in strict liability actions.

Many states have held that the doctrine of comparative negligence (or **comparative fault**) applies to strict liability actions. Under this doctrine, a plaintiff who is contributorily negligent for his or her injuries is responsible for a *proportional share* of the damages. In other words, the damages are apportioned between the plaintiff and the defendant.

Consider This Example   Suppose an automobile manufacturer produces a car with a hidden defect and a consumer purchases the car from an automobile dealer. Assume that the consumer is injured in an automobile accident in which the defect is found to be 75 percent responsible for the accident and the consumer's own reckless driving is found to be 25 percent responsible. The plaintiff suffers $1 million worth of injuries. Under the doctrine of *contributory negligence*, the plaintiff would recover nothing from the defendants. Under the doctrine of *comparative negligence*, the plaintiff would recover $750,000 from the defendants.

International Law

Product Liability Law in Japan

Japanese manufacturers sell many of the same products in Japan and the United States. In the United States, the products are subject to product liability laws. In Japan, they enjoy near-immunity from product liability claims. For example, in almost 50 years, consumers have won few product liability cases in Japan and recovered meager damages. Product liability claims are rare in Japan for several reasons:

1. The plaintiff has the difficult burden of proving that the company was negligent. Japan has not adopted the U.S. doctrine of strict liability.

2. Japanese courts do not allow discovery. It is often impossible to prove a product was defective if the plaintiff cannot obtain access to the defendant's files.

3. Win or lose, claimants must pay a percentage of any damages requested (not won) as court fees. This keeps damage requests low.

4. Awards that are granted by courts are small (at least by U.S. standards), and punitive damages are not available.

The attitude of Japanese consumers is changing, however, and more injured consumers are suing to recover damages for their injuries. ■

Chapter Summary

Warranties of Quality, p. 362

Express Warranty

An express warranty is an affirmation by a seller or lessor that the goods he or she is selling or leasing meet certain standards of quality, description, performance, or condition.

Implied Warranty of Merchantability

1. ***Implied warranty of merchantability.*** This warranty is implied by law in sales and lease transactions. It requires that the goods:
   a. Be fit for the ordinary purposes for which they are used.
   b. Be adequately contained, packaged, and labeled.
   c. Be of an even kind, quality, and quantity within each unit.
   d. Conform to any promise or affirmation of fact made on the container or label.
   e. Pass without objection in the trade.
   f. Meet a fair or middle range of quality if the goods are fungible.

2. ***Implied warranty of fitness for human consumption.*** This is a warranty implied by law that food products are fit for human consumption. States apply one of the two following tests:
   a. *Foreign substance test.* A food is unmerchantable if a foreign object in the food caused the plaintiff's injury.
   b. *Consumer expectation test.* A food is unmerchantable if an object in the food that a consumer would not expect to be there caused the plaintiff's injury.
   The UCC incorporates this warranty within the implied warranty of merchantability.

Implied Warranty of Fitness for a Particular Purpose

Implied warranty of fitness for a particular purpose. This is a warranty by a seller or lessor that the goods will meet the buyer's or lessee's expressed needs.

Warranty Disclaimers

1. ***Express warranties.*** Express warranties can be limited if the warranty and disclaimer can be reasonably construed with each other.

2. ***Implied warranties:***

   a. *Disclaimer.* An implied warranty can be disclaimed by expressions like *as is, with all faults,* or such language. If such language is not used, implied warranties are disclaimed as follows:

      i. *Implied warranty of merchantability.* This is an oral or written disclaimer that mentions the word *merchantability.*

      ii. *Implied warranty of fitness for a particular purpose.* This is a written disclaimer of general language.

3. ***Conspicuousness.*** Written disclaimers must be conspicuously displayed to be enforceable.

Magnuson–Moss Warranty Act

This act is a federal statute that covers written warranties that apply to *consumer* products.

1. ***Full and limited warranties.*** If a good costs more than $10 and the warrantor makes an express warranty, the warranty must be labeled *full* or *limited.*

   a. *Full warranty.* A full warranty guarantees free repair or replacement of a defective product. A time limit may be placed on the warranty.

   b. *Limited warranty.* A limited warranty limits the scope of a full warranty in some way (e.g., return of the purchase price).

2. ***Limitation on disclaiming implied warranties.*** If a seller or lessor makes an express warranty, he or she cannot disclaim or modify the implied warranties of merchantability and fitness for a particular purpose. A time limit may be placed on implied warranties but must correspond to the duration of the express warranty.

Product Liability Based on Fault, p. 368

Misrepresentation

A seller or lessor fraudulently misrepresents the quality of a product, and the plaintiff relies on the misrepresentation and is injured thereby.

Negligence

A seller or lessor breaches his or her duty of due care by producing a defective product that causes injury to the plaintiff. Privity of contract between the seller or lessor and the plaintiff is not required.

Strict Liability, p. 369

Strict Liability in Tort

A manufacturer or seller who sells a defective product is liable to the ultimate user who is injured thereby. All in the chain of distribution are liable, irrespective of fault. Sometimes called *vertical liability.*

The Concept of Defect, p. 372

The Concept of Defect

1. Defect in manufacture
2. Defect in design
3. Failure to warn
4. Defect in packaging
5. Failure to provide adequate instructions for assembly of a product
6. Other defects

Defenses to Product Liability

A manufacturer or seller is not liable for damages caused by a product it manufactures or sells if one of the following defenses applies:

1. *Supervening event.* The product was materially altered or modified after it left the seller's possession and the alteration or modification caused an injury. Also called *intervening event.*

2. *Generally known dangers.* A seller is not liable for failing to warn about inherent dangers in products that are know to the general population.

3. *Government contractor defense.* A manufacturer produces a product to government specifications and warns the government of any known defects in the specific design.

4. *Correction of a defect.* A manufacturer or seller who learns about a defect in a product it has sold notifies purchasers and users of the defect and corrects the defect.

5. *Assumption of the risk.* The plaintiff knew and appreciated the risk and voluntarily assumed the risk.

6. *Misuse of the product:*

   a. *Abnormal misuse.* The seller is not liable for injuries caused by the abnormal misuse of the product by the plaintiff. Also called *unforeseeable misuse.*

   b. *Foreseeable misuse.* The seller is liable for injuries caused by the foreseeable misuse of a product. The manufacturer must design products to be safe for foreseeable misuses.

Statutes of Limitations and Repose

1. *Statute of limitations.* An injured person must bring a product liability lawsuit within a specified period of time after being injured by a defective product.

2. *Statute of repose.* A person must bring a product liability lawsuit within a specified period of time after a defective product was first purchased or leased.

Contributory and Comparative Negligence

1. *Contributory negligence.* A person who is partially responsible for causing his or her own injuries may not recover anything from the manufacturer or seller of a defective product that caused the remainder of the person's injuries.

2. *Comparative negligence.* A person who is partially responsible for causing his or her own injuries is responsible for a proportional share of the damages. The manufacturer or seller of the defective product is responsible for the remainder of the plaintiff's damages. Also called *comparative fault.*

Internet Exercises and Case Questions

Working the Web Internet Exercises

Activities

1. Review an example of Colorado's UCC provisions, at **www.law.du.edu/russell/contracts/ucc**, and study the warranty provisions and how they work.

2. UCC Article 2 provides for disclaimers of warranties. Find the provisions of the Magnuson–Moss Warranty Act and review the various disclaimers. Do you think disclaimers are a good idea? See "LII: Law About . . . Sales of Goods" at **www.law.cornell.edu/topics/sales.html** for a summary of the warranties under UCC Article 2.

3. Find statistics on the most frequent type of product liability cases filed in your jurisdiction. Start with "Consumer Product Safety Data," at **www.cpsc.gov/library/data.html**.

4. What is the statute of limitations on product liability in your jurisdiction? Does it matter if your case is filed under UCC Article 2 warranties, negligence, or strict liability under Section 402A of the *Restatement (Second) of Torts*? See *Restatement of Torts* Section 402A, at **www.ali.org/ali/Tortpl.htm**. See also **www.law.cornell.edu/topics/products_liability.html**, which contains an overview of products liability law, with links to key primary and secondary sources.

5. Does your state have a statute of repose for product liability cases?

Critical Legal Thinking Cases

18.1 Express Warranty   The House of Zog manufactures and sells the "Golfing Gizmo," a training device designed to help golfers improve their swing. The device consists of a golf ball attached to one end of a cotton string, with the other end of the string tied to the middle of an elastic cord. The elastic cord is then stretched between two stakes placed in the ground, forming a "T" configuration. This allows the ball to return automatically after it has been struck. The "Golfing Gizmo" is sold in a package that states "COMPLETELY SAFE—BALL WILL NOT HIT PLAYER." In 1966, Louise Hauter gave a Golfing Gizmo to her 13-year-old son, Fred, for Christmas. One afternoon, Fred decided to use the device, which had been set up in his front yard. Having used the Gizmo before, Fred felt no apprehension as he took his normal swing at the ball. The last thing he remembered was pain and dizziness. Fred had been hit in the head by the ball and had suffered serious injuries. Fred Hauter sued the House of Zog. Who wins? [*Hauter v. Zogarts*, 14 Cal.3d 104, 120 Cal.Rptr. 681, 1975 Cal. Lexis 280 (Cal. 1975)]

18.2 Implied Warranty of Fitness for Human Consumption   Tina Keperwas went to a Publix Supermarket in Florida and bought a can of Doxsee Brand Clam Chowder. Keperwas opened the can of soup and prepared it at home. While eating the chowder, she bit down on a clam shell and injured one of her molars. Keperwas filed suit against Publix and Doxsee for breach of an implied warranty. In the lawsuit, Keperwas alleged that the clam chowder "was not fit for use as food, but was defective, unwholesome, and unfit for human consumption" and "was in such condition as to be dangerous to life and health." At the trial, Doxsee's general manager testified as to the state-of-the-art methods Doxsee uses in preparing its chowder. Are Publix Supermarkets and Doxsee liable for the injury to Keperwas's tooth? [*Keperwas v. Public Supermarkets, Inc.*, 534 S.2d 872, 1988 Fla.App. Lexis 5306 (Fla. App. 1988)]

18.3 Implied Warranty of Fitness for a Particular Purpose   Dennis Walker is the owner of several pizza parlors in Nebraska. The stores operate under the name El Fredo Pizza Restaurants, Inc. Walker planned to open a new restaurant in 1973. A business associate suggested that Walker purchase an oven from the Roto-Flex Oven Co. Walker contacted an agent of Roto-Flex and negotiated to buy a new oven. Walker told the agent the particular purpose for which he was buying the oven—to cook pizza—and that he was relying on the agent's skill and judgment in selecting a suitable oven. Based on the agent's suggestions, Walker entered into a contract to purchase a custom-built Roto-Flex "Pizza Oven Special." The oven was installed in the new restaurant, and problems immediately ensued. The oven failed to bake pizzas properly because of uneven heating. Constant monitoring of the oven was required, and delays occurred in serving customers. Roto-Flex was notified of the problem and attempted to fix the oven. However, the oven continued to bake pizzas improperly. El Fredo Pizza, Inc., sued Roto-Flex Oven Co. Was a warranty of fitness for a particular purpose created in this case? [*El Fredo Pizza, Inc. v. Roto-Flex Oven Co.*, 261 N.W.2d 358, 1978 Neb. Lexis 625 (Neb. 1978)]

18.4 Disclaimer of Warranties   Cole Energy Company wanted to lease a gas compressor for use in its business of pumping and selling natural gas. Cole Energy began negotiating with the Ingersoll-Rand Company. On December 5, 1983, the two parties entered into a lease agreement for a KOA gas compressor. The lease agreement contained a section labeled "WARRANTIES." Part of the section read "THERE ARE NO IMPLIED WARRANTIES OF MERCHANTABILITY OR FITNESS FOR A PARTICULAR PURPOSE CONTAINED HEREIN." The gas compressor that was installed failed to function properly. As a result, Cole Energy lost business. Cole Energy sued Ingersoll-Rand for the breach of an implied warranty of merchantability. Is Ingersoll-Rand liable? [*Cole Energy Development Company v. Ingersoll-Rand Company*, 678 F.Supp. 208, 1988 U.S. Dist. Lexis 923 (C.D.Ill. 1988)]

18.5 Strict Liability   Jeppesen and Company produces charts that graphically display approach procedures for airplanes landing at airports. These charts are drafted from tabular data supplied by the Federal Aviation Administration (FAA), a federal agency of the U.S. government. By law, Jeppesen cannot construct charts that include information different from that supplied by the FAA. On September 8, 1973, the pilot of an airplane owned by World Airways was on descent to land at the Cold Bay, Alaska, airport. The pilot was using an instrument approach procedure chart published by Jeppesen. The airplane crashed into a mountain near Cold Bay, killing all six crew members and destroying the aircraft. Evidence showed that the FAA data did not include the mountain. The heirs of the deceased crew members and World Airways brought a strict liability action against Jeppesen. Does the doctrine of strict liability apply to this case? Is Jeppesen liable? [*Brockleshy v. Jeppesen and Company*, 767 F.2d 1288, 1985 U.S. App. Lexis 21290 (9th Cir. 1985)]

18.6 Defect   The Emerson Electric Co. manufactures and sells a product called the Weed Eater XR-90. The Weed Eater is a multipurpose weed-trimming and brush-cutting device. It consists of a handheld gasoline-powered engine connected to a long drive shaft, at the end of which can be attached various tools for cutting weeds and brush. One such attachment is a 10-inch circular sawblade capable of cutting through growth up to 2 inches in diameter. When this sawblade is attached to the Weed Eater, approximately 270 degrees of blade edge are exposed when in use. The owner's manual contained the following warning: "Keep children away. All people and pets should be kept at a safe distance from the work area, at least 30 feet, especially when using the blade." Donald Pearce, a 13-year-old boy, was helping his uncle clear an overgrown yard. The uncle was operating a Weed Eater XR-90 with the circular sawblade attachment. When Pearce stooped to pick up something off the ground about 6 to 10 feet behind and slightly to the left of where his uncle was operating the Weed Eater, the sawblade on the Weed Eater struck something near the ground. The Weed Eater kicked back to the left and cut off Pearce's right arm to the elbow. Pearce, through his mother, Charlotte Karns, sued Emerson to recover damages under strict liability. Is Emerson liable? [*Karns v. Emerson Electric Co.*, 817 F.2d 1452, 1987 U.S. App. Lexis 5608 (1987)]

18.7 Crashworthiness Doctrine   At 11 P.M. on April 10, 1968, Verne Prior, driving on U.S. 101 under the influence of alcohol and drugs at a speed of 65 to 85 miles per hour, crashed his 1963 Chrysler into the left rear of a 1962 Chevrolet station wagon stopped on the shoulder of the freeway because of a flat tire. Christine Smith was sitting in the passenger seat of the parked car when the accident occurred. In the crash, the Chevrolet station wagon was knocked into a gully, where its fuel tank ruptured. The vehicle caught fire, and Smith suffered severe burn injuries. The Chevrolet station wagon was manufactured by General Motors Corporation. Evidence showed that the fuel tank was located in a vulnerable position in the back of the station wagon, outside the crossbars of the frame. Evidence further showed that if the fuel tank had been located underneath the body of the station wagon, between the crossbars of the frame, it would have been well protected in the collision. Smith sued General Motors for strict liability. Was the Chevrolet station wagon a defective product? [*Smith v. General Motors Corporation*, 42 C.A.3d 1, 116 Cal.Rptr. 575, 1974 Cal.App. Lexis 1199 (Cal. App. 1974)]

18.8 Defect   Virginia Burke purchased a bottle of "Le Domaine" champagne that was manufactured by Almaden Vineyards, Inc. At home, she removed the wine seal from the top of the bottle but did not remove the plastic cork. She set the bottle on the counter, intending to serve it in a few minutes. Shortly thereafter, the plastic cork spontaneously ejected from the bottle, ricocheted off the wall, and struck Burke in the left lens of her eyeglasses, shattering the lens and driving pieces of glass into her eye. The champagne bottle did not contain any warning of this danger. Evidence showed that Almaden had previously been notified of the spontaneous ejection of the cork from its champagne bottles. Burke sued Almaden to recover damages for strict liability. Is Almaden liable? [*Burke v. Almaden Vineyards, Inc.*, 86 C.A.3d 768, 150 Cal.Rptr. 419, 1978 Cal.App. Lexis 2123 (Cal. App. 1978)]

18.9 Assumption of Risk   Lillian Horn was driving her Chevrolet station wagon, which was designed and manufactured by General Motors Corporation, down Laurel Canyon Boulevard in Los Angeles, California. Horn swerved to avoid a collision when a car coming toward her crossed the center line and was coming at her. In doing so, her hand knocked the horn cap off of the steering wheel, which exposed the area underneath the horn cap, including three sharp prongs that had held the horn cap to the steering wheel. A few seconds later, when her car hit an embankment, Horn's face was impaled on the three sharp exposed prongs, causing her severe facial injuries. Horn sued General Motors for strict liability. General Motors asserted the defense of assumption of the risk against Horn. Who wins? [*Horn v. General Motors Corporation*, 17 C.3d 359, 131 Cal.Rptr. 78, 1976 Cal. Lexis 283 (Cal. 1975)]

18.10 Misuse   The Wilcox-Crittendon Company manufactured harnesses, saddles, bridles, leads, and other items commonly used for horses, cattle, and other ranch and farm animals. One such item was a stallion or cattle tie, a five-inch-long iron hook with a one-inch ring at one end. The tongue on the ring opened outward to allow the hook to be attached to a rope or another object. In 1964, a purchasing agent for United Airlines, who was familiar with this type of hook because of earlier experiences on a farm, purchased one of these hooks from Keystone Brothers, a harness and saddlery wares outlet located in San Francisco, California. Four years later, on March 28, 1968, Edward Dosier, an employee of United Airlines, was working to install a new grinding machine at a United Airlines maintenance plant. As part of the installation process, Dosier attached the hook to a 1,700-pound counterweight and raised the counterweight into the air. While the counterweight was suspended in the air, Dosier reached under the counterweight to retrieve a missing bolt. The hook broke, and the counterweight fell and crushed Dosier's arm. Dosier sued Wilcox-Crittendon for strict liability. Who wins? [*Dosier v. Wilcox-Crittendon Company*, 45 Cal.App.3d. 74, 119 Cal.Rptr. 135, 1975 Cal.App. Lexis 1665 (Cal. App. 1975)]

Business Ethics Cases

18.11 Business Ethics   During October 1978, Brian Keith, an actor, attended a boat show in Long Beach, California. At the boat show Keith obtained sales literature on a sailboat called the "Island Trader 42" from a sales representative of James Buchanan, a seller of sailboats. One sales brochure described the vessel as "a picture of sure-footed seaworthiness." Another brochure called the sailboat "a carefully well-equipped and very seaworthy live-aboard vessel." In November 1978, Keith purchased an Island Trader 41 sailboat from Buchanan for a total purchase price of $75,610. After delivery of the sailboat, a dispute arose in regard to the seaworthiness of the vessel. Keith sued Buchanan for breach of warranty. Buchanan defended, arguing that no warranty had been made. Was it ethical for Buchanan to try to avoid being held accountable for statements of quality about its product that were made in the sales brochures given Keith? Should sales "puffing" be considered to create an express warranty? Why or why not? Who wins this case? [*Keith v. Buchanan*, 173 Cal.App.3d 13, 220 Cal.Rptr. 392, 1985 Cal.App. Lexis 2603 (Cal. App. 1985)]

18.12 Business Ethics   Celestino Luque lived with his cousins Harry and Laura Dunn in Millbrae, California. The Dunns purchased a rotary lawn mower from Rhoads Hardware. The lawn mower was manufactured by Air Capital Manufacturing Company and was distributed by Garehime Corporation. On December 4, 1965, neighbors asked Luque to mow their lawn. While Luque was cutting the lawn, he noticed a small carton in the path of the lawn mower. Luque left the lawn mower in a stationary position with its motor running and walked around the side of the lawn mower to remove the carton. As he did so, he suddenly slipped on the wet grass and fell backward. Luque's left hand entered the unguarded hole of the lawn mower and was caught in its revolving blade, which turns at 175 miles per hour and 100 revolutions per second. Luque's hand was severely mangled and lacerated. The word *Caution* was printed above the unguarded hole on the lawn mower. Luque sued Rhoads Hardware, Air Capital, and Garehime Corporation for strict liability. The defendants argued that strict liability does not apply to *patent* (obvious) defects. Was it ethical for the defendants to argue that they were not liable for patent defects? Would patent defects ever be corrected if the defendants' contention was accepted by the court? Who wins? [*Luque v. McLean, Trustee*, 8 Cal.3d 136, 104 Cal.Rptr. 443, 1972 Cal. Lexis 245 (Cal. 1972)]

Briefing the Case Writing Assignment

Read Case A.18 in the Case Appendix [*Johnson v. Chicago Pneumatic Tool Company*]. Review and brief this case. In your brief, be sure to answer the following questions.

1. Who was the plaintiff? Who was the defendant?

2. What law did the plaintiff assert was violated by the defendant?

3. What was the defendant's defense? Explain.

4. Was this defense effective in this case?

Endnotes

1. 15 U.S.C. § 2301–2312.
2. *Restatement (Second) of Torts*, § 395.
3. 111 N.E. 1050, 217 N.Y. 382, 1916 N.Y. Lexis 1324 (N.Y. App. 1916).
4. 59 Cal.2d 57, 27 Cal.Rptr. 697, 1963 Cal. Lexis 140 (1963).
5. *Restatement (Second) of Torts*, § 402A(1)(b).

Creation and Transfer of Negotiable Instruments

19

"The great object of the law is to encourage commerce."

—Judge Chambre
Beale v. Thompson (1803)

Chapter Objectives

After studying this chapter, you should be able to:

1. Distinguish between negotiable and nonnegotiable instruments.

2. Describe drafts, checks, promissory notes, and certificates of deposit, and identify the parties to these instruments.

3. List the formal requirements of a negotiable instrument.

4. Distinguish between instruments payable to order and payable to bearer.

5. Describe how negotiable instruments are indorsed and transferred.

Chapter Contents

■ Negotiable Instruments

■ Types of Negotiable Instruments

■ Creating a Negotiable Instrument

■ Transfer by Assignment and Transfer by Negotiation

■ Indorsements

■ Forged Indorsement

Negotiable instruments (or **commercial paper**) are important for the conduct of business and personal affairs. In this country, modern commerce could not continue without them. Examples of negotiable instruments include checks (such as the one that may have been used to pay for this book) and promissory notes (such as the one executed by a borrower of money to pay for tuition).

The types, creation, and transfer of negotiable instruments are discussed in this chapter.

Negotiable Instruments

To qualify as a negotiable instrument, a document must meet certain requirements established by Article 3 of the Uniform Commercial Code (UCC). If these requirements are met, a transferee who qualifies as a *holder in due course* (HDC) takes the instrument free of many defenses that can be asserted against the original payee. In addition, the document is considered an ordinary contract that is subject to contract law.

The concept of *negotiation* is important to the law of negotiable instruments. The primary benefit of a negotiable instrument is that it can be used as a substitute for money. As such, it must be freely transferable to subsequent parties. Technically, a negotiable instrument is negotiated when it is originally issued. The term *negotiation*, however, is usually used to describe the transfer of negotiable instruments to subsequent transferees.

Revised Article 3 (Negotiable Instruments) of the UCC

Although negotiable instruments have been used in commerce since medieval times, the English law courts did not immediately recognize their validity. To compensate for this failure, the merchants developed rules governing their use. These rules, which were enforced by local private merchant courts, became part of what was called the **Law Merchant**. Eventually, in 1882, England enacted the Bills of Exchange Act, which codified the rules of the Law Merchant.

In 1886, the National Conference of Commissioners of Uniform State Laws promulgated the **Uniform Negotiable Instruments Law (NIL)** in the United States. By 1920, all of the states had enacted the NIL as law, but the rapid development of commercial paper soon made the law obsolete.

Article 3 (Commercial Paper) of the Uniform Commercial Code, which was promulgated in 1952, established rules for the creation of, transfer of, enforcement of, and liability on negotiable instruments. All the states and the District of Columbia have replaced the NIL with Article 3 of the UCC.

In 1990, the American Law Institute and the National Conference of Commissioners on Uniform State Laws repealed Article 3 and replaced it with **Revised Article 3**. The new article, which is called "Negotiable Instruments" instead of "Commercial Paper," was a comprehensive revision of Article 3.

Functions of Negotiable Instruments

Negotiable instruments serve the following functions:

1. ***Substitute for money.*** Merchants and consumers often do not carry cash for fear of loss or theft. Further, it would be almost impossible to carry enough cash for large purchases (e.g., a can, a house). Thus certain forms of negotiable instruments—for example, checks—serve as *substitute's for money*.

2. ***Credit device.*** Some forms of negotiable instruments extend credit from one party to another. For example, a seller may sell goods to a customer on a customer's promise to

pay for the goods at a future time, or a bank may lend money to a buyer who signs a note promising to repay the money. Both these examples represent *extensions of credit*. Without negotiable instruments, the "credit economy" of the United States and other modern industrial countries would not be possible.

3. *Record-keeping device.* Negotiable instruments often serve as a *record-keeping device*. For example, banks may return canceled checks to checking-account customers each month. These act as a record-keeping device for the preparation of financial statements, tax returns, and the like.

Types of Negotiable Instruments

The term **instrument** means negotiable instrument [UCC 3-104(b)]. These terms are often used interchangeably.

Revised Article 3 recognizes four kinds of instruments: (1) drafts, (2) checks, (3) promissory notes, and (4) certificates of deposit. Each of these is discussed in the following paragraphs.

Drafts

A **draft** which is a three-party instrument, is an unconditional written order by one party (the **drawer**) that orders a second party (the **drawee**) to pay money to a third party (the **payee**) [UCC 3-104(e)]. The drawee must be obligated to pay the drawer money before the drawer can order the drawee to pay this money to a third party (the payee).

For the drawee to be liable on a draft, the drawee must accept the drawer's written order to pay it. Acceptance is usually shown by the written word *accepted* on the face of the draft, along with the drawee's signature and the date. The drawee is called the **acceptor** of the draft because his or her obligation changes from that of having to pay the drawer to that of having to pay the payee. After the drawee accepts the draft, it is returned to the drawer or the payee. The drawer or the payee, in turn, can freely transfer it as a negotiable instrument to another party.

Advertisement on Building.
Commerce is facilitated by the use of negotiable instruments, such as checks and promissory notes.

Consider This Example   Mary Owens owes Hector Martinez $1,000. Martinez writes out a draft that orders Owens to pay this $1,000 to Cindy Choy. Owens agrees to this change of obligation and accepts the draft. Martinez is the drawer, Owens is the drawee, and Choy is the payee.

A draft can be either a time draft or a sight draft. A **time draft** is payable at a designated future date. For example, language such as "pay on January 1, 1994" or "pay 120 days after date" creates a time draft (see Exhibit 19.1). A **sight draft** is payable on sight. A sight draft is also called a **demand draft**. For example, language such as "on demand pay" or "at sight pay" creates a sight draft. A draft can be both a time and a sight draft. Such a draft would provide that it is payable at a stated time after sight. For example, this type of draft is created by language such as "payable 90 days after sight."

A **trade acceptance** is a sight draft that arises when credit is extended with the sale of goods. In this type of draft, the seller is both the drawer and the payee. The buyer to whom credit is extended is the drawee. Even though only two actual parties are involved, it is considered a three-party instrument because three legal positions are involved.

Checks

A **check** is a distinct from of draft. It is unique in that it is drawn on a financial institution (the drawee) and is payable on demand [UCC 3-104(f)]. In other words, a check is an order to pay (see Exhibit 19.2). Most businesses and many individuals have checking accounts at financial institutions.

Like other drafts, a check is a three-party instrument. A customer who has a checking account and writes (draws) a check is the **drawer**. The financial institution upon which the check is written is the **drawee**. And the party to whom the check is written is the **payee**.

In addition to traditional checks, there are several forms of special checks, including certified checks, cashier's checks, and traveler's checks. These special checks are discussed in Chapter 21.

Promissory Notes

A **promissory note** (or **note**) is an unconditional written promise by one party to pay money to another party [UCC 3-104(e)]. It is a two-party instrument (see Exhibit 19.3), not an

Exhibit 19.1

A Time Draft

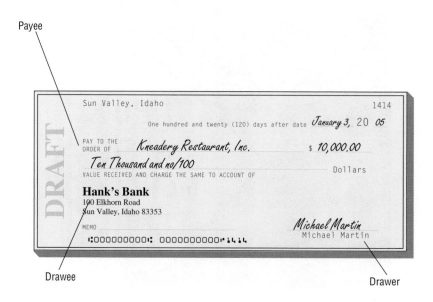

Payee

Drawee

Drawer

Sun Valley, Idaho   1414

One hundred and twenty (120) days after date *January 3*, 20 *05*

PAY TO THE ORDER OF   *Kneadery Restaurant, Inc.* $ *10,000.00*

Ten Thousand and no/100   Dollars

VALUE RECEIVED AND CHARGE THE SAME TO ACCOUNT OF

Hank's Bank
190 Elkhorn Road
Sun Valley, Idaho 83353

MEMO   *Michael Martin*
                                                        Michael Martin

Payee

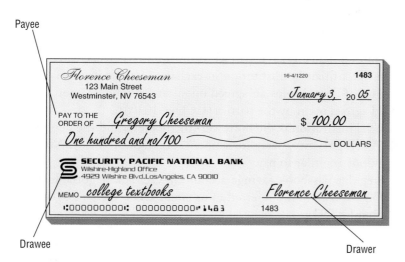

Exhibit 19.2

A Check

Drawee

Drawer

order to pay. Promissory notes usually arise when one party borrows money from another. The note is evidence of (1) the extension of credit and (2) the borrower's promise to repay the debt.

A party who makes a promise to pay is the **maker** of a note (i.e., the borrower). The party to whom the promise to pay is made is the **payee** (i.e., the lender). A promissory note is a negotiable instrument that the payee can freely transfer to other parties.

The parties are free to design the terms of the note to fit their needs. For example, notes can be payable at a specific time (**time note**) or on demand (**demand note**). Notes can be made payable to a named payee or to "bearer." They can be payable in a single payment or in installments. The latter are called **installment notes**. Most notes require the borrower to pay interest on the principal.

Lenders sometimes require the maker of a note to post security for the repayment of the note. This security, which is called **collateral**, may be in the form of automobiles, houses, securities, or other property. If the maker fails to repay the note when it is due, the lender can foreclose and take the collateral as payment for the note. Notes are often named after the security that underlies the note. For example, notes that are secured by real estate are called **mortgage notes**, and notes that are secured by personal property are called **collateral notes**.

Business Brief

Commerce is facilitated by the use of negotiable instruments, such as checks and promissory notes.

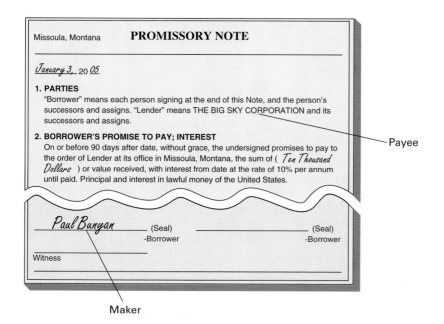

Payee

Maker

Exhibit 19.3

A Promissory Note

Certificates of Deposit

A **certificate of deposit (CD)** is a special form of note that is created when a depositor deposits money at a financial institution in exchange for the institution's promise to pay back the amount of deposit plus an agreed upon rate of interest upon the expiration of a set time period agreed upon by the parties [UCC 3-104(j)].

The financial institution is the borrower (the **maker**), and the depositor is the lender (the **payee**). A CD is a two-party instrument (see Exhibit 19.4). Note that a CD is a promise to pay, not an order to pay.

Unlike a regular passbook savings account, a CD is a negotiable instrument. CDs under $100,000 are commonly referred to as **small CDs**. CDs of $100,000 or more are usually called **jumbo CDs**.

Concept Summary   Types of Negotiable Instruments

Type of Instrument	Party	Description of Party
A. Orders to Pay		
1. Draft	Drawer	Person who issues the draft.
	Drawee	Person who owes money to the drawer; person who is ordered to pay the draft and accepts the draft.
	Payee	Person to whom the draft is made payable.
2. Check	Drawer	Owner of a checking account at a financial institution; person who issues the check.
	Drawee	Financial institution where drawer's checking account is located; party who is ordered to pay the check.
	Payee	Person to whom the check is made payable.
B. Promises to Pay		
1. Promissory note	Maker	Party who issues the promissory note; this is usually the borrower.
	Payee	Party to whom the promissory note is made payable; this is usually the lender.
2. Certificate of deposit (CD)	Maker	Financial institution that issues the CD.
	Payee	Party to whom the CD is made payable; this is usually the depositor.

Exhibit 19.4

A Certificate of Deposit

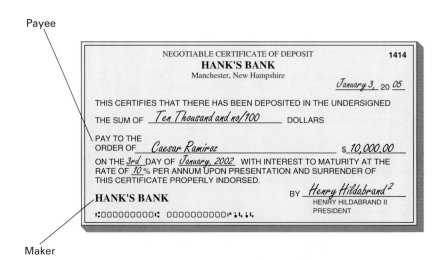

Payee

Maker

NEGOTIABLE CERTIFICATE OF DEPOSIT   1414

HANK'S BANK
Manchester, New Hampshire

January 3, 20 *05*

THIS CERTIFIES THAT THERE HAS BEEN DEPOSITED IN THE UNDERSIGNED

THE SUM OF *Ten Thousand and no/100* DOLLARS

PAY TO THE
ORDER OF *Caesar Ramiroz* $ *10,000.00*

ON THE *3rd* DAY OF *January, 2002* WITH INTEREST TO MATURITY AT THE
RATE OF *10* % PER ANNUM UPON PRESENTATION AND SURRENDER OF
THIS CERTIFICATE PROPERLY INDORSED.

HANK'S BANK   BY *Henry Hildabrand²*
                              HENRY HILDABRAND II
                              PRESIDENT

⑆000000000⑆ 0000000000⑈1414

Creating a Negotiable Instrument

According to UUC 3-104(a), a **negotiable instrument** must:

- Be in writing
- Be signed by the maker or drawer
- Be an unconditional promise or order to pay
- State a fixed amount of money
- Not require any undertaking in addition to the payment of money
- Be payable on demand or at a definite time
- Be payable to order or to bearer

These requirements must appear on the *face* of the instrument. If they do not, the instrument does not qualify as negotiable. Each of these requirements is discussed in the paragraphs that follow. A promise or order that conspicuously states that it is not negotiable or is not subject to Article 3 is not a negotiable instrument [UCC 3-104(d)].

Writing

A negotiable instrument must be (1) in writing and (2) *Permanent and portable*. Often the requisite writing is on a preprinted form, but typewritten, handwritten, or other tangible agreements are also acceptable [UCC 1-201(46)]. In addition, the instrument can be a combination of different kinds of writing. For example, a check is often a preprinted form on which the drawer hand writes the amount of the check, the name of the payee, and the date of the check. Oral promises do not qualify as negotiable instruments because they are not clearly transferable in a manner that will prevent fraud. Tape recordings and videotapes are not negotiable instruments because they are not considered writings.

Most writings on paper meet the **permanency requirement**, although a writing on tissue paper does not because of its impermanence. For example, the courts have held that writings on other objects (e.g., baseballs, shirts) meet this requirement. A promise or an order to pay that is written in snow or sand is not permanent and, therefore, is not a negotiable instrument. A photograph of such a writing that was signed by the maker or drawer would qualify as a negotiable instrument, however. The picture meets the requirements of permanence.

The **portability requirement** is intended to ensure free transfer of the instrument. For example, a promise to pay chiseled in a California redwood tree would not qualify as a negotiable instrument because the tree is not freely transferable in commerce. Writing the same promise or order to pay on a small block of wood could qualify as a negotiable instrument, however.

The best practice is to place the written promise or order to pay on traditional paper. This method ensures that the permanency and portability requirements are met so that transferees will readily accept the instrument.

Signed by the Maker or the Drawer

The UCC **signature requirement** requires that a negotiable instrument must be *signed* by the maker if it is a note or CD and by the drawer if it is a check or draft. The maker or drawer is not liable on the instrument unless his or her signature appears on it. The signature can be placed on the instrument by the maker or drawer or by an authorized agent [UCC 3-401(a)]. Although the signature of the maker, drawer, or agent can be located anywhere on the face of the negotiable instrument, it is usually placed in the lower-right corner.

Business Brief

A negotiable instrument must be in writing; oral promises or orders do not qualify as negotiable instruments. (They are enforceable, however, under ordinary contract law.)

The UCC broadly defines **signature** as any symbol executed or adopted by a party with a present intent to authenticate a writing [UCC 1-201(39)]. A signature is made by the use of any name, including a trade or assumed name, or by any word or mark used in lieu of a written signature [UCC 3-401(b)]. For example, the requisite signature can be the maker's or drawer's formal name (Henry Richard Cheeseman), informal name (Hank Cheeseman), initials (HRC), or nickname (The Big Cheese). Any other symbol or device (e.g., an *X*, a thumbprint) adopted by the signer as his or her signature also qualifies. The signer's intention to use the symbol as his or her signature is controlling. Typed, printed, lithographed, rubber-stamped, or other mechanical means of signing instruments are recognized as valid by the UCC.

Contemporary Environment
Signing As an Authorized Representative

A maker or drawer can appoint an *agent* to sign a negotiable instrument on his or her behalf. For example, corporations and other organizations use agents, usually corporate officers or employees, to sign the corporation's negotiable instruments. Individuals can also appoint agents to sign their negotiable instruments.

A maker or drawer is liable on a negotiable instrument signed by an authorized agent. The agent is not personally liable on the negotiable instrument if his or her signature properly unambiguously discloses (1) his or her agency status and (2) the identity of the maker or drawer [UCC 3-402(b)]. In the case of an organization, the agent's signature is proper if the organization's name is preceded or followed by the name of the authorized agent. ◼

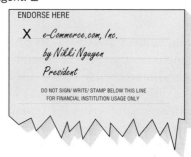

Unconditional Promise or Order to Pay

To be a negotiable instrument under the requirements of UCC 3-104(a), a writing must contain either an **unconditional promise to pay** (note or CD) or an ***unconditional* order to pay** (draft or check). The term *unconditional*, which is discussed shortly, is key.

Promise or Order To be negotiable, a **promise to pay** must be an unconditional and affirmative undertaking. The mere acknowledgment of a debt is not sufficient to constitute a negotiable instrument. In other words, an implied promise to pay is not negotiable, but an expressly stated promise to pay is negotiable. For example, the statement "I owe you $100" is merely an I.O.U. It acknowledges a debt, but it does not contain an express promise to repay the money. If the I.O.U. used language such as "I promise to pay" or "the undersigned agrees to pay," however, a negotiable instrument would be created because the note would contain an affirmative obligation to pay.

Certificates of deposit (CDs) are an exception to this rule. CDs do not require an express promise to pay because the bank's acknowledgment of the payee's bank deposit and other terms of the CD clearly indicate the bank's promise to repay the certificate holder. Nevertheless, most CDs contain an express promise to pay.

To be negotiable, a draft or check must contain the drawer's unconditional **order for the drawee to pay** a payee. An order is a direction to pay and must be more than an authorization or a request to pay. The language of the order must be precise and contain the word *pay*. For example, the printed word *pay* on a check is a proper order that is sufficient to make a check negotiable. The order can be in a courteous form, such as "please pay" or "kindly pay." A mere request or acknowledgment, such as "I wish you would pay," is not sufficient because it lacks a direction to pay.

An order to pay a draft or check must identify the drawee who is directed to make the payment. The name of the drawee financial institution that is preprinted on a check is sufficient. The order can be directed to one or more parties jointly, such as "to A *and* B," or in the alternative, such as "to A *or* B." The order cannot, however, be in succession, such as "to A, and if she does not pay, then to B."

Unconditional Promise or Order   To be negotiable, the promise or order must be **unconditional** [UCC 3-104(a)]. A promise or order that is **conditional** on another promise or event is not negotiable because the risk of the other promise or event not occurring would fall on the person who held the instrument. A conditional promise is subject to normal contract law.

Consider This Example   Suppose American Airlines buys a $10 million airplane from Boeing Aircraft. American signs a promissory note that promises to pay Boeing if it is "satisfied" with the airplane. This promise is a conditional promise. The condition—that American is satisfied with the airplane—destroys the negotiability of the note.

A promise or an order is conditional and, therefore, not negotiable if it states (1) an express condition to payment, (2) that the promise or order is subject to or governed by another writing, or (3) the rights or obligations with respect to the promise or order are stated in another writing. The mere reference to another writing does not make the promise or order conditional [UCC 3-106(a)].

Consider This Example   Dow Chemical purchases equipment from Illinois Tool Works and signs a sales contract. Dow Chemical borrows the purchase price from Citibank and executes a promissory note evidencing this debt and promising to repay the borrowed money plus interest. The note contains the following reference: "sales contract—purchase of equipment." This reference does not affect the negotiability of the note. The note would not be negotiable, however, if the reference stated, "This note hereby incorporates by this reference the terms of the sales contract between Dow Chemical and Illinois Tool Works of this date."

A promise or an order remains unconditional even though it refers to another writing for rights to collateral, prepayment, or acceleration (e.g., "see collateral agreement dated January 15, 2004"). A promise or an order may also stipulate that payment is limited to a particular fund or source (e.g., "payable out of the proceeds of the Tower Construction Contract") [UCC 3-106(b)].

Fixed Amount of Money

To be negotiable, an instrument must contain a promise or an order to pay a **fixed amount of money** [UCC 3-104(a)]. This phrase can be analyzed as two promises or orders: (1) to pay a *fixed amount* and (2) to pay in money.

Fixed Amount   The **fixed amount** requirement ensures that the value of the instrument can be determined with certainty. The principal amount of the instrument must appear on the face of the instrument.

An instrument does not have to be payable with interest, but if it is, the amount of interest being charged may be expressed as either a *fixed* or *variable* rate. The amount or rate of interest may be stated or described in the instrument or may require reference to information not contained in the instrument. If an instrument provides for interest but the amount of interest cannot be determined from the description, interest is payable at the judgment rate (legal rate) in effect at the place of payment of the instrument [UCC 3-112].

For example, a note that contains a promise to pay $10,000 in one year at a stated rate of 10 percent interest is a negotiable instrument because the value of the note can be determined at any time. A note that contains a promise to pay in goods or services is not a negotiable instrument because the value of the note would be difficult to determine at any given time.

Payable in Money UCC 3-104(a) provides that the fixed amount must be payable in "money". The UCC defines **money** as a "medium of exchange authorized or adopted by a domestic or foreign government as part of its currency" [UCC 1-201(24)]. For example, an instrument that is "payable in $10,000 U.S. currency" is a negotiable instrument.

Instruments that are fully or partially payable in a medium of exchange other than money are not negotiable. Thus, an instrument that is "payable in $10,000 U.S. gold" is not negotiable. Although the stated amount is a fixed amount, it is not payable in a medium of exchange of the U.S. government. Likewise, instruments that are payable in diamonds, commodities, goods, services, stocks, bonds, and such do not qualify as negotiable instruments.

Variable Interest Rate Loan Many lending institutions offer **variable interest rate loans**. These loans tie the interest rate to some set measure, such as a major bank's prime rate (e.g., Citibank's prime) or another well-known rate (e.g., Freddie Mac rate). Thus, the interest changes during the life of the loan. Some lenders make loans that are fixed for a period of time (i.e., the first seven years) and become variable for the remaining period of the loan.

Revised Article 3 of the UCC expressly provides that variable interest rate notes are negotiable instruments. UCC 3-112(b) provides: "Interest may be stated in an instrument as a fixed or variable amount of money or it may be expressed as a fixed or variable rate or rates." UCC 3-112(b) also provides that the amount or rate of interest may be determined by reference to information not contained in the instrument.

Not Require Any Undertaking in Addition to the Payment of Money

To qualify as a negotiable instrument, a promise or an order to pay cannot state any other undertaking by the person promising or ordering payment to do any act in addition to the payment of money [UCC 3-104(a)(3)]. For example, if a note required the maker to pay a stated amount of money *and* perform some type of service, it would not be negotiable.

A promise or an order may include authorization or power to protect collateral, dispose of collateral, and waive any law intended to protect the obligee.

International Law

Negotiable Instruments Payable in Foreign Currency

The UCC expressly provides that an instrument may state that it is payable in foreign money [UCC 3-107]. For example, an instrument "payable in 10,000 yen in Japanese currency" is a negotiable instrument that is governed by Article 3 of the UCC.

Unless the instrument states otherwise, an instrument that is payable in foreign currency can be satisfied by the equivalent in U.S. dollars, as determined on the due date. The conversion rate is the current bank-offered spot rate at the place of payment on the due date. The instrument can expressly provide that it is payable only in the stated foreign currency. In this case, the instrument cannot be paid in U.S. dollars. ■

Payable on Demand or at a Definite Time

For an instrument to be negotiable, it is necessary to know when the maker, drawee, or acceptor is required to pay it. UCC 3-104(a)(2) requires the instrument to be **payable either on demand or at a definite time**, as noted on the face of the instrument.

Payable on Demand Instruments that are payable on demand are called **demand instruments**. Demand instruments are created by (1) language such as "payable on demand," "payable at sight," or "payable on presentment" or (2) silence regarding when payment is due [UCC 3-108(a)].

By definition, checks are payable on demand [UCC 3-104(f)]. Other instruments, such as notes, CDs, and drafts can be, but are not always, payable on demand.

Payable at a Definite Time Instruments that are payable at a definite time are called **time instruments**. UCC 3-108(b) and (c) states that an instrument is payable at a definite time if it is payable:

1. At a fixed date (for example, "payable on January 1, 2006").
2. On or before a stated date (for example, "payable on or before January 1, 2006"). The maker or drawee has the option of paying the note before—but not after—the stated maturity date.
3. At a fixed period after sight (for example, "payable 60 days after sight"). Drafts often contain this type of language. The holder must formally present this type of instrument for acceptance so that the date of sight can be established.
4. At a time readily ascertainable when the promise or order is issued (for example, "payable 60 days after January 1, 2006").

Instruments that are payable upon an uncertain act or event are not negotiable. For example, suppose Sarah Smith's father executes a promissory note stating, "I promise to pay to the order of my daughter, Sarah, $100,000 on the date she marries Bobby Boggs." This note is nonnegotiable because the act and date of marriage are uncertain.

Prepayment, Acceleration, and Extension Clauses The inclusion of prepayment, acceleration, or extension clauses in an instrument does not affect its negotiability. Such clauses are commonly found in promissory notes.

A **prepayment clause** permits the maker to pay the amount due prior to the due date of the instrument. An **acceleration clause** allows the payee or holder to accelerate payment of the principal amount of an instrument, plus accrued interest, upon the happening of an event (e.g., default). An **extension clause** is the opposite of an acceleration clause. It allows the date of maturity of an instrument to be extended to some time in the future.

> The great source of the flourishing state of this kingdom is its trade, and commerce, and paper currency, guarded by proper regulations and restrictions, is the life of commerce.
>
> Ashhurst, J.
> *Jordaine v. Lashbrooke (1798)*

Contemporary Environment
Payable to Order or to Bearer

Because negotiable instruments are primarily intended to act as a substitute for money, they must be freely transferable to other persons or entities. The UCC requires that negotiable instruments be either **payable to order** or **payable to bearer** [UCC 3-104(a)(1)]. Promises or orders to pay that do not meet this requirement are not negotiable. They may, however, be assignable under contract law.

Order Instruments

An instrument is an **order instrument** if it is payable (1) to the order of an identified person or (2) to an identified person or orders [UCC 3-109(b)]. For example, an instrument that states "payable to the order of IBM" or "payable to IBM or order" is negotiable. It would not be negotiable if it stated either "payable to IBM" or "pay to IBM" because it is not payable to *order*.

An instrument can be payable to the order of the maker, the drawer, the drawee, the payee, two or more payees together, or, alternatively, to an office, an officer by his or her title, a corporation, a partnership, an unincorporated association, a trust, an estate, or another legal entity. A person to whom an instrument is payable may be identified in any way, including by name, identifying number, office, or account number. An instrument is payable to the person intended by the signer of the instrument even if that person is identified in the instrument by a name or other identification that is not that of the intended person [UCC 3-110].

Contemporary Environment

(continued)

For example, an instrument made "payable to the order of Lovey" is negotiable. The identification of "Lovey" may be determined by evidence. On the other hand, an instrument made "payable to the order of my loved ones" is not negotiable because the payees are not ascertainable with reasonable certainty.

Bearer Instruments

A **bearer instrument** is payable to anyone in physical possession of the instrument who presents it for payment when it is due. The person in possession of the instrument is called the **bearer**.

Bearer paper results when the drawer or maker does not make the instrument payable to a specific payee.

For example, an instrument is payable to bearer when any of the following language is used: "payable to the order of bearer," "payable to bearer," "payable to Xerox or bearer," "payable to cash," or "payable to the order of cash." In addition, any other indication that does not purport to designate a specific payee creates bearer paper [UCC 3-109(a)]. For example, an instrument "payable to my dog Fido" creates a bearer instrument. ■

■ *Concept Summary* *Formal Requirements for a Negotiable Instrument*

Requirement	Description
Writing	Writing must be permanent and portable. Oral or implied instruments are nonnegotiable [UCC 3-104(d)].
Signed by maker or drawer	Signature must appear on the face of the instrument. It may be any mark intended by the signer to be his or her signature. Signature may be by an authorized representative [UCC 3-104(a)].
Unconditional promise or order to pay	Instrument must be an unconditional promise or order to pay [UCC 3-104(a)]. Permissible notations listed in UCC 3-106(a) do not affect the instrument's negotiability. If payment is conditional on the performance of another agreement, the instrument is nonnegotiable.
Fixed amount of money	Fixed amount: Amount required to discharge the instrument must be on the face of the instrument [UCC 3-104(a)]. Amount may include payment of interest and costs of collection. Revised Article 3 provides that variable interest rate notes are negotiable instruments. In money: Amount must be payable in U.S. or foreign country's currency. If payment is to be made in goods, services, or nonmonetary items, the instrument is nonnegotiable [UCC 3-104(a)].
Cannot require any undertaking in addition to the payment of money	A promise or an order to pay cannot state any other undertaking to do an act in addition to the payment of money [UCC 3-104(a)(3)]. A promise or an order may include authorization or power to protect collateral, dispose of collateral, waive any law intended to protect the obligee, and the like.
Payable on demand or at a definite time	Payable on demand: Payable at sight, upon presentation, or when no time for payment is stated [UCC 3-108(a)]. Payable at a definite time: Payable at a definite date or before a stated date, a fixed period after a stated date, or at a fixed period after sight [UCC 3-108(b) and (c)]. An instrument payable only upon the occurrence of an uncertain act or event is nonnegotiable.

Nonnegotiable Contracts

If a promise or an order to pay does not meet one of the previously discussed requirements of negotiability, it is **nonnegotiable contract**. As such, it is not subject to the provisions of UCC Article 3. However, the contract is not rendered either nontransferable or nonenforceable. A nonnegotiable contract can be enforced under normal contract law. If the maker or drawer of a nonnegotiable contract fails to pay it, the holder of the contract can sue the nonperforming party for breach of contract.

Transfer by Assignment and Transfer by Negotiation

After they have been issued, negotiable instruments can be transferred to subsequent parties by *assignment* or by *negotiation*. The rights acquired by subsequent transferees differ according to the method of transfer. The different methods of transfer are discussed in the following paragraphs.

Transfer by Assignment

An **assignment** is the transfer of rights under a contract. It transfers the rights of the transferor (**assignor**) to the transferee (**assignee**). Because normal contract principles apply, the assignee acquires only the rights that the assignor possessed. Thus, any defenses to the enforcement of the contract that could have been raised against the assignor can also be raised against the assignee.

An assignment occurs when a nonnegotiable contract is transferred. In the case of a negotiable instrument, assignment occurs when the instrument is transferred but the transfer fails to qualify as a negotiation under Article 3. In this case, the transferee is an *assignee* rather than a *holder*.

Transfer by Negotiation

Negotiation is the transfer of a negotiable instrument by a person other than the issuer. The person to whom the instrument is transferred becomes the holder [UCC 3-201(a)]. The **holder** receives at least the rights of the transferor and may acquire even greater rights than the transferor if he or she qualifies as a holder in due course (HDC) [UCC 3-302]. An HDC has greater rights because he or she is not subject to some of the defenses that could otherwise have been raised against the transferor.

The proper method of negotiation depends on whether the instrument is order paper or bearer paper, as discussed next.

Negotiating Order Paper   An instrument that is payable to a specific payee or indorsed to a specific indorsee is **order paper**. Order paper is negotiated by delivery with the necessary indorsement [UCC 3-201(b)]. Thus, for order paper to be negotiated, there must be delivery and indorsement.

Consider This Example   Sam Bennett receives a weekly payroll check from his employer, Ace Plumbing Corporation. Bennett takes the check to a local store, signs the back of the check (indorsement), gives the check to the cashier (delivery), and receives cash from the check. Bennett has negotiated the check to the store. Delivery and indorsement have occurred.

Negotiating Bearer Paper   An instrument that is not payable to a specific payee or indorsee is **bearer paper**. Bearer paper is negotiated by *delivery*; indorsement is not necessary [UCC 3-201(b)]. Substantial risk is associated with the loss or theft of bearer paper.

Business Brief

There is a substantial risk associated with the loss or theft of bearer paper.

Business Brief

Negotiable instruments can be converted from order paper to bearer paper, and vice versa, depending on the form of the indorsement.

Consider This Example   Suppose Mary draws a check "pay to cash" and gives it to Peter. There has been a negotiation because Mary delivered a bearer instrument (the check) to Peter. Subsequently, Carmen steals the check from Peter. There has not been a negotiation because the check was not voluntarily delivered. That Carmen physically possesses the check is irrelevant. The negotiation is complete, however, if Carmen delivers the check to an innocent third party. The party is a holder and may qualify as an HDC with all the rights in the check [UCC 3-302]. If the holder is an HDC, Peter's only recourse is to recover against Carmen.

Contemporary Environment
Converting Order and Bearer Paper

Instruments can be converted from order paper to bearer paper and vice versa many times until the instrument is paid [UCC 3-109(c)]. The deciding factor is the type of indorsement placed on the instrument at the time of each subsequent transfer. For example, follow the indorsements below to determine whether order or bearer paper has been created. ∎

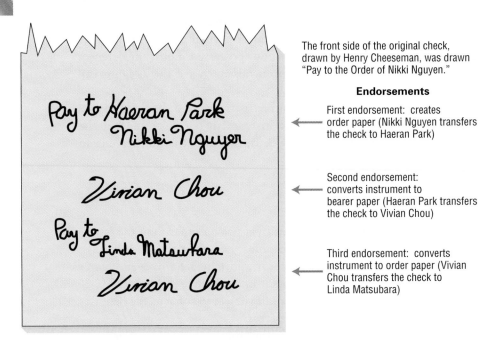

The front side of the original check, drawn by Henry Cheeseman, was drawn "Pay to the Order of Nikki Nguyen."

Endorsements

First endorsement: creates order paper (Nikki Nguyen transfers the check to Haeran Park)

Second endorsement: converts instrument to bearer paper (Haeran Park transfers the check to Vivian Chou)

Third endorsement: converts instrument to order paper (Vivian Chou transfers the check to Linda Matsubara)

Indorsements

An **indorsement** is the signature of a signer (other than as a maker, a drawer, or an acceptor) that is placed on an instrument to negotiate it to another person. The signature may (1) appear alone, (2) name an individual to whom the instrument is to be paid, or (3) be accompanied by other words [UCC 3-204(2)]. The person who indorses an instrument is called the **indorser**. If the indorsement names a payee, this person is called the **indorsee**.

Consider This Example   Nikki Choy receivers a $500 check for her birthday. She can transfer the check to anyone merely by signing her name on the back of the check. Suppose she indorses it "pay to Rob Dewey." Choy is the indorser; Rob Dewey is the indorsee.

Indorsements are usually placed on the reverse side of the instrument, such as on the back of a check (see Exhibit 19.5). If there is no room on the instrument, the indorsement

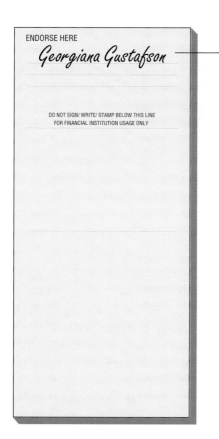

Endorsement should be placed at the top of the back of the check

may be written on a separate piece of paper called an **allonge**. The allonge must be affixed (e.g., stapled, taped) to the instrument [UCC 3-204(a)].

Indorsements are required to negotiate order paper, but they are not required to negotiate bearer paper [UCC 3-201(b)]. For identification purposes and to impose liability on the transferor, however, the transferee often requires the transferor to indorse the bearer paper at negotiation.

Types of Indorsements

Every indorsement is:

1. Blank or special
2. Unqualified or qualified
3. Nonrestrictive or restrictive

These different types of indorsements are discussed in the following paragraphs.

Blank Indorsements

A **blank indorsement** does not specify a particular indorsee. It may consist of a mere signature [UCC 3-205(b)]. For example, suppose Harold Green draw a check "pay to the order of Victoria Rudd" and delivers the check to Victoria. Victoria indorses the check in blank by writing her signature on the back of the check (see Exhibit 19.6).

Order paper that is indorsed in blank becomes bearer paper. As mentioned earlier, bearer paper can be negotiated by delivery; indorsement is not required. For example, if Victoria Rudd loses the check she indorsed in blank and Mary Smith finds it, Mary Smith can deliver it to another person without indorsing it. Thus, the lost check can be presented for payment or negotiated to another holder.

Business Brief

An indorsement is necessary to negotiate order paper but is not required to negotiate bearer paper.

Exhibit 19.6

A Blank Indorsement

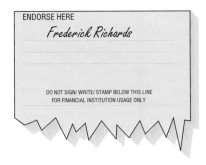

Special Indorsements

A **special indorsement** contains the signature of the indorser and specifies the person (indorsee) to whom the indorser intends the instrument to be payable [UCC 3-205(a)]. Words of negotiation (e.g., "pay the order of . . . ") are not required for a special indorsement. Words such as "pay Emily Ingman" are sufficient to form a special indorsement. For example, a special indorsement would be created if Betsey McKenny indorsed her check and then wrote "pay to Dan Jones" above her signature (see Exhibit 19.7). The check is negotiated when Betsy gives it to Dan. A special indorsement creates *order paper*. As mentioned earlier, order paper is negotiated by indorsement and delivery.

To prevent the risk of loss from theft, a special indorsement (which creates order paper) is preferred over a blank indorsement (which creates bearer paper). A holder can convert a blank indorsement into a special indorsement by writing any contract consistent with the character of the indorsement over the signature of the indorser in blank [UCC 3-205(c)]. For example, words such as "pay to John Jones" written above the indorser's signature are enough to convert bearer paper to order paper.

Unqualified and Qualified Indorsements

Generally, an indorsement is a promise by the indorser to pay the holder or any subsequent indorser the amount of the instrument if the maker, drawer, or acceptor defaults on it. This promise is called an **unqualified indorsement**. Unless otherwise agreed, the order and liability of the indorsers is presumed to be the order in which they indorse the instrument [UCC 3-415(a)].

Consider This Example   Cindy draws a check payable to the order of John. John (indorser) indorses the check and negotiates it to Steve (indorsee). When Steve presents the check for payment, there are insufficient funds in Cindy's account to pay the check. John, as an **unqualified indorser**, is liable on the check. John can recover from Cindy.

Exhibit 19.7

A Special Indorsement

A Special Qualified Indorsement

A Blank Qualified Indorsement

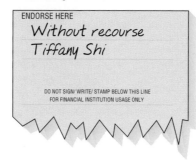

Exhibit 19.8

Qualified Indorsements

The UCC permits **qualified indorsements** that is, indorsements that disclaim or limit liability on the instrument. A **qualified indorser** does not guarantee payment of the instrument if the maker, drawer, or acceptor defaults on it. A qualified indorsement is created by placing a notation such as "without recourse" or other similar language that disclaims liability as part of the indorsement [UCC 3-415(b)] A quantified indorsement protects only the indorser who wrote it on the instrument. Subsequent indorsers must also place a qualified indorsement on the instrument to be protected from liability. An instrument containing a qualified indorsement can be further negotiated.

Qualified indorsements are often used by persons signing instruments in a representative capacity. For example, suppose an insurance company that is paying a claim makes out a check payable to the order of the attorney representing the payee. The attorney can indorse the check to his client (the payee) with the notation "without recourse." This notation ensures that the attorney is not liable as an indorser if the insurance company fails to pay the check.

A qualified indorsement can be either a special qualified indorsement or a blank qualified indorsement. A **special indorsement** creates order paper that can be negotiated by indorsement and delivery. A **blank qualified indorsement** creates bearer paper that can be further negotiated by delivery without indorsement (see Exhibit 19.8).

Nonrestrictive and Restrictive Indorsements

Most indorsements are **nonrestrictive**. Nonrestrictive indorsements do not have any instructions or conditions attached to the payment of the funds. For example, an indorsement is nonrestrictive if the indorsee merely signs his signature to the back of an instrument or includes a notation to pay a specific indorsee ("pay to Sam Smith").

Occasionally, an indorser includes some form of instruction in an indorsement. This instruction is called a **restrictive indorsement**. A restrictive indorsement restricts the indorsee's rights in some manner. An indorsement that purports to prohibit further negotiation of an instrument does not destroy the negotiability of the instrument. For example, a check that is indorsed "pay to Sarah Stein only" can still be negotiated to other transferees. Because of its ineffectiveness, this type of restrictive indorsement is seldom used.

UCC 3-206 recognizes the following types of restrictive indorsements:

- **Indorsement for deposit or collection.** An indorser can indorse an instrument so as to make the indorsee his collecting agent. Such indorsement—called an **indorsement for deposit or collection**—is often done when an indorser deposits a check or other instrument for collection at a bank. Words such as *for collection, for deposit only*, and *pay any bank* create this type of indorsement. Banks use this type of indorsement in the collection process.

Exhibit 19.9

A Trust Indorsement

ENDORSE HERE

Pay to Lana Cheeseman in
trust for Gregory Cheeseman, Jr.
and Nikki Cheeseman
Gregory Cheeseman, Sr.

DO NOT SIGN/ WRITE/ STAMP BELOW THIS LINE
FOR FINANCIAL INSTITUTION USAGE ONLY

■ *Indorsement in trust.* An indorsement can state that it is for the benefit or use of the indorser or another person. For example, checks are often indorsed to attorneys, executors of estates, real estate agents, and other fiduciaries in their representative capacity for the benefit of clients, heirs, or others. These indorsements are called **trust indorsements** or **agency indorsements** (see Exhibit 19.9). The indorser is not personally liable on the instrument if there is a proper trust or agency indorsement.

An indorsee who does not comply with the instructions of a restrictive indorsement is liable to the indorser for all losses that occur because of such noncompliance.

Consider This Example   Suppose a check is drawn "payable to Anne Spencer, Attorney, in trust for Joseph Watkins." If Spencer indorses the check to an automobile dealer in payment for a car that she purchases personally, the automobile dealer (indorsee) has not followed the instructions of the restrictive indorsement. He is liable to Joseph Watkins for any losses that arise because of his noncompliance with the restrictive indorsement.

Misspelled or Wrong Name

Where the name of the payee or indorsee is misspelled in a negotiable instrument, the payee or indorsee can indorse the instrument in the misspelled name, the correct name, or both. For example, if Susan Worth receives a check payable to "Susan Wirth," she can indorse the check "Susan Wirth," "Susan Worth," or both. A person paying or taking the instrument for value or collection may require a signature in both the misspelled and the correct versions [UCC3-204(d)].

> A trader is trusted upon his character, and visible commerce: that credit enables him to acquire wealth. If by secret liens, a few might swallow up all, it would greatly damp that credit.
>
> Lord Mansfield
> *Worseley v. Demattos (1758)*

Contemporary Environment

Multiple Payees or Indorsees

Drawers, makers, and indorsers often make checks, promissory notes, and other negotiable instruments payable to two or more payees or indorsees. The question then arises: Can the instrument be negotiated by the signature of one payee or indorsee, or are all of their signatures required to negotiate the instrument?

Section 3-110(d) of Revised Article 3 of the UCC and cases that have interpreted that section establish the following rules:

■ If an instrument is *payable jointly* using the word *and* (e.g., pay to Shou-Yi Kang *and* Min-Wer Chen), both persons' indorsements are necessary to negotiate the instrument.

■ If the instrument is *payable in the alternative* using the word *or* (e.g., pay to Shou-Yi Kang *or* Min-Wer Chen), either person's indorsement alone is sufficient to negotiate the instrument.

■ If a *virgule*—a slash mark—is used, courts have held that the instrument is payable in the alternative. Thus, if a virgule is used (e.g., pay to Shou-Yi Kang/Min-Wer Chen), either person may individually indorse and negotiate the instrument. [*Mumma v. Rainer National Bank*, 808 P.2d 767 (Wash. App. 1991)] ■

Concept Summary   *Types of Indorsements*

Type of Indorsement	Description
Blank	Does not specify a particular indorsee (e.g.,/s/Mary Jones). This indorsement creates bearer paper.
Special	Specifies the person to whom the indorser intends the instrument to be payable (e.g., "Pay to the order of John Smith" /s/ Mary Jones). This indorsement creates order paper. [If it is not payable to order (e.g., "Pay to John Smith" /s/ Mary Jones), it can be converted to order paper (e.g., "Pay to the order of Fred Roe" /s/ John Smith).]
Unqualified	Does not disclaim or limit liability. The indorsee is liable on the instrument if it is not paid by the maker, acceptor, or drawer.
Qualified	Disclaims or limits the liability of the indorsee. There are two types: 1. Special qualified indorsement (e.g., "Pay to the order of John Smith, without recourse" /s/ Mary Jones). 2. Blank qualified indorsement (e.g., "Without recourse" /s/ Mary Jones).
Nonrestrictive	No instructions or conditions are attached to the payment of funds (e.g., "Pay to John Smith or order" /s/ Mary Jones).
Restrictive	Conditions or instructions restrict the indorsee's rights. There are four types: 1. Conditional indorsement (e.g., "Pay to John Smith if he completes construction of my garage by June 1, 2004" /s/ Mary Jones). 2. Indorsement prohibiting further indorsement (e.g., "Pay to John Smith only" /s/ Mary Jones). 3. Indorsement for deposit or collection (e.g., "For deposit only" /s/ Mary Jones). 4. Indorsement in trust (e.g., "Pay to John Smith, trustee" /s/ Mary Jones).

Forged Indorsement

Article 3 establishes certain rules for assessing liability when a negotiable instrument has been paid over a **forged indorsement**. With few exceptions, unauthorized indorsements are wholly inoperative as the indorsement of the person whose name is signed [UCC 3-401(a)]. Where an indorsement on an instrument has been forged or is unauthorized, the general rule is that the loss falls on the party who first takes the forged instrument after the forgery.

Consider This Example   Suppose Andy draws a check payable to the order of Mallory. Leslie steals the check from Mallory, forges Mallory's indorsement, and cashes the check at the liquor store. The liquor store is liable. Andy, the drawer, is not. The liquor store can recover from Leslie, the forger (if she can be found).

There are two exceptions to this rule: where a drawer or maker bears the loss where an indorsement is forged. The rules governing these circumstances—the imposter rule and the fictitious payee rule—are discussed in the paragraphs that follow.

Contemporary Environment
The Imposter Rule

For purposes of the imposter rule, an **imposter** is one who impersonates a payee and induces the maker or drawer to issue an instrument in the payee's name and give the instrument to the imposter. If the imposter forges the indorsement of the named payee, the drawer or maker is liable on the instrument to any person who, in good faith, pays the instrument or takes it for value or for collection [UCC 3-404(a)]. This rule is called the **imposter rule**.

Consider This Example Suppose Fred purchases goods by telephone from Cynthia. Fred has never met Cynthia. Beverly goes to Fred and pretends to be Cynthia. Fred draws a check payable to the order of Cynthia and gives the check to Beverly,

believing her to be Cynthia. Beverly forges Cynthia's indorsement and cashes the check at a liquor store. Under the imposter rule, Fred is liable and the liquor store is not because Fred was in the best position to have prevented the forged indorsement.

The imposter rule does not apply if the wrongdoer poses as the agent of the drawer or maker. For example, suppose in the preceding example that Beverly lied to Fred and said that she was Cynthia's agent. Believing this, Fred draws the check payable to the order of Cynthia and gives it to Beverly. Beverly forges Cynthia's indorsement and cashes the check at a liquor store. Here, the store is liable because the imposter rule does not apply. The liquor store may recover from Beverly, if she can be found. ■

Contemporary Environment
The Fictitious Payee Rule

A drawer or maker is liable on a forged or unauthorized indorsement under the **fictitious payee rule**. This rule applies when a person signing as or on behalf of a drawer or maker intends the named payee to have no interest in the instrument or when the person identified as the payee is a fictitious person [UCC 3-404(b)].

Consider This Example Marcia is the treasurer of the Weld Corporation. As treasurer, Marcia makes out and signs the payroll checks for the company. Marcia draws a payroll check payable to the order of her neighbor Harold Green, who does not work for the company. Marcia does not intend Harold to receive this money. She indorses Harold's name on the check and names herself as the indorsee. She cashes the check at a liquor store. Under the fictitious payee rule, Weld Corporation is liable because it was in a better position than the liquor store to have prevented the fraud.

The fictitious payee rule also applies if an agent or employee of the drawer or maker supplies the drawer or maker with the name of a fictitious payee [UCC 3-405(c)].

Consider This Example Elizabeth is an accountant for the Baldridge Corporation. She is responsible for drawing up a list of employees who are to receive payroll checks. The treasurer of Baldridge Corporation actually signs the checks. Elizabeth places the name "Annabelle Armstrong" (a fictitious person) on the list. Baldridge Corporation issues a payroll check to this fictitious person. Elizabeth indorses the instrument "Annabelle Armstrong" and names herself as indorsee. She cashes the check at a liquor store. Under the fictitious payee rule, Baldridge Corporation is liable; The liquor store is not. ■

Chapter Summary

Negotiable Instruments, p. 386

Revised Article 3 (Negotiable Instruments) of the UCC

1. *Article 3 of the UCC.* Article 3 of the Uniform Commercial Code was promulgated in 1952 to govern the creation of, transfer of, enforcement of, and liability on negotiable instruments.

2. *Revised Article 3.* In 1990, the American Law Institute and the National Conference of Commissioners on Uniform State Laws approved *Revised Article 3.* This article replaced Article 3. It made substantial changes to the law governing negotiable instruments.

Functions of Negotiable Instruments

A negotiable instrument is a:

1. Substitute for money.
2. Credit device.
3. Record keeping device.

Types of Negotiable Instruments, p. 387

Types of Negotiable Instruments

There are four types of negotiable instruments. They are:

1. *Draft.* An order to pay. A three-party instrument.
2. *Check.* An order to pay. A three-party instrument.
3. *Promissory note.* A promise to pay. A two-party instrument.
4. *Certificate of deposit (CD).* A promise to pay. A two-party instrument.

Drafts

A draft is an unconditional written order by one party (the *drawer*) that orders a second party (the *drawee*) to pay money to a third party (the *payee*). The drawee must owe money to the drawer for the drawer to issue a draft ordering the money to be paid to the payee.

1. *Drawer.* The party who writes the order for a draft.
2. *Drawee.* The party who must pay the money stated in a draft. The drawee is also called the *acceptor*.
3. *Payee.* The party who receives the money from a draft.
4. *Types of drafts.*
   a. *Time draft.* A draft payable at a designated future date.
   b. *Sight draft.* A draft payable on sight. Also called a *demand draft*.
   c. *Trade acceptance.* A sight draft that arises when credit is extended (by a seller to a buyer) with the sale of goods. The seller is both the drawer and the payee, and the buyer is the drawee.

Checks

A check is a form of draft drawn on a financial institution (the *drawee*) and payable on demand. The checking account holder (the *drawer*) orders the financial institution (the *drawee*) to pay money to a third party (the *payee*).

1. *Drawer.* The checking account holder and writer of a check.
2. *Drawee.* The financial institution where the drawer has his or her checking account and pays the money to the payee.
3. *Payee.* The party to whom a check is written.
4. *Types of checks:*
   a. *Ordinary checks*
   b. *Special checks:*
      i. Certified checks
      ii. Cashier's checks
      iii. Traveler's checks

Promissory Notes

An unconditional written promise by one party (the *maker*) to pay money to another party (the *payee*). Promissory notes are also called *notes*:

1. *Maker.* The party who makes the promise to pay (the borrower).
2. *Payee.* The party to whom the promise to pay is made (the lender).

3. ***Types of promissory notes:***
    a. *Time note.* A note payable at a specific time.
    b. *Demand note.* A note payable on demand.
    c. *Installment note.* A note paid in more than one installment.
    d. *Mortgage note.* A note secured by real estate.
    e. *Collateral note.* A note secured by personal property.

Certificates of Deposit

A CD is a special form of note that is created when a depositor (the *payee*) deposits money at a financial institution (the *maker*) in exchange for the institution's promise to pay back the amount of the deposit plus an agreed-upon rare of interest upon the expiration of a set time period agreed upon by the parties.

1. ***Maker.*** The financial institution (the borrower).
2. ***Payee.*** The depositor (the lender).
3. ***Types of CDs:***
    a. *Small CD.* A CD under $100,000.
    b. *Jumbo CD.* A CD of $100,000 or more.

Creating a Negotiable Instrument, p. 391

Creating a Negotiable Instrument

A negotiable instrument must:

1. Be in writing.
2. Be signed by the maker or drawer.
3. Be an unconditional promise or order to pay.
4. State a fixed amount of money.
5. Not require any undertaking in addition to the payment of money.
6. Be payable on demand or at a definite time.
7. Be payable to order or to bearer.

A Writing

1. ***Writing.*** A negotiable instrument must be in writing; oral promises or orders do not qualify as negotiable instruments.
2. ***Requirements of the writing:***
    a. *Permanency requirement.* The writing must be in a permanent state, such as written on ordinary paper.
    b. *Portability requirement.* The writing must be able to be easily transported between areas.

Signed by the Maker or the Drawer

1. ***Signature.*** A negotiable instrument must be signed by the *maker* if it is a note or CD and by the *drawer* if it is a draft or check.
2. ***Type of signature.*** Any symbol executed or adopted by the maker or drawer with a present intent to authenticate a writing qualifies as his or her signature. This signature can be a formal name, an informal name, initials, a nickname, or any symbol or device.
3. ***Signature of authorized agent.*** A maker or drawer can appoint an *agent* to sign a negotiable instrument on his or her behalf. *Liability of the parties:*
    a. *Maker or drawer.* The maker or drawer is liable on a negotiable instrument signed by an authorized agent.
    b. *Agent.* An agent is not personally liable on the negotiable instrument if his or her signature discloses (i) his or her *agency status* and (ii) the *identity of the maker or drawer*. An agent who fails to meet these requirements is personally liable on the instrument.

Unconditional Promise or Order to Pay

1. ***Promise or order.*** A *maker's promise to pay* must be an unconditional and affirmative undertaking to repay the debt evidenced by the note or CD. A *drawer's order to pay* must be an unconditional order to a drawee to pay a payee.

2. ***Unconditional promise or order.*** Promises to pay and orders to pay must be *unconditional* in order to be negotiable.

3. ***Conditional promise or order.*** A promise or an order that is *conditional* on another promise or event is not negotiable. A promise or an order is conditional if it states:

   a. An express condition to payment.

   b. That the promise or order is subject to or governed by another writing.

   c. The rights or obligations with respect to the promise or order are stated in another writing.

   A promise or an order remains *unconditional* if it merely references another writing or refers to another writing for rights as to *collateral, prepayment,* or *acceleration.*

Fixed Amount of Money

1. ***Fixed amount.*** The value of an instrument must be able to be determined with certainty. An instrument does not have to provide for the payment of *interest,* but if it does, interest may be expressed as a *fixed* or *variable* amount or rate. The amount or rate of interest may be determined by reference to information not contained in the instrument (e.g., a bank's prime rate or a government index).

2. ***Payable in money.*** The fixed amount must be payable in *money,* which is any medium of exchange authorized or adopted by a domestic or foreign government. Instruments that are payable in gold, diamonds, commodities, goods, services, stocks, bonds, and such do not qualify as negotiable instruments.

Not Require Any Undertaking in Addition to the Payment of Money

A promise or an order cannot require the person promising or ordering payment to do any act in addition to the payment of money. A note that would require such additional undertaking (e.g., the provision of a service) is not negotiable.

Payable on Demand or at a Definite Time

A negotiable instrument must be payable either on demand or at a definite time.

1. ***Payable on demand.*** An instrument may be payable on demand, at sight, or on presentment or may be silent regarding when payment is due. Called a *demand instrument.*

2. ***Payable at a definite time.*** An instrument is payable at a definite time if it is payable:

   a. At a fixed date.

   b. On or before a stated date.

   c. At a fixed period after sight.

   d. At a time readily ascertainable when the promise or order is issued.

3. ***Prepayment, acceleration, and extension clauses.*** The following clauses in an instrument do not affect its negotiability:

   a. Prepayment clause. A clause that permits a maker or drawee to pay an instrument prior to its due date.

   b. Acceleration clause. A clause that allows the payee or holder to accelerate payment of an instrument upon the happening of an event.

   c. Extension clause. A clause that allows the maturity of an instrument to be extended to some time in the future.

Payable to Order or to Bearer

A negotiable instrument must be payable to order or to bearer.

1. ***Order instruments.*** An instrument payable to the order of an *identified person* or to an identified person or order. The term *order* must be included in the instrument; otherwise, it is not negotiable. For example, an instrument that states "payable to the order of IBM" or "payable to IBM or order" is negotiable; a writing that states "payable to IBM" or "pay to IBM" is not negotiable.

2. *Bearer instruments.* An instrument that is payable to *anyone in physical possession* of the instrument. An instrument is payable to bearer when any of the following language is used; "payable to bearer," "payable to the order of bearer," "payable to IBM or bearer," "payable to cash," or "payable to the order of cash." The person in possession of a bearer instrument is called the *bearer*.

Nonnegotiable Contracts

A writing that fails to qualify as a negotiable instrument is a *nonnegotiable contract*. Nonnegotiable contracts are subject to normal contract law rather than Revised Article 3 of the UCC.

Transfer by Assignment and Transfer by Negotiation, p. 397

Transfer by Assignment or Negotiation

Once issued, negotiable instruments can be transferred by assignment or negotiation. The rights acquired by transferees differ according to the method of transfer.

Transfer by Assignment

1. *Assignment.* Transfer of rights that the transferor (*assignor*) has in a contract to a transferee (*assignee*). Ordinary contracts, writings that do not qualify as negotiable instruments and negotiable instruments that are not transferred by negotiation can be transferred by assignment.

2. *Assignor.* The transferor in an assignment situation.

3. *Assignee.* The transferee in an assignment situation.

4. *Rights acquired under an assignment.* The transferee acquires only the rights that the transferor had and is subject to all the defenses that can be raised against the transferor.

Transfer by Negotiation

1. *Negotiation.* Negotiation involves a transfer of a negotiable instrument by a person other than the issuer to a person who becomes a *holder. Negotiation* is a term signifying that a negotiable instrument has met certain requirements in being transferred.

2. *Transferor.* A transferor is a person who transfers a negotiable instrument by negotiation.

3. *Holder.* A holder is a person who receives a negotiable instrument by negotiation.

4. *Rights acquired under a negotiation.* The holder receives at least the rights of the transferor and may acquire even greater rights than the transferor if he or she qualifies as a *holder in due course (HDC)*.

**5. *Negotiating order paper. Order paper* (an instrument payable to a specific payee or indorsee) is negotiated by *delivery and indorsement.* That is, the transferor signs (indorses) the instrument, with or without other notation, and delivers the instrument to the holder.

**6. *Negotiating bearer paper. Bearer paper* (an instrument that is not payable to a specific payee) is negotiated by *delivery* (indorsement is not required). There is substantial risk associated with the loss or theft of bearer paper.

7. *Converting order and bearer paper.* Negotiable instruments can be *converted from order paper to bearer paper* by the holder indorsing the instrument without naming a specific payee. An instrument can be *converted from bearer paper to order paper* by the holder indorsing the instrument and naming a specific payee.

Indorsements, p. 398

Indorsement

An *indorsement* is the signature of the signer (other than as a maker, a drawer, or an acceptor) that is placed on an instrument to negotiate it to another person—for example, a holder singing the back of a check. An indorsement may be a signature alone (creating bearer paper), be accompanied by the name of a specific payee (creating order paper), or be accompanied by other words (e.g., "without recourse").

1. *Indorser.* An indorser is a person who indorses a negotiable instrument.

2. *Indorsee.* An indorsee is a person to whom a negotiable instrument is indorsed.

3. Allonge. Indorsements are usually placed on the reverse side of the negotiable instrument. If there is no room on the instrument, the indorsement may be placed on a separate sheet of paper called an *allonge.* The allonge must be firmly affixed to the instrument.

4. Instruments requiring indorsement. Indorsements are required to negotiate *order paper* (indorsement and delivery required). Indorsements are not required to negotiate *bearer paper* (only delivery is required).

Types of Indorsements

Every indorsement is:

1. Blank or special.

2. Unqualified or qualified.

3. Nonrestrictive or restrictive.

Blank Indorsements

A blank indorsement is an indorsement that does not specify a particular indorser, which occurs when an indorser merely signs the instrument without naming a payee. This indorsement creates *bearer* paper.

Special Indorsements

A special indorsement is an indorsement that specifies a named payee, which occurs when the indorser signs the instrument and names a particular indorsee. This indorsement creates *order* paper.

Unqualified and Qualified Indorsements

1. Unqualified indorsement. This indorsement does not disclaim or limit the liability of the indorser. An *unqualified indorser* is liable to pay any holder or subsequent indorser if the maker, drawer, or acceptor does not pay the instrument.

2. Qualified indorsement. This indorsement disclaims or limits the liability of the indorser. A *qualified indorser* is not liable to pay any holder or subsequent indorser if the maker, drawer, or acceptor does not pay the instrument. A qualified endorsement is done by adding the words *without recourse* or similar language that disclaims liability.

Nonrestrictive and Restrictive Indorsements

1. Nonrestrictive indorsement. A nonrestrictive indorsement is an indorsement that has no instructions or conditions attached to the payment of the funds. This indorsement occurs when the indorser signs his or her signature to the instrument (either naming a specific payee or not) but does not add any specific condition or instruction concerning the payment of the money.

2. Restrictive indorsement. A restrictive indorsement is an indorsement that contains some sort of instruction from the indorser. The UCC recognizes the following restrictive indorsements:

   a. Conditional indorsement. An indorsement that conditions the payment of an instrument upon the happening or nonhappening of a specified event.

   b. Indorsement for deposit or collection. An indorsement that makes the indorsee the indorser's collection agent (e.g., indorsement "for deposit only").

   c. Indorsement in trust. An indorsement which states that it is for the benefit or use of the indorser or another person.

   An indorsement that purports to prohibit further negotiation of a negotiable instrument (e.g., "pay to Sarah Smith only") is ineffective and does not destroy the negotiability of the instrument.

Misspelled or Wrong Name

If the name of the payee or indorsee is misspelled or is wrong, the payee or indorsee can indorse the instrument in the misspelled or wrong name, the correct name, or both.

Multiple Payees or Indorsees

1. Payable jointly. An instrument that is payable to two or more persons with *and* between their names is payable jointly. All their indorsements are required to negotiate the instrument.

2. Payable in the alternative. An instrument that is payable to two or more persons with *or* between their names is payable in the alternative. Only one of their indorsements is required to negotiate the instrument.

Forged Indorsement, p. 403

Forged Indorsements

1. Forged indorsement. A forged indorsement is a forged signature of a payee or holder on a negotiable instrument.

2. Liability on a forged indorsement. Generally, the person who took the check from the forger is liable on a forged indorsement.

3. Exceptions. There are two exceptions to the general rule: The imposter rule and the fictitious payee rule.

The Imposter Rule

1. An imposter. An imposter is a person who impersonates a payee and induces a maker or drawer to issue an instrument in the payee's name and give it to the imposter.

2. The imposter rule. This rule states that if an imposter forges the indorsement of the named payee, the drawer or maker is liable on the instrument and bears the loss.

The Fictitious Payee Rule

This rule says that a drawer or maker is liable on a forged or unauthorized indorsement of a fictitious payee. This rule applies when a person signing as or on behalf of a drawer or maker intends the named payee to have no interest in the instrument or when the person identified as the payee is a fictitious person.

Internet Exercises and Case Questions
Working the Web Internet Exercises

Activities

1. Find your state laws on financial institutions using the Cornell Web site. Notice that UCC Article 3 is the law of negotiable instruments. Find the imposter rule in your state's version of this article. See "LII: Law About . . . Banking," at **www.law.cornell.edu./topics/banking.html**.

2. Does your state have special laws covering digital signatures? See the law review article "Couriers Without Luggage: Negotiable Instruments and Digital Signature," by Jane Kaufman Winn, at **www.law.sc.edu/sclr/vo149-4-winn.pdf**

3. Read the law review article by Winn. What is the function of negotiable instruments?

Critical Legal Thinking Cases

19.1 Indorsement On November 15, 1979, Katherine Warnock purchased a cashier's check in the amount of $53,541, payable to her order and drawn on the Pueblo Bank and Trust Company (Pueblo Bank). At some time between November 15 and November 30, 1979, Warnock indorsed "Katherine Warnock" on the reverse side of the check. Eventually the check came into the hands of Warnock's attorney, Jerry Quick. Quick added the words *for deposit only* under her indorsement and then had the check deposited into his trust account at the La Junta State Bank. Warnock died on November 10, 1981. The executor of her estate suspected that Quick illegally converted Warnock's funds into his own account. The executor claimed that the cashier's check that Quick deposited should have been payable only to Warnock because it was made to a named payee. When the executor discovered that Quick's trust account had been liquidated, the executor sued La Junta State Bank, where the

deposit had been made. Who wins? [*La Junta Bank v. Travis* 727 p.2d 48, 1986 Colo. Lexis 640 (CO 1986)]

19.2 Note On August 17, 1979, Sandra McGuire and her husband entered into a contract to purchase the inventory, equipment, accounts receivable, and name of "Becca's Boutique" from Pascal and Rebecca Tursi. Becca's Bountique was a clothing store that was owned as a sole proprietorship by the Tursis. The McGuires agreed to purchase the store for $75,000, with a down payment of $10,000 and the balance to be paid by October 5, 1979. The promissory note signed by the McGuires read: "For value received, Thomas J. McGuire and Sandra A. McGuire, husband and wife, do promise to pay to the order of Pascal and Rebecca Tursi the sum of $65,000." Is the note an order to pay or a promise to pay? [*P P Inc. v. McGuire*, 509 F. Supp. 1079, 1981 U.S.Dist. Lexis 17984 (D.N.J. 1981)]

19.3 Bearer or Order Instrument Broadway Management Corporation (Broadway) owned and operated the American Nursing Center. Conan Briggs had received services from the center and had executed an instrument to pay for those services. The instrument read in relevant part: "Ninety days after date, I, we, or either of us, promises to pay to the order of $3,498.45." Briggs refused to pay on the note. Broadway claimed that this note was "bearer paper" and as such was payable to the holder. Briggs claimed that the note was "order paper" and was therefore payable only to a named payee. Can Broadway collect on this note as its bearer? [*Broadway Management Corporation v. Briggs*, 332 N.E.2d 131, 1975 Ill.App. Lexis 2625 (Ill. App. 1975)]

19.4 Formal Requirements Mr. Higgins operated a used car dealership in the state of Alabama. In 1978, Higgins purchased a 1977 Chevrolet Corvette for $8,115. He paid for the car with a draft on his account at the First State Bank of Albertville. Soon after, Higgins resold the car to Mr. Holsonback for $8,225. To pay for the car, Holsonback signed a check that was printed on a standard-sized envelope. The reason the check was printed on an envelope is that this practice made it easier to transfer title and other documents from the seller to the buyer. The envelope on which the check was written contained a certificate of title, a mileage statement, and a bill of sale. Does a check printed on an envelope meet the formal requirements to be classified as a negotiable instrument under the UCC? [*Holsonback v. First State Bank of Albertville*, 394 So.2d 281, 1980 Ala. Civ. App. Lexis 1208 (AL 1980)]

19.5 Unconditional Promise M. S. Horne executed a $100,000 note in favor of R. C. Clark. The note stipulated that it could not be transferred, pledged, or assigned without Horne's consent. Along with the note, Horne signed a letter authorizing Clark to use the note as collateral for a loan. Clark pledged the note as collateral for a $50,000 loan from First State Bank of Gallup (First State). First State telephoned Horne to confirm that Clark could pledge the note, and Horne indicated that it was okay. Clark eventually defaulted on the loan. First State attempted to collect on the note, but Horne refused to pay. Did the restriction written on Horne's promissory note cause it to be nonnegotiable despite the letter or authorization? [*First State Bank of Gallup v. Clark and Horne*, 570 P.2d 1144, 1977 N.M. Lexis 1093 (NM 1977)]

19.6 Negotiable Instrument In 1982, William H. Bailey, M.D., executed a note payable to California Dreamstreet. Dreamstreet is a joint venture that solicits investments for a cattle breeding operation. Bailey's promissory note read: "Dr. William H. Bailey hereby promises to pay to the order of California Dreamstreet the sum of $329,800." In 1986, Dreamstreet negotiated the note to Cooperatieve Centrale Raiffeisen-Boerenleenbank B.A. (Cooperatieve), a foreign bank. A default occurred, and Cooperatieve filed suit against Bailey to recover on the note. Was the note executed by Bailey a negotiable instrument? [*Cooperatieve Centrale Raiffeisen-Boerenleenbank B.A. v. Bailey*, 710 F.Supp. 737, 1989 U.S.Dist. Lexis 4488 (C.D. Cal. 1989)]

19.7 Demand Instrument In July 1977, Stewart P. Blanchard borrowed $50,000 from Progressive Bank & Trust Company (Progressive) to purchase a home. As part of the transaction, Blanchard signed a note secured by a mortgage. The note provided for a 10 percent annual interest rate. Under the terms of the note, payment was "due on demand, if no

demand is made, then $600 monthly beginning 8/1/77." Blanchard testified that he believed Progressive could demand immediate payment only if he failed to make the monthly installments. After one year, Blanchard received notice that the rate of interest on the note would rise to 11 percent. Despite the notice, Blanchard continued to make $600 monthly payments. One year later, Progressive notified Blanchard that the interest rate on the loan would be increased to 12.75 percent. Progressive requested that Blanchard sign a form consenting to the interest rate adjustment. When Blanchard refused to sign the form, Progressive demanded immediate payment of the note balance. Progressive sued Blanchard to enforce the terms of the note. Was the note a demand instrument? [*Blanchard v. Progressive Bank & Trust Company*, 413 So.2d 589, 1982 La.App. Lexis 7213 (La. App. 1982)]

19.8 Order or Bearer Paper Samuel C. Mazilly wrote a personal check that was drawn on Calcasieu-Marine National Bank of Lake Charles, Inc. (CMN Bank). The check was made payable to the order of Lee St. Mary and was delivered to him. St. Mary indorsed the check in blank and delivered it to Leland H. Coltharp, Sr., in payment for some livestock. Coltharp accepted the check and took it to the City Savings Bank & Trust Company (City Savings) to deposit it. He indorsed the check as follows: "Pay to the order of City Savings Bank & Trust Company, DeRidder, Louisianna." City Savings accepted the check and forwarded it to CMN Bank for payment. The check never arrived at CMN Bank. Some unknown person stole the check while it was in transit and presented it directly to CMN Bank for payment. The teller at CMN Bank cashed the check without indorsement of the person who presented it. At the time CMN Bank accepted the check, was it order or bearer paper? [*Coltharp v. Calcasieu-Marine National Bank of Lake Charles, Inc.*, 199 So.2d 568, 1967 La. App. Lexis 5203 (La. App. 1967)]

19.9 Multiple Payees Murray Walter, Inc. (Walter, Inc.), was the general contractor for the construction of a waste treatment plant in New Hampshire. Walter, Inc., contracted with H. Johnson Electric, Inc. (Johnson Electric), to install the electrical system in the treatment plant. Johnson Electric purchased its supplies for the project from General Electric Supply (G.E. Supply). On May 1, 1980, Walter, Inc. issued a check payable to "Johnson Electric and G.E. Supply" in the amount of $54,900, drawn on its account at Marine Midland Bank (Marine Midland). Walter, Inc., made the check payable to both the subcontractor and its material supplier, to be certain that the supplier was paid by Johnson Electric. Despite this precautionary measure, Johnson Electric negotiated the check without G.E. Supply's indorsement, and the check was paid by Marine Midland Bank. Johnson Electric never paid G.E. Supply. G.E. Supply then demanded payment from Walter, Inc. When Walter, Inc., learned that Marine Midland paid the check without G.E. Electric's indorsement, it demanded to be reimbursed. When Marine Midland refused, Walter, Inc., sued Marine Midland to recover for the check. Was Johnson Electric's indorsement sufficient to legally negotiate the check to Marine Midland Bank? [*Murray Walter, Inc. v. Marine Midland Bank*, 480 N.Y.S.2d 631, 1984 N.Y.App.Div. Lexis 19962 (N.Y. Sup.Ct. 1984)]

19.10 Imposter Rule Allan Q. Mowatt was employed as a bookkeeper at the law firm of McCarthy, Kenney & Reidy, P.C. The law firm maintained a primary checking account at First National Bank of Boston (Bank of Boston) and two smaller accounts at other banks to pay operating expenses. One of the law firm's secondary accounts with Union Bank of Lowell, was under the name Clement McCarthy, the name of the firm's senior partner. It was funded by checks drawn on the Bank of Boston account and payable to "Clement McCarthy." The checks used to fund the secondary account were signed by any of four attorneys with check-writing authority. When either of the two accounts was running low, Mowatt would make a check payable to "Clement McCarthy" and have it signed by one of the authorized attorneys. In addition to drawing checks needed to fund the secondary account, Mowatt began making out extra checks on the Bank of Boston account payable to Clement McCarthy. Mowatt would explain that the extra checks were needed to maintain funds in the secondary accounts. Mowatt then forged the indorsement of Clement McCarthy to the extra checks and deposited them into his own bank account. Who is liable for the loss caused by this forgery? [*McCarthy, Kenney & Reidy, P.C. v. First National Bank of Boston*, 524 N.E.2d 390, 1988 Mass. Lexis. 173 (Ma. Sup. Ct. 1986)]

Business Ethics Cases

19.11 Business Ethics Samuel K. Yucht was an attorney practicing law in the state of New Jersey. Yucht specialized in personal injury cases. Over the course of a year, Yucht submitted numerous claims on behalf of his clients against Allstate Insurance Company (Allstate). In each case, Yucht informed Allstate that his client was willing to settle the claim and submitted a signed release. All the signatures on the releases were forged by Yucht. When Allstate issued settlement checks made payable to the client and Yucht as their attorney, Yucht again forged his clients' indorsements. He added his own indorsement and then deposited the checks into his personal account. Yucht never informed his client of the settlements he had made on their behalf or of the money he had received in their names. Did Yucht act ethically in this case? Is Allstate liable for the losses caused by Yucht's actions under the imposter rule? [*Client's Security Fund of the Bar of New Jersey v. Allstate Insurance Company*, 530 A.2d 357, 1987 N.J.Super. Lexis 1273 (N.J. Sup.Ct. 1987)]

19.12 Business Ethics Mullins Enterprises, Inc. (Mullins), was a business operating in the state of Kentucky. To raise capital, Mullins obtained loans from Corbin Deposit Bank & Trust Company (Corbin). Between 1971 and 1975, Corbin made eight loans to Mullins. Mullins executed a promissory note setting out the amount of the debt, the dates and times of installment payments, and the date of final payment and delivered it to the bank each time a loan was made. The notes were signed by an officer of Mullins. In 1980, a dispute arose between Mullins and Corbin as to the proper interpretation of the language contained in the notes. The bank contended that the notes were demand notes. Mullins claimed that the notes were time instruments. Did Corbin on Mullins act unethically in this case? Or was this just a legal dispute? Who wins? [*Corbin Deposit Bank & Trust Co. v. Mullins Enterprises, Inc.*, 641 S.W.2d 760, 1982 Ky.App. Lexis 264 (Ky. App. 1982)]

Briefing the Case Writing Assignment

Read Case A.19 in the Case Appendix [*Federal Deposit Insurance Corporation v. Woodside Construction. Inc.*]. This case is excerpted from the court of appeals opinion. Review and brief the case. In your brief, be sure to answer the following questions.

1. Was Galt acting as an agent when he signed the negotiable instrument? If so, who was his principal?

2. What type of negotiable instrument did Galt sign? How did he sign it?

3. Was Galt's signature proper to notify a holder that his signature was made in a representative capacity?

4. Was Galt found personally liable on the negotiable instrument?

Holder in Due Course and Liability

20

"If one wants to know the real value of money, he needs but to borrow some from his friends."

—Confucius
Analects, c. 500 B. C.

Chapter Objectives

After studying this chapter, you should be able to:

1. Define holder and holder in due course.

2. Describe the signature liability of makers, drawees, drawers, acceptors, and accommodation parties.

3. List the transfer and presentment warranties and describe the liability of parties for breaching them.

4. Identify real defenses that can be asserted against a holder in due course.

5. Describe the Federal Trade Commission rule that prohibits the holder in due course rule in consumer transactions.

Chapter Contents

- Holder Versus Holder in Due Course

- Requirements for HDC Status

- Signature Liability of Parties

- Warranty Liability of Parties

- Defenses

- Discharge

If payment is not made on a negotiable instrument when it is due, the holder can use the court system to enforce the instrument. Various parties, including both signers and nonsigners, may be liable on it. Some parties are primarily liable on the instrument, while others are secondarily liable. Accommodation parties (i.e., guarantors) can also be held liable.

Recall that the primary purpose of commercial paper is to act as a substitute for money. For this to occur, the holder of a negotiable instrument must qualify as a holder in due course (HDC). Commercial paper held by an HDC is virtually as good as money since HDCs take an instrument free of all claims and most defense that can be asserted by other parties.

This chapter discusses the liability of parties on negotiable instruments, the requirements that must be met to qualify as an HDC, the defenses that can be raised against the imposition of liability, and the discharge of liability.

A negotiable bill or note is a courier without luggage.

Chief Justice Gibson
Overton v. Tyler (1846)

Holder Versus Holder in Due Course

Two of the most important concepts of the law of negotiable instruments are those of *holder* and *holder in due course*. A **holder** is a person in possession of an instrument that is payable to bearer or an indentified person who is in possession of an instrument payable to that person [UCC 1-201(20)]. The holder of a negotiable instrument has the same rights as an assignee of an ordinary nonnegotiable contract. That is, the holder is subject to all the claims and defenses that can be asserted against the transferor.

The concept of holder in due course is unique to the area of negotiable instruments. A **holder in due course (HDC)** is a holder who takes an instrument for value, in good faith, and without notice that it is defective or is overdue. An HDC takes a negotiable instrument free of all claims and most defenses that can be asserted against the transferor of the instrument. Only real defenses—and not personal defenses—may be asserted against an HDC. (Defenses are discussed later in this chapter.) Thus, an HDC can acquire greater rights than a transferor.

Consider This Example   John purchases an automobile from Shannen. At the time of sale, Shannen tells John that the car has had only one previous owner and has been driven only 20,000 miles. John, relying on these statement, purchases the car. He pays 10 percent down and signs a promissory note to pay the remainder of the purchase price, with interest, in 12 equal monthly installments. Shannen transfers the note to Patricia.

Taipei. Negotiable instruments facilitate international commerce.

Then John discovers that the car has actually had four previous owners and has been driven 100,000 miles. If Patricia were a holder (but not an HDC) of the note, John could assert Shannen's fraudulent representations against enforcement of the note by Patricia. John could rescind the note and refuse to pay Patricia. Patricia's only recourse would be against Shannen.

If Patricia qualified as an HDC, however, the result would be different. John could not assert Shannen's fraudulent conduct against enforcement of the note by Patricia because this type of fraud is a personal defense that cannot be raised against an HDC. Therefore, Patricia could enforce the note against John. John's only recourse would be against Shannen, if she could be found.

Requirements for HDC Status

To qualify as an HDC, the transferee must meet the requirements established by the UCC: The person must be the *holder* of a negotiable instrument that was taken (1) for value; (2) in good faith; (3) without notice that it is overdue, dishonored, or encumbered in any way; and (4) bearing no apparent evidence of forgery, alterations, or irregularity [UCC 3-302]. These requirements are discussed in the paragraphs that follow. Exhibit 20.1 illustrates the HDC doctrine.

Business Brief

Only a *holder* can qualify as an HDC.

Taking for Value

Under the UCC **taking for value requirement**, the holder must have *given value* for the negotiable instrument to qualify as an HDC [UCC 3-302(a)(2)(i)]. For example, suppose Ted draws a check "payable to the order of Mary Smith" and delivers the check to Mary. Mary indorses it and gives it as a gift to her daughter. Mary's daughter cannot qualify as an HDC because she has not given value for it. The purchaser or a limited interest in a negotiable instrument is an HDC only to the extent of the interest purchased.

Under the UCC, value had been given if the holder [UCC 3-303]:

1. Performs the agreed-upon promise.
2. Acquires a security interest or lien on the instrument.
3. Takes the instrument in payment of or as security for an antecedent claim.
4. Gives a negotiable instrument as payment.
5. Gives an irrevocable obligation as payment.

Exhibit 20.1

Holder in Due Course

Business Brief

If a holder of a negotiable instrument qualifies as a *holder in due course (HDC)*, the HDC takes the instrument free of all claims and most defenses that can be asserted by other parties. In other words, the instrument is almost as good as cash.

If a person promises to perform but has not yet done so, no value has been given, and he or she is not an HDC. For example, Karen executes a note payable to Fred for $3,000 for goods she had purchased from him. Fred transfers the note to Amy for her promise to pay the note in 90 days.. Before Amy pays the note, Karen discovers that the goods she purchased from Fred are defective. Karen can raise this defect against enforcement of the note by Amy because no value has yet been given for the note. If Amy had already paid for the note, she would qualify as an HDC, and Karen could not raise the issue of defect against enforcement of the note by Amy.

Taking in Good Faith

Under the UCC **taking is good faith requirement**, a holder must **take** an instrument in **good faith** to qualify as an HDC [UCC 3-302(a)(2)(ii)]. *Good faith* means honesty in fact in the conduct or transaction concerned [UCC 1-201(19)]. Honesty in fact is a subjective test that examines the holder's actual belief. A holder's subjective belief can be inferred from the circumstances. For example, if a holder acquires an instrument from a stranger under suspicious circumstances and at a deep discount, it could be inferred that the holder did not take the instrument in good faith. A naïve person who acquired the same instrument at the same discount, however, may be found to have acted in good faith and thereby qualify as an HDC. Each case must be reviewed individually

Note that the good faith test applies only to the holder. It does not apply to the transferor of the instrument. For example, suppose a thief steals a negotiable integument and transfers it to Harry. Harry does not know that the instrument is stolen. Harry meets the good faith test and qualifies an an HDC.

Taking Without Notice of Defect

Under the UCC **taking without notice of defect requirement**, a person cannot qualify as an HDC if he or she has notice that the instrument is defective in any of the following ways [UCC 3-302(a)(2)]:

- It is overdue.
- It has been dishonored.
- It contains an unauthorized signature or has been altered.
- There is a claim to it by another person.
- There is a defense against it.

Overdue Instruments If a **time instrument** is not paid on its expressed due date, it becomes overdue the next day. An instrument that has not been paid when due indicates that there is some defect to its payment.

For example, suppose a promissory note is due June 15, 1998. To qualify as an HDC, a purchaser must acquire the note before midnight on June 15, 1998. A purchaser who acquires the note on June 16 or later is only a holder, but not an HDC.

Often, a debt is payable in installments or in a series of notes. If a maker misses an installment payment or fails to pay one note in a series of notes, the purchaser of the instruments is on notice that it is overdue [UCC 3-304(b)].

A **demand instrument** is payable on demand. A purchaser cannot be an HDC if the instrument is acquired either (1) after demand or (2) at an unreasonable length of time after its issue. A "reasonable time" for presenting a check for payment is presumed to be 90 days. Business practices and the circumstances of the case determine a reasonable time for the payment of other demand instruments [UCC 3-304(a)].

Dishonored Instruments An instrument is **dishonored** when it is presented for payment and payment is refused. A holder who takes the instrument with notice of its dishonor cannot qualify as an HDC. For example, a person who takes a check that has been marked by the payor bank "payment refused—not sufficient funds" cannot qualify as an HDC.

Red Light Doctrine A holder cannot qualify as an HDC if he or she has notice that an instrument contains an unauthorized signature or has been altered or that there is any adverse claim against or defense to its payment. This rule is commonly referred to as the **red light doctrine**.

Notice of a defect is given when the holder has (1) actual knowledge of the defect, (2) received a notice or notification of the defect, or (3) reason to know from the facts and circumstances that the defect exists [UCC 1-201(25)]. The filing of a public notice does not of itself constitute notice unless the person actually reads the public notice [UCC 3-302(b)].

No Evidence of Forgery, Alteration, or Irregularity

The UCC has a **no evidence of forgery, alteration, or irregularity requirement**. Under this rule, a holder does not qualify as an HDC if at the time the instrument was issued or negotiated to the holder it bore apparent evidence of forgery or alteration or was otherwise so irregular or incomplete as to call into question its authenticity [UCC 3-302(a)(1)].

Clever and undetectable forgeries and alterations are not classified as obvious irregularities. Determining whether a forgery or an alteration is apparent, and whether the instrument is so irregular or incomplete that its authenticity should be questioned are issues of fact that must be decided on a case-by-case basis.

Payee as an HDC

Payees generally do not meet the requirements for being HDCs because they know about any claims or defenses against the instrument. In a few situations, however, a payee who does not have such knowledge would qualify as an HDC.

Consider This Example   Suppose Kate purchases an automobile from Jake for $5,000. Jake owes Sherry Smith $5,000 from another transaction. Jake has Kate make out the $5,000 check for the automobile "payable to the order of Sherry Smith." Jake gives the check to Sherry. The car Jake sold to Kate is defective, and she wants to rescind the purchase. Sherry (payee), who did not have notice of the defect in the car, is an HDC. As such, Sherry can enforce the check against Kate. Kate's only recourse is to recover from Jake.

> "Bad money drives out good money."
> Sir Thomas Gresham (1560)

Signature Liability of Parties

A person cannot be held contractually liable on a negotiable instrument unless his or her signature appears on it [UCC 3-401(a)]. Therefore, this type of liability is often referred to as **signature liability** or **contract liability**. The signature on a negotiable instrument identify those who are obligated to pay it. If it is unclear who the signer is, parol evidence can identify the signer. This liability does not attach to bearer paper because no indorsement is needed.

Signers of instruments sign in many different capacities, including as makers of notes and certificates of deposit, drawers of drafts and checks, drawees who certify or accept checks and drafts, indorsers who indorse instruments, agents who sign on behalf of others, and accommodation parties. The location of the signature on an instrument generally determines the singer's capacity. For example, a signature in the lower-right corner of a check indicates that the signer is the drawer of the check, and a signature in the lower-right corner of a promissory note indicates that the signer is the maker of the note. The signature of the drawee named in a draft on the face of the draft or other location on the draft indicates that the signer is an acceptor of the draft. Most indorsements appear on the back or reverse side of an instrument. Unless the instrument clearly indicates that such a signature is made in some other capacity, it is presumed to be that of the indorser.

Every party that signs a negotiable instrument (except qualified indorsers and agents that properly sign the instrument) is either primarily or secondarily liable on the instrument. The following discussion outlines the particular liability of signers.

Signature Defined

The **signature** on a negotiable instrument can be any name, word, or mark used in lieu of a written signature [UCC 3-401(b)]. In other words, a signature is any symbol that is (1) handwritten, typed, printed, stamped, or made in almost any other manner and (2) executed or adopted by a party to authenticate a writing [UCC 1-201(39)]. This rule permits trade names and other assumed names to be used as signatures on negotiable instruments.

The unauthorized signature of a person on an instrument is ineffective as that person's signature. It is effective as the signature of the unauthorized signer in favor of an HDC, however. For example, a person who forges a signature on a check may be held liable to an HDC. An unauthorized signature may be ratified [UCC 3-403(a)].

Agent's Signatures

A person may either sign a negotiable instrument him- or herself or authorize a representative to sign the instrument on his or her behalf [UCC 3-401(a)]. The representative is the **agents** and the represented person is the **principal**. The authority of an agent to sign an instrument is established under general agency law, No special form of appointment is necessary.

Authorized Signature If an authorized agent signs an instrument by signing either the principal's name or the agent's own name, the principal is bound as if the signature were made on a simple contract. It does not matter whether the principal is identified in the instrument [UCC 3-402(2)].

For example, suppose Anderson was the agent for Puttkammer. The following signatures on a negotiable instrument would bind Puttkammer on the instrument:

1. Puttkammer, by Anderson, agent
2. Puttkammer
3. Puttkammer, Anderson
4. Anderson

Business Brief

To avoid personal liability on a negotiable instrument, the agent should properly sign the instrument to indicate his or her agency status and the identity of the principal.

An authorized agent's personal liability on an instrument he or she signs on behalf of a principal depends on the information disclosed in the signature. The agent has no liability if the signature shows unambiguously that it is made on behalf of a principal who is identified in the instrument [UCC 3-402(b)(1)]. Signature Number 1 ("Puttkammer, by Anderson, agent") satisfies this requirement.

If the authorized agent's signature does not show unambiguously that the signature was made in a representative capacity and the agent cannot prove that the original parties did not intend him or her to be liable, the agent is liable (1) to an HDC who took the instrument without notice that the agent was not intended to be liable on the instrument and (2) to any other person other than an HDC [UCC 3-402(b)(2)]. Signature Number 2 ("Puttkammer") shows such a signature.

Signatures Number 3 ("Puttkammer, Anderson") and 4 ("Anderson") place the agent at risk of personal liability to an HDC that does not have notice that the agent was not intended to be liable on the instrument. To avoid liability to a non-HDC for these signatures, the agent would have to prove that the third-party non-HDC did not intend to hold the agent liable on the instrument.

There is one exception to these rules. If an agent signs his or her name as the drawer of a check without indicating the agent's representative status and the check is payable from the account of the principal who is identified on the check, the agent is not liable on the check [UCC 3-402(c)].

Unauthorized Signature An **unauthorized signature** is a signature made by a purported agent without authority from the purported principal. Such a signature arises if (1) a person signs a negotiable instrument on behalf of a person for whom he or she is not an agent or (2) an authorized agent exceeds the scope of his or her authority. An unauthorized signature by a purported agent does not act as the signature of the purported principal. The purported agent is liable to any person who in good faith pays the instrument or takes it for value [UCC 3-403(a)].

The purported principal is liable if he or she ratifies the unauthorized signature [UCC 3-403(a)]. For example, a purported agent signs a contract and promissory note to purchase a building for a purported principal. Suppose that the purported principal likes the deal and accepts it. She has ratified the transaction and is liable on the note.

Primary Liability

Makers of promissory notes and certificates of deposit have **primary liability** for the instrument. Upon signing a promissory note, the maker unconditionally promises to pay the amount stipulated in the note when it is due. Makers are absolutely liable to pay the instrument, subject only to certain real defenses. The holder need not take any action to give rise to this obligation. Generally, the maker is obligated to pay the note according to its original terms. If the note was incomplete when it was issued, the marker is obligated to pay the note as completed as long as he or she authorized the terms as they were filled in [UCC 3-412].

A draft or a check is an order from a drawer to pay the instrument to a payee (or other holder) according to its terms. No party is primarily liable when the draft or check is issued because such instruments are merely orders to pay. Thus, a drawee who refuses to pay a draft or a check is not liable to the payee or holder. If there has been a wrongful dishonor of the instrument, the drawee may be liable to the drawer for certain damages.

On occasion, a drawee is requested to accept a draft or check. Acceptance of a draft occurs when the drawee writers the word *accepted* across the face of the draft. The acceptor—that is, the drawee—is primarily liable on the instrument. A check, which is a special form of draft, is accepted when it is certified by a bank. The bank's certification discharges the drawer and all prior indorsers from liability on the check. Note that the bank may choose to refuse to certify the check without liability. The issuer of a cashier's check is also primarily liable on the instrument [UCC 3-411].

In the following case, the court held that a comaker was primarily liable on a promissory note.

Business Brief

The unauthorized signature of a person on a negotiable instrument is ineffective as that person's signature unless he or she *ratifies* the unauthorized signature.

Business Brief

The following parties are *primarily liable* on negotiable instruments: (1) *makers* of promissory notes and certificates of deposit and (2) *acceptors* of drafts and checks.

Grand Island Production Credit Assn. v. Humphrey
388 N.W.2d 807, 1986 Neb. Lexis 1185 (1986)
Supreme Court of Nebraska

Case 20.1
Primary Liability

Background and Facts

The Grand Island Production Credit Association (Grand Island) is a federally chartered credit union. On November 25, 1980, Carl M. and Beulah C. Humphrey, husband and wife, entered into a loan arrangement with Grand Island for a $50,000 line of credit. Mr. and Mrs. Humphrey signed a line of credit promissory note that provided in part: "As long as the Borrower is not in default, the Association will lend to the Borrower, and the Borrower may borrow and repay and reborrow at any time from date of said 'Line of Credit' Promissory Note in accordance with the terms thereof and prior to maturity thereof, up to an aggregate maximum amount of principal at any one time outstanding of $50,000."

Mr. Humphrey borrowed money against the line of credit to purchase cattle. In January 1981, Mrs. Humphrey went to Grand Island's office and told the loan officer that she had left Mr. Humphrey and filed for a divorce. She told the loan officer not to advance any more money to Mr. Humphrey for cattle purchases. When the Humphreys failed to pay the outstanding balance on the line of credit, Grand Island sued Mr. and Mrs. Humphrey to recover the unpaid balance of $13,936.71. A default judgment was entered against Mr. Humphrey. The district court held Mrs. Humphrey not liable for the full outstanding balance. Grand Island appealed.

Issue

Was Mrs. Humphrey a comaker of the line of credit promissory note and, therefore, primarily liable for the outstanding principal balance of the note, plus interest?

Court's Reasoning

The court stated, "Under the provision of the Nebraska UCC, the maker of a note engages that he or she will pay the instrument according to its tenor at the time of his or her engagement." Mrs. Humphrey admits that she signed the promissory note and the supplemental agreement. Consequently, as a comaker of the note, she is jointly and severally liable for the obligations of the note. If Mrs. Humphrey was to be relieved of this obligation, it was a matter that she needed to arrange and take up with her husband in the divorce action. No such arrangement could, however, be binding upon Grand Island, which entered into this transaction in reliance upon the promise of both Mr. Humphrey and Mrs. Humphrey that they would be liable and would pay the amounts so advanced.

Decision and Remedy

The state supreme court held that Mrs. Humphrey was a comaker on the line of credit promissory note and was therefore primarily liable to Grand Island in the amount of $13,936.71 plus interest. The supreme court reversed the district court's decision.

Case Questions

Critical Legal Thinking   Should family problems, such as the separation and divorce action in this case, take precedence over the commercial law rules of the UCC? Why or why not?

Business Ethics   Was it ethical for Mrs. Humphrey to deny liability on the promissory note in this case?

Contemporary Business   What would have been the economic effects if the district court's decision had been upheld in this case?

Secondary Liability

Business Brief

The following parties are *secondarily liable* on negotiable instruments: (1) *drawers* on unaccepted drafts and checks and (2) *unqualified indorsers.*

Under the UCC's **indorsers' liability** rules, drawers of checks and drafts and unqualified indorsers of negotiable instruments have **secondary liability** on the instruments. This liability is similar to that of a guarantor of a simple contract. It arises when the party primarily liable on the instrument defaults and fails to pay the instrument when due.

If an unaccepted draft or check is dishonored by the drawee or acceptor, the drawer is obliged to pay it according to its terms, either when it is issued or, if incomplete when issued, when it is properly completed [UCC 3-414(a)].

Consider This Example   Elliot draws a check on City Bank "payable to the order of Phyllis Jones." When Phyllis presents the check for payment, City Bank refuses to pay it. Phyllis can collect the amount of the check from Elliot because Elliot—the drawer—is secondarily liable on the check when it is dishonored.

Unqualified indorsers have secondary liability on negotiable instruments. In other words, they must pay any dishonored instrument to the holder or to any subsequent indorser according to its terms, when issued or properly completed. Unless otherwise agreed, indorsers are liable to each other in the order in which they indorsed the instrument [UCC 3-415(a)].

Consider This Example   Dara borrows $10,000 from Todd and signs a promissory note promising to pay Todd this amount plus interest in one year. Todd indorses the note and negotiates it to Frank. Frank indorses the note and negotiates it to Linda. Dara refuses to pay the note when it is presented for payment by Linda. Since Frank became secondarily liable on the note when he indorsed it to Linda, he must pay the note to her. He can then require Todd to pay the note because Todd (as payee) became secondarily liable on the note when he indorsed it to Frank. Todd can then enforce the note against Dara. Linda could have skipped over Frank and required the payee, Todd, to pay the note. In this instance, Frank would have been relived of any further liability because he indorsed the instrument after the payee.

Qualified indorsers (i.e., indorsers who indorse the instruments "without recourse" or similar language that disclaims liability) are not secondarily liable on the instrument because they have expressly disclaimed liability [UCC 3-415(b)]. The drawer can disclaim all liability on a draft (but not a check) by drawing the instrument "without recourse." In this instance, the drawer becomes a qualified drawer [UCC 3-414(e)]. Many payees, however, will not accept a draft or check that has been drawn without recourse.

Requirements for Imposing Secondary Liability   A party is secondarily liable on a negotiable instrument only if the following requirements are met:

1. *The instrument is properly presented for payment.* **Presentment** is a demand for acceptance or payment of an instrument made upon the maker, acceptor, drawee, or other payor by or on behalf of the holder. Presentment may be made by any commercially reasonable means, including oral, written, or electronic communication. Presentment is effective when it is received by the person to whom presentment is made [UCC 3-501].

2. *The instrument is dishonored.* An instrument is **dishonored** when acceptance or payment of the instrument is refused or cannot be obtained from the party required to accept or pay the instrument within the prescribed time after presentment is duly made [UCC 3-502].

3. *Notice of the dishonor is timely given to the person to be held secondarily liable on the instrument.* A secondarily liable party cannot be compelled to accept or pay an instrument unless proper **notice of dishonor** has been given. Notice may be given by any commercially reasonable means. The notice must reasonably identify the instrument and indicate that it has been dishonored. Return of an instrument given to a bank for collection is sufficient notice of dishonor. Banks must give notice of dishonor before midnight of the next banking day following the day that presentment is made. Others must give notice of dishonor within 30 days following the day on which the person receives notice of dishonor [UCC 3-503.]

In the following case, the court held that an indorser was not secondarily liable on a check because he had not received proper notice of dishonor.

Clements v. Central Bank of Georgia
270 S.E.2d 194, 1980 Ga.App. Lexis 3235 (1980)
Count of Appeals of Georgia

Case 20.2
Secondary Liability

Background and Facts
On September 19, 1978, Mr. Ridley drew a check on a Tennessee bank made payable to the order of Mr. Clements. On September 25, 1978, Clements indorsed the check and negotiated it to Continental Equity Corporation (Continental). Continental indorsed the check and deposited it in the Central Bank of Georgia (Central Bank) for collection. Central Bank sent the check to the Tennessee bank for payment. On September 29, 1978, the branch manager of the Tennessee bank informed Central Bank by telephone that Ridley's check was "no good" because of insufficient

Clements v. Central Bank of Georgia

270 S.E.2d 194, 1980 Ga.App. Lexis 3235 (1980)
Count of Appeals of Georgia

(continued)

funds. Central Bank authorized the Tennessee bank to hold the check. During October, Central Bank made several unsuccessful attempts to collect the check from Ridley. On October 21, 1978, Central Bank requested the Tennessee bank to return the check. On November 3, Central Bank received the check, and on that date it sent written notice to Clements that Ridley's check had been dishonored. Central Bank sued Clements (the indorser) to recover on the check. The court granted summary judgement to Central Bank. Clements trial appealed.

Issue

Did the Central Bank of Georgia give timely notice of dishonor of the check to Clements, the indorser, in order to hold Clements secondarily liable on Ridley's check?

Court's Reasoning

Every indorser engages that upon dishonor and any necessary notice of dishonor and protest he will pay the instrument according to its tenor at the time of his indorsement to the holder. Unless excused, notice of any dishonor is necessary to charge any indorser. The notice of dishonor to the indorser Clements, on November 3 came too late as a matter of law. The delay in notice of dishonor to the indorser was not due to circumstances beyond Central Bank's control but simply to the bank's failure to give it once the bank itself had notice of the dishonor and was under obligation to take action.

Decision and Remedy

The court of appeals held that Central Bank did not give timely notice to the indorser, Clements. Therefore, he is not secondarily liable on the check he indorsed. The count of appeals reversed the trial court's decision.

Case Questions

Critical Legal Thinking   Should indorsers be held secondarily liable on a negotiable instrument that is drawn or made by another party? Why or why not?

Business Ethics   Was it ethical for Central Bank to try to hold the indorser Clements liable on the check?

Contemporary Business   Who bore the loss of the uncollected check in this case?

Accommodation Party

The party who signs an instrument for the purpose of lending his or her name (and credit) to another party to the instrument is the **accommodation party**. The accommodation party, who may sign the instrument as maker, drawer, acceptor, or indorser, is obliged to *pay* the instrument in the capacity in which he or she signs [UCC 3-419(a) and (b)]. An accommodation party who pays an instrument can recover reimbursement from the accommodated party and enforce the instrument against him or her [UCC 3-419(e)].

There are two types of liability of an accommodation party:

1. *Guarantee of payment.* The accommodation party may sign an instrument guaranteeing either payment or collection. An accommodation party who signs an instrument **guaranteeing payment** is *primarily liable* on the instrument. That is, the debtor can seek payment on the instrument directly from the accommodation maker without first seeking payment from the maker.

   Consider This Example   Sonny, a college student, wants to purchase an automobile on credit from ABC Motors. He does not have a sufficient income or credit history to justify the extension of credit to him alone. Sonny asks his mother to cosign the note to ABC Motors, which she does. Sonny's mother is an accommodation maker and is primarily liable on the note.

2. *Guarantee of collection.* An accommodation party may sign an instrument **guaranteeing collection** rather than payment of an instrument. In this situation, the accommodation party is only *secondarily liable* on the instrument. To reserve this type of liability, the signature of the accommodation party must be accompanied by words indicating that he or she is guaranteeing collection rather than payment of the obligation.

An accommodation party that guarantees collection is obligated to pay the instrument only if (1) execution of judgment against the other party has been returned unsatisfied, (2) the other party is insolvent or in an insolvency proceeding, (3) the other party cannot be served with process, or (4) it is otherwise apparent that payment cannot be obtained from the other party [UCC 3-419(d)].

Concept Summary   Liability of Accommodation Makers and Accommodation Indorsers Compared

Accommodation Party	Contract Liability
Accommodation maker	Primarily liable on the instrument
Accommodation indorser	Secondarily liable on the instrument

Warranty Liability of Parties

In addition to signature liability, transferors can be held liable for breaching certain **implied warranties** when negotiating instruments. Warranty liability is imposed whether or not the transferor signed the instrument. Note that transferors make implied warranties; implied warranties are not made when the negotiable instrument is originally issued.

There are two types of implied warranties: transfer warranties and presentment warranties. Transfer and presentment warranties shift the risk of loss to the party who was in the best position to prevent the loss. This party is usually the one who dealt face-to-face with the wrongdoer. These implied warranties are discussed in the paragraphs that follow.

Transfer Warranties

Any passage of an instrument other than its issuance and presentment for payment is considered a **transfer**. Any person who transfer a negotiable instrument for consideration makes the following five warranties to the transferee. If the transfer is by indorsement, the transferor also makes these warranties to any subsequent transferee [UCC 3-416(a):]

1. The transferor has good title to the instrument or is authorized to obtain payment or acceptance on behalf of one who does have good title.
2. All signatures are genuine or authorized.
3. The instrument has not been materially altered.
4. No defenses of any party are good against the transferor.
5. The transferor has no knowledge of any insolvency proceeding against the maker, the acceptor, or the drawer of an unaccepted instrument.

Transfer warranties cannot be disclaimed with respect to checks, but they can be disclaimed with respect to other instruments. An indorsement that states "without recourse" disclaims the transfer warranties [UCC 3-419(c)].

A transferee who took the instrument in good faith my recover damages for breach of transfer warranty from the warrantor equal to the loss suffered. The amount recovered cannot exceed the amount of the instrument plus expenses and interest [UCC 3-416(b)].

Consider This Example   Jill issues a $1,000 note to Adam. Adam cleverly raises the note to $10,000 and negotiates the note to Nick. Nick indorses the note and negotiates it to Matthew. When Matthew presents the note to Jill for payment, she has to pay only the original amount of the note, $1,000. Matthew can collect the remainder of the note ($9,000) from Nick based on a breach of the transfer warranty. If Nick is lucky, he can recover the $9,000 from Adam.

Presentment Warranties

Any person who **presents** a draft or check for payment or acceptance makes the following **presentment warranties** to a drawee or an acceptor who pays or accepts the instrument in good faith [UCC 3-417(a)]:

1. The presenter has good title to the instrument or is authorized to obtain payment or acceptance of the person who has good title.
2. The instrument has not been materially altered.
3. The presenter has no knowledge that the signature of the maker or drawer is unauthorized.

A drawee who pays an instrument may recover damages for breach of presentment warranty from the warrantor. The amount that can be recovered is limited to the amount paid by the drawee less the amount the drawee received or is entitled to receive from the drawer because of the payment plus expenses and interest [UCC 3-147(b)].

Consider This Example   Suppose Maureen draws a $1,000 check on City Bank "payable to the order of Paul." Paul cleverly raises the check to $10,000 and indorses and negotiates the check to Neal. Neal presents the check for payment to City Bank. As the presenter of the check, Neal makes the presentment warranties of UCC 3-417(1) to City Bank. City Bank pays the check as altered ($10,000) and debits Maureen's account. when Maureen discovers the alteration, she demands that the bank recredit her account, which the bank does. City Bank can recover against the presenter (Neal) based on breach of the presentment warranty that the instrument was not altered when it was presented. Neal can recover against the wrongdoer (Paul) based on breach of the transfer warranty that the instrument was not altered.

Defenses

The creation of negotiable instruments may give rise to a defense against their payment. Many of these defenses arise from the underlying transaction. There are two general types of defenses: real defenses and personal defense. An HDC (or a holder through an HDC) takes the instrument free from personal defenses but not real defenses. Personal and real defenses can be raised against a normal holder of a negotiable instrument. Both of these types of defenses are discussed in the paragraphs that follow.

Real Defenses

Real (or universal) defenses can be raised against both holders and HDCs [UCC 3-305(b)]. If a real defense is proven, the holder or HDC cannot recover on the instrument. Real defenses are discussed in the following paragraphs:

- *Minority.* Infancy, or **minority**, is a real defense to a negotiable instrument to the extent that it is a defense to a simple contract [UCC 3-305(a)(1)(i)]. In most states, a minor who does not misrepresent his or her age can disaffirm contracts, including negotiable instruments. Usually, minors must pay the reasonable value of necessities of life.

- *Extreme duress.* Ordinary duress is a personal defense (discussed later in this chapter). **Extreme duress** is a real defense against the enforcement of a negotiable instrument by a holder or an HDC [UCC 3-305(a)(1)(ii)]. Extreme duress usually requires some form of force or violence (e.g., a promissory note signed at gunpoint).

- *Mental incapacity.* Adjudicated mental incompetence is a real defense that can be raised against holders and HDCs [UCC 3-305(a)(1)(ii)]. Such a person cannot issue a negotiable instrument; the instrument is void from is inception. Nonadjudicated mental incompetence, which is usually only a personal defense, is discussed later.

- *Illegality.* If an instrument arises out of an illegal transaction, the illegality is a real defense if the law declares the instrument void [UICC 3-305(a)(1)(ii)]. For example, assume that a state's law declares gambling to be illegal and gambling contracts to be void. Gordon wins $1,000 from Jerry in an illegal poker game. He signs a promissory note promising to pay Gordon this amount plus interest in 30 days. Gordon negotiates this note to Dawn, an HDC. When Dawn presents the note to Jerry for payment, Jerry can raise the real defense of illegality against the enforcement of the note. Dawn's recourse is against Gordon. If the law makes an illegal contract voidable instead of void, it is only a personal defense. (This situation is discussed later in this chapter.)

- *Discharge in bankruptcy.* Bankruptcy law is intended to relieve debtors of burdensome debts, including obligations to pay negotiable instruments. Thus, **discharge in bankruptcy** is a real defense against the enforcement of a negotiable instrument by a holder or an HDC [UCC 3-305(a)(1)(iv)]. For example, suppose Hunt borrows $10,000 from Amy and signs a note promising to pay Amy this amount plus interest in one year. Amy negotiates the note to Richard, and HDC. Before the note is due, Hunt declares bankruptcy and receives a discharge of his unpaid debts. Richard cannot thereafter enforce the note against Hunt, but he can recover against Amy.

- *Fraud in the inception.* **Fraud in the inception** (also the called **fraud in the factum** or **fraud in the execution**) is a real defense against the enforcement of a negotiable instrument by a holder or an HDC [UCC 3-305(a)(1)(iii)]. It occurs when a person is deceived into signing a negotiable instrument, thinking that it is something else.

  For example, suppose Sam, a door-to-door salesman, convinces Lance, an illiterate consumer, to sign a document purported to be an agreement to use a set of books on a 90-day trial basis. In actuality, the document is a promissory note in which Lance has agreed to pay $1,000 for the books. Sam negotiates the note to Stephanie, and HDC. Lance can raise the real defense of fraud in the inception against the enforcement of the note by Stephanie. Stephanie, in turn, can recover from Sam.

  A person is under a duty to use reasonable efforts to ascertain what he or she is signing. The court inquires into a person's age, experience, education, and other factors before allowing fraud in the inception to be asserted as a real defense to defeat an HDC. Fraud in the inducement (discussed later) is only a personal defense.

- *Forgery.* Another real defense to the payment of a negotiable instrument is **forgery**. The unauthorized signature of a maker, drawer, or indorser is wholly inoperative as that of the person whose name is signed unless that person either ratifies it or is precluded from denying it. In the latter case, a person can be estopped from raising the defense of forgery if his or her negligence substantially contributes to the forgery. A forged signature operates as the signature of the forger. Thus, the forger is liable on the instrument [UCC 3-403(a)].

- *Material alteration.* An instrument that has been fraudulently and **materially altered** cannot be enforced by an ordinary holder. Material alteration consists of adding to any part of a signed instrument, removing any part of a signed instrument making changes in the number or relations of the parties, or the completing an incomplete instrument without the authority to do so.

Business Brief

Distinguishing between fraud *in the inception* (real defense) and fraud *in the inducement* (personal defense) can be difficult.

Under the UCC rule that words control figures, correcting the figure on a check to correspond to the written amount on the check is not a material alteration [UCC 3-118(c)]. If an alteration is not material, the instrument can be enforced by any holder in the original amount for which the drawer wrote the check [UCC 3-407(b)].

Material alteration of a negotiable instrument is only a partial defense against an HDC. Subsequent holders in due course can enforce any instrument, including an altered instrument, according to its original terms, if the alteration is not apparent. An obvious change puts the holder on notice of the alteration and disqualifies him or her as an HDC [UCC 3-407(c)].

Personal Defenses

Although **personal defenses** cannot be raised against an HDC, they can be raised against enforcement of a negotiable instrument by an ordinary holder. Personal defenses are discussed in the paragraphs that follow:

- *Breach of contract.* Breach of contract is one of the most common defenses raised by a party to a negotiable instrument. This personal defense is effective only against an ordinary holder. For example, when Brian purchases a used car on credit from Karen, he signs a note promising to pay Karen the $10,000 purchase price plus interest in 36 equal monthly installments. The sales agreement warrants that the car in the perfect working condition. A month later, the car's engine fails; the cost of repair is $3,000. Brian, the maker of the note, can raise breach of warranty as a defense against enforcement of the note by Karen.

  The outcome would be different if Karen negotiated the promissory note to Max (an HDC) immediately after the car was sold to Brian. Max would be an HDC, and Brian could not raise the breach of warranty defense against him. Max could enforce the note against Brian. Brian's only recourse would be to seek recovery for breach of warranty from Karen.

- *Fraud in the inducement.* **Fraud in the inducement** occurs when a wrongdoer makes a false statement (i.e., misrepresentation) to another person to lead that person to enter into a contract with the wrongdoer. Negotiable instruments often arise out of such transactions. Fraud in the inducement is a personal defense that is not effective against HDCs. It is effective against ordinary holders, however.

  For example, Morton represents to investor that he will accept funds to drill for oil and that the investors will share in the profits from the oil wells. He plans to use these funds himself, however. Relying on Morton's statements, Mimi draws a $50,000 check payable to him. Morton absconds with the funds. Because Morton is an ordinary holder, Mimi can raise the personal defense of fraud in the inducement and, if she stops payment on the check before Morton receives payment, not pay the check.

  If Morton had negotiated the check to Tim, an HDC, Tim could enforce the check against Mimi. Because personal defenses are not effective against Tim (an HDC), Mini's only recourse is to recover against the wrongdoer (Morton) if he can be found.

- *Other personal defenses.* The following personal defenses can be raised against enforcement of a negotiable instrument by an ordinary holder.

  1. Mental illness that makes a contract voidable instead of void (usually a nonadjudicated mental illness).
  2. Illegality of a contract that makes the contract voidable instead of void.
  3. Ordinary duress or undue influence [UCC 3-305(a)(1)(ii)].
  4. Discharge of an instrument by payment or cancellation [UCC 3-602 and 3-604].

Concept Summary *Real and Personal Defenses*

Defense	Effect
Real Defenses	Real defenses can be raised against a holder in due course.

1. Minority
2. Extreme duress
3. Mental incapacity
4. Illegality
5. Discharge in bankruptcy
6. Fraud in the inception
7. Forgery
8. Material alteration

Personal Defenses	Personal defenses cannot be raised against a holder in due course.

1. Breach of contract
2. Fraud in the inducement
3. Mental illness that makes a contract voidable instead of void (usually a nonadjudicated mental illness)
4. Illegality of a contract that makes the contract voidable instead of void
5. Ordinary duress or undue influence [UCC 3-305(a)(1)(ii)]
6. Discharge of an instrument by payment or cancellation [UCC 3-602 and 3-604]

Contemporary Environment

HDC Status Eliminated with Respect to Consumer Credit Transactions

In certain situations, the HDC rule can cause a hardship for the consumer. To illustrate, Greg, a consumer, purchases a stereo on credit from Lou's Stereo. He signs a note promising to pay the purchase price plus interest to Lou's Stereo in 12 equal monthly installments. Lou's Stereo immediately negotiates the note at a discount to City Bank for cash. City Bank is an HDC. The stereo is defective. Greg would like to stop paying on it, but the HDC rule prevents him from asserting any personal defenses against City Bank. Under the UCC, Greg's only recourse is to sue Lou's Stereo. However, this is often an unsatisfactory result because Greg has no leverage against Lou's Stereo, and bringing a court action is expensive and time-consuming.

To correct this harsh result, the Federal Trade Commission (FTC), a federal administrative agency in change of consumer protection, adopted a rule that eliminates HDC status with regard to negotiable instruments arising out of certain *consumer* credit transactions [16 C.F.R. 433.2 (1987)]. This federal law takes precedence over state UCCs.

Thus, sellers of goods and services are prevented from separating the consumer's duty to pay the credit and the seller's duty to perform. This subjects the HDC of a consumer credit instrument to *all* the defenses and claims of the consumer. In the prior example,

Greg can raise the defect in the stereo as a defense against enforcement of the promissory note by City Bank, an HDC.

The FTC rules applies to consumer credit transactions in which (1) the buyer signs a sales contract that includes a promissory note, (2) the buyer signs an installment sales contract that contains a waiver of defenses clause, and (3) the seller arranges consumer financing with a third-party lender. Note that payment for goods and services with a check is not covered by this rule because it is not a credit transaction.

The FTC rule requires that the following clause be included in the bold type in covered consumer credit sales and installment contracts:

Notice. Any holder of this consumer credit contract is subject to all claims and defenses which the debtor could assert against the seller of the goods or services obtained pursuant hereto or with the proceeds hereof. Recovery hereunder by the debtor shall not exceed amounts paid by the debtor hereunder.

A consumer creditor may assert the FTC rule to prevent enforcement of a note that arose from a covered transaction. The FTC can impose monetary fines for violations. ∎

Discharge

The UCC specifies when and how certain parties are **discharged** (relieved) from liability on negotiable instruments. Generally, all parties to a negotiable instrument are discharged from liability if (1) the party primarily liable on the instrument pays it in full to the holder of the instrument or (2) a drawee in good faith pays an unaccepted draft or check in full to the holder. When a party other than a primary obligor (e.g., an indorser) pays a negotiable instrument, that party and all subsequent parties to the instrument are discharged from liability [UCC 3-602].

The holder of a negotiable instrument can discharge the liability of any party to the instrument by **cancellation** [UCC 3-604]. Cancellation can be accomplished by (1) any manner apparent on the face of the instrument or the indorsement (e.g., writing "canceled" on the instrument) or (2) destroying or mutilating a negotiable instrument with the intent of eliminating the obligation.

Intentionally striking out the signature of an indorser cancels that party's liability on the instrument and the liability of all subsequent indorsers. Prior indorsers are not discharged from liability. The instrument is not canceled if it is destroyed or mutilated by accident or by an unauthorized third party. The holder can bring suit to enforce the destroyed or mutilated instrument.

A party to a negotiable instrument sometimes posts collateral as security for the payment of the obligation. Other parties (e.g., holders. indorsers, accommodation parties) look to the credit standing of the party primarily liable on the instrument, the collateral (if any) that is posted, and the liability of secondary parties for the payment of the instrument when it is due. A holder owes a duty not to impair the rights of others when seeking recourse against the liable parties or the collateral. Thus, a holder who either (1) releases an obligor from liability or (2) surrenders the collateral without the consent of the parties who would benefit thereby discharges those parties from their obligation on the instrument [UCC 3-605(e)]. This discharge is called **impairment of the right of recourse**.

Chapter Summary

Holder Versus Holder in Due Course, p. 414

Holder Versus Holder in Due Course

1. **Holder.** A holder is a person who is in possession of a negotiable instrument that is drawn, issued, or indorsed to that person or his or her order, or to bearer, or in blank.
   a. **Rights of a holder.** A holder has the same rights as the assignee of an ordinary contract. A holder is subject to all claims and defenses that can be asserted against the transferor.
2. **Holder in due course (HDC).** An HDC is a holder who takes a negotiable instrument for value, in good faith, and without notice that it is defective or overdue.
   a. **Rights of an HDC.** An HDC takes a negotiable instrument free of all claims and most defenses that can be asserted against the transferor. Thus, an HDC can acquire greater rights than a transferor.

Requirements for HDC Status, p. 415

Requirements for HDC Status

To quality as an HDC, the transferee must meet the following requirements:

1. Be a holder.
2. Take the negotiable instrument for value.

3. Take the instrument in good faith.

4. Take the instrument without notice that it is overdue, dishonored, or encumbered in any way. Also, the instrument must bear no apparent evidence of forgery, alteration, or irregularity.

Taking for Value

Value has been given for a negotiable instrument if the holder:

1. Performs the agreed-upon promise.

2. Acquires a security interest or lien on the instrument.

3. Takes the instrument in payment of or as security for an antecedent claim.

4. Gives a negotiable instrument as payment.

5. Gives an irrevocable obligation as payment.

Taking in Good Faith

A holder must take the instrument in good faith to qualify as an HDC. Good faith means honesty in fact in the conduct or transaction. The holder's subjective belief can be inferred from the circumstances.

Taking Without notice

A person cannot qualify as an HDC if he or she has notice that the instrument is defective in any of the following ways:

1. It is overdue.

2. It has been dishonored.

3. It contains an unauthorized signature or has been altered.

4. There is a claim to it by another person.

5. There is a defense against it.

No Evidence of Forgery, Alteration, or Irregularity

A holder cannot become an HDC to an instrument that is apparently forged or altered or is so otherwise irregular or incomplete as to call into question its authenticity.

Signature Liability of Parties, p. 417

Signature Liability of Parties

1. *Signature liability.* A person cannot be held contractually liable on a negotiable instrument unless his or her signature appears on the instrument. Also called *contract liability.*

2. *Signers.* A person can sign an instrument in the capacity of a(n).

    a. *Maker* of notes and certificates of deposit

    b. *Drawer* of drafts and checks

    c. *Drawee* who certifies or accepts checks and drafts

    d. *Indorser* who indorses instruments

    e. *Agent* who signs on behalf of others

    f. *Accommodation party*

3. *Liability of signers.* Every party that signs a negotiable instrument (except qualified indorsers and agents that properly sign the instrument) is either *primarily* or *secondarily* liable on the instrument.

Signature Defined

The signature on a negotiable instrument can be any name, word, or mark used in lieu of a written signature. A signature may be (a) handwritten, typed, stamped, or made in almost any other manner and (b) executed or adopted by a party to authenticate a writing.

Agent's Signatures

1. *Agent.* An agent is a person who has been authorized to sign a negotiable instrument on behalf of another person.

2. *Principal.* A principal is a person who authorizes an agent to sign a negotiable instrument on his or her behalf.

3. *Authorized signature.* An authorized signature is an agent's signature on a negotiable instrument that is authorized by the principal.

 a. *Principal's liability.* A principal is liable on a negotiable instrument signed on his or her behalf by an authorized agent if either the name of the principal or the name of the agent (or both) appears on the instrument.

 b. *Agent's liability:*

  i. *Unambiguous signature.* An authorized agent is not personally liable on a negotiable instrument he or she signs on behalf of a principal if the signature shows unambiguously that it is made on behalf of a principal who is identified in the instrument.

  ii. *Ambiguous signature.* An authorized agent is personally liable to the following parties on a negotiable instrument if the signature does not show unambiguously that it is made in a representative capacity or the principal is not identified in the instrument:

   a. To an HDC who took the instrument without notice that the agent was not intended to be liable on the instrument

   b. To any other person other than an HDC unless the agent proves that the original parties did not intend the agent to be liable on the instrument

   Special rule for checks. An agent who signs a *check* from the account of a principal who is identified on the check without indicating the agent's representative capacity is not personally liable on the check.

4. *Unauthorized signature.* A signature made by a *purported agent* on behalf of a *purported principal* without the purported principal's authority.

 a. *Liability of the purported principal.* An unauthorized signature by a purported agent does not act as the signature of the purported principal. The purported principal is not liable on the instrument.

 b. *Liability of the purported agent.* The purported agent is liable to any person who in good faith pays the instrument or takes it for value.

Primary Liability

Primary liability is absolute liability of certain signers to pay a negotiable instrument, subject to certain real defenses.

 Parties who have primary liability. The following signers have *primary liability* to pay a negotiable instrument:

1. *Makers* of promissory notes and certificates of deposit

2. *Acceptors* of drafts and checks (e.g., a bank that certifies a check)

Secondary Liability

Secondary liability is liability on a negotiable instrument that is imposed on a party only when the party primarily liable on the instrument defaults and fails to pay the instrument when due.

1. *Parties who have secondary liability.* The following signers have *secondary liability* to pay a negotiable instrument:

 a. *Drawers* of drafts and checks if the check is dishonored by the drawee or acceptor.

 b. *Unqualified indorsers* if the primary obligor fails to pay the instrument.

2. *Qualified indorsers.* Qualified indorsers (i.e., indorsers who indorse instruments "*without recourse*" or similar language that disclaims liability) are not secondarily liable on the instrument.

3. *Requirements for imposing secondary liability.* Parties are secondarily liable on a negotiable instrument only if the following requirements are met:

 a. The instrument is properly *presented* for payment. *Presentment* is a demand for acceptance or payment of an instrument made upon the maker, acceptor, drawee, or other payor by or on behalf of the holder.

b. The instrument is *dishonored. Dishonor* occurs when acceptance or payment of the instrument is refused or cannot be obtained from the party required to accept or pay the instrument within the prescribed time after presentment is duly made.

c. *Notice of dishonor* is timely given to the person to be held secondarily liable on the instrument. *Notice of dishonor* may be given by any commercially reasonable means.

Accommodation Party

1. *Accommodation.* An accomodation occurs when a party signs a negotiable instrument to lend his or her name (and credit) to another party to the instrument.

2. *Accommodation party.* The accomodation party is the party who signs an instrument and lends his or her name (and credit) to another party to the instrument.

3. *Accommodated party.* The accomodated party is the party to whom an accommodation party lends his or her name (and credit) on a negotiable instrument.

4. *Types of liability.* An accommodation party may sign an instrument guaranteeing either *payment* or *collection*:

a. *Guaranteeing payment.* In this form of accommodation, the accommodation party *guarantees payment* of a negotiable instrument. The accommodation party is *primarily liable* on the instrument with the accommodated party. For example, an *accommodation maker* is primarily liable on a promissory note he or she signs. The debtor can seek payment from the accommodation maker without first seeking payment from the maker.

b. *Guaranteeing collection.* In this form of accommodation, the accommodation party *guarantees collection* of a negotiable instrument. The accommodation party is secondarily liable on the instrument. For example, an *accommodation indorser* is secondarily liable on a check he or she indorses. The holder cannot seek payment from the accommodation indorser unless he or she first seeks to recover payment from the primary obligor and is unsuccessful. To reserve this type of liability, the accommodation party's signature must be accompanied by words indicating that he or she is guaranteeing collection rather than payment of the obligation.

Warranty Liability of Parties, p. 423

Warranty Liability of Parties

The law *implies* certain warranties on transferors of negotiable instruments. There are two types of *implied warranties*:

1. Transfer warranties

2. Presentment warranties

Transfer Warranties

1. *Transfer.* Transfer means any passage of an instrument other than its issuance and presentment for payment.

2. *Transfer warranties.* Any person who transfers a negotiable instrument for consideration makes the following five warranties to the transferee:

a. The transferor has good title to the instrument or is authorized to obtain payment or acceptance on behalf of one who does have good title.

b. All signatures are genuine or authorized.

c. The instrument has not been materially altered.

d. No defenses of any party are good against the transferor.

e. The transferor has no knowledge of any insolvency proceeding against the maker, or acceptor, or the drawer of an unaccepted instrument.

3. *Breach of transfer warranty.* A transferee who takes an instrument in good faith may recover damages for *breach of transfer warranty* from the warrantor equal to the loss suffered. The amount cannot exceed the amount of the instrument plus expenses and interest.

Presentment Warranties

1. *Presentment.* Presentment is the demand for acceptance or payment of the instrument made upon the maker, acceptor, drawee, or other party by or on behalf of the holder.

2. **Presentment warranties.** Any person who presents a draft or check for payment or acceptance makes the following three warranties to a drawee or acceptor who in good faith pays or accepts the instrument:

   a. The presenter has good title to the instrument or is authorized to obtain payment or acceptance of the person who has good title.

   b. The instrument has not been materially altered.

   c. The presenter has no knowledge that the signature of the maker or drawer is unauthorized.

3. **Breath of presentment warranty.** A drawee who pays an instrument may recover damages for breach of presentment warranty from the warrantor. The amount that can be recovered is limited to the amount paid by the drawee less the amount the drawee received or is entitled to receive from the drawer because of the payment plus expenses and interest.

Defenses, p. 424

Defenses

Types of defenses. The creation of negotiable instruments may give rise to a defense against payment of the instrument. There are two types of defenses:

1. **Real defenses.** Real defenses can be raised against holders and HDCs.

2. **Personal defenses.** Personal defenses can be raised against holders but not against HDCs.

Real Defenses

Real defenses are defenses against the enforcement of a negotiable instrument that *can be raised against both holders and HDCs*. Real defenses include:

1. **Minority.** In most states, minors who do not misrepresent their age can disaffirm contracts, including negotiable instruments.

2. **Extreme duress.** A person who has signed a negotiable instrument under *extreme duress* (e.g., because of force or violence or threat of force or violence) may raise duress as a defense of the enforcement of the instrument.

3. **Mental incapacity.** An instrument that was signed by a person who has been adjudicated mentally incompetent is void.

4. **Illegality.** If an instrument arises out of an illegal transaction, the illegality is a real defense if the law declares the instrument void.

5. **Discharge in bankruptcy.** If an obligor's duty to pay a negotiable instrument has been discharged in bankruptcy, that person is relieved of the obligation to pay the instrument.

6. **Fraud in the inception.** This type of fraud occurs when a person is deceived into signing a negotiable instrument thinking that it is something else. Fraud in the inception, also called *fraud in the factum* or *fraud in the execution*, is a real defense against enforcement of an instrument.

7. **Forgery.** In forgery, the unauthorized signature of a maker, drawer, or indorser is wholly inoperative as that of the person whose name is signed. Forgery is a real defense unless the person whose name has been signed ratifies it or is precluded from raising the defense (e.g., his or her negligence substantially contributed to the forgery).

8. **Material alteration.** Material alteration of a negotiable instrument is a partial defense against an HDC. An HDC can enforce an altered instrument according to its original tenor but not to the raised amount.

Personal Defenses

Personal defenses are defenses against the enforcement of a negotiable instrument that can be raised against holders but cannot be raised against HDCs. Personal defenses include:

1. **Breach of contract.** The breach of contract by one of the original parties at the time of contracting can be raised against the enforcement of an instrument by holder. This defense is not effective against an HDC, however.

2. **Fraud in the inducement.** This type of fraud occurs when a wrongdoer makes a false representation to another person to lead that person to enter into a contract with the wrongdoer. This type of fraud may be raised as a defense against a holder but not against an HDC.

3. *Other personal defenses.* The following additional personal defenses can be raised against enforcement of a negotiable instrument by an ordinary holder but not against an HDC:

a. *Mental illness* that makes the contract voidable instead of void (usually a nonadjudicated mental illness)

b. *Illegality* of a contract that makes the contact voidable instead of void

c. *Ordinary* duress or undue influence

d. *Discharge* of an instrument by *payment* or *cancellation*

The FTC Eliminates HDC Status with Respect to Consumer Credit Transactions

1. *Consumer credit transaction.* This is a transaction whereby a consumer purchases goods or services on credit and signs a negotiable instrument (note) agreeing to pay the remainder of the purchase price.

2. *FTC rule.* The Federal Trade Commission (FTC) has adopted a rule that *eliminates HDC status* with regard to negotiable instruments that arise out of certain consumer credit transactions.

3. *Effect of the rule.* All defenses and claims that can be raised by the consumer purchaser against holders can also be raised against HDCs. Thus, both personal and real defenses can be raised against an HDC in this situation.

Discharge, p. 428

Discharge

Discharge involves actions or events that relieve certain parties from liability on negotiable instruments. The three methods of discharge are:

1. *Payment.* Generally, all parties to an instrument are discharged from liability if (a) the party primarily liable on the instrument pays it in full to the holder or (b) the drawee pays an unaccepted draft or check in full to the holder.

2. *Cancellation.* Cancellation of the instrument discharges the liability of any party to the instrument. Cancellation can be accomplished by (a) any manner apparent on the face of the instrument or the indorsement (e.g., writing "canceled" on the instrument) or (b) destroying or mutilating the instrument with the intent of eliminating the obligation.

3. *Impairment of the right of recourse.* Certain parties (holders, accommodation parties) are discharged from liability on an instrument if the holder (a) releases an obligor from liability or (b) surrenders collateral without the consent of the parties who would benefit by it.

 Internet Exercises and Case Questions

Working the Web Internet Exercises

Activities

1. Go to the FTC web site, at **www.ftc.gov**, and find "Federal Trade Commission Agency: Federal Trade Commission, 16 CFR Part 433 Regulatory Flexibility Act

Review of the Trade Regulation Rule Concerning Preservation of Consumer's Claims and Defenses." Review this regulation.

Critical Legal Thinking Cases

20.1 Holder in Due Course On May 8, 1974, Royal Insurance Company Ltd. (Royal) issued a draft in the amount of $12,000 payable through the Morgan Guaranty Trust Company (Morgan Guaranty). The draft was made payable to Gary E. Terrell in settlement of a claim in an insurance policy for fire damage to premises located at 3031 North 11th Street, Kansas City, Kansas. On May 9, the attorney for Mr. and Mrs. Louis Wexler notified Royal that Terrell's clients had an insurable

interest in the damaged property. As a result, Royal immediately stopped payment on the draft. On the same day, the draft was indorsed by Gary E. Terrell and deposited in his account at the UAW-CIO Local #31 Federal Credit Union (Federal). Over the next two days, Terrell withdrew $9,000 from this account. Immediately upon receiving the draft, Federal indorsed it and forwarded it to Morgan Guaranty for payment. The draft was returned to Federal on May 14 with the notation "payment stopped." When Royal refused to pay Federal the amount of the draft, Federal sued. The basis of the suit was whether Federal was a holder in due course. Who wins? [*UAW-CIO Local #31 Federal Credit Union v. Royal Insurance Company, Ltd.*, 594 S.W.2d 276, 1980 Mo. Lexis 446 (MO 1980)]

20.2 Taking for Value On September 30, 1976, Betty Ellis and her then husband W. G. Ellis executed and delivered to the Standard Finance Company (Standard) a promissory note in the amount of $2,800. After receiving the note, Standard issued a check to the couple for $2,800. The check was made payable to "W. G. Ellis and Betty Ellis." The check was cashed after both parties indorsed it. Shortly thereafter, the Ellises were divorced. Mrs. Ellis claims that (1) she never saw or used the money and (2) Standard understood that all the money went to her ex-husband. W. G. Ellis was declared bankrupt. When the note became due in 1980, Betty Ellis refused to pay it. Standard sued her, seeking payment as a holder in due course. She claimed that Standard is not a holder in due course in regard to her because she never received consideration for the note and, therefore, Standard did not take the note for value. Who wins? [*Standard Finance Company, Ltd. v. Ellis*, 657 P.2d 1056, 1983 Haw.App. Lexis 83 (Hawaii App. 1983)]

20.3 Fraud in the Factum John Wade was employed by Mike Fazzari. Fazzari was an immigrant who was unable to speak or read English. In December 1957, Wade prepared a promissory note in the amount of $400. The instrument was payable at the Glen National Bank, Watkins Glen, New York. Wade took the note to Fazzari and told him that the document was a statement of wages earned by Wade during the course of his employment. Fazzari signed the instrument after Wade told him it was necessary for income tax purposes. Fazzari was not in debt to Wade and there was no consideration given for the note. On April 10, 1958, the note was presented to the First National Bank of Odessa by Wellington Doane, a customer of the bank and an indorsee of the payee, Wade. Doane indorsed the check in blank and accepted a $400 cashier's check in exchange for the note. Fazzari and Glen National Bank refused payment of the note. Can the First National Bank of Odessa enforce payment of the note as a holder in due course? [*First National Bank of Odessa v. Fazzari*, 179 N.E. 2d 493, 223 N.Y.S. 2d 483, 1961 N.Y. Lexis 857 (N.Y. App. 1961)]

20.4 Fraud in the Inducement J. H. Thompson went to the Central Motor Company (Central), an automobile dealership, to purchase a car. With the assistance of Central's sales manager, Ed Boles, Thompson selected a 1966 Imperial automobile. Boles drew up a loan agreement that stipulated 35 monthly installments of $125 and a final installment of $5,265. Under this agreement, Thompson would be charged an annual interest rate of 8 percent. Boles assured Thompson that when the $5,265 installment became due he would be allowed to sign a second note to cover that amount. Thompson was told that the interest rate on this second note would also be 8 percent. With this assurance, Thompson signed the original loan agreement and note and made all the payments except the final one. When Thompson went to Central to sign the second note he was told that the interest rate on the second installment note would be 12 percent, not 8 percent. Thompson refused to sign the second note or make the balloon payment on the original note. Instead, he returned the car. Central was able to sell the car, but it sued Thompson to recover a deficiency judgement. Who wins?

[*Central Motor Company v. J. H. Thompson*, 465 S.W. 2d 405, 1971 Tex.App. Lexis 2634 (Tex. App. 1971)]

20.5 Federal Trade Commission Rule Warren and Kristina Mahaffey were approached by a salesman from the Five Star Solar Screens Company (Five Star). The salesman offered to install insulation in their home at a cost of $5,289. After being told that the insulation would reduce their heating bills by 50 percent, the Mahaffeys agreed to the purchase. To pay for the work, the Mahaffeys executed a note promising to pay the purchase price with interest, in installments. The note, which was secured by a deed of trust on the Mahaffeys' home, contained the following language: "Notice: Any holder of this consumer credit contract is subject to all claims and defenses which the debtor could assert against the seller of goods or services obtained pursuant hereto or with the proceeds thereof." Several days after Five Star finished working at the Mahaffeys' home, it sold the installment note to Mortgage Finance Corporation (Mortgage Finance).

There were major defects in the way the insulation was installed in the Mahaffey home. Large holes were left in the walls, and heater blankets and roof fans were never delivered as called for by the purchase contract. Because of these defects, the Mahaffeys refused to make the payments due on the note. Mortgage Finance instituted foreclosure proceedings to collect the money owed. Can the Mahaffeys successfully assert the defense of breach of contract against the enforcement of the note by Mortgage Finance? [*Mahaffey v. Investor's National Security Company*, 747 P.2d 890, 1987 Nev. Lexis 1875 (NV 1987)]

20.6 Presentment Warranties John Waddell Construction Company (Waddell) maintained a checking account at the Longview Bank & Trust Company (Longview Bank). Waddell drafted a check from this account made payable to two payees, Engineered Metal Works (Metal Works) and E. G. Smith Construction (Smith Construction). The check was sent to Metal Works, which promptly indorsed the check and presented it to the First National Bank of Azle (Bank of Azle) for payment. The Bank of Azle accepted the check with only Metal Works's indorsement and credited Metal Works's account. The Bank of Azle subsequently presented the check to Longview Bank through the Federal Reserve System. Longview Bank accepted and paid the check. When Waddell received the check along with its monthly checking statements from Longview Bank, a company employee noticed the missing indorsement and notified Longview Bank. Longview Bank returned the check to the Bank of Azle, and the Bank of Azle's account was debited the amount of the check at the Federal Reserve. Did the Bank of Azle breach its warranty of good title? [*Longview Bank & Trust Company v. First National Bank of Azle*, 750 S.W.2d 297, 1988 Tex.App. Lexis 1377 (Tex. App. 1988)]

20.7 Drawer's Liability Carlisle Distributing Company, Inc. (Carlisle), owed William Paladino $10,000. To pay this debt, Carlisle delivered a $10,000 check drawn on an Arkansas bank made payable to Paladino. Paladino indorsed the check and delivered it to Wildman Stores, Inc. (Wildman), as security for an $8,000 loan he had received from that company. Seventeen months after receiving the check, Wildman presented it for payment at the bank upon which it had been drawn. The payor bank dishonored the check due to insufficient funds. Wildman informed Carlisle of the dishonor and demanded payment of the $10,000. Carlisle refused Wildman's demand. Wildman sued Carlisle to collect the $10,000. The statute of limitations for enforcing a negotiable instrument in Arkansas is five years. Who wins? [*Wildman Stores, Inc. v. Carlisle Distributing Co., Inc.*, 688 S.W.2d 748, 1985 Ark.App. Lexis 1926 (Ark. App. 1985)]

20.8 Liability of Accommodation Makers   John Valenti wanted to operate an Amoco service station. He contracted with American oil Company (Amoco), the licensor of Amoco service Stations, to lease a service station and become a dealer of Amoco products. The documents that made up the lease agreement included a promissory note and guaranty. Since Valenti had no established credit history, Amoco required that his father be a cosignor. Both Valentis signed the lease and note. After about one year, the younger Valenti abandoned the operation. Amoco sued both Valentis to recover on the note and guaranty. The suit against the son was dropped when Amoco learned that he had no assets from which to satisfy a judgement. The father claimed that Amoco could not go after him because it was not suing his son. Who wins? [*American Oil Company v. Valenti*, 426 A.2d 305, 1979 Conn. Lexis 973 (Conn. Sup. 1979)]

20.9 Principal's Liability   John Smith was the corporate secretary for Carriage House Mobile Homes, Inc. (Carriage House). Beginning on November 9, 1973, Smith signed a series of checks totalling $13,900 made payable to Danube Carpet Mills (Danube). The checks were in payment for carpet ordered by Carriage House. Each check was signed in the following manner: "Carriage House Mobile homes, Inc., General Account, By: /s/ John Smith." When Danube presented the checks for payment to the drawee bank, the First State Bank of Phil Campbell, Alabama (First State Bank), payment was refused. The reason for the refusal was that the checks were drawn against uncollected funds. The holder of these checks, Southeastern Financial Corporation, sued Smith and Carriage House to recover the $13,900. Who is liable on the Checks? [*Southeastern Financial Corporation v. Smith*, 397 F.Supp. 649, 1975 U.S.Dist. Lexis 12624 (N.D. Ala.1975)]

20.10 Authorized Agent's Liability   Richard G. Lee was the president of Village Homes, Inc. (Village Homes). Village Homes had several loans from Farmers & Merchants National Bank of Hattan, North Dakota (Farmers Bank) that were in default. Lee and Farmers Bank worked out an arrangement to consolidate the delinquent loans and replace them with a new loan. The new loan would be secured by a promissory note. The parties drafted a note in the amount of $85,000 with a 17 percent annual interest rate. Lee signed the note without indicating that he was signing as an agent of Village Homes. The name "Village Homes, Inc." did not appear on the note. Six months after the note was signed, Village Home defaulted on it. Farmers Bank sued Lee, seeking to hold him personally liable for the note. Who wins? [*Farmers & Merchants National Bank of Hattan, North Dakota v. Lee*, 333 N.W.2d 792, 1983 N.D. Lexis 289 (ND 1983)]

Business Ethics Cases

20.11 Business Ethics   Anthony and Dolores Angelini entered into a contract with Lustro Aluminum Products, Inc. (Lustro). Under the contract, Lustro agreed to replace exterior veneer on the Angelini home with Gold Bond Plasticrylic avocado siding. The cash price for the job was $3,600, and the installment plan price was $5,363.40. The Angelinis chose to pay on the installment plan and signed a promissory note as security. The note's language provided that it would not mature until 60 days after a certificate of completion was signed. Ten days after the note was executed, Lustro assigned it for consideration to General Investment Corporation (General), an experienced home improvement lender. General was aware that Lustro (1) was nearly insolvent at the time of the assignment and (2) had engaged in questionable business practices in the past. Lustro never completed the installation of siding at the Angelini home. General demanded payment of the note from the Angelinis as a holder in due course. Did General act morally in this case? Who wins? [*General Investment Corporation v. Angelini*, 278 A.2d 193, 1971 N.J. Lexis 263 (NJ 1971)]

20.12 Business Ethics   In 1976, Gerald Tinker purchased for investment purposes a used 1972 Jaguar from De Maria Porsche Audi, Inc. (De Maria). De Maria represented to Tinker, prior to making the sale, that the automobile was in good operating condi-

tion, was powered by its original engine, and had never been involved in a major collision. Tinker relied on these representations and executed a retail installment contract and note with De Maria. The contract and note contained the FTC-required notice. De Maria assigned the contract and note to Central Bank of Miami (Central Bank), which provided floor financing for De Maria.

Tinker had problems with the automobile immediately after its purchase. The car operated poorly, and Tinker soon discovered that it was not powered by its original engine, had previously been involved in a major collision, and had been determined to be a total loss by its previous owner's insurance company. The title held by the owner preceding De Maria stated that it was a "parts car." The title obtained by Tinker from De Maria did not contain this disclaimer. When De Maria failed to replace or successfully repair the automobile after it became totally inoperable, Tinker ceased making payments on the note and sued De Maria and Central Bank for fraud. Central Bank counterclaimed for the amount due on the note. Is it ethical for a third-party lender to assert its HDC status to collect on note when the seller has engaged in fraud or other misconduct? Does the FTC rule prevent Central Bank from being a holder in due course? [*Tinker v. De Maria Porsche Audi, Inc.*, 459 So.2d 487, 1984 Fla.App. Lexis 16028 (Fla. App. 1984)]

Briefing the Case Writing Assignment

Read Case A.20 in the Case Appendix [*Kedzie & 103rd Currency Exchange, Inc. v. Hodge*]. This case is excerpted from the appellate court opinion. Review and brief the case. In your brief, be sure to answer the following questions.

1. Who was the drawer of the check? Who was the payee of the check?

2. What firm cashed the check? Did it qualify as an HDC?

3. What defense did the defendant assert?

4. Was the defense effective against enforcement of the negotiable instrument?

21

Checks and Digital Banking

> "Bankers have no right to establish a customary law among themselves, at the expense of other men."
>
> —Justice Foster
> Hankey v. Trotman, I Black W.I (I746)

Chapter Objectives

After studying this chapter, you should be able to:

1. Describe the difference between certified, cashier's, and traveler's checks.

2. Describe the system of processing and collecting checks through the banking system.

3. Identify when a bank engages in a wrongful dishonor of a check.

4. Describe electronic fund transfer systems.

5. Define wire transfer and describe the main provisions of Article 4A of the Uniform Commercial Code (UCC).

Chapter Contents

- The Bank–Customer Relationship
- Ordinary Checks
- Special Types of Checks
- Honoring Checks
- Forged Signatures and Altered Checks
- The Collection Process
- Commerical Wire Transfers

Checks are the most common form of negotiable instrument used in this country. More than 70 billion checks are written annually. Checks act both as substitutes for money and as record-keeping devices, but they do not serve a credit function. In addition, billions of dollars are transferred each day by **wire transfer** between businesses and banks. This chapter discusses the various forms of checks, the procedure for paying and collecting on checks through the banking system, the duties and liabilities of banks and other parties in the collection process, and the process of electronic fund transfers.

Money speaks sense in a language all nations understand.

Aphra Behn (1640-1689)
The Rover

The Bank–Customer Relationship

When a customer makes a deposit into a bank, a **creditor–debtor relationship** is formed. The customer is the creditor, and the bank is the debtor. In effect, the customer is loaning money to the bank.

A **principal–agent relationship** is created if (1) the deposit is a check that the bank must collect for the customer or (2) the customer writes a check against his or her account. The customer is the principal, and the bank is the agent. The bank is obligated to follow the customer's order to collect or pay the check. The rights and duties of a bank and a checking account and wire transfer customer are contractual. The signature card and other bank documents signed by the customer form the basis of the contract.

The Uniform Commercial Code Banking Provisions

Various articles of the Uniform Commercial Code (UCC) establish rules for creating, collecting, and enforcing checks and wire transfers. These articles are:

- **Article 3 (Negotiable Instruments)** establishes the requirements for finding a negotiable instrument. Because a check is a negotiable instrument, the provisions of Article 3 apply. **Revised Article 3** was promulgated in 1990. The provisions of Revised Article 3 serve as the basis of the discussion of Article 3 in this chapter.

- **Article 4 of the UCC (Bank Deposits and Collections)** establishes the rules and principles that regulate bank deposit and collection procedures for checking accounts offered by commercial banks, NOW (negotiable orders of withdrawal) accounts, and other check-like accounts offered by savings and loan associations, savings banks, credit unions, and other financial institutions. Article 4 controls if the provisions of Articles 3 and 4 conflict [UCC 4-102(a)]. Article 4 was substantially amended in 1990. The amended Article 4 serves as the basis of the discussion of Article 4 in this chapter.

- **Article 4A (Funds Transfer)** establishes rules that regulate the creation and collection of and liability for wire transfers. Article 4A was added to the UCC in 1989.

Ordinary Checks

Most adults and businesses have at least one checking account at a bank. A customer opens a checking account by going to the bank, completing the necessary forms (including a signature card), and making a **deposit** to the account. The bank issues checks to the customer. The customer then uses the checks to purchase goods and services.

Parties to a Check

UCC 3-104(f) defines a **check** as an order by the drawer to the drawee bank to pay a specified sum of money from the drawer's checking account to the named payee (or holder). There are three parties to an ordinary check:

1. *Drawer.* The **drawer** is the customer who maintains the checking account and writes (draws) checks against the account.
2. *Drawee (or payor bank).* The **drawee** is the bank on which the check is drawn.
3. *Payee.* The **payee** is the party to whom the check is written.

Consider This Example The Kneadery Restaurant has a checking account at Mountain Bank. The Kneadery writes a check for $1,500 from this account to Sun Valley Bakery to pay for food supplies. The Kneadery Restaurant is the drawer, Mountain Bank is the drawee, and Sun Valley Bakery is the payee.

Indorsement of a Check

The payee is a *holder* of the check. As such, the payee has the right to either (1) demand payment of the check or (2) *indorse* the check to another party by signing the back of the check. This latter action is called **indorsement** of a check. The payee is the **indorser**, and the person to whom the check is indorsed is the **indorsee**. The indorsee in turn becomes a holder who can either demand payment of the check or indorse it to yet another party. Any subsequent holder can demand payment of the check or further transfer the check [UCC 3-204(a)].

Consider This Example Referring to the previous example, the Sun Valley Bakery may either present the Kneadery Restaurant's check to Mountain Bank for payment or it can indorse the check to another party. Assume that Sun Valley Bakery indorses the check to the Flour Company in payment for flour; Sun Valley Bakery is the indorser, and the Flour Company is the indorsee. The Flour Company may either present the check for payment or indorse it to another party, and so on.

Online Commerce & Internet Law
Electronic Fund Transfer Systems

Computers and electronic technology have made it possible for banks to offer electronic payment and collection systems to bank customers. This technology is collectively referred to as **electronic fund transfer systems (EFTS)**. EFTS are supported by contracts among and between customers, banks, private clearinghouses, and other third parties. The most common forms of EFTS are discussed in the following paragraphs.

Automated Teller Machines

An **automated teller machine (ATM)** is an electronic machine that is located either on a bank's premises or at some other convenient location, such as a shopping center or supermarket. These devices are connected online to the bank's computers. Each bank customer is issued a secret personal identification number (PIN) to access his or her bank accounts through ATMs.

ATMs are commonly used when the bank is not open. They are also used as an alternative means of conducting banking when the bank is open. They are used to withdraw cash from bank accounts, cash checks, make deposits to checking or savings accounts, and make payments owed to the bank.

Point-of-Sale Terminals

Many banks issue *debit cards* to customers. Debit cards replace checks in that customers can use them to make purchases. No credit is extended. Instead, the customer's bank account is immediately debited for the amount of the purchase.

Debit cards can be used only at merchants that have **point-of-sale (POS) terminals** at the checkout counters. These terminals are connected online to the bank's computers. To make a purchase, a customer inserts the debit card into the terminal for the amount of the purchase. If there are sufficient funds in the customer's account, the transaction will debit the customer's account and credit the merchant's account for the amount of the purchase. If there are insufficient funds in the customer's account, the purchase is rejected unless the customer has overdraft protection. Some POS terminals allow for the extension of credit in the transaction. Gasoline station POS terminals are one example. At many POS terminals, customers can also obtain cash back above the amount of their purchase.

Direct Deposits and Withdrawals

Many banks provide the service of paying recurring payments and crediting recurring deposits on behalf of customers. Commonly, payments are for utilities, insurance premiums, mortgage payments, and the like. Social Security checks, wages, and dividend and interest checks are examples of recurring deposits. To provide this service, the customer's bank and the payee's bank must belong to the same clearinghouse.

Pay-by-Internet

Many banks permit customers to pay bills from their bank accounts by use of personal computer by using the Internet. To do so, the customer must enter his or her PIN and account name or number, the amount of the bill to be paid, and the account number of the payee to whom the funds are to be transferred. Internet banking is expected to increase dramatically in the future. ■

Special Types of Checks

If a payee fears there may be insufficient funds in the drawer's account to pay a check when it is presented for payment or that the drawer has stopped payment of the check, the payee may be unwilling to accept an ordinary check from the drawer. However, the payee might be willing to accept a **bank check**—that is, a certified check, a cashier's check, or a traveler's check. These types of checks are usually considered "as good as cash" because the bank is solely or primarily liable for payment. These forms of checks are discussed in the following paragraphs.

Certified Checks

When a bank **certifies a check**, it agrees in advance to (1) accept the check when it is presented for payment and (2) pay the check out of funds set aside from the customer's account and either placed in a special certified check account or held in the customer's account. Certified checks do not become stale. Thus, they are payable at any time from the date they are issued.

Exhibit 21.1

A Certified Check

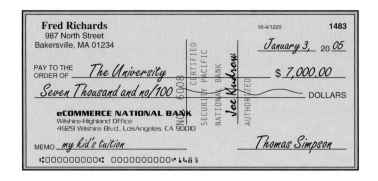

A check is **certified** when the bank writes or stamps the word *certified* across the face of an ordinary check. The certification should also contain the date and the amount being certified and the name and title of the person at the bank who certifies the check (see Exhibit 21.1). Note that a bank is not obligated to certify a check. A bank's refusal to do so is not a dishonor of a check [UCC 3-409(d)].

Business Brief

The drawer is discharged from liability if the drawee bank certifies a check.

Liability on a Certified Check Either the drawer or the payee (or holder) can present the check to the drawee's bank for certification. If the drawee's bank certifies the check, the drawer is discharged from liability on the check, regardless of who obtained the certification [UCC 3-414(c)]. The holder must recover from the certifying bank. The obligated bank can be held liable for the amount of the check, expenses, and loss of interest resulting from nonpayment. If the bank refuses to pay after receiving notice of particular circumstances giving rise to such damages, it can also be held liable for consequential damages [UCC 3-413].

Problems may arise if a certified check was altered (e.g., the amount of the check increased). If the alteration occurred before the check was certified, the certifying bank is liable for the certified amount. If the check was altered after certification, the bank is liable for only the certified amount, not the raised amount. The drawer cannot stop payment on a certified check. Because certification constitutes acceptance of the check, the certifying bank can revoke its certification only in limited circumstances [UCC 3-413].

Cashier's Checks

A person can purchase a **cashier's check** from a bank by paying the bank the amount of the check plus a fee for issuing the check. Usually, a specific payee is named. The purchaser does not have to have a checking account at the bank. The check is a noncancellable negotiable instrument upon issue.

Business Brief

Many businesses require payment by certified or cashier's checks because these are "as good as cash." By doing so, businesses avoid the problem of being paid by normal checks that may "bounce."

A cashier's check is a two-party check for which (1) the issuing bank serves as both the drawer and the drawee and (2) the holder serves as payee [UCC 3-104(g)]. The bank, which has been paid for the check, guarantees its payment. When the check is presented for payment, the bank debits its own account [UCC 3-412]. (See Exhibit 21.2 for a sample cashier's check.)

Exhibit 21.2

A Cashier's Check

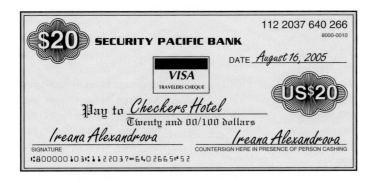

Exhibit 21.3
A Traveler's Check

An obligated bank that wrongfully refuses to pay a cashier's check is liable to the person asserting the right to enforce the check for expenses and loss of interest resulting from nonpayment and consequential damages [UCC 3-411].

Traveler's Checks

Traveler's checks are so named because individuals often purchase them to use as a safe substitute for cash while on vacations or other trips. They may be issued by banks or by companies other than banks (e.g., American Express). A traveler's check is a two-party instrument, where the issuing bank serves as both the drawer and the drawee. It is drawn by the bank upon itself.

Traveler's checks may be purchased in many denominations, including $10, $20, $50, and $100. Unlike cashier's checks, traveler's checks are issued without a named payee. The checks have two signature blanks. The purchaser signs one blank when the traveler's checks are issued. The purchaser enters the payee's name and signs the second blank when he or she uses a check to purchase goods or services. A traveler's check is not a negotiable instrument until it is signed the second time [UCC 3-104(i)] (see Exhibit 21.3).

Purchasers of traveler's checks do not have to have a checking account at the issuing bank. The purchaser pays the bank the amount of the checks to be issued. When a traveler's check is presented for payment, the bank debits its own account. Most banks charge a fee for this service, but some banks merely earn interest on the "float" while the checks are not written. If a traveler's check is stolen or lost prior to its use, the purchaser can stop payment on the check. Payment cannot be stopped once the check has been negotiated.

Business Brief

Travelers checks are used in place of cash when people are on vacation or business trips. Credit cards are replacing the use of traveler's checks.

Online Commerce & Internet Law
Bank Debit Cards

Computers have made it much easier and faster for banks and their customers to conduct banking transactions. For example, bank customers can now use **debit cards** to pay for goods and services. When a bank customer uses a debit card to pay, the money is immediately deducted electronically from his or her bank account. There is no extension of credit as there is when a credit card is used; using a debit card is like writing an electronic check.

Congress enacted the **Electronic Fund Transfer Act** [15 U.S.C. §§ 1693 et seq.] to regulate consumer electronic fund transfers. The Federal Reserve Board, which is empowered to enforce the provisions of the act, adopted **Regulation E** to further interpret it. Regulation E has the force of law. The Electronic Fund Transfer Act and Regulation E establish the following consumer rights:

1. **Unsolicited cards.** A bank can send unsolicited EFTS debit cards to a consumer only if the cards are not valid for use. Unsolicited cards can be validated for use by a consumer's specific request.

2. **Lost or stolen debit cards.** Debit cards are sometimes lost or stolen. If a customer notifies the issuer bank within two days of learning that his or her debit card has been lost or stolen, the customer is liable for only $50 for unauthorized use. If a customer does not notify the bank within this two-day period, the customer's liability increases to $500. If the customer fails to notify the bank within 60 days after an unauthorized use appears on the customer's bank statement, the customer can be held liable for more than $500.

Online Commerce & Internet Law
(continued)

Federal law allows states to impose a lesser liability on customers for lost or stolen debit cards.

3. *Evidence of transaction.* Other than for a telephone transaction, a bank must provide a customer with a written receipt of a transaction made through a computer terminal. This receipt is prima facie evidence of the transaction.

4. *Bank statements.* A bank must provide a monthly statement to an electronic funds transfer customer at the end of the month in which the customer conducts a transaction. Otherwise, a quarterly statement must be provided to the customer. The statement must include the date and amount of the transfer, the name of the retailer, the location or identification of the terminal, and the fees charged for the transaction. Bank statements must also contain the address and telephone number where inquiries or errors can be reported.

Banks are required to disclose the foregoing information to their customers. A bank is liable for wrongful dishonor when it fails to pay an electronic fund transfer when there are sufficient funds in the customer's account to do so. ■

Honoring Checks

When a customer opens a checking account at a bank, the customer impliedly agrees to keep sufficient funds in the account to pay any checks written against it. Thus, when the drawee bank receives a properly drawn and payable check, the bank is under a duty to **honor** the check and charge (debit) the drawer's account the amount of the check [UCC 4-401(a)].

Stale Checks

Occasionally, payees or other holders in possession of a check fail to present the check immediately to the payor bank for payment. A check that has been outstanding for more than six months is considered **stale**, and the bank is under no obligation to pay it. A bank that pays a stale check in good faith may charge the drawer's account [UCC 4-404].

Incomplete Checks

Drawers sometimes write checks that omit certain information, such as the amount of the check or the payee's name, either on purpose or by mistake. In such cases, the payee or any holder can complete the check, and the payor bank that in good faith makes payment on the completed check can charge the customer's account the amount of the completed check unless it has notice that the completion was improper [UCC 3-407(c) and 4-401(d)(2)]. The UCC places the risk of loss of an incomplete item on the drawer.

Consider This Example   Suppose Richard, who owes Sarah $500, draws a check payable to Sarah on City Bank. Richard signs the check but leaves the amount blank. Sarah fraudulently fills in "$1,000" and presents the check to City Bank, which pays it. City Bank can charge Richard's account $1,000. Richard's only recourse is to sue Sarah. If Richard had telephoned the bank to tell them that he owed Sarah only $500, however, City Bank would be liable for paying any greater amount to Sarah.

Death or Incompetence of a Drawer

Checks may be paid against the accounts of deceased customers or customers who have been adjudicated incompetent until the bank has actual knowledge of such condition and had reasonable opportunity to act on the information. In the case of a deceased customer, the bank may pay or certify checks drawn on the deceased customer's account on or prior to the date of death for 10 days after the date of death. This rule applies unless a person claiming an interest in the account, such as an heir or a taxing authority, orders the bank to stop payment. A bank that pays such a check when it should not have is liable for the amount improperly paid [UCC 4-405].

Postdated Checks

On occasion, a drawer of a check does not want a check he or she writes to be cashed until sometime in the future. Under UCC 4-401(c), to require a bank to abide by a postdated check, the drawer must take the following steps:

1. The drawer must postdate the check to some date in the future.
2. The drawer must give *separate written notice* to the bank, describing the check with reasonable certainty and notifying the bank not to pay the check until the date on the check.

If these steps are taken and the bank pays the check before its date, the bank is liable to the drawer for any losses resulting from its act.

Consider This Example   On May 1, Gion writes a check to Tina and postdates the check June 1. Suppose Gion sent a separate written notice to his bank notifying the bank of this fact. If Tina cashes the check on May 2 and Gion's bank pays the check, the bank is liable to Gion if Gion suffers any loss.

Stop-Payment Orders

A **stop-payment order** is an order by a drawer of a check to the payor bank not to pay or certify a check. Only the drawer can order a stop payment. If the signature of more than one person is required to draw on an account, any of these persons may stop payment on the account. The bank must be given a reasonable opportunity to act on a stop-payment order. The order is ineffectual if the bank has already accepted or certified the check.

A stop-payment order can be given orally or in writing. An **oral order** is binding on the bank for only 14 calendar days, unless confirmed in writing during this time. A **written order** is effective for six months. It can be renewed in writing for additional six-month periods [UCC 4-403].

If the payor bank fails to honor a valid stop-payment order, it must recredit the customer's account. The bank is subrogated to the rights of the drawer. In addition, the bank is liable only for the actual damages suffered by the drawer. The drawer must prove the fact and amount of loss resulting from the payment of a check on which a stop-payment order was issued.

Business Brief

An oral stop-payment order is binding on the bank for only 14 days, unless confirmed in writing during the 14-day period.

Consider This Example   Suppose Karen buys a car from Silvio. She pays for the car by drawing a $10,000 check on City Bank, payable to the order of Silvio. Karen thinks the car is defective and stops payment on the check. If City Bank mistakenly pays Silvio over the stop-payment order, it is liable and must recredit Karen's account. If it is determined that the car is not defective, however, City Bank does not have to recredit Karen's account because Karen has suffered no actual loss; she owes Silvio for the car.

Overdrafts

If the drawer does not have enough money in his or her account when a properly payable check is presented for payment, the payor bank can either (1) dishonor the check or (2) honor the check and create an overdraft in the drawer's account [UCC 4-401(a)]. The bank notifies the drawer of the dishonor and returns the check to the holder, marked "insufficient funds." The holder often resubmits the check to the bank, hoping that the drawer has deposited more money into the account and the check will clear. If the check does not clear, the holder's recourse is against the drawee of the check.

If the bank chooses to pay the check even though there are insufficient funds in the drawer's account, it can later charge the drawer's account for the amount of the **overdraft** [UCC 4-401(a)] because there is an implied promise that the drawer will reimburse the bank for paying checks the drawer orders the bank to pay. If the drawer does not fulfill this commitment, the bank can sue him or her to recover payment for the overdrafts and overdraft fees. A bank cannot charge interest on the amount of the overdraft without the drawer's permission. Therefore, many banks offer optional overdraft protection to their customers.

Wrongful Dishonor

If the bank does not honor a check when there are sufficient funds in a drawer's account to pay a properly payable check, it is liable for **wrongful dishonor**. The payor bank is liable to the drawer for damages proximately caused by the wrongful dishonor as well as for consequential damages, damages caused by criminal prosecution, and such. A payee or holder cannot sue the bank for damages caused by the wrongful dishonor of a drawer's check. The only recourse for the payee or holder is to sue the drawer to recover the amount of the check [UCC 4-402].

Contemporary Environment

Federal Currency Reporting Law

Federal currency reporting law requires financial institutions and other entities (e.g., retailers, car and boat dealers, antique dealers, jewelers, travel agencies, real estate brokers, and other businesses) to file a **Currency Transaction Report (CTR)** with the Internal Revenue Service (IRS), reporting:

- The receipt in a single transaction or a series of related transactions of cash in an amount greater than $10,000. "Cash" is not limited to currency, but includes cashier's checks, bank drafts, traveler's checks, and money orders (but not ordinary checks) [26 U.S.C. § 60501].
- Suspected criminal activity by bank customers involving a financial transaction of $1,000 or more in funds [12 C.F.R. § 21.11(b)(3)].

The law also stipulates that it is a crime to structure or assist in structuring any transaction for the purpose of evading these reporting requirements [31 U.S.C. § 5324]. Financial institutions and entities may be fined for negligent violations of the currency reporting requirements. A $50,000 fine may be levied for a pattern of negligent violations. Willful failure to file reports may subject the violator to civil money penalties, charges of aiding and abetting the criminal activity, and prosecution for violating the money-laundering statutes. ■

Forged Signatures and Altered Checks

Major problems associated with checks are that (1) certain signatures are sometimes forged and (2) the check itself may have been altered prior to presentment for payment. The UCC rules that apply to these situations are discussed in the following paragraphs.

These rules apply to all types of negotiable instruments but are particularly important concerning checks.

Forged Signature of the Drawer

When a check is presented to the payor bank for payment, the bank is under a duty to verify the drawer's signature. This is usually done by matching the signature on the signature card on file at the bank to the signature on the check.

A check with a *forged drawer's signature* is called a **forged instrument**. A forged signature is wholly inoperative as the signature of the drawer. The check is not "properly payable" because it does not contain an order of the drawer. The payor bank cannot charge the customer's account if it pays a check over the forged signature. If the bank has charged the customer's account, it must recredit the account, and the forged check must be dishonored [UCC 3-401].

The bank can recover from the party who presented the check to it for payment only if that party had knowledge that the signature of the drawer on the check was unauthorized [UCC 3-417(a)(3)]. The forger is liable on the check because the forged signature acts as the forger's signature [UCC 3-403(a)]. Although the payor bank can sue the forger, the forger usually cannot be found or is judgment-proof.

Consider This Example   Suppose Gregory has a checking account at Country Bank. Lana steals a check, completes it, and forges Gregory's signature. She indorses it to Mike, who knows that Gregory's signature has been forged. Mike indorses it to Barbara, who is innocent and does not know of the forgery. She presents it to Country Bank, the payor bank, which pays the check. Country Bank may recover from the original forger, Lana, and from Mike, who knew of the forgery. It cannot recover from Barbara because she did not have knowledge of the forgery.

Altered Checks

Sometimes a check is altered before it is presented for payment. This is an unauthorized change in the check that modifies the legal obligation of a party [UCC 3-407(a)]. The payor bank can dishonor an **altered check** if it discovers the alteration.

If the payor bank pays the altered check, it can charge the drawer's account for the **original tenor** of the check but not the altered amount [UCC 3-407(c) and 4-401(d)(1)].

If the payor bank has paid the altered amount, it can recover the difference between the altered amount and the original tenor from the party who presented the altered check for payment. This is because the presenter of the check for payment and each prior transferor *warrant* that the check has not been altered [UCC 3-417(a)(2)]. This is called the **presentment warranty**. If there has been an alteration, each party in the chain of collection can recover from the preceding transferor based on a breach of this warranty. The ultimate loss usually falls on the party that first paid the altered check because that party was in the best position to identify the alteration. The forger is liable for the altered amount—if he or she can be found and is not judgement-proof.

Consider This Example   Father draws a $100 check on City Bank made payable to his daughter. The daughter alters the check to read "$1,000" and cashes the check at a liquor store. The liquor store presents the check for payment to City Bank. City Bank pays the check. Father is liable only for the original tenor of the check ($100), and City Bank can charge the father's account this amount. City Bank is liable for the $900 difference, but it can recover this amount from the liquor store for breach of presentment warranty. The liquor store can seek to recover the $900 from the daughter.

Business Brief

The ultimate loss for the payment of a check over the *forged signature* of the drawer usually falls on the bank that paid the check. The payor bank may recover from the forger, if he or she can be found.

Business Brief

A payor bank that has paid a check over the forged signature of a drawer can recover only from (1) prior transferors who had knowledge that the signature of the drawer was unauthorized or (2) the forger.

Business Brief

If the payor bank pays an altered check, it can charge the drawer's account the *original tenor* of the check but not the altered amount.

Business Brief

A checking account customer owes a duty to examine bank statements promptly and with reasonable care to determine if any payment was made because of alteration of a check or forged signature of the customer.

If the same wrongdoer engages in a *series of forgeries* or *alterations* on the same account, the customer must report that to the payor bank within a reasonable period of time, not exceeding 30 calendar days from the date that the bank statement was made available to the customer [UCC 4-406(d)(2)]. The customer's failure to do so discharges the bank from liability on all similar forged or altered checks after this date and prior to notification.

The drawer's failure to report a forged or altered check to the bank within *one year* of receiving the bank statement and canceled checks containing it relieves the bank of any liability for paying the instrument [UCC 4-406(3)]. Thus, the payor bank is not required after this time to recredit the customer's account for the amount of the forged or altered check even if the customer later discovers the forgery or alteration.

The Collection Process

A bank is under a duty to accept deposits into a customer's account. This includes collecting checks that are drawn on other banks and made payable or indorsed to the depositor. The collection process, which may involve several banks, is governed by **Article 4 of the UCC**.

When a payee or holder receives a check, he or she can either go to the drawer's bank (the **payor bank**) and present the check for payment in cash or—as is more common—deposit the check into a bank account at his or her own bank, called the **depository bank**. (The depository bank may also serve as the payor bank if both parties have accounts at the same bank.)

The depository bank must present the check to the payor bank for collection. At this point in the process, the Federal Reserve System (discussed next) and other banks may be used in the collection of a check. The depository bank and these other banks are called **collecting banks**. Banks in the collection process that are not the depository or payor bank are called **intermediary banks**. A bank can have more than one role during the collection process [UCC 4-105]. The collection process is illustrated in Exhibit 21.4.

Contemporary Environment
The Federal Reserve System

The **Federal Reserve System**, which consists of 12 regional Federal Reserve banks located in different geographic areas of the country, assists banks in the collection of checks. Rather than send a check directly to another bank for collection, member banks may submit paid checks to the Federal Reserve banks for collection.

Most banks in this country have accounts at the regional Federal Reserve banks. The Federal Reserve banks debit and credit the accounts of these banks daily to reflect the collection and payment of checks. Banks pay the Federal Reserve banks a fee for this service. In large urban areas, private clearinghouses may provide a similar service [UCC 4-110 and 4-213(a)]. ∎

Deferred Posting

The **deferred posting rule** applies to all banks in the collection process. This rule allows banks to fix an afternoon hour of 2:00 P.M. or later as a cutoff hour for the purpose of processing checks. Any check or deposit of money received after this cutoff hour is treated as received on the next banking day [UCC 4-108]. Saturdays, Sundays, and holidays are not *banking days* unless the bank is open to the public for carrying on substantially all banking functions [UCC 4-104(a)(3)].

Exhibit 21.4

The Check Collection Process

Provisional Credits

When a customer deposits a check into a checking account for collection, the depository bank does not have to pay the customer the amount of the check until the check "clears"— that is, until final settlement occurs. The depository bank may **provisionally credit** the customer's account. Each bank in the collection process provisionally credits the account of the prior transferor [UCC 4-201(a)]. If the check is dishonored by the payor bank (e.g., for insufficient funds, a stop-payment order, or a closed account), the check is returned to the payee or holder, and the provisional credits are reversed. The collecting bank must either return the check to the prior transferor or notify that party within a reasonable time that provisional credit is being revoked. If the collecting bank fails to do this, it is liable for any losses caused by its delay [UCC 4-214].

Depository banks often allow their customers to withdraw the funds prior to final settlement. If the bank later learns that the check was dishonored, it can debit the customer's account for the amount withdrawn. If this is not possible (e.g., the payee or holder does not have sufficient funds in his or her account or has closed the account), the depository bank can sue the customer to recover the funds.

Final Settlement

A check is finally paid when the payor bank (1) pays the check in cash, (2) settles for the check without having a right to revoke the settlement, or (3) fails to dishonor the check within certain statutory time periods. These time periods are discussed in the following paragraphs.

When a check is finally settled, the provisional credits along the chain of collecting banks "firm up" and become **final settlements** [UCC 4-215(a)].

"On Us" Checks If the drawer and the payee or holder have accounts at the *same* bank, the depository bank is also the payor bank. The check is called an **"on us" item** when it is presented for payment by the payee or holder. In this case, the bank has until the opening of business on the second banking day following the receipt of the check to dishonor it. If it fails to do so, the check is considered paid. The payee or holder can withdraw the funds at this time [UCC 4-215(e)(2)].

Consider This Example   Christine and Jim both have checking accounts at Country Bank. On Tuesday morning, Christine deposits a $1,000 check from Jim into her account. Country Bank issues a provisional credit to Christine's account for this amount. On Thursday morning when the bank opens for business, the check is considered honored.

"On Them" Checks   If the drawer and the payee or holder have accounts at *different* banks, the payor and depository bank are not the same bank. In this case, the check is called an **"on them" item**.

Each bank in the collection process, including the payor bank, but excepting the collecting bank, must take proper action on the check prior to its "midnight deadline." The **midnight deadline** is the midnight of the next banking day following the banking day on which the bank received an "on them" check for collection [UCC 4-104(a)(10)]. Collecting banks are permitted to act within a reasonably longer time, but the bank then has the burden of establishing the timeliness of its action [UCC 4-202(b)].

This deadline is of particular importance to the payor bank: If the payor bank does not dishonor a check by its midnight deadline, the bank is *accountable* (liable) for the face amount of the check. It does not matter whether the check is properly payable or not [UCC 4-302(a)].

Consider This Example   If on Wednesday morning a payor bank receives an "on them" check drawn on an account at the bank, it has until midnight of the next banking day, Thursday, to dishonor the check. If it does not, the check is considered paid by the bank. This deadline does not apply to "on us" checks, which clear when the bank opens on the second business day following receipt of the checks (unless they are dishonored).

Instead of depositing an "on them" check for collection, a depositor can physically present the check for payment at the payor bank. This is called **presentment across the counter**. In this case, the payor bank has until the end of that banking day to dishonor the check. If it fails to do so, it must pay the check [UCC 4-301(a)].

Deposit of Money   A deposit of money to an account becomes available for withdrawal at the opening of the next banking day following the deposit [UCC 4-215(a)].

The "Four Legals" That Prevent Payment of a Check

Sometimes the payor bank will receive some form of notice that affects the payment of a check that has been presented for collection and is in the process of being *posted*. The following types of notices or actions—known as the **four legals**—effectively prevent payment of the check:

1. Receipt of a notice affecting the account, such as a notice of the customer's death, adjudgment of incompetence, or bankruptcy.
2. Receipt of service of a court order or other legal process that "freezes" the customer's account, such as a writ of garnishment.
3. Receipt of a stop-payment order from the drawer.
4. The payor bank's exercise of its right of setoff against the customer's account (i.e., notice to pay a debt the customer owes to the bank).

If one of these four legals is received before the payor bank has finished its process of posting, the check cannot be paid contrary to the legal notice or action. However, the account is not affected if the check was paid or the process of posting was completed before the notice was received. The **process of posting** is considered completed when (1) the responsible bank officer has made a decision to pay the check and (2) the proper book entry has been made to charge the drawer's account the amount of the check.

Failure to Examine Bank Statements in a Timely Manner

Ordinarily, banks send their checking account customers monthly statements of account. The canceled checks usually accompany the statement, although banks are not required to send them. If the canceled checks are not sent to the customer, the statement of account must provide sufficient information to allow the customer to identify the checks paid (e.g., check number, amount, date of payment) [UCC 4-406(a)]. In addition, if the checks are not returned to the customer, the bank must retain either the original checks or legible copies for seven years. A customer may request a check or a copy of it during this period [UCC 4-406(b)].

The customer owes a duty to examine the statements (and canceled checks, if received) promptly and with reasonable care to determine if any payment was not authorized because of alteration of a check or a forged signature. The customer must promptly notify the bank of unauthorized payments [UCC 4-406(c)]. The customer is liable if the payor bank suffers a loss because of the customer's failure to perform these duties [UCC 4-406(d)(1)].

Most banks provide images of checks online.

Business Brief

Banks are no longer required to return canceled checks to customers with their monthly statements. Instead, they are required to keep each check or a legible copy for seven years and to provide a check or a copy of it to customers upon request.

Liability of Collecting Banks for Their Own Negligence

The collecting bank owes a **duty to use ordinary care** in presenting and sending a check for collection, sending notices of dishonor, and taking other actions in the collection process. Failure to do so constitutes *negligence*. A collecting bank that takes proper action on a check prior to its midnight deadline is deemed to have exercised ordinary care. A bank is liable only for losses caused by its own negligence [UCC 4-202].

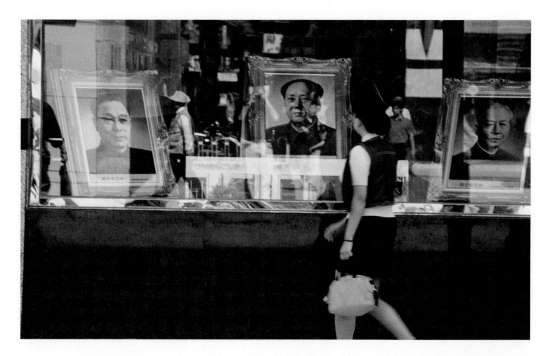

Beijing, China. The financing of international trade is made easier by the fast same-day use of commercial wire transfers. Trillions of dollars are transferred each day between banks and businesses in different countries to pay for the sale of goods and services.

Online Commerce & Internet Law
Commercial Wire Transfers

Commercial or **wholesale wire transfers** are often used to transfer payments between businesses and financial institutions. Trillions of dollars per day are transferred over the two principal wire payment systems—the **Federal Reserve wire transfer network (Fedwire)** and the **New York Clearing House Interbank Payments System (CHIPS)**. A wire transfer often involves a large amount of money (multimillion-dollar transactions are commonplace). The benefits of using wire transfers are their speed—most transfers are completed in the same day—and low cost. Banks sometimes require a customer to pay for a fund transfer in advance. On other occasions, however, a bank will extend credit to a customer and pay for the fund transfer. The customer is liable to pay the bank for any properly paid fund transfer.

UCC Article 4A—Fund Transfers, which was promulgated in 1989, governs wholesale wire transfers. Most states have adopted this article. Where adopted, Article 4A governs the rights and obligations between parties to a fund transfer unless they have entered into a contrary agreement. Article 4A applies only to *commercial* electronic fund transfers; consumer electronic fund transfers subject to the Electronic Fund Transfer Act are not subject to Article 4A.

Fund transfers are not complex transactions. For example, suppose Diebold Corporation wants to pay Bethlehem Steel for supplies it purchased. Instead of delivering a negotiable instrument such as a check to Bethlehem, Diebold instructs its bank to wire the funds to Bethlehem's bank, with instructions to credit Bethlehem's account. Diebold's order is called a *payment order*. Diebold is the *originator* of the wire transfer, and Bethlehem is the *beneficiary*. Diebold's bank is called the *originator's bank*, and Bethlehem's bank is called *beneficiary's bank*. In more complex transactions, there may be one or more additional banks, known as *intermediary banks*, between the originator's bank and the beneficiary's bank [UCC 4A-103(a)].

If a receiving bank mistakenly pays a greater amount to the beneficiary than ordered, the originator is liable for only the amount he or she instructed to be paid. The receiving bank that erred has the burden of recovering any overpayment from the beneficiary [UCC 4A-303(a)]. If a wrong beneficiary is paid, the originator is not obliged to pay his or her payment order. The bank that issued the erroneous payment order has the burden of recovering the payment from the improper beneficiary [UCC 4A-303(c)].

Banks and customers usually establish security procedures (e.g., codes, identifying numbers, words) to prevent unauthorized electronic payment orders. To protect the bank from liability for unauthorized payment orders, the security procedure must be commercially reasonable. If the bank verifies the authenticity of a payment order by complying with such a security procedure and pays the order, the customer is bound to pay the order, even if it was not authorized [UCC 4A-202]. The customer is not liable if it can prove that the unauthorized order was not initiated by an employee or another agent or by a person who obtained that information from a source controlled by the customer [UCC 4A-203]. ∎

Chapter Summary

The Bank–Customer Relationship, p. 437

The Bank–Customer Relationship

1. **Creditor–debtor relationship.** This relationship occurs when a customer (the *depositor*) deposits money into his or her account at a financial institution. In effect, the customer is loaning money to the financial institution. The customer is the *creditor*, and the financial institution is the *debtor*.
2. **Principal–agent relationship.** This relationship occurs when a customer writes a check against his or her checking account or deposits a check into his or her account for collection by the financial institution. The customer is the *principal*, and the financial institution is the *agent*.

The Uniform Commercial Code

The following *articles* of the Uniform Commercial Code (UCC) govern the creation, collection, and enforcement of checks and wire transfers:

1. **Article 3.** This article sets forth the requirements for creating negotiable instruments including checks. *Revised Article 3* was promulgated in 1990.
2. **Article 4.** This article establishes rules and principles that regulate the deposit and collection of *checks* by the banking system.
3. **Article 4A.** This article establishes rules and principles regulating the creation and collection of and liability for *wire transfers*. This article was promulgated in 1989.

Ordinary Checks, p. 437

Ordinary Checks

1. **Check.** A check is an order by a checking account holder (the *drawer*) to the financial institution at which the account is located (the *drawee*) to pay a named person (the *payee*) the amount of the check.
2. **Drawer.** The drawer is the checking account holder and writer of a check.
3. **Drawee.** The drawee is the financial institution on which a check is drawn.
4. **Payee.** The payee is the party to whom a check is written.

Special Types of Checks, p. 439

Special Types of Checks

Bank checks. Bank checks are special types of checks for which the bank is solely or primarily liable. *Bank checks* include certified checks, cashier's checks, and traveler's checks. These bank checks are considered "as good as cash" because the issuing bank has guaranteed their payment.

Certified Check

A bank agrees in advance (*certifies*) to accept and pay a certified check when it is presented for payment. The issuer or holder takes an ordinary check to the bank and the bank writes "certified" on the check. The bank sets aside funds from the issuer's account to pay the check when it is presented for payment.

Cashier's Check

A person pays a bank the amount of a cashier's check and a fee, and the bank guarantees that it will pay the check when it is presented for payment. The person purchasing a cashier's check does not have to have a checking account at the bank.

Traveler's Check

A traveler's check is a form of check sold by banks and other issuers. The purchaser of a traveler's check signs it at the time of purchase. When the check is used to purchase goods or services, the purchaser again signs the check and fills in the payee's name. Purchasers of traveler's checks do not have to have an account at the issuing bank.

Honoring Checks, p. 442

Honoring Checks

Honor. When a drawee bank receives a properly drawn check and there are sufficient funds in the drawer's account to pay the check, the bank must *honor* the check and pay it.

Stale Check

A check that has been outstanding for more than six months before it is presented for payment is stale.
   Payment of a stale check. A bank is under no obligation to pay a stale check. A bank that pays a stale check in good faith may charge the drawer's account.

Incomplete Check

A check that omits certain information, such as the amount of the check or the payee's name is incomplete.
   Payment of an incomplete check. A bank may pay an incomplete check *as completed* by the payee as long as it acts in good faith and without notice that the completion was improper.

Death or incompetence of a Drawer

1. **Death of drawer.** A bank may pay or certify checks drawn on a deceased customer's account for 10 days after receiving actual notice of the customer's death, unless a person claiming an interest in the account (e.g., heir, taxing authority) stops payment on the checks.

2. **Incompetence of drawer.** A bank may pay checks of a customer adjudicated incompetent until the bank has received actual notice of the customer's adjudication of incompetence.

Stop-Payment Orders

A stop-payment order is an order by a drawer of a check to the payor bank not to pay or certify a check. An oral stop-payment order is binding on the bank for only 14 days; a written stop-payment order is binding for six months and may be renewed for additional six-month periods.

Payment over a stop-payment order. If the payor bank fails to honor a stop-payment order and pays the check, it must recredit the customer's account the amount paid. The bank is subrogated to the rights of the drawer.

Overdraft

Insufficient funds. When a drawer does not have sufficient funds in his or her account to cover a check the drawer has written, the check is said to have "bounced."

Overdraft. When a check is presented for payment and there are insufficient funds in the drawer's account to pay the check, the payor bank may either (1) dishonor the check or (2) honor the check and create an *overdraft* in the drawer's account. The bank can later charge the drawer's account the amount of the overdraft or sue the drawer to recover this amount.

Postdated Check

A postdated check is dated with a date in the future.

Payment of a postdated check. A bank may pay a postdated check and charge the drawer's account, even though payment is made before the date on the check, *unless* the drawer has given the bank *separate notice* (notice in addition to the date on the check) stating not to pay the postdated check until its date and describing the check with reasonable certainty. Oral notice is good for 14 days, and written notice is good for six months, which may be renewed for additional six-month periods. A bank that pays a postdated check over such notice is liable for damages resulting therefrom.

Wrongful Dishonor

Wrongful dishonor occurs when a payor bank dishonors a drawer's properly payable check when it is presented for payment even though there are sufficient funds in the account to honor the check.

Liability for wrongful dishonor. The payor bank is liable to the drawer for damages proximately caused by the wrongful dishonor of a check plus consequential damages and damages caused by criminal prosecution.

Forged Signatures and Altered Checks, p. 444

Forged Signature of the Drawer

1. **Forged instrument.** A forged instrument is a check on which the *drawer's signature* has been forged.

2. **Liability on a forged instrument:**

   a. *Drawer.* A forged signature is wholly inoperative as the signature of the drawer. Therefore, the drawer is not liable on a forged instrument, and the bank cannot charge the drawer's account the amount paid. If the bank has charged the drawer's account, the account must be recredited.

   b. *Forger.* The forger is liable on the check because the forged signature acts as the forger's signature.

   c. *Prior transferors.* Prior transferors who had *knowledge* that the signature of a drawer was forged are liable on the forged instrument.

d. *Payor bank.* A payor bank that has charged the drawer's account for a forged instrument must seek recovery from the forger and prior transferors who had knowledge of the forged signature. The ultimate loss for the payment of a forged check usually falls on the payor bank (unless it can recover from the forger).

Altered Check

An altered check is a check that has been altered without authorization of the drawer that modifies the legal obligation of a party.

Liability on an altered check:

1. **Drawer.** If a payor bank pays an altered check, it can charge the drawer's account the *original tenor* (original amount) of the check. The drawer is not liable for the altered amount.

2. **Forger.** The person who altered the check is liable on the check for the amount above the original tenor.

3. **Prior transferors.** The presenter of the check for payment and all prior transferors *warrant* that the check has not been altered. This is called a *presentment warranty*. Therefore, the payor bank can recover from the presenter for breach of this warranty, and each party in the chain of collection can recover from the preceding transferor based on the breach of this warranty. The ultimate loss usually falls on the party that first paid the altered check (unless that party can recover from the forger).

4. **Payor bank.** The payor bank can recover from the presenter of the altered check, any prior transferor, or the forger.

The Collection Process, p. 446

The Collection Process

1. **Bank's duty to accept deposits.** A bank owes a duty to accept deposits into a customer's account. This includes collecting checks that are drawn on other banks and made payable or indorsed to the customer.

2. **Collection process.** If a customer deposits a check drawn on another bank into his or her account at a bank, his or her bank may send the check directly to the payor bank or through other banks until it is received by the payor bank for payment.

3. **Banks in the collection process.** The *banks* that may be involved in the collection process are:

   a. *Depository bank.* The bank at which the *payee* or *holder* has an account and deposits a check into this account to be collected.

   b. *Payor bank.* The bank where the *drawer* has a checking account and that will pay the check if properly payable. (The payor bank and depository bank will be the same bank if the drawer and the payee or holder have accounts at the same bank.)

   c. *Collecting bank.* Any bank in the collection process other than the payor bank. The depository bank is also a collecting bank.

   d. *Intermediary bank.* A bank in the collection process other than the depository and payor banks.

The Federal Reserve System

A series of 12 regional Federal Reserve banks assist banks in the collection of checks. The Federal Reserve banks act as collecting banks by debiting and crediting the accounts of banks at the Federal Reserve banks daily to reflect the collection and payment of checks.

Deferred Posting

1. **Deferred posting rule.** This rule allows banks to fix an afternoon hour of 2:00 P.M.; or later as a *cutoff hour* for the purpose of processing checks. Any check or deposit received after this cutoff hour is treated as being received the next banking day.

2. **Banking days.** Banking days are days that a bank is open to the public for carrying on substantially all banking functions.

Provisional Credit

Provisional credit occurs when a bank in the collection process credits a customer's account with the amount of a deposited check before the check has cleared by final settlement.

Reversal of provisional credits. If a deposited check does not clear (e.g., for insufficient funds, stop-payment order), all provisional credits may be reversed.

Final Settlement

Final settlement occurs when the payor bank either (1) pays the check in cash, (2) settles for the check without having a right to revoke the settlement, or (3) fails to dishonor the check within certain statutory time periods. When a check is finally settled, all provisional credits "firm up" and become final settlements.

Statutory deadlines. Article 4 of the UCC establishes the following *statutory deadlines* for collecting and payor banks to act on checks:

1. ***"On us" check.*** An "on us" check is a check that is presented for payment where the drawer and payee or holder have accounts at the *same bank*. That is, the payor bank is also the depository bank. In this case, the bank has until the opening for business on the second banking day following the receipt of the check to dishonor it. If it fails to do so, the check is considered paid.

2. ***"On them" check.*** An "on them" check is a check that is presented for payment where the drawer and payee or holder have accounts at *different banks*. That is, the payor bank and the depository bank are different banks. In this case, each bank in the collection process, including the payor bank, must take proper action on the check (particularly the payor bank to dishonor the check) prior to its "midnight deadline." The *midnight deadline* is the midnight of the next banking day following the banking day on which the bank received the "on them" check for collection.

3. ***Presentment across the counter.*** This occurs when a payee or holder physically presents an "on them" check for payment at the payor bank rather than using the collection process. In this case, the payor bank has until the end of that banking day to dishonor the check. If it fails to do so, it must pay the check.

The "Four Legals" That Prevent Payment of a Check

Four notices or actions can prevent the payment of a check if they are received by the payor bank before it has finished its *process of posting* the check for payment. The four legals are:

1. Receipt of a notice affecting the account, such as a notice of the customer's death, adjudgment of incompetence, or bankruptcy.
2. Receipt of service of a court order or other legal process that "freezes" the customer's account, such as a writ of garnishment.
3. Receipt of a stop-payment order from the drawer.
4. The payor bank's exercise of its right of *setoff* against the customer's account.

Failure to Examine Bank Statements in a Timely Manner

1. ***Duty to examine bank statements.*** A bank customer owes a duty to examine bank statements (and canceled checks, if received) *promptly* and with *reasonable care* to determine if any payment was not authorized because of the forged signature of the customer or alteration of a check. The customer must notify the bank of unauthorized payments.

2. ***Failure to examine bank statements.*** A customer who fails to examine bank statements promptly and reasonably and notify the bank of unauthorized payments is liable for any losses suffered by the bank because of this failure.

3. ***Series of forgeries or alterations.*** If the *same wrongdoer* engages in a series of forgeries or alterations on the same account, the customer must report that to the payor bank within a reasonable period of time, not exceeding 30 calender days from the date that the bank statement was made available to the customer. The customer's failure to do so discharges the bank from liability on all similar forged or altered checks after this date and prior to notification.

Liability of Collecting Banks for Their Own Negligence

1. **Duty of ordinary care.** Collecting banks are required to exercise *ordinary care* in presenting for and sending checks for collection.

2. **Liability for negligence.** A collecting bank that fails to exercise ordinary care in the collection of checks is negligent. A collecting bank is liable for losses caused by its *negligence* in the collection process.

Commercial Wire Transfers, p. 450

Commercial Wire Transfers

A commercial wire transfer involves the transfer of funds electronically by wire between business and financial institutions.

1. **Wire payment systems.** The two principal wire payment systems in this country are the Federal Reserve wire transfer network (*Fedwire*) and the New York Clearing House Interbank Payments Systems (*CHIPS*).

2. **Article 4A of the UCC.** This article of the UCC governs the creation of, transfer, and collection of and liability for commercial wire transfers.

Internet Exercises and Case Questions
Working the Web Internet Exercises

Activities

1. Go to the FAQ page of the Federal Reserve site, at **www.frbsf.org/tools/ faq.html**. Confirm your understanding of how the banking system works.

2. Which article of the UCC provides for *provisional credit?* See **www.law.cornell.edu/uniform/ucc.html**.

3. Which section of 15 U.S.C. 1693 protects credit card holders with the $50 charge limitation on lost or stolen cards? See "LII: Law About . . . Banking," at **www.law. cornell.edu/topics/banking.html**, which is an overview of banking law with links to key primary and secondary sources.

Critical Legal Thinking Cases

21.1 Cashier's Check   In October 1978, Dr. Graham Wood purchased a cashier's check in the amount of $6,000 from Central Bank of the South (Bank). The check was made payable to Ken Walker and was delivered to him. In September 1979, Bank's branch manager informed Wood that the cashier's check was still outstanding. Wood subsequently signed a form requesting that payment be stopped and a replacement check issued. He also agreed to indemnify Bank for any damages resulting from the issuance of the replacement check. Bank issued a replacement check to Wood. In April 1980, Walker deposited the original cashier's check in his bank, which was paid by Bank. Bank requested that Woods repay the bank $6,000. When he refused, Bank sued Woods to recover this amount. Who wins? [*Wood v. Central Bank of the South*, 435 So.2d 1287, 1982 Ala. Civ. App. Lexis 1362 (Ala. App. 1982)]

21.2 Overdraft   Louise Kalbe maintained a checking account at the Pulaski State Bank (Bank) in Wisconsin. In December 1981, Kalbe made out a check for $7,260, payable in cash. Thereafter, she misplaced it but did not report the missing check to the bank or stop payment on it. In January

1982, some unknown person presented the check to a Florida bank for payment. The Florida bank paid the check and sent it to the Bank for collection. Bank paid the check even though it created a $6,542.12 overdraft in Kalbe's account. Bank requested Kalbe pay this amount. When she refused, Bank sued Kalbe to collect the overdraft. Who wins? [*Pulaski State Bank v. Kalbe*, 364 N.W.2d 162, 1985 Wisc.App. Lexis 3034 (Wis. App. 1985)]

21.3 Wrongful Dishonor   Larry J. Goodwin and his wife maintained a checking and savings account at City National Bank of Fort Smith (Bank). Bank also had a customer named Larry K. Goodwin. In November 1985, two loans of Larry K. Goodwin were in default. Bank mistakenly took money from Larry J. Goodwin's checking account to pay the loans. On Saturday, November 30, 1985, the Goodwins received written notice that four of their checks, which were written to merchants, had been dishonored for insufficient funds. When the Goodwins investigated, they discovered that their checking account balance was zero, and the bank had placed their savings account on hold. After being informed of the error, Bank promised to send letters of apology to the four merchants and to correct the error. Bank, however, subsequently "bounced" several other checks of the Goodwins. Eventually, Bank notified all the parties of its error. On January 14, 1986, the Goodwins closed their accounts at Bank and were paid the correct balances due. They sued the bank for consequential and punitive damages for wrongful dishonor. Who wins? [*City National Bank of Fort Smith v. Goodwin*, 783 S.W.2d 335, 1990 Ark. Lexis 49 (AR 1990)]

21.4 Stale Check   On June 30, 1972, Charles Ragusa & Son (Ragusa), a partnership consisting of Charles and Michael Ragusa, issued a check in the amount of $5,000, payable to Southern Masonry, Inc. (Southern). The check was drawn on Community State Bank (Bank). Several days later, Southern informed Ragusa that the check had been lost. Ragusa issued a replacement check for the same amount and sent it to Southern, and that check was cashed. At the same time, Ragusa gave a verbal stop-payment order to Bank regarding the original check. In July 1975, the original check was deposited by Southern into its account at the Bank of New Orleans. When the check was presented to Bank, it paid it and charged $5,000 against Ragusa's account. The partnership was not made aware of this transaction until August 4, 1975, when it received its monthly bank statement. Ragusa demanded that Bank recredit its account $5,000. When Bank refused to do so, Ragusa sued. Who wins? [*Charles Ragusa & Son v. Community State Bank*, 360 So.2d 231, 1978 La.App. Lexis 3435 (La. App. 1978)]

21.5 Postdated Check   David Siegel maintained a checking account with the New England Merchants National Bank (Bank). On September 14, 1973, Siegel drew and delivered a $20,000 check payable to Peter Peters. The check was dated November 14, 1973. Peters immediately deposited the check in his own bank, which forwarded it for collection. On September 17, 1973, Bank paid the check and charged it against Siegel's account. Siegel discovered that the check had been paid when another of his checks was returned for insufficient funds. Siegel informed Bank that the check to Peters was postdated November 14 and requested that the bank return the $20,000 to his account. When Bank refused, Siegel sued for wrongful debit of his account. Must Bank recredit Siegel's account? [*Siegel v. New England Merchants National Bank*, 437 N.E.2d 218, 1982 Mass. Lexis 1559 (Mass. Sup. 1982)]

21.6 Stop Payment   Dynamite Enterprises, Inc. (Dynamite), a corporation doing business in Florida, maintained a checking account at Eagle National Bank of Miami (Bank). Sometime in 1985, Dynamite drew a check on this account, payable to one of its business associates. Before the check had been cashed or deposited, Dynamite issued a written stop-payment order to the Bank. Bank informed Dynamite that it would not place a stop-payment order on the check because there were insufficient funds in the account to pay the check. Several weeks later the check was presented to Bank for payment. By this time, sufficient funds had been deposited in the account to pay the check. Bank paid the check and charged Dynamite's account. When Dynamite learned that the check had been paid, it requested Bank to recredit its account. When Bank refused, Dynamite sued to recover the amount of the check. Who wins? [*Dynamite Enterprises, Inc. v. Eagle National Bank of Miami*, 517 So.2d 112, 1987 Fla.App. Lexis 11791 (Fla. App. 1987)]

21.7 Examining Bank Statements   Mr. Gennone maintained a checking account at Peoples National Bank & Trust Company of Pennsylvania (Bank). In June 1965, Gennone noticed that he was not receiving his bank statements and canceled checks. When Gennone contacted Bank, he was informed that the statements had been mailed to him. Bank agreed to hold future statements so that he could pick them up in person. Gennone picked up the statements but did not reconcile the balance of the account. As a result, it was not until March 1967 that he discovered that beginning in January 1966 his wife had forged his signature on 25 checks. Gennone requested Bank to reimburse him for the amount of these checks. When Bank refused, Gennone sued Bank to recover. Who wins? [*Gennone v. Peoples National Bank & Trust Co.*, 9 U.C.C. Rep.Serv. 707, 1971 Pa. D. & C. Lexis 160 (PA 1971)]

21.8 Deferred Posting   Dr. Robert L. Pracht received a check in the amount of $6,571.25 from Northwest Feedyards in payment for three loads of corn. The check was drawn on a checking account at Oklahoma State Bank (Bank). Pracht also maintained an account at Bank. On Friday, January 17, 1975, Pracht indorsed the check and gave it to an associate to deposit to Pracht's account at the bank. When the associate arrived at the bank around 3:00 P.M., he discovered that the bank's doors were locked. After gaining the attention of a bank employee, the associate was allowed into the bank, where he gave the check and deposit slip to a teller. Because the bank's computer had shut down at 3:00 P.M., the teller put the check aside. The associate testified that several bank employees were working at their desks as he left the bank. The bank was not open on Saturday or Sunday. On Monday, January 20, 1975, Bank dishonored the check due to insufficient funds. Pracht sued to recover the amount of the check from Bank. Who wins? [*Pracht v. Oklahoma State Bank*, 592 P.2d 976, 1979 Okla. Lexis 209 (OK 1979)]

21.9 Right of Setoff   On November 28, 1978, States Steamship Company (States Steamship) drew a check for $35,948 on its checking account at Crocker National Bank (Crocker). The check was made payable to Nautilus Leasing Services, Inc. (Nautilus). Nautilus deposited the check in its account at Chartered Bank of London, which forwarded the check to Crocker for collection. The check was received at Crocker's processing center at 8:00 A.M. on Friday, December 1, 1978.

At the time the check was presented for payment, States Steamship was indebted to Crocker for loans in the amount of $2 million. These loans were payable on demand. During the latter part of 1978, States Steamship was in severe financial difficulty and was conducting merger negotiations with another steamship company. On the morning of Monday, December 4, 1978, Crocker learned that these merger negotiations had broken down and demanded immediate payment of the $2 million. Crocker then seized the $1,726,032 in States Steamship's checking account at the bank. This action left State Steamship's account with a zero balance. State Steamship's check to Nautilus, as well as other checks that had been presented for payment, were returned unpaid. Nautilus sued Crocker to recover the amount of the check. Who wins? [*Nautilus Leasing Services, Inc. v. Crocker National Bank*, 195 Cal.Rptr. 478, 1983 Cal.App. Lexis 2257 (Cal. App. 1983)]

Business Ethics Cases

21.10 Business Ethics   In 1982, Actors Equity, a union that represents 37,000 stage actors, sought to hire a new comptroller. A man named Nicholas Scotti applied for the position and submitted an extensive resume, showing that he was currently employed by Paris Maintenance Company as its comptroller. Scotti also stated that he had held various financial positions with Equitable Life Assurance Society and the Investors Funding Corporation. Officers of Actors Equity interviewed Scotti and offered him the job. No attempt was made to verify Scotti's background or prior employment history.

Actors Equity maintained a checking account at the Bank of New York. During the first six months as comptroller, Scotti forged the signature of the appropriate company employee on four Actors Equity checks totaling $100,000. The checks were made payable to N. Piscotti and were cashed by Scotti and paid by the Bank of New York. The forged signatures were of professional quality. After Scotti resigned as comptroller, the forgeries were discovered. Subsequent investigation revealed that Scotti's real name was Piscotti, that the information on his resume was false, and that he had an extensive criminal record. Actors Equity sued the drawee bank to recover the $100,000. Did Scotti act ethically in this case? Should Actors Equity have sued the bank to recover on the forged checks? Who wins? [*Fireman's Fund Insurance Co. v. The Bank of New York*,

539 N.Y.S.2d 339, 1989 N.Y.App.Div. Lexis 4172 (N.Y. Sup. 1989)]

21.11 Business Ethics   Golden Gulf, Inc. (Golden Gulf), opened a checking account at AmSouth Bank, N.A. (AmSouth). On August 27, 1988, Golden Gulf entered into a subscription agreement wherein Albert M. Rossini agreed to pay $250,000 for stock in the company. Rossini tendered a check drawn on the Mark Twain Bank in Kansas City, Missouri, to Golden Gulf for that amount. Golden Gulf deposited the check in its checking account at AmSouth on August 30, 1988. On September 2, 1988, Golden Gulf contacted AmSouth and asked if the funds were "available." AmSouth said the funds were available for use. Golden Gulf requested AmSouth to wire transfer the funds to it in New York for use in that state. AmSouth complied with the request. On September 7, 1988, AmSouth received notice from the Mark Twain Bank that Rossini's check would not be paid due to insufficient funds. On September 8, 1988, AmSouth notified Golden Gulf that the check had been dishonored. AmSouth revoked the credit it had given to Golden Gulf's account, resulting in an overdraft of $248,965.69. AmSouth sued to recover this amount. Did Golden Gulf act ethically in this case? Did AmSouth extend a provisional or final settlement to Golden Gulf's account? [*Golden Gulf, Inc. v. AmSouth Bank, N. A.*, 565 So.2d 114, 1990 Ala. Lexis 436 (AL 1990)]

Briefing the Case Writing Assignment

Read Case A.21 in the Case Appendix [*First American Bank and Trust v. Rishoi*]. This case is excerpted from the court of appeals opinion. Review and brief the case. In your brief, be sure to answer the following questions.

1. Who was the plaintiff? Who was the defendant?

2. What type of negotiable instrument was at issue in this case?

3. Was the issuer's dishonor of the negotiable instrument proper or wrongful?

22

Credit, Secured Transactions, and Surety Agreements

"Creditors have better memories than debtors."

—Benjamin Franklin
Poor Richard's Almanack (1758)

Chapter Objectives

After studying this chapter, you should be able to:

1. Distinguish between unsecured and secured credit.

2. Describe security interests in real property, such as mortgages.

3. Define a secured transaction in personal property and the scope of Article 9 of the UCC.

4. Describe the perfection of a security interest through the filing of a financing statement.

5. Define and distinguish between surety and guaranty contracts.

Chapter Contents

- Unsecured and Secured Credit
- Security Interests in Real Property
- Security Interests in Personal Property
- Surety and Guaranty Arrangements

The U.S. economy is a credit economy. Consumers borrow money to make major purchases (e.g., homes, automobiles, appliances) and use credit cards (e.g., Visa, Master Card) to purchase goods and services at restaurants, clothing stores, and the like. Businesses use credit to purchase equipment, supplies, and other goods and services. In a credit transaction, the borrow is the **debtor** and the lender is the **creditor**.

Because lenders are reluctant to lend large sums of money simply on the borrower's promise to repay, many of them take a *security interest* in either the item purchased or some other property of the debtor. The property in which the security interest is taken is called *collateral*. If the debtor does not pay the debt, the creditor can foreclose on and recover the collateral.

A lender who is unsure whether a debtor will have sufficient income or assets to repay a loan may require another person to guarantee payment. If the borrower fails to repay the loan, that person is responsible for paying it. This responsibility is called *suretyship*.

This chapter discusses types of credit, secured transactions in personal property, and suretyship.

Business Brief

The United States is a credit economy. Businesses and individuals use credit to purchase many goods and services.

Unsecured and Secured Credit

Credit may be extended on either an *unsecured* or a *secured* basis. The following paragraphs discuss these types of credit.

Debt is the prolific mother of folly and of crime.

Benjamin Disraeli
Henrietta Temple (1837)

Unsecured Credit

Unsecured credit does not require any security (collateral) to protect the payment of the debt. Instead, the creditor relies on the debtor's promise to repay the principal (plus any interest) when it is due. If the debtor fails to make the payments, the creditor may bring legal action and obtain a judgment against him or her. If the debtor is *judgment-proof* (i.e., has little or no property or no income that can be garnished), the creditor may never collect.

Store Window. Many consumer purchases are made with credit cards. This creates a debtor-creditor relationship between the consumer-borrower and the issuer of the credit card.

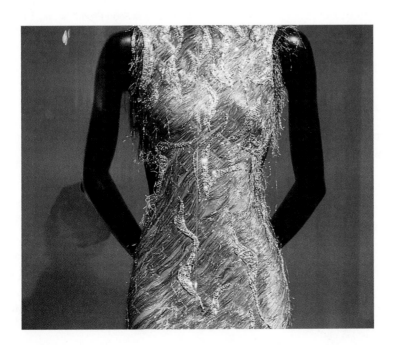

Secured Credit

To minimize the risk associated with extending unsecured credit, a creditor may require a security interest in the debtor's property (collateral). The collateral secures payment of the loan. This type of credit is called **secured credit**. Security interests may be taken in real, personal, intangible, and other property.

If the debtor fails to make the payments when due, the collateral may be repossessed to recover the outstanding amount. Generally, if the sale of the collateral is insufficient to repay the amount of the loan (plus any interest), the creditor may bring a lawsuit against the debtor to recover a **deficiency judgment** for the difference. Some states prohibit or limit deficiency judgments with respect to certain types of loans.

Contemporary Environment
Klondike Bar's Unsecured Claim Melts

Generally, a creditor would rather be a secured creditor than an unsecured creditor because of the extra protection and priority status the secured position gives the creditor. The following case shows why.

Sunstate Dairy & Food Products Co. (Sunstate) distributed dairy products in Florida. It had the following two debts among its other debts:

1. On November 19, 1990, Sunstate borrowed money from Barclays Business Credit, Inc. (Barclays), and signed a security agreement granting Barclays a continuing security interest in and lien upon substantially all of Sunstate's personal property, including all of Sunstate's inventory, equipment, accounts receivable, and general intangibles then existing or thereafter acquired. Barclays perfected its security interest by filing a financing statement with the proper state government authorities.
2. On February 14, 1992, Sunstate purchased $49,512 of Klondike ice cream bars from Isaly Klondike Company

(Klondike) on credit. Klondike did not take a security interest in the ice cream bars.

On February 19, 1992, Sunstate filed for bankruptcy. At that time, Sunstate owed Barclays $10,050,766, and $47,731 worth of unpaid-for Klondike bars remained in Sunstate's possession. Barclays and Klondike fought over the Klondike bars. Klondike filed a motion with the court, seeking to reclaim the Klondike bars. Barclays sought to enforce its security agreement against Sunstate and recover the Klondike bars in Sunstate's possession.

The court sided with Barclays because it was a secured creditor with a perfected security interest. The court found that Klondike, as an unsecured creditor, had no legal right to reclaim the Klondike bars. Klondike was merely one of many unsecured general creditors that would receive but pennies on the dollar in Sunstate's bankruptcy. Klondike learned a costly lesson: It is better to be a secured creditor than an unsecured creditor. [*In the Matter of Sunstate Dairy & Food Products Co.*, 145 B.R. 341, 1992 Bankr. Lexis 1496 (1992) (Bk. M.D. Fla.)] ■

Security Interests in Real Property

Owners of real estate can create security interests in their property. This occurs if the owner borrows money from a lender and pledges real estate as security for repayment of the loan.

Mortgages

A person who owns a piece of real property has an ownership interest in that property. A property owner who borrows money from a creditor may use his or her real estate as collateral for repayment of the loan. This type of collateral arrangement, known as a **mortgage**, is a *two-party instrument*. The *owner-debtor* is the **mortgagor**, and the *creditor* is the **mortgagee**. The parties to a mortgage are illustrated in Exhibit 22.1.

Exhibit 22.1

Parties to a Mortgage

Consider This Example   Suppose General Electric purchases a manufacturing plant for $10 million, pays $2 million cash as a down payment, and borrows the remaining $8 million from City Bank. To secure the loan, City Bank requires General Electric to give it a mortgage on the plant. If General Electric defaults on the loan, the bank may take action under state law to foreclose on the property.

Notes and Deeds of Trust

Some states' laws provide for the use of a *deed of trust* and *note* in place of a mortgage. The **note** is the instrument that evidences the borrower's debt to the lender; the **deed of trust** is the instrument that gives the creditor a security interest in the debtor's property that is pledged as collateral.

A deed of trust is a *three-party instrument*. Under it, legal title to the real property is placed with a **trustee** (usually a trust corporation) until the amount borrowed has been paid. The *owner-debtor* is called the **trustor**. Although legal title is vested in the trustee, the trustor has full legal rights to possession of the real property. The *creditor* is called the **beneficiary**. Exhibit 22.2 illustrates the relationship between the parties.

Recording Statutes

Most states have enacted **recording statutes** that require a mortgage or deed of trust to be recorded in the county recorder's office in the county in which the real property is located. This record gives potential lenders or purchasers of real property the ability to determine whether there are any existing liens (mortgages) on the property.

The nonrecordation of a mortgage or deed of trust does not affect either the legality of the instrument between the mortgagor and the mortgagee or the rights and obligations of the parties. In other words, the mortgagor is obligated to pay the amount of the mortgage according to the terms of the mortgage, even if the document is not recorded. However, an improperly recorded document is not effective against either (1) subsequent purchasers of the real property or (2) other mortgagees or lienholders who have no notice of the prior mortgages.

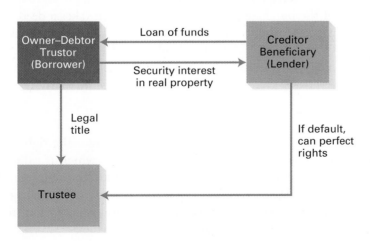

Exhibit 22.2

Parties to a Note and Deed of Trust

Consider This Example   Suppose Debbie Brown purchases a house for $100,000. She borrows $75,000 from Country Bank and gives the bank a mortgage on the house for this amount. Country Bank fails to record the mortgage. Brown contracts to sell the house to Edward Johnson. He reviews the recordings and finds no mortgage against the property. Johnson pays $125,000 cash to Brown for the house. Brown defaults on her loan from Country Bank. In this case, Country Bank cannot foreclose on the real property because it failed to record the mortgage. Johnson owns the house free of Country Bank's mortgage. The bank's only recourse is to sue Brown to recover the amount of the loan (if she can be found).

Foreclosure

If a mortgagor defaults on a mortgage, the mortgagee can declare the entire debt due and payable immediately. This right can be enforced through a procedure called **foreclosure**.

All states permit *foreclosure sales*. Under this method, the debtor's defaulting may trigger a legal court action for foreclosure. Any party having an interest in the property—including owners of the property and other mortgagees or lienholders—must be named as a defendant. If the mortgagee's case is successful, the court will issue a judgment that orders the real property to be sold at a judicial sale. The procedures for a foreclosure action and sale are mandated by state statute. Any surplus must be paid to the mortgagor.

Most states permit foreclosure by *power of sale*, although this must be expressly conferred in the mortgage or deed of trust. Under a power of sale, the procedure for that sale is contained in the mortgage or deed of trust itself. No court action is necessary. Some states have enacted statutes that establish the procedure for conducting the sale. Such a sale must be by auction for the highest price obtainable. Any surplus must be paid to the mortgagor.

Deficiency Judgments

Some states permit a mortgagee to bring a separate legal action to recover a deficiency from the mortgagor. If the mortgagee is successful, the court will award a *deficiency judgment* that entitles the mortgagee to recover the amount of the judgment from the mortgagor's property.

Several states have enacted statutes that prohibit deficiency judgments regarding certain types of mortgages, such as those on residential property. These statutes are called **antideficiency statutes**.

Consider This Example   Kaye buys a house in San Francisco, puts $100,000 down, and borrows $300,000 of the purchase price from a bank, which takes a deed of trust on the property to secure the loan. Suppose that Kaye defaults, and when the bank forecloses on the property, it is worth only $240,000. The bank cannot recover the $60,000 deficiency from Kaye because California has an antideficiency statute.

Right of Redemption

The common law and many state statutes give the mortgagor the right to redeem real property after default and before foreclosure. This right, which is called the **right of redemption**, requires the mortgagor to pay the full amount of the debt—that is, principal, interest, and other costs—incurred by the mortgagee because of the mortgagor's default. Redemption of a partial interest is not permitted. Upon redemption, the mortgagor receives title to the property, free and clear of the mortgage debt.

Some states allow the mortgagor to redeem real property only for a specified period (usually six months or one year) after foreclosure. This is called the *statutory period of redemption*. If this right exists, the deed to the real property is not delivered to the purchaser at the foreclosure sale until after the statutory period of redemption has expired.

Most state laws provide that any party in interest—such as a second mortgage holder or another lienholder—may redeem the property during the redemption period.

Contemporary Environment
Material Person's Lien

Owners of real property often hire contractors and laborers (e.g., painters, plumbers, roofers, bricklayers, furnace installers) to make improvements to that property. The contractors and laborers expend the time to provide their services as well as money to provide the materials for the improvements. Their investments are protected by state statutes that permit them to file a **material person's lien** (sometimes called a mechanic's lien) against the improved real property.

When a lien is properly filed, the real property to which the improvements have been made becomes security for the payment of these services and materials. In essence, the lienholder has the equivalent of a mortgage on the property. If the owner defaults, the lienholder may foreclose on the lien, sell the property, and satisfy the debt plus interest and costs out of the proceeds of the sale. Any surplus must be paid to the owner-debtor.

Generally, the lien must be foreclosed on during a specific period of time (commonly 6 months to 2 years) from the date the lien is filed. Material person's liens are usually subject to the debtor's right of redemption.

Procedure for Obtaining a Material Person's Lien
Although the procedures for obtaining a material person's lien vary from state to state, the following requirements generally must be met:

1. The lienholder must file a *notice of lien* with the county recorder's office in the county in which the real property subject to the lien is located.
2. The notice must state the amount of the claim, the name of the claimant, the name of the owner of the real property, and a description of the real property.

3. The notice must be filed within a specified time period (commonly 30 to 120 days) after the services have been performed or materials delivered.
4. Notice of the lien must be given to the owner of the real property.

Lien Release
If the contractor, laborer, or material person has been paid, the property owner should obtain a *release of lien* (also called a **lien release**), which is an affidavit attesting to receipt of the payment. The release of lien should be signed by all subcontractors, laborers, and material persons who have contributed services or materials to the project. The release can be used to defeat a lienholder's attempt to obtain payment.

Consider This Example Suppose Travis Company, which owns an undeveloped piece of property, hires Mason Corporation, a general contractor, to build a warehouse on the lot. Mason builds the warehouse and hires Rouse Company, a roofer, as a subcontractor to put the roof on the warehouse. When the warehouse is complete, Travis pays Mason the full contract price for the warehouse but fails to obtain a release of lien. Mason does not pay Rouse. Rouse files a material person's lien against the warehouse and demands payment from Travis. Here, Travis must pay Rouse for the roofing work. If he does not, Rouse may foreclose on the warehouse, have it sold, and satisfy the debt out of the proceeds of the sale. Travis's only recourse is to sue Mason. Travis ends up paying twice for the roofing work. ■

Security Interests in Personal Property

When a creditor extends credit to a debtor and takes a security interest in some personal property of the debtor, it is called a **secured transaction**. The **secured party** is the seller, lender, or other party in whose favor there is a security interest. If the debtor defaults and does not repay the loan, generally the secured party can foreclose and recover the collateral.

Exhibit 22.3

Two-Party Secured
Transaction

Article 9 of the Uniform Commercial Code (UCC) governs secured transactions in personal property. Article 9 has been adopted in one form or another by all states except Louisiana. Although there may be some variance among states, most of the basics of Article 9 are the same.

Exhibit 22.3 illustrates a two-party secured transaction. Such transactions occur, for example, when a seller sells goods to a buyer on credit and retains a security interest in the goods.

A *three-party secured transaction* is illustrated in Exhibit 22.4. This type of situation occurs when a seller sells goods to a buyer who has obtained financing from a third-party lender (e.g., bank) that takes a security interest in the goods sold.

Debtors are liars.

George Herbert
Jacula Prudentum (1651)

Business Brief

Article 9 of the UCC governs secured transactions in *personal property*.

Business Brief

A security interest may be given in various types of personal property, including (1) goods, (2) instruments, (3) chattel paper, (4) documents of title, (5) accounts, and (6) general intangibles.

Personal Property Subject to a Security Agreement

A security interest may be given in various types of **personal property**, including:

■ **Goods,** including (1) *consumer goods* bought or used primarily for personal, family, or household purposes; (2) *equipment* bought or used primarily for business; (3) *farm products*, including crops, livestock, and supplies, used or produced in farming operations; (4) *inventory* held for sale or lease, including work in progress and materials; and (5) *fixtures* affixed to real estate so as to become part thereof.

■ **Instruments,** such as checks, notes, stocks, bonds, and other investment securities.

■ **Chattel paper** (i.e., a writing or writings that evidence both a monetary obligation and a security interest), such as a conditional sales contract.

■ **Documents of title,** including bills of lading, ware house receipts, and such.

■ **Accounts** (i.e., any right of payment not evidenced by an instrument or chattel paper), such as accounts receivable.

■ **General intangibles,** such as patents, copyrights, money franchises, royalties, and the like.

Article 9 of the UCC does not apply to transactions involving real estate mortgages, landlord's liens, artisan's or mechanic's liens, liens on wages, judicial liens, and the like [UCC 9-104]. These types of liens are usually covered by other laws.

Exhibit 22.4

Three-Party Secured
Transaction

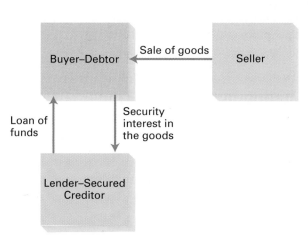

Creating a Security Interest in Personal Property

A secured party must meet the requirements discussed in the following paragraphs to have an enforceable secured interest in collateral.

Unless the creditor has possession of the collateral, there must be a written security agreement. To be valid, a written **security agreement** must (1) clearly describe the collateral so that it can be readily identified, (2) contain the debtor's promise to repay the creditor, including terms of repayment (e.g., the interest rate, time of payment), (3) set forth the creditor's rights upon the debtor's default, and (4) be signed by the debtor [UCC 9-203(1)].

Consider This Example   Suppose Ashley borrows $1,000 from Chris and gives Chris her gold ring as security for the loan. This agreement does not have to be in writing because the creditor is in possession of the collateral. This oral security agreement is enforceable. If Ashley retained possession of the ring, however, a written security interest describing the collateral (the ring) signed by Ashley would be required.

The debtor must have a current or future legal right in or the right to possession of the collateral. For example, a debtor may give a creditor a security interest in goods currently owned or in the possession of the debtor or in goods to be later acquired by the debtor. A debtor who does not have ownership or possessory rights to property cannot give a security interest in that property.

If these requirements are met, the rights of the secured party **attach** to the collateral. **Attachment** means that the creditor has an enforceable security interest against the debtor and can satisfy the debt out of the designated collateral (subject to the priority rules discussed later in this chapter) [UCC 9-203(2)].

The Floating-Lien Concept

A security agreement may provide that the security interest attaches to **property** that was not originally in the possession of the debtor when the agreement was executed. This interest is usually referred to as a **floating lien**. A floating lien can attach to the types of property discussed in the following paragraphs.

Store Window, Brentwood California. Businesses often purchase goods on credit from suppliers. A supplier often takes a security interest in personal property to secure the loan, such as the inventory in this store.

Many security agreements contain a clause that gives the secured party a security interest in **after-acquired property** of the debtor. After-acquired property is property that the debtor acquires after the security agreement is executed [UCC 9-204(1)].

Consider This Example Manufacturing Corporation borrows $100,000 from First Bank and gives the bank a security interest in both its current and after-acquired inventory. If Manufacturing Corporation defaults on its loan to First Bank, the bank can claim any available original inventory as well as enough after-acquired inventory to satisfy its secured claim.

Unless otherwise stated in the security agreement, if a debtor sells, exchanges, or disposes of collateral subject to such an agreement, the secured party automatically has the right to receive the **proceeds** of the sale, exchange, or disposition [UCC 9-203(3) and 9-306].

Consider This Example Zip, Inc., is a retail automobile dealer. To finance its inventory of new automobiles, Zip borrows money from First Bank and gives the bank a security interest in the inventory. Zip sells an automobile subject to the security agreement to Phyllis, who signs an installment sales contract, agreeing to pay Zip for the car in 24 equal monthly installments. If Zip defaults on its payment to First Bank, the bank is entitled to receive the remaining payments from Phyllis.

Contemporary Environment
Revised Article 9—Secured Transactions

In 1999, the National Conference of Commissioners on Uniform State Laws (Commissioners) promulgated **Revised Article 9—Secured Transactions** of the UCC. Revised Article 9, which is the result of almost a decade of study by the Commissioners, is designed to supercede Article 9 of the UCC. Revised Article 9:

- Provides that collateral for secured transactions can include deposit accounts at banks and other financial institutions, promissory notes, permits, franchises, licenses, letters of credit, and payment intangibles where the principal obligation is monetary.
- Clarifies the law and expressly brings agricultural liens within the scope of Article 9.
- Changes the place to file for perfection purposes to the jurisdiction where the debtor is located. For a "registered

organization" such as a corporation or limited liability company (LLC), that location is the state under whose laws the debtor-organization is organized (e.g., a corporation's state of incorporation). For Article 9 purposes, an individual debtor is located at his or her principal residence.
- Allows persons other than the debtor to file a financing statement or any given record, as long as the debtor authorizes the filing.

Revised Article 9 is a comprehensive proposed statute that incorporates most of the principles and concepts of the law of Article 9, and it also updates and clarifies many of these principles. The Commissioners recommend that Revised Article 9 be adopted by states to replace existing Article 9. ■

Perfecting a Security Interest

The concept of **perfection of a security interest** establishes the right of a secured creditor against other creditors who claim an interest in the collateral. Perfection is a legal process. The three main methods of perfecting a security interest under the UCC are discussed in the following paragraphs.

Perfection by Filing a Financing Statement

Often, a creditor's physical possession of the collateral is impractical because it would deprive the debtor of use of the collateral (e.g., farm equipment, industrial machinery, consumer goods). At other times, it is simply impossible (e.g., accounts receivable). Filing a **financing statement** in the appropriate government office is the most common method of perfecting a creditor's security interest in such collateral. The person who files the financing statement should request the filing officer to note on his or her copy of the document the file number, date, and hour of filing [UCC 9-402(1)]. A financing statement covering fixtures is called a *fixture filing*.

Financing statements are available for review by the public. They serve as constructive notice to the world that the creditor claims an interest in the property. Financing statements are effective for five years from the date of filing. A *continuation statement* may be filed up to six months prior to the expiration of the financing statement's five-year term. Such statements are effective for a new five-year term. Succeeding continuation statements may be filed [UCC 9-403(2) and (3)].

To be enforceable, a financing statement must contain (1) the debtor's name and mailing address, (2) the name and address of the secured party from whom information concerning the security interest can be obtained, and (3) a statement (preferably exactly as shown in the security agreement) indicating the types, or describing the items, of collateral. The secured party can file the security agreement as a financing statement [UCC 9-402(1)].

State law specifies where the financing statement must be filed. The UCC provides that a state may choose either the secretary of state or the county clerk in the county of the debtor's residence or, if the debtor is not a resident of the state, in the county where the goods are kept or in another county office or both. Most states require financing statements covering farm equipment, farm products, accounts, and consumer goods to be filed with the county clerk [UCC 9-401].

In the following case, the court found that there was a defective filing of the financing statement.

Business Brief

It is good practice for a creditor who plans on taking a security interest in personal property to check whether any previous financing statements have been filed concerning the property and, if not, to properly file a financing statement covering his or her interest in the property.

In re Greenbelt Cooperative, Inc.

124 B.R. 465, 1991 Bankr. Lexis 233 (1991)
Untied States Bankruptcy Court, Maryland

Case 22.1
Financing Statement

Background and Facts

Greenbelt Cooperative, Inc. (Greenbelt), was a consumer-owned cooperative engaged in the retail furniture business. It engaged in the business under the trade name SCAN, and it was well known among consumers by that name. On May 4, 1987, Greenbelt executed an Equipment Lease and Security Agreement with Raymond Leasing Corporation (Raymond) to lease forklifts, racking, and other items. At the conclusion of the lease term, Greenbelt could purchase the equipment for $1. On July 6, 1987, Raymond filed a financing statement covering the equipment in the proper state government office. Raymond listed "SCAN Furniture" as the debtor on the financing statement. On December 4, 1988, Greenbelt filed for bankruptcy. The bankruptcy trustee made a motion to avoid Raymond's claimed security interest in the equipment.

Issue

Did Raymond properly identify the debtor on the financing statement?

Court's Reasoning

For a financing statement to be effective, the UCC requires that it be filed under the legal name of the debtor or under a name that is substantially similar to the legal name of the debtor so that it

would not mislead a reasonably diligent creditor searching the financing records. The court held that a filing under SCAN Furniture would not be found by those looking for security interests in the assets of Greenbelt Cooperative, Inc. Consequently, Raymond's financing statement was not sufficient to perfect its security interests in Greenbelt's assets.

Decision and Remedy

The bankruptcy court held that Raymond failed to identify the actual debtor in its financing statement. The court voided Raymond's lien on the equipment.

Case Questions

Critical Legal Thinking   Should creditors searching financing records be required to search for financing statements filed under the debtor's trade names as well as its legal name?

Business Ethics   Did the bankruptcy trustee act ethically in avoiding the secured creditor's security interest?

Contemporary Business   Was the filing of the financing statement under the wrong name an error that could have easily been prevented?

Perfection by Possession of Collateral

No financing statement has to be filed if the creditor has physical **possession of the collateral**. The rationale behind this rule is that if someone other than the debtor is in possession of the property, a potential creditor is on notice that another may claim an interest in the debtor's property. A secured creditor who holds the debtor's property as collateral must use reasonable care in its custody and preservation [UCC 9-207].

Consider This Example Suppose Karen borrows $3,000 from Alan and gives her motorcycle to him as security for the loan. Alan does not file a financing statement. Another creditor obtains a judgment against Karen. This creditor cannot recover the motorcycle from Alan. Even though Alan has not filed a financing statement, his security interest in the motorcycle is perfected because he has possession of the motorcycle.

Perfection by a Purchase Money Security Interest in Consumer Goods

Sellers and lenders often extend credit to consumers to purchase consumer goods. **Consumer goods** include furniture, television sets, home appliances, and other goods used primarily for personal, family, or household purposes.

A creditor who extends credit to a consumer to purchase a consumer good under a written security agreement obtains a **purchase money security interest** in the good. This agreement automatically perfects the creditor's security interest at the time of the sale. The creditor does not have to file a financing statement or take possession of the goods to perfect his or her security interest. This interest is called **perfection by attachment** or the **automatic perfection rule**.

Two types of consumer goods are excepted from this rule. Financing statements must be filed to perfect a security interest in motor vehicles and fixtures [UCC 9-302(1)(d)].

Consider This Example Assume that Marcia buys a $3,000 HDTV plasma television for her home on credit extended by the seller, Circuit City. Circuit City requires Marcia to sign a security agreement. Circuit City has a purchase money security interest in the television that is automatically perfected at the time of the credit sale. Now suppose Marcia borrowed the money from Country Bank to buy the television for cash from Circuit City. If the bank requires Marcia to sign a security agreement, its security interest in the television is automatically perfected at the time Marcia buys the television from Circuit City.

Concept Summary Methods for Perfecting a Security Interest

Perfection Method	How Created
Financing statement	Creditor files a financing statement with the appropriate government office.
Possession of collateral	Creditor obtains physical possession of the collateral.
Purchase money security interest	Creditor extends credit to a debtor to purchase consumer goods and obtains a security interest in the goods.

Termination

Once a secured consumer debt is paid, the secured party must file a **termination statement** with each filing officer with whom the financing statement was filed. The termination statement must be filed within one month after the debt is paid or 10 days after receipt of the debtor's written demand, whichever occurs first. In all other cases, the secured party must either file a termination statement with each filing officer with whom the financing statement has been filed or send the termination statement to the debtor within 10 days of receipt of a written demand by the debtor. If the affected secured party fails to file or send the termination statement as required, he or she is liable to the debtor for $100. In addition, the secured party is liable for any other losses caused to the debtor [UCC 9-404(1)].

Priority of Claims

Often, two or more creditors claim an interest in the same collateral or property. The priority of the claims is determined according to (1) whether the claim is unsecured or secured and (2) the time at which secured claims were attached or were perfected.

UCC Rules for Determining Priority

The UCC establishes the following set of rules for determining **priority** among *conflicting claims* of creditors [UCC 9-301(1)(a), UCC 9-312(5), UCC 9-315(2)]:

1. *Secured versus unsecured claims.* A creditor who has the only secured interest in the debtor's collateral has priority over unsecured interests.
2. *Competing unperfected secured claims.* If two or more secured parties claim an interest in the same collateral but neither has a perfected claim, the first to attach has priority.
3. *Perfected versus unperfected claims.* If two or more secured parties claim an interest in the same collateral but only one has perfected his or her security interest, the perfected security interest has priority.
4. *Competing perfected secured claims.* If two or more secured parties have perfected security interests in the same collateral, the first to perfect (e.g., by filing a financing statement or taking possession of the collateral) has priority.
5. *Perfected secured claims in fungible, commingled goods.* If a security interest in goods is perfected but the goods are later commingled with other goods in which there are perfected security interests and the goods become part of a product or mass and lose their identity, the security interests rank equally according to the ratio that the cost of goods to which each interest originally attached bears to the cost of the total product or mass.

> Creditor: One of a tribe of savages dwelling beyond the Financial Straits and dreaded for their desolating excursions.
>
> Ambrose Bierce.
> *The Devil's Dictionary (1911)*

Exceptions to the Perfection-Priority Rule

Perfection does not always protect a secured party from third-party claims. As discussed in the paragraphs that follow, the UCC recognizes several exception to the perfection-priority rule:

- *Purchase money security interest: Inventory as collateral.* In certain circumstances, a perfected purchase money security interest prevails over perfected nonpurchase money security interests in after-acquired property. The order of perfection is irrelevant. If the collateral is inventory, the perfected purchase money security interest prevails if the purchase money secured party gives written notice of the perfection to the perfected nonpurchase money secured party before the debtor receives possession of the inventory [UCC 9-312(3)].

Business Brief

Perfection does not always protect a secured party from third-party claims. Consider the following exceptions, as discussed: (1) purchase money security interests involving inventory, (2) purchase money security interests involving goods other than inventory, (3) buyers in the ordinary course of business, (4) secondhand consumer goods, (5) artisan's and mechanic's liens.

Consider This Example Toy Shops, Inc., a retailer, borrows money from First Bank for working capital. In return, First Bank gets a security interest in all Toy Shops's current and after-acquired inventory. First Bank perfects its security interest by filing a financing statement. Later, Toy Shops purchases new inventory on credit from Mattel, a toy manufacturer. Mattel perfects its purchase money security interest by filing a financing statement. It notifies First Bank of this fact prior to delivery of the new inventory. Toy Shops defaults on its loans. Mattel's lien has priority.

■ ***Purchase money security interest: Noninventory as collateral.*** If the collateral is something other than inventory, a perfected purchase money security interest would prevail over a perfected nonpurchase money security interest in after-acquired property if it was perfected before or within 10 days after the debtor receives possession of the collateral [UCC 9-312(4)].

Consider This Example On September 1, Matco, a manufacturer, borrows money for working capital from First Bank and gives First Bank a security interest in its current and after-acquired equipment. First Bank perfects its security interest by filing a financing statement. On September 20, Matco purchases a new piece of equipment on credit from Allegheny Industries, an equipment manufacturer. On September 30, Allegheny perfects its purchase money security interest by filing a financing statement. Matco defaults on its loans. Here, Allegheny's perfected purchase money security interest prevails because the lien was perfected within 10 days after the debtor received the collateral. If Allegheny had waited until October 1 to perfect its purchase money security interest, First Bank would have prevailed.

■ ***Buyers in the ordinary course of business.*** A **buyer in the ordinary course of business** who purchases goods from a merchant takes the goods free of any perfected or unperfected security interest in the merchant's inventory, even if the buyer knows of the existence of the security interest. This rule is necessary because buyers would be reluctant to purchase goods if the merchant's creditors could recover the goods if the merchant defaulted on loans owed to secured creditors [UCC 9-307(1)].

Consider This Example Suppose Central Car Sales, Inc., a new car dealership, finances all its inventory of new automobiles at First Bank. First Bank takes a security interest in Central's inventory of cars and perfects this security interest. Kim, a buyer in the ordinary course of business, purchases a car from Central for cash. The car cannot be recovered from Kim even if Central defaults on its payments to the bank.

■ ***Secondhand consumer goods.*** Buyers of secondhand consumer goods take the goods free of security interest if they do not have actual or constructive knowledge about the security interest, give value, and buy the goods for personal, family, or household purposes. The filing of a financing statement by a creditor provides constructive notice of the security interest [UCC 9-307(2)].

Consider This Example Suppose Anne purchases a microwave oven on credit from Stearns, a retailer, to be used for household purposes. Pursuant to a security agreement, Stearns acquires an automatically perfected purchase money security interest in the oven. Suppose Stearns does not file a financing statement. Anne sells the microwave oven to her neighbor, Jeff, for cash. Anne defaults on her loan payments to Stearns. Stearns cannot recover the microwave oven from Jeff. Note, however, that Stearns

$13,250. First Bank repossesses the automobile and sells it at a public auction for $11,000. The selling expenses and sales commission are $1,250. This amount is deducted from the proceeds. The remaining $9,750 is applied to the $13,250 balance of the debt. Sean remains personally liable to First Bank for the $3,500 deficiency.

Redemption Rights The debtor or another secured party may **redeem** the collateral before the priority lienholder has disposed of it, entered into a contract to dispose of it, or discharged the debtor's obligation by exercising a right to retain the collateral. The **right of redemption** may be accomplished by payment of all obligations secured by the collateral, all expenses reasonably incurred by the secured party in retaking and holding the collateral, and any attorneys' fees and legal expenses provided for in the security agreement and not prohibited by law [UCC 9-506].

Online Commerce & Internet Law
Revised Article 9 Recognizes E-Commerce

Revised Article 9 of the UCC, which was promulgated in 1999 as a model act to replace Article 9—Secured Transactions, recognizes many aspects of e-commerce and the digital world. The modern e-commerce features of Revised Article 9 include the following:

- Filing of financing statements and other records with the secretary of state, county recorder's office, or other filing office may be made electronically as well as in writing.
- To facilitate electronic filings, the debtor's signature or other authorized signature does not have to appear on the financing statement or other electronic record.
- Electronic chattel paper, which is a record consisting of information stored in an electronic medium (i.e., not written), can be collateral for Article 9 purposes. Perfection of a security interest in electronic chattel paper may be by filing.
- The seller of software is given a purchase money security interest (PMSI) in its software that has priority over other secured interests. For example, if software with a PMSI is placed on the licensee's computer system that is subject to a security interest itself, the software PMSI takes precedence over the security interest in the computer hardware.

Revised Article 9 reflects the drafters' concern for upgrading commercial law to recognize the increased use of digital information and e-commerce. ∎

Surety and Guaranty Arrangements

Sometimes a creditor refuses to extend credit to a debtor unless a third person agrees to become liable on the debt. The third person's credit becomes the security for the credit extended to the debtor. This relationship may be either a surety or a guaranty arrangement. Each of these arrangements is discussed in the following paragraphs.

Surety Arrangement

In a strict **surety arrangement**, a third person—known as the **surety** or **co-debtor**—promises to be liable for the payment of another person's debt. A person who acts as a surety is commonly called an **accommodation party** or **cosigner**. Along with the principal debtor, the surety is primarily liable for paying the principal debtor's debt when it is due.

The principal debtor does not have to be in default on the debt, and the creditor does not have to have exhausted all its remedies against the principal debtor before seeking payment from the surety.

Guaranty Arrangement

In a **guaranty arrangement**, a third person (the **guarantor**) agrees to pay the debt of the principal debtor if the debtor defaults and does not pay the debt when it is due. In this type of arrangement, the guarantor is secondarily liable on the debt. In other words, the guarantor is obligated to pay the debt only if the principal debtor defaults and the creditor has attempted unsuccessfully to collect the debt from the debtor.

In the following case, the court had to decide whether there was a surety or guaranty contract.

General Motors Acceptance Corporation v. Daniels
492 A.2d 1306, 1985 Md. Lexis 596 (1985)
Court of Appeals of Maryland

Case 22.2
Surety Contract

Background and Facts

In June 1981, John Daniels agreed to purchase a used automobile from Lindsay Cadillac Company (Lindsay Cadillac). Because John had a poor credit rating, his brother, Seymour, agreed to cosign with him. General Motors Acceptance Corporation (GMAC), a company engaged in the business of financing automobiles, agreed to finance the purchase. On June 23, 1981, Seymour accompanied John to Lindsay Cadillac. John signed the contract on the line designated "Buyer." Seymour signed the contract on the line designated "Co-Buyer." In May 1982, GMAC declared the contract in default. After attempting to locate the automobile for several months, GMAC brought this action against the Daniels brothers. Because service of process was never effected upon John, the case proceeded to trial against only Seymour. The trial court found that Seymour had entered into a guaranty contract and that Seymour was not liable because GMAC had not yet proceeded against John. GMAC appealed.

Issue

Was the contract Seymour signed a guaranty or surety contract?

Court's Reasoning

If the contract Seymour signed was a guaranty contract, he would have been only secondarily liable on his brother's loan. This situation was not true in this case, however, because Seymour signed the contract on the line on the contract designated "Co-Buyer." The contract clearly stated that all buyers agreed to be jointly and severally liable for the purchase of the vehicle. Seymour executed the same contract as his brother, thereby making himself a party to the original contract. These facts establish the existence of a surety contract upon which Seymour became primarily liable.

Decision and Remedy

The court of appeals held that Seymour signed a surety contract and thus agreed to be primarily liable with his brother John for the purchase of the automobile. GMAC was therefore not required to proceed against John in the first instance. The court of appeals reversed the decision of the trial court, and held that Seymour was a surety co-buyer liable to GMAC for his brother John's car loan.

Case Questions

Critical Legal Thinking What purposes do guaranty and surety contracts serve? Explain.

Business Ethics Did Seymour act ethically in trying to avoid liability for his brother's loan?

Contemporary Business As a lender, would you rather have a third party sign as a surety or guarantor?

Defenses of a Surety or Guarantor

Business Brief

Many businesses will not sell goods and services to a minor or a person with a bad credit history unless a competent adult cosigns or guarantees payment.

Generally, the defenses the principal debtor has against the creditor may also be asserted by a surety or guarantor. For example, if credit has been extended for the purchase of a piece of machinery that proves to be defective, the debtor and surety both can assert the defect as a defense to liability. The defenses of fraudulent inducement to enter into the surety or guaranty agreement and duress may also be cited as personal defenses to liability. The surety or guarantor cannot assert the debtor's incapacity (i.e., minority or insanity) or bankruptcy as a defense against liability. The surety's or guarantor's own incapacity or bankruptcy may be asserted, however.

Concept Summary *Liability of Sureties and Guarantors Compared*

Type of Arrangement	Party	Liability
Surety contract	Surety	Primarily liable. The surety is a co-debtor who is liable to pay the debt when it is due.
Guaranty contract	Guarantor	Secondarily liable. The guarantor is liable to pay the debt if the debtor defaults and does not pay the debt when it is due.

Contemporary Environment
Collection Remedies

When a debt is past due, the creditor may bring a legal action against the debtor. If the creditor is successful, the court will award a **judgment** against the debtor. The judgment will state that the debtor owes the creditor a specific sum of money. The amount usually consists of principal and interest past due on the debt, other costs resulting from the debtor's default, and court costs.

The most common collection remedies are:

1. **Attachment.** This is a prejudgment court order that permits the seizure of the debtor's property while the lawsuit is pending. To obtain a *writ of attachment*, a creditor must follow the procedures of state law, give the debtor notice and post a bond with the court.
2. **Execution.** This is a postjudgment court order that permits the seizure of the debtor's property that is in the possession of the debtor. Certain property that is exempt from levy (e.g., tools of trade, clothing, homestead exemption). A *writ of execution* is a court order directing the sheriff to seize the debtor's property and authorizing a judicial sale of that prop-

erty. The proceeds are used to pay the creditor the amount of the final judgement. Any surplus must be paid to the debtor.

3. **Garnishment.** This is a postjudgment court order that permits the seizure of the debtor's property in the possession of third parties. The creditor (also known as the **garnishor**) must go to court to seek a *writ of garnishment*. The third person is called the **garnishee**. Common garnishees are employers who possess wages due a debtor, banks in possession of funds belonging to the debtor, and other third parties in the possession of property of the debtor.

To protect debtors from abusive and excessive garnishment actions by creditors, Congress enacted Title III of the Consumer Credit Protection Act [15 U.S.C.§ 1601 et seq.]. This law allows debtors who are subject to a writ of garnishment to retain the greater of (1) 75 percent of their weekly disposable earnings (after taxes) or (2) an amount equal to 30 hours of work paid at federal minimum wage. State law limitations on garnishment control are more stringent than federal law. ■

Chapter Summary

Unsecured and Secured Credit, p. 459

Unsecured Credit

Unsecured credit does not require any security (collateral) to protect the payment of the loan.
Recovery of unpaid loan. If the debtor does not pay the loan, the creditor may bring a legal action and obtain a *judgment* against the debtor. The debtor is called *judgment-proof* if he or she has no money to pay the judgment.

Secured Credit

Secured credit requires security (collateral) that secures the payment of the loan.
Collateral. The property that is pledged as security for a loan is called collateral.

Security Interests in Real Property, p. 460

Mortgage

1. ***Mortgage.*** A mortgage is an instrument that represents a security interest in real property.
2. ***Mortgagor.*** A mortgagor is an owner-debtor who pledges his or her real property as security for a loan.
3. ***Mortgagee.*** A mortgagee is a creditor who holds a security interest in the owner-debtor's real property.

Note and Deed of Trust

Some states use a note and deed of trust as an alternative to a mortgage.

1. ***Note.*** A note is an instrument that evidences the debt.
2. ***Deed of trust.*** A deed of trust is an instrument that gives the creditor a security interest in the owner-debtor's real property.

Foreclosure

Foreclosure is a method whereby if a mortgagor defaults on the payment on a mortgage, the mortgagee can declare the entire debt due and proceed to acquire title to the property that is collateral for the loan.

Deficiency Judgment

If, after foreclosure of the property, there is a deficiency owing, the mortgagee can sue the mortgagor to recover the amount of the deficiency.

Antideficiency Statute

Some states have enacted antideficiency statutes that prohibit a mortgagee form recovering a deficiency owned on a loan.

Material Person's Lien

A material person's lien is given by law to contractors and laborers on real property they made improvement on until the amount they are owed is paid.

Security Interests in Personal Property, p. 463

Article 9 of the UCC

This article of the Uniform Commercial Code governs secured transactions in personal property.

Secured Transactions

Secured transactions are created when a creditor makes a loan to a debtor in exchange for the debtor's pledge of personal property as security.

1. ***Two-party secured transaction.*** In this type of transaction, a seller sells goods to a buyer on credit and retains a security interest in the goods.
2. ***Three-party secured transaction.*** In this type of transaction, a seller sells goods to a buyer who has obtained financing from a third-party lender (e.g., bank) that takes a security interest in the goods sold.

Requirements for Creating a Security Interest

1. ***Requirements***
   a. Written security agreement
   b. Value given to the debtor
   c. Debtor has rights in collateral
      If these requirements are met, the rights of the secured creditor *attach* to the collateral.
2. ***Attachment.*** With attachment, the creditor has an enforceable security interest against the debtor and can satisfy the debt out of the designated collateral.

Personal Property Subject to a Security Agreement

1. *Goods*
2. *Instruments* (i.e., checks, notes, stocks, bonds)
3. *Chattel paper* (i.e., conditional sales contracts)
4. *Documents of title* (i.e., bills of lading, warehouse receipts)
5. *Accounts* (i.e., accounts receivable)
6. *General intangibles* (i.e., patents, copyrights, royalties, franchises)

The Floating-Lien Concept

Floating lien. A floating lien occurs when a security agreement provides that the security interest attaches to personal property that was not originally in the possession of the debtor when the agreement was executed. This property may include:

1. *After acquired property.* Property acquired after the security agreement is executed.
2. *Sale proceeds.* Proceeds from the sale, exchange, or disposal of collateral subject to the security agreement.
3. *Future advances.* Personal property of the debtor that is designated as collateral for future loans taken against a line of credit.

Perfection of a Security Interest

Perfection of a security interest establishes the right of the secured creditor against other creditors who claim an interest in the collateral. The UCC provides the following three methods of perfecting a security interest:

1. *Perfection by Filing a Financing Statement.* The creditor files a *financing statement* with the appropriate government recording office. This statement puts the world on notice of the creditor's security interest in the property. This method is the most common form of perfecting a security interest.
2. *Perfection by Possession of Collateral.* If the creditor has physical possession of the collateral, no financing statement has to be filed. This method is the least common form of perfecting a security interest.
3. *Perfection by a Purchase Money Security Interest in Consumer Goods.* A creditor (seller or lender) who extends credit to a consumer to purchase a *consumer good* under a written security agreement obtains a *purchase money security interest* in the goods. This agreement automatically perfects the creditor's security interest at the time of the sale. The creditor does not have to file a financing statement to perfect his or her security interest. This method is called *perfection by attachment* or the *automatic perfection rule.*

Information Requests and Certificate of Filing

Certificate of filing. A certificate of filing is a document that a person can request of the government filing officer that states (1) whether any presently effective financing statement naming a particular debtor is on file, (2) the date and hour of any such filing, and (3) the names and addresses of the secured parties.

Assignment, Amendment, and Release

1. *Statement of assignment.* This document shows that the secured party has transferred all or part of his or her rights under a financing statement to another party.
2. *Amendment.* An amendment is a writing that is signed by both the debtor and the secured creditor, showing that the financing statement has been amended.
3. *Release.* A release is a document showing that the secured creditor has released all or part of any collateral described in a financing statement.

   All these documents must be filed where the original financing statement has been filed.

Termination

Termination statement. A termination statement is a document that must be filed by a secured creditor within a specified number of days after a secured consumer debt has been paid. This statement must be filed where the original financing statement was filed.

UCC Rules for Determining Priority

The UCC establishes the following rules for determining *priority* among conflicting claims of creditors to the collateral:

1. *Secured versus unsecured claims.* Secured claims have priority over unsecured claims.
2. *Competing unperfected secured claims.* The first claim to attach has priority.
3. *Perfected versus unperfected claims.* The perfected claim has priority.
4. *Competing perfected secured claims.* The first to perfect has priority.
5. *Perfected secured claims in fungible, commingled goods.* The security interests rank equally according to the ratio that the cost of goods to which each interest originally attached bears to the cost of the total product or mass.

Exceptions to the Perfection-Priority Rule

Perfection does not always protect a secured creditor from third-party claims. The UCC recognizes the following *exceptions to the perfection-priority rule*:

1. *Purchase money security interest—collateral as inventory.* A perfected *purchase* money security interest in *inventory* prevails over a perfected *nonpurchase* money security interest in after acquired property.
2. *Purchase money security interest—noninventory as collateral.* A perfected *purchase* money security interest in *noninventory* prevails over a perfected *nonpurchase* money security interest in after-acquired property if it was perfected before or within 10 days after the debtor receives possession of the collateral.
3. *Buyers in the ordinary course of business.* A buyer in the ordinary course of business who purchases goods from a merchant takes the goods free of any perfected or unperfected security interest in the merchant's inventory, even if the buyer knows of the existence of the security interest.
4. *Secondhand consumer goods.* Buyers of secondhand consumer goods take the goods free of security interests if they do not have actual or constructive knowledge about the security interest, give value, and buy the goods for personal, family, or household purposes.

Artisan's and Mechanic's lien

This type of lien is given by law to artisans and mechanics on personal property they made repairs or improvements on until the amount they are owed is paid. Artisan's and mechanic's liens for services or materials provided prevail over all other security interests in goods unless a statute provides otherwise.

Default

The parties may define the actions or inactions that cause default under an agreement. These actions usually include failure to make scheduled payments when due, bankruptcy of the debtor, and breach of other terms of the agreement.

Secured Creditor's Remedies

Article 9 of the UCC provides the secured creditor with certain remedies upon the debtor's default. These remedies are:

Taking Possession of the Collateral

Repossession. The secured creditor can use self-help to take physical possession of the collateral as long as it does not cause a *breach of peace*.

1. *Deficiency judgment.* If the proceeds from the disposition of the collateral are not sufficient to satisfy the debt, the secured party may obtain a *deficiency judgment* against the debtor, holding the debtor personally liable for the difference.
2. *Redemption rights.* The debtor may *redeem* the collateral within a statutorily stipulated period of time after repossession by payment of all obligations owed on the debt and all expenses reasonably incurred by the secured creditor in repossessing and holding the collateral.

Relinquishing the Security Interest and Proceeding to Judgment on the Underlying Debt

This course of action is usually taken only when the value of the collateral has been reduced below the amount of the secured interest and the debtor has other assets from which to satisfy the debt.

Surety and Guaranty Arrangements, p. 473

Surety and Guaranty Arrangements

Surety and guaranty arrangements both occur when a creditor refuses to extend credit to a debtor without further security and a third person agrees to provide that security by agreeing to become liable on the debt.

Surety Arrangement

A third party—called the *surety* or *co-debtors*—promises to be liable for another person's debt. The surety is *primarily liable* for payment of the debt when it is due, along with the principal debtor. The creditor does not have to attempt to collect the debt from the principal debtor before demanding payment from the surety.

Guaranty Arrangement

A third party—called the *guarantor*—agrees to pay the debt of the principal debtor if the debtor *defaults* and does not pay the debt when it is due. The guarantor is *secondarily liable* and has to pay the debt only if the creditor has attempted unsuccessfully to collect the debt from the debtor.

Right of Subrogation

When a surety or guarantor has been made to pay a debt owed by the principal debtor, the surety or guarantor acquires all the creditor's rights against the debtor and may recover the amount it paid on the debtor's behalf.

Collection Remedies

If a creditor sues a debtor or obtains a *judgment* against a debtor, the creditor can use the following collection remedies to recover from the debtor.

Attachment. This is a *prejudgment* court order that permits the seizure of the debtor's property while the lawsuit is pending. The creditor must follow the procedures established by state law, give the debtor notice, and post a bond with the court.

Execution. This is a *postjudgment* court order that permits the seizure of the debtor's property that is in the *possession of the debtor*. Certain property is exempt from levy (e.g., homestead exemption).

Garnishment. This is a *postjudgment* court order that permits the seizure of the debtor's property in the *possession of third parties* (e.g., wages to be paid to the debtor by his or her employer). Garnishment is subject to limitations established by federal and state law.

 Internet Exercises and Case Questions

Working the Web Internet Exercises

Activities

1. For an overview of the pervasiveness and importance of credit in the United States and the world economy, see **www.equifax.com**.

2. For a definition and examples of suretyship, see **www.lectlaw.com/def2/s208.htm**.

3. Using the Cornell site, at **www.law.cornell.edu/topics/secured_transactions.html**, find which part of the UCC provides for secured transactions.

Critical Legal Thinking Cases

22.1 Financing Statement In 1984, C&H Trucking, Inc. (C&H), borrowed $19,747.56 from S&D Petroleum Company, Inc. (S&D). S&D hired Clifton M. Tamsett to prepare a security agreement naming C&H as the debtor and giving S&D a security interest in a 1984 Mack truck. The security agreement prepared by Tamsett declared that the collateral also secured

any other indebtedness or liability of the debtor to the secured party direct or indirect, absolute or contingent, due or to become due, now existing or hereafter arising, including all future advances or loans which may be made at the option of the secured party.

Tamsett failed to file a financing statement or the executed agreement with the appropriate government office. C&H subsequently paid off the original debt, and S&D continued to extend new credit to C&H. In March 1986, when C&H owed S&D over $17,000, S&D learned that (1) C&H was insolvent, (2) the Mack truck had been sold, and (3) Tamsett had failed to file the security agreement. Does S&D have a security interest in the Mack truck? Is Tamsett liable to S&D? [*S&D Petroleum Company, Inc. v. Tamsett*, 534 N.Y.S.2d 800, 1988 N.Y.App.Div. Lexis 11258 (N.Y. Sup.Ct.App. 1988)]

22.2 Priority of Security Agreements On July 15, 1980, World Wide Tracers, Inc. (World Wide), sold certain of its assets and properties, including equipment, furniture, uniforms, accounts receivable, and contract rights, to Metropolitan Protection, Inc. (Metropolitan). To secure payment of the purchase price, Metropolitan executed a security agreement and financing statement in favor of World Wide. The agreement, which stated that "all of the property listed on Exhibit A (equipment, furniture, and fixtures) together with any property of the debtor acquired after July 15, 1980" was collateral, was filed with the Minnesota secretary of state on July 16, 1980.

In February 1982, State Bank (Bank) loaned money to Metropolitan, which executed a security agreement and financing statement in favor of the Bank. The Bank filed the financing statement with the Minnesota secretary of state's office on March 3, 1982. The financing statement contained the following language describing the collateral:

All accounts receivable and contract rights owned or hereafter acquired. All equipment now owned and hereafter acquired, including but not limited to, office furniture and uniforms.

When Metropolitan defaulted on its agreement with World Wide in the fall of 1982, World Wide brought suit asserting its alleged security agreement in Metropolitan's accounts receivable. The Bank filed a counterclaim, asserting its perfected security interest in Metropolitan's accounts receivable. Who wins? [*World Wide Tracers, Inc. v. Metropolitan Protection, Inc.*, 384 N.W.2d 442, 1986 Minn. Lexis 753 (MN 1986)]

22.3 Floating Lien On March 17, 1973, Joseph H. Jones and others (debtors) borrowed money from Columbus Junction State Bank (Bank) and executed a security agreement

in favor of the Bank. On March 29, 1973, the Bank perfected its security interest by filing financing statements covering "equipment, farm products, crops, livestock, supplies, contract rights, and all accounts and proceeds thereof" with the Iowa secretary of state. On January 28, 1978, the Bank filed a continuation statement with the Iowa secretary of state. On February 10, 1983, the Bank filed a second continuation statement with the Iowa secretary of state. On January 31, 1986, the debtors filed for Chapter 7 (liquidation) bankruptcy. The bankruptcy collected $10,073 from the sale of the debtor's 1985 crops and an undetermined amount of soybeans harvested in 1986 on farmland owned by the debtors. The bankruptcy trustee claimed the funds and soybeans on behalf of the bankruptcy estate. The Bank claimed the funds and soybeans as a perfected secured creditor. Who wins? [*In re Jones*, 79 B.R. 839, 1987 Bankr. Lexis 1825 (Bk.N.D.Iowa 1987)]

22.4 Sale Proceeds Murphy Oldsmobile, Inc. (Murphy), operated an automobile dealership that sold new and used automobiles. General Motors Acceptance Corporation (GMAC) loaned funds to Murphy to finance the purchase of new automobiles as inventory. The loan was secured by a duly perfected security agreement in all existing and after-acquired inventory and the proceeds therefrom. Section 9-306 of the New York UCC provides that a security interest in collateral continues in "identifiable proceeds." During the first week of May 1980, Murphy received checks and drafts from the sale of the secured inventory in the amount of $97,888, which it deposited in a general business checking account at Norstar Bank (Bank). During that week, Murphy defaulted on certain loans it had received from Bank. Bank exercised its right of setoff and seized the funds on deposit in Murphy's checking account. GMAC sued to enforce its security claim against these funds. Who wins? [*General Motors Acceptance Corporation v. Norstar Bank, N.A.*, 532 N.Y.S.2d 685, 1988 N.Y.Misc. Lexis 595 (N.Y. Sup.Ct. 1988)]

22.5 Priority of Security Interests Clyde and Marlys Trees, owners of the Wine Shop, Inc., borrowed money from the American Heritage Bank & Trust Company (Bank). They personally and on behalf of the corporation executed a promissory note, security agreement, and financing statement to Bank. Bank properly filed a security agreement and financing statement naming the Wine Shop's inventory, stock in trade, furniture, fixtures, and equipment "now owned or hereafter to be acquired" as collateral. The Trees also borrowed money from a junior lienholder, whose promissory note was secured by the same collateral. The Wine Shop subsequently defaulted on both notes. Without informing Bank, the junior lienholder took over the assets of the Wine Shop and transferred them to a corporation, O&E, Inc. Fearing that its security interest would not be adequately protected, Bank filed a motion to enforce its security interest. Can Bank enforce its security interest even though the collateral was transferred to another party? [*American Heritage Bank & Trust Company v. O&E, Inc.*, 576 P.2d 566, 1978 Colo.App. Lexis 667 (Colo. App. 1978)]

22.6 Priority of Security Interests On October 8, 1980, Paul High purchased various items of personal property and livestock from William and Marilyn McGowen (McGowens). To secure the purchase price, High granted the McGowens a security interest in the personal property and livestock. On December 18, 1980, High borrowed $86,695 from Nebraska State Bank (Bank) and signed a promissory note granting Bank a security interest in all his farm products, including but not limited to all his livestock. On December 20, 1980, Bank perfected its security agreement by filing a financing statement with the county clerk in Dakota County, Nebraska. The McGowens perfected their security interest by filing a financing statement and security agreement with the county clerk on April 28, 1981. In 1984, High defaulted on the obligations owed to the McGowens and Bank. Whose security interest has priority? [*McGowen v. Nebraska State Bank*, 427 N.W.2d 772, 1988 Neb. Lexis 290 (NE 1988)]

22.7 Purchase Money Security Interest In 1974, Prior Brothers, Inc. (PBI), began financing its farming operations through Bank of California, N.A. (Bank). Bank's loans were secured by PBI's equipment and after-acquired property. On March 22, 1974, Bank filed a financing statement perfecting its security interest. On April 8, 1976, PBI contacted the International Harvester dealership in Sunnyside, Washington, about the purchase of a new tractor. A retail installment contract for a model 1066 International Harvester tractor was executed. PBI took delivery of the tractor "on approval," agreeing that if it decided to purchase the tractor it would inform the dealership of its intention and send a $6,000 down payment. On April 22, 1976, the dealership received a $6,000 check. The dealership filed a financing statement concerning the tractor on April 27, 1976. Later, when PBI went into receivership, the dealership filed a complaint asking the court to declare that its purchase money security interest in the tractor had priority over Bank's security interest. Did it? [*In the Matter of Prior Brothers, Inc.*, 632 P.2d 522, 1981 Wash.App. Lexis 2507 (Wash. App. 1981)]

22.8 Purchase Money Security Interest In 1973, Sandwich State Bank (Sandwich) made general farm loans to David Klotz and Hinckley Grain Company. The loan was secured by the assets of Klotz's farm and after-acquired property. Sandwich filed a financing statement with the Kane County Recorder to perfect its security interest. Sandwich filed the necessary continuation statements so its security interest remained in effect up to and during the time of trial. On February 3, 1984, DeKalb Bank (DeKalb) loaned Klotz funds for the particular purpose of purchasing certain cattle. DeKalb filed a financing statement on February 3, 1984, to perfect its security interest in the cattle. The cattle in question were all purchased using funds loaned to

Klotz by DeKalb. When Klotz defaulted on its loan to DeKalb, DeKalb sued to enforce its security interest and to recover possession of the cattle. Does DeKalb's security interest have priority over Sandwich's security interest? [*DeKalb Bank v. Klotz*, 502 N.E.2d 1256, 1986 Ill.App. Lexis 3351 (Ill. App. 1987)]

22.9 Buyer in the Ordinary Course of Business Heritage Ford Lincoln Mercury, Inc. (Heritage), was in the business of selling new cars. In April 1978, Heritage entered into an agreement with Ford Motor Credit Company (Ford) whereby Ford extended a continuing line of credit to Heritage to purchase vehicles. Heritage granted Ford a purchase money security interest in all motor vehicles it owned and thereafter acquired and in all proceeds from the sale of such motor vehicles. Ford filed its financing statement with the secretary of state of Kansas on May 11, 1978. When the dealership experienced financial trouble, two Heritage officers decided to double finance certain new cars by issuing dealer papers to themselves and obtaining financing for two new cars from First National Bank & Trust Company of El Dorado (Bank). The loan proceeds were deposited in the dealership's account to help its financial difficulties. The cars were available for sale. When the dealership closed its doors and turned over the car inventory to Ford, Bank alleged that it had priority over Ford because the Heritage officers were buyers in the ordinary course of business. Who wins? [*First National Bank and Trust Company of El Dorado v. Ford Motor Credit Company*, 646 P.2d 1057, 1982 Kan. Lexis 280 (KS 1982)]

22.10 Artisan's Lien On April 25, 1985, Ozark Financial Services (Ozark) loaned money to Lonnie and Patsy Turner to purchase a tractor truck unit. The Turners signed a security agreement giving Ozark a security interest in the tractor truck. Ozark properly filed a financing statement giving public notice of its security interest. In June 1985, the Turners took the truck to Pete & Sons Garage, Inc. (Pete & Sons), for repairs. When the Turners arrived to pick up the truck, they could not pay for the repairs. Pete & Sons returned the truck to the Turners upon their verbal agreement that if they did not pay for the repairs, they would return the truck to Pete & Sons. The Turners did not pay Pete & Sons for the repair services and defaulted on the loan payments due Ozark. Ozark brought this action to recover the truck under its security agreement. Pete & Sons asserted that it had a common law artisan's lien on the truck for the unpaid repair services that it claimed took priority over Ozark's security interest. Who wins? [*Ozark Financial Services v. Turner*, 735 S.W.2d 374, 1987 Mo.App. Lexis 4273 (Mo.App. 1987)]

Business Ethics Cases

22.11 Business Ethics On February 26, 1982, Jessie Lynch became seriously ill and needed medical attention. Her sister, Ethel Sales, took her to the Forsyth Memorial Hospital in North Carolina for treatment. Lynch was admitted for hospitalization. Sales signed Lynch's admission form, which included the following section:

The undersigned, in consideration of hospital services being rendered or to be rendered by Forsyth County Memorial Hospital Authority, Inc., in Winston-Salem, N.C., to the above patient, does hereby guarantee payment to Forsyth

County Hospital Authority, Inc., on demand all charges for said services and incidentals incurred on behalf of such patient.

Lynch received the care and services rendered by the hospital until her discharge over 30 days later. The total bill during her hospitalization amounted to $7,977. When Lynch refused to pay the bill, the hospital instituted an action against Lynch and Sales to recover the unpaid amount. Is Sales liable? Did Sales act ethically in denying liability? Did she have a choice when she signed the contract? [*Forsyth County Memorial Hospital Authority, Inc.*, 346 S.E.2d 212, 1986 N.C.App. Lexis 2432 (N.C.App. 1986)]

22.12 Business Ethics On February 25, 1975, Harder & Sons, Inc., an International Harvester dealership in Ionia, Michigan, sold a used International Harvester 1066 diesel tractor to Terry Blaser on an installment contract. Although the contract listed Blaser's address as Ionia County, Blaser informed Harder at the time of purchase that he was going to work and live in Barry County. Blaser took delivery of the tractor at his Ionia County address on February 28, 1975. On the same day, Harder filed a financing statement, which was executed by Blaser with the installment contract, in Barry County. The state of Michigan UCC requires an Article 9 financing statement to be filed in the debtor's county of residence. The contract and security agreement were immediately assigned to International Harvester Credit Corporation (International Harvester).

Blaser subsequently moved to Barry County for about three months, then to Ionia County for a few months, then to Kent County for three weeks, and then to Muskegon County, where he sold the tractor to Jay and Dale Vos. At the time of sale, Blaser informed the Vos brothers that he owned the tractor. He did not tell them that it was subject to a lien. The Vos brothers went to First Michigan Bank & Trust Company (Bank) to obtain a loan to help purchase the tractor. When the Bank checked the records of Ionia County and found that no financing statement was filed against the tractor, it made a $7,000 loan to the Vos brothers to purchase the tractor. On May 19, 1977, International Harvester filed suit to recover the tractor from the Vos brothers on the grounds that it had a prior perfected security interest. Did Blaser act ethically in this case? Who wins? [*International Harvester Credit Corporation v. Vos*, 290 N.W.2d 401, 1980 Mich. App. Lexis 2430 (Mich.App. 1980)]

Briefing the Case Writing Assignment

Read Case A.22 in the Case Appendix [*General Motors Acceptance Corporation v. Daniels*]. This case is excerpted from the court of appeals opinion. Review and brief the case. In your brief, be sure to answer the following questions.

1. What is the difference between a surety and a guarantor?

2. Why did this difference matter in this case?

3. Which was the defendant found to be, a surety or a guarantor?

23

Bankruptcy and Reorganization

" A trifling debt makes a man your debtor, a large one makes him your enemy. "

—Seneca
Epistulae Morales and Lucilium, 63–65

Chapter Objectives

After studying this chapter, you should be able to:

1. Describe the procedure for filing for bankruptcy.

2. Describe a Chapter 7 liquidation bankruptcy.

3. Describe secured and unsecured creditors' rights in bankruptcy.

4. Describe how a business is reorganized in Chapter 11 bankruptcy.

5. Describe a Chapter 13 consumer debt adjustment bankruptcy.

Chapter Contents

- ■ Federal Bankruptcy Code
- ■ Chapter 7 Liquidation Bankruptcy
- ■ Chapter 11 Reorganization Bankruptcy
- ■ Chapter 13 Consumer Debt Adjustment
- ■ Chapter 12 Family Farmer Bankruptcy

Small debts are like small shot; they are rattling on every side, and can scarcely be escaped without a wound; great debts are like cannon; of loud noise, but little danger.

Samuel Johnson
Letter to Joseph Simpson (1759)

The extension of credit from creditors to debtors in commercial and personal transactions is important to the viability of the U.S. and world economics. On occasion, however, borrowers become overextended and are unable to meet their debt obligations.

Years ago in Britain and Europe, persons who could not meet their debts were sentenced to debtors' prisons or indentured to their creditors until the debts were "worked off." To avoid such harsh results, many countries adopted bankruptcy laws that were intended to achieve a better balance between debtor's rights and creditors' rights.

The founders of our country thought the plight of debtors was so important that they included a provision in the U.S. Constitution giving Congress the authority to establish uniform bankruptcy laws. The goal of federal bankruptcy law is to give debtors a "fresh start" by relieving them from legal responsibility for past debts. This chapter discusses federal bankruptcy law, which is the exclusive law that governs throughout this country.

Federal Bankruptcy Code

Business Brief

Bankruptcy law is *federal law*. There are no state bankruptcy laws.

Article I, section 8, clause 4 of the U.S. Constitution provides that "The Congress shall have the power . . . to establish . . . uniform laws on the subject of bankruptcies throughout the United States." Federal bankruptcy law establishes procedures for filing for bankruptcy, resolving creditors' claims, and protecting debtors' rights. Bankruptcy law is exclusively federal law; there are no state bankruptcy laws.

Congress enacted the original **Bankruptcy Act** in 1878. It was amended in 1938 by the **Chandler Act**, and that law was completely revised by the **Bankruptcy Reform Act of 1978**.[1] The 1978 act, which became effective on October 1, 1979, substantially changed—and eased—the requirements for filing bankruptcy. The Bankruptcy Reform Act of 1978, as amended, is referred to as the **Bankruptcy Code**. The Bankruptcy Code establishes rules and procedures for filing and completing bankruptcy.

Bankruptcy Courts

Congress enacted the **Bankruptcy Amendments and Federal Judgeship Act of 1984** which created federal bankruptcy courts. Bankruptcy courts are part of the federal district court systems and one bankruptcy court is attached to each district court. Bankruptcy judges are appointed by the president for 14-year terms. Other provisions of the 1984 amendments clarified procedures for filing bankruptcy.

Business Brief

Only federal bankruptcy courts can hear *core proceedings* regarding bankruptcy cases.

Bankruptcy judges decide *core proceedings* (e.g., allowing creditor claims, deciding preferences, confirming plans of reorganization) regarding **bankruptcy** cases. *Noncore proceedings* concerning the debtor (e.g., decisions on personal injury, divorce, and other civil proceedings) are resolved in federal or state court.

Types of Bankruptcy

Poor bankrupt.

William Shakespeare
Romeo and Juliet (1595)

The Bankruptcy Code is divided into chapters. The most common forms of bankruptcy are provided by the following chapters: Chapter 7 (liquidation), Chapter 11 (reorganization), Chapter 13 (consumer debt adjustment), and Chapter 12 (family farmer bankruptcy). The remaining chapters of the Bankruptcy Code govern the bankruptcies of municipalities, stockbrokers, and railroads.

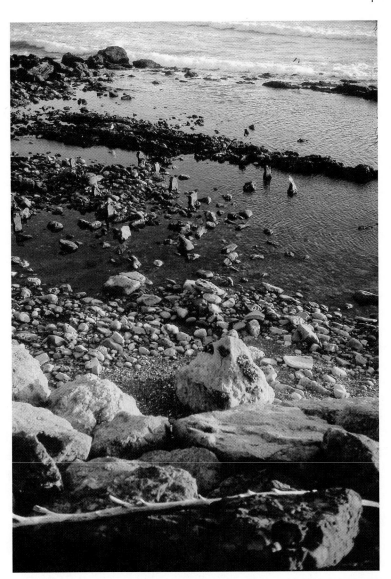

Shoreline, Santa Barbara, California. Federal bankruptcy law provides a method for individuals and businesses to discharge all or a portion of their debt and obtain a fresh start, free of certain debts.

"Fresh Start"

The primary purpose of federal bankruptcy law is to discharge the debtor from burdensome debts. The law gives debtors a **fresh start** by freeing them from legal responsibility for past debts by (1) protecting debtors from abusive activities by creditors in collecting debts, (2) preventing certain creditors from obtaining an unfair advantage over other creditors, (3) protecting creditors from actions of the debtor that would diminish the value of the bankruptcy estate, (4) providing for the speedy, efficient, and equitable distribution of the debtor's nonexempt property to claim holders, and (5) preserving existing business relations.

Chapter 7 Liquidation Bankruptcy

Chapter 7 liquidation bankruptcy (also called **straight bankruptcy**) is the most familiar form of bankruptcy. In this type of proceeding, the debtor's nonexempt property is sold for cash, the cash is distributed to the creditors, and any unpaid debts are **discharged**. Any person, including individuals, partnerships, and corporations, may be a debtor in a Chapter 7 proceeding.

The filing and maintenance of a Chapter 7 case must follow certain procedures.

Filing a Petition

A Chapter 7 bankruptcy is commenced when a **petition** is filed with the bankruptcy court. Two types of petitions can be filed:

1. **Voluntary petition. A voluntary petition** is filed by the debtor. The petition only has to state that the debtor has debts; insolvency (i.e., that debts exceed assets) need not be declared. The petition must include the following schedules: (1) a list of secured and unsecured creditors, including their addresses and the amount of debt owed to each, (2) a list of all property owned by the debtor, including property claimed to be exempt by the debtor, (3) a statement of the financial affairs of the debtor, and (4) a list of the debtor's current income and expenses. The petition must be signed and sworn to under oath. Married couples may file a joint petition.

2. **Involuntary petition. An involuntary petition** is filed by a creditor or creditors and places the debtor into bankruptcy. The petition can be filed against any debtors who can file a voluntary petition under Chapter 7. An involuntary petition must allege that the debtor is not paying his or her debts as they become due. If the debtor has more that 12 creditors, the petition must be signed by at least 3 of them. If there are 12 or fewer creditors, any creditor can sign the petition. The creditor or creditors who sign the petition must have valid unsecured claims of at least $10,000 (in the aggregate).

Order for Relief

The filing of either a voluntary petition or an unchallenged involuntary petition constitutes an **order for relief**. If the debtor challenges an involuntary petition, a trial will be held to determine whether an order for relief should be granted. If the order is granted, the case is accepted for further bankruptcy proceedings. In the case of an involuntary petition, the debtor must file the same schedules filed by voluntary debtors.

Meeting of the Creditors

Within a reasonable time (not less than 10 days nor more than 30 days) after the court grants an order for relief, the court must call a **meeting of the creditors** (also called the **first meeting of the creditors**). The judge cannot attend this meeting. The debtor, however, must appear and submit to questioning by creditors. Creditors may ask questions regarding the debtor's financial affairs, disposition of property prior to bankruptcy, possible concealment of assets, and such. The debtor may have an attorney present at this meeting.

Appointment of a Trustee

A trustee must be appointed in a Chapter 7 proceeding. An interim trustee is appointed by the court when an order for relief is entered. A **permanent trustee** is elected at the first meeting of the creditors. Trustees, who are often lawyers or accountants, are entitled to receive reasonable compensation for their services and reimbursement for expenses. Once appointed, the trustee becomes the legal representative of the bankrupt debtor's estate. Generally, the trustee must:

- Take immediate possession of the debtor's property.
- Separate secured and unsecured property.
- Set aside exempt property.
- Investigate the debtor's financial affairs.
- Employ disinterested professionals (e.g., attorneys, accountants, appraisers) to assist in the administration of the estate.
- Examine proof of claims.
- Defend, bring, and maintain lawsuits on behalf of the estate.
- Invest the property of the estate.
- Sell or otherwise dispose of property of the estate.
- Distribute the proceeds of the estate.
- Make reports to the court, creditors, and debtor regarding the administration of the estate.

Business Brief

Beginning April 1, 1998, the dollar amount stated in the Bankruptcy Code is adjusted every three years based on changes in the Consumer Price Index.

Proof of Claims

Unsecured creditors must file **proof of claims** stating the amounts of their claims against the debtor. The form for this statement is provided by the court. The proof of claim must be "timely filed," which generally means within six months of the first meeting of the creditors. Secured creditors are not required to file proof of claim. A secured creditor whose claim exceeds the value of the collateral, however, may submit a proof of claim and become an unsecured claimant as to the difference.

The claim must be allowed by the court before a creditor is permitted to participate in the bankruptcy estate. Any party of interest may object to a claim. If an objection to a claim is raised, the court will hold a hearing to determine the validity and amount of the claim.

Property of the Bankruptcy Estate

The **bankruptcy estate** is created upon the commencement of a Chapter 7 proceeding. It includes all the debtor's legal and equitable interests in real, personal, tangible, and intangible property, wherever located, that exist when the petition is filed. The debtor's separate and community property are included in the estate.

Property acquired after the petition is filed does not become part of the bankruptcy estate. The only exceptions are gifts, inheritances, life insurance proceeds, and property from divorce settlements that the debtor is entitled to receive within 180 days after the petition if filed. Earnings from property of the estate—such as rents, dividends, and interest payments— are property of the estate.

Exempt Property

Because the Bankruptcy Code is not designed to make the debtor a pauper, certain property is exempt from the bankruptcy estate. The debtor may retain **exempt property**.

The Bankruptcy Code establishes a *federal* exemption scheme[2] (see Exhibit 23.1).

Exhibit 23.1

Federal Exemptions from
the Bankruptcy Estate

EXEMPTIONS AS OF APRIL 1, 2001:

1. Interest up to $17,425 in equity in property used a residence and burial plots (called the "homestead exemption")
2. Interest up to $2,775 in value in one motor vehicle
3. Interest up to $450 per item in household goods and furnishings, wearing apparel, appliances, books, animals, crops, or musical instruments, up to an aggregate value of $9,300 for all items
4. Interest in jewelry up to $1,150
5. Interest in any property the debtor chooses (including cash) up to $925, plus up to $8,725 of any unused portion of the $17,425 homestead exemption
6. Interest up to $1,750 in value in implements, tools, or professional books used in the debtor's trade
7. Any unmatured life insurance policy owned by the debtor
8. Professionally prescribed health aids
9. Many government benefits, regardless of value, including Social Security benefits, welfare benefits, unemployment compensation, veteran's benefits, disability benefits, and public assistance benefits
10. Certain rights to receive income, including alimony and support payments, certain pension benefits, profit sharing, and annuity payments
11. Interests in wrongful death benefits, life insurance proceeds, and personal injury awards (up to $17,425)

Federal exemptions are adjusted every three years to reflect changes in the Consumer Price Index.

State Law Exemptions

Business Brief

States that provide liberal exemptions (e.g., California, Florida, Texas) are called "debtors' havens."

The Bankruptcy Code permits states to enact their own exemptions. States that do so may (1) give debtors the option of choosing between federal and state exemptions or (2) require debtors to follow state law. The exemptions available under state law are often quite liberal. For example, homestead exemptions are often higher under state law than under the federal exemption scheme. Many states require the debtor to file a **Declaration of Homestead** prior to bankruptcy. This document is usually filed in the county recorder's office in the county in which the property is located.

If the debtor's equity in property (above liens and mortgages) exceeds the exemption limits, the trustee may liquidate the property to realize the excess value for the bankruptcy estate.

Neither a borrower nor a lender be:
For loan oft loses both itself and
friend. And borrowing dulls the edge
of husbandry.

William Shakespeare
Hamlet 1.13 (1600)

Consider This Example   Assume that a debtor owns a home worth $500,000 that is subject to a $700,000 mortgage. The trustee may sell the home, pay off the mortgage, pay the debtor $17,425 (applying the federal exemption), and use the remaining proceeds ($85,000) for distribution to the debtor's creditors.

In the following case, the court found that an asset was exempt from the debtor's bankruptcy estate.

In re Witwer

163 B.R. 614, 1994 Bankr. Lexis 75
United States Bankruptcy Appellate Panel of the Ninth Circuit

Case 23.1
Bankruptcy Estate

Background and Facts

Dr. James J. Witwer is the sole stockholder, sole employee, and president of James J. Witwer, M.D., Inc., a California corporation under which he practices medicine. He is also the sole beneficiary of the corporation's retirement plan, which was established in 1970. On October 21, 1991, Witwer filed a voluntary petition for relief under Chapter 7 (liquidation). At the time, the value of the assets in his retirement plan was $1.8 million. California law exempted retirement plans from a debtor's bankruptcy estate. When Witwer claimed that his retirement plan was exempt from

the bankruptcy estate, several creditors filed objections. The bankruptcy court held in favor of Witwer. The creditor appealed.

Issue

Is Witwer's retirement plan exempt from the bankruptcy estate?

Court's Reasoning

Under California law, the assets of a retirement plan are entirely exempt if the plan was designed and used for retirement purposes. The bankruptcy court found that the retirement plan established by Witwer fit this exemption. The court stated that although allowing the debtor to retain over $1.8 million in retirement benefits in bankruptcy while being discharged from debts legitimately owed to creditors seems fundamentally unfair, under the law, Witwer's retirement plan was beyond the reach of his creditors.

Decision and Remedy

The appellate panel upheld the bankruptcy court's decision that Witwer's retirement plan was fully exempt from his bankruptcy estate.

Case Questions

Critical Legal Thinking Do you think bankruptcy law was intended to reach the result in this case?

Business Ethics Was it ethical for the debtor to declare bankruptcy and wipe out his unsecured creditors while retaining $1.8 million in his retirement account?

Contemporary Business Should businesspeople establish and fund retirement programs?

Contemporary Environment
Homestead Exemptions

Long ago, many states enacted laws that protected a debtor's homestead from creditors. Depending on state law, at least a portion of the equity in a debtor's home may still be protected from creditors if the owner declares bankruptcy. Many states exempt between $20,000 and $70,000 of equity in a single person's or a married couple's home from a bankruptcy estate. The largest exemptions are in the following states:

■ **Florida** The Florida constitution and statutes give a homestead exemption from bankruptcy without dollar limit. The homestead is 160 acres outside a municipality and one-half acre inside a municipality.

■ **Texas** The Texas homestead exemption is even bigger than Florida's. Texas has an urban homestead of one acre and a rural homestead of up to 200 acres, without any dollar limit.

Florida and Texas are known as "debtors' havens" because of their generous homestead exemptions from bankruptcy. ■

Voidable Transfers

The Bankruptcy Code prevents debtors from making unusual payments or **transfers** of property on the eve of bankruptcy that would unfairly benefit the debtor or some creditors at the expense of others. The following paragraphs discuss the transfers that may be avoided by the bankruptcy court.

Preferential Transfers Within 90 Days Before Bankruptcy

A **preferential transfer** occurs when (1) a debtor transfers property to a creditor within 90 days before the filing of a petition in bankruptcy, (2) the transfer is made for an antecedent (preexisting) debt, and (3) the creditor would receive more from the transfer than it would from Chapter 7 liquidation. The Bankruptcy Code presumes that the debtor is insolvent during this 90-day period.

Consider This Example Assume that six months prior to filing for bankruptcy, a debtor purchases $10,000 of equipment on credit from a supplier. Within 90 days of filing the petition, the debtor still owes the money to this creditor, which is not due for 120 days. The debtor pays the creditor the $7,000 before filing the petition. In a Chapter 7 liquidation proceeding, the creditor would have received $1,000. This payment is a voidable preference because it was made within 90 days of filing the petition, was made to pay an antecedent debt, and gives the creditor more than he or she would receive in liquidation.

Business Brief

Sometimes prior to declaring bankruptcy, debtors transfer property to others as gifts or for less than fair market value, perhaps with a promise that the property will be returned to the debtor after the bankruptcy is over. This is *bankruptcy fraud.*

There are exceptions to the 90-day rule. They include (1) transfers for current consideration (e.g., equipment purchased for cash within 90 days of the petition), (2) credit payments made in the ordinary course of the debtor's business (e.g., supplies purchased on credit and paid for within the normal payment term of 30 days after purchase), and (3) payment of up to $600 by a consumer-debtor to a creditor within 90 days of the petition.

Preferential Liens

Debtors sometimes attempt to favor certain unsecured creditors on the eve of bankruptcy by giving them a secured interest in property. This type of interest is called a **preferential lien**. Preferential liens occur when (1) the debtor gives the creditor a secured interest in property within 90 days of petition, (2) the secured interest is given for preexisting debt, and (3) the creditor would receive more because of this lien than it would as an unsecured creditor in liquidation.

Consider This Example   On January 2, Debbie borrows $20,000 from her mother, which is an unsecured debt. Debbie later realizes she is not doing well financially and will have to declare Chapter 7 bankruptcy. On June 1, Debbie changes her mother from an unsecured creditor to being a secured creditor by giving her mother a lien on Debbie's car. Debbie files for Chapter 7 bankruptcy on July 1. This is a preferential lien that is voidable by the bankruptcy court.

Preferential Transfers to Insiders

The Bankruptcy Code provides that **preferential transfers and liens made to "insiders"** within one year of the filing of the petition in bankruptcy may be voided by the court. **Insiders** are defined as relatives, partners, partnerships, officers and directors of a corporation, corporations, and others who have a relationship with the debtor. To void a transfer to an insider within one-year period (other than the first 90 days prior to the petition), the trustee must prove that the debtor was insolvent at the time of the transfer.

Fraudulent Transfers

Section 548 of the Bankruptcy Code gives the court the power to avoid **fraudulent transfers** of property that occur within one year of the filing of the petition in bankruptcy. Any transfer of property by the debtor made with actual intent to "hinder, delay, or defraud" creditors is considered a voidable fraudulent transfer. The debtor's actual intent must be proved, although it may be inferred from the circumstances. For example, a transfer of property by an insolvent debtor for substantially less than fair market value would be voidable as a fraudulent transfer. In addition, Section 544(b) of the Bankruptcy Code gives the trustee the power to void fraudulent transfers made in violation of state fraudulent conveyances acts. Because these acts usually contain a longer statute of limitations (e.g., six years), a court can void any fraudulent transfer made during this period.

If a transfer is voided, a bona fide good faith purchaser must receive the value he or she paid for the property. Thus, if an insolvent debtor sold property worth $50,000 to a bona fide purchaser for $30,000 within the one-year period and the court rescinds the transfer, the trustee must return the $30,000 to the bona fide purchaser.

Business Ethics

Voidable Transfers

Often, a debtor who knows in advance that he or she is heading for bankruptcy will try to get assets out of his or her possession. That way, when bankruptcy comes, the only things left are the debts. Consider the following case.

Blair and Marie Woodfield and Parley and Deanna Pearce (Debtors), as partners, operated two "Wendy's Famous Hamburger" restaurants in Washington and Oregon, pursuant to a franchise from Wendy's International, Inc. On March, 10, 1989, Debtors filed their petitions for bankruptcy under Chapter 7.

Within 10 days prior to filing for bankruptcy, Debtors had formed a new corporation called Quality Foods, Inc. (QFI), in which they each held a 50 percent interest. They then transferred the franchise operating rights, equipment, fixtures, inventory, and restaurant supplies of the two restaurants to QFI. In addition, Woodfield transferred $10,000 cash and Pearce $6,954 cash to QFI within this 10-day period.

Associates (EVA), objected. Nevertheless, the bankruptcy court approved the abandonment, and the district court affirmed.

A creditor protested. The court of appeals held that Debtors transferred property with the intent to hinder, delay, and defraud their creditors. The court of appeals stated:

> The transaction here carried many badges of fraud. The relationship between the Debtors and QFI could not have been closer, the Debtors created and operated the transferee corporation. The transfer was admittedly made in anticipation of the bankruptcy filing. The partnership was admittedly in poor financial condition at the time, having defaulted on several obligations. Substantially all of the partnership's property relating to the Wendy's franchises was transferred, leaving nothing to satisfy the judgments. Because of this fraud, the court denied Debtors discharge. [*In re Woodfield*, 978 F.2d 516, 1992 U.S.App. Lexis 26902 (9th Cir. 1992)]

1. Did the debtors act unethically in this case? Did they act legally?
2. Do you think many debtors engage in insider and fraudulent transfers prior to declaring bankruptcy? ■

Statutory Distribution to Secured Creditors

Under Chapter 7, the nonexempt property of the bankruptcy estate must be **distributed** to the debtor's secured and unsecured creditors. The claim of a secured creditor to the debtor's property has priority over the claims of unsecured creditors. The secured creditor may (1) accept the collateral in full satisfaction of the debt, (2) foreclose on the collateral and use the proceeds to pay the debt, or (3) allow the trustee to retain the collateral, dispose of it at a sale, and remit the proceeds of the sale to him or her.

If the value of the collateral exceeds the secured interest, the excess becomes available to satisfy the claims of the debtor's unsecured creditors. Before the excess funds are released, however, the secured creditor is allowed to deduct reasonable fees and costs resulting from the default. If the value of the collateral is less than the secured interest, the secured creditor becomes an unsecured creditor to the difference.

Business Brief

Secured creditors are made whole in a Chapter 7 bankruptcy if the value of the collateral equals or exceeds the amount of their security interest.

Statutory Distribution to Unsecured Creditors

The Bankruptcy Code stipulates that unsecured claims are to be satisfied out of the bankruptcy estate in the order of their statutory priority. The statutory priority of an unsecured claim is as follows:

1. Fees and expenses of administering the estate, including court costs, trustee fees, attorneys' fees, appraisal fees, and other costs of administration.
2. In an involuntary bankruptcy, secured claims of "gap" creditors who sold goods or services on credit to the debtor in the ordinary course of the debtor's business between

Business Brief

The fees and expenses of administering the estate, including court costs, trustee fees, attorneys' fees, appraised fees, and other costs of administering the bankruptcy are the first unsecured claims to be paid.

the date of the filing of the petition and the date of the appointment of the trustee or issuance of the order for relief (whichever occurred first).

3. Unsecured claims for wages, salary, or commissions earned by the debtor's employees within 90 days immediately preceding the filing of the petition, up to $4,000 per employee; any claim exceeding $4,000 is treated as a claim of a general unsecured creditor (see item 9).

4. Unsecured claims for contributions to employee benefit plans based on services performed within 180 days immediately preceding the filing of the petition, up to $4,000 per employee.

5. Farm producers and fishermen against debtors who operate grain storage facilities or fish storage or processing facilities, up to $4,000 per claim.

6. Unsecured claims for cash deposited by a consumer with the debtor prior to the filing of the petition in connection with the purchase, lease, or rental of property or the purchase of services that were not delivered or provided by the debtor, up to $1,800 per claim.

7. Debts owed for child support, paternity, alimony, and spousal support.

8. Certain tax obligations owed by the debtor to federal, state, and local governmental units.

9. Claims of general unsecured creditors.

10. If there is any balance remaining after the allowed claims of the creditors are satisfied, it is returned to the debtor.

Each class must be paid in full before any lower class is paid anything. If a class cannot be paid in full, the claims of that class are paid *pro rata* (proportionately).

Business Brief

Generally, unsecured creditors after receive little, if anything, in a Chapter 7 bankruptcy.

Discharge

In a Chapter 7 bankruptcy, after the property is distributed to satisfy the allowed claims, the remaining unpaid claims are **discharged** (i.e., the debtor is no longer legally responsible for them). Only individuals may be granted a discharge. Discharge is not available to partnerships and corporations. These entities must liquidate under state law before or upon completion of the Chapter 7 proceeding. A debtor can be granted a discharge in a Chapter 7 proceeding only once every six years.

Consider This Example   Maryjane files for Chapter 7 bankruptcy. At the time of filing, she has many unsecured creditors. Nordstrom Department Store is one of them. She owes Nordstrom $3,000. The bankruptcy estate has only enough assets to pay unsecured creditors $.10 on the dollar. Nordstrom receives $300, and the remaining $2,700 is discharged. Nordstrom cannot thereafter collect this money and will write it off as a bad debt.

Nondischargeable Debts

Business Brief

Not all debts are dischargeable in bankruptcy.

The following debts are not dischargeable in a Chapter 7 proceeding:

■ Claims for taxes accrued within three years prior to the filing of the petition in bankruptcy

■ Certain fines and penalties payable to federal, state, and local governmental units

■ Claims based on the debtor's liability for causing willful or malicious injury to a person or property

- Claims arising from the fraud, larceny, or embezzlement by the debtor while acting in a fiduciary capacity

- Alimony, maintenance, and child support

- Unscheduled claims

- Claims based on the consumer-debtor's purchase of luxury goods of more than $1,000 from a single creditor within 60 days of the order for relief

- Cash advances in excess of $1,000 obtained by a consumer-debtor by use of a revolving line of credit or credit cards within 60 days of the order for relief

- Judgments and consent decrees against the debtor for liability incurred as a result of the debtor's operation of a motor vehicle while legally intoxicated

Creditors who have nondischargeable claims against the debtor may participate in the distribution of the bankruptcy estate. The nondischarged balance may be pursued by the creditor against the debtor after bankruptcy.

In the following case, the U.S. Supreme Court ruled that a debt was dischargeable in bankruptcy.

> *Beggars can never be bankrupt.*
>
> Thomas Fuller
> *Gnomologia (1732)*

U.S. SUPREME COURT CASE
Kawaauhau v. Geiger
523 U.S. 57, 118 S.Ct. 974, 1998 U.S. Lexis 1595 (1998)
Supreme Court of the United States

Case 23.2
Discharge of Debts

Background and Facts

Margaret Kawaauhau sought treatment from Dr. Paul Geiger for a foot injury. Geiger examined Kawaauhau and admitted her to the hospital to attend to the risks of infection. Although Geiger knew that intravenous penicillin would have been the more effective treatment, he prescribed oral penicillin, explaining that he thought that his patient wished to minimize the cost of her treatment. Geiger then departed on a business trip, leaving Kawaauhau in the care of other physicians. When Geiger returned, he discontinued all antibiotics because he believed that the infection had subsided. Kawaauhau's condition deteriorated over the next few days, requiring the amputation of her right leg below the knee. Kawaauhau and her husband sued Geiger for medical malpractice. The jury found Geiger liable and awarded the Kawaauhaus $355,000 in damages. Geiger, who carried no malpractice insurance, filed for bankruptcy in an attempt to discharge the judgment. The bankruptcy court denied discharge, and the district court agreed. The court of appeals reversed and allowed discharge, and the Kawaauhaus appealed to the U.S. Supreme Court.

Issue

Is a debt arising from a medical malpractice judgment that is attributable to negligent or reckless conduct dischargeable in bankruptcy?

Court's Reasoning

Section 523(a)(b) of the Bankruptcy Code provides that a debt "for willful and malicious injury by the debtor to another" is not dischargeable. The question before the Supreme Court was whether a debt arising from a medical malpractice judgment, attributable to negligent or reckless conduct, fell within this statutory exception. The Supreme Court held that the exception that prohibits willful and malicious acts from being discharged in bankruptcy does not apply to debts arising from negligent or reckless conduct. Therefore, the Kawaauhaus' medical malpractice judgment against Dr. Geiger in this case could be discharged in Dr. Geiger's bankruptcy proceeding

Decision and Remedy

The U.S. Supreme Court ruled that a medical malpractice judgment based on negligent or reckless conduct—and not intentional conduct—is dischargeable in bankruptcy. The Supreme Court affirmed the decision of the court of appeals.

Case Questions

Critical Legal Thinking   What public policy is promoted by denying discharge for "willful" injurious conduct? Do you think Geiger's conduct was willful?

Business Ethics   Was it ethical for Geiger to avoid liability to the Kawaauhaus by declaring bankruptcy?

Contemporary Business   What purpose is served by allowing individuals and business to declare bankruptcy? What are the business implications of bankruptcy laws?

Acts That Bar Discharge

Any party of interest may file an objection to the discharge of a debt. The court will then hold a hearing. Discharge of the unsatisfied debts will be denied if the debtor:

- Made false representations about his or her financial position when he or she obtained an extension of credit.
- Transferred, concealed, or removed property from the estate with the intent to hinder, delay, or defraud creditors.
- Falsified, destroyed, or concealed records of his or her financial condition.
- Failed to account for any assets.
- Failed to submit to questioning at the meeting of the creditors (unless excused).

If the discharge is obtained through the fraud of the debtor, a party of interest may bring a motion to have the bankruptcy revoked. The bankruptcy court may revoke a discharge within one year after it is granted.

Discharge of Student Loans

For any bankruptcy case commenced after October 7, 1998, Section 523 (a)(8)(A) of the Bankruptcy Code mandates that **student loans** can be **discharged** in bankruptcy only if nondischarge would cause an "undue hardship" to the debtor and his or her dependents [Higher Education Amendments of 1998, P.L. 105–244]. Undue hardship is construed strictly and would include not being able to pay for food or shelter for the debtor or the debtor's family.

Cosigners (e.g., parents who guarantee their child's student loan) must also meet the heightened undue hardship test to discharge their obligation.

Chapter 11 Reorganization Bankruptcy

Chapter 11 of the Bankruptcy Code provides a method for reorganizing a debtor's financial affairs under the supervision of the bankruptcy court.[3] Its goal is to reorganize the debtor with a new capital structure so that it will emerge from bankruptcy as a viable concern. This option, which is referred to as **reorganization bankruptcy**, is often in the best interests of the debtor and its creditors.

Reorganization Proceeding

Chapter 11 is available to individuals, partnerships, corporations, nonincorporated associations, and railroads. It is not available to banks, savings and loan associations, credit unions, insurance companies, stockbrokers, or commodities brokers. The majority of Chapter 11 proceedings are filed by corporations.

A Chapter 11 petition may be filed voluntarily by the debtor or involuntarily by its creditors. The principles discussed earlier under Chapter 7 regarding the filing of petitions, the first meeting of creditors, the entry of the order for relief, automatic stay, and relief from stay also apply to Chapter 11 proceedings.

Debtor-in-Possession

In most Chapter 11 cases, the debtor is left in place to operate the business during the reorganization proceeding. In such cases, the debtor is called a **debtor-in-possession**. The court may appoint a trustee to operate the debtor's business only upon a showing of cause, such as fraud, dishonesty, or gross mismanagement by the debtor or its management. Even if a trustee is not appointed, however, the court may appoint an examiner to investigate the debtor's financial affairs.

The debtor-in-possession (or the trustee, if one is appointed) has the same powers and duties as a trustee in a Chapter 7 proceeding. In addition, the debtor-in-possession (or trustee) is empowered to operate the debtor's business during the bankruptcy proceeding. This power includes authority to enter into contracts, purchase supplies, incur debts, and so on. Some suppliers will accept only cash for their goods or services during this time, whereas others will extend credit. Credit extended by postpetition unsecured creditors in the ordinary course of business is given automatic priority as an administrative expense in bankruptcy. Further, upon notice and hearing, the court may create a secured interest by granting a postpetition unsecured creditor a lien on the debtor-in-possession's property.

Creditors' Committees

Business Brief

In 2002, the telecommunications company WorldCom, Inc., filed for Chapter 11 bankruptcy. This was the largest bankruptcy filing in U.S. history.

Once an order for relief is granted, the court will appoint **a creditors' committee** composed of representatives of the class of unsecured claims. Generally, the creditors holding the seven largest claims are appointed to the committee. The court may also appoint a committee of secured creditors and a committee of equity holders. Committee members owe a fiduciary duty to represent the interest of the class. Committees may appear at bankruptcy court hearings, participate in the negotiation of a plan of reorganization, assert objections to proposed plans, and the like.

Automatic Stay

The filing of a voluntary or an involuntary petition automatically stays—that is, suspends—certain action by creditors against the debtor or the debtor's property. This is called an **automatic stay**. The stay, which applies to collection efforts of both secured and unsecured creditors, is designed to prevent a scramble of the debtor's assets in a variety of court proceedings. The following creditor actions are stayed:

1. Instituting or maintaining legal actions to collect prepetition debts
2. Enforcing judgments obtained against the debtor
3. Obtaining, perfecting, or enforcing liens against property of the debtor
4. Attempting to set off debts owed by the creditor to the debtor against the creditor's claims in bankruptcy.
5. Nonjudicial collection efforts, such as self-help activities (e.g., repossession of a car)

The court also has the authority to issue injunctions preventing creditor activity not covered by the automatic stay provision. Actions to recover alimony and child support are not stayed in bankruptcy. The automatic stay does not preclude collection efforts by creditors against co-debtors and guarantors of the bankrupt debtor's debts, except (1) in a Chapter 13 bankruptcy (discussed later in this chapter) or (2) if the co-debtor is also in bankruptcy.

Business Brief

The importance of the automatic stay in bankruptcy should not be underestimated. For example, in *Pennzoil v. Texaco*, Texaco filed a voluntary petition in bankruptcy to stay any attempt by Pennzoil to perfect its $10 billion judgment against Texaco.

Relief from Stay A secured creditor may petition the court for a **relief from stay**, which usually occurs in situations involving depreciating assets where the secured property is not adequately protected during the bankruptcy proceeding. The court may opt to provide adequate protection rather than grant relief from stay. In such cases, the court may (1) order cash payments equal to the amount of the depreciation, (2) grant an additional or replacement lien, or (3) grant an "indubitable equivalent" (e.g., a guarantee from a solvent party).

Contemporary Environment
Small Business Bankruptcy

Large firms, such as Macy's, Continental Airlines, and Dow Corning, have reorganized under Chapter 11 of the Bankruptcy Code. These large firms have resources to hire lawyers, investment bankers, and other professionals, to assist them in the time-consuming and expensive Chapter 11 reorganization process. Smaller firms often do not have the resources or the luxury of the time necessary to use a Chapter 11 proceeding, however.

To address this problem, Congress enacted the **Bankruptcy Reform Act of 1994**, which amended Chapter 11. **Section 217**

of this act permits business with total debts of less than $2 million to elect a "fast-track" for processing its Chapter 11 case. This procedure makes creditors' committees optional and sets up deadlines aimed at concluding the Chapter 11 case within 160 days of the bankruptcy filing. Section 217 "small business bankruptcy" provides an efficient and cost-saving method for smaller firms to seek bankruptcy protection and reorganize as a going concern using Chapter 11 of the Bankruptcy Code. ■

Plan of Reorganization

The debtor has the exclusive right to file a **plan of reorganization** with the bankruptcy court within the first 120 days after the date of the order for relief. The debtor also has the right to obtain creditor approval of the plan within the first 180 days after the date of the order. After that, any party of interest (i.e., a trustee, a creditor, an equity holder) may propose a plan. The court has discretion to extend the 120- and 180-day periods in complex cases.

The plan of reorganization sets forth the debtor's proposed new capital structure. In a Chapter 11 proceeding, creditors have claims and equity holders have interests. The plan must designate the different classes of claims and interests. The reorganization plan may propose altering the rights of creditors and equity holders. For example, it might require the reduction of claims and interests, the conversion of unsecured creditors to equity holders, the sale of assets, or the like.

> **Business Brief**
>
> In a Chapter 11 proceeding, creditors have *claims* and equity holders have *interests*.

Disclosure Statement

The debtor must supply the creditors and equity holders with a **disclosure statement** that contains adequate information about the proposed plan of reorganization. The court must approve the disclosure statement before it is distributed.

Executory Contracts

Under the Bankruptcy Code, the debtor-in-possession (or trustee) is given the authority to assume or reject **executory contracts** (i.e., contracts that are not fully performed by both sides). In general, unfavorable executory contracts will be rejected and favorable executory contracts will be assumed. For example, a debtor-in-possession may reject an unfavorable lease. Court approval is necessary to reject an executory contract. Executory contracts may also be rejected in Chapter 7 and Chapter 13 proceedings.

> **Business Brief**
>
> Chapter 11 reorganization bankruptcy permits a debtor to assume or reject executory contracts, such as leases for office space, and sales and purchase contracts.
>
> **Business Brief**
>
> A collective bargaining agreement may be rejected or modified as an executory contract if (1) it is necessary to the reorganization, (2) the debtor acted in good faith, and (3) the balance of the equities favors rejection or modification of the agreement.

Rejection of Collective Bargaining Agreements   Companies that file for Chapter 11 reorganization sometimes argue that agreements with labor unions that still have years to run are executory contracts that may be rejected in bankruptcy. The U.S. Supreme Court has upheld the right of companies to reject union contracts in bankruptcy.[4] In one case, the Court held that rejection was permitted if necessary for the successful rehabilitation of the debtor.

Subsequently, labor unions lobbied Congress for a change in the law. Congress responded by enacting Section 1113 of the 1984 amendments to the Bankruptcy Code.

Section 1113 established the following multistep process that must be followed before a collective bargaining agreement may be rejected or modified:

1. The debtor must make a proposal to the union regarding the modification of the agreement.
2. The debtor must meet with the union to discuss the proposal.
3. The court must hold a hearing if the union refuses to accept the proposal.

If these requirements are met, the court may order the modification or rejection of the labor agreement if (1) such rejection or modification is necessary to the reorganization, (2) the debtor acted in good faith, and (3) the balance of equities favor rejection or modification of the collective bargaining agreement.

Confirmation of a Plan of Reorganization

The final step in Chapter 11 bankruptcy is **confirmation** of the plan of reorganization by the court. A plan of reorganization must be confirmed by the court before it becomes effective. If more than one plan is proposed, the court may confirm only one plan. Classes of creditors and interests must be given the opportunity to vote to accept or reject the plan before the court considers its confirmation. Under **Section 1129(a)**—that is, the **acceptance method**—the court must confirm a plan of reorganization if the following tests are met:

1. The plan must be in the best interests of each class of claims and interests, as indicated by either (a) a unanimous vote of acceptance by the members of the class or (b) the property received by the class members under the plan being worth at least as much as they would receive upon liquidation.
2. The plan must be feasible. That is, the debtor must have a good probability of surviving as a going concern. The court examines the debtor's estimated earnings and expenses as proposed by the plan before making this determination.
3. At least one class of claims must vote to accept the plan. A plan is deemed accepted by a class of claims if at least one-half the number of creditors who vote to accept the plan and the accepting creditors represent two-thirds the dollar amount of allowed claims who vote.
4. Each class of claims and interests is nonimpaired. A class is nonimpaired if (a) its legal, equitable, and contractual rights are unaltered by the plan or (b) the class votes to accept the plan. A class of claims accepts the plan if one-half the number who vote accept the plan and they represent two thirds the dollar amount of allowed claims that vote to accept the plan. A class of interests accepts a plan if at least two-thirds of the number of interests that vote accept the plan.

> **Business Brief**
>
> Creditors and equity holders are given the opportunity to vote on the confirmation of a plan of reorganization.

A plan of reorganization cannot discriminate unfairly against members of a class. For example, no members of any class can receive more than any other member of that class. No class of claims or interests may be paid more than the full amount of its claim.

Cram Down   If a dissenting class of claims is impaired, the plan of reorganization cannot be confirmed for the dissenting class via the acceptance method. The court can, however, force an impaired class to participate in a plan of reorganization under the **cram down method** of **Section 1129(b)**. As discussed in the following paragraphs, to be crammed down, the plan must be fair and equitable to the impaired class:

■ *Secured creditors.* A plan is fair and equitable to an impaired class of secured creditors if the reorganization allows the class to (1) retain its lien on the collateral (whether the property is retained by the debtor or transferred to another party), (2) place a lien on the proceeds from the sale of the collateral, or (3) receive an "indubitable equivalent," such as a lien on other property.

> **Business Brief**
>
> The term *cram down* derives from the notion that the plan of reorganization is being "crammed down the throats" of the impaired dissenting class

■ *Unsecured creditors.* A reorganization plan is fair and equitable to an impaired class of unsecured creditors if (1) that class is paid cash or property that has a discounted present value equal to the allowed amount of the claim or (2) no class below it receives anything in the plan (the **absolute priority rule**).[5]

■ *Equity holders.* A plan is fair and equitable to an impaired class of equity holders if that class is paid the greater of (1) the fixed liquidation preference (if any), (2) the fixed redemption preference (if any), or (3) the discounted present value of their equity interest. Alternatively, the absolute priority rule can be applied to an impaired equity class if no class below it receives anything.

Consider This Example   Assume that in a Chapter 11 case there is a class of secured creditors, a class of unsecured creditors, and a class of equity holders. The secured creditors vote to accept the plan. The unsecured creditors, who are impaired because they are given only 10 percent of their claim, vote to reject the plan. Nevertheless, the plan can be crammed down on the unsecured class under the absolute priority rule if the plan does not give the equity holders anything.

Discharge

Upon confirmation of a plan of reorganization, the debtor is granted a **discharge** of all claims not included in the plan. The plan is binding on all parties once it is confirmed.

Contemporary Environment
Kmart Emerges from Bankruptcy

The Kmart Corporation was founded in 1899 and became one of the most successful retailers in America. The company offered goods for sale at low prices and was famous for its spontaneous "Blue Light Special" sales offered to consumers while they were in Kmart stores. Kmart's business model consisted of building stores bigger than its competitors and offering goods for sale that it purchased at volume discounts from vendors. By 2000, Kmart had more than 2,100 stores nationwide.

Kmart's strategy worked for most of the twentieth century, until formidable competition appeared—Wal-Mart and Target stores. Wal-Mart's larger warehouse stores and lower prices stole customers from Kmart. And Target offered more trendy brand names than Kmart. Kmart fought back but eventually lost the battle to these competitors. Kmart's shelves became emp-

tier as many vendors refused to deliver goods to Kmart unless they were paid in cash.

In 2002, Kmart filed for Chapter 11 bankruptcy. It was the largest bankruptcy filed by a retailer in America. Once under the protection of the federal bankruptcy laws, Kmart used the executory contract rule, shed more than 300 leases on its worst-performing stores, and closed these stores. Kmart also used its bankruptcy reorganization to discharge billions of dollars of unpaid unsecured credit owed to creditors.

Kmart is a good example of how a financially troubled company can use Chapter 11 reorganization bankruptcy to rid itself of problem debts and obligations and have a "fresh start." Kmart emerged from bankruptcy with a leaner balance sheet and the ability to make a profit again. Once out of bankruptcy, creditors and vendors again sold goods to Kmart. ■

Chapter 13 Consumer Debt Adjustment

Chapter 13, which is called **consumer debt adjustment**, is a rehabilitation form of bankruptcy for natural persons. Chapter 13 permits the court to supervise the debtor's plan for the payment of unpaid debts by installments.

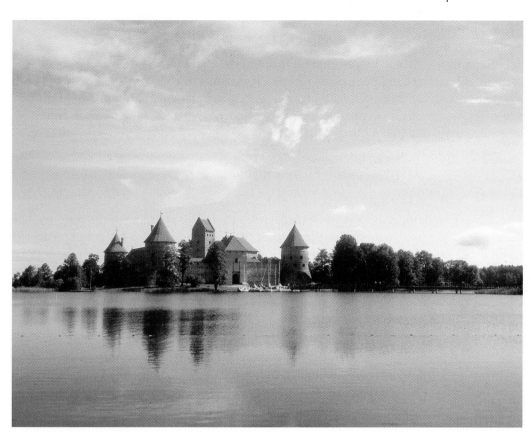

Lithuania. Other countries of the world have developed credit and bankruptcy laws.

The debtor has several advantages under Chapter 13. These include avoiding the stigma of Chapter 7 liquidation, retaining more property than is exempt under Chapter 7 and incurring less expense than in a Chapter 7 proceeding. The creditors have advantages, too: They may recover a greater percentage of the debts owed them than they would under a Chapter 7 proceeding.

Filing the Petition

A Chapter 13 proceeding can be initiated only by the voluntary filing of a petition by a debtor who alleges that he or she is (1) insolvent or (2) unable to pay his or her debts when they become due. The petition must state that the debtor desires to effect an extension or composition of debts, or both. An **extension** provides for a longer period of time for the debtor to pay his or her debts. A **composition** provides for a reduction of debts.

Only individuals (including sole proprietors) with regular income who owe individually (or with their spouses) noncontingent, liquidated, unsecured debts of less than $250,000 and secured debts of less than $750,000 may file such a petition. The key is the debtor's regular income, which may be from any source, including wages, salary, commissions, income from investments, Social Security, pension income, or public assistance. The amount of the debtor's assets is irrelevant. Most Chapter 13 petitions are filed by home owners who want to protect nonexempt equity in their residences.

When (or shortly after) the petition is filed, the debtor must file a list of creditors, assets, and liabilities with the court. The court then schedules a meeting of creditors. The debtor must appear at this meeting. Creditors may submit proof of claims, which will be allowed or disallowed by the court. No creditor committees are appointed, but the court must appoint a trustee upon confirmation of the plan.

Business Brief

A Chapter 13 proceeding can be initiated only by the voluntary filing of a petition by the debtor. Creditors cannot file an involuntary petition to place a debtor in Chapter 13 bankruptcy.

Business Brief

Chapter 13 is a form of reorganization bankruptcy. The debtor must file a proposed *plan of payment* for how the debts are to be rescheduled.

Automatic Stay

The filing of a Chapter 13 petition automatically stays (1) liquidation bankruptcy proceedings, (2) judicial and nonjudicial actions by creditors to collect prepetition debts from the debtor, and (3) collection activities against co-debtors and guarantors of consumer debts. The automatic stay continues until the Chapter 13 plan is completed or dismissed. The stay does not apply to business debts.

Plan of Payment

The debtor's plan of payment must be filed within 15 days of the filing of the petition. The debtor must file information about his or her finances, including a budget of estimated income and expenses during the period of the plan. The plan period cannot exceed three years unless the court approves a longer period (of up to five years). During the plan period, the debtor retains possession of his or her property, may acquire new property and incur debts, and so on.

The debtor must begin making the planned installment payments to the trustee within 30 days after the plan is filed. These interim payments must continue until the plan is confirmed or denied. If the plan is denied, the trustee must return the interim payments to the debtor less any administrative costs. If the plan is converged, the debtor must continue making payments to the trustee. The trustee is responsible for remitting these payments to the creditors. The trustee is paid 10 percent of the debts paid under the plan.

A Chapter 13 plan may be modified if the debtor's circumstances materially change. For example, if the debtor's income subsequently decreases, the court may decrease the debtor's payments under the plan. A request for the modification of a plan may be made by the debtor, the trustee, or a creditor. If an interested party objects to the modification, the court must hold a hearing to determine whether it should be approved.

Confirmation of the Plan

The plan of payment may modify the rights of unsecured creditors and some secured creditors. Any objections they have may be voiced at the confirmation hearing held by the court. The plan must (1) be proposed in good faith, (2) pass the feasibility test (e.g., the debtor must be able to make the proposed payments, and (3) be in the best interests of the creditors (i.e., the present value of the payments must equal or exceed the amount that the creditors would receive in a Chapter 7 liquidation proceeding).

Secured Creditors The plan must be submitted to the secured creditors for acceptance. The plan will be confirmed if the secured creditors unanimously accept it. If a secured creditor does not accept the plan, the court may still confirm the plan if (1) it permits the secured creditor to retain its lien and the value of the plan's distribution to the creditor is more than its secured interest or (2) the debtor surrenders the property securing the claim to the secured creditor.

Unsecured Creditors Although a vote of unsecured creditors is not required for confirmation of a Chapter 13 plan, their objection to the plan can delay or defeat confirmation. The court cannot confirm the plan unless (1) it proposes to pay the objecting unsecured creditor the present value of his or her claim or (2) the debtor agrees to commit all of his or her disposable income during the plan period to pay his or her creditors. (Disposable income is all income not necessary to maintain the debtor and his or her dependents.)

Law cannot persuade, where it cannot punish.

Thomas Fuller
Gnomologia (1732)

Consider This Example   Suppose a debtor earns $1,800 per month, of which $1,200 is reasonably necessary to support the debtor and his or her family. If the $400 per month disposable income is committed to pay prepetition debts, the court may confirm the plan even if the debts of the unsecured creditors are substantially modified or liquidated.

Discharge

The court will grant an order **discharging** the debtor from all unpaid debts covered by the plan after all the payments required under the plan are completed. All debts are dischargeable under Chapter 13 except alimony and child support and priority debts such as trustee fees.

Dischargeable debts include student loans, fraudulently incurred debts, and debts arising from malicious or willful injury from drunken driving. Thus, a Chapter 13 discharge may be more beneficial to a debtor than a Chapter 7 liquidation discharge. A discharge can be revoked within one year if it was obtained by fraud. Thus, a debtor may file successive petitions for Chapter 13 bankruptcy.

Hardship Discharge   Even if the debtor does not complete the payments called for in the plan, the court may grant the debtor a **hardship discharge**. Such a discharge will be granted if (1) the debtor fails to complete the payments due to unforeseeable circumstances (e.g., the debtor loses his or her job through no fault of his or her own), (2) the unsecured creditors have been paid as much as they would have been paid in a Chapter 7 liquidation proceeding, and (3) it is not practical to modify the plan.

Chapter 12 Family Farmer Bankruptcy

In the 1980s, farms across the United States experienced financial difficulty as farm prices and real estate values fell. Many farmers who found it difficult to meet their financial obligations and faced bankruptcy lobbied Congress for help. In 1986, Congress responded and added **Chapter 12** to the Bankruptcy Code. Chapter 12 gives "family farmers"— defined as farmers whose total debt does not exceed $1.5 million and are at least 80 percent farm related—a special form of bankruptcy protection.

Chapter 12 is a reorganization provision that allows family farmers to reorganize financially. Upon filing, an automatic stay goes into place against creditors' actions against the family farmer. The farmer-debtor must file a plan of reorganization within 90 days of the order for relief. Creditors cannot vote on the plan of reorganization.

The major provision of Chapter 12 allows family farmers to have mortgage loans rewritten to the fair market value of the property in cases where the value of the farm land has decreased below the value of the loan. For example, assume that a farm is worth $1,000,000 at the time a family farmer borrows $800,000 from Rural Bank, which takes back a mortgage on the farm for this amount. After several years, the farmer suffers financial difficulty and files Chapter 12 bankruptcy. At the time of the bankruptcy filing, the farm land is worth only $500,000. Under Chapter 12, the mortgage is reduced to $500,000 under the plan of reorganization.

Contemporary Environment

Sarbanes-Oxley Act Imposes Criminal Penalties for Bankruptcy Fraud

When Congress enacted the **Sarbanes-Oxley Act of 2002** to revise the corporate governance rules in this country, Congress included **Section 802** in the act to address the issue of hiding fraud that led to bankruptcies. Section 802 makes it a crime for anyone to knowingly alter, destroy, mutilate, conceal, cover up, falsify, or make a false entry in any record, document, or tangible object with the intent to impede, obstruct, or influence the investigation or proper administration of any matter in any bankruptcy case, or in relation to or in contemplation of a bankruptcy filing. A violation is punishable by a fine or imprisonment for not more than 20 years, or both. ■

Chapter Summary

Federal Bankruptcy Code, p. 484

Bankruptcy

1. *Bankruptcy Reform Act of 1978; as amended.* This federal statute establishes the requirements and procedures for filing bankruptcy. Called the *Bankruptcy Code.*
2. *Bankruptcy courts.* Bankruptcy courts have exclusive jurisdiction to hear bankruptcy cases. A bankruptcy court is attached to each federal district court. Bankruptcy judges are appointed for 14 year terms.

The "Fresh Start"

The purpose of a bankruptcy is to discharge the debtor from burdensome debts.

Chapter 7 Liquidation Bankruptcy, p. 485

Chapter 7 Bankruptcy

In Chapter 7 bankruptcy, the debtor's nonexempt property is sold for cash, the cash is distributed to the creditors, and any unpaid debts are discharged. Also called *liquidation bankruptcy.*

Bankruptcy Procedure

1. *Filing a petition.* The filing of a petition commences a bankruptcy case.
   a. *Voluntary petition.* A voluntary petition is filed by the debtor.
   b. *Involuntary petition.* An involuntary petition is filed by a creditor or creditors.
2. *Order for relief.* An order for relief designates that the bankruptcy court has accepted a case for further proceedings.
3. *Meeting of the creditors.* The debtor must appear at this meeting and answer questions by the creditors. Also called the *first meeting of the creditors.*
4. *Appointments of a trustee.* A *permanent trustee* is elected at the first meeting of the creditors in a Chapter 7 case.
5. *Proof of claims.* Unsecured creditors must file proof of claim, stating the amount of their claims against the debtors.

Automatic Stay

The filing of a bankruptcy petition *stays* (suspends) certain legal actions against the debtor or the debtor's property.

Relief from stay. A secured creditor may petition the court for a relief from stay in situations involving depreciating assets and when the creditor is not adequately protected during the bankruptcy proceeding.

Property of the Bankruptcy Estate

The *bankruptcy estate* includes:

1. All the debtor's legal and equitable interests in real, personal, tangible, and intangible property at the time the petition if filed.
2. Gifts, inheritances, life insurance proceeds, and property from divorce settlements that the debtor is entitled to receive within 180 days after the petition is filed.

Exempt Property

The Bankruptcy Code permits the debtor to retain certain property that does not become part of the bankruptcy estate. Exemptions are stipulated in federal and state law.

Voidable Transfers

The following transfers and preferences are voidable by the trustee:

1. *Preferential transfer within 90 days before bankruptcy.* Transfer is for an antecedent debt and gives the creditor more than he or she would receive in bankruptcy.
2. *Preferential liens within 90 days before bankruptcy.* Transfer is for an antecedent debt, and the creditor receives more because of this lien than he or she would as an unsecured creditor in bankruptcy.
3. *Preferential transfer to an insider within one year before bankruptcy.* The transferee is an "insider" (e.g., relative, business associate), and the creditor is insolvent.
4. *Fraudulent transfer within one year before bankruptcy.* The debtor transfers property with the actual intent to hinder, delay, or defraud creditors.

Priority of Distribution

Nonexempt property of the bankruptcy estate is distributed to the creditors in the following statutory priority:

1. *Secured creditors.* Either a secured creditor obtains the collateral or the collateral is sold and the secured creditor is paid. If the value of the collateral exceeds the secured interest, the excess becomes available to pay other creditors. If the value of the collateral is less than the secured interest, the secured creditor becomes an unsecured creditor to the difference.
2. *Unsecured creditors.* Unsecured creditors are paid in the priority established by the Bankruptcy Code. Each class must be paid in full before any lower class is paid anything. If a class cannot be paid in full, the claims of that class are paid *pro rata* (proportionately).

Discharge

After the nonexempt property is distributed, the remaining unpaid claims of the debtor are *discharged*, the debtor's legal obligation to pay these unpaid debts is terminated. Discharge is available only to individuals.

Nondischargeable Debts

The Bankruptcy Code stipulates that certain debts are not dischargeable.

Acts That Bar Discharge

A bankruptcy court may deny discharge of debts if the debtor has engaged in prohibited conduct.

Discharge of Student Loans

A student loan may be discharged after it is due only if nondischarge would cause an *undue hardship* on the debtor or his or her family.

Chapter II Reorganization Bankruptcy, p. 494

Chapter 11 Reorganization Bankruptcy

Chapter 11 bankruptcy provides a method for reorganizing the debtor's financial affairs under the supervision of the bankruptcy court.

Reorganization Proceeding

The principles discussed for Chapter 7 regarding the filing of petitions, the first meeting of the creditors, the entry for the order of relief, and automatic stay also apply to Chapter 11 proceedings.

Debtor-In-Possession

In most Chapter 11 cases, the debtor is left in place to operate the business during the reorganization proceeding. In such cases, the debtor is called *debtor-in-possession*.

Trustee The court may appoint a trustee to operate the debtor's business only upon a showing of cause, such as fraud, dishonesty, or gross mismanagement by the debtor or its management.

Creditors' Committees

The court will appoint a committee of unsecured creditors (usually creditors holding the seven largest claims). The court may also appoint committees of secured creditors and equity holders. Committees participate in the bankruptcy proceeding and in the negotiation of a plan of reorganization.

Small Business Bankruptcy

Bankruptcy Reform Act of 1994. This federal statute provides a less-costly and faster procedure for small businesses to file, maintain, and emerge from a Chapter 11 bankruptcy proceeding.

Plan of Reorganization

This plan sets forth the debtor's proposed new capital structure. The debtor has the exclusive right to file a plan within the first 120 days after the date of the order for relief.

Disclosure Statement

The debtor must supply the creditors and equity holders with a disclosure statement that contains adequate information about the proposed plan of reorganization.

Executory Contracts

The debtor-in-possession (or trustee) may assume or reject executory contracts. A special procedure has been established for rejecting union collective bargaining agreements.

Confirmation of a Plan of Reorganization

A plan of reorganization must be confirmed by the bankruptcy court before it becomes effective. Confirmation may be by either of the following methods:

Confirmation by the acceptance method. This type of confirmation is established by Section 1129(a) of the Bankruptcy Code.

Confirmation by the cram down method. This type of confirmation is provided for by Section 1129(b) of the Bankruptcy Code.

Discharge

Upon confirmation of a plan of reorganization, the debtor is granted a discharge of all claims not included in the plan. The debtor's legal obligation to pay the discharged debts is terminated.

Chapter 13 Consumer Debt Adjustment, p. 498

Chapter 13 Consumer Debt Adjustment

Chapter 13 is a rehabilitation form of bankruptcy that permits bankruptcy courts to supervise the debtor's plan for the repayment of unpaid debts by installment. Called *consumer debt adjustment* or *Chapter 13 bankruptcy*.

The Plan of Payment

The debtor must file a plan of payment. The plan period cannot exceed three years unless the court approves a longer period (of up to five years). A plan may be modified if the debtor's circumstances materially change.

Trustee. A permanent trustee will be appointed by the court. The debtor makes payments to the trustee, who is responsible for remitting payments to the creditors.

Discharge

The court will grant an order discharging the debtor from all unpaid debts covered by the plan only after all the payments required under the plan are completed.

Hardship discharge. The court can grant the debtor a hardship discharge even if the debtor does not complete the payments called for by the plan if (1) the failure to make the payments was caused by an unforeseeable circumstance, (2) the creditors have been paid as much as they would have been paid in a Chapter 7 liquidation proceeding, and (3) it is not practical to modify the plan.

Chapter 12 Family Farmer Bankruptcy, p. 501

Chapter 12 Family Farmer Bankruptcy

Chapter 12 is a rehabilitation form of bankruptcy that provides a method for reorganizing the family farmer debtor's financial affairs under the supervision of the bankruptcy court.

Family Farmer

A family farmer is defined by the Bankruptcy Code as a farmer whose total debts do not exceed $1.5 million and are at least 80 percent farm related.

Plan of Reorganization

A plan of reorganization can only be filed by the farmer-debtor. The plan provides that mortgage loans will be rewritten to the fair market value of the farm land if the value of the farm land has decreased below the value of the loan.

Internet Exercises and Case Questions
Working the Web Internet Exercises

Activities

1. Check on current statistics on the number of bankruptcies filed at **www. abiworld.org/stats/newstatsfront.html** and "InterNet Bankruptcy Library—Worldwide Troubled Company Resources and Daily Source of Bankruptcy News," at **www.bankrupt.com**.

2. What is the amount of your state's homestead exemption? More theory may be found in "The Outer Boundaries of

the Bankruptcy Estate," at **www.law.emory.edu/ELJ/ volumes/fall98/plank.html**.

3. The FTC has practical advice for debtors at **www.ftc.gov/ bcp/conline/pubs/credit/kneedeep.htm**.

4. Why do we have bankruptcy? Theoretical underpinnings of bankruptcy are explored in "Bankruptcy's Organizing Principle," by David Gray Carlson, at **www.law.fsu.edu/ journals/lawreview/downloads/263/carl.pdf**.

Critical Legal Thinking Cases

23.1 Petition   In March 1988, Daniel E. Beren, John M. Elliot, and Edward F. Mannino formed Walnut Street Four, a general partnership, to purchase and renovate an office building in Harrisburg, Pennsylvania. They borrowed more than $200,000 from Hamilton Bank to purchase the building and begin renovation. Disagreements among the partners arose when the renovation costs exceeded their estimates. When Beren was unable to obtain assistance from Elliot and Mannino regarding obtaining additional financing, the partnership quit paying its debts. Beren filed an involuntary petition to place the partnership into Chapter 7 bankruptcy. The other partners objected to the bankruptcy filing. At the time of the filing, the partnership owed debts of more than $380,000

and had approximately $550 in the partnership bank account. Should the petition for involuntary bankruptcy be granted? [*In re Walnut Street Four*, 106 B.R. 56, 1989 Bankr. Lexis 1806 (Bk.M.D. Pa. 1989]

23.2 Bankruptcy Estate   In 1983, Bill K. and Marilyn E. Hargis, husband and wife, filed a Chapter 11 bankruptcy proceeding. In 1984, more than 120 days after the bankruptcy petition was filed, Bill died. His life was insured for $700,000. His wife was the beneficiary of the policy. The bankruptcy trustee moved to recover the $700,000 as property of the bankruptcy estate. Who gets the insurance proceeds? [*In re Hargis*, 887 F.2d 77, 1989 U.S.App. Lexis 16246 (5th Cir. 1989)]

23.3 Automatic Stay In 1985, James F. Kost filed a voluntary petition for relief under Chapter 11 of the Bankruptcy Code. First Interstate Bank of Greybull (First Interstate) held a first mortgage on the debtor's residence near Basin, Wyoming. Appraisals and other evidence showed that the house was worth $116,000. The debt owed to First Interstate was almost $103,000 and was increasing at the rate of $32.46 per day. The debtor had only an 11.5 percent equity cushion in the property. Further evidence showed that the (1) Greybull/Basin area was suffering from tough economic times, (2) there were more than 90 homes available for sale in the area, (3) the real estate market in the area was declining, (4) the condition of the house was seriously deteriorating and the debtor was not financially able to make the necessary improvements, and (5) the insurance on the property had lapsed. First Interstate moved for a relief from stay so that it could foreclose on the property and sell it. Should the motion be granted? [*In re Kost*, 102 B.R.829, 1989 U.S.Dist. Lexis 8316 (Bk.D. Wyo. 1989)]

23.4 Fraudulent Transfer In November 1974, Peter and Geraldine Tabala (Debtors), husband and wife, purchased a house in Clarkstown, New York. In November 1976, they purchased a Carvel ice cream business for $70,000 with a loan obtained from People's National Bank. In addition, the Carvel Corporation extended trade credit to Debtors. On October 23, 1978, Debtors conveyed their residence to their three daughters, ages 9, 19, and 20, for no consideration. Debtors continued to reside in the house and to pay maintenance expenses and real estate taxes due on the property. On the date of transfer, Debtors owed obligations in excess of $100,000. On March 28, 1980, Debtors filed a petition for Chapter 7 bankruptcy. The bankruptcy trustee moved to set aside Debtors' conveyance of their home to their daughters as a fraudulent transfer. Who wins? [*In re Tabala*, 11 B.R. 405, 1981 Bankr. Lexis 3663 (Bk.S.D.N.Y. 1981)]

23.5 Preferential Payment Air Florida System, Inc. (Air Florida), an airline company, filed a voluntary petition to reorganize under Chapter 11 of the Bankruptcy Code. Within 90 days prior to the commencement of the case, Air Florida paid $13,575 to Compania Panamena de Aviacion, S.A. (COPA), in payment of an antecedent debt. This payment enabled COPA to receive more than it would have received if Air Florida were liquidated under Chapter 7. Is the payment to COPA an avoidable preferential transfer? [*In re Jet Florida System, Inc. f/k/a Air Florida System, Inc.*, 105 B.R. 137, 1989 Bankr. Lexis 1629 (Bk.S.D. Fla. 1989)]

23.6 Executory Contract On October 15, 1980, The Record Company, Inc. (The Record Company), entered into a purchase agreement to buy certain retail record stores from Bummbusiness, Inc. (Bummbusiness). All assets and inventory were included in the deal. The Record Company agreed to pay Bummbusiness $20,000 and to pay the $380,000 of trade debt owed by the stores. In exchange, Bummbusiness agreed not to compete with the new buyer for two years within a 15-mile radius of the stores and to use its best efforts to obtain an extension of the due dates for the trade debt. The Record Company began operating the stores but shortly thereafter filed a petition for Chapter 11 bankruptcy. At the time of the bankruptcy filing, (1) The Record Company owed Bummbusiness $10,000 and owed the trade debt of $380,000 and (2) Bummbusiness was obligated not to compete with The Record Company. Can The Record Company reject the purchase agreement? [*In re The Record Company*, 8 B.R. 57, 1981 Bankr. Lexis 5157 (Bk.S.D. Ind. 1981)]

23.7 Plan of Reorganization Richard P. Friese (Debtor) filed a voluntary petition for Chapter 11 bankruptcy. In May 1989,

Debtor filed a plan of reorganization that divided his creditors into three classes. The first class, administrative creditors, were to be paid in full. The second class, unsecured creditors, were to receive 50 percent on their claims. The IRS was the third class. It was to receive $20,000 on confirmation and the balance in future payments. No creditors voted to accept the plan. The unsecured creditors were impaired because their legal, equitable, and contractual rights were being altered. Can the bankruptcy court confirm Debtor's plan of reorganization? [*In re Friese*, 103 B.R. 90, 1989 Bankr. Lexis 1309 (Bk.S.D. N.Y. 1989)]

23.8 Consumer Debt Adjustment Manuel Guadalupe (Debtor) was a tool and die machinist who was employed at Elco Industries for more than five years. He accumulated more then $19,000 in unsecured debt, including deficiencies owed after secured creditors repossessed a van (leaving a deficiency of $1,066) and a car (leaving a deficiency of $3,130). Shortly after the second automobile was repossessed, Debtor borrowed approximately $19,000 from Elco Credit Union to purchase a 1988 four-wheel-drive Chevrolet Blazer. The $472 monthly payment was to be taken directly from Debtor's earnings.

On February 28, 1989, Debtor filed a voluntary petition for Chapter 13 consumer debt adjustment. The schedule listed total secured debts of $22,132, which included the debt for the Blazer, furniture, and a camcorder. Total unsecured debt was $19,575, which included $2,160 owed to General Finance Corporation (General). Debtor's budget projected that $700 per month would be left over for funding the Chapter 13 plan after his monthly expenses were deducted from his $25,000 gross income. Secured creditors were to be paid in full; unsecured creditors would receive 10 percent of their claims. General objected to the plan. Should Debtor's Chapter 13 plan be confirmed? [*In re Reyes*, 106 B.R. 155, 1989 Bankr. Lexis 1731 (Bk.N.D. Ill. 1989)]

23.9 Student Loan Donald Wayne Doyle (Debtor) obtained a guaranteed student loan to enroll in a school for training truck drivers. Due to his impending divorce, Debtor never attended the program. The first monthly installment of approximately $50 to pay the student loan became due on September 1, 1988. On September 16, 1988, Debtor filed a voluntary petition for Chapter 7 bankruptcy.

Debtor was a 29-year-old man who earned approximately $1,000 per month at an hourly wage of $7.70 as a truck driver, a job that he had held for 10 years. Debtor resided on a farm where he performed work in lieu of paying rent for his quarters. Debtor was paying monthly payments of $89 on a bank loan for his former wife's vehicle, $200 for his truck, $40 for health insurance, $28 for car insurance, $120 for gasoline and vehicular maintenance, $400 for groceries and meals, and $25 for telephone charges. In addition, a state court had ordered Debtor to pay $300 per month to support his children, ages four and five. Debtor's parents were assisting him by buying him $130 of groceries per month. Should Debtor's student loan be discharged in bankruptcy? [*In re Doyle*, 106 B.R. 272, 1989 Bankr. Lexis 1772 (Bk.N.D. Ala. 1989)]

23.10 Preference Rule On December 17, 1986, ZZZZ Best Co., Inc. (Debtor), borrowed $7 million from Union Bank. On July 8, 1987, Debtor filed a voluntary petition under Chapter 7 (liquidation). During the preceding 90-day period, Debtor had made two interest payments on its loan to Union Bank totaling $100,000. The trustee of Debtor's estate filed a complaint against Union Bank to recover those interest payments as preferential transfers made within 90 days of the bankruptcy filing. Can payments on long-term debt qualify as payments within the ordinary course of business exception to the 90-day preference rule? [*Union Bank v. Wolas*, 502. U.S. 151, 112 S.Ct. 527, 1991 U.S. Lexis 7174 (1991)]

Business Ethics Cases

23.11 Business Ethics   Scott Greig Keebler (Debtor) became indebted, and his debts exceeded his assets. The Internal Revenue Service (IRS) had levied his wages for nonpayment of taxes. Debtor was healthy and capable of earning a substantial income. Evidence showed that Debtor did not try his best to pay his debts, lived an affluent lifestyle, and determined not to pay his principal creditors. Debtor voluntarily quit his job and filed a voluntary petition for Chapter 7 bankruptcy. The petition stated that he was unemployed. Shortly after filing for bankruptcy, the petitioner resumed work. Should Debtor's Chapter 7 case be dismissed because he filed the petition in bad faith? [*In re Keebler*, 106 B.R. 662, 1989 Bankr. Lexis 1919 (Bk.D. Hawaii 1989]

23.12 Business Ethics   On February 3, 1983, Douglas G. and Aleta Brantz (Debtor's), husband and wife, borrowed $40,000 from Meritor Financial Services, Inc. (Meritor), and signed a promissory note evidencing the debt. The proceeds of the loan were used in a business operated by Douglas.

After a portion of the debt had been paid, the business began to fail, and the Brantzes defaulted on the loan. Debtors made several attempts to cure the default but failed. On August 11, 1988, Meritor filed a collection action and obtained a judgment lien against Debtors' residence.

On August 16, 1988, a $40,000 mortgage on Debtors' home in favor of Aleta's parents, Philip and Sondra Schley, was recorded. The mortgage was dated February 1, 1988. On May 25, 1989, Debtors filed a voluntary petition for bankruptcy. The parties stipulated that Debtors' home was worth $65,000 and was subject to unvoidable mortgages of $38,000. The Schleys asserted that their mortgage of $40,000 preceded Meritor's judicial lien of $28,441. Debtors also claimed an exemption of $15,800 in the premises. Who wins? Was Debtors' behavior unethical? [*In re Brantz*, 106 B.R. 62, 1989 Bankr. Lexis 1662 (Bk.E.D. Pa. 1989)]

Briefing the Case Writing Assignment

Read Case A.23 in the Case Appendix [*Dewsnup v. Timm*]. This case is excerpted from the U.S. Supreme Court opinion. Review and brief the case. In your brief, be sure to answer the following questions.

1. Who was the debtor? Who was the creditor? What was the collateral for the secured loan?

2. What amount did the debtor owe on the loan when he filed for bankruptcy? What was the value of the collateral at that time?

3. Succinctly state the issue that was presented to the U.S. Supreme Court.

4. How did the Supreme Court decide this issue? Explain.

Endnotes

1. 11 U.S.C. § § 101–1330.
2. 11 U.S.C. § 522.
3. 11 U.S.C. § § 1101–1174.
4. *National Labor Relations Board v. Bildisco and Bildisco*, 465 U.S. 513, 104 S.Ct. 1188, 1984 U.S. Lexis 6 (1984).
5. The absolute priority rule was announced in *Consolidated Rock Products Co. v. Du Bois*, 312 U.S. 510, 61 S.Ct. 675, 1941 U.S. Lexis 1215 (1941). The doctrine was codified in the Bankruptcy Reform Act of 1978.

Agency

24

"Let every eye negotiate for itself, and trust no agent."

—William Shakespeare
Much Ado About Nothing (1598)

Chapter Objectives

After studying this chapter you should be able to:

1. Define agency.

2. Identify and define a principal–independent contractor relationship.

3. List and describe the agent's duties to the principal and the principal's duties to the agent.

4. Describe the principal's and agent's liability on third-party contracts.

5. Identify and describe the principal's liability for the tortious conduct of an agent.

Chapter Contents

- Agency
- Formation of an Agency Relationship
- Principal's and Agent's Duties
- Contract Liability to Third Parties
- Tort Liability to Third Parties
- Termination of an Agency
- Independent Contractor

If businesspeople had to personally conduct all their business, the scope of their activities would be severely curtailed. Partnerships would not be able to operate; corporations could not act through managers and employees; and sole proprietorships would not be able to hire employees. The use of agents (or agency), which allows one person to act on behalf of another, solves this problem.

There are many examples of agency relationships. They include a salesperson who sells goods for a store, an executive who works for a corporation, a partner who acts on behalf of a partnership, an attorney who is hired to represent a client, a real estate broker who is employed to sell a house, and so on. Agency is governed by a large body of common law, known as **agency law**. This law, which is a mixture of contract law and tort law, is discussed in this chapter.

Agency

Agency relationships are formed by the mutual consent of a principal and an agent. Section 1(1) of the *Restatement (Second) of Agency* defines *agency* as a *fiduciary relationship* "which results from the manifestation of consent by one person to another that the other shall act in his behalf and subject to his control, and consent by the other so to act." The *Restatement (Second) of Agency* is the reference source for the rules of agency. A party who employs another person to act on his or her behalf is called a **principal**. A party who agrees to act on behalf of another is called an **agent**. The principal–agent relationship is commonly referred to as an **agency**. This relationship is depicted in Exhibit 24.1.

Persons Who Can Initiate an Agency Relationship

Any person who has the capacity to contract can appoint an agent to act on his or her behalf. Generally, persons who lack **contractual capacity**, such as insane persons and minors, cannot appoint an agent. However, the court can appoint a legal guardian or another representative to handle the affairs of insane persons, minors, and others who lack capacity to contract. With court approval, these representatives can enter into enforceable contracts on behalf of the persons they represent.

An agency can be created only to accomplish a lawful purpose. Agency contracts that are created for illegal purposes or are against public policy are void and unenforceable. For example, a principal cannot hire an agent to kill another person. Some agency relationships are prohibited by law. For example, unlicensed agents cannot be hired to perform the duties of certain licensed professionals (e.g., doctors, lawyers).

Business Brief

Some agency relationships are prohibited by law.

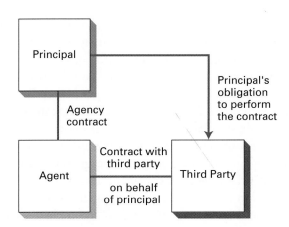

Exhibit 24.1

Principal–Agent Relationship

Principal–Agent Relationship

A **principal–agent relationship** is formed when an employer hires an employee and gives that employee authority to act and enter into contracts on his or her behalf. The extent of this authority is governed by any express agreement between the parties and implied from the circumstances of the agency. For example, the president of a corporation usually has the authority to enter into major contracts on the corporation's behalf, and a supervisor on the corporation's assembly line may have the authority only to purchase the supplies necessary to keep the line running.

Employer–Employee Relationship   An **employer–employee relationship** exists when an employer hires an employee to perform some form of physical service. For example, a welder on General Motors Corporation's assembly line is employed in an employer–employee relationship because he performs a physical task.

An employee is not an agent unless he or she is specifically empowered to enter into contracts on the principal employer's behalf. Employees may only enter into contracts that are within the scope of their employment. The welder in the previous example is not an agent because he cannot enter into contracts on behalf of General Motors Company. If the company empowered him to enter into contracts, he would become an agent.

Concept Summary   Kinds of Employment Relationships

Type of Relationship	Description
Principal–agent	The agent has authority to act on behalf of the principal as authorized by the principal and implied from the agency. An employee is often the agent of his employer.
Employer–employee	The employer has the right to control the physical conduct of the employee.

Formation of an Agency Relationship

An agency and the resulting authority of an agent can arise in any of these four ways: (1) express agency, (2) implied agency, (3) apparent agency, and (4) agency by ratification. Each of these types of agencies is discussed in the paragraphs that follow.

Express Agency

Express agency is the most common form of agency. In an express agency, the agent has the authority to contract or otherwise act on the principal's behalf, as expressly stated in the agency agreement. In addition, the agent may also possess certain implied or apparent authority to act on the principal's behalf (as discussed later in this chapter).

Express agency occurs when a principal and an agent expressly agree to enter into an agency agreement with each other. Express agency contracts can be either oral or written, unless the Statute of Frauds stipulates that they must be written. For example, in most states, a real estate broker's contract to sell real estate must be in writing.

If a principal and an agent enter into an **exclusive agency contract**, the principal cannot employ any agent other than the exclusive agent. If the principal does so, the exclusive agent can recover damages from the principal. If an agency is not an exclusive agency, the principal can employ more than one agent to try to accomplish a stated purpose. When

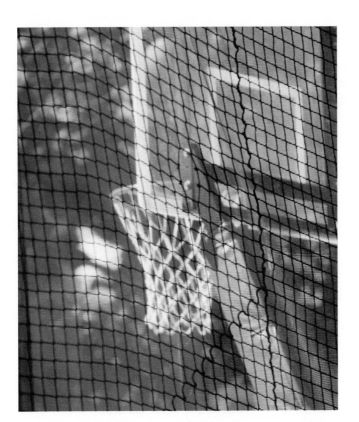

multiple agents are employed, the agencies with all the agents terminate when any one of the agents accomplishes the stated purpose.

Power of Attorney   A **power of attorney** is one of the most formal types of express agency agreements. It is often used to give an agent the power to sign legal documents, such as deeds to real estate, on behalf of the principal. There are two kinds of powers of attorney: *general*, which confers broad powers on the agent to act in any matters on the principal's behalf; and *special*, which limits the agent to those acts specifically enumerated in an agreement. The agent is called an **attorney-in-fact** even though he or she does not have to be a lawyer. Powers of attorney must be written. Usually, they must be notarized.

Implied Agency

In many situations, a principal and an agent do not expressly create an agency. Instead, the agency is implied from the conduct of the parties. This type of agency is referred to as **implied agency**. The extent of the agent's authority is determined from the particular facts and circumstances of the particular situation. Implied authority can be conferred by either industry custom, prior dealing between the parties, the agent's position, the acts deemed necessary to carry out the agent's duties, and other factors the court deems relevant. Implied authority cannot conflict with express authority or with stated limitations on express authority.

Incidental Authority   Often, even an express agency agreement does not provide enough detail to cover all contingencies that may arise in the future regarding the performance of the agency. In this case, the agent possesses certain implied authority to act. This implied authority is sometimes referred to as *incidental authority*.

Certain emergency situations may arise in the course of an agency. If the agent cannot contact the principal for instructions, the agent has implied emergency powers to take all actions reasonably necessary to protect the principal's property and rights.

Apparent Agency

Apparent agency (or **agency by estoppel**) arises when a principal creates the appearance of an agency that in actuality does not exist. Where an apparent agency is established, the principal is estopped from denying the agency relationship and is bound to contracts entered into by the apparent agent while acting within the scope of the apparent agency. Note that it is the principal's actions—not the agent's—that create an apparent agency.

Ethics Brief

Where an apparent agency is established, the principal is *estopped* from denying the agency relationship.

Consider This Example   Suppose Georgia Pacific, Inc., interviews Albert Iorio for a sales representative position. Mr. Iorio, accompanied by Jane Franklin, the national sales manager, visits retail stores located in the open sales territory. While visiting one store, Jane tells the store manager, "I wish I had more sales reps like Albert." Nevertheless, Albert is not hired. If Albert later enters into contracts with the store on behalf of Georgia Pacific and Jane has not controverted the impression of Albert she left with the store manager, the company will be bound to the contract.

Business Ethics

Apparent Agency

Franchising has become a major form of conducting business in the United States. In a franchise agreement, one company (called the franchisor) licenses another company (called the franchisee) to use its trade name, trademarks and service marks, and trade secrets. Many fast-food restaurants, gasoline stations, motels and hotels, and other businesses operate in this fashion.

The franchisor and franchisee are independently owned businesses. A principal–agent relationship usually is not created by the franchise. If no express or implied agency is created, the franchisor would not normally be civilly liable for the tortious conduct (e.g., negligence) of the franchisee. Liability could be imposed on the franchisor, however, if an apparent agency is shown. Consider the following case.

The Howard Johnson Company (HJ) operates a chain of hotels, motels, and restaurants across the United States. Approximately 75 percent of the HJ motor lodges are owned and operated by franchisees that are licensed by HJ to do business under the "Howard Johnson" trade name and trademarks. The rest are company owned.

Orlando Executive Park, Inc. (OEP), is a corporate franchisee that owns and operates an HJ motor lodge franchise in Orlando, Florida. The motor lodge is part of a large complex known as "Howard Johnson's Plaza," located off Interstate 4. The motor lodge contains approximately 300 guest rooms in six separate buildings.

P.D.R. (name withheld by the court), a 35-year-old married woman and mother of a small child, worked as a supervisor for a restaurant chain. Her work occasionally required her to travel and stay overnight in Orlando. On October 22, 1975, P.D.R. stopped to stay at the HJ motor lodge in Orlando. At approximately 9:30 P.M., P.D.R. registered for her previously reserved room at the lodge. The registration form did not inform her that the hotel was an HJ franchisee. P.D.R. parked her car in the motor lodge parking lot and proceeded with her suitcase to her ground-floor room in Building A, which was located directly behind the registration office. P.D.R. then went back to her car to get some papers. After obtaining the papers from her car, P.D.R. returned to Building A. As she proceeded down an interior hallway of the building toward her room, she was accosted by a man she had previously seen standing behind the registration office. The man struck her in the throat and neck and choked her until she became semiconscious. When P.D.R. fell to the floor, her assailant sat on top of her and stripped her of her jewelry. He then dragged her down the hallway and beneath a secluded stairway, where he brutally beat her. The assailant then disappeared into the might and has never been identified.

P.D.R. suffered serious physical and psychological injury, including memory loss, mental confusion, and an inability to tolerate and communicate with people. P.D.R. suffers permanent injury that requires expensive, long-term medical and psychiatric treatment. P.D.R. brought a tort action against OEP and HJ and sought actual and punitive damages against both of them.

Negligence of the Independent Contractor

The jury had little trouble finding that OEP had breached its duty of care and was liable. Evidence showed that other criminal activity had occurred previously on the premises but that OEP failed to warn guests, including P.D.R., of the danger. In fact, OEP management actively discouraged criminal investigations by the sheriff's deputies, thus minimizing any deterrent effect they may have had. Further evidence showed that the dark and secluded stairwell area where P.D.R. was dragged was a security hazard that should have been boarded up or better lit.

Liability of the Principal

The jury also found HJ liable to P.D.R. under the doctrine of **apparent agency**. The appellate court stated: "While OEP might not be HJ's agent for all purposes, the signs, national advertising, uniformity of building design and color schemes allow the public to assume that this and other similar motor lodges are under the same ownership. An HJ official testified that it was the HJ marketing strategy to appear as a 'chain that sells a product across the nation.'" The court continued, "There was sufficient evidence for the jury to reasonably conclude that HJ represented to the traveling public that it could expect a particular level of service at a Howard Johnson Motor Lodge. The uniformity of signs, design and color schemes easily leads the public to believe that each motor lodge is under common ownership or

conforms to common standards, and the jury could find they are intended to do so." The appellate court upheld an award of $750,000 compensatory damages against OEP and HJ jointly. [*Orlando Executive Park, Inc. v. P.D.R.*, 402 So.2d 442, 1981 Fla. App. Lexis 20565 (Fla. App. 1981)]

1. Should the doctrine of apparent agency be recognized by the law?
2. Should the Howard Johnson Company have been found liable in this case? Explain. ■

Agency by Ratification

Agency by ratification occurs when (1) a person misrepresents himself or herself as another's agent when in fact he or she is not and (2) the purported principal ratifies (accepts) the unauthorized act. In such cases, the principal is bound to perform, and the agent is relieved of any liability for misrepresentation.

Consider This Example   Bill Levine sees a house for sale and thinks his friend Sherry Maxwell would want it. Bill Levine enters into a contract to purchase the house from the seller and signs the contract "Bill Levine, agent for Sherry Maxwell." Because Bill is not Sherry Maxwell's agent, she is not bound to the contract. However, if Sherry agrees to purchase the house, there is an agency by ratification. The ratification "relates back" to the moment Bill Levine entered into the contract. Upon ratification of the contract, Sherry Maxwell is obligated to purchase the house.

Concept Summary   Formation of Agency Relationships

Type of Agency	Definition	Enforcement of the Contract
Express	Authority is expressly given to the agent by the principal.	Principal and third party are bound to the contract.
Implied	Authority is implied from the conduct of the parties, custom and usage of trade, or act incidental to carrying out the agent's duties.	Principal and third party acts are bound to the contract.
Apparent	Authority created when the principal leads a third party into believing that the agent has authority.	Principal and third party are bound to the contract.
By ratification	Acts of the agent committed outside the scope of his authority.	Principal and third party are not bound to the contract unless the principal ratifies the contract.

Principal's and Agent's Duties

The principal and the agent owe each other certain duties. These duties are discussed in the paragraphs that follow.

Principal's Duty of Compensation

A principal owes a **duty to compensate** an agent for services provided. Usually, the agency contract (whether written or oral) specifies the compensation to be paid. The principal must pay this amount either upon the completion of the agency or at some other mutually agreeable time.

If there is no agreement as to the amount of compensation, the law implies a promise that the principal will pay the agent the customary fee paid in the industry. If the compensation cannot be established by custom, the principal owes a duty to pay the reasonable value of the agent's services.

There is no duty to compensate a gratuitous agent. However, gratuitous agents who agree to provide their services free of charge may be paid voluntarily.

Certain types of agents traditionally perform their services on a *contingency-fee* basis. Under this type of arrangement, the principal owes a duty to pay the agent the agreed-upon contingency fee only if the agency is completed. For example, real estate brokers, finders, lawyers, and salespersons often work on this basis.

Business Brief

Many plaintiffs' lawyers agree to take cases on a contingency fee basis.

Principal's Duties of Reimbursement and Indemnification

In carrying out an agency, an agent may spend his or her own money on the principal's behalf. Unless otherwise agreed, the principal owes a **duty to reimburse** the agent for all such expenses if they were (1) authorized by the principal, (2) within the scope of the agency, and (3) necessary to discharge the agent's duties in carrying out the agency. For example, a principal must reimburse an agent for authorized business trips taken on the principal's behalf.

A principal also owes a **duty to indemnify** the agent for any losses the agent suffers because of the principal. This duty usually arises where an agent is held liable for the principal's misconduct. For example, suppose an agent enters into an authorized contract with a third party on the principal's behalf, the principal fails to perform on the contract, and the third party recovers a judgment against the agent. The agent can recover indemnification of this amount from the principal.

Principal's Duty of Cooperation

Unless otherwise agreed, the principal owes a **duty to cooperate** with and assist the agent in the performance of the agent's duties and the accomplishment of the agency. For example, unless otherwise agreed, a principal who employs a real estate agent to sell her house owes a duty to allow the agent to show the house to prospective purchasers during reasonable hours.

Agent's Duty of Performance

An agent who enters into a contract with a principal has two distinct obligations: (1) performing the lawful duties expressed in the contract and (2) meeting the standards of reasonable care, skill, and diligence implicit in all contracts. Collectively, these duties are referred to as the agent's **duty of performance**.

Normally, an agent is required to render the same standard of care, skill, and diligence that a fictitious reasonable agent in the same occupation would render in the same locality and under the same circumstances. For example, a general medical practitioner in a rural area would be held to the standard of a reasonable general practitioner in rural areas. That standard might be different for a general medical practitioner in a big city. In some professions, such as accounting, a national standard of performance (such as the "generally accepted accounting principle") is imposed. If an agent holds himself or herself as possessing higher-than-customary skills, the agent will be held to this higher standard of performance. For example, a lawyer who claims to be a specialist in securities law will be held to a reasonable specialist-in-securities-law standard.

An agent who does not perform his or her express duties or fails to use the standard degree of care, skill, or diligence is liable to the principal for breach of contract. An agent who has negligently (or intentionally) failed to perform properly is also liable in tort.

Agent's Duty of Notification

In the course of an agency, the agent usually learns information that is important to the principal. This information may come from third parties or other sources. The agent's duty to notify the principal of such information is called the **duty of notification**. The agent is liable to the principal for any injuries resulting from a breach of this duty.

Imputed Knowledge Most information learned by an agent in the course of an agency is **imputed** to the principal. This means that the principal is assumed to know what the agent knows. This is so even if the agent does not tell the principal certain relevant information.

Agent's Duty of Accountability

Unless otherwise agreed, an agent owes a duty to maintain an accurate accounting of all transactions undertaken on the principal's behalf. This **duty of accountability** includes keeping records of all property and money received and expended during the course of the agency. A principal has a right to demand an accounting from the agent at any time, and the agent owes a legal duty to make the accounting. This duty also requires the agent to (1) maintain a separate account for the principal and (2) use the principal's property in an authorized manner.

Any property, money, or other benefit received by the agent in the course of an agency belongs to the principal. For example, all secret profits received by the agent are the property of the principal. If an agent breaches the agency contract, the principal can sue the agent to recover damages caused by breach. The court can impose a *constructive trust* on any secret profits on property purchased with secret profits for the benefit of the principal.

Ethics Brief

A "constructive trust" is created by law, rather than agreement, to impose a duty to transfer property to another.

Agent's Duty of Loyalty

Because the agency relationship is based on trust and confidence, an agent owes the principal a **duty of loyalty** in all agency-related matters. Thus, an agent owes a fiduciary duty not to act adversely to the interests of the principal. If this duty is breached, the agent is liable to the principal. The most common types of breaches of loyalty by an agent are discussed in the following paragraphs:

- *Self-dealing.* Agents are generally prohibited from undisclosed self-dealing with the principal. For example, a real estate agent who is employed to purchase real estate for a principal cannot secretly sell his own property in the transaction. However, the deal is lawful if the principal agrees to buy the property after the agent discloses his or her ownership.

- *Usurping an opportunity.* An agent cannot usurp an opportunity that belongs to the principal. For example, a third-party offer to an agent must be conveyed to the principal. The agent cannot appropriate the opportunity for himself or herself unless the principal rejects it after due consideration. Opportunities to purchase real estate, businesses, products, ideas, and other property are subject to this rule.

■ ***Competing with the principal.*** Agents are prohibited from competing with the principal during the course of an agency unless the principal agrees. The reason for this rule is that an agent cannot meet his or her duty of loyalty when his or her personal interests conflict with the principal's interests. If the parties have not entered into an enforceable covenant-not-to-compete, an agent is free to compete with the principal once the agency has ended.

■ ***Misuse of confidential information.*** In the course of an agency, the agent often acquires confidential information about the principal's affairs (e.g., business plans, technological innovations, customer lists, trade secrets. The agent is under a legal duty not to disclose or misuse such information either during or after the course of the agency. There is no prohibition against using general information, knowledge, or experience acquired during the course of the agency.

■ ***Dual agency.*** An agent cannot meet a duty of loyalty to two parties with conflicting interests. Dual agency occurs when an agent acts for two or more different principals in the same transaction. This practice generally is prohibited unless all the parties involved in the transaction agree to it. If an agent acts as an undisclosed dual agent, he or she must forfeit all compensation received in the transaction. Some agents, such as middlemen and finders, are not considered dual agents. This is because they only bring interested parties together; they do not take part in any negotiations.

Red Square, Moscow, Russia.
Multinational companies often use agents to represent them to conduct business in foreign countries.

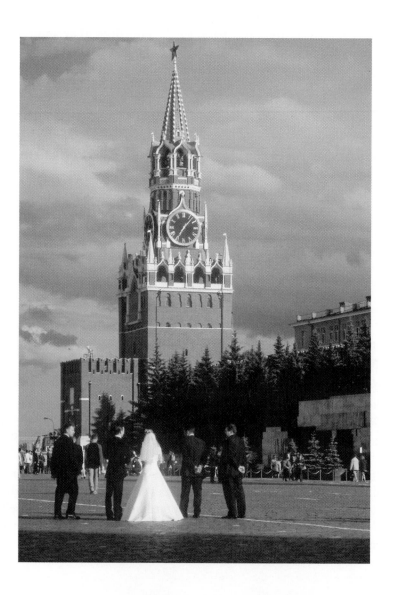

Contract Liability to Third Parties

A principal who authorizes an agent to enter into a contract with a third party is liable on the contract. Thus, the third party can enforce the contract and recover damages if the principal fails to perform it.

The agent can also be held liable on the contract in certain circumstances. Imposition of such liability depends on whether the agency is classified as (1) *fully disclosed*, (2) *partially disclosed*, or (3) *undisclosed*.

Fully Disclosed Agency

A **fully disclosed agency** results if the third party entering into the contract knows (1) that the agent is acting as an agent for a principal and (2) the actual identity of the principal.[1] The third party has the requisite knowledge if the principal's identity is disclosed to the third party by either the agent or some other source.

In a fully disclosed agency, the contract is between the principal and the third party. Thus, the principal, who is called a *fully disclosed principal*, is liable on the contract. The agent, however, is not liable on the contract because the third party relied on the principal's credit and reputation when the contract was made. An agent is liable on the contract if he or she guarantees that the principal will perform the contract.

The agent's signature on a contract entered into on the principal's behalf is important. It can establish the agent's status and, therefore, his or her liability. For instance, in a fully disclosed agency, the agent's signature must clearly indicate that he or she is acting as an agent for a specifically identified principal. Examples of proper signatures include "Allison Adams, agent for Peter Perceival," "Peter Perceival, by Allison Adams, agent," and "Peter Perceival, by Allison Adams."

Consider This Example   Poran Kawamara decides to sell her house and hires Mark Robbins, a real estate broker, to list and sell the house for a price of $1 million. They agree that Mark will disclose the existence of the agency and the identity of the principal to interested third parties. This is a fully disclosed agency. Mark shows the house to Heather, a prospective buyer, and discloses to Heather that he is acting as an agent for Poran. Heather makes an offer for the house at the $1 million asking price. Mark signs the contract with Heather on behalf of Poran by signing "Mark Robbins, agent for Poran Kawamara." Poran is liable on the contract with Heather, but Mark is not liable on the contract with Heather.

Partially Disclosed Agency

A **partially disclosed agency** occurs if the agent discloses his or her agency status but does not reveal the principal's identity and the third party does not know the principal's identity from another source. The nondisclosure may be because (1) the principal instructs the agent not to disclose his or her identity to the third party or (2) the agent forgets to tell the third party the principal's identity. In this kind of agency, the principal is called a *partially disclosed principal*.

In a partially disclosed agency, both the principal and the agent are liable on third-party contracts.[2] This is because the third party must rely on the agent's reputation, integrity, and credit because the principal is unidentified. If the agent is made to pay the contract, the agent can sue the principal for indemnification. The third party and the agent can agree to relieve the agent's liability. A partially disclosed agency can be created either expressly or by mistake.

Business Brief
In a fully disclosed agency, the principal is liable to the third party on the contract; the agent is not liable.

Business Brief
In a partially disclosed agency, both the principal and the agent are liable to the third party if the principal fails to perform the contract.

Consider These Examples   Assume that a principal employs an agent to purchase a business on its behalf. The principal and agent expressly agree that the agent will disclose the existence of the agency to third parties but will not disclose the identity of the principal. The agent finds a business that is for sale, and he discloses to the seller that he is acting as an agent but does not disclose the identity of the principal. The seller agrees to sell the business, and the agent signs "Allison Adams, agent." Here, there is a partially disclosed agency. The principal is liable on the contract with the third-party seller; the agent is also liable on the contract with the third-party seller.

If instead a principal and an agent agree that the agent will represent the principal to purchase a business and that the agent will disclose the existence of the agency and the identity of the principal to third parties, this is a fully disclosed agency. Suppose the agent finds a suitable business for the principal and contracts to purchase the business on behalf of the principal, but the agent mistakenly signs the contract with the third party "Allison Adams, agent." This is a partially disclosed agency. The principal is liable on the contract with the third party, but the agent is also liable.

Undisclosed Agency

An **undisclosed agency** occurs when the third party is unaware of either the existence of an agency or the principal's identity. The principal is called an **undisclosed principal**. Undisclosed agencies are lawful. They are often used when the principal feels that the terms of the contract would be changed if his or her identity were known. For example, a wealthy person may use an undisclosed agency to purchase property if he thinks that the seller would raise the price of the property if his identity were revealed.

In an undisclosed agency, both the principal and the agent are liable on the contract with the third party. This is because the agent, by not divulging that he or she is acting as an agent, becomes a principal to the contract. The third party relies on the reputation and credit of the agent in entering into the contract. If the principal fails to perform the contract, the third party can recover against the principal of the agent. If the agent is made to pay the contract, he or she can recover indemnification from the principal. An undisclosed agency can be created either expressly or by mistake.

Consider These Examples   Assume that The Walt Disney Company wants to open a new theme park in Chicago but needs to first acquire land for the park. Disney employs an agent to work on its behalf to acquire the needed property, with an express agreement that the agent will not disclose the existence of the agency to a third-party seller. If a seller agrees to sell the needed land, and the agent signs her name "Allison Adams," without disclosing the existence of the agency, it is an undisclosed agency. Disney is liable on the contract with the third-party seller and so is the agent.

Suppose instead that Disney hires an agent to purchase land on its behalf and they agree that the agent will represent Disney in a fully disclosed agency—that is, the agent is to disclose the existence of the agency and the identity of the principal to the third-party seller. If the agent locates a third-party seller who is willing to enter into a contract to sell the land, but the agent mistakenly signs the contract "Allison Adams," without disclosing the agency to the third party, it is an undisclosed agency. Disney is liable on the contract with the third-party seller, but the agent is also liable.

Agent Exceeding the Scope of Authority

An agent who enters into a contract on behalf of another party impliedly warrants that he or she has the authority to do so. This is called the agent's **implied warranty of authority**. If the agent exceeds the scope of his or her authority, the principal is not liable on the contract unless the principal **ratifies** it. The agent, however, is liable to the third party for breaching the implied warranty of authority. To recover, the third party must show (1) reliance on the agent's representation and (2) ignorance of the agent's lack of status.

Consider This Example   Suppose Sam, Sara, Satchel, Samantha, and Simone form a rock band called SSSS. SSSS is just a voluntary association without any legal status. Sam enters into a contract with Rocky's Musical Instruments to purchase instruments and equipment for the band on credit and signs the contract, "Sam, for SSSS." When SSSS fails to pay the debt, Rocky's can sue Sam and recover. Sam must pay the debt because he breached his implied warranty of authority when he acted as an agent for a *nonexistent principal*; that is, the purported principal was not a legal entity on which liability could be imposed.

Concept Summary *Contract Liability of Principals and Agents to Third Parties*

Type of Agency	Principal Liable	Agent Liable
Fully disclosed	Yes,	No, unless the agent (1) acts as a principal or (2) guarantees the performance of the contract
Partially disclosed	Yes,	Yes, unless the third party relieves the agent's liability
Undisclosed	Yes,	Yes
Nonexistent	No, unless the principal ratifies the contract,	Yes, the agent is liable for breaching the implied warranty of authority

Tort Liability to Third Parties

A principal and an agent are each personally liable for their own tortious conduct. The principal is liable for the tortious conduct of an agent who is acting within the scope of his or her authority. The agent, however, is liable, for the tortious conduct of the principal only if he or she directly or indirectly participates in or aids and abets the principal's conduct.

The courts have applied a broad and flexible standard in interpreting scope of authority in the context of employment. Although other factors may also be considered, the courts rely on the following factors to determine whether an agent's conduct occurred within the scope of his or her employment:

■ Was the act specifically requested or authorized by the principal?
■ Was it the kind of act that the agent was employed to perform?
■ Did the act occur substantially within the time period of employment authorized by the principal?
■ Did the act occur substantially within the location of employment authorized by the employer?
■ Was the agent advancing the principal's purpose when the act occurred?

Where liability is found, tort remedies are available to the injured party. These remedies include recovery for medical expenses, lost wages, pain and suffering, emotional distress, and, in some cases, punitive damages. As discussed in the following paragraphs, the three main sources of tort liability for principals and agents are misrepresentation, negligence, and intentional torts.

Business Brief

The use of agents creates tort liability exposure for principals. A principal is only liable for the tortious conduct of agents committed within their scope of employment, however.

An agent's scope of authority was at issue in the following case.

Edgewater Motels, Inc. v. Gatzke and Walgreen Co.
277 N.W.2d 11, 1979 Minn. Lexis 1381 (1979)
Supreme Court of Minnesota

Case 24.1
Tort Liability

Background and Facts

Arlen Gatzke (Gatzke) was a district manager for the Walgreen Company (Walgreen). In August 1979, Gatzke was sent to Duluth, Minnesota, to supervise the opening of a new Walgreen store. In Duluth, Gatzke stayed at the Edgewater Motel (Edgewater). While in Duluth, Gatzke was "on call" 24 hours a day to other Walgreen stores located in his territory. About midnight on the evening of August 23, 1979, Gatzke, after working 17 hours that day, went with several other Walgreen employees to a restaurant and bar to drink. Within 1 hour's time, Gatzke had consumed three doubles and one single brandy Manhattan. About 1:30 A.M., he went back to the Edgewater Motel and filled out his expense report. Soon thereafter, a fire broke out in Gatzke's motel room. Gatzke escaped, but the fire spread and caused extensive damage to the motel. Evidence showed that Gatzke smoked two packs of cigarettes a day. An expert fire reconstruction witness testified that the fire started from a lit cigarette in or next to the wastepaper basket in Gatzke's room. Edgewater sued Gatzke and Walgreen. The parties stipulated that the damage to the Edgewater Motel was $330,360. The jury returned a verdict against defendants Gatzke and Walgreen. The court granted Walgreen's posttrial motion for judgment notwithstanding the verdict. Plaintiff Edgewater and defendant Gatzke appealed.

Issue

Was Gatzke's act of smoking within his "scope of employment," making his principal, the Walgreen Company, vicariously liable for his negligence?

Court's Reasoning

In reaching its decision, the supreme court stated:

> After careful consideration of the issue we are persuaded that smoking can be an act within an employee's scope of employment. It seems only logical to conclude that an employee does not abandon his employment as a matter of law while temporarily acting for his personal comfort when such activities involve only slight deviations from work that are reasonable under the circumstances, such as eating, drinking, or smoking. The record indicates that Gatzke was an executive type of employee who had no set working hours. His room at the Edgewater Motel was his 'office away from home.'

Decision and Remedy

The state supreme court held that Gatzke's negligent act of smoking was within the scope of his employment while acting as an employee of the Walgreen Company. The supreme court reinstated the jury's verdict awarding damages to plaintiff Edgewater Motels, Inc.

Case Questions

Critical Legal Thinking   Should smoking cigarettes be held to be within an employee's scope of employment? Why or why not?

Business Ethics   Do employers owe a duty to police the personal habits of their employees?

Contemporary Business   Because of the dangers of smoking, would employers be justified in hiring only nonsmokers as employees?

Misrepresentation

Intentional misrepresentations are also known as **fraud** or **deceit**. They occur when an agent makes statements that he or she knows are not true. An **innocent misrepresentation** occurs when an agent negligently makes a misrepresentation to a third party.

A principal is liable for the intentional and innocent misrepresentations made by an agent acting within the scope of employment. The third party can either (1) rescind the contract with the principal and recover any consideration paid or (2) affirm the contract and recover damages.

Consider This Example   Assume that (1) a car salesman is employed to sell the principal's car and (2) the principal tells the agent that the car was repaired after it was involved in a major accident. If the agent intentionally tells the buyer that the car was never involved in an accident, the agent has made an intentional misrepresentation. Both the principal and the agent are liable for this misrepresentation.

Negligence

Principals are liable for the negligent conduct of agents acting within the scope of their employment. This liability is based on the common law doctrine of **respondent superior** ("let the master answer"), which, in turn, is based on the legal theory of *vicarious liability* (liability without fault). In other words, the principal is liable because of his or her employment contract with the negligent agent, not because the principal was personally at fault.

This doctrine rests on the principle that if someone (i.e., the principal) expects to derive certain benefits from acting through others (i.e., an agent), that person should also bear the liability for injuries caused to third persons by the negligent conduct of an agent who is acting within the scope of his or her employment.

Frolic and Detour Agents sometimes do things during the course of their employment to further their own interests rather than the principal's. For example, an agent might take a detour to run a personal errand while on assignment for the principal. This is commonly referred to as a **frolic and detour**. Negligence actions stemming from frolic and detour are examined on a case-by-case basis. Agents are always personally liable for their tortious conduct in such situations. Principals are generally relieved of liability if the agent's frolic and detour is substantial. However, if the deviation is minor, the principal is liable for the injuries caused by the agent's tortious conduct.

Consider This Example A salesperson stops home for lunch while on an assignment for his principal. While leaving his home, the agent hits and injures a pedestrian with his automobile. The principal would be liable if the agent's home was not too far out of the way from the agent's assignment. However, the principal would not be liable if an agent who is supposed to be on assignment to Los Angeles flies to San Francisco to meet a friend and is involved in an accident. The facts and circumstances of each case determine its outcome.

The "Coming and Going" Rule Under the common law, a principal is generally not liable for injuries caused by its agents and employees while they are on their way to or from work. This so-called **"coming and going" rule** applies even if the principal supplies the agent's automobile or other transportation or pays for gasoline, repairs, and other automobile operating expenses. This rule is quite logical. Because principals do not control where their agents and employees live, they should not be held liable for tortious conduct of agents on their way to and from work.

Dual-Purpose Mission Sometimes, principals request that agents run errands or conduct other acts on their behalf while the agent or employee is on personal business. In this case, the agent is on a **dual-purpose mission**. That is, he or she is acting partly for himself or herself and partly for the principal. Most jurisdictions hold both the principal and the agent liable if the agent injures someone while on such a mission.

Consider This Example Suppose a principal asks an employee to drop off a package at a client's office on the employee's way home. If the employee negligently injures a pedestrian while on this dual-purpose mission, the principal is liable to the pedestrian.

Intentional Torts

Intentional torts include such acts as assault, battery, false imprisonment, and other intentional conduct that cause injury to another person. A principal is not liable for the intentional torts of agents and employees that are committed outside the principal's scope of business. For example, if an employee attends a sporting event after working hours and gets into a fight with another spectator at the event, the employer is not liable.

However, a principal is liable under the doctrine of vicarious liability for intentional torts of agents and employees committed within the agent's scope of employment. The courts generally apply one of the tests discussed in the following paragraphs in determining whether an agent's intentional torts were committed within the agent's scope of employment.

The Motivation Test   Under the **motivation test**, if the agent's motivation in committing the intentional tort is to promote the principal's business, the principal is liable for any injury caused by the tort. However, if the agent's motivation in committing the intentional tort was personal, the principal is not liable, even if the tort took place during business hours or on business premises. For example, a principal is not liable if his agent was motivated by jealousy to beat up someone on the job who dated her boyfriend.

The Work-Related Test   Some jurisdictions have rejected the motivation test as too narrow. These jurisdictions apply the **work-related test** instead. Under this test, if an agent commits an intentional tort within a work-related time or space—for example, during working hours or on the principal's premises—the principal is liable for any injuries caused by the agent's intentional torts. Under this test, the agent's motivation is immaterial.

In the following case, the court applied the work-related test in determining whether an employer was liable for an agent's intentional tort.

Desert Cab Inc. v. Marino
823 P.2d 898, 1992 Nev. Lexis 6 (1992)
Supreme Court of Nevada

Case 24.2
Intentional Tort

Background and Facts

On October 6, 1986, Maria Marino, a cab driver with Yellow-Checkered Cab Company (Yellow Cab), and James Edwards, a cab driver with Desert Cab Inc. (Desert Cab), parked their cabs at the taxicab stand at the Sundance Hotel and Casino in Las Vegas to await fares. Marino's cab occupied the first position in the line, and Edwards's cab occupied the third. As Marino stood alongside her cab, conversing with the driver of another taxi, Edwards began verbally harassing her from inside his cab. When Marino approached Edwards to inquire as to the reason for the harassment, a verbal argument ensued. Edwards jumped from his cab, grabbed Marino by her neck and shoulders, began choking her, and threw her in front of his taxicab. A bystander pulled Edwards off Marino and escorted her back to her cab. Marino sustained injuries that rendered her unable to work for a time. Edwards was convicted of misdemeanor assault and battery. Marino brought a personal injury action against Desert Cab. The jury found Desert Cab liable and awarded Marino $65,000. Desert Cab appealed.

Issue

Is Desert Cab liable for the intentional tort of its employee?

Court's Reasoning

Under the doctrine of *respondeat superior*, an employer is liable for the intentional torts committed by its employees within the scope of their employment. For liability to be imposed on the employer, the intentional tort must be work-related. The court held that Edward's intentional conduct of assault and battery against Marino was work-related, and Desert Cab was, therefore, liable to Marino.

Decision and Remedy

The appellate court held that Desert Cab was liable for the intentional tort committed by its employee.

Case Questions

Critical Legal Thinking   Should employers be held liable for the intentional torts of their employees?

Business Ethics   Did Desert Cab act ethically in denying liability?

Contemporary Business   Should employers give prospective employees psychological examinations to determine if they have any dangerous propensities?

Concept Summary   Tort Liability of Principals and Agents to Third Parties

Agent's Conduct	Agent Liable	Principal Liable
Misrepresentation	Yes	The principal is liable for the intentional and innocent misrepresentations made by an agent acting within the scope of her authority.
Negligence	Yes	The principal is liable under the doctrine of *respondeat superior* if the agent's negligent act was committed within his or her scope of employment.
Intentional tort	Yes	Motivation test: The principal is liable if the agent's motivation in committing the intentional tort was to promote the principal's business.
	Yes	Work-related test: The principal is liable if the agent committed the intentional tort within work-related time and space.

Termination of an Agency

An agency contract is similar to other contracts in that it can be terminated either by an act of the parties or by operation of law. These different methods of termination are discussed next. Note that once an agency relationship is terminated, the agent can no longer represent the principal or bind the principal to contracts.

Termination by Acts of the Parties

The parties to an agency contract can terminate an agency contract by agreement or by their actions. The four methods of **termination** of an agency relationship by **acts of the parties** are:

- **Mutual agreement.** As with any contract, the parties to an agency contract can mutually agree to terminate their agreement. By doing so, the parties relieve each other of any further rights, duties, obligations, or powers provided for in the agency contract. Either party can propose the termination of an agency contract.

- **Lapse of time.** Agency contracts are often written for a specific period of time. The agency terminates when the specified time period elapses. Suppose, for example, that the principal and agent enter into an agency contract "beginning January 1, 2005, and ending December 31, 2007." The agency automatically terminates on December 31, 2007. If the agency contract does not set forth a specific termination date, the agency terminates after a reasonable time has elapsed. The courts often look to the custom of an industry in determining the reasonable time for the termination of the agency.

- **Purpose achieved.** A principal can employ an agent for the time it takes to accomplish a certain task, purpose, or result. Such agencies automatically terminate when they are completed. For example, suppose a principal employs a licensed real estate broker to sell his house. The agency terminates when the house is sold and the principal pays the broker the agreed-upon compensation.

■ ***Occurrence of a specified event.*** An agency contract can specify that the agency exists until a specified event occurs. The agency terminates when the specified event happens. For example, if a principal employs an agent to take care of her dog until she returns from a trip, the agency terminates when the principal returns from the trip.

Notification Required at the Termination of an Agency

If an agency is terminated by agreement between the parties, the principal is under a duty to give certain third parties notification of the termination. Unless otherwise required, the notice can be from the principal or some other source (e.g., the agent). If an agency terminates by operation of law, there is no duty to notify third parties about the termination, however.

The termination of an agency extinguishes an agent's actual authority to act on the principal's behalf. However, if the principal fails to give the proper notice of termination to a third party, the agent still has apparent authority to bind the principal to contracts with these third parties. If this happens, the contract is enforceable against the principal. The principal's only recourse is against the agent to recover damages caused by these unauthorized contracts.

The following notification requirements must be met:

■ ***Parties who dealt with the agent.*** Direct notice of termination must be given to all persons with whom the agent dealt. Although the notice may be either written or oral, it is better practice to give written notice.

■ ***Parties who have knowledge of the agency.*** The principal must give direct or constructive notice to any third party who has knowledge of the agency but with whom the agent has not dealt. Direct notice is often in the form of a letter. Constructive notice usually consists of placing a notice of the termination of the agency in a newspaper serving the relevant community. This notice is effective even against persons who do not see it.

■ ***Parties who have no knowledge of the agency.*** Generally, a principal is not obligated to give notice of termination to strangers who have no knowledge of the agency. However, a principal who has given the agent written authority to act but fails to recover the writing upon termination of the agency may be liable to strangers who later rely on this writing and deal with the agent. The laws of most states provide that this liability can be avoided by giving constructive notice (e.g., newspaper announcement) of the termination of the agency.

Contemporary Environment
Irrevocable Agency

An agency coupled with an interest is a special type of agency relationship that is created for the agent's benefit. This type of agency is irrevocable by the principal (i.e., the principal cannot terminate it). An agency coupled with an interest is commonly used in security agreements to secure loans. An agency coupled with an interest is not terminated by the death or incapacity of either the principal or the agent. It terminates only when the agent's obligations are performed. However, the parties can expressly agree that an agency coupled with an interest is terminated.

Consider This Example Heidi Norville owns a piece of real estate. She goes to Wells Fargo Bank to obtain a loan on the property. The bank makes the loan but requires her to sign a security agreement (e.g., a mortgage) pledging the property as collateral for the loan. The security agreement contains a clause that appoints that bank as Ms. Norville's agent and permits the bank to sell the property and recover the amount of the loan from the sale proceeds if she defaults on her payments. This agency is irrevocable by Ms. Norville, the principal. ■

Termination by Operation of Law

Agency contracts can be **terminated by operation of law** as well as by agreement. The six methods of terminating an agency relationship by operation of law are:

1. **Death.** The death of either the principal or the agent terminates an agency relationship. This rule is based on the old legal principle that, because a dead person cannot act, no one can act for him or her. Note that the agency terminates even if one party is unaware of the other party's death. An agent's actions that take place after the principal's death do not bind the principal's estate.

2. **Insanity.** The insanity of either the principal or the agent generally terminates an agency relationship. A few states have modified this rule to provide that a contract entered into by an agent on behalf of an insane principal is enforceable if (1) the insane person has not been adjudged insane, (2) the third party does not have knowledge of the principal's insanity at the time of contracting, and (3) the enforcement of the contract will prevent injustice.

3. **Bankruptcy.** An agency relationship is terminated if the principal is declared bankrupt. Bankruptcy requires the filing of a petition for bankruptcy under federal bankruptcy law. With few exceptions, neither the appointment of a state court receiver nor the principal's financial difficulties or insolvency terminates the agency relationship. The agent's bankruptcy usually does not terminate an agency unless the agent's credit standing is important to the agency relationship.

4. **Impossibility.** An agency relationship terminates if a situation arises that makes its fulfillment impossible. The following circumstances can lead to termination on this ground:

   - **The loss or destruction of the subject matter of the agency.** For example, assume that a principal employs an agent to sell his horse, but the horse dies before it is sold. The agency relationship terminates at the moment the horse dies.

   - **The loss of a required qualification.** For example, suppose a principal employs a licensed real estate agent to sell her house, and the real estate agent's license is revoked. The agency terminates at the moment the license is revoked.

   - **A change in the law.** For example, suppose that a principal employs an agent to trap alligators. If a law is passed that makes trapping alligators illegal, the agency contract terminates when the law becomes effective.

5. **Changed circumstances.** An agency terminates when there is an unusual change in circumstances that would lead the agent to believe that the principal's original instructions should no longer be valid. For example, a principal employs a licensed real estate agent to sell a farm for $100,000. The agent thereafter learns that oil has been discovered on the property and makes it worth $1 million. The agency terminates because of this change in circumstances.

6. **War.** The outbreak of a war between the principal's country and the agent's country terminates an agency relationship between the parties. Such an occurrence usually makes the performance of the agency contract impossible.

Wrongful Termination of an Agency or Employment Contract

Generally, agency and employment contracts that do not specify a definite time for their termination can be terminated at will by either the principal or the agent without liability to the other party. When a principal terminates an agency contract, it is called a **revocation of authority**. When an agent terminates an agency, it is called a **renunciation of authority**.

Unless an agency is irrevocable, both the principal and the agent have an individual power to unilaterally terminate any agency contract. Note that having the power to terminate an agency agreement is not the same as having the right to terminate it. The unilateral termination of an agency contract may be wrongful. If the principal's or agent's termination of an agency contract breaches the contract, the other party can sue for damages for **wrongful termination**.

Business Brief

The distinction between the *power* and the *right* to terminate an agency is critical. Be certain it is clear.

Consider This Example   A principal employs a licensed real estate agent to sell his house. The agency contract gives the agent an exclusive listing for three months. After one month, the principal unilaterally terminates the agency. The principal has the power to do so, and the agent can no longer act on behalf of the principal. However, because the principal did not have the right to terminate the contract, the agent can sue him and recover damages (i.e., lost commission) for wrongful termination.

Independent Contractor

Business Brief

Persons and businesses often employ independent contractors to perform certain tasks on their behalf.

Principals often employ outsiders—that is, persons and businesses who are not employees—to perform certain tasks on their behalf. These persons and businesses are called **independent contractors**. For example, lawyers, doctors, dentists, consultants, stockbrokers, architects, certified public accountants, real estate brokers, and plumbers are examples of people who commonly act as independent contractors. The party that employs an independent contractor is called a **principal**.

A principal–independent contractor relationship is depicted in Exhibit 24.2.

Exhibit 24.2

Principal–Independent Contractor Relationship

Principal

Contract

Independent Contractor

Consider This Example   Jin is a lawyer who has her own law firm and specializes in real estate law. Raymond, a real estate developer, hires Jin to represent him in the purchase of land. Raymond is the principal, and Jin is the independent contractor.

Factors for Determining Independent Contractor Status

Section 2 of the *Restatement (Second) of Agency* defines an **independent contractor** as "A person who contracts with another to do something for him who is not controlled by the other nor subject to the other's right to control with respect to his physical conduct in the performance of the undertaking." Independent contractors usually work for a number of clients, have their own offices, hire employees, and control the performance of their work.

The crucial factor in determining whether someone is an independent contractor or an employee is the *degree of control* that the principal has over the agent. Critical factors in determining independent contractor status include:

- Whether the worker is engaged in a distinct occupation or an independently established business
- The length of time the agent has been employed by the principal.
- The amount of time that the agent works for the principal
- Whether the principal supplies the tools and equipment used in the work
- The method of payment, whether by time or by the job
- The degree of skill necessary to complete the task
- Whether the worker hires employees to assist him or her
- Whether the employer has the right to control the manner and means of accomplishing the desired result

If an examination of these factors shows that the principal asserts little control, the person is an independent contractor. Substantial control indicates an employer–employee relationship. Labeling someone an "independent contractor" is only one factor in determining whether independent contractor status exists.

> **Business Brief**
>
> The crucial factor in determining whether a person is an employee or an independent contractor is the *degree of control* that the principal has over that person.

Liability for an Independent Contractor's Contracts

A principal can authorize an independent contractor to enter into contracts. Principals are bound by the authorized contracts of their independent contractors. For example, suppose a client hires a lawyer as an independent contractor to represent her in a civil lawsuit against a defendant to recover monetary damages. If the client authorizes the lawyer to settle a case within a certain dollar amount and the lawyers does so, the settlement agreement is binding.

If an independent contractor enters into a contract with a third party on behalf of the principal without express or implied authority from the principal to do so, the principal is not liable on the contract.

Liability for an Independent Contractor's Torts

Generally, a principal is not liable for the torts of its independent contractors. Independent contractors are personally liable for their own torts. The rationale behind this rule is that principals do not control the means by which the results are accomplished.

Consider This Example   Qixia hires Harold, a lawyer and independent contractor, to represent her in a court case. While driving to the courthouse to represent Qixia at trial, Harold negligently causes an automobile accident in which Mildred is severely injured. Harold is liable to Mildred because he caused the accident. Qixia is not liable to Mildred because Harold was an independent contractor when he caused the accident.

> **Business Brief**
>
> A principal is generally not liable for the tortious conduct of independent contractors it hires. However, there are several exceptions.

Staples Center, Los Angeles, California. A general contractor who constructs a building is an independent contractor of the owner. The general contractor usually hires other independent contractors, called subcontractors, to do much of the work on the project.

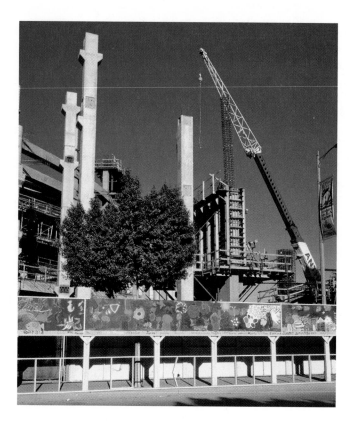

Business Brief

There are several situations where the law imposes liability on a principal for the tortious conduct of an independent contractor he or she has hired.

Exceptions Where a Principal Is Liable for the Torts of an Independent Contractor There are several exceptions where the law imposes liability on a principal for the tortious conduct of an independent contractor he or she has hired. These exceptions are:

- *Inherently dangerous activities.* Principals cannot avoid strict liability for inherently dangerous activities assigned to independent contractors. For example, the use of explosives, clearing land by fire, crop dusting, and such involve special risks that are shared by the principal.

- *Negligence in the selection of an independent contractor.* A principal who hires an unqualified or knowingly dangerous person as an independent contractor is liable if that person injures someone while on the job.

In the following case, the court found a principal liable for the negligence of an independent contractor.

Maldonado v. Gateway Hotel Holdings, L.L.C.

2003 Mo.App. Lexis 1577 (2003)
Court of Appeals of Missouri

Case 24.3

Inherently Dangerous Activity

Background and Facts

Doug Hartmann Productions, L.L.C. (Hartmann Productions), was a promoter of sporting events. Hartmann Productions entered into a contract with Gateway Hotel Holdings, L.L.C., to hold a kickboxing match at the Regal Riverfront Hotel owned by Gateway. It was agreed in the contract that Hartmann Productions would provide

an ambulance at the hotel the night of the match. Fernando Ibarra Maldonado was one of the kickboxers the night of the match; his contract was not with Gateway.

On the night of the match, Maldonado was knocked out. He was revived and left the ring and walked to his dressing room. Maldonado later lost consciousness in his dressing room. There was no ambulance on site. An ambulance was called, and Maldonado was taken to a hospital. He suffered severe brain damage and partial paralysis as a result of his injuries. Maldonado sued Gateway to recover damages for his injuries. Maldonado alleged that Hartmann Productions was negligent in not providing an ambulance the night of the kickboxing match, that Hartmann Productions was an independent contractor of Gateway, that kickboxing is an inherently dangerous activity, and that Gateway, as the principal, was liable for his injuries. The jury returned a verdict in favor of Maldonado and ordered Gateway to pay $13.7 million in compensatory damages. Gateway appealed.

Issue

Is kickboxing an inherently dangerous activity that made Gateway liable for the negligence of its independent contractor, Hartmann Productions?

Court's Reasoning

The court of appeals found that Hartmann Productions was an independent contractor of Gateway. The general rule of agency law is that a principal is not liable for the negligence of an independent contractor. However, an exception to this rule exists if there is an inherently dangerous activity, and then the principal cannot delegate its responsibility and duties to avoid liability. The court of appeals held that kickboxing was an inherently dangerous activity and that Gateway owed a duty to provide safe conditions for

Maldonado's kickboxing match, including having an ambulance at the hotel the night of the kickboxing match. The court held that Gateway could not avoid this responsibility by delegating it to Hartmann Productions. Therefore, Gateway was held liable for the negligence of Hartmann Productions for failing to provide an ambulance for Maldonado's kickboxing match.

Decision and Remedy

The court of appeals held that Hartmann Productions was an independent contractor of Gateway, that kickboxing was an inherently dangerous activity, and that Gateway was responsible for the negligence of Hartmann Productions in not providing an ambulance the night of the kickboxing match. The court of appeals upheld the judgment against Gateway that awarded Maldonado $13.7 million in compensatory damages.

Case Questions

Critical Legal Thinking   Why does the law provide an "inherently dangerous activity" exception to the general rule that principals are not liable for the negligence of their independent contractors? Explain.

Business Ethics   Did Gateway act ethically in denying liability in this case? Should Maldonado been denied recovery against Gateway in this case?

Contemporary Business   What should Gateway have done to protect itself from liability in this case?

Business Ethics

Principal Liable for Repo Man's Tort

Yvonne Sanchez borrowed money from MBank El Paso (MBank) to purchase an automobile. She gave MBank a security interest in the vehicle to secure the loan. When Sanchez defaulted on the loan, MBank hired El Paso Recovery Service, an independent contractor, to repossess the automobile. The two men who were dispatched to Sanchez's house found the car parked in the driveway and hooked it to a tow truck. Sanchez demanded that they cease their efforts and leave the premises, but the men nonetheless continued with the repossession. Before the men could tow the automobile into the street, Sanchez jumped into the car, locked the doors, and refused to leave. The men towed the car at a high rate of speed to the repossession yard. They parked the car in the fenced repossession yard, with Sanchez inside, and padlocked the gate. Sanchez was left in the repossession lot with a Doberman Pinscher guard dog loose in the yard. Later, she was rescued by the police. The law prohibits the repossession of a vehicle if a breach of peace would occur. Sanchez filed suit against MBank, alleging that it was liable for the tortious conduct of El Paso Recovery Service. The trial court granted summary

judgment to MBank, but the court of appeals reversed. MBank appealed.

The supreme court of Texas held that MBank, the principal, was liable for the tortious conduct of El Paso Recovery Service, an independent contractor. The court held that the act of repossessing an automobile from a defaulting debtor is an inherently dangerous activity and a nondelegable duty. The court concluded that El Paso Recovery Service had breached the peace in repossessing the car from Sanchez and caused her physical and emotional harm. The court held that MBank, the principal, could not escape liability by hiring an independent contractor to do this task. The court found MBank liable to Sanchez. [*MBank El Paso, N.A. v. Sanchez*, 836 S.W.2d 151, 1992 Tex. Lexis 97 (1992)]

1. Did the independent contractor act responsibly in this case?
2. Should the principal bank have been held liable in this case? Why or why not? ∎

Chapter Summary

Agency, p. 509

The Nature of Agency

1. Agency. Agency is a fiduciary relationship that results from the manifestation of consent by one person to act on behalf of another person, with that person's consent.

2. Parties.

  a. Principal. A principal is a party who employs another person to act on his or her behalf.

  b. Agent. An agent is a party who agrees to act on behalf of another person.

Principal–Agent Relationship

In this type of relationship, an employer hires an employee and authorizes the employee to enter into contracts on the employer's behalf.

Employer–Employee Relationship

In this type of relationship, an employer hires an employee to perform some form of physical service. An employee is not an agent unless the principal authorizes him or her to enter into contracts on the principal's behalf.

Formation of an Agency Relationship, p. 510

Express Agency

In an express agency, the principal and agent expressly agree in words to enter into an agency agreement. The agency contract may be oral or written, unless the Statute of Frauds requires it to be in writing.

Implied Agency

In an implied agency, the agency is implied (inferred) from the conduct of the parties.

Apparent Agency

Apparent agency arises when a principal creates the appearance of an agency that in actuality does not exist. Also called *agency by estoppel* or *ostensible agency*.

Agency by Ratification

Agency by ratification occurs when a person misrepresents him- or herself as another's agent when he or she is not and the purported principal ratifies (accepts) the unauthorized act.

Principal's and Agent's Duties, p. 513

Principal's Duties

Duty of compensation. A principal must pay the agent the agreed-upon compensation. If there is no agreement, the principal must pay what is customary in the industry or, if there is no custom, then the reasonable value of the services.

  Duties of reimbursement and indemnification. A principal must *reimburse* an agent for all expenses paid that were authorized by the principal, within the scope of the agency, and necessary to discharge the agent's duties. The principal must *indemnify* the agent for any losses suffered because of the principal's misconduct.

  Duty of cooperation. A principal must cooperate with and assist the agent in the performance of the agent's duties and the accomplishment of the agency.

Agent's Duties

Duty of performance. An agent must perform the lawful duties expressed in the agency contract with reasonable care, skill, and diligence.

Duty of notification. An agent owes a duty to notify the principal of any information he or she learns that is important to the agency. Information learned by the agent in the course of the agency is *imputed* to the principal.

Duty of accountability. An agent must maintain an accurate accounting of all transactions undertaken on the principal's behalf. A principal may demand an accounting from the agent at any time.

Duty of loyalty. An agent owes a duty not to act adversely to the interests of the principal. The most common breaches of loyalty are:

1. **Self dealing.** The agent cannot deal with the principal unless his or her position is disclosed and the principal agrees to deal with the agent.

2. **Usurping an opportunity.** An agent cannot usurp (take) an opportunity belonging to the principal as his or her own.

3. **Competing with the principal.** An agent is prohibited from competing with the principal during the course of an agency unless the principal agrees.

4. **Misuse of confidential information.** An agent is under a legal duty not to disclose or misuse confidential information learned within the course of an agency.

5. **Dual agency.** An agent cannot act on behalf of two different principals in the same transaction unless the principals agree.

Contract Liability to Third Parties, p. 517

Fully Disclosed Agency

In fully disclosed agency, the third party entering into the contract knows that the agent is acting for a principal and knows the identity of the principal. The principal is liable on the contract; the agent is not liable on the contract.

Partially Disclosed Agency

In partially disclosed agency, the third party knows that the agent is acting for a principal but does not know the identity of the principal. Both the principal and the agent are liable on the contract.

Undisclosed Agency

In undisclosed agency, the third party does not know that the agent is acting for a principal. Both the principal and the agent are liable on the contract.

Tort Liability to Third Parties, p. 519

Tort Liability

A principal is liable for the *tortious conduct* of an agent who is acting within the *scope of his or her authority*. Liability is imposed for misrepresentation, negligence, and intentional torts.

Misrepresentation

A principal is liable for intentional and innocent misrepresentations made by an agent acting within the scope of his or her employment.

Negligence

A principal is liable for the negligent conduct of agents acting within the scope of their employment. Special negligence doctrines include:

1. **Frolic and detour.** A principal is generally relieved of liability if the agent's negligent act occurred on a substantial frolic and detour from the scope of employment.

2. **"Coming and going" rule.** A principal is not liable if the agent's tortious conduct occurred while on the way to or from work.

3. *Dual purpose mission.* If an agent is acting on his or her own behalf and on behalf of the principal, the principal is generally liable for the agent's tortious conduct.

Intentional Torts

States apply one of the following rules to determine liability for intentional torts:

1. *Motivation test.* The principal is liable if the agent's intentional tort was committed to promote the principal's business.
2. *Work-related test.* The principal is liable if the agent's intentional tort was committed within a work-related time or space.

Agents are personally liable for their own tortious conduct.

Termination of an Agency, p. 523

Termination by Acts of the Parties

The following *acts of the parties* terminate agency contracts:

1. *Mutual agreement.* Parties mutually agree to terminate an agency contract.
2. *Lapse of time.* The stipulated time period of the agency expires.
3. *Purpose achieved.* The stipulated purpose of the agency is achieved.
4. *Occurrence of a specified event.* The occurrence of a stipulated event happens.

Notification of Termination

If an agency is terminated by agreement between the parties, the principal must notify third parties as follows:

1. *Parties who dealt with the agent.* Direct notice must be given to these parties.
2. *Parties who have knowledge of the agency.* Direct or constructive (e.g., public notice in newspapers) notice must be given to these parties.
3. *Parties who have no knowledge of the agency.* No notice needs to be given to these parties.

If the proper notice of termination of an agency is not given, the agent has *apparent authority* to bind the principal to contracts.

The principal and agent both have the *power* to terminate an agency at any time. After termination, the agent can no longer act on behalf of the principal. The terminating party may not, however, have had the *right* to terminate the agency and may be held liable for damages caused by *wrongful termination* of the agency.

Termination by Operation of Law

Agency contracts can be terminated by *operation of law*. This includes the following methods:

1. *Death.* Either the principal or the agent dies.
2. *Insanity.* Either the principal or the agent is insane.
3. *Bankruptcy.* The principal is bankrupt.
4. *Impossibility.* A situation arises that makes the performance of the agency contract impossible.
5. *Changed circumstances.* An unusual circumstance would lead the agent to believe that the principal's original instructions are no longer valid.
6. *War.* War breaks out between the principal's country and the agent's country.

Irrevocable Agency

An *agency coupled with an interest* is a special type of agency that is irrevocable by the principal. This type of agency is commonly used in security interests to secure loans.

Wrongful Termination of an Agency Contract

If an agency is for an agreed-upon term or purpose, the *unilateral termination* of the agency contract by either the principal or the agent constitutes the *wrongful termination* of the agency. The breaching party is liable to the other party for damages caused by the breach.

Independent Contractor, p. 526

Principal–Independent Contractor Relationship

In this type of relationship, a principal employs a person who is not an employee of the principal. The independent contractor has authority only to enter into contracts authorized by the principal.

Liability for Independent Contractor's Torts

Generally, principals are not liable for the tortious conduct of independent contractors. Exceptions to the rule are for:

1. Inherently dangerous activities
2. Negligence in selecting an independent contractor

Independent contractors are personally liable for their own torts.

Internet Exercises and Case Questions

Working the Web Internet Exercises

Activities

1. A quick overview of the topic of agency from a practical business perspective can be found at **consumer.pub. findlaw.com/newcontent/consumerlaw/chp2_h.html**. See also "Law About . . . Agency," at **www.law.cornell. edu/topics/agency.html**.

2. One way to create an agency is to execute a power of attorney. See **smallbiz.biz.findlaw.com/bookshelf/**

sblg/sblgchp13_f.html for information and **consumer. pub.findlaw.com/nllg/forms/128.html** for a form.

3. Agency law is very important and widely used in international business ventures. For an example of how the law is applied in another country, Iran, see **www.nourlaw.com/ guide_to_iranian_market/Agency.html**.

Critical Legal Thinking Cases

24.1 Creation of an Agency   Renaldo, Inc., d/b/a Baker Street, owns and operates a nightclub in Georgia. On the evening in question, plaintiff Ginn became "silly drunk" at the nightclub and was asked by several patrons and the manager to leave the premises. The police were called, and Ginn left the premises. When Ginn realized that his jacket was still in the nightclub, he attempted to reenter the premises. He was met at the door by the manager, who refused him admittance. When Ginn persisted, an unidentified patron, without the approval of the manager, pushed Ginn, who lost his balance and fell backward. To break his fall, Ginn put his hand against the door jamb. The unidentified patron slammed the door on Ginn's hand and held it shut for several minutes. Ginn, who suffered severe injuries to his right hand, sued the nightclub for damages. Was the unidentified patron an agent of the nightclub? [*Ginn v. Renaldo, Inc.*, 359 S.E.2d 390, 1987 Ga.App. Lexis 2023 (Ga. App. 1987)]

24.2 Independent Contractor   The Butler Telephone Company, Inc. (Butler), contracted with the Sandidge Construction Company to lay 18 miles of telephone cable in a rural area. In the contract, Butler reserved the right to inspect the work for compliance with the terms of the contract. Butler did not control how Sandidge performed the work. Johnnie Carl Pugh, an employee of Sandidge, was killed on the job when the sides to an excava-

tion in which he was working caved in on top of him. Evidence disclosed that the excavation was not properly shored or sloped and that it violated general safety standards. Pugh's parents and estate brought a wrongful death action against Butler. Is Butler liable? [*Pugh v. Butler Telephone Company, Inc.*, 512 So.2d 1317, 1987 Ala. Lexis 4468 (AL 1987)]

24.3 Ratification   After Francis Pusateri retired, he met with Glibert J. Johnson, a stockbroker with E. F. Hutton & Co., Inc., and informed Johnson that he wished to invest in tax-free bonds and money market accounts. Pusateri opened an investment account with E. F. Hutton and checked the box stating his objective was "tax-free income and moderate growth." During the course of a year, Johnson churned Pusateri's account to make commissions and invested Pusateri's funds in volatile securities and options. Johnson kept telling Pusateri that his account was making money, and the monthly statement from E. F. Hutton did not indicate otherwise. The manager at E. F. Hutton was aware of Johnson's activities but did nothing to prevent them. When Johnson left E. F. Hutton, Pusateri's account—which had been called the "laughingstock" of the office—had shrunk from $196,000 to $96,880, Pusateri sued E. F. Hutton for damages. Is E. F. Hutton liable? [*Pusateri v. E. F. Hutton & Co., Inc.*, 180 Cal.App.3d 247, 225 Cal.Rptr. 526, 1986 Cal.App. Lexis 1502 (Cal. App. 1986)]

24.4 Reasonable Care and Skill   Norman R. Barton and his wife decided to vacation in Florida in November 1984. In March 1984, they contacted Wonderful World of Travel, Inc., a travel agency licensed by the state of Ohio, to make the arrangements. They requested a room with a view of the ocean, a kitchenette so they would be saved the expense of dining out, free parking, and a free spa. In August, with the Bartons' approval, the travel agency made reservations at the Beau Rivage motel in Bal Harbour, Florida. The travel agency did not confirm the reservations prior to the Bartons' departure in November. When the Bartons arrived at the motel, they found it closed, chained, and guarded. The only other hotel or motel in the area was a Sheraton, which was almost triple the room cost of the Beau Rivage. The Sheraton overlooked the ocean, but it did not have a kitchenette, free parking, or free spa privileges. The Bartons stayed at the Sheraton. They sued the travel agent upon their return. Is the travel agent liable for the increased cost incurred by the Bartons? [*Barton v. Wonderful World of Travel, Inc.*, 502 N.E.2d 715, 1986 Ohio Misc. Lexis 57 (Ohio Mun. 1986)]

24.5 Imputed Knowledge   On March 31, 1981, Iota Management Corporation entered into a contract to purchase the Bel Air West Motor Hotel in the City of St. Louis from Boulevard Investment Company. The agreement contained the following warranty: "Seller has no actual notice of any substantial defect in the structure of the Hotel or in any of its plumbing, heating, air-conditioning, electrical, or utility systems."

When the buyer inspected the premises, no leaks in the pipes were visible. Iota purchased the hotel for $2 million. When Iota removed some of the walls and ceilings during remodeling, it found evidence of prior repairs to leaking pipes and ducts, as well as devices for catching water (e.g., milk cartons, cookie sheets, buckets). The estimate to repair these leaks was $500,000. Evidence at trial showed that Cecil Lillibridge, who was Boulevard's maintenance supervisor from 1975 until the sale of the hotel in 1981, had actual knowledge of these problems and had repaired some of the pipes. Iota sued Boulevard to rescind the contract. Is Boulevard liable? [*Iota Management Corporation v. Boulevard Investment Company*, 731 S.W.2d 399, 1987 Mo.App. Lexis 4027 (Mo.App. 1987)]

24.6 Dual Agency   Chemical Bank is the primary bank for Washington Steel Corporation. As an agent for Washington Steel, Chemical Bank expressly and impliedly promised that it would advance the best interests and welfare of Washington Steel. During the course of the agency, Washington Steel provided the bank with comprehensive and confidential financial information, other data, and future business plans.

At some point during the agency, TW Corporation and other approached Chemical Bank to request a loan of $7 million to make a hostile tender offer for the stock of Washington Steel. Chemical Bank agreed and became an agent for TW. Management at Chemical Bank did not disclose its adverse relationship with TW to Washington Steel, did not request Washington Steel's permission to act as an agent for TW, and directed employees of the bank to conceal the bank's involvement with TW from Washington Steel. After TW commenced its public tender offer, Washington Steel filed suit, seeking to obtain an injunction against Chemical Bank and TW. Who wins? [*Washington Steel Corporation v. TW Corporation*, 465 F.Supp. 1100, 1979 U.S.Dist. Lexis 14391 (W.D. Pa. 1979)]

24.7 Duty of Loyalty   Peter Shields was the president and a member of the board of directors of Production Finishing Corporation from 1974 through August 1981. The company provided steel polishing services. It did most, if not all, of the polishing work in the Detroit area, except for that of the Ford Motor Company. (Ford did its own polishing.) Shields discussed this matter with Ford on behalf of Production Finishing on a number of occasions. When Shields learned that Ford was discontinuing its polishing operation, he incorporated Flat Rock Metal and submitted a confidential proposal to Ford that provided that he would buy Ford's equipment and provide polishing services to Ford. It was not until he resigned from Production Finishing that he informed the board of directors that he was pursuing the Ford business himself. Production Finishing sued Shields. Did Shields breach his fiduciary duty of loyalty to Production Finishing? [*Production Finishing Corporation v. Shields*, 405 N.W.2d 171, 1987 Mich.App. Lexis 2379 (Mich. App. 1987)]

24.8 Personal Guaranty   In May 1978, Sebastian International, Inc., entered into a five-year lease for a building in Chadsworth, California. In September 1980, with the consent of the master lessors, Sebastian sublet the building to West Valley Grinding, Inc. In conjunction with the execution of the sublease, the corporate officers of West Valley, including Kenneth E. Peck, each signed a guaranty of lease, personally ensuring the payment of West Valley's rental obligations. The guaranty contract referred to Peck in his individual capacity; however, on the signature line he was identified as "Kenneth Peck, Vice President." In May 1981, West Valley went out of business, leaving 24 months remaining on the sublease. After unsuccessful attempts to secure another sublease, Sebastian surrendered the leasehold back to the master lessors and brought suit against Peck to recover the unpaid rent. Peck argued that he was not personally liable because his signature was that of an agent for a disclosed principal and not that of a principal himself. Who wins? [*Sebastian International, Inc. v. Peck*, 195 Cal.App.3d 803, 240 Cal.Rptr. 911, 1987 Cal.App. Lexis 2237 (Cal.App. 1987)]

24.9 Contract Liability   G. Elvin Grinder of Marbury, Maryland, was a building contractor who, prior to May 1, 1973, did business as an individual and traded as "Grinder Construction." Grinder maintained an open account, on his individual credit, with Bryans Road Building & Supply Co., Inc. Grinder would purchase materials and supplies from Bryans on credit and later pay the invoices. On May 1, 1973, G. Elvin Grinder Construction, Inc., a Maryland corporation, was formed, with Grinder personally owning 52 percent of the stock of the corporation. Grinder did not inform Bryans that he had incorporated and continued to purchase supplies on credit from Bryans under the name "Grinder Construction." In May 1978, after certain invoices were not paid by Grinder, Bryans sued Grinder personally to recover. Grinder asserted that the debts were owed by the corporation. Bryans amended its complaint to include the corporation as a defendant. Who is liable to Bryans? [*Grinder v. Bryans Road Building & Supply Co., Inc.*, 432 A.2d 453, 1981 Md. Lexis 246 (Md.App. 1981)]

24.10 Tort Liability   Intrastate Radiotelephone, Inc., is a public utility that supplies radiotelephone utility service to the general public for radiotelephones, pocket pagers, and beepers. Robert Kranhold, an employee of Intrastate, was authorized to use his personal vehicle on company business. On the morning of March 9, 1976, when Kranhold was driving his vehicle to

Intrastate's main office, he negligently struck a motorcycle being driven by Michael S. Largey, causing severe and permanent injuries to Largey. The accident occurred at the intersection where Intrastate's main office is located. Evidence showed that Kranhold acted as a consultant to Intrastate, worked both in and out of Intrastate's offices, had no set hours of work, often attended meetings at Intrastate's offices, and went to Intrastate's offices to pick things up or drop things off. Largey sued Intrastate for damages. Is Intrastate liable? [*Largey v. Radiotelephone, Inc.*, 136 Cal.App.3d 660, 186 Cal.Rptr. 520, 1982 Cal.App. Lexis 2049 (Cal.App. 1982)]

Ethics Cases

24.11 Business Ethics   The Hagues, husband and wife, owned a 160-acre tract that they decided to sell. On March 19, 1976, they entered into a listing agreement with Harvey C. Hilgendorf, a licensed real estate broker, which gave Hilgendorf the exclusive right to sell the property for a period of 12 months. The Hagues agreed to pay Hilgendorf a commission of 6 percent of the accepted sale price if a bona fide buyer was found during the listing period.

By letter on August 13, 1976, the Hagues terminated the listing agreement with Hilgendorf. Hilgendorf did not acquiesce to the Hagues' termination, however. On September 30, 1976, Hilgendorf presented an offer to the Hagues from a buyer willing to purchase the property at the full listing price. The Hagues ignored the offer and sold the property to another buyer. Hilgendorf sued the Hagues for breach of the agency agreement. Did the Hagues act ethically in this case? Who wins the lawsuit? [*Hilgendorf v. Hague*, 293 N.W.2d 272, 1980 Iowa Sup. Lexis 882 (IA 1980)]

24.12 Business Ethics   The National Biscuit Company (Nabisco) is a corporation that produces and distributes cookies and other food products to grocery stores and other outlets across the nation. In October 1968, Nabisco hired Ronnell Lynch as a cookie salesman-trainee. On March 1, 1969, Lynch was assigned to his own sales territory. Lynch's duties involved making sales calls, taking orders, and making sure that shelves of stores in his territory were stocked with Nabisco products. During the period March 1 to May 1, 1969, Nabisco received numerous complaints from store owners in Lynch's territory that Lynch was overly aggressive and was taking shelf space for Nabisco products that was reserved for competing brands.

On May 1, 1969, Lynch visited a grocery store that was managed by Jerome Lange. Lynch was there to place previously delivered merchandise on the store's shelves. An argument developed between Lynch and Lange. Lynch became very angry and started swearing. Lange, the store manager, told Lynch to stop swearing or leave the store because children were present. Lynch became uncontrollably angry and went behind the counter and dared Lange to a fight. When Lange refused to fight, Lynch proceeded to viciously assault and batter Lange, causing severe injuries. Lange sued Nabisco. Was it ethical for Nabisco to deny liability in this case? Do you think the prior complaints against Lynch had an effect on the decision reached in this case? Is Nabisco liable for the intentional tort (assault and battery) of its employee, Lynch? [*Lange v. National Biscuit Company*, 211 N.W.2d 783, 1973 Minn. Lexis 1106 (MN 1983)]

Briefing the Case Writing Assignment

Read Case A.24 in the Case Appendix [*District of Columbia v. Howell*]. This case is excerpted from the court of appeals opinion. Review and brief the case. In your brief, be sure to answer the following questions.

1. Was A. Louis Jagoe hired by the District of Columbia as an employee or as an independent contractor?

2. Describe the accident that occurred. Who was injured?

3. Normally, an employer is not liable for the tortious conduct of an independent contractor it has hired. Describe the "special risks" exception to this rule.

4. What damages were awarded to the plaintiff?

Endnotes

1. *Restatement (Second) of Agency*, § 4.
2. *Restatement (Second) of Agency*, § 321.

25

Sole Proprietorships and Partnerships

*"*There are a great many of us who will adhere to that ancient principle that we prefer to be governed by the power of laws, and not by the power of men.*"*

—Woodrow Wilson
Speech, September 25, 1912

Chapter Objectives

After studying this chapter, you should be able to:

1. Define sole proprietorship and the liability of a sole proprietor.

2. Define general partnership.

3. Explain the contract and tort liability of general partners.

4. Define limited partnership and describe the liability of general and limited partners.

5. Define limited liability partnership (LLP) and describe the limited liability of partners of an LLP.

Chapter Contents

- Entrepreneurship
- Sole Proprietorship
- General Partnership
- Limited Partnership
- Limited Liability Partnership (LLP)

A person who wants to start a business must decide whether the business should operate as one of the major forms of business organization—*sole proprietorship*, *general partnership*, *limited partnership*, *limited liability partnership*, *limited liability company*, and *corporation*—or under some other available legal business form. The selection depends on many factors, including the ease and cost of formation, the capital requirements of the business, the flexibility of management decisions, government restrictions, the extent of personal liability, tax considerations, and the like.

This chapter discusses entrepreneurship, sole proprietorships, general partnerships, limited partnerships, and limited liability partnerships, limited liability companies are discussed in Chapter 29, and corporations are discussed in Chapters 26–28.

Entrepreneurship

An **entrepreneur** is a person who forms and operates a new business. An entrepreneur may start the business by him or herself or cofound the business with others. Most businesses started by entrepreneurs are small, although some grow into substantial organizations. For example, Bill Gates started Microsoft Corporation, which grew into the giant software and Internet company. Michael Dell started Dell Computers as a mail-order business; it has become a leader in computer sales. Entrepreneurs in this country and around the world create new businesses daily that hire employees, provide new products and services, and make economies of countries grow.

Entrepreneurial Forms of Conducting Business

Entrepreneurs contemplating starting a business have many options when choosing the legal form in which to conduct the business. Each of these forms of business has

> It has been uniformly laid down in this Court, as far back as we can remember, that good faith is the basis of all mercantile transactions.
>
> Buller, J.
> *Salomons v. Nissen (1788)*

> It is the privilege of a trader in a free country, in all matters not contrary to law, to regulate his own mode of carrying it on according to his own discretion and choice.
>
> B. Alderson
> *Hilton v. Eckersly (1855)*

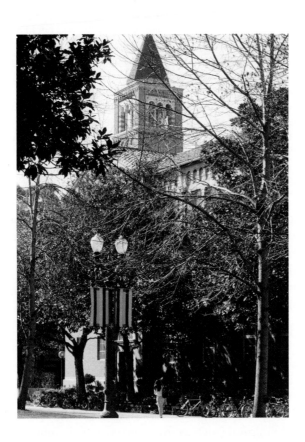

University Campus. Many of today's students will become tomorrow's entrepreneurs.

advantages and disadvantages for the entrepreneur. The major forms for conducting businesses and professions are:

1. Sole proprietorship
2. General partnership
3. Limited partnership
4. Limited liability partnership
5. Limited liability company
6. Corporation

Certain requirements must be met to form and operate each of these forms of business.

Contemporary Environment

The Entrepreneurial Spirit: The Creation of Amazon.com

In 1994, Jeff Bezos, the son of a Cuban immigrant to the United States, graduated from Princeton University. Bezos then saw an opportunity: online commerce. Bezos drew up a list of 20 products that he figured he could sell online, and then he narrowed it to books. Bezos settled on books for two reasons. First, there are lots to sell (about 1.3 million books in print). Second, there were thousands of bookstores, the largest of which was Barnes & Noble, with 12 percent of the industry's $25 billion annual sales.

Bezos and his wife settled in Seattle, Washington. They rented a house, hired four employees, and started Amazon.com out of their garage. Bezos and his family incorporated the business, sold some stock to friends and other investors, and kept the rest of the stock for themselves. Bezos took a traditional business—bookselling—online. He reasoned that books were fungible—everyone sold the same product—and that a portion of a traditional bookseller's cost represented the real estate on which the store sat. So Bezos began taking orders in cyberspace. Amazon.com sold its first book in July 1995.

Amazon.com became a success, at least at selling books. Bezos's business plan called for building a client base and making "Amazon.com" a readily recognized e-commerce name. He accomplished these goals, attracting a client base of loyal book-buying customers and getting the Amazon.com brand name to be recognized.

Following on the heels of its book-selling success, Amazon.com began selling other products over the Internet, including CDs, videos, gifts, greeting cards, and thousands of other items. Amazon.com entered the world of online auctions and linked with other companies selling pet supplies, drugstore goods, and more. Purchasers pay Amazon.com by credit card, submitted over the telephone or the Web, and the transaction is guarded by encryption. Amazon.com offers one-click ordering, which lets buyers store credit cards and addresses after their first purchase.

In May 1997, Amazon.com went public, raising over $40 million by selling stock for $18 per share. The price of Amazon.com doubled on the first day of trading. Bezos became a billionaire before the age of 34. Bezos and his family own about 40 percent of Amazon.com. In the span of less than five years, Bezos had taken his business plan and created the largest, most recognized e-commerce company in the world. This entrepreneur's dream became reality. But when asked if he feared Barnes & Noble's entry into online bookselling, Bezos replied that he feared "two guys or girls in a garage" more because they represented the most dangerous of competitors—entrepreneurs. ■

Sole Proprietorship

Sole proprietorships are the simplest form of business organization. The owner is the business. There is no separate legal entity. Sole proprietorships are the most common form of business organization in the United States. Many small businesses—and a few large ones—operate in this way.

There are several major advantages to operating a business as a sole proprietorship. They include the following:

> It is the spirit and not the form of law that keeps justice alive.
>
> Earl Warren
> *The Law and the Future (1955)*

1. Forming a sole proprietorship is easy and does not cost a lot.
2. The owner has the right to make all management decisions concerning the business, including those involving hiring and firing employees.
3. The sole proprietor owns all of the business and has the right to receive all of the business's profits.
4. A sole proprietorship can be easily transferred or sold if and when the owner desires to do so; no other approval (such as from partners or shareholders) is necessary.

There are important disadvantages to this business form, too. For example, (1) the sole proprietor's access to the capital is limited to personal funds plus any loans he or she can obtain, and (2) the sole proprietor is legally responsible for the business's contracts and the torts he/she or any of his or her employees commit in the course of employment.

Creation of a Sole Proprietorship

It is easy to create a sole proprietorship. There are no formalities, and no federal or state government approval is required. Some local governments require all businesses, including sole proprietorships, to obtain a license to do business within the city. If no other form of business organization is chosen, the business is by default a sole proprietorship.

Contemporary Environment
d.b.a—"Doing Business As"

A sole proprietorship can operate under the name of the sole proprietor or a *trade name*. For example, the author of this book can operate a sole proprietorship under the name "Henry R. Cheeseman" or under a trade name such as "The Big Cheese." Operating under a trade name is commonly designated as **d.b.a. (doing business as)** (e.g., Henry R. Cheeseman, doing business as "The Big Cheese").

Most states require all businesses that operate under a trade name to file a **fictitious business name statement** (or **certificate of trade name**) with the appropriate government agency. The statement must contain the name and address of the applicant, the trade name, and the address of the business. Most states also require notice of the trade name to be published in a newspaper of general circulation serving the area in which the applicant does business.

These requirements are intended to disclose the real owner's name to the public. Noncompliance can result in a fine. Some states prohibit violators from maintaining lawsuits in the state's courts. ∎

Personal Liability of Sole Proprietors

The sole proprietor bears the risk of loss of the business; that is, the owner will lose his or her entire capital contribution if the business fails. In addition, the sole proprietor has *unlimited personal liability* (see Exhibit 25.1). Therefore, creditors may recover claims against the business from the sole proprietor's personal assets (e.g., home, automobile, bank accounts).

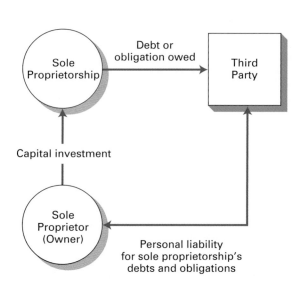

Exhibit 25.1

Sole Proprietorship

There shall be one law for the native and for the stranger who sojourns among you.

Moses
Exodus 12:49

Consider This Example Suppose Ken Smith opens a clothing store called The Rap Shop and operates it as a sole proprietorship. Smith files the proper statement and publishes the necessary notice of the use of the trade name. He contributes $25,000 of his personal funds to the business and borrows $100,000 in the name of the business from a bank. Assume that after several months Smith closes the business because it was unsuccessful. At the time it is closed, the business has no assets, owes the bank $100,000, and owes rent, trade credit, and other debts of $25,000. Here, Smith is personally liable to pay the bank and all the debts from his personal assets.

In the following case, The court addressed the liability of a sole proprietor.

Vernon v. Schuster, d/b/a Diversity Heating and Plumbing
688 N.E.2d 1172, 1997 Ill. Lexis 482 (1997)
Supreme Court of Illinois

Case 25.1
Sole Proprietor

Background and Facts

James Schuster was a sole proprietor doing business as (d.b.a.) "Diversity Heating and Plumbing." Diversity Heating was in the business of selling, installing, and servicing heating and plumbing systems. George Vernon and others (Vernon) owned a building that needed a new boiler. In November 1989, Vernon hired Diversity Heating to install a new boiler in the building. Diversity Heating installed the boiler and gave a warranty that the boiler would not crack for 10 years. On October 20, 1993, James Schuster died. On that date, James's son, Jerry Schuster, inherited his father's business and thereafter ran the business as a sole proprietorship under the d/b/a "Diversity Heating and Plumbing." In February 1994, the boiler installed in Vernon's building broke and could not be repaired. Vernon demanded that Jerry Schuster honor the warranty and replace the boiler. When Jerry Schuster refused to do so, Vernon had the boiler replaced at the cost of $8,203 and sued Jerry Schuster to recover this amount for breach of warranty. The trial court dismissed Vernon's complaint, but the appellate court reinstated the case. Jerry Schuster appealed to the supreme court of Illinois.

Issue

Is Jerry Schuster liable for the warranty made by his father?

Court's Reasoning

The court noted that common identity of ownership is lacking when one sole proprietorship succeeds another. It is well settled that a sole proprietorship has no legal identity separate from that of the individual who owns it. The sole proprietor may do business

under a fictitious name if he or she chooses. However, doing business under another name does not create an entity distinct from the person operating the business. The court stated that there is generally no continuity of existence because on the death of the sole proprietor, the sole proprietorship obviously ends.

In this case, therefore, it must be remembered that "Diversity Heating" has no legal existence. Diversity Heating was only a pseudonym for James Schuster. Once he died, Diversity Heating ceased to exist. Now, Diversity Heating is only a pseudonym for the defendant, Jerry Schuster. Even though defendant Jerry Schuster inherited Diversity Heating from his father, defendant would not have continued his father's sole proprietorship, but rather would have started a new sole proprietorship.

Decision and Remedy

The Illinois supreme court held that Jerry Schuster, as a sole proprietor, was not liable for the warranty previously made by his father, who was also a sole proprietor. The supreme court reversed the decision of the appellate court.

Case Questions

Critical Legal Thinking Is a sole Proprietorship a separate legal entity? Explain.

Business Ethics Did Jerry Schuster act unethically by failing to honor the warranty made by his father?

Contemporary Business Do you think many businesses are run as sole proprietorships? What are the benefits and detriments of doing so?

General Partnership

General, or *ordinary*, *partnerships* have been recognized since ancient times. The English common law of partnerships governed early U.S. partnerships. The individual states expanded the body of partnership law.

A **general partnership**, or partnership, is a voluntary association of two or more persons for carrying on a business as co-owners for profit. The formation of a partnership creates certain rights and duties among partners and with third parties. These rights and duties are established in the partnership agreement and by law. **General partners**, or **partners**, are personally liable for the debts and obligations of the partnership (see Exhibit 25.2).

Uniform Partnership Act (UPA)

In 1914, the National Conference of Commissioners on Uniform State Laws (a group of lawyers, judges, and legal scholars) promulgated the **Uniform Partnership Act (UPA)**. The UPA codifies partnership law. Its goal was to establish consistent partnership law that was uniform throughout the United States. The UPA has been adopted in whole or in

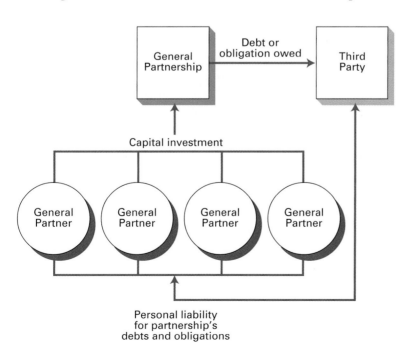

Exhibit 25.2

General Partnership

part by 48 states,[1] the District of Columbia, Guam, and the Virgin Islands. Because it is so important, the UPA form's the basis of the study of general partnerships in this chapter.

The UPA covers most problems that arise in the formation, operation, and dissolution of ordinary partnerships. Other rules of law or equity govern if there is no applicable provision of the UPA [UPA § 5].

The UPA adopted the **entity theory** of partnership, which considers partnerships as separate legal entities. As such, partnerships can hold title to personal and real property, transact business in the partnership name, and the like.

Partnership Name

An ordinary partnership can operate under the names of any one or more of the partners or under a fictitious business name. If the partnership operates under a fictitious name, it must file a *fictitious business name statement* with the appropriate government agency and publish a notice of the name in a newspaper of general circulation where the partnership does business. The name selected by the partnership cannot indicate that it is a corporation (e.g., it cannot contain the term *Inc.*) and cannot be similar to the name used by any existing business entity.

Formation of a Partnership

A business must meet four criteria to qualify as a partnership under the UPA [UPA § 6(1)]. It must be (1) an association of two or more persons (2) carrying on a business (3) as co-owners (4) for profit. Partnerships are voluntary associations of two or more persons. All partners must agree to the participation of each co-partner. A person cannot be forced to be a partner or to accept another person as a partner. The UPA definition of *person* includes natural persons, partnerships (including limited partnerships), corporations, and other associations. A business—trade, occupation, or profession—must be carried on. The organization or venture must have a profit motive in order to qualify as a partnership, even though the business does not actually have to make a profit.

A general partnership may be formed with little or no formality. Co-ownership of a business is essential to create a partnership. The most important factor in determining co-ownership is whether the parties share the business's profits and management responsibility.

Receipt of a share of business profits is prima facie evidence of a partnership because nonpartners usually are not given the right to share in the business's profits. No inference of the existence of a partnership is drawn if profits are received in payment of (1) a debt owed to a creditor in installments or otherwise, (2) wages owed to an employee, (3) rent owed to a landlord, (4) an annuity owed to a widow, widower, or representative of a deceased partner, (5) interest owed on a loan, or (6) consideration for the sale of goodwill of a business [UPA § 7]. An agreement to share losses of a business is strong evidence of a partnership.

The right to participate in the management of a business is important evidence for determining the existence of a partnership, but it is not conclusive evidence because the right to participate in management is sometimes given to employees, creditors, and others. It is compelling evidence of the existence of a partnership if a person is given the right to share in profits, losses, and management of a business.

The Partnership Agreement

The agreement to form a partnership may be oral, written, or implied from the conduct of the parties. It may even be created inadvertently. No formalities are necessary, although a few states require general partnerships to file certificates of partnership with an appropri-

One of the most fruitful sources of ruin to men of the world is the recklessness or want of principle of partners, and it is one of the perils to which every man exposes himself who enters into partnership with another.

Malins, V.G.
Mackay v. Douglas, 14 Eq. 106 at 118 (1872)

Business Brief

Partnerships often operate under a fictitious business name. Those that do must file a fictitious business name statement with the appropriate government agency.

Business Brief

A partnership is a *voluntary* association. A person cannot be forced to be a partner or to accept another person as a partner.

The partner of my partner is not my partner.

Legal Maxim

ate government agency. Partnerships that exist for more than one year or are authorized to deal in real estate must be in writing under the Statute of Frauds.

It is good practice for partners to put their partnership agreement in writing. A written document is important evidence of the terms of the agreement, particularly if a dispute arises among the partners.

A written partnership agreement is called a **partnership agreement** or **articles of partnership**. The partners can agree to almost any terms in their partnership agreement, except terms that are illegal. The articles of partnership can be short and simple or long and complex. If the agreement fails to provide for an essential term or contingency, the provisions of the UPA control. Thus, the UPA acts as a gap-filling device to the partners' agreement.

In the following case, the court had to decide whether a partnership had been created.

> It is the privilege of a trader in a free country, in all matters not contrary to law, to regulate his own mode of carrying it on according to his own discretion and choice.
>
> B. Alderson
> *Hilton v. Eckersley (1855)*

Case 25.2
General Partnership

Vohland v. Sweet
435 N.E. 2d 860, 1982 Ind.App. Lexis 1145 (1982)
Court of Appeals of Indiana

Background and Facts

Norman E. Sweet began working for Charles Vohland as an hourly employee at a garden nursery owned by Vohland in 1956, when he was a youngster. Upon completion of military service (from 1958 to 1960), Sweet resumed his former employment. In 1963, Charles Vohland retired, and his son Paul Vohland (Vohland) commenced what became known as Vohland's Nursery, the business of which was landscape gardening. Vohland purchased the interests of his brothers and sisters in the nursery. At that time, Sweet's status changed: He was to receive a 20 percent share of the net profit of the business after all expenses were paid, including labor, supplies, plants, and other expenses. Sweet contributed no capital to the enterprise. The compensation was paid on an irregular basis— every several weeks, Vohland and Sweet would sit down, compute the income received and expenses paid, and Sweet would be issued a check for 20 percent of the balance. No Social Security or income taxes were withheld from Sweet's checks.

Vohland and Sweet did not enter into a written agreement. No partnership income tax returns were filed by the business. Sweet's tax returns declared that he was a self-employed salesman. He paid self-employment Social Security taxes. Vohland handled all the finances and books of the nursery and borrowed money from the bank solely in his own name for business purposes. Vohland made most of the sales for the business. Sweet managed the physical aspects of the nursery, supervised the care of the nursery stock, and oversaw the performance of the contracts for customers. Sweet testified that in the early 1970s, Vohland told him:

> He was going to take me in and that I wouldn't have to punch a time clock anymore, that I would be on a commission basis and that I would be—have more of an interest in the business if I had an interest in the business. He referred to it as a "piece of the action."

Vohland denied making this statement. Sweet brought this action for dissolution of the alleged partnership and for an accounting. He sought payment for 20 percent of the business's inventory. The trial court held in favor of Sweet and awarded him $58,733. Vohland appealed.

Issue

Did Vohland and Sweet enter into a partnership?

Court's Reasoning

Receipt by a person of a share of the profits is prima facie evidence that he or she is a partner in a business. Here, Sweet shared in the profits of the nursery. Although the parties called Sweet's sharing in the profits a "commission," the court stated that the term "when used by landscape gardeners and not lawyers, should not be restricted to its technical definition." The court found that the absence of a capital contribution by Sweet was not controlling and that his contribution of labor and skill would suffice.

Decision and Remedy

The court of appeals held that partnership had been created between Vohland and Sweet. The court of appeals affirmed the decision of the trial court in favor of Sweet.

Case Questions

Critical Legal Thinking   Do you think a partnership was formed in this case? Should all partnership agreements be required to be in writing?

Business Ethics   Do you think either party acted unethically in this case?

Contemporary Business   What are the economic consequences of founding a partnership?

Right to Participate in Management

In the absence of an agreement to the contrary, all partners have equal rights in the management and conduct of the partnership business. In other words, each partner has one vote, regardless of the proportional size of his or her capital contribution or share in the partnership's profits. Under the UPA, a simple majority decides most ordinary partnership matters [UPA § 18]. If the vote is tied, the action being voted on is considered to be defeated. The partners may agree to modify the majority rule by delegating management responsibility to a committee of partners or to a managing partner.

Right to an Accounting

Partners are not permitted to sue the partnership or other partners at law. Instead, they are given the right to bring an **action for an accounting** against other partners. An accounting is a formal judicial proceeding in which the court is authorized to (1) review the partnership and the partners' transactions and (2) award each partner his or her share of the partnership assets [UPA § 24]. It results in a money judgment for or against partners, according to the balance struck.

Partners' Rights to Share in Profits

Unless otherwise agreed, the UPA mandates that a partner has the right to an equal share in the partnership's profits and losses [UPA § 18(a)]. Partnership agreements often provide that profits and losses are to be allocated in proportion to the partners' capital contributions. The right to share in the profits of the partnership is considered to be the right to share in the earnings from the investment of capital.

For example, suppose LeAnn Pearson and Mark Butler form a partnership. Pearson contributes $75,000 capital and Butler contributes $25,000 capital. They do not have an agreement as to how profits or losses are to be shared. Assume the partnership makes $100,000 in profits. Under the UPA, Pearson and Butler share the profits equally— $50,000 each.

Where a partnership agreement provides for the sharing of profits but is silent as to how losses are to be shared, losses are shared in the same proportion as profits. The reverse is not true, however. If a partnership agreement provides for the sharing of losses but is silent as to how profits are to be shared, profits are shared equally.

Expressly providing how profits and losses are to be shared by partners can increase the benefits to partners. For example, partners with high incomes from other sources can benefit most from the losses generated by a partnership.

Tort Liability

While acting on partnership business, a partner or an employee of the partnership may commit a tort that causes injury to a third person. This tort could be caused by a negligent act, a breach of trust (such as embezzlement from a customer's account), a breach of fiduciary duty, defamation, fraud, or another intentional tort. The partnership is liable if the act is committed while the person is acting within the ordinary course of partnership business or with the authority of his or her co-partners.

Under the UPA, partners are **jointly and severally liable** for torts and breaches of trust [UPA § 15(a)]. This is so even if a partner did not participate in the commission of the act. This type of liability permits a third party to sue one or more of the partners separately. Judgment can be collected only against the partners who are sued. The partnership and partners who are made to pay tort liability may seek indemnification from the partner who committed the wrongful act. A release of one partner does not discharge the liability of other partners.

Consider This Example   Suppose Nicole, Jim, and Maureen form a partnership. Assume that Jim, while on partnership business, causes an automobile accident that injures Kurt, a pedestrian. Kurt suffers $100,000 in injuries. Kurt, at his option, can sue Nicole, Jim, or Maureen separately, or any two of them, or all of them.

The court applied the doctrine of joint and several liability in the following case.

> It is when merchants dispute about their own rules that they invoke the law.
>
> J. Brett
> *Robinsone v. Mollett* (1875)

Zuckerman v. Antenucci
478 N.Y.S,2d 578, 1984 N.Y.Misc. Lexis 3283 (1984)
Supreme Court of New York

Case 25.3
Tort Liability

Background and Facts

Jose Pena and Joseph Antenucci were both medical doctors who were partners in a medical practice. Both doctors treated Elaine Zuckerman during her pregnancy. Her son, Daniel Zuckerman, was born with severe physical problems. Elaine, as Daniel's mother and natural guardian, brought this medical malpractice suit against both doctors. The jury found that Pena was guilty of medical malpractice but that Antenucci was not. The amount of the verdict totaled $4 million. The trial court entered judgment against Pena but not against Antenucci. The plaintiffs made a posttrial motion for judgment against both defendants.

Issue

Is Antenucci jointly and severally liable for the medical malpractice of his partner, Pena?

Court's Reasoning

The court noted that a general partnership is liable for the tortious act of a partner, and a partner is jointly and severally liable for tortious acts chargeable to the partnership. When a tort is committed by the partnership, the wrong is imputable to all the partners jointly and severally, and an action may be brought against all or any of them in their individual capacities or against the partnership as an entity. The court held that even though the jury found that defendant Antenucci was not guilty of any malpractice in his treatment of the patient but that defendant Pena, his partner, was guilty of malpractice in his treatment of the patient, they were then both jointly and severally liable for the malpractice committed by defendant Pena by operation of law.

Decision and Remedy

The court held that both partners were jointly and severally liable for the judgment. The supreme court reversed the decision of the trial court and held that Antenucci was liable for the tort of his partner Pena.

Case Questions

Critical Legal Thinking   What is joint and several liability? How does it differ from joint liability?

Business Ethics   Is it ethical for a partner to deny liability for torts of other partners?

Contemporary Business   What types of insurance should a partnership purchase? Why?

Contract Liability

As a legal entity, a partnership must act through its agents—that is, its partners. Contracts entered into with suppliers, customers, lenders, or others on the partnership's behalf are binding on the partnership.

Under the UPA, partners are **jointly liable** for the contracts and debts of the partnership [UPA § 15(b)]. This means that a third party who sues to recover on a partnership contract or debt must name all the partners in the lawsuit. If such a lawsuit is successful, the plaintiff can collect the entire amount of the judgment against any or all of the partners. If the third party's suit does not name all the partners, the judgment cannot be collected against any of the partners or the partnership assets. Similarly, releasing any partner from the lawsuit releases them all.

A partner who is made to pay more than his or her proportionate share of contract liability may seek **indemnification** from the partnership and from those partners who have not paid their share of the loss.

In the following case, the court found partners jointly liable on a partnership contract.

Edward A. Kemmler Memorial Foundation v. Mitchell
584 N.E.2d 695, 1992 Ohio Lexis 205 (1992)
Supreme Court of Ohio

Case 25.4
Contract Liability

Background and Facts

Clifford W. Davis and Dr. William D. Mitchell formed a general partnership to purchase and operate rental properties for investment purposes. The partnership purchased a parcel of real property from the Edward A. Kemmler Memorial Foundation (Foundation) on credit. Davis signed a $150,000 promissory note to the Foundation as "Cliff W. Davis, Partner." Prior to executing the note, Davis and Mitchell entered into an agreement that provided that only Davis, and not Mitchell, would be personally liable on the note to the Foundation. They did not inform the Foundation of this side agreement, however. When the partnership defaulted on the note, the Foundation sued the partnership and both partners to recover on the note. Mitchell asserted in defense that the side agreement with Davis relieved him of personal liability. The trial court found Davis and Mitchell jointly liable. The appellate court reversed, excusing Mitchell from liability. The Foundation appealed.

Issue

Are both partners, Davis and Mitchell, jointly liable on the note?

Court's Reasoning

The court stated the following legal principle:

> Every partner is an agent of the partnership for the purpose of its business, and the act of every partner, including the execution in the partnership name of any instrument, for apparently carrying on in the usual way the business of the partnership of which he is a member binds the partnership, unless the partner so acting has in fact no authority to act for the partnership in the particular matter, and the person with whom he is dealing has knowledge of the fact that he has no such authority.

The court stated that if a promissory note is executed in the name of the partnership, the partnership is bound, unless a contradictory agreement between the partners is known to the parties with whom they are dealing. The trial court found that the Foundation had no knowledge of the agreement between Davis and Mitchell regarding Mitchell's liability for the note.

Decision and Remedy

The supreme court of Ohio held that both partners were jointly liable on the note. The supreme court reversed the decision of the appellate court.

Case Questions

Critical Legal Thinking   What is joint liability? Should one general partner be liable to pay a judgment against the partnership?

Business Ethics   Should Davis and Mitchell have notified the Foundation of their side agreement?

Contemporary Business   Is it financially dangerous to be a partner in a general partnership? Explain.

Concept Summary   Personal Liability of General Partners

Issue	Joint Liability	Joint and Several Liability
Type of lawsuit	Joint liability applies to contract actions	Joint and several liability applies to tort actions.
Defendants	Plaintiff must name all partners as defendants	Plaintiff can sue partners individually.
Recovery	If successful, the plaintiff can recover the judgment against all or any of the defendants.	If successful, the plaintiff can recover the judgment against all or any of the named defendants.
Indemnification	Partner who pays judgment can recover contribution from other partners for their share of the judgment.	Partner who pays judgment can recover contribution from other partners for their share of the judgment.

Liability of Incoming Partners

A new partner who is admitted to a partnership is liable for the existing debts and obligations (**antecedent debts**) of the partnership only to the extent of his or her capital contribution. The new partner is personally liable for debts and obligations incurred by the partnership after becoming a partner.

Consider This Example   Bubble.com is a general partnership with four partners. On May 1, Frederick is admitted as a new general partner by investing $100,000 capital contribution. As of May 1, Bubble.com owes $800,000 of debt. After Frederick becomes a partner, the general partnership borrows $1 million of new debt. If the general partnership goes bankrupt and out of business still owing both debts, Frederick's capital contribution of $100,000 will go toward paying the $800,000 of existing debt owed by the partnership when he joined the partnership, but he is not personally liable for this debt. However, Frederick is personally liable for the $1 million of unpaid debt that the partnership borrowed after he became a partner.

Dissolution of Partnerships

The duration of a partnership can be a fixed term (e.g., five years) or until a particular undertaking is accomplished (e.g., until a real estate development is completed) or it can be an unspecified term. A partnership with a fixed duration is called a **partnership for a term**. A partnership with no fixed duration is called a **partnership at will**.

A partner has the *power* to withdraw and dissolve the partnership at any time, but he or she may not have the *right* to do so. For example, a partner who withdraws from a partnership before the expiration of the term stated in the partnership agreement does not have the right to do so. The partner's action causes a **wrongful dissolution** of the partnership. The partner is liable for damages caused by the wrongful dissolution of the partnership.

Notice of Dissolution   The dissolution of a partnership terminates the partners' actual authority to enter into contracts or otherwise act on behalf of the partnership. Notice of dissolution must be given to certain third parties. The degree of notice depends on the relationship of the third party with the partnership [UPA § 35]:

1. Third parties who have actually dealt with the partnership must be given **actual notice** (verbal or written) of dissolution or have acquired knowledge of the dissolution from another source.
2. Third parties who have not dealt with the partnership but have knowledge of it must be given either actual or **constructive notice** of dissolution. Constructive notice consists of publishing a notice of dissolution in a newspaper of general circulation serving the area where the business of the partnership was regularly conducted.
3. Third parties who have not dealt with the partnership and do not have knowledge of it do not have to be given notice.

If proper notice is not given to a required third party after the dissolution of a partnership, and a partner enters into a contract with the third party, liability may arise on the grounds of *apparent authority*.

Continuation of a Partnership After Dissolution

The surviving or remaining partners have the right to continue a partnership after dissolution. It is good practice for the partners of a partnership to enter into a *continuation agreement* that expressly sets forth the events that allow for continuation of the partnership, the amount to be paid out going partners, and other details.

Business Brief

A new partner who is admitted to a partnership is liable for existing debts and obligations of the partnership only to the extent of his or her capital contribution.

Business Brief

A new partner who is admitted to a partnership is personally liable for the debts and obligations incurred by the partnership after becoming a partner.

Business Brief

If a partnership is dissolved, notice of the dissolution must be given to certain third parties. Partners may be liable for debts and obligations incurred on behalf of the partnership after the dissolution if the required notice is not given.

Business Brief

The surviving or remaining partners have the right to continue the partnership after dissolution.

When a partnership is continued, the old partnership is dissolved and a new partnership is created. The new partnership is composed of the remaining partners and any new partners admitted to the partnership. The creditors of the old partnership become creditors of the new partnership and have equal status with the creditors of the new partnership [UPA § 41].

Liability of Outgoing Partners

The dissolution of a partnership does not of itself discharge the liability of outgoing partners for existing partnership debts and obligations.

For example, if a partnership consisting of four partners is dissolved, each partner is personally liable for debts and obligations of the partnership that exist at the time of dissolution. If a partnership is dissolved because a partner leaves the partnership and the partnership is continued by the remaining partners, the outgoing partner is personally liable for the debts, and obligations of the partnership at the time of dissolution. The outgoing partner is not liable for any new debts and obligations incurred by the partnership after the dissolution as long as proper notification of his or her withdrawal from the partnership has been given to the creditor.

Contemporary Environment
Right of Survivorship

A partner is a co-owner with the other partners of the specific partnership property as a *tenant in partnership* [UPA § 25(1)]. This is a special legal status that exists only in a partnership. Upon the death of a partner, the deceased partner's right in specific partnership property vests in the remaining partner or partners—it does not pass to his or her heirs or next of kin. This is called the **right of survivorship**. Upon the death of the last surviving partner, the rights in specific partnership property vest in the deceased partner's legal representative [UPA § 25(2)C]. The *value* of the deceased partner's interest in the partnership passes to his or her beneficiaries or heirs upon his or her death, however.

Consider This Example   Jaime, Harold, Shou-Ju, and Jesus form a general partnership to operate a new restaurant. After their first restaurant is successful, they expand until the partnership owns 100 restaurants. At that time Jaime dies. None of the partnership assets transfer to Jaime's heirs; for example, they do not get 25 of the restaurants. Instead, under the right of survivorship, they inherit Jaime's ownership interest, and his heirs now have the right to receive Jaime's one-quarter of the partnership's profits each year. ■

Limited Partnership

Limited partnerships are statutory creations that have been used since the Middle Ages. They include both general (manager) and limited (investor) partners. Today, all states have enacted statutes that provide for the creation of limited partnerships. In most states these partnerships are called **limited partnerships** or **special partnerships**. Limited partnerships are used for such business ventures as investing in real estate, drilling oil and gas wells, investing in movie productions, and the like.

The Revised Uniform Limited Partnership Act

In 1916 the National Conference of Commissioners on Uniform State Laws, a group composed of lawyers, judges, and legal scholars, promulgated the **Uniform Limited Partnership Act (ULPA)**. The ULPA contains a uniform set of provisions for the formation, operation, and dissolution of limited partnerships. Most states originally enacted this law.

In 1976, the National Conference of Commissioners on Uniform State Laws promulgated the **Revised Uniform Limited Partnership Act (RULPA)**, which provides a more modern comprehensive law for the formation, operation, and dissolution of limited partnerships. This law supersedes the ULPA in the states that have adopted it. The RULPA provides the basic foundation for the discussion of limited partnership law in the following text.

General and Limited Partners

Limited partnerships have two types of partners: (1) **general partners**, who invest capital, manage the business, and are personally liable for partnership debts, and (2) **limited partners**, who invest capital but do not participate in management and are not personally liable for partnership debts beyond their capital contributions (see Exhibit 25.3).

A limited partnership must have one or more general partners and one or more limited partners [RULPA § 101(7)]. There are no upper limits on the number of general or limited partners allowed in a limited partnership. Any person may be a general or limited partner. This includes natural persons, partnerships, limited partnerships, trusts, estates, associations, and corporations. A person may be both a general and a limited partner in the same limited partnership.

The RULPA permits a corporation to be the sole general partner of a limited partnership. Where this is permissible, it affects the liability of the limited partnership. This is because the limited partners are liable only to the extent of their capital contributions, and the corporation acting as general partner is liable only to the extent of its assets.

Formation of Limited Partnerships

The creation of a limited partnership is formal and requires public disclosure. The entity must comply with the statutory requirements of the RULPA or other state statutes.

Exhibit 25.3

Limited Partnership

Under the RULPA, two or more persons must execute and sign **a certificate of limited partnership** [RULPA §§ 201 and 206]. The certificate must contain the following information:

1. Name of the limited partnership
2. General character of the business
3. Address of the principal place of business and name and address of the agent to receive service of legal process
4. Name and business address of each general and limited partner
5. Latest date on which the limited partnership is to dissolve
6. Amount of cash, property, or services (and description of property or services) contributed by each partner, and any contributions of cash, property, or services promised to be made in the future
7. Any other matters that the general partners determine to include

The certificate of limited partnership must be filed with the secretary of state of the appropriate state and, if required by state law, with the county recorder in the county or counties in which the limited partnership carries on business. The limited partnership is formed when the certificate of limited partnership is filed.

Limited Partnership Agreement

Although not required by law, the partners of a limited partnership often draft and execute a **limited partnership agreement** (also called the **articles of limited partnership**) that sets forth the rights and duties of the general and limited partners, the terms and conditions regarding the operation, termination, and dissolution of the partnership, and so on. Where there is no such agreement, the certificate of limited partnership serves as the articles of limited partnership.

The limited partnership agreement may specify how profits and losses from the limited partnership are to be allocated among the general and limited partners. If there is no such agreement, the RULPA provides that profits and losses from a limited partnership are shared on the basis of the value of the partner's capital contribution [RULPA § 503]. A limited partner is not liable for losses beyond his or her capital contribution.

In addition, it is good practice to establish voting rights in the limited partnership agreement or certificate of limited partnership. The limited partnership agreement can provide which transactions must be approved by which partners (i.e., general, limited, or both). General and limited partners may be given unequal voting rights.

Liability of General and Limited Partners

The **general partners** of a limited partnership have unlimited liability for the debts and obligations of the limited partnerships. This liability extends to debts that cannot be satisfied with the existing capital of the limited partnership.

Generally, **limited partners** are liable only for the debts and obligations of the limited partnership up to their capital contributions.

As a trade-off for limited liability, limited partners give up their right to participate in the control and management of the limited partnership. This means, in part, that limited partners have no right to bind the partnership to contracts or other obligations. Under the RULPA, a limited partner is liable as a general partner if his or her participation in the control of the business is substantially the same as that of a general partner, but the limited partner is liable only to persons who reasonably believed him or her to be a general partner [RULPA § 303(a)].

Defective Formation

Defective formation occurs when (1) a certificate of limited partnership is not properly filed, (2) there are defects in a certificate that is filed, or (3) some other statutory requirement for the creation of a limited partnership is not met. If there is a substantial defect in the creation of a limited partnership, persons who thought they were limited partners can find themselves liable as general partners. Such partners who erroneously but in good faith believe they have become limited partners can escape liability as general partners by either (1) causing the appropriate certificate of limited partnership (or certificate of amendment) to be filed or (2) withdrawing from any future equity participation in the enterprise and causing a certificate showing this withdrawal to be filed. Nevertheless, the limited partner remains liable to any third party who transacts business with the enterprise before either certificate is filed if the third person believed in good faith that the partner was a general partner at the time of the transaction [RULPA § 304].

Business Brief

A limited partner may be held liable as a general partner if the limited partnership is defectively formed.

Liability on Personal Guarantee

On some occasions when limited partnerships apply for an extension of credit from a bank, a supplier, or another creditor, the creditor will not make the loan based on the limited partnership's own credit history or ability to repay the credit. The creditor may require a limited partner to guarantee the repayment of the loan in order to extend credit to the limited partnership. If a limited partner personally guarantees a loan made by a creditor to the limited partnership, and the limited partnership defaults on the loan, the creditor may enforce the personal guarantee and recover payment from the limited partner who personally guaranteed the repayment of the credit.

Concept Summary   Liability of Limited Partners

General rule	Limited partners are not individually liable for the obligations or conduct of the partnership beyond the amount of their capital contribution.
Exceptions to the general rule	Limited partners are individually liable for the debts, obligations, and tortious acts of the partnership in three situations: 1. **Defective formation.** There has not been substantial compliance in good faith with the statutory requirements to create a limited partnership. *Exception:* Persons who erroneously believed themselves to be limited partners either (1) caused the appropriate certificate of limited partnership or amendment thereto to be filed or (2) withdrew from any future equity participation in the profits of the partnership and caused a certificate of withdrawal to be filed. 2. **Participation in management.** The limited partner participated in the management and control of the partnership. *Exception:* The limited partner was properly employed by the partnership as a manager or executive. 3. **Personal guarantee.** The limited partner signed an enforceable personal guarantee that guarantees the performance of the limited partnership.

Limited Liability Partnership (LLP)

Many states have enacted legislation to permit the creation of **limited liability partnerships (LLPs)**. In an LLP, there does not have to be a general partner who is personally liable for the debts and obligations of the partnership. Instead, *all* partners are limited partners who stand to lose only their capital contribution should the partnership fail. None of the partners is personally liable for the debts and obligations of the partnership beyond his or her capital contribution (see Exhibit 25.4).

LLPs enjoy the "flow-through" tax benefit of other types of partnerships—that is, there is no tax paid at the partnership level, and all profits and losses are reported on the individual partners' income tax returns.

Articles of Partnership

LLPs must be created formally by filing **articles of partnership** with the secretary of state of the state in which the LLP is organized. This is a public document. The LLP is a **domestic LLP** in the state in which it is organized. The LLP law of the state governs the operation of the LLP. An LLP may do business in other states, however. To do so, the LLP must register as a **foreign LLP** in any state in which it wants to conduct business.

Liability Insurance Required

In most state, LLP law restricts the use of the LLPs to certain types of professionals, such as accountants and lawyers. Many state laws require LLPs to carry a minimum of $1 million of liability insurance that covers negligence, wrongful acts, and misconduct by partners or employees of the LLP. This requirement guarantees that injured third parties will have compensation to recover for their injuries and is a quid pro quo for permitting partners to have limited liability.

> Justice is the end of government. It is the end of civil society. It ever has been, and ever will be pursued, until it be obtained, or until liberty be lost in the pursuit.
>
> James Madison
> *The Federalist No. 51 (1788)*

Exhibit 25.4

Limited Liability
Partnership (LLP)

Contemporary Environment
Accounting Firms Operate as LLPs

Prior to the advent of the limited liability partnership (LLP) form of doing business, accounting firms operated as general partnerships. As such, the general partners were personally liable for the debts and obligations of the general partnership. In large accounting firms, this personal liability was rarely imposed. This was because the general partnership usually carried sufficient liability insurance to cover most awards to third-party plaintiffs in negligence tort actions. Creditors usually extended credit to the large accounting firms based on the reputation of the firms and the fact that these large accounting firms had sufficient capital in the partnership to meet most loan obligations.

Beginning in the early 1980s, large accounting firms were hit with many large court judgments. These cases were brought in conjunction with the failure of large savings banks and commercial banks and the failure of other large firms that accountants had audited. Many of these firms failed because of fraud by their major owners and officers. The shareholders and creditors of these failed companies sued the auditors, alleging that the auditors had been negligent in not catching the fraud. Many juries agreed and awarded large sums against the accounting firms.

Sometimes the accounting firm's liability insurance was not enough to cover the judgment, thus imposing personal liability on partners. General partners in accounting firms became worried that the inability of the profession to shield itself from such liability jeopardized the profession.

In response, in the 1990s state legislatures created a new form of business, the LLP. This entity was particularly created for accountants, lawyers, and other professionals to offer their services under an umbrella of limited liability. The partners of an LLP have limited liability up to their capital contribution; the partners do not have personal liability for the debts and liabilities of the LLP, however.

Once LLPs were permitted by law, all of the Big Five accounting firms changed their status from general partnerships to LLPs. The signs and letterhead of each Big Five accounting firm prominently announces that the firm is an "LLP." Many accounting firms other than the Big Five have also changed over to LLP status, as have many law firms. The LLP form of business has changed how accountants, lawyers, and other professionals offer their services. ■

International Law
Partnerships Outside the United States

The English forms of business organizations are essentially the same as those in the United States. Partnership law, in particular, is virtually identical. Thus, in both countries (and in countries following the English model), a partnership is an association of two or more persons carrying on a business with the intent to make a profit.

In the civil law countries, including France and Germany, every form of business organization, including a partnership, is a "company" (*société* in French, *Gesellschaft* in German). A French partnership, because it is a company, is considered as having separate legal or juridical personality independent from its partners and thus can own property or sue or be sued in its own name. In Germany, by comparison, a partnership does not have a separate juridical personality. Therefore, even though a German partnership is a company, the partners own the property, and the partners must sue or be sued.

Although partnerships are categorized as companies in both France and Germany, they remain associations of persons who have full individual liability for the actions of their company.

Similarly, because they are associations, they must have two or more partners.

A specialized form of partnership, the limited partnership, is recognized in the civil law countries. At least one partner must be a general partner (with personal unlimited liability) and one must be a limited partner. In both types of countries persons can be either general or limited partners, but they cannot be both. In France, limited partners can participate in the internal administration of the partnership. In Germany, they can participate in internal administration and be given broad powers to deal with third parties on behalf of the partnership.

Germany recognizes another type of partnership, known as the silent partnership. This is a secret relationship between the partners that is unknown to third parties. The active partner conducts the business in his or her name alone, never mentioning the silent partner. So long as the silent partner's participation is not disclosed, the silent partner's risk is limited to the amount he or she invested. ■

Chapter Summary

Entrepreneurship, p. 537

Entrepreneurship

Entrepreneur. An entrepreneur is a person who forms and operates a new business.

Forms of Conducting Business

Entrepreneurs may choose to conduct business using any of the following forms:

1. Sole proprietorship
2. General partnership
3. Limited partnership
4. Limited liability partnership (LLP)
5. Limited liability company (LLC)
6. Corporation

   Certain requirements must be met to form and operate each of these forms of business.

Sole Proprietorship, p. 538

Sole Proprietorship

Sole proprietorship is form of business in which the owner and the business are one. The business is not a separate legal entity.

1. ***d.b.a. (doing business as).*** A sole proprietorship can operate under the name of the sole proprietor or a *trade name*. Operating under a trade name is commonly designated as a *d.b.a.* (*doing business as*). If a trade name is used, a *fictitious business name statement* must be filed with the appropriate state government office.
2. ***Personal liability of sole proprietors.*** A sole proprietor is personally liable for the debts and obligations of the sole proprietorship.

General Partnership, p. 540

General Partnerships

1. ***General partnership.*** A general partnership is an association of two or more persons to carry on as co-owners of a business for profit [UPA § 6(1)].
2. ***Uniform Partnership Act (UPA).*** This model act codifies partnership law. Most states have adopted all or part of the UPA.
3. ***Entity theory of partnerships.*** This theory holds that partnership are *separate legal entities* that can hold title to personal and real property, transact business in the partnership name, and the like.
4. ***Taxation of partnerships.*** Partnerships do not pay federal income taxes. The income and losses of partnership flow onto individual partners' federal income tax returns.
5. ***Partnership name.*** A general partnership can operate under the names of any one or more of the partners of under a fictitious business name.

The Partnership Agreement

A partnership agreement establishes a general partnership. It sets forth the terms of the partnership. It is good practice to have a written partnership agreement that the partners sign.

   Certificate of partnership. General partnerships must file this document with the appropriate state government agency in some states.

Contract Liability

1. *Partners' contract authority.* A contract entered into by a partner with a third party on behalf of a partnership is binding on the partnership.

2. *Ratification.* The partners can decide to *ratify* an unauthorized contract. The ratification binds the partnership to the contract from the time of execution.

3. *Partnership liability.* A partnership is liable for the contracts entered into on its behalf by partners acting with express, implied, or apparent authority, or where unauthorized contracts have been ratified by the partners.

Tort Liability

1. *Tort.* A tort occurs when a partner causes injury to a third party by his or her negligent act, breach of trust, breach of fiduciary duty, or intentional tort.

2. *Partnership liability.* The partnership is liable to third persons who are injured by torts committed by a partner while he or she is acting within the ordinary course of partnership business.

3. *Joint and several liability of partners.* Partners are *personally liable* for torts committed by partners acting on partnership business. This liability is *joint and several.* This means that the plaintiff can sue *one or more* of the partners separately. If successful, the plaintiff can recover the entire amount of the judgment from any or all of the defendant-partners.

Liability of Incoming Partners

A new partner who is admitted to the partnership is liable for the existing debts and obligations (*antecedent debts*) of the partnership only to the extent of his or her capital contribution. The new partner is personally liable for debts and obligations incurred by the partnership after becoming a partner.

Dissolution of Partnerships

The dissolution of a partnership is a change in the relationship of the partners caused by any partner ceasing to be associated in the carrying on of the business [UPA § 29].

Wrongful Dissolution

Wrongful dissolution occurs when a partner withdraws from a partnership without having the *right* to do so at the time. The partner is liable for damages caused by the wrongful dissolution of the partnership.

Notice of Dissolution

1. *Notice of dissolution to partners.* Notice of dissolution must be given to all partners. If a partner who has not received notice of dissolution enters into a contract on behalf of the partnership in the course of partnership business, the contract is binding on all the partners.

2. *Notice of dissolution to third parties.* The following notice must be given to third parties when a partnership has been dissolved other than by operation of law:

   a. *Actual notice.* Actual notice must be given to third parties who have actually dealt with the partnership.

   b. *Constructive notice.* Constructive notice must be given to third parties who have not dealt with the partnership but have knowledge of it. Constructive notice is given by publishing a notice of dissolution in a newspaper of general circulation serving the area where the business of the partnership is conducted.

   c. *No notice.* Parties who have not dealt with the partnership and do not have knowledge of it do not have to be given notice.

Continuation of a Partnership After Dissolution

The surviving or remaining partners have the right to continue a partnership after dissolution. When a partnership is continued, the old partnership is dissolved and a new partnership is created.

1. *Continuation agreement.* This document expressly sets forth the events that allow for continuation of the partnership, the amount to be paid to outgoing partners, and other details.

2. *Creditors' status.* The creditors of the old partnership become creditors of the new partnership and have equal status with the creditors of the new partnership.

3. Liability of outgoing partners. An outgoing partner is liable for existing partnership debts unless the creditor, other partners, and the outgoing partner enter into a *novation agreement* that expressly relieves the outgoing partner of liability to the creditor.

Limited Partnership, p. 548

Uniform Limited Partnership Act

1. *Uniform Limited Partnership Act (ULPA).* This 1916 model act contains a uniform set of provisions for the formation, operation, and dissolution of limited partnerships.
2. *Revised Uniform Limited Partnership Act (RULPA).* This 1976 revision of the ULPA provides a more modern comprehensive law for the formation, operation, and dissolution of limited partnerships.

Limited Partnerships

1. *Limited partnership.* This is a special form of partnership that has both limited and general partners.
   a. *General partners.* General partners in a limited partnership invest capital, manage the business, and are personally liable for partnership debts.
   b. *Limited partners.* Limited partners in a limited partnership invest capital but do not participate in management and are not personally liable for partnership debts beyond their capital contributions.
2. *Corporation as sole general partner.* A corporation may be the sole general partner of a limited partnership. Shareholders of corporations are liable only up to their capital contributions.

Formation of Limited Partnerships

1. *Certificate of limited partnership.* This certificate is a document that two or more persons must execute and sign that establishes a limited partnership. The certificate of limited partnership must be filed with the secretary of state of the appropriate state.
2. *Limited partnership agreement.* This document acts forth the rights and duties of general and limited partners, the terms and conditions regarding the operation, termination, and dissolution of the partnership, and so on.
3. *Offering circular.* This document is provided to investors of limited partnership interests and it describes the issuer, its business the terms of the partnership agreement, and other relevant information.
4. *Defective formation.* Defective formation occurs when (a) a certificate of limited partnership is not properly filed, (b) there are defects in a certificate that is filed, or (c) some other statutory requirement for the creation of a limited partnership is not met. A limited partner may be held liable as a general partner if the limited partnership is defectively formed.

Share of Profits and Losses

Unless otherwise agreed, profits and losses from a limited partnership are shared on the basis of the value of the partner's capital contributions. A limited partner is not liable for losses beyond his or her capital contribution. The limited partnership agreement may specify how profits and losses are to be allocated among the general and limited partners.

Liability of General and Limited Partners

1. *General partners.* General partners of a limited partnership have *unlimited personal liability* for the debts and obligations of the limited partnership.
2. *Limited partners.* Limited partners of a limited partnership are liable only for the debts and obligations of the limited partnership up to their capital contributions.
3. *Limited partners and management.* Limited partners have no right to participate in the management of a partnership. A limited partner is *liable as a general partner* if his or her participation in the control of the business is substantially the same as that of a general partner, but the limited partner is liable only to persons who reasonably believed him or her to be a general partner.

Limited Liability Partnership (LLP), p. 552

Limited Liability Partnership

1. *Limited liability partnership (LLP).* LLP is a relatively new form of business in which there does not have to be a general partner who is personally liable for debts and obligations of the partnership. All partners are limited partners and stand to lose only their capital contributions should the partnership fail. LLPs are formed by accountants and other professionals, as allowed by LLP law.

2. *Partners.* The partners are the owners of an LLP.

3. *Articles of partnership.* This is a document that the partners of an LLP must execute, sign, and file with the secretary of state of the appropriate state to form an LLP.

4. *Taxation.* An LLP does not pay federal income taxes unless it elects to do so. If an LLP is taxed as a partnership, the income and losses of the LLP flow onto individual partners' federal income tax returns.

Internet Exercises and Case Questions

Working the Web Internet Exercises

Activities

1. Review the materials at **smallbiz.biz.findlaw.com/ planning/index.html?planning/wa**. Compare this information with the text discussion of partnerships. Can you see why lawyers generally advise business clients *not* to do business in a partnership form?

2. A large, rambling, and self-consciously offbeat site is the Lectric Law Library, **www.lectlaw.com/bus.html**. There you will find a business law section with numerous items of interest, including an overview of (business) partnership law, with links to key primary and secondary sources.

3. A checklist of questions about partnership can be found at **www.nolo.com/lawcenter/faqs/detail.cfm/objectID/ D2C7200B-28A8-49FB-9EA5E2B7E7F15CB5**. Use it as a self-test.

4. Study the provisions of the Uniform Limited Partnership Act at **www.law.upenn.edu/bll/ulc/ulpa/final2001.htm**.

5. Check your state statute on LLPs. Are LLPs permitted in your jurisdiction? Are there any limitations on the type of businesses allowed to operate as an LLP? See "LII: Law About . . . Partnership," at **www.law.cornell.edu/ topics/partnership.html**.

Critical Legal Thinking Cases

25.1 General Partnership   In early 1986, Thomas Smithson, a house builder and small-scale property developer, decided that a certain tract of undeveloped land in Franklin, Tennessee, would be extremely attractive for development into a subdivision. Smithson contacted the owner of the property, Monsanto Chemical Company, and was told that the company would sell the property at the "right price."

Smithson did not have the funds with which to embark unassisted in the endeavor, so he contacted Frank White, a co-owner of the Andrews Realty Company, and two agents of the firm, Dennis Devrow and Temple Ennis. Smithson showed them a sketch map with the proposed layout of the lots, roads, and so forth. Smithson testified that they all orally agreed to develop the property together, and in lieu of a financial investment, Smithson would oversee the engineering of the property. Subsequently, H. R. Morgan was brought into the deal to provide additional financing.

Smithson later discovered that White had contacted Monsanto directly. When challenged about this, White assured Smithson that he was still "part of the deal" but refused to put the agreement in writing. White, Devrow, Ennis, and Morgan purchased the property from Monsanto. They then sold it to H. A. H. Associates, a corporation, for a $184,000 profit. When they refused to pay Smithson, he sued to recover an equal share of the profits. Was a partnership formed between Smithson and the defendants? [*Smithson v. White*, 1988 Tenn.App. Lexis 221 (Tenn. App. 1988)]

25.2 General Partnership   Richard Filip owned Trans Texas Properties. Tracy Peoples was an employee of the company. In order to obtain credit to advertise in the *Austin American-Statesman* newspaper, which was owned by Cox Enterprises, Inc., Peoples completed a credit application that listed Jack Elliot as a partner in Trans Texas. Evidence showed that Elliot did not own an interest in Trans Texas and did not consent to or authorize Peoples to make this representation to Cox. Cox made no effort to verify the accuracy of the representation and extended credit to Trans Texas. When Trans Texas defaulted on payments owed Cox, Cox sued both Filip and Elliot to recover the debt. Is Elliot liable? [*Cox Enterprises, Inc. v. Filip and Elliot*, 538 S.W.2d 836, 1976 Tex.App. Lexis 2947 (Tex. App. 1976)]

25.3 Tort Liability   In January 1977, Charles Fial and Roger J. Steeby entered into a partnership called Audit Consultants to perform auditing services. Pursuant to the agreement, they shared equally the equity, income, and profits of the partnership. Originally, they performed the auditing services themselves, but as business increased, they engaged independent contractors to do some of the audit work. Fial's activities generated approximately 80 percent of the partnership's revenues. Unhappy with their agreement to divide the profits equally, Fial wrote a letter to Steeby on July 11, 1984, dissolving the partnership.

Fial asserted that the clients should be assigned based on who brought them into the business. Fial formed a new business called Audit Consultants of Colorado, Inc. He then terminated the original partnership's contracts with many clients and put them under contract with his new firm. Fial also terminated the partnership's contracts with the independent-contractor auditors and signed many of these auditors with his new firm. The partnership terminated on May 24, 1985. Steeby brought an action against Fial, alleging breach of fiduciary duty and seeking a final accounting. Who wins? [*Steeby v. Fial*, 765 P.2d 1081, 1988 Colo.App. Lexis 409 (Colo. App. 1988)]

25.4 Fiduciary Duty   Edgar and Selwyn Husted, attorneys, formed Husted and Husted, a law partnership. Herman McCloud, who was the executor of his mother's estate, hired them as attorneys for the estate. When taxes were due on the estate, Edgar told McCloud to make a check for $18,000 payable to the Husted and Husted Trust Account and that he would pay the IRS from this account. There was no Husted and Husted trust account. Instead, Edgar deposited the check into his own personal account and converted the funds to his own personal use. When Edgar's misconduct was uncovered, McCloud sued the law firm for conversion of estate funds. Is the partnership liable for Edgar's actions? [*Husted v. McCloud*, 436 N.E.2d 341, 1982 Ind.App. Lexis 1244 (Ind. App. 1982)]

25.5 Tort Liability   Thomas McGrath was a partner in the law firm Torbenson, Thatcher, McGrath, Treadwell & Schoonmaker. At approximately 4:30 P.M. on February 11, 1980, McGrath went to a restaurant-cocktail establishment in Kirkland, Washington. From that time until about 1:00 A.M. he imbibed considerable alcohol while socializing and discussing personal and firm-related business. After 11:00 A.M. McGrath did not discuss firm business but continued to socialize and drink until approximately 1:45 A.M., when he and Frederick Hayes, another bar patron, exchanged words. Shortly thereafter, the two encountered each other outside, and after another exchange, McGrath shot Hayes. Hayes sued McGrath and the law firm for damages. Who is liable? [*Hayes v. Tarbenson, Thatcher, McGrath, Treadwell & Schoonmaker*, 749 P.2d 178, 1988 Wash.App. Lexis 27 (Wash. App. 1988)]

25.6 Notice of Dissolution   In 1976, Leonard Sumter, Sr., entered into a partnership agreement with his son, Michael T. Sumter, to conduct a plumbing business in Shreveport, Louisiana, under the name Sumter Plumbing Company. On June 18, 1976, the father, on behalf of the partnership, executed a credit application with Thermal Supply of Louisiana, Inc., for an open account to purchase supplies on credit. From that date until the spring of 1980, the Sumters purchased plumbing supplies from Thermal on credit and paid their bills without fail. Both partners and one employee signed for supplies at Thermal.

In May 1980, the partnership was dissolved, and all outstanding debts to Thermal were paid in full. The Sumters did not, however, notify Thermal that the partnership had been dissolved.

A year later, the son decided to reenter the plumbing business. He used the name previously used by the former partnership, listed the same post office address for billing purposes, and hired the employee of the former partnership who signed for supplies at Thermal. The father decided not to become involved in this venture. The son began purchasing supplies on credit from Thermal on the open credit account of the former partnership. Thermal was not informed that he was operating a new business. When the son defaulted on payments to Thermal, it sued the original partnership to recover the debt. Is the father liable for these debts? [*Thermal Supply of Louisiana, Inc. v. Sumter*, 452 So.2d 312, 1984 La.App. Lexis 8975 (La. App. 1984)]

25.7 Liability of General Partners   Pat McGowan, Val Somers, and Brent Robertson were general partners of Vermont Place, a limited partnership formed on January 20, 1984, for the purpose of constructing duplexes on an undeveloped tract of land in Fort Smith, Arkansas. The general partners appointed McGowan and his company, Advance Development Corporation, to develop the project, including contracting with materials people, mechanics, and other suppliers. None of the limited partners took part in the management or control of the partnership.

On September 3, 1984, Somers and Robertson discovered that McGowan had not been paying the suppliers. They removed McGowan from the partnership and took over the project. The suppliers sued the partnership to recover the money owed them. The partnership assets were not sufficient to pay all their claims. Who is liable to the suppliers? [*National Lumber Company v. Advance Development Corporation*, 732 S.W. 2d 840, 1987 Ark. Lexis 2225 (AK 1987)]

25.8 Limited Partners   Union Station Associates of New London (USANL) is a limited partnership formed under the laws of Connecticut. Allen M. Schultz, Anderson Nolter Associates, and the Lepton Trust were limited partners. The limited partners did not take part in the management of the partnership. The National Railroad Passenger Association (NRPA) entered into an agreement to lease part of an railroad facility from USANL. NRPA sued USANL for allegedly breaching the lease and also named the limited partners as defendants. Are the limited partners liable? [*National Railroad Passenger Association v. Union Station Associates of New London*, 643 F.Supp. 192, 1986 U.S.Dist. Lexis 22190 (D.D.C. 1986)]

25.9 Limited Partnership   8 Brookwood Fund (Brookwood) is a limited partnership that was formed to invest in securities. The original certificate of limited partnership, which was filed with the Westchester County, New York, clerk on April 24, 1987, listed Kenneth Stein as the general partner and Barbara Stein as the limited partner. Between May and August 1987, additional investors joined Brookwood as limited partners. However, no certificate amending the original certificate was filed to reflect the newly admitted limited partners. The newly added partners conducted themselves at all times as limited partners.

The partnership purchased securities on margin (i.e., it borrowed a percentage of the purchase price of the securities) from the securities firms of Sloate, Weisman, Murray & Co., Inc. (Sloate), and Bear Stearns & Co., Inc. (Bear Stearns). On October 19, 1987, the stock market crashed, causing many of the securities that Brookwood purchased to go down in value. The securities firms made margin calls on Brookwood to pay more money to cover the losses. When the margin calls were not met, Sloate and Bear Stearns immediately initiated arbitration proceedings to recover the balance of $1,849,183 allegedly due after Brookwood's accounts were liquidated. On October 28, 1987, Brookwood filed a certificate amending the original certificate of limited partnership to reflect the recently added limited partners.

Upon receiving the notice of arbitration, the recently added limited partners renounced their interest in the profits of the limited partnership. Can these limited partners be held individually liable for the partnership debts owed to Sloate and Bear Stearns? [*8 Brookwood Fund v. Bear Stearns & Co., Inc.*, 539 N.Y.S.2d 411, 1989 N.Y.App.Dist. Lexis 4208 (N.Y. A.D. 2dDept. 1989)]

25.10 Limited Partnership Raugust-Mathwig, Inc., a corporation, was the sole general partner of a limited partnership. Calvin Raugust was the major shareholder of this corporation. The three limited partners were (1) Cal-Lee Trust, (2) W. J. Mathwig, Inc.,

and (3) W. J. Mathwig, Inc., and Associates. All three of the limited partners were valid corporate entities. Although the limited partnership agreement was never executed and a certificate of limited partnership was not filed with the state, the parties opened a bank account and began conducting business.

On May 9, 1973, John Molander, an architect, entered into an agreement with the limited partnership to design a condominium complex and professional office building to be located in Spokane, Washington. The contract was signed on behalf of the limited partnership by its corporate general partner. Molander provided substantial architectural services to the partnership, but neither project was completed because of a lack of financing. Molander sued the limited partnership, its corporate general partner, the corporate limited partners, and Calvin Raugust individually to recover payments allegedly due him. Against whom can Molander recover? [*Molander v. Raugust-Mathwig, Inc.*, 722 P.2d 103, 1986 Wash.App. Lexis 2992 (Wash. App. 1986)]

Business Ethics Cases

25.11 Business Ethics Harriet Hankin, Samuel Hankin, Moe Henry Hankin, Perch P. Hankin, and Pauline Hankin, and their spouses, for many years operated a family partnership composed of vast real estate holdings. Some of the properties included restaurants, industrial buildings, shopping centers, golf courses, a motel chain, and hundreds of acres of developable ground, estimated to be worth $72 million in 1977. In that year, because of family disagreement and discontent, the Hankin family agreed to dissolve the partnership. When they could not agree on how to liquidate the partnership assets, in August 1977, Harriet and Samuel (collectively called Harriet) initiated this equity action.

Based on assurances from Moe and Perch that they would sell the partnership assets as quickly as possible and at the highest possible price, the court appointed them as liquidators of the partnership during the winding-up period. Based on similar assurances, the court again appointed them liquidators for the partnership in 1979. But by 1981, only enough property had been sold to retire the debt of the partnership. Evidence showed that Moe and Perch had not aggressively marketed the remaining properties and that Moe wished to purchase some of the properties for himself at a substantial discount from their estimated value. Six years and three appeals to the superior court later, Harriet brought this action, seeking the appoint-

ment of a receiver to liquidate the remaining partnership assets.

Did the winding-up partners breach their fiduciary duties? Should the court appoint a receiver to liquidate the remaining partnership assets? Did Moe Henry Hankin act ethically in this case? [*Hankin v. Hankin*, 493 A.2d 675, 1985 Pa. Lexis 337 (PA 1985)]

25.12 Business Ethics Robert K. Powers and Lee M. Solomon were among other limited partners of the Cosmopolitan Chinook Hotel (Cosmopolitan), a limited partnership. On October 25, 1972, Cosmopolitan entered into a contract to lease and purchase neon signs from Dwinell's Central Neon (Dwinell's). The contract identified Cosmopolitan as a "partnership" and was signed on behalf of the partnership, "R. Powers, President." At the time the contract was entered into, Cosmopolitan had taken no steps to file its certificate of limited partnership with the state, as required by limited partnership law. The certificate was not filed with the state until several months after the contract was signed. When Cosmopolitan defaulted on payments due under the contract, Dwinell's sued Cosmopolitan and its general and limited partners. The limited partners denied liability. Did the limited partners act ethically in denying liability on the contract? Are the limited partners liable? [*Dwinell's Central Neon v. Cosmopolitan Chinook Hotel*, 587 P.2d 191, 1978 Wash.App. Lexis 2735 (Wash. App. 1978)]

Briefing the Case Writing Assignment

Read Case A.25 in the Case Appendix [*Catalina Mortgage Company, Inc. v. Monier*]. This case is excerpted from the supreme court of Arizona's opinion. Review and brief the case. In your brief, be sure to answer the following questions.

1. Who was the plaintiff? Who were the defendants?

2. What business arrangement were the defendants engaged in? How did this lead to the lawsuit?

3. What is joint and several liability?

4. Did the court impose joint and several liability in this case?

Endnote

1. Georgia and Louisiana have not adopted the UPA. These states have enacted their own partnership statutes.

26

Formation and Operation of Domestic and Multinational Corporations

"A corporation is an artificial being, invisible, intangible, and existing only in the contemplation of law. Being the mere creature of the law, it possesses only those properties which the charter of its creation confers upon it, either expressly or as incidental to its very existence. These are such as supposed best calculated to effect the object for which it was created. Among the most important are immortality, and, if the expression may be allowed, individuality; properties by which a perpetual succession of many persons are considered as the same, and may act as a single individual."

—John Marshall, Chief Justice, U.S. Supreme Court
Dartmouth College v. Woodward
4 Wheaton 518, 636 (1819)

Chapter Objectives

After studying this chapter, you should be able to:

1. Define corporation and list the major characteristics of a corporation.
2. Describe the process of forming a corporation.
3. Define common stock and preferred stock.
4. Define S corporation and describe its tax benefits.
5. Describe the organization and operation of multinational corporations.

Chapter Contents

- Nature of a Corporation
- Incorporation Procedures
- Financing the Corporation
- Corporate Powers
- Dissolution and Termination of Corporations

Corporations are the most dominant form of business organization in the United States, generating over 85 percent of the country's gross business receipts. Corporations range in size from one owner to thousands of owners. Owners of corporations are called *shareholders*.

Corporations were first formed in medieval Europe. Great Britain granted charters to certain trading companies from the 1500s to the 1700s. The English law of corporations applied in most of the colonies until 1776. After the War of Independence, the states of the United States developed their own corporation law.

Originally, corporate charters were individually granted by state legislatures. In the late 1700s, however, the states began enacting *general corporation statutes* that permitted corporations to be formed without the separate approval of the legislature. Today, most corporations are formed pursuant to general corporation laws of the states.

The formation and financing of corporations are discussed in this chapter.

Nature of the Corporation

Corporations can only be created pursuant to the laws of the state of incorporation. These statutes—commonly referred to as **corporations codes**—regulate the formation, operation, and dissolution of corporations. The state legislature may amend its corporate statute at any time. Such changes may require the corporation's articles of incorporation to be amended.

The courts interpret state corporation statutes to decide individual corporate and shareholder disputes. As a result, a body of common law has evolved concerning corporate and shareholder rights and obligations.

The Corporation as a Legal "Person"

A corporation is a separate *legal entity* (or *legal person*) for most purposes. Corporations are treated, in effect, as artificial persons created by the state that can sue or be sued in their own names, enter into and enforce contracts, hold title to and transfer property, and be found civilly and criminally liable for violations of law. Because corporations cannot be put in prison, the normal criminal penalty is the assessment of a fine, loss of a license, or other sanction.

Business Brief

A corporation is a separate legal entity—an *artificial person*—that can own property, sue and be sued, enter into contracts, and such.

Characteristics of Corporations

Corporations have the following unique characteristics:

1. *Limited liability of shareholders.* As separate legal entities, corporations are liable for their own contracts and debts. Generally, the shareholders have only **limited liability**. That is, they are liable only to the extent of their capital contributions. (see Exhibit 26.1).
2. *Free transferability of shares.* Corporate shares are freely transferable by the shareholder by sale, assignment, pledge, or gift unless they are issued pursuant to certain exemptions from securities registration. Shareholders may agree among themselves on restrictions on the transfer of shares. National securities markets, such as the New York Stock Exchange, the American Stock Exchange, and NASDAQ, have been developed for the organized sale of securities.

Exhibit 26.1

Corporation

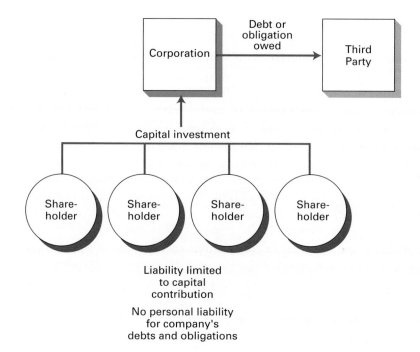

3. *Perpetual existence.* Corporations exist in perpetuity unless a specific duration is stated in the corporation's articles of incorporation. The existence of a corporation can be voluntarily terminated by the shareholders. Corporations may be involuntarily terminated by the corporation's creditors if an involuntary petition for bankruptcy against the corporation is granted. The death, insanity, or bankruptcy of a shareholder, a director, or an officer of the corporation does not affect its existence.

4. *Centralized management.* The *board of directors* makes policy decisions concerning the operation of the corporation. The members of the board of directors are elected by the shareholders. The directors, in turn, appoint corporate *officers* to run the corporation's day-to-day operations. Together, the directors and the officers form the corporate "management."

Revised Model Business Corporation Act (RMBCA)

The Committee on Corporate Laws of the American Bar Association first drafted the **Model Business Corporation Act (MBCA)** in 1950. The model act was intended to provide a uniform law regulating the formation, operation, and termination of corporations.

In 1984, the committee completely revised the MBCA and issued the **Revised Model Business Corporation Act (RMBCA)**. Certain provisions of the RMBCA have been amended since 1984. The RMBCA arranges the provisions of the act more logically, revises the language of the act to be more consistent, and makes substantial changes in the provisions of the model act. Many states have adopted all or part of the RMBCA. The RMBCA serves as the basis for the discussion of corporations law in this book.

There is no general federal corporations law governing the formation and operation of private corporations. Many federal laws regulate the operation of private corporations, however. These include federal securities laws, labor laws, antitrust laws, consumer protection laws, environmental protection laws, bankruptcy laws, and the like. These federal statutes are discussed in other chapters in this book.

Public and Private Corporations

Government-owned (or **public**) **corporations** are formed to meet a specific governmental or political purpose. For example, most cities and towns are formed as corporations, as are most water, school, sewage, and park districts. Local government corporations are often called *municipal corporations*.

Private corporations are formed to conduct privately owned business. They are owned by private parties, not by the government. Most corporations fall into this category.

Profit and Nonprofit Corporations

Private corporations may be classified as either for profit or nonprofit. **Profit corporations** are created to conduct a business for profit and can distribute profits to shareholders in the form of dividends. Most private corporations fit this definition.

Not-for-profit corporations are formed for charitable, educational, religious, or scientific purposes. Although nonprofit corporations may make a profit, they are prohibited by law from distributing this profit to their members, directors, or officers. About a dozen states have enacted the **Model Nonprofit Corporation Act**, which governs the formation, operation, and termination of nonprofit corporations. All other states have their own individual statutes that govern the formation, operation, and dissolution of such corporations.

Publicly Held and Closely Held Corporations

Publicly held corporations have many shareholders. Often, they are large corporations with hundreds or thousands of shareholders whose shares are traded on organized securities markets. IBM Corporation and General Motors Corporation are examples of publicly held corporations. The shareholders rarely participate in the management of such corporations.

A **closely held** (or **close**) **corporation** is one whose shares are owned by a few shareholders who are often family members, relatives, or friends. Frequently, the shareholders are involved in the management of the corporation. The shareholders sometimes enter into buy-and-sell agreements that prevent outsiders from becoming shareholders.

Professional Corporations

Professional corporations are formed by professionals such as lawyers, accountants, physicians, and dentists. The abbreviations *P.C.* (professional corporation), *P.A.* (professional association), and *S.C.* (service corporation) often identify professional corporations. Shareholders of professional corporations are often called *members*. Generally, only licensed professionals may become members.

All states permit the incorporation of professional corporations, although some states allow only designated types of professionals to incorporate. Professional corporations have normal corporate attributes and are formed like other corporations.

Members of a professional corporation are not usually liable for the torts committed by its agents or employees. Some states impose liability on members for the malpractice of other members of the corporation.

The doctrine of limited liability of shareholders was an issue in the following case.

We're Associates Company v. Cohen, Stracher & Bloom, P.C.
478 N.Y.S.2d 670, 1984 N.Y.App.Div. Lexis 19254 (1984)
Supreme Court of New York, Appellate Division

Case 26.1
Limited Liability
of Shareholders

Background and Facts

Three lawyers, Howard R. Cohen, Richard L. Stracher, and Paul J. Bloom, formed a professional corporation, Cohen, Stracher & Bloom, P.C., to engage in the practice of law. The three men were the sole shareholders, directors, and officers of the corporation. The corporation entered into an agreement to lease office space from We're Associates Company (We're Associates) in a building in Lake Success, New York. The lease was executed on behalf of the corporation "by Paul J. Bloom, Vice President." We're Associates sued Cohen, Stracher & Bloom, P.C., and its three shareholders to recover $9,000 allegedly due and owing under the lease. The trial court dismissed we're Associates case, Plaintiff We're Associates appealed.

Issue

Are the three shareholders of the professional corporation liable for the lease obligation of the corporation?

Court's Reasoning

The appellate court held that the shareholders of a professional corporation may not be sued in their individual capacities for rents due under a lease executed solely in the name of the corporation.

The court stated that the shareholders of a corporation are not liable for its contractual obligations and that parties who contract with the corporation must look to the corporation itself and not to the shareholders for payment of their claims. The court added, "Any analysis of the possible ethical considerations or moral obligations of attorneys in this situation is a separate matter and does not bear upon the substantive legal issue of the scope of liability."

Decision and Remedy

The appellate court held that members of professional corporations enjoy the same benefits of limited liability afforded to shareholders of any other form of corporation. The appellate court affirmed the dismissal of We're Associates's complaint against the three shareholders of the legal professional corporation.

Case Questions

Critical Legal Thinking   Why does the law provide limited liability for shareholders of corporations? Explain.

Business Ethics   Did the attorneys act ethically in denying personal liability in this case?

Contemporary Business   What could We're Associates have done to have assured recovery against the three shareholders?

Incorporation Procedures

Corporations are creatures of statute. Thus, the organizers of a corporation must comply with the state's corporations code to form a corporation. Although relatively similar, the procedure for *incorporating* a corporation varies somewhat from state to state. The procedure for incorporating a corporation is discussed in the following paragraphs.

Promoters' Liability

The **promoter** is the person or persons who organize and start a corporation, find the initial investors to finance the corporation, and so on. Promoters often enter into contracts on behalf of the corporation prior to its actual incorporation. **Promoters' contracts** include leases, sales contracts, contracts to purchase property, employment contracts, and the like. The liability of a promoter and the corporation on promoters' contracts follow these rules:

- If the corporation never comes into existence, the promoters have joint personal liability on the contract unless the third party specifically exempts them from such liability.

- If the corporation is formed, it becomes liable on a promoters' contract only if it agrees to become bound to the contract. This requires a resolution of the board of directors to be bound by the promoter's contract.

■ Even if the corporation agrees to be bound to the contract, the promoter remains liable on the contract unless the parties enter into a novation. A *novation* is a three-party agreement whereby the corporation agrees to assume the contract liability of the promoter with the consent of the third party. After a novation, the corporation is solely liable on the promoter's contract.

In the following case, the court found a promoter liable on a promoter's contract.

Coopers & Lybrand v. Fox
758 P.2d 683, 1988 Colo.App. Lexis 258 (1988)
Colorado Court of Appeals

Case 26.2
Promoter's Contract

Background and Facts

On November 3, 1981, Garry J. Fox met with a representative of Coopers & Lybrand (Coopers), a national accounting firm. Fox informed Coopers that he was acting on behalf of a corporation he was in the process of forming, G. Fox and Partners, Inc., and requested a tax opinion and other accounting services for the corporation. Coopers accepted the engagement with the knowledge that the corporation was not yet in existence. The corporation was incorporated on December 4, 1981. Coopers completed its work by mid-December and billed the corporation and Fox $10,827 for services rendered. When neither Fox nor the corporation paid the bill, Coopers sued Fox as a promoter to recover the debt. The trial court held in favor of Fox. Coopers appealed.

Issue

Is Fox liable on the Coopers & Lybrand contract as a promoter?

Court's Reasoning

The uncontroverted facts place Fox squarely within the definition of a promoter. As a general rule, promoters are personally liable for the contracts they make, although made on behalf of a corpo-

ration to be formed. The well-recognized exception to the general rule of promoter liability is that if the contracting party agrees to look solely to the corporation and not to the promoter for payment, the promoter incurs no personal liability. As the proponent of an alleged agreement to release the promoter from liability, the promoter has the burden of proving the release agreement. Here, Fox did not prove that such an agreement existed.

Decision and Remedy

The court of appeals held that Fox was liable, as a matter of law, under the doctrine of promoter liability. The court of appeals reversed the decision of the trial court.

Case Questions

Critical Legal Thinking Should promoters be held liable on their contracts even if the corporation is subsequently formed and accepts the contract as its own?

Business Ethics Did Fox act ethically in this case?

Contemporary Business To avoid promoters' liability, when should contracts on behalf of a proposed corporation be executed?

Selecting a State for Incorporating a Corporation

A corporation can be incorporated in only one state, even though it can do business in all other states in which it qualifies to do business. In choosing a state for incorporation, the incorporators, directors, and/or shareholders must consider the corporations law of the states under consideration.

For the sake of convenience, most corporations (particularly small ones) choose the state in which the corporation will be doing most of its business as the state for incorporation. Large corporations generally opt to incorporate in the state with the laws that are most favorable to the corporation's internal operations (e.g., Delaware).

Incorporators

One or more persons, partnerships, domestic or foreign corporations, or other associations may act as an **incorporator** of a corporation [RMBCA § 2.01]. The incorporator's primary duty is to sign the articles of incorporation. Incorporators often become shareholders, directors, or officers of the corporation.

Japan. Multinational corporations have grown to immense size and power in recent years. For example, the Mitsubishi Group of Japan operates subsidiary corporations in many nations of the world.

Domestic, Foreign, and Alien Corporations

A corporation is a **domestic corporation** in the state in which it is incorporated. It is a **foreign corporation** in all other states and jurisdictions. For example, suppose a corporation is incorporated in Texas and does business in Montana. The corporation is a domestic corporation in Texas and a foreign corporation in Montana.

A state can require a foreign corporation to *qualify* to conduct intrastate commerce within the state. Where a foreign corporation is required to qualify to do intrastate commerce in a state, it must obtain a *certificate of authority* from the state [RMBCA § 15.01(a)]. This requires the foreign corporation to file certain information with the secretary of state, pay the required fees, and appoint a registered agent for service of process.

Conduct that usually constitutes "doing business" includes maintaining an office to conduct intrastate business, selling personal property in intrastate business, entering into contracts involving intrastate commerce, using real estate for general corporate purposes, and the like. Activities that are generally *not* considered doing business within the state include maintaining, defending, or settling a lawsuit or an administrative proceeding; maintaining bank accounts; effectuating sales through independent contractors; soliciting orders through the mail; securing or collecting debts; transacting any business in interstate commerce; and the like [RMBCA § 15.01(b) and (c)].

Conducting intrastate business in a state in which it is not qualified subjects a corporation to fines. In addition, the corporation cannot bring a lawsuit in the state, although it can defend itself against lawsuits and administrative proceedings brought by others [RMBCA § 15.02].

An **alien corporation** is a corporation that is incorporated in another country. In most instances, alien corporations are treated as foreign corporations.

Concept Summary Types of Corporations

Type of Corporation	Description
Domestic	A corporation is a domestic corporation in the state in which it is incorporated.
Foreign	A corporation is a foreign corporation in states other than the one in which it is incorporated.
Alien	A corporation is an alien corporation in the United States if it is incorporated in another country.

Contemporary Environment

Selecting a Corporate Name

When starting a new corporation, the organizers must choose a name for the entity. To ensure that the name selected is not already being used by another business, the organizers should take the following steps [RMBCA § 4.01]:

- Choose a name (and alternative names) for the corporation. The name must contain the words *corporation*, *company*, *incorporated*, or *limited* or an abbreviation of one of these words (i.e., *Corp., Co., Inc., Ltd.*).
- Make sure that the name chosen does not contain any word or phrase that indicates or implies that the corporation is organized for any purpose other than those stated in the articles of incorporation. For example, a corporate name cannot contain the word *Bank* if it is not authorized to conduct the business of banking.

- Determine whether the name selected is federally trademarked by another company and is therefore unavailable for use. Trademark lawyers and specialized firms will conduct trademark searches for a fee.
- Determine whether the chosen name is similar to other non-trademarked names and is therefore unavailable for use. Lawyers and specialized firms will conduct such searches for a fee.
- Determine whether the name selected is available as a domain name on the Internet. If the domain name is already owned by another person or business, the new corporation cannot use this domain name to conduct e-commerce over the Internet. Therefore, it is advisable to select another corporate name. ■

Articles of Incorporation

The **articles of incorporation** (or **corporate charter**) are the basic governing documents of a corporation. They must be drafted and filed with, and approved by, the state before the corporation can be officially incorporated. Under the RMBCA, the articles of incorporation must include [RMBCA § 2.02(a)]:

1. The name of the corporation
2. The number of shares the corporation is authorized to issue
3. The address of the corporation's initial registered office and the name of the initial registered agent
4. The name and address of each incorporator

The articles of incorporation may also include provisions concerning (1) the period of duration (which may be perpetual), (2) the purpose or purposes for which the corporation is organized, (3) limitation or regulation of the powers of the corporation, (4) regulation of the affairs of the corporation, or (5) any provision that would otherwise be contained in the corporation's bylaws.

Exhibit 26.2 illustrates sample articles of incorporation.

Business Brief

Over half of the corporations listed on the New York Stock Exchange are incorporated in Delaware because of its laws that favor management.

Exhibit 26.2

Sample Articles of Incorporation

ARTICLES OF INCORPORATION
OF
THE BIG CHEESE CORPORATION

ONE: The name of this corporation is:

THE BIG CHEESE CORPORATION

TWO: The purpose of this corporation is to engage in any lawful act or activity for which a corporation may be organized under the General Corporation Law of California other than the banking business, the trust company business, or the practice of a profession permitted to be incorporated by the California Corporations Code.

THREE: The name and address in this state of the corporation's initial agent for service of process is:

Nikki Nguyen, Esq.
1000 Main Street
Suite 800
Los Angeles, California 90010

FOUR: This corporation is authorized to issue only one class of shares which shall be designated common stock. The total number of shares it is authorized to issue is 1,000,000 shares.

FIVE: The names and addresses of the persons who are appointed to act as the initial directors of this corporation are:

Shou-Yi Kang	100 Maple Street Los Angeles, California 90005
Frederick Richards	200 Spruce Road Los Angeles, California 90006
Jessie Qian	300 Palm Drive Los Angeles, California 90007
Richard Eastin	400 Willow Lane Los Angeles, California 90008

SIX: The liability of the directors of the corporation from monetary damages shall be eliminated to the fullest extent possible under California law.

SEVEN: The corporation is authorized to provide indemnification of agents (as defined in Section 317 of the Corporations Code) for breach of duty to the corporation and its stockholders through bylaw provisions or through agreements with the agents, or both, in excess of the indemnification otherwise permitted by Section 317 of the Corporations Code, subject to the limits on such excess indemnification set forth in Section 204 of the Corporations Code.

IN WITNESS WHEREOF, the undersigned, being all the persons named above as the initial directors, have executed these Articles of Incorporation.

Dated: January 2, 2005

> The corporation is, and must be, the creature of the state, into its nostrils the state must breathe the breath of a fictitious life for otherwise it would be no animated body but individualistic dust.
>
> Frederic Wm. Maitland
> *Introduction to Gierke, Political Theories of the Middle Ages*

Business Brief

The filing of the articles of incorporation is *conclusive proof* that a corporation exists. After that, only the state can challenge the status of the corporation; third parties cannot.

Amending the Articles of Incorporation   The articles of incorporation can be amended to contain any provision that could have been lawfully included in the original document [RMBCA § 10.01]. Such an amendment must show that (1) the board of directors adopted a *resolution* recommending the amendment and (2) the shareholders voted to approve the amendment [RMBCA § 10.03]. The board of directors of a corporation may approve an amendment to the articles of incorporation without shareholder approval if the amendment does not affect rights attached to shares [RMBCA § 10.02]. After the amendment is approved by the shareholders, the corporation must file *articles of amendment* with the secretary of state [RMBCA § 10.06].

Corporate Status   The RMBCA provides that corporate existence begins when the articles of incorporation are filed. The secretary of state's filing of the articles of incorporation is *conclusive proof* that the incorporators satisfied all conditions of incorporation. After that, only the state can bring a proceeding to cancel or revoke the incorporation or involuntarily dissolve the corporation. Third parties cannot thereafter challenge the existence of the corporation or raise it as a defense against the corporation [RMBCA § 2.03]. The corollary to this rule is that failure to file articles of incorporation is conclusive proof of the nonexistence of the corporation.

Purpose

A corporation can be formed for "any lawful purpose." Many corporations include a **general-purpose clause** in their articles of incorporation. Such a clause allows the corporation to engage in any activity permitted corporations by law. A corporation may choose to limit its purpose or purposes by including a *limited-purpose clause* in the articles of incorporation [RMBCA § 3.01]. For example, a corporation may be organized "to engage in the business of real estate development."

Registered Agent

The articles of incorporation must identify a **registered office** with a designated **registered agent** (either an individual or a corporation) in the state of incorporation [RMBCA § 5.01]. The registered office does not have to be the same as the corporation's place of business. A statement of change must be filed with the secretary of state of the state of incorporation if either the registered office or the registered agent is changed.

The registered agent is empowered to accept service of process on behalf of the corporation. For example, if someone were suing the corporation, the complaint and summons would be served on the registered agent. If no registered agent is named or the registered agent cannot be found at the registered office with reasonable diligence, service may be made by mail or alternative means [RMBCA § 5.04].

Corporate Bylaws

In addition to the articles of incorporation, corporations are governed by their **bylaws**. Either the incorporators or initial directors can adopt the bylaws of the corporation. The bylaws are much more detailed than are the articles of incorporation. Bylaws may contain any provisions for managing the business and affairs of the corporation that are not inconsistent with law or the articles of incorporation [RMBCA § 2.06]. They do not have to be filed with any government official. The bylaws are binding on the directors, officers, and shareholders of the corporation.

The bylaws govern the internal management structure of the corporation. For example, they typically specify the time and place of the annual shareholders' meeting, how special meetings of shareholders are called, the time and place of annual and monthly board of directors' meetings, how special meetings of the board of directors are called, the notice required for meetings, the quorum necessary to hold a shareholders' or board of directors' meeting, the required vote necessary to enact a corporate matter, the corporate officers and their duties, the committees of the board of directors and their duties, where the records of the corporation are kept, directors' and shareholders' inspection rights of corporate records, the procedure for transferring shares of the corporation, and such. Sample provisions of corporate bylaws are set forth in Exhibit. 26.3.

The board of directors has the authority to amend the bylaws unless the articles of incorporation reserve that right for the shareholders. The shareholders of the corporation have the absolute right to amend the bylaws even though the bylaws may also be amended by the board of directors [RMBCA § 10.20].

Business Brief

The bylaws, which are much more detailed than the articles of incorporation, regulate the internal management structure of the corporation.

Exhibit 26.3

Sample Provisions from Corporate Bylaws

BYLAWS
of
THE BIG CHEESE CORPORATION

ARTICLE I   Offices

Section 1. Principal Executive Office.   The corporation's principal executive office shall be fixed and located at such place as the Board of Directors (herein called the "Board") shall determine. The Board is granted full power and authority to change said principal executive office from one location to another.

Section 2. Other Offices.   Branch or subordinate offices may be established at any time by the Board at any place or places.

ARTICLE II   Shareholders

Section 1. Annual Meetings.   The annual meetings of shareholders shall be held on such date and at such time as may be fixed by the Board. At such meetings, directors shall be elected and any other proper business may be transacted.

Section 2. Special Meetings.   Special meetings of the shareholders may be called at any time by the Board, the Chairman of the Board, the President, or by the holders of shares entitled to cast not less than ten percent of the votes at such meeting. Upon request in writing to the Chairman of the Board, the President, any Vice President or the Secretary by any person (other than the Board) entitled to call a special meeting of shareholders, the officer forthwith shall cause notice to be given to the shareholders entitled to vote that a meeting will be held at a time requested by the person or persons calling the meeting, not less than thirty-five nor more than sixty days after the receipt of the request. If the notice is not given within twenty days after receipt of the request, the persons entitled to call the meeting may give the notice.

Section 3. Quorum.   A majority of the shares entitled to vote, represented in person or by proxy, shall constitute a quorum at any meeting of shareholders. If a quorum is present, the affirmative vote of a majority of the shares represented and voting at the meeting (which shares voting affirmatively also constitute at least a majority of the required quorum) shall be the act of the shareholders, unless the vote of a greater number or voting by classes is required by law or by the Articles, except as provided in the following sentence. The shareholders present at a duly called or held meeting at which a quorum is present may continue to do business until adjournment, notwithstanding the withdrawal of enough shareholders to leave less than a quorum, if any action taken (other than adjournment) is approved by at least a majority of the shares required to constitute a quorum.

ARTICLE III   Directors

Section 1. Election and term of office.   The directors shall be elected at each annual meeting of the shareholders, but if any such annual meeting is not held or the directors are not elected thereat, the directors may be elected at any special meeting of shareholders held for that purpose. Each director shall hold office until the next annual meeting and until a successor has been elected and qualified.

Section 2. Quorum.   A majority of the authorized number of directors constitutes a quorum of the Board for the transaction of business. Every act or decision done or made by a majority of the directors present at a meeting duly held at which a quorum is present shall be regarded as the act of the Board, unless a greater number be required by law or by the Articles. A meeting at which a quorum is initially present may continue to transact business notwithstanding the withdrawal of directors, if any action taken is approved by at least a majority of the required quorum for such meeting.

Section 3. Participation in Meetings by Conference Telephone.   Members of the Board may participate in a meeting through use of conference telephone or similar communications equipment, so long as all members participating in such meeting can hear one another.

Section 4. Action Without Meeting.   Any action required or permitted to be taken by the Board may be taken without a meeting if all members of the board shall individually or collectively consent in writing to such action. Such consent or consents shall have the same effect as a unanimous vote of the Board and shall be filed with the minutes of the proceedings of the Board.

Corporate Seal

Most corporations adopt a **corporate seal** [RMBCA § 3.02(2)]. Generally, the seal is a design that contains the name of the corporation and the date of incorporation. It is imprinted by the corporate secretary on certain legal documents (e.g., real estate deeds) that are signed by corporate officers or directors. The seal is usually affixed by a metal stamp.

Organizational Meeting

An **organizational meeting** of the initial directors of the corporation must be held after the articles of incorporation are filed. At this meeting, the directors must adopt the bylaws, elect corporate officers, and transact such other business as may come before the meeting [RMBCA § 2.05]. The last category includes such matters as accepting share subscriptions, approving the form of the stock certificate, authorizing the issuance of the shares, ratifying or adopting promoters' contracts, authorizing the reimbursement of promoters' expenses, selecting a bank, choosing an auditor, forming committees of the board of directors, fixing the salaries of officers, hiring employees, authorizing the filing of applications for government licenses to transact the business of the corporation, and empowering corporate officers to enter into contracts on behalf of the corporation. Exhibit 26.4 contains sample corporate resolutions from an organizational meeting of a corporation.

Exhibit 26.4

Sample Corporate Resolutions from an Organizational Meeting

**MINUTES OF FIRST MEETING
OF
BOARD OF DIRECTORS
OF
THE BIG CHEESE CORPORATION
January 2, 2005
10:00 A.M.**

The Directors of said corporation held their first meeting on the above date and at the above time pursuant to required notice.

The following Directors, constituting a quorum of the Board of Directors, were present at such meeting:

Shou-Yi Kang
Frederick Richards
Jessie Quian
Richard Eastin

Upon motion duly made and seconded, Shou-Yi was unanimously elected Chairman of the meeting and Frederick Richards was unanimously elected Secretary of the meeting.

1. Articles of Incorporation and Agent for Service of Process

The Chairman stated that the Articles of Incorporation of the Corporation were filed in the office of the California Secretary of State. The Chairman presented to the meeting a certified copy of the Articles of Incorporation. The Secretary was directed to insert the copy in the Minute Book. Upon motion duly made and seconded, the following resolution was unanimously adopted:

RESOLVED, that the agent named as the initial agent for service of process in the Articles of Incorporation of this corporation is hereby confirmed as this corporation's agent for the purpose of service of process.

2. Bylaws

The matter of adopting Bylaws for the regulation of the affairs of the corporation was next considered. The Secretary presented to the meeting a form of Bylaws, which was considered and discussed. Upon motion duly made and seconded, the following recitals and resolutions were unanimously adopted:

WHEREAS, there has been presented to the directors a form of Bylaws for the regulation of the affairs of this corporation; and

WHEREAS, it is deemed to be in the best interests of this corporation that said Bylaws be adopted by this Board of Directors as the Bylaws of this corporation;

NOW, THEREFORE, BE IT RESOLVED, that Bylaws in the form presented to this meeting are adopted and approved as the Bylaws of this corporation until amended or repealed in accordance with applicable law.

RESOLVED FURTHER, that the Secretary of this corporation is authorized and directed to execute a certificate of the adoption of said Bylaws and to enter said Bylaws as so certified in the Minute Book of this corporation, and to see that a copy of said Bylaws is kept at the principal executive or business office of this corporation in California.

3. Corporate Seal

The secretary presented for approval a proposed seal of the corporation. Upon motion duly made and seconded, the following resolution was unanimously adopted:

RESOLVED, that a corporate seal is adopted as the seal of this corporation in the form of two concentric circles, with the name of this corporation between the two circles and the state and date of incorporation within the inner circle.

4. Stock Certificate

The Secretary presented a proposed form of stock certificate for use by the corporation. Upon motion duly made and seconded, the following resolution was unanimously adopted:

RESOLVED, that the form of stock certificate presented to this meeting is approved and adopted as the stock certificate of this corporation.

The secretary was instructed to insert a sample copy of the stock certificate in the Minute Book immediately following these minutes.

5. Election of officers

The Chairman announced that it would be in order to elect officers of the corporation. After discussion and upon motion duly made and seconded, the following resolution was unanimously adopted:

RESOLVED, that the following persons are unanimously elected to the offices indicated opposite their names

Title	Name
Chief Executive Officer	Shou-Yi Kang
President	Frederick Richards
Secretary and Vice President	Jessie Quian
Treasurer	Richard Eastin

There being no further business to come before the meeting, on motion duly made, seconded and unanimously carried, the meeting was adjourned.

Contemporary Environment

C Corporations and S Corporations

A C corporation is a corporation that does not qualify to or does not elect to be taxed as an S corporation. Any corporation with more than 75 shareholders is automatically a C corporation. A C corporation must pay federal income tax at the corporate level. In addition, if a C corporation distributes its profits to shareholders in the form of dividends, the shareholders must pay personal income tax on the dividends. This causes *double taxation*: one tax paid at the corporate level and another paid at the shareholder level.

In 1982, Congress enacted the **Subchapter S Revision Act** [26 U.S.C. §§ 6242 et seq.]. The act allows some corporations and their shareholders to avoid double taxation by electing to be an S corporation.

If a corporation elects to be taxed as an S corporation, it pays no federal income tax at the corporate level. As in a partnership, the corporation's income or loss flows to the shareholders' individual income tax returns. Thus, this election is particularly advantageous if (1) the corporation is expected to have losses that can be offset against other income of the shareholders or (2) the corporation is expected to make profits and the shareholders' income tax brackets are lower than the corporation's. Profits are taxed to the shareholders even if the income is not distributed. The shares retain other attributes of the corporate form, including limited liability.

Election to be an S Corporation

Corporations that meet the following criteria can elect to be taxed as S corporations:

1. The corporation must be a domestic corporation.
2. The corporation cannot be a member of an affiliated group of corporations.
3. The corporation can have no more than 75 shareholders.
4. Shareholders must be individuals, estates, or certain trusts. Corporations and partnerships cannot be shareholders.
5. Shareholders must be citizens or residents of the United States. Nonresident aliens cannot be shareholders.
6. The corporation cannot have more than one class of stock. Shareholders do not have to have equal voting rights.

An S corporation election is made by filing *form 2553* with the Internal Revenue Service (IRS). The election can be rescinded by shareholders who collectively own at least a majority of the shares of the corporation. However, if the election is rescinded, another S corporation election cannot be made for five years. ■

Financing the Corporation

A corporation needs to finance the operation of its business. The most common way to do this is by selling *equity securities* and *debt securities*. **Equity securities** (or **stocks**) represent ownership rights in the corporation. Equity securities can be *common stock* and *preferred stock*. These are discussed in the following paragraphs.

Common Stock

Common stock is an equity security that represents the residual value of the corporation. Common stock has no preferences. That is, creditors and preferred shareholders must receive their required interest and dividend payments before common shareholders receive anything. Common stock does not have a fixed maturity date. If the corporation is liquidated, the creditors and preferred shareholders are paid the value of their interests first, and the common shareholders are paid the value of their interests (if any) last. Corporations may issue different classes of common stock [RMBCA § 6.01(a) and (b)].

Persons who own common stock are called **common stockholders**. A common stockholder's investment in the corporation is represented by a **common stock certificate**. Common stockholders have the right to elect directors and to vote on mergers and other important matters. In return for their investment, common stockholders receive *dividends* declared by the board of directors.

Par Value and No Par Shares Common shares are sometimes categorized as either par or no par. *Par share* is a value assigned to common shares by the corporation, usually in the articles of incorporation, which sets the lowest price at which the shares may be issued by the corporation. It does not affect the market value of the shares. Most shares that are issued by corporations are *no par shares*. No par shares are not assigned a par value. The RMBCA has eliminated the concept of par value.

Preferred Stock

Preferred stock is an equity security that is given certain *preferences and rights over common stock* [RMBCA § 6.01(c)]. The owners of preferred stock are called **preferred stockholders**. Preferred stockholders are issued **preferred stock certificates** to evidence their ownership interest in the corporation.

Preferred stock can be issued in classes or series. One class of preferred stock can be given preferences over another class of preferred stock. Like common stockholders, preferred stockholders have limited liability. Preferred stockholders generally are not given the right to vote for the election of directors or such. However, they are often given the right to vote if there is a merger or if the corporation has not made the required dividend payments for a certain period of time (e.g., three years).

Preferences Preferences of preferred stock must be set forth in the articles of incorporation. Preferred stock may have any or all of the following preferences or rights:

- *Dividend preference.* A **dividend preference** is the right to receive a *fixed dividend* at set periods during the year (e.g., quarterly). The dividend rate is usually a set percentage of the initial offering price. For example, suppose a stockholder purchases $10,000 of a preferred stock that pays an 8 percent dividend annually. The stockholder has the right to receive $800 each year as a dividend on the preferred stock.

- *Liquidation preference.* The right to be paid before common stockholders if the corporation is dissolved and liquidated is called a **liquidation preference**. A liquidation preference is normally a stated dollar amount. For example, a corporation issues a preferred stock that has a liquidation preference of $200. This means that if the corporation is dissolved and liquidated, the holder of each preferred share will receive at least $200 before the common shareholders receive anything. Note that because the corporation must pay its creditors first, there may be insufficient funds to pay this preference.

- *Cumulative dividend right.* Corporations must pay a preferred dividend if they have the earnings to do so. **Cumulative preferred stock** provides that any missed dividend payments must be paid in the future to preferred shareholders before the common shareholders can receive any dividends. The amount of unpaid cumulative dividends is called dividend *arrearages*. Usually, arrearages can be accumulated for only a limited period of time (e.g., three years). If the preferred stock is **noncumulative**, there is no right of accumulation. In other words, the corporation does not have to pay any missed dividends.

- *Right to participate in profits.* **Participating preferred stock** allows the stockholder to participate in the profits of the corporation along with the common stockholders. Participation is in addition to the fixed dividend paid on preferred stock. The terms of participation vary widely. Usually, the common stockholders must be paid a certain amount of dividends before participation is allowed. **Nonparticipating preferred stock** does not give the holder a right to participate in the profits of the corporation beyond the fixed dividend rate. Most preferred stock falls into this category.

- *Conversion right.* **Convertible preferred stock** permits the stockholders to convert their shares into common stock. The terms and exchange rate of the conversion are established when the shares are issued. The holders of the convertible preferred stock usually exercise this option if the corporation's common stock significantly increases in value. Preferred stock without a conversion feature is called **nonconvertible preferred stock**. Nonconvertible stock is more common.

Business Brief

Preferred stock is given certain *preferences*, and its value is based on these preferences.

This list of preferences and rights is not exhaustive [RMBCA § 6.01(d)]. Corporations may establish other preferences and rights for preferred stock.

Redeemable Preferred Stock **Redeemable preferred stock** (or **callable preferred stock**) permits a corporation to redeem (i.e., buy back) the preferred stock at some future date. The terms of the redemption are established when the shares are issued. Corporations usually redeem the shares when the current interest rate falls below the dividend rate of the preferred shares. Preferred stock that is not redeemable is called **nonredeemable preferred stock**. Nonredeemable stock is more common.

Authorized, Issued, and Outstanding Shares

The number of shares provided for in the articles of incorporation is called **authorized shares** [RMBCA § 6.01]. The shareholders may vote to amend the articles of incorporation to increase this amount. Authorized shares that have been sold by the corporation are called **issued shares**. Not all authorized shares have to be issued at the same time. Authorized shares that have not been issued are called *unissued shares*. The board of directors can vote to issue unissued shares at any time without shareholder approval.

A corporation is permitted to repurchase its own shares [RMBCA § 6.31]. Repurchased shares are commonly called **treasury shares**. Treasury shares cannot be voted by the corporation, and dividends are not paid on these shares. Treasury shares can be reissued by the corporation. The shares that are in shareholder hands, whether originally issued or reissued treasury shares, are called **outstanding shares**. Only outstanding shares have the right to vote [RMBCA § 6.03].

Concept Summary   Types of Shares

Type of Share	Description
Authorized	Shares authorized in the corporation's articles of incorporation.
Issued	Shares sold by the corporation.
Treasury	Shares repurchased by the corporation. They do not have the right to vote.
Outstanding	Issued shares minus treasury shares. These shares have the right to vote.

Consideration to Be Paid for Shares

Business Brief

Shares of a corporation may be sold in exchange for any property or benefit to the corporation, as determined by the board of directors.

The RMBCA allows shares to be issued in exchange for any benefit to the corporation, including cash, tangible property, intangible property, promissory notes, services performed, contracts for services performed, or other securities of the corporation. In the absence of fraud, the judgment of the board of directors or shareholders as to the value of consideration received for shares is conclusive [RMBCA § 6.21 (b) and (c)].

Debt Securities

A corporation often raises funds by issuing debt securities [RMBCA § 3.02(7)]. **Debt securities** (also called **fixed income securities**) establish a debtor–creditor relationship in which the corporation borrows money from the investor to whom the debt security is issued. The corporation promises to pay interest on the amount borrowed and to repay the principal at some stated maturity date in the future. The corporation is the *debtor*, and the holder is the *creditor*. The three classifications of debt securities are:

1. *Debenture.* A **debenture** is a *long-term* (often 30 years or more), *unsecured* debt instrument that is based on the corporation's general credit standing. If the corporation encounters financial difficulty, unsecured debenture holders are treated as general creditors of the corporation (i.e., they are paid only after the secured creditors' claims are met).
2. *Bond.* A **bond** is a *long-term* debt security that is *secured* by some form of *collateral* (e.g., real estate, personal property). Thus, bonds are the same as debentures except that they are secured. Secured bondholders can foreclose on the collateral in the event of non-payment of interest, principal, or other specified events.
3. *Note.* A **note** is a *short-term* debt security with a maturity of five years or less. Notes can be either *unsecured* or *secured*. They usually do not contain a conversion feature. They are sometimes made redeemable.

Indenture Agreement The terms of a debt security are commonly contained in a contract between the corporation and the holder known as an **indenture agreement** (or simply an **indenture**). The indenture generally contains the maturity date of the debt security, the required interest payment, the collateral (if any), conversion rights into common or preferred stock, call provisions, any restrictions on the corporation's right to incur other indebtedness, the rights of holders upon default, and such. It also establishes the rights and duties of the indenture trustee. Generally, a trustee is appointed to represent the interest of the debt security holders. Bank trust departments often serve in this capacity.

Contemporary Environment

Stock Options and Stock Warrants

A corporation can grant **stock options** (options) and stock warrants (warrants) that permit parties to purchase common or preferred shares at a certain price for a set time [RMBCA § 6.24].

A stock option gives the recipient the right to purchase shares of the corporation from the corporation at a stated price (called the *striking price*) for a specified period of time (called the *option period*). If the profitability of the corporation and the market value of its securities increase during the option period, the holder of the option is likely to *exercise the option*—that is, purchase the shares subject to the option. Stock options are nontransferable.

Corporations commonly grant **stock options** to top-level managers. Stock options are often issued to attract executive talent to work for the corporation. Shareholders sometimes criticize their corporations for being too generous in granting stock options.

A **stock warrant** is a stock option that is evidenced by a certificate. Warrants are commonly issued in conjunction with other securities. A warrant holder can exercise the warrant and purchase the common stock at the strike price anytime during the warrant period. Warrants can be transferable or nontransferable. ∎

Corporate Powers

A corporation has the same basic rights to perform acts and enter into contracts as a physical person [RMBCA § 3.02]. The express and implied powers of a corporation are discussed in the following paragraphs.

Express Powers

A corporation's **express powers** are found in (1) the U.S. Constitution, (2) state constitutions, (3) federal statutes, (4) state statutes, (5) articles of incorporation, (6) bylaws, and (7) resolutions of the board of directors. Corporation statutes normally state the express powers granted to the corporation.

Generally, a corporation has the power to purchase, own, lease, sell, mortgage, or otherwise deal in real and personal property; make contracts; lend money; borrow money; incur liabilities; issue notes, bonds, and other obligations; invest and reinvest funds; sue and be sued in its corporate name; make donations for the public welfare or for charitable, scientific, or educational purposes; and the like. RMBCA § 3.02 provides a list of express corporate powers.

Corporations formed under general incorporation laws cannot engage in certain businesses, such as banking, insurance, or operating public utilities. Corporations must obtain a corporate charter under special incorporation statutes and receive approval of special government administrative agencies before engaging in these businesses.

Implied Powers

Neither the governing laws nor the corporate documents can anticipate every act necessary for a corporation to carry on its business. **Implied powers** allow a corporation to exceed its express powers in order to accomplish its corporate purpose. For instance, a corporation has the implied power to open a bank account, reimburse its employees for expenses, engage in advertising, purchase insurance, and the like.

Ultra Vires Act

An act by a corporation that is beyond its express or implied powers is called an ***ultra vires act***. The following remedies are available if an *ultra vires* act is committed:

1. Shareholders can sue for an injunction to prevent the corporation from engaging in the act.
2. The corporation (or the shareholders, on behalf of the corporation) can sue the officers or directors who caused the act for damages.
3. The attorney general of the state of incorporation can bring an action to enjoin the act or to dissolve the corporation [RMBCA § 3.04].

Business Brief

Today, the doctrine of *ultra vires* has lost significance because most corporations select general-purpose clauses (making very few acts *ultra vires*).

Dissolution and Termination of Corporations

The life of a corporation may be terminated voluntarily or involuntarily. The methods for dissolving and terminating corporations are discussed in the following paragraphs.

Voluntary Dissolution

A corporation can be **voluntarily dissolved**. If the corporation has not commenced business or issued any shares, it may be dissolved by a vote of the majority of the incorporators or initial directors [RMBCA § 14.01]. After that, the corporation can be voluntarily dissolved if the board of directors recommends dissolution and a majority of shares entitled to vote (or a greater number, if required by the articles of incorporation or bylaws) votes for dissolution as well [RMBCA § 14.02]. For a voluntary dissolution to be effective, **articles of dissolution** must be filed with the secretary of state of the state of incorporation. A corporation is dissolved upon the effective date of the articles of dissolution [RMBCA § 14.03].

Administrative Dissolution

The secretary of state can obtain **administrative dissolution** of a corporation if (1) it failed to file an annual report, (2) it failed for 60 days to maintain a registered agent in the state, (3) it failed, for 60 days after a change of its registered agent, to file a statement of such change with the secretary of state, (4) it did not pay its franchise fee, or (5) the period of duration stated in the corporation's articles of incorporation has expired [RMBCA § 14.20]. Administrative dissolution is simple. If the corporation does not cure the default within 60 days of being notified of it, the secretary of state issues a *certificate of dissolution* that dissolves the corporation [RMBCA § 14.21].

Judicial Dissolution

A corporation can be involuntarily dissolved by a judicial proceeding. **Judicial dissolution** can be instituted by the attorney general of the state of incorporation if the corporation (1) procured its articles of incorporation through fraud or (2) exceeded or abused the authority conferred on it by law [RMBCA § 14.30(1)]. If a court judicially dissolves a corporation, it enters a *decree of dissolution* that specifies the date of dissolution [RMBCA § 14.33].

Winding-Up, Liquidation, and Termination

A dissolved corporation continues its corporate existence but may not carry on any business except as required to **wind up and liquidate** its business and affairs [RMBCA § 14.05].

In a voluntary dissolution, the liquidation is usually carried out by the board of directors. If (1) the dissolution is involuntary or (2) the dissolution is voluntary but the directors refuse to carry out the liquidation, a court-appointed receiver carriers out the winding-up and liquidation of the corporation [RMBCA § 14.32].

Termination occurs only after the winding-up of the corporation's affairs, the liquidation of its assets, and the distribution of the proceeds to the claimants. The liquidated assets are paid to claimants according to the following priority: (1) expenses of liquidation and creditors according to their respective liens and contract rights, (2) preferred shareholders according to their liquidation preferences and contract rights, and (3) common stockholders.

The dissolution of a corporation does not impair any rights or remedies available against the corporation or its directors, or officers, or shareholders for any right or claim existing or incurred prior to dissolution.

International Law

International Branch Offices and Subsidiary Corporations

A corporation can conduct business in a foreign country by using either a *branch office* or a *subsidiary corporation*. Different liability rules apply to each of these forms of conducting international business.

Branch Office

A corporation can conduct business in another country by using a **branch office** (see Exhibit 26.5). A branch office is not a separate legal entity but is merely an office of the corporation. As such, the corporation is liable for the contracts of the branch office and is also liable for the torts committed by personnel of the branch office. There is no liability shield between the corporation and the branch office.

Consider This Example Ford Motor Company, a U.S. corporation incorporated under the laws of Delaware, opens a branch office in Delhi, India, to sell its automobiles there. If an employee at the branch office in India negligently injures an Indian citizen in India while on a test drive, Ford Motor Company in the United States is wholly liable for the injured person's damages.

Subsidiary Corporation

A corporation can conduct business in another country by using a **subsidiary corporation** (see Exhibit 26.6). The subsidiary corporation is organized under the laws of the foreign country. The **parent corporation** usually owns all or the majority of the subsidiary corporation. A subsidiary corporation is a separate legal entity. Therefore, the parent corporation is not liable for the contracts of or torts committed by the subsidiary corporation. There is a liability shield between the parent corporation and the subsidiary corporation.

Exhibit 26.5

Conducting International Business Using a Branch Office

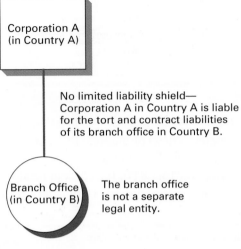

Exhibit 26.6

Conducting International Business Using a Subsidiary Corporation

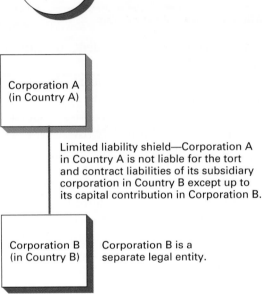

Consider This Example Ford Motor Company, a U.S. corporation incorporated under the laws of Delaware, forms a subsidiary corporation called Ford.India Corporation, an Indian corporation formed under the laws of India, to sell automobiles in India. Ford Motor Company is the parent corporation, and Ford.India

Corporation is the subsidiary corporation. If an employee of Ford.India Corporation negligently injures an Indian citizen while on a test drive, only Ford.India Corporation is liable; Ford Motor Company in the United States is not liable other than that it may lose its capital contribution in Ford.India Corporation. ■

Chapter Summary

Nature of the Corporation, p. 561

Name of the Corporation

1. ***Corporation.*** A corporation is a legal entity created pursuant to the laws of the state of incorporation.
2. ***Corporation codes.*** State statutes govern the formation, operation, and dissolution of corporations.

The Corporation as a Legal "Person"

A corporation is a separate legal entity—an *artificial person*—that can own property, sue and be sued, enter into contracts, and such.

Characteristics of Corporations

1. *Limited liability of shareholders.* Shareholders are liable for the debts and obligations of the corporation only to the extent of their capital contributions.
2. *Free transferability of shares.* Shares of a corporation are freely transferable by shareholders unless they are expressly restricted.
3. *Perpetual existence.* Corporations exist in perpetuity unless a specific duration is stated in the corporation's articles of incorporation.
4. *Centralized management.* The *board of directors* of the corporation makes policy decisions for the corporation. Corporate *officers* appointed by the board of directors run the corporation's day-to-day operations. Together, the directors and officers form the corporation's "management."

The Revised Model Business Corporation Act

1. *Model Business Corporation Act (MBCA).* This model act, drafted in 1950, was intended to provide a uniform law for the regulation of corporations.
2. *Revised Model Business Corporation Act (RMBCA).* RMBCA is a revision of the MBCA promulgated in 1984 that arranges the provisions of the model act more logically, revises the language to be more consistent, and makes substantial changes that modernize the provisions of the act.

Public and Private Corporations

1. *Public corporation.* A public corporation is a corporation formed to meet a specific governmental or political purpose. Also called a *government-owned* corporation. *Municipal corporations* (i.e., cities) are an example.
2. *Private corporation.* A private corporation is a corporation formed to conduct privately owned businesses. It may be large or small.

Profit and Nonprofit Corporations

1. *Profit corporation.* A profit corporation is created to conduct a business for profit that can distribute profits to shareholders in the form of dividends.
2. *Nonprofit corporation.* A nonprofit corporation is formed to operate charitable institutions, colleges, universities, and other not for profit entities. There are no shareholders of these corporations.

Publicly Held and Closely Held Corporations

1. *Publicly held corporation.* A publicly held corporation has many shareholders, and its securities are often traded on national stock exchanges. General Motors Corporation is an example.
2. *Closely held corporation.* A closely held corporation is owned by one or a few shareholders. Examples are family-owned corporations. They are also called *close corporations*.

Professional Corporations

Professional corporations are formed by lawyers, doctors, and other professionals. Shareholders of professional corporations are usually called *members*. Members must be licensed to practice the profession for which the corporation is formed.

Incorporation Procedures, p. 564

Incorporation Procedures

1. *Incorporation.* Incorporation is the process of incorporating (forming) a new corporation.
2. *Corporations code.* Corporations are creatures of statute, they can be formed only if certain statutory formalities contained in the state's corporations code are followed.

Promoters' Liability

1. *Promoter.* A promoter is a person or persons who organize and start a corporation, negotiate and enter into contracts in advance of formation, find the initial investors to finance the corporation, and so forth.

2. *Promoter's contract.* A promoter's contract is entered into by a promoter on behalf of a proposed corporation prior to its actual incorporation. These contracts often include leases, sales contracts, contracts to purchase property, and so forth.

3. *Liability of promoters for promoters' contracts.* Promoters are personally liable for promoters' contracts unless (a) the corporation ratifies the contract as its own once it is formed and (b) the corporation, the promoter, and the third party with whom the contract is made enter into a *novation* agreement that expressly releases the promoter from liability.

Selecting a State of Incorporation

A corporation can be incorporated in only one state, although it can conduct business in other states.

Incorporators

Incorporators are the person or persons, partnerships, or corporations who are responsible for incorporating a new corporation.

Domestic, Foreign, and Alien Corporations

1. *Domestic corporation.* A domestic corporation is a corporation in the state in which it is incorporated.

2. *Foreign corporation.* A foreign corporation is a corporation in any state other than the one in which it is incorporated. A domestic corporation often transacts business in states other than its state of incorporation; hence, it is a foreign corporation in these states. A foreign corporation must obtain a *certificate of authority* from these other states to transact intrastate business in those states.

3. *Alien corporation.* An alien corporation is a corporation that is incorporated in another country. Alien corporations are treated as foreign corporations for most purposes.

Articles of Incorporation

The articles of incorporation is the basic governing document of a corporation. This document must be filed with the secretary of state of the state of incorporation. It is a public document. It is also called the *corporate charter*.

1. *Information to be set forth in the articles of incorporation.* The corporations code of each state sets out the information that must be included in the articles of incorporation. Additional information may be included in the articles of incorporation as deemed necessary or desirable by the incorporators.

2. *Amending the articles of incorporation.* The articles of incorporation can be amended to contain any provision that could have been lawfully included in the original articles of incorporation. After an amendment is approved by the shareholders, the corporation must file *articles of amendment* with the secretary of state in the state in which it is incorporated.

Corporate Status

RMBCA rule. The filing of the articles of incorporation is *conclusive proof* that a corporation exists. After that, only the state can challenge the status of the corporation; third parties cannot. Failure to file articles of incorporation is conclusive proof that the corporation does not exist. The state and third parties may challenge the existence of the corporation.

Other Issues Concerning Incorporation

1. *Corporate name.* A corporate name selected for a new corporation must be distinguishable from existing corporate names. A corporate name may be reserved for a limited period of time while the corporation is being formed.

2. *Purpose.* A corporation can be formed for "any lawful purpose." Corporations can limit the purposes of the corporation by including in the articles of incorporation a *limited-purpose clause* that stipulates the purposes and activities the corporation can engage in.

3. *Registered agent.* A new corporation must designate a person or corporation that is empowered to accept *service of process* on behalf of the corporation. A new designation must be made annually.

Corporate Bylaws

Bylaws are a detailed set of rules that are adopted by the board of directors after a corporation is formed that contain provisions for managing the business and affairs of the corporation. This document does not have to be filed with the secretary of state.

Corporate Seal

A corporate seal is a design that contains the name of the corporation and the date of incorporation. It is imprinted by the corporate secretary on certain legal documents, using a metal stamp containing the design.

Organization Meeting

An organization meeting must be held by the initial directors of a corporation after the articles of incorporation are filed. At this meeting, the directors adopt the bylaws, elect corporate officers, ratify promoters' contracts, adopt a corporate seal, and transact such other business as may come before the meeting.

Minutes. Minutes are the written recording of the actions taken by the directors at the organizational and other directors' meetings.

S Corporations

An S corporation is a corporation that has elected to be taxed as an S corporation for federal income tax purposes. An S corporation pays no federal income tax at the corporate level, and the S corporation's income or loss flows to the shareholders and must be reported on the shareholders' individual income tax returns. A corporation must meet certain requirements to elect to be an S corporation.

C Corporation

A C corporation is a corporation that either does not qualify to be on S corporation or elects not to be an S corporation. C corporations must pay federal income tax at the corporate level. If a C corporation distributes its profits to shareholders in the forms of dividends, the shareholders must pay personal income tax on the dividends.

Financing the Corporation, p. 572

Financing the Corporation

Equity securities. These securities represent the ownership rights to the corporation. They are also called *stocks*. Equity securities consist of *common stock* and *preferred stock*.

Common Stock

Common stock is a type of equity security that represents the *residual value* of the corporation. Common stock has no preferences, and its shareholders are paid dividends and assets upon liquidation only after creditors and preferred shareholders have been paid.

1. *Common stockholder.* A common stockholder is a person who owns common stock.
2. *Common stock certificate.* A common stock certificate represents the common shareholder's investment in the corporation.
3. *Par value.* A par value is assigned by the corporation to common shares that sets the lowest price at which the shares may be issued by the corporation. *No par shares* are not assigned a par value. The RMBCA has eliminated the concept of par value.

Preferred Stock

A type of equity security that is given certain preferences and rights over common stock.

1. *Preferred stockholder.* A preferred stockholder is a person who owns preferred stock.
2. *Preferred stock certificate.* A preferred stock certificate represents the preferred stockholder's investment in the corporation.

3. **Preferences and rights.** Preferred stock may have any or all of the following preferences or rights:

    a. *Dividend preference.* This preference gives the right to receive a fixed dividend at stipulated periods during the year (e.g., quarterly).

    b. *Liquidation preference.* This preference gives the right to be paid a stated dollar amount if the corporation is dissolved and liquidated. The corporation must pay its creditors first, however.

    c. *Cumulative dividend right. Cumulative preferred stock* is stock that provides that any missed dividend payments must be paid in the future to the preferred shareholders before the common shareholders can receive any dividends.

    d. *Right to participate in profits. Participating preferred stock* is preferred stock that allows the stockholder to participate in the profits of the corporation along with the common stockholders on an expressly stated basis.

    e. *Conversion right. Convertible preferred stock* is preferred stock that permits stockholders to convert their shares into common stock at a stipulated conversion price.

4. **Redeemable preferred stock.** Preferred stock that may be bought back by the corporation at a specified price at some future date. This stock is also called *callable preferred stock.*

Authorized, Issued, and Outstanding Shares

1. **Authorized shares.** This is the number of shares provided for in the articles of incorporation. The shareholders may amend the articles of incorporation to increase this amount.

2. **Issued shares.** Issued shares are authorized shares that have been sold by the corporation.

3. **Unissued shares.** Unissued shares are authorized shares that have not been sold by the corporation.

4. **Treasury shares.** Treasury shares are issued shares that have been repurchased by the corporation. They may be resold by the corporation.

5. **Outstanding shares.** Outstanding shares are shares that are in shareholder hands, whether originally issued or reissued treasury shares. Only outstanding shares have the right to vote.

Consideration to Be Paid for Shares

Shares may be issued in exchange for any benefit to the corporation, including cash, tangible property, intangible property, promissory notes, services performed, contracts for services to be performed, or other securities of the corporation.

Debt Securities

Debt securities establish a *debtor–creditor* relationship in which the corporation borrows money from the investor to whom the debt security is issued.

1. **Debenture.** A debenture is a *long-term unsecured* debt instrument that is based on the corporation's general credit rating.

2. **Bond.** A bond is a *long-term* debt security that is *secured* by some form of property. The property securing the bond is called *collateral.* In the event of nonpayment of interest or principal or other specified events, bondholders can foreclose on and obtain the collateral.

3. **Note.** A note is a *short-term* debt instrument with a maturity of five years or less. Notes can be either unsecured or secured.

4. **Indenture agreement.** The indenture agreement is the contract between the corporation and debt security holders that contains the terms of the agreement between the corporation and the holders.

Stock Options and Stock Warrants

1. **Stock option.** A stock option is a nontransferable right to purchase shares of the corporation from the corporation at a stated price for a specific period of time.

    a. *Striking price.* The striking price is the stated price at which the stock may be bought at a future date.

    b. *Option period.* The option period is the specified period of time for exercising a stock option.

c. *Exercising the option.* Exercising the option is the act of purchasing the shares subject to the option by the holder of the option. Stock options are usually granted to the management of a corporation.

2. **Stock warrant.** A stock warrant is a stock option that is represented by a certificate. Stock warrants are commonly issued in conjunction with another security. Warrants may be transferable or nontransferable.

Corporate Powers, p. 575

Corporate Powers

1. **Express powers.** A corporation has the express powers granted to it by the U.S. Constitution, state constitutions, federal statutes, state statutes (particularly the state's corporation code), articles of incorporation, bylaws, and resolutions of the board of directors.

2. **Implied powers.** Implied powers allow a corporation to accomplish its corporate purpose.

Ultra Vires Acts

Acts by a corporation that are beyond its express or implied powers.
    Remedies. The following remedies are available if an *ultra vires* act is committed:

1. Shareholders can sue for an *injunction* to prevent the corporation from engaging in the act.

2. The corporation (or shareholders, on behalf of the corporation) can sue the officers and directors who caused the act for *damages*.

3. The attorney general of the state of incorporation can bring an action to enjoin the act or to dissolve the corporation.

Dissolution and Termination of Corporations, p. 576

Voluntary Dissolution

Voluntary dissolution is dissolution of a corporation by the incorporators or initial directors if the corporation has not begun business or issued shares and by the majority vote of shareholders if the corporation has begin business or issued shares.
    Articles of dissolution. This document is filed with the secretary of state of the state of incorporation when a corporation is voluntarily dissolved.

Administrative Dissolution

Administrative dissolution is involuntary dissolution of a corporation that is ordered by the secretary of state if the corporation has failed to comply with certain procedures required by law (e.g., failure to pay franchise tax).
    Certificate of dissolution. This document is filed by the secretary of state when a corporation is administratively dissolved.

Judicial Dissolution

Judicial dissolution is dissolution of a corporation by a court proceeding instituted by:

1. **The state.** If the corporation (a) procured its articles of incorporation through fraud or (b) exceeded or abused the authority conferred upon it by law.

2. **Decree of dissolution.** Order issued by the court when a corporation has been judicially dissolved.

Winding-Up, Liquidation, and Termination

1. **Winding-up and liquidation.** A dissolved corporation's assets are collected, liquidated, and distributed to creditors, shareholders and other claimants.

2. **Termination.** The ending of a corporation occurs only after the winding up of the corporation's affairs, the liquidation of its assets, and the distribution of the proceeds and property to the claimants.

Internet Exercises and Case Questions

Working the Web Internet Exercises

Activities

1. Create a hypothetical corporation by preparing articles of incorporation, bylaws, and a shareholder agreement, using forms suitable for your state. For a list of state corporation statutes, see **www.law.cornell.edu/topics/state_statutes. html#corporations**.

2. Prepare minutes of the organizational meeting for your newly formed corporation. See Findlaw's compilation of state corporation and business forms, at **www.findlaw. com/11stategov/indexcorp.html**.

3. Using your state's database of corporations, find the last field annual report of a local corporation and determine who the officers are and who is designated as the registered agent for service of process. See the "Legal Information Institute's Corporate Law Page," at **www. law.cornell.edu/topics/corporations.html**. See also "The Corporate Library," at **www.thecorporatelibrary.com**.

4. Assume that you have decided to form a nonprofit corporation. What other steps do you need to take to properly create such an entity? See "U.S. Incorporation and Nonprofits Online Directory; Charities, Secretary of State, Corporations Division, Foundation Directories, UCC, Trademarks 1996," at **www.internet-prospector.org/ secstate.html**.

Critical Legal Thinking Cases

26.1 Legal Entity   Jeffrey Sammak was the owner of a contracting business known as Senaco. In the early part of 1980, Sammak decided to enter the coal reprocessing business. In April 1980, Sammak attended the "Coal Show" in Chicago, Illinois, at which he met representatives of the Deister Co., Inc. (Deister). Deister was incorporated under the laws of Pennsylvania. Sammak began negotiating with Deister to purchase equipment to be used in his coal reprocessing business. Deister sent Sammak literature guaranteeing a certain level of performance for the equipment. On April 3, 1981, Sammak purchased the equipment. After the equipment was installed, Sammak became dissatisfied with its performance. Sammak believes that Deister breached an express warranty and wants to sue. Can a suit be brought against a corporation such as Deister? [*Blackwood Coal v. Deister Co., Inc.*, 626 F.Supp. 727, 1985 U.S.Dist. Lexis 12767 (E.D. Pa. 1985)]

26.2 Limited Liability of Shareholders   Joseph M. Billy was an employee of the USM Corporation (USM). USM is a publicly held corporation. On October 21, 1976, Billy was at work when a 4,600-pound ram from a vertical boring mill broke lose and crushed him to death. Billy's widow brought suit against USM, alleging that the accident was caused by certain defects in the manufacture and design of the vertical boring mill and the two moving parts directly involved in the accident, a metal lifting arm and the 4,600-pound ram. If Mrs. Billy's suit is successful, can the shareholders of USM be held personally liable for any judgment against USM? [*Billy v. Consolidated Mach. Tool. Corp.*, 412 N.E.2d 934, 51 N.Y.2d 152, 1980 N.Y. Lexis 2638 (N.Y. App. 1980)]

26.3 Type of Corporation   William O'Donnel and Vincent Marino worked together as executives of a shipping container repair company known as Marine Trailers. Marine Trailer's largest customer was American Export Lines (American Export). When American Export became unhappy with the owners of Marine Trailers, it let O'Donnel and Marino know that if they formed their own company, American Exports would give them its business. O'Donnel and Marino decided to take American Export's suggestion, and they bought the major-

ity of shares of a publicly traded corporation known as Marine Repair Service, Inc. (Repair Services). O'Donnel and Marino operated Repair Services as a container repair company at the Port of New York. The company prospered, expanding to five other states and overseas. O'Donnel and Marino's initial $12,000 investment paid off. Ten years after buying the company, each man was earning over $150,000 a year in salary alone. What type of corporation is Repair Service? [*O'Donnel v. Marine Repair Services, Inc.*, 530 F.Supp. 1199, 1982 U.S.Dist. Lexis 10456 (S.D. N.Y.1982)]

26.4 Type of Corporation   Hutchinson Baseball Enterprises, Inc. (Hutchinson, Inc.), was incorporated under the laws of Kansas on August 31, 1980. Among the purposes of the corporation, according to its bylaws, are to "promote, advance, and sponsor baseball, which shall include Little League and Amateur baseball, in the Hutchinson, Kansas, area." The corporation is involved in a number of activities, including the leasing of a field for American Legion teams, furnishing instructors as coaches for Little League teams, conducting a Little League camp, and the leasing of a baseball field to a local junior college for a nominal fee. Hutchinson, Inc., raises money through ticket sales to amateur baseball games, concessions, and contributions. Any profits are used to improve the playing fields. Profits are never distributed to the corporation's directors or members. What type of corporation is Hutchinson, Inc.? [*Hutchinson Baseball Enterprises, Inc. v. Commissioner of Internal Revenue*, 696 F.2d 757, 1982 U.S.App. Lexis 23179 (10th Cir. 1982)]

26.5 Type of Corporation   In November 1979, Elmer Balvik and Thomas Sylvester formed a partnership, named Weldon Electric, for the purpose of engaging in the electrical contracting business. Balvik contributed $8,000 and a vehicle worth $2,000, and Sylvester contributed $25,000 to the partnership's assets. The parties operated the business as a partnership until 1984, when they decided to incorporate. Stock was issued to Balvik and Sylvester in proportion to their partnership ownership interests, with Sylvester receiving 70 percent and Balvik 30 percent of the stock. Balvik and his wife and Sylvester and his wife were the four directors of the corporation. Sylvester was elected president of the corporation. Balvik was vice president. The corporation's bylaws stated that "sales of shares of stock by any shareholder shall be as set forth in a 'Buy Sell Agreement' entered into by the shareholders." What type of corporation is Weldon Electric? [*Balvik v. Sylvester*, 411 N.W.2d 383, 1987 N.D. Lexis 392 (ND 1987)]

26.6 Type of Corporation   Leo V. Mysels was the president of Florida Fashions of Interior Design, Inc. (Florida Fashions). Florida Fashions, which was a Pennsylvania corporation, had never registered to do business in the state of Florida. In 1973, while acting in the capacity of a salesman for the corporation, Mysels took an order for goods from Francis E. Barry. The transaction took place in Florida. Barry paid Florida Fashions for the goods ordered. When Florida Fashions failed to perform its obligations under the sales agreement, Barry brought suit in Florida. What type of corporation was Florida Fashions in regards to the state of Pennsylvania and to the state of Florida? Can Florida Fashions defend itself in a lawsuit? [*Mysels v. Barry*, 332 So.2d 38, 1976 Fla.App. Lexis 14344 (Fla. App. 1976)]

26.7 Promoter's Liability   On December 27, 1972, the Homes Corporation (Homes), a closely held corporation whose sole stockholders were Jerry and Beverly Ann Allen, purchased 10 acres of real estate near Kahaluu on the island of Oahu, Hawaii. Homes made a down payment of $50,000. It was the Allens' intention to obtain approval for a planned unit development (PUD) from the city and county of Honolulu and then develop the property with some 60 condominium townhouses. To further this project, the Allens sought an outside investor. Herbert Hadley, a real estate developer from Texas, decided to join the Allens' project. The two parties entered an agreement whereby a new Hawaiian corporation would be formed to build the condominiums, with Handley owning 51 percent of the corporation's stock and the Allens the remaining 49 percent. The two parties began extensive planning and design of the project. They also took out a $69,500 loan from the Bank of Hawaii. After a year had gone by, Handley informed the Allens that he was no longer able to advance funds to the project. Soon thereafter, the city and county denied their PUD zoning application. The new corporation was never formed. Who is liable for the failed condominium project's contractual obligations? [*Handley v. Ching*, 627 P.2d 1132, 1981 Haw.App. Lexis 192 (Hawaii App. 1981)]

26.8 Promoter's Contracts   Martin Stern, Jr., was an architect who worked in Nevada. In January 1969, Nathan Jacobson asked Stern to draw plans for Jacobson's new hotel/casino, the Kings Castle at Lake Tahoe. Stern agreed to take on the project and immediately began preliminary work. At this time, Stern dealt directly with Jacobson, who referred to the project as "my hotel." In February 1969, Stern wrote to Jacobson, detailing, among other things, the architect's services and fee. Stern's plans were subsequently discussed by the two men, and Stern's fee was set at $250,000. On May 9, 1969, Jacobson formed Lake Enterprises, Inc. (Lake Enterprises), a Nevada corporation of which Jacobson was the sole shareholder and president. Lake Enterprises was formed for the purpose of owning the new casino. During this period, Stern was paid monthly by checks drawn on an account belonging to another corporation controlled by Jacobson. Stern never agreed to contract with any of these corporations and always dealt exclusively with Jacobson. When Stern was not paid the full amount of his architectural fee, he sued Jacobson to recover. Jacobson claimed that he was not personally liable for any of Stern's fee because a novation had taken place. Who wins? [*Jacobson v. Stern*, 605 P.2d 198, 1980 Nev. Lexis 522 (NV 1980)]

26.9 Preferred Stock   On June 24, 1970, Commonwealth Edison Co. (Commonwealth Edison), through its underwriters, sold one million shares of preferred stock at an offering price of $100 per share. commonwealth Edison wanted to issue the stock with a dividend rate of 9.26 percent, but its major underwriter, First Boston Corporation (First Boston), advised that a rate of 9.44 percent should be paid. According to First Boston, a shortage of investment funds existed and a higher dividend rate was necessary for a successful stock issue. Commonwealth Edison's management was never happy with the high dividend rate being paid on this preferred stock. On April 2, 1971, Commonwealth Edison's vice chairman was quoted in the report of the annual meeting of the corporation as saying "we were disappointed at the 9.44 percent dividend rate on the preferred stock we sold last August, but we expect to refinance it when market conditions make it feasible." On March 20, 1972, Commonwealth Edison, pursuant to the terms under which the stock was sold, bought back the one million shares of preferred stock at a price of $110 per share. What type of preferred stock is this? [*The Franklin Life Insurance Company v. Commonwealth Edison Company*, 451 F.Supp. 602, 1978 U.S.Dist. Lexis 17604 (S.D. Ill. 1978)]

26.10 Debt Securities   United Financial Corporation of California (United Financial) was incorporated in the state of Delaware on May 8, 1959. United Financial owned the majority of a California savings and loan association as well as three insurance agencies. In 1960, the original investors in United Financial decided to capitalize on an increase in investor interest in savings and loans. In June 1960, the first public offering of United Federal stock was made. The stock was sold as a unit, with 60,000 units being offered. Each unit consisted of two shares of United Financial stock and one $100, 5 percent interest-bearing debenture bond. This initial offering was a success. It provided $7.2 million to the corporation, of which $6.2 million was distributed as a return of capital to the original investors. What is the difference between the stock offered for sale by United Financial and the debenture bonds? [*Jones v. H.F. Abmanson & Company*, 1 Cal. 3d 93, 81 Cal.Rptr. 592, 1969 Cal.Lexis 195 (CA 1969)]

Business Ethics Cases

26.11 Business Ethics   John A. Goodman was a real estate salesman in the state of Washington. In 1979, Goodman sold an apartment building that needed extensive renovation to Darden, Doman & Stafford Associates (DDS), a general partnership. Goodman represented that he personally had experience in renovation work. During the course of negotiations on a renovation contract, Goodman informed the managing partner of DDS that he would be forming a corporation to do the work. A contract was executed in August 1979 between DDS and "Building Design and Development (In Formation), John A. Goodman, President." The contract required the renovation work to be completed by October 15. Goodman immediately subcontracted the work, but the renovation was not completed on time. DDS also found that the work that was completed was of poor quality. Goodman did not file the articles of incorporation for his new corporation until November 1. The partners of DDS sued Goodman to hold him liable for the renovation contracts. Goodman denied personal liability. Was it morally correct for Goodman to deny liability? Is Goodman personally liable? [*Goodman v. Darden, Doman & Stafford Associates*, 670 P.2d 648, 1983 Wash. Lexis 1776 (WA 1983)]

26.12 Business Ethics In 1983, pursuant to a public offering, Knoll International, Inc. (Knoll), issued debentures to investors. The debentures bore interest at 8 1/8 percent, matured in 30 years, and were subordinated, convertible into common stock at the rate of each $19.20 of principal amount for one share of common stock, and redeemable. Section 8.08 of the indenture agreement provided that no debenture holder could sue unless the holders of 35 percent of the debentures requested the trustee to sue. The indenture also gave the trustee the authority to amend the indenture agreement.

Knoll was controlled through a series of subsidiaries by Knoll International Holdings, Inc. (Holdings), which, in turn, was controlled by Marshall S. Cogan. On January 22, 1987, Knoll merged into Holdings and paid its common shareholders $12 cash per share. Knoll and the indenture trustee executed a supplemental indenture that provided that each debenture holder would receive $12 cash for each $19.20 principal amount of debentures. Simons, a debenture holder who did not own 35 percent of the debentures, brought this suit against Knoll and Cogan. Does Knoll International, Inc., or Cogan owe a fiduciary duty to the debenture holders? Is Cogan breaching an ethical duty to the debenture holders? [*Simons v. Cogan*, 542 A.2d 785, 1987 Del.Ch. Lexis 520 (Del. Ch. 1987)]

Briefing the Case Writing Assignment

Read Case A.26 in the Case Appendix [*Johnson v. Dodgen*]. This case is excerpted from the state supreme court's opinion. Review and brief the case. In your brief, be sure to answer the following questions.

1. Who were the plaintiffs? Who were the defendants?

2. Describe the contract alleged to have been breached in this case.

3. Was the contract signed by a corporation?

4. Did the court find the individual defendant liable on the contract?

27

Corporate Directors, Officers, and Shareholders

> " Corporation, n. An ingenious device for obtaining individual profit without individual responsibility. "
>
> —Ambrose Bierce
> The Devil's Dictionary (1911)

Chapter Objectives

After studying this chapter, you should be able to:

1. Describe the functions of shareholders, directors, and officers in managing the affairs of a corporation.

2. Distinguish between straight and cumulative voting for directors.

3. Describe a director's and an officer's duty of care and the business judgment rule.

4. Describe a director's and an officer's duty of loyalty and how this duty is breached.

5. Define piercing of the corporate veil or alter ego doctrine.

Chapter Contents

- Shareholders
- Board of Directors
- Corporate Officers
- Liability of Corporate Directors and Officers
- Sarbanes-Oxley Act of 2002

Shareholders, directors, and officers have different rights in managing a corporation. The shareholders elect the directors and vote on other important issues affecting the corporation. The directors are responsible for making policy decisions and employing officers. The officers are responsible for the corporation's day-to-day operations.

As a legal entity, a corporation can be held liable for the acts of its directors and officers and for authorized contracts entered into on its behalf. The directors and officers of a corporation have certain rights and owe certain duties to the corporation and its shareholders. A director or an officer who breaches any of these duties can be held personally liable to the corporation, to its shareholders, or to third parties. Insurance is available against certain of these losses. Except in a few circumstances, shareholders do not owe a fiduciary duty to other shareholders or the corporation.

This chapter discusses the rights, duties, and liability of corporate shareholders, directors, and officers.

Shareholders

A corporation's shareholders own the corporation. Nevertheless, they are not agents of the corporation (i.e., they cannot bind the corporation to any contracts), and the only management duties they have is the right to vote on matters such as the election of directors and the approval of fundamental changes in the corporation.

Shareholders' Meetings

Annual shareholders' meetings are held to elect directors, choose an independent auditor, or take other actions. These meetings must be held at the times fixed in the bylaws [RMBCA § 7.01]. If a meeting is not held within either 15 months of the last annual meeting or 6 months after the end of the corporation's fiscal year, whichever is earlier, a shareholder may petition the court to order the meeting held [RMBCA § 7.03].

Special shareholders' meetings may be called by the board of directors, the holders of at least 10 percent of the voting shares of the corporation, or any other person authorized to do so by the articles of incorporation or bylaws (e.g., the president) [RMBCA § 7.02]. Special meetings may be held to consider important or emergency issues, such as a merger or consolidation of the corporation with one or more other corporations, the removal of directors, amendment of the articles of incorporation, or dissolution of the corporation.

Any act that can be taken at a shareholders' meeting can be taken without a meeting if all of the corporate shareholders sign a written consent approving the action [RMBCA § 7.04].

Notice of Meetings A corporation is required to give the shareholders written *notice* of the place, day, and time of annual and special meetings. For a special meeting, the purpose of the meeting must also be stated. Only matters stated in the notice of a special meeting can be considered at the meeting. The notice, which must be given not less than 10 days or more than 50 days before the date of the meeting, may be given in person or by mail [RMBCA § 7.05]. If the required notice is not given or is defective, any action taken at the meeting is void.

Proxies

Shareholders do not have to attend a shareholders' meeting to vote. Shareholders may vote by *proxy*; that is, they can appoint another person (the proxy) as their agent to vote at the shareholders' meeting. The proxy may be directed exactly how to vote the shares or may be authorized to vote the shares at his or her discretion. Proxies may be in writing or posted online. The written document itself is called the **proxy** (or **proxy card**). Unless otherwise stated, a proxy is valid for 11 months [RMBCA § 7.22].

Voting Requirements

At least one class of shares of a corporation must have voting rights. The Revised Model Business Corporation Act (RMBCA) permits corporations to grant more than one vote per share to some classes of stock and less than one vote per share to others [RMBCA § 6.01].

Only those shareholders who own stock as of a set date may vote at a shareholders' meeting. This date, which is called the **record date**, is set forth in the corporate bylaws. The record date may not be more than 70 days before the shareholders' meeting [RMBCA § 7.07].

The corporation must prepare a *shareholders' list* that contains the names and addresses of the shareholders as of the record date and the class and number of shares owned by each shareholder. This list must be available for inspection at the corporation's main office [RMBCA § 7.20].

Quorum and Vote Required

Unless otherwise provided in the articles of incorporation, if a majority of shares entitled to vote are represented at the meeting in person or by proxy, there is a **quorum** to hold the meeting. Once a quorum is present, the withdrawal of shares does not affect the quorum of the meeting [RMBCA § 7.25(a) and (b)].

The affirmative **vote** of the majority of the **voting** shares represented at a shareholders' meeting constitutes an act of the shareholders for actions other than for the election of directors [RMBCA § 7.25(c)].

Consider This Example   Suppose there are 20,000 shares of a corporation outstanding. Assume that a shareholders' meeting is duly called to amend the articles of incorporation and that 10,001 shares are represented at the meeting. A quorum is present because a majority of the shares entitled to vote are represented. Suppose that 5,001 shares are voted in favor of the amendment. The amendment passes. In this example, just over 25 percent of the shares of the corporation bound the other shareholders to the action taken at the shareholders' meeting.

Election of Directors by Straight and Cumulative Voting

The election of directors by shareholders may be by one of the following two methods.

Straight (Noncumulative) Voting   Unless otherwise stated in the corporation's articles of incorporation, voting for the election of directors is by the **straight voting** method. This voting method is quite simple: Each shareholder votes the number of shares he or she owns on candidates for each of the positions open for election. Thus, a majority shareholder can elect the entire board of directors.

Consider This Example   Assume that a corporation has 10,000 outstanding shares. Erin Caldwell owns 5,100 shares (or 51 percent), and Michael Rhodes owns 4,900 shares (49 percent). Suppose that three directors of the corporation are to be elected. Caldwell casts 5,100 votes each for her chosen candidates. Rhodes votes 4,900 shares for each of his chosen candidates, who are different from those favored by Caldwell. Each of the three candidates whom Caldwell voted for wins, with 5,100 votes.

Cumulative Voting A corporation's articles of incorporation may provide for **cumulative voting** for the election of directors. Under this method, a shareholder can accumulate all of his or her votes and vote them all for one candidate or split them among several candidates. This means that each shareholder is entitled to multiply the number of shares he or she owns by the number of directors to be elected and cast the product for a single candidate or distribute the product among two or more candidates [RMBCA § 7.28]. Cumulative voting gives a minority shareholder a better opportunity to elect someone to the board of directors.

Consider This Example   Suppose Lisa Monroe owns 1,000 shares. Assume that four directors are to be elected to the board. Under cumulative voting, Monroe can multiply the number of shares she owns by the number of directors to be elected. She can take the resulting number of votes (4,000) and cast them all for one candidate or split them. Examples of cumulative voting are set forth in Exhibit 27.1.

Supramajority Voting Requirement

The articles of incorporation or the bylaws of a corporation can require a greater than majority of shares to constitute a quorum or the vote of the shareholders [RMBCA § 7.27]. This is called a **supramajority voting requirement** (or **supermajority**). Such votes are often required to approve mergers, consolidation, the sale of substantially all the assets of a corporation, and such. To add a supramajority voting requirement, the amendment must be adopted by the number of shares of the proposed increase. For example, to increase a majority voting requirement to an 80 percent supramajority voting requirement would require an 80 percent affirmative vote.

Exhibit 27.1

Examples of Cumulative Voting

Formula for Cumulative Voting. A shareholder can use the following formula to determine whether or not he or she owns a sufficient number of shares to elect a director to the board of directors using cumulative voting:

$$\frac{S \times T}{D + 1} + 1 = X$$

where X is the number of shares needed by a shareholder to elect a director to the board, S is the number of shares that actually vote at the shareholders' meeting, T is the number of directors the shareholder wants to elect, and D is the number of directors to be elected at the shareholders' meeting.

Example 1 Suppose there are 9,000 outstanding shares of a corporation. Shareholder 1 owns 1,000 shares, Shareholder 2 owns 4,000 shares, and Shareholder 3 owns 4,000 shares. Assume nine directors are to be elected to the board of directors. All the shares are voted. Under cumulative voting, does Shareholder 1 have enough votes to elect a director to the board? The answer is yes:

$$\frac{9,000 \times 1}{9 + 1} + 1 = 901$$

Example 2 If a board of directors is divided into classes and elected by staggered elections, the ability of a minority shareholder to elect a director to the board is diminished. Suppose in Example 1 that the corporation staggered the election of the board of directors so that three directors are elected each year to serve three-year terms. How many shares would a shareholder have to own to elect a director to the board?

$$\frac{9,000 \times 1}{3 + 1} + 1 = 2,251$$

Because of the staggered election of the board of directors, Shareholder 1 (who owns 1,000 shares) would not be able to elect a director to the board without the assistance of another shareholder.

Voting Agreements

Sometimes shareholders agree in advance as to how their shares will be voted. The two major forms of shareholder agreements are discussed in the following paragraphs:

1. *Voting trusts.* A **voting trust** is an arrangement whereby shareholders transfer their stock certificates to a trustee. Legal title to these shares is held in the name of the trustee. In exchange, *voting trust certificates* are issued to the shareholders. The trustee of the voting trust is empowered to vote the shares held by the trust. The trust may either specify how the trustee is to vote the shares or authorize the trustee to vote the shares at his or her discretion. The members of the trust retain all other incidents of ownership of the stock.

   A voting trust agreement must be in writing and cannot exceed 10 years. It must be filed with the corporation and is open to inspection by shareholders of the corporation [RMBCA § 7.30].

2. *Shareholder voting agreements.* Two or more shareholders may enter into an agreement that stipulates how they will vote their shares for the election of directors or other matters that require shareholder vote. **Shareholder voting agreements** are not limited in duration and do not have to be filed with the corporation. They are specifically enforceable [RMBCA § 7.31]. Shareholder voting agreements can be either revocable or irrevocable [RMBCA § 7.22(d)].

Transfer of Shares

Generally, shareholders have the right to transfer their shares. Shareholders may enter into agreements with one another to prevent unwanted persons from becoming owners of the corporation [RMBCA § 6.27]. The following are the two most common forms of agreements:

- *Right of first refusal.* A **right of first refusal** is an **agreement** entered into by shareholders whereby they grant each other the right of first refusal to purchase shares they are going to sell. A selling shareholder must offer his or her shares for sale to the other parties to the agreement before selling them to anyone else. If the shareholders do not exercise their right of first refusal, the selling shareholder is free to sell his or her shares to another party. A right of first refusal may be granted to the corporation as well.

- *Buy-and-sell agreement.* A **buy-and-sell agreement** is one entered into by shareholders that requires selling shareholders to sell their shares to the other shareholders or to the corporation at the price specified in the agreement. The price of the shares is normally determined by a formula that considers, among other factors, the profitability of the corporation. The purchase of shares of a deceased shareholder pursuant to a buy-and-sell agreement is often funded by proceeds from life insurance.

Preemptive Rights

The articles of incorporation can grant shareholders preemptive rights. **Preemptive rights** give existing shareholders the option of subscribing to new shares being issued by the corporation in proportion to their current ownership interests [RMBCA § 6.30]. Such a purchase can prevent a shareholder's interest in the corporation from being *diluted*. Shareholders are given a reasonable period of time (such as 30 days) to exercise their preemptive rights. If a shareholder does not exercise his or her preemptive rights during this time, shares can then be sold to anyone.

Consider This Example Suppose that the ABC Corporation has 10,000 outstanding shares and that Linda Norton owns 1,000 shares (10 percent). Assume that the corporation plans to raise more capital by issuing another 10,000 shares of stock. With preemptive rights, Norton must be offered the option to purchase 1,000 of the 10,000 new shares before they are offered to the public. If she does not purchase them, her ownership in the corporation will be diluted from 10 percent to 5 percent.

Right to Receive Information and Inspect Books and Records

Shareholders have the right to be informed about the affairs of the corporation. A corporation must furnish its shareholders with an **annual financial statement** containing a balance sheet, an income statement, and a statement of changes in shareholder equity [RMBCA § 16.20].

Shareholders have an absolute **right to inspect** the shareholders' list, the articles of incorporation, the bylaws, and the minutes of shareholders' meetings held within the past three years. To inspect accounting and tax records, minutes of board of directors' and committee meetings, and minutes of shareholders' meetings held more than three years in the past, a shareholder must demonstrate a "proper purpose," such as deciding how to vote in a shareholder election, identifying fellow shareholders to communicate with them regarding corporate matters, investigating the existence of corporate mismanagement or improper action, and the like [RMBCA § 16.02].

Dividends

Profit corporations operate to make a profit. The objective of the shareholders is to share in those profits, either through capital appreciation, the receipt of dividends, or both. **Dividends** are paid at the discretion of the board of directors [RMBCA § 6.40]. The directors are responsible for determining when, where, how, and how much will be paid in dividends. They may opt to retain the profits in the corporation to be used for corporate purposes instead of as dividends. This authority cannot be delegated to a committee of the board of directors or to officers of the corporation.

When a corporation declares a dividend, it sets a date, usually a few weeks prior to the actual payment, that is called the **record date**. Persons who are shareholders on that date are entitled to receive the dividend, even if they sell their shares before the payment date, Once declared, a cash or property dividend cannot be revoked. Shareholders can sue to recover declared but unpaid dividends.

Stock Dividends Corporations may use additional shares of stock as a dividend. **Stock dividends** are not a distribution of corporate assets. They are paid in proportion to the existing ownership interests of shareholders, so they do not increase a shareholder's proportionate ownership interest.

Consider This Example Suppose Betty owns 1,000 shares (10 percent) of the 10,000 outstanding shares of the ABC Corporation. If the ABC Corporation declares a stock dividend of 20 percent, Betty will receive a stock dividend of 200 shares. She now owns 1,200 shares—or 10 percent—of a total of 12,000 outstanding shares.

Derivative Lawsuits

If a corporation is harmed by someone, the directors of the corporation have the authority to bring an action on behalf of the corporation against the offending party to recover damages or other relief. If the corporation fails to bring the lawsuit, shareholders have the right to bring the lawsuit on behalf of the corporation. This is called a **derivative action**, or **derivative lawsuit** [RMBCA § 7.40].

A shareholder can bring a derivative action if he or she (1) was a shareholder of the corporation at the time of the act complained of; (2) fairly and adequately represents the interests of the corporation; and (3) made a written demand upon the corporation to take suitable actions and either the corporation rejected the demand or 90 days have expired from the date of the demand.

A derivative lawsuit will be dismissed by the court if either a majority of independent directors or a panel of independent persons appointed by the court determines that the lawsuit is not in the best interests of the corporation. This decision must be reached in good faith and only after conducting a reasonable inquiry.

If a shareholder derivative action is successful, any award goes into the corporate treasury. The plaintiff-shareholder is entitled to recover payment for reasonable expenses, including attorneys' fees, incurred in bringing and maintaining the derivative action. Any settlement of a derivative action requires court approval.

Piercing the Corporate Veil

Shareholders of a corporation generally have **limited liability** (i.e., they are liable for the debts and obligations of the corporation only to the extent of their capital contribution), and they are not personally liable for the debts and obligations of the corporation. However, if a shareholder or shareholders dominate a corporation and misuse it for improper purposes, a court of equity can *disregard the corporate entity* and hold the shareholders of a corporation personally liable for the corporation's debts and obligations. This doctrine is commonly referred to as **piercing the corporate veil**. It is often resorted to by unpaid creditors who are trying to collect from shareholders a debt owed by the corporation. The piercing the corporate veil doctrine is also called the *alter ego doctrine* because the corporation has become the *alter ego* of the shareholder.

Courts will pierce the corporate veil if (1) the corporation has been formed without sufficient capital (i.e., *thin capitalization*) or (2) separateness has not been maintained between the corporation and its shareholders (e.g., commingling of personal and corporate assets, failure to hold required shareholders' meetings, failure to maintain corporate records and books). The courts examine this doctrine on a case-by-case basis.

The piercing the corporate veil doctrine was raised in the following case.

> **Business Brief**
>
> Shareholders are generally not personally liable for debts and obligations of the corporation.

Kinney Shoe Corp. v. Polan
939 F.2d 209 (1991)
United States Court of Appeals, Fourth Circuit

Case 27.1
Piercing the Corporate Veil

Background and Facts

In 1984, Lincoln M. Polan formed Industrial Realty Company (Industrial), a West Virginia corporation. Polan was the sole shareholder of Industrial. Although a certificate of incorporation was issued, no organizational meeting was held, and no officers were elected. Industrial issued no stock certificates because nothing was ever paid in to the corporation. Other corporate formalities were not observed. Polan, on behalf of Industrial, signed a lease to sublease commercial space in a building controlled by Kinney Shoe Corporation (Kinney). The first rental payment to Kinney was made out of Polan's personal funds, and no further payments were made on the lease. Kinney filed suit against Industrial and obtained a judgment of $66,400 for unpaid rent. When the amount was unpaid by Industrial, Kinney

sued Polan individually and sought to pierce the corporate veil to collect from Polan. The district court held for Polan. Kinney appealed.

Issue

Is Polan personally liable for Industrial's debts?

Court's Reasoning

The court of appeals found that Industrial's corporate veil should be pierced because the corporation was undercapitalized, corporate formalities were not observed, and Polan commingled his funds with those of the corporation. The court stated that Polan tried to limit his liability by "setting up a paper curtain constructed of nothing more than Industrial's certificate of incorporation." The court allowed Kinney to pierce the corporate veil to reach the responsible party and produce an equitable result.

Decision and Remedy

The court of appeals pierced the corporate veil and held Polan personally liable on Industrial's debt to Kinney. The court of appeals reversed the district court's judgment.

Case Questions

Critical Legal Thinking   Is the doctrine of piercing the corporate veil needed? Should parties such as Kinney bear the risk of dealing with corporations like Industrial?

Business Ethics   Is it ethical for persons to form corporations to avoid personal liability? Should this be allowed?

Contemporary Business   What is the risk if corporate formalities are not observed? Explain.

Contemporary Environment
Close Corporations

Many of the formal rules in state corporation statutes are designed to govern the management of large, publicly held corporations. These rules may not be relevant for regulating the management of **close corporations**—that is, corporations formed by entrepreneurs with few shareholders who often work for the corporation and manage its day-to-day operations.

The **Model Statutory Close Corporation Supplement (Supplement)** was added to the RMBCA to permit entrepreneurial corporations to choose to be **close corporations**. Only corporations with 50 or fewer shareholders may elect statutory close corporation (SCC) status. To choose this status, two-thirds of the shares of each class of shares of the corporation must approve the election. The articles of incorporation must contain a statement that the corporation is a statutory close corporation, and the share certificates must conspicuously state that the shares have been issued by a statutory close corporation.

A close corporation may dispense with some of the formalities of operating a corporation. For example, if all the shareholders approve, a close corporation may operate without a board of directors, and the articles of incorporation should contain a

statement to that effect. The powers and affairs of the corporation are then managed by the shareholders. A close corporation need not adopt bylaws if the provisions required by law to be contained in bylaws are contained in the articles of incorporation or a shareholders' agreement. The corporation need not hold annual shareholders' meetings unless one or more shareholders demand in writing that such meetings be held. The shareholders may enter into a shareholders' agreement about how the corporation will be managed. In effect, the shareholders can treat the corporation as a partnership for governance purposes [Supp. § 20(b)(3)]. Selecting statutory close corporation status does not affect the limited liability of shareholders [Supp. § 25].

The articles of incorporation of a close corporation may authorize one or more shareholders to dissolve the corporation at will or upon the occurrence of a specified event or contingency. Judicial dissolution may be ordered by a court if there is an unbreakable deadlock in the management of the corporation; if the directors have acted in an illegal, oppressive, or fraudulent manner; or in the case of other such statutory grounds. ■

Board of Directors

Business Brief

The directors of a corporation are responsible for formulating the *policy* decisions affecting the corporation.

The **board of directors** of a corporation is responsible for formulating the *policy decisions* affecting the management, supervision, and control of the operation of the corporation [RMBCA § 8.01]. Such policy decisions include deciding what business or businesses in which the corporation should be engaged, selecting and removing the top officers of the corporation, determining the capital structure of the corporation, declaring dividends, and the like.

The board may initiate certain actions that require shareholders' approval. These actions are initiated when the board of directors adopts a *resolution* that approves a transaction and recommends that it be submitted to the shareholders for a vote. Examples of such transactions include mergers, sale of substantially all of the corporation's assets outside the course of ordinary business operations, amendment of the articles of incorporation, and the voluntary dissolution of the corporation.

Corporate directors are required to have access to the corporation's books and records, facilities, and premises, as well as any other information affecting the operation of the corporation. This right of inspection is absolute. It cannot be limited by the articles of incorporation, the bylaws, or board resolution.

Compensating Directors Originally, it was considered an honor to serve as a director. No payment was involved. Today, directors are often paid an annual retainer and an attendance fee for each meeting attended. Unless otherwise provided in the articles of incorporation, the directors are permitted to fix their own compensation [RMBCA § 8.11].

Contemporary Environment
States Enact Constituency Statutes

Under this classical theory of the corporation, the board of directors owed a fiduciary duty to act in the best interest of the shareholders of the corporation. The rights of other constituents—such as employees, bondholders and creditors, and suppliers and customers—exist by contract, period.

In recent years, more than 30 states have enacted **constituency statutes** that allow directors to consider constituents other than shareholders when making decisions. Constituency statutes recognize the complex nature of the modern corporation and the modern view that shareholders are not the only "owners" of corporations. These statutes acknowledge the rights of a variety of participants, including lenders, employees, managers, suppliers, distributors, customers, and the local communities in which corporations are located.

For example, Minnesota adopted the following statute:

In discharging the duties of the position of director, a director may, in considering the best interests of the corporation, consider the interests of the corporation's employees, customers, suppliers, and creditors, the economy of the state and nation, community and societal considerations, and the long-term as well as short-term interests of the corporation and its shareholders, including the possibility that these interests may be best served by the continued independence of the corporation. [Minn. Stat. § 302A.251(5)]

Most constituency statutes are permissive, not mandatory. That is, directors may take into account nonstockholder interests but are not required to do so. ■

Selecting Directors

Boards of directors are typically composed of inside and outside directors. An **inside director** is a person who is also an officer of the corporation. For example, the president of the corporation often sits as a director of the corporation.

An **outside director** is a person who sits on the board of directors of a corporation but is not an officer of that corporation. Outside directors are often officers and directors of other corporations, bankers, lawyers, professors, and others. Outside directors are often selected for their business knowledge and expertise.

There are no special qualifications that a person must meet to be elected a director of a corporation. A director need not be a resident of the state of incorporation or a shareholder of the corporation. The articles of incorporation or bylaws may prescribe qualifications for directors, however [RMBCA § 8.02].

A board of directors can consist of one or more individuals. The number of initial directors is fixed by the articles of incorporation. This number can be amended in the articles of incorporation or the bylaws. The articles of incorporation or bylaws can establish a variable range for the size of the board of directors. The exact number of directors within the range may be changed from time to time by the board of directors or the shareholders [RMBCA § 8.03].

Term of Office

The term of a director's office expires at the next annual shareholders' meeting following his or her election, unless terms are staggered [RMBCA § 8.05]. The RMBCA allows boards of directors that consist of nine or more members to be divided into two or three classes (each class to be as nearly equal in number as possible) that are elected to serve *staggered terms* of two or three years [RMBCA § 8.06]. The specifics of such an arrangement must be outlined in the articles of incorporation.

Consider This Example   Suppose a board of directors consists of nine directors. The board can be divided into three classes of three directors each, each class to be elected to serve a three-year term. Only three directors of the nine-member board would come up for election each year. This nine-member board could also be divided into two classes of five and four directors, each class to be elected to two-year terms.

Vacancies on a board of directors can occur because of death, illness, the resignation of a director before the expiration of his or her term, or an increase in the number of positions on the board. Such vacancies can be filled by the shareholders or the remaining directors [RMBCA § 8.10].

> The director is really a watch-dog, and the watch-dog has no right, without the knowledge of his master, to take a sop from a possible wolf.
>
> L.J. Bowen
> *Re The North Australian Territory Co. Ltd.* (1891)

Meetings of the Board of Directors

The directors of a corporation can act only as a board. They cannot act individually on the corporation's behalf. Every director has the right to participate in any meeting of the board of directors. Each director has one vote. Directors cannot vote by proxy.

Regular meetings of the board of directors are held at the times and places established in the bylaws. Such meetings can be held without notice. The board can call **special meetings** as provided in the bylaws [RMBCA § 8.20(a)]. They are usually convened for such reasons as issuing new shares, considering proposals to merge with other corporations, adopting maneuvers to defend against hostile takeover attempts, and the like.

The board of directors may act without a meeting if all of the directors sign written consents that set forth the actions taken. The RMBCA permits meetings of the board to be held via conference calls [RMBCA § 8.20(b)].

Quorum and Voting Requirement

A simple majority of the number of directors established in the articles of incorporation or bylaws usually constitutes a **quorum** for transacting business. However, the articles of incorporation and the bylaws may increase this number. If a quorum is present, the approval or disapproval of a majority of the quorum binds the entire board. The articles of incorporation or the bylaws can require a greater than majority of directors to constitute a quorum or the vote of the board [RMBCA § 8.24].

Committees of the Board of Directors

In the current complex business world, the demands on directors have increased. To help handle this increased work load, boards of directors have turned to creating committees of their members to handle specific duties. Board members with special expertise or interests are appointed to the various committees.

Unless the articles of incorporation or bylaws provide otherwise, the board of directors may create committees of the board and delegate certain powers to those committees [RMBCA § 8.25]. All members of these committees must be directors. An act of a committee pursuant to delegated authority is the act of the board of directors.

Committees commonly appointed by the board of directors include:

- *Executive committee.* This committee has authority to (1) act on certain matters on behalf of the board during the interim period between board meetings and (2) conduct preliminary investigations of proposals on behalf of the full board. Most members of the committee are inside directors because it is easier for them to meet to address corporate matters.

- *Audit committee.* This committee recommends independent public accountants and supervises the audit of the financial records of the corporation by the accountants.

- *Nominating committee.* This committee nominates the management slate of directors to be submitted for shareholder vote.

- *Compensation committee.* This committee approves management compensation, including salaries, bonuses, stock option plans, fringe benefits, and such.

- *Investment committee.* This committee is responsible for investing and reinvesting the funds of the corporation.

- *Litigation committee.* This committee reviews and decides whether to pursue requests by shareholders for the corporation to sue persons who have allegedly harmed the corporation.

> The law does not permit the stockholders to create a sterilized board of directors.
>
> Collins, J.
> *Manson v. Curtis (1918)*

The following powers cannot be delegated to committees but must be exercised by the board itself: (1) declaring dividends, (2) initiating actions that require shareholders' approval, (3) appointing members to fill vacancies on the board, (4) amending the bylaws, (5) approving a plan of merger that does not require shareholder approval (short-form merger), and (6) authorizing the issuance of shares.

Business Ethics

The Sarbanes-Oxley Act of 2002 Regulates Accounting Practices

During the late 1990s and early 2000s, many corporations in the United States engaged in fraudulent accounting in order to report inflated earnings or to conceal losses. Many public accounting firms that were hired to audit the financial statements of these companies conspired with the companies to conceal this fraudulent conduct.

In response, Congress enacted the federal **Sarbanes-Oxley Act of 2002**. This act imposes new rules that establish independence between public accounting firms and the public companies they audit, and it creates government oversight over public corporations and the public accountants who audit them. Several major provisions of the act that addresses accounting issues are:

- **Audit committee.** A public company must have an audit committee. Members of the audit committee must be members of the board of directors and must be independent—that is, not employed or receive compensation from the company or any of its subsidiaries for services other than as a board member and member of the audit committee. At least one

member of the audit committee must be a financial expert, based on either education or prior experience, so as to understand generally accepted accounting principles, preparation of financial statements, and audit committee functions.

The audit committee is responsible for the appointment, payment of compensation, and oversight of public accounting firms employed to audit the company. The audit committee must preapprove all audit and permissible nonaudit services to be performed by a public accounting firm. The audit committee has authority to employ independent legal counsel and other advisors.

- **Establishment of the Public Company Accounting Oversight Board.** The act creates the Public Company Accounting Oversight Board. This board consists of five financially literate members who are appointed by the Securities and Exchange Commission (SEC) for five-year terms. Two of the members must be certified public accountants (CPAs), and three must not be CPAs. The SEC has oversight and enforcement authority over the board. The board has the authority to adopt rules concerning auditing, accounting quality control,

Business Ethics

(continued)

independence, and ethics of public companies and public accountants.

- **Public accounting firms must register with the board.** In order to audit a public company, a public accounting firm must register with the board. Registered accounting firms that audit more than 100 public companies annually are subject to inspection and review by the board once a year; all other public accounting firms must be audited by the board every three years. The board may discipline public accountants and accounting firms and order sanctions for intentional or reckless conduct, including suspending or revoking registration with the board, placing temporary limitations on activities, and assessing civil money penalties.

- **Separation of audit and nonaudit services.** The act makes it unlawful for a registered public accounting firm to simultaneously provide audit and certain nonaudit services to a public company. If a public accounting firm audits a public company, the accounting firm may not provide the following nonaudit services to the client: (1) bookkeeping services; (2) financial information systems; (3) appraisal or valuation services; (4) internal audit services; (5) management functions; (6) human resources services; (7) broker, dealer, or investment services; (8) investment banking services; (9) legal services; (10) or any other services the board determines. A certified public accounting firm may provide tax services to audit clients if such tax services are preapproved by the audit committee of the client.

- **Audit reports sign-offs.** Each audit by a certified public accounting firm is assigned an audit partner of the firm to supervise the audit and approve the audit report. The act requires that a second partner of the accounting firm review and approve audit reports prepared by the firm. All audit papers must be retained for at least seven years. The lead audit partner and reviewing partner must rotate off an audit every five years.

- **Prohibited employment.** Any person who is employed by a public accounting firm that audits a client cannot be employed by that client as the chief executive officer (CEO), chief financial officer (CFO), controller, chief accounting officer, or equivalent position for a period of one year following the audit.

- **Internal control procedures of public companies.** The act requires public companies to establish and maintain adequate internal controls and procedures for financial reporting. The act required public companies to prepare an assessment of the effectiveness of its internal quality controls at the end of each fiscal year.

- **Off-balance-sheet items.** Annual and quarterly reports of public companies must disclose material off-balance-sheet transactions and relationships with other entities that may have a material effect on the financial condition of the public company.

The goals of these rules are to improve financial reporting, eliminate conflicts of interest, and provide government oversight of accounting and audit services.

1. Do you think that public accounting firms sometimes become too close to their clients to be nonbiased? Explain.
2. Will the Sarbanes-Oxley Act's accounting rules lead to increased investor confidence in public companies' financial statements? Explain. ▪

Corporate Officers

The board of directors has the authority to appoint the **officers** of the corporation. The officers are elected by the board of directors at such time and by such manner as prescribed in the corporation's bylaws. The directors can delegate certain management authority to the officers of the corporation.

At minimum, most corporations have the following officers: (1) a president, (2) one or more vice presidents, (3) a secretary, and (4) a treasurer. The bylaws or the board of directors can authorize duly appointed officers the power to appoint assistant officers. The same individual may simultaneously hold more than one office in the corporation [RMBCA § 8.40]. The duties of each officer are specified in the bylaws of the corporation.

An officer of a corporation may be removed by the board of directors. The board only has to determine that the best interests of the corporation will be served by such removal [RMBCA § 8.43(b)]. Officers who are removed in violation of an employment contract can sue the corporation for damages.

Business Brief

Although theoretically shareholders own the corporation and directors make the policy decisions, officers are often more powerful than the shareholders and the directors. Officers are often criticized for operating corporations for their own self-interest.

Agency Authority of Officers

Officers and agents of a corporation have such authority as may be provided in the bylaws of the corporation or as determined by resolution of the board of directors [RMBCA § 8.41]. As agents, the authority of officers to bind a corporation to contracts is derived from express authority, implied authority, and apparent authority.

A corporation can *ratify* an unauthorized act of a corporate officer or agent. For example, suppose an officer acts outside the scope of his or her employment and enters into a contract with a third person. If the corporation accepts the benefits of the contract, it has ratified the contract and is bound by it. Officers are liable on an unauthorized contract if the corporation does not ratify it.

Concept Summary *Management of a Corporation*

Management Group	Function
Shareholders	Owners of the corporation. They vote on the directors and other major actions to be taken by the corporation.
Board of directors	Responsible for making policy decisions and employing the major officers for the corporation. They also make recommendations regarding actions to be taken by the shareholders.
Officers	Responsible for the day-to-day operation of the corporation. Includes acting as agents for the corporation, hiring other officers and employees, and the like.

Online Commerce & Internet Law

Delaware Amends Corporation Code to Recognize Electronic Communications

The state of Delaware leads the nation as the preferred site for incorporation of the largest corporations in the United States. This is the result of the Delaware corporations code itself, as well as the expertise of the Delaware courts in resolving corporate disputes. In order to keep this leadership position, in 2000 the state legislature amended the Delaware General Corporation law to recognize evolving electronic technology. The major changes to the law are:

■ Delivery of notices to stockholders may be made electronically if the stockholder consents to the delivery of notice in this form.
■ Proxy solicitation for shareholder votes may be made by electronic transmission.
■ The shareholder list of a corporation that must be made available during the 10 days prior to a stockholder meeting may be made available either at the principal place of business of the corporation or by posting the list on an electronic network.
■ Stockholders who are not physically present at a meeting may be deemed present, participate in, and vote at the meeting by electronic communication; a meeting may be held solely by electronic communication, without a physical location.
■ The election of directors of the corporation may be held by electronic transmission.
■ Directors' actions by unanimous consent may be taken by electronic transmission.

The use of electronic transmissions, electronic networks, and communications by e-mail will make the operation and administration of corporate affairs more efficient in Delaware. Other states are amending their corporations codes to recognize the importance of electronic communications. ■

Liability of Corporate Directors and Officers

A corporation's directors and officers owe the **fiduciary duties** of trust and confidence to the corporation and its shareholders. More specifically, they owe the (1) *duty of obedience*, (2) *duty of care*, and (3) *duty of loyalty*. Each of these is discussed in detail in the paragraphs that follow.

Duty of Obedience

The directors and officers of a corporation must act within the authority conferred upon them by the state corporation statute, the articles of incorporation, the corporate bylaws, and the resolutions adopted by the board of directors. This duty is called the **duty of obedience**. Directors and officers who either intentionally or negligently act outside their authority are personally liable for any resultant damages caused to the corporation or its shareholders.

Consider This Example Suppose its articles of incorporation authorize a corporation to invest in real estate only. If a corporate officer invests corporate funds in the commodities markets, the officer is liable to the corporation for any losses suffered.

Duty of Care

The **duty of care** requires corporate directors and officers to use *care and diligence* when acting on behalf of a corporation. To meet this duty, the directors and officers must discharge their duties (1) in good faith, (2) with the care that an *ordinary prudent person* in a like position would use under similar circumstances, and (3) in a manner he or she reasonably believes to be in the best interests of the corporation [RMBCA §§ 8.30(a) and 8.42(a)].

A director or an officer who breaches this duty of care is personally liable to the corporation and its shareholders for any damages caused by the breach. Such breaches, which are normally caused by **negligence**, often involve a director's or an officer's failure to (1) make a reasonable investigation of a corporate matter, (2) attend board meetings on a regular basis, (3) properly supervise a subordinate who causes a loss to the corporation through embezzlement and such, or (4) keep adequately informed about corporate affairs. **Breaches** are examined by the courts on a case-by-case basis.

The Business Judgment Rule The determination of whether a corporate director or officer has met his or her duty of care is measured as of the time the decision is made—the benefit of hindsight is not a factor. Therefore, the directors and officers are not liable to the corporation or its shareholders for honest mistakes of judgment. This is called the **business judgment rule**. Were it not for the protection afforded by the business judgment rule, many high-risk but socially desirable endeavors might not be undertaken.

Consider This Example Suppose that after conducting considerable research and investigation, the directors of a major automobile company decide to produce a large and expensive automobile. When the car is introduced to the public for sale, few of the automobiles are sold because of the public's interest in buying smaller, less expensive automobiles. Because this was an honest mistake of judgment on the part of corporate management, their judgment is shielded by the business judgment rule.

The court had to decide whether directors were protected by the business judgment rule in the following case.

Smith v. Van Gorkom
488 A.2d 858, 1985 Del. Lexis 421 (1985)
Supreme Court of Delaware

Case 27.2
Business Judgment Rule

Background and Facts

Trans Union Corporation (Trans Union) was a publicly traded, diversified holding company that was incorporated in Delaware. Its principal earnings were generated by its railcar leasing business. Jerome W. Van Gorkom was a Trans Union officer for more than 24 years, its chief executive officer for more than 17 years, and the chairman of the board of directors for 2 years. Van Gorkom, a lawyer and certified public accountant, owned 75,000 shares of Trans Union. He was approaching 65 years of age and mandatory retirement. Trans Union's board of directors was composed of 10 members—5 inside directors and 5 outside directors.

In September 1980, Van Gorkom decided to meet with Jay A. Pritzker, a well-known corporate takeover specialist and a social acquaintance of Van Gorkom's, to discuss the possible sale of Trans Union to Pritzker. Van Gorkom met Pritzker at Pritzker's home on Saturday, September 13, 1980. He did so without consulting Trans Union's board of directors. At this meeting, Van Gorkom proposed a sale of Trans Union to Pritzker at a price of $55 per share. The stock was trading at about $38 in the market. On Monday, September 15, Pritzker notified Van Gorkom that he was interested in the $55 cash-out merger proposal. Van Gorkom, along with two inside directors, privately met with Pritzker on September 16 and 17. After meeting with Van Gorkom on Thursday, September 18, Pritzker notified his attorney to begin drafting the merger documents.

On Friday, September 19, Van Gorkom called a special meeting of Trans Union's board of directors for the following day. The board members were not told the purpose of the meeting. At the meeting, Van Gorkom disclosed the Pritzker offer and described its terms in a 20-minute presentation. Neither the merger agreement nor a written summary of the terms of agreement was furnished to the directors. No valuation study as to the value of Trans Union was prepared for the meeting. After two hours, the board voted in favor of the cash-out merger with Pritzker's company at $55 per share for Trans Union's stock. The board also voted not to solicit other offers. The merger agreement was executed by Van Gorkom during the evening of September 20 at a formal social event he hosted for the opening of the Chicago Lyric Opera's season. Neither he nor any other director read the agreement prior to its signing and delivery to Pritzker.

Trans Union's board of directors recommended the merger be approved by its shareholders and distributed proxy materials to the shareholders stating that the $55 per share price for their stock was fair. In the meantime, Trans Union's board of directors took steps to dissuade two other possible suitors who showed an interest in purchasing Trans Union. On February 10, 1981, 69.9 percent of the shares of Trans Union stock was voted in favor of the merger. The merger was consummated. Alden Smith and other Trans Union

shareholders sued Van Gorkom and the other directors for damages. The plaintiffs alleged that the defendants were negligent in their conduct in selling Trans Union to Pritzker. The Delaware court of chancery held in favor of the defendants. The plaintiffs appealed.

Issue

Did Trans Union's directors breach their duty of care?

Court's Reasoning

The supreme court explained that the business judgment rule exists to protect and promote the full and free exercise of the managerial power granted to Delaware directors. The rule itself is a presumption that in making a business decision, the directors of a corporation acted (1) on an informed basis, (2) in good faith, and (3) in the honest belief that the action taken was in the best interests of the company. Thus, the party attacking a board decision as uninformed must rebut the presumption that its business judgment was an informed one. Under the business judgment rule, there is no protection for directors who have made an unintelligent or unadvised judgment.

The supreme court held that the business judgment rule did not protect the directors' actions in this case. The court stated, "The directors (1) did not adequately inform themselves as to Van Gorkom's role in forcing the sale of the company and in establishing the per share purchase price; (2) they were uninformed as to the intrinsic value of the company; and (3) given these circumstances, at a minimum, they were grossly negligent in approving the sale of the company upon two hours' consideration, without prior notice, and without the exigency of a crisis or emergency."

Decision and Remedy

The supreme court of Delaware held that the defendant directors had breached their duty of care. The supreme court reversed the judgment of the court of chancery and remanded the case to the court of chancery to conduct an evidentiary hearing to determine the fair value of the shares represented by the plaintiffs' class. If that value was higher than $55 per share, the difference was to be awarded to the plaintiffs as damages.

Case Questions

Critical Legal Thinking   What does the business judgment rule provide? Is this a good rule? Explain.

Business Ethics   Do you think Van Gorkom and the other directors had the shareholders' best interests in mind? Were the plaintiff-shareholders being greedy?

Contemporary Business   Is there any liability exposure for sitting on a board of directors?

Reliance on Others Corporate directors and officers usually are unable to personally investigate every corporate matter brought to their attention. Under the RMBCA, directors and officers are entitled to rely on information, opinions, reports, or statements, including financial statements and other financial data, prepared or presented by [RMBCA §§ 8.30(b) and 8.42(b)]:

- Officers and employees of the corporation whom the director believes are reliable and competent in the matter presented.

- Lawyers, public accountants, and other professionals as to any matters that the director believes to be within their professional or expert competence.

- A committee of the board of directors upon which the director does not serve as to matters within the committee's designated authority and which committee the director reasonably believes to merit confidence.

A director is not liable if such information is false, misleading, or otherwise unreliable unless he or she has knowledge that would cause such reliance to be unwarranted [RMBCA §§ 8.30(c) and 8.42(c)]. The degree of an officer's reliance on such sources is more limited than that given to directors because they are more familiar with corporate operations.

Dissent to Directors' Action On some occasions, individual directors may oppose the action taken by the majority of the board of directors. To avoid liability for such action, the dissenting director must either resign from the board or register his or her **dissent**. Dissent may be registered by (1) entering it in the minutes of the meeting, (2) filing a written dissent with the secretary before the adjournment of the meeting, or (3) forwarding a written dissent by registered mail to the secretary immediately following the adjournment of the meeting [RMBCA § 8.24(d)]. A dissenting director who has not attended the meeting must follow the latter course of action to register his or her dissent.

Indemnification and D&O Insurance Protection

Directors and officers of corporations are sometimes personally named in lawsuits that involve actions they have taken on behalf of the corporation. Such lawsuits are often brought by disgruntled shareholders or third parties who claim they have suffered damages because of the director's or officer's negligence or other conduct.

Directors and officers can protect themselves against personal liability by making sure the corporation does the following:

- Purchase **directors' and officers' liability insurance (D&O insurance)**. Corporations can purchase D&O insurance from private insurance companies by paying an annual premium for the insurance. The insurance company is required to defend a corporate director or officer who has been sued in his or her corporate capacity. The insurance company is also required, subject to the terms of the insurance coverage, to pay the litigation costs incurred in defending the lawsuit (e.g., attorneys' fees, court costs) and any judgments or settlement costs. Most D&O policies contain deductible clauses and maximum coverage limits [RMBCA § 8.57].

- Provide **indemnification**. Corporations may provide that directors and officers who are sued in their corporate capacities will be **indemnified** by the corporation for the costs of the litigation as well as any judgments or settlements stemming from the lawsuit. Indemnification means that the corporation—and not the director or officer personally—pays these costs. The RMBCA provides that a court may order indemnification if a director or an officer is found to be fairly and reasonably entitled to such indemnification [RMBCA § 8.54 and 8.56(1)].

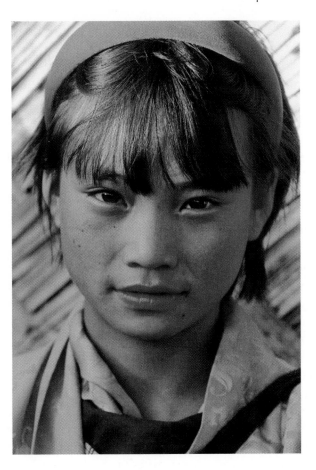

Bhutan. The opportunities for U.S.-based multinational companies will increase as other countries of the world open up their markets to free trade.

Duty of Loyalty

The **duty of loyalty** requires directors and officers to subordinate their personal interests to those of the corporation and its shareholders. Justice Benjamin Cardozo defined this duty of loyalty as follows:

> [A corporate director or officer] owes loyalty and allegiance to the corporation— a loyalty that is undivided and an allegiance that is influenced by no consideration other than the welfare of the corporation. Any adverse interest of a director [or officer] will be subjected to a scrutiny rigid and uncompromising. He may not profit at the expense of his corporation and in conflict with its rights; he may not for personal gain divert unto himself the opportunities that in equity and fairness belong to the corporation.
>
> Many forms of conduct permissible in a workaday world for those acting at arm's length are forbidden to those bound by fiduciary ties. Not honesty alone, but the punctilio of an honor the most sensitive, is then the standard of behavior. As to this there has developed a tradition that is unbending and inveterate.[1]

If a director or an officer breaches his or her duty of loyalty and makes a secret profit on a transaction, the corporation can sue the director or officer to recover the secret profit. Some of the most common breaches of the duty of loyalty are:

Business Brief

Breach of the *duty of care* usually occurs because of accident or mistake. Breach of the *duty of loyalty* usually occurs because of intentional conduct.

- ■ *Usurping a corporate opportunity.* Directors and officers may not personally usurp (steal) a corporate opportunity for themselves. **Usurping a corporate opportunity** constitutes a violation of a director's or an officer's duty of loyalty. If usurping is proven, the corporation can (1) acquire the opportunity from the director or officer and (2) recover any profits made by the director or officer.

The following elements must be shown to prove usurping:

1. The opportunity was presented to the director or officer in his or her corporate capacity.
2. The opportunity is related to or connected with the corporation's current or proposed business.
3. The corporation has the financial ability to take advantage of the opportunity.
4. The corporate officer or director took the corporate opportunity for him- or herself.

However, the director or officer is personally free to take advantage of a corporate opportunity if it was fully disclosed and presented to the corporation and the corporation rejected it.

- **Self-dealing.** Under the RMBCA, a contract or transaction with a corporate director or officer is voidable by the corporation if it is unfair to the corporation [RMBCA § 8.31]. Contracts of a corporation to purchase property from, sell property to, or make loans to corporate directors or officers where the directors or officers have not disclosed their interest in the transaction are often voided under this standard. Contracts or transactions with corporate directors or officers are enforceable if their interest in the transaction has been disclosed to the corporation and the disinterested directors or the shareholders have approved the transaction.

- **Competing with the corporation.** Directors and officers cannot engage in activities that *compete* with the corporation unless full disclosure is made and a majority of the disinterested directors or shareholders approve the activity. The corporation can recover any profits made by nonapproved competition and any other damages caused to the corporation.

Business Brief

Directors and officers may not compete with their corporation unless the competitive activity has been fully disclosed and approved.

Disgorgement of Secret Profits If a director or an officer breaches his or her duty of loyalty and makes a secret profit on a transaction, the corporation can sue the director or officer to recover the secret profit. For example, suppose Maxine Chambers is the purchasing agent for the Roebolt Corporation. Her duties require her to negotiate and execute contracts to purchase office supplies and equipment for the corporation. Assume that Bruce Nevel, a computer salesperson, pays Chambers a $10,000 kickback to purchase computers needed by the Roebolt Corporation. The Roebolt Corporation can sue and recover the $10,000 secret profit from Chambers.

In the following case, the court held that a corporate officer had usurped a corporate opportunity.

Hill V. Southeastern Floor Covering Co., Inc.
596 So.2d 874, 1992 Miss. Lexis 124 (1992)
Supreme Court of Mississippi

Case 27.3
Usurping a Corporate Opportunity

Background and Facts

Danny Hill was an officer and the general manager of Southeastern Floor Covering Company, Inc. (Southeastern). Southeastern did jobs in floor covering and ceilings for general contractors. Southeastern did much of its own work, and it subcontracted out the work it could

not do. Southeastern often subcontracted asbestos removal work to Southern Interiors (Interiors). In 1983, Southeastern bid on a job with Chata Construction Company for various work, including asbestos removal work. Hill secretly made a deal with the owner of Interiors to bid on the asbestos work on the Chata project without telling Southwestern. Interiors bid for the work, and Chata awarded the asbestos work to Interiors. Hill made $90,000 secret profits on the transaction. When Southeastern discovered this fact, it sued Hill to recover his secret profits. The trial court held that Hill had breached his duty of loyalty to Southeastern by usurping a corporate opportunity, and it awarded Southeastern $90,000. Hill appealed.

Issue

Did Hill violate his duty of loyalty to his corporate employer?

Court's Reasoning

The Supreme Court stated that the doctrine of corporate opportunity prohibits directors and officers from appropriating for themselves business opportunities that in fairness should belong to

the corporation. The supreme court held that Hill diverted an opportunity that could have been Southeastern's and thereby violated his duty of loyalty.

Case Questions

Critical Legal Thinking   When can a corporate director or officer take an opportunity for himself or herself? Explain.

Business Ethics   Did Hill act ethically in this case? Do you think he usurped a corporate opportunity?

Contemporary Business   Do you think the award in this case is sufficient to deter breaches of loyalty by corporate directors and officers?

Concept Summary   *Fiduciary Duties of Corporation Directors and Officers*

Duty	Description	Violation
Duty of obedience	Duty to act within the authority conferred by law and the corporation.	Acts outside the corporate officer's or director's authority.
Duty of care	Duty to use care and diligence when acting on behalf of the corporation. This duty is discharged if an officer or a director acts: 1. In good faith. 2. With the care that an ordinary prudent person in a like position would use under similar circumstances. 3. In a manner he or she reasonably believes to be in the best interests of the corporation.	Acts of negligence and mismanagement. Such acts include failure to: 1. Make a reasonable investigation of a corporate matter. 2. Attend board meetings on a regular basis. 3. Properly supervise a subordinate who causes a loss to the corporation. 4. Keep adequately informed about corporate matters. 5. Take other actions necessary to discharge duties.
Duty of loyalty	Duty to subordinate personal interests to those of the corporation and its shareholders.	Acts of disloyalty. Such acts include unauthorized: 1. Self-dealing with the corporation. 2. Usurping of a corporate opportunity. 3. Competition with the corporation. 4. Making a secret profit that belongs to the corporation.

Liability for Crimes

Corporate directors, officers, employees, and agents are personally liable for the crimes they commit while acting on behalf of the corporation. Criminal law sanctions include fines and imprisonment.

Under the law of agency, a corporation is liable for the crimes committed by its directors, officers, employees, or agents while acting within the scope of their employment. Because a corporation cannot be placed in prison, the criminal penalty imposed on a corporation is usually the assessment of a monetary fine or the loss of some legal privilege (such as a license).

Business Ethics

The Sarbanes-Oxley Act of 2002 Improves Corporate Governance

During the late 1990s and early 2000s, the U.S. economy was wracked by a number of business and accounting scandals. Companies such as Enron, Tyco, and Worldcom engaged in fraudulent conduct, leading to the conviction of many corporate officers of financial crimes. Many of these companies went bankrupt, causing huge losses to their shareholders, employees, and creditors. Boards of directors were complacent, not keeping a watchful eye over the conduct of their officers and employees.

In response, Congress enacted the federal **Sarbanes-Oxley Act of 2002**. This act establishes far-reaching new rules regarding corporate governance. The goals of the Sarbanes-Oxley Act are to improve corporate governance rules, eliminate conflicts of interest, and instill confidence in investors and the public that management will run public companies in the best interests of all constituents.

Several Major provisions of the Act are:

■ *CEO and CFO certification.* The CEO and CFO of a public company must file a statement accompanying each annual and quarterly report, certifying that the signing officer has reviewed the report, based on the officer's knowledge that the report does not contain any untrue statement of a material fact or omit to state a material fact that would make the statement misleading and that the financial statement and disclosures fairly present, in all material aspects, the operation and financial condition of the company. A knowing and willful violation is punishable for up to 20 years in prison and a fine of not more than $5 million.

■ *Reimbursement of bonuses and incentive pay.* If a public company is required to restate its financial statements because of material noncompliance with financial reporting requirements, the CEO and CFO must reimburse the company for any bonuses, incentive pay, or securities trading profits made because of the noncompliance.

■ *Prohibition on personal loans.* The act prohibits public companies from making personal loans to its directors or executive officers.

■ *Tampering with evidence.* The act makes it a crime for any person to knowingly alter, destroy, mutilate, conceal, or create any document to impair, impede, influence, or obstruct any federal investigation. A violation is punishable for up to 20 years in prison and a monetary fine.

■ *Bar from acting as an officer or a director.* The Securities and Exchange Commission (SEC), a federal government agency, may issue an order prohibiting any person who has committed securities fraud from acting as an officer or a director of a public company.

Although the Sarbanes-Oxley Act applies only to public companies, private companies and nonprofit organizations are also influenced by the act's accounting and corporate governance rules.

1. Will the CEO and CFO certification requirement reduce corporate fraudulent conduct? Explain.
2. Will the Sarbanes-Oxley Act encourage ethical behavior by corporate officers and directors? ■

Chapter Summary

Shareholders, p. 588

Rights of Shareholders

Ownership rights. Shareholders of a corporation own the corporation.

Shareholder's Meetings

1. *Annual shareholders' meeting.* This meeting of the shareholders of a corporation must be held annually by the corporation to elect directors and vote on other matters.
2. *Special shareholders' meeting.* This meetings of shareholders may be called to consider and vote on important or emergency matters, such as a proposed merger or amending the articles of incorporation.

3. *Notice of shareholders' meetings.* The corporation must notify shareholders of the place, day, and time of annual and special shareholder meetings. If the required notice is not given or is defective, any action taken at the meeting is void.

Proxies

1. *Proxy.* Shareholders may appoint another person (the *proxy*) as their agent to vote their shares at shareholders' meetings.

2. *Proxy card.* A proxy card is a written document that a shareholder signs that authorizes another person to vote his or her shares at a shareholders' meeting.

Voting Requirements

1. *Record date.* The record date is a date specified in the corporate bylaws that determines whether a shareholder may vote at a shareholders' meeting. Only persons who are shareholders on the record date are permitted to vote at the meeting.

2. *Shareholders' list.* This list contains the names and addresses of the shareholders as of the record date and the class and number of shares owned by each shareholder. This list must be made available to all shareholders.

3. *Quorum.* A quorum is the required number of shares that must be represented in person or by proxy to hold a shareholders' meeting. The RMBCA establishes a majority of outstanding shares as a quorum.

4. *Vote required for elections other than for directors.* The affirmative vote of the *majority* of the voting shares represented at a shareholders' meeting constitutes an act of the shareholders for actions other than for the elections of directors.

5. *Voting methods for electing directors:*
   a. *Straight (noncumulative) voting.* Unless otherwise stated, each shareholder votes the number of shares he or she owns on candidates for each of the positions open for election. The candidate or candidates with the most votes win the open position or positions.
   b. *Cumulative voting.* The articles of incorporation may provide for cumulative voting. Under this method, a shareholder is entitled to multiply the number of shares he or she owns by the number of directors to be elected and cast the product for a single candidate or distribute the product among two or more candidates.

6. *Supramajority voting requirement.* The articles of incorporation or bylaws can require a greater than majority of shares to constitute quorum or the vote of the shareholders (e.g., 80 percent). Also called *supermajority voting requirement.*

Voting Agreements

1. *Voting trust.* In this arrangement, participating shareholders transfer their shares to a trustee who is then empowered to vote the shares held by the trust. Shareholders are issued *voting trust certificates* that evidence their interest in the trust.

2. *Voting agreements.* This agreement is between two or more shareholders, agreeing on how they will vote their shares. Voting agreements are enforceable.

Right to Transfer Shares

Shareholders have the right to transfer their shares. Shareholders can enter into the following agreements to restrict the transfer of shares:

1. *Right of first refusal.* This agreement requires the selling shareholder to offer his or her shares for sale to the other parties to the agreement before selling them to anyone else.

2. *Buy-and-sell agreement.* This agreement requires selling shareholders to sell their shares to the other shareholders or to the corporation at the price specified in the agreement.

Preemptive Rights

These rights give existing shareholders the option of subscribing to new shares being issued by the corporation in proportion to their current ownership interest.

Right to Receive Information and Inspect Books and Records

1. ***Annual financial statement.*** A corporation must furnish its shareholders with an annual *financial statement* containing a balance sheet, an income statement, and a statement of changes in shareholder equity.

2. ***Inspection rights.*** Shareholders have the *absolute right to* inspect the shareholders' list, the articles of incorporation, the bylaws, and the minutes of shareholders' meetings held within the past three years. They have the right to inspect accounting and tax records, minutes of board of directors' and committee meetings, and minutes of shareholders' meetings held more than three years in the past if they demonstrate a *proper purpose*.

Directors' Authority to Pay Dividends

1. ***Directors' authority to pay dividends.*** The board of directors has the *discretion* to pay *dividends* to shareholders.

2. ***Record date.*** When a corporation declares a dividend, it sets a date, usually a few weeks prior to the actual payment, that establishes the *record date* for payment of the dividend. Shareholders as of that date will be paid the dividend.

3. ***Stock dividends.*** Additional shares of stock may be issued to the shareholders as a dividend. They are paid in proportion to the existing ownership interests of shareholders so they do not increase a shareholder's proportionate ownership interest.

Derivative Lawsuits

A shareholder may bring a derivative lawsuit on behalf of the corporation against an offending party who has injured the corporation when the directors of the corporation fail to bring the suit. The shareholder must make a written *demand* upon the corporation to bring the lawsuit, and the corporation either rejects it or 90 days expire without the corporation bringing the requested lawsuit.

Liability of Shareholders

Limited liability. Shareholders of corporations generally have *limited liability*; that is, they are liable for the debts and obligations of the corporation only to the *extent of their capital contribution* to the corporation.

Piercing the Corporate Veil

Courts can *disregard the corporate entity* and hold shareholders personally liable for the debts and obligations of the corporation if (a) the corporation has been formed without sufficient capital (*thin capitalization*) or (b) separateness has not been maintained between the corporation and its shareholders (e.g., commingling of personal and corporate assets, failure to hold required shareholders' meetings). Also called the *alter ego doctrine*.

Close Corporations

1. ***Election.*** A corporation with 50 or fewer shareholders may elect to be a *statutory close corporation*.

2. ***Dispensing with corporate formalities.*** A close corporation may dispense with some of the formalities of operating as a corporation. In effect, the shareholders can treat the corporation as a *partnership* for governance purposes.

3. ***Limited liability.*** Selecting close corporation statue does not affect the limited liability of shareholders.

Board of Directors, p. 594

Rights of Directors

1. ***Board of directors.*** The board is a panel of decision makers for the corporation, the members of which are elected by the shareholders.

2. ***Policy decisions.*** The directors of a corporation are responsible for formulating the *policy* decisions affecting the corporation, such as deciding what business to engage in, determining the capital structure of the corporation, and selecting and removing top officers of the corporation.

3. **Resolutions.** The board of directors can adopt a resolution that approves a transaction that requires shareholder vote and recommend it to shareholders.

4. **Right of Inspection.** Corporate directors have an *absolute right* to have access to the corporation's books, records, facilities, premises, and any other information affecting the operation of the corporation.

Compensation of Directors

Directors are usually paid an annual retainer and an attendance fee for each meeting attended.

Selecting Directors

1. **Inside director.** Inside director is an member of the board of directors who is also an officer of the corporation.

2. **Outside director.** An outside director is a member of the board of directors who is not an officer of the corporation.

3. **Qualifications.** There are no qualifications to serve as a director unless the articles of incorporation or bylaws prescribe qualifications.

4. **Number of directors.** A board of directors can consist of one or more individuals. The articles of incorporation fix the number of initial directors. This number can be amended by the articles of incorporation or bylaws.

5. **Variable range.** The articles of incorporation or bylaws can establish a *variable range* for the size of the board of directors. The exact number of directors within the range may be changed from time to time by the board or directors or the shareholders.

Term of Office

1. **Annual term.** The term of a director's office expires at the next annual shareholders' meeting following his or her election unless terms are staggered.

2. **Staggered terms.** If a board of directors consists of nine or more members, it may be divided into two or three *classes* (each class to be as nearly equal in number as possible), and classes can be elected to serve *staggered terms* of two or three years.

3. **Vacancies.** Vacancies on a board of directors can be filled by the shareholders or the remaining directors.

Meeting of the Board of Directors

1. **Regular meeting.** A regular meeting of the board of directors is held at the time and place scheduled in the bylaws.

2. **Special meeting.** A special meeting of the board of directors may be convened to discuss an important or emergency matter such as a proposed merger or a hostile takeover attempt.

3. **Written consents.** The board of directors may act without a meeting if all the directors sign written consents that set forth the action taken.

4. **Conference call.** The board of directors may meet via conference call if all the directors can hear and participate in the call.

5. **Quorum.** A simple *majority* of the number of directors established in the articles of incorporation or bylaws constitutes a quorum for transacting business.

6. **Vote.** The approval or disapproval of a *majority* of the quorum binds the entire board.

7. **Supramajority vote.** The articles of incorporation or bylaws may require a greater then majority of directors to constitute quorum or the vote of the board.

Committees of the Board of Directors

Unless the articles of incorporation or bylaws provide otherwise, the board of directors may create committees of its members and delegate certain powers to those committees. The most common committees are:

1. **Executive committee.** This committee has authority to (1) act on certain matters during the interim period between board meetings and (2) conduct preliminary investigations of proposals on behalf of the board.

2. *Audit committee.* This committee recommends independent public accountants and supervises the audit of the financial records of the corporation by the accountants.

3. *Nominating committee.* This committee nominates the management slate of directors to be submitted for shareholder vote.

4. *Compensation committee.* This committee approves management compensation, including salaries, bonuses, stock option plans, fringe benefits and such.

5. *Investment committee.* This committee is responsible for investing and reinvesting the funds of the corporation.

6. *Litigation committee.* This committee reviews and decides whether to pursue requests by shareholders for the corporation to sue persons who have allegedly harmed the corporation.

Corporate Officers, p. 598

Rights of Officers

Officers. Officers are employees of the corporation who are appointed by the board of directors to manage the *day-to-day operations* of the corporation.

Removal of Officers

Unless an employment contract provides otherwise, any officer of a corporation may be removed by the board of directors.

Agency Authority of Officers

Officers and agents of the corporation have express, implied, and apparent authority to bind the corporation to contracts with third parties.

Liability of Corporate Directors and Officers, p. 600

Liability of Corporate Directors and Officers

Fiduciary duties. Corporate directors and officers owe the fiduciary duties of trust and confidence to the corporation and its shareholders. They owe the duties of *obedience, care*, and *loyalty*.

Duty of Obedience

Directors and officers of a corporation have a duty to act within the authority conferred upon them by the state corporation statute, the articles of incorporation, the corporate bylaws, and the resolutions adopted by the board of directors.

Duty of Care

Corporate directors and officers have a duty to use care and diligence when acting on behalf of the corporation. This duty is discharged if they perform their duties (a) in good faith, (b) with the care that an *ordinary prudent person* in a like position would use under similar circumstances, and (c) in a manner he or she reasonably believes to be in the best interests of the corporation.

1. *Negligence.* Negligence is the failure of a corporate director or officer to exercise this duty of care when conducting the corporation's business.

2. *Business judgment rule.* This rule says that directors and officers are not liable to the corporation or its shareholders for honest mistakes of judgment.

3. *Reliance on others.* Directors and officers may rely on information and reports prepared by competent and reliable officers and employees, lawyers, public accountants, and other professionals as well as on committees of the board of directors as long as such reliance is warranted.

4. *Dissent to directors' action.* When an individual director opposes the action taken by the majority of the board of directors, he or she should register his or her dissent by (a) entering it in the minutes of the meeting, (b) filing a written dissent with the secretary before the adjournment

of the meeting, or (c) forwarding a written dissent by registered mail to the secretary immediately following the adjournment of the meeting if the director has not attended the meeting.

Indemnification

The corporation must indemnify (*pay back*) any director or officer for litigation expenses incurred in a lawsuit won by the director or officer. The corporation may indemnify a director or officer who loses a lawsuit as long as the director or officer was not adjudged liable to the corporation or did not improperly obtain personal benefit for himself or herself in the challenged transaction. Directors and officers may not be paid insurance or indemnification for intentional conduct that harmed third parties.

Insurance

Corporations can purchase *directors' and officers' liability insurance (D&O insurance)* that pays the cost to defend litigation against directors and officers and pays any judgment or settlement of the lawsuit.

Duty of Loyalty

Directors and officers have a duty not to act adversely to the interests of the corporation and to subordinate their personal interests to those of the corporation and its shareholders.

Common examples of breaches of the duty of loyalty:

1. *Usurping a corporate opportunity.* A director or an officer may not personally *usurp* (*steal*) an opportunity that belongs to the corporation. The corporation can acquire the opportunity from the director or officer and recover any profits made by the director or officer.

2. *Self-dealing.* The corporation may void any transaction with a director or an officer if it is *unfair to the corporation.* Such transactions usually involve undisclosed self-dealing by a director or officer with the corporation.

3. *Competing with the corporation.* Directors and officers may not compete with their corporation unless the competitive activity has been fully disclosed to the corporation and approved by a majority of disinterested directors or shareholders.

4. *Secret profits.* The corporation can sue and recover any secret profits made by an officer or a director's breach of his or her duty of loyalty.

Liability for Crimes

1. *Liability of directors and officers.* Corporate directors and officers are *personally liable* for the crimes they commit while acting on behalf of the corporation. Criminal sanctions include fines and imprisonment.

2. *Liability of the corporation.* Under the law of *agency*, corporations are liable for the crimes committed by its directors and officers while acting within the scope of their authority. Criminal sanctions include monetary fines and loss of legal privileges (e.g., loss of a license).

Sarbanes-Oxley Act of 2002, p. 606

Sarbanes-Oxley Act of 2002

This act is a federal statute enacted by Congress to improve corporate governance rules, establish independence between public accounting firms and the public companies they audit, and eliminate conflicts of interest.

Auditing and Accounting Rules

1. *Audit committee.* A public company must have an audit committee that is responsible for the appointment, payment to, and oversight of public accounting firms employed to audit the company.

2. *Public company accounting oversight board.* A board regulated by the Securities and Exchange Commission (SEC) has the authority to adopt rules concerning auditing, accounting, independence, and ethics of public companies and public accountants.

3. *Registration with board.* Public accounting firms must register with the board and are subject to audits by the board.

4. *Separation of audit and nonaudit services.* It is unlawful for a registered public accounting firm to simultaneously provide audit and certain nonaudit services to a public company.

5. *Audit report sign-offs.* Each audit by a certified public accounting firm must be supervised by a partner who must approve the audit report. A second partner must review and approve the audit report.

6. *Prohibited employment.* Any person employed by a public accounting firm that audits a client cannot be employed by that client for certain positions for a period of one year following the audit.

7. *Internal control procedures.* Public companies must establish and maintain adequate internal controls and procedures for financial reporting.

8. *Off-balance sheet items.* Annual and quarterly reports of public companies must disclose material off-balance sheet transactions and relationships with other entities.

Corporate Governance Rules

1. *CEO and CFO certification.* The CEO and CFO of a public company must file a statement accompanying each annual and quarterly report certifying that the signing officer has reviewed the report and based on the officer's knowledge the report:

   a. Does not contain any untrue statement of a material fact or omit to state a material fact that would make the statement misleading.

   b. The financial statement and disclosures fairly present, in all material aspects, the operation and financial condition of the company.

   A knowing and willful violation is punishable for up to 20 years in prison and a fine of not more than $5 million.

2. *Reimbursement of bonuses and incentive pay.* The CEO and CFO must reimburse the company for any bonuses, incentive pay, or securities trading profits if the company is required to restate its financial statements because of material noncompliance with financial reporting requirements.

3. *Prohibition on personal loans.* Public companies cannot make personal loans to its directors or executive officers.

4. *Tampering with evidence.* It is a crime for any person to tamper with evidence to impede, influence, or obstruct any federal investigation. A violation is punishable for up to 20 years in prison and a monetary fine.

5. *Bar from acting as an officer or a director.* The SEC may issue an order prohibiting any person who has committed securities fraud from acting as an officer or a director of a public company.

Internet Exercises and Case Questions

Working the Web Internet Exercises

Activities

1. Find your state statute on indemnification for corporate officers and directors. Why do you think this concept was included in the statute? See **www.law.cornell.edu/topics/corporations.html** for an overview of corporations law with links to key primary and secondary sources.

2. Review the sample indemnification agreement at **www.lawvantage.com/description/corporate_law/director_and_officer_benefits_incentives_and_indemnification/summaries/CODO1000S.shtml**.

3. For more coverage of the background on directors and officers liability, see **www.griffincom.com/docont.htm**. For a lengthy list of topics, see **guide.lp.findlaw.com/01topics/08corp/index.html**. For a quick overview of corporate law, see **www.nolo.com/category/sb_home.html**.

4. Go to **lawcrawler.findlaw.com**. Type in the search term *piercing the corporate veil*. Note how many articles are written from the perspective of an attorney representing a small business owner against claims seeking personal assets.

Note: For socially responsible investing information, see **www.socialinvest.org**.

Critical Legal Thinking Cases

27.1 Shareholder Meeting   Ocilla Industries, Inc. (Ocilla), owned 40 percent of the stock of Direct Action Marketing, Inc. (Direct Action). Direct Action was a New York corporation that specialized in the marketing of products through billing inserts. In 1985, Ocilla helped place Howard Katz and Joseph Esposito on Direct Action's five-member board of directors. A dispute between Ocilla and the two directors caused Ocilla to claim that Katz and Esposito wanted excess remuneration in exchange for leaving the board at the end of their terms. As a result, no shareholders' meeting was held between September 19, 1986, and January 27, 1988. Under the Model Business Corporations Act, can Ocilla compel Direct Action to hold the meeting earlier? [*Ocilla Industries, Inc. v. Katz*, 677 F.Supp. 1291, 1987 U.S.Dist. Lexis 12741 (E.D. N.Y. 1987)]

27.2 Special Meeting   Jack C. Schoenholtz was a shareholder and member of the board of directors of Rye Psychiatric Hospital Center, Inc. (Rye Hospital). The hospital was incorporated in 1973. By 1977, a split had developed among the board of directors concerning the operation of the facility. Three directors stood on one side of the dispute and three directors on the other. In an attempt to break the deadlock, Schoenholtz, who owned over 10 percent of the corporation's voting stock, asked the corporation's secretary to call a special meeting of the shareholders. In response, the secretary sent a notice to the shareholders stating that a special meeting of the shareholders would be held on November 12, 1982, "for the purpose of electing directors." The meeting was held as scheduled. Some stockholders brought suit claiming that the special shareholders' meeting was not called properly. Who wins? [*Rye Psychiatric Hospital Center, Inc. v. Schoenholtz*, 476 N.Y.S.2d 339, 1984 N.Y.App.Div. Lexis 17818 (A.D. 2 Dept. 1984)]

27.3 Irrevocable Proxy   George Gibbons, William Smith, and Gerald Zollar were all shareholders in GRG Operating, Inc. (GRG). On May 13, 1983, Zollar contributed $1,000 of his own funds so that the corporation could begin to do business. In exchange for this contribution, Gibbons and Smith both granted Zollar the right to vote their shares of GRG stock. They gave Zollar a signed form that stated that "Gibbons and Smith, for a period of 10 years from the date hereof, appoint Zollar as their proxy. This proxy is solely intended to be an irrevocable proxy." A year after the agreement was signed, Gibbons and Smith wanted to revoke their proxies. Can they? [*Zollar v. Smith*, 710 S.W.2d 155, 1986 Tex.App. Lexis 12900 (Tex. App. 1986)]

27.4 Right to Inspect Records   On July 20, 1983, Helmsman Management Services, Inc. (Helmsman), became a 25 percent stockholder of A&S Consultants, Inc. (A&S), a Delaware corporation. Helmsman paid $50,000 for its interest in A&S. At the time of the stock purchase, Helmsman was also a customer of A&S, paying the company for the use of a computer software program. Since 1983, Helmsman verified A&S's billings by a periodic review of certain of A&S's books and records. In January 1986, Helmsman conducted a review of A&S's records over a six-day period. The review showed that A&S had never paid any dividends on the stock held by Helmsman and that Helmsman had never received notice of A&S's stockholder meetings. Suspecting that A&S was being mismanaged, Helmsman sent a letter to A&S asking to inspect all A&S's records. The letter stated several purposes for the inspection, including to (1) determine the reasons for nonpayment of dividends and (2) gain information to be used in

determining how to vote in stockholders' elections. Under the Model Business Corporations Act, should Helmsman's request be honored? [*Helmsman Management Services, Inc. v. A&S Consultants, Inc.*, 525 A.2d 160, 1987 Del.Ch. Lexis 397 (Del. Ch. 1987)]

27.5 Dividends   Gay's Super Markets, Inc. (Super Markets) was a corporation formed under the laws of the state of Maine. Hannaford Bros. Company held 51 percent of the corporation's common stock. Lawrence F. Gay and his brother Carrol were both minority shareholders in Super Markets. Lawrence Gay was also the manager of the corporation's store at Machias, Maine. On July 5, 1971, he was dismissed from his job. At the January 1972 meeting of Super Markets's board of directors, a decision was made not to declare a stock dividend for 1971. The directors cited expected losses from increased competition and the expense of opening a new store as reasons for not paying a dividend. Lawrence Gay claims that the reason for not paying a dividend was to force him to sell his shares in Super Markets. Lawrence sued to force the corporation to declare a dividend. Who wins? [*Gay v. Gay's Super Markets, Inc.*, 343 A.2d 577, 1975 Me. Lexis 391 (Maine Sup. 1975)]

27.6 Duty of Loyalty   Edward Hellenbrand ran a comedy club known as the Comedy Cottage in Rosemont, Illinois. The business was incorporated, with Hellenbrand and his wife as the corporation's sole shareholders. The corporation leased the premises in which the club was located. In 1978, Hellenbrand hired Jay Berk as general manager of the club. In 1980, Berk was made vice president of the corporation and given 10 percent of its stock. Hellenbrand experienced health problems and moved to Nevada, leaving Berk to manage the daily affairs of the business. In June 1984, the ownership of the building where the Comedy Cottage was located changed hands. Shortly thereafter, the club's lease on the premises expired. Hellenbrand instructed Berk to negotiate a new lease. Berk arranged a month-to-month lease but had the lease agreement drawn up in his name instead of that of the corporation. When Hellenbrand learned of Berk's move, he fired him. Berk continued to lease the building in his own name and opened his own club there, known as the Comedy Company, Inc. Hellenbrand sued Berk for an injunction to prevent Berk from leasing the building. Who wins? [*Comedy Cottage, Inc. v. Berk* 495 N.E.2d 1006, 1986 Ill.App. Lexis 2486 (Ill. App. 1986)]

27.7 Duty of Loyalty   Lawrence Gaffney was the president and general manager of Ideal Tape Company (Ideal). Ideal, which was a subsidiary of Chelsea Industries, Inc. (Chelsea), was engaged in the business of manufacturing pressure sensitive tape. In 1975, Gaffney recruited three other Ideal executives to join him in starting a tape manufacturing business. The four men remained at Ideal for the two years it took them to plan the new enterprise. During this time, they used their positions at Ideal to travel around the country to gather business ideas, recruit potential customers, and purchase equipment for their business. At no time did they reveal to Chelsea their intention to open a competing business. In November 1977, the new business was incorporated as Action Manufacturing Company (Action). When executives at Chelsea discovered the existence of the new venture, Gaffney and the others resigned from Chelsea. Chelsea sued them for damages. Who wins? [*Chelsea Industries, Inc. v. Gaffney*, 449 N.E.2d 320, 1983 Mass. Lexis 1413 (Mass. Sup. 1983)]

27.8 Indemnification William G. Young was a director of Pool Builders Supply, Inc. (Pool Builders). Pool Builders experienced financial difficulties and was forced to file for bankruptcy. Eddie Lawson was appointed the receiver for the creditors of the corporation. Lawson believed that Young had mismanaged the corporation. Lawson filed a suit against Young and Pool Builders, alleging that Young had used Pool Builders personally to obtain money, goods, and property from creditors on the credit of the corporation. Lawson's suit also alleged that Young attempted to convert corporate assets for his own use. Young defended the suit for himself and the corporation. At trial, the judge found insufficient evidence to support Lawson's charges, and the suit was dismissed. Young then sought to have Pool Builders pay the legal fees he incurred while defending the suit. Can Young recover this money from the corporation? [*Lawson v. Young*, 486 N.E.2d 1177, 1984 Ohio App. Lexis 12678 (Ohio App. 1984)]

27.9 Derivative Lawsuit In 1948, four brothers—Monnie, Mechel, Merko, and Sam Dotlich—formed a partnership to run a heavy equipment rental business. By 1957, the company had been incorporated as Dotlich Brothers, Inc. Each brother owned 25 percent of the corporation's stock, and each served on the board of directors. In 1951, the business acquired a 56-acre tract of land in Speedway, Indiana. This land was held in the name of Monnie Dotlich. Each of the brothers was aware of this agreement. By 1976, the corporation had purchased six other pieces of property, all of which were held in Monnie's name. Sam Dotlich was not informed that Monnie was the record owner of these other properties. In 1976, Sam discovered this irregularity and requested the board of directors take action to remedy the situation. When the board refused to do so, Sam initiated a lawsuit on behalf of the corporation. Can Sam bring this lawsuit? [*Dotlich v. Dotlich*, 475 N.E.2d 331, 1985 Ind.App. Lexis 2233 (Ind. App. 1985)]

27.10 Piercing the Corporate Veil M. R. Watters was the majority shareholder of several closely held corporations, including Wildhorn Ranch Inc. (Wildhorn). All these businesses were run out of Watter's home in Rocky Ford, Colorado. Wildhorn operated a resort called the Wildhorn Ranch Resort in Teller County, Colorado. Although Watters claimed that the ranch was owned by the corporation, the deed for the property listed Watters as the owner. Watters paid little attention to corporate formalities, holding corporate meetings at his house, never taking minutes of these meetings, and paying the debts of one corporation with the assets of another. During August 1986, two guest of Wildhorn Ranch Resort drowned while operating a paddleboat at the ranch. The family of the deceased guests sued for damages. Can Watters be held personally liable? [*Geringer v. Wildhorn Ranch, Inc.*, 706 F.Supp. 1442, 1988 U.S.Dist. Lexis 15701 (D. Colo. 1988)]

Business Ethics Cases

27.11 Business Ethics Alfred S. Johnson, Incorporated (Corporation), was incorporated in 1955 by Alfred S. Johnson, who owned 70 shares of the corporation. Two employees of the corporation, James DeBaun and Walter Stephens, owned 20 and 10 shares, respectively. When Johnson died in 1965, his will created a testamentary trust in which his 70 shares were placed. Johnson's will named First Western Bank and Trust Company (Bank) trustee for the trust. Several years later, Bank decided to sell the 70 shares but did not tell anyone associated with Corporation of its decision. An appraisal was obtained that valued the corporation at $326,000 as a going concern.

On May 27, 1968, Raymond J. Mattison submitted an offer to purchase the 70 shares for $250,000 payable in $50,000 in securities of companies Mattison owned and the $200,000 balance over a five-year period. Bank obtained a Dun & Bradstreet report that showed several outstanding tax liens against Mattison. Bank accepted Mattison's explanation that they were not his fault. At the time, Mattison owed Bank a judgment for fraud. Bank was also aware that Mattison owed unpaid debts and that several entities in which he was involved were insolvent. Bank did not investigate these matters. If it had, the public records of Los Angeles County would have revealed 38 unsatisfied judgments against Mattison and his entities totaling $330,886, 54 pending lawsuits claiming damages of $373,588, and 18 tax liens aggregating $20,327. Bank agreed to sell the 70 shares to Mattison and accepted the assets of Corporation as security for the repayment of the $200,000 balance. As part of the transaction Bank required Mattison to agree to have Corporation give its banking business to Bank.

At the time of sale, Corporation was a successful going business with a bright future. It had cash of $76,000 and other liquid assets of over $120,000. Its net worth was about $220,000. Corporation was profitable, and its trend of earnings indicated a pattern of growth. Mattison immediately implemented a systematic scheme to loot Corporation. He (1) diverted $73,000 in corporate cash to himself and a shell company he owned, (2) caused Corporation to assign all its assets, including accounts receivable, to the shell company, (3) diverted all corporate mail to a post office box and extracted incoming checks to Corporation, (4) refused to pay corporate creditors on time or at all, (5) issued payroll checks without sufficient corporate funds, and (6) removed Corporation's books and records. On June 20, 1969, hopelessly insolvent, Corporation shut down operations and was placed in receivership. At that time, its debts exceeded its assets by over $200,000. DeBaun's and Stephens's shares were worthless. They sued Bank for damages, alleging that Bank, as the majority shareholder of Corporation, breached its fiduciary duty to the minority shareholders.

Did Bank have knowledge of the dangerous situation in which it placed Corporation? Did Bank, as the controlling shareholder of Corporation, breach its fiduciary duty to the minority shareholders? [*DeBaun v. First Western Bank and Trust Co.*, 46 Cal.App.3d 791, 120 Cal.Rptr. 354, 1975 Cal.App. Lexis 1801 (Cal. App. 1975)]

27.12 Business Ethics Jon-T Chemicals, Inc. (Chemicals), was an Oklahoma corporation engaged in the fertilizer and chemicals business. John H. Thomas was its majority shareholder and its president and board chairman. In April 1971, Chemicals incorporated Jon-T Farms, Inc. (Farms), as a wholly owned subsidiary to engage in the farming and land-leasing business. Chemicals invested $10,000 to establish Farms. All the directors and officers of Farms were directors and officers of Chemicals, and Thomas was its president and board chairman. In addition, Farms used officers, computers, and accountants of Chemicals without paying a fee, and Chemicals paid the salary of Farms' only employee.

Chemicals made regular informal advances to pay Farms' expenses. These payments reached $7.5 million by January 1975.

Thomas and Farms engaged in a scheme whereby they submitted fraudulent applications for agricultural subsidies from the federal government under the Uplands Cotton Program. As a result of these applications, the Commodity Credit Corporation, a government agency, paid over $2.5 million in subsidies to Thomas and Farms. After discovering the fraud, the federal government obtained criminal convictions against Thomas and Farms. In a separate civil action, the federal government obtained a $4.7 million judgment against Thomas and Farms, finding them jointly and severally liable for the tort of fraud. Farms declared bankruptcy, and Thomas was unable to pay the judgment. Because Thomas and Farms were insolvent, the federal government sued Chemicals to recover the judgment. Was Farms the alter ego of Chemicals, permitting the United States to pierce the corporate veil and recover the judgment from Chemicals? Did Thomas act ethically in this case? [*United States of America v. Jon-T Chemicals, Inc.*, 768 F.2d 686, 1985 U.S.App. Lexis 21255 (5th Cir. 1985)]

Briefing the Case Writing Assignment

Read Case A.27 in the Case Appendix [*United States v. WRW Corporation*]. This case is excerpted from the court of appeals opinion. Review and brief the case. In your brief, be sure to answer the following questions.

1. Who was the plaintiff? What was it suing for?

2. Who were the defendants?

3. Explain the doctrine of piercing the corporate veil.

4. Did the court find the defendants personally liable?

Endnote

1. *Meinhard v. Salmon*, 164 N.E.2d 545, 546, 1928 N.Y. Lexis 830 (N.Y. App. 1928).

28

Corporate Mergers and Acquisitions

"To supervise wisely the great corporations is well; but to look backward to the days when business was polite pillage and regard our great business concerns as piratical institutions carrying letters of marque and reprisal is a grave error born in the minds of little men. When these little men legislate they set the brakes going uphill."

—Elbert Hubbard (1856–1915)
Notebook, p. 16

Chapter Objectives

After studying this chapter, you should be able to:

1. Describe the process for soliciting proxies from shareholders and engaging in proxy contests.
2. Define shareholder proposal and identify when a shareholder can include a proposal in proxy materials.
3. Describe the process for approving a merger or share exchange.
4. Define tender offer and describe poison pills, white knight mergers, greenmail, and other defensive maneuvers to prevent hostile takeover.
5. Analyze the lawfulness of state antitakeover statutes.

Chapter Contents

- Proxy Solicitation
- Mergers and Acquisitions
- Tender Offers
- State Antitakeover Statutes

During the course of its existence, a corporation may go through certain *fundamental changes*. A corporation must seek shareholder approval for many changes. This requires the solicitation of votes or proxies from shareholders. Persons who want to take over the management of a corporation often conduct proxy contests to try to win over shareholder votes.

Corporations often engage in acquisitions of other corporations or businesses. This may occur by friendly merger or consolidation or by hostile tender offer. In defense, a corporation may erect certain barriers or impediments to a hostile takeover.

This chapter discusses fundamental changes to a corporation, including the solicitation of proxies, mergers and consolidations, hostile tender offers, and defensive strategies of corporations.

> The usual trade and commerce is cheating all round by consent.
>
> Thomas Fuller
> *Gnomologia (1732)*

Proxy Solicitation

Corporate shareholders have the right to vote on the election of directors, mergers, charter amendments, and the like. They can exercise their power to vote either in person or by proxy [RMBCA § 7.22]. Voting by proxy is common in large corporations with thousands of shareholders located across the country and the world.

A *proxy* is a written document (often called **proxy card**) that is completed and signed by the shareholder and sent to the corporation. The proxy authorizes another person—the proxy holder—to vote the shares at the shareholders' meeting as directed by the shareholder. The proxy holder is often a director or an officer of the corporation. Exhibit 28.1 shows a proxy card.

Exhibit 28.1

Proxy: E. du Pont de Nemours and Company

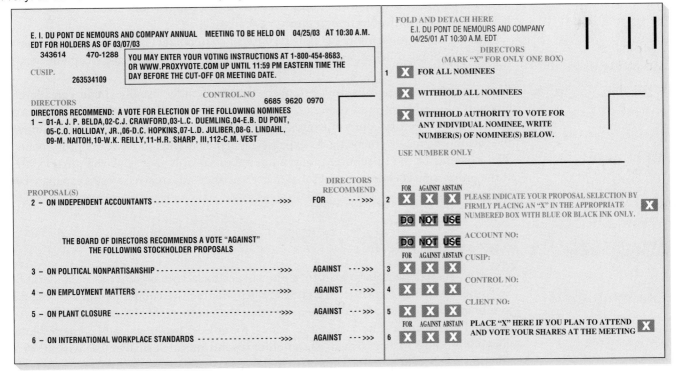

Federal Proxy Rules

Section 14(a) of the Securities Exchange Act of 1934 gives the Securities and Exchange Commission (SEC) the authority to regulate the solicitation of proxies.[1] The federal proxy rules promote full disclosure. In other words, management or any other party soliciting proxies from shareholders must prepare a **proxy statement** that fully describes (1) the matter for which the proxy is being solicited, (2) who is soliciting the proxy, and (3) any other pertinent information.

A copy of the proxy, the proxy statement, and all other solicitation material must be filed with the SEC at least 10 days before the materials are sent to the shareholders. If the SEC requires additional disclosures, the solicitation can be held up until these disclosures are made.

Antifraud Provision

Section 14(a) of the Securities Exchange Act of 1934 prohibits material misrepresentations or omissions of a material fact in the proxy materials. Known false statements of facts, reasons, opinions, or beliefs in proxy solicitation materials are actionable. Violations of this rule can result in civil and criminal actions by the SEC and the Justice Department, respectively. The courts have implied a private cause of action under this provision. Thus, shareholders who are injured by a material misrepresentation or omission in proxy materials can sue the wrongdoer and recover damages. The court can also order a new election if a violation is found.

Proxy Contests

Shareholders sometimes oppose the actions taken by the *incumbent directors* and management. These *insurgent shareholders* may challenge the incumbent management in a **proxy contest**, in which both sides solicit proxies from the other shareholders. The side that receives the greatest number of votes wins the proxy contest. Such contests are usually held with regard to the election of directors.

Management must either (1) provide a list of shareholders to the dissenting group or (2) mail the proxy solicitation materials of the challenging group to the shareholders.

Reimbursement of Expenses In a proxy contest, both sides usually spend considerable amounts of money on legal expenses, media campaigns, mailers, telephone solicitations, and the like. If a proxy contest involves an issue of policy, the corporation must reimburse the incumbent management for its expenses, whether it wins or loses the proxy contest. The expenses of the dissenting group are reimbursed only if it wins the proxy contest. If the proxy contest concerns a personal matter, neither side may recover its expenses from the corporation.

Shareholder Resolution

At times, shareholders may wish to submit issues for a vote to other shareholders. The Securities Exchange Act of 1934 and SEC rules adopted thereunder permit a shareholder to submit a resolution to be considered by other shareholders if (1) the shareholder owned at least 1,000 shares of the corporation's stock for at least two years and (2) the resolution does not exceed 550 words. Such **shareholder resolutions** are usually made when the corporation is soliciting proxies from its shareholders.

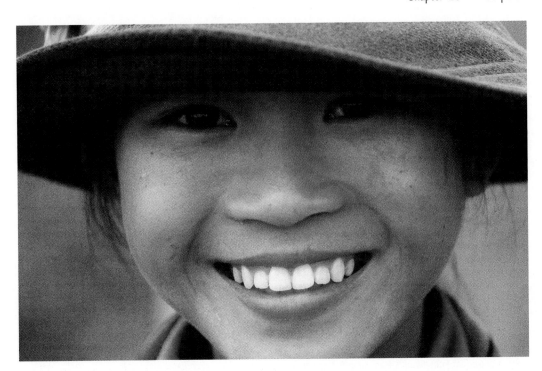

Vietnam. Shareholder resolutions often challenge corporate policies. For example, is it socially responsible for U.S. businesses to have goods made in countries that do not have substantial worker protection laws?

If management does not oppose the resolution, it may be included in the proxy materials issued by the corporation. Even if management is not in favor of the resolution, the shareholder has the right to have the shareholder resolution included in the corporation's proxy materials if it (1) relates to the corporation's business, (2) concerns a *policy issue* (and not the day-to-day operations of the corporation), and (3) does not concern the payment of dividends. The SEC rules on whether a resolution can be submitted to shareholders.

Shareholder resolutions have recently been presented concerning protecting the environment, reducing global warming, preventing the overcutting of the rain forests in Brazil, and prohibiting U.S. corporations from purchasing goods manufactured in developing countries under poor working conditions, including the use of forced and child labor.

Most shareholder resolutions have a slim chance of being enacted because large-scale investors usually support management. They can, however, cause a corporation to change the way it does business. For example, to avoid the adverse publicity such issues can create, some corporations voluntarily adopt the changes contained in shareholder resolutions. Others negotiate settlements with the sponsors of resolutions to get the measures off the agenda before the annual shareholders' meetings.

Business Ethics
Shareholder Resolution

The E. I. du Pont de Nemours and Company (DuPont), organized under the laws of the state of Delaware, is one of the largest chemical and consumer products companies in the world. As such, DuPont has manufacturing and production facilities located in many foreign countries. Several of these countries have been criticized because child labor and forced

labor are alleged to be used to produce goods in those countries.

At its annual meeting in April 2001, the International Brotherhood of Teamsters General Fund, owner of 90 shares of DuPont common stock, proposed the following shareholder resolution to the shareholders of DuPont.

Business Ethics

(continued)

Stockholder Proposal on International Workplace Standards

RESOLVED: *That the Board of Directors of E. I. du Pont de Nemours and Company (Du Pont) shall adopt, implement and enforce the workplace Code of Conduct (Code) as based on the International Labor Organization's (ILO) Conventions on workplace human rights, which include:*

- *No use of child labor.*
- *No discrimination or intimidation in employment.*
- *All workers have the right to form and join unions and to bargain collectively.*
- *No use of forced labor.*

Stockholder's (Teamster's) Statement in support of the proposal:

The Teamsters, in support of its proposal, provided the following statement in Du Pont's annual Proxy Statement submitted to Du Pont shareholders.

As a global institution, Du Pont and its international operations and sourcing arrangements are exposed to sundry risks. Adoption of this proposal manages the risk of being a party to serious human rights violations in the workplace. Du Pont operates or has business relationships in a number of countries, including China, Indonesia, and Thailand, where the U.S. State Department, Amnesty International, and Human Rights Watch indicate law and public policy do not adequately protect human rights. To wit: Forced labor, illegal child labor, and violence against women.

The success of Du Pont's operations depends on consumer and governmental good will. Brand name is a significant asset. Du Pont benefits from adopting and enforcing the Code ensuring that it isn't associated with human rights violations. This protects Du Pont's brand names and its relationships with customers and the numerous governments under which Du Pont operates and with which it does business.

Position of the Board of Directors in Opposition to the Proposal

In response, Du Pont included the following statement in the Proxy Statement, recommending that Du Pont shareholders vote against the shareholder resolution.

Du Pont is committed to conducting its business affairs with the highest ethical standards, and works diligently to be a respected corporate citizen throughout the world. The company has had in place for many years an Ethics Policy, Mission Statement and Code of Business Conduct addressing many of the issues covered in the standards proposed for adoption. These corporate policies are applicable to all employees in all Du Pont businesses around the world.

The company is supportive of the general intent of the proposal and similar international workplace standards suggested by other organizations for adoption. The company reviews on an ongoing basis codes offered by other organizations, and examines its own policies and practices in light of the provisions of the proposed codes. The company also meets with advocates of codes to explore issues of mutual concern. These efforts will continue. The company therefore believes adoption of the proposed code is unnecessary.

The shareholder resolution for the adoption of International Workplace Standards was defeated by an overwhelming majority of DuPont shareholders at the annual meeting.

1. Why do you think the International Brotherhood of Teamsters introduced this shareholder resolution?

2. Do you think the reasons DuPont asserted for recommending that its shareholders vote against the proposal were legitimate? Explain. ■

Business Brief

Mergers, consolidations, share exchanges, and sales of assets are *friendly* in nature. That is, both corporations have agreed to the combination of corporations or acquisition of assets.

Mergers and Acquisitions

Corporations may agree to friendly acquisitions or combinations of one another. This may be by (1) merger, (2) consolidation, (3) share exchange, or (4) sale of assets. These types of combinations are discussed in the following paragraphs.

Exhibit 28.2
Example of a Merger

Mergers

A **merger** occurs when one corporation is absorbed into another corporation and ceases to exist. The corporation that continues to exist is called the *surviving corporation*. The other is called the *merged corporation* [RMBCA § 11.01]. The surviving corporation gains all the rights, privileges, powers, duties, obligations, and liabilities of the merged corporation. Title to property owned by the merged corporation transfers to the surviving corporation, without formality or deeds. The shareholders of the merged corporation receive stock or securities of the surviving corporation or other consideration, as provided in the plan of merger.

Suppose, for example, that Corporation A and Corporation B merge and it is agreed that Corporation A will absorb Corporation B. Corporation A is the surviving corporation. Corporation B is the merged corporation. A symbolic representation of this merger is A + B = A (see Exhibit 28.2).

Consolidations

A **consolidation** occurs when two or more corporations combine to form an entirely new corporation (i.e., there is no surviving corporation). The new corporation is called the *consolidated corporation*, and the articles of incorporation of the new corporation replace the articles of incorporation of the component corporations.

Consider This Example   Corporation A and Corporation B consolidate to form a new organization called Corporation C. A symbolic representation of this combination is A + B = C (see Exhibit 28.3).

The new corporation accedes to all the rights, privileges, powers, duties, obligations, and liabilities of the constituent corporations. Title to property owned by the component corporations transfers to the new corporation, without any formality. The shareholders receive stock of other securities in the consolidated corporation or other agreed-upon consideration. Today, consolidations are not used very often because it is generally advantageous for one of the corporations to survive.

Share Exchanges

One corporation can also acquire all the shares of another corporation through a **share exchange**. In a share exchange, both corporations retain their separate legal existence. After the exchange, one corporation (*parent corporation*) owns all the shares of the other corporation (*subsidiary corporation*) [RMBCA § 1102]. (See Exhibit 28.4.) Such exchanges are often used to create holding company arrangements (e.g., bank or insurance holding companies).

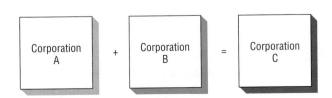

Exhibit 28.3
Example of a Consolidation

Exhibit 28.4

Example of a Share
Exchange

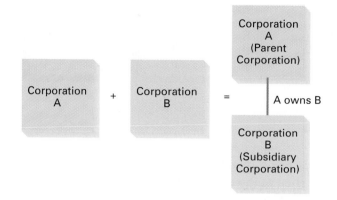

Consider This Example   Suppose Corporation H is a bank holding company that wishes to acquire First Bank. Assume that Corporation H offers to exchange its shares for those of First Bank and that First Bank's shareholders approve of the transaction. After the share exchange, Corporation H is the parent corporation, and First Bank is the wholly owned subsidiary of Corporation H.

Required Approvals for a Merger or Share Exchange

An ordinary merger or share exchange requires (1) the recommendation of the board of directors of each corporation and (2) an affirmative vote of the majority of shares of each corporation that is entitled to vote [RMBCA § 11.03]. The articles of incorporation or corporate bylaws can require the approval of a *supramajority*, such as 80 percent of the voting shares.

The approval of the surviving corporation's shareholders is not required if the merger or share exchange increases the number of voting shares of the surviving corporation by 20 percent or less [RMBCA § 11.03(g)].

The approved *articles of merger or share exchange* must be filed with the secretary of state. The state normally issues a *certificate of merger or share exchange* to the surviving corporation after all the formalities are met and the requisite fees are paid [RMBCA § 11.05].

If one corporation (called the *parent corporation*) owns 90 percent or more of the outstanding stock of another corporation (known as the *subsidiary corporation*), a **short-form merger** procedure may be followed to merge the two corporations. The short-form merger procedure is simpler than an ordinary merger because neither the approval of the shareholders of either corporation nor the approval of the board of directors of the subsidiary corporation is needed. All that is required is the approval of the board of directors of the parent corporation [RMBCA § 11.04].

Sale or Lease of Assets

A corporation may sell, lease, or otherwise dispose of all or substantially all of its property in other than the usual and regular course of business. Such a sale or lease transaction requires (1) the recommendation of the board of directors and (2) an affirmative vote of the majority of the shares of the selling or leasing corporation that is entitled to vote (unless greater vote is required) [RMBCA § 12.02]. This rule prevents the board of directors from selling all or most of the assets of the corporation without shareholder approval.

Dissenting Shareholder Appraisal Rights

Specific shareholders sometimes object to a proposed ordinary or short-form merger, share exchange, or sale or lease of all or substantially all of the property of a corporation, even though the transaction received the required approvals. Objecting shareholders are provided a statutory right to dissent and obtain payment of the fair value of their shares [RMBCA §

13.02]. This is referred to as a **dissenting shareholder appraisal right** or **appraisal right**. Shareholders have no other recourse unless the transaction is unlawful or fraudulent.

The corporation must notify shareholders of the existence of their appraisal rights before the transaction can be voted on [RMBCA § 13.20]. To obtain appraisal rights, a dissenting shareholder must (1) deliver written notice of his or her intent to demand payment of his or her shares to the corporation before the vote is taken and (2) not vote his or her shares in favor of the proposed action [RMBCA § 13.23]. The shareholder must deposit his or her share certificates with the corporation [RMBCA § 13.23]. Shareholders who fail to comply with these statutory procedures lose their appraisal rights.

As soon as the proposed action is taken, the corporation must pay each dissenting shareholder the amount the corporation estimates to be the fair value of his or her shares, plus accrued interest [RMBCA § 13.25]. If the dissenter is dissatisfied, the corporation must petition the court to determine the fair value of the shares [RMBCA § 13.30].

After a hearing, the court will issue an order declaring the fair value of the shares. Appraisers may be appointed to help in determining this value. Court costs and appraisal fees are usually paid by the corporation. However, the court can assess these costs against the dissenters if they acted arbitrarily, vexatiously, or in bad faith [RMBCA § 13.31].

The court had to determine the appraisal value of a company's shares in the following case.

Business Brief

The court must determine the "fair value" of the shares of dissenting shareholders. Courts usually use appraisers to assist in determining this value.

In the Matter of the Appraisal of Shell Oil Company
607 A.2d 1213, 1992 Del. Lexis 193 (1992)
Supreme Court of Delaware

Case 28.1
Dissenting Shareholder Appraisal Rights

Background and Facts

Royal Dutch Petroleum Company (Royal Dutch), a large natural resource conglomerate, owned 94.6 percent of the stock of Shell Oil Company (Shell). The remaining shares of Shell were held by minority, public shareholders. On June 7, 1985, Royal Dutch effectuated a short-form merger with Shell and offered $60 cash per share for the outstanding shares of Shell that it did not own. After the merger was complete, 1,005,001 shares had not accepted the offer and qualified for appraisal rights. The Delaware chancery court conducted an appraisal hearing. The parties offered extensive evidence through expert witnesses. These experts gave the following estimated per share value for Shell's shares:

Valuation Method	Shell's Expert	Shareholder's Expert
Liquidation value	$57	$100
Comparative value	$60	$106
Market value	$43–$45	$92–$143

Liquidation value was the estimated value if Shell were dissolved and its assets sold. Comparative value was an estimate based on a price reflected by prices in similar transactions in the oil and gas industry. Market value was an estimated price that Shell shares would sell for without the effect of merger speculation.

The chancery court determined that the fair value was $71.20 per share. It further held that the shareholders were entitled to 10 percent interest on that amount from the date of the merger to the date of payment. Both parties appealed.

Issue

What price should Shell be required to pay its minority shareholders who demanded appraisal rights?

Court's Reasoning

The chancery court assigned little or no weight to the valuations reached by the experts because it found that they lacked objectivity. The court stated: "In this case, each party's valuation evidence was replete with deficiencies and so susceptible to bias that indiscriminate endorsement of either would have been indefensible. The opinions expressed by the expert witnesses significantly reflected the desires of their clients." The chancery court reviewed the evidence and used its broad discretion to arrive at a valuation of $71.20 per share.

Decision and Remedy

The supreme court of Delaware affirmed the award granted by the chancery court.

Case Questions

Critical Legal Thinking   Should the law provide dissenting shareholder appraisal rights? Why or why not?

Business Ethics   Do you think expert witnesses act objectively?

Contemporary Business   Is there a temptation for a company to "low-ball" the cash-out price offered to shareholders in a merger? Explain.

Tender Offers

Recall that a merger, a consolidation, a share exchange, and a sale of assets all require the approval of the board of directors of the corporation whose assets or shares are to be acquired. If the board of directors of the target corporation does not agree to the merger or acquisition, the acquiring corporation can make a **tender offer** for the shares directly to the shareholders of the **target corporation**. The shareholders each make an individual decision about whether to sell their shares to the **tender offeror** (see Exhibit 28.5). Such offers are often referred to as *hostile tender offers*.

The tender offeror's board of directors must approve the offer, although the shareholders do not have to approve. The offer can be made for all or a portion of the shares of the target corporation.

In a tender offer, the tendering corporation and the target corporation retain their separate legal status. However, a successful tender offer is sometimes followed by a merger of the two corporations.

The Williams Act

Prior to 1968, tender offers were not federally regulated. However, securities that were issued in conjunction with such offers had to be registered with the SEC or qualify for an exemption from registration. Tender offers made with cash were not subject to any federal disclosure requirements

In 1968, Congress enacted the **Williams Act** as an amendment to the Securities Exchange Act of 1934 [15 U.S.C. 78n(d) and (e)]. This act specifically regulates all tender offers, whether they are made with securities, cash, or other consideration, and establishes certain disclosure requirements and antifraud provisions.

Tender Offer Rules

The **Williams Act** does not require the tender offeror to notify either the management of the target company or the SEC until the offer is made.[2] Detailed information regarding the terms, conditions, and other information concerning the tender offer must be disclosed at that time.

Exhibit 28.5

Illustration of a Tender Offer

Tender offer is made to the shareholders of the target corporation. The tender offeror offers to purchase the shareholders' shares in the target corporation.

Tender offers are governed by the following rules:

1. The offer cannot be closed before 20 business days after the commencement of the tender offer.
2. The offer must be extended for 10 business days if the tender offeror increases the number of shares that it will take or the price that it will pay for the shares.
3. The **fair price rule** stipulates that any increase in price paid for shares tendered must be offered to all shareholders, even those who have previously tendered their shares.
4. The **pro rata rule** holds that the shares must be purchased on a pro rata basis if too many shares are tendered.

A shareholder who tenders his or her shares has the absolute right to withdraw them at any time prior to the closing of the tender offer. The dissenting shareholder appraisal rights are not available.

Contemporary Environment
Leveraged Buyouts

Many tender offerors do not have the hundreds of millions or billions of dollars necessary to purchase the stock from the shareholders of the target corporation. Instead, the tender offeror relies on the fact that the money can be raised from creditors. Many tender offers are not possible without such loans. Because of the use of borrowed money, these acquisitions are called. **leveraged buyouts (LBOs).**

A typical LBO works as follows. The tender offeror identifies a potential target and then contacts a large commercial bank and an investment banker. The commercial bank, for a large fee, agrees to supply some of the funds necessary to make the initial acquisition. The bank will be paid off at a later date, after the acquisition is successful.

Most of the rest of the purchase price comes from money raised by the investment banker by selling **junk bonds** of the

acquiring firm to investors. Junk bonds are nothing more than risky bonds that pay a higher rate of interest than normal corporate bonds. Generally, the buyers are banks, pension funds, investment pools, and wealthy individuals. The investment banker is paid a huge fee by the raider for raising this money.

With this borrowed money in hand, the raider commences its hostile tender offer for the shares of the target corporation.

After the tender offer is completed, the tender offeror usually merges with the target corporation. The resulting entity is a highly leveraged corporation. The tender offeror usually sells off some of the assets to pay the bank loans, fees, and other expenses of the takeover. ■

Antifraud Provision

Section 14(e) of the Williams Act prohibits fraudulent, deceptive, and manipulative practices in connection with a tender offer.[3] Violations of this section may result in civil charges brought by the SEC or criminal charges brought by the Justice Department. The courts have implied a private civil cause of action under Section 14(e). Therefore, a shareholder who has been injured by a violation of Section 14(e) can sue the wrongdoer for damages.

Fighting a Tender Offer

The incumbent management of the target of a hostile tender offers may not want the corporation taken over by the tender offeror. Therefore, it may engage in varied activities to impede and defeat the tender offer. Some of the strategies and tactics used by incumbent management in defending against hostile tender offers are described as follows:

Business Brief

Target corporations initiate and implement a variety of defensive maneuvers and tactics to defend against unwanted hostile tender offers.

1. *Persuasion of shareholders.* Media campaigns are organized to convince shareholders that the tender offer is not in their best interests.

2. *Delaying lawsuits.* Lawsuits are filed, alleging that the tender offer violates securities laws, antitrust laws, or other laws. The time gained by this tactic gives management the opportunity to erect or implement other defensive maneuvers.

3. *Selling a crown jewel.* Such assets as profitable divisions or real estate that are particularly attractive to outside interests—that is, **crown jewels**—are sold. This tactic makes the target corporation less attractive to the tender offeror.

4. *Adopting a poison pill.* Poison pills are defensive strategies that are built into the target corporation's articles of incorporation, corporate bylaws, or contracts and leases. For example, contracts and leases may provide that they will expire if the ownership of the corporation changes hands. These tactics make the target corporation more expensive to the tender offeror.

5. *White knight merger.* White knight mergers are mergers with friendly parties,— that is, parties that promise to leave the target corporation and/or its management intact.

6. *Pac-Man (or reverse) tender offer.* The target corporation makes a **tender offer** on the tender offeror. Thus, the target corporation tries to purchase the tender offeror.

7. *Issuing additional stock.* Placing additional stock on the market increases the number of outstanding shares that the tender offeror must purchase in order to gain control of the target corporation.

8. *Creating an employee stock ownership plan (ESOP).* A company creates an ESOP and places a certain percentage of the corporation's securities (e.g., 15 percent) in it. The ESOP is then expected to vote the shares it owns against the potential acquirer in a proxy contest or tender offer because the beneficiaries (i.e., the employees) have a vested interest in keeping the company intact.

9. *Flip-over and flip-in rights plans.* These plans provide that existing shareholders of the target corporation may convert their shares for a greater amount (e.g., twice the value) of shares of the acquiring corporation (*flip-over rights plan*) or debt securities of the target company (*flip-in rights plan*). Rights plans are triggered if the acquiring firm acquires a certain percentage (e.g., 20 percent) of the shares of the target corporation. They make it more expensive for the acquiring firm to take over the target corporation.

10. *Greenmail and standstill agreements.* Most tender offerors purchase a block of stock in the target corporation before making an offer. Occasionally, the tender offeror will agree to give up its tender offer and agree not to purchase any further shares if the target corporation agrees to buy back the stock at a premium over fair market value. This payment is called **greenmail**. The agreement of the tender offeror to abandon its tender offer and not purchase any additional stock is called a *standstill agreement*.

There are many other strategies and tactics that target companies initiate and implement in defending against a tender offer.

Business Judgment Rule

The members of the board of directors of a corporation owe a **fiduciary duty** to the corporation and its shareholders. This duty, which requires the board to act carefully and honestly, is truly tested when a tender offer is made for the stock of the company. That is because shareholders and others then ask whether the board's initiation and implementation or defensive measures were taken in the best interests of the shareholders or to protect the board's own interests and jobs.

The legality of defensive strategies is examined using the **business judgment rule**. This rule protects the decisions of a board of directors that acts on an informed basis, in good faith, and in the honest belief that the action taken was in the best interests of the corporation and its shareholders.[4] In the context of a tender offer, the defensive measures chosen by the board must be reasonable in relation to the threat posed.[5]

In the following case, the court found that certain defensive tactics by a target corporation violated the law.

Paramount Communications Inc. v. QVC Network Inc.

637 A.2d 34, 1994 Del. Lexis 57 (1994)
Supreme Court of Delaware

Case 28.2
Tender Offer

Background and Facts

In September 1993, Viacom, Inc. (Viacom), and Paramount Communications, Inc. (Paramount), announced a friendly merger agreement. Basically, Viacom was taking over Paramount. Viacom controlled national cable networks, including Showtime and The Movie Channel. Paramount's holdings included Paramount Pictures, the Simon & Schuster publishing house, Madison Square Garden, the New York Knicks basketball team, and the New York Rangers hockey team. Both sides touted the synergism of the marriage of these two companies into a media colossus.

Five days later, QVC Network, Inc. (QVC), a rival cable operator, made a $90 per share hostile bid for Paramount that topped Viacom's merger offer. Paramount's board of directors, which did not want Paramount to be taken over by QVC, adopted the following antitakeover strategies:

1. A **no-shop provision** whereby the Paramount board guaranteed Viacom that it would not investigate QVC's offer or meet with QVC.
2. A **lockup option** that granted Viacom (but not QVC) the right to buy 23.7 million shares of Paramount at $69.14 each if a bidder other than Viacom bought Paramount.
3. An agreement to drop certain **poison pill** defenses as to Viacom but not as to QVC. (Thus, Viacom could pursue its acquisition of Paramount, but QVC could not.)

QVC sued Paramount in Delaware chancery court, alleging that these tactics violated the fiduciary duty of the Paramount board of directors to the corporation and its shareholders. The Delaware chancery court agreed with QVC that Paramount's defensive strategies were unlawful. Paramount appealed.

Issue

Do the defensive tactics adopted by Paramount's board of directors violate their fiduciary duties?

Court's Reasoning

The Delaware supreme court ruled that the "no shop" provision was unlawful, stating that Paramount directors "had a duty to continue their search for the best value available to shareholders." The court invalidated the less-than fair market value "lockup option" stock purchase plan as being an illegal transfer of corporate wealth to Viacom at the expense of Paramount shareholders.

The Delaware supreme court held that the poison pills Paramount had erected must be dismantled for QVC (and any other bidder) as they had been for Viacom. The court ordered that Paramount be put on the block and auctioned to the highest bidder.

Decision and Remedy

The Delaware supreme court invalidated Paramount's no-shop provision and lockup option. The court held that once a Delaware corporation has put itself "in play," it must remove all poison pills as to all possible bidders and put itself up for auction to be purchased by the highest bidder.

Note: In February 1994, after escalating bids from both Viacom and QVC, the five-month saga ended when Viacom won the right to buy Paramount with a $10-billion-plus bid.

Case Questions

Critical Legal Thinking   Can the management of a target company fight a tender offer? Explain.

Business Ethics   Did the board of directors of Paramount act in their shareholders' best interests?

Contemporary Business   Are many corporations safe from being taken over by a tender offer? Explain.

Business Ethics

Golden Parachutes

The term *golden parachute* has been coined to describe the large severance payments received by top executives when they leave their employment at a corporation. They are called "golden" because of their lucrative nature. They are called "parachutes" because they are "pulled" when an executive leaves or is fired from a company that has been taken over.

Golden parachutes are long-term employment contracts. They usually provide that all cash payments and stock options due under the contract become due and payable immediately upon the occurrence of the trigger—the takeover of the company.

For example, a company enters into an employment contract with its president and agrees to pay a $1 million salary annually

Business Ethics

(continued)

and grant options to purchase 1,000,000 shares of the company stock at $50 per share. The contract includes a golden parachute clause in the event of a takeover. Suppose the company is taken over in a $75-per-share tender offer when there are three years left on the president's contract. The president can "pull" his or her parachute and demand $3 million in salary as well as making a $25 million profit by exercising his stock options.

Some companies have added "silver parachutes" to protect lower-level managers and "tin parachutes" to protect wage-earning workers in case of a takeover. As the names indicate, the compensation paid under these plans is much lower than that paid under golden parachutes.

1. Do you think top executives' compensation is too high? Explain.
2. Are golden parachutes a legitimate compensation scheme? Or are they an egregious example of management greed? ■

State Antitakeover Statutes

Many states have enacted **antitakeover statutes** that are aimed at protecting corporations that are either incorporated in or do business within the state from hostile takeovers. Many of these state statutes have been challenged as being unconstitutional because they violate the Williams Act and the Commerce and Supremacy Clauses of the U.S. Constitution. In the following case, the U.S. Supreme Court held that a state antitakeover law was constitutional.

U.S. SUPREME COURT CASE

CTS Corporation v. Dynamics Corporation of America

481 U.S. 69, 107 S.Ct. 1637, 1987 U.S. Lexis 1811 (1987)
Supreme Court of the United States

Case 28.3
State Antitakeover
Statute

Background and Facts

On March 4, 1986, Indiana enacted the Control Share Acquisitions Chapter. This act covers corporations that (1) are incorporated in Indiana and have at least 100 shareholders, (2) have their primary place of business or substantial assets in Indiana, and (3) have either 10 percent of their shareholders in Indiana or 10 percent of their shares owned by Indiana residents. The act provides that if an entity acquires 20 percent or more of the voting shares of a covered corporation, the acquirer loses voting rights to these shares unless a majority of the disinterested shareholders of the acquired corporation vote to restore such voting rights. The acquirer can request that such vote be held within 50 days after its acquisition. If the shareholders do not restore the voting rights, the target corporation may redeem the shares from the acquirer at fair market value, but it is not required to do so.

On March 10, 1986, Dynamics Corporation of America (Dynamics), a Delaware corporation, announced a tender offer for one million shares of CTS Corporation, an Indiana corporation covered by the act. The purchase of these shares would have brought Dynamics's voting interest in CTS to 27.5 percent. Dynamics sued in federal court, alleging that Indiana's Control Share Acquisitions Chapter was unconstitutional. The U.S. district court held for Dynamics. The court of appeals affirmed. CTS appealed.

Issue

Does the Indiana Control Share Acquisitions Chapter conflict with the Williams Act or violate the Commerce Clause of the U.S. Constitution by unduly burdening interstate commerce?

Court's Reasoning

The U.S. Supreme Court found that the Indiana antitakeover statute did not conflict with the Williams Act. The Supreme Court stated that the state law, which allows shareholders to vote as a group, protects them from the coercive aspects of some tender offers. The shareholders as a group, acting in the corporation's best interest, could reject a tender offer although individual shareholders might be inclined to accept it. The desire of the Indiana legislature to protect shareholders of Indiana corporations from a coercive offer does not conflict with the Williams Act.

The Supreme Court also held that Indiana's antitakeover statute did not unduly burden interstate commerce. The Court stated: "Every state in this country has enacted laws regulating corporate governance. By prohibiting certain transactions and regulating others, such laws necessarily affect certain aspects of interstate commerce." Large corporations that are listed on national exchanges, or even regional exchanges, will have shareholders in many states and shares that are traded frequently. The

Supreme Court held that it is an accepted part of the business landscape in this country for states to create corporations, to prescribe their powers, and to define the rights that are acquired by purchasing their shares.

Decision and Remedy

The U.S. Supreme Court held that the Indiana Control Share Acquisitions Chapter neither conflicted with the Williams Act nor violated the Commerce Clause of the U.S. Constitution. The Supreme Court reversed the decision of the court of appeals.

Case Questions

Critical Legal Thinking   Should states be permitted to adopt antitakeover statutes? Why or why not? Whom do you think these statutes actually protect?

Business Ethics   Is it ethical for a target corporation's management to assert a state antitakeover statute?

Contemporary Business   What are the economic effects of a state antitakeover statute?

International Law

The Exon-Florio Law

The **Exon-Florio Law** of 1988 [50 U.S.C. 2170], as amended, mandates the president of the United States to suspend, prohibit, or dismantle the acquisition of U.S. businesses by foreign investors if there is credible evidence that the foreign investor might take action that threatens to impair the "national security."

The act apply to mergers, acquisitions, takeovers, stock purchases, asset purchases, joint ventures, and proxy contests that would result in foreign control of U.S. businesses engaged in interstate commerce in the United States. The U.S. business could be a corporation, a partnership, a sole proprietorship, or another business. The size of the U.S. operation is irrelevant.

Exon-Florio and the regulations adopted thereunder do not define the term *national security*. The Treasury Department has interpreted the term broadly to include not only defense contractors but also technology and other businesses. The term *control* includes any investment exceeding 10 percent ownership in a U.S. business by a foreign investor.

When a foreign investor proposes to acquire an interest in a U.S. business, it may voluntarily notify the U.S. government of its intention. If the president finds a threat to the national security, the acquisition may be prohibited. If the foreign investor does not notify the U.S. government and completes the acquisition, it remains indefinitely subject to divestment if the president subsequently determines that the acquisition threatens the national security. The president's decision is not subject to judicial review. ■

Chapter Summary

Proxy Solicitation, p. 617

Solicitation of Proxies

1. **Proxy.** Shareholders can exercise their rights to vote on the election of directors, mergers, charter amendments, and the like either in person or by *proxy*.

2. **Proxy card.** A proxy card is a written document signed by a shareholder that authorizes another person to vote the shareholder's shares.

Federal Proxy Rules

Section 14(a). This provision of the Securities Exchange Act of 1934 authorizes the *Securities and Exchange Commission (SEC)* to regulate the solicitation of proxies.

1. **Solicitation of proxies.** This occurs when management or others seek to obtain proxies from a corporation's shareholders.

2. **Proxy statement.** A proxy statement is a written document that must be given to shareholders by management and others who are soliciting shareholder proxies. The statement must fully

describe (a) the matter for which the proxy is being solicited, (b) who is soliciting the proxy, and (c) any other pertinent information.

3. *Filing with the SEC.* Proxy statements must be filed with the SEC at least 10 days before the materials are sent to shareholders.

Antifraud Provision

Section 14(a) of the 1934 Securities Exchange act prohibits misrepresentations or omissions of a material fact in proxy materials. The SEC, the U.S. Justice Department, shareholders, and others may sue the wrongdoer.

Proxy Contests

Proxy contests occur when opposing factions of shareholders and managers solicit proxies from other shareholders, the side that receives the greatest number of votes wins the proxy contest.

1. *Opposing groups:*
   a. *Incumbent group.* This is the management-sponsored slate of proposed directors.
   b. *Insurgent group.* This is the slate of proposed directors sponsored by the group that is challenging the incumbent group.

2. *Reimbursement of expenses.* In a proxy contest that involves a *policy issue*, the corporation pays the incumbent management's expenses, whether they win or lose the proxy contest. If the insurgent group wins the proxy contest, the corporation must reimburse its expenses, too. If the proxy contest concerned a *personal matter*, neither side may recover its expenses from the corporation.

Shareholder Resolution

These resolutions are submitted by a shareholder or group of shareholders to be considered and voted by the corporation's shareholders. Most shareholder resolutions concern social issues (e.g., protection of the environment, discontinuation of the manufacture and sale of dangerous products).

1. *Inclusion in proxy materials.* If management does not oppose the proposal, it may be included in the proxy materials issued by the corporation. If management opposes the shareholder resolution, the SEC rules on whether the proposal must be submitted to the shareholders in the corporation's proxy materials.

2. *Requirements.* To be included in the corporation's proxy materials, the shareholder resolution must (a) relate to the corporation's business, (b) concern policy issues (and not the day-to-day operations of the corporation), and (c) not concern the payment of dividends.

Mergers and Acquisitions, p. 620

Mergers and Acquisitions

Mergers, consolidations, and share exchanges are *friendly* combinations of corporations.

1. *Merger.* A merger occurs when one corporation is absorbed into another corporation and ceases to exist. The corporation that continues to exist after a merger is called the *surviving corporation*. The corporation that is absorbed in the merger and ceases to exist as a separate entity is called the *merged corporation*.

2. *Consolidation.* A consolidation occurs when two or more corporations combine to form an entirely new corporation. The new corporation is called the *consolidated corporation*.

3. *Share exchange.* A share exchange occurs when one corporation acquires all the shares of another corporation while both corporations retain their separate legal existence. The corporation that owns the shares of the other corporation is called the *parent corporation*. The corporation that is owned by the other corporation is called the *subsidiary corporation*.

Required Approvals

1. ***Required approvals.*** An ordinary merger or share exchange requires (a) the recommendation of the board of directors of each corporation and (b) an affirmative vote of the majority of shares of each corporation that is entitled to vote (unless a greater vote is required).

2. ***No shareholder vote required.*** The approval of the surviving corporation's shareholders is not required if the merger or share exchange increases the number of voting shares of the surviving corporation by 20 percent or less.

3. ***Articles of merger or share exchange.*** This document must be filed with the secretary of state when the merger or share exchange is completed.

Short-Form Mergers

A short-form merger is a merger between a *parent corporation* and a *subsidiary corporation* where the parent corporation owns 90 percent or more of the subsidiary corporation.

Required approval. Only the approval of the board of directors of the parent corporation is required to effectuate a short-form merger. The votes of the shareholders of either corporation and the board of directors of the subsidiary corporation are not required.

Sale or Lease of Assets

1. ***Sale or lease of assets not in the usual and regular course of business.*** This involves the sale, lease, or disposition by a corporation of all or substantially all its assets not in the usual and regular course of business.

2. ***Required approval.*** Such a sale requires (a) the recommendation of the board of directors and (b) an affirmative vote of the majority of the shares of the selling or leasing corporation that is entitled to vote (unless a greater vote is required).

Dissenting Shareholder Appraisal Rights

Shareholders who object to a proposed merger, share exchange, or sale or lease of all or substantially all the property of a corporation have a statutory right to have their shares valued by the court and receive cash payment of this value from the corporation.

1. ***Procedures.*** The corporation must notify shareholders of their appraisal rights. To obtain appraisal rights, the shareholder must (a) deliver written notice to the corporation of his or her intent to demand payment of his or her shares before the vote is taken and (b) not vote his or her shares in favor of the proposed action.

2. ***Fair value.*** If the shareholder does not accept the value offered by the corporation, the court will determine the *fair value* of the shares. The court may hire appraisers to assist in making this determination. Costs of this proceeding are usually borne by the corporation.

Tender Offers, p. 624

Tender Offers

A tender offer is an offer that an acquirer makes directly to a *target corporation's shareholders* in an effort to acquire the target corporation or control of the target corporation.

1. ***Tender offeror.*** The tender offeror is the party that makes a tender offer.

2. ***Target corporation.*** The target corporation is the corporation that is proposed to be acquired in a tender offer situation.

The Williams Act

This federal statute regulates all tender offers. The Securities and Exchange Commission (SEC) is empowered to administer the Williams Act.

Tender Offer Rules

1. *Notification.* The tender offeror does not have to notify the SEC or the target corporation's management until the tender offer is made.
2. *Completion.* The tender offer cannot be closed before 20 business days after the commencement of the offer.
3. *Extension.* The offer must be extended for 10 business days if the tender offeror increases the number of shares it will take or the price it will pay for the shares.
4. *Fair price rule.* This rule stipulates that any increase in price paid for shares tendered must be offered to all shareholders, even those who have previously tendered their shares.
5. *Pro rata rule.* This rule provides that shares must be purchased on a *pro rata basis* if too many shares are tendered.
6. *Withdrawal rights.* Shareholders who tender their shares have an absolute right to withdraw them at any time prior to the closing of the tender offer.

Antifraud Provision

Section 14(e). This provision of the Williams Act prohibits fraudulent, deceptive, and manipulative practices in connection with a tender offer.

Fighting a Tender Offer

The management of the target corporation often takes one or more of the following steps to try to defeat a hostile tender offer:

1. Persuade the shareholders not to tender their shares.
2. File delaying lawsuits (e.g., antitrust lawsuits).
3. Sell the *crown jewel* (e.g., a valuable asset that the tender offeror is particularly interested in acquiring).
4. Adopt *poison pills* (e.g., contract provisions that make contracts and leases expire).
5. Find a *white knight* to purchase the corporation in a friendly acquisition.
6. Conduct a *Pac-man tender offer* (i.e., a reverse tender offer to acquire the tender offeror).
7. Issue additional stock to friendly parties.
8. Create an *employee stock ownership plan (ESOP)* and issue stock to the ESOP.
9. Adopt *flip-over* and *flip-in rights plans* that make it more expensive for the tender offeror to acquire shares.
10. Pay *greenmail* by purchasing the shares held by the tender offeror at a premium.
11. Obtain a *standstill agreement* whereby the offeror agrees not to purchase shares of the target corporation for a stipulated period of time.
12. Engage in other strategies and tactics that make it more difficult for a tender offeror to complete its tender offer.

Business Judgment Rule

This rule protects the decisions of a board of directors that acts on an *informed basis*, in *good faith*, and in the *honest belief that the action taken was in the best interests of the corporation and its shareholders.*

Tender offers. The actions of the management of a target corporation in fighting a tender offer are judged by the business judgment rule. The defensive measure must be reasonable in relation to the threat posed.

State Antitakeover Statutes, p. 628

State Antitakeover Statutes

These statutes enacted by state legislatures are aimed at protecting corporations that are either incorporated in or doing business within the state from hostile takeovers.

Lawfulness. State antitakeover statutes are lawful if they do not conflict with the federal *Williams Act* or unduly burden interstate commerce in violation of the *Commerce Clause* of the U.S. Constitution.

Internet Exercises and Case Questions

Working the Web Internet Exercises

Activities

1. Research your own state law on antitakeover statutes. Compile examples. See **www.law.cornell.edu/topics/state_statutes.html#corporations**.

2. What is a *Phantom Stock?* For a set of definitions see **www.investopedia.com/categories/buzzwords.asp**.

3. Review your own state statutes on termination of corporations. Why do you think some lawyers advise their corporate clients who are planning to terminate to just allow the secretary of state to cause an administrative dissolution for failure to file the annual renewal application? See **www.law.cornell.edu/topics/state_statutes.html#corporations**.

4. Find state statutes that control the distribution of corporate assets at termination for nonprofit corporations. How does this differ from the rules in for-profit corporations? See **www.law.cornell.edu/topics/state_statutes.html#corporations**.

Critical Legal Thinking Cases

28.1 Proxy Disclosure   Western Maryland Company (Western) was a timbering and mining concern. A substantial portion of its stock was owned by CSX Minerals (CSX), its parent corporation. The remaining shares were owned by several minority shareholders, including Sanford E. Lockspeiser. Western's stock was not publicly traded. In 1983, the board of directors of Western voted to merge the company with CSX. Western distributed a proxy statement to the minority shareholders that stated that CSX would vote for the merger and recommended approval of the merger by the other shareholders. The proxy materials disclosed Western's natural resource holdings in terms of acreage of minerals and timber. It also stated real property values as carried on the company's books—that is, a book value of $17.04 per share. It included an opinion of the First Boston Corporation, an investment banking firm, that the merger was fair to shareholders; First Boston did not undertake an independent evaluation of Western's physical assets. Lockspeiser sued, alleging that the proxy materials were misleading because they did not state tonnage of Western's coal reserves, timber holdings in board feet, and actual value of Western's assets. Did Lockspeiser state a claim for relief? [*Lockspeiser v. Western Maryland Company*, 768 F.2d 558, 1985 U.S.App. Lexis 20476 (4th Cir. 1985)]

28.2 Proxy Contest   The Medfield Corporation (Medfield) was a publicly held corporation engaged in operating hospitals and other health care facilities. Medfield established March 1, 1974, as the date for its annual shareholders' meeting, at which time the board of directors would be elected. In its proxy statement, management proposed the incumbent slate of directors. A group known as the Medfield Shareholders Committee nominated a rival slate of candidates and also solicited proxies. Medfield sent proxy solicitation material to shareholders that:

1. Failed to disclose that Medfield had been overpaid more than $1.8 million by Blue Cross and this amount was due and owing Blue Cross.
2. Failed to disclose that Medicare funds were being withheld because of Medfield's nonpayment.
3. Failed to adequately disclose self-dealing by one of the directors with Medfield who owned part of a laboratory used by Medfield.
4. Failed to disclose that Medfield was attempting to sell two nursing homes.

5. Impugned the character, integrity, and personal reputation of one of the rival candidates by stating that he had previously been found liable for patent infringement when, in fact, the case had been reversed on appeal.

At the annual meeting, the incumbent slate of directors received 50 percent of the votes cast, against 44 percent of the insurgent slate of directors. The Gladwins, who own voting stock, sued to have the election overturned. Who wins? [*Gladwin v. Medfield Corporation*, 540 F.2d 1266, 1976 U.S.App. Lexis 6548 (5th Cir. 1976)]

28.3 Reimbursement for Expenses Incurred in a Proxy Contest   The Fairchild Engine and Airplane Corporation (Fairchild) was a privately held corporation whose management proposed the incumbent slate of directors for election at its annual shareholders' meeting. An insurgent slate of directors challenged the incumbents for election to the board. After the solicitation of proxies and a hard-fought proxy contest, the insurgent slate of directors was elected. Evidence showed that the proxy contest was waged over matters of corporate policy and for personal reasons. The old board of directors had spent $134,000 out of corporate funds to wage the proxy contest. The insurgents had spent $127,000 of their personal funds in their successful proxy contest and sought reimbursement from Fairchild for this amount. The payment of these expenses was ratified by a 16-to-1 majority vote of the stockholders. Mr. Rosenfeld, an attorney who owned 25 of the 2,300,000 outstanding shares of the corporation, filed an action to recover the amounts already paid by the corporation and to prevent any further payments of these expenses. Who wins? [*Rosenfeld v. Fairchild Engine and Airplane Corporation*, 128 N.E.2d 291, 1955 N.Y. Lexis 947 (N.Y. App. 1955)]

28.4 Shareholder Resolution   The Medical Committee for Human Rights (Committee), a nonprofit corporation organized to advance concerns for human life, received a gift of shares of Dow Chemical (Dow) stock. Dow manufactured napalm, a chemical defoliant that was used during the Vietnam conflict. Committee objected to the sale of napalm by Dow primarily because of its concerns for human life. Committee owned sufficient shares for a long enough time to propose a shareholders' resolution as long as it met the other requirements to propose such a resolution. Committee proposed that the following resolution be included in the proxy materials circulated by management for the 1969 annual shareholders' meeting:

RESOLVED, that the shareholders of the Dow Chemical company request that the Board of Directors, in accordance with the law, consider the advisability of adopting a resolution setting forth an amendment to the composite certificate of incorporation of the Dow Chemical Company that the company shall not make napalm.

Dow's management refused to include the requested resolution in its proxy materials. Committee sued, alleging that its resolution met the requirements to be included in the proxy materials. Who wins? [*Medical Committee for Human Rights v. Securities and Exchange Commission,* 432 F.2d 659, 1970 U.S.App. Lexis 8284 (D.C. Cir. 1970)]

28.5 Merger   During the last six months of 1980, the board of directors of Plant Industries, Inc. (Plant), under the guidance of Robert B. Bregman, the chief executive officer of the corporation, embarked on a course of action that resulted in the sale of several unprofitable subsidiaries. Bregman then engaged in a course of action to sell Plant National (Quebec) Ltd., a subsidiary that constituted Plant's entire Canadian operations. This was a profitable subsidiary that comprised over 50 percent of Plant's assets, sales, and profits. Do Plant's shareholders have to be accorded voting and appraisal rights regarding the sale of this subsidiary? [*Katz v. Bregman,* 431 A.2d 1274, 1981 Del.Ch. Lexis 449 (Del. Ch. 1981)]

28.6 Dissenting Shareholder Appraisal Rights   Over a period of several years, the Curtiss-Wright Corporation (Curtiss-Wright) purchased 65 percent of the stock of Dorr-Oliver Incorporated (Dorr-Oliver). In early 1979, Curtiss-Wright's board of directors decided that a merger with Dorr-Oliver would be beneficial to Curtiss-Wright. The board voted to approve a merger of the two companies and to pay $23 per share to the stockholders of Dorr-Oliver. The Dorr-Oliver board and 80 percent of Dorr-Oliver's shareholders approved the merger. The merger became effective on May 31, 1979. John Bershad, a minority shareholder of Dorr-Oliver, voted against the merger, but thereafter tendered his 100 shares and received payment of $2,300. Bershad subsequently sued, alleging that the $23 per share paid to Dorr-Oliver shareholders was grossly inadequate. Can Bershad obtain minority shareholder appraisal rights? [*Bershad v. Curtiss-Wright Corporation,* 535 A.2d 840, 1987 Del. Lexis 1313 (DE 1987)]

28.7 Fighting a Tender Offer   On October 30, 1981, Mobil Corporation (Mobil) made a tender offer to purchase up to 40 million outstanding common shares of stock in Marathon Oil Company (Marathon) for $85 per share in cash. It further stated its intentions to follow the purchase with a merger of the two companies. Mobil was primarily interested in acquiring Marathon's oil and mineral interests in certain properties, including the Yates Field. Marathon directors immediately held a board meeting and determined to find a white knight. Negotiations developed between Marathon and United States Steel Corporation (U.S. Steel). On November 18, 1981, Marathon and U.S. Steel entered into an agreement whereby U.S. Steel would make a tender offer for 30 million common shares of Marathon stock at $125 per share, to be followed by a merger of the two companies.

The Marathon–U.S. Steel agreement was subject to the following two conditions: (1) U.S. Steel was given an irrevocable option to purchase 10 million authorized but unissued shares of Marathon common stock for $90 per share (or 17 percent of Marthon's outstanding shares), and (2) U.S. Steel was given an option to purchase

Marathon's interest in oil and mineral rights in Yates Field for $2.8 billion (Yates Field option). The latter option could be exercised only if U.S. Steel's offer did not succeed and if a third party gained control of Marathon. Evidence showed that Marathon's interest in the Yates Field was worth up to $3.6 billion. Marathon did not give Mobil either of these two options. Mobil sued, alleging that these two options violated Section 14(e) of the Williams Act. Who wins? [*Mobil Corporation v. Marathon Oil Company,* 669 F.2d 366, 1981 U.S.App. Lexis 14958 (6th Cir. 1981)]

28.8 Fighting a Tender Offer   The Fruehauf Corporation (Fruehauf) is engaged in the manufacture of large trucks and industrial vehicles. The Edelman group (Edelman) made a cash tender offer for the shares of Fruehauf for $48.50 per share. The stock sold in the low $20-per-share range a few months earlier. Fruehauf's management decided to make a competing management-led leveraged buyout (MBO) tender offer for the company in conjunction with Merrill Lynch. The MBO would be funded using $375 million borrowed from Merrill Lynch, $375 million borrowed from Manufacturers Hanover Bank, and $100 million contributed by Fruehauf. Total equity contribution to the new company under the MBO would be only $25 million: $10 million to $15 million from management and the rest from Merrill Lynch. In return for their equity contributions, management would receive between 40 and 60 percent of the new company.

Fruehauf's management agreed to pay $30 million to Merrill Lynch for brokerage fees that Merrill Lynch could keep even if the deal did not go through. Management also agreed to a no-shop clause whereby they agreed not to seek a better deal with another bidder. Incumbent management received better information about the goings-on. They also gave themselves golden parachutes that would raise the money for management's equity position in the new company.

Edelman informed Fruehauf's management that it could top their bid, but Fruehauf's management did not give them the opportunity to present their offer. Management's offer was accepted. Edelman sued, seeking an injunction. did Fruehauf's management violate the business judgment rule? [*Edelman v. Fruehauf Corporation,* 798 F.2d 882, 1986 U.S.App. Lexis 27911 (6th Cir. 1986)]

28.9 Poison Pill Defense   Household International, Inc. (Household), is a diversified holding company with its principal subsidiaries engaged in financial services, transportation, and merchandising. On August 14, 1984, the board of directors of Household adopted a 48-page "Rights Plan" by a 14-to-2 vote. Basically, the plan provides that Household common stockholders are entitled to the issuance of one irrevocable right per common share if any party acquires 20 percent of Household's shares. The right permitted Household shareholders to purchase $200 of the common stock of the tender offeror for $100. In essence, this forced any party interested in taking over Household to negotiate with Household's directors. Dyson-Kissner-Moran Corporation (DKM), which was interested in taking over Household, filed suit, alleging that this flip-over rights plan violated the business judgment rule. Who wins? [*Moran v. Household International, Inc.,* 500 A.2d 1346, 1985 Del. Lexis 557 (DE 1985)]

28.10 State Antitakeover Statute   The state of Wisconsin enacted an antitakeover statute that protects corporations that are incorporated in Wisconsin and have their headquarters, substantial operations, or 10 percent of their shares of shareholders in the state. The statute prevents any party that acquires a 10 percent interest in a covered corporation from engaging in a business combination (e.g., merger) with the covered corporation for three years unless approval of the management is obtained in advance of the combination. Wisconsin firms cannot opt out of the law. This statute effectively eliminates hostile leveraged buyouts because buyers must rely on the assets and income of the target company to help pay off the debt incurred in effectuating the takeover.

Business Ethics Cases

28.11 Business Ethics   MCA, Inc. (MCA), a corporate holding company, owned 92 percent of the stock of Universal Pictures Company (Universal) and 100 percent of the stock of Universal City Studios, Inc. (Universal City). On March 25, 1966, these two subsidiaries merged pursuant to Delaware's short-form merger statute. The minority shareholders of Universal were offered $75 per share for their shares. Francis l. Du Pont & Company and other minority shareholders (Plaintiffs) rejected the offer and then perfected their dissenting shareholder appraisal rights. On March 29, 1973, the appraiser filed a final report in which he found the value of Universal stock to be $91.47 per share. Both parties filed exceptions to this report.

The parties' ultimate disagreement, of course, was over the value of the stock. Plaintiffs submitted that the true value was $131.89 per share; the defendant said it was $52.36. The computations were as follows:

Plaintiffs

Value Factor	Value	Weight	Result
Earnings	$129.12	70%	$90.38
Market	144.36	20	28.87
Assets	126.46	10	12.64
	Value per share		**$131.89**

Defendants

Value Factor	Value	Weight	Result
Earnings	$51.93	70%	$36.35
Dividends	41.66	20	8.33
Assets	76.77	10	7.68
	Value per share		**$52.36**

Appraiser

Value Factor	Value	Weight	Result
Earnings	$92.89	80%	$74.31
Assets	85.82	20	17.16
	Value per share		**$91.47**

The defendant took exception to the appraiser's failure to find that, in the years prior to merger, the industry was declining and that Universal was ranked near its bottom. And it argued that Universal was in the business of producing and distributing feature motion pictures for theatrical exhibition. It contended that such business, generally, was in a severe decline at the time of merger and that Universal, in particular, was in a vulnerable position because it had failed to diversify, its feature

Universal Foods (Universal) was a Wisconsin corporation covered by the statute. On December 1, 1988, Amanda Acquisition Corporation (Amanda) commenced a cash tender offer for up to 75 percent of the stock of Universal. Universal asserted the Wisconsin law. Is Wisconsin's antitakeover statute lawful? [*Amanda Acquisition Corporation v. Universal Foods*, 877 F.2d 496, 1989 U.S.App. Lexis 9024 (7th Cir. 1989)]

films were of low commercial quality, and, unlike other motion picture companies, substantially all of its film library had already been committed to distributors for television exhibition. In short, defendant pictures Universal was a weak "wasting asset" corporation in a sick industry with poor prospects for revival.

The stockholders saw a different company. They said that Universal's business was indeed the production and distribution of feature films, but not merely for theatrical exhibition. They argued that there was a dramatic increase in the television market for such feature films at the time of the merger. This new market, they contended, gave great new value to a fully amortized film library and significantly enhanced the value of Universal's current and future productions. They equated the television market to the acquisition of a new and highly profitable business whose earnings potential was just beginning to be realized at the time of the merger. Finally, said plaintiffs, the theatrical market itself was recovering in 1966. Thus, they painted the portrait of a well-situated corporation in a rejuvenated industry.

Did the parties act ethically in arriving at their proposed value of the company? What is the value of the minority shareholders' shares of Universal Pictures Company? [*Francis I. Du Pont & Company v. Universal City Studios, Inc.*, 312 A.2d 344, 1973 Del.Ch. Lexis 123 (Del. Ch. 1973)]

28.12 Business Ethics   Realist, Inc. (Realist), is a Delaware corporation that has its principal place of business in Wisconsin. In March 1988, Royal Business Group, Inc. (Royal), a New Hampshire corporation, acquired eight percent of the outstanding voting stock of Realist. Royal sent a series of letters to Realist, declaring its intention to acquire all of Realist's outstanding shares at an above-market premium. Realist repulsed Royal's overtures. Unbeknownst to Royal, Realist began negotiations to acquire Ammann Laser Technik AG (Ammann), a Swiss-based company.

Royal instituted a proxy contest and nominated two candidates for the two Realist directorships to be filed at Realist's June 6, 1989, annual shareholders' meeting. Realist and Royal both submitted proxy statements to Realist's shareholders.

The insurgent Royal nominees prevailed. On June 30, 1989, Realist announced that it had acquired Ammann. This acquisition made Realist much less attractive as a takeover target. Royal immediately withdrew its offer to acquire Realist and sued Realist to recover the $350,000 it had spent in connection with the proxy contest. Royal alleged that Realist had engaged in fraud in violation of Section 14(a) of the Securities Exchange Act of 1934 by failing to disclose its secret negotiations with Ammann in its proxy materials. The basis of Royal's complaint was that if Realist had disclosed that it intended to acquire Ammann, Royal would not have engaged in the costly proxy contest. Is Realist liable to Royal? Did Realist act unethically in seeking to acquire Ammann to thwart Royal's takeover attempt? [*Royal Business Group, Inc. v, Realist, Inc.*, 933 F.2d 1056, 1991 U.S.App. Lexis 10389 (1st Cir. 1991)]

Briefing the Case Writing Assignment

Read Case A.28 in the Case Appendix [*Neal v. Alabama By-Products Corporation*]. This case is excerpted from the court of chancery's opinion. Review and brief the case. In your brief, be sure to answer the following questions:

1. What are dissenting shareholder appraisal rights?

2. What type of transaction occurred that triggered these rights in this case?

3. What value were the dissenting shareholders offered in the original transaction? What value was offered by the corporation in the court proceeding? What value were the dissenting shareholders seeking in the court proceeding?

4. What amount did the court determine to be the fair value of the shares?

Endnotes

1. 15 U.S.C. 78n(a).
2. Section 13(d) of the Securities Exchange Act of 1934 requires that any party that acquires 5 percent or more of any equity security of a company registered with the SEC must report the acquisition to the SEC and disclose its intentions regarding the acquisition. This is public information.

3. 15 U.S.C. 78n(e).
4. *Smith v. Van Gorkum*, 488 A.2d 858, 1985 Del. Lexis 421 (Del. 1985).
5. *Unocal Corporation v. Mesa Petroleum Company*, 493 A.2d 946, 1985 Del. Lexis 482 (DE 1985).

Limited Liability Companies

29

"Justice is the end of government. It is the end of civil society. It ever has been, and ever will be pursued, until it be obtained, or until liberty be lost in the pursuit."

—James Madison
The Federalist No. 51 (1788)

Chapter Objectives

After studying this chapter, you should be able to:

1. Define limited liability company (LLC).
2. Describe the process of organizing an LLC.
3. Describe the limited liability shield provided by an LLC.
4. Compare a member-managed LLC to a manager-managed LLC.
5. Determine when members and managers owe fiduciary duties of loyalty and care to an LLC.

Chapter Contents

- Limited Liability Company (LLC)
- Formation of an LLC
- Member-Managed and Manager-Managed LLCs
- Dissolution of an LLC

Owners may choose to operate a business as a **limited liability company (LLC)**. The use of the LLCs as a form of conducting business in the United States is of rather recent origin. In 1977, Wyoming was the first state in the United States to enact legislation creating an LLC as a legal form for conducting business. This new form of business received little attention until the early 1990s, when several more states enacted legislation to allow the creation of LLCs. The evolution of LLCs then grew at blinding speed, with all the states having enacted LLC statues by 1998. Most LLC laws are quite similar, although some differences do exist between these state statutes.

An LLC is an unincorporated business entity that combines the most favorable attributes of general partnerships, limited partnerships, and corporations. An LLC may elect to be taxed as a partnership, the owners can manage the business, and the owners have limited liability. Many entrepreneurs who begin new businesses choose the LLC as their legal form for conducting business. The formation and operation of LLCs are discussed in this chapter.

Limited Liability Company (LLC)

Limited liability companies are creatures of state law, not federal law. LLCs can only be created pursuant to the laws of the state in which the LLC is being organized. These statutes, commonly referred to as **limited liability company codes**, regulate the formation, operation, and dissolution of LLCs. The state legislature may amend its LLC statute at any time. The courts interpret state LLC statutes to decide LLC and member disputes.

A limited liability company is a separate **legal entity** (or legal person) distinct from its members [ULLCA § 201]. Limited liability companies are treated as artificial persons who can sue or be sued, enter into and enforce contracts, hold title to and transfer property, and be found civilly and criminally liable for violations of law.

The Uniform Limited Liability Company Act

Business Brief

An LLC combines the tax benefits of a partnership with the limited personal liability attributes of a corporation.

In 1995, the National Conference of Commissioners of Uniform State Laws (a group of lawyers, judges, and legal scholars) issued the **Uniform Limited Liability Company Act (ULLCA)**. The ULLCA codifies limited liability company law. Its goal is to estab-

London, England. Great Britain and many European countries offered forms of limited liability businesses long before the United States developed the limited liability company (LLC).

lish comprehensive LLC law that is uniform throughout the United States. The ULLCA covers most problems that arise in the formation, operation, and termination of LLCs. The ULLCA is not law unless a state adopts it as its LLC statute. Many states have adopted all or part of the ULLCA as their limited liability company law. Because it is so important, the ULLCA forms the basis of the study of limited liability companies in this chapter.

Member's Limited Liability

The owners of LLCs are usually called **members**. The general rule is that members are not personally liable to third parties for the debts, obligations, and liabilities of an LLC beyond their capital contribution. Members are said to have **limited liability** (see Exhibit 29.1). The debts, obligations, and liabilities of an LLC, whether arising from contracts, torts, or otherwise, are solely those of the LLC [ULLCA § 303(a)].

Consider This Example   Jasmin, Shan-Y1, and Vanessa form an LLC, and each contributes $25,000 in capital. The LLC operates for a period of time, during which it borrows money from banks and purchases goods on credit from suppliers. After some time, the LLC experiences financial difficulty and goes out of business. If the LLC fails with $500,000 in debts, each of the members will lose her capital contribution of $25,000 but will not be personally liable for the rest of the unpaid debts of the LLC.

The failure of an LLC to observe the usual company formalities is not ground for imposing personal liability on the members of the LLC [ULLCA § 303(b)]. For example, if the LLC does not keep minutes of the company's meetings, the members do not become personally liable for the LLC's debts.

In the following case, the court addressed the issue of the limited liability of a member of an LLC.

> There shall be one law for the native and for the stranger who sojourns among you.
>
> Moses
> *Exodus 12:49*

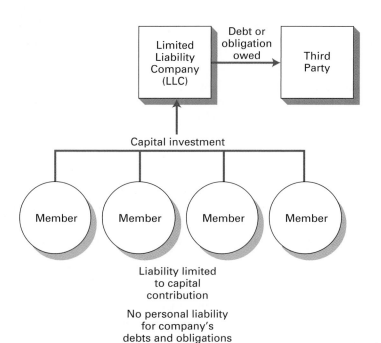

Exhibit 29.1

Limited Liability Company (LLC)

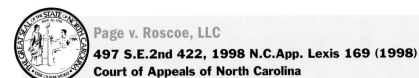

Page v. Roscoe, LLC

497 S.E.2nd 422, 1998 N.C.App. Lexis 169 (1998)

Court of Appeals of North Carolina

Background and Facts

Dale C. Bone was a member of Roscoe, LLC, an LLC organized under the laws of North Carolina. In August 1994, Roscoe, LLC, purchased two acres of land near the town of Apex, North Carolina. In January 1995, Apex approved Roscoe, LLC's plan to construct and operate a propane gas bulk storage and distribution facility on the land. This use was permitted under Apex's zoning ordinance. In April 1995. Daylene Page and other homeowners in the area sued Roscoe, LLC, and Dale C. Bone, alleging that the gas storage facility, if constructed, would constitute a nuisance. In December 1995, after the trial court denied the plaintiffs' motion to obtain a preliminary injunction against construction of the facility, the plaintiffs dismissed the lawsuit. Subsequently, Bone sued the plaintiffs for sanctions to recover attorneys' fees he had spent in defending against the plaintiffs' lawsuit. The trial court ordered the plaintiffs to pay Bone's attorneys' fees. The plaintiffs appealed.

Issue

Were the sanctions warranted against the plaintiffs for naming an individual member of an LLC in the lawsuit they brought against the LLC?

Court's Reasoning

The court of appeals found that the allegations against Bone individually were not well-grounded in law. N.C. Gen.Stat. § 57C-3-30 (1993) provides in pertinent part:

(a) A person who is a member or manager, or both, of a limited liability company is not liable for the obligations of a limited lia-

bility company solely by reason of being a member or manager or both, and does not become so by participating, in whatever capacity, in the management or control of the business.

(b) A member of a limited liability company is not a proper party to proceedings by or against a limited liability company.

The court of appeals held that the record sustained the conclusion that no acts by Bone, individually, were properly alleged. Therefore, under the above statute, it was improper to name an individual member of an LLC as a party defendant without any evidence to support it.

Decision and Remedy

The court of appeals held that Bone, as a member of Roscoe, LLC, was not liable as a matter of law for the acts of the LLC and was therefore improperly named as a defendant in the lawsuit filed by the plaintiffs. The plaintiffs were held liable for sanctions and were required to pay Bone's attorneys' fees that he expended in defending against the plaintiffs' lawsuit. The court of appeals affirmed the trial court's judgment in favor of Bone.

Case Questions

Critical Legal Thinking   Should members of an LLC be released from personal liability for the debts and obligations incurred by the LLC?

Business Ethics   Did the plaintiff homeowners act ethically in naming Bone as a defendant? Why do you think they named Bone as a defendant?

Contemporary Business   Is this case good precedent for businesspersons wishing to conduct business as LLCs?

Personal Guarantees

A member is personally liable for the debts of an LLC only if he or she agrees to be in either the articles of organization or other writing, or if he or she personally guarantees the repayment of the LLC's debts [ULLCA § 303(c)].

Business Brief

A member is personally liable if he or she personally guarantees repayment of the debts of LLC.

Consider This Example   Patricia, Arnold, and Emory form a new LLC. When they go to a bank to have the LLC borrow money from the bank, the bank refuses to make the loan to such a new LLC unless the members personally guarantee the loan. To obtain the loan, Patricia, Arnold, and Emory sign personal guarantees with the bank, agreeing to repay the loan if the LLC does not. In this case, if the LLC fails to repay the loan, the bank may enforce the personal guarantees and recover the amount of the loan from the members.

Business Brief

An LLC is liable for any loss or injury caused to anyone as a result of a wrongful act or omission by a member, a manager, an agent, or an employee of the LLC who commits the wrongful act while acting within the ordinary course of business of the LLC or with authority of the LLC.

Liability of an LLC

An LLC is liable for any loss or injury caused to anyone as a result of a wrongful act or omission by a member, a manager, an agent, or an employee of the LLC who commits the wrongful act while acting within the ordinary course of business of the LLC or with authority of the LLC [ULLCA § 302].

Consider This Example   Sable, Silvia, and Samantha form the SSS, LLC, to own and operate a business. Each member contributes $10,000 capital. While on LLC business, Sable drives her automobile and accidently hits and injures Damon. Damon can recover damages for his injuries from Sable personally because she committed the negligent act. Damon can also recover damages from the SSS, LLC, because Sable was acting within the scope of the ordinary business of the LLC when the accident occurred. Silvia and Samantha have limited liability only up to their capital contribution in the SSS, LLC.

Liability of Managers

Managers of LLCs are not personally liable for the debts, obligations, and liabilities of the LLC they manage [ULLCA § 303(a)].

Consider This Example   An LLC that does real estate development hires Sarah Goldstein, a nonmember, to be its president. While acting within the scope of her LLC authority, Sarah signs a loan agreement whereby the LLC borrows $1 million from a bank to complete the construction of an office building. If the LLC subsequently suffers financial difficulty and defaults on the bank loan, Sarah is not personally responsible for the loan. The LLC is liable for the loan, but Sarah is not because she is the manager of the LLC.

In the following case, the court enforced a personal guarantee against a manager of an LLC.

> **Business Brief**
>
> Managers of LLCs are not personally liable for the debts, obligations, and liabilities of the LLCs they manage.

Case 29.2
Personal Guarantee

Creative Resource Management, Inc. v. Soskin
1998 Tenn.App. Lexis 788 (1998)
Court of Appeals of Tennessee

Background and Facts

Nashville Pro Hockey, LLC, was a limited liability company organized under the laws of Tennessee. The LLC owned and operated the Nashville Nighthawks, a minor league professional hockey team. On September 4, 1996, Nashville Pro Hockey, LLC, contracted with Creative Resource Management, Inc. (CRM), whereby CRM, for fees and other consideration, would provide employee leasing services to Nashville Pro Hockey, LLC. The contract was signed by Barry Soskin, the president of Nashville Pro Hockey, LLC. A paragraph in the contract provided "By affixing my hand and seal to this agreement, I personally guarantee any and all payments payable as represented and outlined in this agreement."

Nashville Pro Hockey, LLC, failed, owing CRM $29,626. CRM sued Nashville Pro Hockey, LLC, and Barry Soskin to recover the unpaid compensation. Soskin defended, alleging that his signature on the contract was in his representative capacity only and not in his individual capacity as a guarantor. The trial court agreed and granted summary judgment to Soskin. CRM appealed.

Issue

Did Soskin's signature on the contract constitute a personal guarantee for the payment of the debt of Nashville Pro Hockey, LLC, to CRM?

Court's Reasoning

The court of appeals noted that the words "I personally guarantee any and all payments payable as represented and outlined in this agreement" reflect indisputably a guarantee by someone. Soskin insisted that he signed only as a representative of the LLC. The stark fact was that the words "I personally guarantee" were meaningless if applied to Nashville Pro Hockey, LLC, and not to Barry Soskin individually. The court of appeals held that because the words "I personally guarantee" cannot refer to Nashville Pro Hockey, LLC, and retain any meaning at all in the context of the agreement, they must of necessity reflect the personal guarantee of Barry Soskin.

Decision and Remedy

The court of appeals held that Soskin was a guarantor and that he was liable to repay the money owed to CRM by Nashville Pro Hockey, LLC. The court of appeals reversed the judgment of the trial court and granted summary judgment to CRM.

Case Questions

Critical Legal Thinking   In this case, a contracting party, CRM, was able to break the limited liability shield of an LLC and have a manager of the LLC personally guarantee its contract with the LLC. Are tort victims of negligent conduct of an LLC's employees and agents granted the same benefit?

Business Ethics   Did Soskin act ethically in arguing that he was not liable on the contract? Was the language of the contract clear?

Contemporary Business   What purpose do personal guarantees serve in business transactions?

Liability of the Tortfeasors

A person who intentionally or unintentionally (negligently) causes injury or death to another person is called a **tortfeasor**. A tortfeasor is personally liable to persons he or she injures, and to the heirs of persons who die because of his or her conduct. This rule applies to members and managers of LLCs. Thus, if a member or a manager of an LLC negligently causes injury or death to another person, he or she is personally liable to the injured person or the heirs of a deceased person.

Taxation of LLCs

Business Brief

For federal income tax purposes, an LLC is taxed as a partnership unless it elects to be taxed as a corporation.

Under the Internal Revenue Code and regulations adopted by the Internal Revenue Service (IRS), for federal income tax purposes, an LLC is taxed as a partnership unless it elects to be taxed as a corporation. Thus, an LLC is not taxed at the entity level, but its income or losses "flow through" to the members' individual income tax returns. This avoids double taxation. Most LLCs accept the default status of being taxed as a partnership instead of electing to be taxed as a corporation.

Powers of an LLC

Morality cannot be legislated, but behavior can be regulated. Judicial decrees may not change the heart, but they can restrain the heartless.

Martin Luther King, Jr.
Strength to Love (1963)

An LLC has the same powers as an individual to do all things necessary or convenient to carry on its business or affairs. These include the power to own and transfer personal property; sell, lease, and mortgage real property; make contracts and guarantees; borrow and lend money; issue notes and bonds; sue and be sued; and take other actions to conduct the affairs and business of the LLC [ULLCA § 112].

Contemporary Environment

Why Operate a Business as a Limited Liability Company (LLC)?

Why should an LLC be used instead of an S corporation or a partnership? S corporations and partnerships are subject to many restrictions and adverse consequences that do not exist with an LLC. Some differences are:

- S corporations cannot have shareholders other than estates, certain trusts, and individuals (who cannot be nonresident aliens). S corporations can have no more than 75 shareholders and one class of stock and may not own more than 80 percent of another corporation. LLCs have no such restrictions.

- In a general partnership, the partners are personally liable for the obligations of the partnership. Members of LLCs have limited liability.

- A limited partnership must have at least one general partner who is personally liable for the obligations of the partnership (although this partner can be a corporation). Limited partners are precluded from participating in the management of the business. An LLC provides limited liability to all members, even though they participate in management of the business. ■

Formation of an LLC

The great can protect themselves, but the poor and humble require the arm and shield of the law.

Andrew Jackson

Most LLCs are organized to operate businesses, real estate developments, and such. LLCs cannot operate the practices of certain professionals, such as accountants, lawyers, and doctors who can operate as a limited liability partnerships (LLPs), as discussed in Chapter 25.

An LLC can be organized in only one state, even though it can conduct business in all other states. When choosing a state for organization, the members should consider the LLC codes of the states under consideration. For the sake of convenience, most LLCs, particularly smaller ones, choose the state in which the LLC will be doing most of its business as the state of organization.

When starting a new LLC, the organizers must choose a name for the entity. The name must contain the words "limited liability company" or "limited company" or the abbreviation "L.L.C.," "LLC," "L.C.," or "LC." "Limited" may be abbreviated as "Ltd.," and "company" may be abbreviated as "Co." [ULLCA § 105(a)].

Articles of Organization

LLCs are creatures of statute. As such, certain formalities must be taken and statutory requirements met to form an LLC.

Under the ULLCA, an LLC may be organized by one or more persons. Some states require at least two members to organize an LLC. In states where an LLC may be organized by only one member, sole proprietors can obtain the benefit of the limited liability shield of an LLC.

An LLC is formed by delivering **articles of organization** to the office of the secretary of state of the state of organization for filing. If the articles are in proper form, the secretary of state will file the articles. The existence of an LLC begins when the articles of organization are filed. The filing of the articles of organization by the secretary of state is conclusive proof that the organizers have satisfied all conditions necessary to create the LLC [ULLCA § 202].

Under the ULLCA, the articles of organization of an LLC must set forth [ULLCA § 203]:

1. The name of the LLC.
2. The address of the LLC's initial office.
3. The name and address of the initial agent for service of process.
4. The name and address of each organizer.
5. Whether the LLC is a term LLC and, if so, the term specified.
6. Whether the LLC is to be a manager-managed LLC and, if so, the name and address of each manager.
7. Whether one or more of the members of the LLC are to be personally liable for the LLC's debts and obligations.

The articles of organization may set forth provisions from the members' operating agreement and any other matter not inconsistent with law. A sample articles of organization document is set forth in Exhibit 29.2. The articles of organization may be amended at any time by filing *articles of amendment* with the secretary of state [ULLCA § 204].

Duration

An LLC is an at-will LLC unless it is designated as a **term LLC** and the duration of the term is specified in the articles of organization [ULLCA § 203(a)(5)]. The duration of a term LLC may be specified in any manner that sets forth a specific and final date for the dissolution of the LLC. For example, periods specified as "50 years from the date of filing of the articles of organizations end "the period ending January 1, 2050" are valid to create a term LLC. An **at-will LLC** has no specified term.

Exhibit 29.2

Sample Articles of
Organization

**ARTICLES OF ORGANIZATION
FOR FLORIDA LIMITED LIABILITY COMPANY**

ARTICLE I - NAME
The name of the Limited Liability Company is
iCitrusSystems.com

ARTICLE II - ADDRESS
The mailing address and street address of the principal office of the Limited Liability
Company is

3000 Dade Boulevard
Suite 200
Miami Beach, Florida 33139

ARTICLE III - DURATION
The period of duration for the Limited Liability Company shall be
50 years

ARTICLE IV - MANAGEMENT
The Limited Liability Company is to be managed by a manager and the name and
address of such manager is

Susan Escobar
1000 Collins Avenue
Miami Beach, Florida 33141

_____
Thomas Blandford

_____
Pam Rosales

Capital Contribution

Business Brief

A member's capital contribution may
be money, tangible or intangible
property, services performed or
promised to be performed, promissory notes, or other agreements to
contribute cash or property.

A member's capital contribution to an LLC may be in the form of money, personal property, real property, other tangible property, intangible property (e.g., a patent), services
performed, contracts for services to be performed, promissory notes, or other agreements
to contribute cash or property [ULLCA § 401].

A member's obligation to contribute capital is not excused by the member's death, disability, or other inability to perform. If a member cannot make the required contribution of
property or services, he or she is obligated to contribute money equal to the value of the
promised contribution. The LLC or any creditor who extended credit to the LLC in reliance
on the promised contribution may enforce the promised obligation [ULLCA § 402].

Certificate of Interest

An LLC's operating agreement may provide that a member's ownership interest may be
evidenced by a **certificate of interest** issued by the LLC [ULLCA § 501(c)]. The certificate of interest acts the same as a stock certificate issued by a corporation.

Operating Agreement

Members of an LLC may enter into an **operating agreement** that regulates the affairs of
the company and the conduct of its business and governs relations among the members,
managers, and company [ULLCA § 103(a)]. The operating agreement may be amended
by the approval of all members unless otherwise provided in the agreement. The operating
agreement and amendments may be oral but are usually written. Sample provisions from
an operating agreement appear in Exhibit 29.3.

Exhibit 29.3

Sample Provisions from an LLC Operating Agreement

Management

1. Management by Managers The management of the Company's shall be vested in Managers designated by the Members. The Members hereby designate each of Nikki Nguyen, Frederick Richards, and Sylvia Maiorescu to be the initial Managers of the Company.

2. Powers of Managers The property, business, and affairs of the company will be managed, and the conduct of its business will be controlled by, the Managers. The Managers shall have the following rights, powers, and obligations as provided in the Limited Liability Company Act and as otherwise provided by law. The Managers shall have the following powers and the Managers are authorized on behalf of the Company to do or cause to be done the following:

(i) To supervise with respect to the property, business, and affairs of the Company and hire, on behalf of the Company, such professionals or other experts as may be necessary or desirable in connection therewith.

(ii) To determine, in their sole judgment, the amount, manner of payment, and date of any Distributions to be made to the Members hereunder.

(iii) To make any and all filings on behalf of the Company and its Members as they shall deem necessary, including, without limitation, filings of articles or certificates with the Secretary of State and the filing of such documents, forms, and requests for exemption as may be required pursuant to federal and state securities laws.

(iv) To make such filings with governmental and other authorities and to take any and all other actions as may be necessary to maintain the limited liability of the Members of the Company.

(v) To establish and maintain bank accounts, including savings accounts and demand deposit accounts, and cash management accounts.

(vi) To do generally all things in connection with any of the foregoing, generally manage, oversee, and administer the property, business, and affairs of the Company and execute all documents on behalf of the Company in connection therewith and sign or accept all checks, notes, and drafts on the Company's behalf and, except as expressly restricted herein, pay as Company expenses all costs or expenses connected with the operation or management of the Company.

3. Managers as Agents The Managers shall be agents of the Company for the purpose of transacting its business, and the acts of the Managers, including the execution in the name of the Company of any instrument, for apparently carrying on in the usual way the business of the Company shall bind the Company, unless (1) the the Manager acting has in fact no authority to act for the Company in the particular matter and (2) the Person with whom such Manager is dealing has knowledge of the fact that such Manager has no such authority. No Member, solely by reason of being a Member, shall be an agent of the Company for the purpose of transacting its business except to the extent that authority has been expressly delegated to such Member in writing by the Managers or by the provisions in this Operating Agreement. An act of a Member or the Managers that is not apparently for the carrying on of the business of the Company in the usual way shall not bind the Company unless authorized in fact by the Company in the particular matter. No act of a Member, a Manager or other agent of the Company in contravention of a restriction on authority shall bind the Company to Persons having knowledge of such restriction.

4. Duties of Managers Each Manager shall perform his or her duties in good faith and with that degree of care that an ordinarily prudent person in a like position would use under similar circumstances. In performing their duties, each Manager shall be entitled to rely on information, opinions, reports, or statements, including financial statements and other financial data, in each case prepared or presented by: (1) one or more agents or employees of the Company or (2) counsel, accountants or other Persons as to matters that such Manager believes to be within such Person's professional or expert competence, provided such Manager has no knowledge concerning the matter in question that would cause such reliance to be unwarranted. A Person who so performs his or her duties in accordance with this Section shall have no liability by reason of being or having been a Manager of the Company.

5. Qualification of Managers A Manager may, but need not, be a Member of the Company.

6. Term of Managers Each Manager shall hold office and have the terms and responsibilities accorded to him or her by this Operating Agreement until resignation or removal by the Members.

7. Election of Managers Each initial Manager shall hold office until the earlier of the first annual meeting of the Company or until resignation or removal by the Members. The Members shall thereafter vote to elect or designate any subsequent Managers of the Company. Any Manager of the Company may be removed or replaced with or without cause by a vote of a Majority in Interest of the Members entitled to vote thereon.

8. Action by Managers The Managers shall manage the Company by the affirmative vote of a majority of the Managers. Any action required or permitted to be taken by the Managers may be taken without a vote if all of the Managers consent thereto in writing and such writing is filed with the records of the Company. The Managers may participate in a meeting by means of conference telephone or similar communications equipment by means of which all persons participating in the meeting hear each other. Such participation shall constitute presence in person at such meeting.

9. Resignation of Managers A Manager may resign at any time by giving written notice to the Company. However, if such resignation violates any provision contained in this Operating Agreement or the provision of any contractual agreement between such Manager and the Company, the Company may recover from such Manager damages for such breach as provided in this Operating Agreement or by contract or law. The election of a Manager shall not of itself create contract rights in favor of any such party.

10. Vacancies Vacancies occurring among the Managers shall be filled by the vote of a Majority in Interest of the Members entitled to vote thereon. Any Manager chosen to fill a vacancy shall serve the unexpired term of his or her predecessor.

11. Fees and Compensation The Company may pay the Managers, or any accountants, agents, attorneys, consultants or advisors to the Company, compensation, and fees in compensation for services rendered to the Company. Any such fees shall be treated as expenses of the Company and shall not be deemed to constitute Distributions to the recipient of any Profit, Loss or capital of the Company.

12. Reimbursement The Company shall reimburse the Managers for all ordinary and necessary out-of-pocket expenses incurred by them on behalf of the Company. Such reimbursement shall be treated as an expense of the Company that shall be deducted in computing the Net Cash Flow and shall not be deemed to constitute a distributive share of Profits or a Distribution or return of capital to the Managers, and such reimbursement shall be made out of the assets of the Company. The Managers' sole determination of which expenses may be reimbursed and the amount thereof shall be conclusive.

13. Indemnification To the fullest extent permitted by law, the Company shall indemnify and hold harmless each Manager from and against any and all losses, claims, damages, liabilities, or expenses of whatever nature, as incurred, arising out of or relating to the fact that such party was or is a Manager of the Company. Notwithstanding the foregoing, no indemnification may be made to such a Manager if a judgment or other final adjudication adverse to such Manager establishes (1) that his or her acts were commited in bad faith or were the result of active and deliberate dishonesty and were material to the cause of action so adjudicated or (2) that he or she personally gained in fact a financial profit or other advantage to which he or she was not legally entitled.

14. Interested Managers No contract or other transaction between the Company and one or more of the Managers or between the Company and any other limited liability company or other business entity in which one or more of the Managers are managers, directors, or officers or have a substantial financial interest, shall be either void or voidable for this reason alone or by reason alone that such Manager or Managers were present at the meeting of Managers which approved such contract or transaction or that his or her or their votes were counted for such purposes, (i) if the material facts as to such Manager's interest in such contract or transaction and as to any such common managership, directorship, officership, or financial interest are disclosed in good faith or known to the other Managers, and the Managers approve such contract or transaction by a vote sufficient for such purpose without counting the vote of such interested Manager or, if the votes of the disinterested Managers are insufficient to constitute an act of the Managers by unanimous vote of the disinterested Managers or (ii) if the material facts as to such Manager's interest in such contract or transaction and as to any common managership, directorship, officership, or financial interest are disclosed in good faith or known to the Members entitled to vote thereon, and such contract or transaction is approved by the vote of such Members.

Conversion of an Existing Business to an LLC

Many LLCs are formed by entrepreneurs to start new businesses. In addition, an existing business may want to convert to an LLC to obtain its tax benefits and limited liability shield. General partnerships, limited partnerships, and corporations may be converted to LLCs if the following requirements are met [ULLCA § 902]:

1. An **agreement of conversion** is drafted that sets forth the terms of the conversion.
2. The terms of the conversion are approved by all the parties or by the number or percentage of owners required for conversion.
3. Articles of organization of the LLC are filed with the secretary of state. The articles must state that the LLC was previously another form of business and the prior business's name.

The conversion takes effect when the articles of organization are filed with the secretary of state or at any later date specified in the articles of organization. When the conversion takes effect, all property owned by the prior business vests in the LLC, and all debts, obligations, and liabilities of the prior business become those of the LLC [ULLCA § 903].

Dividing an LLC's Profits and Losses

Unless otherwise agreed, the ULLCA mandates that a member has the right to an equal share in the LLC's profits [ULLCA § 405(a)]. This is a default rule that the members can override by agreement and is usually a provision in their operating agreement. For example, in many instances, the members may not want the profits of the LLC to be shared equally. This would normally occur if the capital contributions of the members were unequal. If the members want the profits divided in the same proportion as their capital contributions, that should be specified in the operating agreement.

Consider This Example   Lilly and Harrison form an LLC. Lilly contributes $75,000 capital, and Harrison contributes $25,000 capital. They do not have an agreement as to how profits are to be shared. If the LLC makes $100,000 in profits, under the ULLCA, Lilly and Harrison will share the profits equally—$50,000 each. To avoid this outcome, Lilly and Harrison should agree in their operating agreement how they want the profits to be divided.

Losses from an LLC are shared equally unless otherwise agreed. Sometimes members will not want to divide losses equally and maybe not even in the same way as their capital contributions. If the LLC has chosen to be taxed as a partnership, the losses from an LLC flow to the members' individual income tax returns. Losses from an LLC can sometimes be offset against members' gains from other sources. Therefore, the members may want to agree to divide the losses so that the members who can use them to offset other income will receive a greater share of the losses.

Profits and losses from an LLC do not have to be distributed in the same proportion. For example, a member who has the right to a 10 percent share of profits may be given the right to receive 25 percent of the LLC's losses.

Distributional Interest

A member's ownership interest in an LLC is called a **distributional interest**. A member's distributional interest in an LLC is personal property and may be transferred in whole or in part [ULLCA § 501(b)]. Unless otherwise provided in the operating agreement a transfer of an interest in an LLC does not entitle the transferee to become a member of the LLC or to exercise any right of a member. A transfer entitles the transferee to receive only distributions from the LLC to which the transferor would have been entitled [ULLCA § 502]. A transferee of a distributional interest becomes a member of the LLC if it is so provided in the operating agreement or if all the other members of the LLC consent [ULLCA § 503(a)].

Consider This Example   Cleveland, Heather, and Archibald are members of the Boston Tea Party, LLC; each owns a one-third interest in the LLC, and the members agree to divide the distributions equally in one-third portions. The LLC's operating agreement does not provide that a transferee of a distributional interest will become a member. Cleveland sells his one-third interest to Theodore. The members do not consent to allow Theodore to become a member. The LLC makes $99,999 in profits. Theodore is entitled to receive one-third of the distributions ($33,333). Theodore is not a member of the LLC, however.

A transferee who transfers his or her distributional interest is not released from liability for the debts, obligations, and liabilities of the LLC [ULLCA § 503(c)].

> **Business Brief**
>
> A transferee of a distributional interest in an LLC receives the right to receive profit and other distributions of the LLC.

> **Business Brief**
>
> Members of member-managed LLCs and managers of manager-managed LLCs owe fiduciary duties of loyalty and care to the LLC.

Contemporary Environment

DreamWorks SKG, LLC: Script for a Movie Company

In 1995, Steven Spielberg, Jeffrey Katzenberg, and David Geffen formed **Dream Works SKG**, which is a major movie and recording production company. Spielberg's fame and money came from directing films, Katzenberg had been a leading executive at Disney, and Geffen built and sold a major record company. These multimillionaire, multimedia giants combined their talents to form a formidable entertainment company.

DreamWorks was formed as a Delaware LLC. The organizers chose an LLC because it is taxed as a partnership, and the profits (or losses) flow directly to the owners, but like a corporation, the owners are protected from personal liability beyond their capital contributions.

DreamWorks issued several classes of interests. The three principals put up $100 million ($33.3 million each) for **"SKG" stock**, which grants the principals 100 percent voting control and 67 percent of the firm's profits. In addition, each principal has multiyear employment contracts plus other benefits.

DreamWorks raised the other $900 million of its $1 billion capital from other investors, who received one-third of future profits. The other investors were issued the following classes of stock:

Class	Investment
A	Outside investors. Class A stock was sold to big investors with over $20 million to invest. Microsoft's confounder, Paul Allen, purchased $500 million of Class A stock. Class A investors got seats on the board of directors.
S	Outside investors. Class S stock was issued for smallish, "strategic" investments with other companies for cross-marketing purposes.
E	Employees. Employees were granted the right to participate in an employee stock purchase plan. ∎

Member-Managed and Manager-Managed LLC's

An LLC can be either a **member-managed LLC** or a **manager-managed LLC**. An LLC is a member-managed LLC unless it is designated as a manager-managed LLC in its articles of organization [ULLCA § 203(a)(b)]. The distinctions between these two are:

- **Member-managed LLC.** In this type of LLC, the members of the LLC have the right to manage the LLC.

■ *Manager-managed LLC.* In this type of LLC, the members designate a manager or managers to manager the LLC, and by doing so they delegate their management rights to the manager or managers, designated manager or managers have the authority to manage the LLC, and the members no longer have the right to manage the LLC.

A manager may be a member of an LLC or a nonmember.

Whether an LLC is a member-managed or manager-managed LLC has important consequences on the right to bind the LLC to contracts and on determining the fiduciary duties owed by members to the LLC. These important distinctions are discussed in the paragraphs that follow.

Management of a Member-Managed LLC

In a member-managed LLC, each member has equal rights in the management of the business of the LLC, irrespective of the size of his or her capital contribution. Any matter relating to the business of the LLC is decided by a majority vote of the members [ULLCA § 404(a)].

Consider This Example Allison, Jaeson, Stacy, Lan-Wei, and Ivy form NorthWest.com, LLC. Allison contributes $100,000 capital, and the other four members each contributes $25,000 capital. When deciding whether to add another line of products to the business, Stacy, Lan-Wei, and Ivy vote to add the line, and Allison and Jaeson vote against it. The line of new products is added to the LLC's business because three members voted yes while two members voted no. It does not matter that the two members who voted no contributed $125,000 in capital collectively versus $75,000 in capital contributed by the three members who voted yes.

Management of a Manager-Managed LLC

In a manager-managed LLC, the members and nonmembers who are designated managers control the management of the LLC. The members who are not managers have no rights to manage the LLC unless otherwise provided in the operating agreement. In a manager-managed LLC, each manager has equal rights in the management and conduct of the company's business. Any matter relating to the business of the LLC may be exclusively decided by the managers by a majority vote of the managers [ULLCA § 403(b)].

A manager must be appointed by a vote of a majority of the members; managers may also be removed by a vote of the majority of the members [ULLCA § 404(b)(3)].

Certain actions cannot be delegated to managers but must be voted on by all members of the LLC. These include (1) amending the articles of organization, (2) amending the operating agreement, (3) admitting new members, (4) consenting to dissolve the LLC, (5) consenting to merge the LLC with another entity, and (6) selling, leasing, or disposing of all or substantially all of the LLC's property [ULLCA § 404(c)].

Compensation and Reimbursement

A nonmanager member of an LLC is not entitled to remuneration for services performed for the LLC (except for winding-up the business of the LLC). Managers of an LLC, whether they are members or not, are paid compensation and benefits as specified in their employment agreements with the LLC [ULLCA § 403(d)].

An LLC is obligated to reimburse members and managers for payments made on behalf of the LLC (e.g., business expenses) and to indemnify members and managers for liabilities incurred in the ordinary course of LLC business or in the preservation of the LLC's business or property [ULLCA § 403(a)].

Agency Authority to Bind an LLC to Contracts

The designation of an LLC as member-managed or manager-managed is important in determining who has authority to bind the LLC to contracts. The following rules apply:

- **Member-managed LLC.** In a member-managed LLC, all members have agency authority to bind the LLC to contracts. For example, if Theresa, Artis, and Yolanda form a member-managed LLC, each one of them can bind the LLC to a contract with a third party such as a supplier, purchaser, landlord, and others.

- **Manager-managed LLC.** In a manager-managed LLC, the managers have authority to bind the LLC to contracts, but nonmanager members cannot bind the LLC to contracts. For example, Alexis, Derek, Ashley, and Sadia form an LLC. They designate the LLC as a manager-managed LLC and name Alexis and Ashley as the managers. Alexis, a manager, enters into a contract to purchase goods from a supplier for the LLC. Derek, a nonmanager member, enters into a contract to lease equipment on behalf of the LLC. The LLC is bound to the contract entered into by Alexis, a manager, but is not bound to the contract entered into by Derek, a nonmanager member.

An LLC is only bound to contracts that are in the ordinary course of business or that the LLC has authorized [ULLCA § 301].

Business Brief

In a member-managed LLC, all members can bind the LLC to authorized contracts.

Business Brief

In a manager-managed LLC, only the managers can bind the LLC to authorized contracts.

Duty of Loyalty Owed to an LLC

A member of a member-managed LLC and a manager of a manager-managed LLC owe a *fiduciary* **duty of loyalty** to the LLC. This means that these parties must act honestly in their dealings with the LLC. The duty of loyalty includes the duty not to usurp the LLC's opportunities, make secret profits, secretly deal with the LLC, secretly compete with the LLC, or represent any interests adverse to those of the LLC [ULLCA § 409(b)].

Consider These Examples   Ester, Yi, Maria, and Enrique form the member-managed LLC Big.Business.com, LLC, which conducts online auctions over the Internet. Ester secretly starts a competing business to conduct online auctions over the Internet. Ester is liable for breaching her duty of loyalty to the LLC with Yi, Maria, and Enrique. Ester is liable for any secret profits she made, and her business will be shut down.

Suppose that instead, Ester, Yi, Maria, and Enrique designated their LLC as a manager-managed LLC and named Ester and Yi managers. In this case, only the managers owe a duty of loyalty to the LLC, but nonmanager members do not. Therefore, Ester and Yi, the named managers, could not compete with the LLC; Maria and Enrique, nonmanager members, could compete with the LLC without any legal liability.

Business Brief

Members of member-managed LLCs and managers of manager-managed LLCs owe a duty of loyalty to the LLC.

Business Brief

Breaches of the duty of loyalty by a covered member or manager include (1) usurping an LLC opportunity, (2) making secret profits, (3) secretly dealing with the LLC, (4) secretly competing with the LLC, and (5) representing any interests adverse to those of the LLC.

Limited Duty of Care Owed to an LLC

A member of a member-managed LLC and a manager of a manager-managed LLC owe a *fiduciary* **duty of care** to the LLC not to engage in (1) a known violation of law, (2) intentional conduct, (3) reckless conduct, or (4) grossly negligent conduct that injures the LLC. A member of a member-managed LLC or a manager of a manager-managed LLC are liable to the LLC for any damages the LLC incurs because of such conduct.

This duty is a **limited duty of care** because it does not include ordinary negligence. Thus, if a covered member or manager commits an *ordinarily negligent* act that is not grossly negligent, he or she is not liable to the LLC.

Consider This Example   Charlene is a member of a member-managed LLC. While engaging in LLC business, Charlene is driving an automobile and accidently hits Zubin, a pedestrian, and severely injures him. Under agency theory, Zubin sues the LLC and recovers $1 million in damages. If the court determines that Charlene was ordinarily negligent when she caused the accident—for example, she was driving the speed limit and did not see Zubin because the sun was in her eyes—she will not be liable to the LLC for any losses caused to the LLC by her ordinary negligence. If instead the court determines that Charlene was driving 65 mph in a 35 mph zone and thus was grossly negligent, Charlene is liable to the LLC for the $1 million it was ordered to pay Zubin.

No Fiduciary Duty Owed by a Nonmanager Member

A member of a manager-managed LLC who is not a manager owes no fiduciary duty of loyalty or care to the LLC or its other members [ULLCA § 409(h)(1)]. Basically, a nonmanager member of a manager-managed LLC is treated equally to a shareholder in a corporation.

Consider This Example   Felicia is a member of a 30-person manager-managed LLC that is engaged in buying, developing, and selling real estate. Felicia is not a manager of the LLC but is just a member-owner. If a third party approaches Felicia with the opportunity to purchase a large and valuable piece of real estate that is ripe for development, and the price is below fair market value, Felicia owes no duty to offer the opportunity to the LLC. She may purchase the piece of real estate for herself without violating any duty to the LLC.

Dissolution of an LLC

Unless the operating agreement provides otherwise, a member has the *power* to withdraw from both an at-will LLC and a term LLC [ULLCA § 602(a)]. The disassociation of a member from an at-will LLC is not wrongful unless the power to withdraw is eliminated in the operating agreement [ULLCA § 602(b)]. The disassociation of a member from a term LLC before the expiration of the specified term is wrongful. A member who wrongfully disassociates him- or herself from an LLC is liable to the LLC and to the other members for any damages caused by his or her **wrongful disassociation** [ULLCA § 602(c)].

A member's disassociation from an LLC terminates that member's right to participate in the management of the LLC, act as an agent of the LLC, or conduct the LLC's business [ULLCA § 603(b)(3)]. Disassociation also terminates the disassociating member's duties of loyalty and care to the LLC [ULLCA § 603(b)(3)].

Payment of Distributional Interest

If a member disassociates from an at-will LLC without causing a wrongful disassociation, the LLC must purchase the disassociated member's **distributional interest** [ULLCA § 701(a)(1)]. The price and terms of a distributional interest may be fixed in the operating agreement [ULLCA § 701(c)]. If the price is not agreed upon in the operating agreement, the LLC must pay the fair market value of the distributional interest.

If a member disassociates him- or herself from a term LLC, the LLC must only purchase the disassociating member's distributional interest on the expiration of the specified term of the LLC [ULLCA § 701(a)(2)]. Any damages caused by wrongful withdrawal must be offset against the purchase price [ULLCA § 701(f)].

This trial is a travesty; it's a travesty of a mockery of a sham of a mockery of a travesty of two mockeries of a sham. I move for a mistrial.

Woody Allen
Bananas (1971)

Notice of Disassociation

For two years after a member disassociates him- or herself from an LLC that continues in business, the disassociating member has apparent authority to bind the LLC to contracts in the ordinary course of business except to parties who either (1) know of the disassociation or (2) are given notice of the disassociation [ULLCA § 703].

An LLC can give *constructive notice* of a member's disassociation by filing a **statement of disassociation** with the secretary of state, stating the name of the LLC and the name of the member disassociated from the LLC [ULLCA § 704]. This notice is effective against any person who later deals with the disassociated member, whether the person was aware of the notice or not.

Consider This Example   William, Jesse, and Sandy are members of a member-managed LLC that operates an automobile dealership. Jesse disassociates from the LLC. The LLC fails to file a statement of disassociation with the secretary of state. Although Jesse has no express agency authority to bind the LLC to contracts because she is no longer a member of the LLC, Jesse has apparent authority to bind the LLC to contracts in the ordinary course of business for two years after the disassociation or until the LLC files a statement of disassociation with the secretary of state.

Continuation of an LLC

At the expiration of the term of a term LLC, some of its members may want to continue the LLC. At the expiration of its term, a term LLC can be continued in two situations. First, the members of the LLC may vote prior to the expiration date to continue the LLC for an additional specified term. This requires the unanimous vote of all of the members and the filing of an amendment to the articles of organization with the secretary of state, stating this fact. Second, absent the unanimous vote to continue the term LLC, the LLC may be continued as an at-will LLC by a simple majority vote of the members of the LLC [ULLCA § 411(b)].

Winding-Up an LLC's Business

If an LLC is not continued, the LLC is wound up. The **winding-up** of an LLC is the process of preserving and selling the assets of the LLC and distributing the money and property to creditors and members.

The assets of the LLC must be applied to first pay off the creditors; thereafter the surplus amount is distributed to the members in equal shares, unless the operating agreement provides otherwise [ULLCA § 806]. It is good practice for members to specify in the operating agreement how distributions will be made to members.

Business Brief

When winding-up and distributing the assets of an LLC, creditors are paid first; thereafter surplus amounts are distributed to members in equal amounts, unless the operating agreement provides otherwise.

After dissolution and winding-up, an LLC may terminate its existence by filing **articles of termination** with the secretary of state [ULLCA § 805].

International Law

Limited Liability Companies in Foreign Countries

The United States did not invent the LLC as a form of business. An LLC form of business has been used in different countries of the world for a long time. The *limitada*, a form of business used in Latin America, has many similarities to the LLC. *Limitadas* have been used in Argentina, Brazil, Mexico, and other Latin American countries for a century. These entities share the features of limited liability of owners and centralized management with the LLC.

On the European continent, an equivalent form of business to the LLC has existed for centuries. In Spain it was called the *sociedad de responsibilidades limitada*. Modern continental LLCs provide for limited liability of owners and centralized management. Germany was one of the last European countries to add the LLC as a form of business—one century ago. In England, an antecedent to the LLC, called the **stock company**, was developed around 1555. These companies, while technically partnerships, had limited liability of owners, free transferability of ownership interests, and centralized management similar to those of modern LLCs. ∎

Chapter Summary

Limited Liability Company (LLC), p. 638

Limited Liability Company (LLC)

1. ***Limited liability company (LLC).*** An LLC is a special form of unincorporated business entity that combines the tax benefits of a partnership and limited liability attribute of a corporation.
2. ***Uniform Limited Liability Company Act (ULLCA).*** This model act provides comprehensive and uniform rules for the formation, operation, and dissolution of LLCs.
3. ***Members.*** Members are owners of LLCs.

Liability

1. ***Limited liability of members.*** Members are liable for an LLC's debts, obligations, and liabilities only to the extent of their capital contributions. Members are not personally liable for the debts, obligations, and liabilities of the LLC.
2. ***Personal guarantee.*** A member is personally liable for the debts of an LLC if he or she personally guarantees the repayment of the LLC's debts.
3. ***Liability of the LLC.*** An LLC is liable for any loss or injury caused to anyone as a result of a wrongful act or omission by a member, a manager, an agent, or an employee of the LLC who commits the wrongful act while acting within the ordinary course of business of the LLC or with authority of the LLC.
4. ***Liability of managers.*** Managers of LLCs are not personally liable for the debts, obligations, and liabilities of the LLC they manage.
5. ***Liability of a tortfeasor.***
   a. *Tortfeasor.* A tortfeasor is a person who intentionally or unintentionally (negligently) causes injury or death to another person.
   b. *Liability of a tortfeasor.* A member or manager of an LLC who intentionally or unintentionally (negligently) causes injury or death to another person is personally liable to the injured person or the heirs of a deceased person.

Taxation

"Flow-through" taxation. For federal income tax purposes, an LLC is taxed as a partnership unless it elects to be taxed as a corporation.

Formation of an LLC, p. 642

Organization Procedures

1. ***Name.*** The name of an LLC must contain the words "limited liability company" or "limited company" or the abbreviation "L.L.C.," "LLC," "L.C.," or "LC." "Limited" may be abbreviated as "Ltd.," and "company" may be abbreviated as "Co."

2. ***Articles of organization.*** The articles of organization is a document that owners of an LLC must execute, sign, and file with the secretary of state of the appropriate state to form an LLC.

3. ***Duration.*** An LLC is an *at-will LLC* unless it is designated as a *term LLC* and the duration of the term is specified in the articles of organization.

4. ***Certificate of interest.*** This document evidences a member's ownership interest in an LLC.

5. ***Distributional interest.*** Distributional interest is a member's ownership interest in an LLC. This interest is personal property that may be transferred in whole or part.

6. ***Operating agreement.*** An operating agreement is an agreement entered into among members that governs the affairs and business of the LLC and relations among members, managers, and the LLC.

7. ***Agreement of conversion.*** This document sets forth the terms for converting general partnerships, limited partnerships, and corporations to an LLC.

Profits and Losses

1. ***No agreement.*** Unless otherwise agreed, the ULLCA mandates that a member has the right to an equal right to share in an LLC's profits and losses.

2. ***Agreement.*** Members may agree in their operating agreement how profits and losses of an LLC will be shared by the members.

Member-Managed and Manager-Managed LLCs, p. 647

Management of an LLC

1. ***Member-managed LLC.*** In this type of LLC, the members have not designated managers to manage the LLC. A member-managed LLC is managed by its members.

2. ***Manager-managed LLC.*** In this type of LLC, the members have designated certain members or nonmembers to manage the LLC. A manager-managed LLC is managed by the designated managers; nonmanager members have no right to manage the LLC.

Agency Authority

1. ***Member-managed LLC.*** In a member-managed LLC, all members have agency authority to bind the LLC to contracts.

2. ***Manager-managed LLC.*** In a manager-managed LLC, the managers have authority to bind the LLC to contracts; The nonmanager members cannot bind the LLC to contracts.

3. ***Liability for contracts.*** An LLC is bound to contracts that members or managers have properly entered into on its behalf in the ordinary course of business or that the LLC has authorized.

Fiduciary Duties of Loyalty and Care

1. ***Duty of loyalty.*** A member of a member-managed LLC and a manager of a manager-managed LLC owe a duty of care to the LLC. This means that these parties must act honestly in their dealings with the LLC. These parties are liable to the LLC for any secret profits made by them and damages caused to the LLC by a violation of their duty of loyalty.

2. ***Duty of care.*** A member of a member-managed LLC and a manager of a manager-managed LLC owe a duty of care to the LLC not to engage in:

   a. A known violation of law.

   b. Intentional conduct.

   c. Reckless conduct.

   d. Grossly negligent conduct.

   A covered member or manager is liable to the LLC for any damages the LLC suffers because of such breaches of the duty of care.

3. *Limited duty of care.* A covered member or manager is not liable to the LLC for damages caused to the LLC because of their *ordinary negligence.*

4. *No fiduciary duty owed by nonmanager members.* A member of a manager-managed LLC who is not a manager owes no fiduciary duty of loyalty or care to the LLC.

Dissolution of an LLC, p. 650

Disassociation from an LLC

1. *Member's power to disassociate.* Unless the operating agreement provides otherwise, members have the power to withdraw from both at-will and term LLCs.

2. *Wrongful disassociation.*
    a. *Term LLC.* The disassociation of a member from a term LLC before the expiration of the specified term is wrongful.
    b. *At-will LLC.* The disassociation of a member from an at-will LLC is not wrongful unless the power to withdraw is eliminated in the operating agreement.
    c. *Liability for wrongful disassociation.* A member who wrongfully disassociates himself or herself from an LLC is liable to the LLC and to the other members for any damages caused by his or her wrongful disassociation.

3. *Notice of disassociation.*
    a. *Statement of disassociation.* This document, filed with the secretary of state, states the name of the member disassociated from the LLC. This statement is *constructive notice* that is effective against persons, whether those person's are aware of the notice or not.
    b. *Apparent authority.* A disassociated member has apparent authority to bind an LLC to contracts in the ordinary course of business for two years after disassociation, unless either
        i. The other party knew of the disassociation.
        ii. Constructive notice of the disassociation was given.

4. *Continuation of an LLC.* At the expiration of a term LLC, the LLC can be continued by all or some of its members.

5. *Winding-up.* If an LLC is not continued, an LLC's business is wound up. This consists of preserving and selling the assets of the LLC and distributing the money and property to creditors and members.

 Internet Exercises and Case Questions

Working the Web Internet Exercises

Activities

1. Review business associations at **jurist.law.pitt.edu/ sg_bus.htm**. to determine why the LLC is an increasingly popular form of doing business.

2. Check your state statute on LLCs. How many persons are required to form an LLC? Try **www.4inc.com/llcfaq.htm**.

3. For an overview of partnerships and LLCs in the context of a state law, see "Florida's New Partnership Law," at **www. law.fsu.edu/journals/lawreview/issues/232/larson.html**.

Critical Legal Thinking Cases

29.1 Liability Harold, Jasmine, Caesar, and Yuan form Microhard.com, LLC, a limited liability company, to sell computer hardware and software over the Internet. Microhard.com, LLC, hires Heather, a recent graduate of the University of Chicago and a brilliant software designer, as an employee. Heather's job is to design and develop software that will execute a computer command when the computer user thinks of the next command he or she wants to execute on the computer. Using Heather's research, Microhard.com, LLC, develops the "Third Eye" software program that does this. Microhard.com, LLC, sends Heather to the annual Comdex Computer Show in Las Vegas, Nevada, to unveil this revolutionary software. Heather goes to Las Vegas, and while there, she rents an automobile to get from the hotel to the computer show and to meet interested buyers at different locations in Las Vegas. While Heather is driving from her hotel to the site of the Comdex Computer Show, she negligently causes an accident in which she runs over Harold Singer, a pedestrian.

Singer, who suffers severe personal injuries, sues Microhard.com, LLC, Heather, Harold, Jasmine, Caesar, and Yuan to recover monetary damages for his injuries. Who is liable?

29.2 Liability Isabel, Koshi, and Winchester each contribute $50,000 capital and form a limited liability company called Fusion Restaurant, LLC, which operates an up-scale restaurant serving "fusion" cuisine, combining foods from cultures around the world. Fusion Restaurant, LLC, as a business, borrows $1 million from Melon Bank for operating capital. Isabel, Koshi, and Winchester are so busy cooking, serving, and running the restaurant that they forget to hold members' meetings, keep minute books, or otherwise observe any usual company formalities for the entire first year of business. After this one year of hard work, Fusion Restaurant, LLC, suffers financial difficulties and defaults on the $1 million bank loan from Melon Bank. Melon Bank sues Fusion Restaurant, LLC, Isabel, Koshi, and Winchester to recover the unpaid bank loan. Who is liable?

29.3 Personal Guarantee Tran, Donald, and Elvira form a limited liability company called Real Estate Developers, LLC. Each of the three owners contributes $50,000 capital to the LLC, and the LLC then purchases a 400-acre parcel of vacant land 75 miles from Chicago, Illinois. Real Estate Developers, LLC, wants to build a tract of homes on the site. The owners of Real Estate Developers, LLC, go to City Bank and ask to borrow $100 million to complete the development and construction of the homes. City Bank agrees to make the loan, but only if Donald agrees to personally guarantee the LLC's loan and give security for the loan by pledging his 12-story penthouse in Manhattan, worth $100 million, as collateral for the loan. Donald agrees and signs the personal guarantee that pledges his penthouse as collateral for the loan; City Bank makes the $100 million loan to the LLC. Real Estate Developers, LLC, makes regular interest payments on the loan for one year and then defaults on the loan, with $100 million still owed to City Bank. At the time of default, Real Estate Developers, LLC's only asset is the 400-acre parcel of land that is still worth $150,000. City Bank sues Real Estate Developers, LLC, Tran, Donald, and Elvira to recover the amount of the unpaid loan. Who is liable to City Bank?

29.4 Member-Managed LLC Jennifer, Martin, and Edsel form a limited liability company called Big Apple, LLC, to operate a bar in New York City. Jennifer, Martin, and Edsel are member-managers of the LLC. One of Jennifer's jobs as a member-manager is to drive the LLC's truck and pick up certain items of supply for the bar each Wednesday. On the way back to the bar one Wednesday after picking up the supplies for that week, Jennifer negligently runs over a pedestrian, Tilly Tourismo, on a street in Times Square. Tilly is severely injured and sues Big Apple, LLC, Jennifer, Martin, and Edsel to recover monetary damages for her injuries. Who is liable?

29.5 Contract Liability Maria, Richard, and Dakota form a limited liability company called Ummmmm, LLC, to operate a spa in Santa Fe, New Mexico. Each member contributes $100,000 in capital to start the LLC. Ummmmm, LLC, is a member-managed LLC. Maria enters into a contract on behalf of the LLC where she contracts to have a new hot tub installed at the spa by Hot Tubs, Inc., for $80,000. Hot Tubs, Inc., installs the hot tub and sends a bill for $80,000 to Ummmmm, LLC. When Ummmmm, LLC, fails to pay the bill, Hot Tub, Inc., sues Ummmmm, LLC, to recover the unpaid $80,000. Is Ummmmm, LLC, liable?

29.6 Manager-Managed LLC Juan, Min-Yi, and Chelsea form Unlimited, LLC, a limited liability company that operates a chain of women's retail clothing stores that sell eclectic women's clothing. The company is a manager-managed LLC, and Min-Yi has been designated in the articles of organization filed with the secretary of state as the manager of Unlimited, LLC. Min-Yi sees a store location on Rodeo Drive in Beverly Hills, California, that she thinks would be an excellent location for an Unlimited Store. Min-Yi enters into a five-year lease on behalf of Unlimited, LLC, with Landlord, Inc., the owner of the store building, to lease the store at $100,000 rent per year. While visiting Chicago, Chelsea sees a store location on North Michigan Avenue in Chicago that she thinks is a perfect location for an Unlimited store. Chelsea enters into a five-year lease on behalf of Unlimited, LLC, with Real Estate, Inc., the owner of the store building, to lease the store location at $100,000 rent per year. Is Unlimited, LLC, bound to either of these leases?

29.7 Projects Donna, Arnold, Jose, and Won-Suk form a limited liability company called Millennium Foods, LLC, to operate an organic foods grocery store in Portland, Oregon. Donna and Arnold each contribute $25,000 capital, Jose contributes $50,000, and Won-Suk contributes $100,000. The LLC's articles of organization are silent as to how profits and losses of the LLC are to be divided. The organic foods grocery store is an immediate success, and Millennium Foods, LLC, makes $200,000 profit the first year. Jose and Won-Suk want the profits distributed based on the amount of the members' capital contribution. Arnold and Donna think the profits should be distributed equally. Who is correct?

29.8 Distributional Interest Daniel is one of five members of Blue Note, LLC, a limited liability company that operates a jazz club in New Orleans, Louisiana. The LLC's operating agreement provides that Daniel has the right to receive 20 percent of the LLC's profits. Daniel also owns another business as a sole proprietorship and has taken out a $100,000 loan from River Bank to operate this other business. Daniel defaults on his loan from River Bank, and River Bank sues Daniel and obtains a charging order against Daniel's ownership interest in Blue Note, LLC. What rights does River Bank have with regard to Blue Note, LLC, and Daniel's interest in Blue Note, LLC?

29.9 Duty of Loyalty Ally is a member and a manager of the manager-managed limited liability company called Movers & You, LLC, a moving company. Movers & You, LLC's main business is moving large corporations from old office space to new office space in other buildings. After Ally has been a member-manager of Movers & You, LLC, for several years, she decides to join her friend Lana and form another LLC, called Lana & Me, LLC. This new LLC provides moving services that move large corporations from old office space to new office space. Ally becomes a member-manager of Lana & Me, LLC, while retaining her member-manager position at Movers & You, LLC, Ally does not disclose her new position at Lana & Me, LLC, to the other members or managers of Movers & You, LLC. Several years later, the other members of Movers & You, LLC, discover Ally's other ownership and management position at Lana & Me, LLC. Movers & You, LLC, sues Ally to recover damages for her working for Lana & Me, LLC. Is Ally liable?

29.10 Duty of Care   Jonathan is a member of a member-managed limited liability company called Custom Homes, LLC. Custom Homes, LLC, is hired by an owner of a piece of vacant land located on Hilton Head Island, South Carolina, to build a new custom home on the site. Custom Homes, LLC, begins work on the house. Jonathan is responsible for making sure that flashing warning lights are placed in front of the house while it is being constructed to mark open holes in the ground and other dangerous conditions. One night Jonathan leaves the site and forgets to place a flashing warning light marking a hole in front of the house that the LLC is building.

That night, Candy, a neighbor who lives in one of the houses in the housing tract where the new house is being built, takes her dog for a walk. As Candy is walking by the unmarked area in front of the new house, she falls into the hole and is severely injured. Candy sues Custom Homes, LLC, to recover damages for her injuries. The jury finds that Jonathan had been ordinarily negligent when he failed to place the flashing warning lights to mark the hole that Candy fell in, and awards Candy $1 million for her injuries. Custom Homes, LLC, pays Candy the $1 million and then sues Jonathan to recover the $1 million. Is Jonathan liable?

Business Ethics Cases

29.11 Business Ethics   Angela, Yoko, Cherise, and Serena want to start a new business that designs and manufactures toys for children. At a meeting where the owners want to decide what type of legal form to use to operate the business, Cherise states

> We should use a limited liability company to operate our business because this form of business provides us, the owners, with a limited liability shield, which means that if the business gets sued and loses, we the owners are not personally liable to the injured party except up to our capital contribution in the business.

The others agree and form a limited liability company called Fuzzy Toys, LLC, to conduct the member-managed business. Each of the four owners contributes $50,000 as her capital contribution to the LLC. Fuzzy Toys, LLC, purchases $800,000 of liability insurance from Allied Insurance Company and starts business. Fuzzy Toys, LLC, designs and produces "Heidi," a new toy doll and female action figure. The new toy doll is an instant success, and Fuzzy Toys, LLC, produces and sells millions of these female action figures. After a few months, however, the LLC starts getting complaints that one of the parts of the female action figure is breaking off quite regularly, and some children are swallowing the part. The concerned member-managers of Fuzzy Toys, LLC, issue an immediate recall of the female action figure, but before all of the dolls are returned for a refund, Catherine, a seven-year-old child, swallows the toy's part and is severely injured. Catherine, through her mother, sues Fuzzy Toys, LLC, Allied Insurance Company, Angela, Yoko,

Cherise, and Serena to recover damages for product liability. At the time of suit, Fuzzy Toys, LLC, has $200,000 of assets. The jury awards Catherine $10 million for her injuries. Who is liable to Catherine and for how much? How much does Catherine recover? Did Angela, Yoko, Cherise, and Serena act ethically in using an LLC as a form of conducting their toy business? Explain.

29.12 Business Ethics   Christopher, Melony, Xie, and Ruth form iNet.com, LLC, a limited liability company. The four members are all Ph.D. scientists who have been working together in a backyard garage to develop a handheld wireless device that will let you receive and send e-mail, surf the Internet, use a word processing program that can print to any printer in the world, view cable television stations, and keep track of anyone you want anywhere in the world and let you zoom in on the person being tracked without that person knowing you are doing so. This new device, called Eros, costs only $29 but makes the owners $25 profit per unit sold. The owners agree that they will buy a manufacturing plant and start producing the unit in six months. Melony, who owns a one-quarter interest in iNet.com, LLC, decides she wants "more of the action" and soon, so she secretly sells the plans and drawings for the new Eros unit to a competitor for $100 million. The competitor comes out with the exact same device, called Zeus, in one month and beats iNet.com, LLC, to the market. The LLC, which later finds out about Melony's action, suffers damages of $100 million because of Melony's action. Is Melony liable to iNet.com, LLC? Explain. Did Melony act ethically in this case?

Briefing the Case Writing Assignment

Read Case A.29 in the Case Appendix [*Water, Waste, and Land, Inc. v. Preferred Income Investors, L.L.C.*]. This case is excerpted from the appellate court opinion. Review and brief the case. In your brief, be sure to answer the following questions:

1. What was the liability of the disclosed agent and the undisclosed agent for the LLC's contracts?
2. Did the notice provision of LLC law change the law of agency in this case?

Franchises, Licensing, and Strategic Alliances

30

"It has been uniformly laid down in this Court, as far back as we can remember, that good faith is the basis of all mercantile transactions."

—J. Buller
Salomons v. Nisson (1788)

Chapter Objectives

After studying this chapter, you should be able to:

1. Define franchise and describe the various forms of franchises.

2. Describe the rights and duties of the parties to a franchise agreement.

3. Identify the contract tort liability of franchisors and franchisees.

4. Define licensing and describe how trademarks and intellectual property is licensed.

5. Describe how international franchising, partnering, and strategic alliances are used in global commerce.

Chapter Contents

- Franchise
- Liability of Franchisors and Franchisees
- Licensing
- Joint Venture
- Strategic Alliance

Business Brief

Franchising is an important method of distributing goods and services to the public.

Franchising is an important method for distributing goods and services to the public. Originally pioneered by the automobile and soft drink industries, franchising today is used in many other forms of business. The 700,000-plus franchise outlets in the United States account for over 25 percent of retail sales and about 15 percent of the gross domestic product (GDP).

The special forms of business are used in domestic and international commerce. **Licensing** permits one business to use another business' trademarks, service marks, trade names and other intellectual property in selling goods or services. **Joint ventures** allow two or more businesses to combine their resources to pursue a single project or transaction. **Strategic alliances** are often used to enter foreign markets.

This chapter discusses franchises, licensing, joint ventures, and strategic alliances used in domestic and international commerce.

Franchise

A **franchise** is established when one party (the **franchisor** or **licensor**) licenses another party (the *franchisee* or *licensee*) to use the franchisor's trade name, trademarks, commercial symbols, patents, copyrights, and other property in the distribution and selling of goods and services. Generally, the franchisor and the franchisee are established as separate corporations. The term *franchise* refers to both the agreement between the parties and the franchise outlet.

There are several advantages to franchising, including (1) the franchisor can reach lucrative new markets, (2) the franchisee has access to the franchisor's knowledge and resources while running an independent business, and (3) consumers are assured of uniform product quality.

A typical franchise arrangement is illustrated in Exhibit 30.1.

Types of Franchises

There are four basic forms of franchises. They are:

- *Distributorship franchise.* In a **distributorship franchise**, the franchisor manufactures a product and licenses a retail dealer to distribute the product to the public. For example, the Ford Motor Company manufactures automobiles and franchises independently owned automobile dealers (franchisees) to sell them to the public.

Exhibit 30.1

Parties to a Typical Franchise Arrangement

Franchisor (Licensor)

Grant of franchise and license to use trademarks, service marks, and trade secrets

Franchisee (Licensee)

- *Processing plant franchise.* In a **processing plant franchise**, the franchisor provides a secret formula or the like to the franchisee. The franchisee then manufactures the product at its own location and distributes it to retail dealers. For example, the Coca-Cola Corporation, which owns the secret formulas for making Coca-Cola and other soft drinks, licenses regional bottling companies to manufacture and distribute soft drinks under the "Coca-Cola" and other brand names.

- *Chain-style franchise.* In a **chain-style franchise**, the franchisor licenses the franchisee to make and sell its products or services to the public from a retail outlet serving an exclusive geographical territory. Most fast-food franchises use this form. For example, the Pizza Hut Corporation franchises independently owned restaurant franchises to make and sell pizzas to the public under the "Pizza Hut" name.

- *Area franchise.* In an **area franchise**, the franchisor authorizes the franchisee to negotiate and sell franchises on behalf of the franchisor. The are franchisee is called a **subfranchisor** (see Exhibit 30.2). An area franchise is granted for a certain designated geographical area, such as a state, a region, or another agreed-upon area.

State Disclosure Laws

Prior to the 1970s, franchising was not highly regulated by either state or federal governments. In 1971, California enacted its *Franchise Investment Law*[1] which requires franchisors to register and deliver disclosure documents to prospective franchisees. Since then, many other states have enacted franchise disclosure statutes. For a while, franchisors struggled to comply with the various state statutes. Finally, in the mid-1970s, state franchise administrators developed a uniform disclosure document called the **Uniform Franchise Offering Circular (UFOC)**.

The UFOC and state laws require a franchisor to make specific presale disclosures to prospective franchisees. Information that must be disclosed includes a description of

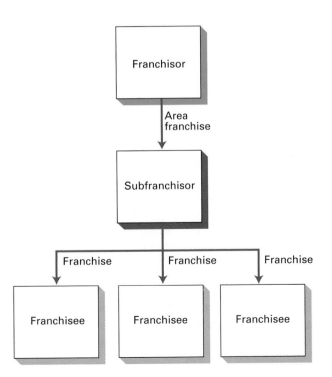

Exhibit 30.2

Example of an Area Franchise

the franchisor's business, balance sheets and income statements of the franchisor for the preceding three years, material terms of the franchise agreement, any restrictions on the franchisee's territory, grounds for termination of the franchise, and other relevant information.

FTC's Franchise Rule

In 1979, the Federal Trade Commission (FTC), a federal administrative agency, adopted the **FTC franchise rule**. The FTC rule requires franchisors to make full presale disclosure nationwide to prospective franchisees.[2] The FTC does not require the registration of the disclosure document prior to its use. The UFOC satisfies both state regulations and the FTC. The FTC rule requires the following disclosures:

1. ***Sales or earnings projections based on actual data.*** If a franchisor makes sales or earnings projections for a potential franchise location that are based on the actual sales, income, or profit figures of an existing franchise, the franchisor must disclose the following:

   - The number and percentage of its actual franchises that have obtained such results; and

   - A cautionary statement in at least 12-point boldface type that reads, "Caution: Some outlets have sold (or earned) this amount. There is no assurance you'll do as well. If you rely upon our figures, you must accept the risk of not doing so well."

2. ***Sales or earnings projections based on hypothetical data.*** If a franchisor makes sales or earnings projections based on hypothetical examples, the franchisor must disclose the following:

   - The assumptions underlying the estimates;

   - The number and percentage of actual franchises that have obtained such results; and

   - A cautionary statement in at least 12-point boldface print that reads, "Caution: These figures are only estimates of what we think you may earn. There is no assurance you'll do as well. If you rely upon our figures, you must accept the risk of not doing so well."

3. ***FTC notice.*** The FTC requires that the following statement, called the **FTC notice**, appear in at least 12-point boldface type on the cover of a franchisor's required disclosure statement to prospective franchisees:

   > To protect you, we've required your franchisor to give you this information.
   >
   > We haven't checked it, and don't know if it's correct. It should help you make up your mind. Study it carefully. While it includes some information about your contract, don't rely on it alone to understand your contract. Read all of your contract carefully. Buying a franchise is a complicated investment. Take your time to decide. If possible, show your contract and this information to an adviser, like a lawyer or an accountant. If you find anything you think may be wrong or anything important that's been left out, you should let us know about it. It may be against the law. There may also be laws on franchising in your state. Ask your state agencies about them.

If a franchisor violates FTC disclosure rules, the wrongdoer is subject to an injunction against further franchise sales, civil fines, and an FTC civil action on behalf of injured franchisees to recover damages from the franchisor that were caused by the violation.

Franchise Outlet. Franchising is a major form of business in the United States.

Trademarks and Trade Secrets

A franchisor's ability to maintain the public's perception of the quality of the goods and services associated with its trade name, **trademarks**, and **service marks** is the essence of its success. The **Lanham Trademark Act**, which was enacted in 1946, provides for the registration of trademarks and service marks with the federal **Patent and Trademark Office** in Washington, DC, by franchisors and others. Most franchisors license the use of their trade names, trademarks, and service marks and prohibit their franchisees from misusing these marks. Anyone who uses a mark without authorization may be sued for *trademark infringement*. The trademark holder can sue to recover damages and obtain an injunction prohibiting further unauthorized use of the mark.

Franchisors are often owners of **trade secrets**, including product formulas, business plans and models, and other ideas. Franchisors license and disclose many of their trade secrets to franchisees. The misappropriation of a trade secret is called *unfair competition*. The holder of the trade secret can sue the offending party for damages and obtain an injunction to prohibit further unauthorized use of the trade secret.

The Franchise Agreement

A prospective franchisee must apply to the franchisor for a franchise. The application often includes detailed information about the applicant's previous employment, financial and educational history, credit status, and so on. If an applicant is approved, the parties enter into a **franchise agreement** that sets forth the terms and conditions of the franchise. Although some states permit oral franchise agreements, most have enacted a Statute of Frauds that requires franchise agreements to be in writing. To prevent unjust enrichment, the courts will occasionally enforce oral franchise agreements that violate the Statute of Frauds.

Common Terms of a Franchise Agreement

Franchise agreements do not usually have much room for negotiation. Generally, the agreement is a standard form contract prepared by the franchisor. Franchise agreements cover the following topics:

1. *Quality control standards.* The franchisor's most important assets are its name and reputation. The quality control standards set out in the franchise agreement—such as the franchisor's right to make periodic inspections of the franchisee's premises and operations—are intended to protect these assets. Failure to meet the proper standards can result in loss of the franchise.

2. *Training requirements.* Franchisees and their personnel are usually required to attend training programs either on-site or at the franchisor's training facilities.

3. *Covenant not to compete.* Covenants not to compete prohibit franchisees from competing with the franchisor during a specific time and in a specified area after the termination of the franchise. Unreasonable (overextensive) covenants not to compete are void.

4. *Arbitration clause.* Most franchise agreements contain an arbitration clause that provides that any claim or controversy arising from the franchise agreement or an alleged breach thereof is subject to arbitration. The U.S. Supreme Court has held such clauses to be enforceable.[3]

5. *Other terms and conditions.* Capital requirements—restrictions on the use of the franchisor's trade name, trademarks, and logo; standards of operation; duration of the franchise; record-keeping requirements; sign requirements; hours of operation; prohibition as to the sale or assignment of the franchise; conditions for the termination of the franchise; and other specific terms pertinent to the operation of the franchise and the protection of the parties' rights—are included in the agreement.

Franchise Fees

Franchise fees payable by the franchisee are usually stipulated in the franchise agreement. The franchisor may require the franchisee to pay any or all of the following fees:

1. *Initial license fee.* An initial license fee is a lump-sum payment for the privilege of being granted a franchise.

2. *Royalty fees.* A royalty fee is a fee for the continued use of the franchisor's trade name, property, and assistance that is often computed as a percentage of the franchisee's gross sales.

3. *Assessment fee.* An assessment fee is a fee for such things as advertising and promotional campaigns and administrative costs, billed either as a flat monthly or annual fee or as a percentage of gross sales.

4. *Lease fees.* Lease fees are payment for any land or equipment leased from the franchisor, billed either as a flat monthly or annual fee or as a percentage of gross sales or other agreed-upon amount.

5. *Cost of supplies.* Cost of supplies involves payment for supplies purchased from the franchisor.

Breach of the Franchise Agreement

A lawful franchise agreement is an enforceable contract. Each party owes a duty to adhere to and perform under the terms of the franchise agreement. If the agreement is breached, the aggrieved party can sue the breaching party for rescission of the agreement, restitution, and damages.

In the following case, the court found that there had not been a breach of a franchise agreement.

Case 30.1
Franchise Agreement

Carlock v. Pillsbury Company
719 F.Supp. 791, 1989 U.S.Dist. Lexis 9370 (1989)
United States District Court, Minnesota

Background and Facts

In the late 1950s, Reuben Mattus developed a "super premium" ice cream and named it "Häagen-Dazs" to give the product a Scandinavian flair. Mattus began selling Häagen-Dazs ice cream in prepackaged pints to small stores and delicatessens in the New York metropolitan area.

In 1976, Mattus's daughter, Doris Mattus-Hurley, opened the first "Häagen-Dazs Shoppe" in Brooklyn Heights, New York. After this shop prospered, Mattus-Hurley began franchising other shops to independent franchisees throughout the country. Häagen-Dazs ice cream is manufactured, distributed, and franchised through a variety of corporate entities (collectively referred to as Häagen-Dazs). The franchise agreement, which has been the same since 1978, had granted a limited license to the franchisee to operate a single shop under the Häagen-Dazs trademark at a specific location. The franchisee agrees to purchase all its ice cream from the franchisor at prices set by Häagen-Dazs.

In 1983, the Pillsbury Company (Pillsbury), a diversified international food and restaurant company headquartered in Minneapolis, Minnesota, purchased the Häagen-Dazs Company, including its franchise operations. The franchise agreements were assigned to Pillsbury as part of the sale. Pillsbury decided that it could maximize sales of Häagen-Dazs ice cream by expanding sales through methods of distribution that did not involve franchises. Pillsbury substantially increased sales of Häagen-Dazs products to national grocery store chains, convenience stores such as 7-Eleven, and other retail outlets.

This change severely harmed sales at existing franchises. Franchisees located in many states sued Pillsbury, alleging breach of the franchise agreement. Plaintiffs claimed that the defendant breached the franchise agreement by distributing Häagen-Dazs ice cream through nonfranchised outlets that were not "upscale" and by mass distribution of prepackaged pints that competed with franchise outlet sales.

Issue

Did Pillsbury breach the franchise agreement?

Court's Reasoning

The court found that the franchise agreement expressly reserved the right of the franchisor to distribute Häagen-Dazs products "through not only Häagen-Dazs Shoppes, but through any other distribution method, which may from time to time be established." The court held that this language gave Pillsbury the right to aggressively distribute prepackaged pints of Häagen-Dazs ice cream through nonfranchise outlets even though that distribution adversely affected retail sales by franchisees.

Decision and Remedy

The U.S. district court held that the express terms of the franchise agreement had not been violated and granted Pillsbury's motion for summary judgment.

Case Questions

Critical Legal Thinking   Who has the most power in drafting the terms of a franchise agreement, the franchisor or the franchisee?

Business Ethics   Even though the express terms of the franchise agreement allowed Pillsbury to distribute Häagen-Dazs ice cream through nonfranchise outlets, do you think Pillsbury acted ethically in doing so?

Contemporary Business   Should the contract in this case have been enforced as written? Explain.

Termination "For Cause"

Most franchise agreements permit a franchisor to terminate the franchise "for cause." For example, the continued failure of a franchisee to pay franchise fees or meet legitimate quality control standards would be deemed just cause. Unreasonably strict application of a just cause termination clause constitutes wrongful termination. A single failure to meet a quality control standard, for example, is not cause for termination.

Business Brief

A franchisor can terminate a franchise agreement for "just cause" (e.g., nonpayment of franchise fees by the franchisee, continued failure to meet quality control standards).

Wrongful Termination

Termination-at-will clauses in franchise agreements are generally held to be void on the grounds that they are unconscionable. The rationale for this position is that the franchisee has spent time, money, and effort developing the franchise.

If a franchise is terminated without just cause, the franchisee can sue the franchisor for **wrongful termination**. The franchisee can then recover damages caused by the unlawful termination and recover the franchise.

International Law

International Franchising

The international market presently offers a great opportunity for U.S. franchisors to expand their businesses. Many U.S. franchisors view international expansion as their number one priority. However, in addition to providing lucrative new markets, international franchising also poses difficulties and risks.

The expansion into other countries through franchising means that U.S. franchisors can expand internationally without the huge capital investments that would be required if they tried to penetrate these markets with company-owned stores or branches. In addition, a foreign franchisee will know things about the cultural and business traditions of the foreign country that the franchisor will not. Consequently, the franchisee will be better able to serve the consumers and customers in the particular market.

Foreign franchising is not without difficulties, however. For example, the host country's laws may differ from U.S. laws. Foreign cultures may also require different advertising, marketing, and promotional approaches. In addition, the franchisor may be subjecting itself to government regulation in the host country. Finally, different dispute settlement procedures may be in place that will have to be used if there is a dispute between the U.S. franchisor and the foreign franchisee.

In addition to U.S. franchisors' expanding to other countries, foreign franchisors also view the United States as a potential market. This will provide an opportunity for U.S. entrepreneurs to become franchisees for foreign franchisors. ■

Liability of Franchisors and Franchisees

Business Brief

A franchisor and franchisee are liable for their own contracts and torts.

If properly organized and operated, the franchisor and franchisee are separate legal entities. Therefore, the franchisor deals with the franchisee as an *independent contractor*.

Franchisees are liable on their own contracts and are liable for their own tort, (e.g., negligence). Franchisors are liable for their own contracts and torts. Generally, however, neither party is liable for the contracts or torts of the other.

Business Brief

If properly organized and operated as separate businesses, generally a franchisor and franchisee are not liable for each other's contracts and torts.

Consider These Examples   The McDonald's Corporation, a fast-food restaurant franchisor, grants a restaurant franchise to Tina Corporation. Tina Corporation opens the franchise restaurant. One day a customer at the franchise spills a chocolate shake on the floor. The employees at the franchise fail to clean up the spilled shake, and one hour later another customer slips on the spilled shake and suffers severe injuries. The injured customer can recover damages from the franchisee, Tina Corporation, because it was negligent. It cannot recover damages from the franchisor, McDonald's Corporation.

The McDonald's Corporation, the franchisor, grants a franchise to Gion Corporation, the franchisee. McDonald's Corporation enters into a loan agreement with City Bank, whereby it borrows $100 million. Gion Corporation, the franchisee, is not liable on the loan. McDonald's Corporation, the franchisor and debtor, is liable on the loan.

In the first case that follows, the court found the franchisee directly liable for its own negligent conduct. In the second case that follows, the court imposed liability on a franchisor for its own negligent conduct.

Cislaw v. Southland Corporation

4 Cal.App.4th 1384, 6 Cal.Rptr.2d 386, 1992 Cal.App. Lexis 375 (1992)

Court of Appeals of California

Case 30.2
Franchisee's Liability

Background and Facts

The Southland Corporation (Southland) owns the "7-Eleven" trademark and licenses franchisees to operate convenience stores using this trademark. Each franchise is independently owned and operated. The franchise agreement stipulates that the franchisee is an independent contractor who is authorized to make all inventory, employment, and operational decisions for the franchise.

Timothy Cislaw, 17 years old, died of respiratory failure on May 10, 1984. His parents filed a wrongful death action against the franchise and Southland, alleging that Timothy's death resulted from his consumption of Djarum Specials (clove cigarettes) sold at a Costa Mesa, California, 7-Eleven franchise store. The Costa Mesa 7-Eleven was franchised to Charles Trujillo and Patricia Colwell-Trujillo. After answering the complaint, Southland moved for summary judgment, arguing that it was not liable for the alleged tortious conduct of its franchisee because the franchisee was an independent contractor. The plaintiffs alleged that the franchisee was Southland's agent, and therefore Southland was liable for its agent's alleged negligence of selling the clove cigarettes to their son. The trial court granted Southland's motion. The Cislaws appealed.

Issue

Was the Costa Mesa franchisee an agent of Southland?

Court's Reasoning

The franchisor—franchisee arrangement does not create a principal—agent relationship unless the franchisor has the right to exercise substantial control over the operations of the franchisee. Although the franchise agreement gave Southland the right to establish the hours of operation of its franchises, to protect its "7-Eleven" trademark from misuse by the franchisee, and to set cleanliness and quality control standards at its franchises, the agreement did not give Southland the right to control the day-to-day operations of its Costa Mesa franchise. The court found that because the franchisee made all inventory, employment, and day-to-day operational decisions, it was an independent contractor.

Decision and Remedy

The court of appeals held that the Costa Mesa 7-Eleven franchise was not an agent of Southland, but was an independent contractor. The court of appeals affirmed the judgment of the trial court.

Case Questions

Critical Legal Thinking   Should franchisors be automatically held liable for the tortious conduct of their franchisees? Why or why not?

Business Ethics   Did the Cislaws act ethically in suing Southland?

Contemporary Business   How careful must a franchisor be to retain enough control to protect the quality of the goods and services sold by its franchisees, but not to retain too much control so as to become liable for the actions of its franchisees?

Martin v. McDonald's Corporation

572 N.E.2d 1073, 1991 Ill.App. Lexis 715 (1991)

Appellate Court of Illinois

Case 30.3
Franchisor's Liability

Background and Facts

McDonald's Corporation (McDonald's) is a franchisor that licenses franchisees to operate fast-food restaurants and to use McDonald's trademarks and service marks. One such franchise, which was located in Oak Forest, Illinois, was owned and operated by McDonald's Restaurants of Illinois, the franchisee.

Recognizing the threat of armed robbery at its franchises, especially in the time period immediately after closing, McDonald's established an entire corporate division to deal with security problems at franchises. McDonald's prepared a manual for restaurant security operations and required its franchisees to adhere to these procedures.

Jim Carlson was the McDonald's regional security manager for the area in which the Oak Forest franchise was located. Carlson visited the Oak Forest franchise on October 31, 1979, to inform the manager of security procedures. He specifically mentioned these rules: (1) No one should throw garbage out the backdoor after dark, and (2) trash and grease were to be taken out the side glass door at least one hour prior to closing. During his inspection, Carlson noted that the locks had to be changed at the restaurant and an alarm system needed to be installed for the backdoor. Carlson never followed up to determine whether these security measures had been taken.

Martin v. McDonald's Corporation

572 N.E.2d 1073, 1991 Ill.App. Lexis 715 (1991)
Appellate Court of Illinois
(continued)

On the evening of November 29, 1979, a six-woman crew, all teenagers, was working to clean up and close the Oak Forest restaurant. Laura Martin, Therese Dudek, and Maureen Kincaid were members of that crew. A person later identified as Peter Logan appeared at the back of the restaurant with a gun. He ordered the crew to open the safe and get him the money and then ordered them into the refrigerator. In the course of moving the crew into the refrigerator, Logan shot and killed Martin and assaulted Dudek and Kincaid. Dudek and Kincaid suffered severe emotional distress from the assault.

Evidence showed that Logan had entered the restaurant through the backdoor. Trial testimony proved that the work crew used the backdoor exclusively, both before and after dark, and emptied garbage and grease through the backdoor all day and all night. In addition, there was evidence that the latch on the backdoor did not work properly. Evidence also showed that the crew had not been instructed about the use of the backdoor after dark and had never received copies of the McDonald's security manual, and that the required warning about not using the backdoor after dark had not been posted at the restaurant.

Martin's parents, Dudek, and Kincaid sued McDonald's to recover damages for negligence. The trial court awarded damages of $1,003,445 to the Martins for the wrongful death of their daughter and awarded $125,000 each to Dudek and Kincaid. McDonald's appealed.

Issue

Is McDonald's liable for negligence?

Court's Reasoning

The appellate court held that McDonald's had voluntarily assumed a duty to the crew at the Oak Forest franchise by establishing and requiring the franchisee to implement certain security measures and by obligating itself to inspect the restaurant to see that the required security measures were implemented. The court held that McDonald's was liable for its own negligence due to the failure of security measures and the failure of its employee, Carlson, to follow up to determine that the security deficiencies at the Oak Forest franchise had been corrected. The appellate court held that there was ample evidence for the jury to determine that McDonald's had breached its assumed duty to the plaintiffs.

Decision and Remedy

The appellate court held that McDonald's was negligent for not following up and making sure that the security deficiencies it had found at the Oak Forest franchise had been corrected. The appellate court affirmed the judgment of the trial court, holding McDonald's liable.

Case Questions

Critical Legal Thinking   Should businesses be held liable for criminal actions of others? Why or why not?

Business Ethics   Should McDonald's have denied liability in this case?

Contemporary Business   What is the benefit to a franchisor to establish and require its franchisees to adhere to security rules? Is there any potential detriment? Explain.

Tokeyo, Japan. The major growth in franchising opportunities for U.S. franchisors, such as McDonald's, is in international markets.

Apparent Agency

If the franchisee is the *actual* or *apparent agent* of the franchisor, the franchisor is responsible for the torts and contracts the franchise committed or entered into within the scope of the agency. Franchisors very seldom appoint franchisees as their agents.

Apparent agency is created when a franchisor leads a third person into believing that the franchisee is its agent. For example, a franchisor and franchisee who use the same trade name and trademarks and make no effort to inform the public of their separate legal status may find themselves in such a situation. However, mere use of the same name does not automatically make the franchisor liable for the franchisee's actions. The court's decision whether an apparent agency has been created depends on the facts and circumstances of the case.

In the following case, the court found that a franchisee was the apparent agent of the franchisor, thereby making the franchisor liable for the tortious conduct of the franchisee.

Holiday Inns, Inc. v. Shelburne
576 So.2d 322, 1991 Fla.App. Lexis 585 (1991)
District Court of Appeals of Florida

Case 30.4
Apparent Agency

Background and Facts

Holiday Inns, Inc. (Holiday Inns), is a franchisor that licenses franchisees to operate hotels using its trademarks and service marks. Holiday Inns licensed Hospitality Venture to operate a franchised hotel in Fort Pierce, Florida. The Rodeo Bar, which had a reputation as the "hottest bar in town," was located in the hotel.

The Fort Pierce Holiday Inn and Rodeo Bar did not have sufficient parking, so security guards posted in the Holiday Inn parking lot required Rodeo Bar patrons to park in vacant lots that surrounded the hotel but that were not owned by the hotel. The main duty of the guards was to keep the parking lot open for hotel guests. Two unarmed security guards were on duty on the night in question. One guard was drinking on the job, and the other was an untrained temporary fill-in.

The record disclosed that although the Rodeo Bar had a capacity of 240 people, the bar regularly admitted 270 to 300 people, with 50 to 75 people waiting outside. Fights occurred all the time in the bar and the parking lots, and often there were three or four fights a night. Police reports involving 58 offenses, including several weapons charges and battery and assault charges, had been filed during the previous 18 months.

On the night in question, the two groups involved in the altercation did not leave the Rodeo Bar until closing time. According to the record, these individuals exchanged remarks as they moved toward their respective vehicles in the vacant parking lots adjacent to the Holiday Inn. Ultimately, a fight erupted. The evidence shows that during the course of physical combat, Mr. Carter shot David Rice, Scott Turner, and Robert Shelburne. Rice died from his injuries.

Rice's heirs, Turner, and Shelburne sued the franchisee, Hospitality Venture, and the franchisor, Holiday Inns, for damages. The trial court found Hospitality Venture negligent for not providing sufficient security to prevent the foreseeable incident that took the life of Rice and injured Turner and Shelburne. The court also found that Hospitality Venture was the apparent agent of Holiday Inns, and therefore Holiday Inns was vicariously liable for its franchisee's tortious conduct. Turner was awarded $3,825,000 for his injuries, Shelburne received $1 million, and Rice's interests were awarded $1 million. Hospitality Venture and Holiday Inns appealed.

Issue

Are the franchisee and the franchisor liable?

Court's Reasoning

A franchisee is always liable for its own tortious conduct. A franchisor may be held liable for the tortious conduct of a franchisee if the franchisee is the "apparent agent" of the franchisor. This "apparent agent" occurs when the franchisor misleads the public into believing that the franchise is really owned and operated by the franchisor, even though it is not. Here, the court held that Holiday Inns led the public into believing that its franchisees were part of the Holiday Inns system and not independently owned businesses. The trial court held that Holiday Inns reservation system, as well as the signs at the Fort Pierce franchise hotel, gave this appearance to the public. Therefore, Holiday Inns was determined to be vicariously liable for the tortious conduct of its franchisee.

Decision and Remedy

The court of appeals held that the franchisee was negligent and that the franchisee was the apparent agent of the franchisor. The court of appeals affirmed the judgment of the trial court.

Case Questions

Critical Legal Thinking   What does the doctrine of apparent agency provide? How does it differ from actual agency?

Business Ethics   Did Hospitality Venture act ethically in denying liability? Did Holiday Inns act ethically in denying liability?

Contemporary Business   Why do you think the plaintiffs included Holiday Inns as a defendant in their lawsuit? Do you think the damages that were awarded were warranted?

Exhibit 30.3

Parties to a Typical
Licensing Arrangement

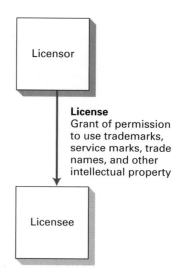

Licensor

License
Grant of permission
to use trademarks,
service marks, trade
names, and other
intellectual property

Licensee

Licensing

Licensing is an important business arrangement in both domestic and international markets. **Licensing** occurs when one business or party that owns trademarks, service marks, trade names, and other intellectual property (the licensor) contracts to permit another business or party (the licensee) use its trademarks, service marks, trade names, and other intellectual property in the distribution of goods, services, software, and digital information. A licensing arrangement is illustrated in Exhibit 30.3.

Consider This Example   The Walt Disney Company owns the merchandising rights to "Winnie the Pooh" stories and all of the characters associated with the Winnie the Pooh stories. The Walt Disney Company enters into an agreement whereby it permits the Beijing Merchandising Company, a business formed under Chinese law, to manufacture and distribute a line of clothing, children's toys, and other items bearing the likeness of the Winnie the Pooh characters. This is a license. The Walt Disney Company is the licensor, and the Beijing merchandising Company is the licensee.

Joint Venture

A **joint venture** is an arrangement whereby two or more business entities combine their resources to pursue a single project or transaction. The parties to a joint venture are called **joint venturers**. Joint ventures resemble partnerships, except that partnerships are usually formed to pursue ongoing business operations rather than to focus on a single project or transaction.

Unless otherwise agreed, joint venturers have equal rights to manage the joint venture. Joint venturers owe each other the fiduciary duties of loyalty and care. If a joint venturer violates these duties, it is liable for the damages the breach causes.

International Law

Starbucks Invades the World

Starbucks Coffee has been a tremendous success in the United States. Beginning with a single outlet in Seattle, Washington, Starbucks Coffee Company has expanded Starbucks Coffee shops across the United States. The company expanded in the United States through company-owned stores.

When Starbucks wanted to enter overseas markets, however, it realized it could not expand solely through company-owned outlets. This was because (1) government restrictions in some countries prohibit 100 percent ownership of a business by a foreign investor and (2) the company lacked the business expertise and cultural knowledge necessary to enter many foreign markets. To enter foreign markets, Starbucks turned to joint ventures.

For example, Starbucks entered the markets of Spain and France using a 50–50 joint venture with Grupo Vips, a Spanish company. Starbucks is expanding its operations in China by using a 50–50 joint venture with Shanghai President Coffee Corporation, a Chinese company. ■

Strategic Alliance

A **strategic alliance** is an arrangement between two or more companies in the same industry whereby they agree to ally themselves to accomplish a designated objective. A strategic alliance allows the companies to reduce risks, share costs, combine technologies, and extend their markets. For example, companies often enter into strategic alliances when they decide to expand internationally into foreign countries.

Strategic alliances do not have the same protection as mergers, joint ventures, or franchising, and sometimes are dismantled. Consideration must always be given to the fact that a strategic alliance partner is also a potential competitor.

Business Brief

Strategic alliances are often used by companies internationally to enter a foreign market.

Online Commerce & Internet Law
Strategic Internet Alliances in China

Leading Internet companies in the United States have eyed the China market for its tremendous growth potential. But China prohibits complete ownership of Internet companies in China by foreigners. In addition, the legendary Chinese "connections" method of conducting business places another hurdle in the way of foreign companies wishing to do business there. So what is the main way to tap into this Internet market? Strategic alliances.

A major strategic alliance by U.S. companies in China was their tie-in and investment in China.com. China.com is a Chinese-language Web portal backed by investments by U.S. companies Time Warner, Inc., Sun Microsystems and Nortel Networks. China.com became China's largest Internet company when it went public in 1999. Intel Corp., another major U.S. company, has aligned itself with Sohu.com, a Chinese Internet company located in Beijing. CMGI Inc., a U.S. Internet holding company, has joined with Pacific Century Cyber-Works (PCCW), a Hong Kong company, to sell Web content and e-commerce services to the exploding Chinese Internet market from its base in Hong Kong.

The Chinese government has permitted these strategic alliances. Based on the communist government's rules in China and a culture that favors business connections, U.S. Internet companies will continue to enter the Chinese Internet market through strategic alliances with Chinese Internet firms. These strategic alliances bring together the expertise of all the parties. ■

Chapter Summary

Franchise, p. 658

Franchise

A franchise is established when one party licenses another party to use the franchisor's trade name, trademarks, commercial symbols, patents, copyrights, and other property in the distribution and selling of goods and services.

1. *Franchisor.* The franchisor is the party who does the licensing in a franchise arrangement. Also called the *licensor.*

2. *Franchisee.* The franchisee is the party who is licensed by the franchisor in a franchise arrangement. Also called the *licensee.*

Types of Franchises

1. ***Distributorship franchise.*** The franchisor manufactures a product and licenses a retail franchisee to distribute the product to the public.

2. ***Processing plant franchise.*** The franchisor provides a secret formula or process to the franchisee, and the franchisee manufactures the product and distributes it to retail dealers.

3. ***Chain-style franchise.*** The franchisor licenses the franchisee to make and sell its products or distribute its services to the public from a retail outlet serving an exclusive territory.

4. ***Area franchise.*** The franchisor authorizes the franchisee to negotiate and sell franchises on behalf of the franchisor in designated areas. The area franchisee is called a *subfranchisor*.

State Disclosure Laws

Many states have enacted statutes that require franchisors to make specific presale disclosures to prospective franchisees. Some states use a uniform disclosure document called the *Uniform Franchise Offering Circular (UFOC)*.

FTC's Franchise Rule

The *FTC* requires franchisors to make presale disclosures to prospective franchisees. If the franchisor uses actual or hypothetical sales or income data in its sales materials, the franchisor must disclose assumptions underlying any estimates and how many franchises have obtained such results, and it must provide a mandated precautionary statement.

Trademarks

1. ***Trademarks and service marks.*** A distinctive mark, symbol, name, word, motto, or device may identify the goods or services of a particular franchisor.

2. ***Licensing of marks.*** A franchisor *licenses* the use of its trademarks and service marks to its franchisees in the franchise agreement.

3. ***Trademark infringement.*** Anyone who uses a mark without authorization from the franchisor may be sued for *trademark infringement*. The franchisor can recover damages and obtain an injunction prohibiting further unauthorized use of the mark.

Trade Secrets

1. ***Trade secrets.*** Trade secrets are ideas, formulas, and methods of doing business that make a franchise successful but do not qualify for trademark, patent, or copyright protection.

2. ***Misappropriation of trade secrets.*** Anyone who steals and uses a franchisor's trade secret is liable for misappropriation of a trade secret. The franchisor can recover damages and obtain an injunction prohibiting further unauthorized use of the trade secret.

The Franchise Agreement

A franchise agreement is an agreement that the franchisor and franchisee enter into that sets forth the terms and conditions of the franchise (e.g., quality control standards, covenants-not-to-compete). Common terms in a franchise agreement include:

1. Quality control standards
2. Training requirements
3. Covenant-not-to-compete
4. Arbitration clause
5. Other terms and conditions

Franchise Fees

A franchisee may be required to pay any or all of the following franchise fees to the franchisor:

1. ***Initial license fee.*** This is a lump-sum payment for the privilege of being granted a franchise.

2. ***Royalty fee.*** This is a fee for the continued use of the franchisor's trade name, property, and assistance, and it is often computed as a percentage of the franchisee's gross sales.

3. *Assessment fee.* This is a fee for such things as advertising and promotional campaigns, administrative costs, and the like, billed either as a flat monthly fee or annual fee or as a percentage of gross sales.

4. *Lease fees.* These fees are payment for any land or equipment leased from the franchisor, billed either as a flat monthly or annual fee or as a percentage of gross sales or other agreed-upon amount.

5. *Cost of supplies.* These fees are payment for supplies purchased from the franchisor.

Termination of Franchises

Termination "for cause." Most franchise agreements, and state and federal laws, permit a franchisor to terminate the franchise "for cause" (e.g., nonpayment of franchise fees by the franchisee, continued failure of the franchisee to meet quality control standards).

Wrongful Termination

1. *Termination at will.* Most state and federal laws regulating franchising prohibit franchisors from terminating franchises at will. This is to prevent a franchisor from taking advantage of the good will developed at the franchise location by the franchisee.

2. *Wrongful termination.* If a franchisor terminates a franchise agreement without just cause, the franchisee can sue the franchisor for *wrongful termination*. The franchisee can recover damages caused by the wrongful termination and recover the franchise.

Liability of Franchisors and Franchisees, p. 664

Contract and Tort Liability

1. **Liability.** Franchisors and franchisees are liable for their own contracts and torts.

2. **Independent contractor.** An independent contractor is a separately organized and operated business that is not the agent of another party with whom it does business. This is the typical franchisor–franchisee arrangement. There is no agency relationship, so neither party is liable for the other's contracts or torts.

3. **Actual agency.** This arrangement occurs where a franchisor expressly or implicitly by its conduct makes a franchisee its agent. The franchisor is liable for the contracts entered into and torts committed by the franchisee while acting within the scope of the agency.

4. **Apparent agency.** This agency arises when a franchisor creates the appearance that a franchisee is its agent when in fact an actual agency does not exist. The franchisor is liable for the contracts entered into and torts committed by the franchisee acting as an apparent agent.

Licencing, p. 668

Licensing

1. **License.** In a licensing arrangement, the owner of trademarks, service marks, trade names, and other intellectual property grants another party the right to use these in the manufacture and sale of goods, services, softwares or digital information.

2. **Licensor.** The licensor is the party who grants the license.

3. **Licensee.** The licensee is the party to whom the license is granted.

Joint Venture, p. 668

Joint Venture

1. **Joint venture.** A joint venture is an arrangement whereby two or more business entities combine their resources to pursue a single project or transaction.

2. **Joint Venturer.** A joint venturer is a party to a joint venture.

Strategic Alliance

1. **Strategic alliance.** A strategic alliance is an arrangement between two or more companies in the same industry whereby they agree to accomplish a designated objective.

2. **International strategic alliance.** A strategic alliance may be used by companies to enter a foreign market.

Internet Exercises and Case Questions

Working the Web Internet Exercises

Activities

1. Review the FTC cases of alleged abusive practices of franchisors at **www.ftc.gov/bcp/franchise/1999-2000cases. htm**. How would you advise a franchisee client to protect against such practices? For information on federal law regarding franchising, see **www.ftc.gov/bcp/franchise/ netfran.htm**.

2. Franchising makes extensive use of licensing of intellectual property, especially trademarks and trade secrets. Use the Web sites listed below to find examples of licensing agreements and the disputes that they can sometimes produce:

- The Trade Secrets home page, at **www.execpc.com/ mhallign**
- All About Trademarks, at **www.ggmark.com**
- Intellectual Property Digital Library, at **ipdl.wipo.int**
- Intellectual Property Mall, at **www.fplc.edu/ipmall/ pointbox/pb_copy.htm**
- JurisNotes.Com—A source for all aspects of intellectual property law, at **www.jurisnotes.com**
- Marksonline—For free trademark search and domain name search, at **www.marksonline.com**

Critical Legal Thinking Cases

30.1 Franchise Agreement   H&R Block, Inc. (Block), is a franchisor that licenses franchisees to provide tax preparation services to customers under the "H&R Block" service mark. In 1975, June McCart was granted a Block franchise at 900 Main Street, Rochester, New York. From 1972 to 1979, her husband, Robert, was involved in the operation of a Block franchise in Rensselaer, New York. After that, he assisted June in the operation of her Block franchise. All the McCarts' income during the time in question came from the Block franchises.

The Block franchise agreement that June signed contained a provision whereby she agreed not to compete (1) in the business of tax preparation (2) within 250 miles of the franchise (3) for a period of two years after the termination of the franchise. Robert did not sign the Rochester franchise agreement. On December 31, 1981, June wrote a letter to Block, giving notice that she was terminating the franchise. Shortly thereafter, the McCarts sent a letter to people who had been clients of the Rochester Block office, informing them that June was leaving Block and that Robert was opening a tax preparation service in which June would assist him. Block granted a new franchise in Rochester to another franchisee. It sued the McCarts to enforce the covenant not to compete against them. Who wins? [*McCart v. H&R Block, Inc.*, 470 n.E.2d 756, 1984 Ind.App. Lexis 3039 (Ind. App. 1984)]

30.2 Franchise Agreement   Libby-Broadway Drive-In, Inc. (Libby), is a corporation licensed to operate a McDonald's fast-food franchise restaurant by the McDonald's System, Inc. (McDonald's). Libby was granted a license to operate a McDonald's in Cleveland, Ohio, and was granted an exclusive

territory in which McDonald's could not grant another franchise. The area was described as "bound on the north by the south side of Miles Avenue, on the west and south side by Turney Road, on the east by Warrensville Center Road." In December 1976, McDonald's granted a franchise to another franchisee to operate a McDonald's restaurant on the west side of Turney Road. Libby sued McDonald's, alleging a breach of the franchise agreement. Is McDonald's liable? [*Libby-Broadway Drive-In, Inc. v. McDonald's System, Inc.*, 391 N.E.2d 1, 1979 Ill.App. Lexis 2698 (Ill. App. 1979)]

30.3 Disclosure   My Pie International, Inc. (My Pie), an Illinois corporation, is a franchisor that licenses franchisees to open pie shops under its trademark name. My Pie licensed 13 restaurants throughout the country, including one owned by Dowmont, Inc. (Dowmont), in Glen Ellyn, Illinois. The Illinois Franchise Disclosure Act requires a franchisor that desires to issue franchises in the state to register with the state or qualify for an exemption from registration and to make certain disclosures to prospective franchisees. My Pie granted the license to Dowmont without registering with the state of Illinois or qualifying for an exemption from registration and without making the required disclosures to Dowmont. Dowmont operated its restaurant as a "My Pie" franchise between July 1976 and May 1980, and since then it has operated it under the name "Arnold's." Dowmont paid franchise royalty fees to My Pie prior to May 1980. My Pie sued Dowmont for breach of the franchise agreement to recover royalties it claimed were due from Dowmont. Dowmont filed a counter-claim seeking to rescind the franchise agreement and recover the royalties it paid to My Pic. Who wins? [*My Pie International, Inc. v. Dowmont, Inc.*, 687 F.2d 919, 1982 U.S. App. Lexis 16537 (7th Cir. 1982)]

30.4 Tort Liability   Georgia Girl Fashions, Inc. (Georgia Girl), is a franchisor that licenses franchisees to operate women's retail clothing stores under the "Georgia Girl" trademark. Georgia Girl granted a franchise to a franchisee to operate a store on South Cobb Drive in Smyrna, Georgia. Georgia Girl did not supervise or control the day-to-day operations of the franchisee. Melanie McMullan entered the store to exchange a blouse that she had previously purchased at the store. When she found nothing that she wished to exchange the blouse for, she began to leave the store. At that time, she was physically restrained and accused of shoplifting the blouse. McMullan was taken to the local jail, where she was held until her claim of prior purchase could be verified. The store then dropped the charges against her, and she was released from jail. McMullan filed an action against the store owner and Georgia Girl to recover damages for false imprisonment. Is Georgia Girl liable? [*McMullan v. Georgia Girl Fashions, Inc.*, 348 S.E.2d 748, 1986 Ga.App. Lexis 2093 (Ga. App. 1988)]

30.5 Tort Liability   The Seven-Up Company (Seven-Up) is a franchisor that licenses local bottling companies to manufacture, bottle, and distribute soft drinks using the "7-Up" trademark. The Brooks Bottling Company (Brooks) is a Seven-Up franchisee that bottles and sells 7-Up soft drinks to stores in Michigan. Under the franchise agreement, the franchisee is required to purchase the 7-Up syrup from Seven-Up, but it can purchase its bottles, cartons, and other supplies from independent suppliers if Seven-Up approves the design of these articles.

Brooks used cartons designed and manufactured by Olinkraft, Inc., using a design that Seven-Up had approved. Sharon Proos Kosters, a customer at Meijers Thrifty Acre Store in Holland, Michigan, removed a cardboard carton containing six bottles of 7-Up from a grocery store shelf, put it under her arm, and walked toward the checkout counter. As she did so, a bottle slipped out of the carton, fell on the floor, and exploded, causing a piece of glass to strike Kosters in her eye as she looked down; she was blinded in that eye. Evidence showed that the 7-Up carton was designed to be held from the top and was made without a strip on the side of the carton that would prevent a bottle from slipping out if held underneath. Kosters sued Seven-Up to recover damages for her injuries. Is Seven-Up liable? [*Kosters v. Seven-Up Company*, 595 F.2d 347, 1979 U.S.App. Lexis 15945 (6th Cir. 1979)]

30.6 Trademark   The Kentucky Fried Chicken Corporation (KFC) is the franchisor of Kentucky Fried Chicken restaurants. Franchisees must purchase equipment and supplies from manufacturers approved in writing by KFC. Equipment includes cookers, fryers, ovens, and the like; supplies include carry-out boxes, napkins, towelettes, and plastic eating utensils known as "sporks." These products are not trade secrets. KFC may not "unreasonably withhold" approval of any suppliers who apply and whose goods are tested and found to meet KFC's quality control standards. The 10 manufacturers who went through KFC's approval process were approved. KFC also sells supplies to franchisees in competition with these independent suppliers. All supplies, whether produced by KFC or the independent suppliers, must contain "Kentucky Fried Chicken" trademarks.

Upon formation in 1972, Diversified Container Corporation (Diversified) began manufacturing and selling supplies to KFC franchisees without applying for or receiving KFC's approval. All the items sold by Diversified contained KFC trademarks. Diversified represented to franchisees that its products met "all standards" of KFC and that it sold "approved supplies." Diversified even affixed KFC trademarks to the shipping boxes in which it delivered supplies to franchisees. Evidence showed that Diversified's products did not meet the quality control standards set by KFC. KFC sued Diversified for trademark infringement. Who wins? [*Kentucky Fried Chicken Corporation v. Diversified Container Corporation*, 549 F.2d 368, 1977 U.S. App. Lexis 14128 (5th Cir. 1977)]

30.7 Trademarks   Ramada Inns, Inc. (Ramada Inns), is a franchisor that licenses franchisees to operate motor hotels using the "Ramada Inns" trademarks and service marks. In August 1977, the Gadsden Motor Company (Gadsden), a partnership, purchased a motel in Attalla, Alabama, and entered into a franchise agreement with Ramada Inns to operate it as a Ramada Inns motor hotel. In 1982, the motel began receiving poor ratings from Ramada Inns inspectors, and Gadsden fell behind on its monthly franchise fee payments. Despite proddings from Ramada Inns, the motel never met Ramada Inns's operational standards again. On November 17, 1983, Ramada Inns properly terminated the franchise agreement, citing quality deficiencies and Gadsden's failure to pay past-due franchise fees. The termination notice directed Gadsden to remove any materials or signs identifying the motel as a Ramada Inns. Gadsden continued using Ramada Inn's signage, trademarks, and service marks inside and outside the motel. In September 1984, Ramada Inns sued Gadsden for trademark infringement. Who wins? [*Ramada Inns, Inc. v. Gadsden Motel Company*, 804 F.2d 1562, 1986 U.S. App. Lexis 34279 (11th Cir.)]

30.8 Termination of a Franchise   Kawasaki Motors Corporation (Kawasaki), a Japanese corporation, manufactures motorcycles that it distributes in the United States through its subsidiary, Kawasaki Motors Corporation, U.S.A. (Kawasaki USA). Kawasaki USA is a franchisor that grants franchises to dealerships to sell Kawasaki motorcycles. In 1971, Kawasaki USA granted the Kawasaki Shop of Aurora, Inc. (Dealer), a franchise to sell Kawasaki motorcycles in Aurora, Illinois. The franchise changed locations twice. Both moves were within the five-mile exclusive territory granted Dealer in the franchise agreement.

Dealer did not obtain Kawasaki USA's written approval for either move, as required by the franchise agreement. Kawasaki USA acquiesced to the first move but not the second. At the second new location, Dealer also operated Honda and Suzuki motorcycle franchises and was negotiating to operate a Yamaha franchise. The Kawasaki franchise agreement expressly permitted multiline dealerships. Kawasaki USA objected to the second move, asserting that Dealer had not received written approval for the move, as required by the franchise agreement. Evidence showed, however, that the real reason Kawasaki objected to the move was because it did not want its motorcycles to be sold at the same location as other manufacturers' motorcycles. Kawasaki terminated Dealer's franchise. Dealer sued Kawasaki USA for wrongful termination. Who wins? [*Kawasaki Shop of Aurora, Inc. v. Kawasaki Motors Corporation, U.S.A.*, 544 N.E.2d 457, 1989 Ill. App. Lexis 1442 (Ill. App. 1989)]

Business Ethics Cases

30.9 Business Ethics Southland Corporation (Southland) owned the "7-Eleven" trademark and licenses franchisees throughout the country to operate 7-Eleven stores. The franchise agreement provides for fees to be paid to Southland by each franchisee based on a percentage of gross profits. In return, franchisees receive a lease of premises, a license to use the 7-Eleven trademark and trade secrets, advertising merchandise, and bookkeeping assistance. Vallerie Campbell purchased an existing 7-Eleven store in Fontana, California, and became a Southland franchisee. The franchise was designated #13974 by Southland. As part of the purchase, she applied to the state of California for transfer of the beer and wine license from the prior owner. Southland also executed the application. California approved the transfer and issued the license to "Campbell Vallerie Southland #13974."

On September 9, 1978, an employee of Campbell's store sold beer to Jesse Lewis Cope, a minor who was allegedly intoxicated at the time. After drinking the beer, Cope drove his vehicle and struck another vehicle. Two occupants of the other vehicle, Denise Wickham and Tyrone Crosby, were severely injured, and a third occupant, Cedrick Johnson, was killed. Johnson (through his parents), Wickham, and Crosby sued Southland—but not Campbell—to recover damages. Is Southland legally liable for the tortious acts of its franchisee? Is it morally responsible? [*Wickham v. The Southland Corporation*, 168 Cal.App.3d 49, 213 Cal.Rptr. 825, 1985 Cal.App. Lexis 2070 (Cal.App. 1985)]

30.10 Business Ethics The Kentucky Fried Chicken Corporation (KFC), with its principal place of business in Louisville, Kentucky, is the franchisor of Kentucky Fried Chicken restaurants. KFC's registered trademarks and service marks include "Kentucky Fried Chicken," "It's Finger Lickin' Good," and the portrait of Colonel Harlan Sanders. KFC grants a license to its franchisees to use these marks in connection with the preparation and sale of "Original Recipe Kentucky Fried Chicken." Original Recipe Kentucky Fried Chicken, which is sold only by KFC franchisees, is prepared by a special cooking process featuring the use of a secret recipe seasoning known as "KFC Seasonings." This blend of seasoning was developed by KFC's founder, Colonel Harlan Sanders. As a condition of each franchise agreement, KFC requires that its franchisees use only KFC Seasoning in connection with the preparation and sale of Kentucky Fried Chicken.

KFC Seasoning is a trade secret. To make the seasoning, KFC has entered into contracts with two spice blenders, the John W. Sexton Company, Inc. (Sexton), and Strange Company (Strange). Each of these companies blends approximately one-half the spices of KFC Seasoning; neither has knowledge of the complete formulation of KFC Seasoning, and both entered into secrecy agreements to maintain the confidentiality of their formulation. After the seasoning is blended by Sexton and Strange, it is mixed together and sold directly to all KFC franchisees. KFC does not receive a royalty or other economic benefit from the sale of KFC Seasoning. KFC's relationship with Sexton and Strange has existed for more than 25 years; no other companies are licensed to blend KFC Seasoning.

Marion-Kay Company, Inc. (Marion-Kay), is a spice blender engaged in the manufacture of chicken seasoning known as "Marion-Kay Seasoning." In 1973, Marion-Kay requested permission from KFC to sell its seasoning products to KFC franchisees. KFC refused the request. In 1977, KFC learned that Marion-Kay was supplying some KFC franchisees with Marion-Kay seasoning and demanded it cease this practice. When Marion-Kay refused, KFC sued it for interference with contractual relations. Marion-Kay filed a counterclaim, alleging violation of antitrust law. Who wins? Was KFC justified in preventing Marion-Kay from blending its seasonings? Did Marion-Kay act morally in selling seasoning to KFC franchisees? [*KFC Corporation v. Marion-Kay Company, Inc.*, 620 F.Supp. 1160, 1985 U.S. Dist. Lexis 14766 (S.D. Ind. 1985)]

Briefing the Case Writing Assignment

Read Case A.30 in the Case Appendix [*Little v. Howard Johnson Company*]. This case is excerpted from the court of appeals opinion. Review and brief the case. In your brief, be sure to answer the following questions.

1. Describe how the plaintiff was injured. Whom did she sue?

2. Was Howard Johnson Company directly liable for the plaintiff's injuries? Explain.

3. Was the franchisee an actual agent of Howard Johnson Company?

4. Did Howard Johnson's actions create an apparent agency between it and the franchisee?

Endnotes

1. Cal. Corp. Code §§ 31000–31019.
2. 16 CFR Part 436.

3. *Southland Corporation v. Keating*, 465 U.S. 1, 104 S.Ct. 852, 1984 U.S. Lexis 2 (1985).

31

Investor Protection and Online Securities Transactions

Chapter Objectives

After studying this chapter, you should be able to:

1. Describe the procedure for "going public" and how securities are registered with the Securities and Exchange Commission.

2. Describe the requirements for qualifying for private placement, intrastate, and small offering exemptions from registration.

3. Define insider trading that violates Section 10(b) of the Securities Exchange Act of 1934.

4. Describe the liability of tippers and tippees for insider trading.

5. Describe short-swing profits that violate Section 16(b) of the Securities Exchange Act of 1934.

Chapter Contents

- The Securities and Exchange Commission (SEC)

- The Securities Act of 1933—Going Public

- Private and Other Transactions Exempt from Registration

- Violations of the Securities Act of 1933

- The Securities Exchange Act of 1934—Trading in Securities

- Violations of the Securities Exchange Act of 1934

- Short-Swing Profits

- State Securities Laws

Prior to the 1920s and 1930s, the securities markets in this country were not regulated by the federal government. Securities were sold to investors with little, if any, disclosure. Fraud in these transactions was common.

Following the stock market crash of 1929, Congress enacted a series of statutes designed to regulate securities markets. The *Securities Act of 1933* requires disclosure by companies and others who wish to issue securities to the public. The *Securities Exchange Act of 1934* was enacted to prevent fraud in the subsequent trading of securities, including insider trading. Securities are now sold online. The SEC also regulates the sale of securities online.

These federal and state statutes are designed to (1) require disclosure of information to investors and (2) prevent fraud. This chapter discusses federal and state securities laws and regulations that provide investor protection, as well as the sale of securities online.

The Securities and Exchange Commission (SEC)

The Securities Exchange Act of 1934 created the **Securities and Exchange Commission (SEC)** and empowered it to administer federal securities laws. The SEC is an administrative agency composed of five members who are appointed by the president. The major responsibilities of the SEC are:

1. Adopting rules (also called regulations) that further the purpose of the federal securities statutes. These rules have the force of law.
2. Investigating alleged securities violations and bringing enforcement actions against suspected violators. This may include a recommendation of criminal prosecution. Criminal prosecutions of violations of federal securities laws are brought by the U.S. Department of Justice.
3. Regulating the activities of securities brokers and advisors. This includes registering brokers and advisors and taking enforcement action against those who violate securities laws.

Definition of Security

A **security** must exist before securities laws apply. Securities are defined as:

1. Interests or instruments that are commonly known as securities (e.g., common stock, preferred stock, bonds, debentures, warrants).
2. Interests or instruments that are expressly mentioned in securities acts (e.g., preorganization subscription agreements; interests in oil, gas, and mineral rights; deposit receipts for foreign securities).
3. Investment contracts—that is, any contract whereby an investor invests money or other consideration in a common enterprise and expects to make a profit from the significant efforts of others. Limited partnership interests, pyramid sales schemes, and investments in farm animals accompanied by care agreements have been found to be securities under this test, which is known as the *Howery test*.[1]

In the following case, the U.S. Supreme Court held that a financial scheme constituted a security subject to federal securities laws.

Case 31.1

Definition of Security

Background and Facts

Charles Edwards was the chairman, chief executive officer (CEO), and sole shareholder of ETS Payphones, Inc. (ETS). ETS sold payphones to the public via independent distributors. The payphones were sold to buyers in a $7,000 package deal, consisting of a payphone site lease, a 5-year leaseback by ETS, and an agreement whereby ETS would install the equipment at the site, arrange for connection and long-distance telephone service, collect coin revenues, and maintain and repair the payphones. Under the ETS contract, each payphone investor was guaranteed to receive $82 per month on his or her investment. ETS guaranteed to refund the full purchase price at the end of the lease. ETS enrolled over 10,000 people in the payphone program, and they invested over $300 million.

In actuality, the payphone did not generate enough revenues for ETS to make the guaranteed monthly payments. After ETS defaulted on hundreds of millions of dollars of payments to investors, it filed for bankruptcy. The Securities and Exchange Commission (SEC) brought a civil action against Edwards and ETS, alleging that the defendants had failed to register the payphone sale-and-leaseback arrangement with the SEC as a "security" prior to selling the phones to the public and had committed securities fraud. The U.S. District Court held that the payphone arrangement constituted a "security" and was therefore subject to federal securities laws. The U.S. Court of Appeals reversed, finding no security because the sale-and-leaseback provided for a fixed rate of return rather than capital appreciation or participation in the earnings of the enterprise. The SEC appealed to the U.S. Supreme Court.

Issue

Is the payphone sale-and-leaseback arrangement that guaranteed a fixed rate of return a security and therefore subject to federal securities laws?

Court's Reasoning

The U.S. Supreme Court mocked ETS; promotional brochure that stated "Opportunity doesn't always knock, sometimes it rings" by stating "And sometimes it hangs up." The Supreme Court stated that that is exactly what Edwards and ETS did to the 10,000 investors who lost $300 million on the payphone investment scheme. The Supreme Court held that Congress, by enacting federal securities laws, intended to regulate investments in whatever form they are made and by whatever name they are called. The Court stated:

> There is no reason to distinguish between promises of fixed returns and promises of variable returns. In both cases, the investing public is attracted by representations of investment income. Moreover, investments pitched as low risk (such as those offering a guaranteed fixed return) are particularly attractive to individuals more vulnerable to investment fraud, including older and less sophisticated investors.

The Court noted that under the reading respondent Edwards advances, unscrupulous marketers of investments could evade the securities laws by picking a fixed rate of return to promise.

Decision and Remedy

The U.S. Supreme Court held that an investment arrangement that offers a fixed rate of return is a security subject to the provisions of federal securities laws. The Supreme Court reversed the decision of the Court of Appeals and remanded the case for further proceedings based on violations of securities laws and securities fraud.

Case Questions

Critical Legal Thinking   If a financial arrangement that guaranteed a fixed rate of return is not found to be a security, what would be the result for society? Explain.

Business Ethics   Did Edwards act ethically in this case? Is there any evidence that he acted fraudulently? Explain.

Contemporary Business   If Edwards had to disclose the truth about his and ETS's investment scheme, would many people have invested? Explain.

The Securities Act of 1933—Going Public

The **Securities Act of 1933** primarily regulates the issuance of securities by a corporation, a limited partnership, other businesses, or an individual.[2] **Section 5** of the Securities Act of 1933 requires securities offered to the public through the use of the mails or any facility of interstate commerce to be registered with the SEC by means of a registration statement and an accompanying prospectus.

The business or party selling the securities to the public is called the **issuer**. The issuer may be a relatively new company (e.g., Google, Inc.) selling securities to the

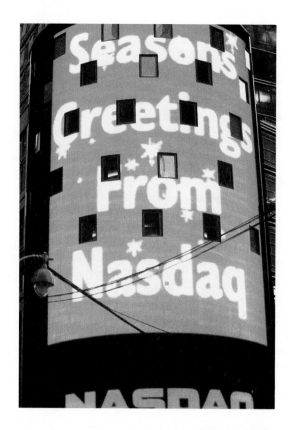

public through an *initial public offering* (*IPO*), or it may be an established company (e.g., Microsoft Corporation) selling new securities to the public. Many issuers of securities employ **investment bankers**, which are independent securities companies, to sell their securities to the public. Issuers pay a fee to investment bankers for this service.

Registration Statement

A covered issuer must file a written **registration statement** with the SEC. The issuer's lawyer normally prepares the statement, with the help of the issuer's management, accountants, and underwriters.

A registration statement must contain descriptions of (1) securities being offered for sale, (2) the registrant's business, (3) the management of the registrant, including compensation, stock options and benefits, and material transactions with the registrant, (4) pending litigation, (5) how the proceeds from the offering will be used, (6) government regulation, (7) the degree of competition in the industry, and (8) any special risk factors. In addition, a registration statement must be accompanied by financial statements certified by certified public accountants.

Registration statements usually become effective 20 business days after they are filed, unless the SEC requires additional information to be disclosed. A new 20-day period begins each time the registration statement is amended. At the registrant's request, the SEC may "accelerate the *effective date*" (i.e., not require the registrant to wait 20 days after the last amendment is filed).

The SEC does not pass judgment on the merits of the securities offered. It decides only whether the issuer has met the disclosure requirements.

Prospectus

A **Prospectus** is a written disclosure document that must be submitted to the SEC along with the registration statement. A prospectus is used as a selling tool by the issuer. It is provided to prospective investors to enable them to evaluate the financial risk of an investment.

A prospectus must contain the following language in capital letters and boldface (usually red) type:

THESE SECURITIES HAVE NOT BEEN APPROVED OR DISAPPROVED BY THE SECURITIES AND EXCHANGE COMMISSION OR ANY STATE SECURITIES COMMISSION NOR HAS THE SECURITIES AND EXCHANGE COMMISSION OR ANY STATE SECURITIES COMMISSION PASSED UPON THE ACCURACY OR ADEQUACY OF THIS PROSPECTUS. ANY REPRESENTATION TO THE CONTRARY IS A CRIMINAL OFFENSE.

Online Commerce & Internet Law
Company Goes Public over the Internet

The SEC permits companies to issue securities over the Internet. The same federal securities laws that regulate the traditional issuance of securities also apply to the issuance of securities using the Internet. One company's Internet initial public offering (IPO) follows. ■

The information in this prospectus is not complete and may be changed. We may not sell these securities until the registration statement filed with the Securities and Exchange Commission is effective. This prospectus is not an offer to sell these securities and is not soliciting an offer to buy these securities in any state where the offer or sale is not permitted.

SUBJECT TO COMPLETION, DATED DECEMBER 21, 2000

PEET'S COFFEE & TEA, INC.

3,300,000 Shares
of Common Stock

This is our initial public offering and no public market currently exists for our shares. We expect that the public offering price will be between $10.00 and $14.00 per share. This price may not reflect the market price of our shares after this offering.

THE OFFERING	PER SHARE	TOTAL
Public Offering Price	$	$
Underwriting Discount	$	$
Proceeds to Peet's	$	$
Proceeds to Selling Shareholders	$	$

Of the 3,300,000 shares being offered, we are selling 2,500,000 shares and the selling shareholders identified in this prospectus are selling 800,000 shares. We will not receive any of the proceeds from the sale of shares by the selling shareholders. We have granted the underwriters the right to purchase up to 182,623 additional shares from us and 312,377 additional shares from the selling shareholders within 30 days to cover any over- allotments. The underwriters expect to deliver shares of common stock to purchasers on _____ , 2001.

Proposed Nasdaq National Market Symbol: PEET

OPENIPO: The method of distribution being used by the underwriters in this offering differs somewhat from that traditionally employed in firm commitment underwritten public offerings. In particular, the public offering price and allocation of shares will be determined primarily by an auction process conducted by the underwriters and other securities dealers participating in this offering. A more detailed description of this process, known as an OpenIPO, is included in "Plan of Distribution."

THIS OFFERING INVOLVES A HIGH DEGREE OF RISK. YOU SHOULD PURCHASE SHARES ONLY IF YOU CAN AFFORD A COMPLETE LOSS OF YOUR INVESTMENT. SEE "RISK FACTORS" BEGINNING ON PAGE 5.

NEITHER THE SECURITIES AND EXCHANGE COMMISSION NOR ANY STATE SECURITIES COMMISSION HAS APPROVED OR DISAPPROVED OF THESE SECURITIES OR DETERMINED IF THIS PROSPECTUS IS TRUTHFUL OR COMPLETE. ANY REPRESENTATION TO THE CONTRARY IS A CRIMINAL OFFENSE.

WRHAMBRECHT+CO

Pacific Growth Equities, Inc.

The date of this prospectus is _____ , 2001

Limitations on Activities During the Registration Process

Section 5 of the Securities Act of 1933 limits the types of activities that an issuer, an underwriter, and a dealer may engage in during the registration process. These limitations are divided into the following three time periods:

- *The prefiling period.* The **prefiling period** begins when the issuer first contemplates issuing the securities and ends when the registration statement is filed. During this time, the issuer cannot either sell or offer to sell the securities. The issuer also cannot *condition the market* for the upcoming securities offering. This rule makes it illegal for an issuer to engage in a public relations campaign (e.g., newspaper and magazine articles and advertisements) that touts the prospects of the company and the planned securities issue. However, sending annual reports to shareholders and making public announcements of factual matters (such as the settlement of a strike) are permissible because they are considered normal corporate disclosures.

- *The waiting period.* The **waiting period** begins when the registration statement is filed with the SEC and continues until the registration statement is declared effective.

    The issuer is encouraged to condition the market during this time. Thus, the issuer may (1) make oral offers to sell (including face-to-face and telephone conversations), (2) distribute a *preliminary prospectus* (usually called a red herring), which contains most of the information to be contained in the final prospectus except for price, (3) distribute a *summary prospectus*, which is a summary of the important terms contained in the prospectus, and (4) publish *tombstone ads* in newspapers and other publications. Unapproved writings (which are considered illegal offers to sell) as well as actual sales are prohibited during the waiting period.

- *The posteffective period.* The **posteffective period** begins when the registration statement becomes effective and runs until the issuer either sells all of the offered securities or withdraws them from sale. Thus, the issuer and its underwriter and dealers may close the offers received prior to the effective date and solicit new offers and sales.

    Prior to or at the time of confirming a sale or sending a security to a purchaser, the issuer (or its representative) must deliver a **final prospectus** (also called a **statutory prospectus** to the investor. Failure to do so is a violation of Section 5. Tombtone ads are often used during this period.

    The investor may rescind his or her purchase if the issuer violates any of the prohibitions on activities during these periods. If an underwriter or a dealer violates any of these prohibitions, the SEC may issue sanctions, including the suspension of securities licenses.

Sale of Unregistered Securities

Sale of securities that should have been registered with the SEC but are not, violates the Securities Act of 1933. Investors can rescind their purchase and recover damages. The U.S. government can impose criminal penalties on any person who willfully violates the Securities Act of 1933.

Regulation A Offerings

Regulation A permits issuers to sell up to $5 million of securities to the public during a 12-month period pursuant to a simplified registration process. Such offerings may have an unlimited number of purchasers who do not have to be accredited investors. Offerings exceeding $100,000 must file an **offering statement** with the SEC. The offering statement requires less disclosure than a registration statement and is less costly to prepare. Investors must be provided with an offering circular prior to the purchase of securities. There are no resale restrictions on the securities.

Small Corporate Offering Registration Form (SCOR) Small businesses often need to raise capital and must find public investors to buy company stock. In 1992, after years of investigation, the SEC amended Regulation A by adopting the **Small Corporate Offering Registration Form (SCOR)**. The SCOR form—**Form U-7**—is a question-and-answer disclosure form that small businesses can complete and file with the SEC if they plan on raising $1 million or less from the public issue of securities. An issuer must answer the questions on Form U-7, which then becomes the offering circular that must be given to prospective investors.

Form U-7 questions are so clearly and specifically drawn that they can be answered by the issuer without the help of an expensive securities lawyer. The SCOR questions require the issuer to develop a business plan that states specific company goals and how it plans to reach them. SCOR is limited to domestic businesses. The SCOR offering cannot exceed $1 million, and the offering price of the common stock or its equivalent may not be less than $5 per share. SCOR offerings are a welcomed addition for entrepreneur-owners who want to raise money through a small public offering.

Contemporary Environment
Securities Offerings Must Be Written in Plain English

Nonlawyers have always been frustrated by the legalese used by lawyers in contracts, court documents, and regulatory disclosures. There has been no wider use of arcane legal language than in prospectuses offering securities for sale to the public.

These documents, which are supposed to provide relevant information to potential investors before they invest in company stock and securities, are usually barely skimmed, let alone read, by potential investors.

The SEC decided to change this practice in 1998 when it adopted a "plain English" rule for securities offerings. Under this rule, issuers of securities must use plain English language on the cover page, in the summary, and in the risk factors sections of their prospectuses. Issuers must now use:

■ Active voice.
■ Short sentences.

■ "Everyday" words.
■ Bullet lists for complex information.
■ No legal jargon or highly technical terms.
■ No multiple negatives.

The plain English rule has required a major cultural change by issuers, underwriters, and securities lawyers, who are used to using complicated and confusing language. The SEC has stated that it will not be the "grammar police," but will instead focus on the clarity of disclosures to potential investors by issuers. The SEC hopes that its new rule will encourage issuers to use plain English throughout the entire prospectus. [Rule 421(d) of Regulation C] ■

Private and Other Transactions Exempt from Registration

Certain *transactions* in securities are exempt from registration. Exempt transactions are subject to the antifraud provisions of the federal securities laws. Therefore, the issuer must provide investors with adequate information—including annual reports, quarterly reports, proxy statements, financial statements, and so on—even though a registration statement is not required. The exempt transactions are discussed in the paragraphs that follow.

Business Brief

If a business plans to issue nonexempt securities, it must either (1) register the securities with the SEC or (2) qualify for an exemption from registration.

Nonissuer Exemption

Nonissuers, such as average investors, do not have to file a registration statement prior to reselling securities they have purchased. This is because the Securities Act of 1933 exempts securities transactions not made by an issuer, an underwriter, or a dealer from registration. For example, an investor who owns shares of IBM can resell these shares to another at any time without having to register with the SEC.

Intrastate Offerings

The purpose of the **intrastate offerings exemption** is to permit local businesses to raise from local investors capital to be used in the local economy without the need to register with the SEC.[3] There is no limit on the dollar amount of capital that can be raised pursuant to an intrastate offering exemption. An issuer can qualify for this exemption in only one state.

Three requirements must be met to qualify for this exemption[4]:

1. The issuer must be a resident of the state for which the exemption is claimed. A corporation is a resident of the state in which it is incorporated.
2. The issuer must be doing business in that state. This requires that 80 percent of the issuer's assets be located in the state, 80 percent of its gross revenues be derived from the state, its principal office be located in the state, and 80 percent of the proceeds of the offering be used in the state.
3. The purchasers of the securities all must be residents of that state.

Private Placements

An issue of securities that does not involve a public offering is exempt from the registration requirements.[5] This exemption—known as the **private placement exemption**—allows issuers to raise capital from an unlimited number of accredited investors without having to register the offering with the SEC.[6] There is no dollar limit on the amount of securities that can be sold pursuant to this exemption.

An *accredited investor* may be[7]:

1. Any natural person (including spouse) who has a net worth of at least $1 million.
2. Any natural person who has had an annual income of at least $200,000 for the pervious two years and reasonably expects to make $200,000 income in the current year.
3. Any corporation, partnership, or business trust with total assets in excess of $5 million.
4. Insiders of the issuers, such as executive officers and directors of corporate issuers and general partners of partnership issuers.
5. Certain institutional investors, such as registered investment companies, pension plans, colleges and universities, and the like.

No more than 35 *nonaccredited investors* may purchase securities pursuant to a private placement exemption. Nonaccredited investors must be sophisticated investors, however, either through their own experience and education or through representatives (such as accountants, lawyers, and business managers). General selling efforts, such as advertising to the public, are not permitted.

Small Offerings

Securities offerings that do not exceed a certain dollar amount are exempt from registration.[8] Rule 504 exempts the sale of securities not exceeding $1 million during a 12-month period from registration. The securities may be sold to an unlimited number of accredited and unaccredited investors, but general selling efforts to the public are not permitted. This is called the **small offering exemption**.

Resale Restrictions

Certain *resale restrictions* are placed on securities issued pursuant to exemptions from registration. These restrictions are discussed in the following paragraphs.

Restricted Securities Securities sold pursuant to the intrastate, private placement, or small offering exemptions are called **restricted securities** because they cannot be resold for a limited period of time after their initial issue. The following restrictions apply:

- Rule 147 stipulates that securities sold pursuant to an intrastate offering exemption cannot be sold to nonresidents for a period of nine months.

- Rule 144 provides that securities sold pursuant to the private placement or small offering exemption must be held for one year from the date when the securities are last sold by the issuer. After that time, investors may sell the greater of (1) one percent of the outstanding securities of the issuer or (2) the average weekly volume of trading in the securities (i.e., the four-week moving average) in any three-month period. Information about the issuer must be available to the public. Generally, all restrictions are lifted after two years.

Preventing Transfer of Restricted Securities To protect the nontransferability of restricted shares, the issuer must:

1. Require the investors to sign an *affidavit* stating that they are buying the securities for investment, acknowledging that they are purchasing restricted securities, and promising not to transfer the shares in violation of the restriction.
2. Place a *legend* on the stock certificate describing the restriction.
3. Notify the *transfer agent* not to record a transfer of the securities that would violate the restriction.

If the issuer has taken these precautions, it will not lose its exemption from registration even if isolated transfers of stock occur in violation of the restricted periods. If these precautions are not taken, the issuer may lose its exemption from registration. In that event, it has sold unregistered securities in violation of Section 5, permitting all purchasers to rescind their purchases of the securities.

Ethics Brief
An issuer must take certain actions to ensure that restricted securities are not sold in violation of the restrictions imposed by Rules 144 and 147.

Rule 144A

To establish a more liquid and efficient secondary market in unregistered securities, the SEC adopted Rule 144A in 1990. This rule permits "qualified institutional investors"—defined as institutions that own and invest at least $100 million in securities—to buy unregistered securities without being subject to the holding periods of Rule 144. This rule is designed to create an institutional market in unregistered securities as well as to permit foreign issuers to raise capital in this country from sophisticated investors without making registration process disclosures.

Business Brief
To increase the liquidity of registered securities, the SEC adopted Rule 144A in 1990. It permits "qualified institutional investors" to buy unregistered securities without being subject to the holding periods of Rule 144.

Securities Exempt from Registration

Certain *securities* are exempt from registration. Once a security is exempt, it is exempt forever. It does not matter how many times the security is transferred. Exempt securities include:

1. Securities issued by any government in the United States (e.g., municipal bonds issued by city governments).
2. Short-term notes and drafts that have a maturity date that does not exceed nine months (e.g., commercial paper issued by corporations).

Business Brief
Certain types of *securities* do not have to be registered with the SEC.

3. Securities issued by nonprofit issuers, such as religious institutions, charitable institutions, and colleges and universities.
4. Securities of financial institutions (e.g., banks and savings associations) that are regulated by the appropriate banking authorities.
5. Securities issued by common carriers (railroads and trucking companies) that are regulated by the Interstate Commerce Commission (ICC).
6. Insurance and annuity contracts issued by insurance companies.
7. Stock dividends and stock splits.
8. Securities issued in a corporate reorganization where one security is exchanged for another security.

Violations of the Securities Act of 1933

Violations of the Securities Act of 1933 may result in various penalties and remedies against the perpetrator. These penalties and remedies are discussed in the following paragraphs.

SEC Actions   The SEC may (1) issue a *consent order* whereby a defendant agrees not to violate securities laws in the future but does not admit to having violated securities laws in the past, (2) bring an action in federal district court to obtain an *injunction*, or (3) request the court to grant ancillary relief, such as *disgorgement of profits* by the defendant.

Private Actions

Private parties who have been injured by violations of the Securities Act of 1933 have recourse against the violator under the following two sections:

1. **Section 12** of the 1933 act imposes *civil liability* on any person who violates the provisions of Section 5 of the act. Violations include selling securities pursuant to an unwarranted exemption and making misrepresentations concerning the offer or sale

Singing Sand Mountains, Dunhuang, China. Foreign securities markets have developed in many countries. Each country has its own securities laws.

of securities. The purchaser's remedy for a violation of Section 12 is either to rescind the purchase or to sue for damages.

2. **Section 11** of the 1933 act provides for civil liability for damages when a registration statement on its effective date misstates or omits a material fact. Liability under Section 11 is imposed on those who (1) intentionally defraud investors or (2) are negligent in not discovering the fraud. Thus, the issuer, certain corporate officers (chief executive officer, chief financial officer, chief accounting officer), directors, signers of the registration statement, underwriters, and experts (accountants who certify financial statements and lawyers who issue legal opinions that are included in a registration statement) may be liable.

All defendants except the issuer may assert a **due diligence defense** against the imposition of Section 11 liability. If this defense is proven, the defendant is not liable. To establish a due diligence defense, the defendant must prove that after reasonable investigation, he or she had reasonable grounds to believe and did believe that, at the time the registration statement became effective, the statements contained therein were true and there was no omission of material facts.

Criminal Liability

Section 24 of the Securities Act of 1933 imposes *criminal liability* on any person who *willfully* violates either the act or the rules and regulations adopted thereunder.[9] A violator may be fined up to $10,000 or imprisoned up to five years, or both. Criminal actions are brought by the Department of Justice.

Business Ethics

Sarbanes-Oxley Act Erects a Wall Between Investment Bankers and Security Analysis

Investment banking is a service provided by many securities firms, whereby they assist companies to "go public" when issuing shares to the public and otherwise selling securities. The securities firms are paid lucrative fees for providing investment banking services in assisting companies to sell their securities and finding customers to purchase these securities. These same securities firms often provide securities analysis, whereby they provide investment advice, recommending securities listed on the stock exchanges and other securities to be purchased by the public.

In the late 1990s and early 2000s, many conflicts of interest were uncovered. Investment bankers and securities analysts of the same firm shared information, and the analysts were paid or pressured by the securities firms to write glowing reports of companies that the investment bankers of the firm were earning fees from.

Congress sought to remedy this problem by enacting Section 501 of the Sarbanes-Oxley Act of 2002. Section 501 established rules for separating the investment banking and securities advice functions of securities firms, thus eliminating many conflicts of interest:

■ Securities firms must establish structural and institutional "walls" between their investment banking and securities analysis areas. These walls must protect analysts from review, pressure, and oversight by persons employed by the investment banking area of the securities firm.
■ Securities analysts must disclose in each research report or public appearance any conflicts of interest that are known or should have been known to exist at the time of publication or public appearance.

The SEC is empowered to adopt rules to enforce the provisions of Section 501.

1. Why did investment bankers of a securities firm put pressure on analysts to issue positive reports on certain companies? Was this conduct ethical?
2. Do you think Section 501 will prevent such conduct in the future? Why or why not? ■

The Securities Exchange Act of 1934— Trading in Securities

Unlike the Securities Act of 1933, which regulates the original issuance of securities, the **Securities Exchange Act of 1934** primarily regulates subsequent trading.[10] It provides for the registration of certain companies with the SEC, the continuous filing of periodic reports by these companies to the SEC, and the regulation of securities exchanges, brokers, and dealers. It also contains provisions that assess civil and criminal liability on violators of the 1934 act and rules and regulations adopted thereunder.

Continuous Reporting Requirements

The **Securities Exchange Act of 1934** requires issuers (1) with assets of more than $5 million and at least 500 shareholders, (2) whose equity securities are traded on a national securities exchange, or (3) who have made a registered offering under the Securities Act of 1933 to file periodic reports with the SEC. These issuers, called *reporting companies*, must file an annual report (*Form 10-K*), quarterly reports (*Form 10-Q*), and monthly reports within 10 days of the end of the month in which a material event (such as a merger) occurs (*Form 8-K*). These reports are electronically filed with the SEC.

Section 10(b) and Rule 10b-5

Section 10(b) is one of the most important sections in the entire 1934 act. It prohibits the use of manipulative and deceptive devices in contravention of the rules and regulations prescribed by the SEC.

Pursuant to its rule-making authority, the SEC has adopted **Rule 10b-5**, which provides that:

> It shall be unlawful for any person, directly or indirectly, by use of any means or instrumentality of interstate commerce or of the mails, or of any facility of any national securities exchange,
>
> a. to employ any device, scheme, or artifice to defraud,
>
> b. to make any untrue statement of a material fact or to omit to state a material fact necessary in order to make the statements made, in light of the circumstances under which they were made, not misleading, or
>
> c. to engage in any act, practice, or course of business that operates or would operate as a fraud or deceit upon any person, in connection with the purchase or sale of any security.

Rule 10b-5 is not restricted to purchases and sales of securities of reporting companies.[11] All transfers of securities, whether made on a stock exchange, in the over-the-counter market, in a private sale, or in connection with a merger, are subject to this rule.[12] The U.S. Supreme Court has held that only conduct involving **scienter** (intentional conduct) violates Section 10(b) and Rule 10b-5. Negligent conduct is not a violation.[13]

Section 10(b) and Rule 10b-5 require reliance by the injured party on the misstatement. However, many sales and purchases of securities occur in open market transactions (e.g., over stock exchanges) where there is no direct communication between the buyer and the seller.

Insider Trading

One of the most important purposes of Section 10(b) and Rule 10b-5 is to prevent **insider trading**. Insider trading occurs when a company employee or company advisor uses material nonpublic information to make a profit by trading in the securities of the company. This practice is considered illegal because it allows insiders to take advantage of the investing public.

In the *Matter of Cody, Roberts & Co.*,[14] the SEC announced that the duty of an insider who possesses material nonpublic information is to either (1) abstain from trading in the securities of the company or (2) disclose the information to the person on the other side of the transaction before the insider purchases the securities from or sells the securities to him or her.

Insiders For Purposes of Section 10(b) and Rule 10b-5, *insiders* are defined as (1) officers, directors, and employees at all levels of the company; (2) lawyers, accountants, consultants, and other agents and representatives who are hired by the company on a temporary and non-employee status to provide services or work to the company; and (3) others who owe a fiduciary duty to the company.

Consider This Example The Widget Corporation has its annual audit done by its outside CPAs, Ernest & Old, CPAs. Peter is one of the CPAs who conduct the audit. The audit discloses that the Widget Corporation's profits have doubled since last year, and Peter rightfully discloses this fact to Martha, the chief financial officer (CFO) of Widget Corporations. Both Martha and Peter are *insiders*. The earnings information is definitely *material*, and it is *nonpublic* until the corporation publicly announce its earnings in two days. Prior to the earnings information being made public, Peter and Martha buy stock in Widget Corporation at $100 per share. After the earnings information is made public, the stock of Widget Corporation increases to $150 per share. Both Peter and Martha are liable for insider trading in violation of Section 10(b) and Rule 10b-5 because they traded in the securities of Widget Corporation while in possession of inside information.

The following two cases illustrate insider trading.

Securities and Exchange Commission v. Texas Gulf Sulphur Co.

401 F.2d 833 1968 U.S.App. Lexis 5797 (1968)
United States Court of Appeals, Second Circuit

Case 31.2
Insider Trading

Background and Facts

On November, 12, 1963, Texas Gulf Sulphur Co. (TGS) a mining company, drilled an exploratory hole—Kidd 55—near Timmins, Ontario. Assay reports showed that the core from this drilling proved to be remarkably high in copper, zinc, and silver. TGS kept the discovery secret, camouflaged the drill site, and diverted drilling efforts to another site to allow TGS to acquire land around Kidd 55. In November, 1963, TGS stock traded at $18 per share.

Eventually, rumors of a rich mineral strike began circulating. On Saturday, April 11, 1964, the *New York Times* published an unauthorized report of TGS drilling efforts in Canada and its rich mineral strike. On Sunday, April 12, officers of TGS drafted a press release that was issued that afternoon. The press release appeared in morning newspapers of general circulation on Monday, April 13. It read in pertinent part: "The work done to date has not been sufficient to reach definite conclusions and any statement as to size and grade of ore would be premature and possibly misleading."

The rumors persisted. On April 16, 1964, at 10:00 A.M., TGS held a press conference for the financial media. At the time of the press conference, TGS stock was trading at $37 per share. At this press conference, which lasted about 10 minutes, TGS disclosed

the richness of the Timmins mineral strike and that the strike should run to at least 25 million tons in ore. Several officers, directors, and other employees of TGS who had knowledge of the mineral strike at Timmins traded in the stock of TGS during the period November 13, 1963, to April 16, 1964. By May 15, 1964, the stock was selling at $58.

The SEC brought an action against several of these executives for insider trading in violation of section 10(b) of the Securities Exchange Act of 1934. The SEC sought to rescind their stock purchases. The district court held against most of these executives, who then appealed.

Issue

Are the defendant executives liable for engaging in insider trading?

Court's Reasoning

The U.S. Court of appeals stated that the insiders in this case were not trading on an equal footing with the outside investors. They alone were in a position to evaluate the probability and magnitude of what seemed from the outset to be a major ore strike. The Court stated, "Before insiders may act upon material information, such

Securities and Exchange Commission v. Texas Gulf Sulphur Co.

401 F.2d 833 1968 U.S.App. Lexis 5797 (1968)
United States Court of Appeals, Second Circuit
(continued)

information must have been effectively disclosed in a manner sufficient to ensure its availability to the investing public. We hold, therefore, that all transactions in TGS stock by individuals appraised of the drilling results were made in violation of Rule 10b-5."

Decision and Remedy

The Court of Appeals held that the executives in this case had engaged in illegal insider trading.

Case Questions

Critical Legal Thinking   Should insider trading be illegal? Why or why not?

Business Ethics   Did the inside executives act ethically in this case?

Contemporary Business   How can businesses protect against their employees engaging in insider trading? Explain.

U.S. SUPREME COURT CASE
United States v. O'Hagan

521 U.S. 642, 117 S.Ct. 2199, 1997 U.S. Lexis 4033 (1997)
Supreme Court of the United States

Case 31.3

Misappropriation Theory

Background and Facts

James O'Hagan was a partner in the law firm Dorsey & Whitney in Minneapolis, Minnesota. In July 1988, Grand Metropolitan PLC (Grand Met), a company based in London, England, hired Dorsey & Whitney to represent it in a secret tender offer for the stock of the Pillsbury Company, headquartered in Minneapolis. On August 18, 1988, O'Hagan began purchasing call options for Pillsbury stock. Each call option gave O'Hagan the right to purchase 100 shares of Pillsbury stock at a specified price. O'Hagan continued to purchase call options in August and September, and he became the largest holder of call options for Pillsbury stock. In September, O'Hagan also purchased 5,000 shares of Pillsbury common stock at $39 per share. These purchases were all made while Grand Met's proposed tender offer for Pillsbury remained secret to the public. When Grand Met publicly announced its tender offer in October 1988, Pillsbury stock increased to nearly $60 per share. O'Hagan sold his Pillsbury call options and common stock, making a profit of more than $4.3 million.

The U.S. Department of Justice charged O'Hagan with criminally violating Section 10(b) and Rule 10b-5. Because this was not a case of classic insider trading because O'Hagan did not trade in the stock of his law firm's client, Grand Met, the government alleged that O'Hagan was liable under the "misappropriation theory" for trading in Pillsbury stock by engaging in deceptive conduct by misappropriating the secret information about Grand Met's tender offer from his employer, Dorsey & Whitney, and from its client, Grand Met. The district court found O'Hagan guilty and sentenced him to 41 months in prison. The Eighth Circuit Court of Appeals reversed, finding that liability under Section 10(b) and Rule 10b-5 cannot be based on the

misappropriation theory. The government appealed to the U.S. Supreme Court.

Issue

Can a defendant be criminally convicted of violating Section 10(b) and Rule 10b-5 based on the misappropriation theory?

Court's Reasoning

The U.S. Supreme Court explained that the misappropriation theory holds that a person commits fraud in connection with a securities transaction, and thereby violates Section 10(b) and Rule 10b-5, when he or she misappropriates confidential information for securities trading purposes, in breach of a duty owed to the source of the information. Under this theory, a fiduciary's undisclosed, self-serving use of a principal's information to purchase or sell securities, in breach of a duty of loyalty and confidentiality, defrauds the principal of the exclusive use of that information. The Supreme Court noted that the classical theory of insider trading targets a corporate insider's breach of duty to shareholders with whom the insider transacts; the misappropriation theory outlaws trading on the basis of nonpublic information by a corporate "outsider" in breach of a duty owed not to a trading party, but to the source of the information.

The misappropriation theory comports with Section 10(b)'s language, which requires deception "in connection with the purchase or sale of any security." The Supreme Court stated that it makes no sense to hold a lawyer such as O'Hagan a Section 10(b) violator if he works for a law firm representing the target of a tender offer (e.g., if he had worked for Pillsbury), but not if he works for a law firm representing the bidder (Grand Met). The text of the statute requires no such result.

Decision and Remedy

The Supreme Court held that a defendant can be criminally convicted of violating Section 10(b) and Rule 10b-5 under the misappropriation theory. The Supreme Court reversed the decision of the Court of Appeals, which held otherwise.

Case Questions

Critical Legal Thinking   Should the misappropriation theory be recognized as a basis for criminal liability under Section 10(b) and Rule 10b-5? Do you agree with the Supreme Court's decision?

Business Ethics   If the Supreme Court had upheld the circuit court's decision, would ethics alone be enough to prevent persons like O'Hagan from trading on secret information?

Contemporary Business   Will the securities markets be more or less honest because of the Supreme Court's ruling in this case?

Tipper–Tippee Liability

A person who discloses material nonpublic information to another person is called a **tipper**. A person who receives such information is known as a **tippee**. A tippee is liable for acting on material information that he or she knew or should have known was not public. The tipper is liable for the profits made by the tippee. If the tipee tips other persons, both the tippee (who is now a tipper) and the original tipper are liable for the profits made by these remote tippees. The remote tippees are liable for their own trades if they knew or should have known that they possessed material inside information.

Business Ethics

Reg FD Requires Fair Disclosure to All

Prior to 2000, publicly held companies routinely announced crucial earnings and other significant information to securities analysts and other Wall Street insiders before making the information public. This meant that the analysts and others on Wall Street could profit from the information before it was made available to the general public. They did this by purchasing securities of the disclosing companies on good news and selling securities on bad news, before others could act. The SEC felt that this so-called "front-running" gave an unfair advantage to the investment professionals.

In 2000, the SEC adopted **Regulation Fair Disclosure**, or **Reg FD**, which prohibits companies from leaking important information to securities professionals before the information is disclosed to the public. Reg FD forces companies, by law, to reveal sensitive information to the general public at the same time that the information is released to stock analysts. Reg FD has taken away a lucrative advantage that the Wall Street professionals had over the general investing public.

1. Was it ethical for securities professionals to "front run" by trading securities before the public had the same information?
2. Do the FD rules level the playing field? Explain.

Violations of the Securities Exchange Act of 1934

The civil and criminal penalties that may be assessed for violations of the Securities Exchange Act of 1934 are discussed in the following paragraphs.

SEC Actions

The SEC may investigate suspected violations of the Securities Exchange Act of 1934 and the rules and regulations adopted thereunder. The SEC may enter into *consent orders* with defendants, seek *injunctions* in federal district court, or seek court orders requiring defendants to *disgorge* illegally gained profits.

In 1984, Congress enacted the **Insider Trading Sanctions Act**,[15] which permits the SEC to obtain a *civil penalty* of up to three times the illegal profits gained or losses avoided on insider trading. The fine is payable to the U.S. Treasury.

Private Actions

Business Brief

Courts have implied a private right of action under Section 10(b) and Rule 10b-5 whereby private parties can obtain rescission of a securities contract or recover monetary damages from liable defendants.

Although Section 10(b) and Rule 10b-5 do not expressly provide for a private right of action, courts have implied such a right. Generally, a private plaintiff may seek rescission of the securities contract or recover damages (e.g., disgorgements of the illegal profits by the defendants). Private securities fraud claims must be brought within two years after discovery or five years after the violation occurs, whichever is shorter.

Criminal Liability

Section 32 of the Securities Exchange Act of 1934 makes it a criminal offense to violate willfully the provisions of the act or the rules and regulations adopted thereunder.[16] Under the Sarbanes-Oxley Act of 2002, a person who willfully violates the Securities Exchange Act of 1934 can be fined up to $5 million or imprisoned for up to 25 years, or both. A corporation or another entity may be fined up to $2.5 million.

Sarbanes-Oxley Act

The SEC may issue an order prohibiting any person who has committed securities fraud from acting as an officer or a director of a public company.

Short-Swing Profits

Section 16(a) of the 1934 act defines any person who is an executive officer, a director, or a 10 percent shareholder of an equity security of a reporting company as a *statutory insider* for Section 16 purposes. Statutory insiders must file reports with the SEC, disclosing their ownership and trading in the company's securities.[17] These reports must be filed with the SEC and made available on the company's Web site within two days after the trade occurs.

Section 16 (b)

Section 16(b) requires that any profits made by a statutory insider on transactions involving *short-swing profits*—that is, trades involving equity securities occurring within six months of each other—belong to the corporation.[18] The corporation may bring a legal action to recover these profits. Involuntary transactions, such as forced redemption of securities by the corporation or an exchange of securities in a bankruptcy proceeding, are exempt. Section 16(b) is a strict liability provision. Generally, no defenses are recognized. Neither intent nor the possession of inside information need be shown.

Consider This Example   Rosanne is the president of a corporation and statutory insider who does not possess any inside information. On February 1, she purchases 1,000 shares of her employer's stock at $10 per share. On June 1, she sells the stock for $14 per share. The corporation can recover the $4,000 profit because the trades occurred within six months of each other. Rosanne would have to wait until after August 1 to sell the securities.

SEC Rules

The SEC has adopted the following rules concerning Section 16:

- Clarify the definition of *officer* to include only executive officers who perform policy-making functions. This would include the president, the chief executive officer, the vice presidents in charge of business units or divisions, the principal financial officer, the principal accounting officer, and the like. Officers who run day-to-day operations but are not responsible for policy decisions are not included.

- Relieve insiders of liability for transactions that occur within six months before becoming an insider. For example, if a noninsider buys shares of his or her company January 15, becomes an insider March 15, and sells the shares May 15, the January 15 purchase is not matched against the May 15 sale.

- Continue the rule that insiders are liable for transactions that occur within six months of the last transaction engaged in while an insider. For example, if an insider buys shares in his or her company April 30 and leaves the company May 15, this purchase must be matched against any sale of the company's shares that occurs on or before October 30.

Business Brief

The SEC has issued rules that clarify the persons and transactions subject to Section 16's short-swing profit rule.

Concept Summary: Section 10(b) and Section 16(b) Compared

Element	Section 10(b) and Rule 10b-5	Section 16(b)
Covered securities	All securities.	Securities required to be registered with the SEC under the 1934 act.
Inside information	Defendant made a misrepresentation or traded on inside (or perhaps misappropriated) information.	Short-swing profits recoverable whether or not they are attributable to misappropriation or inside information.
Recovery	Belongs to the injured purchaser or seller.	Belongs to the corporation.

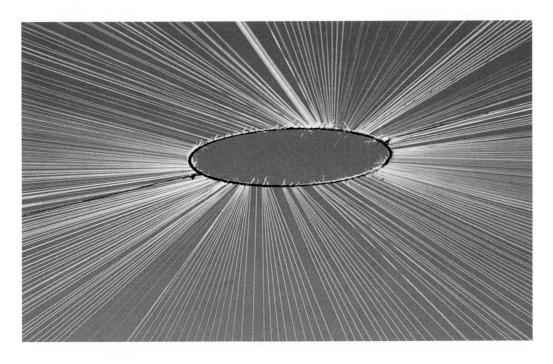

Blue Sky. State securities laws are often referred to as "blue-sky" laws because they help prevent investors from purchasing a piece of the blue sky.

State Securities Laws

Most states have enacted securities laws. These laws, which are often called *blue-sky laws*, generally require the registration of certain securities and provide exemptions from registration. They also contain broad antifraud provisions. The **Uniform Securities Act** has been adopted by many states. This act is drafted to coordinate state securities laws with federal securities laws.

Chapter Summary

The Securities and Exchange Commission (SEC), p. 676

The Securities and Exchange Commission (SEC)

Created in 1934, the SEC is a federal administrative agency empowered to administer federal securities laws. The SEC can adopt rules and regulations to interpret and implement federal securities.

Definition of a Security

Security. A security must be found before federal securities laws apply. A *security* is defined as:

1. **Common securities.** Interests or instruments that are commonly known as securities, such as common stock, preferred stock, debentures, and warrants.
2. **Statutorily defined securities.** Interests and instruments that are expressly mentioned in securities acts as being securities, such as interests in oil, gas, and mineral rights.
3. **Investment contracts.** A flexible standard for defining a security. Under the *Howey* test; a security exists if (1) an investor invests money (2) in a common enterprise, and (3) expects to make a profit off the significant efforts of others.

The Securities Act of 1933—Going Public, p. 677

The Securities Act of 1933

This act is a federal statute that primarily regulates the *issuance* of securities by corporations, partnerships, associations, and individuals.

Registration Statement

1. **Section 5.** This provision of the 1933 act requires an issuer to register its securities with the SEC prior to selling them to the public if the securities or transaction does not qualify for an exemption from registration.
2. **Registration statement.** This is a document that an issuer of securities files with the SEC to register its securities. It must contain information about the issuer, the securities to be issued, and other relevant information.

Prospectus

A prospectus is a written disclosure document that is submitted to the SEC with the registration statement. It is distributed to prospective investors to enable them to evaluate the financial risk of the investment.

Limitations on Activities During the Registration Process

1. **Prefiling period.** This period begins when the issuer first contemplates issuing securities and ends when the registration statement is filed with the SEC. During this period, the issuer cannot (1) offer to sell securities, (2) sell securities, or (3) *condition the market*.

2. **Waiting period.** This period begins when the registration statement is filed with the SEC and ends when the registration statement becomes effective. During this time, the issuer cannot (1) sell securities or (2) use unapproved writing to offer to sell the securities. The issuer may make oral offers, distribute *preliminary* and *summary prospectuses*; and publish *tombstone ads*.

3. **Posteffective period.** This period begins when the registration statement becomes effective and runs until the issuer either sells all of the offered securities or withdraws them from sale. The issuer may offer to sell and sell the securities during this period. The issuer must deliver a *final prospectus* (*statutory prospectus*) to a purchaser prior to or at the time of confirming the sale or sending the security to the purchaser.

Regulation A Offerings

Regulation A. This regulation permits an issuer to sell up to $5 million of securities to the public during a 12-month period pursuant to a simplified registration process.

Small Business offerings

1. **Small Corporate Offering Registration Form (SCOR).** This regulation permits businesses to sell up to $1 million to the public pursuant to a simplified registration process:

2. **Form, U-7.** This is a question-and-answer disclosure form that a business can complete and file with the SEC to sell securities pursuant to SCOR.

Private and Other Transactions Exempt from Registration, p. 681

Transactions Exempt from Registration

The following *transactions* are exempt from the SEC registration process: (1) nonissuer transactions, (2) intrastate offerings, (3) private placements, and (4) small offerings.

Nonissuer Exemption

Securities transactions *not* by an issuer, an underwriter, or a dealer are exempt from SEC registration. This covers normal purchases of securities by investors.

Intrastate Offerings

A local business can issue securities without dollar limit without registering with the SEC if the following requirements are met:

1. The issuer is a resident of the state (e.g., the corporation is incorporated in the state).

2. The issuer is doing business in the state. This requires that:

   a. 80 percent of the issuer's assets are located in the state.

   b. 80 percent of the issuer's gross revenues are derived from the state.

   c. The issuer's principal office is located in the state.

   d. 80 percent of the proceeds of the offering will be used in the state.

3. The purchasers of the securities are all residents of the state.

Private Placements

An issue of securities that does not involve a public offering is exempt from SEC registration. There is no dollar limit on the amount of securities that can be issued pursuant to this exemption. Securities can be sold to any number of *accredited investors*, but to no more than 35 *nonaccredited investors*.

1. **Accredited investors.** These include:

   a. Any natural person (including spouse) who has a net worth of at least $1 million.

   b. Any natural person who has had an annual income of at least $200,000 for the previous two years and reasonably expects to make $200,000 income in the current year.

   c. Any corporation, partnership, or business trust with total assets in excess of $5 million.

   d. Insiders of the issuers, such as executive officers and directors of corporate issuers and general partners of partnership issuers.

    e. Certain institutional investors, such as registered investment companies, pension plans, colleges and universities, and the like.

Small Offerings

An offering of securities that does not exceed $1 million during a 12-month period is exempt from SEC registration. The securities may he sold to any number of purchasers.

Resale Restrictions

1. **Restricted securities.** Securities sold pursuant to the intrastate, private placement, or small offering exemptions are called *restricted securities*.
2. **Rule 147.** This SEC rule stipulaties that securities sold pursuant to an *intrastate offering exemption* cannot he sold to nonresidents for a period of nine months.
3. **Rule 144.** This SEC rule stipulaties that securities sold pursuant to the *private placement or small offering exemption* must be held for two years; limited sales may be made between years two and three; then unlimited sales are permitted.
4. **Preventing transfer of restricted securities.** To prevent the illegal transfer of restricted securities, the issuer must take the following precautions:
   a. Affidavit. The issuer must require investors to sign an affidavit stating that they are buying the securities for investment, and promising not to transfer the restricted securities until the restrictions no longer apply.
   b. Legend: The issuer must place a legend on the stock certificate describing the restriction.
   c. Transfer agent. The issuer must appoint and notify the transfer agent not to record a transfer of the securities that would violate the restriction.
5. **Rule 144A.** This SEC rule permits *qualified institutional investors*—defined as institutions—that own and invest at least $100 million in securities—to buy unregistered securities without being subject to the holding periods of Rule 144.

Integration of Exempt Offerings

Separate exempt offerings of securities will be *integrated* (added together) if they occur within six months of each other and they are found to be similar and part of the same offering.

1. **Safe harbor rule.** Exempt securities offerings made more than six months before or after the current offering are not integrated with the current offering.
2. **Integrated offering.** If two or more exempt offerings are integrated, they are considered one offering. This *integrated offering* must be examined to determine whether it qualifies for any exemption from SEC registration.

Securities Exempt from Registration

The following *securities* are exempt from the SEC registration process:

1. Securities issued by any government in the United States (e.g., municipal bonds issued by city governments)
2. Short-term notes and drafts that have a maturity date that does not exceed nine months (e.g., commercial paper issued by corporations)
3. Securities issued by nonprofit issuers, such as religious institutions, charitable institutions, and colleges and universities.
4. Securities of financial institutions (e.g., banks, savings associations) that are regulated by the appropriate banking authorities
5. Securities issued by common carriers (e.g., railroads, trucking companies) that are regulated by the Interstate Commerce Commission (ICC)
6. Insurance and annuity contracts issued by insurance companies
7. Stock dividends and stock splits
8. Securities issued in a corporate reorganization where one security is exchanged for another security

Violations of the Securities Act of 1933, p. 684

SEC Actions

The SEC may seek the following remedies:

1. **Consent order.** The SEC may issue a consent order whereby a defendant agrees not to violate securities laws in the future but does not admit to violating securities laws in the past.
2. **Injunction.** The SEC may bring an action in federal district court to obtain an injunction.
3. **Disgorgement of profits.** The SEC may request the court to order the defendant to disgorge illegally gained profits.

Private Actions

Private parties who have been injured by a violation of the 1933 act may sue the violator to rescind the securities contract or recover damages. The plaintiff may sue under:

1. **Section 12.** This provision of the 1933 act imposes civil liability on any person who violates the provisions of Section 5 of the act (e.g., sells unregistered securities).
2. **Section 11.** This provision of the 1933 act imposes civil liability on persons who intentionally defraud investors by making misrepresentations or omissions of material facts in the registration statement or are negligent in not discovering the fraud.
   a. *Due diligence defense.* This is a defense to a Section 11 action that, if proven, makes the defendant not liable. It requires the defendant to have made a reasonable investigation and had reasonable grounds to believe and did believe that the statements made in the registration statement were true.

Criminal Liability

Section 24 of the 1933 act imposes criminal liability on any person who willfully violates either the act or the rules and regulations adopted thereunder. Criminal actions are brought by the U.S. Justice Department.

The Securities Exchange Act of 1934—Trading in Securities, p. 686

The Securities Exchange Act of 1934

This federal statute primarily regulates the *trading* of securities.

Continuous Reporting Requirements

1. **Reporting companies.** Reporting companies are issuers (1) with assets of more than $5 million and at least 500 shareholders, (2) whose equity securities are traded on a national securities exchange, or (3) who have made a registered offering under the Securities Act of 1933.
2. **Reporting requirements.** Reporting companies must file the following reports with the SEC: (1) annual reports (*Form 10-K*), (2) quarterly reports (*Form 10-Q*), and (3) monthly reports (*Form 8 K*) within 10 days of the end of the month in which a material event (e.g., merger) occurs.

Section 10(b) and Rule 10b-5

1. **Section 10(b).** This provision of the 1934 act prohibits the use of manipulative and deceptive devices in the purchase or sale of securities in contravention of the rules and regulations prescribed by the SEC.
2. **Rule 10b-5.** This rule adopted by the SEC clarifies the reach of Section 10(b) against deceptive and frandulent activities in the purchase and sale of securities.
3. **Scienter.** Only conduct involving *scienter* (intentional conduct) violates Section 10(b) and Rule 10b-5. Negligent conduct is not a violation.

Insider Trading

Insider trading occurs when an insider makes a profit by purchasing shares of the commodity prior to public release of favorable information or selling shares of the corporation prior to public disclosure of unfavorable information. Insider trading violates Section 10(b) and Rule 10b-5.

1. ***Cady, Roberts rule.*** An insider who possesses material information must either (1) abstain from trading in the securities of the company or (2) disclose the information to the person from whom he or she purchases or to whom he or she sells the securities.

Insiders

Insiders for Section 10(b) and Rule 10b-5 purposes include all employees of a company, independent contractors hired by the company on a temporary basis to provide services or work to the company, and others who owe a fiduciary duty to the company.

Tipper–Tippee Liability

1. ***Tipper.*** A tipper is a person who discloses material nonpublic information to another person.
2. ***Tippee.*** A tippee is a person who receives material nonpublic information from a tipper.
3. ***Tippee's liability.*** The tippee is liable for acting on material information received from a tipper if he or she knew or should have known that the information was not public. The tippee must disgorge profits made on the tip.
4. ***Tipper's liability.*** The tipper is liable for his or her own profits and the profits made by the tippee.

Violations of the Securities Exchange Act of 1934, p. 689

SEC Actions

The SEC may enter into *consent orders* with defendants, seek *injunctions* in federal district court, or seek orders requiring defendants to *disgorge* illegally gained profits.

Private Actions

Section 10(b). A private plaintiff has an *implied right* under Section 10(b) and Rule 10b-5 to sue to rescind the securities contract or recover damages from a defendant who has engaged in manipulative and deceptive practices that have caused the plaintiff injury.

Criminal Liability

Section 32 of the 1934 act imposes criminal liability on any person who willfully violates the 1934 act or the rules and regulations adopted thereunder. Criminal actions are brought by the U.S. Justice Department.

Short-Swing Profits, p. 690

Short-Swing Profits

Statutory insiders. Section 16(a) of the Securities Exchange Act of 1934 defines a *statutory insider* for Section 16 purposes as any person who is an executive officer, a director, or a 10-percent shareholder of an equity security of a reporting company.

Section 16(b)

1. ***Short-swing profits.*** Short swing profits are profits made by statutory insiders on trades involving equity securities that occur within six months of each other.
2. ***Section 16(b).*** This provision of the 1934 act requires that any profits made by a statutory insider on transactions involving short-swing profits belong to the corporation.

1991 SEC Rules

These rules issued by the SEC clarify the persons and transactions subject to Section 16 short-swing profit rules.

State Securities Laws, p. 692

State Securities Laws

Most states have enacted securities laws that regulate the issuance and trading of securities. These acts are often patterned after, and are designed to coordinate with, federal securities laws. The *Uniform Securities Act*, which is a model state securities act, has been adopted by many states.

Internet Exercises and Case Questions

Working the Web Internet Exercises

Activities

Note: For socially responsible investing information, see **www. socialinvest.org**.

1. Using the Stanford Securities Class Action Clearinghouse site, at **securities.stanford.edu**, identify the leading sector, industry, and companies targeted in securities class action litigation.

2. Investigate the modern varieties of fraud by reading the following law review articles:

   "Internet Securities Fraud: Old Trick, New Medium," at **www.law.duke.edu/journals/dltr/ARTICLES/2001 dltr0006.html**

   "Software Disclosure and Liability Under the Securities Acts," at **www.law.duke.edu/journals/dltr/ARTICLES/ 2001dltr0016.html**

"The Future of Corporate Disclosure: The Internet, Securities Fraud, and Rule 10B-5," at **www.law.emory. edu/ELJ/volumes/win98/prentice.html**

3. Determine whether an athletic club membership can be a *security* by using the U.S. Securities & Exchange Commission site, at **www.sec.gov**.

4. Who qualifies as *accredited investors?* Seé Bloomberg Online Financial Market Info, at **bloomberg.com**.

5. What is Rule 144 stock? See The Motley Fool, at **www.fool.com**.

6. What constitutes insider trading? See Microsoft Investor Version 4.0, at **moneycentral.msn.com/investor/ home.asp**.

Critical Legal Thinking Cases

31.1 Definition of Security   Dare To Be Great, Inc. (Dare), was a Florida corporation that was wholly owned by Glenn W. Turner Enterprises, Inc. Dare offered self-improvement courses aimed at improving self-motivation and sales ability. In return for an investment of money, the purchaser received certain tapes, records, and written materials. In addition, depending on the level of involvement, the purchaser had the opportunity to help sell the Dare courses to others and to receive part of the purchase price as a commission. There were four different levels of involvement.

The task of salespersons was to bring prospective purchasers to "Adventure Meetings." The meetings, which were conducted by Dare people and not the salespersons, were conducted in a preordained format that included great enthusiasm, cheering and charming, exuberant handshaking, standing on chairs, and shouting. The Dare people and the salespersons dressed in modern, expensive clothes, displayed large sums of cash, drove new expensive automobiles, and engaged in "hard-sell" tactics to induce prospects to sign their name and part with their money. In actuality, few Dare purchasers ever attained the wealth promised. The tape recordings and materials distributed by Dare were worthless. In this sales scheme a "security" that should have been registered with the SEC? [*Securities and Exchange Commission v. Glenn W. Turner Enterprises, Inc.*, 474 F.2d 476, 1973 U.S. Lexis 11903 (9th Cir. 1973)]

31.2 Definition of Security   The Farmer's Cooperative of Arkansas and Oklahoma (Co-Op) was an agricultural cooperative that had approximately 23,000 members. To raise money to support its general business operations, the Co-Op sold promissory notes to investors that were payable upon demand. The Co-Op offered the notes to both members and nonmembers, advertised the notes as an "investment program" and offered an interest rate higher than that available on savings accounts at financial institutions. More than 1,600 people purchased the notes, worth a total of $10 million. Subsequently, the Co-Op filed for bankruptcy. A class of

holders of the notes filed suit against Ernst & Young, a national firm of certified public accountants that had audited the Co-Op's financial statements, alleging, that Ernst & Young had violated Section 10(b) of the Securities Exchange Act of 1934. Are the notes issued by the Co-Op "securities"? [*Reeves v. Ernst & Young*, 494 U.S. 56, 110 S.Ct. 945, 1990 U.S. Lexis 1051 (1990)]

31.3 Intrastate Offering Exemption   The McDonald Investment Company was a corporation organized and incorporated in the state of Minnesota. The principal and only place of business from which the company conducted operations was located in Rush City, Minnesota. More than 80 percent of the company's assets were located in Minnesota and more than 80 percent of its income was derived from Minnesota. On January 18, 1972, McDonald sold securities to Minnesota residents only. The proceeds from the sale were used entirely to make loans and other investments in real estate and other assets located outside the state of Minnesota. The company did not file a registration statement with the SEC. Does this offering qualify for an intrastate offering exemption from registration? [*Securities and Exchange Commission v. McDonald Investment Company*, 343 F.Supp. 343, 1972 U.S. Dist. Lexis 13547 (D. Minn. 1972)]

31.4 Transaction Exemption   Continental Enterprises, Inc., had 2,510,000 shares of stock issued and outstanding. Louis E. Wolfson and members of his immediate family and associates owned in excess of 40 percent of those shares. The balance was in the hands of approximately 5,000 outside shareholders. Wolfson was Continental's largest shareholder and the guiding spirit of the corporation who gave direction to and controlled the company's officers. Between August 1, 1960, and January 31, 1962, without public disclosure, Wolfson and his family and associates sold 55 percent of their stock through six brokerage houses. Wolfson and his family and associates did not file a registration statement with the SEC with respect to these sales. Do the securities sales by Wolfson and his family and associates qualify for an exemption for registration as a sale "not by an issuer, an underwriter, or a dealer"? [*United States v. Wolfson*, 405 F.2d 779, 1968 U.S. App. Lexis 4342 (2nd Cir. 1968)]

31.5 Insider Trading Chiarella worked as a "markup man" in the New York composing room of Pandick Press, a financial printer. Among the documents that Chairella handled were five secret announcements of corporate takeovers. The tender offerors had hired Pandick Press to print the offers, which would later be made public when the tender offers were made to the shareholders of the target corporations. When the documents were delivered to Pandick Press, the identities of the acquiring and target corporations were concealed by blank spaces or false names. The true names would not be sent to Pandick Press until the night of the final printing.

Chiarella was able to deduce the names of the target companies before the final printing. Without disclosing this knowledge, he purchased stock in the target companies and sold the shares immediately after the takeover attempts were made public. Chiarella realized a gain of $30,000 in the course of 14 months. The federal government indicted Chiarella for criminal violations of Section 10(b) of the Securities Exchange Act of 1934. Is Chiarella guilty? [*Chiarella v. United States*, 445 U.S. 222, 100 S.Ct. 1108, 1980 U.S. Lexis 88 (1980)]

31.6 Section 10(b) Leslie Neadeau was the president of T.O.N.M. Oil & Gas Exploration Corporation (TONM). Charles Lazzaro was a registered securities broker employed by Batemen Eichler, Hill Richards, Inc. (Bateman Eichler). The stock of TONM was traded in the over-the-counter market. Lazzaro made statements to potential investors that he had "inside information" about TONM, including that (1) vast amounts of gold had been discovered in Surinam and that

TONM had options on thousands of acres in the gold-producing regions of Surinam; (2) the discovery was "not publicly known, but would be subsequently announced"; and (3) when this information was made public, TONM stock, which was then selling from $1.50 to $3.00 per share, would increase to $10.00 to $15.00 within a short period of time and might increase to $100.00 per share within a year.

The potential investors contacted Neadeau at TONM, and he confirmed that the information was not public knowledge. In reliance on Lazzaro's and Neadeau's statements, the investors purchased TONM stock. The so-called "inside information" turned out to be false, and the shares declined substantially below the purchase price. The investors sued Lazzaro, Bateman Eichler, Neadeau, and TONM, alleging violations of Section 10(b) of the Securities Exchange Act of 1934. The defendants asserted that the plaintiffs' complaint should be dismissed because they participated in the fraud. Who wins? [*Bateman Eichler, Hill Richards, Inc. v Berner*, 472 U.S. 299, 105 S.Ct. 2662, 1985 U.S. Lexis 95 (1985)]

31.7 Insider Trading Donald C. Hoodes was the chief executive officer of the Sullair Corporation. As an officer of the corporation, he was regularly granted stock options to purchase stock of the company at a discount. On July 20, 1982, Hoodes sold 6,000 shares of Sullair common stock for $38,350. On July 31, 1982, Sullair terminated Hoodes as an officer of the corporation. On August 20, 1982, Hoodes exercised options to purchase 6,000 shares of Sullair stock that cost Hoodes $3.01 per share ($18,060) at the time they were trading at $4.50 per share ($27,000). Hoodes did not possess material nonpublic information about Sullair when he sold or purchased the securities of the company. The corporation brought suit against Hoodes to recover the profits Hoodes made on these trades. Who wins? [*Sullair Corporation v. Hoodes*, 672 F.Supp. 337, 1987 U.S.Dist. Lexis 10152 (N.D. Ill. 1987)]

Business Ethics Cases

31.8 Business Ethics Stephen Murphy owned Intertie, a California company that was involved in financing and managing cable television stations. Murphy was both an officer of the corporation and chairman of the board of directors. Intertie would buy a cable television station, make a small cash down payment, and finance the remainder of the purchase price. It would than create a limited partnership and sell the cable station to the partnership for a cash down payment and a promissory note in favor of Intertie. Finally, Intertie would lease the station back from the partnership. Intertie purchased more than 30 stations and created an equal number of limited partnerships, from which it received more than $7.5 million from approximately 400 investors.

Evidence showed that most of the limited partnerships were not self-supporting but that this fact was not disclosed to investors. Intertie commingled partnership funds, taking funds generated from the sale of new partnership offerings to meet debt service obligations of previously sold cable systems; Intertie also used funds from limited partnerships that were formed but that never acquired cable systems. Intertie did not keep any records regarding the qualifications of investors to purchase the securities and also refused to make its financial statements available to investors.

Intertie suffered severe financial difficulties and eventually filed for bankruptcy. The limited partners suffered substantial

losses. Did each of the limited partnership offerings alone qualify for the private placement exemption from registration? Should the 30 limited partnership offerings be integrated? [*Securities and Exchange Commission v. Murphy*, 626 F.2d 633, 1980 U.S. App. Lexis 15483 (9th Cir. 1980)]

31.9 Business Ethics R. Foster Winans, a reporter for the *Wall street Journal*, was one of the writers of the "Heard on the Street" column, a widely read and influential column in the *Journal*. This column frequently included articles that discussed the prospects of companies listed on national and regional stock exchanges and the over-the-counter market. David Carpenter worked as a news clerk at the *Journal*. The *Journal* had a conflict of interest policy that prohibited employees from using nonpublic information learned on the job for their personal benefit. Winans and Carpenter were aware of this policy.

Kenneth P. Felis and Peter Brant were stockbrokers at the brokerage house of Kidder Peabody. Winans agreed to provide Felis and Brant with information that was to appear in the "Heard" column in advance of its publication in the *Journal*. Generally, Winans would provide this information to the brokers the day before it was to appear in the *Journal*. Carpenter served as a messenger between the parties. Based on this advance information, the brokers bought and sold securities of companies discussed in the "Heard" column.

During 1983 and 1984, prepublication trades of approximately 27 "Heard" columns netted profits of almost $690,000. The parties used telephones to transfer information. The *Wall Street Journal* is distributed by mail to many of its subscribers.

Eventually, Kidder Peabody noticed a correlation between the "Heard" column and trading by the brokers. After an SEC investigation, criminal charges were brought against defendants Winans, Carpenter, and Felis in U.S. district court. Brant became the government's key witness. Winans and Felis were convicted of conspiracy to commit securities, mail, and wire fraud. Carpenter was convicted of aiding and abetting the commission of securities, mail, and wire fraud. The defendants appealed their convictions. Can the defendants be held criminally liable for conspiring to violate, and aiding and abetting the violation of, Section 10(b) and Rule 10b-5 of securities law? Did Winans act ethically in this case? Did Brant act ethically by turning government's witness? [*United States v. Carpenter*, 484 U.S. 19, 108 S.Ct. 316, 1987 U.S. Lexis 4815 (1987)]

Briefing the Case Writing Assignment

Read Case A.31 in the Case Appendix [*Lampf, Pleva, Lipkind, Prupis & Petigrow v. Gilbertson*]. This case is excerpted from the U.S. Superme Court opinion. Review and brief the case. In your brief, be sure to answer the following questions.

1. Were the limited partnership interests securities"?

2. What statute did the plaintiffs allege that the defendants had violated?

3. Succinctly state the issue presented to the U.S. Supreme Court.

4. How did the U.S. Supreme Court decide the issue?

Endnotes

1. *Securities and Exchange Commission v. W. J. Howey Co.*, 328 U.S. 293, 66 S. Ct. 1100, 1946 U.S. Lexis 3159 (1946).
2. 15 U.S.C. § § 77a-77aa.
3. Securities Act of 1933, § 3(a)(11).
4. SEC Rule 147.
5. Securities Act of 1933,§ 4(2).
6. SEC Rule 506.
7. SEC Rule 501.
8. Securities Act of 1933, § 3(b).
9. 15 U.S.C. § 77x.
10. 15 U.S.C. § § 78a–78 mm.
11. Litigation instituted pursuant to § 10(b) and Rule 10b-5 must be commenced within one year after the discovery of the violation and within three years after such violation [*Lampf, Pleva, Lipkind, Prupis & Petigrow v. Gilbertson*, 501 U.S. 350, 111 S.Ct. 2773, 1991 U.S. Lexis 3629 (1991)].
12. The U.S. Supreme Court has held that the sale of a business is a sale of securities that is subject to Section 10(b). *See Gould v. Ruefenacht*, 471 U.S. 701, 105 S.Ct. 2308, 1985 U.S. Lexis 21 (1985) (where 50 percent of a business was sold) and *Landreth Timber Co. v. Landreth*, 471 U.S. 681, 105 S.Ct. 2297, 1985 U.S. Lexis 20 (1985) (where 100 percent of a business was sold).
13. *Ernst & Ernst v. Hochfelder*, 425 U.S. 185, 96 S.Ct. 1375, 1976 U.S. Lexis 2 (1976).
14. 40 SEC 907 § (1961).
15. 15 U.S.C. § § 78 ff.
16. P.L. 98-376.
17. 15 U.S.C. § 78l.
18. 15 U.S.C. § 78p(b).

Antitrust Law

32

" While competition cannot be created by statutory enactment, it can in large measure be revived by changing the laws and forbidding the practices that killed it, and by enacting laws that will give it heart and occasion again. We can arrest and prevent monopoly. "

—Woodrow Wilson
Speech, August 7, 1912

Chapter Objectives

After studying this chapter, you should be able to:

1. Describe the enforcement of federal antitrust laws.

2. Describe the horizontal and vertical restraints of trade that violate Section 1 of the Sherman Act.

3. Identify acts of monopolization that violate Section 2 of the Sherman Act.

4. Explain how the lawfulness of mergers is examined under Section 7 of the Clayton Act.

5. Apply Section 5 of the Federal Trade Commission Act to antitrust cases.

Chapter Contents

- Federal Antitrust Laws

- Section 1 of the Sherman Act—Restraints of Trade

- Section 2 of the Sherman Act—Monopolization

- Section 7 of the Clayton Act—Mergers

- Section 3 of the Clayton Act—Tying Arrangements

- Section 2 of the Clayton Act—Price Discrimination

- Section 5 of the Federal Trade Commission Act—Unfair Methods of Competition

- Exemptions from Antitrust Laws

- State Antitrust Laws

The U.S. economic system was built on the theory of freedom of competition. After the Civil War, however, the American economy changed from a rural and agricultural economy to an industrialized and urban one. Many large industrial trusts were formed during this period. These arrangements resulted in a series of monopolies in basic industries such as oil and gas, sugar, cotton, and whiskey.

Because the common law could not deal effectively with these monopolies, Congress enacted a comprehensive system of **antitrust laws** to limit anticompetitive behavior. Almost all industries, businesses, and professions operating in the United States were affected. Although many states have also enacted antitrust laws, most actions in this area are brought under federal law.

This chapter discusses federal and state antitrust laws.

Federal Antitrust Laws

The **Sherman Act**, enacted in 1890, made certain restraints of trade and monopolistic acts illegal. Both the **Clayton Act** and the **Federal Trade Commission Act (FTC Act)** were enacted in 1914. The Clayton Act regulates mergers and prohibits certain exclusive dealing arrangements. The FTC Act prohibits unfair methods of competition. The **Robinson-Patman Act**, which prohibits price discrimination, was enacted in 1930.

Antitrust Enforcement

The federal antitrust statutes are broadly drafted to reflect the government's enforcement policy and to allow it to respond to economic, business, and technological changes. Each administration that occupies the White House adopts an enforcement policy for antitrust laws. From the 1940s through the 1970s, antitrust enforcement was quite stringent. During the 1980s, government enforcement of antitrust laws was more relaxed. During the 2000s, antitrust enforcement increased.

Antitrust Penalties

Federal antitrust laws provide for both government and private lawsuits.

Government Actions The federal government is authorized to bring actions to enforce federal antitrust laws. Government enforcement of federal antitrust laws is divided between the Antitrust Division of the Department of Justice and the Bureau of Competition of the Federal Trade Commission (FTC).

The Sherman Act is the only major antitrust act with *criminal* sanctions. Intent is the prerequisite for criminal liability under this act. Penalties for individuals include fines of up to $350,000 per violation and up to three years in prison; corporations may be fined up to $10 million per violation.[1]

The government may seek *civil* damages, including treble damages, for violations of antitrust laws.[2] Broad remedial powers allow the courts to order a number of civil remedies, including orders for divestiture of assets, cancellation of contracts, liquidation of businesses, licensing of patents, and such. Private parties cannot intervene in public antitrust actions brought by the government.

Private Actions **Section 4** of the **Clayton Act** permits any person who suffers antitrust injury in his or her "business or property" to bring a *private civil action* against the offenders.[3] Consumers who have to pay higher prices because of an antitrust violation have recourse under this provision.[4] To recover damages, plaintiffs must prove that they suffered *antitrust injuries* caused by the prohibited act. The courts have required that consumers must have dealt *directly* with the alleged violators to have standing to sue; indirect injury resulting from higher prices being "passed on" is insufficient.

The notion that a business is clothed with a public interest and has been devoted to the public use is little more than a fiction intended to beautify what is disagreeable to the sufferers.

Holmes, Jr.
Tyson & Bro-United Theatre Ticket Offices v. Banton (1927)

Business Brief
Each administration that occupies the White House adopts an enforcement policy for antitrust laws.

Business Brief
The Sherman Act is the only major federal antitrust act that provides for *criminal* penalties.

Ethics Brief
Businesses or individuals who are found to violate federal antitrust laws may be assessed *treble* (triple) damages in private civil lawsuit by any person who suffers injury in his or her business or property because of the violation.

Successful plaintiffs may recover **treble damages** (i.e., triple the amount of the damages), plus reasonable cots and attorneys' fees. Damages may be calculated as lost profits, an increase in the cost of doing business, or a decrease in the value of tangible or intangible property caused by the antitrust violation. This rule applies to all violations of the Sherman Act, the Clayton Act, and the Robinson-Patman Act. Only actual damages—not treble damages—may be recovered for violations of the FTC Act.

A private plaintiff has four years from the date on which an antitrust injury occurred to bring a private civil treble damage action. Only damages incurred during this four-year period are recoverable. This statute is *tolled* (i.e., does not run) during a suit by the government.

Ethics Brief

Many defendants settle government-brought antitrust lawsuits by entering pleas of *nolo contendere* in criminal actions and *consent decree* in civil actions. These pleas cannot be used as evidence in a subsequent private civil action.

Effect of a Government Judgment   A government judgment against a defendant for an antitrust violation may be used as prima facie evidence of liability in a private civil treble damage action. Antitrust defendants often opt to settle government-brought antitrust actions by entering a plea of *nolo contendere* in a criminal action or a *consent decree* in a government civil action. These pleas usually subject the defendant to penalty without an admission of guilt or liability.

Section 16 of the **Clayton Act** permits the government or a private plaintiff to obtain an injunction against anticompetitive behavior that violates antitrust laws.[5] Only the FTC may obtain an injunction under the FTC Act.

Section 1 of the Sherman Act—Restraints of Trade

In 1890 Congress enacted the **Sherman Antitrust Act**. The purpose of the act was to outlaw anticompetitive behavior. The Sherman Act has been called the "Magna Carta of free enterprise."[6] **Section 1 of the Sherman Act** is intended to prohibit certain concerted anticompetitive activities. It provides that:

> Every contract, combination in the form of trust or otherwise, or conspiracy, in restraint of trade or commerce among the several states, or with foreign nations, is hereby declared to be illegal. Every person who shall make any contract or engage in any combination or conspiracy hereby declared to be illegal shall be deemed guilty of a felony.[7]

Business Brief

Note that for a Section 1 violation it is essential to show concerted activity, one party acting alone cannot be liable.

In other words, Section 1 outlaws **contracts, combinations**, and **conspiracies** in restraint of trade. Thus, it applies to unlawful conduct by two or more parties. The agreement may be written, oral, or inferred from the conduct of the parties. The two tests the U.S. Supreme Court has developed for determining the lawfulness of a restraint—the *rule of reason* and the *per se rule*—are discussed in the following paragraphs.

Rule of Reason

Landmark Law

In *Standard Oil Company of New Jersey v. United States* (1911), the U.S. Supreme Court adopted the "rule of reason" standard for analyzing Sherman Act Section 1 cases.

If Section 1 of the Sherman Act were read literally, it would prohibit almost all contracts. In the landmark case *Standard Oil Company of New Jersey v. United States*,[8] the Supreme Court adopted the **rule of reason** standard for analyzing Section 1 cases. This rule holds that only *unreasonable restraints of trade* violate Section 1 of the Sherman Act. Reasonable restraints are lawful. The courts examine the following factors in applying the rule of reason:

- The pro- and anticompetitive effects of the challenged restraint
- The competitive structure of the industry
- The firm's market share and power
- The history and duration of the restraint
- Other relevant factors

Per Se Rule

The Supreme Court adopted the **per se rule**, which is applicable to those restraints of trade considered inherently anticompetitive. No balancing of pro- and anticompetitive effects is necessary in such cases: The restraint is automatically in violation of Section 1 of the Sherman Act. Once a restraint is characterized as a *per se* violation, no defenses or justifications for the restraint will save it, and no further evidence need be considered. Restraints that are not characterized as *per se* violations are examined under the rule of reason.

Horizontal Restraints of Trade

A **horizontal restraint of trade** occurs when two or more competitors at the *same level of distribution* enter into a contract, combination, or conspiracy to restrain trade (see Exhibit 32.1). Many horizontal restraints fall under the *per se* rule; others are examined under the rule of reason. The most common forms of horizontal restraint are discussed in the following paragraphs.

Price-Fixing   Horizontal **price-fixing** occurs when the competitors in the same line of business agree to set the price of goods or services they sell. Price-fixing is defined as raising, depressing, fixing, pegging, or stabilizing the price of a commodity or service. Illegal price-fixing includes setting minimum or maximum prices or fixing the quantity of a product or service to be produced or provided. Although most price-fixing agreements occur between sellers, an agreement among buyers to set the price they will pay for goods or services is also price-fixing. The plaintiff bears the burden of proving a price-fixing agreement.

Price-fixing is a *per se violation* of Section 1 of the Sherman Act. No defenses or justifications of any kind—such as "the price-fixing helps consumers or protects competitors from ruinous competition"—can prevent the *per se* rule from applying.

Consider These Examples   If the three largest automobile manufactures agreed among themselves as to what prices to charge automobile dealers for this year's models, this would be sellers' illegal *per se* price-fixing. If the same automobile manufactures agreed among themselves as to what price they would pay to purchase tires from tire manufactures, this would be buyers' illegal *per se* price-fixing.

Business Ethics

The Department of Justice Flunks the Ivy League Schools

For years, the administrators of the Ivy League schools (Brown, Columbia, Cornell, Dartmouth, Harvard, Princeton, the University of Pennsylvania, and Yale) and the Massachusetts Institute of Technology (M.I.T.) met annually to trade information about student applicants seeking admission and scholarships at their universities. The universities than divided up the applicants and agreed to offer scholarships to the students they thought would attend their schools; scholarships were not offered to those less likely to attend. The schools defended this practice as preventing "overlap"—that is, certain students getting scholarship offers from many schools and other applicants receiving no scholarship offers.

The U.S. Department of Justice sued the universities, alleging that they engaged in the horizontal restraint of trade of price-fixing, in violation of Section 1 of the Sherman Act.

The Department of Justice lawyers pointed to what they learned in Economics 101 and asserted that this collegiate cartel was no different from any other cartel—it denied customers (students) the right to "comparison shop" just as they would for other services.

The eight Ivy League schools agreed to settle the case with the Department of Justice. Under the terms of the consent decree, the schools agreed not to share financial aid information or discuss future tuition levels with other schools. M.I.T. chose to fight the case in court and lost. The court found M.I.T. guilty of price-fixing and enjoined the challenged practices. [*United States v. Brown University*, 5 F.3d 658, 1993 U.S. App. Lexis 23895 (3d Cir. 1993)]

1. Do you think the schools acted ethically in this case?
2. Did their "overlap" argument justify their actions? ■

Exhibit 32.1

Horizontal Restraint
of Trade

Division of Markets Competitors who agree that each will serve only a designated portion of the market are engaging in a **division of markets** (or **market sharing**), which is a *per se* violation of Section 1 of the Sherman Act. Each market segment is considered a small monopoly served only by its designated "owner." Horizontal market-sharing arrangements include division by geographical territory, customers, and products.

Consider These Examples Suppose three national breweries agreed among themselves that each one would be assigned one-third of the country as its geographical "territory" and each agreed not to sell beer in the other two companies' territories. This would be a *per se* illegal geographical division of markets. If the three largest sellers of media software agreed that each could only sell media software to one designated media software purchaser and not to any other media software purchasers, this would be a *per se* illegal product division of markets.

Group Boycotts A **group boycott** (or **refusal to deal**) occurs when two or more competitors at one level of distribution agree not to deal with others at a different level of distribution. Although in the past the U.S. Supreme Court has held that group boycotts were *per se* illegal, recent Supreme Court decisions have held that only certain group boycotts are *per se* illegal. Others are to be examined under the rule of reason. Nevertheless, most group boycotts are found to be illegal.

Consider These Examples A boycott would occur if a group of television manufacturers agreed not to sell their products to certain discount retailers (see Exhibit 32.2). A boycott would also occur if a group of rental car companies agreed not to purchase Chrysler automobiles for their fleets (see Exhibit 32.3).

Other Horizontal Agreements Some agreements entered into by competitors at the same level of distribution—including trade association activities and rules, exchange of non-price information, participation in joint ventures, and the like—are examined using the rule of reason. Reasonable restraints are lawful; unreasonable restraints violate Section 1 of the Sherman Act.

> People of the same trade seldom meet together, even for merriment and diversion, but that the conversation ends in a conspiracy against the public, or in some contrivance to raise prices.
>
> Adam Smith
> *The Wealth of Nations (1776)*

Business Brief

Note that for a Sherman Act Section 1 violation, it is *essential* to show *concerted activity*; one party, acting alone, cannot be liable.

Exhibit 32.2

Group Boycott by Sellers

AGREEMENT NOT TO DEAL WITH A CUSTOMER

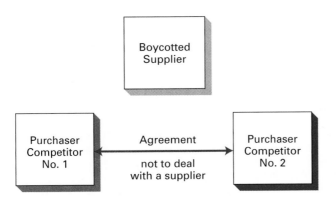

Exhibit 32.3

Group Boycott by Purchasers

Vertical Restraints of Trade

A **vertical restraint of trade** occurs when two or more parties on *different levels of distribution* enter into a contact, combination, or conspiracy to restrain trade (see Exhibit 32.4). The Supreme Court has applied both the *per se* rule and the rule of reason in determining the legality of vertical restraints of trade under Section 1 of the Sherman Act. The most common forms of vertical restraint are discussed in the following paragraphs.

Resale Price Maintenance   **Resale pricing maintenance** (or **vertical price-fixing**) occurs when a party at one level of distribution enters into an agreement with a party at another level to adhere to a price schedule that either sets or stabilizes prices. For example, a computer manufacturer that sells its computers only to retailers that agree to resell them at the prices set by the manufacturer is engaged in this practice.

Setting *minimum* resale prices is a *per se* violation of Section 1 of the Sherman Act as an unreasonable restraint of trade.[9] Consider this example: Integral Camera Corporation manufactures digital cameras and sets a *minimum* price below which the cameras cannot be sold by retailers (e.g., the cameras cannot be sold for less than $1,000 by retailers. This constitutes per se illegal minimum resale price maintenance.

In the following case, the Supreme Court had to decide whether the setting of a *maximum* resale price was a *per se* violation of Section 1 of the Sherman Act.

Exhibit 32.4

Vertical Restraint of Trade

Case 32.1

Resale Price Maintenance

Background and Facts

Barkat U. Khan and his corporation entered into an agreement with State Oil Company to lease and operate a gas station and convenience store owned by State Oil. The agreement provided that Khan would obtain his station's gasoline supply from State Oil. The agreement provided that Khan could charge any price for the gasoline he sold to the station's customers, but if the price charged was higher than State Oil's "suggested retail price," the excess was to be rebated to State Oil; Khan could choose to sell gasoline for less than State Oil's suggested retail price. Khan sued State Oil, alleging that the maximum resale price required by State Oil was a *per se* violation of Section 1 of the Sherman Act. The district court entered summary judgment for State Oil, but the court of appeals reversed and held that the maximum resale price set by State Oil was a *per se* violation of Section 1. The court of appeals cited a previous U.S. Supreme Court case—*Albrecht v. Herald Co.*, 390 U.S. 145 (1968)—which held that the setting of maximum resale prices was a *per se* violation of Section 1. State Oil appealed to the U.S. Supreme Court.

Issue

Is the setting of a maximum resale price by a supplier a *per se* violation of Section 1 of the Sherman Act?

Court's Reasoning

The U.S. Supreme Court noted that a previous Supreme Court—in *Albrecht v. Herald Co.*, 390 U.S. 145, 88 S.Ct. 869, 1968 U.S. Lexis 3126 (1968)—had held that the setting of maximum

resale prices also was a *per se* violation of Section 1. In the present case of *State Oil Company v. Khan*, the Supreme Court decided to reverse the *Albrecht* decision and held that the setting of maximum resale prices is no longer a *per se* violation of Section 1. The Supreme Court concluded, "There is insufficient economic justification for *per se* invalidation of vertical maximum price fixing." The Supreme Court announced that the rule of reason—a balancing of pro- and anticompetitive effects—would now be used to examine the lawfulness of maximum vertical price fixing. Minimum resale price fixing, however, would still be *per se* illegal.

Decision and Remedy

The U.S. Supreme Court reversed *Albrecht*. The Supreme Court held that the setting of a maximum resale price is not a *per se* violation of Section 1 of the Sherman Act, but instead its legality would be analyzed using the rule of reason test. The Supreme Court remanded the current case for trial, using the new rule of reason standard.

Case Questions

Critical Thinking   How often do you think the U.S. Supreme Court reverses itself? Do you think it should have done so in this case?

Business Ethics   Was the State Oil contract that set a maximum resale price in this case lawful under the rule of reason standard?

Contemporary Business   How will this decision affect suppliers and the retailers they sell to? Explain.

Nonprice Vertical Restraints   The legality of **nonprice vertical restraints** of trade under Section 1 of the Sherman Act is examined using the rule of reason.[10] Nonprice restraints are unlawful under this analysis if their anticompetitive effects outweigh their procompetitive effects. Nonprice vertical restraints include situations where a manufacturer assigns exclusive territories to retail dealers or limits the number of dealers that may be located in a certain territory.

Defenses to Section 1 of the Sherman Act

The courts have recognized several defenses to alleged violations of Section 1 of the Sherman Act. These defenses are discussed in the following paragraphs.

Unilateral Refusal to Deal   The U.S. Supreme Court has held that a firm can unilaterally choose not to deal with another party without being liable under Section 1 of the Sherman Act. A **unilateral refusal to deal** is not a violation of Section 1 because there is no concerted action with others. This rule was announced in *United States v. Colgate & Co.* and is therefore often referred to as the "**Colgate doctrine**."[11]

Consider This Example   If Louis Vuitton, a maker of expensive women's clothing, shoes, handbags, and accessories, refuses to sell its merchandise to Wal-Mart stores, this is a lawful unilateral refusal to deal.

Conscious Parallelism   If two or more firms act the same, but no concerted action is shown, there is no violation of Section 1 of the Sherman Act. This doctrine is often referred to as **conscious parallelism**. Thus, if two competing manufacturers of a similar product both separately reach an independent decision not to deal with a retailer, there is no violation of Section 1 of the Sherman Act. The key is that each of the manufacturers acted on its own.

Consider This Example   If Louis Vuitton, Gucci, and Chanel, makers of expensive women's clothing, shoes, handbags, and accessories, each independently make a decision not to sell their products to Wal-Mart, this is lawful conscious parallelism. There is no violation of Section 1 of the Sherman Act because the parties did not agree with one another in making their decisions.

Noerr Doctrine   The *Noerr doctrine* holds that two or more persons may petition the executive, legislative, or judicial branch of the government or administrative agencies to enact laws or to take other action without violating the antitrust laws. The rationale behind this doctrine is that the right to petition the government has precedence because it is guaranteed by the Bill of Rights.[12] For example, General Motors and Ford could collectively petition Congress to pass a law that would limit the import of foreign automobiles into this country.

There is an exception to this doctrine. Under, the *"sham" exception*, petitioners are not protected if their petition or lawsuit is baseless—that is, if a reasonable petitioner or litigant could not realistically expect to succeed on the merits of the petition or lawsuit. If the protection of the Noerr doctrine is lost, an antitrust action may be maintained against the parties who had asserted its protection.

Contemporary Environment
How Trade Association Members Can Avoid Antitrust Liability

Trade associations are organizations that are formed by industry members to promote the industry, provide education to members, formulate rules for self-regulation of the industry, and conduct lobbying and other activities.

Trade associations usually hold annual and other meetings that industry members attend. To avoid antitrust problems, attendees should avoid sharing and discussing certain information with each other. Here are some activities to avoid:

- Do not discuss or exchange price information about current or future sales to customers
- Do not agree to share or split customers or geographical areas
- Do not agree to operate only during agreed-upon hours ■

Section 2 of the Sherman Act—Monopolization

By definition, monopolies have the ability to affect the price of goods and services. **Section 2 of the Sherman Act** was enacted in response to widespread concern about the power generated by this type of anticompetitive activity. Section 2 of the Sherman Act prohibits the act of monopolization. It provides that

Every person who shall monopolize, or attempt to monopolize, or combine or conspire with any other person or persons, to monopolize any part of the trade or commerce among the several States, or with foreign nations, shall be deemed guilty of a felony.[13]

Proving that a defendant is in violation of Section 2 means proving that the defendant (1) possesses monopoly power in the relevant market and (2) engaged in a willful act of monopolization to acquire or maintain that power. Each of these elements is discussed in the following paragraphs.

Defining the Relevant Market

Identifying the **relevant market** for a Section 2 action requires defining the relevant product or service market and geographical market. The definition of the relevant market often determines whether the defendant has monopoly power. Consequently, this determination is often litigated.

The **relevant product or service market** generally includes substitute products or services that are reasonably interchangeable with the defendant's products or services. Defendants often try to make their market share seem smaller by arguing for a broad definition of the product or service market. Plaintiffs, on the other hand, usually argue for a narrow definition.

Consider This Examples   If the Anheuser-Busch Corporation, which is the largest beer producer in the United States, is sued by the government for violating Section 2 of the Sherman Act, the government would argue that the relevant product market is beer sales. Anheuser-Busch, on the other hand, would argue that the relevant product market is all alcoholic beverages, or even all drinkable beverages.

The **relevant geographical market** is usually defined as the area in which the defendant and its competitors sell the product or service. This may be a national, regional, state, or local area, depending on the circumstances.

Consider These Examples   If the Coca-Cola Corporation is sued by the government for violating Section 2 of the Sherman Act, the relevant geographical market would be the nation. If the largest owner of automobile dealerships in south Florida were sued for violating Section 2, the geographical market would be the counties of south Florida.

Monopoly Power

For an antitrust action to be sustained, the defendant must possess **monopoly power** in the relevant market. Monopoly power is defined by the courts to be the power to control prices or exclude competition. The courts generally apply the following guidelines: Market share above 70 percent is monopoly power; market share under 20 percent is not monopoly power. Otherwise, the courts generally prefer to examine the facts and circumstances of each case before making this determination.

Willful Act of Monopolizing

Section 2 of the Sherman Act outlaws the **act of monopolizing**, not monopolies. Any act that otherwise violates any other antitrust law (such as illegal restraints of trade in violation of Section 1 of the Sherman Act) is an act of monopolizing that violates Section 2. When coupled with monopoly power, certain otherwise lawful acts have been held to constitute an act of monopolizing. For example, *predatory pricing*—that is, pricing below average or marginal cost—that is intended to drive out competition has been held to violate Section 2.[14]

A monopoly granted either to an individual or to a trading company has the same effect as a secret in trade or manufacture. The monopolists, by keeping the market constantly understocked, by never fully supplying the effectual demand, sell their commodities much above the natural price, and raise their emoluments greatly above their natural rate.

Adam Smith
Wealth of Nations (1776)

Defenses to Monopolization

Only two narrow defenses to a charge of monopolizing have been recognized: (1) innocent acquisition (e.g., acquisition because of a *superior business acumen*, skill, foresight, or industry) and (2) *natural monopoly* (e.g., a small market that can support only one competitor, such as a small-town newspaper). If a monopoly that fits into one of these categories exercises its power in a predatory or exclusionary way, the defense is lost.

Attempts and Conspiracies to Monopolize

Firms that *attempt* or *conspire* to monopolize a relevant market may be found liable under Section 2 of the Sherman Act. A single firm may be found liable for monopolizing or attempting to monopolize. Two or more firms may be found liable for conspiring to monopolize.

Business Brief

Note carefully that, in contrasts to Section 1, which requires *concerted action*, Section 2 may apply to individual behavior.

Concept Summary The Sherman Act

Section	Description
1	Prohibits contracts, combinations, and conspiracies in restraint of trade. To violate Section 1, the restraint must be found to be unreasonable under either of two tests: 1. Rule of reason 2. *Per se* rule Requires the concerted action of two or more parties.
2	Prohibits the act of monopolizing and attempts or conspiracies to monopolize. Can be violated by the conduct of one firm.

Online Commerce & Internet Law
United States v. Microsoft Corporation

In less than 25 years, Microsoft Corporation grew from a startup company into the world's largest software company, whose products touch the lives of virtually everyone who uses a personal computer. Microsoft dominates the software market with its Windows operating system, which is used on most of the world's personal computers.

Netscape a competing company, developed its Navigator Internet Web browser, and by 1994 it controlled over 80 percent of that market. Microsoft began a campaign to defeat Netscape. Microsoft developed its own browser, called *Explorer*, and attached it to its Windows operating system for free. Microsoft warned Apple, a manufacturer of personal computers, that it would cancel Microsoft's all-important Office software unless Apple used Explorer; Apple capitulated and made Explorer its Web browser. Microsoft muscled AOL into offering Explorer in return for a small placement on the Windows desktop if it would not offer Netscape anywhere on its online service. AOL agreed. Microsoft gave Compaq, a maker of personal computers, a lower price for Windows in return for placing a Microsoft icon for the Explorer Web browser on Compaq's computers.

After investigating, the U.S. government and 19 states sued Microsoft in a civil antitrust case. After a nine-month trial and four months of failed settlement negotiations, the U.S. District Court held that Microsoft had used predatory and anticompetitive conduct to illegally maintain its monopoly in the Windows operating system in violation of Section 2 of the Sherman Act. The judge issued an order that prohibited Microsoft from engaging in such conduct in the future and ordered that Microsoft be split into two separate companies, one company to own the operating systems such as Windows, and a second company to own software, Internet browsers, and other computer applications.

Microsoft appealed. On appeal, the U.S. Court of Appeals upheld the finding that Microsoft had engaged in monopolization in violation of Section 2, but it ruled that Microsoft did not have to be broken up. The case was remanded for further proceedings.

A new district court judge ordered Microsoft Corporation to refrain from engaging in coercive practices and to make some of the code for its operating systems available to other software companies under reasonable licensing arrangement so that they could design their software to be used in conjunction with Microsoft's operating system. Many commentators believe that Microsoft basically "won" this case. [*United States v. Microsoft Corporation*, 2002 U.S. Dist. Lexis 22864 (District Court, D.C. 2002)] ■

Section 7 of the Clayton Act—Mergers

In the late 1800s and early 1900s, *mergers* led to increased concentration of wealth in the hands of a few wealthy individuals and large corporations. In response, in 1914 Congress enacted **Section 7 of the Clayton Act**, which gave the federal government the power to check anticompetitive mergers. Originally, Section 7 of the Clayton Act applied only to stock mergers. The Celler *Kefauver* Act, which was enacted in 1950, widened Section 7's scope to include asset acquisitions.

Today, Section 7 applies to all methods of external expansion, including technical mergers, consolidations, purchases of assets, subsidiary operations, joint ventures, and other combinations.

Section 7 of the Clayton Act provides that it is unlawful for a person or business to acquire stock or assets of another "where in any line of commerce or in any activity affecting commerce in any section of the country, the effect of such acquisition may be substantially to lessen competition, or to tend to create a monopoly."[15] In determining whether a merger is lawful under Section 7 of the Clayton Act, the courts must examine the elements discussed in the following paragraphs.

Line of Commerce

Determining the **line of commerce** that will be affected by a merger involves defining the relevant *product or service market*. Traditionally, the courts have done this by applying the functional interchangeability test. Under this test, the relevant line of commerce includes products or services that consumers use as substitutes. If two products are substitutes for each other, they are considered as part of the same line of commerce. For example, suppose a price increase for regular coffee causes consumers to switch to Sanka (decaffeinated coffee). The two products are part of the same line of commerce because they are interchangeable.

Section of the Country

Defining the relevant **section of the country** consists of determining the relevant *geographical market*. The courts traditionally identify this market as the geographical area that will feel the direct and immediate effects of the merger. It may be a local, state, or regional market, the entire country, or some other geographical area. For example, Anheuser-Busch and the Miller Brewing Company sell beer nationally, whereas a local brewery, such as Upper Steam, sells beer only in Michigan. If Anheuser-Busch and the Miller Brewing Company plan to merge, the relevant section of the country is the nation; if Anheuser-Busch intends to acquire a local brewery that sells beer in the West, the relevant section of the country is the western states.

Probability of a Substantial Lessening of Competition

After the relevant product or service and geographical market have been defined, the court must determine whether a merger or an acquisition is **likely to substantially lessen competition or create a monopoly**. If the court feels that a merger is likely to do either, it may prevent the merger. Section 7 tries to prevent potentially anticompetitive mergers before they occur. It deals in probabilities; an actual showing of the lessening of competition is not required.

In applying Section 7, mergers are generally classified as one of the following: *horizontal merger*, *vertical merger*, *market extension merger*, or *conglomerate merger*. Each of these is discussed in the paragraphs that follow.

Horizontal Mergers   A **horizontal merger** is a merger between two or more companies that compete in the same business and geographical market. The merger of two grocery store chains that serve the same geographical market fits this definition. Such mergers are subjected to strict review under Section 7 because they clearly result in an increase in concentration in the relevant market. For example, if General Motors Corporation and Ford Motor Company tried to merge, this horizontal merger would clearly violate Section 7.

In the landmark case *United States v. Philadelphia National Bank*,[16] the U.S. Supreme Court adopted the *presumptive illegality test* for determining the lawfulness of horizontal mergers. This test finds horizontal mergers presumptively illegal under Section 7 if (1) the merged firm would have a 30 percent or more market share in the relevant market and (2) the merger would cause an increase in concentration of 33 percent or more in the relevant market. This presumption is rebuttable—that is, the defendants may overcome it by introducing evidence that shows that the merger does not violate Section 7.

This test is not the only criterion for evaluating the lawfulness of a merger. The court must also examine factors such as the trend toward concentration in the relevant market, the past history of the firms involved, the aggressiveness of the merged firms, the economic efficiency of the proposed merger, and consumer welfare.

Vertical Mergers   A **vertical merger** is a merger that integrates the operations of a supplier and a customer. For example, if Prentice Hall, Inc., a textbook publisher, acquired a paper mill, it would be a **backward vertical merger**. If a book publisher, such as Doubleday, acquired a retail bookstore chain, such as B. Dalton Bookstores, it would be a **forward vertical merger**. In examining the legality of vertical mergers, the courts usually consider such factors as the past history of the firms, the trend toward concentration in the industries involved, the barriers to entry, the economic efficiencies of the merger, and the elimination of potential competition caused by the merger.

Vertical mergers do not create an increase in market share because the merging firms serve different markets. They may, however, cause anticompetitive effects such as *foreclosing* competitors from either selling goods or services to or buying them from the merged firm. Assume that a furniture manufacturer acquires a chain of retail furniture stores. The merger is unlawful if it is likely that the merged firm will not buy furniture from other manufacturers or sell furniture to other retailers.

Market Extension Mergers   A **market extension merger** is a merger between two companies in similar fields whose sales do not overlap. The merger may expand the acquiring firm's geographical or product market. For example, a merger between two regional brewers that do not sell beer in the same geographical area is called a *geographical market extension merger*. A merger between sellers of similar products, such as a soft drink manufacturer and an orange juice producer, is called a *product market extension merger*. The legality of market extension mergers is examined under Section 7 of the Clayton Act. Market extension mergers are treated like conglomerate mergers.

Conglomerate Mergers   **Conglomerate mergers** are mergers that do not fit into any other category. That is, they are mergers between firms in unrelated businesses. For example, if an oil company such as Exxon merged with a clothing retailer such as Neiman-Marcus, the result would be a conglomerate merger.

The **unfair advantage theory** holds that a conglomerate merger may not give the acquiring firm an unfair advantage over its competitors in finance, marketing, or expertise. This rule is intended to prevent wealthy companies from overwhelming the competition in a given market. For example, Wal-Mart Stores, Inc., a giant discount warehouse store and one of the largest and wealthiest companies, may be prevented from acquiring Polo Ralph Lauren Corporation, a high-end clothing manufacturer and retailer, under this theory.

Defenses to Section 7 Actions

There are two primary defenses to Section 7 actions. These defenses can be raised even if the merger would otherwise violate Section 7. The defenses are:

1. *The failing company doctrine.* According to this defense, a competitor may merge with a failing company if (1) there is no other reasonable alternative for the failing company, (2) no other purchaser is available, and (3) the assets of the failing company would completely disappear from the market if the anticompetitive merger were not allowed to go through.

2. *The small company doctrine.* The courts have permitted two or more small companies to merge without liability under Section 7 if the merger allows them to compete more effectively with a large company.

Premerger Notification

In 1976, premerger notification rules were enacted pursuant to the **Hart-Scott-Rodino Antitrust Improvement Act**.[17] These rules require certain firms to notify the FTC and the Department of Justice of any proposed merger. This gives those agencies time to investigate and challenge any mergers they deem anticompetitive. If the merger is reportable, the parties must file the notification form and wait 30 days. If within the waiting period the government sues, the suit is entitled to expedited treatment in the courts.

Art Center, Paris, France. The European Union (EU) has enacted and enforces very strong antitrust laws. The EU antitrust authorities have denied mergers of multinational companies that had been previously approved by antitrust authorities in the United States.

Section 3 of the Clayton Act—Tying Arrangements

Section 3 of the Clayton Act prohibits tying arrangements involving sales and leases of goods (tangible personal property).[18] **Tying arrangements** are vertical trade restraints that involve the seller's refusal to sell a product (the *tying* item) to a customer unless the customer purchases a second product (the *tied* item). **Section 1 of the Sherman Act** (restraints of trade) forbids tying arrangements involving goods, services, intangible property, and real property.

The defendant must be shown to have had sufficient economic power in the tying product market to restrain competition in the tied product market.

A tying arrangement is lawful if there is some justifiable reason for it. For example, the protection of quality control coupled with a trade secret may save a tie-in arrangement.

Consider These Examples   Suppose, for example, that a manufacturer makes one patented product and one unpatented product. An illegal tie-in arrangement occurs if the manufacturer refuses to sell the patented product to a buyer unless the buyer also purchases the unpatented product. Coca-Cola Company owns the right to the formula for the syrup to make Coca-Cola, which is a trade secret. Now, suppose Coca-Cola requires its distributors to purchase the syrup to make Coca-Cola from it. The tying product is the Coca-Cola franchise distributorship, and the tied product is the syrup. Here, the tying arrangement is lawful because a trade secret is involved and quality control must be preserved.

Section 2 of the Clayton Act—Price Discrimination

Businesses in the U.S. economy survive by selling their goods and services at prices that allow them to make a profit. Sellers often offer favorable terms to their preferred customers. **Price discrimination** occurs if a seller does this without just cause. The rules regarding this type of unlawful trade practices are found in **Section 2 of the Clayton Act**, which is commonly referred to as the **Robinson-Patman Act**. **Section 2(a) of the Robinson-Patman Act** contains the following basic prohibition against price discrimination in the sale of goods.

> It shall be unlawful for any person engaged in commerce, either directly or indirectly, to discriminate in price between different purchases of commodities of like grade and quality, where either or any of the purchases involved in such discrimination are in commerce, where the effect of such discrimination may be substantially to lessen competition or tend to create a monopoly in any line of commerce, or to injure, destroy, or prevent competition with any person who either grants or knowingly receives the benefit of such discrimination, or with customers of either of them.[19]

This section does not apply to the sale of services, real estate, intangible property, securities, leases, consignments, or gifts. Mixed sales (i.e., those involving both services and commodities) are controlled by the dominant nature of the transaction.

Direct Price Discrimination

To prove a violation of **Section 2(a) of the Robinson-Patman Act**, the following elements of price discrimination must be shown:

- **Sales to two or more purchasers.** To violate Section 2(a), the price discrimination must involve sales to at least two different purchasers at approximately the same time. It is legal to make two or more sales of the same product to the same purchaser at different prices. The Robinson-Patman act requires that the discrimination occur "in commerce."

Business Brief

To prove a violation of Section 2(a), the following elements must be shown: (1) The defendant sold commodities of like grade and quality (2) to two or more purchasers at different prices at approximately the same time, and (3) the plaintiff suffered injury because of the price discrimination.

- ■ *Commodities of like grade and quality.* A Section 2(a) violation must involve goods of "like grade and quality." To avoid this rule, sellers sometimes try to differentiate identical or similar products by using brand names. Nevertheless, as one court stated, "Four roses under any other name would still swill the same."[20]
- ■ *Injury.* To recover damages, the plaintiff must have suffered actual injury because of the price discrimination. The injured party may be the purchaser who did not receive the favored price (*primary line injury*), that party's customers to whom the lower price could not be passed along (*secondary line injury*), and so on down the line (*tertiary line injury*).

A plaintiff who has not suffered injury because of the price discrimination cannot recover. For example, assume that a wholesaler sells Michelin tires to General Motors more inexpensively than to Ford Motor Company. If Ford could have purchased comparable Michelin tires elsewhere at the lower price, it cannot recover.

Indirect Price Discrimination

Because direct forms of price discrimination are readily apparent, sellers of goods have devised sophisticated ways to provide discriminatory prices to favored customers. Favorable credit terms, freight charges, and such are examples of **indirect price discrimination** that violate the Robinson-Patman Act.

Defenses to Section 2(a) Actions

The Robinson-Patman Act establishes three statutory defenses to Section 2(a) liability:

1. *Cost justification.* Section 2(a) provides that a seller's price discrimination is not unlawful if the price differential is due to "differences in the cost of manufacture, sale, or delivery" of the product. This is called the **cost justification defense**. For example, quantity or volume discounts are lawful to the extent that they are supported by cost savings. Sellers may classify buyers into various broad groups and compute an average cost of selling to the group. The seller may then charge members of different groups different prices without being liable for price discrimination. The seller bears the burden of proving this defense.

   For example, if the Procter & Gamble Company can prove that bulk shipping rates make it less costly to deliver 10,000 boxes of Tide than lesser quantities, it may charge purchasers accordingly. However, Procter & Gamble may not simply lower its price per box because the buyer is a good customer.

2. *Changing conditions.* Price discrimination is not unlawful if it is in response to "changing conditions in the market for or the marketability of the goods." For example, the price of goods can be lowered to subsequent purchasers to reflect the deterioration of perishable goods (e.g., fish), obsolescence of seasonable goods (e.g., winter coats sold in the spring), a distress sale pursuant to court order, or discontinuance of a business. This is called the **changing conditions defense**.

3. *Meeting the competition.* The **meeting the competition defense** to price discrimination is stipulated in **Section 2(b) of the Robinson-Patman Act**.[21] This defense holds that a seller may lawfully engage in price discrimination to meet a competitor's price. For example, assume that Rockport sells its "Pro Walker" shoe nationally at $100 per pair, while the Great Lakes Shoe Co. (Great Lakes), which produces and sells a comparable walking shoe, sells its product only in Michigan and Wisconsin. If Great Lakes sells its walking shoes at $75 per pair, Rockport can do the same in Michigan and Wisconsin. Rockport does not have to reduce the price of the shoe in the other 48 states. The seller can only meet, not beat, the competitor's price, however.

Section 5 of the Federal Trade Commission Act— Unfair Methods of Competition

In 1914, Congress enacted the **FTC Act** and created the FTC. **Section 5 of the FTC Act** prohibits *unfair methods of competition and unfair or deceptive acts or practices* in or affecting commerce.[22]

Section 5, which is broader than the other antitrust laws, covers conduct that (1) violates any provision of the Sherman Act or the Clayton Act, (2) violates the "spirit" of those acts, (3) fills the gaps of those acts, and (4) offends public policy, or is immoral, oppressive, unscrupulous, or unethical, or causes substantial injury to competitors or consumers.

The FTC is exclusively empowered to enforce the FTC Act. It can issue interpretive rules, general statements of policy, trade regulation rules, and guidelines that define unfair or deceptive practices, and it can conduct investigations of suspected antitrust violations. It can also issue cease-and-desist orders against violators. These orders are appealable to federal court. The FTC Act provides for a private civil cause of action for injured parties. Treble damages are not available.

Online Commerce & Internet Law
Unfair and Deceptive Acts Prohibited over the Internet

Little did Congress know over 90 years ago when it passed the FTC Act that Section 5 of the act would be used to prosecute fraud over the internet. Section 5 prohibits "unfair and deceptive" acts affecting commerce. The FTC has demonstrated recently that old laws can learn new tricks. Consider the following case.

Powerful search engines have been developed to allow surfers to browse the Internet and connect to Web sites in which they are interested. Certain scammers came up with a scheme in which they entice unwitting surfers to connect to their porn sites and not allow them to get out. The scheme worked as follows. The scammers made fake copies of more than 25 million popular Web sites, such as the *Harvard Business Review*, *Japanese Friendship Gardens*, and others. Search engines trolling the Web for new pages found these Web sites and added them

to their listings. The scammers added to the faked Web pages an extra bit of coding so that as soon as surfers found the bogus Web page, it rerouted—"page-jacked"—them to the scammer's porn Web site. Once there, the user was "mouse-trapped" at the porn site, and efforts to escape led only to new porn pages appearing. The porn site operators made money by selling advertisements, and ad prices were often based on the number of "hits" on the site.

The FTC, a federal government agency, investigated and sued porn site operators in federal court for violating Section 5 of the FTC Act. The court found that the porn site operators had engaged in unfair and deceptive practices in violation of Section 5 and issued an injunction to shut down the porn sites and ordered the operators not to engage in such conduct in the future. ∎

Exemptions from Antitrust Laws

Certain industries and businesses are exempt from federal antitrust laws. The three categories of exemptions are:

1. ***Statutory exemptions.*** Certain statutes expressly exempt some forms of business and other activities from the reach of antitrust laws. **Statutory exemptions** include labor unions,[23] agricultural cooperatives,[24] export activities of American companies,[25] and insurance business that is regulated by a state.[26] Other statutes exempt railroad, utility, shipping, and securities industries from most of the reach of antitrust laws.

Oriole Park at Camden Yards, Baltimore, Maryland. In 1922, the U.S. Supreme Court held that professional baseball was exempt from federal antitrust law.

2. *Implied exemptions.* The federal courts have implied several exemptions from antitrust laws. Examples of **implied exemptions** include professional baseball (but not other professional sports) and airlines.[27] The airline exemption was granted on the ground that railroads and other forms of transportation were expressly exempt. The Supreme Court has held that professionals such as lawyers do not qualify for an implied exemption from antitrust laws.[28] The Supreme Court strictly construes implied exemptions from antitrust laws.

3. *State action exemptions.* The U.S. Supreme Court has held that economic regulations mandated by state law are exempt from federal antitrust laws. The **state action exemption** extends to businesses that must comply with these regulations.

Consider This Example States may set the rates that public utilities (e.g., gas, electric, and cable television companies) may charge their customers. The states that set these rates and the companies that must abide by them are not liable for price-fixing in violation of federal antitrust law.

Contemporary Environment
The NFL Sacks Maurice Clarett

Maurice Clarett was a star high school football player who was given a football scholarship at Ohio State University (OSU) of the Big Ten college football conferences. As a freshman running back at OSU, Clarett led his team to an undefeated (14-0) season that was capped by a victory over the University of Miami in a bowl game, winning OSU's first national championship in 35 years. As a result of his freshman season's success, Clarett was named the Big Ten freshman of the year and was voted the best running back in college football by *The Sporting News.*

OSU and the Big Ten suspended Clarette for his sophomore year. At the end of that year, Clarett decided that he would like to turn professional and play for a team in the National Football League (NFL) beginning in the 2004–2005 season. There was only one problem: The 32 member teams of the NFL, each owned by different owners, had agreed to a rule that limited eligibility to players three years removed from their high school graduation date (the Rule). Because Clarett had only been out of high school two years, under the Rule he was ineligible to put himself in the NFL draft to be selected to play in the NFL.

Clarett decided to go on the offense and filed an antitrust lawsuit against the NFL. Clarett alleged that the NFL's three-year rule constituted a group boycott that was an unreasonable restraint of trade in violation of Section 1 of the Sherman Act. The U.S. district court found that the Rule constituted an illegal group boycott and ordered the NFL to allow Clarett to be able to be drafted in the NFL draft. The NFL appealed.

The U.S. Court of Appeals held that the NFL and the NFL Players Association, a labor union that represents the football players of the NFL, had engaged in collective bargaining and had agreed to the eligibility rules that included the three-year rule at issue in this case. The Court of Appeals held that the three-year rule, as agreed to by the NFL and players' labor union, is shielded from antitrust laws by the labor exemption. The Court of Appeals stated, "The NFL argues that federal labor law favoring and governing the collective bargaining process precludes the application of the antitrust laws to its eligibility rules. We agree." [*Clarett v. National Football League*, 369 F.3d 124, 2004 U.S.App. Lexis 10171 (2nd Cir. 2004)] ■

State Antitrust Laws

Most states have enacted antitrust statutes. These statutes are usually patterned after the federal antitrust statutes. They often contain the same language as well. State antitrust laws are used to attack anticompetitive activity that occurs in intrastate commerce. When federal antitrust laws are laxly applied, plaintiffs often bring lawsuits under state antitrust laws.

International Law

Japanese *Keiretsus* Ignore Antitrust Laws

In the past 50 years, Japan has grown into an economic superpower. Much of this success has to do with the relationship between Japan's federal government and the *keiretsu* (industrial groupings). *Keiretsu* cartels are considered a key factor behind the country's economic success. After World War II, American-style antitrust laws were enacted in Japan; since then, though, they have been virtually ignored. The Japan Fair Trade Commission (JFTC), which is empowered to enforce antitrust laws, rarely does so.

Japan's industry and commerce are rife with cartels—more than 250 are legally permitted. These cartels blatantly engage in anticompetitive conduct. Price fixing permeates the beer, cosmetics, over-the-counter drug, and construction industries, among others. The cartels are politically entrenched and lobby against the passage of laws that would curtail their monopolistic positions.

This protectionist attitude has helped Japanese *keiretsus* become giants that have a substantial advantage in the international marketplace. This has come at the expense of Japanese consumers, however, who have to pay higher-than-competitive prices for goods and services sold by these cartels in Japan. This helps Japanese cartels compete abroad. Today, Japanese *keiretsus* retain their monopolistic positions with little interference from the Japanese government. ■

Chapter Summary

Federal Antitrust Laws, p. 701

Federal Antitrust Law

Congress has enacted a series of laws to limit anticompetitive behavior in business. Federal antitrust laws include:

1. *Sherman Act.* This act, enacted in 1890, made certain restraints of trade and monopolistic acts illegal.
2. *Clayton Act.* This act, enacted in 1914, regulates mergers and prohibits certain exclusive dealing arrangements.
3. *Federal Trade Commission (FTC) Act.* This act, enacted in 1914, prohibits unfair methods of competition.
4. *Robinson-Patman Act.* This act, enacted in 1930, prohibits price discrimination.

Antitrust Enforcement

Each administration adopts an enforcement policy for antitrust laws. Antitrust laws are enforced more stringently at some times than at other times.

Antitrust Penalties

Federal antitrust laws provide the following penalties:

1. *Criminal sanctions.* Criminal penalties may be assessed for violations of the Sherman Act.
2. *Civil penalties.* The federal government may seek civil damages, including treble damages, for violations of federal antitrust laws. Courts may issue orders for divestiture of assets, cancellation of contracts, and other remedies.
3. *Private civil actions.* Section 4 of the Clayton Act provides that anyone injured in his or her business or property by the defendant's violation of any federal antitrust law (except the FTC Act) may bring a civil action and recover *treble damages*, plus reasonable costs and attorney's fees, from the defendant.
4. *Effect of government judgment.* A government judgment against a defendant for an antitrust violation may be used as prima facie evidence of liability in a private, civil treble-damage action. A plea of *nolo contendere* or a *consent decree* cannot be used as evidence in a subsequent private, civil antitrust action.

Section I of the Sherman Act—Restraints of Trade, p. 702

Restraints of Trade

Section 1 of the Sherman Act. This section prohibits contracts, combinations, or conspiracies that cause *unreasonable restraints of trade*. It requires *concerted activity* between two or more parties. The courts apply one of the following two tests in determining the lawfulness of a restraint of trade.

1. *Rule of reason.* This requires a balancing of pro- and anticompetitive effects of the restraint. Restraints found to be unreasonable are unlawful, violating Section 1 of the Sherman Act.
2. *Per se rule.* The *per se* rule is applied to restraints that are inherently anticompetitive. No justification for the restraint is permitted.

Horizontal Restraints of Trade

Horizontal restraint of trade occurs when two or more competitors at the *same level of distribution* enter into a contract, combination, or conspiracy to restrain trade. Horizontal restraints include:

1. *Price fixing.* Competitors in the same line of business agree to set the price of the goods or services they sell. This is a *per se violation*.
2. *Division of markets.* Competitors agree that each will serve only a designated portion of a market. Also called *market sharing*. This is a *per se violation*.
3. *Group boycott.* Competitors agree not to deal with others at another level of distribution (e.g., customer, supplier). Most group boycotts are examined using the *rule of reason*.
4. *Other horizontal agreements.* These agreements are examined using the *rule of reason*.

Vertical Restraints of Trade

Vertical restraint of trade occurs when two or more parties on *different levels of distribution* enter into a contract, combination, or conspiracy to restrain trade. Vertical restraints include:

1. *Resale price maintenance.* A party at one level of distribution (e.g., a manufacturer) requires a party at another level of distribution (e.g., a retailer) to sell a good or service at a designated price. Also called *vertical price fixing*. This is a *per se violation*.
2. *Nonprice vertical restraints.* There restraints are examined using the *rule of reason*.

Defenses to Section 1 of the Sherman Act

The following defenses may be raised against an alleged violation of Section 1 of the Sherman Act:

1. *Unilateral refusal to deal.* A party may unilaterally refuse to deal with another party. This does not violate Section 1 because there has been no concerted action.

2. *Conscious parallelism.* This occurs when two or more firms act the same but without concerted action; they reached their decisions independently.

3. *The Noerr doctrine.* Two or more parties may petition the executive, legislative, or judicial branches of government to enact laws or take other action. *Sham exception*: The *Noerr* doctrine does not protect petitioners or plaintiffs if their petition or lawsuit is without merit.

Section 2 of the Sherman Act—Monopolization, p. 707

Monopolization

Section 2 of the Sherman Act. This section prohibits the act of *monopolizing* and attempts, combinations, and conspiracies to monopolize trade or commerce in a relevant market. The following elements are necessary to prove a defendant in violation of Section 2 of the Sherman Act:

1. *Relevant market.* The relevant market is defined as:

   a. *Relevant product or service market.* This market includes substitute products or services that are reasonably interchangeable with the defendant's products or services.

   b. *Relevant geographical market.* This is the geographical area in which the defendant and its competitors sell the product or service.

2. *Monopoly power.* The defendant must possess monopoly power in the relevant market. This is defined as the power to control prices or exclude competition.

3. *Act of monopolizing.* The defendant must have engaged in a willful act of monopolizing. Mere possession of a monopoly is not enough.

Defenses to Monopolization

The following defenses may be raised against an alleged violation of Section 2 of the Sherman Act:

1. *Superior business acumen.* A monopoly may be acquired by superior skill, foresight, or industry.

2. *Natural monopoly.* A monopoly may be thrust upon the defendant (e.g., only newspaper in a small town).

Section 7 of the Clayton Act—Mergers, p. 710

Elements of a Section 7 Action

Section 7 of the Clayton Act. This section prohibits acquisitions that may substantially lessen competition in any line of commerce in any section of the country. The following elements are necessary to prove a violation of Section 7 of the Clayton Act:

1. *Line of commerce.* The line of commerce is defined as the market that will be affected by the merger. It includes products or services that consumers use as substitutes for those produced or sold by the merging firms.

2. *Section of the country.* The section of the country is the geographical market that will be affected by the merger. It includes the area that will feel the direct and immediate impact of the merger.

3. *Probability of a substantial lessening of competition.* If the court determines that the merger would have a probability of a substantial lessening of competition, the merger may be prohibited. The statute deals with probabilities: A showing of actual lessening of competition is not required.

Horizontal Mergers

A horizontal merger is a merger between two or more firms that compete in the same business and geographical market; it is a merger between competitors at the same level of distribution.

Vertical Mergers

A vertical merger is a merger between firms at different levels of distribution that integrates the operations of a supplier and a customer.

Market Extension Mergers

A market extension merger is a merger of two firms in similar fields whose sales do not overlap.

1. *Geographical market extension merger.* This is a merger of two firms that sell the same product or service but in different geographical markets.
2. *Product market extension merger.* This is a merger of two firms that sell similar products or services in the same geographical market.

Conglomerate Mergers

A conglomerate merger is a merger of firms in totally unrelated businesses. Conglomerate mergers may be challenged under:

1. *Unfair advantage theory.* A merger may not give the acquiring firm an unfair advantage over its competitors in finance, marketing, or expertise.

Defenses to Section 7 Actions

The following defenses may be raised against a violation of Section 7 of the Clayton Act:

1. *Failing company doctrine.* A competitor may merge with a failing company if (1) there is no other reasonable alternative for the failing company, (2) no other purchaser is available, and (3) the assets of the failing company would completely disappear from the market if the anticompetitive merger were not allowed to go through.
2. *Small company doctrine.* Two or more small companies may merge if the merger allows them to compete more effectively with a large company.

Premerger Notification

Hart-Scott-Rodino Antitrust Improvement Act. This federal act requires certain firms to notify the FTC and Justice Department in advance of a proposed merger. Unless the government challenges the proposed merger within 30 days, the merger may proceed.

Section 3 of the Clayton Act—Tying Arrangements, p. 713

Section 3 of the Clayton Act

1. *Tying arrangement.* A tying arrangement occurs when a seller refuses to sell a product (the *tying* product) to a customer unless the customer purchases a second product (the *tied* product).
2. *Section 3 of the Clayton Act.* This section prohibits tying arrangements involving sales and leases of *goods*.
3. *Section 1 of the Sherman Act.* This section prohibits trying arrangements involving goods, *services*, intangible property, and real property.

Section 2 of the Clayton Act—Price Discrimination, p. 713

Section 2 of the Clayton Act

This section is commonly referred to as the *Robinson-Patman Act*. It prohibits price discrimination and discriminatory fees, payments, and services. The act applies only to products, not services.

Price Discrimination

Section 2(a). This section prohibits a seller from discriminating in price between two or more different purchasers of commodities of *like grade and quality* where the effect may be to substantially lessen competition. *Direct* and *indirect* price discrimination are unlawful.

Defenses to Section 2(a) Actions

A seller's price discrimination is not unlawful if the price differential is due to:

1. *Cost justification.* Differences in the cost of maintenance, sale, or delivery of a product to different purchasers can justify cost discrimination.

2. *Changing conditions.* The seller is allowed to respond to changing conditions in the market (e.g., deterioration of perishable goods).

3. *Meeting the competition.* Section 2(b) permits a seller to have a lower price in one market than in another market to meet the price of a competitor in the lower-priced market.

Section 5 of the Federal Trade Commission Act—Unfair Methods of Competition, p. 715

Sections 5 of the FTC Act

This section prohibits *unfair methods of competition and unfair or deceptive acts or practices.* Section 5 covers conduct that (1) violates any provision of the Sherman Act or the Clayton Act, (2) violates the "spirit" of those acts, (3) fills the gaps of those acts, and (4) causes substantial injury to competitors or consumers.

Exemptions from Antitrust Laws, p. 715

Statutory Exemptions

Statutes expressly exempt labor unions, agricultural cooperatives, export activities of U.S. companies, insurance business regulated by states, and railroad, utility, shipping, and securities industries from federal antitrust laws.

Implied Exemptions

The courts have held that certain industries, including professional baseball and airlines, are implicitly exempt from federal antitrust laws.

State Action Exemptions

Businesses' activities that are mandated by state law are exempt from federal antitrust laws.

State Antitrust Laws, p. 717

State Antitrust Laws

Most states have enacted state antitrust laws that attack anticompetitive activity that occurs in intrastate commerce.

Internet Exercises and Case Questions

Working the Web Internet Exercises

Activities

1. The largest antitrust case of our time, *United States v. Microsoft Corporation*, leaves a long and rich trail of documents for study. See, for example, **www.ssrn.com/update/lsn/lsn_microsoft-case.html**, which contains a lengthy list of links to articles about the famous case. List the specific sections of the antitrust laws that Microsoft was alleged to have violated.

2. Find your state's laws relating to unfair competition and restraint of trade. Are they consistent with federal law?

See "Law About . . . Antitrusts at," **www.law.cornell. edu/topics/antitrust.html**, for an overview of antitrust law, with links to key primary and secondary sources.

3. Antitrust is an area of law deeply connected with economic theory. The intent of the law is to protect competition. So how can mergers be permitted under the Clayton Act? Section 7 of the Clayton Act [15 U.S.C. 18].

4. Where does the United States derive its purported authority to enforce its antitrust laws extraterritorially? See **www.usdoj.gov/atr/public/guidelines/internat.htm**.

Critical Legal Thinking Cases

32.1 Price-Fixing   The Maricopa County Medical Society (Society) is a professional association that represents doctors of medicine, osteopathy, and podiatry in Maricopa County, Arizona. The society formed the Maricopa Foundation for Medical Care (Foundation), a nonprofit Arizona corporation. Approximately 1,750 doctors, who represent 70 percent of the practitioners in the country, belong to the foundation. The foundation acts as an insurance administrator between its member doctors and insurance companies that pay patients' medical bills.

The foundation established a maximum fee schedule for various medical services. The member doctors agreed to abide by this fee schedule when providing services to patients. The state of Arizona brought this action against the Society and the Foundation and its members, alleging price-fixing in violation of Section 1 of the Sherman Act. Who wins? [*Arizona v. Maricopa County Medical Society*, 457 U.S. 332, 102 S.Ct. 2466, 1982 U.S. Lexis 5 (1982)]

32.2 Division of Markets   Topco Associates, Inc., was founded in the 1940s by a group of small, local grocery store chains to act as a buying cooperative for the member stores. In this capacity, Topco procured and distributed more than 1,000 different food and related items to its members. Topco did not itself own any manufacturing or processing facilities, and the items it procured were shipped directly from the manufacturer or packer to Topco members. Topco members agreed to sell only Topco brand products within an exclusive territory. The United States sued Topco and its members, alleging a violation of Section 1 of the Sherman Act. Who wins? [*United States v. Topco Associates, Inc.*, 405 U.S. 596, 92 S.Ct. 1126, 1972 U.S. Lexis 167 (1972)]

32.3 Tying Arrangement   Mercedes-Benz of North America (MBNA) was the exclusive franchiser of Mercedes-Benz dealerships in the United States. MBNA's franchise agreements required each dealer to establish a customer service department for the repair of Mercedes-Benz automobiles and for dealers to purchase Mercedes-Benz replacement parts from MBNA. At least eight independent wholesale distributors, including Metrix Warehouse, Inc., sold replacement parts for Mercedes-Benz automobiles. Because they were precluded from selling parts to Mercedes-Benz dealers, these parts distributors sold their replacement parts to independent garages that specialized in the repair of Mercedes-Benz automobiles. Evidence showed that Metrix sold replacement parts for Mercedes-Benz automobiles of equal quality and at a lower price than those sold by MBNA. Metrix sued MBNA, alleging a violation of Section 1 of the Sherman Act. Who wins? [*Metrix Warehouse, Inc. v. Mercedes-Benz of North America, Inc.*, 828 F.2d 1033, 1987 U.S. App. Lexis 12341 (4th Cir. 1987)]

32.4 Resale Price Maintenance   The Union Oil Company was a major oil company that operated a nationwide network of franchised service station dealers who sold Union Oil gasoline and other products throughout the United States. The franchise dealers leased their stations from Union Oil; they also signed a franchise agreement to purchase gasoline and other products on assignment from Union Oil. Both the lease and the franchise agreement were one year contracts that could be canceled by Union Oil if a dealer did not adhere to the contract.

The franchise agreement provided that all dealers must adhere to the retail price of gasoline as set by Union Oil. The retail price fixed by Union Oil for gasoline during the period in question was 29.9 cents per gallon. Simpson, a franchised dealer, violated this provision in the franchise agreement and sold gasoline at 27.9 cents per gallon to meet competitive prices. Because of this, Union Oil canceled Simpson's lease and franchise agreement. Simpson sued Union Oil, alleging a violation of Section 1 of the Sherman Act. Who wins? [*Simpson v. Union Oil Company*, 377 U.S. 13, 84 S.Ct. 1051, 1964 U.S. Lexis 2378 (1964)]

32.5 Monopolization   The International Business Machine Corporation (IBM) manufactured entire computer systems, including mainframes and peripherals, and provided software and support services to customers. IBM both sold and leased computers. Greyhound Computer Corporation, Inc., was a computer leasing company that bought older computers from IBM and then leased them to businesses. Thus, Greyhound was both a customer and a competitor of IBM. Prior to 1963, IBM sold its second-generation equipment at a 10 percent discount per year, up to a maximum of 75 percent. Thus, equipment on the market for several years could be purchased at a substantial discount from its original cost.

IBM's market share of this leasing market was 82.5 percent. The portion of the leasing market not controlled by IBM was dispersed among many companies, including Greyhound. IBM officials became concerned that the balance between sales and leases was turned too heavily toward sales and that the rapid increase in leasing companies occurred because of their ability to purchase second-generation computers from IBM at a substantial discount. In 1963, IBM reduced the annual discount to 5 percent per year, with a maximum of 35 percent. In 1964, the discount was changed to 12 percent after the fist year, with no further discounts. Greyhound sued IBM, alleging that IBM engaged in monopolization in violation of Section 2 of the Sherman Act. Who wins? [*Greyhound v. International Business Machine Corporation*, 559 F.2d 488, 1977 U.S. App. Lexis 11957 (9th Cir. 1977)]

32.6 Merger   The Lipton Tea Co. was the second largest U.S. producer of herbal teas, controlling 32 percent of the national market. Lipton announced that it would acquire Celestial Seasonings, the largest U.S. producer of herbal teas, which controlled 52 percent of the national market. R.C. Bigelow, Inc., the third largest producer of herbal teas, with 13 percent of the national market, brought this action, alleging that the merger would violate Section 7 of the Clayton Act and seeking an injunction against the merger. What type of merger was proposed? What was the relevant market? Should the merger be enjoined? [*R. C. Bigelow, Inc., v. Unilever, N.V.*, 867 F.2d 102, 1989 U.S. App. Lexis 574 (2nd Cir. 1989)]

32.7 Antitrust Injury   The Brunswick Corporation was the second largest manufacturer of bowling equipment in the United States. In the late 1950s, the bowling industry expanded rapidly. Brunswick's sales of lanes, automatic pinsetters, and ancillary equipment to bowling alley operators rose accordingly. Because the equipment required a major capital expenditure by bowling center operators, Brunswick extended credit for all of the purchase price except a cash down payment. It took a security interest in the equipment.

Brunswick's sales dropped in the early 1960s, when the bowling industry went into a sharp decline. In addition, many of the bowling center operators defaulted on their loans. By the end of 1964, Brunswick was in financial difficulty. It met with limited success when it foreclosed on its security interests and attempted to lease or sell the repossessed equipment and bowling centers. To avoid complete loss, Brunswick started running those that would provide a positive cash flow. This made Brunswick the largest operator of bowling centers in the country, with more than five times as many bowling centers as its next largest competitor. Because the bowling industry was so deconcentrated, however, Brunswick controlled fewer than 2 percent of the bowling centers in the country.

Pueblo Bowl-O-Mat, Inc., operated three bowling centers in markets where Brunswick had repossessed bowling centers and began operating them. Pueblo Bowl sued Brunswick, alleging that Brunswick had violated Section 7 of the Clayton Act. Pueblo Bowl alleged that it had suffered injury in the form of lost profits that it would have made had Brunswick allowed the bowling centers to go bankrupt, and it requested treble damages. Is Brunswick liable? [*Brunswick Corporation v. Pueblo Bowl-O-Mat, Inc.*, 429 U.S. 477, 97 S.Ct. 690, 1977 U.S. Lexis 37 (1977)]

32.8 Price Discrimination Corn Products Refining Company manufactured corn syrup, or glucose, at two plants, one located in Chicago, Illinois, and the other in Kansas City, Missouri. Glucose was a principal ingredient of low-priced candy. Corn Products sold glucose at the same retail price to all purchasers but charged separately for freight charges. Instead of charging actual freight charges, Corn Products charged every purchaser the freight that it would have cost if the glucose were shipped from Chicago, even if the glucose was shipped from its Kansas City plant. This "base point pricing" system created a favored price zone for Chicago-based purchasers. This put them in a better position to compete for business. The FTC sued Corn Products, alleging that it engaged in price discrimination in violation of Section 2(a) of the Robinson-Patman Act. Did it? [*Corn Products Refining Company v. Federal Trade Commission*, 324 U.S. 726, 65 S.Ct. 961, 1945 U.S. Lexis 2749 (1945)]

Business Ethics Cases

32.9 Business Ethics E. I. du Pont de Nemours & Co. (du Pont) is a manufacturer of chemicals, paints, finishes, fabrics, and other products. General Motors Corporation is a major manufacturer of automobiles. During the period 1917–1919, du Pont purchased 23 percent of the stock of General Motors. du Pont became a major supplier of finishes and fabrics to General Motors.

Du Pont's commanding position as a General Motors supplier was not achieved until shortly after its purchase of a sizable block of General Motors stock in 1917. The company's interest in buying into General Motors was stimulated by John J. Raskob, du Pont's treasurer, and Pierre S. du Pont, du Pont's president, who acquired personal holdings of General Motors stock in 1914. General Motors had been organized six years earlier by William C. Durant to acquire previously independent automobile manufacturing companies—Buick, Cadillac, Oakland, and Oldsmobile. Durant later brought in Chevrolet, organized by him when he was temporarily out of power, during 1910–1915, and a bankers' group controlled General Motors. In 1915, when Durant and the bankers deadlocked on the choice of a board of directors, they resolved the deadlock by an agreement under which Pierre S. du Pont was named chairman of the General Motors Board and Pierre S. du Pont, Raskob, and two nominees of Mr. du Pont were named neutral directors. By 1916, Durant settled his differences with the bankers and resumed the presidency and his controlling position in General Motors. He prevailed upon Pierre S. du Pont and Raskob to continue their interest in General Motors's affairs, which both did as members of the finance committee, working closely with Durant in matters of finances and operations and plans for future expansion.

Raskob foresaw the success of the automobile industry and the opportunity for great profit in a substantial purchase of General Motors stock. On December 19, 1917, Raskob submitted a treasurer's report to the du Pont finance committee, recommending a purchase of General Motors stock in the amount of $25 million. That report made it clear that more than just a profitable investment was contemplated. A major consideration was that an expanding General Motors would provide a substantial market needed by the burgeoning du Pont organization. Raskob's summary of reasons in support of the purchase included this statement: "Our interest in the General Motors Company will undoubtedly secure for us the entire Fabrikoid, Pyralin (celluloid), paint and varnish business of those companies, which is a substantial factor."

General Motors was the colossus of the giant automobile industry. It accounted annually for upwards of two-fifths of the total sales of automotive vehicles in the nation. Expressed in percentages, du Pont supplied 67 percent of General Motors's requirements for finishes in 1946 and 68 percent in 1947. In fabrics, du Pont supplied 52.3 percent of requirements in 1946 and 38.5 percent in 1947. Because General Motors accounted for almost one-half of the automobile industry's annual sales, its requirements for automotive finishes and fabrics must have represented approximately one-half of the relevant market for these materials.

In 1949, the United States brought an antitrust action against du Pont, alleging violation of Section 7 of the Clayton Act and seeking the divestiture of du Pont's ownership of stock in General Motors. Did du Pont's ownership of 23 percent of the stock of General Motors constitute a vertical merger that gave du Pont illegal preferences over competitors in the sale of finishes and fabrics to General Motors in violation of Section 7 of the Clayton Act? Did the du Ponts act ethically in this case? [*United States v. E. I. du Pont de Nemours & Co.*, 353 U.S. 586, 77 S.Ct. 872, 1957 U.S. Lexis 1755 (1955)]

32.10 Business Ethics Falls City Industries, Inc., (Falls City), was a regional brewer located in Nebraska. It sold its "Falls City" brand beer in 13 states, including Indiana and Kentucky. In Indiana, Falls City sold its beer to Vanco Beverage, Inc., a beer wholesaler located in Vanderburgh County. In Kentucky, Falls City sold its beer to wholesalers located in Henderson County. The two counties are directly across from each other and are separated only by the Indiana–Kentucky state line. A four-lane interstate highway connects the two counties. When other brewers raised their wholesale prices in Indiana, Falls City also raised its prices. Falls City also raised its wholesale prices in Kentucky, but less than it raised its prices in Indiana. Vanco brought a treble damages action against Falls City, alleging that Falls City had engaged in price discrimination in violation of Section 2(a) of the Robinson-Patman Act by raising prices less in Kentucky than in Indiana.

Does the meeting-the-competition defense protect Falls City Industries from liability for price discrimination? Did Falls City act unethically in this case? [*Falls City Industries, Inc. v. Vanco Beverage, Inc.*, 460 U.S. 428, 103 S.Ct. 1282, 1983 U.S. Lexis 148 (1983)]

Briefing the Case Writing Assignment

Read Case A.32 in the Case Appendix [*Texaco Inc. v. Hasbrouck, dba Rick's Texaco*]. This case is excerpted from the U.S. Supreme Court opinion. Review and brief the case. In your brief, be sure to answer the following questions.

1. Who were the plaintiffs? Who was the defendant?

2. Describe the activities that the defendant engaged in that the plaintiffs alleged were unlawful.

3. What law did the plaintiffs assert was violated? What does this law prohibit?

4. Did the U.S. Supreme Court find a violation? Explain the reasoning the Supreme Court used in reaching its decision.

Endnotes

1. Antitrust Amendments Act of 1990, P.L. 101–588.
2. Antitrust Amendments Act of 1990, P.L. 101–588.
3. 15 U.S.C. § 15.
4. *Reiter v. Sonotone Corporation*, 442 U.S. 330, 99 S.Ct. 2326, 1979 U.S. Lexis 108 (1979).
5. 15 U.S.C. § 26.
6. Justice Marshall, *United States v. Topco Associates, Inc.*, 405 U.S. 596, 92 S.Ct. 1126, 1972 U.S. Lexis 167 (1972).
7. 15 U.S.C. § 1.
8. 221 U.S. 1, 31 S.Ct. 502, 1911 U.S. Lexis 1725 (1911). The Court found that Rockefeller's oil trust violated the Sherman Act and ordered the trust broken up into 30 separate companies.
9. *Dr. Miles Medical Co. v. John D. Park & Sons, Co.*, 220 U.S. 373, 31 S.Ct. 376, 1911 U.S. Lexis 1685 (1911).
10. *Continental T.V., Inc. v. GTE Sylvania, Inc.*, 433 U.S. 36, 97 S.Ct. 2549, 1977 U.S. Lexis 134 (1977), reversing *United States v. Arnold Schwinn & Co.*, 388 U.S. 365, 87 S.Ct. 1856, 1967 U.S. Lexis 2965 (1969).
11. 250 U.S. 300, 39 S.Ct. 465, 1919 U.S. Lexis 1748 (1919).
12. This doctrine is the result of two U.S. Supreme Court decisions: *Eastern R.R. President's Conference v. Noerr Motor Freight, Inc.*, 365 U.S. 127, 81 S.Ct. 523, 1961 U.S. Lexis 2128 (1961), and *United Mine Workers v. Pennington*, 381 U.S. 657, 85 S.Ct. 1585, 1965 U.S. Lexis 2207 (1965).
13. 15 U.S.C. § 2.
14. *William Inglis & Sons Baking Company v. ITT Continental Baking Company, Inc.*, 668 F.2d 1014, 1982 U.S. App. Lexis 21926 (9th Cir. 1982).
15. 15 U.S.C. § 18.
16. 374 U.S. 321, 83 S.Ct. 1715, 1963 U.S. Lexis 2413 (1963).
17. 15 U.S.C. § 18(a).
18. 15 U.S.C. § 14.
19. 15 U.S.C. § 13(a).
20. *Hartley & Parker, Inc. v. Florida Beverage Corp.*, 307 F.2d 916, 923, 1962 U.S. App. Lexis 4196 (5th Cir. 1952).
21. 15 U.S.C. § 13(b).
22. 15 U.S.C. § 45.
23. Section 6 of the Clayton Act, 15 U.S.C. § 17; the Norris-LaGuardia Act of 1932, 29 U.S.C. §§ 101–155; and the National Labor Relations Act of 1935, 29 U.S.C. §§ 141 et seq. Labor unions that conspire or combine with nonlabor groups to accomplish a goal prohibited by federal antitrust law lose their exemption.
24. Capper-Volstrand Act of 1922, 7 U.S.C. § 291; Cooperative Marketing Act of 1926, 15 U.S.C. § 521.
25. Webb-Pomerene Act, 15 U.S.C. §§ 61–65.
26. McCarran-Ferguson Act of 1945, 15 U.S.C. §§ 1011–1015.
27. *Community Communications Co., Inc. v. City of Boulder*, 455 U.S. 40, 102 S.Ct. 835, 1982 U.S. Lexis 65 (1982).
28. *Goldfarb v. Virginia State Bar*, 421 U.S. 773, 95 S.Ct. 2004, 1975 U.S. Lexis 13 (1975).

Consumer and Environmental Protection

33

Chapter Objectives

After studying this chapter, you should be able to:

1. Define administrative law and explain the functions of administrative agencies.

2. List the responsibilities of the federal Food and Drug Administration and describe its regulation of food, drugs, cosmetics, and medicinal devices.

3. Explain the coverage of consumer product safety acts.

4. Describe the national ambient air quality standards required by the Clean Air Act and the effluent water standards required by the Clean Water Act.

5. Explain how environmental laws regulate the use of toxic substances and the disposal of hazardous wastes.

Chapter Contents

- Administrative Law
- Food, Drugs, and Cosmetics Safety
- Product Safety
- Unfair and Deceptive Practices
- Environmental Protection
- State Environmental Protection Laws

Federal and state governments enact laws that regulate business. The legislative and executive branches of government have created numerous administrative agencies to assist in implementing and enforcing these laws. The operation of these administrative agencies is governed by a body of **administrative law**. Because of their importance, administrative agencies are informally referred to as the *fourth branch of government*.

Originally, sales transactions in this country were guided by the principle of *caveat emptor* ("let the buyer beware"). To promote the safety of foods, cosmetics, drugs, products, and services, and to prohibit abusive, unfair, and deceptive selling practices, federal and state governments have enacted a variety of statutes that regulate the behavior of businesses that deal with consumers. These laws are collectively referred to as **consumer protection laws**.

In producing and consuming products, businesses and consumers generate air pollution, water pollution, and hazardous and toxic wastes that cause harm to the environment and to human health. Pollution has now reached alarming rates in this country and the world. In response, federal and state governments have enacted **environmental protection laws** to contain the levels of pollution and to clean up hazardous waste sites in this country.

This chapter examines administrative law and consumer and environmental laws that are applicable to businesses and individuals.

Administrative Law

Congress and the executive branch of government have created more than 100 federal **administrative agencies**. These agencies are intended to provide resources and expertise in dealing with complex commercial organizations and businesses. In addition, state governments have created many state administrative agencies. Thousands of *rules and regulations* regulating business operations have been adopted and enforced by federal and state administrative agencies.

Business Brief

Businesses spend billions of dollars each year complying with government regulation.

Administrative law is a combination of *substantive* and *procedural* law. Each federal administrative agency is empowered to administer a particular statute or statutes. For example, the federal Securities and Exchange Commission (SEC) is authorized to enforce the Securities Act of 1933 and the Securities Exchange Act of 1934; the federal Food and Drug Administration (FDA) is empowered to enforce the Federal Food, Drug and Cosmetics Act; and the federal Environmental Protection Agency is authorized to enforce federal environmental protection laws. These statutes are the *substantive law* that is enforced by the agency.

General Government Regulation

Most government regulation, which is **general government regulation**, applies to many businesses and industries collectively. For example, the National Labors Relations Board (NLRB) is empowered to regulate the formation and operation of labor unions in most industries, the Occupational Safety and Health Administration (OSHA) is authorized to formulate and enact safety and health standards for the workplace, and the Consumer Product Safety Commission (CPSC) is empowered to establish mandatory safety standards for products sold in this country.

Specific Government Regulation

Congress and the executive branch created some administrative agencies to monitor certain regulated industries with **specific government regulation**. For example, the Federal Communications Commission (FCC) regulates the operation of television and radio stations, the Interstate Commerce Commission (ICC) regulates railroads, the Federal Aviation Administration (FAA) regulates commercial airlines, and the Office of the Comptroller of the Currency (OCC) regulates national banks.

Administrative Agencies

Administrative agencies are generally established with the goal of creating a body of professionals who are experts in a particular field.

Many administrative agencies are given the authority to adopt **rules and regulations** that enforce and interpret statutory law. The most pervasive government regulations have developed from the statutes enforced by and the rules and regulations adopted by **federal administrative agencies**. Federal administrative agencies include the Department of Homeland Security, the Department of Justice, the Department of Labor, the Department of Commerce, and other agencies.

All states have created **state administrative agencies** to enforce and interpret state law. For example, most states have a corporations department to enforce state corporations law, a banking department to regulate the operation of banks, fish and game departments, and workers' compensation boards. Local governments and municipalities create administrative agencies, such as zoning commissions, to administer local law.

Delegation of Powers

When an administrative agency is created, it is delegated certain powers. The agency has only the legislative, judicial, and executive powers that are delegated to it. This is called the **delegation doctrine**. Thus, an agency can adopt a rule or regulation (a legislative function), prosecute a violation of the statute or rule (an executive function), and adjudicate the dispute (a judicial function). The courts have upheld this combined power of administrative agencies as being constitutional. If an administrative agency acts outside the scope of its delegated powers, it is an unconstitutional act.

Administrative Procedure Act

In 1946, Congress enacted the **Administrative Procedure Act (APA)**.[1] This act establishes certain administrative procedures that federal administrative agencies must follow in connecting their affairs. For example, the APA establishes notice and hearing requirements, rules for conducting agency adjudicative actions, and procedures for rule making. Most states have enacted administrative procedural acts that govern state administrative agencies.

Administrative law Judges (ALJs) preside over administrative proceedings. They decide questions of law and fact concerning the case. There is no jury. An ALJ is an employee of the administrative agency. Both the administrative agency and the respondent may be represented by counsel. Witnesses may be examined and cross-examined, evidence may be introduced, objections may be made, and such.

The ALJ's decision is issued in the form of an **order**. The order must state the reasons for the ALJ's decision. The order becomes final if it is not appealed. An appeal consists of a review by the agency. Further appeal can be made to the appropriate federal court (in federal agency actions) or state court (in state agency actions).

Business Ethics

Do-Not-Call Registry

Two federal administrative agencies—the **Federal Trade Commission (FTC)** and the **Federal Communications Commission (FCC)**—are accorded heroes' status by consumers for creating the **"Do-Not-Call" Registry**, on which consumers can place their names and free themselves from most unsolicited commercial telephone calls. The FTC and FCC found their authority to adopt their coordinated do-not-call rules in several federal statutes. The first is the **Telephone Consumer Protection Act of 1991**, which authorized the FCC to establish a national database of consumers who objected to receiving commercial sales calls.

Business Ethics

(continued)

The second is the **Telemarketing and Consumer Fraud and Abuse Prevention Act of 1994**, which authorized the FTC to prohibit sales calls that a reasonable consumer would consider abusive to his or her privacy. And just to wrap things up, after the do-not-call registry was put in place, in 2003 Congress enacted an **Act to Ratify the Authority of the Federal Trade Commission to Establish a Do-Not-Call Registry**.

In 2003, the FTC and the FCC promulgated administrative rules that created the Do-Not-Call Registry. A person can place himself or herself on the Do-Not-Call Registry by calling toll-free 888-382-1222 or registering online, at **www.donotcall.gov**. Both wire-connected phones and wireless cell phones can be registered. Telemarketers have three months from the date on which a consumer signs up for the registry to remove the customer's phone number from their sales call list. Customer registration remains valid for five years and can be renewed. Charitable and political organizations are exempt from the registry. Also, there is an "established business relationship" exception that allows businesses to call customers for 10 months after they sell or lease goods or services to that person or conduct a financial transaction with that person. The Do-Not-Call Registry allows consumers to designate specific companies not to call them, including those that otherwise qualify for the established business relationship exemption.

Telemarketers, who claimed they would lose substantial business and have to fire millions of workers, sued to have the Do-Not-Call Registry declared unconstitutional as a violation of their constitutional right to free speech. A U.S. district court in Colorado agreed with the telemarketers. On appeal, however, the

U.S. Court of Appeals for the Tenth Circuit reversed, holding that the Do-Not-Call Registry did not violate telemarketers' free speech rights. The Court of Appeals justified its decision by finding that the Do-Not-Call Registry:

- Restricts only core commercial speech (i.e., sales calls).
- Targets speech that invades the privacy of the home, a personal sanctuary.
- Is an opt-in program that puts the choice on whether to restrict commercial calls in the hands of consumers.
- Furthers the government's interest in combating fraudulent and abusive telemarketing.

The Court of Appeals held that the Do-Not-Call Registry was narrowly tailored and did not prevent marketers from reaching consumers by direct mail, advertisements, and other lawful methods. The Court upheld the lawfulness of the charitable and political organizations exception and the established business relationship exception. In reaching its decision, the Court stated, "The Do-Not-Call Registry is a valid commercial speech regulation because it directly advances the government's important interests in safeguarding personal privacy and reducing the danger of telemarketing abuse without burdening an excessive amount of speech. The Do-Not-Call Registry lets consumers avoid unwanted sales pitches that invade the home via telephone." [*Mainstream Marketing Services, Inc. v. Federal Trade Commission*, 358 F.3d 1228, 2004 U.S. App. Lexis 2564 (2004)]

1. Do many telemarketers act unethically? Explain.

2. Do you think that the Do-Not-Call Registry was warranted? ■

Food, Drugs, and Cosmetics Safety

The federal **Food, Drug, and Cosmetic Act (FDCA)** was enacted in 1938.[2] This act, as amended, regulates the testing, manufacture, distribution, and sale of foods, drugs, cosmetics, and medicinal products and devices in the United States. The **Food and Drug Administration (FDA)** is the federal administrative agency empowed to enforce the FDCA.

Before certain food additives, drugs, cosmetics, and medicinal devices can be sold to the public, they must receive FDA approval. An applicant must submit an application to the FDA that contains relevant information about the safety and uses of the product. The FDA, after considering the evidence, will either approve or deny the application.

The FDA can seek search warrants and conduct inspections; obtain orders for the seizure, recall, and condemnation of products; seek injunctions; and turn over suspected criminal violations to the U.S. Department of Justice for prosecution.

Regulation of Food

The **FDCA** prohibits the shipment, distribution, or sale of *adulterated food*. Food is deemed adulterated if it consists in whole or in part of any "filthy, putrid, or decomposed substance" or if it is otherwise "unfit for food." Note that food does not have to be entirely pure to be distributed or sold—it only has to be unadulterated.

Cattle. The **United States Department of Agriculture (USDA)**, a federal administrative agency, administers and enforces numerous federal statutes that regulate the safety of agricultural and food products.

The FDCA also prohibits *false and misleading labeling* of food products. In addition, it mandates affirmative disclosure of information on food labels, including the name of the food, the name and place of the manufacturer, a statement of ingredients and nutrition content. A manufacturer may be held liable for deceptive labeling or packaging.

Business Brief

The FDA prohibits the shipment, distribution, or sale of *adulterated* food and the *false and misleading labeling* of food.

Contemporary Environment
A Hidden Source of Protein in Peanut Butter

You take a big bite of a peanut butter sandwich and savor the taste. It has been processed by a food manufacturer and inspected by the federal government, so you think it is pure peanut butter. Not necessarily. Under federal FDA guidelines, peanut butter may contain up to 30 insect fragments per 3 ounces and still be considered "safe" for human consumption.

The FDA has set ceilings, or "action levels," for certain contaminants, or "defects," as the FDA likes to call them, for various foods. Several of these action levels are

- Golden raisins—35 fly eggs per 8 ounces
- Popcorn—two rodent hairs per pound
- Shelled peanuts—20 insects per 100 pounds
- Canned mushrooms—20 maggots per 3 1/2 ounces
- Tomato juice—10 fly eggs per 3 1/2 ounces

The FDA can mount inspections and raids to enforce its action levels. If it finds that the federal tolerance system has been violated, it can seize the offending food and destroy it at the owner's expense.

The courts have upheld the presence of some contamination in food as lawful under the federal FDCA. For example, in one case the court found that 28 insect parts in 9 pounds of butter did not violate the act. The court stated, "Few foods contain no natural or unavoidable defects. Even with modern technology, all defects in foods cannot be eliminated." [*United States v. Capital City Foods, Inc.*, 345 F.Supp. 277, 1972 U.S.Dist. Lexis (N.D. Dist. 1972)]. ■

Food Labeling In late 1990, Congress passed a sweeping truth-in-labeling law called the **Nutrition Labeling and Education Act**. The statute requires food manufacturers and processors to provide more nutritional information on most foods and prohibits them from making scientifically unsubstantiated health claims.

Morocco. Many other countries of the world have different means of distributing and regulating the production and sale of food products than the United States.

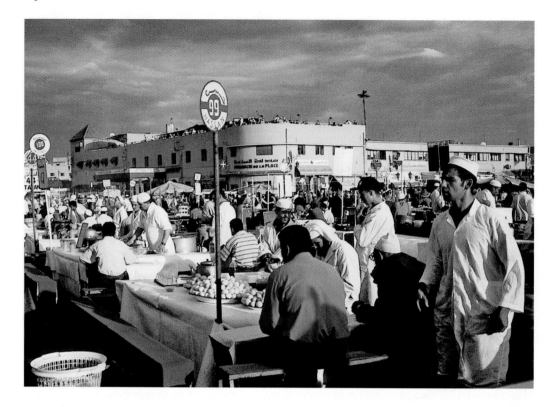

The law requires the more than 20,000 food labels found on grocery store shelves to disclose the number of calories derived from fat and the amount of dietary fiber, saturated fat, cholesterol, and a variety of other substances. The law applies to packaged foods as well as fruits, vegetables, and raw seafood. Meat, poultry, and egg products, which are regulated by the Department of Agriculture, are exempt from the act.

The FDA announced final regulations to implement the act. The regulations require food processors to provide uniform information about serving sizes and nutrients on labels of the food products they sell and establish standard definitions for *light, low fat, natural*, and other terms routinely bandied about by food processors.

Regulation of Drugs

The FDCA gives the FDA the authority to regulate the testing, manufacture, distribution, and sale of drugs. The **Drug Amendment to the FDCA**,[3] enacted in 1962, gives the FDA broad powers to license new drugs in the United States. After a new drug application is filed, the FDA holds a hearing and investigates the merits of the application. This process can take many years. The FDA may withdraw approval of any previously licensed drug.

This law requires all users of prescription and nonprescription drugs to receive proper directions for use (including the method and duration of use) and adequate warnings about any related side effects. The manufacture, distribution, or sale of adulterated or misbranded drugs is prohibited.

Business Brief

The FDA may speed up the process for experimental drugs that hold promise in treating incurable diseases (e.g., AIDS).

Regulation of Cosmetics

The FDA's definition of *cosmetics* includes substances and preparations for cleansing, altering the appearance of, and promoting the attractiveness of a person. Eye shadow and other facial makeup products are examples of cosmetics subject to FDA regulation. Ordinary household soap is expressly exempted from this definition.

The FDA has issued regulations that require cosmetics to be labeled, to disclose ingredients, and to contain warnings if they are carcinogenic (cancer-causing) or otherwise dangerous to a person's health. The manufacture, distribution, or sale of adulterated or misbranded cosmetics is prohibited. The FDA may remove from commerce any cosmetics that contain unsubstantiated claims of preserving youth, increasing virility, growing hair, and such.

Regulation of Medicinal Devices

In 1976, Congress enacted the **Medicinal Device Amendment to the FDCA**.[4] This amendment gives the FDA authority to regulate medicinal devices, such as heart pacemakers, kidney dialysis machines, defibrillators, surgical equipment, and other diagnostic, therapeutic, and health devices. The mislabeling of such devices is prohibited. The FDA is empowered to remove "quack" devices from the market.

International Law

United Nations Biosafety Protocol for Genetically Altered Foods

Many food processors in the United States and across the world genetically modify some foods by adding genes from other organisms to help crops grow faster or ward off pests. In the past, food processors did not notify consumers that they were purchasing genetically modified agricultural products. Although the companies insist that genetically altered foods are safe, consumers and many countries began to demand that such foods be clearly labeled so that buyers could decide for themselves.

The most concerned countries in the world regarding this issue were in Europe. Led by Germany, many European countries wanted to require genetically engineered food products to be labeled as such and be transported separately from nonaltered agricultural products. Some European countries wanted genetically altered foods to be banned completely. The United States, a major exporter of agricultural products and the leader in the development of biotech foods, argued that these countries were using this issue to erect trade barriers to keep U.S.–produced food products out of their countries in violation of international trade treaties and conventions administered by the World Trade Organization (WTO), which had reduced or eliminated many international trade restrictions.

In January 2000, a compromise was reached when 138 countries, including the United States, agreed to the United Nations–sponsored **Biosafety Protocol**. After much negotiation, the countries agreed that all genetically engineered foods would be clearly labeled with the phrase "May contain living modified organisms." This allows consumers to decide on their own whether to purchase such altered food products. In addition, the boxes and containers in which such goods are shipped must also be clearly marked as containing genetically altered food products. ■

Product Safety

In 1972, Congress enacted the **Consumer Product Safety Act (CPSA)**[5] and created the **Consumer Product Safety Commission (CPSC)**. The CPSC is an independent federal regulatory agency empowered to (1) adopt rules and regulations to interpret and enforce the CPSA, (2) conduct research on the safety of consumer products, and (3) collect data regarding injuries caused by consumer products.

Because the CPSC regulates potentially dangerous consumer products, it issues product safety standards for consumer products that pose an unreasonable risk of injury. If a consumer product is found to be imminently hazardous—that is, its use can cause an unreasonable risk of death or serious injury or illness—the manufacturer can be required to recall, repair, or replace the product or take other corrective action. Alternatively, the CPSC can seek injunctions, bring actions to seize hazardous consumer products, seek civil penalties for knowing violations of the act or of CPSA rules, and seek criminal penalties for knowing and willful violations of the act or of CPSC rules. A private party can sue for an injunction to prevent violations of the act or of CPSC rules and regulations.

Certain consumer products, including motor vehicles, boats, aircraft, and firearms, are regulated by other government agencies.

Business Ethics

Lemon Laws Protect Consumers from Sour Deals

In the past, consumers who purchased automobiles and other vehicles that developed nagging mechanical problems had to try to convince the dealer or manufacturer to correct the problem. If the problem was not corrected, the consumer's only recourse was to seek redress through costly and time-consuming litigation. Today, most states have enacted **lemon laws**, which give consumers a new weapon in this battle.

Lemon laws provide a procedure for consumers to follow to correct recurring problems in vehicles. Lemon laws establish an administrative procedure that is less formal than a court proceeding. Most of these laws require that an arbitrator decide the dispute between a consumer and a car dealer. Lemon laws stipulate that if the dealer or manufacturer does not correct a recurring defect in a vehicle within a specified number of tries (e.g., four tries) within a specified period of time (e.g., two years), the purchaser can rescind the purchase and recover a full refund of the vehicle's purchase price.

To properly invoke a state's lemon law, a consumer should take the following steps:

- Notify the car dealer immediately of any mechanical or other problems that develop in the vehicle.
- Take the vehicle back to the dealer for the statutory number of times to give the dealer the opportunity to correct the defect.
- File a claim with the appropriate state agency, seeking arbitration of the claim if the defect is not corrected during the number of times and time period established by the state's lemon law.
- Attend the arbitration hearing and present evidence to substantiate the claim that the vehicle suffered from a defect that was not corrected by the dealer or manufacturer within the statutorily prescribed period.

1. In general, do you think automobile dealerships are very scrupulous?
2. Are lemon laws needed to protect consumers? ■

Unfair and Deceptive Practices

The **FTC Act** was enacted in 1914.[6] The **Federal Trade Commission (FTC)** was created the following year. The FTC is empowered to enforce the FTC Act as well as other federal consumer protection statutes.

Section 5 of the FTC Act, as amended, prohibits *unfair and deceptive practices*. It has been used extensively to regulate business conduct. This section gives the FTC the authority to bring an administrative proceeding to attack a deceptive or unfair practice. If, after a public administrative hearing, the FTC finds a violation of Section 5, it may order a cease-and-desist order, an affirmative disclosure to consumers, corrective advertising, or the like. The FTC may sue in state or federal court to obtain compensation on behalf of consumers. The decision of the FTC may be appealed to federal court.

False and Deceptive Advertising

Advertising is false and deceptive under Section 5 of the FTC Act if it (1) contains misinformation or omits important information that is likely to mislead a "reasonable consumer" or (2) makes an unsubstantiated claim (e.g., "This product is 33 percent better than our competitor's"). Proof of actual deception is not required. Statements of opinion and "sales talk" (e.g., "This is a great car") do not constitute false and deceptive advertising.

> Like a gun that fires at the muzzle and kicks over at the breach, a cheating transaction hurts the cheater as much as the man cheated.
>
> Henry Ward Beecher
> *Proverbs from Plymouth Pulpit*
> (1887)

Bait and Switch

Bait and switch is another type of deceptive advertising under Section 5 of the FTC Act. It occurs when a seller advertises the availability of a low-cost discounted item (the "bait") to attract customers to its store. Once the customers are in the store, however, the seller pressures them to purchase more expensive merchandise (the "switch"). The FTC states that a bait and switch occurs if the seller refuses to show consumers the advertised merchandise, discourages employees from selling the advertised merchandise, or fails to have adequate quantities of the merchandise available.

Door-to-Door Sales

Some salespersons sell merchandise and services door-to-door. In some situations, these salespersons use aggressive sales tactics to overcome a consumer's resistance to the sale. To protect consumers from ill-advised decisions, many states have enacted laws that give the consumer a certain number of days to rescind (cancel) a door-to-door sales contract. The usual period is three days. The consumer must send a required notice of cancellation to the seller. An FTC regulation requires the salesperson to permit cancellation of the contract within the stipulated time.

Business Brief

Many states have enacted statutes that permit consumers to rescind contracts made at home with door-to-door sales representatives within a three-day period after signing the contract.

Unsolicited Merchandise

The **Postal Reorganization Act**[7] makes the mailing of unsolicited merchandise an unfair trade practice. The act permits persons who receive unsolicited merchandise through the mail to retain, use, discard, or otherwise dispose of the merchandise without incurring any obligation to pay for it or return it. Unsolicited mailings by charitable organizations and mailings made by mistake are excepted from this rule.

The following is a classic case of false and deceptive advertising.

U.S. SUPREME COURT CASE

Federal Trade Commission v. Colgate-Palmolive Company

380 U.S. 374, 85 S.Ct. 1035, 1965 U.S. Lexis 2300 (1965)
Supreme Court of the United States

Case 33.1
False and Deceptive Advertising

Background and Facts

The Colgate-Palmolive Co. (Colgate) manufactured and sold a shaving cream called "Rapid Shave." Colgate hired Ted Bates & Company (Bates), an advertising agency, to prepare television commercials designed to show that Rapid Shave could shave the toughest beards. With Colgate's consent, Bates prepared a television commercial that included the sandpaper test. The announcer informed the audience, "To prove Rapid Shave's super-moisturizing power, we put it right from the can onto this tough, dry sandpaper. And off in a stroke."

While the announcer was speaking, Rapid Shave was applied to a substance that appeared to be sandpaper, and immediately a razor was shown shaving the substance clean. Evidence showed that the substance resembling sandpaper was in fact a simulated prop or "mock-up" made of Plexiglas to which sand had been glued. The Federal Trade Commission (FTC) issued a complaint against Colgate and Bates, alleging a violation of Section 5 of the

FTC Act. The FTC held against the defendants. The Court of Appeals reversed. The FTC appealed to the U.S. Supreme Court.

Issue

Did the defendants engage in false and deceptive advertising in violation of Section 5 of the FTC Act?

Court's Reasoning

The Supreme Court agreed with the FTC that the undisclosed use of plexiglass in the commercial was a material deceptive practice. The Court found unpersuasive respondents' objections to this conclusion. Respondents' claimed that it would have been impractical to inform the viewing public that it was not seeing an actual test, experiment, or demonstration, but the Court Stated that it was inconceivable that the ingenious advertising world would be unable, if it so desired to conform to the FTC's insistence that the public be not misinformed. The Supreme Court concluded that there was no

Federal Trade Commission v. Colgate-Palmolive Company

380 U.S. 374, 85 S.Ct. 1035, 1965 U.S. Lexis 2300 (1965)

Supreme Court of the United States

(continued)

defect in the provision of the order which prohibits respondents from engaging in similar practices with respect to any product they advertise. The Supreme Court concluded, "Having been caught violating the Act, respondents must expect some fencing in."

Decision and Remedy

The U.S. Supreme Court held that Colgate and Bates had engaged in false and deceptive advertising. The Supreme Court reversed the decision of the Court of Appeals and remanded the case for further proceedings.

Case Questions

Critical Legal Thinking   Does the government owe a duty to protect consumers from false and misleading business practices?

Business Ethics   Did Colgate and Bates act ethically in this case? Do you think the viewing public believed the commercial?

Contemporary Business   Do you think many companies engage in false and deceptive advertising? Can you think of any examples?

Environmental Protection

Good government is an empire of laws.

John Adams
Thoughts on Government (1776)

In the 1970s, the federal government began enacting statutes to protect our nation's air and water from pollution, to regulate hazardous wastes, and to protect wildlife. In many instances, states enacted their own environmental laws that now coexist with federal law. These laws provide both civil and criminal penalties. **Environmental protection** is one of the most important, and costly, issues facing business and society today.

Environmental Protection Agency

In 1970, Congress created the **Environmental Protection Agency (EPA)** to coordinate the implementation and enforcement of the federal environmental protection laws. The EPA has broad rule-making powers to adopt regulations to advance the laws that it is empowered to administer. The agency also has adjudicative powers to hold hearings, make decisions, and order remedies for violations of federal environmental laws. In addition, the EPA can initiate judicial proceedings in court against suspected violators of federal environmental laws.

Environmental Impact Statement

The **National Environmental Policy Act (NEPA)** became effective January 1, 1970.[8] The NEPA mandates that the federal government consider the "adverse impact" of proposed legislation, rule making, or other federal government action on the environment before the action is implemented.

The NEPA and rules adopted thereunder require that an **Environmental Impact Statement (EIS)** must be prepared for any proposed legislation or major federal action that significantly affects the quality of the human environment. The purpose of the EIS is to provide enough information about the environment to enable the federal government to determine the feasibility of the project. The EIS is also used as evidence in court whenever a federal action is challenged as violating the NEPA or other federal environmental protection laws. Examples of actions that require an EIS include proposals to build a new federally funded highway, to license nuclear plants, and the like.

The EIS must (1) describe the affected environment, (2) describe the impact of the proposed federal action on the environment, (3) identify and discuss alternatives to the proposed action, (4) list the resources that will be committed to the action, and (5) contain a cost–

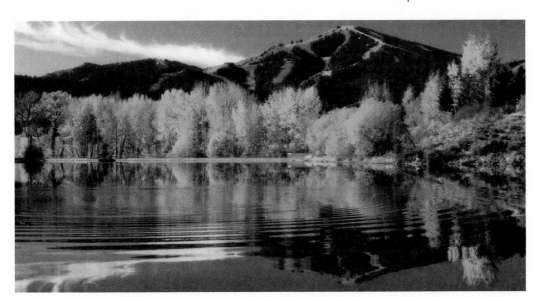

Baldy Mountain, Sun Valley, Idaho. An environmental impact statement (EIS) must be prepared to consider the adverse impact any federal government action will have on the environment.

benefit analysis of the proposed action and alternative actions. Expert professionals, such as engineers, geologists, and accountants, may be consulted during the preparation of the EIS.

Once an EIS is prepared, it is subject to public review, and the public has 30 days in which to submit comments to the EPA. After the comments have been received and reviewed, the EPA will issue an order that states whether the proposed federal action may proceed. Decisions of the EPA are appealable to the appropriate U.S. court of appeals.

Most states and many local governments have enacted laws that require an EIS to be prepared regarding proposed state and local government action as well as private development.

Air Pollution

One of the major problems facing the United States is **air pollution**. The **Clean Air Act** was enacted in 1963 to assist states in dealing with air pollution. The act was amended in 1970 and 1977 and, most recently, by the **Clean Air Act Amendments of 1990**.[9] The Clean Air Act, as amended, provides comprehensive regulation of air quality in this country.

Substantial amounts of air pollution are emitted by **stationary sources** (e.g., industrial plants, oil refineries, public utilities). The Clean Air Act requires states to identify major stationary sources and develop plans to reduce air pollution from these sources. Automobile and other vehicle emissions are one of the major sources of air pollution in this country. In an effort to control emissions from these **mobile sources**, the Clean Air Act requires air pollution controls to be installed on motor vehicles. Emission standards have been set for automobiles, trucks, buses, motorcycles, and airplanes. In addition, the Clean Air Act authorizes the EPA to regulate air pollution caused by fuel and fuel additives.

National Ambient Air Quality Standards   The Clean Air Act directs the EPA to establish **national ambient air quality standards (NAAQS)** for certain pollutants. These standards are set at two different levels: primary (to protect human beings) and secondary (to protect vegetation, matter, climate, visibility, and economic values). Specific standards have been established for carbon monoxide, nitrogen oxide, sulfur oxide, ozone, lead, and particulate matter.

Although the EPA establishes air quality standards, the states are responsible for their enforcement. The federal government has the right to enforce these air pollution standards if the states fail to do so. Each state is required to prepare a *state implementation plan* (SIP) that sets out how the state plans to meet the federal standards. The EPA has divided each state into *air quality control regions (AQCRs)*. Each region is monitored to ensure compliance.

Nonattainment Areas   Regions that do not meet the air quality standards are designated **nonattainment areas**. Nonattainment areas are classified into one of five categories—(1) marginal, (2) moderate, (3) serious, (4) severe, and (5) extreme—based on the degree to which they exceed the ozone standard. Deadlines are established for areas to meet the attainment level. States must submit compliance plans that (1) identify major sources of air pollution and require them to install pollution control equipment, (2) institute permit systems for new stationary sources, and (3) implement inspection programs to monitor mobile sources. States that fail to develop or implement an approved plan are subject to the following sanctions: (1) loss of federal highway funds and (2) limitations on new sources of emissions (e.g., the EPA can prohibit the construction of a new pollution-causing industrial plant in the nonattainment area).

The Clean Air Act was at issue in the following case.

U.S. SUPREME COURT CASE

Whitman, Administrator of Environmental Protection Agency v. American Trucking Association

Case 33.2
Clean Air Act

531 U.S. 457, 121 S. Ct. 903, 2001 U.S. Lexis 1952 (2001)
Supreme Court of the United States

Background and Facts

Section 109 of the Federal Clean Air Act requires the administrator of the EPA, a federal administrative agency, to set NAAQS for air pollutants. Section 109 instructs the EPA to set NAAQS at levels "to protect the public health" with "an adequate margin of safety." Pursuant to Section 109, the EPA issued new standards for ozone and particular matter emitted from the operation of trucks. The American Trucking Association sued the EPA, arguing that the EPA must consider the cost caused to trucking firms before issuing the NAAQS. The EPA argued that it did not have to do so under the statute. The district court held for the American Trucking Association, but the court of appeals held for the EPA on this issue. The U.S. Supreme Court granted review.

Issue

Under Section 109 of the Federal Clean Air Act, must the EPA consider the cost imposed on trucking firms before setting NAAQS for ozone and particulate matter emissions from trucks?

Court's Reasoning

Section 109 instructs the EPA to set primary ambient air quality standards "the attainment and maintenance of which are requisite to protect the public health" with "an adequate margin of safety." The Supreme Court held that it is clear that this text does not permit the EPA to consider costs in setting the standards. The language "is absolute." The Supreme Court stated that the EPA,

based on the information about health effects contained in the technical criteria documents, is to identify the maximum airborne concentration of a pollutant that the public health can tolerate, decrease the concentration to provide an adequate margin of safety, and set the standard at that level. Nowhere are the costs of achieving such a standard made part of that initial calculation. The respondent argued that the economic cost of implementing a very stringent standard might close down whole industries and thereby impoverish the workers and consumers dependent upon those industries. That is unquestionably true.

Decision and Remedy

The U.S. Supreme Court held that the statutory language of Section 109 of the Clean Air Act does not require the EPA to consider the cost to trucking firms for implementing the NAAQS set by the EPA. The Supreme Court affirmed the decision of the court of appeals in favor of the EPA.

Case Questions

Critical Legal Thinking   Do you think the statutory language of Section 109 was clear in this case?

Business Ethics   Would the "public health" be compromised under the trucking firms' argument? Why did the trucking firms resist the NAAQS set by the EPA?

Contemporary Business   What are the economic consequences of the Supreme Court's ruling? Explain.

Contemporary Environment
Indoor Air Pollution

According to officials of the EPA, the air inside some buildings may be 100 times more polluted than outside air. Doctors increasingly attribute a wide range of symptoms to **indoor air pollution**, or **sick building syndrome**. Indoor air pollution has two primary causes. In an effort to reduce dependence on foreign oil, many recently constructed office buildings were overly insulated and built with sealed windows and no outside air ducts. As a result, no fresh air enters many workplaces. This absence of fresh air can cause headaches, fatigue, and dizziness among workers.

The other chief cause of sick building syndrome, which is believed to affect up to one-third of U.S. office buildings, is hazardous chemicals and construction materials. In the office, these include everything from asbestos to noxious fumes emitted from copy machines, carbonless paper, and cleaning fluids. In the home, radon, an odorless gas that is emitted from the natural breakdown of uranium in soil, poses a particularly widespread danger. Radon gas damages and may destroy lung tissue. The costs of eliminating these conditions can be colossal.

Experts predict that sick building syndrome is likely to spawn a flood of litigation and that a wide range of parties will be sued. Manufacturers, employers, home sellers, builders, engineers, and architects will increasingly be forced to defend themselves against tort and breach of contract actions filed by homeowners, employees, and others affected by indoor air pollution. Insurance companies will undoubtedly be drawn into costly lawsuits stemming from indoor air pollution. ■

Water Pollution

Water pollution affects human health, recreation, agriculture, and business. Pollution of waterways by industry and humans has caused severe ecological and environmental problems, including making water sources unsafe for drinking water, fish, birds, and animals. The federal government has enacted a comprehensive scheme of statutes and regulations to prevent and control water pollution.

In 1948, Congress enacted the **Federal Water Pollution Control Act (FWPCA)** to regulate water pollution. This act has been amended several times. As amended, it is simply referred to as the **Clean Water Act**.[10] This act is administered by the EPA.

Pursuant to the Clean Water Act, the EPA has established water quality standards that define which bodies of water can be used for public drinking water, recreation (such as swimming), propagation of fish and wildlife, and agricultural and industrial uses.

La Jolla, California. The federal and state governments have enacted many statutes to protect the environment from pollution.

States are primarily responsible for enforcing the provisions of the Clean Water Act and EPA regulations adopted thereunder. If a state fails to do so, the federal government may enforce the act.

The Clean Water Act regulates the following types of water pollution:

- *Point sources of water pollution.* The Clean Water Act authorizes the EPA to establish water pollution control standards for **point sources** of water pollution (i.e., mines, manufacturing plants, paper mills, electric utility plants, municipal sewage plants, other stationary sources of water pollution). Dischargers of pollutants are required to keep records, maintain monitoring equipment, and keep samples of discharges.

- *Thermal pollution.* The Clean Water Act expressly forbids **thermal pollution** because the discharge of heated waters or materials into the nation's waterways may upset the ecological balance; decrease the oxygen content of water; and harm fish, birds, and animals that use the waterways.[11] Sources of thermal pollution (such as electric utility companies and manufacturing plants) are subject to the provisions of the Clean Water Act and regulations adopted by the EPA.

- *Wetlands.* **Wetlands** are defined as areas that are inundated or saturated by surface water or ground water that support vegetation typically adapted for life in saturated soil conditions. Wetlands include swamps, marshes, bogs, and similar areas that support birds, animals, and vegetative life. The Clean Water Act forbids the filling or dredging of wetlands unless a permit has been obtained from the **Army Corps of Engineers (Corps)**. The Corps is empowered to adopt regulations and conduct administrative proceedings to enforce the act.

Safe Drinking Water Act The **Safe Drinking Water Act**,[12] which was enacted in 1974 and amended in 1986, authorizes the EPA to establish national primary drinking water standards (minimum quality of water for human consumption). The act also prohibits the dumping of wastes into wells used for drinking water. The states are primarily responsible for enforcing the act. If a state fails to do so, the federal government can enforce the act.

St. Ignace, Michigan. Federal environmental protection statutes control water pollution.

Ocean Dumping The **Marine Protection, Research, and Sanctuaries Act,**[13] enacted in 1972, extended environmental protection to the oceans. It (1) requires a permit for dumping wastes and other foreign materials into ocean waters and (2) establishes marine sanctuaries in ocean waters as far seaward as the edge of the Continental Shelf and in the Great Lakes and their connecting waters.

The Clean Water Act authorizes the U.S. government to clean up oil spills and spills of other hazardous substances in ocean waters within 12 miles of the shore and on the Continental Shelf and to recover the cleanup costs from responsible parties.

Ethics Brief

When the oil tanker *Exxon Valdez* ran aground off Alaska in 1989, the oil industry was not prepared to respond to the emergency.

Toxic Substances

Many chemicals used for agriculture, industry, and mining contain **toxic substances** that cause cancer, birth defects, and other health-related problems in human beings, as well as injury or death to birds, fish, other animals, and vegetation. Many chemical compounds that are used in the manufacture of products are toxic (e.g., PCBs, asbestos). Hundreds of new chemicals and chemical compounds that may be toxic are discovered each year.

In 1976, Congress enacted the **Toxic Substances Control Act**[14] and gave the EPA authority to administer the act. The act requires manufacturers and processors to test new chemicals to determine the effect on human health and the environment and to report the results to the EPA before they can be marketed. The EPA may limit or prohibit the manufacture and sale of toxic substances, and it can remove them from commerce, if it finds that they pose an imminent hazard or an unreasonable risk of injury to human health or the environment. The EPA also requires special labeling of toxic substances.

Insecticides, Fungicides, and Rodenticides Farmers and ranchers use chemical pesticides, herbicides, fungicides, and rodenticides to kill insects, pests, and weeds. Evidence shows that the use of some of these chemicals on food, and their residual accumulation in soil, poses health hazards. In 1947, Congress enacted the **Insecticide, Fungicide, and Rodenticide Act,** which gave the federal government authority to regulate pesticides and related chemicals. This act, which was substantially amended in 1972,[15] is administered by the EPA. Under the act, pesticides must be registered with the EPA before they can be sold. The EPA may suspend the registration of a registered pesticide that it finds poses an imminent danger or emergency.

International Law

Kyoto Protocol Reduces Greenhouse Gases

For decades, scientists have been concerned that *greenhouse gases*—particularly from carbon dioxide created by burning coal, oil, and gas—were causing a global warming effect and creating a hole in the ozone layer around the earth. In 1997, after much debate, the countries of the world met in Kyoto, Japan, and proposed the **Kyoto Protocol**, an international treaty to reduce greenhouse gases. The deal almost fell apart; but in 2001, 178 countries agreed to abide by the rules of the Kyoto Protocol.

The Kyoto Protocol calls for the reduction of greenhouse gases worldwide to 5.2 percent below 1990 levels, with this goal to be reached by 2012. The protocol originally set targets for 39 industrialized countries; however, developing nations are not covered by the initial emission control standards. The protocol calls for member nations to create a $400 million fund to help developing nations adopt technology to reduce greenhouse gases. The United States was not a signatory to the Kyoto Protocol, but instead chose to adopt its own laws to control greenhouse gas emissions. ■

Hazardous Waste

Wastes, which often contain hazardous substances that can harm the environment or pose a danger to human health, are generated by agriculture, mining, industry, other businesses, and households. Wastes consist of garbage, sewage, industrial discharges, old equipment, and such. The mishandling and disposal of **hazardous wastes** can cause air, water, and **land pollution**.

The disposal of hazardous wastes sometimes causes **land pollution**. In 1976, Congress enacted the **Resource Conservation and Recovery Act (RCRA)**[16] which regulates the disposal of new hazardous wastes. This act, which has been amended several times, authorizes the EPA to regulate facilities that generate, treat, store, transport, and dispose of hazardous wastes. States have primary responsibility for implementing the standards established by the act and EPA regulations.

The act defines hazardous waste as a solid waste that may cause or significantly contribute to an increase in mortality or serious illness or pose a hazard to human health or the environment if improperly managed. The EPA has designated substances that are toxic, radioactive, or corrosive or that ignite as hazardous and can add to the list of hazardous wastes as needed.

The EPA also establishes standards and procedures for the safe treatment, storage, disposal, and transportation of hazardous wastes. Under the act, the EPA is authorized to regulate underground storage facilities, such as underground gasoline tanks.

Contemporary Environment
The Superfund

In 1980, Congress enacted the **Comprehensive Environmental Response, Compensation, and Liability Act (CERCLA)**, which is commonly called the **Superfund** [42 U.S.C. § 9601 et seq.]. The act, which was significantly amended in 1986, is administered by the EPA. The act gave the federal government a mandate to deal with hazardous wastes that have been spilled, stored, or abandoned. The Superfund provides for the creation of a government fund to finance the cleanup of hazardous waste sites (hence the name *Superfund*). The fund is financed through taxes on chemicals, feedstocks, motor fuels, and other products that contain hazardous substances.

The Superfund requires the EPA to (1) identify sites in the United States where hazardous wastes have been disposed, stored, abandoned, or spilled and (2) rank these sites regarding the severity of the risk. When it ranks the sites, the EPA considers factors such as the types of hazardous waste, the toxicity of the wastes, the types of pollution (air, water, land, or other pollu-

tion), the number of people potentially affected by the risk, and other factors. The hazardous waste sites with the highest ranking are put on the National Priority List. The sites on this list receive first consideration for cleanup. The EPA has the authority to clean up hazardous priority or nonpriority sites quickly to prevent fire, explosion, contamination of drinking water, or other imminent danger.

The EPA can order a responsible party to clean up a hazardous waste site. If that party fails to do so, the EPA can clean up the site and recover the cost of the cleanup. The Superfund imposes strict liability—that is, liability without fault. The EPA can recover the cost of the cleanup from (1) the generator who deposited the wastes, (2) the transporter of the wastes to the site, (3) the owner of the site at the time of the disposal, and (4) the current owner and operator of the site. The Superfund permits states and private parties who clean up hazardous waste sites to seek reimbursement from the fund. ■

Nuclear Waste

Nuclear-powered fuel plants create radioactive wastes that maintain a high level of *radioactivity*. Radioactivity can cause injury and death to humans and other life and can also cause severe damage to the environment. Accidents, human error, faulty construction, and such all can be causes of **radiation pollution**.

Regulation of nuclear energy in the United States is primarily placed with the following two federal agencies:

1. *Nuclear Regulatory Commission.* The **Nuclear Regulatory Commission (NRC)**, which was created by Congress in 1977, licenses the construction and opening of commercial nuclear power plants. It continually monitors the operation of nuclear power plants and may close a plant if safety violations are found.
2. *EPA.* The EPA is empowered to set standards for radioactivity in the environment and to regulate the disposal of radioactive waste. The EPA also regulates thermal pollution from nuclear power plants and emissions from uranium mines and mills.

Currently, nuclear wastes are stored on an interim basis at the power plants that generated the wastes or other temporary sites. The **Nuclear Waste Policy Act of 1982**[17] mandates that the federal government select and develop a permanent site for the disposal of nuclear wastes.

Endangered Species

Many species of animals are endangered or threatened with extinction. The reduction of certain species of wildlife may be caused by environmental pollution, real estate development, or hunting. The **Endangered Species Act** was enacted in 1973.[18] The act, as amended, protects *endangered* and *threatened* species of animals. The secretary of the interior is empowered to declare a form of wildlife as *endangered* or *threatened*. The act requires the EPA and the Department of Commerce to designate *critical habitats* for each endangered and threatened species. Real estate and other development in these areas is prohibited or severely limited. The secretary of commerce is empowered to enforce the provisions of the act as to marine species.

In addition, the Endangered Species Act, which applies to both government and private persons, prohibits the *taking* of any endangered species. *Taking* is defined as an act intended to "harass, harm, pursue, hunt, shoot, wound, kill, trap, capture, or collect" an endangered animal.

Numerous other federal laws protect wildlife. These include (1) the Migratory Bird Treaty Act, (2) the Bald Eagle Protection Act, (3) the Wild Free-Roaming Horses and Burros Act, (4) the Marine Mammal Protection Act, (5) the Migratory Bird Conservation Act, (6) the Fishery Conservation and Management Act, (7) the Fish and Wildlife Coordination Act, and (8) the National Wildlife Refuge System. Many states have enacted statutes that protect and preserve wildlife.

Monterey, California. Greenpeace international is an organization that engages in activism to protect animals, including fish and birds, and the environment.

In the following case, the U.S. Supreme Court enjoined the operation of a dam to save an endangered species of fish.

U.S. SUPREME COURT CASE

Tennessee Valley Authority v. Hill, Secretary of the Interior

437 U.S. 153, 98 S.Ct. 2279, 1978 U.S. Lexis 33 (1978)
Supreme Court of the United States

Case 33.3

Endangered Species Act

Background and Facts

The Tennessee Valley Authority (TVA) is a wholly owned public corporation of the United States. It operates a series of dams, reservoirs, and water projects that provide electric power, irrigation, and flood control to areas in several southern states. In 1967, with appropriations from Congress, the TVA began construction of the Tellico Dam on the Little Tennessee River. When completed, the dam would impound water covering 16,500 acres, thereby converting the river's shallow, fast-flowing waters into a deep reservoir over 30 miles in length. Construction of the dam continued until 1977, when it was completed.

In 1973, a University of Tennessee ichthyologist found a previously unknown species of perch called the *Percina (Imostoma) Tansai*—or "snail darter"—in the Little Tennessee River. After further investigation, it was determined that approximately 10,000 to 15,000 of these three-inch, tannish colored fish existed in the river's waters that would be flooded by the operation of the Tellico Dam. The snail darter is not found anywhere else in the world. It feeds exclusively on snails and requires substantial oxygen, both supplied by the fast-moving waters of the Little Tennessee River. The impounding of the water behind the Tellico Dam would destroy the snail darter's food and oxygen supplies, thus causing its extinction. Evidence was introduced showing that the TVA could not, at that time, successfully transplant the snail darter to any other habitat.

Also in 1973, Congress enacted the Endangered Species Act. This act authorizes the secretary of the interior to declare species of animal life "endangered" and to identify the "critical habitat" of these creatures. When a species or its habitat is so listed, Section 7 of the act mandates that the secretary take such action as is necessary to ensure that actions of the federal government do not jeopardize the continued existence of such endangered species. The secretary declared the snail darter an endangered species and the area that would be affected by the Tellico Dam its critical habitat.

Congress continued to appropriate funds for the construction of the dam, which was completed at a cost of over $100 million. In 1976, a regional association of biological scientists, a Tennessee conservation group, and several individuals filed an action seeking to enjoin the TVA from closing the gates of the dam and impounding the water in the reservoir on the grounds that those actions would violate Section 7 of the act by causing the extinction of the snail darter. The district court held in favor of the TVA. The court of appeals reversed and remanded with instructions to the district court to issue a permanent injunction halting the operation of the Tellico Dam. The TVA appealed to the U.S. Supreme Court.

Issue

Would the TVA be in violation of the Endangered Species Act if it operated the Tellico Dam?

Court's Reasoning

In reaching its decision, the Supreme Court stated: "Examination of the language, history, and structure of the legislation under review here indicates beyond doubt that Congress intended endangered species to be afforded the highest of priorities." As it was passed, the Endangered Species Act of 1973 represented the most comprehensive legislation for the preservation of endangered species ever enacted by any nation. Virtually all dealings with endangered species, including taking, possession, transportation, and sale, were prohibited. Section 7 of the act provides a particularly good gauge of congressional intend. "The Supreme Court concluded, it is abundantly clear that the result we reach today is wholly in accord with both the words of the statute and the intent of Congress. The plain intent of Congress in enacting this statute was to halt and reverse the trend toward species extinction, whatever the cost."

Decision and Remedy

The U.S. Supreme Court held that the Endangered Species Act prohibited the impoundment of the Little Tennessee River by the Tellico Dam. The Supreme Court affirmed the decision of the court of appeals that enjoined the operation of the dam.

Comment

Eventually, after substantial research and investigation, it was determined that the snail darter could live in another habitat that was found for it. After the snail darter was removed, at government expense, to this new location, the TVA was permitted to close the gates of the Tellico Dam and begin its operation.

Case Questions

Critical Legal Thinking Should the law protect endangered species? Why or why not?

Business Ethics Did the TVA act ethically in this case by completing construction of the dam?

Contemporary Business Do you think the cost of constructing the Tellico Dam ($100 million) should have been considered by the Court in reaching its decision?

Tibet. Many areas of the world must protect the environment from pollution.

State Environmental Protection Laws

Many state and local governments have enacted statutes and ordinances to protect the environment. For example, most states require that an EIS or report be prepared for any proposed state action. In addition, under their police power to protect the "health, safety, and welfare" of their residents, many states require private industry to prepare EISs for proposed developments.

   Some states have enacted special environmental statutes to protect unique areas within their boundaries. For example, Florida has enacted laws to protect the Everglades, and California has enacted laws to protect its Pacific Ocean coastline.

Business Brief

States are entitled to set pollution standards that are stricter than federal requirements.

Chapter Summary

Administrative Law, p. 726

Government Regulation of Business

1. *General government regulation.* General government regulation applies to many industries (e.g., antidiscrimination laws).
2. *Specific government regulation.* Specific government regulation applies to a specific industry (e.g., banking laws).

Administrative Agencies

1. *Administrative agencies.* These agencies are created by federal and state legislative and executive branches. They consist of professionals having an area of expertise in a certain area of commerce, who interpret and apply designated statutes.
2. *Administrative rules and regulations.* Administrative agencies are empowered to adopt rules and regulations that interpret and advance the laws they enforce.
3. *Administrative Procedure Act.* This act establishes procedures (i.e., notice, hearing) to be followed by federal agencies in conducting their affairs. States have enacted their own procedural acts to govern state agencies.

Foods, Drugs, and Cosmetics Safety, p. 728

Federal Food, Drug, and Cosmetic Act (FDCA)

This federal statute regulates the testing, manufacture, distribution, and sale of foods, food additives, drugs, cosmetics, and medicinal products.

Federal Food and Drug Administration (FDA)

This federal administrative agency is empowered to interpret and enforce the Federal Food, Drug, and Cosmetic Act and other federal consumer protection laws.

Required FDA Approval

The FDA has the power to approve or deny applications by private companies to distribute drugs, food additives, and medicinal devices to the public.

Regulation of Food, Drugs, and Cosmetics

Adulterated or misbranded items. The FDA prohibits the shipment, distribution, or sale of *adulterated* or *misbranded* food, drugs, cosmetics, or medicinal devices.

Nutrition Labeling and Education Act of 1990

This federal statute (1) requires food manufacturers and processors to provide nutritional information on food products and (2) prohibits the making of scientifically unsubstantiated health claims.

United Nations Biosafety Protocol for Genetically Altered Foods

This United Nations–sponsored protocol requires Signatory countries to place the label "May contain living modified organisms" on all genetically engineered foods.

Product Safety, p. 731

Consumer Product Safety Act (CPSA)

This federal statute regulates the safety of consumer products. It created the Consumer Product Safety Commission.

1. ***Consumer Product Safety Commission (CPSC).*** The CPSC is a federal administrative agency that is empowered to:
   a. Interpret and enforce the Consumer Product Safety Act.
   b. Conduct research on safety.
   c. Collect data regarding injuries.

Unfair and Deceptive Practices, p. 732

Section 5 of the Federal Trade Commission Act (FTC Act)

This federal statute prohibits unfair and deceptive practices, including false and deceptive advertising, abusive sales tactics, consumer fraud, and other unfair business practices.

Federal Trade Commission (FTC)

This federal administrative agency is empowered to enforce the FTC Act and other federal consumer protection statutes.

Environmental Protection, p. 734

Environmental Protection

Environmental protection laws. Federal and state governments have enacted environmental protection statutes to control pollution and to penalize those who violate these statutes.

The Environmental Protection Agency (EPA)

This federal administrative agency is empowered to implement and enforce federal environmental protection statutes. The EPA can adopt regulations to interpret and enforce the laws it is authorized to administer.

National Environmental Policy Act (NEPA)

This federal statute mandates that the federal government consider the *adverse impact* a federal government action would have on the environment before the action is implemented.

Environmental Impact Statement (EIS)

An EIS is a document that must be prepared for all proposed legislation or major federal action that significantly affects the quality of the human environment.

The EIS must (1) describe the affected environment, (2) describe the impact of the proposed federal action on the environment, (3) identify and discuss alternatives to the proposed action, (4) list the resources that will be committed to the action, and (5) contain a cost–benefit analysis of the proposed action and alternative actions.

Air Pollution

Air pollution is caused by factories, homes, vehicles, and the like.

1. ***Clean Air Act.*** This federal statute, enacted in 1963 and amended several times, regulates air pollution.
2. ***National Ambient Air Quality Standards (NAAQS).*** These standards for certain pollutants set by the EPA protect (1) human beings (*primary*) and (2) vegetation, matter, climate, visibility, and economic values (*secondary*).
   a. *State implementation plan (SIP).* An SIP is a document issued by a state that explains how the state plans to meet federal air pollution standards.
   b. *Air quality control regions (AQCRs).* AQCRs are divisions by the EPA of each state into geographical areas that are monitored to ensure compliance with federal air pollution standards.
   c. *Nonattainment areas.* These regions do not meet federal air quality standards. They are classified into one of five categories—(1) marginal, (2) moderate, (3) serious, (4) severe, and (5) extreme—based on the degree to which they exceed federal air quality standards. States that fail to develop or implement an approved plan to correct deficiencies are subject to sanctions.

Sources of Air Pollution

1. ***Stationary sources.*** Stationary sources are sources of air pollution such as industrial plants, oil refineries, and public utilities.
2. ***Mobile sources.*** Mobile sources are sources of air pollution such as automobiles, trucks, buses, motorcycles, and airplanes.

Water Pollution

Water pollution is pollution of lakes, rivers, oceans, and other bodies of water.

1. ***Clean Water Act.*** This federal statute regulates water pollution. As amended, it is called the *Clean Water Act.*
2. ***Point sources of water pollution.*** These are sources of water pollution such as paper mills, manufacturing plants, electric utility plants, and sewage plants.
3. ***Pollution controls.*** Point sources are required to install pollution control equipment.

Thermal Pollution

Thermal pollution involves heated water or material being discharged into waterways and upsetting the ecological balance and decreases the oxygen content. Thermal pollution is subject to the provisions of the Clean Water Act.

Wetlands

Wetlands are areas that are inundated or saturated by surface or groundwater that support vegetation typically adapted for life in such conditions. The Clean Water Act forbids the filling or dredging of wetlands unless a permit has been obtained from the *Army Corps of Engineers*.

Safe Drinking Water

The *Safe Drinking Water Act of 1974* authorizes the EPA to establish national minimum quality of water standards for human consumption. States are primarily responsible for enforcing the act. If a state fails to do so, the federal government can enforce the act.

Ocean Dumping

Marine Protection, Research, and Sanctuaries Act of 1972. This federal statute extends environmental protection to oceans. It requires a permit for dumping wastes and other foreign materials into ocean waters.

Oil Spills

The Clean Water Act authorizes the U.S. government to clean up oil spills and spills of other hazardous substances in ocean waters within 12 miles of the shore and on the Continental Shelf.

Toxic Substances

Toxic substances are chemicals used for agricultural, industrial, and mining uses that cause injury to humans, birds, animals, fish, and vegetation.

1. ***Toxic Substances Control Act.*** This federal statute requires manufacturers and processors to test new chemicals to determine their effect on human health and the environment before the EPA will allow them to be marketed. The EPA requires special labeling of toxic substances.

2. ***Federal Insecticide, Fungicide, and Rodenticide Act.*** This federal statute requires pesticides, herbicides, fungicides, and rodenticides to be registered with the EPA. The EPA may deny, suspend, or cancel registration.

Hazardous Waste

Hazardous waste is solid waste that may cause or significantly contribute to an increase in mortality or serious illness, or pose a hazard to human health or the environment, if improperly managed.

1. ***Land pollution.*** Pollution of the land is generally caused by hazardous waste being disposed of in an improper manner.

2. ***Resource Conservation and Recovery Act.*** This federal statute authorizes the EPA to regulate facilities that generate, treat, store, transport, and dispose of hazardous wastes.

Comprehensive Environmental Response, Compensation, and Liability Act (Superfund)

This federal statute gives the federal government a mandate to deal with hazardous wastes that have been spilled, stored, or abandoned. This act is commonly called the *Superfund*.

1. ***Hazardous waste sites.*** The Superfund requires the EPA to identify sites in the United States where hazardous wastes have been disposed of, stored, spilled, or abandoned, and to rank these sites regarding the severity of the risk.

2. ***Superfund.*** The act created a fund to finance the cleanup of hazardous waste sites (hence, the name Superfund).

3. ***Liability for cleanup costs.*** The EPA can order a responsible party to clean up a hazardous waste site. If that party fails to do so, the EPA can clean up the site and recover the cost of the cleanup from the responsible parties.

Nuclear Waste

Nuclear waste is radioactive wastes generated by nuclear-powered fuel plants.

1. ***Radioactive pollution.*** Emissions from radioactive wastes can cause injury and death to humans and other life and can cause severe damage to the environment.

2. ***Nuclear Regulatory Commission (NRC).*** The NRC is a federal agency that licenses the construction and opening of commercial nuclear power plants. The NRC may deny or revoke a license.

3. Nuclear Waste Policy Act of 1982. This federal statute says that the federal government must select and develop a permanent site for the disposal of nuclear wastes.

Endangered Species Act

This federal statute protects *endangered* and *threatened* species of animals.

1. Critical habitat. The act requires the EPA to designate *critical habits* for each endangered and threatened species.

2. Taking. The act prohibits the *taking* (e.g., hunting, trapping, harming) of any endangered species.

Other Federal Laws That Protect Wildlife

Other federal laws that protect wildlife include:

1. Migratory Bird Treaty Act
2. Bald Eagle Protection Act
3. Wild Free-Roaming Horses and Burros Act
4. Marine Mammal Protection Act
5. Migratory Bird Conservation Act
6. Fishery Conservation and Management Act
7. Fish and Wildlife Coordination Act
8. National Wildlife Refuge System

State Environmental Protection Laws, p. 743

State Environmental Protection Laws

Many state and local governments have enacted statutes and ordinances to protect the environment. States and local governments are entitled to set pollution control standards that are stricter than federal requirements.

Internet Exercises and Case Questions

Working the Web Internet Exercise

Activities

1. Check the Consumer Product Safety Commission site for information on window blinds and/or batteries for notebook computers. See the U.S. Consumer Product Safety Commission site, at **www.cpsc.gov**.

2. Review the FDA Enforcement Reports for a detailed list of recent violators. Are any of your favorite foods listed? See the U.S. Food & Drug Administration site, at **www.fda.gov**.

3. Go to the FTC site and find the "Top Ten Dot Cons," at **www.ftc.gov/bcp/menu-credit.htm**. See also **www.law.cornell.edu/topics/consumer_credit.html** for an overview of consumer credit law, with links to key primary and secondary sources.

4. Find the EPA Superfund toxic waste clean-up sites in your state. See the U.S. Environmental Protection Agency site, at **www.epa.gov**.

5. Compare the positions of Greenpeace, the Sierra Club, and others on drilling in the Arctic National Wildlife Refuge:

- Greenpeace
  www.greenpeace.org
- National Audubon Society
  www.audubon.org
- Natural Resources Defense Council
  www.nrdc.org
- Sierra Club
  www.sierraclub.org
- Earth Watch Institute
  www.earthwatch.org/index.html
- World Environmental Law
  www.hg.org/environ.html

6. Is your state home to any of the animals protected by the Endangered Species Act? Which ones? See the Earth Justice Legal Defense Fund site, at **www.earthjustice.org**, and the Environmental Defense Fund site, at **www.edf.org**.

Critical Legal Thinking Cases

33.1 Adulterated Food Barry Engel owned and operated the Gel Spice Co., Inc., which specialized in the importation and packaging of various food spices for resale. All the spices Gel Spice imported were unloaded at a pier in New York City and taken to a warehouse on McDonald Avenue. Storage and repackaging of the spices took place in the warehouse. Between July 1976 and January 1979, the McDonald Avenue warehouse was inspected four times by investigators from the FDA. The investigators found live rats in bags of basil leaves, rodent droppings in boxes of chili peppers, and mammalian urine in bags of sesame seeds. The investigators produced additional evidence that showed that spices packaged and sold from the warehouse contained insects, rodent excreta pellets, rodent hair, and rodent urine. The FDA brought criminal charges against Engel and Gel Spice. Are they guilty? [*United States v. Gel Spice Co., Inc.*, 601 F.Supp. 1205, 1984 U.S.Dist. Lexis 21041 (E.D. N.Y. 1984)]

33.2 Food Additive Coco Rico, Inc., manufactures a coconut concentrate called "Coco Rico" for use as an ingredient in soft drinks. The concentrate that is sold to beverage bottlers in Puerto Rico contains potassium nitrate, which is added for the purpose of developing and fixing a desirable color and flavor. Puerto Rico is subject to U.S. federal laws, including those administered by the FDA. The FDA had not approved the use of potassium nitrate as a food additive in soft drinks. The FDA learned of the use of the Coco Rico concentrate in soft drinks and on March 10, 1982, obtained a warrant from a federal district court to search the premises of a Puerto Rican bottler. On March 24, 1982, government investigators discovered three lots of soft drinks containing Coco Rico on the premises of the bottler and seized them pursuant to the warrant. Coco Rico, Inc., sued to reclaim the soft drinks. Who wins? [*United States v. An Article of Food*, 752 F.2d 11, 1985 U.S.App. Lexis 27849 (1st Cir. 1985)]

33.3 Regulation of Drugs Dey Laboratories, Inc., is a drug manufacturer operating in the state of Texas. In 1983, Dey scientists created an inhalant know as ASI. The only active ingredient in ASI is atropine sulfate. The inhalant is sold to physicians, who then prescribe the medication for patients suffering from asthma, bronchitis, and other pulmonary diseases. In May 1983, Dey filed a new drug application with the FDA. By September 1983, Dey was advised that its application would not be approved. In spite of the lack of FDA approval, Dey began marketing ASI in November 1983. On August 25, 1985, the United States filed a complaint for forfeiture of all ASI manufactured by Dey. The inhalant was seized, and Dey sued to have the FDA's seizure declared illegal. Who wins? [*United States v. Atropine Sulfate 1.0 MG (Article of Drug)*, 843 F.2d 860, 1988 U.S.App. Lexis 5819 (5th Cir. 1988)]

33.4 Cosmetics FBNH Enterprises, Inc., is a distributor of a product know as French Bronze Tablets. The purpose of the tablets is to allow a person to achieve an even tan without exposure to the sun. When ingested, the tablets impart color to the skin through the use of various ingredients, one of which is canthaxanthin, a coloring agent. Canthaxanthin has not been approved for use by the FDA as a coloring additive. The FDA became aware that FBNH was marketing the tablets and that each contains 30 milligrams of canthaxanthin. On June 16, 1988, the FDA filed a lawsuit, seeking the forfeiture and condemnation of eight cases of the tablets in the possession of FBNH. FBNH challenged the government's right to seize the tablets. Who wins? [*United States v. Eight Unlabeled Cases of an Article of Cosmetic*, 888 F.2d 945, 1989 U.S.App. Lexis 15589 (2nd Cir. 1989)]

33.5 Environmental Impact Statement The U.S. Forest Service is responsible for managing the country's national forests for recreational and other purposes. This includes issuing special use permits to private companies to operate ski areas on federal lands. Sandy Butte is a 6,000-foot mountain located in the Okanogan National Forest in Okanogan County, Washington. Sandy Butte, like the Methow Valley it overlooks, is a pristine, unspoiled, sparsely populated area located within the North Cascades National Park. Large populations of mule deer and other animals exist in the park.

In 1978, Methow Recreation, Inc. (MRI), applied to the Forest Service for a special use permit to develop and operate its proposed Early Winters Ski Resort on Sandy Butte and a 1,165-acre parcel of private land it had acquired adjacent to the national forest. The proposed development would make use of approximately 3,900 acres of Sandy Butte to provide up to 16 ski lifts capable of accommodating 10,500 skiers at one time. Is an Environmental Impact Statement required? [*Robertson v. Methow Valley Citizens Council*, 490 U.S. 332, 109 S.Ct. 1835, 1989 U.S. Lexis 2160 (1989)]

33.6 Clean Air Act Pursuant to the Clean Air Act, the state of New Mexico divided its territory into eight air quality control regions, one of which consisted of the city of Albuquerque and parts of three counties (AQCR 2). AQCR 2 was a nonattainment area for purposes of carbon monoxide. The act requires states to prepare and submit a state implementation plan (SIP) showing how they will attain compliance and have the plan approved by the EPA. As part of the plan, the state must implement a vehicle emission control inspection and maintenance program (I/M program). New Mexico filed an SIP but failed to implement an enforceable I/M program. The EPA engaged in formal, public rule making, disapproved New Mexico's SIP, and imposed sanctions by cutting off certain federal funds that New Mexico would have otherwise received. New Mexico challenged the EPA's action. Who wins? [*New Mexico Environmental Improvement Division v. Thomas, Administrator, U.S. Environmental Protection Agency*, 789 F.2d 825, 1986 U.S.App. Lexis 24575 (10th Cir. 1986)]

33.7 Clean Water Act Placer mining is a method used to mine for gold in streambeds of Alaska. The miner removes soil, mud, and clay from the streambed, places it in an on-site sluice box, and separates the gold from the other matter by forcing water through the paydirt. The water in the sluice box is discharged into the stream, causing aesthetic and water quality impacts on the water both in the immediate vicinity and downstream. Toxic metals, including arsenic, cadmium, lead, zinc, and copper, are found in higher concentrations in streams where mining occurs than in nonmining streams.

In 1988, after public notice and comment, the EPA issued rules that require placer miners to use the best practical control technology (BPCT) to control discharges of nontoxic pollutants and the best available control technology (BACT) to control discharges of toxic pollutants. The BACT standard requires miners to construct settling ponds and recycle water through these ponds before discharging the water into the streambed. This method requires substantial expenditure. The Alaska Miners Association challenged the EPA's rule making. Who wins? [*Rybachek v. U.S. Environmental Protection Agency*, 904 F.2d 1276, 1990 U.S.App. Lexis 7833 (9th Cir. 1990)]

33.8 Water Pollution The Reserve Mining Company owns and operates a mine in Minnesota that is located on the shores of Lake Superior and produces hazardous waste. In 1947, Reserve obtained a permit from the state of Minnesota to dump its wastes into Lake Superior. The permits prohibited discharges that would "result in any clouding or discoloration of the water outside the specific discharge zone" or "result in any material adverse affects on public water supplies." Reserve discharged its wastes into Lake Superior for years, until they reached 67,000 tons per day in the early 1970s. Evidence showed that the discharges caused discoloration of surface waters outside the zone of discharge and contained carcinogens that adversely affected public water supplies. The United States sued Reserve for engaging in unlawful water pollution. Who wins? [*United States v. Reserve Mining Co.*, 543 F.2d 1210, 1976 U.S.App. Lexis 6503 (8th Cir. 1976)]

33.9 Hazardous Waste Douglas Hoflin was the director of the Public Works Department for Ocean Shores, Washington. From 1975 to 1982, the department purchased 3,500 gallons of paint for road maintenance. As painting jobs were finished, the 55-gallon drums that had contained the paint were returned to the department's yard. Paint contains hazardous substances such as lead. When 14 of the drums were discovered to still contain unused paint, Hoflin instructed employees to haul the paint drums to the city's sewage treatment plant and bury them. The employees took the drums, dug a hole on the grounds of the treatment plant, and dumped the drums in. Some of the drums were rusted and leaking. The hole was not deep enough, so the employees crushed the drums with a front-end loader to make them fit. The refuse was then covered with sand. Almost two years later, one of the city's employees reported the incident to state authorities, who referred the matter to the EPA. Investigation showed that the paint had contaminated the soil. The United States brought criminal charges against Hoflin for aiding and abetting the illegal dumping of hazardous waste. Who wins? [*United States v. Hoflin*, 880 F.2d 1033, 1989 U.S.App. Lexis 10169 (9th Cir. 1989)]

33.10 Endangered Species The red-cockaded woodpecker is a small bird that lives almost exclusively in the old pine forests throughout the southern United States. Its survival depends on a very specialized habitat of pine trees that are at least 30, if not 60, years old in which they build their nests and forage for insects. The population of this bird decreased substantially between 1978 and 1987 as pine forests were destroyed by clearcutting. The secretary of the interior has named the red-cockaded woodpecker as an endangered species.

The Forest Service, which is under the authority of the secretary of agriculture, manages federal forests and is charged with duties to provide recreation, protect wildlife, and provide timber. To accomplish the charge of providing timber, the Forest Service leases national forest lands to private companies for lumbering. When the Forest Service proposed to lease several national forests in Texas, where the red-cockaded woodpecker lives, to private companies for lumbering, the Sierra Club sued. The Sierra Club sought to enjoin the Forest Service from leasing these national forests for lumbering. Who wins? [*Sierra Club v. Lyng, Secretary of Agriculture*, 694 F.Supp. 1260, 1988 U.S.Dist Lexis 9203 (E.D. Tex. 1990)]

Business Ethics Cases

33.11 Business Ethics Charles of the Ritz Distributors Corporation is a New York corporation that was engaged in the sale and distribution of a product called Rejuvenescence Cream. The extensive advertising campaign that accompanied the sale of the cream placed emphasis upon the supposed rejuvenating powers of the product. The ads claimed that the cream would bring to the user's "skin quickly the clear radiance" and "the petal-like quality and texture of youth." Another advertisement claimed that the product would "restore natural moisture necessary for alive, healthy skin," with the result that "your face need not know drought years." The FTC learned of the ads and asked several experts to investigate application of cosmetics to overcome skin conditions that result from physiological changes occurring with the passage of time. The FTC issued a cease-and-desist order in regard to the advertising. Ritz appealed the FTC's decision to a federal court. Did Ritz act ethically in making its advertising claims? Who wins? [*Charles of the Ritz Distributing Corp. v. FTC*, 143 F.2d 676, 1944 U.S.App. Lexis 3172 (2nd Cir. 1944)]

33.12 Business Ethics The state of Michigan owns approximately 57,000 acres of land that comprise the Pigeon River County State Forest in southwestern Michigan. On June 12, 1977, Shell Oil Company applied to the Michigan Department of Natural Resources (DNR) for a permit to drill 10 exploratory oil wells in the forest. Roads had to be constructed to reach the proposed drill sites. Evidence showed that the only sizable elk herd east of the Mississippi River annually used the forest as their habitat and returned to this range every year to breed. Experts testified that elk avoid roads, even when there is no traffic, and that the construction of the roads and wells would destroy the elk's habitat. Michigan law prohibits activities that adversely affect natural resources. The West Michigan Environmental Action Council sued the DNR, seeking to enjoin the DNR from granting the drilling permits to Shell. Did Shell Oil Company act socially responsibly in this case? Who wins? [*West Michigan Environmental Action Council, Inc. v. Natural Resources Commission*, 275 N.W.2d 538, 1979 Mich. Lexis 347 (MI 1979)]

Briefing the Case Writing Assignment

Read Case A.33 in the Case Appendix [*X-Tra Art, Inc. v. Consumer Product Safety Commission*]. This case is excerpted from the district court opinion. Review and brief the case. In your brief, be sure to answer the following questions:

1. Who were the plaintiffs? Who were the defendants?

2. What product was being sold by the plaintiffs?

3. What act was alleged to have been violated by the plaintiffs?

4. In whose favor did the district court decide the case?

Endnotes

1. 5 U.S.C. §§ 551 et seq.
2. 21 U.S.C. § 301.
3. 21 U.S.C. § 321.
4. 21 U.S.C. §§ 360(c) et seq.
5. 15 U.S.C. § 2051.
6. 15 U.S.C. §§ 41–51.
7. 39 U.S.C. § 3009.
8. 42 U.S.C. §§ 4321 et seq.
9. 42 U.S.C. §§ 7401 et seq.
10. 33 U.S.C. §§ 1251 et seq.
11. 33 U.S.C. § 1254(t).
12. 21 U.S.C. § 349; 42 U.S.C. §§ 201 and 300F et seq.
13. 16 U.S.C. §§ 1431 et seq.; 33 U.S.C. §§ 1407 et seq.
14. 15 U.S.C. §§ 2601 et seq.
15. 7 U.S.C. §§ 135 et seq.
16. 42 U.S.C. §§ 6901 et seq.
17. 42 U.S.C. §§ 10101 et seq.
18. 16 U.S.C. §§ 1531 et seq.

34

Labor and Employment Law

*"*Strong responsible unions are essential to industrial fair play. Without them the labor bargain is wholly one-sided.*"*

—Louis D. Brandeis
(1935)

Chapter Objectives

After studying this chapter, you should be able to:

1. Describe how a union is organized and the process of collective bargaining.

2. Describe employees' rights to strike and picket.

3. Explain how state workers' compensation programs work and describe the benefits available.

4. Describe employers' duty to provide safe working conditions under the Occupational Safety and Health Act.

5. List the benefits provided by unemployment compensation and Social Security laws.

Chapter Contents

- Labor Law
- Workers' Compensation Acts
- Occupational Safety and Health Act
- Fair Labor Standards Act (FLSA)
- Other Worker Protection Laws
- Government Programs

Business Brief

Prior to this century, the doctrine of laissez-faire governed the employment relationship. Since then, federal and state governments have enacted a multitude of statutes that regulate employment.

Before the Industrial Revolution, the doctrine of laissez-faire governed the employment relationship in this country. Generally, this meant that employment was subject to the common law of contracts and agency law. In most instances, employees and employers had somewhat equal bargaining power.

This changed dramatically when the country became industrialized in the late 1800s. For one thing, large corporate employers had much more bargaining power than their employees. For another, the issues of child labor, unsafe working conditions, long hours, and low pay caused concern. Both federal and state legislation sought to protect workers' rights, and labor unions were made lawful. Today, employment law is a mixture of contract law, agency law, and government regulation.

This chapter discusses employment laws, labor unions, worker safety, and security and immigration laws.

Labor Law

Business Brief

Unions in the United States have not formed their own political party as they have in many other countries.

In the 1880s, few laws protected workers against employment abuses. The workers reacted by organizing unions in an attempt to gain bargaining strength. Unlike unions in many European countries, unions in the United States did not form their own political party. By the early 1900s, employers used violent tactics against workers who were trying to organize into unions. The courts generally sided with employers in such disputes.

The **American Federation of Labor (AFL)** was formed in 1886, under the leadership of Samuel Gompers. Only skilled craft workers such as silversmiths and artisans were allowed to belong. In 1935, John L. Lewis formed the **Congress of Industrial Organizations (CIO)**. The CIO permitted semiskilled and unskilled workers to become members. In 1955, the AFL and CIO combined to form the **AFL-CIO**. Individual unions (such as the United Auto Workers and United Steel Workers) may choose to belong to the AFL-CIO, but not all unions opt to join.

Today, approximately 15 percent of private-sector wage and salary workers belong to labor unions. Many government employees also belong to unions.

Federal Labor Union Statutes

Management and union may be likened to that serpent of the fables who on one body had two heads that fighting with poisoned fangs, killed themselves.

Peter Drucker
The New Society (1951)

In the early 1900s, members of the labor movement lobbied Congress to pass laws to protect their rights to organize and bargain with management. During the Great Depression of the 1930s, several statutes that were enacted gave workers certain rights and protections. Other statutes have been added since then. The major federal statutes in this area are:

Business Brief

An employer may not sponsor or control a union.

- *Norris-LaGuardia Act.* Enacted in 1932, this act stipulates that it is legal for employees to organize.[1]

- *National Labor Relations Act (NLRA).* This act, also known as the Wagner Act, was enacted in 1935.[2] The NLRA establishes the right of employees to form, join, and assist labor organizations; to bargain collectively with employers; and to engage in concerted activity to promote these rights.

- *Labor–Management Relations Act.* In 1947, Congress enacted the Labor–Management Relations Act (the Taft-Hartley Act).[3] This act (1) expands the activities that labor unions can engage in, (2) gives employers the right to engage in free-speech efforts against unions prior to a union election, and (3) gives the president of the United States the right to seek an injunction (for up to 80 days) against a strike that would create a national emergency.

- *Labor–Management Reporting and Disclosure Act.* Congress enacted the Labor–Management Reporting and Disclosure Act of 1959 (the Landrum-Griffin Act).[4] This act regulates internal union affairs and establishes the rights of union members.

- *Railway Labor Act.* The Railway Labor Act of 1926, as amended in 1934, covers employees of railroad and airline carriers.[5]

Business Brief

The right of workers to form, join, and assist labor unions is a statutorily protected right in the United States.

National Labor Relations Board (NLRB)

The National Labor Relations Act created the **National Labor Relations Board (NLRB)**. The NLRB is an administrative body comprised of five members appointed by the president and approved by the Senate. The NLRB oversees union elections, prevents employers and unions from engaging in illegal and unfair labor practices, and enforces and interprets certain federal labor laws. The decisions of the NLRB are enforceable in court.

Organizing a Union

Section 7 of the NLRA gives employees the right to join together and form a union.[6] The group that the union is seeking to represent—which is called the **appropriate bargaining unit** or **bargaining unit**—must be defined before the union can petition for an election. This group can be the employees of a single company or plant, a group within a single company (e.g., maintenance workers at all of a company's plants), or an entire industry (e.g., nurses at all hospitals in the country). Managers and professional employees may not belong to unions formed by employees whom they manage.

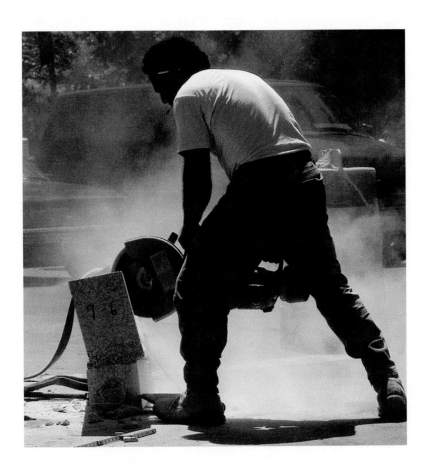

Washington D.C. Federal labor laws protect the rights of workers to form and join unions.

Types of Union Elections

If it can be shown that at least 30 percent of the employees in the bargaining unit are interested in joining or forming a union, the NLRB can be petitioned to investigate and set an election date. The following types of elections are possible.

- **Contested election.** Most union elections are contested by the employer. The NLRB is required to supervise all *contested elections*. A simple majority vote (over 50 percent) wins the election. For example, if 51 of 100 employees vote for the union, the union is certified as the bargaining agent for all 100 employees.

- **Consent election.** If management does not contest the election, a *consent election* may be held without NLRB supervision.

- **Decertification election.** If employees no longer want to be represented by a union, a *decertification election* will be held. Such elections must be supervised by the NLRB.

Union Solicitation on Company Property

If union solicitation is being conducted by employees, an employer may restrict solicitation activities to the employees' free time (e.g., coffee breaks, lunch hours, before and after work). The activities may also be limited to nonworking areas such as the cafeteria, rest room, or parking lot. Off-duty employees may be barred from union solicitation on company premises, and nonemployees (e.g., union management) may be prohibited from soliciting on behalf of the union anywhere on company property. Employers may dismiss employees who violate these rules.

An exception to this rule applies if the location of the business and the living quarters of the employees place the employees beyond the reach of reasonable union efforts to communicate with them. This so-called **inaccessibility exception** applies to logging camps, mining towns, company towns, and the like.

In the following case, the U.S. Supreme Court addressed the issue of whether an employer had to allow nonemployee union organizers on its property.

U.S. SUPREME COURT CASE
Lechmere, Inc. v. National Labor Relations Board

Case 34.1
Organizing a Union

502 U.S. 527, 112 S.Ct. 841, 1992 U.S. Lexis 555 (1992)
Supreme Court of the United States

Background and Facts

Lechmere, Inc. (Lechmere), owned and operated a retail store in the Lechmere Shopping Plaza in Newington, Connecticut. Thirteen smaller stores were located between Lechmere's store and the parking lot, which was owned by Lechmere. In June 1987, the United Food and Commercial Workers Union, AFL-CIO (Union), attempted to organize Lechmere's 200 employees, none of whom belonged to a union. After a full-page advertisement in a local newspaper drew little response, nonemployee Union organizers entered Lechmere's parking lot and began placing handbills on windshields of cars parked in the employee section of the parking lot. Lechmere's manager informed the organizers that Lechmere prohibited solicitation or handbill distribution of any kind on the property and asked them to leave. They did so, and Lechmere personnel removed the handbills. Union organizers renewed their handbill effort in the parking lot on several subsequent occa-

sions, but each time, they were asked to leave, and the handbills were removed. Union filed a grievance with the NLRB. The NLRB ruled in favor of Union and ordered Lechmere to allow handbill distribution in the parking lot. The court of appeals affirmed. Lechmere appealed to the U.S. Supreme Court.

Issue

May a store owner prohibit nonemployee union organizers from distributing leaflets in a shopping mall parking lot owned by the store?

Court's Reasoning

The U.S. Supreme Court cited the general rule that an employer cannot be compelled to allow distribution of union literature by nonemployee union organizers on its property. The Supreme Court noted, however, that an exception applies if the employees would otherwise live and work beyond the reach of reasonable union efforts to communicate with them. The Court held that this exception did not apply in this case. The Court cited the fact that the employees lived in a metropolitan area and that the union could advertise in the media and could stand on the public area adjoining Lechmere's parking lot to inform the employees of the union's organizational effort. The Supreme Court concluded, "Access to employees, not success in winning them over, is the critical issue."

Decision and Remedy

The U.S. Supreme Court held that under the facts of this case, Lechmere could prohibit nonemployee union organizers from dis-

tributing leaflets to employees in the store's parking lot. The Supreme Court reversed the decision of the court of appeals.

Case Questions

Critical Legal Thinking   Should property rights take precedence over a union's right to organize employees?

Business Ethics   Is it ethical for an employer to deny union organizers access to company property to conduct their organization efforts? Is it ethical for union organizers to demand this as a right?

Contemporary Business   What implications does this case have for business? Is this a pro- or antibusiness decision?

Illegal Interference with an Election

Section 8(a) of the NLRA makes it an **unfair labor practice** for an employer to interfere with, coerce, or restrain employees from exercising their statutory right to form and join unions. Threats of loss of benefits for joining the union, statements such as "I'll close this plant if a union comes in here," and the like are unfair labor practices. Also, an employer may not form a company union.

Section 8(b) of the NLRA prohibits unions from engaging in unfair labor practices that interfere with a union election. Coercion, physical threats, and such are unfair labor practices.

Where an unfair labor practice has been found, the NLRB (or the courts) may issue a cease-and-desist order or an injunction to restrain unfair labor practices and may set aside an election and order a new election.

In the following case, the U.S. Supreme Court found that an employer had engaged in an unfair labor practice and ordered a new election.

U.S. SUPREME COURT CASE

National Labor Relations Board v. Exchange Parts Co.

375 U.S. 405, 84 S.Ct. 457, 1964 U.S. Lexis 2263 (1964)
Supreme Court of the United States

Case 34.2
Unfair Labor
Practice

Background and Facts

Exchange Parts Co. (Exchange Parts) is engaged in the business of rebuilding automobile parts in Fort Worth, Texas. Prior to November 1959, its employees were not represented by a union. On November 9, 1959, the International Brotherhood of Boilermakers, Iron Shipbuilders, Blacksmiths, Forgers and Helpers, AFL-CIO (Union), advised Exchange Parts that it was going to conduct a campaign to organize the workers at the plant. After obtaining sufficient support from members of the appropriate bargaining unit. Union petitioned the NLRB to set an election date. After completing its investigation on February 19, 1960, the NLRB issued an order setting March 18, 1960, as the election date. On February 25, 1960, Exchange Parts held a dinner for its employees at which management announced a new company benefit allowing employees to have an extra holiday (their birthday). On March 4, Exchange Parts sent a letter to its employees that announced new increased wages for overtime pay and an extended vacation plan for employees. Union subsequently lost

the election. Union filed a complaint with the NLRB, and the NLRB held in favor of Union and ordered a new election. The court of appeals reversed. The NLRB appealed to the U.S. Supreme Court.

Issue

Is it an unfair practice for an employer to confer new economic benefits on its employees on the eve of a union election?

Court's Reasoning

The U.S. Supreme Court noted that the broad purpose of Section 8(a) is to establish the right of employees to organize for mutual aid without employer interference. This prohibits not only intrusive threats but also conduct immediately favorable to employees that is undertaken with the express purpose of impinging upon their freedom of choice for or against unionization and is reasonably calculated to have that effect. The danger inherent in well-timed increases in benefits is the suggestion of a "fist inside a velvet glove." Employees are not likely to miss the inference

National Labor Relations Board v. Exchange Parts Co.

375 U.S. 405, 84 S.Ct. 457, 1964 U.S. Lexis 2263 (1964)

Supreme Court of the United States

(continued)

that the source of benefits now conferred is also the source from which future benefits must flow and which may dry up if it is not obliged.

Decision and Remedy

The U.S. Supreme Court held that an employer's conferral of benefits on employees on the eve of a union election, which are designed to affect the outcome of that election, is an unfair labor practice. The Supreme Court reversed the decision of the court of appeals.

Case Questions

Critical Legal Thinking   Should a company be prohibited from taking away (or giving) economic benefits in its fight with a union?

Business Ethics   Was it ethical for the employer in this case to increase employee benefits on the eve of the union election?

Contemporary Business   Do you think the employer's conduct in this case constituted a "fist in a velvet glove"? Were the benefits conferred in this case likely to be ephemeral?

Collective Bargaining

Once a union has been elected, the employer and the union discuss the terms of employment of union members and try to negotiate a contract that embodies these terms. The act of negotiating is called **collective bargaining**, and the resulting contract is called a **collective bargaining agreement**. The employer and the union must negotiate with each other in good faith. Among other things, this prohibits making take-it-or-leave-it proposals.

The subjects of collective bargaining are classified as follows:

- *Compulsory subjects.* Wages, hours, and other terms and conditions of employment are compulsory subjects of collective bargaining. Fringe benefits, health benefits, retirement plans, work assignments, safety rules, and the like are included in this category.

- *Illegal subjects.* Subjects such as closed shops and discrimination are illegal subjects and may not be negotiated.

- *Permissive subjects.* Subjects that are not compulsory or illegal are permissive subjects of collective bargaining. These include such issues as the size and composition of the supervisory force, location of plants, corporate reorganizations, and the like. These subjects may be bargained for if the company and union agree to do so.

Union Security Agreements

To obtain the greatest power possible, elected unions sometimes try to install a *union security agreement*. The two types of security agreements are:

- *Union shop.* Under a **union shop** agreement, an employee must join the union within a certain time period (e.g., 30 days) after being hired. Employees who do not join must be discharged by the employer upon notice from the union. Union members pay union dues to the union. Union shops are lawful.

- *Agency shop.* Under an **agency shop** agreement, employees do not have to become union members, but they do have to pay an agency fee (an amount equal to dues) to the union. Agency shops are lawful.

Upon proper notification by the union, union and agency shop employers are required to (1) deduct union dues and agency fees from employees' wages and (2) forward these dues to the union.

Contemporary Environment

State Right-to-Work Laws

In 1947, Congress is amended the Taft-Hartley Act by enacting Section 14(b), which provides: "Nothing in this Act shall be construed as authorizing the execution or application of agreements requiring membership in a labor organization as a condition of employment in any State or Territory in which such execution or application is prohibited by State or Territorial Law." In other words, states can enact **right-to-work laws**—either by constitutional amendment or statute—that outlaw union and agency shops.

If a state enacts a right-to-work law, individual employees cannot be forced to join a union or pay union dues and fees even though a union has been elected by other employees. Right-to-work laws are often enacted by states to attract new businesses to a nonunion and low-wage environment. Unions vehemently oppose the enactment of right-to-work laws because they substantially erode union power.

Today, the following 22 states have enacted right-to-work laws:

Alabama	Nevada
Arizona	North Carolina
Arkansas	North Dakota
Florida	Oklahoma
Georgia	South Carolina
Idaho	South Dakota
Iowa	Tennessee
Kansas	Texas
Louisiana	Utah
Mississippi	Virginia
Nebraska	Wyoming

The remedies for violation of right-to-work laws vary from state to state but usually include damages to persons injured by the violation, injunctive relief, and often criminal penalties. ∎

Strikes

The NLRA gives union management the right to recommend that the union call a **strike** if a collective bargaining agreement cannot be reached. Before there can be a strike, though, a majority vote of the union's members must agree to the action.

Picketing

Striking union members often engage in **picketing** in support of their strike. Picketing usually takes the form of the striking employees and union representatives walking in front of the employer's premises carrying signs announcing their strike. It is used to put pressure on an employer to settle a strike. The right to picket is implied from the NLRA.

Picketing is lawful unless it (1) is accompanied by violence, (2) obstructs customers from entering the employer's place of business, (3) prevents nonstriking employees from entering the employer's premises, or (4) prevents pickups and deliveries at the employer's place of business. An employer may seek an injunction against unlawful picketing.

Secondary Boycott Picketing Unions sometimes try to bring pressure against an employer by picketing the employer's suppliers or customers. Such **secondary boycott picketing** is lawful only if it is product picketing (i.e., if the picketing is against the primary employer's product). The picketing is illegal if it is directed against the neutral employer instead of the struck employer's product.

Consider This Example Suppose the apple pickers' union in the state of Washington goes on strike against its primary employers, the apple growers. Picketing the apple orchards may do little to draw attention of the strike to the public. Therefore, members of the apple pickers' union may picket grocery stores in metropolitan areas that sell Washington apples. If the signs the picketers carry ask shoppers at the grocery stores not to buy Washington apples, the secondary boycott is lawful. However, it is unlawful if the signs ask customers not to shop at the grocery stores.

Illegal Strikes

Several types of strikes have been held to be illegal and are not protected by federal labor law. Illegal strikes are:

- **Violent strikes.** In violent strikes, striking employees cause substantial damage to property of the employer or a third party. Courts usually tolerate a certain amount of isolated violence before finding that the entire strike is illegal.

- **Sit-down strikes.** In sit-down strikes, striking employees continue to occupy the employer's premises. Such strikes are illegal because they deny the employer's statutory right to continue its operations during the strike.

- **Partial or intermittent strikes.** In these strikes, employees strike part of the day or workweek and work the other part. This type of strike is illegal because it interferes with the employer's right to operate its facilities at full operation.

- **Wildcat strikes.** In wildcat strikes, individual union members go on strike without proper authorization from the union. The courts have recognized that a wildcat strike becomes lawful if it is quickly ratified by the union.

- **Strikes during the 60-day cooling-off period.** These strikes begin during the mandatory 60-day **cooling-off period.** This time is designed to give the employer and the union time to negotiate a settlement of the union grievances and avoid a strike. Any strike without a proper 60-day notice is illegal.

- **Strikes in violation of a no-strike clause.** These strikes take place in violation of a negotiated no-strike clause, under which an employer gives economic benefits to the union and, in exchange, the union agrees that no strike will be called for a set time.

Illegal strikers may be discharged by the employer, with no rights to reinstatement.

Crossover and Replacement Workers

Individual members of a union do not have to honor a strike. They may (1) choose not to strike or (2) return to work after joining the strikers for a time. Employees who choose either of these options are known as **crossover workers**.

Once a strike begins, the employer may continue operations by using management personnel and hiring **replacement workers** to take the place of the striking employees. Replacement workers can be hired on either a temporary or permanent basis. If replacement workers are given permanent status, they do not have to be dismissed when the strike is over.

Employer Lockout

If an employer reasonably anticipates a strike by some of its employees, it may prevent those employees from entering the plant or premises. This is called an **employer lockout**.

Internal Union Affairs

Unions may adopt **internal union rules** to regulate the operation of the union, acquire and maintain union membership, and the like. The undemocratic manner in which many unions were formulating these rules prompted Congress in 1959 to enact **Title I of the Landrum-Griffin Act**. Title I, which is often referred to as **labor's "bill of rights,"** gives each union member equal rights and privileges to nominate candidates for union office, vote in elections, and participate in membership meetings. It further guarantees union members the right of free speech and assembly, provides for due process (notice and hearing), and permits union members to initiate judicial or administrative action.

A union may discipline members for participating in certain activities, including (1) walking off the job in a nonsanctioned strike, (2) working for wages below union scale, (3) spying for an employer, and (4) any other unauthorized activity that has an adverse economic impact on the union. A union may not punish a union member for participating in a civic duty, such as testifying in court against the union.

Contemporary Environment
Plant Closing Act

Often, a company would choose to close a plant without giving its employees prior notice of the closing. To remedy this situation, on August 4, 1988, Congress enacted the **Worker Adjustment and Retraining Notification (WARN) Act**, also called the **Plant Closing Act** (29 U.S.C. § 2102). The act, which covers employers with 100 or more employees, requires employers to give their employees 60 days' notice before engaging in certain plant closings or layoffs.

If the employees are represented by a union, the notice must be given to the union; if they are not, the notice must be given to the employees individually.

The actions covered by the act are:

- *Plant closings.* A plant closing is a permanent or temporary shut-down of a single site that results in a loss of employment of 50 or more employees during any 30-day period.

- *Mass layoffs.* A mass layoff is a reduction of 33 percent of the employees or at least 50 employees during any 30-day period.

An employer is exempted from having to give such notice if:

1. The closing or layoff is caused by business circumstances that were not reasonably foreseeable as of the time that the notice would have been required.
2. The business was actively seeking capital or business that, if obtained, would have avoided or postponed the shutdown and the employer in good faith believed that giving notice would have precluded it from obtaining the needed capital or business. ■

Workers' Compensation Acts

Many types of employment are dangerous, and each year many workers are injured on the job. Under common law, employees who were injured on the job could sue their employer for negligence. This time-consuming process placed the employee at odds with his or her employer. In addition, there was no guarantee that the employee would win the case. Ultimately, many injured workers—or the heirs of deceased workers—were left uncompensated.

Workers' compensation acts were enacted by states in response to the unfairness of that result. These acts create an administrative procedure for workers to receive compensation for injuries that occur on the job. First, the injured worker files a claim with the appropriate state government agency (often called the workers' compensation board or commission). Next, that entity determines the legitimacy of the claim. If the worker disagrees with the agency's findings, he or she may appeal the decision through the state court system. Workers' compensation benefits are paid according to preset limits established by statute or regulation. The amounts that are recoverable vary from state to state.

Workers' Compensation Insurance

States usually require employers to purchase insurance from private insurance companies or state funds to cover workers' compensation claims. Some states permit employers to self-insure if they demonstrate that they have the ability to pay workers' compensation claims. Many large companies self-insure. Workers can sue their employers in court to recover damages for employment-related injuries if the employer does not carry workers' compensation insurance or does not self-insure if permitted to do so.

Business Brief

Depending on the state, employers are required either to pay for workers' compensation insurance or to self-insure by making payments into a contingency fund. This is a substantial expense for businesses.

It is difficult to imagine any grounds, other than our own personal economic predilections, for saying that the contract of employment is any the less an appropriate subject of legislation than are scores of others, in dealing with which this Court has held that legislatures may curtail individual freedom in the public interest.

Justice Stone
*Dissenting Opinion, Morehead v.
New York (1936)*

Mackinac Bridge, Michigan. Workers on this bridge are covered by workers' compensation, occupational safety, and other labor and worker protection laws.

Employment-Related Injury

For an injury to be compensable under workers' compensation, the claimant must prove that the injury arose out of and in the course of his or her employment. An accident that occurs while an employee is actively working is clearly within the scope of this rule. Accidents that occur at a company cafeteria or while on a business lunch for an employer are covered. Accidents that happen while the employee is at an off-premises restaurant during his or her personal lunch hour are not covered. Many workers' compensation acts include stress as a compensable work-related injury.

Exclusive Remedy

Workers' compensation is an exclusive remedy. Thus, workers cannot sue their employers in court for damages. There is one exception to this rule: If an employer intentionally injures a worker, the worker can collect workers' compensation benefits and sue the employer. Workers' compensation acts do not bar injured workers from suing responsible third parties to recover damages.

In the following case, the court had to decide whether an accident was work related.

Smith v. Workers' Compensation Appeals Board
191 Cal.App.3d 127, 236 Cal.Rptr. 248,
1987 Cal.App. Lexis 1587 (1987)
Court of Appeals of California

Case 34.3
Workers' Compensation

Background and Facts

Ronald Wayne Smith was employed by Modesto High School as a temporary math instructor. In addition, he coached the girls baseball and basketball teams. The contract under which he was employed stated that he "may be required to devote a reasonable amount of time to other duties" in addition to instructional duties. The teachers in the school system were evaluated once a year regarding both instructional duties and noninstructional duties, including "sponsorship or the supervision of out-of-classroom student activities."

The high school's math club holds an annual end-of-year outing. For the 1983–1984 school year, a picnic was scheduled for June 7, 1984, at the Modesto Reservoir. The students invited their math teachers, including Smith, to attend. The food was paid for by math club members' dues. Smith attended the picnic with his wife and three children. One of the students brought along a windsurfer. Smith watched the students as they used it before and after the picnic. When Smith tried it himself, he fell and was seriously injured. He died shortly thereafter. Mrs. Smith filed a claim for workers' compensation benefits, which was objected to by the employer. The workers' compensation judge denied benefits. The Workers' Compensation Appeals Board affirmed. Mrs. Smith appealed.

Issue

Was Smith engaged in employment-related activities when the accident occurred?

Court's Reasoning

The court of appeals held that the decedent believed that his participation in the math club picnic was expected by his employer and that this belief was objectively reasonable. The court stated, "The school was more than minimally involved in the picnic." Teachers were encouraged to involve themselves in extracurricu-lar activities of the school, thus conferring the benefit of better teacher–student relationships. The court noted that teachers were evaluated on whether they shared equally in the sponsorship or the supervision of out-of-classroom student activities. The court concluded that the decedent's engagement in the recreational activities was causally connected to his employment.

Decision and Remedy

The court of appeals held that the decedent's accident was causally connected to his employment for purposes of awarding workers' compensation benefits to his heirs. The court of appeals reversed the decision of the Workers' Compensation Appeals Board and remanded the case for further proceedings.

Case Questions

Critical Legal Thinking Should workers' compensation benefits be awarded only for accidents that occur at the job site? Why or why not?

Business Ethics Did the employer act ethically in objecting to the payment of benefits in this case?

Contemporary Business How costly is workers' compensation for business? Do you think that many fraudulent workers' compensation claims are filed?

Occupational Safety and Health Act

In 1970, Congress enacted the **Occupational Safety and Health Act**[7] to promote safety in the workplace. Virtually all private employers are within the scope of the act, but federal, state, and local governments are exempt. Industries regulated by other federal safety legislation are also exempt.[8] The act also established the **Occupational Safety and Health Administration (OSHA)**, a federal administrative agency within the Department of Labor, that is empowered to enforce the act. The act imposes recordkeeping and reporting requirements on employers and requires them to post notices in the workplace, informing employees of their rights under the act.

Specific and General Duty Standards

OSHA is empowered to adopt rules and regulations to interpret and enforce the Occupational Safety and Health Act. OSHA has adopted thousands of regulations to enforce the safety standards established by the act. These include the following:

- *Specific duty standards.* Many of the OSHA standards address safety problems of a **specific duty** nature. For example, OSHA standards establish safety requirements for equipment (e.g., safety guards), set maximum exposure levels to hazardous chemicals, regulate the location of machinery, establish safety procedures for employees, and the like.
- *General duty standards.* The act imposes a **general duty** on an employer to provide a work environment free from recognized hazards that are causing or are likely to cause death or serious physical harm to his employees. This is so even if no specific regulation applies to the situation.

OSHA is empowered to inspect places of employment for health hazards and safety violations. If a violation is found, OSHA can issue a *written citation* that requires the employer to abate or correct the situation. Contested citations are reviewed by the Occupational Safety and Health Review Commission. Its decision is appealable to the Federal Circuit Court of Appeals. Employers who violate the act, OSHA rules and regulations, or OSHA citations are subject to both civil and criminal penalties.

Fair Labor Standards Act (FLSA)

In 1938, Congress enacted the **Fair Labor Standards Act (FLSA)** to protect workers.[9] The FLSA applies to private employers and employees engaged in the production of goods for interstate commerce.

Child Labor

The FLSA forbids the use of oppressive child labor and makes it unlawful to ship goods produced by businesses that use oppressive child labor. The Department of Labor has adopted the following regulations that define lawful child labor: (1) children under the age of 14 cannot work except as newspaper deliverers; (2) children ages 14 and 15 may work limited hours in nonhazardous jobs approved by the Department of Labor (e.g., restaurants and gasoline stations); and (3) children ages 16 and 17 may work unlimited hours in nonhazardous jobs. The Department of Labor determines which occupations are hazardous (e.g., mining, roofing, working with explosives). Children who work in agricultural employment and child actors and performers are exempt from these restrictions. Persons age 18 and older may work at any job, whether it is hazardous or not.

Minimum Wage and Overtime Pay Requirements

The FLSA establishes minimum wage and overtime pay requirements for workers. Managerial, administrative, and professional employees are exempt from the act's wage and hour provisions. As outlined in the following paragraphs, the FLSA requires employers to pay covered workers at least the minimum wage for their regular work hours and to provide overtime pay:

- *Minimum wage.* The minimum wage is set by Congress and can be changed. As of 2005, it was set at $5.15 per hour. The Department of Labor permits employers to pay less than the minimum wage to students and apprentices. An employer may reduce minimum wages by an amount equal to the reasonable cost of food and lodging provided to employees.
- *Overtime pay.* Under the FLSA, an employer cannot require nonexempt employees to work more than 40 hours per week unless they are paid one-and-a-half times their regular pay for each hour worked in excess of 40 hours. Each week is treated separately. For example, if an employee works 50 hours one week and 30 hours the next, the employer owes the employee 10 hours of overtime pay for the first week.

Business Ethics

Microsoft Violates Employment Law

Microsoft Corporation is the world's largest provider of computer operating systems, software programs, and Internet browsers. The company has grown into a monopoly and made one of its founders, Bill Gates, the richest person in the world. But the company has been caught nickel-and diming some of its

workers. It all started with an Internal Revenue Service (IRS) investigation.

Microsoft is headquartered in the state of Washington. In addition to having regular employees, Microsoft used the services of other workers who are classified as *independent contrac-*

tors (called *freelancers*) and temporary agency employees (called *temps*). Most of these special employees worked full time for Microsoft, doing jobs that were identical to jobs performed by Microsoft's regular employees. Microsoft paid the special employees by check as outside workers. In 1990, the IRS conducted an employment tax examination and determined that Microsoft had misclassified these special workers as independent contractors and that the workers in these positions needed to be reclassified as "employees" for federal tax purposes.

But the IRS investigation was not the end of the story. Plaintiff Donna Vizcaino and other freelancers sued Microsoft in a class action lawsuit, alleging that they were denied employment benefits, especially employee stock options, that were paid to regular employees. Microsoft contributed 3 percent of an employee's salary to the stock option plan. The court of appeals agreed with the plaintiffs, citing the Internal Revenue Code that requires such stock option plans to be available to all employees. Thus, Microsoft's attempts to define certain full-time employees as freelancers and temps was rebuffed by the courts [*Vizcaino v. United States District Court for the Western District of Washington*, 173 F.3d 713, 1999 U.S. App.Lexis 9057 (9th Cir. 1999)].

1. Did Microsoft act ethically in this case?
2. Why did Microsoft classify full-time workers as freelancers and temps? Explain. ■

Other Worker Protection Laws

Congress has enacted other major federal statutes that provide employees with certain rights. These statutes include the Family and Medical Leave Act, the Consolidated Omnibus Budget Reconciliation Act (COBRA), Employee Retirement Income Security Act (ERISA), and Immigration Reform and Control Act (IRCA). Each of these statutes is discussed in the following paragraphs.

Family and Medical Leave Act

In February 1993, Congress enacted the **Family and Medical Leave Act**.[10] This act guarantees workers unpaid time off from work for medical emergencies. The act, which applies to companies with 50 or more workers as well as federal, state, and local governments, covers about half of the nation's workforce. To be covered by the act, an employee must have worked for the employer for at least one year and have performed more than 1,250 hours of service during the previous 12 month period.

Covered employers are required to provide up to 12 weeks of unpaid leave during any 12-month period due to:

1. The birth of, and care for, a child.
2. The placement of a child with an employee for adoption or in foster care.
3. A serious health condition that makes the employee unable to perform his or her duties.
4. Care for a spouse, child, or parent with a serious health problem.

Leave because of the birth of a child or the placement of a child for adoption or foster care cannot be taken intermittently unless the employer agrees. Other leaves may be taken on an intermittent basis. The employer may require medical proof of claimed serious health conditions.

An eligible employee who takes leave must, upon returning to work, be restored to either the same or an equivalent position with equivalent employment benefits and pay. The restored employee is not entitled to the accrual of seniority during the leave period, however. A covered employer may deny restoration to a salaried employee who is among the highest-paid 10 percent of that employer's employees if the denial is necessary to prevent "substantial and grievous economic injury" to the employer's operations.

Consolidated Omnibus Budget Reconciliation Act (COBRA)

The **Consolidated Omnibus Budget Reconciliation Act of 1985 (COBRA)**[11] provides that an employee of a private employer or the employee's beneficiaries must be offered the opportunity to continue his or her group health insurance after the voluntary or involuntary termination of a worker's employment or the loss of coverage due to certain qualifying events defined in the law. The employer must notify covered employees and their beneficiaries of their rights under COBRA. To continue coverage, a person must pay the required group rate premium. Government employees are subject to parallel provisions found in the Public Health Service Act.

Employee Retirement Income Security Act (ERISA)

Employers are not required to establish pension plans for their employees. If they do, however, they are subject to the recordkeeping, disclosure, and other requirements of the **Employee Retirement Income Security Act (ERISA).**[12] ERISA is a complex act designed to prevent fraud and other abuses associated with private pension funds. Federal, state, and local government pension funds are exempt from its coverage. ERISA is administered by the Department of Labor and the IRS.

Among other things, ERISA requires pension plans to be in writing and to name a pension fund manager. The plan manager owes a fiduciary duty to act as a "prudent person" in managing the fund and investing its assets. No more than 10 percent of a pension fund's assets can be invested in the securities of the sponsoring employer.

Vesting occurs when an employee has a nonforfeitable right to receive pension benefits. First, ERISA provides for immediate vesting of each employee's own contributions to the plan. Second, it requires employers' contributions to be either (1) completely forfeitable for a set period of up to five years and totally vested after that (*cliff vesting*) or (2) gradually vested over a seven-year period and completely vested after that time.

Immigration Reform and Control Act (IRCA)

The **Immigration Reform and Control Act of 1986 (IRCA)**[13] and the **Immigration Act of 1990**[14] are administered by the U.S. Immigration and Naturalization Service (INS). These acts make it unlawful for employers to hire illegal immigrants. As of June 1, 1987, all U.S. employers must complete **INS Form I-9** for each employee. The form attests that the employer has inspected documents of the employee and has determined that he or she is either a U.S. citizen or otherwise qualified to work in the country (e.g., has a proper work visa). Employers must maintain records and post in the workplace notices of the contents of the law. Violators are subject to both civil and criminal penalties.

Government Programs

The U.S. government has established several programs that provide benefits to workers and their dependants. Two of these programs, unemployment compensation and Social Security, are discussed in the following paragraphs.

Unemployment Compensation

In 1935, Congress established an unemployment compensation program to assist workers who were temporarily unemployed. Under the **Federal Unemployment Tax Act (FUTA)**[15] and state laws enacted to implement the program, employers are required to pay unemployment contributions (taxes). The tax rate and unemployment wage level are subject to change. Employees do not pay unemployment taxes.

State governments administer unemployment compensation programs under general guidelines set by the federal government. Each state establishes its own eligibility requirements and the amount and duration of the benefits. To collect benefits, applicants must be able and available for work and seeking employment. Workers who have been let go because of bad conduct (e.g., illegal activity, drug use on the job) or who voluntarily quit work without just cause are not eligible to receive benefits.

Social Security

In 1935, Congress established the federal **Social Security** system to provide limited retirement and death benefits to certain employees and their dependents. The Social Security system is administered by the Social Security Administration. Today, Social Security benefits include (1) retirement benefits, (2) survivors' benefits to family members of deceased workers, (3) disability benefits, and (4) medical and hospitalization benefits (Medicare).

Under the **Federal Insurance Contributions Act (FICA)**,[16] employees and employers must make contributions (pay taxes) into the Social Security fund. The employer must pay a matching amount. Social Security does not operate like a savings account. Instead, current contributions are used to fund current claims. The employer is responsible for deducting employees' portions from their wages and remitting the entire payment to the IRS.

Under the **Self-Employment Contributions Act**,[17] self-employed individuals must pay Social Security contributions, too. The amount of taxes self-employed individuals must pay is equal to the combined employer–employee amount.

Failure to submit Social Security taxes subjects the violator to interest payments, penalties, and possible criminal liability. Social Security taxes may be changed by act of Congress.

Tibet. Workers in many other countries are not accorded the same worker protection laws as those provided by many state and federal laws in the United States.

Chapter Summary

Labor Law, p. 752

Federal Labor Statutes

Federal labor statutes include:

1. *Norris-LaGuardia Act.* This act made it legal for employees to organize.
2. *National Labor Relations Act.* This act established the right of employees to form, join, and assist labor unions. Also called the *Wagner Act* or *NLRA*.
3. *Labor-Management Relations Act.* This act expanded the activities labor unions could engage in, gave employers free speech rights to oppose unionization, and gave the president the right to seek injunctions against strikes that would create a national emergency. Also called the *Taft-Hurley Act*.
4. *Labor-Management Reporting and Disclosure Act.* Called labor's "bill of rights," this act gives union members the right to nominate candidates for union offices and vote in union elections. Also called the *Landrum-Griffin Act*.
5. *Railway Labor Act.* This act governs union rights of railroad and airline employees.

National Labor Relations Board (NLRB)

This federal administrative agency is empowered to administer federal labor law, oversee union elections, and decide labor disputes.

Organizing a Union

1. *Section 7 of the NLRA.* This section gives employees the right to join together and form a union.
2. *Appropriate bargaining union.* An appropriate bargaining union is a group of employees that a union is seeking to represent.

Types of Union Elections

1. *Contested election.* Management may contest a union. The NLRB must supervise the election.
2. *Consent election.* In a consent election, management does not contest the union election.
3. *Decertification election.* This is an election to determine if the employees want to reject a union as their representative. The NLRB must supervise the election.

Union Solicitation on Company Property

1. *Employees.* An employer may restrict solicitation activities to the employees' free time (e.g., breaks, lunch hours, before and after work).
2. *Nonemployee union representatives.* An employer may prohibit solicitation on company property unless the employees cannot otherwise be contacted.

Illegal Interference with an Election

1. *Section 8(a) of the NLRA.* This section makes it an *unfair labor practice* for an employer to interfere with, coerce, or restrain employees from exercising their right to form and join unions.
2. *Section 8(b) of the NLRA.* This section makes it an unfair labor practice for a *union* to interfere with a union election.

Collective Bargaining

Collective bargaining is a process whereby the union and employer negotiate the terms and conditions of employment for the covered employee union members.

1. *Collective bargaining agreement.* This is a contract resulting from collective bargaining.

Subjects of Collective Bargaining

1. *Compulsory subjects.* Compulsory subjects are wages, hours, and other terms and conditions of employment (e.g., vacations, medical benefits).
2. *Illegal subjects.* Illegal subjects are subjects that may not be negotiated (e.g., discrimination).
3. *Permissive subjects.* Permissive subjects are not compulsory or illegal (e.g., closing of plants).

Union Security Agreements

1. *Union shop.* A union shop is an establishment where an employee must join a union within a certain number of days after being hired.
2. *Agency shop.* In an agency shop, employees do not have to join the union but must pay an *agency fee* equal to union dues.
3. *Check-off provision.* This provision requires employers to deduct union and agency dues from employees' wages and remit these payments to the union.

State Right-to-Work Laws

States may enact statutes that make union shops and agency shops illegal. In such a case, individual employees may choose not to join the union.

Strikes

A strike is a cessation of work by union members in order to obtain economic benefits, to correct an unfair labor practice, or to preserve their work. The NLRA gives union employees the right to strike.

Picketing

Striking employees and union organizers may predect—that is, walk around the employer's premises, usually carrying signs, notifying the public of their grievance against the employer.

1. *Illegal picketing.* Picketing is illegal if it is accompanied by violence or obstructs customers, nonstriking workers, or suppliers from entering the employer's premises.
2. *Secondary boycott.* A Secondary boycott is picketing conducted at a third party's premises. *Product picketing* against the products of the struck employer is lawful. It is illegal if it is directed against the neutral employer.

Illegal Strikes

1. *Violent strike.* In this type of strike, striking employees cause substantial damage to the employer's or a third party's property.
2. *Sit-down strike.* In this type of strike, employees occupy and refuse to leave the employer's premises.
3. *Partial or intermittent strike.* In this type of strike, employees strike for only parts of each day or week.
4. *Wildcat strike.* A wildcat strike is not sanctioned by the union.
5. *Strike during the 60-day cooling-off period.* In this type of strike, the union has not given the employer at lest 60 days' prior notice of the strike.
6. *Strike in violation of a no-strike clause.* This type of strike violates a no-strike clause in a collective bargaining agreement.

Crossover Workers and Replacement Workers

Crossover worker. A crossover worker is an employee who does not honor a strike who either (1) chooses not to strike or (2) returns to work after joining strikers for a time.
Replacement worker. Persons who are hired to take the place of striking workers. The employer may offer these employees permanent positions.

Employer Lockout

An employer may lock employees out of its premises if it reasonably anticipates a strike.

Internal Union Rules

Title I of the Landrum-Griffin Act. This federal law gives each union member equal rights and privileges to nominate candidates for union office, vote in union elections, and participate in membership meetings. Commonly called *labor's "bill of rights."*

Plant Closings

Worker Adjustment and Retraining Notification (WARN) Act. This federal law requires employers with 100 or more employees to give their employees 60 days' notice before engaging in certain plant closings or layoffs. Also called the *Plant Closing Act* and *Warn Act.*

Workers' Compensation Acts, p. 759

Workers' Compensation Acts

These state statutes create an administrative procedure for workers to receive payments for job-related injuries.

1. *Workers' compensation insurance.* Most states require employers to carry private or government-sponsored workers' compensation insurance. Some states permit employers to self-insure.

Employment-Related Injury

To be compensable under workers' compensation, a claimant must prove that his or her injury arose out of and in the course of his or her employment.

Exclusive Remedy

Workers' compensation is an exclusive remedy. Thus, workers cannot sue their employers to recover damages for job-related injuries.

1. *Exceptions to exclusive-remedy rule.* Workers may recover damages from their employers for job-related injuries if the employer:
   a. Does not provide workers' compensation.
   b. Intentionally causes the worker's injuries.
2. *Lawsuits against third parties.* Workers' compensation acts do not bar injured workers from suing responsible third parties to recover damages (e.g., the manufacturer of a defective machine that caused a worker's injuries).

Occupational Safety and Health Act, p. 761

Occupational Safety and Health Act

This federal statute requires employers to provide safe working conditions.

1. *Occupational Safety and Health Administration (OSHA).* This federal administrative agency administers and enforces the Occupational Safety and Health Act.

Specific and General Duty Standards

1. *Specific duty standards.* These are safety standards for specific equipment (e.g., lathe) or a specific industry (e.g., mining).
2. *General duty standards.* These standards impose a general duty on employers to provide safe working conditions.

Fair Labor Standards Act (FLSA), p. 762

Fair Labor Standards Act (FLSA)

This federal statute protects workers.

Child Labor

The FLSA forbids the use of illegal child labor. The U.S. Department of Labor defines illegal child labor.

Minimum Wage and Overtime Pay Requirements

1. *Minimum wage.* The minimum wage is set by Congress and can be changed. The minimum wage, as of 2005, is $5.15 per hour.

2. *Overtime pay.* An employer cannot require employees to work more than 40 hours per week unless they are paid 1.5 times their regular pay for each hour worked in excess of 40 hours.

Other Worker Protection Laws, p. 763

Family and Medical Leave Act

This federal statute guarantees covered workers unpaid time off from work for the birth or adoption of a child, serious health problems of the worker, and serious health problems of a spouse, child, or parent.

Consolidated Omnibus Budget Reconciliation Act (COBRA)

This federal statute requires an employer to offer an employee or the employee's beneficiaries the opportunity to continue health benefits (upon payment of the premium) after termination of employment due to dismissal or death.

Employee Retirement Income Security Act (ERISA)

This federal statute governs the establishment and administration of private pension programs to prevent fraud and other abuses.

Immigration Reform and Control Act (IRCA)

This federal statute prohibits employers from employing illegal immigrant. Employers must require workers to prove that they are U.S. citizens or have proper work visas to work in this country.

Government Programs, p. 764

Unemployment Compensation

This state and federal program pays compensation to unemployed persons who meet certain qualifying standards. Employers are required to pay unemployment compensation payments to the government to fund the program. Authorized by the *Federal Unemployment Tax Act (FUTA)* and state laws.

Social Security

This federal government program provides limited retirement, disability, and medical and hospitalization to covered employees and their dependents. Employers and employees pay taxes to fund the program.

 Internet Exercises and Case Questions

Working the Web Internet Exercises

Activities

1. For an overview of labor law, see "Labor and Employment Law," at **jurist.law.pitt.edu/sg_lab.htm**.

2. Visit the Web site of one of the largest labor unions, at **www.aflcio.org**.

3. Check the current unemployment rate at the Department of Labor: **www.dol.gov**. Is it higher or lower than it was one year ago?

Critical Legal Thinking Cases

34.1 Unfair Labor Practice   In July 1965, the Teamsters Union began a campaign to organize the employees at a Sinclair Company plant. When the president of Sinclair learned of the Teamsters' drive, he talked with all of his employees and emphasized the results of a long 1952 strike that he claimed "almost put our company out of business" and expressed worry that the employees were forgetting the "lessons of the past." He emphasized that the company was on "thin ice" financially, that the Teamsters' "only weapon is to strike," and that a strike "could lead to the closing of the plant" because the company had manufacturing facilities elsewhere. He also noted that because of the employees' ages and the limited usefulness of their skills, they might not be able to find reemployment if they lost their jobs. Finally, he sent literature to the employees, stating that "the Teamsters Union is a strike happy outfit" and that they were under "hoodlum control," and he included a cartoon showing the preparation of a grave for the Sinclair Company and other headstones containing the names of other plants allegedly victimized by unions. The Teamsters lost the election 7 to 6 and then filed an unfair labor practice charge with the NLRB. Did the company violate labor law? [*N.L.R.B. v. Gissel Packing Co.*, 395 U.S. 575, 89 S.Ct. 1918, 1969 U.S. Lexis 3172 (1969)]

34.2 Work Preservation   The Frouge Corporation was the general contractor on a housing project in Philadelphia. The carpenter-employees of Frouge were represented by the Carpenters' International Union. Traditional jobs of carpenters included mortising blank wooden doors for doorknobs, routing them for hinges, and beveling them to fit between the door jambs. The union had entered into a collective bargaining agreement with Frouge that provided that no member of the union would handle any doors that had been fitted prior to being furnished to the job site. The housing project called for 3,600 doors. Frouge contracted for the purchase of premachined doors that were already mortised, routed, and beveled. When the union ordered its members not to hang the prefabricated doors, the National Woodwork Manufacturers Association filed an unfair labor practice charge against the union with the NLRB. Was the union's refusal to hang prefabricated doors lawful? [*National Woodwork Manufacturers Association v. N.L.R.B.*, U.S. 612, 87 S.Ct. 1250, 1967 U.S. Lexis 2858 (1967)]

34.3 Illegal Strike   In September 1966, the employees of the Shop Rite Foods, Inc.'s, warehouse in Lubbock, Texas, elected the United Packinghouse, Food and Allied Workers (Union) as its bargaining agent. Negotiations for a collective bargaining agreement began in late November 1966. In February and March 1967, when an agreement had not yet been reached, the company found excess amounts of damage to merchandise in its warehouse and concluded that it was being intentionally caused by dissident employees as a pressure tactic to secure concessions from the company. The company notified the union representative that employees caught doing such acts would be terminated; the Union representative in turn notified the employees. On March 31, 1967, a Shop Rite manager observed an employee in the flour section—where he had no business to be—making quick motions with his hands. The manager found that several bags of flour had been cut. The employee was immediately fired. Another employee and fellow union member led about 30 other employees in an immediate walkout. The company discharged

these employees and refused to rehire them. The employees filed a grievance with the NLRB. Can they get their jobs back? [*N.L.R.B. v. Shop Rite Foods, Inc.*, 430 F.2d 786, 1970 U.S. App. Lexis 7613 (5th Cir. 1970)]

34.4 Employer Lockout   The American Shipbuilding Company operated a shipyard in Chicago, Illinois, where it repaired Great Lakes ships during the winter months, when freezing on the Great Lakes renders shipping impossible. The workers at the shipyard was represented by several unions. On May 1, 1961, the unions notified the company of their intention to seek modification of the current collective bargaining agreement when it expired on August 1, 1961. On five previous occasions, agreements had been preceded by strikes (including illegal strikes) that were called just after the ships had arrived in the shipyard for repairs so that the unions increased their leverage in negotiations with the company.

Based on this prior history, the company displayed anxiety about the unions' strike plans and possible work stoppage. On August 1, 1961, after extended negotiations, the company and the unions reached an impasse in their collective bargaining. In response, the company decided to lay off most of the workers at the shipyard. It sent them the following notice: "Because of the labor dispute which has been unresolved since August 1, 1961, you are laid off until further notice." The unions filed unfair labor practice charges with the NLRB. Were the company's actions legal? [*American Ship Building Company v. N.L.R.B.*, 380 U.S. 300, 85 S.Ct. 955, 1965 U.S. Lexis 2310 (1965)]

34.5 Secondary Boycott   Safeco Title Insurance Company is a major insurance company that underwrites title insurance for real estate in the state of Washington. Five local title companies act as insurance brokers who exclusively sell Safeco insurance. In 1972, Local 1001 of the Retail Store Employees Union, AFL-CIO, was elected as the bargaining agent for certain Safeco employees. When negotiations between Safeco and the union reached an impasse, the employees went on strike. The union did not confine its picketing to Safeco's office in Seattle but also picketed each of the five local title companies. The picketers carried signs declaring that Safeco had no contract with the union and distributed handbills asking consumers to support the strike by canceling their Safeco insurance policies. The local title companies filed a complaint with the NLRB. Was the picketing of the neutral title insurance companies lawful? [*N.L.R.B. v. Retail Store Employees Union, Local 1001, Retail Clerks International Association, AFL-CIO*, 447 U.S. 607, 100 S.Ct. 2372, 1980 U.S. Lexis 133 (1980)]

34.6 Workers' Compensation   John B. Wilson was employed by the City of Modesto, California, as a police officer. He was a member of the special emergency reaction team (SERT), a tactical unit of the city's police department that is trained and equipped to handle highly dangerous criminal situations. Membership in SERT is voluntary for police officers. No additional pay or benefits are involved. To be a member of SERT, each officer is required to pass physical tests four times a year. One such test requires members to run two miles in 17 minutes. Other tests call for a minimum number of pushups, pullups, and situps. Officers who do not belong to SERT are not required to undergo these physical tests. On June 27, 1984, Wilson completed his patrol shift, changed clothes, and drove to the

Modesto Junior College track. While running there, he injured his left ankle. Wilson filed a claim for workers' compensation benefits, which was contested by his employer. Who wins? [*Wilson v. Workers' Compensation Appeals Board*, 196 Cal.App.3d 902, 239 Cal.Rptr. 719, 1987 Cal.App. Lexis 2382 (Cal.App. 1987)]

34.7 Occupational Safety   Getty Oil Company operates a separation facility where it gathers gas and oil from wells and transmits them to an outgoing pipeline under high pressure. Getty engineers designed and produced a pressure vessel, called a fluid booster, that was to be installed to increase pressure in the system. Robinson, a Getty engineer, was instructed to install the vessel. Robinson picked up the vessel from the welding shop without having it tested. After he completed the installation, the pressure valve was put into operation. When the pressure increased from 300 to 930 pounds per square inch, an explosion occurred. Robinson died from the explosion, and another Getty employee was seriously injured. The secretary of labor issued a citation against Getty for violating the general duty provision for worker safety contained in the Occupational Safety and Health Act. Getty challenged the citation. Who wins? [*Getty Oil Company v. Occupational Safety and Health Review Commission*, 530 F.2d 1143, 1976 U.S. App. Lexis 11640 (5th Cir. 1976)]

34.8 ERISA   United Artists is a Maryland corporation doing business in the state of Texas. United Pension Fund (Plan) is a defined-contribution, employee pension-benefit plan sponsored by United Artists for its employees. Each employee has his or her own individual pension account, but Plan assets are pooled for investment purposes. The Plan is administered by a board of trustees. During the period 1977 through 1986, seven of the trustees caused the Plan to make a series of loans to themselves. The trustees did not (1) require the borrowers to submit written applications for the subject loans, (2) assess the prospective borrowers' ability to repay the loans, (3) specify a period in which the loans were to be repaid, or (4) call the loans when they remained unpaid. The trustees also charged less than fair-market-value interest rates for the loans. The secretary of labor sued the trustees, alleging that they breached their fiduciary duty in

violation of ERISA. Who wins? [*McLaughlin v. Rowley*, 698 F.Supp. 1333, 1988 U.S. Dist. 12674 (N.D. Tex. 1988)]

34.9 Unemployment Benefits   Devon Overstreet worked as a bus driver for the Chicago Transit Authority (CTA) for more than six years. She took a sick leave from January 30 to March 15, 1985. Because she had been on sick leave for more than seven days, the CTA required her to take a medical examination. The blood and urine analysis indicated the presence of cocaine. A second test confirmed this finding. On March 20, 1985, the CTA suspended her and placed her in the Employee's Assistance Program for substance abuse for not less than 30 days, with a chance of reassignment to a nonoperating job if she successfully completed the program. The program is an alternative to discharge and is available at the election of the employee. Overstreet filed for unemployment compensation benefits. The CTA contested her claim. Who wins? [*Overstreet v. Illinois Department of Employment Security*, 522 N.E.2d 185, 1988 Ill.App. Lexis 269 (Ill. App. 1988)]

34.10 Plant Closing Act   Arrow Automotive Industries, Inc. (Arrow), is engaged in the remanufacture and distribution of automobile and truck parts. All of its operating plants produce identical product lines. Arrow is planning to open a new facility in Santa Maria, California. The employees at the Arrow plant in Hudson, Massachusetts, are represented by the United Automobile, Aerospace, and Agricultural Implement Workers of America (Union). The Hudson plant has a history of unprofitable operations. The union called a strike when the existing collective bargaining agreement expired and a new agreement could not be reached. After several months, the board of directors of the company voted to close the striking plant. The closing gave Arrow a 24 percent increase in gross profits and freed capital and equipment for the new Santa Maria plant. In addition, the existing customers of the Hudson plant could be serviced by the Spartanburg plant, which was at that time being underutilized. What would have to be done if the Plant Closing Act applied to this situation? [*Arrow Automotive Industries, Inc., v. N.L.R.B.*, 853 F.2d 223, 1988 U.S. App. Lexis 10091 (4th Cir. 1988)]

Business Ethics Cases

34.11 Business Ethics   Whirlpool Corporation operates a manufacturing plant in Marion, Ohio, for the production of household appliances. Overhead conveyors transport appliance components throughout the plant. To protect employees from objects that occasionally fall from the conveyors, Whirlpool installed a horizontal wire-mesh guard screen approximately 20 feet above the plant floor. The mesh screen is welded to angle-iron frames suspended from the building's structural steel skeleton.

Maintenance employees spend several hours each week removing objects from the screen, replacing paper spread on the screen to catch grease drippings from the materials on the conveyors, and performing occasional maintenance work on the conveyors. To perform these duties, maintenance employees are usually able to stand on the iron frames, but sometimes they find it necessary to step onto the steel-mesh screen itself. Several employees have fallen partly through the screen. On June 28, 1974, a maintenance employee fell to his death through the guard screen.

On July 7, 1974, two maintenance employees, Virgil Deemer and Thomas Cornwell, met with the plant supervisor to voice their concern about the safety of the screen. Unsatisfied with the supervisor's response, on July 9 they met with the plant safety director and voiced similar concerns. When they asked him for the name, address, and telephone number of the local OSHA office, he told them they "had better stop and think about" what they were doing. The safety director then furnished them with the requested information, and later that day one of the men contacted the regional OSHA office and discussed the guard screen.

The next day, Deemer and Cornwell reported for the night shift at 10:45 P.M. Their foreman directed the two men to perform their usual maintenance duties on a section of the screen. Claiming that the screen was unsafe, they refused to carry out the directive. The foreman sent them to the personnel office, where they were ordered to punch out without working or being paid for the remaining six hours of the shift. The two men subsequently received written reprimands, which were placed in their employment files.

The secretary of labor filed suit, alleging that Whirlpool's actions constituted discrimination against the two men in violation of the Occupational Safety and Health Act. Did Whirlpool act ethically in this case? Can employees engage in self-help in certain circumstances under OSHA regulations? [*Whirlpool Corporation v. Marshall, Secretary of Labor*, 445 U.S. 1, 100 S.Ct. 883, 1980 U.S. Lexis 81 (1980)]

34.12 Business Ethics On April 23, 1971, the International Association of Machinists and Aerospace Workers, AFL-CIO (Union), began soliciting the employees of Whitcraft Houseboat Division to organize a union. On April 26, 27, and 28, Whitcraft management dispersed congregating groups of employees. During these three days, production was down almost 50 percent. On April 28, Whitcraft adopted the following no-solicitation rule and mailed a copy to each employee and posted it around the workplace:

As you well know working time is for work. No one will be allowed to solicit or distribute literature during our working time, that is, when he or she should be working. Anyone doing so and neglecting his work or interfering with the work of another employee will be subject to discharge.

On April 30, a manager of Whitcraft found that two employees of the company were engaged in union solicitation during working hours in a working area. The company discharged them for violating the no-solicitation rule. Was their discharge lawful? Did the company act ethically in discharging the employees? [*Whitcraft Houseboat Division, North American Rockwell Corporation v. International Association of Machinists and Aerospace Workers, AFL-CIO*, 195 N.L.R.B. 1046 (1972)]

Briefing the Case Writing Assignment

Read Case A.34 in the Case Appendix [*Wiljef Transportation, Inc. v. National Labor Relations Board*]. This case is excerpted from the court of appeals opinion. Review and brief the case. In your brief, be sure to answer the following questions.

1. Who was the plaintiff? Who was the defendant?

2. What did the defendant do that caused the plaintiff to file this action?

3. What is an unfair labor practice?

4. Did the court find an unfair labor practice in this case?

Endnotes

1. 29 U.S.C. §§ 101–110, and 113–115.
2. 29 U.S.C. §§ 151–169.
3. 29 U.S.C. §§ 141 et seq.
4. 29 U.S.C. §§ 401 *et seq.*
5. 45 U.S.C. §§ 151–162, and 181–188.
6. Section 7 of the NLRA provides that employees shall have the right to self-organization; to form, join, or assist labor organizations; to bargain collectively through representatives of their own choosing; and to engage in other concerted activities for the purpose of collective bargaining or other mutual aid protection.
7. 29 U.S.C. §§ 553, and 651–678.

8. For example, the Railway Safety Act and the Coal Mine Safety Act regulate workplace safety of railway workers and coal miners, respectively.
9. 29 U.S.C. §§ 201–206.
10. 29 U.S.C. §§ 2601, 2611–2619, and 2651–2654.
11. 26 U.S.C. §§ 1161–1169.
12. 29 U.S.C. §§ 1001 *et seq.*
13. 29 U.S.C. § 1802.
14. 8 U.S.C. §§ 1101 *et seq.*
15. 26 U.S.C. §§ 3301–3310.
16. 26 U.S.C. §§ 3101–3125.
17. 26 U.S.C. §§ 1401–1403.

Equal Opportunity in Employment

35

> "What people have always sought is equality of rights before the law. For rights that were not open to all equally would not be rights."
>
> —Cicero (106–43 B.C.)
> De officilis, Bk. II. Ch. XII

Chapter Objectives

After studying this chapter, you should be able to:

1. Describe the scope of coverage of Title VII of the Civil Rights Act of 1964.

2. Identify race, color, and national origin discrimination that violates Title VII.

3. Identify sex discrimination—including sexual harassment—that violates Title VII.

4. Describe the scope of coverage of the Age Discrimination in Employment Act.

5. Describe the protections afforded by the Americans with Disabilities Act of 1990.

Chapter Contents

- Equal Employment Opportunity Commission (EEOC)
- Title VII of the Civil Rights Act of 1964
- Equal Pay Act of 1963
- Age Discrimination in Employment Act of 1967
- Americans with Disabilities Act of 1990
- Affirmative Action
- State and Local Government Antidiscrimination Laws

Under common law, employers could terminate an employee at any time and for whatever reason. In this same vein, employers were free to hire and promote anyone they chose without violating the law. This often created unreasonable hardship on employees and erected employment barriers to certain minority classes.

Starting in the 1960s, Congress began enacting a comprehensive set of federal laws that eliminated major forms of employment discrimination. These laws, which were passed to guarantee **equal employment opportunity** to all employees and job applicants, have been broadly interpreted by the federal courts, particularly the U.S. Supreme Court. States have also enacted antidiscrimination laws.

This chapter discusses federal and state equal opportunity in employment laws.

Equal Employment Opportunity Commission (EEOC)

The **Equal Employment Opportunity Commission (EEOC)** is the federal agency responsible for enforcing most federal antidiscrimination laws. The members of the EEOC are appointed by the U.S. president. The EEOC is empowered to conduct investigations, interpret the statutes, encourage conciliation between employees and employers, and bring suit to enforce the law. The EEOC can also seek injunctive relief.

Title VII of the Civil Rights Act of 1964

> Racial discrimination in any form and in any degree has no justifiable part whatever in our democratic way of life. It is unattractive in any setting but it is utterly revolting among a free people who have embraced the principles set forth in the Constitution of the United States.
>
> Murphy, J., dissenting opinion
> *Korematsu v. U.S. (1944)*

After substantial debate, Congress enacted the **Civil Rights Act of 1964**. **Title VII of the Civil Rights Act of 1964** (called the **Fair Employment Practices Act**) was intended to eliminate job discrimination based on the following *protected classes: (1) race, (2) color, (3) national origin, (4) sex, and (5) religion.*

As amended by the **Equal Employment Opportunity Act of 1972**, Section 703(a)(2) of Title VII provides in pertinent part that

> It shall be an unlawful employment practice for an employer
>
> (1) to fail or refuse to hire or to discharge any individual, or otherwise to discriminate against any individual with respect to his compensation, terms, conditions, or privileges of employment, because of such individual's race, color, religion, sex, or national origin; or
>
> (2) to limit, segregate, or classify his employees or applicants for employment in any way which would deprive or tend to deprive any individual of employment opportunities or otherwise adversely affect his status as an employee, because of such individual's race, color, religion, sex, or national origin.

Scope of Coverage of Title VII

Title VII of the Civil Rights Act of 1964, also called the **Fair Employment Practices Act**, applies to (1) employers with 15 or more employees, (2) all employment agencies, (3) labor unions with 15 or more members, (4) state and local governments and their agencies, and (5) most federal government employment. Indian tribes and tax-exempt private clubs are expressly excluded from coverage.[1]

Title VII prohibits discrimination in hiring, decisions regarding promotion or demotion, payment of compensation and fringe benefits, availability of job training and apprenticeship opportunities, referral systems for employment, decisions regarding dismissal, work rules, and any other *"term, condition, or privilege"* of employment. Any employee of covered employers, including undocumented aliens,[2] may bring actions for employment discrimination under Title VII.

Business Brief

Title VII applies to any term, condition, or privilege of employment, including but not limited to hiring, firing, promotion, and payment of fringe benefits decisions.

Forms of Title VII Actions

Title VII prohibits the following forms of employment discrimination based on any of the five prohibited factors listed previously:

1. *Disparate-treatment discrimination.* **Disparate-treatment discrimination** occurs when an employer treats a specific *individual* less favorably than others because of that person's race, color, national origin, sex, or religion. In such situations, the complainant must prove that (1) he or she belongs to a Title VII protected class, (2) he or she applied for and was qualified for the employment position, (3) he or she was rejected despite this, and (4) the employer kept the position open and sought applicants from persons with the complainant's qualifications.[3]

   Consider This Example   A member of a minority race applies for a promotion to a position advertised as available at his company. The minority applicant, who is qualified for the position, is rejected by the company, which hires a non-minority applicant for the position. The minority applicant sues under Title VII. He has a *prima facie* case of illegal discrimination. The burden of proof shifts to the employer to prove a nondiscriminatory reason for its decision. If the employer offers a reason, such as saying that the minority applicant lacked sufficient experience, the burden shifts back to the minority applicant to prove that this was just a *pretext* (not the real reason) for the employer's decision.

2. *Disparate-impact discrimination.* **Disparate-impact discrimination** occurs when an employer discriminates against an entire protected *class*. Many disparate-impact cases are brought as class action lawsuits. Often, this type of discrimination is proven through statistical data about the employer's employment practices. The plaintiff must demonstrate a *causal link* between the challenged practice and the statistical imbalance. Showing a statistical disparity between the percentage of protected class employees versus the percentage of the population that the protected class makes within the surrounding community is not enough, by itself, to prove discrimination.

   Consider This Example   Disparate-impact discrimination occurs when an employer adopts a work rule that is neutral on its face but is shown to cause an adverse impact on a protected class. If an employer has a rule that all applicants for a position of executive must be at least 5'8" tall, this looks like a neutral rule because it applies to both males and females. However, because this rule is unrelated to the performance of an executive position and eliminates many more females than males from being hired or promoted to an executive position, it is disparate-impact sex discrimination in violation of Title VII.

Procedure for Bringing a Title VII Action

To bring an action under Title VII, a private complainant must first file a complaint with the EEOC.[4] The EEOC is given the opportunity to sue the employer on the complainant's behalf. If the EEOC chooses not to bring suit, it will issue a *right to sue letter* to the complainant. This gives the complainant the right to sue the employer.

Remedies for Violations of Title VII

A successful plaintiff in a Title VII action can recover back pay and reasonable attorneys' fees. The courts also have broad authority to grant equitable remedies. For instance, the courts can order reinstatement, grant fictional seniority, and issue injunctions to compel the hiring or promotion of protected minorities.

God . . . hath made of one blood all nations of men for to dwell on the face of the earth.

Bible, Acts 17:26

Business Brief

As originally proposed, sex discrimination was not included in Title VII. The amendment (Equal Employment Opportunity Act), designed to kill the entire legislation, backfired when the Civil Rights Act of 1964 passed.

In a case involving intentional discrimination, the aggrieved party can recover compensatory damages. A court can award punitive damages against an employer in a case involving an employer's malice or reckless indifference to federally protected rights. The sum of compensatory and punitive damages is capped at up to $50,000 for employers with 100 or fewer employees, $100,000 for employers with 101 to 200 employees, $200,000 for employers with 201 to 500 employees, and $300,000 for employers with more than 500 employees.

Race, Color, and National Origin Discrimination

Rights matter most when they are claimed by unpopular minorities.

Michael Kirby, J.
Sydney Morning Herald, November 30, 1985

Title VII of the Civil Rights Act of 1964 was primarily enacted to prohibit employment discrimination based on *race, color, and national origin*. *Race* refers to broad categories such as black, Caucasian, Asian, and Native American. *Color* refers to the color of a person's skin. *National origin* refers to the country of a person's ancestors or cultural characteristics.

The following case demonstrates race discrimination.

National Association for the Advancement of Colored People, Newark Branch v. Town of Harrison, New Jersey

Case 35.1
Race Discrimination

907 F.2d 1408, 1990 U.S. App. Lexis 11793 (1990)
United States Court of Appeals, Third Circuit

Background and Facts

The town of Harrison, New Jersey (Harrison), adopted Ordinance 747, which stipulated that "all officers and employees of the Town shall, as a condition of employment, be bona fide residents of the Town." Because of the implementation of this ordinance for years, none of the 51 police officers, 55 firefighters, or 80 nonuniformed employees of the town were black. Although Harrison is a small primarily white community located in Hudson County, New Jersey, it is clearly aligned with Essex County to the west and is considered an extension of the city of Newark, which it abuts. Adjacent counties are within an easy commute of Harrison. Only 0.2 percent of Harrison's population is black. Several blacks who were members of the National Association for the Advancement of Colored People, Newark Branch (NAACP) applied for employment with Harrison but were rejected because they did not meet the residency requirement. The NAACP sued Harrison for race discrimination in violation of Title VII. The U.S. District Court dismissed the plaintiff's complaint. The NAACP appealed.

Issue

Does the residency requirement of the town of Harrison violate Title VII of the Civil Rights Act of 1964?

Court's Reasoning

The court noted that Harrison's geographical location and transportation facilities allowed the town to be viewed as a functional component of the city of Newark and a part of Essex County. Newark's population is approximately 60 percent black. Essex County's civilian labor force is 33.3 percent black. Of the persons employed by private industry, 22.1 percent are black. Because so few black persons live in Harrison, most of these persons must have commuted from elsewhere in the labor market that serves Harrison. The court held that the otherwise socially neutral employment rule caused an adverse impact on blacks and therefore constituted race discrimination in violation of Title VII.

Decision and Remedy

The court held that the plaintiffs had established that the ordinance constituted disparate-impact race discrimination in violation of Title VII of the Civil Rights Act of 1964. The court issued an injunction against enforcement of the ordinance.

Case Questions

Critical Legal Thinking   Would the same residency requirement rule cause disparate impact discrimination if it were adopted by New York City or Los Angeles? Explain.

Business Ethics   Did the town of Harrison act ethically when it adopted the residency requirements?

Contemporary Business   Could a private business impose a residency requirement on its employees?

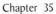

Jin, Santa Monica, California.
Title VII guarantees equal opportunity in employment based on sex, race, national origin, color, and religion.

Sex Discrimination

Although the prohibition against **sex discrimination** applies equally to men and women, the overwhelming majority of Title VII sex discrimination cases are brought by women. The old airline practice of ignoring the marital status of male flight attendants but hiring only single female flight attendants is an example of such discrimination.

In 1978, the **Pregnancy Discrimination Act** was enacted as an amendment to Title VII.[5] This amendment forbids employment discrimination because of "pregnancy, childbirth, or related medical conditions." Thus, a work rule that prohibits the hiring of pregnant women violates Title VII.

In the following case, the court found sex discrimination in violation of Title VII.

Barbano v. Madison County
922 F.2d 139, 1990 U.S. App. Lexis 22494 (1990)
United States Court of Appeals, Second Circuit

Case 35.2
Sex Discrimination

Background and Facts
In February 1980, the position of director of the Madison County Veterans Service Agency became vacant. The Madison County Board of Supervisors (Board) appointed a committee of five men to hold interviews. Maureen E. Barbano applied for the position and was interviewed by the committee. Upon entering the interview, Barbano heard someone say, "Oh, another woman." When the interview began, Donald Greene, a committee member, said he would not consider "some woman" for the position. He then asked Barbano personal questions about her plans on having a family and whether her husband would object to her transporting male veter-

ans. Barbano said the questions were irrelevant and discriminatory. No committee member asked Barbano any substantive questions. Ultimately, the Board acted on the committee's recommendation and hired a male candidate. Barbano sued Madison County for sex discrimination in violation of Title VII. The district court held in favor of Barbano and awarded her $55,000 in back pay, prejudgment interest, and attorneys' fees. Madison County appealed.

Issue
Did the defendant engage in sex discrimination in violation of Title VII?

Barbano v. Madison County

922 F.2d 139, 1990 U.S. App. Lexis 22494 (1990)
United States Court of Appeals, Second Circuit
(continued)

Court's Reasoning

The Court of Appeals held that the record supported a finding that the committee and Board engaged in sex discrimination against Barbano in making the hiring decision. The Court of Appeals held that the questions asked of Barbano were unrelated to a bona fide occupational qualification and that Greene's questions were discriminatory and tainted the decision process.

Decision and Remedy

The Court of Appeals held that the defendant, Madison County, had engaged in sex discrimination in violation of Title VII. The

Court of Appeals affirmed the district court's decision and award of damages to plaintiff Barbano.

Case Questions

Critical Legal Thinking   Why are questions concerning family obligations made illegal by Title VII?

Business Ethics   Was Greene's conduct morally reprehensible?

Contemporary Business   What actions should employers take to make sure their interviewers and other personnel understand Title VII and other antidiscrimination laws?

Sexual Harassment

In the modern work environment, coworkers sometimes become sexually interested or involved with each other voluntarily. On other occasions, though, a coworker's sexual advances are not welcome.

Refusing to hire or promote someone unless he or she has sex with the manager or supervisor is sex discrimination that violates Title VII. Other forms of conduct, such as lewd remarks, touching, intimidation, posting of indecent materials and other verbal or physical conduct of a sexual nature, constitute **sexual harassment** and violate Title VII.[6]

To determine what conduct creates a hostile work environment, the Supreme Court stated:

> We can say that whether an environment is "hostile" or "abusive" can be determined only by looking at all the circumstances. These may include the frequency of the discriminatory conduct; its severity; whether it is physically threatening or humiliating, or a mere offensive utterance; and whether it unreasonably interferes with an employee's work performance.[7]

In the following case, the U.S. Supreme Court decided that the challenged conduct created a hostile work environment.

Business Brief

To prevent future lawsuits, employers should be fully aware of federal and state equal employment opportunity laws and implement policies and procedures to adhere to them.

U.S. SUPREME COURT CASE

Harris v. Forklift Systems, Inc.

510 U.S. 17, 114 S.Ct. 367, 1993 U.S. Lexis 7155 (1993)
Supreme Court of the United States

Case 35.3
Sexual Harassment

Background and Facts

Teresa Harris worked as a manager at Forklift Systems, Inc. (Forklift), an equipment rental company, from April 1985 until October 1987. Charles Hardy was Forklift's president. Throughout Harris's time at Forklift, Hardy often insulted her because of her sex and made her the target of unwanted sexual innuendos. Hardy told Harris on several occasions, in the presence of other employees, "You're a woman, what do you know"

and "We need a man as the rental manager"; at least once, he told her she was "a dumb ass woman." Again in front of others, he suggested that the two of them "go to the Holiday Inn to negotiate Harris's raise." He made sexual innuendos about Harris's and other women's clothing.

In mid-August 1987, Harris complained to Hardy about his conduct. Hardy said he was surprised that Harris was offended, claimed he was only joking, and apologized. He also promised he would stop, and based on this assurance, Harris stayed on the job. But in early September, Hardy began anew: While Harris was arranging a deal with one of Forklift's customers, he asked her, again in front of other employees, "What did you do, promise the guy some sex Saturday night?" On October 1, Harris collected her paycheck and quit.

Harris then sued Forklift, claiming that Hardy's conduct had created an abusive work environment for her because of her gender. The district court held that because Harris had not suffered severe psychological injury, she could not recover. The court of appeals affirmed. Harris appealed to the U.S. Supreme Court.

Issue

Must conduct, to be actionable as abusive work environment harassment, seriously affect the victim's psychological well-being?

Court's Reasoning

The U.S. Supreme Court noted that Title VII certainly bars conduct that would seriously affect a reasonable person's psychological well-being but that the statute was not just limited to such conduct. The Supreme Court held that as long as the work environment would reasonably be perceived as hostile or abusive, there was no need for it also to be psychologically injurious. The Supreme Court stated:

When the workplace is permeated with discriminatory intimidation, ridicule, and insult, that is sufficiently severe or pervasive to alter the conditions of the victim's employment and create an abusive working environment, Title VII is violated. The very fact that the discriminatory conduct was so severe or pervasive that it created a work environment abusive to employees because of their race, gender, religion, or national origin, offends Title VII's broad rule of workplace equality.

Decision and Remedy

The Supreme Court held that Title VII does not require a victim to prove that the challenged conduct seriously affected her psychological well-being. The Supreme Court reversed the decision of the court of appeals and remanded the case to the district court for trial.

Case Questions

Critical Legal Thinking   Should an employer be held liable for sexual harassment committed by one of its employees?

Business Ethics   What penalty should be assessed against Hardy for his conduct?

Contemporary Business   How can businesses eliminate sexual harassment on the job?

Same-Sex Discrimination

For years, it was unclear whether same-sex sexual harassment and sex discrimination in employment were actionable under Title VII. In 1998, in *Omcale v. Sundowner Offshore Services, Incorporated*,[8] the U.S. Supreme Court held that same-sex discrimination and harassment violated Title VII. Many state and local antidiscrimination laws outlaw same-sex discrimination and harassment in the workplace.

Business Brief

Same-sex employment discrimination and harassment violate Title VII.

Contemporary Environment
Affirmative Defense in Sexual Harassment Cases

In two cases, *Faragher v. City of Boca Raton* and *Burlington Industries, Inc. v. Ellerth*, female plaintiffs sued their employers, proving that their supervisors had engaged in unconsented physical touching and verbal sexual harassment. In both cases, the female employee quit her job and sued her employer for sexual harassment in violation of Title VII. In the first case, the employer had never disseminated a policy against sexual harassment to its employees. In the second case, the employer had disseminated its policy against sexual harassment to its employees and had put into place a complaint system that was not used by the female employee. After trials and appeals, the U.S. Supreme Court accepted these two cases for review.

The U.S. Supreme Court, in these two decisions, held that an employer is not strictly liable for sexual harassment. The Supreme Court held that an employer may raise an *affirmative defense* against liability by proving two elements:

1. The employer exercised reasonable care to prevent, and promptly correct, any sexual-harassing behavior.
2. The plaintiff employee unreasonably failed to take advantage of any preventive or corrective opportunities provided by the employer or to otherwise avoid harm.

The defendant employer has the burden of proving this affirmative defense. In determining whether the defense has been proven, a court must consider (1) whether the employer has an antiharassing policy, (2) whether the employer had a complaint mechanism in place, (3) whether employees were informed of the antiharassment policy and complaint procedure, and (4) other factors that the court deems relevant. [*Faragher v. City of Boca Raton*, 524 U.S. 775, 118 S.Ct. 2275, 1998 U.S. Lexis 4216 (1998); *Burlington Industries, Inc. v. Ellerth*, 524 U.S. 742, 118 S.Ct. 2257, 1998 U.S. Lexis 4217 (1998)] ■

Online Commerce & Internet Law
E-Mail Can Create a Hostile Work Environment

The use of e-mail in business has dramatically increased efficiency and information sharing among employees. E-mail often sets the social tone of an office. At some point, however, e-mail can become actionable sexual or racial harassment. The standard of whether e-mail creates an illegal hostile work environment is the same as that for measuring harassment in any other context. The offensive conduct must be severe and not isolated or trivial remarks and incidents.

E-mail differs from many other incidents of harassment because it is subtle and insidious. Unlike with paper pin-up calendars in plain view, an employer does not readily see e-mail messages. Obscenity pulled off the Internet or scanned into a computer can be sent as an attachment to an e-mail message. Because e-mail is hidden, to detect offensive messages, an employer must take action to review e-mail messages on its network. Courts have generally held that an employee does not have an expectation of privacy of e-mail. Stored e-mail is the property of the employer, which may review it freely. Employers can also use software to scan and filter e-mail messages that contain any of a predefined list of objectionable words or phrases or certain "to" or "from" headers. Employers can also use software programs to scan graphics and block X-rated pictures.

E-mail has increased the possibility of there being sexual or racial harassment on the job. Therefore, employers must adopt policies pertaining to the use of e-mail by their employees and make their employees aware that certain e-mail messages constitute sexual or racial harassment and violate the law. ■

Religious Discrimination

Title VII prohibits employment discrimination based on a person's religion. Religions include traditional religions, other religions that recognize a supreme being, and religions based on ethical or spiritual tenets. Many **religious discrimination** cases involve a conflict between an employer's work rule and an employee's religious beliefs (e.g., when an employee is required to work on his or her religious holiday).

The right of an employee to practice his or her religion is not absolute. Under Title VII, an employer is under a duty to *reasonably accommodate* the religious observances, practices, or beliefs of its employees if doing so does not cause an *undue hardship* on the employer. The courts must apply these general standards to specific fact situations. In making their decisions, the courts must consider such factors as the size of the employer, the importance of the employee's position, and the availability of alternative workers.

Title VII expressly permits religious organizations to give preference in employment to individuals of a particular religion. For example, if a person applies for a job with a reli-

Ethics Brief

Employers owe a duty to *reasonably accommodate* an employee's religious practices, observances, or beliefs if doing so does not cause *undue hardship* to the employer.

Vietnam. In some countries, females do not have equality of rights under the law, as provided in the United States and other countries.

gious organization but does not subscribe to its religious tenets, the organization may refuse to hire that person.

Defenses to a Title VII Action

Title VII and case law recognize the following defenses to a charge of discrimination under Title VII:

- **Merit.** Employers can select or promote employees based on *merit*. Merit decisions are often based on work, educational experience, and professionally developed ability tests. To be lawful under Title VII, the requirement must be job related. For example, requiring a person to pass a typing test to be hired as a typist would be lawful. Requiring a person to pass a college-level English composition test to be employed as a maintenance worker would violate Title VII.

- **Seniority.** Many employers maintain *seniority* systems that reward long-term employees. Higher wages, fringe benefits, and other preferential treatment (e.g., choice of working hours and vacation schedule) are examples of such rewards. Seniority systems provide an incentive for employees to stay with the company. Such systems are lawful if they are not the result of intentional discrimination.

- **Bona Fide Occupational Qualification (BFOQ).** Discrimination based on protected classes (other than race or color) is permitted if it is shown to be a **bona fide occupational qualification (BFOQ)**. To be legal, a BFOQ must be both *job related* and a *business necessity*. For example, allowing only women to be locker room attendants in a women's gym is a valid BFOQ, but prohibiting males from being managers or instructors at the same gym would not be a BFOQ.

As the following U.S. Supreme Court case shows, BFOQ exceptions are narrowly interpreted by the courts.

U.S. SUPREME COURT CASE

International Union, United Automobile, Aerospace and Agricultural Implement Workers of America, UAW v. Johnson Controls, Inc.

499 U.S. 187, 111 S.Ct. 1196, 1991 U.S. Lexis 1715 (1991)
Supreme Court of the United States

Case 35.4
Bona Fide Occupational Qualification

Background and Facts

Johnson Controls, Inc. (Johnson Controls), manufacturers batteries. Lead is the primary ingredient in the manufacturing process. Exposure to lead entails health risks, including risk of harm to any fetus carried by a female employee. To protect unborn children from such risk, Johnson Controls adopted an employment rule that prevented pregnant women and women of childbearing age from working at jobs involving lead exposure. Only women who were sterilized or could prove they could not have children were not affected by the rule. Consequently, most female employees were relegated to lower-paying clerical jobs at the company. Several female employees filed a class action suit, challenging Johnson Controls's fetal-protection policy as sex discrimination in violation of Title VII. The district court held that the policy was justified as a bona fide occupational qualification (BFOQ) and granted summary judgment to Johnson Controls, and

the court of appeals affirmed. The plaintiffs appealed to the U.S. Supreme Court.

Issue

Is Johnson Controls's fetal protection policy a BFOQ?

Court's Reasoning

The U.S. Supreme Court found that Johnson Controls's policy created a bias: Fertile men—but not fertile women—were given a choice as to whether they wished to risk their reproductive health for a particular job. Despite evidence about the debilitating effect of lead exposure on the male reproductive system, Johnson Controls was only concerned with the harms that may befall the unborn offspring of its female employees. The Supreme Court stated, "Johnson Controls' professed moral and ethical concerns about the welfare of the next generation do not suffice to establish a BFOQ of female sterility. Decisions about the welfare of future

International Union, United Automobile, Aerospace and Agricultural Implement Workers of America, UAW v. Johnson Controls, Inc.

499 U.S. 187, 111 S.Ct. 1196, 1991 U.S. Lexis 1715 (1991)
Supreme Court of the United States
(continued)

children must be left to the parents who conceive, bear, support, and raise them rather than to the employers who hire those parents."

Decision and Remedy

The U.S. Supreme Court held that Johnson Controls's fetal protection policy was not a BFOQ. Instead, it was sex discrimination in violation of Title VII. The Supreme Court reversed the decision of the court of appeals and remanded the case for further proceedings.

Case Questions

Critical Legal Thinking   Should any BFOQ exceptions to Title VII actions be permitted? Why or why not?

Business Ethics   Should Johnson Controls's moral and ethical concerns about the welfare of the next generation justify its actions?

Contemporary Business   Does Johnson Controls have any tort liability to children who are born injured by exposure to lead? How can Johnson Controls limit such liability?

■ *Concept Summary* **Title VII of the Civil Rights Act of 1964**

Covered employers and employment decisions	1. **Employers.** Employers with 15 or more employees for 20 weeks in the current or preceding year, all employment agencies, labor unions with 15 or more members, state and local governments, and most federal agencies. 2. **Employment decisions.** Decisions regarding hiring; promotion; demotion; payment of salaries, wages, and fringe benefits; dismissal; job training and apprenticeships; work rules; or any other *term*, *condition*, or *privilege* of employment. Decisions to admit partners to a partnership are also covered.
Protected classes	1. **Race.** A broad class of individuals with common characteristics (e.g., black, Caucasian, Asian, Native American). 2. **Color.** The color of a person's skin (e.g., light-skinned person, dark-skinned person). 3. **National origin.** A person's country of origin or national heritage (e.g., Italian, Hispanic). 4. **Sex.** A person's sex, whether male or female. Includes sexual harassment and discrimination against females who are pregnant. 5. **Religion.** A person's religious beliefs. An employer has a duty to reasonably accommodate an employee's religious beliefs if doing so does not cause an undue hardship on the employer.
Types of discrimination	1. **Disparate-treatment discrimination.** Discrimination against a specific individual because that person belongs to a protected class. 2. **Disparate-impact discrimination.** Discrimination in which an employer discriminates against a protected class. This is a neutral-looking employment rule that causes discrimination against a protected class is disparate-impact discrimination.
Defenses	1. **Merit.** Job-related experience, education, or unbiased employment test. 2. **Seniority.** Length of time an employee has been employed by the employer. Intentional discrimination based on seniority is unlawful. 3. **Bona fide occupational qualification (BFOQ).** Discrimination based on sex, religion, or national origin is permitted if it is a valid BFOQ for the position. Qualification based on race or color is not a permissible BFOQ.
Remedies	1. The court may order the payment of back pay, issue an injunction awarding reinstatement, grant fictional seniority, or order some other equitable remedy. 2. The court can award compensatory damages in cases of intentional discrimination. The court can award punitive damages in cases involving an employer's malice or reckless indifference to federally protected rights.

Civil Rights Act of 1866

The **Civil Rights Act of 1866** was enacted after the Civil War. **Section 1981** of this act states that all persons "have the same right . . . to make and enforce contracts . . . as is enjoyed by white persons" [42 U.S.C. § 1981]. This law was enacted to give African-Americans, just freed from slavery, the same right to contract as caucasions. Section 1981 expressly prohibits racial discrimination; it has also been held to forbid discrimination based on national origin.

Employment decisions are covered by Section 1981 because the employment relationship is contractual. Although most racial and national origin employment discrimination cases are brought under Title VII, there are two reasons that a complainant would bring the action under Section 1981: (1) A private plaintiff can bring an action without going through the procedural requirements of Title VII, and (2) there is no cap on the recovery of compensatory or punitive damages.

Equal Pay Act of 1963

Discrimination often takes the form of different pay scales for men and women performing the same job. The **Equal Pay Act of 1963** protects both sexes from pay discrimination based on sex.[9] This act covers all levels of private-sector employees and state and local government employees. Federal workers are not covered, however.

The act prohibits disparity in pay for jobs that require *equal skill* (i.e., equal experience), *equal effort* (i.e., mental and physical exertion), *equal responsibility* (i.e., equal supervision and accountability), or *similar working conditions* (e.g., dangers of injury, exposure to the elements). To make this determination, the courts examine the actual requirements of jobs to determine whether they are equal and similar. If two jobs are determined to be equal and similar, an employer cannot pay disparate wages to members of different sexes.

Employees can bring a private cause of action against an employer for violating the act. Back pay and liquidated damages are recoverable. In addition, the employer must increase the wages of the discriminated-against employee to eliminate the unlawful disparity of wages. The wages of other employees may not be lowered.

> By what justice can an association of citizens be held together when there is no equality among the citizens?
>
> Cicero
> *De Re Publia De Legibus J XXXII 49*

Criteria That Justify a Differential in Wages

The Equal Pay Act expressly provides four criteria that justify a differential in wages. These defenses include payment systems that are based on

- **Seniority**
- **Merit** (as long as there is some identifiable measurement standard)
- **Quantity or quality of product** (commission, piecework, or quality-control–based payment systems are permitted)
- **"Any factor other than sex"** (including shift differentials, i.e., night versus day shifts)

The employer bears the burden of proving these defenses.

Business Brief

The Equal Pay Act expressly provides four criteria that justify a differential in wages. The employer bears the burden of proving these defenses.

Age Discrimination in Employment Act of 1967

Some employers have discriminated against employees and prospective employees based on their age. Primarily, employers have often refused to hire older workers. The **Age Discrimination in Employment Act (ADEA)**, which prohibits certain *age discrimination* practices, was enacted in 1967.[10]

The ADEA covers nonfederal employers with at least 20 employees, labor unions with at least 25 members, and all employment agencies. State and local government employees except those in policy-making positions are covered, as are employees of certain sectors of the federal government.

The ADEA prohibits age discrimination in all employment decisions, including hiring, promotions, payment of compensation, and other terms and conditions of employment. The **Older Workers Benefit Protection Act (OWBPA)** amended the ADEA to prohibit age discrimination with regard to employee benefits. Employers cannot use employment advertisements that discriminate against applicants covered by the ADEA. The same defenses that are available in a Title VII action are also available in an ADEA action.

Protected Age Categories

Business Brief

Originally, the ADEA protected employees from ages 40 to 65 only. The act has been amended to protect employees who are 40 and older.

Originally, the ADEA prohibited employment discrimination against persons between the ages of 40 and 65. In 1978, its coverage was extended to persons up to the age of 70. Further amendments completely eliminated an age ceiling, so the ADEA now applies to employees who are 40 and older. As a result, covered employers cannot establish mandatory retirement ages for their employees.

Because persons under 40 are not protected by the ADEA, an employer can maintain an employment policy of hiring only workers who are 40 years of age or older without violating the ADEA. However, the employer could not maintain an employment practice whereby it hired only persons 50 years of age and older because it would discriminate against persons aged 40 to 49.

The ADEA is administered by the EEOC. Private plaintiffs can also sue under the ADEA. A successful plaintiff in an ADEA action can recover back wages, attorney's fees, and equitable relief, including hiring, reinstatement, and promotion. Where a violation of the ADEA is found, the employer must raise the wages of the discriminated-against employee. It cannot lower the wages of other employees.

The following U.S. Supreme Court case raises the issue of age discrimination.

U.S. SUPREME COURT CASE

Reeves v. Sanderson Plumbing Products, Inc.

530 U.S. 133, 120 S.Ct. 2097,
2000 U.S. Lexis 3966 (2000)
Supreme Court of the United States

Case 35.5
Age Discrimination

Background and Facts

In October 1995, Roger Reeves was 57 years old and had spent 40 years employed by Sanderson Plumbing Products, Inc., a manufacturer of toilet seats and covers. Reeves worked as a supervisor of a production line, where his responsibilities included recording the attendance and hours of the workers under his supervision. In the summer of 1995, the president of Sanderson Plumbing fired Reeves, asserting that Reeves had failed to maintain accurate attendance records. Sanderson Plumbing replaced Reeves with a worker in his 30s. Reeves sued Sanderson Plumbing for violating the Age Discrimination in Employment Act of 1967 (ADEA), alleging that Sanderson's stated reason for discharging him was false and the real reason was to discriminate against him because of his age. The jury held in favor of Reeves, but the court of appeals reversed. The U.S. Supreme Court granted certiorari to hear Reeve's appeal.

Court Issue

Did Sanderson discriminate against Reeves based on his age?

Court's Reasoning

The U.S. Supreme Court held that Reeves first established a prima facie case of discrimination: (i) At the time he was fired, he was a member of the class protected by the ADEA (individuals who are at least 40 years of age), (ii) he was otherwise qualified for the position of supervisor, (iii) he was discharged by respondent, and (iv) respondent hired a person in his 30s to fill Reeves's position. The burden then shifted to the employer to produce evidence that the plaintiff was rejected for a legitimate, nondiscriminatory reason.

The Supreme Court noted that the ultimate burden of persuading the trier of fact that the employer intentionally discriminated against the plaintiff remains at all times with the plaintiff. Once the employer produces evidence to support a nondiscriminatory explanation for its decision, the plaintiff must be afforded the opportunity to prove by a preponderance of the evidence that the reasons offered by the defendant are not true reasons but are a mere pretext for discrimination. Reeves offered evidence that he had properly maintained the attendance records. The Supreme Court held that it is permissible for the trier of fact to infer the ultimate fact of discrimination from the falsity of the employer's explanation.

Decision and Remedy

The U.S. Supreme Court held that plaintiff Reeves had presented sufficient evidence to the jury that Sanderson Plumbing's asserted justification for dismissing him was false and thus per-

mitted the jury to conclude that Sanderson Plumbing had unlawfully discriminated against him. The Supreme Court reversed the decision of the court of appeals.

Case Questions

Critical Legal Thinking   Does the Supreme Court's back-and-forth burden-shifting approach in employment discrimination lawsuits work well? Do you think it leads to fair decisions in most cases?

Business Ethics   Did Sanderson Plumbing act ethically in this case? Why do you think it used a false pretense to fire Reeves?

Contemporary Business   Are there economic reasons for employers to prefer to discharge older employees? Explain.

Americans with Disabilities Act of 1990

The **Americans with Disabilities Act of 1990 (ADA),**[11] which was signed into law July 26, 1990, is the most comprehensive piece of civil rights legislation since the Civil Rights Act of 1964. The ADA imposes obligations on employers and providers of public transportation, telecommunications, and public accommodations to accommodate individuals with disabilities.

Title I of the ADA

Title I of the ADA prohibits employment discrimination against qualified individuals with disabilities in regard to job application procedures, hiring, compensation, training, promotion, and termination. Title I covers employers with 15 or more employees. The United States, corporations wholly owned by the United States, and bona fide tax-exempt private membership clubs are exempt from Title I coverage.

Title I requires an employer to make reasonable accommodations to individuals with disabilities that do not cause undue hardship to the employer. *Reasonable accommodations* may include making facilities readily accessible to individuals with disabilities, providing part-time or modified work schedules, acquiring equipment or devices, modifying examination and training materials, and providing qualified readers or interpreters.

Handicap Parking Space. Title I of the Americans with Disabilities Act (ADA) requires employers to make reasonable accommodations for individuals with disabilities that do not cause undue hardship to the employer.

Employers are not obligated to provide accommodations that would impose an *undue burden*. This means actions that would require significant difficulty or expense. Factors such as the nature and cost of accommodation, the overall financial resources of the employer, and the employer's type of operation are considered by the EEOC and the courts. Obviously, what may be a significant difficulty or expense for a small employer may not be an undue hardship for a large employer.

Qualified Individual with a Disability

A **qualified individual with a disability** is a person who, with or without reasonable accommodation, can perform the essential functions of the job that person desires or holds. A disabled person is someone who (1) has a physical or mental impairment that substantially limits one or more of his or her major life activities, (2) has a record of such impairment, or (3) is regarded as having such impairment. Mental retardation, paraplegia, schizophrenia, cerebral palsy, epilepsy, diabetes, muscular dystrophy, multiple sclerosis, cancer, infection with HIV (human immunodeficiency virus), and visual, speech, and hearing impairments are covered under the ADA. A current user of illegal drugs or an alcoholic who uses alcohol or is under the influence of alcohol at the workplace is not covered. However, recovering alcoholics and former users of illegal drugs are protected.

Forbidden Conduct

Title I of the ADA limits an employer's ability to inquire into or test for an applicant's disabilities. Title I forbids an employer from asking a job applicant about the existence, nature, and severity of a disability. An employer may, however, inquire about the applicant's ability to perform job-related functions. Preemployment medical examinations are forbidden before a job offer. Once a job offer has been made, an employer may require a medical examination and may condition the offer on the examination results, as long as all entering employees are subject to such an examination. The information must be kept confidential.

Procedure and Remedies

Title I of the ADA is administered by the EEOC. An aggrieved individual must first file a charge with the EEOC, which may take action against the employer or permit the individual to pursue a private cause of action. Relief can take the form of an injunction, hiring or reinstatement (with back pay), payment of attorneys' fees, and recovery of compensatory and punitive damages (subject to the same caps as Title VII damages).

In the following cases, the U.S. Supreme Court was called upon to interpret and apply the ADA.

U.S. SUPREME COURT CASE
PGA Tour, Inc. v. Martin
532 U.S. 661, 121 S.Ct. 1879, 2001 U.S. Lexis 4115 (2001)
Supreme Court of the United States

Case 35.6

Americans with Disabilities Act

Background and Facts

The PGA Tour, Inc., is a nonprofit entity that sponsors professional golf tournaments. The PGA has adopted a set of rules that apply to its golf tour. One rule requires golfers to walk the golf course during PGA-sponsored tournaments. Casey Martin is a talented amateur golfer who won many high school and university golf championships. Martin has been afflicted with Klippel-Trenaunay-Weber

Syndrome, a degenerative circulatory disorder that obstructs the flow of blood from his right leg to his heart. The disease is progressive and has atrophied his right leg. Walking causes Martin pain, fatigue, and anxiety, with significant risk of hemorrhaging.

When Martin turned professional, he qualified for the PGA Tour. He made a request to use a golf cart while playing in PGA tournaments. When the PGA denied his request, Martin sued the PGA for violation of the Americans with Disabilities Act (ADA) for not making reasonable accommodations for his disability. The district court sided with Martin and ordered the PGA to permit Martin to use a golf cart, and the court of appeals affirmed. The U.S. Supreme Court agreed to hear the PGA's appeal.

Issue

Does the ADA require the PGA Tour, Inc., to accommodate Casey Martin, a disabled professional golfer, by permitting him to use a golf cart while playing in PGA-sponsored golf tournaments?

Court's Reasoning

The U.S. Supreme Court held that Martin is an individual with a disability, as defined by the ADA. The Supreme Court then noted that the dispute in this case was whether allowing Martin to use a golf cart, despite the walking requirement that applies to the PGA Tour tournaments, is a modification that would "fundamentally alter the nature" of those events. As an initial matter, the Court observed that the use of golf carts is not itself inconsistent with the fundamental character of the game of golf. Today they are everywhere.

The Supreme Court stated that the force of petitioner PGA Tour's argument is, first of all, mitigated by the fact that golf is a game in which it is impossible to guarantee that all competitors will play under exactly the same conditions or that an individual's ability will be the sole determinant of the outcome. For example, changes in the weather may produce harder greens and more head winds for the tournament leader than for his closest pursuers. A lucky bounce may save a shot or two. Whether such happenstance events are more or less probable than the likelihood that a golfer afflicted with Klippel-Trenaunay-Weber Syndrome would one day qualify for the PGA Tour, they at least demonstrate that pure chance may have a greater impact on the outcome of elite golf tournaments than the fatigue resulting from the enforcement of the walking rule.

Decision and Remedy

The U.S. Supreme Court held that the ADA requires that the PGA Tour, Inc., accommodate Casey Martin, a disabled professional golfer, by allowing him to use a golf cart while competing in PGA-sponsored professional golf tournaments. The Supreme Court affirmed the judgment of the court of appeals.

Case Questions

Critical Legal Thinking   Do you agree with U.S. Supreme Court's decision? Will the decision open a floodgate of similar lawsuits?

Business Ethics   Was Casey Martin just asking for "fairness," or was he asking for an advantage when competing in professional golf tournaments?

Contemporary Business   Is the PGA Tour a lucrative business? Will the Supreme Court's ruling have any effect on the revenues generated by the PGA Tour?

International Law

International Reach of U.S. Antidiscrimination Laws

The **Civil Rights Act of 1991** protects *U.S. citizens*—but not for-eign nationals—employed in a foreign country by U.S.-controlled employers. An employer of a U.S. citizen abroad is subject to claims under Title VII in the following two situations:

1. An employer that is incorporated in the United States and operates a branch office in a foreign country is liable for Title VII violations against U.S. citizens that occur in its foreign operation.
2. If a U.S. parent corporation owns a foreign corporation that is incorporated in another country, the foreign-controlled

subsidiary is subject to Title VII because the 1991 act expressly states that discriminatory practices of "controlled foreign corporations" are presumed to be acts engaged in by the parent corporation.

If required conduct under Title VII would cause the employer to violate the law of a foreign nation (e.g., foreign law does not permit the employment of female workers), compliance with Title VII is excused. The 1991 act also extends its international reach to disabilities and age discrimination. ■

Affirmative Action

Employers often adopt **affirmative action plans** that provide that certain job preferences will be given to members of minority racial and ethnic groups, females, and other protected-class applicants when an employer makes an employment decision. Such plans can be voluntarily adopted by employers, undertaken to settle a discrimination action, or ordered by the courts.

To be lawful, an affirmative action plan must be narrowly tailored to achieve some compelling interest. Employment quotas based on a specified number or percentage of minority applicants or employees are unlawful. If a person's minority status is only one factor of many factors considered is an employment decision, that decision will be considered lawful.

Forbidden City, Beijing, China.
Foreign nationals employed in foreign countries by U.S.-controlled companies are not covered by Title VII; U.S. citizens employed by U.S.-controlled companies in foreign countries are covered by Title VII, however.

Affirmative action plans are often controversial. Proponents of such plans argue that the plans are necessary to address imbalances in the workforce and to remedy past discrimination against protected classes. Some argue that affirmative action plans cause work hardship on other employees.

Reverse Discrimination

Title VII not only applies to members of minority groups, but it also protects members of majority classes from discrimination. Lawful affirmative action plans have an effect on members of majority classes. The courts have held that this effect is not actionable by the members of the majority class who are affected.

The courts have held, however, that if an affirmative action plan is based on preestablished numbers or percentage quotas for hiring on promoting minority applicants, then it causes illegal **reverse discrimination**. In this case, the members of the majority class may sue under Title VII and recover damages and other remedies for reverse discrimination.

State and Local Government Antidiscrimination Laws

Many state and local governments have adopted laws that prevent discrimination in employment. These laws usually include classes protected by federal equal opportunity laws, as well as classes of persons not protected by federal laws.

International Law

Japan Adopts an Equal Opportunity in Employment Law

Prior to April 1, 1999, job openings in Japan were restricted by sex; that is, jobs could be reserved for men without violating the law. Classified advertisements in major Japanese newspapers typically listed "men only" jobs, which were executive positions and high-paying blue-collar jobs. "Women only" listings tended to be for nursing, secretarial, food-service, and other low-paying jobs.

All this changed with Japan's enactment of the **Equal Employment Opportunity and Labor Standard Law** in 1999. This statute grants equal opportunity rights to females in being hired for jobs and promoted to higher positions. The law bans the use of gender-specific advertising, so the "men only" and "women only" job listings have disappeared. Women may compete equally, under the law, for jobs and promotions. This law

also makes other gender-based discrimination illegal. For example, prior to the new law, women were banned from working after 10:00 P.M. or putting in more than six hours of overtime per week. Both of these restrictions have been removed, allowing females to earn higher wages from working night shifts and overtime.

The equal opportunity law prohibits sexual harassment in the workplace. Prior to the passage of the law, companies could veto any sexual harassment complaint brought against them, which helped explain why fewer than a dozen cases were even ruled on during the 1990s. Under the law, a woman can file a complaint with the Labor Ministry, a government administrative agency empowered to investigate such charges. ■

Chapter Summary

Equal Employment Opportunity Commission (EEOC), p. 774

Equal Employment Opportunity Commission (EEOC)

The EEOC is a federal administrative agency responsible for administering, interpreting, and enforcing most federal equal employment opportunity (antidiscrimination) laws.

Title VII of the Civil Rights Act of 1964, p. 774

Title VII of the Civil Rights Act of 1964

This federal statute prohibits job discrimination based on the (1) race, (2) color, (3) religion, (4) sex, or (5) national origin of the job applicant.

Scope of Coverage of Title VII

1. **Employers subject to Title VII.** Employers who had 15 or more employees for at least 20 weeks in the current or preceding year, all employment agencies, labor unions with 15 or more members, state and local governments, and most federal agencies are subject to Title VII.
2. **Employment decisions subject to Title VII.** Decisions regarding hiring; promotion; demotion; payment of salaries, wages, and fringe benefits; job training and apprenticeships; work rules; or any other "term, condition, or privilege of employment" are subject to Title VII.

Forms of Title VII Actions

1. **Disparate-treatment discrimination.** This type of discrimination occurs when an employer treats a specific *individual* less favorably than others because of that person's race, color, national origin, sex, or religion.
   To be successful, the complainant must prove:
   a. He or she belongs to a Title VII protected class.
   b. He or she applied for and was qualified for the employment position.
   c. He or she was rejected despite these qualifications.
   d. The employer kept the position open and sought applicants from persons with the complainant's qualifications.
2. **Disparate-impact discrimination.** This type of discrimination occurs when an employer discriminates against an entire protected *class*. Its may be proven by statistical data that demonstrate a causal link between the challenged practice and the statistical imbalance. *Neutral employment rules* that have an adverse impact on a protected class constitute disparate-impact discrimination.

Procedure for Bringing a Title VII Action

1. **Complaint.** A private complainant must file a complaint with the EEOC. The EEOC is given the opportunity to sue the employer on the complainant's behalf.
2. **Right to sue letter.** If the EEOC chooses not to bring suit, it will issue a *right to sue letter* that authorizes the complaint to sue the employer.

Remedies for Violations of Title VII

A successful plaintiff in a Title VII action can recover back pay, compensatory and punitive damages (subject to certain caps, based on the size of the defendant employer), reasonable attorneys' fees, and equitable remedies such as reinstatement, fictional seniority, and injunctions.

Protected Classes

Employment discrimination based on the following protected classes is forbidden by Title VII:

1. *Race*
2. *Color*
3. *National origin*
4. *Sex*
5. *Religion*

Race, Color, and National Origin Discrimination

1. ***Race.*** Race is a broad class of individuals with common physical characteristics (e.g., black, Caucasian, Asian, Native American).
2. ***Color.*** *Color* refers to the color of a person's skin (e.g., light-skinned person, dark-skinned person).
3. ***National origin.*** National origin is a person's country of origin or national heritage (e.g., Italian, Hispanic).

Sex Discrimination

1. ***Sex.*** Sex refers to a person's sex, whether male or female.
2. ***Pregnancy.*** The *Pregnancy Discrimination Act of 1978* amended Title VII to forbid employment discrimination because of "pregnancy, childbirth, or related medical conditions."
3. ***Sexual harassment.*** Sexual harassment is lewd remarks, touching, intimidation, posting of pinups, and other verbal or physical conduct of a sexual nature that occurs on the job. Sexual harassment that creates *a hostile work environment* violates Title VII.
4. ***Sexual preference.*** Title VII applies to employment discrimination based on sexual preference.

Title VII: Religious Discrimination

Religious discrimination is discrimination solely because of a person's religious beliefs or practices. An employer has a duty to *reasonably accommodate* an employee's religious beliefs if doing so does not cause an *undue hardship* on the employer.

Defenses to a Title VII Action

1. ***Merit.*** Merit includes job-related experiences, education, or unbiased employment tests.
2. ***Seniority.*** Seniority is the length of time an employee has been employed by the employer. Intentional discrimination based on seniority is unlawful.
3. ***Bona fide occupational qualification (BFOQ).*** Employment discrimination based on the sex, religion, or national origin of an applicant is permitted if it is a valid *bona fide occupational qualification (BFOQ)* for the position. To be legal, a BFOQ must be *job related* and a *business necessity*. BFOQ exceptions are narrowly interpreted by the courts.

Civil Rights Act of 1866

1. ***Section 1981 of the Civil Rights Act of 1866.*** This federal statute, enacted after the Civil War, states that all persons "have the same right . . . to make and enforce contracts . . . as is enjoyed by white persons."
2. ***Protected class.*** Section 1981 prohibits *race* and *national origin* discrimination concerning employment contracts.
3. ***Remedies.*** A successful plaintiff can recover back pay, equitable remedies, compensatory and punitive damages, and reasonable attorneys' fees. There are no monetary caps on compensatory and punitive damages.

Equal Pay Act of 1963, p. 783

Equal Pay Act

This federal statute forbids pay discrimination for the same job based on the sex of the employee performing the job. There cannot be pay disparity based on sex for jobs that require equal skill, equal effort, equal responsibility and similar working conditions.

1. Criteria that justify a differential in wages. The Equal Pay Act stipulates that the following four criteria justify a differential in wages:

   a. Seniority

   b. Merit

   c. Quantity or quality of work (commission, piecework, or quality control–based pay systems)

   d. Any factor other than sex (e.g., night versus day shifts)

Age Discrimination in Employment Act of 1967, p. 783

Age Discrimination in Employment Act (ADEA)

Federal statute that prohibits employment discrimination against applicants and employees who are 40 years of age or older.

1. Older Workers Benefit Protection Act (OWBPA). This federal statute amended the ADEA to prohibit age discrimination with respect to employment benefits.

2. Defenses. The same defenses that are available in a Title VII action are also available in an ADEA action.

3. Remedies. A successful plaintiff can recover back wages, attorney's fees, and equitable relief, including hiring, reinstatement, and promotion.

Americans with Disabilities Act of 1990, p. 785

Americans with Disabilities Act of 1990 (ADA)

This federal statute imposes obligations on employers and providers of public transportation, telecommunications, and public accommodations to accommodate individuals with disabilities.

Title I of the ADA

This federal law prohibits employment discrimination against qualified individuals with disabilities.

1. Reasonable accommodation. Title I requires employers to make *reasonable accommodations* to accommodate employees with disabilities that do not cause *undue hardship* to the employer.

Qualified Individual with a Disability

A qualified individual with a disability is a person who (1) has a physical or mental impairment that substantially limits one or more of his or her major life functions, (2) has a record of such impairment, or (3) is regarded as having such impairment.

Procedure and Remedies

A successful plaintiff can recover back pay, compensatory and punitive damages (subject to certain caps, based on the size of the defendant employer), reasonable attorney's fees, and equitable remedies, such as hiring, reinstatement, or promotion.

Affirmative Action, p. 787

Affirmative Action and Reverse Discrimination

Affirmative action is a policy that provides that certain job preferences will be given to minority or other protected-class applicants when an employer makes an employment decision.

1. Lawfulness of affirmative action plans. An employer may adopt a voluntary affirmative action plan that uses race or other protected-class status as a "*plus factor*" in making employment decisions. *Race norming*—the practice of altering or adjusting test scores on the basis of race—is unlawful.

2. Reverse discrimination. Reverse discrimination is discrimination against a person who is a member of a group that is usually thought of as a majority. Very few reverse discrimination lawsuits are successful.

State and Local Government Antidiscrimination Laws, p. 788

State and Local Government Antidiscrimination Laws

Many state and local governments have adopted laws that prevent discrimination in employment. These laws usually include classes protected by federal equal opportunity laws (e.g., race, color, national origin, sex religion, age, disability), as well as classes not protected by federal laws (e.g., homosexuals).

Internet Exercises and Case Questions
Working the Web Internet Exercises

Activities

1. Review the case *Gupta v. Florida Bd. of Regents* (5/17/2000, No. 98-5392) via the Cornell Discrimination Web site, at **www.law.cornell.edu/topics/employment_discrimination.html**. According to the 11th Circuit Court of Appeals, is it sexual harassment to make comments to coworkers such as "You are looking very beautiful"?

2. Review Congress's statement of purpose in the ADEA. Has this law served to accomplish that purpose? See the U.S. Equal Employment Opportunity Commission site, at **www.eeoc.gov**, and the Law About . . . Employment

Discrimination site, at **www.law.cornell.edu/topics/employment_discrimination.html**.

3. For a discussion of the courts' definition of *disability*, see "The Supreme Court's Definition of Disability Under the ADA: A Return to the Dark Ages," at **www.law.ua.edu/lawreview/tucker521.htm**.

4. Find the case *PGA Tour, Inc. v. Martin* involving the ADA and a professional golfer. Do you agree with the court's decision? Try the Law About . . . Employment Discrimination site.

Critical Legal Thinking Cases

35.1 Equal Pay Act For years, New York law prevented females from working at night. Therefore, Coming Glass Works employed male workers for night inspection jobs and female workers for day inspection jobs. Males working the night shift were paid higher wages than were females who worked the day shift. When the federal Equal Pay Act was enacted, Corning began hiring females for night shift jobs, but it instituted a "red circle" wage rate that permitted previously hired male night shift workers to continue to receive higher wages than newly hired night shift workers. Does this violate the Equal Pay Act? [*Corning Glass Works v. Brennan, Secretary of Labor*, 417 U.S. 188, 94 S.Ct. 2223, 1974 U.S. Lexis 62 (1974)]

35.2 Sex Discrimination The Los Angeles Department of Water and Power maintains a pension plan for its employees that is funded by both employer and employee contributions. The plan pays men and women retirees pensions with the same monthly benefits. However, because statistically women on average live several years longer than men, female employees are required to make monthly contributions to the pension fund that are 14.84 percent higher than the contributions required of male employees. Because employee contributions are withheld from paychecks, a female employee takes home less pay than a male employee earning the same salary. Does this practice violate Title VII? [*City of Los Angeles Department of Water and Power v. Manhart*, 435 U.S. 702, 98 S.Ct. 1370, 1978 U.S. Lexis 23 (1978)]

35.3 Hostile Work Environment Shirley Huddleston became the first female sales representative of Roger Dean Chevrolet, Inc. (RDC), in West Palm Beach, Florida. Shortly after she began working at RDC, Philip Geraci, a fellow sales representative, and other male employees began making derogatory comments to and about her, expelled gas in her presence, called her a

bitch and a whore, and such. Many of these remarks were made in front of customers. The sales manager of RDC participated in the harassment. On several occasions, Huddleston complained about this conduct to RDC's general manager. Was Title VII violated? [*Huddleston v. Roger Dean Chevrolet, Inc.*, 845 F.2d 900, 1988 U.S. App. Lexis 6823 (11th Cir. 1988)]

35.4 National Origin Discrimination The Federal Bureau of Investigation (FBI) engaged in a pattern and practice of discrimination against Hispanic FBI agents. Job assignments and promotions were areas that were especially affected. Bernardo M. Perez, a Hispanic, brought this Title VII action against the FBI. Did the FBI violate Title VII? [*Perez v. Federal Bureau of Investigation*, 714 F.Supp. 1414, 1989 U.S. Dist. Lexis 8426 (W.D. Tex 1989)]

35.5 Religious Discrimination Trans World Airlines (TWA), an airline, operates a large maintenance and overhaul base for its airplanes in Kansas City, Missouri. Because of its essential role, the stores department at the base must operate 24 hours per day, 365 days per year. The employees at the base are represented by the International Association of Machinists and Aerospace Workers (Union). TWA and Union entered into a collective bargaining agreement that includes a seniority system for the assignment of jobs and shifts.

Larry Hardison was hired by TWA to work as a clerk in the stores department. Soon after beginning work, Hardison joined the Worldwide Church of God, which does not allow its members to work from sunset on Friday until sunset on Saturday and on certain religious holidays. Hardison, who had the second lowest seniority within the stores department, did not have enough seniority to observe his Sabbath regularly. When Hardison asked for special consideration, TWA offered to allow him to take his Sabbath off if he could switch shifts with another employee-union member. None of the other employees would do so. TWA refused Hardison's request for a four-day workweek because it would have to either hire and train a part-time worker to work on Saturdays or incur the cost of paying overtime to an existing full-time worker on Saturdays. Hardison sued TWA for religious discrimination in violation of Title VII. Did TWA's actions violate Title VII? [*Trans World Airlines v. Hardison*, 432 U.S. 63, 97 S.Ct. 2264, 1977 U.S. Lexis 115 (1977)]

35.6 Bona Fide Occupational Qualification   At the age of 60, Manuel Fragante emigrated from the Philippines to Hawaii. In response to a newspaper ad, Fragante applied for an entry-level civil service clerk job with the City of Honolulu's Division of Motor Vehicles and Licensing. The job required constant oral communication with the public, either at the information counter or on the telephone. Fragante scored the highest of 731 test takers on a written examination that tested word usage, grammar, and spelling. As part of the application process, two civil service employees who were familiar with the demands of

the position interviewed Fragante. They testified that his accent made it difficult to understand him. Fragante was not hired for the position, which was filled by another applicant. Fragante sued, alleging national origin discrimination in violation of Title VII. Who wins? [*Fragante v. City and County of Honolulu*, 888 F.2d 591, 1989 U.S. App. Lexis 2636 (9th Cir. 1989)]

35.7 Age Discrimination   Walker Boyd Fite was an employee of First Tennessee Production Credit Association for 19 years. He had attained the position of vice president–credit. During the course of his employment, he never received an unsatisfactory review. On December 26, 1983, at the age of 57, Fite was hospitalized with a kidney stone. On January 5, 1984, while Fite was recovering at home, an officer of First Tennessee called to inform him that he had been retired as of December 31, 1983. A few days later, Fite received a letter stating that he had been retired because of poor job performance. Fite sued First Tennessee for age discrimination. Who wins? [*Fite v. First Tennessee Production Credit Association*, 861 F.2d 884, 1988 U.S. App. Lexis 14759 (6th Cir. 1989)]

Business Ethics Cases

35.8 Business Ethics

Dianne Rawlinson, 22 years old, was a college graduate whose major course of study was correctional psychology. After graduation, she applied for a position as a correctional counselor (prison guard) with the Alabama Board of Corrections. Her application was rejected because she failed to meet the minimum 120-pound weight requirement of an Alabama statute that also established a height minimum of 5 feet 2 inches. In addition, the Alabama Board of Corrections adopted Administrative Regulation 204, which established gender criteria for assigning correctional counselors to maximum-security prisons for "contact positions." These are correctional counselor positions that require continual close physical proximity to inmates. Under this rule, Rawlinson did not qualify for contact positions with male prisoners in Alabama maximum-security prisons. Rawlinson brought this class action lawsuit against Dothard, who was the director of the Department of Public Safety of Alabama. Does either the height–weight requirement or the

contact position rule constitute a bona fide occupational qualification that justifies the sexual discrimination in this case? Does society owe a duty of social responsibility to protect women from dangerous job positions? Or is this "romantic paternalism"? [*Dothard, Director, Department of Public Safety of Alabama v. Rawlinson*, 433 U.S. 321, 97 S.Ct. 2720, 1977 U.S. Lexis 143 (1977)]

35.9 Business Ethics

Rita Machakos, a white female, worked for the Civil Rights Division (CRD) of the Department of Justice. During her employment, she was denied promotion to certain paralegal positions. In each instance, the individual selected was a black female. Evidence showed that the CRD maintained an institutional and systematic discrimination policy that favored minority employees over white employees. Machakos sued the CRD for race discrimination under Title VII. Who wins? [*Machakos v. Attorney General of the United States*, 859 F.2d 1487, 1988 U.S. App. Lexis 14672 (D.C. Cir. 1988)]

Briefing the Case Writing Assignment

Read Case A.35 in the Case Appendix [*Robinson v. Jacksonville Shipyards, Inc.*]. This case is excerpted from the district court opinion. Review and brief the case. In your brief, be sure to answer the following questions.

1. Who is the plaintiff? Who is the defendant?

2. What is sexual harassment?

3. Did the court find sexual harassment in this case?

4. What remedy did the court order?

Endnotes

1. 42 U.S.C. §§ 2000e et seq. Other portions of the Civil Rights Act of 1964 prohibit discrimination in housing, education, and other facets of life.
2. *Equal Employment Opportunity Commission v. Tortilleria "La Mejor,"* 758 F.Supp. 585, 1991 U.S. Dist. Lexis 5754 (E.D. Cal. 1991).
3. *McDonnell Douglas v. Green*, 411 U.S. 792, 93 S.Ct. 1817, 1973 U.S. Lexis 154 (1973).
4. In some states, the complaint must be filed with the appropriate state agency rather than the EEOC.
5. 42 U.S.C. § 2000e(K).
6. *Meritor Savings Bank v. Vinson*, 477 U.S. 57, 106 S.Ct. 2399, 1986 U.S. Lexis 108 (1986).
7. *Harris v. Forklift Systems, Inc.*, 510 U.S. 17, 114 S.Ct. 367, 1993 U.S. Lexis 7155 (1993).
8. 523 U.S. 75, 118 S.Ct. 998, 1998 U.S. Lexis 1599 (1998).
9. 29 U.S.C. § 206(d).
10. 29 U.S.C. §§ 621–634
11. 42 U.S.C. §§ 1201 et seq.

Personal Property and Bailments

36

" Property and law are born and must die together. "

Jeremy Bentham
Principles of the Civil Code, I Works 309

Chapter Objectives

After studying this chapter, you should be able to:

1. Define personal property.

2. Describe the methods for acquiring and transferring ownership in personal property.

3. Describe and apply rules regarding ownership rights in mislaid, lost, and abandoned property.

4. List and describe the elements for creating a bailment.

5. Explain the liability of bailees for lost, damaged, or destroyed goods.

Chapter Contents

■ The Nature of Personal Property

■ Acquiring Ownership of Personal Property

■ Mislaid, Lost, and Abandoned Property

■ Bailments

Private ownership of property forms the foundation of our economic system. As such, a comprehensive body of law has been developed to protect property rights. The law protects the rights of property owners to use, sell, dispose of, control, and prevent others from trespassing on their rights.

The first part of this chapter discusses the kinds of personal property, methods of acquiring ownership in personal property, and property rights in mislaid, lost, and abandoned property. The second part of this chapter discusses bailment, situations where possession of (but not title to) personal property is delivered to another party for transfer, safekeeping, or some other purpose.

> Property is the most ambiguous of categories. It covers a multitude of rights which have nothing in common except that they are exercised by persons and enforced by the state.
>
> R. H. Tawney
> *The Acquisitive Society, Ch. V (1921)*

The Nature of Personal Property

There are two kinds of property: *real property* and *personal property*. Real property includes land and property that is permanently attached to it. For example, minerals, crops, timber, and buildings that are attached to land are generally considered real property. **Personal property** (sometimes referred to as goods or chattels) consists of everything that is not real property. Real property can become personal property if it is removed from the land. For example, a tree that is part of a forest is real property; a tree that is cut down is personal property.

Personal property that is permanently affixed to land or buildings is called a fixture. Such property, which includes things like heating systems and storm windows, is categorized as real property. Unless otherwise agreed, fixtures remain with a building when it is sold. Personal property (e.g., furniture, pictures, other easily portable household items) may be removed by the seller prior to sale.

Personal property can be either tangible or intangible. **Tangible property** includes physically defined property such as goods, animals, and minerals. **Intangible property** represents rights that cannot be reduced to physical form; stock certificates, certificates of deposit, bonds, and copyrights are examples of intangible property.

Real and personal property may be owned by one person or by more than one person. If property is owned concurrently by two or more persons, there is concurrent ownership.

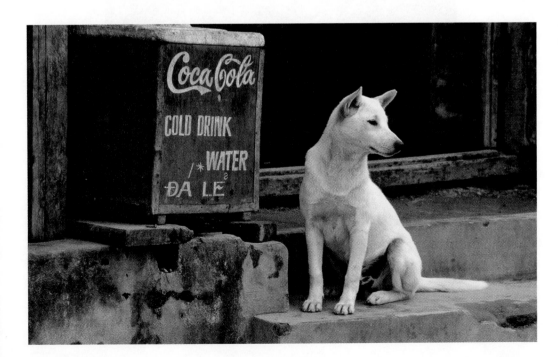

Domestic Animal. Domestic animals are an example of personal property.

Acquiring Ownership of Personal Property

Personal property may be acquired or transferred with a minimum of formality. Commerce would be severely curtailed if the transfer of such items were difficult. The methods for acquiring ownership in personal property are discussed in the following paragraphs.

The right of property enables an industrious man to reap where he has sown.

Anonymous

By Possession or Capture

A person can acquire ownership in unowned personal property by **taking possession** of it or **capturing** it. The most notable unowned objects are things in their natural state. For example, people who obtain the proper fishing license acquire ownership of all the fish they catch. This type of property acquisition was important when this country was being developed. In today's urbanized society, however, there are few unowned objects, and this method of acquiring ownership in personal property has become less important.

By Purchase or Production

The most common method of acquiring title to personal property is by **purchasing** the property from its owner. For example, Urban Concrete Corporation owns a large piece of equipment. City Builders, Inc., purchases the equipment from Urban Concrete for $50,000. Urban Concrete signs over the title to the equipment to City Builders. City Builders is now the owner of the equipment.

Production is another common method of acquiring ownership in personal property. Thus, a manufacturer that purchases raw materials and produces a finished product owns that product.

Bicycle Shop. Personal property is often transferred by gift. The person who makes the gift is called the donor, and the person who receives the gift is called the donee.

By Gift

A **gift** is a voluntary transfer of property without consideration. The lack of consideration is what distinguishes a gift from a purchase. The person making a gift is called the **donor**. The person who receives the gift is called the **donee**. There are three elements of a valid gift:

1. ***Donative intent.*** For a gift to be effective, the donor must have intended to make a gift. Donative intent can be inferred from the circumstances or language used by the donor. The courts also consider such factors as the relationship of the parties, the size of the gift, and the mental capacity of the donor.

2. ***Delivery.*** Delivery must occur for there to be a valid gift. Although **physical delivery** is the usual method of transferring personal property, it is sometimes impracticable. In such circumstances, **constructive delivery** (or **symbolic delivery**) is sufficient. For example, if the property being gifted is kept in a safe-deposit box, physically giving the key to the donee is enough to signal the gift. Most intangible property is transferred by written conveyance (e.g., conveying a stock certificate represents a transfer of ownership in a corporation).

3. ***Acceptance.*** Acceptance is usually not a problem because most donees readily accept gifts. In fact, the courts presume acceptance unless there is proof that the gift was refused. Nevertheless, a person cannot be forced to accept an unwanted gift.

Business Brief
The donee must accept a gift for the gift to be effective.

Gift *Inter Vivos* and Gift *Causa Mortis* A gift made during a person's lifetime that is an irrevocable present transfer of ownership is a **gift *inter vivos***. A **gift *causa mortis*** is a gift made in contemplation of death. A gift *causa mortis* is established when (1) the donor makes a gift in anticipation of approaching death from some existing sickness or peril and (2) the donor dies from such sickness or peril without having revoked the gift. A gift *causa mortis* can be revoked by the donor up until the time he or she dies. A gift *causa mortis* takes precedence over a prior conflicting will.

Consider This Example Suppose Sandy is a patient in the hospital. She is to have a major operation from which she may not recover. Prior to going into surgery, Sandy removes her diamond ring and gives it to her friend Pamela, stating, "In the event of my death, I want you to have this." This gift is a gift *causa mortis*. If Sandy dies from the operation, the gift is effective and Pamela owns the ring. If Sandy lives, the requisite condition for the gift (her death) has not occurred; therefore, the gift is not effective and Sandy can recover the ring from Pamela.

In the following case, the court had to determine whether a gift of a valuable painting had been made.

Gruen v. Gruen
505 N.Y.S.2d 849, 1986 N.Y. Lexis 19366 (1986)
Court of Appeals of New York

Case 36.1
Gift of Personal Property

Background and Facts

Victor Gruen was a successful architect. In 1959, Victor purchased a painting titled *Schloss Kammer am Attersee II* by a noted Austrian modernist, Gustav Klimt, and paid $8,000 for the painting. In 1963, Victor wrote a letter to his son Michael, then an undergraduate student at Harvard University, giving the painting to Michael but reserving a life estate in the painting. The letter stated

Dear Michael:

The 21st birthday, being an important event in life, should he celebrated accordingly. I therefore wish to give you as a present the oil painting by Gustav Klimt of Schloss Kammer which now hangs in the New York living room.

Happy birthday again.

Love,

s/Victor

Because Victor retained a life interest in the painting, Michael never took possession of the painting. Victor died on February 14, 1980. The painting was appraised at $2.5 million. When Michael requested the painting from his stepmother, Kemija Gruen, she refused to turn it over to him. Michael sued to recover the painting. The trial court held in favor of the stepmother. The appellate division reversed in favor of Michael. The stepmother appealed.

Issue

Did Victor Gruen make a valid gift *inter vivos* of the Klimt painting to his son Michael?

Court's Reasoning

The appellate court held that the elements necessary to create a valid gift *inter vivos* had been met. First, the court held that the evidence was conclusive that Victor had the requisite *donative intent* to transfer ownership of the painting to Michael in 1963. Second, the court stated that physical *delivery* of the painting was not required in this case because Victor intended to retain a life estate in the painting. The court held that Victor's letter consti-

tuted constructive delivery of the painting. Third, the court found that Michael had *accepted* the gift. Evidence showed that Michael had told several of his friends and classmates about the gift when it was made in 1963 and that he had retained the letter for more than 17 years to verify the gift after his father died.

Decision and Remedy

The appellate court held that Victor Gruen had made a valid gift *inter vivos* of the Klimt painting to his son Michael. The court affirmed the judgment of the appellate division in favor of Michael Gruen.

Case Questions

Critical Legal Thinking   Should a donor who makes a gift *Inter vivos* be required to relinquish physical possession of the property to the donee?

Business Ethics   Did the stepmother act ethically in refusing to turn the painting over to Michael?

Contemporary Business   What could Victor Gruen had done to make his donative intent more clear? Explain.

Uniform Gift to Minors Act   All states have adopted in whole or part the **Uniform Gift to Minors Act** or the **Revised Uniform Gift to Minors Act**. These laws establish procedures for adults to make irrevocable gifts of money and securities to minors. Gifts of money can be made by depositing the money in an account in a financial institution with the donor or another trustee (such as another adult or bank) as custodian for the minor. Gifts of securities can be made by registering the securities in the name of a trustee as custodian for the minor. The laws give custodians broad discretionary powers to invest the money or securities for the benefit of the minor.

By Will or Inheritance

Title to personal property is frequently acquired by **will or inheritance**. If the person who dies has a valid will, the property is distributed to the **beneficiaries**, pursuant to the provisions of that will. Otherwise, the property is distributed to the **heirs**, as provided in the relevant state's inheritance statute.

By Accession

Accession occurs when the value of personal property increases because it is added to or improved by natural or manufactured means. Accession that occurs naturally belongs to the owner (e.g., a colt that is born to a mare belongs to the mare's owner).

If the improvement was made wrongfully, the owner acquires title to the improved property and does not have to pay the improver for the value of the improvements. For example, suppose a thief steals a car and puts a new engine in it. The owner is entitled to recover the car as improved, without having to pay the thief for the improvements.

If the improvement was mistakenly made by the improver, the courts generally follow these rules:

1. If the improvements can be easily separated from the original article, the improver must remove the improvements and pay any damages caused by such removal. For example, a builder who puts the wrong door on a house must replace that door with the correct door at his own cost.

Only a ghost can exist without material property.

Ayn Rand
Atlas Shrugged (1957)

2. If the improvements cannot be removed, the owner owns title to the improved property and does not have to pay the improver for the improvements. For example, if a builder misreads blueprints and extends an addition to a building too far, the building owner is entitled to keep the improvement at no extra cost.

By Confusion

Confusion occurs if two or more persons commingle fungible goods (i.e., goods that are exactly alike, such as the same grade of oil, grains, or cattle). Title to goods can be acquired by confusion.

The owners share ownership in the commingled goods in proportion to the amount of goods contributed. It does not matter whether the goods were commingled by agreement or by accident. For example, if three farmers agree to store the same amount of Grade B winter wheat in a silo, each of them owns one-third. When the grain is sold, the profits are divided into three parts; if the silo burns to the ground, each suffers one-third of the loss. If goods are wrongfully or intentionally commingled without permission, the innocent party acquires title to them.

By Divorce

When a marriage is dissolved by a divorce, the parties obtain certain rights in the property of the marital estate. Often, a settlement of property rights is reached. If not, the court must decide the property rights of the spouses.

In the following case, the court decided the spouse's ownership right to personal property upon divorce.

> Laws are always useful to persons of property, and hurtful to those who have none.
>
> Jean-Jacques Rousseau
> *Du Contrat Social* (1761)

Giha v. Giha
609 A.2d 945, 1992 R.I. Lexis 133 (1992)
Supreme Court of Rhode Island

Case 36.2
Acquiring Personal Property

Background and Facts

On October 7, 1987, Nagib Giha (husband) filed a complaint for divorce from Nelly Giha (wife) on the grounds of irreconcilable differences. On May 20, 1988, the parties reached an agreement for the disposition of their property which provided that they would divide equally the net proceeds from the sale of their marital assets. There was a statutory waiting period before the divorce was final. On December 25, 1988, the husband learned that he had won $2.4 million in the Massachusetts MEGABUCKS state lottery. The husband kept this fact secret. After the waiting period was over, the family court entered its final judgment, severing the parties' marriage on April 27, 1989. The husband claimed his lottery prize on October 6, 1989. In December 1990, after learning of the lottery winnings, the wife sued to recover her portion of the lottery prize. She alleged that the lottery prize was a marital asset because her husband had won it before their divorce was final. The trial court dismissed her complaint. The wife appealed.

Issue

Was the $2.4 million lottery prize personal property of the marital estate?

Court's Reasoning

The supreme court held that the marital agreement did not sever either the matrimonial or economic ties between the husband and the wife. Because the parties' marriage remained in effect during the statutory waiting period, so did the property rights of each spouse during that period. The court concluded that the lottery prize was a marital asset.

Decision and Remedy

The supreme court of Rhode Island held that the parties remained as husband and wife until the entry of final judgment of divorce in April 1989. Therefore, the lottery prize was a marital asset. The court reversed the decision of the trial court and remanded the case for a division of the lottery prize.

Case Questions

Critical Legal Thinking   Should a spouse's lottery winnings be considered separate property? Why or why not?

Business Ethics   Did the husband act ethically in this case?

Contemporary Business   Can couples who are getting married agree on what property is marital property and what property is their separate property in advance of marriage? Explain.

Mislaid, Lost, and Abandoned Property

Personal property has no locality.

Lord Loughborough C.J.
Sill v. Worswick (1971)

Often, people find another person's personal property. Ownership rights to the property differ depending on whether the property is mislaid, lost, or abandoned. The following paragraphs discuss these legal rules.

Mislaid Property

Property is **mislaid** when its owner voluntarily places the property somewhere and then inadvertently forgets it. It is likely that the owner will return for the property upon realizing that it was misplaced.

The owner of the premises where the property is mislaid is entitled to take possession of the property against all except the rightful owner. This right is superior to the rights of the person who finds it. Such possession does not involve a change of title. Instead, the owner of the premises becomes an involuntary bailee of the property (bailments are discussed later in this chapter) and owes a duty to take reasonable care of the property until it is reclaimed by the owner.

Business Brief

The owner of the premises where personal property is *mislaid* is entitled to take possession of the property against all except the rightful owner.

Consider This Example   Suppose Felicity is on a business trip and stays in a hotel during her trip. Felicity accidentally leaves her diamond engagement ring in the hotel room she has stayed in and checks out of the hotel. The engagement ring is mislaid property, and the hotel has a duty to return it to Felicity, its rightful owner.

Lost Property

Property is considered **lost** when its owner negligently, carelessly, or inadvertently leaves it somewhere. The finder obtains title to such property against the whole world except the true owner. The lost property must be returned to its rightful owner, whether he or she discovers the loser's identity or the loser finds him or her. A finder who refuses to return the property is liable for the tort of conversion and the crime of larceny. Many states require the finder to conduct a reasonable search (e.g., place advertisements in newspapers) to find the rightful owner.

Business Brief

The finder of *lost property* obtains title to the found property against everyone except the true owner.

Consider This Example   If a commuter finds a laptop computer on the floor of a subway station in New York City, the computer is considered lost property. The finder can claim title to the computer against the whole world except the true owner. If the true owner discovers that the finder has her computer, she may recover it from the finder. If there is identification of the owner on the computer (e.g., name, address, and telephone number), the finder owes a duty to contact the rightful owner and give the computer book.

Contemporary Environment
Estray Statutes

Most states have enacted **estray statutes** that permit a finder of *mislaid* or *lost* property to clear title to the property if:

1. The finder reports the found property to the appropriate government agency and then turns over possession of the property to this agency,
2. Either the finder or the government agency posts notices and publishes advertisements describing the lost property, and
3. A specified time (usually a year or a number of years) has passed without the rightful owner's reclaiming the property.

Many state estray statutes provide that the government receive a portion of the value of the property. Some statutes provide that title cannot be acquired in found property that is the result of illegal activity. For example, title has been denied to finders of property and money deemed to have been used for illegal drug purchases.

The following case demonstrates the application of an estray statute. ■

Willsmore v. Township of Oceola, Michigan

308 N.W.2d 796, 1981 Mich.App. Lexis 2993 (1981)
Court of Appeals of Michigan

Background and Facts

While hunting on unposted and unoccupied property in Oceola Township, Michigan, Duane Willsmore noticed an area with branches arranged in a crisscross pattern. When he kicked aside the branches and sod, he found a watertight suitcase in a freshly dug hole. Willsmore informed the Michigan State Police of his find. A state trooper and Willsmore together pried open the suitcase and discovered $383,840 in cash. The state police took custody of the money, which was deposited in an interest-bearing account. Michigan's "Lost Goods Act" provides that the finder and the township in which the property was found must share the value of the property if the finder publishes required notices and the true owner does not claim the property within one year.

Willsmore published the required notices and brought a declaratory judgment action seeking a determination of the ownership of the money. Thomas Powell, the owner of the land on which the suitcase was found, claimed he was the owner of the suitcase. After Powell incorrectly named the amount of money in the suitcase, he asserted his Fifth Amendment right not to testify at his deposition and at trial. The trial court awarded the money equally to Willsmore and the Township of Oceola. Powell appealed.

Issue

Who is the owner of the lost briefcase and its contents?

Court's Reasoning

First, the court held that Powell had not met his burden of proving that he was the true owner of the suitcase of money. Then, the court held that the requirements of Michigan's estray law had been met. The money was awarded to the finder, Willsmore, and the township. The court stated that the Lost Goods Act encourages the goals that the court considers important. It provides certainty of title to property by eventually investing clear title after a set period of time. It encourages honesty in finders by providing incentives for compliance. The act provides notice to potential true owners and publication to seek them out. And the public obtains a portion of the benefit of a find through the receipt of one-half of the value by the township.

Decision and Remedy

The court of appeals held that Willsmore and the Township of Oceola were the owners of the briefcase and its contents. The court of appeals affirmed the judgment of the trial court and ordered that Willsmore and the township each receive one-half the proceeds of the find after Willsmore's costs were deducted.

Case Questions

Critical Legal Thinking Do estray statutes serve a useful social purpose? Explain.

Business Ethics If you had found the suitcase, would you have turned it in to the government?

Contemporary Business Should the government be entitled to half the find? Explain.

Abandoned Property

Property is classified as **abandoned** if (1) an owner discards the property with the intent to relinquish his or her rights in it or (2) an owner of mislaid or lost property gives up any further attempts to locate it. Anyone who finds abandoned property acquires title to it. The title is good against the whole world, including the original owner. For example, property left at a garbage dump is abandoned property. It belongs to the first person who claims it.

Concept Summary *Rules Regarding Ownership Rights in Mislaid, Lost, and Abandoned Property*

Type of Property	Ownership Rights
Mislaid property	The owner of the premises where property is mislaid is entitled to possession but does not acquire title. He or she holds the property as an involuntary bailee until the owner reclaims it.
Lost property	The finder acquires title to the property against the whole world except the true owner, the owner may reclaim his or her property from the finder.
Abandoned property	The finder acquires title to the property, even against its original owner.

International Law

Who Owns the Treasure Trove on the *SS Central America*?

On Saturday, September 12, 1857, the *SS Central America*, a luxurious steamship, sank 169 miles off the coast of South Carolina. The ship carried 587 passengers, many of whom were returning from California, where they had recovered gold from newly discovered mines. Only 166 passengers survived. Insurance companies paid many claims for gold coins and bricks that sank with the ship.

For nearly 130 years, the *SS Central America* lay peacefully in the icy waters off the East Coast. In 1981, Thomas G. Thompson organized an expedition called the Columbus–America Discovery Group to find the sunken ship and recover its bounty. Finally, in 1987, by using a 5,000-pound robot with a video camera, Thompson found the submerged *SS Central America* and its undisturbed cargo of thousands of rare gold coins and even rarer gold

bars. When the jubilant Thompson and crew returned to port, they were greeted by more than just well-wishers. Representatives of several insurance companies immediately claimed that some of the *SS Central America's* loot belonged to them as compensation for the claims they had paid 130 years earlier. Thompson argued that the gold belonged to him and his group.

The federal court applied the maritime **Law of Salvage**. Under the doctrine, original owners retain ownership interest, although the salvager is entitled to a very liberal salvage award. The court determined that Thompson and his group were entitled to 90 percent of the gold coins and other treasure found on the *SS Central America*. [*Columbus-America Discovery Group v. Atlantic Mutual Insurance Company*, 56 F.3d 556, 1995 U.S.App. Lexis 14607 (4th Cir. 1995)] ■

Bailments

A **bailment** occurs when the owner of personal property delivers his or her property to another person, either to be held, stored, or delivered or for some other purpose. In a bailment, the owner of the property is the **bailor**. The party to whom the property is delivered for safekeeping, storage, or delivery (e.g., warehouse, common carrier) is the **bailee** (see Exhibit 36.1). The law of bailments establishes the rights, duties, and liabilities of parties to a bailment.

A bailment is different from a sale or a gift because title to the goods does not transfer to the bailee. Instead, the bailee must follow the bailor's directions concerning the goods. For example, suppose Hudson Corporation is relocating offices and hires American Van Lines to move its office furniture and equipment to the new location. American Van Lines (the bailee) must follow Hudson's (the bailor's) instructions regarding delivery.

Elements Necessary to Create a Bailment Three **elements** are necessary *to create a bailment*:

1. *Personal property.* *Only personal property* can be bailed. The property can be **tangible** (e.g., automobiles, jewelry, animals) or *intangible* (e.g., stocks, bonds, promissory notes).
2. *Delivery of possession.* Delivery of possession involves two elements: (1) The bailee has exclusive control over the personal property, and (2) the bailee must knowingly accept the personal property. For example, no bailment is created if a patron goes

Exhibit 36.1

Parties to a Bailment

into a restaurant and hangs her coat on an unattended coat rack because other patrons have access to the coat. However, a bailment is created if the patron checks her coat with a checkroom attendant because the restaurant has assumed exclusive control over the coat. If valuable property was left in the pocket of the coat, there would be no bailment of that property because the checkroom attendant did not knowingly accept it. Most bailments are created by *physical delivery*. For example, Great Lakes Shipping, Inc., delivers a vessel to Marina Repairs, Inc., for repairs. *Constructive delivery* can create a bailment, too. For example, there has been constructive delivery of an automobile if the owner gives someone the keys and registration to his car.

3. **Bailment agreement.** The creation of a bailment does not require any formality. A bailment may be either express or implied. Most *express bailments* can be either written or oral. Under the Statute of Frauds, however, a bailment must be in writing if it is for more than one year. An example of an *implied bailment* is the finding and safeguarding of lost property.

In the following case, the court found that no bailment had been created.

Sisters of Charity of the Incarnate Word v. Meaux
122 S.W.3d 428, 2003 Tex. App. Lexis 10189 (2003)
Court of Appeals of Texas

Case 36.4
Bailment

Background and Facts

The Sisters of Charity of the Incarnate Word, d/b/a/ St. Elizabeth Hospital of Beaumont, operates a health and wellness center. Phil Meaux was a paying member of the health center. The rules of the center, which Meaux had been given, state, "The Health & Wellness Center is not responsible for lost or stolen items." A sign stating "We cannot assure the safety of your valuables" was posted at the check-in desk. The wellness center furnished a lock and key to each member, but had a master key to open lockers in case a member forgot or lost his or her key. On January 19, 2000, Meaux went to the wellness center, placed his clothes and an expensive Rolex watch and a money clip with $400 cash in the locker assigned him. Upon returning from swimming, Meaux discovered that his locker had been pried open, and his watch and money had been stolen by some unknown person. Meaux sued the Sisters of Charity, alleging that a bailment had been created between him and the Sisters and that the Sisters, as bailee, were negligent and therefore liable to him for the value of his stolen property. The trial court held in favor of Meaux and awarded him $19,500 as the value of the stolen property, plus interest and attorneys' fees. The Sisters of Charity appealed.

Issue

Was a bailment created between Meaux and the Sisters of Charity?

Court's Reasoning

The court of appeals stated that in order to create a bailment, there must be delivery of personal property by one person (the bailor) to another (the bailee) in trust for a specific purpose. If there is a bailment, the bailee owes a duty to exercise ordinary care over the goods and is therefore responsible for their loss if the bailee is negligent. The court of appeals held that no bailment was created between Meaux and the Sisters of Charity. Instead, the court of appeals held that a landlord–tenant relationship had been created between the Sisters of Charity and Meaux. In a landlord–tenant agreement, the landlord does not possess dominion and control over the lessee's property and is therefore not responsible for the loss of the lessee's property. The court stated, "There is no evidence of a bailment agreement."

Decision and Remedy

The court of appeals held that a landlord–tenant agreement, and not a bailment, had been created between Meaux and the Sisters of Charity. The court held that the Sisters of Charity were not liable for Meaux's loss. The court of appeals reversed the trial court's judgment in favor of Meaux and rendered a decision in favor of the Sisters of Charity.

Case Questions

Critical Legal Thinking   What is the difference between a bailment and a landlord–tenant relationship? Explain.

Business Ethics   Did Meaux act ethically in arguing that a bailment had been created in this case?

Contemporary Business   Do you think the fact that the Sisters of Charity had a public rule that it was "not responsible" for the loss of items had much bearing on the outcome of this case?

Ordinary Bailments

There are three classifications of **ordinary bailments**. The difference among these categories is the degree of care owed by the bailee in protecting the bailed property. The three types of ordinary bailments are:

1. **Bailments for the sole benefit of the bailor** are *gratuitous bailments* that benefit only the bailor. They arise when the bailee is requested to care for the bailor's property as a favor. The bailee owes only a **duty of slight care** to protect the bailed property—that is, he or she owes a duty not to be grossly negligent in caring for the bailed goods.

   Consider This Example   The Watkins family is going on vacation and asks the neighbors, the Smiths, to feed its dog, which is allowed to run free. The Smiths diligently feed the dog, but the dog runs away and does not return. The Smiths are not liable for the loss of the dog.

2. **Bailments for the sole benefit of the bailees** are *gratuitous bailments* that solely benefit the bailee. They generally arise when a bailee requests to use the bailor's property for personal reasons. In this situation, the bailee owes a **duty of great care** (or **utmost care**) to protect the bailed property—that is, he or she owes a duty not to be slightly negligent in caring for the bailed goods.

   Consider This Example   Suppose Mitch borrows Courtney's lawn mower (free of charge) to mow his own lawn. Mitch is the bailee, and Courtney is the bailor. This bailment is for the sole benefit of the bailee. Suppose Mitch, while mowing his lawn, leaves the lawn mower in his front yard while he goes into his house to answer the telephone. While he is gone, the lawn mower is stolen. Here, Mitch will be held liable to Courtney for the loss of the lawn mower because Mitch breached his duty of great care to protect the lawn mower.

3. **Mutual benefit bailments** are bailments that *benefit both parties*. The bailee owes a **duty of reasonable care** (or **ordinary care**) to protect the bailed goods. This means that the bailee is liable for any goods that are lost, damaged, or destroyed because of his or her negligence.

   Consider This Example   Suppose ABC Garment Co. delivers goods to Lowell, Inc., a commercial warehouseman, for storage. A fee is charged for this service. ABC Garments Co. receives the benefit of having its goods stored, and Lowell, Inc., receives the benefit of being paid compensation for storing the goods. In this example, Lowell, Inc. (the bailee), owes a duty of ordinary care to protect the goods.

   Some states have eliminated these three categories of ordinary bailments, ruling that all bailees owe a duty of reasonable care, regardless of whether they benefit from the bailment.

Concept Summary   Ordinary Bailee's Duty of Care

Type of Bailment	Duty of Care Owed by Bailee	Bailee Liable to Bailor for
For the sole benefit of the bailor	Slight	Gross negligence
For the sole benefit of the bailee	Great	Slight negligence
For the mutual benefit of the bailor and bailee	Ordinary	Ordinary negligence

Contemporary Environment

Parking Lots Liability

Who is liable when a car is stolen or damaged while parked in a commercial lot or garage? The answer to this question depends on whether the parking lot is considered to be a bailee of an automobile or merely a lessor of parking space.

It is clear that parking lots and garages are bailees of automobiles once they assume control and possession of the automobile. Thus, if a valet parking attendant parks the car and keeps the keys, it is relatively certain that a court will recognize the existence of a bailment and hold the garage liable if the vehi-

cle is stolen or damaged. Disclaimers to the contrary (either on the ticket or posted at the parking lot) are usually held to be ineffective.

On the other hand, if the owner of a car parks his or her own car in a parking lot and takes the keys, this is considered a lease. The general rule in this case is that the "landlord"—the parking lot—is not responsible for the safety of the car.

A provision in the parking contract requiring that damage be reported prior to leaving the parking lot is enforceable, however. ∎

Duration and Termination of Bailments

Bailments generally expire at a specified time or when a certain purpose is accomplished. A **bailment for a fixed term** terminates at the end of the term or sooner by mutual consent of the parties. A party who terminates a bailment in breach of the bailment agreement is liable to the innocent party for damages resulting from the breach. Bailments without a fixed term are called **bailments at will**. A bailment at will can be terminated at any time by either party. Gratuitous bailees can generally terminate a fixed-term bailment prior to expiration of the term.

Upon termination of the bailment, the bailee is legally obligated to do as the bailor directs with the property. Unless otherwise agreed, the bailee is obligated to return the identical goods bailed. Where commingled *fungible goods* are involved (e.g., grain), identically equivalent goods may be returned by the bailee.

Special Bailments

Special (or **extraordinary**) **bailees** include *common carriers*, *innkeepers*, and *warehouse companies*. Special bailees must follow most of the rules applicable to ordinary bailees. In addition, they are subject to special liability rules contained in **Article 7 of the Uniform Commercial Code (UCC)**. These special bailment situations are discussed in the following paragraphs.

Common Carriers   **Common carriers** offer transportation services to the general public. For example, commercial airlines, railroads, public trucking companies, public pipeline companies, and such are common carriers. The delivery of goods to a **common** carrier creates a mutual benefit bailment. The person shipping the goods is the **shipper** or **consignor** (the bailor). The transportation company is called the **common carrier** (the bailee). The person to whom the goods are to be delivered is called the **consignee**.

Common carriers are held to a **duty of strict liability**.[1] Thus, if the goods are lost, damaged, destroyed, or stolen, the common carrier is liable even if it was not at fault for the loss. Common carriers are not liable for the loss, damage, or destruction of goods caused by (1) an act of God (e.g., a tornado), (2) an act of a public enemy (e.g., a terrorist activity), (3) an order of the government (e.g., statutes, court decisions, government regulations), (4) an act of the shipper (e.g., improper packaging), or (5) the inherent nature of the goods (e.g., perishability).

Common carriers can limit their liability to a stated dollar amount by expressly stating that in the bailment agreement. Federal law requires common carriers who take advantage of such limitation to offer shippers the opportunity to pay a premium and declare a higher value for the goods.[2]

Bills of Lading A **bill of lading** is a document of title that is issued by a carrier-bailee to the bailor when goods are received for transportation.

A carrier has a lien on the goods in its possession covered by a bill of lading for necessary charges and expenses. If the charges are not paid, the carrier can sell the goods at public or private sale and apply the proceeds to pay the charges. Any excess proceeds must be held for the person who had the right to demand delivery of the goods.[3]

Warehouse Companies A **warehouser**, or **warehouse company**, is a bailee engaged in the business of storing property for compensation. Warehousers are subject to the rights, duties, and liability of an ordinary bailee. As such, they owe a **duty of reasonable care** to protect the bailed property in their possession from harm or loss.[4] Warehousers are liable only for loss or damage to the bailed property caused by their own negligence. They are not liable for loss or damage caused to bailed goods by another person's negligence or conduct. Warehousers can limit the dollar amount of their liability if they offer the bailor the opportunity to increase the liability limit for the payment of an additional charge.

Warehouse Receipt A **warehouse receipt** is a document of title issued by a warehouse company that is engaged in the business of storing goods for hire, such as a warehouse company or a storage company.[5] The warehouse receipt which is issued to the bailor, is often a preprinted form drafted by the warehouse company. Warehouse receipts include the date of issue, a description of the goods or of the packages containing them, the location of the warehouse where the goods are stored, and other terms relating to the bailment. A warehouse company has a *lien* on the goods in its possession for necessary expenses incurred in storing and handling the goods. If the charges are not paid, the warehouse company may sell the goods at a public or private auction and apply the proceeds to pay the charges. Any excess proceeds must be held for the persons who had the right to demand delivery of the goods.

Innkeepers An **innkeeper** is the owner of a facility that provides lodging to the public for compensation (e.g., hotel, motel). Under the common law, innkeepers are held to a **strict liability standard** regarding loss caused to the personal property of transient guests. Permanent lodgers are not subject to this rule.

However almost all states, have enacted **innkeepers' statutes** that change the common law and limit the liability of innkeepers. These statutes allow innkeepers to avoid liability for loss caused to guests' property if a safe is provided in which the guests' valuable property may be kept and the guests are aware of the safe's availability. Most state laws also allow innkeepers to limit the dollar amount of their liability by notifying their guests of this limit (e.g., by posting a notice on each guest room door).

Consider This Example Hospitality Hotel, Inc., operates a hotel. The hotel is located in a state that has an innkeepers' statute that (1) eliminates a hotel's liability for guests' property not placed in the safe located at the hotel's registration desk, and (2) limits a hotel's liability to $500 for any guest's property stored in the hotel's safe. The hotel has proper notices posted at the registration counter and in guests' rooms, notifying guests of these limitations on liability. Suppose Gion, a guest at the hotel, leaves expensive jewelry and cameras in his room when he temporarily leaves the hotel. Upon return, Gion's jewelry and cameras have been stolen. Because of the innkeepers' statute, the hotel is not liable for

Gion's loss. Suppose instead that Gion had taken items to the hotel's registration desk and had the hotel place them in the hotel's safe. If the items had been stolen from the hotel's safe, the innkeepers' statute, would have limited the hotel's liability to $500.

Concept Summary   *Special Bailee's Duty of Care*

Type of Bailee	Liability	Limitation on Liability
Common carrier	Strictly liable except for 1. Act of God 2. Act of a public enemy 3. Order of the government 4. Act of the shipper 5. Inherent nature of the goods	May limit the dollar amount of liability by offering the bailor the right to declare a higher value for the bailed goods for an additional charge.
Warehouse company	Ordinary negligence	May limit the dollar amount of liability by offering the bailor the right to declare a higher value for the bailed goods for an additional charge.
Innkeeper	Strictly liable	State innkeepers' statutes limit the liability of an innkeeper for others' negligence.

Chapter Summary

The Nature of Personal Property, p. 795

Personal Property

Personal property consists of everything that is not real property. It is sometimes referred to as goods or *chattels*. Types of personal property:

1. *Tangible property.* Tangible property is physically defined property such as goods, animals, and minerals.
2. *Intangible property.* Intangible property is rights that cannot be reduced to physical form, such as stock certificates, bonds, and copyrights.

Acquiring Ownership of Personal Property, p. 796

Methods of Acquiring Ownership in Personal Property

1. *Possession or capture.* A person can take possession of or capture unowned property, such as wild animals.
2. *Purchase.* A person can purchase property from its rightful owner.
3. *Production.* A person can produce a finished product from raw materials and supplies.
4. *Gift.* A gift is a voluntary transfer of property by its owner to a donee without consideration.
   a. Three elements are necessary to create a valid gift:
      i. *Donative intent.* The donor must have intended to make a gift. This intent can be inferred from the circumstances.
      ii. *Delivery.* Delivery of the personal property must be made to the donee by *physical delivery* or, where impracticable, by *constructive* (or *symbolic*) *delivery*.
      iii. *Acceptance.* The donee must accept the gift. Donees are free to reject gifts that they do not want.

    b. Types of gifts.

        i. *Gifts inter vivos.* These gifts are made during a donor's lifetime and are irrevocable present transfers of ownership.

        ii. *Gifts causa mortis.* These gifts are made in anticipation of death. A gift *causa mortis* is established if:

            a. The donor makes a gift in anticipation of approaching death from an existing illness or peril.

            b. The donor dies from such illness or peril without having revoked the gift.

5. *Will.* Gifts are made to beneficiaries named in a will.

6. *Inheritance.* Heirs are stipulated in an inheritance statute.

7. *Accession.* Accession occurs when the value of personal property increases because it is added to or improved by natural or manufactured means.

8. *Confusion.* Where fungible goods are commingled, the owners share title to the commingled goods in proportion to the amount of goods contributed.

9. *Divorce.* When a marriage is dissolved by a divorce, the parties obtain certain rights in the property of the marital estate.

Mislaid, Lost, and Abandoned Property, p. 800

Mislaid, Lost, and Abandoned Property

1. *Mislaid property.* Mislaid property is personal property that an owner voluntarily places somewhere and then inadvertently forgets. The owner of the premises where the property is mislaid does not acquire title to the property but has the right of possession against all except the rightful owner. The rightful owner can reclaim the property.

2. *Lost property.* Lost property is personal property that an owner leaves somewhere because of negligence or carelessness. The finder obtains title to the property against the whole world except the true owner. The rightful owner can reclaim the property.

    a. Estray statutes. These state statutes permit a finder of mislaid or lost property to obtain title to the property. To obtain clear title, the finder must:

        i. Report the find to the appropriate government agency and turn over possession of the property to the agency.

        ii. Post and publish required notices.

        iii. Wait the statutorily required time (e.g., one year) without the rightful owner claiming the property.

3. *Abandoned property.* Abandoned property is personal property that an owner has discarded, or mislaid or lost property that the owner gives up any further attempt to locate. The finder acquires title to the property. The prior owner cannot reclaim the property.

Bailments, p. 802

Bailment

Bailment occurs when the owner of personal property delivers the property to another person to be held, stored, or delivered, or for some other purpose.

1. Parties to a bailment:

    a. Bailor. The bailor is the owner of the property.

    b. Bailee. The bailee is the party to whom the property is delivered.

2. Three elements are necessary to create a bailment:

    a. Personal property. Only personal property can be bailed.

    b. Delivery of possession. The bailee must knowingly accept the property and have exclusive control over it.

    c. Bailment agreement. There must be a bailment agreement. *Express bailments* may be oral or written unless required to be in writing by the Statute of Frauds. A bailment may be *implied* from the circumstances.

Ordinary Bailments

1. **Bailments for the sole benefit of the bailor:**
   a. *Gratuitous bailment.* This type of bailment arises when the bailee is requested to care for the bailor's property as a favor.
   b. *Voluntary bailment.* This type of bailment arises when the bailee finds lost or misplaced property and decides to protect it.
   c. *Duty of care.* The bailee owes a duty of *slight care*, that is, the bailee is liable for *gross negligence*.

2. **Bailments for the sole benefit of the bailee:**
   a. *Gratuitous bailment.* A gratuitous bailment arises when the bailee uses the bailor's property for personal reasons without paying compensation.
   b. *Duty of care.* The bailee owes a duty of *great care* (or *utmost care*) and is liable for *slight negligence*.

3. **Bailments for the mutual benefit of the bailor and the bailee:**
   a. *Mutual benefit bailment.* This type of bailment arises when both parties benefit from the bailment. This includes commercial bailments.
   b. *Duty of care.* The bailee owes a duty of *reasonable care* (or *ordinary care*) and is liable for *ordinary negligence*.

Duration and Termination of Bailments

1. **Bailment for a fixed term.** This type of bailment terminates at the end of a stipulated term. It may be terminated prior to the end of the term by mutual assent of the bailor and bailee.

2. **Bailments at will.** They are bailments without a fixed term. They may be terminated at any time by either party.

Special Bailees

1. **Common carriers.** Common carriers are companies that offer transportation services to the public, such as airlines, railroads, and trucking firms. The parties are:
   a. *Cosignor or shipper.* The cosignor is the person shipping the goods, the bailor.
   b. *Common carrier.* The common carrier is the transportation company, the bailee.
   c. *Cosignee.* The cosignee is the party to whom the goods are to be delivered.
   d. *Duty of care.* Common carriers owe a duty of *strict liability*; that is, if the goods are lost, damaged, destroyed, or stolen, the common carrier is liable even if the loss or damage was not its fault.
   e. *Bill of lading.* This document of title is issued by a common carrier to the bailor when goods are received by the common carrier for transportation.

2. **Warehouse companies.** Warehouse companies engage in the business of storing property for compensation. *Duty of care.* Warehouse companies owe a duty of reasonable care (or ordinary care) to protect the bailed goods from loss or damage.
   a. *Warehouse receipt.* This document is issued by a warehouse company to the bailor when goods are received by the warehouse company for storage.

3. **Innkeepers.** An innkeeper is the owner of a facility that provides lodging to the public for compensation (e.g., hotel, or motel).
   a. *Duty of care.* Under the common law, innkeepers owe a duty of *strict liability* regarding loss caused to guests' property.
   b. *Innkeepers' statutes.* These laws have been enacted to limit the liability of innkeepers for loss or damage to guests' property. The innkeeper must post required notices to be covered by the law.

Internet Exercises and Case Questions

Working the Web Internet Exercises

Activities

1. Review your state's laws on innkeepers' liability for lost or stolen property of hotel guests. What is the statutory limitation on losses?

Critical Legal Thinking Cases

36.1 Uniform Gift to Minors Act   Between 1972 and 1984, Theodore Alexander Buder's father made substantial gifts to his minor grandchildren. The Buders divorced during this period. The cash gifts, typically in the form of checks made directly payable to the children, were given to Buder with the understanding that he would safeguard the money and invest it on behalf of the children. Buder invested various amounts of the children's money in "blue chip" stocks traded over the New York and American stock exchanges. In 1974, he began investing substantial sums of the children's money in speculative penny stocks. The stocks were purchased in Buder's name as custodian for the children, as required by the Uniform Gifts to Minors Act (UGMA). At one point, almost half of the children's money was invested in penny stocks. All the penny stocks except one suffered substantial losses. Buder's ex-wife, Sartore, sued him, alleging that he had breached his fiduciary owed to the children under the UGMA. She sought to recover the funds lost by Buder's investment of the children's funds in penny stocks. Who wins? [*Buder v. Sartore*, 774 P.2d 1383, 1989 Colo. Lexis 227 (Co. 1989)]

36.2 Lost Property   In June 1983, Danny Lee Smith and his brother, Jeffrey Allen Smith, found a 16-foot fiberglass boat lying beside the roadway in Mobile County, Alabama. Seeing two sheriff's deputies, they stopped them to discuss the boat. Over the Smiths' objections, the deputies impounded the boat. The Smiths made it clear that if the true owner of the boat was not found, they wanted the boat. The true owner did not claim the boat. Mobile County claimed the boat and wanted to auction it off for sale to raise money for county recreational programs. The Smiths claimed the boat as finders. Alabama did not have an estray statute that applied to the situation. Who gets the boat? [*Smith v. Sheriff Purvis*, 474 So.2d 1131, 1985 Ala.Civ.App. Lexis 1280 (Ala. App. 1985)]

36.3 Abandoned Property   Late in 1975, police officers of the city of Miami, Florida, responded to reports of a shooting at the apartment of Carlos Fuentes. Fuentes had been shot in the neck and shoulder, and shortly after the police arrived, he was removed to a hospital. In an ensuing search of the apartment, the police found assorted drug paraphernalia, a gun, and cash in the amount of $58,591. The property was seized, taken to the police station, and placed in custody. About nine days later, the police learned that Fuentes had been discharged from the hospital. All efforts by police to locate Fuentes and his girlfriend, a co-occupant of Fuentes's apartment, were unsuccessful. Neither Fuentes nor his girlfriend ever came forward to claim any of the items taken by the police from his apartment. About four years later, in 1979, James W. Green and Walter J. Vogel, the owners of the apartment building in which Fuentes was a tenant, sued the city of Miami to recover the cash found in Fuentes's apartment. The state of Florida intervened in the case, also claiming an interest in the money. Who wins? [*State of Florida v. Green*, 456 So.2d 1309 1984 Fla.App. Lexis 15340 (Fla. App. 1984)]

36.4 Bailment   On February 4, 1976, James D. Merritt leased a storage locker from Nationwide Warehouse Co., Ltd. (Nationwide), and agreed to pay $16 per month lease for the locker. Merritt placed various items in the leased premises but never informed Nationwide as to the nature or quantity of articles stored therein. Merritt was free to store or remove whatever he wished without consultation with, permission from, or notice to Nationwide. Merritt locked the leased premises with his own lock and key. Nationwide was not furnished with a key. Subsequently, certain personal property belonging to Merritt disappeared from the storage space. Merritt sued Nationwide to recover damages of $5,275. Was a bailment created between Merritt and Nationwide? [*Merritt v. Nationwide Warehouse Co., Ltd.*, 605 S.W.2d 250, 1980 Tenn.App. Lexis 338 (Tenn. App. 1980)]

36.5 Liability for Lost Goods   On May 14, 1980, Clarence Williams took his wife's fur coat to Debonair Cleaners for cleaning and storage. The clerk told him that the cleaners was experienced in such matters and that the charge would be 3 percent of the stated value of the coat. Williams stated that the coat was worth $13,000, and the clerk gave Williams a claim check and informed Williams that the total fee for storage would be $390, to be paid when the coat was retrieved. That evening Williams related the substance of his conversation with the clerk to his wife, America, and gave her the claim check. Approximately eight months later, America Williams went to Debonair Cleaners to retrieve her coat. She presented the claim check to the clerk who, after searching the premises for the coat, told her that it could not be located. Williams was informed that the coat had probably been stolen during a break-in and burglary. Williams sued Debonair Cleaners to recover the value of the coat. Who wins? [*Mahallati v. Williams*, 479 A.2d 300, 1984 D.C.App. Lexis 419 (D.C. App. 1984)]

36.6 Gratuitous Bailment   Marsha Hamilton and Andrea Morris were guests at a dinner party attended by approximately 25 people. The party began about 7:00 P.M. and ended at approximately 1:00 A.M. Alcoholic beverages were served throughout the evening. At approximately 11:30, while working in the kitchen, Hamilton removed her watch and placed it on the counter. About midnight, Hamilton left the kitchen and went outside. After about 15 minutes, she became ill and fled to the bathroom. Shortly after Hamilton left the kitchen, Morris saw the watch on the counter and, fearing for its safety, picked it up and carried it in her hand as she looked for Hamilton. When Hamilton came out of the bathroom, she and her fiancé left the party. Morris was unable to find Hamilton and could not recall precisely what she did with the watch. She testified that she either gave it to Hamilton's fiancé or put it somewhere in the host's house for safekeeping. Hamilton's fiancé testified that Morris did not give him the watch. The next day Hamilton discovered that she did not have her watch, but in a search of the host's home, the watch was not recovered. Hamilton sued Morris for damages. Who wins? [*Morris v. Hamilton*, 302 S.E.2d 51, 1983 Va. Lexis 231 (VA 1983)]

36.7 Parking Lot's Liability   Allright, Inc., is a parking lot operator in Houston, Texas. On January 18, 1980, Kirkland Strauder drove his 1978 Buick Regal automobile to a Houston Allright parking lot and placed it in a row of cars to be parked by the attendant. When Strauder returned two hours later to reclaim his car, it could not be found. Strauder reported the car stolen. Allright could not explain the loss of the car, which was found 1 1/2 weeks later, wrecked and stripped. Strauder sued Allright, Inc., for damages. Who wins? [*Allright, Inc. v. Strauder*, 679 S.W.2d 81, 1984 Tex.App. Lexis 6006 (Tex. App. 1984)]

36.8 Disclaimer of Liability On January 23, 1982, Joseph Conboy, his wife, and a group of friends convened in Manhattan, New York, for a party at Studio 54, a discotheque where patrons dance to recorded music played on high-fidelity sound equipment. The Conboy party checked their coats, 14 in all, with the coatroom attendant. After paying a $0.75 charge per coat, they received seven check stubs. A small sign in the coatroom stated "Liability for lost property in this coat/check room is limited to $100 per loss of misplaced article." Conboy testified that he did not notice it when he checked his coat and that the coatroom attendant did not call his attention to the sign. At the end of the evening, Conboy and the other guests of the party attempted to reclaim their coats. Conboy's one-month-old $1,350 leather coat was missing. Conboy sued Studio 54 for damages. Is the disclaimer of liability enforceable? [*Conboy v. Studio 54, Inc.* 449 N.Y.S.2d 391, 1982 N.Y.Misc. Lexis 3309 (N.Y. Civ. Ct. 1982)]

Business Ethics Cases

36.9 Business Ethics When Dr. Arthur M. Edwards died, leaving a will disposing of this property, he left the villa-type condominium in which he lived, its "contents," and $10,000 to his stepson, Ronald W. Souders. Edwards left the residual of his estate to other named legatees. In administering the estate, certain stock certificates, passbook savings accounts, and other bank statements were found in Edwards' condominium. Souders claimed that these items belonged to him because they were "contents" of the condominium. The other legatees opposed Souders's claim, alleging that the disputed property was intangible property and not part of the contents of the condominium. The value of the property was as follows: condominium, $138,000; furniture in condominium, $4,000; stocks, $377,000; and passbook and other bank accounts, $124,000. Who is entitled to the stocks and bank accounts? Do you think Souders acted ethically in this case? [*Souders v. Johnson*, 501 So.2d 745, 1987 Fla.App. Lexis 6579 (Fla. App. 1987)]

36.10 Business Ethics Darryl Kulwin was employed by Nova Stylings, Inc. (Nova), as a jewelry salesman. In that capacity, he traveled throughout the country, carrying with him jewelry owned and manufactured by Nova to show to prospective buyers. Kulwin was visiting Panoria Ruston, who was a guest registered with the Red Roof Inn in Overland Park, Kansas. Ruston and Kulwin met at the Red Roof Inn and later made plans to leave to go to dinner. Kulwin asked Ruston to make arrangements with the desk clerk to leave his sample case in the office of the Red Roof Inn while they went out to dinner. Ruston asked the clerk if she could leave the bag in the manager's office of the Red Roof Inn and the clerk agreed. Ruston advised the clerk that the contents of the case were valuable but did not descibe the contents of the bag.

Kansas Statute § 36-402(b) provides:

No hotel or motel keeper in this state shall be liable for the loss of, or damage to, merchandise for sale or samples belonging to a guest, lodger, or boarder unless the guest, lodger, or boarder upon entering the hotel or motel, shall give notice of having merchandise for sale or samples in his possession, together with an itemized list of such property, to the hotel or motel keeper, or his authorized agent or clerk in the registration office of the hotel or motel office.

No hotel or motel keeper shall be liable for any loss of such property designated in this subsection (b), after notice an itemized statement having been given and delivered as aforesaid, in an amount in excess of two hundred fifty dollars ($250), unless such hotel or motel keeper, by specific agreement in writing, individually, or by an authorized agent or clerk in charge of the registration office of the hotel or motel, shall voluntarily assume liability for a larger amount with reference to such property. The hotel or motel keeper shall not be compelled to receive such guests, lodgers, or boarders with merchandise for sale or samples.

The inn posted the proper notice of the provisions of this act in all of the guests' rooms, including that of Ruston. An unidentified person obtained access to the manager's office and removed the case from the office. Nova sued Red Roof Inns for the alleged value of the jewelry, $650,000. Is Red Roof Inns liable? Did either party act unethically in this case? [*Nova Stylings v. Red Roof Inns, Inc.*, 747 P.2d 107, 1987 Kan. Lexis 469 (KS 1987)]

Briefing the Case Writing Assignment

Read Case A.36 in the Case Appendix [*Michigan Mutual Insurance Co. v. Marriot Corporation*]. This case is excerpted from the district court's opinion. Review and brief the case. In your brief, be sure to answer the following questions.

1. Who is the plaintiff and who is the defendant?
2. What elements must be proven to establish a bailment?
3. Was a bailment found in this case? Why or why not?

Endnotes

1. UCC § 7-301(1).
2. UCC § 7-309(2).
3. UCC § 7-308(1).
4. UCC §§ 7-204(1) and 7-403(1).
5. UCC § 1-201(45).

Real Property and Landlord–Tenant Relationship

37

> "Without that sense of security which property gives, the land would still be uncultivated."
>
> —Francois Quesnay
> Maximes, IV

Chapter Objectives

After studying this chapter, you should be able to:

1. List and describe the different types of real property.

2. Describe the different types of freehold estates, concurrent ownership, and future interests in land.

3. Explain how ownership interests in real property can be transferred.

4. Explain how a landlord–tenant relationship is created and describe landlords' and tenants' rights and duties.

5. Describe the various forms of private and public land use regulation.

Chapter Contents

- Real Property
- Transfer of Ownership of Real Property
- Nonpossessory Interests
- Landlord–Tenant Relationship
- Land Use Regulation

Property and ownership rights in **real property** play an important part in the U.S. society and economy. The concept of real property is concerned with the legal rights to the property rather than the physical attributes of the tangible land. Thus, real property includes some items of personal property that are affixed to real property (e.g., fixtures) and other rights (e.g., minerals, air).

The area covered by laws concerning real property is very broad. It includes **landlord–tenant relationships** and **land use regulation**, among other things.

Individuals and families own or rent houses, farmers and ranchers own farmland and ranches, and businesses own or lease commercial and office buildings. In addition, (1) over half of the population rents their homes, and (2) many businesses lease office space, stores, manufacturing facilities, and other commercial property. The parties to a **landlord–tenant** relationship have certain legal rights and duties that are governed by a mixture of real estate and contract law.

Although the United States has the most advanced private property system in the world, the ownership and possession of real estate are not free from government regulation. Pursuant to constitutional authority, federal, state, and local governments have enacted myriad laws that regulate the ownership, possession, and use of real property. These laws, which are collectively referred to as **land use regulation**, include zoning laws, building codes, antidiscrimination laws, and the like.

This chapter covers the law concerning the ownership and transfer of real property, landlord–tenant relationships, and land use control.

> Property is an instrument of humanity. Humanity is not an instrument of property.
>
> Woodrow Wilson
> *Speech (1912)*

Real Property

Property is usually classified as either real or personal property. **Real property** is immovable or attached to immovable land or buildings, whereas personal property is movable. The various types of real property are:

1. ***Land and buildings.*** **Land** is the most common form of real property. A landowner usually purchases the *surface rights* to the land—that is, the right to occupy the land. The owner may use, enjoy, and develop the property as he or she sees fit, subject to any applicable government regulation.

   Buildings constructed on land are real property. For example, houses, apartment buildings, manufacturing plants, and office buildings constructed on land are real property. Such things as radio towers and bridges are usually considered real property as well.

2. ***Subsurface rights.*** The owner of land possesses **subsurface rights**, or **mineral rights**, to the earth located beneath the surface of the land. These rights can be very valuable. For example, gold, uranium, oil, or natural gas may lie beneath the surface of the land. Theoretically, mineral rights extend to the center of the earth. In reality, mines and oil wells usually extend only several miles into the earth. Subsurface rights may be sold separately from surface rights.

3. ***Plant life and vegetation.*** **Plant life and vegetation** growing on the surface of land are considered real property. Such vegetation includes both natural plant life (e.g., trees) and cultivated plant life (e.g., crops). When land is sold, any plant life growing on the land is included unless the parties agree otherwise. Plant life that is severed from the land is considered personal property.

4. ***Fixtures.*** Certain personal property is so closely associated with real property that it becomes part of the realty. Such items are called **fixtures**. For example, kitchen cabinets, carpeting, and doorknobs are fixtures, but throw rugs and furniture are personal property.

   Unless otherwise provided, if a building is sold, the fixtures are included in the sale. If the sale agreement is silent as to whether an item is a fixture, the courts make their determination on the basis of whether the item can be removed without causing substantial damage to the realty.

5. *Air Rights.* Common law provided that the owners of real property owned that property from the center of the earth to the heavens. This rule has been eroded by modern legal restrictions such as land use regulation laws, environmental protection laws, and air navigation requirements. Even today, however, the owners of land may sell or lease air space parcels above their land.

An **air space parcel** is the air space above the surface of the earth of an owner's real property. Air space parcels are valuable property rights, particularly in densely populated metropolitan areas where building property is scarce. For example, many developments have been built in air space parcels in New York City. More developments are expected to be built in air space parcels in the future.

A person's ownership right in real property is called an **estate in land** (or **estate**). An estate is defined as the bundle of **legal rights** that the owner has to possess, use, and enjoy the property. The type of estate that an owner possesses is determined from the deed, will, lease, or other document that transferred the ownership rights to him or her.

Freehold Estates

A **freehold estate** is an estate where the owner has a *present possessory interest* in the real property; that is, the owner may use and enjoy the property as he or she sees fit, subject to any applicable government regulation or private restraint. The two types of freehold estates are *estates in fee* and *life estates*.

Estates in Fee A **fee simple absolute** (or **fee simple**) is the highest form of ownership of real property because it grants the owner the fullest bundle of legal rights that a person can hold in real property. It is the type of ownership most people connect with "owning" real property. A fee simple owner has the right to exclusively possess and use his or her property to the extent that the owner has not transferred any interest in the property (e.g., by lease).

If a person owns real property in fee simple, his or her ownership:

- Is infinite in duration (fee).
- Has no limitation on inheritability (simple).
- Does not end upon the happening of any event (absolute).

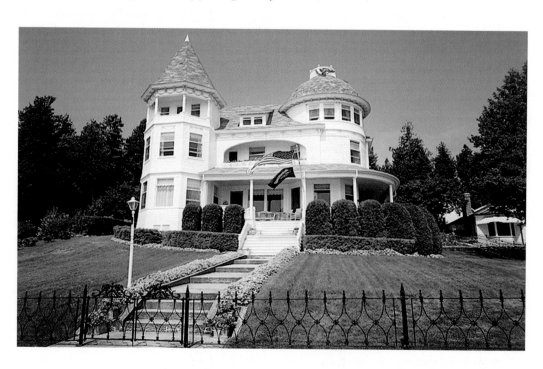

Mackinac Island, Michigan. The most valuable asset of many families is the home they own, such as this cottage on Mackinac Island, Michigan.

A **fee simple defeasible** (or **qualified fee**) grants the owner all the incidents of a fee simple absolute except that it may be taken away if a specified *condition* occurs or does not occur. For example, a conveyance of property to a church "as long as the land is used as a church or for church purposes" creates a qualified fee. The church has all the rights of a fee simple absolute owner except that its ownership rights are terminated if the property is no longer used for church purposes.

Life Estate A **life estate** is an interest in real property that lasts for the life of a specified person, usually the grantee. For example, a conveyance of real property "to Anna for her life" creates a life estate. A life estate may also be measured by the life of a third party (e.g., "to Anna for the life of Benjamin"). This is called an **estate pour autre vie**. A life estate may be defeasible (e.g., "to John for his life but only if he continues to occupy this residence"). Upon the death of the named person, the life estate terminates, and the property reverts to the grantor or the grantor's estate or other designated person.

A life tenant is treated as the owner of the property during the duration of the life estate. He or she has the right to possess and use the property except to the extent that it would cause permanent *waste* of the property. A life tenant may sell, transfer, or mortgage his or her estate in the land. However, the mortgage cannot exceed the duration of the life estate. A life tenant is obligated to keep the property in repair and to pay property taxes.

Concept Summary *Freehold Estates*

Estate	Description
Fee simple absolute	Is the highest form of ownership of real property. Ownership (1) is infinite in duration, (2) has no limitation on inheritability, and (3) does not end upon the occurrence or nonoccurrence of an event.
Fee simple defeasible	Grants the owner all the incidents of a fee simple absolute except that it may be taken away if a specified condition occurs or does not occur.
Life estate	Is an interest in property that lasts for the life of a specified person. A life estate terminates upon the death of the named person and reverts back to the grantor or his or her estate or other designated person.

Concurrent Ownership

Two or more persons may own a piece of real property. This is called **co-ownership** or **concurrent ownership**. The following forms of co-ownership are recognized: *joint tenancy, tenancy in common, tenancy by the entirety, community property, condominiums,* and *cooperatives*.

Joint Tenancy To create a joint tenancy, words that clearly show a person's intent to create a joint tenancy must be used. Language such as "Marsha Leest and James Leest, as joint tenants" is usually sufficient. The most distinguished feature of a **joint tenancy** is the co-owners' *right of survivorship*. This means that upon the death of one of the co-owners (or **joint tenants**), the deceased person's interest in the property automatically passes to the surviving joint tenants. Any contrary provision in the deceased's will is ineffective.

Consider This Example   Jones, one of four people who own a piece of property in joint tenancy, executes a will leaving all of his property to a university. Jones dies. The surviving joint tenants—not the university—acquire his interest in the piece of property. Each joint tenant has a right to sell or transfer his or her interest in the property, but such conveyance terminates the joint tenancy. The parties then become tenants in common.

Business Brief

Upon the death of a joint tenant, the deceased's interest in the property automatically passes to the surviving joint tenants, not to the deceased's heirs or beneficiaries.

In the following case, the court had to decide how to split the proceeds from the sale of real property owned by co-owners.

Cunningham v. Hastings
556 N.E.2d 12, 1990 Ind.App. Lexis 764 (1990)
Court of Appeals of Indiana

Case 37.1
Joint Tenancy

Background and Facts

On August 30, 1984, Warren R. Hastings and Joan L. Cunningham, who were unmarried, purchased a house together. Hastings paid $45,000 down payment toward the purchase price out of his own funds. The deed referred to Hastings and Cunningham as "joint tenants with the right of survivorship." Hastings and Cunningham occupied the property jointly. After their relationship ended, Hastings took sole possession of the property. Cunningham filed a complaint seeking partition of the real estate. Based on its determination that the property could not be split, the trial court ordered it to be sold. The trial court further ordered that $45,000 of the sale proceeds be paid to Hastings to reimburse him for his down payment and that the remainder of the proceeds be divided equally between Hastings and Cunningham. Cunningham appealed, alleging that Hastings should not have been given credit for the down payment.

Issue

Is Cunningham entitled to an equal share of the proceeds of the sale of the real estate?

Court's Reasoning

The court of appeals stated that the determination of the parties' interests in the present case was simple. There were only two parties involved in the joint tenancy. Once a joint tenancy relationship is found to exist between two people in a partition action, it is axiomatic that each person owns a one-half interest. The court held that regardless of who provided the money to purchase the land, the creation of a joint tenancy relationship entitles each party to an equal share of the proceeds of the sale upon partition.

Decision and Remedy

The court of appeals held that Cunningham was entitled to an equal share of the proceeds of the sale because she and Hastings owned the property as joint tenants. The court of appeals reversed the trial court's judgment and remanded the case to the trial court, with instructions to order the entire proceeds of the sale to be divided equally between Cunningham and Hastings.

Case Questions

Critical Legal Thinking Should the law recognize so many different forms of ownership of real property? Do you think most people understand the legal consequences of taking title in the various forms?

Business Ethics Did Cunningham act ethically in demanding one-half the value of the down payment even though she did not contribute to it?

Contemporary Business Could Hastings have protected the $45,000 he paid for the down payment? If so, how could he have done it?

Tenancy in Common In a **tenancy in common**, the interests of a surviving *tenant in common* pass to the deceased tenant's estate and not to the co-tenants. A tenancy in common may be created by express words, such as "Ian Cespedes and Joy Park, as tenants in common." Unless otherwise agreed, a tenant in common can sell, give, devise, or otherwise transfer his or her interest in the property without the consent of the other co-owners.

Consider This Example Lopez, who is one of four tenants in common who own a piece of property, has a will that leaves all his property to his granddaughter. When Lopez dies, the granddaughter receives his interest in the tenancy in common, and the granddaughter becomes a tenant in common with the three other owners.

Tenancy by the Entirety **Tenancy by the entirety** is a form of co-ownership of real property that can be used only by married couples. This type of tenancy must be created by express words, such as "Harold Jones and Maude Jones, husband and wife, as tenants by the entireties." A surviving spouse has the right of survivorship.

Tenancy by the entirety is distinguished from a joint tenancy because neither spouse may sell or transfer his or her interest in the property without the other spouse's consent. Only about half of the states recognize tenancy by the entirety.

Community Property Nine states—Arizona, California, Idaho, Louisiana, Nevada, New Mexico, Texas, Washington, and Wisconsin—recognize a form of co-ownership known as

community property. This method of co-ownership applies only to married couples. It is based on the notion that a husband and wife should share equally in the fruits of the marital partnership. Under these laws, each spouse owns an equal one-half share of the *income* both spouses earned during the marriage and one-half of the *assets acquired by this income during the marriage*, regardless of who earns the income. Property that is acquired through gift or inheritance either before or during marriage remains **separate property**. Interest payments, dividends, and appreciation of separate property received or accrued during marriage is also separate property.

When a spouse dies, the surviving spouse automatically receives one-half the community property. The other half passes to the heirs of the deceased spouse as directed by will or by state intestate statute if there is no will.

During the marriage, neither spouse can sell, transfer, or gift community property without the consent of the other spouse. Upon a divorce, each spouse has a right to one-half the community property.

The location of the real property determines whether community property law applies. For example, if a married couple who lives in a noncommunity property state purchases real property located in a community property state, community property laws apply to that property.

Consider This Example   Elma is a successful brain surgeon who makes $500,000 income per year. She meets and marries Brad, a struggling actor who makes $10,000 per year. When Elma gets married, she owns $1 million of real estate and $2 million in securities, which she retains as her separate property. Brad has no separate property when he and Elma are married. After three years, Elma and Brad get a divorce. Assume that Elma has made $500,000 and Brad has made $10,000 each of the three years of their marriage, their living expenses were $110,000 per year and they have $1,200,000 of earned income saved in a bank account. During the marriage, Elma's real estate has increased is value to $1.5 million, and her securities have increased in value to $3 million. Upon divorce, Elma receives her $1.5 million in real estate and $3 million in securities as her separate property. Elma and Brad each receive $600,000 from the community property bank account.

Concept Summary   *Concurrent Ownership*

Form of Ownership	Right of Survivorship	Tenant May Unilaterally Transfer His or Her Interest
Joint tenancy	Yes, deceased tenant's interest automatically passes to co-tenants.	Yes, tenant may transfer his or her interest without the consent of co-tenants. Transfer severs joint tenancy.
Tenancy in common	No, deceased tenant's interest passes to his or her estate.	Yes, tenant may transfer his or her interest without the consent of co-tenants. Transfer does not sever tenancy in common.
Tenancy by the entirety	Yes, deceased tenant's interest automatically passes to his or her spouse.	No, neither spouse may transfer his or her interest without the other spouse's consent.
Community property	Yes, when a spouse dies the surviving spouse automatically receives one-half of the community property. The other half passes to the heirs of the deceased spouse, as directed by a valid will or by state interstate statute if there is no will.	No, neither spouse may transfer his or her interest without the other spouse's consent.

Condominiums **Condominiums** are a common form of ownership in multiple-dwelling buildings. Purchasers of a condominium (1) have title to their individual units and (2) own the common areas (e.g., hallways, elevators, parking areas, recreational facilities) as tenants in common with the other owners. Owners may sell or mortgage their units without the permission of the other owners. Owners are assessed monthly fees for the maintenance of common areas. In addition to dwelling units, the condominium form of ownership is offered for office buildings, boat docks, and such.

Cooperatives A **cooperative** is a form of co-ownership of a multiple-dwelling building where a corporation owns the building, and the residents own shares in the corporation. Each cooperative owner leases a unit in the building from the corporation under a renewable, long-term, proprietary lease. Individual residents may not secure loans with the units they occupy. The corporation may borrow money on a blanket mortgage, and each shareholder is jointly and severally liable on the loan. Usually, cooperative owners may not sell their shares or sublease their units without the approval of the other owners.

Future Interests

A person may be given the right to possess property in the *future* rather than in the present. This right is called a **future interest**. The two forms of future interests are:

1. *Reversion.* A **reversion** is a right of possession that returns to the *grantor* after the expiration of a limited or contingent estate. Reversions do not have to be expressly stated because they arise automatically by law. For example, if a grantor conveys property "to M. R. Harrington for life," the grantor has retained a reversion in the property. That is, when Harrington dies, the property reverts to the grantor or, if he or she is not living, then to his or her estate.

2. *Remainder.* If the right of possession returns to a *third party* upon the expiration of a limited or contingent estate, it is called a **remainder**. The person who is entitled to the future interest is called a **remainderman**. For example, a conveyance of property "to Joe for life, remainder to Meredith" is a vested remainder—the only contingency to Meredith's possessory interest is Joe's death.

Concept Summary Future Interests

Future Interest	Description
Reversion	Right to possession of real property returns to the grantor after the expiration of a limited or contingent estate.
Remainder	Right to possession of real property goes to a third person upon the expiration of a limited or contingent estate.

Transfer of Ownership of Real Property

Ownership of real property may be transferred from one person to another. Title to real property may be transferred by sale; tax sale; gift, will, or inheritance; and adverse possession. The different methods of transfer provide different degrees of protection to the transferee.

Sale of Real Estate

A **sale** or **conveyance** is the most common method for transferring ownership rights in real property. An owner may offer his or her real estate for sale either by himself or herself or by using a real estate broker. Once a buyer has been located and the parties have negotiated the terms of the sale, a **real estate sales contract** is executed by the parties. The Statute of Frauds in most states requires this contract to be in writing.

The seller delivers a deed to the buyer, and the buyer pays the purchase price at the **closing** or **settlement**. Unless otherwise agreed, it is implied that the seller is conveying fee simple absolute title to the buyer. If either party fails to perform, the other party may sue for breach of contract and obtain either monetary damages or specific performance.

Deeds

Deeds are used to convey real property by sale or gift. The seller or donor is called the **grantor**. The buyer or recipient is called the **grantee**. A deed may be used to transfer a fee simple absolute interest in real property or any lesser estate (e.g., life estate).

State laws recognize different types of deeds that provide differing degrees of protection to grantees. A **warranty deed** (deed in which the grantor warrants that he or she has sold title to the real property) contains the greatest number of warranties and provides the most protection to grantees. A **quitclaim deed** (deed in which the grantor transfers only whatever interest he or she has in the real property) provides the least amount of protection because only the grantor's interest is conveyed.

Recording Statutes

Every state has a **recording statute** that provides that copies of deeds and other documents concerning interests in real property (e.g., mortgages, liens, easements) may be filed in a government office, where they become public records open to viewing by the public. Recording statutes are intended to prevent fraud and to establish certainty in the ownership and transfer of property. Instruments are usually filed in the **county recorder's office** of the country in which the property is located. A fee is charged to record an instrument.

Persons interested in purchasing the property or lending on the property should check these records to determine whether the grantor or borrower actually owns the property and whether any other parties (e.g., lienholders, mortgages, easement holders) have an interest in the property. The recordation of a deed is not required to pass title from the grantor to the grantee. Recording the deed gives **constructive notice** to the world of the owner's interest in the property.

A party who is concerned about his or her ownership rights in a parcel of real property can bring a **quiet title action** which is a lawsuit, to have a court determine the extent of those rights. Public notice of the hearing must be given so that anyone claiming an interest in the property may appear and be heard. After the hearing, the judge declares who has title to the property; that is, the court "quiets title" by its decision.

Business Brief

Anyone interested in purchasing property or lending on the property should check the county recorder's records of the county in which the real property is located to determine if the grantor or borrower actually owns the property and whether any other parties have an interest in the property.

Marketable Title

A grantor has the obligation to transfer **marketable title**, or **good title**, to the grantee. Marketable title means that the title is free from any encumbrances, defects in title, or other defects that are not disclosed but would affect the value of the property. The three most common ways of assuring marketable title are as follows:

- *Attorney's opinion.* An attorney examines an **abstract of title** (i.e., a chronological history of the chain of title and encumbrances affecting the property) and renders an opinion concerning the status of the title. The attorney may be sued for any losses caused by his or her negligence in rendering the opinion.

- *Torrens system.* The Torrens system is a method of determining title to real property in a judicial proceeding at which everyone claiming an interest in the property may appear and be heard. After the evidence is heard, the court issues a **certificate of title** to the person who is determined to be the rightful owner.

- *Title insurance.* The best way for a grantee to be sure that he or she has obtained marketable title is to purchase **title insurance** from an insurance company. The title insurer must reimburse the insured for any losses caused by undiscovered defects in the title. Each time a property is transferred or refinanced a new title insurance policy must be obtained.

Tax Sale

If an owner of real property fails to pay property taxes, the government may obtain a *lien* on the property for the amount of the taxes. If the taxes remain unpaid for a statutory period of time, the government may sell the property at a **tax sale** to satisfy the lien. Any excess proceeds are paid to the taxpayer. The buyer receives title to the property.

Many states provide a *period of redemption* after a tax sale during which the taxpayer may redeem the property by paying the unpaid taxes and penalties. In these states, the buyer at a tax sale does not receive title to the property until the period of redemption has passed.

Gift, Will, or Inheritance

Ownership of real property may be transferred by **gift**. The gift is made when the deed to the property is delivered by the donor to the donee or to a third party to hold for the donee. No consideration is necessary. For example, suppose a grandfather wants to give his farm to his granddaughter. To do so, he only has to execute a deed and give the deed to her or to someone to hold for her, such as her parents.

Real property may also be transferred by **will**. For example, a person may leave a piece of real estate to his best friend by will when he dies. This transfer does not require the transfer of a deed during the testator's lifetime. A deed will be issued to the beneficiary when the will is probated. If a person dies without a valid will, his or her property is distributed to the heirs pursuant to the applicable state intestacy statute.

Ranch, Idaho. This ranch land is an example of real property.

Adverse Possession

In most states, a person who wrongfully possesses someone else's real property obtains title to that property if certain statutory requirements are met. This is called **adverse possession**. Property owned by federal and state governments is not subject to adverse possession.

Under this doctrine, the transfer of the property is involuntary and does not require the delivery of a deed. To obtain title under adverse possession, the wrongful possession must be

- **For a statutorily prescribed period of time.** In most states, this period is between 10 and 20 years.

- **Open, visible, and notorious.** The adverse possessor must occupy the property so as to put the owner on notice of the possession.

- **Actual and exclusive.** The adverse possessor must physically occupy the premises. The planting of crops, grazing of animals, or building of a structure on the land constitutes physical occupancy.

- **Continuous and peaceful.** The occupancy must be continuous and uninterrupted for the required statutory period. Any break in normal occupancy terminates the adverse possession. This means that the adverse possessor may leave the property to go to work, to the store, on a vacation, and such. The adverse possessor cannot take the property by force from an owner.

- **Hostile and adverse.** The possessor must occupy the property without the express or implied permission of the owner. Thus, a lessee cannot claim title to property under adverse possession.

If the elements of adverse possession are met, the adverse possessor acquires clear title to the land. However, title is acquired only as to the property actually possessed and occupied during the statutory period, and not the entire tract. For example, an adverse possessor who occupies 1 acre of a 200,000-acre ranch for the statutory period of time acquires title only to the 1 acre. In the following case, the court held that adverse possession had occurred.

Business Brief

Owners of property should check their property every so many years to determine if anyone is attempting to acquire title by adverse possession. If anyone is found to be doing so, the owner should take appropriate action to prevent the adverse possession.

Good fences make good neighbors.
Robert Frost
"Mending Wall" (1914)

Witt v. Miller
845 S.W.2d 665, 1993 Mo.App. Lexis 20 (1993)
Court of Appeals of Missouri

Case 37.2
Adverse Possession

Background and Facts

Edward and Mary Shaughnessey purchased a 16-acre tract in St. Louis county in 1954. Subsequently, they subdivided 12 acres into 18 lots offered for sale and retained possession of the remaining 4-acre tract. In 1967, Charles and Elaine Witt purchased lot 12, which is adjacent to the 4-acre tract. The Witts constructed and moved into a house on their lot. In 1968, they cleared an area of land that ran the length of their property and extended 40 feet onto the 4-acre tract. The Witts constructed a pool and a deck, planted a garden, made a playground for their children, set up a dog run, and built a fence along the edge of the property line, which included the now-disputed property. Neither the Witts nor the Shaughnesseys realized that the Witts had encroached on the Shaughnesseys' property.

In February 1988, the Shaughnesseys sold the 4-acre tract to Thomas and Rosanne Miller. When a survey showed the encroachment, the Millers demanded that the Witts remove the pool and cease using the property. When the Witts refused to do so, the Millers sued to quiet title. The Witts defended, arguing that they had obtained title to the disputed property by adverse possession. The trial court held that there was no adverse possession and ruled in favor of the Millers. The Witts appealed.

Issue

Had the elements for adverse possession been met?

Court's Reasoning

The court of appeals held that the Witts had proven the necessary elements for adverse possession under state law. The Witts'

Witt v. Miller
845 S.W.2d 665, 1993 Mo.App. Lexis 20 (1993)
Court of Appeals of Missouri
(continued)

occupation of the land was open and notorious, actual and exclusive, hostile and adverse, continuous and peaceful, and had been for over the statutory period of 10 years.

Decision and Remedy

The court of appeals held that the elements of adverse possession had been proven. The court of appeals reversed the decision of the trial court and issued an order quiting title to the disputed property in the Witts' favor.

Case Questions

Critical Legal Thinking   What does the doctrine of adverse possession provide? What elements need to be proven?

Business Ethics   Did the Witts act ethically in claiming title to someone else's land? Should they be allowed to benefit from their own mistake?

Contemporary Business   What should owners of property do to protect themselves from adverse possession claims? Explain.

Nonpossessory Interests

A person may own a **nonpossessory interest** in another's real estate. The three nonpossessory interests—*easements*, *licenses*, and *profits*—are discussed in the following paragraphs.

Easements

An **easement** is an interest in land that gives the holder the right to make limited use of another's property without taking anything from it. Typical easements are common driveways, party walls, and rights-of-ways. Easements may be expressly created by *grant* (where an owner gives another party an easement across his or her property) or *reservation* (where an owner sells land that he or she owns but reserves an easement on the land). Easement can also be implied by (1) *implication*, where an owner subdivides a piece of property with a well, path, road, or other beneficial appurtenant that serves the entire parcel or by (2) *necessity*—for example, where "landlocked" property has an implied easement across surrounding property to enter and exit the landlocked property. Easements can also be created by *prescription*—that is, adverse possession.

There are two types of easements:

- *Easements appurtenant.*   An **easement appurtenant** is created when the owner of one piece of land is given an easement over an adjacent piece of land. The land over which the easement is granted is called the **servient estate**. The land that benefits from the easement is called the **dominant estate**. Adjacent land is defined as two estates that are in proximity to each other, but do not necessarily abut each other. An appurtenant easement runs with the land. For example, if an owner sells the servient estate, the new owner acquires the benefit of the easement. If an owner sells the dominant estate, the buyer-purchases the property subject to the easement.

- *Easements in gross.*   An **easement in gross** authorizes a person who does not own adjacent land the right to use another's land. An easement in gross is a personal right because it does not depend on the easement holder owning adjacent land. Thus, there is no dominant estate. Examples of easements in gross include those granted to run power, telephone, and cable television lines across an owner's property. Commercial easements in gross run with the land.

The easement holder owes a duty to maintain and repair the easement. The owner of the estate can use the property as long as it does not interfere with the easement. For example, if a piece of property is subject to an easement for an underground pipeline, the owner of the property could graze cattle or plant crops on the land above the easement, subject to the easement holder's right to repair the pipeline.

In the following case, the court had to decide whether an easement had been created.

Case 37.3
Easement

Walker v. Ayres
1993 Del. Lexis 105 (1993)
Supreme Court of Delaware

Background and Facts

Elizabeth Star Ayres and Clara Louise Quillen own in fee simple absolute a tract of land in Sussex County known as "Bluff Point." The tract is surrounded on three sides by Reboboth Bay and is landlocked on the fourth side by land owned by Irvin C. Walker. At one time, the two tracts were held by a common owner. In 1878, Bluff Point was sold in fee simple absolute apart from the other holdings, thereby landlocking the parcel. A narrow dirt road, which traverses Walker's land, connects Bluff Point to a public road and is its only means of access. Ayres and Quillen sought an easement to use this road, and Walker objected. This lawsuit ensued. The trial court granted an easement. Walker appealed.

Issue

Should Ayres and Quillen's estate be granted an easement against Walker's estate?

Court's Reasoning

The supreme court held that an easement appurtenant had been created between two adjacent parcels of property. The court held that the easement was created by implication in 1878 when Bluff Point was separated from the rest of the holdings and landlocked at that time. The court also held that an easement was created by necessity because Bluff Point was landlocked and its only access was over Walker's property. The court found that water access, even if a reasonable substitute for land access, was not feasible because of the shallowness of the water surrounding Bluff Point.

Decision and Remedy

The supreme court held that an easement had been created. The supreme court affirmed the trial court's judgment granting an easement to Ayres and Quillen.

Case Questions

Critical Legal Thinking   Should easements be recognized by the law? Why or why not?

Business Ethics   Did Walker act ethically in denying the easement? Did Ayres and Quillen act ethically in seeking to use Walker's property?

Contemporary Business   Does an easement increase or decrease the value of the servient estate? of the dominant estate?

Licenses

A **license** grants a person the right to enter upon another's property for a specified and usually short period of time. The person granting the license is called the **licensor**; the person receiving the license is called the **licensee**. For example, a common license is a ticket to a movie theater or sporting event that grants the holder the right to enter the premises for the performance. A license does not transfer any interest in the property. A license is a personal privilege that may be revoked by the licensor at any time.

Concept Summary   Nonpossessory Interests

Nonpossessory Interest	Description
Easement appurtenant	Is an easement over a servient estate that benefits a dominant estate. The easement runs with the land.
Easement in gross	Is an easement that grants a person a right to use another's land. It is a personal right that does not run with the land.
License	Grants a person the right to enter upon another's real property for a specified event or time (e.g., for a concert).
Profit	Grants the holder the right to remove something from another's real property (e.g., timber, grain).

Landlord–Tenant Relationship

A **landlord–tenant relationship** is created when the owner of a freehold estate (i.e., an estate in fee or a life estate) transfers a right to exclusively and temporarily possess the owner's property. The tenant receives a **nonfreehold estate** in the property; that is, the tenant has a right to possession of the property but not title to the property.

The tenant's interest in the property is called a **leasehold estate**, or **leasehold**. The owner who transfers the leasehold estate is called the **landlord**, or **lessor**. The party to whom the leasehold estate is transferred is called the **tenant**, or **lessee**.

The Lease

The rental agreement between a landlord and a tenant is called the **lease**. Leases can generally be either oral or written, except that most Statutes of Frauds require written leases for periods of time longer than one year. The lease must contain the essential terms of the parties' agreement. The lease is often a form contract that is prepared by the landlord and presented to the tenant. This practice is particularly true of residential leases. Other leases are negotiated between the parties. For example, Bank of America's lease of a branch office would be negotiated with the owner of the building.

Types of Tenancy

There are four types of *tenancies*:

1. *Tenancy for years.* A **tenancy for years** is created when a landlord and a tenant agree on a specific duration for a lease. Any lease for a stated period—no matter how long or short—is called a tenancy for years. Examples of such arrangements include office space leased in a high-rise office building on a 30-year lease and a cabin leased for a summer. A tenancy for years terminates automatically, without notice, upon the expiration of the stated term.

2. *Periodic tenancy.* A **periodic tenancy** is created when a lease specifies intervals at which payments are due but does not specify how long the lease is for. A lease that states, "Rent is due on the first day of the month" establishes a periodic tenancy. Many such leases are created by implication. A periodic tenancy may be terminated by either party at the end of any payment interval, but adequate notice of the termination must be given. Under common law, the notice period equaled the length of the payment period. That is, a month-to-month tenancy required a one-month notice of termination.

3. *Tenancy at will.* A lease that may be terminated at any time by either party is a **tenancy at will**. A tenancy at will may be created expressly (e.g., "to tenant as long as landlord wishes") but is more likely to be created by implication. Most states have enacted statutes requiring minimum advance notice for the termination of a tenancy at will. The death of either party terminates a tenancy at will.

4. *Tenancy at sufferance.* A **tenancy at sufferance** is created when a tenant retains possession of property after the expiration of another tenancy or a life estate without the owner's consent. That is, the owner suffers the *wrongful possession* of his or her property by the holdover tenant. This is not really a true tenancy but merely the possession of property without right. Technically, a tenant at sufferance is a trespasser. A tenant at sufferance is liable for the payment of rent during the period of sufferance. Most states require an owner to go through certain legal proceedings, called *eviction proceedings* or *unlawful detainer actions*, to evict a holdover tenant. A few states allow owners to use self-help to evict a holdover tenant if force is not used.

Concept Summary *Types of Tenancies*

Types of Tenancy	Description
Tenancy for years	Continues for the duration of the lease and then terminates automatically without notice. It does not terminate upon the death of either party.
Periodic tenancy	Continues from payment interval to payment interval. It may be terminated by either party with adequate notice. It does not terminate upon the death of either party.
Tenancy at will	Continues at the will of the parties and may be terminated by either party at any time with adequate notice. It terminates upon the death of either party.
Tenancy at sufferance	Arises when a tenant wrongfully occupies real property after the expiration of another tenancy or life estate. It continues until the owner either evicts the tenant or holds him or her over for another term. It terminates upon the death of the tenant.

Landlord's Duties

A landlord owes the following duties to the tenant:

1. ***Duty to deliver possession.*** A lease grants the tenant *exclusive* **possession** of the leased premises until (1) the term of the lease expires or (2) the tenant defaults on the obligations under the lease. The landlord is obligated to deliver possession of the leased premises to the tenant on the date the lease term begins. A landlord may not enter leased premises unless the right is specifically reserved in the lease.

2. ***Duty not to interfere with the tenant's right to quiet enjoyment.*** The law implies a **covenant of quiet enjoyment** in all leases. Under this covenant, the landlord may not interfere with the tenant's quiet and peaceful possession, use, and enjoyment of the leased premises. The covenant is breached if the landlord, or anyone acting with the landlord's consent, interferes with the tenant's use and enjoyment of the property. This interference is called **wrongful**, or **unlawful**, **eviction**. It may occur if the landlord actually evicts the tenant by physically preventing him or her from possessing or using the leased premises or if the landlord **constructively evicts** the tenant by causing the leased premises to become unfit for their intended use (e.g., by failing to provide electricity). If the landlord refuses to cure the defect after a reasonable time, a tenant who has been constructively evicted may (1) sue for damages and possession of the premises or (2) treat the lease as terminated, vacate the premises, and cease paying rent. The landlord is not responsible for wrongful acts of third persons that were done without his or her authorization.

3. ***Duty to maintain the leased premises.*** At common law, the doctrine of *caveat lessee*— "lessee beware"—applied to leases. The landlord made no warranties about the quality of leased property and had no duty to repair it. The tenant took the property "as is." Modern real estate law, however, imposes certain statutory and judicially implied duties on landlords to repair and maintain leased premises.

   States and local municipalities have enacted statutes called **building**, or **housing**, **codes**. These statutes impose specific standards on property owners to maintain and repair leased premises. They often provide certain minimum standards regarding heat, water, light, and other services. Depending on the statute, violators may be subject to fines by the government, loss of their claim for rent, and imprisonment for serious violations.

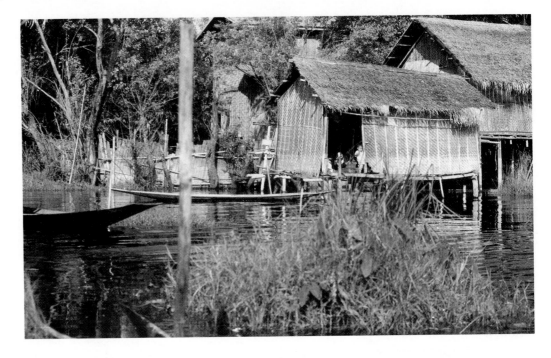

Inle Lake, Myanmar. Houses in many parts of the world differ from those in the United States. This house on the Inle Lake in Myanmar is built on stilts.

Tenant's Duties

The tenant owes the following duties to the landlord:

1. **Duty to Pay Rent.** A commercial or residential tenant owes a duty to pay the agreed-upon amount of **rent** for the leased premises to the landlord at the agreed-upon time and terms. Generally, rent is payable in advance (e.g., on the first day of the month for use that month), although the lease may provide for other times and methods for payment. Reasonable late charges may be assessed on rent that is overdue. In a *gross lease* the tenant pays a gross sum to the landlord. The landlord is responsible for paying the property taxes and assessments on the property.

    Several of the most common commercial rental arrangements are:

    ■ *Net lease.* In this arrangement, the tenant is responsible for paying rent and property taxes.

    ■ *Double net lease.* In this arrangement, the tenant is responsible for paying rent property taxes, and utilities.

    ■ *Net, net, net lease (or triple net lease).* In this arrangement, the tenant is responsible for paying rent, property taxes, utilities, and insurance.

    Upon nonpayment of rent, the landlord is entitled to recover possession of the leased premises from the tenant. This may require the landlord to *evict* the tenant. Most states provide a summary procedure called **unlawful detainer action** that a landlord can bring to evict a tenant. The landlord may also sue to recover the unpaid rent from the tenant. The more modern rule requires the landlord to make reasonable efforts to *mitigate damages* (i.e., to make reasonable efforts to re-lease the premises).

2. **Duty not to use leased premises for illegal or nonstipulated purposes.** A tenant may use the leased property for any lawful purposes permitted by the lease. Leases often stipulate that the leased premises can be used only for specific purposes. If the tenant uses the leased premises for unlawful purposes (e.g., operating an illegal gambling casino) or nonstipulated purposes (e.g., operating a restaurant in a residence), the landlord may terminate the lease, evict the tenant, and sue for damages.

Business Brief

Various types of commercial leases make the tenant responsible for paying rent and other specified items.

3. ***Duty not to commit waste.*** A tenant is under a duty not to commit **waste** to the leasehold. Waste occurs when the tenant causes substantial and permanent damage to the leased premises that decreases the value of the property and the landlord's reversionary interest in it. Waste does not include ordinary wear and tear. For example, it would be waste if the floor of the premises buckled because a tenant permitted heavy equipment to be placed on the premises. It would not be waste if the paint chipped from the walls because of the passage of time. The landlord can recover damages from the tenant for waste.

4. ***Duty not to disturb other tenants.*** A tenant owes a duty not to disturb the use and enjoyment of the leased premises by other tenants in the same building. For example, a tenant in an apartment building breaches this duty if he or she disturbs the sleep of other tenants by playing loud music throughout the night. A landlord may evict a tenant who interferes with the quiet enjoyment of other tenants.

Implied Warranty of Habitability

The courts of many jurisdictions hold that an **implied warranty of habitability** applies to residential leases for their duration. This warranty provides that the leased premises must be fit, safe, and suitable for ordinary residential use. For example, unchecked rodent infestation, leaking roofs, unworkable bathroom facilities, and the like have been held to breach the implied warranty of habitability. On the other hand, a small crack in the wall or some paint peeling from a door does not breach this warranty.

If the landlord's failure to maintain or repair the leased premises affects the tenant's use or enjoyment of the premises, state statutes and judicial decisions provide various remedies. Generally, the tenant may (1) withhold from his or her rent the amount by which the defect reduced the value of the premises to him or her, (2) repair the defect and deduct the cost of repairs from the rent due for the leased premises, (3) cancel the lease if the failure to repair constitutes constructive eviction, or (4) sue for damages in the amount by which the landlord's failure to repair the defect reduced the value of the leasehold.

> Property has its duties as well as its rights.
>
> Benjamin Disraelli
> *Sybil, Bk. II, Ch. XI*
> *(1845)*

Transferring Rights to Leased Property

Landlords may sell, gift, devise, or otherwise transfer their interests in the leased property. For example, a landlord can sell either the right to receive rents, his or her reversionary interest, or both. If complete title is transferred, the property is subject to the existing lease. The new landlord cannot alter the terms of the lease (e.g., raise the rent) during the term of the lease unless the lease so provides.

The tenant's right to transfer possession of the leased premises to another depends on the terms of the lease. Many leases permit the tenants to *assign* or *sublease* his or her rights in the property. Assignment and subleases are discussed in the following paragraphs.

> The right of property has not made poverty, but it has powerfully contributed to make wealth.
>
> J. R. McCulloch
> *Principles of Political Economy*

Assignment of the Lease   If a tenant transfers all of his or her interests under a lease, it is an **assignment**. The original tenant is the **assignor**, and the new tenant is the **assignee**. Under an assignment, the assignee acquires all the rights that the assignor had under the lease. The assignee is obligated to perform the duties that the assignor had under the lease. That is, the assignee must pay the rent and perform other covenants contained in the original lease. The assignor remains responsible for his or her obligations under the lease unless specifically released from doing so by the landlord. If the landlord recovers from the assignor, the assignor has a course of action to recover from the assignee.

Sublease   If a tenant transfers only some of his or her rights under the lease, it is a **sublease**. The original tenant is the **sublessor**, and the new tenant is the **sublessee**. The sublessor is not released from his or her obligations under the lease unless specifically

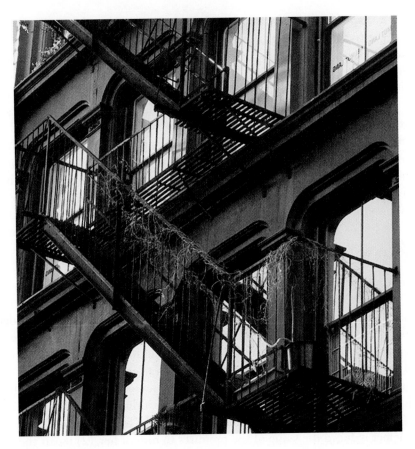

Soho, New York City. Many people rent apartments from landlords. The landlord and tenant owe each other certain dues.

released by the landlord. Subleases differ from assignments in important ways. In a sublease, no legal relationship is formed between the landlord and the sublessee. Therefore, the sublessee does not acquire rights under the original lease. For example, a sublessee would not acquire the sublessor's option to renew a lease. Further, the landlord cannot sue the sublessee to recover rent payments or enforce duties under the original lease.

In most cases, tenants cannot assign or sublease their leases without the landlord's consent. This right protects the landlord from the transfer of the leasehold to someone who might damage the property or not have the financial resources to pay the rent. Most states, either by statute or by judicial decision, hold that the owner's consent cannot be unreasonably withheld.

Land Use Regulation

Generally, the ownership of property entitles the owner to use his or her property as he or she wishes. Such use, however, is subject to limitations imposed by government regulation. These limitations are collectively referred to as **land use control**, or **land use regulation**. Several forms of land use regulation are discussed in the following paragraphs.

Zoning

Most countries and municipalities have enacted **zoning ordinances** to regulate land use. Zoning ordinances generally (1) establish use districts within the municipality (i.e., areas are generally designated residential, commercial, or industrial); (2) restrict the height, size, and location of buildings on a building site; and (3) establish aesthetic requirements or limitations for the exterior of buildings.

A **zoning commission** usually formulates zoning ordinances, conducts public hearings, and makes recommendations to the city council, which must vote to enact an ordinance. Once a zoning ordinance is enacted, the zoning ordinance commission enforces it. If landowners believe that a zoning ordinance is illegal or that it has been applied unlawfully to them or their property, they may institute a court proceeding seeking judicial review of the ordinance or its application.

An owner who wishes to use his or her property for a use different from that permitted under a current zoning ordinance may seek relief from the ordinance by obtaining a **variance**. To obtain a variance, the landowner must prove that the ordinance causes an undue hardship by preventing him or her from making a reasonable return on the land as zoned. Variances are usually difficult to obtain.

Zoning laws act prospectively; that is, uses and buildings that already exist in the zoned area are permitted to continue even though they do not fit within new zoning ordinances. Such uses are called **nonconforming uses**. For example, if a new zoning ordinance is enacted, making an area a residential zone, an existing funeral parlor is a nonconforming use.

Civil Rights Act

Federal and state governments have enacted statutes that prohibit discrimination in the sale and rental of real property. The **Civil Rights Act**, a federal statute, prohibits racial discrimination in the transfer of real property, including housing, commercial, and industrial property.[1] The act prohibits private and public discrimination and permits lawsuits to recover damages and obtain injunctions against offending conduct.

Many states and local communities have also enacted statutes and ordinances that prohibit discrimination in the sale or lease of real property. These laws usually prohibit discrimination based on race, color, national origin, sex, or religion but also often prohibit discrimination based on other protected classes, such as age, sexual preference, and persons receiving government assistance.

Fair Housing Act

The **Fair Housing Act**, a federal statute, makes it unlawful for a party to refuse to rent or sell a dwelling to any person because of his or her race, color, national origin, sex, or religion.[2] The act also prohibits discrimination by real estate brokers, mortgage lenders, and advertisers concerning the sale or rental of real property. The law does not apply to the following: (1) a person who owns a building of four or fewer units and occupies one of the units and leases the others and (2) a person who leases a single-family dwelling and does not own more than three single-family dwellings. To qualify for either exemption, the lessor cannot use a real estate broker or advertise in a discriminating manner.

Title III of the Americans with Disabilities Act

The **Americans with Disabilities Act (ADA)**, a federal statute, became effective on January 26, 1992.[3] The ADA is a broad civil rights statute that prohibits discrimination against disabled individuals in employment, public services, public accommodations and services, and telecommunications. **Title III** of the ADA prohibits discrimination on the basis of disability in places of public accommodation operated by private entities. The attorney general of the United States is empowered to issue regulations that interpret and enforce the ADA.

Title III of the ADA applies to public accommodations and commercial facilities such as motels, hotels, restaurants, theaters, recreation facilities, colleges and universities, department stores, retail stores, and office buildings. It does not generally apply to residential facilities (single- and multifamily housing).

Title III requires covered facilities to be designed, constructed, and altered in compliance with specific accessibility requirements established by regulations issued pursuant to the ADA. This includes constructing ramps to accommodate wheelchairs, installing railings next to steps, placing signs written in Braille in elevators and at elevator call buttons, and so on.

New construction must be built in such a manner as to be readily accessible to and usable by disabled individuals. Any alterations made to existing buildings must be made so that the altered portions of the building are readily accessible to disabled individuals to the maximum extent feasible. With respect to existing buildings, architectural barriers must be removed if such removal is readily achievable. In determining when an action is readily achievable, the factors to be considered include the nature and cost of the action, the financial resources of the facility, and the type of operations of the facility.

The ADA provides for both private right of action and enforcement by the attorney general. Individuals may seek injunctive relief and monetary damages, while the attorney general may seek equitable relief and civil fines for any violation.

Building owners, managers, architects, and others involved in the design, construction, ownership, and management of public accommodations and commercial buildings must be knowledgeable about, and comply with, the provisions of Title III of the ADA.

Compensable Taking of Real Property

The government may use its power of **eminent domain** to acquire private property for public purposes. However, the Due Process Clause of the U.S. Constitution (and state constitutions, where applicable) requires the government to allow the owner to make a case for keeping the property. The **Just Compensation Clause** of the Fifth Amendment to the U.S. Constitution mandates that the government must compensate the property owner (and possibly others, such as lessees) when it exercises the power of eminent domain. Anyone who is not satisfied with the compensation offered by the government can bring an action to have the court determine the compensation to be paid. Often, the government's action is not considered a "taking," even if it causes economic losses to property owners and others.

Consider This Example   Assume that ITT has acquired a large piece of property, with the intention of erecting a commercial building at some future time. Now suppose the government wants to build a new highway that passes through the property owned by ITT. The government can use its power of eminent domain to acquire the property. There has been a "taking," so the government must pay ITT just compensation. Suppose, instead, that the government enacts a zoning law that affects ITT's property by restricting building in the area to single-family housing. Although ITT would suffer a substantial economic loss, the zoning law, nevertheless, would probably not constitute a "taking" that required the payment of compensation.

Chapter Summary

Real Property, p. 813

Nature of Real Property

Real property is immovable. It includes land, buildings, subsurface rights, air rights, plant life, and fixtures.

Freehold Estates

Freehold estates are estates where the owner has a present possessory interest in the real property.

1. *Estate in fee:*
   a. *Fee simple absolute (or fee simple).* This is the highest form of ownership.
   b. *Fee simple defeasible (or qualified fee).* This is an estate that ends if a specified condition occurs.
2. *Life estate.* This is an interest in real property that lasts for the life of a specified person. Called an *estate pour autre vie* if the time is measured by the life of a third person.

Concurrent Ownership

In concurrent ownerships two or more persons jointly own real property. Types of concurrent ownership are:

1. *Joint tenancy.* Owners may transfer their interests without the consent of co-owners. Transfer severs the joint tenancy. Under the *right of survivorship*, the interest of a deceased owner passes to his or her co-owners.
2. *Tenancy in common.* Owners may transfer their interests without the consent of co-owners. Transfer does not sever the tenancy in common. Interest of a deceased owner passes to his or her estate.
3. *Tenancy by the entirety.* This form of co-ownership can be used only by a married couple. Neither spouse may transfer his or her interest without the other spouse's consent. A surviving spouse has the right of survivorship.
4. *Community property.* This form of co-ownership that applies only to a married couple. Neither spouse may transfer his or her interest without the other spouse's consent. When a spouse dies, the surviving spouse automatically receives one-half the community property.
5. *Condominium.* Condominium owners have title to their individual units and own the common areas as tenants in common. Owners may transfer their interests without the consent of other owners.
6. *Cooperative.* A corporation owns the building, and the residents own shares of the corporation. Usually, owners may not transfer their shares without the approval of the other owners.

Future Interests

A future interest is a right to possess real property in the future rather than currently. Types of future interests are:

1. *Reversion.* The right to possession returns to the grantor after the expiration of a limited or contingent estate.
2. *Remainder.* The right to possession goes to a third person after the expiration of a limited or contingent estate. The third person is called a *remainderman*.

Transfer of Ownership of Real Property, p. 818

Sale of Real Estate

An owner sells his or her property to another for consideration.

The government may obtain a lien on property for nonpayment of taxes and sell the property at a tax sale to a buyer. The buyer takes the title subject to the taxpayer's right of redemption.

Deeds

Instrument used to convey real property by sale or gift:

1. *Warranty deed.* This type of deed provides the most protection to the grantee because the grantor makes warranties against defect in title.
2. *Quitclaim deed.* This type of deed provides the least amount of protection to the grantee because the grantor transfers only the interest he or she has in the property.

Recording Statutes

Recording statutes permit copies of deeds and other documents concerning interests in real property (e.g., mortgages, liens) to be filed in a government office, where they become public record. This puts third parties on notice of recorded interests.

Marketable Title

A marketable title is free from any undisclosed encumbrances, defects in title, or other defects. Methods of assuring marketable title:

1. *Attorney's opinion.* An attorney renders an opinion concerning the status of the title.
2. *Torrens system.* A court issues a *certificate of title* to the rightful owner of the property.
3. *Title insurance.* A title insurer agrees to reimburse the insured for losses caused by undiscovered defects in title.

Gift, Will, or Inheritance

Owners may give their property to another during their lifetime or leave their property by will to a beneficiary when they die. If a person dies without a will, his or her property is distributed to the heirs pursuant to state intestacy statutes.

Adverse Possession

A person who occupies another's property acquires title to the property if the occupation has been:

1. For a statutory period of time (in many states, 10 to 20 years)
2. Open, visible, and notorious
3. Actual and exclusive
4. Continuous and peaceful
5. Hostile and adverse

Nonpossessory Interests, p. 822

Easements

An easement is an interest in land that gives the holder the right to make limited use of another's property without taking anything from it (e.g., driveways, party walls).

1. *Easement appurtenant.* An owner of land is given an easement over an adjacent piece of land.
2. *Easement in gross.* This type of easement authorizes a person who does not own adjacent land the right to use another's land.

Licenses

A license is a right to enter upon another's property for a specified and usually short period of time (e.g., ticket to a sporting event).

Landlord–Tenant Relationship, p. 824

Landlord–Tenant Relationship

This relationship is created when an owner of a freehold estate transfers a right to another to exclusively and temporarily possess the owner's property.

The Lease

A lease is a rental agreement between a landlord and a tenant that contains the essential terms of the parties' agreement.

Types of Tenancy

Four types of tenancy are:

1. *Tenancy for years.* This is tenancy for a specified period of time.
2. *Periodic tenancy.* This is tenancy for a period of time determined by the payment interval.
3. *Tenancy at will.* This is tenancy that may be terminated at any time by either party.
4. *Tenancy at sufferance.* This is tenancy created by the wrongful possession of property.

Landlord's Duties

Duty to deliver possession. A landlord is obligated to deliver possession of the leased premises to the tenant on the date the lease term begins.

Duty not to interfere with the tenant's right to quiet enjoyment. A landlord may not interfere with the tenant's quiet and peaceful possession, use, and enjoyment of the leased premises.

Duty to maintain the leased premises. A landlord owes contractual and statutory duties to repair and maintain the leased premises. The *implied warranty of habitability* requires leased premises to be fit, safe, and suitable for ordinary residential use.

Tenant's Duties

Duty to pay rent. A tenant owes a duty to pay the agreed-upon rent to the landlord. Reasonable late charges may be assessed on overdue rent. Common rental agreements are:

1. **Gross lease.** This requires the tenant to pay a stated sum to the landlord. The landlord is responsible for paying property taxes and assessments on the property.
2. **Net lease.** The tenant is responsible for paying rent and property taxes.
3. **Double net lease.** The tenant is responsible for paying rent, property taxes, and utilities.
4. **Triple net lease.** The tenant is responsible for paying rent, property taxes, utilities, and insurance.

Duty not to use leased premises for illegal or nonstipulated purposes. A tenant may not use leased premises for any illegal or nonstipulated uses.

Duty not to commit waste. A tenant may not commit waste to the leased premises.

Duty not to disturb other tenants. A tenant may not disturb the use and enjoyment of the premises by other tenants.

Implied Warranty of Habitability

This warranty is implied by law is residential leases. It provides that leased premises must be fit, safe, and suitable for ordinary residential use.

Transferring Rights to Leased Property

Assignment of a lease. Landlords may transfer their ownership interests in leased property. The tenant becomes a tenant of the new owner.

Sublease. Subject to the terms of the lease, tenants may assign or sublease the leased premises to a third party. The original tenant is not relieved of obligations under the lease.

Land Use Regulation, p. 828

Zoning

Zoning ordinances. These are laws adopted by local governments that restrict the use of property, set building standards, and establish architectural requirements.

1. **Variance.** A variance permits an owner to make a nonzoned use of his or her property. A variance requires permission from a zoning board.
2. **Nonconforming use.** A nonconforming use is a nonzoned use that is permitted (grandfathered in) when an area is rezoned.

Civil Rights Act

This federal statute prohibits racial discrimination in the transfer of real property.

Fair Housing Act

This federal statute makes it unlawful for a party to refuse to rent or sell a dwelling to any person because of his or her race, color, national origin, sex, or religion.

The Americans with Disabilities Act (ADA)

Title III. This title of the ADA prohibits discrimination on the basis of disability in places of public accomodation operated by private entities.

Compensable Taking of Property

1. *Eminent domain.* Eminent domain is the power and process by which the government acquires private property for public purposes.
2. *Just Compensation Clause.* This clause of the U.S. Constitution mandates that the government compensate the property owner and possibly others just compensation when the government exercises its power of eminent domain and takes property for government purposes.

Internet Exercises and Case Questions

Working the Web Internet Exercises

Activities

1. Some states have special laws relating to land and Indian tribes. See, for example, Washington state statute RCW 64.20—Alienation of Land by Indians. Does your state have any similar laws? See "Law About . . . Real Estate Transactions," at **www.law.cornell.edu/topics/real_estate.html**, for an overview of real estate law with links to key primary and secondary sources.

2. Although most real estate law is local law, there are important federal controls on certain types of transactions. See 42 U.S.C., Chapter 45—Federal Fair Housing Act.

3. There is an ongoing and vigorous debate about governmental authority to regulate land use without paying compensation to the property owner. Read the cited law review for an overview of the Taking Clause of the Fifth Amendment and related issues. See the Law Review article "Windfalls or Windmills: The Right of a Property Owner to Challenge Land Use Regulations," at **www.law.fsu.edu/journals/landuse/Vol131/ABRA.html**.

4. Is your state one that has adopted the Uniform Landlord—Tenant Act? See **www.law.cornell.edu/uniform/vol7.html#lndtn**.

Critical Legal Thinking Cases

37.1 Subsurface Rights In 1883, Isaac McIlwee owned 100 acres of land in Valley Township, Guernsey County, Ohio. In that year, he sold the property to Akron & Cambridge Coal Company (Akron & Cambridge) in fee simple but reserved in fee simple "the surface of all said lands" to himself. Over the years, the interests in the land were transferred to many different parties. As of 1981, the Mid-Ohio Coal Company owned the rights originally transferred to Akron & Cambridge, and Peter and Irene Minnich owned the rights reserved by Isaac McIlwee in 1883. The Minniches claim they possess subsurface rights to the property except for coal rights. Who wins? [*Minnich v. Guernsey Savings and Loan Company*, 521 N.E.2d 489, 1987 OhioApp. Lexis 10497 (Ohio App. 1987)]

37.2 Life Estate and Remainder Baudilio Bowles died testate. His will devised to his sister, Julianita B. Vigil, "one-half of any income, rents, or profits from any real property located in Bull Creek or Colonias, New Mexico." The will contained another clause that left to his children "my interest in any real property owned by me at the time of my death, located in Bull Creek and/or Colonias, San Miguel County." The property referred to in both devises is the same property. Julianita died before the will

was probated. Her heirs claim a one-half ownership interest in the real property. Bowles's children asserted that they owned all his property. Who wins? [*In the Matter of the Estate of Bowles*, 764 P.2d 510, 1988 N.M.App. Lexis 93 (N.M. App. 1988)]

37.3 Reversion In 1941, W.E. and Jennie Hutton conveyed land they owned to the Trustees of Schools of District Number One of the Town of Allison, Illinois (School District), by warranty deed "to be used for school purpose only; otherwise to revert to Grantor." The School District built a school on the site, commonly known as Hutton School. The Huttons conveyed the adjoining farmland and their reversionary interest in the school site to the Jacqmains, who in turn conveyed their interest to Herbert and Betty Mahrenholz in 1959. The 1.5-acre site sits in the middle of Mahrenhoz's farmland. In May 1973, the School District discontinued holding regular classes at Hutton School. Instead, it used the school building to warehouse and store miscellaneous school equipment, supplies, unused desks, and the like. In 1974, Mahrenholz filed suit to quiet title to the school property to themselves. Who wins? [*Mahrenholz v. County Board of School Trustees of Lawrence County*, 544 N.E.2d 128, 1989 Ill.App. Lexis 1445 (Ill. App. 1989)]

37.4 Easement in Gross   John L. Yutterman died in 1953 and left one piece of property, located in Fort Smith, Arkansas, to his two sons and two daughters. Each child received approximately one fourth of the property in fee simple. A 40-foot driveway divided the property. Concerning the driveway, Yutterman's will provided as follows: "Further, a specific condition of this will and of these devises is that the forty (40) foot driveway from Free Ferry Road, three hundred (300) feet Northward, shall be kept open for the common use of the devisees in this will." In 1982, one of the daughters wanted to sell her property to a third party. If the third party purchases the property, will that party have an easement to use the driveway? [*Merriman v. Yutterman*, 723 S.W.2d 823, 1987 Ark. Lexis 1934 (AK 1987)]

37.5 Adverse Possession   In 1973, Joseph and Helen Naab purchased a tract of land in a subdivision of Williamstown, West Virginia. At the time of purchase, there was both a house and a small concrete garage on the property. Evidence showed that the garage had been erected sometime prior to 1952 by one of the Naabs' predecessors in title. In 1975, Roger and Cynthia Nolan purchased a lot contiguous to that owned by the Naabs. The following year, the Nolans had their property surveyed. The survey indicated that one corner of the Naabs' garage encroached 1.22 feet onto the Nolans' property and the other corner encroached 0.91 feet over the property line. The Nolans requested that the Naabs remove the garage from their property. When the Naabs refused, this lawsuit ensued. Who wins? [*Naab v. Nolan*, 327 S.E.2d 151, 1985 W.Va. Lexis 476 (WV 1985)]

37.6 Recording Statute   On October 13, 1972, Johnnie H. Hill and his wife, Clara Mac, entered into an installment sales contract with Pinelawn Memorial Park (Pinelawn) to purchase a mausoleum crypt. They made it clear they wanted to buy crypt "D" that faced eastward toward Kinston. The Hills paid a $1,035 down payment and continued to make $33.02 monthly payments. On February 13, 1974, William C. Shackelford and his wife, Jennie L., entered into an agreement with Pinelawn to purchase crypt D. They paid a $1,406 down payment and two annual installments of $912. The Hills were first put on notice of the second contract when they visited Pinelawn in February 1977 and saw the Shackelford name on crypt D. The Hills then tendered full payment to Pinelawn for crypt D. On April 25, 1977, the Hills sued Pinelawn and the Shackelfords. They demanded specific performance of the contract and the deed to crypt D. Upon being served with summons, the Shackelfords discovered that they had no deed to the crypt and demanded one from Pinelawn. Pinelawn delivered them a deed dated August 18, 1977, which the Shackelfords recorded in the County Register on September 9, 1977. Who owns crypt D? [*Hill v. Pinelawn Memorial Park, Inc.*, 282 S.E.2d 779, 1981 N.C. Lexis 1326 (NC 1981)]

37.7 Implied Warranty of Habitability   Sharon Love entered into a written lease agreement with Monarch Apartments for apartment 4 at 441 Winfield in Topeka, Kansas. Shortly after moving in, she experienced serious problems with termites. Her walls swelled, clouds of dirt came out, and when she checked on her children one night, she saw termites flying around the room. She complained to Monarch, which arranged for the apartment to be fumigated. When the termite problem persisted, Monarch moved Love and her children to apartment 2.

Upon moving in, Love noticed that roaches crawled over the walls, ceilings, and floors of the apartment. She complained, and Monarch called an exterminator, who sprayed the apartment. When the roach problem persisted, Love vacated the premises. Did Love lawfully terminate the lease? [*Love v. Monarch Apartments*, 771 P.2d 79, 1989 Kan.App. Lexis 219 (Kan. App. 1989)]

37.8 Tenant's Breach of Lease   Susan Nylen, Elizabeth Lewis, and Julie Reed, students at Indiana University, signed a rental agreement as cosigners to lease an apartment from Park Doral Apartments. The rental term was from August 26, 1986, until August 19, 1987, at a monthly rental of $420. The tenants paid a security deposit of $420, constituting prepayment of rent for the last month of the lease term. At the end of the fall semester. Reed moved out of the apartment, and in February 1987, she refused to pay any further rent. Nylen and Lewis remained in possession of the apartment, paying only two-thirds of the total rent due for the month of February. Nylen and Lewis made a payment of $280 for the rent due in March. They vacated the apartment on March 13, 1987. The landlord, who was unable to re-lease the apartment during the lease term, sued Reed, Nylen, and Lewis for the unpaid rent. Who wins? [*Nylen v. Park Doral Apartments*, 535 N.E.2d 178, 1989 Ind.App. Lexis 185 (Ind. App. 1989)]

37.9 Landlord's Tort Liability   William Long, d/b/a Hoosier Homes, owned an apartment building in Indianapolis, Indiana. He rented a second-story apartment to Marvin Tardy. On August 20, 1984, Almedia McLayea visited Tardy with her one-month-old nephew, Garfield Dawson. As McLayea was leaving the apartment, she walked down the stairway, carrying Dawson in an infant seat. As she came down 4 steps to a landing, which led to a flight of 10 stairs, she caught her heel on a stair, slipped, and fell forward. There was no handrail along the stairway (as required by law) by which she could break her fall. Instead, her shoulder struck a window at the landing, the window broke, the rotted screen behind it collapsed, and Dawson fell through the opening to the ground below. He sustained permanent injuries, including brain damage. Dawson (through his mother) sued the landlord to recover damages for negligence. Who wins? [*Dawson v. Long*, 546 N.E.2d 1265, 1989 Ind.App. Lexis 1225 (Ind. App. 1989)]

37.10 Zoning   The city of Ladue is one of the finer suburban residential areas of metropolitan St. Louis. The homes in the city are considerably more expensive than those in surrounding areas and consist of homes of traditional design such as colonial, French provincial, and English. The city set up an architectural board to approve plans for buildings that "conform to certain minimum architectural standards of appearance and conformity with surrounding structures, and that unsightly, grotesque, and unsuitable structures, detrimental to the stability of value and the welfare of surrounding property, structures, and residents, and to the general welfare and happiness of the community, be avoided." The owner of a lot in the city submitted a plan to build a house of ultramodern design. It was pyramid-shaped, with a flat top and triangular-shaped windows and doors. Although the house plans met other city zoning ordinances and building codes, the architectural board rejected the owner's petition for a building permit based on aesthetic reasons. The owner sued the city. Who wins? [*State of Missouri v. Berkeley*, 458 S.W.2d 305, 1970 Mo. Lexis 902 (MO 1970)]

Business Ethics Cases

37.11 Business Ethics On March 19, 1971, Victor and Phyllis Garber acquired a piece of real property by warranty deed. The deed was recorded on December 30, 1971. The property consisted of 80 acres that was enclosed by a fence that had been in place for over 50 years. The enclosed area was used to graze cattle and produce hay. Subsequently, William and Herbert Doenz acquired a piece of real property adjacent to the Garbers'. In March 1981, the Doenzes employed a surveyor to locate their land's boundaries. As a result of the survey, it was discovered that the shared fence was 20 to 30 feet inside the deed line on the Doenz property. The amount of property between the old fence and the deed line was 3.01 acres. In September 1981 the Doenzes removed the old fence and constructed a new fence along the deed line. The Garbers, brought suit to quiet title. Did the Doenzes act ethically in removing the fence? Did the Garbers act ethically in claiming title to property that originally belonged with the adjacent property? Did the Garbers, acquire title to the property between the fence and the deed through adverse possession? [*Doenz v. Garber*, 665 P.2d 932, 1983 Wyo. Lexis 339 (WY 1983)]

37.12 Business Ethics Moe and Joe Rappaport (tenants) leased space in a shopping mall owned by Bermuda Avenue Shopping Center Associates, L.P. (landlord) to use as an indoor golf arcade. The lease was signed in May 1987, and the tenants were given possession of the leased premises on July 23, 1987. The tenants were not told by the landlord of the extensive renovations planned for the mall. From July 23 until August 18, the golf arcade was busy and earned a net profit. On August 18, the renovation of the mall began in front of the arcade. According to the tenants, their store sign was taken down, there was debris and dust in front of the store, the sidewalks and parking spaces in front of the store were taken away, and their business "died." The tenants closed their arcade on September 30 and sued the landlord for damages. The landlord counterclaimed, seeking to recover lost rental income. Did the landlord act ethically in not explaining the planned renovations to the tenants? Did the tenants act ethically in terminating the lease? Were the tenants constructively evicted from the leased premise? [*Bermuda Avenue Shopping Center Associates v. Rappaport*, 565 S.2d 805, 1990 Fla.App. Lexis 5354 (Fla. App. 1990)]

Briefing the Case Writing Assignment

Read Case A.37 in the Case Appendix [*Walker v. Quillen*]. This case is excerpted from the supreme court of Delaware's opinion. Review and brief the case. In your brief, be sure to answer the following questions.

1. Who were the plaintiffs (appellees)? Who was the defendant (appellant)?

2. Describe the tract of land owned by the plaintiffs and defendant.

3. What was the issue in this case? How did the court decide this issue?

Endnotes

1. 42 U.S.C. §§ 1971 et seq.
2. 42 U.S.C. §§ 360 et seq.
3. 42 U.C.C. §§ 1201 et seq.

38

Insurance, Wills, and Estates

> "When you have told someone you have left him a legacy, the only decent thing to do is to die at once."
>
> —Samuel Butler

Chapter Objectives

After studying this chapter, you should be able to:

1. List and describe the various types of life, health and disability, fire and homeowner's, and automobile insurance.

2. List and describe special forms of business insurance.

3. Describe the requirements for making a valid will and identify how property is distributed under intestacy statutes if a person dies without a will.

4. Describe the right to die and define living will.

5. Define trust and living trust and describe the purposes of each.

Chapter Contents

- Insurance
- Wills
- Intestate Succession
- Living Wills
- Trusts
- Living Trusts

Insurance is a means for persons and businesses to protect themselves against the risk of loss. For example, a business may purchase fire insurance to cover its buildings. If there is a fire and the property is damaged, the insurance company will pay for all or part of the loss, depending on the policy. Similarly, an individual who purchases automobile insurance may be reimbursed by the insurer if his or her car is stolen. Insurance is crucial to personal, business, and estate planning.

Wills and trusts are means of transferring property. **Wills** transfer property upon a person's death. They permit people to state exactly where they want their property to go when they die. If a person dies *intestate*—that is, without a will—the deceased's property is distributed to relatives according to state statute. The property escheats (goes) to the state if there are no relatives.

Trusts are used to transfer property that is to be held and managed for the benefit of another person or persons. Although trusts are created during one's lifetime, they may be worded to become effective only upon the trustor's (or grantor's) death. A *living trust* is a special type of trust used for estate planning.

After discussing how insurance is used to protect against risk of loss, this chapter discusses the use of wills and trusts to transfer property.

Insurance

Insurance is defined as a contract whereby one party undertakes to indemnify another against loss, damage, or liability arising from a contingent or unknown event. It is a means of transferring and distributing risk of loss. The risk of loss is *pooled* (i.e., spread) among all the parties (or **insureds**) who pay premiums to a particular insurance company. The insurance company—also called the **insurer**, or **underwriter**—is then obligated to pay insurance proceeds to those members of the pool who experience losses.

The insurance contract is called a **policy**. The money paid to the insurance company is called a **premium**. Premiums are based on an estimate of the number of parties within the pool who will suffer the risks insured against. The estimate is based on past experience.

Sometimes an insurer will spread the risk of loss through **reinsurance**. That is, it will sell a portion of the policy's risk and right to receive premiums to other insurance companies, called **reinsurers**.

Insurance policies are often sold by insurance agents or brokers. An **insurance agent** usually works exclusively for one insurance company and is an agent of that company. An **insurance broker** is an independent contractor who represents a number of insurance companies. The broker is the agent of the insured. Some insurance is sold directly by the insurer to the insured (e.g., by direct mail).

The **McCarran-Ferguson Act**,[1] which was enacted by the federal government in 1945, gave the regulation of insurance to the states. State regulations cover the incorporation, licensing and supervision of insurance companies, as well as the licensing and supervision of insurance agents and brokers.

Insurable Interest

Anyone who would suffer a pecuniary (monetary) loss from the destruction of real or personal property has an **insurable interest** in that property. If the insured does not have an insurable interest in the property being insured, the contract is treated as a wager and cannot be enforced.

Ownership creates an insurable interest. In addition, mortgagees, lienholders, and tenants have an insurable interest in property. The insurable interest in property must exist at the time of loss.

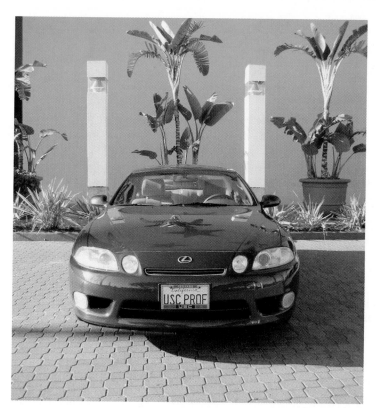

In the case of life insurance, a person must have a close family relationship or an economic benefit from the continued life of another to have an insurable interest in that person's life. Thus, spouses, parents, children, and sisters and brothers may insure each others' lives. Other more remote relationships (e.g., aunts, uncles, cousins) require additional proof of an economic interest (e.g., proof of support). The insurable interest must exist when the life insurance policy is issued but need not exist at the time of death.

A person may insure his or her own life and name anyone as the **beneficiary**. The named beneficiary or beneficiaries receive the proceeds from the life insurance policy when the insured dies. The beneficiary does not have to have an insurable interest in the insured's life.

Exhibit 38.1 lists and describes types of insurance.

No-Fault Automobile Insurance

Until fairly recently, most automobile insurance coverage in this country was based on the principle of "fault," whereby a party injured in an accident relied on the insurance of the at-fault party to pay for his or her injuries. This system led to substantial litigation, but many accident victims were unable to recover because the at-fault party had either inadequate insurance or no insurance at all.

To remedy this problem, over half of the states have enacted legislation that mandates **no-fault insurance** for automobile accidents. Under this system, a driver's insurance company pays for any injuries or death he or she suffered in an accident, no matter who caused the accident. No-fault insurance assures the insureds that coverage is available if they are injured in an automobile accident.

No-fault insurance policies provide coverage for medical expenses and lost wages. Pain and suffering are sometimes covered. No-fault insurance usually covers the insured, members of the insured's immediate family, authorized drivers of the automobile, and passengers.

An insurance policy is like old underwear. The gaps in its cover are only shown by accident.

David Yates (1984)

Exhibit 38.1

Types of Insurance

Life Insurance	
Whole life	Insurance that provides coverage during the life of the insured. It involves an element of savings. The premium is set to cover both the death benefit and an amount for investment. The value of savings grows at a fixed interest rate.
Term	Insurance that covers a limited period of time (e.g., five years). It involves no savings feature.
Universal life	Insurance that combines features of both term and whole life insurance. The value of savings grows at a variable interest rate.
Double indemnity	A provision in many life insurance policies that provides for payment of double the amount of the policy if death is caused by accident.
Key person	Life insurance taken out by businesses that insures the life of key executives. It is also taken out by partners to insure the lives of other partners.
Annuity	Payments made to an insured before death. For the payment of premiums, an insurance company agrees to make period payments (e.g., monthly) to the insured once he reaches a certain age.
Health and Disability Insurance	
Health	Insurance that covers the cost of medical treatment, surgery, and hospital care.
Disability	Insurance that provides monthly income to an insured who is disabled and cannot work. Benefits are based on the degree of disability.
Dental	Insurance that covers the costs of dental care.
Fire and Homeowner's Insurance	
Standard fire insurance policy	Insurance that protects real and personal property against loss resulting from fire, lightning, smoke, water damage, and related perils. Most policies limit recovery to damage caused by *hostile fires* (i.e., fire caused by faulty electrical wiring) and not *friendly fires* (e.g., damage caused by a fire contained in a fireplace). No personal liability coverage is provided.
Homeowners policy	A comprehensive insurance policy that includes coverage for the risks covered by a standard fire insurance policy as well as personal liability insurance. It includes coverage for property damage, personal injury, and medical expenses of persons injured on the insured's property.
Personal articles	Insurance that covers specific valuable items (e.g., jewelry, works of art, furs) that are usually excluded from standard fire and homeowner's policies.
Renters insurance	Insurance that covers loss and damage to a renter's possessions and provides personal liability coverage. Insures against the same perils as a homeowner's policy.
Automobile Insurance	
Collision	Property insurance that covers the insured's vehicle against risk of loss or damage when it is struck by another vehicle.
Comprehensive	Property insurance that covers the insured's vehicle against risk of loss or damage from causes other than collision; namely, fire, theft, explosion, hail, windstorm, falling objects, earthquakes, floods, hurricanes, vandalism, and riots.
Liability	Insurance that covers damage and loss that the insured causes to third parties. This includes both bodily injury and property damage. States often require to carry minimum liability insurance, specified by statute. The following additional coverage may be purchased: Other driver coverage—liability coverage that protects the owner of a vehicle when someone else drives his or her vehicle with his or her permission. Drive-other coverage—liability coverage that protects the insured while driving other vehicles.
Medical payment	Insurance that covers medical expenses incurred by the owner, passengers, and other authorized driver of his or her car who are injured in an automobile accident.
Uninsured motorist	Insurance that provides coverage to the driver and passengers of a vehicle who are injured by an uninsured motorist or a hit-and-run driver.
Other Types of Insurance	
Credit	Pays debtors' debts if they are unable to pay because of some insured peril (e.g., death, disability).
Title	Debtors and creditors may purchase. It insures that a property owner has clear title to real property. It may be purchased by the owner or mortgagees or lienholders of the property.
Marine	Covers loss or damage to a vessel and its cargo caused by perils at sea. Marine insurance is often comprehensive, covering property damage and liability for personal injury.
Umbrella	An insurance that pays only when the basic policy limits of other insurance (e.g., homeowner's, liability, automobile) have been exceeded.

Contemporary Environment

Business Insurance

Businesses purchase insurance to cover myriad risks, including property and liability insurance on buildings and automobiles. In addition, businesses often purchase insurance to cover risks uniquely applicable to businesses. These types of insurance include:

- *Business interruption insurance.* When a business is severely damaged or destroyed by fire or some other peril, it usually takes time to repair or reconstruct the damaged property. During this time, the business is losing money. A business can purchase a **business interruption insurance** policy that will reimburse it for any revenues lost during that period.
- *Workers' compensation insurance.* Employees are sometimes injured while working within the scope of their employment. All states have enacted legislation that compensates employees for such injuries. Employers may purchase **workers' compensation insurance** to cover this risk. Many states require companies to purchase this form of insurance.

- *Fidelity insurance.* An employer can purchase **fidelity insurance** to protect against the dishonesty and defalcation of employees. For example, a bank can purchase fidelity insurance to protect against losses caused by the embezzlement of its employees.
- *Key-person life insurance.* Small businesses, such as partnerships, limited liability companies, and close corporations, often purchase key-person life insurance on the owners of the business. The company pays the premiums for the life insurance policies. The life insurance is usually used to fund buy–sell agreements among the owners of the business. Thus, if an insured owner dies, the insurance proceeds are paid to the deceased's beneficiaries. The deceased's interest in the company then reverts to either the other owners or the business, according to the terms of the buy–sell agreement. ∎

Insurance Contracts

Insurance contracts (**policies**) are governed by the law of contracts. Most policies are prepared on standardized forms. Some states even make that a requirement. Often, state statutes mandate that specific language be included in different types of insurance contracts. These statutes concern coverage for certain losses, how limitations on coverage must be stated in the contract, and the like. The insurance coverage is in place once the insurance policy is issued. Insurance policies often contain the clauses discussed below:

- *Deductible clauses.* **Deductible clauses** provide that insurance proceeds are payable only after the insured has paid a certain amount of the damage or loss. Typical deductibles for automotive collision insurance are $100, $250, and $500.

- *Coinsurance clause.* A **coinsurance clause** permits an owner who insures his or her property to a certain percented of its value (e.g., 80 percent) to recover up to the face value of the policy. An owner who insures the property for less than the stated percentage must bear a proportionate share of the loss. Most fire insurance policies contain coinsurance clauses.

- *Exclusions from coverage clause.* **Exclusion clauses** stipulate certain exclusions from insurance coverage. For example, standard fire insurance policies often exclude coverage for damage caused by the storage of explosives or flammable liquids unless a special premium is paid for this coverage. Insurance policies should be read carefully to determine the extent of coverage.

- *Suicide clause.* Life insurance policies usually contain a **suicide clause** which states that if the insured commits suicide within a certain period after taking out a life insurance policy on himself or herself, the insurance company does not have to pay the life insurance proceeds to the named beneficiary. The insurance company must refund the premium paid to the deceased insureds' estate. The usual time period for the validity of a suicide clause in two years.

Business Brief

Insureds should read insurance contracts carefully so that they fully understand what risks are covered and what risks are not covered.

Business Brief

Insurance contracts cover only certain specified risks. They often contain *exclusions* that identify risks not covered by the policy.

If both the insurer and the insured agree, an insurance contract may be modified. Modification is usually done either by adding an **endorsement** to the policy or by the execution of a document called a **rider**.

In most instances, an insured can cancel an insurance policy at any time. An insurer may cancel an insurance policy for nonpayment of premiums. Many insurance policies provide a *grace period* during which an insured may pay an overdue premium. The insurance usually remains in effect during the grace period.

Duties of Insured and Insurer

The parties to an insurance contract are obligated to perform the duties imposed by the contract. The insured owes the following duties: (1) to pay the premiums stipulated by the policy, (2) to notify the insurer after the occurrence of an insured event within the time period stated in the policy or within a reasonable time, and (3) to cooperate with the insurer in investigating claims made against the insurer.

The insurer owes two primary duties. First, the insurer owes a **duty to defend** against any suit brought against the insured that involves a claim within the coverage of the policy. Thus, the insurer must provide and pay for the lawyers and court costs necessary to defend the lawsuit. Second, the insurer owes the duty to pay legitimate claims up to the policy limit. Insurers who wrongfully refuse to perform these duties are liable for damages.

Subrogation

If an insurance company pays a claim to an insured for liability or property damage caused by a third party, the insurer succeeds to the right of the insured to recover from the third party. This right is called **subrogation**. For example, if a third party negligently injures an insured who had hospital and disability insurance, the insurer can sue to recover the insurance proceeds it paid from the party who caused the injury. Subrogation does not apply to life insurance policies. An insurer has no right of subrogation against his or her own insured.

Airplane. Airline companies purchase substantial liability insurance to cover the possibility of accidents.

Warranty

A **warranty** is a representation of the insured that is expressly incorporated in the insurance contract:

- An **affirmative warranty** is a statement asserting that certain facts are true (e.g., there are no environmental problems currently existing as to the property the insured is insuring).

- A **promissory warranty** stipulates that facts will continue to be true throughout the duration of the policy (e.g., the insured will not store flammable products in the insured building).

An insurer may avoid liability caused by a breach of warranty.

Misrepresentation and Concealment

Insurance companies may require applicants to disclose certain information to help them determine whether they will insure the risk and to calculate the premium. The insurer may avoid liability on the policy (1) if its decision is based on a material misrepresentation on the part of the applicant or (2) if the applicant concealed material information from the insurer. This rule applies whether the misrepresentation was intentional or nonintentional.

Many states have enacted **incontestability clauses** that prevent insurers from contesting statements made by insureds in applications for insurance after the passage of a stipulated number of years (the typical length of time is two to five years). An incontestability clause was at issue in the following case.

> The underwriter knows nothing and the man who comes to him to ask him to insure knows everything.
>
> L. Scrutton
> *Rozanes v. Bowen (1928)*

Amex Life Assurance Company v. Slome Capital Corp.

60 Cal.Rptr.2d 898, 930 P.2d 1264, 1997 Cal. Lexis 404 (1997)
Supreme Court of California

Case 38.1
Incontestability Clause

Background and Facts

In January 1991, Jose Morales applied for a life insurance policy from Amex Life Assurance Company (Amex). Morales knew he was HIV (human immunodeficiency virus) positive, but he lied on the application form and denied having AIDS (acquired immune deficiency syndrome). As part of the application process, Amex required Morales to have a medical examination. In March 1991, a paramedic working for Amex met a man claiming to be Morales and took blood and urine samples from him. On his application, Morales had listed his height as 5 feet 6 inches and his weight as 147 pounds. The examiner registered the man taking the examination as 5 feet 10 inches tall, weighing 172 pounds, and appearing to be "older than the stated age." The blood samples tested HIV negative. Amex issued Morales a life insurance policy on May 1, 1991; the policy included a two-year incontestability clause as required by state law. All premiums were paid. Morales sold the policy to Slome Capital Corporation (Slome), a viatical company that purchased life insurance policies at a discount from AIDS carriers before their death.

On June 11, 1993, Morales died of AIDS-related causes. When Slome presented Morales's policy to Amex for payment, Amex refused to pay, alleging that Morales had engaged in fraud and had had an imposter take his physical examination for him. The trial court denied Amex's summary judgment motion. The court of appeals held that the incontestability clause prevented Amex from denying coverage. Amex appealed.

Issue

Does the two-year incontestability clause prevent Amex from raising the insured's fraud as a reason not to pay the life insurance proceeds?

Court's Reasoning

Most states, including California, have enacted statutes that require that an incontestability clause be part of a life insurance contract. In California, the statute requires a two-year incontestability clause, which was part of the life insurance contract between Morales and Amex. The supreme court noted that incontestability clauses are designed to require the insurer to investigate and act with reasonable promptness if it wishes to deny liability on the grounds of false representation or warranty by the insured. The facts can best be ascertained and proven early, instead of waiting until the death of the insured, who can no longer give testimony or defend himself or herself. The court stated that incontestability

Amex Life Assurance Company v. Slome Capital Corp.

60 Cal.Rptr.2d 898, 930 P.2d 1264, 1997 Cal. Lexis 404 (1997)
Supreme Court of California
(continued)

clauses apply to fraud claims as well as to nonfraud claims. Therefore, Morales's fraudulent statements on the life insurance application form and his having an imposter take the physical exam for him does not prohibit payment of life insurance benefits because the two-year incontestability clause had run out on May 1, 1993, and Morales did not die until six weeks later.

Decision

The California supreme court held that the incontestability clause prevented Amex from denying coverage. The court ordered Amex to pay the proceeds of Morales's life insurance policy to Slome.

Case Questions

Critical Legal Thinking   Should the law contain incontestability clauses? What public policy is served by these clauses?

Business Ethics   Did Morales act ethically in this case? Should unethical conduct be rewarded?

Contemporary Business   Who pays the cost of insurance fraud?

International Law

Lloyd's of London

International businesses are often faced with risks that are not a primary concern for domestic businesses. These risks include such things as damage to businesses from military conflict, loss of assets from expropriation by foreign governments, and losses when currency becomes inconvertible. **Lloyd's of London** is one insurer that is famous for insuring unique international risks. The company, which is based in London, England, has been insuring international business risks for over 300 years.

Lloyd's is organized differently from most insurance companies in that it is really an insurance syndicator. That is, it originates insurance business and then seeks a pool of investors to guarantee payment if the risk occurs. A separate partnership of investors is arranged to insure individual risks. For example, if a business wants to insure against the risk of loss to an oil tanker traveling in international waters, Lloyd's would seek investors for that insurance pool. If enough investors agreed to guarantee payment if the risk occurred, Lloyd's would write the policy.

With more strife in the world and major natural disasters, insurance payouts and thus insurance premiums have soared.

International risk is difficult to insure, but as long as Lloyd's of London is around, there will be a place to purchase such insurance. ■

Wills

A **will** is a declaration of how a person wants his or her property to be distributed upon his or her death. It is a testamentary deposition of property. The person who makes the will is called the **testator** or **testatrix**. The persons designated in the will to receive the testator's property are called **beneficiaries**.

Requirements for Making a Will

Every state has a **Statute of Wills** that establishes the requirements for making a valid will in that state. These requirements are:

- ■ *Testamentary capacity.*   The testator must have been of legal age and "sound mind" when the will was made. The courts determine testamentary capacity on a case-by-case basis. The legal age for executing a will is set by state statute.

- **_Writing._** Wills must be in writing to be valid (except for dying declarations, discussed later in this chapter). The writing may be formal or informal. Although most wills are typewritten, they can be handwritten (see the later discussion of holographic wills). The writing may be on legal paper, other paper, scratch paper, envelopes, napkins, or the like. A will may incorporate other documents by reference.
- **_Testator's signature._** Wills must be signed.

Most jurisdictions require the testator's signature to appear at the end of the will. This step is to prevent fraud that could occur if someone added provisions to the will below the testator's signature. For example, courts have held that initials (_R.K.H._), a nickname (_Buffy_), title (_mother_), and even an _X_ is a valid signature on a will if it can be proven that the testator intended it to be his or her signature.

Attestation by Witnesses

Wills must be **attested** to by mentally competent witnesses. Although state law varies, most states require two or three witnesses. The witnesses do not have to reside in the jurisdiction in which the testator is domiciled. Most jurisdictions stipulate that interested parties (e.g., a beneficiary under the will, the testator's attorney) cannot be witnesses. If an interested party has attested to a will, state law either voids any clauses that benefit such person or voids the entire will.

Witnesses usually sign the will following the signature of the testator. These signatures are called the **attestation clause**. Most jurisdictions require that each witness attest to the will in the presence of the other witnesses.

A will that meets the requirements of the Statute of Wills is called a **formal will**. A sample will is shown in Exhibit 38.2.

Exhibit 38.2

A Sample Will

Last Will and Testament of Florence Winthorpe Blueblood

I, FLORENCE WINTHORPE BLUEBLOOD, presently residing at Boston, County of Suffolk, Massachusetts, being of sound and disposing mind and memory, hereby make, publish, and declare this to be my Last Will and Testament.

FIRST. I hereby revoke any and all Wills and Codicils previously made by me.

SECOND. I direct that my just debts and funeral expenses be paid out of my Estate as soon as practicable after my death.

THIRD. I am presently married to Theodore Hannah Blueblood III.

FOURTH. I hereby nominate and appoint my husband as the Personal Representative of this my Last Will and Testament. If he is unable to serve as Personal Representative, then I nominate and appoint Mildred Yardly Winthorpe as Personal Representative of this my Last Will and Testament. I direct that no bond or other security be required to be posted by my Personal Representative.

FIFTH. I hereby nominate and appoint my husband as Guardian of the person and property of my minor children. In the event that he is unable to serve as Guardian, then I nominate and appoint Mildred Yardly Winthorpe Guardian of the person and property of my minor children. I direct that no bond or other security be required to be posted by any Guardian herein.

SIXTH. I give my Personal Representative authority to exercise all the powers, rights, duties, and immunities conferred upon fiduciaries under law with full power to sell, mortgage, lease, invest, or reinvest all or any part of my Estate on such terms as he or she deems best.

SEVENTH. I hereby give, devise, and bequeath my entire estate to my husband, except for the following specific bequests:

I give my wedding ring to my daughter, Hillary Smythe Blueblood.

I give my baseball card collection to my son, Theodore Hannah Blueblood IV.

In the event that either my above-named daughter or son predeceases me, then and in that event, I give, devise, and bequeath my deceased daughter's or son's bequest to my husband.

EIGHTH. In the event that my husband shall predecease me, then and in that event, I give, devise and bequeath my entire estate, with the exception of the bequests in paragraph SEVENTH, to my beloved children or grandchildren surviving me, per stirpes.

NINTH. In the event I am not survived by my husband or any children or grandchildren, then and in that event, I give, devise, and bequeath my entire estate to Harvard University.

IN WITNESS WHEREOF, I, Florence Winthorpe Blueblood, the Testatrix, sign my name to this Last Will and Testament this 3rd day of January, 2005.

Florence Winthorpe Blueblood
(Signature)

Signed, sealed, published and declared by the above-named Testatrix, as and for her Last Will and Testament, in the presence of us, who at her request, in her presence, and in the presence of one another, have hereunto subscribed our names as attesting witnesses, the day and year last written above.

Witness	Address
Norm Peterson	*100 Beacon Hill Rd* *Boston, Massachusett*
Clifford Claven	*200 Minute Man Drive* *Boston, Massachusetts*
Rebecca Howe	*300 Charles River Place* *Boston, Massachusett*

Codicil

A will cannot be amended by merely striking out existing provisions and adding new ones. Adding **codicils** is the legal way to change an existing will. A codicil is a separate document that must be executed with the same formalities as a will. In addition, it must incorporate by reference the will it is amending. The codicil and the will are then read as one instrument.

Revoking a Will

A will may be **revoked** by acts of the testator. A will is revoked if the testator intentionally burns, tears, obliterates, or otherwise destroys it. A properly executed **subsequent will** revokes a prior will if it specifically states that it is the testator's intention to do so. If the second will does not expressly revoke the prior will, the wills are read together. If any will provisions are inconsistent, the provision in the second will controls.

Wills can also be revoked by operation of law. For example, divorce or annulment revokes disposition of property to the former spouse under the will. The remainder of the will is valid. The birth of a child after a will has been executed does not revoke the will but does entitle the child to receive his or her share of the parents' estate, as determined by state statute.

Business Brief

A will cannot be amended or changed by striking out existing provisions and adding new ones on to the will itself.

Simultaneous Deaths

Sometimes people who would inherit property from each other die simultaneously. If it is impossible to determine who died first, the question becomes one of inheritance. The **Uniform Simultaneous Death Act** provides that each deceased person's property is distributed as though he or she survived.

Consider This Example   Suppose a husband and wife make wills that leave their entire estate to each other. Assume that the husband and wife are killed simultaneously in an airplane crash. Here, the husband's property would go to his relatives, and the wife's property would go to her relatives.

Undue Influence

A will may be found to be invalid if it was made as a result of **undue influence** on the testator. Undue influence can be inferred from the facts and circumstances surrounding the making of a will. For example, if an 85-year-old woman leaves all her property to the lawyer who drafted her will and ignores her blood relatives, the court is likely to presume undue influence.

Undue influence is difficult to prove by direct evidence, but it may be proved by circumstantial evidence. The elements that courts examine to find the presence of undue influence include:

The power of making a will is an instrument placed in the hands of individuals for the prevention of private calamity.

Jeremy Bentham
Principles of the Civil Code (1748)

- The benefactor and beneficiary are involved in a relationship of confidence and trust.
- The will contains substantial benefit to the beneficiary.
- The beneficiary caused or assisted in effecting execution of the will.
- There was an opportunity to exert influence.
- The will contains an unnatural disposition of the testator's property.
- The bequests constitute a change from a former will.
- The testator was highly susceptible to the undue influence.

Angel Statute. It is wise for a person to have a valid will that designates how his or her property will be distributed upon his or her death.

Types of Testamentary Gifts

In a will, a gift of real estate by will is called a **devise**. A gift of personal property by will is called a **bequest** or **legacy**. Gifts in wills can be specific, general, or residuary.

- *Specific gifts.* **Specific gifts** are gifts of specifically named pieces of property, such as a ring, a boat, or a piece of real estate.
- *General gifts.* **General gifts** are gifts that do not identify the specific property from which the gift is to be made, such as a cash amount that can come from any source in the decedent's estate.
- *Residuary gifts.* **Residuary gifts** are gifts that are established by a **residuary clause** in the will. Such a clause might state, "I give my daughter the rest, remainder, and residual of my estate." Thus, any portion of the estate left after the debts, taxes, and specific and general gifts have been paid belongs to the decedent's daughter.

A person who inherits property under a will or intestacy statute takes the property subject to all the outstanding claims against it (e.g., liens, mortgages). A person can **renounce** an inheritance and often does where the liens or mortgages against the property exceed the value of the property.

Ademption and Abatement

If a testator leaves a specific gift of property to a beneficiary, but the property is no longer in the estate of the testator when he or she dies, the beneficiary receives nothing. This doctrine is called the doctrine of **ademption**.

If the testator's estate is not large enough to pay all the devises and bequests, the doctrine of **abatement** applies. The doctrine works as follows:

- If a will provides for both general and residuary gifts, the residuary gifts are abated first. For example, suppose a testator executes a will when he owns $500,000 of property that leaves (1) $100,000 to the Red Cross, (2) $100,000 to a university, and (3) the residue to his niece. Suppose that when the testator dies his estate is worth only $225,000. Here, the Red Cross and the university each receive $100,000 and the niece receives $25,000.

- If a will provides only for general gifts, the reductions are proportionate. For example, suppose a testator's will leaves $75,000 to two beneficiaries, but the estate is only $100,000. Each beneficiary would receive $50,000.

Per Stirpes and Per Capita Distribution

A testator's will may state that property is to be left to his or her **lineal descendants** (children, grandchildren, great-grandchildren, etc.) either **per stirpes** or **per capita**. The difference between these two methods is as follows:

- **Per stirpes.** The lineal descendants inherit by representation of their parent; that is, they split what their deceased parent would have received. If their parent is not deceased, they receive nothing.

- **Per capita.** The lineal descendants equally share the property of the estate without regard to the degree of the relationship to the testator. That is, children of the testator share equally with grandchildren, great-grandchildren, and so forth.

Consider This Example   Suppose Anne dies without a surviving spouse, and she had three children, Bart, Beth, and Bruce. Bart, who survives his mother, has no children. Beth has one child, Carla, and they both survive Anne. Bruce, who predeceased his mother, had two children, Clayton and Cathy; and Cathy, who predeceased Anne, had two children, Deborah and Dominic, both of whom survive Anne.

If Anne leaves her estate to her lineal descendants *per stirpes*, Bart and Beth each get one-third, Carla receives nothing because Beth is alive, Clayton gets one-sixth, and Deborah and Dominic each get one-twelfth. See Exhibit 38.3.

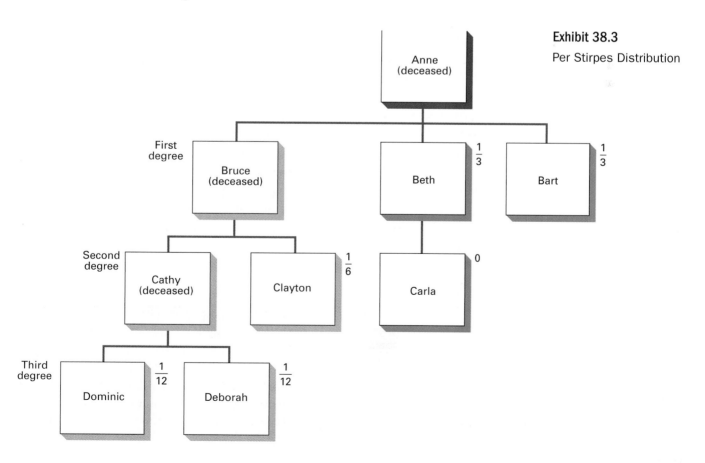

Exhibit 38.3

Per Stirpes Distribution

Exhibit 38.4

Per Capita Distribution

On the other hand, if Anne leaves her estate to her lineal descendants *per capita*, all of the surviving issue—Bart, Beth, Carla, Clayton, Deborah, and Dominic—share equally in the estate. That is, they each get one-sixth of Anne's estate. See Exhibit 38.4.

Special Types of Wills

The law recognizes several types of wills that do not meet all the requirements discussed above. The special types of wills admitted by the courts include:

- *Holographic wills.* **Holographic wills** are entirely handwritten and signed by the testator. The writing may be in ink, pencil, crayon, or some other writing instrument. Many states recognize the validity of such wills even though they are not witnessed.

- *Nuncupative wills.* **Nuncupative wills** are oral wills that are made before witnesses. Such wills are usually valid only if they are made during the testator's last illness. They are sometimes called **dying declarations** or **deathbed wills**.

Joint and Mutual Wills

If two or more testators execute the same instrument as their will, the document is called a **joint will**. A joint will may be held invalid as to one testator but not the other(s).

Mutual, or **reciprocal**, **wills** arise where two or more testators execute separate wills that make testamentary dispositions of their property to each other on the condition that the survivor leave the remaining property on his or her death as agreed by the testators. The wills are usually separate instruments with reciprocal terms. Because of their contractual nature, mutual wills cannot be unilaterally revoked after one of the parties has died.

Contemporary Environment

Videotaped Wills

Many acrimonious will contents involve written wills. The contestors allege such things as mental incapacity of the testator at the time the will was made, undue influence, fraud, or duress. Although the written will speaks for itself, the mental capacity of the testator and the voluntariness of his or her actions cannot be determined from the writing alone.

To prevent unwarranted will contests, a testator can use a videotaped will to supplement a written will. Videotaping a will that can withstand challenges by disgruntled relatives and alleged heirs involves a certain amount of planning.

The following procedures should be followed. A written will should be prepared to comply with the state's Statute of Wills. The video session should not begin until after the testator has become familiar with the document. The video should begin with the testator reciting the will verbatim. Next, the lawyer should ask the testator questions to demonstrate the testator's sound mind and understanding of the implications of his or her actions. The execution ceremony—the signing of the will by the testator and the attestation by the witnesses—should be the last segment on the film. The videotape should then be stored in a safe place.

With the testator's actions crystallized on videotape, a judge or jury will be able to determine the testator's mental capacity at the time the will was made and the voluntariness of his or her testamentary gifts. In addition, fraudulent competing wills will fall in the face of such proof. ■

Intestate Succession

If a person dies without a will, or if his or her will fails for some legal reason, the property is distributed to his or her relatives pursuant to the state's **intestacy statute**.

Relatives who receive property under these statutes are called **heirs**. Although intestacy statutes differ from state to state, the general rule is that the deceased's real property is distributed according to the intestacy statute of the state where the real property is located, and the deceased's personal property is distributed according to the intestacy statute of the state where the deceased had his or her permanent residence.

Intestacy statutes usually leave the deceased's property to his or her heirs in this order: spouse, children, lineal heirs (e.g., grandchildren, parents, brothers and sisters), collateral heirs (e.g., aunts, uncles, nieces, nephews), and other next of kin (e.g., cousins). If the deceased has no surviving relatives, the deceased's property **escheats** (goes) to the state. In-laws do not inherit under most intestacy statutes. If a child dies before his or her parents, the child's spouse does not receive the inheritance.

To avoid the distribution of an estate as provided in an intestacy statute, a person should have a properly written, signed, and witnessed will that distributes the estate property as the testator wishes.

Concept Summary   Comparison of Dying with and Without a Valid Will

Situation	Parties Who Receive Deceased's Property
Deceased dies with a valid will	Beneficiaries named in the will.
Deceased dies without a valid will	Heirs set forth in the applicable state intestacy statute. If there are no heirs, the deceased's property escheats to the state.

Living Wills

Technological breakthroughs have greatly increased the life span of human beings. This same technology, however, permits life to be sustained long after a person is "brain dead." Some people say they have a right to refuse such treatment. Others argue that human life must be preserved at all costs. In 1990, the U.S. Supreme Court was called upon to decide the **right to die** issue. [*Cruzan v. Director, Missouri Department of Health*, 497 U.S. 261, 110 S.Ct. 2841, 1990 U.S. 3301 (1990)]

In the *Guzan* case, the U.S. Supreme Court acknowledged that the right to refuse medical treatment is a personal liberty protected by the due process clause of the U.S. Constitution. The Court stated that this interest must be expressed through clear and convincing proof that the patient did not want to be sustained by artificial means.

The clear message of the Supreme Court's opinion is that people who do not want their lives prolonged indefinitely by artificial means should sign a **living will** that stipulates their wishes before catastrophe strikes and they become unable to express it themselves because of an illness or an accident. The living will should state which life saving measures the signor does and does not want. In addition, the signor can specify that he or she wants any such treatments withdrawn if doctors determine that there is no hope of a meaningful recovery. The living will provides clear and convincing proof of a patient's wishes with respect to medical treatment.

In a living will or in a separate document, the maker should name someone, such as a spouse or another relative or trusted party, to be his or her **health care agent** to make all health care decisions in accordance with his or her wishes in the living will. An alternative person should also be named in case the originally designated health care agent is unable or chooses not to serve in that capacity.

Trusts

A **trust** is a legal arrangement under which one person (the **settlor**, **trustor**, or **transferor**) delivers and transfers legal title to property to another person (the **trustee**) to be held and used for the benefit of a third person (the **beneficiary**). The property held

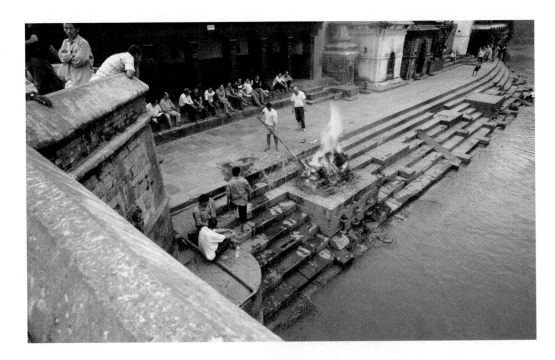

Kathmandu, Nepal. Different countries and cultures around the world have various rituals for honoring their deceased loved ones.

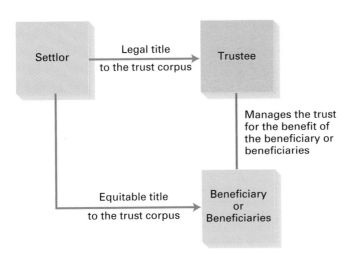

Exhibit 38.5
Parties to a Trust

in trust is called the **trust corpus** or **trust res**. The trust has legal title to the trust corpus, and the beneficiary has equitable title. Unlike wills, trusts are not public documents, so property can be transferred in privacy. Exhibit 38.5 shows the parties to a trust.

Trusts often provide that any trust income is to be paid to a person called the **income beneficiary**. The person to receive the trust corpus upon the termination of the trust is called the **remainder beneficiary**. The income beneficiary and the remainder beneficiary can be the same person or different persons. The designated beneficiary can be any identifiable person, animal (such as a pet), charitable organization, or other institution or cause that the settlor chooses. An entire class of persons—for example, "my grandchildren"—can be named.

A trust can allow the trustee to invade (use) the trust corpus for certain purposes. These purposes can be named (e.g., "for the beneficiary's college education"). The trust agreement usually specifies how the receipts and expenses of the trust are to be divided between the income beneficiary and the remainder beneficiary.

Generally, the trustee has broad management powers over the trust property. Thus the trustee can invest the trust property to preserve its capital and make it productive. The trustee must follow any restrictions on investments contained in the trust agreement or state statute.

Living Trusts

Living trusts have become a popular method for holding property during a person's lifetime and distributing the property upon that person's death. A living trust works as follows. During his or her life, a person establishes a living trust, which is a legal entity used for estate planning. A living trust is also referred to as a **grantor's trust**, a **revocable trust**, or an **inter vivos trust**. The person who creates the trust is called the **grantor** (also the **trustor**).

Benefits of a Living Trust

The primary purpose of using a living trust is to avoid *probate* associated with using a **will**. If a person dies with a will, the will must be probated so the deceased's assets can be properly distributed according to the will. A probate judge is named to oversee the probate process, and all documents, including the will, are public record. A living trust, on the other hand, is private. When the grantor dies, the assets are owned by the living trust and are therefore not subject to probate proceedings. In addition, if real property is owned in more than one state and a will is used, then ancillary probate must be conducted in the other state. If a living trust is used, ancillary probate is avoided.

Disinherit: The prankish action of the ghosts in cutting the pockets out of trousers.

Frank McKinney Hubbard
The Roycroft Dictionary (1923)

Business Brief

The primary purpose of using a living trust is to avoid probate.

Living trusts are often promoted for claimed benefits that do not exist. The true facts are that a living trust:

- Does not reduce estate taxes any more than a will.
- Does not reduce the grantor's income taxes. All the income earned by the trust is attributed to the grantor, who must pay income taxes on the earnings just as if the trust did not exist.
- Does not avoid creditors. Thus, creditors can obtain liens against property in the trust.
- Is subject to property division upon divorce.
- Is usually not cheaper than a will. Both require payments to lawyers and usually to accountants and other professionals to draft and probate a will or draft and to manage a living trust.
- Does not avoid controversies upon the grantor's death. Like wills, living trusts can be challenged for lack of capacity, undue influence, duress, and other legal grounds.

Funding and Operation of a Living Trust

To **fund a living trust**, the grantor transfers title to his or her property to the trust. This property is called the *trust corpus*. Bank accounts, stock certificates, real estate, personal property, intangible property, and other property owned by the grantor must be retitled to the trust's name. For example, the grantor must execute deeds transferring title to real estate to the trust. Once property is transferred to the trust, the trust is considered funded. A living trust is revocable during the grantor's lifetime. Thus, a grantor can later change his or her mind and undo the trust and retake title of the property in his or her own name.

A living trust names a **trustee** who is responsible for maintaining, investing, buying, or selling trust assets. The trustee is usually the grantor. Thus, the grantor who establishes the trust does not lose control of the property placed in the trust and may manage and invest trust assets during his or her lifetime. The trust should name a *successor trustee* to replace the grantor-trustee if the grantor becomes incapacitated or too ill to manage the trust.

"Grains of sand have been ten thousand mountains. Who are we to hold them?"

In memory of my parents, Henry Benjamin and Florence Lorraine Cheeseman.

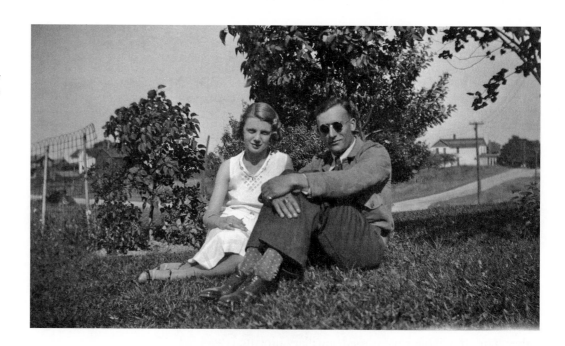

A living trust names a **beneficiary** or **beneficiaries** who are entitled to receive income from the living trust while it is in existence and to receive the property of the trust when the grantor dies. Usually the grantor is the **income beneficiary**, who receives the income from the trust during his lifetime. Upon the death of the grantor, assets of the trust are distributed to the **remainder beneficiary** or beneficiaries named in the trust. The designated trustee has the fiduciary duties of identifying assets, paying creditors, paying income and estate taxes, transferring assets to named beneficiaries, and rendering an accounting.

A **pour-over will** is necessary to distribute any property acquired in the name of the grantor after the living trust is established or any property that was not transferred to the trust in the first place. The pour-over will transfers this property to the trust upon the grantor's death, and it is then distributed to the named beneficiaries of the trust. A pour-over will is subject to probate and is therefore public. A pour-over will is usually created at the same time that the living trust is established.

A living trust is a legitimate planning tool for many people. A person should seek professional advice from, and have the living trust, pour-over will, and other necessary documents drafted by, an attorney.

Chapter Summary

Insurance, p. 838

Insurance

1. Insurance is a contract whereby one party (insurer) undertakes to indemnify another party (insured) against loss, damage, or liability arising from a contingent or unknown event.

2. Insurance is based on the concept of *risk pooling*—that is, transferring and distributing the risk of loss among a large number of persons (insureds).

3. Parties:

  a. Insured. The insured is the person who purchases insurance to cover a risk.

  b. Insurer. The insurance company (or underwriter) is obligated to pay insurance proceeds if an insured risk occurs.

  c. Reinsurer. A reinsurer is an insurance company that purchases insurance contracts from other insurance companies and is obligated to pay insurance proceeds if an insured risk occurs.

  d. Agent. An agent is a party who sells insurance exclusively for one insurance company.

  e. Broker. A broker is a party who is an independent contractor and sells insurance for a number of insurance companies.

  f. Policy. A policy is an insurance contract between an insured and an insurer.

  g. Premium. The premium is the money the insured is obligated to pay the insurer for insurance coverage.

Regulation of the Insurance Industry

The federal McCarran-Ferguson Act gave the regulation of insurance to the states. States have enacted laws that require the licensing of insurance agents and brokers and regulate insurance companies.

Insurable Interest

A person must have an insurable interest in anything he or she insures. That is, the person must benefit from the preservation of the life, health, property, or other interest that is insured.

No-Fault Automobile Insurance

No-fault insurance is an automobile insurance system where the driver's insurance company pays for any injuries or death the driver or other covered persons suffers in an accident, no matter who caused the accident.

Business Insurance

Several types of insurance are uniquely applicable to business. These include:

1. Business interruption insurance
2. Worker's compensation insurance
3. Fidelity insurance
4. Key-person life insurance

The Insurance Contract

Insurance contracts are governed by the law of contracts and statutes enacted to regulate the insurance contract. Insurance policies often contain the following clauses:

1. *Deductible clause.* This clause requires insureds to pay a certain amount of the loss before the insurer is obligated to pay.
2. *Coinsurance clause.* This clause requires an owner to insure his or her property to a certain percentage of its value to recover the face value of the policy.
3. *Exclusions from coverage clause.* This clause stipulates exclusions from insurance coverage (e.g., preexisting conditions).
4. *Suicide clause.* This clause states that if an insured commits suicide within a time period specified in a life insurance contract, the life insurance company does not have to pay the proceeds of the life insurance policy.

Endorsement and Rider

The insurer and insured may modify an insurance contract by adding an *endorsement* to the policy or executing a document called a *rider*.

Cancellation of Insurance

Grace period. A grace period is a time period during which an insured may pay an overdue premium and during which the insurance remains in effect.

Duties of Insured and Insurer

Duties of the insured:

1. Pay premiums stipulated in the policy.
2. Notify the insurer after the occurrence of an insured event.
3. Cooperate with the insurer in the investigation of claims.

Duties of the insurer:

1. Defend against suits brought against the insured that involve a claim within the coverage of the policy.
2. Pay legitimate claims up to the policy limit.

Subrogation

If an insurer pays a claim to an insured for liability or property damage caused by a third party, the insurer succeeds to the right of the insured to recover from the third party.

Warranty

An *affirmative warranty* is a statement asserting facts to be true. A *promissory warranty* stipulates that facts will continue to be true.

Misrepresentation and Concealment

Insureds sometimes misrepresent or conceal material information prior to the running of the incontestability period.

Incontestability Statutes

These statutes prohibit insurers from contesting statements made by insureds after the passage of a stipulated number of years.

Wills, p. 844

Wills

A will is a declaration of how a person wants his or her property to be distributed upon his or her death.

Requirements for Making a Will

1. A statute of wills is a state statute that establishes the requirements for making a valid will.
2. The normal requirements for making a will are:
    a. *Testamentary capacity.* The testator must have been of legal age and "sound mind" when the will was made.
    b. *Writing.* A will must be in writing, except for certain special wills.
    c. *Testator's signature.* A will must be signed by the testator.
    d. *Attestation by witnesses.* A will must be attested to by the stipulated number of mentally competent and uninterested witnesses.

Parties to a Will

Parties to a will:

1. *Testator or testatrix.* This is the person who makes a will.
2. *Beneficiary.* A beneficiary is a person designated in the will to receive the testator's property. There may be multiple beneficiaries.
3. *Executor or executrix.* This is the person named in a will to administer the testator's estate during the settlement of the estate.

Codicil

Adding a codicil is a legal way to change an existing will. A codicil must be executed with the same formalities as a will.

Simultaneous Deaths

The Uniform Simultaneous Death Act provides that if people who would inherit property from each other die simultaneously, each deceased person's property is distributed as though he or she had survived.

Undue Influence

A will may be found to be invalid if it was made under undue influence, where one person takes advantage of another person's mental, emotional, or physical weakness and unduly persuades that person to make a will.

Types of Testamentary Gifts

1. *Specific gift.* A specific gift is a gift of a specifically mentioned piece of property (e.g., a ring).
2. *General gift.* A general gift is a gift that does not identify the specific property from which the gift is to be made (e.g., gift of cash).
3. *Residuary gift.* A residuary gift is a gift of the remainder of the testator's estate after the debts, taxes, and specific and general gifts have been paid.

Ademption and Abatement

1. *Ademption.* If a testator leaves a specific gift but the property is no longer in the estate when the testator dies the beneficiary of that gift receives nothing.
2. *Abatement.* If the testator's estate is insufficient to pay the stated gifts, the gifts are abated (reduced) in the following order: (1) residuary gifts then (2) general gifts proportionately.

Per Stirpes and Per Capita Distribution

1. ***Per stirpes.*** Lineal descendants inherit by representation of their parent—that is, they split what their deceased parent would have received.
2. ***Per capita.*** Lineal descendants equally share the property of the estate without regard to degree.

Special Types of Wills

1. ***Holographic will.*** A holographic will is entirely handwritten and signed by the testator. Most states recognize the validity of these wills even though they are not witnessed.
2. ***Nuncupative will.*** Nuncupative wills are oral wills that are made by dying persons before witnesses. Many states recognize these oral wills. Also called a *dying declaration* or a *deathbed will.*

Joint and Mutual Wills

1. ***Joint will.*** Two or more testators may execute the same instrument as their will. This is called a joint will.
2. ***Mutual, or reciprocal, wills.*** Two or more testators may execute separate wills that leave property in favor of the other on condition that the survivor leave the remaining property on his or her death as agreed by the testators.

Intestate Succession, p. 851

Intestate Succession

1. ***Intestacy statutes.*** There state statutes stipulate how a deceased's property will be distributed if he or she dies without leaving a will or if the will fails for some legal reason.
2. ***Heirs.*** Heirs are relatives who receive property under an intestacy statute.
3. ***Escheat.*** Intestacy statutes provide that if there are no heirs, the deceased's property goes to the state.

Living Wills, p. 852

Living Will

1. ***Right to die.*** The right to die is a personal liberty protected by the U.S. Constitution.
2. ***Living will.*** A living will is a document signed by a person that stipulates his or her wishes to not have his or her life prolonged by artificial means.
3. ***Health care agent.*** A health care agent is a person named in a living will or other document to make health care decisions for the maker of the living will or other document is accordance with the maker's wishes.

Trusts, p. 852

Trust

1. ***Trust.*** A trust is a legal arrangement whereby one person delivers and transfers legal title to property to another person to be held and used for the benefit of a third person.
2. ***Trust corpus.*** The trust corpus is property that is held in trust. Also called *trust res.*
3. ***Parties:***
   a. *Settlor.* A settlor is a person who establishes a trust. Also called a *trustor* or *transferor.*
   b. *Trustee.* A trustee is a person to whom *legal title* of the trust assets is transferred. The trustee is responsible for managing the trust assets as established by the trust and law.
   c. *Beneficiary.* A beneficiary is a person for whose benefit a trust is created. A beneficiary holds *equitable title* to the trust assets. There can be multiple beneficiaries, including:
      i. *Income beneficiary.* This is a person to whom trust income is to be paid.
      ii. *Remainder beneficiary.* This is a person who is entitled to receive the trust corpus upon the termination of the trust.

Living Trusts, p. 853

Living Trust

1. ***Living trust.*** A living trust is a legal entity used for estate planning. Also called a *grantor's trust*, *revocable trust*, or *inter vivos trust*.

2. ***Trust corpus.*** The trust corpus is the property that is placed in a trust to fund the trust.

3. ***Parties:***

   a. *Grantor.* A grantor is a person who establishes a living trust.

   b. *Trustee.* A trustee is a person who is responsible for maintaining, investing, buying, and selling trust assets.

   c. *Income beneficiary.* An income beneficiary is a person who is entitled to receive income from a living trust.

   d. *Remainder beneficiary.* A remainder beneficiary is a person who is entitled to receive the assets of a trust upon the death of the grantor.

   e. *Pour-over will.* A pour-over will is necessary to distribute any of the grantor's property not in the living trust at the time of the grantor's death to the trust upon the grantor's death.

Internet Exercises and Case Questions

Working the Web Internet Exercises

Activities

1. Estate planning is more than just the distribution of decedents' property. Review the issues presented by The Kansas Elder Law Network, at **www.keln.org.**

2. For an overview of trusts, including a link to the draft Uniform Trust Act, see **www.law.cornell.edu/topics/ estates_trusts.html**. Note the historical purposes of a trust. Why are trusts permitted by law?

Critical Legal Thinking Cases

38.1 Exclusion   Richard Usher's home was protected by a homeowner's policy issued by National American Insurance Company of California. The policy included personal liability insurance. A provision in the policy read: "Personal liability and coverage do not apply to bodily injury or property damage arising out of the ownership, maintenance, use, loading, or unloading of a motor vehicle owned or operated by, or rented or loaned to any insured." On August 24, 1984, Usher parked a Chevrolet van he owned in his driveway. He left the van's side door open while he loaded the van in preparation for a camping trip. While Usher was inside his house, several children, including two-year-old Graham Coburn, began playing near the van. One of the children climbed into the driver's seat and moved the shift lever from *park* to *reverse.* The van rolled backward, crushing Coburn and killing him. Coburn's parents sued Usher for negligence. Is the accident covered by Usher's homeowner's policy? [*National American Insurance Company of California v. Coburn*, 209 Cal.App.3d 914, 257 Cal.Rptr. 591, 1989 Cal.App. Lexis 356 (Cal. App. 1989)]

38.2 Duty to Pay Premiums   Mutual Life Insurance Company of New York (Mutual Life) issued a $100,000 life insurance policy on the life of 65-year-old Alex Brecher, effective December 22, 1977. In consideration for the policy, Brecher agreed to pay an annual insurance premium of $7,830 in 12 monthly installments. On July 14, 1983, Brecher made a written request and authorization to have the insurance company withdraw the premiums directly from his checking account at Citibank. The insurance company's first attempt to do so, on July 15, 1983, was returned unpaid. Mutual Life and Brecher were informed that one of Brecher's creditors had placed a restraining order on the bank account. On July 29, 1983, Mutual Life sent Brecher a returned check notice, advising him that the July withdrawal had been dishonored by his bank and that to keep the policy in force, both the July and August premiums would have to be paid before August 28. Mutual Life received Brecher's check for the outstanding amounts on August 26. When Mutual Life tried to cash the check, which was drawn on the Citibank account, the bank returned it unpaid, marked "refer to maker." Brecher made no further attempts to pay the insurance premiums. He died on September 18, 1983. His widow, the beneficiary of the life insurance policy, filed a claim to recover $100,000 from Mutual Life. When Mutual Life refused to pay, the widow sued. Who wins? [*Brecher v. Mutual Life Insurance Company of New York*, 501 N.Y.S.2d 879, 1986 N.Y.App.Div. 56512 (N.Y. App. 1986)]

38.3 Duty to Defend   In February 1983, Judith Isenhart purchased a 1983 Dodge station wagon. She then contacted Ed Carpenter, an agent of the National Automobile and Casualty Insurance Company (National) and told him she was interested in obtaining "full coverage" for the car. The policy that Carpenter provided to Judith provided coverage for bodily injury, property damage, medical costs, and collision damage. The policy specifically exempted coverage for accidents involving "non-owned automobiles." In July 1984, Judith's 16-year-old son Matt purchased a 1969 Volkswagen. Insurance for this car was obtained from Allstate Insurance Company (Allstate). Two months after buying the car, Matt had an accident in which a passenger in the Volkswagen, Thea Stewart, was severely injured. Stewart sued Matt and Judith. Allstate agreed to defend the suit up to the limits of its policy. When National was contacted regarding the accident, the company refused to defend Judith in the suit and denied coverage based on the policy's exclusion. Must National defend Judith? [*National Automobile and Casualty Insurance Company v. Stewart*, 223 Cal.App.3d 452, 272 Cal.Rptr. 625, 1990 Cal.App. Lexis 941 (Cal. App. 1990)]

38.4 Concealment   A federal regulation to the Resource Conservation and Discovery Act required certain manufacturers to insure against pollution hazards. The regulation was adopted on January 12, 1981. Early in September 1981, Advanced Micro Devices, Inc. (AMD), a company covered by the regulation, purchased the required insurance from Great American Surplus Lines Insurance Company (Great American). Before issuing the policy, Great American asked AMD to disclose any preexisting conditions that could give rise to a claim retroactive to August 27, 1981. AMD warranted that there were none. AMD made this statement despite the existence of a company memorandum written by AMD's environmental supervisor on July 21, 1981. The memo warned that toxic waste was escaping from an underground steel tank in AMD's acid neutralization system "C" and that AMD was "far from being in compliance" with environmental laws. Great American issued the insurance policy. In 1982, the government ordered AMD to undertake a $1.5 million cleanup of the toxic contaminants surrounding the steel tank in system "C." AMD filed a claim for this amount with Great American, which refused to pay. AMD sued. Who wins? [*Advanced Micro Devices, Inc. v. Great American Surplus Lines Insurance Company*, 199 Cal.App.3d 791, 245 Cal.Rptr. 44, 1988 Cal.App. Lexis 226 (Cal. App. 1988)]

38.5 Subrogation   In 1977, Home Indemnity Company (Home Indemnity) agreed to insure Liberty Savings Association (Liberty), a savings and loan association, for losses that Liberty might incur through the dishonest or fraudulent acts of its employees. In August 1983, Liberty filed a proof of loss with Home Indemnity, alleging losses of $579,922. The claim was based on the conversion of $98,372 by Richard Doty, the former president and managing officer of Liberty, and loan losses resulting from four unsecured loans Doty made to friends and relatives. None of the borrowers filed financial statements to qualify for the loans. Home Indemnity paid Liberty for the losses and received a general assignment of Liberty's right to recover against Doty and the borrowers. Home Indemnity then sued Liberty's board of directors, claiming they were negligent in their supervision of Doty. Who wins? [*Home Indemnity Company v. Shaffer*, 860 F.2d 186, 1988 U.S.App. Lexis 11953 (6th Cir. 1988)]

38.6 Formalities of a Will   On or about June 10, 1959, Martha Jansa executed a will naming her two sons as executors and leaving all her property to them. The will was properly signed and attested to by witnesses. Thereafter, Martha died. When Martha's safe-deposit box at a bank was opened, the original of this will was discovered, along with two other instruments that were dated after the will. One was a handwritten document that left her home to her grandson, with the remainder of her estate to her two sons; this document was not signed. The second document was a typed version of the handwritten one; this document was signed by Martha but was not attested to by witnesses. Which of the three documents should be admitted to probate? [*In re Estate of Jansa*, 670 S.W.2d 767, 1984 Tex.App. Lexis 5503 (Tex. App. 1984)]

38.7 Mental Capacity   On March 18, 1987, Everett Clark met with William Wham, an attorney, to discuss the preparation of a will. Clark, who had never married and lived with his sister, was to return the following day to execute his will. Clark was hospitalized that evening with a perforated ulcer. He underwent surgery on March 19. Subsequent to the surgery, and until the time of his death, he was in intensive care and unable to communicate verbally. On March 23, Clark's cousin John Bailey retrieved the will prepared by Wham and took it to attorney Frank Walker to have him finalize it. Walker testified that he took the will to the hospital on March 25. Immediately prior to the execution of the will, Walker asked Clark a few questions. Walker testified that Clark knew what he was doing. Dorothy Smith, an attesting witness, testified that Clark could not talk, but answered her questions by nodding yes or no. She asked Clark "if he knew me and if he knew we were all there and he shook his head yes." She testified that he also shook his head yes to the question "Is this your will and testament?" "Is John Bailey your cousin?" and "Do you want to leave everything to John Bailey?" Clark signed the will with an X. On March 26, Clark passed into a coma and died. Bailey introduced the will into probate, but another relative of Clark's challenged it. Is the will valid? [*Bailey v. Bailey*, 561 N.E.2d 367, 1990 Ill.App. Lexis 1541 (Ill. App. 1990)]

38.8 Inheritance   In October 1973, Mr. and Mrs. Pate executed separate wills that followed a common plan in disposing of their respective estates. Each will provided for the establishment of trusts with a life estate to their son Billy, and upon his death, the estate was to be distributed "in equal shares per stirpes to my natural born grandchildren." Mr. and Mrs. Pate had two sons, Billy and Wallace. Billy's first marriage ended in divorce without children. Billy's second marriage also ended in divorce without children, although his second wife had a daughter by her previous marriage. Billy married again, and to the time of this action, no children had been born to his 32-year-old wife. Wallace first married in 1952. Of that marriage five children were born, each before the time that the Pates made their wills. After that marriage ended in divorce, Wallace married his present wife. There were no children of the second marriage, but there were stepchildren by Wallace's second wife. One of Wallace's daughters had two children by her marriage. Mr. Pate died on November 9, 1979, leaving an estate of $1.6 million. Mrs. Pate died on October 21, 1983, leaving an estate of $6.7 million. Who inherits the estate? [*Pate v. Ford*, 360 S.E.2d 145, 1987 S.C.App. Lexis 363 (S.C. App. 1987)]

Business Ethics Cases

38.9 Business Ethics   In 1983, Lewis Coe bought a $500,000 life insurance policy from Farmers New World Life Insurance Company (Farmers) from its authorized agent, Hannify. The policy, which was payable in monthly installments, contained a clause allowing for the insurance to remain in effect for a 31-day grace period if the insured failed to pay a premium by the due date. In February 1984, Lewis informed Hannify that he wanted to cancel the policy. Farmers sent Lewis a cancellation form that he signed and returned on or about March 1, 1984. At the time, Farmer received the written cancellation notice, Lewis had paid the monthly premium for February, covering the period ending March 10, 1984. Lewis died on April 8, 1984. His widow sued Farmers for the policy proceeds, claiming that Lewis died during the 31-day grace period provided by the policy. Farmers claimed that the policy had been canceled and the grace period did not apply. Who wins? Did either party act unethically in this case? [*Coe v. Farmers New World Life Insurance Company*, 209 Cal.App.3d 600, 257 Cal.Rptr. 411, 1989 Cal.App. Lexis 328 (Cal. App. 1989)]

38.10 Business Ethics   In 1967, Homer and Edna Jones, husband and wife, executed a joint will that provided "We will and give to our survivor, whether it be Homer Jones or Edna Jones, all property and estate of which the first of us that dies may be seized and possessed. If we should both die in a common catastrophe, or upon the death of our survivor, we will and give all property and estate then remaining to our children, Leonida Jones Eschman, daughter, Sylvia Marie Jones, daughter, and Grady V. Jones, son, share and share alike."

Homer died in 1975, and Edna Jones received his entire estate under the 1967 will. In 1977, Edna executed a new will that left a substantially larger portion of the estate to her daughter Sylvia Marie Jones than to the other two children. Edna Jones died in 1982. Edna's daughter introduced the 1977 will for probate. The other two children introduced the 1967 will for probate. Did Edna act ethically in this case? Who wins? [*Jones v. Jones*, 718 S.W.2d 416, 1986 Tex.App. Lexis 8929 (Tex. App. 1986)]

Briefing the Case Writing Assignment

Read Case A.38 in the Case Appendix [*Saritejdiam, Inc. v. Excess Insurance Company, Ltd.*]. This case is excerpted from the court of appeals opinion. Review and brief the case. In your brief, be sure to answer the following questions.

1. Was the "close personal custody and control" provision in the insurance policy plain and clear?

2. Summarize the factual details of the case.

3. What public policy is served by the exclusion of coverage in this case?

4. Do you think that the insurance policy met the reasonable expectations of the insured?

Endnote

1. 5 U.S.C. §§ 1011–1015.

39

International and Comparative Law

" International law, or the law that governs between nations, has at times, been like the common law within states, a twilight existence during which it is hardly distinguishable from morality or justice, till at length the imprimatur of a court attests its jural quality. "

—Justice Cardozo
New Jersey v. Delaware, 291 U.S. 361, 54 S.Ct. 407, 1934 U.S. Lexis 973 (1934)

Chapter Objectives

After studying this chapter, you should be able to:

1. Describe the federal government's power under the Foreign Commerce and Treaty Clauses of the U.S. Constitution.

2. List and describe the sources of international law.

3. Describe the functions and governance of the United Nations.

4. Describe the North American Free Trade Agreement (NAFTA) and other regional economic organizations.

5. Describe the World Trade Organization (WTO) and explain how its dispute resolution procedure works.

Chapter Contents

- ■ The United States and Foreign Affairs
- ■ Sources of International Law
- ■ The United Nations
- ■ Regional International Organizations
- ■ The World Trade Organization (WTO)
- ■ National Courts Deciding International Disputes

International law, important to both nations and businesses, has many unique features. First, there is no single legislative source of international law. All countries of the world and numerous international organizations are responsible for enacting international law. Second, there is no single world court that is responsible for interpreting international law. There are, however, several courts or tribunals that hear and decide international legal disputes of parties that agree to appear before them. Third, there is no world executive branch that can enforce international law. Thus, nations do not have to obey international law enacted by other countries or international organizations. Because of these uncertainties, some commentators question whether international law is really "law."

As technology and transportation bring nations closer together and American and foreign firms increase their global activities, international law will become even more important to governments and businesses. This chapter introduces the main concepts of international law and discusses the sources of international law and the organizations responsible for its administration.

The United States and Foreign Affairs

The U.S. Constitution divides the power to regulate the internal affairs of this country between the federal and state governments. On the international level, however, the Constitution gives most of the power to the federal government. Two constitutional provisions establish this authority:

- *Foreign Commerce Clause.* Article I, Section 8, clause 3—the **Foreign Commerce Clause**—vests Congress with the power "to regulate commerce with foreign nations."
- *Treaty Clause.* Article II, Section 2, clause 2—the **Treaty Clause**—states that the president "shall have power, by and with the advice and consent of the Senate, to make treaties, provided two-thirds of the senators present concur."

Indonesia. The federal government of the United States has exclusive power to regulate commerce with foreign nations.

The Constitution does not vest exclusive power over foreign affairs in the federal government, but any state or local law that unduly burdens foreign commerce is unconstitutional under the Foreign Commerce Clause. Under the Treaty Clause, only the federal government may enter into treaties with foreign nations. Under the Supremacy Clause of the Constitution, treaties become part of the "law of the land," and conflicting state or local law is void. The president is the agent of the United States in dealing with foreign countries.

In the following case, the U.S. Supreme Court struck down a state law as violating the Constitution.

U.S. SUPREME COURT CASE
Crosby, Secretary of Administration and Finance of Massachusetts v. National Foreign Trade Council

Case 39.1
Foreign Affairs

530 U.S. 363, 120 S.Ct. 2288, 2000 U.S. Lexis 4153 (2000)
Supreme Court of the United States

Background and Facts

The military regime of the country of Myanmar (called Burma prior to 1989) has been accused of major civil rights violations, including using forced and child labor, imprisoning and torturing political opponents, and harshly repressing ethnic minorities. These inhumane actions have been condemned by human rights organizations around the world. The state legislators in the state of Massachusetts were so appalled at these actions that in June 1996 they enacted a state statute banning the state government from purchasing goods and services from any company that did business with Myanmar.

In the meantime, the U.S. Congress enacted a federal statute that delegated power to the President of the United States to regulate U.S. dealings with Myanmar. The federal statute (1) banned all aid to the government of Myanmar except for humanitarian assistance, (2) authorized the president to impose economic sanctions against Myanmar, and (3) authorized the president to develop a comprehensive multilateral strategy to bring democracy to Myanmar.

The National Foreign Trade Council—a powerful Washington, DC–based trade association with more than 500 member companies—filed a lawsuit against Massachusetts to have the state law declared unconstitutional. The council argued that the Massachusetts "anti-Myanmar" statute was preempted by the Supremacy Clause of the U.S. Constitution, which makes federal law the "supreme law of the land" and gives the federal government the power to regulate foreign affairs. The district court and court of appeals ruled in favor of the council. Massachusetts appealed to the U.S. Supreme Court.

Issue

Did the Massachusetts anti-Myanmar state statute violate the Supremacy Clause of the U.S. Constitution?

Court's Reasoning

The U.S. Supreme Court stated that the federal statute placed the president in a position with as much discretion to exercise economic leverage against Burma, with an eye toward national security, as law will admit. The president has been given this authority not merely to make a political statement but to achieve a political result.

The Supreme Court noted that it was simply implausible that Congress intended both to enable the president to protect national security by giving him the flexibility to suspend or terminate federal sanctions against Myanmar while simultaneously allowing Massachusetts to act at odds with the president's judgment of what national security requires. The Supreme Court held, quite simply, if the Massachusetts law is enforceable the president has less to offer and less economic and diplomatic leverage as a consequence.

Decision and Remedy

The U.S. Supreme Court held that the Massachusetts anti-Myanmar law conflicted with federal law and was therefore preempted by the Supremacy Clause of the Constitution. The Supreme Court affirmed the decisions of the district court and court of appeals in favor of the council.

Case Questions

Critical Legal Thinking Should the federal government have sole power to regulate the foreign affairs of the United States? Or should the states share in this power?

Business Ethics Do you think companies that have goods manufactured in Myanmar violate any ethical principles? Explain.

Contemporary Business Did the Massachusetts anti-Myanmar law have any economic implications for business? What would have been the consequences if the U.S. Supreme Court had held that the Massachusetts anti-Myanmar statute was lawful?

Sources of International Law

The **sources of international law** are those things that international tribunals rely on in deciding international disputes. **Article 38(1) of the Statute of the International Court of Justice** lists the following four sources of international law: *treaties and conventions, custom, general principles of law*, and *judicial decisions and teachings*. Most courts rely on the hierarchy suggested by this list; that is, treaties and conventions are turned to before custom, and so on. Each of these sources of law is discussed in the following paragraphs.

Treaties and Conventions

Treaties and conventions are the equivalents of legislation at the international level. A **treaty** is an agreement or a contract between two or more nations that is formally signed by an authorized representative and ratified by the supreme power of each nation. *Bilateral treaties* are between two nations; *multilateral treaties* involve more than two nations. **Conventions** are treaties that are sponsored by international organizations, such as the United Nations. Conventions normally have many signatories.

Treaties and conventions address such matters as human rights, foreign aid, navigation, commerce, and the settlement of disputes. Most treaties are registered with and published by the United Nations.

Custom

Custom between nations is an independent source of international law. Custom describes a practice followed by two or more nations when dealing with each other. It may be found in official government statements, diplomatic correspondence, policy statements, press releases, speeches, and the like. Two elements must be established to show that a practice has become a custom:

1. Consistent and recurring action by two or more nations over a considerable period of time.
2. Recognition that the custom is binding—that is, followed because of legal obligation rather than courtesy.

International customs evolve as mores, technology, forms of government, political parties, and other factors change throughout the world. Customs that have been recognized for some period of time are often codified in treaties.

Business Brief

Even customs that have not been elevated to the level of international law are still vitally important to the conduct of international business.

General Principles of Law

Courts and tribunals that decide international disputes frequently rely on **general principles of law** that are recognized by civilized nations. These are principles of law that are common to the *national* law of the parties to the dispute. They may be derived from constitutions, statutes, regulations, common law, or other sources of national law. In some cases, however, the countries' laws may differ concerning the matter in dispute.

Judicial Decisions and Teachings

A fourth source of law to which international tribunals can refer is **judicial decisions and teachings** of the most qualified scholars of the various nations involved in the dispute. Although international courts are not bound by the doctrine of *stare decisis* and may decide each case on its own merits, the courts often refer to their own past decisions for guidance. Court decisions of national courts do not create precedent for international courts.

The United Nations

One of the most important international organizations is the **United Nations (UN)**, which was created by a multilateral treaty on October 24, 1945.[1] Most countries of the world are members of the UN. The goals of the UN, which is headquartered in New York City, are to maintain peace and security in the world, promote economic and social cooperation, and protect human rights (see Exhibit 39.1).

Governance of the UN

The UN is governed by:

- **The General Assembly**, composed of all member nations. As the legislative body of the UN, it adopts resolutions concerning human rights, trade, finance and economics, and other matters within the scope of the UN Charter. Although resolutions have limited force, they are usually enforced through persuasion and the use of economic and other sanctions.

- **The Security Council**, composed of 15 member nations, 5 of which are permanent members (China, France, Russia, the United Kingdom, and the United States), and 10 other countries chosen by the members of the General Assembly to serve two-year terms. The council is primarily responsible for maintaining international peace and security and has authority to use armed forces.

- **The Secretariat**, which administers the day-to-day operations of the UN. It is headed by the *secretary-general*, who is elected by the General Assembly. The secretary-general may refer matters that threaten international peace and security to the Security Council and use his office to help solve international disputes.

The International Court of Justice

The **International Court of Justice (ICJ)**, also called the **World Court**, is located in The Hague, the Netherlands. It is the judicial branch of the UN. Only nations, not individuals or businesses, may have cases decided by this court. The ICJ may hear cases that nations refer to it as well as cases involving treaties and the UN Charter. A nation may seek redress

Exhibit 39.1

Selected Provisions from the Charter of the United Nations

Our respective Governments, through representatives assembled in the city of San Francisco, who have exhibited their full powers found to be in good and due form, have agreed to the present Charter of the United Nations and do hereby establish an international organization to be known as the United Nations.

Chapter 1. Purposes and Principles

Article 1 The Purposes of the United Nations are:

(1) To maintain international peace and security, and to that end: to take effective collective measures for the prevention and removal of threats to the peace, and for the suppression of acts of aggression or other breaches of the peace, and to bring about by peaceful means, and in conformity with the principles of justice and international law, adjustment or settlement of international disputes or situations which might lead to a breach of the peace;

(2) To develop friendly relations among nations based on respect for the principle of equal rights and self-determination of peoples, and to take other appropriate measures to strengthen universal peace;

(3) To achieve international co-operation in solving international problems of an economic, social, cultural, or humanitarian character, and in promoting and encouraging respect for human rights and for fundamental freedoms for all without distinction as to race, sex, language, or religion; and

(4) To be a centre for harmonizing the actions of nations in the attainment of these common ends.

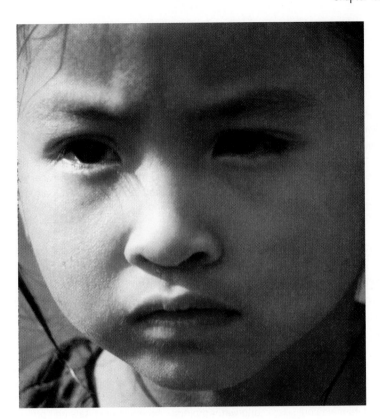

Laos. The United Nations is an international organization created in 1945 to promote peace and provide humanitarian assistance worldwide.

on behalf of an individual or a business that has a claim against another country. The ICJ is composed of 15 judges who serve nine-year terms; not more than 2 judges may be from the same nation. A nation that is a party to a dispute before the ICJ may appoint 1 judge on an ad hoc basis for that case.

UN Agencies

The UN is composed of various autonomous agencies that deal with a wide range of economic and social problems. These include UNESCO (United Nations Educational, Scientific, and Cultural Organization), UNICEF (United Nations International Children's Emergency Fund), the IMF (International Monetary Fund), the World Bank, and IFAD (International Fund for Agricultural Development).

International Law
The International Monetary Fund (IMF)

The IMF, an agency of the United Nations, was established by treaty in 1945 to help promote the world economy following the Great Depression of the 1930s and the end of World War II in 1945. The IMF comprises more than 180 countries that are each represented on the board of directors, which makes the policy decisions of the IMF. The day-to-day operations of the IMF are run by the executive committee, which is composed of the United States, the United Kingdom, Japan, Germany, France, China,

Russia, and Saudi Arabia, and 16 other countries elected from countries other than those already named. The IMF is funded by monetary contributions of member nations, assessed based on the size of each nation's economy. The IMF's headquarters is located in Washington, DC.

The primary function of the IMF is to promote sound monetary, fiscal, and macroeconomic policies worldwide by providing assistance to needy countries. The IMF examines a country's

International Law

(continued)

economy as a whole, its currency accounts, inflation, balance of payments with other countries, employment, consumer and business spending, and other factors to determine whether the country needs assistance. The IMF responds to financial crises across the globe. It does so by providing short-term loans to member countries to help them weather problems caused by unstable currencies, to balance payment problems, and to

recover from the economic policies of past governments. For example, the IMF has played a financial role in helping eastern and central European countries recover since the collapse of the Soviet Union. In return for the financial assistance, a country must agree to meet certain monetary, fiscal, employment, inflation, and other goals established by the IMF. ■

International Law

The World Bank

The **World Bank** is a United Nations agency that comprises more than 180 member nations. The World Bank is financed by contributions from developed countries, with the United States, the United Kingdom, Japan, Germany, and France being its main contributors. The World Bank has employees located in its headquarters in Washington, DC, and regional offices throughout the world. Each member country is represented on a board of governors that meets to determine how the bank's funds will be distributed. The executive directors, comprising directors from the 5 largest donor countries and 19 directors elected by the other countries, is responsible for the conduct of the bank's general operations.

The World Bank provides money to developing countries to fund projects for humanitarian purposes and to relieve poverty. The World Bank provides funds to build roads, construct dams and water projects, establish hospitals and provide medical assistance, develop agriculture, and provide funds for humanitarian aid. The World Bank provides outright grants of funds to developing countries for such projects, and it makes long-term low-interest-rate loans to these countries. The bank routinely grants debt relief for these loans. ■

European Union. The European Union (EU) is a regional trading block comprised of 25 countries of Western and Eastern Europe. The EU treaty creates open borders for trade by providing for the free flow of capital, labor, goods, and services among member nations.

Regional International Organizations

There are several significant regional organizations whose members have agreed to work together to promote peace and security as well as economic, social, and cultural development. The most important of these organizations are discussed in the following paragraphs.

The European Union

One of the most important international regional organizations is the **European Union (EU)**, formerly called the **European Community**, or **Common Market**. The EU was created in 1957. The EU is composed of many countries of western and eastern Europe, including Austria, Belgium, Cyprus (Greek part), Denmark, Estonia, Finland, France, Germany, Greece, Hungary, Ireland, Italy, Latvia, Lithuania, Luxembourg, Malta, Netherlands, Poland, Portugal, Slovakia, Slovenia, Spain, Sweden, The Czech Republic, and the United Kingdom of Great Britain and Northern Ireland. The EU represents more than 400 million people and a gross community product that exceeds that of the United States, Canada, and Mexico combined.

The EU's **Council of Ministers** is composed of representatives from each member country, who meet periodically to coordinate efforts to fulfill the objectives of the treaty. The council votes on significant issues and changes to the treaty. Some matters require unanimity, whereas others require only a majority vote. The member nations have surrendered substantial sovereignty to the EU. The EU **commission**, which is independent of member nations, acts in the best interests of the union. The member nations have delegated substantial powers to the commission, including authority to enact legislation and to take enforcement actions to ensure member compliance with the treaty.

The EU treaty creates open borders for trade by providing for the free flow of capital, labor, goods, and services among member nations. Under the EU, customs duties have been eliminated among member nations. Common customs tariffs have been established for EU trade with the rest of the world. A single monetary unit, the euro, and a common monetary policy have been introduced. An EU central bank, equivalent to the U.S. Federal Reserve Board, has been established.

A unanimous vote of existing EU members is needed to admit a new member. Other nonmember European countries are expected to apply for and be admitted as members of the EU.

A map of the European Union (EU) is shown in Exhibit 39.2.

The North American Free Trade Agreement (NAFTA)

In 1990, Mexico asked the United States to set up a two-country trade pact. Negotiations between the two countries began. Canada joined the negotiations, and on August 12, 1992, the **North American Free Trade Agreement (NAFTA)** was signed by the leaders of the three countries. The treaty creates a free-trade zone stretching from the Yukon to the Yucatan, bringing together over 400 million people in the three countries.

NAFTA eliminates or reduces most of the duties, tariffs, quotas, and other trade barriers between Mexico, the United States, and Canada. Agriculture, automobiles, computers, electronics, energy and petrochemicals, financial services, insurance telecommunications, and many other industries are affected. The treaty contains a safety valve: A country can reimpose tariffs if an import surge from one of the other nations hurts its economy or workers. Like other regional trading agreements. NAFTA allows the bloc to discriminate against outsiders and to cut deals among themselves. NAFTA also includes special protection for favored industries with a lot of lobby muscle. Thus, many economists assert that NAFTA is not a "free trade" pact but a *managed trade* agreement.

When Kansas and Colorado have a quarrel over the water in the Arkansas River they don't call out the National Guard in each state and go to war over it. They bring a suit in the Supreme Court of the United States and abide by the decision. There isn't a reason in the world why we cannot do that internationally.

Harry S. Truman Speech
(1945)

Exhibit 39.2

The European Union

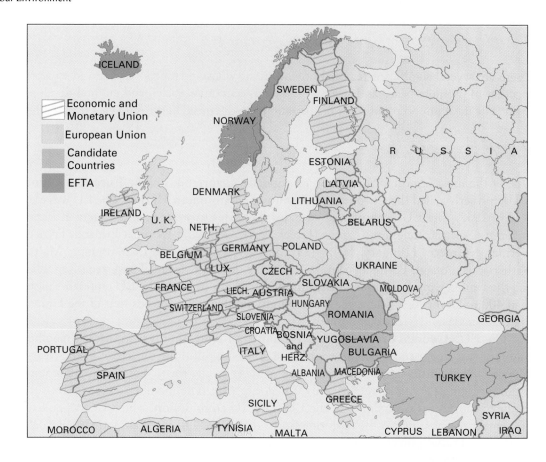

Business Brief

NAFTA removed or reduced tariffs, duties, quotas, and other trade barriers between the United States, Canada, and Mexico.

NAFTA forms a supranational trading region that more effectively competes with Japan and the European Community. Consumers in all three countries pay lower prices on a wide variety of goods and services as trade barriers fell and competition increased. Critics contend that NAFTA shifted American jobs—particularly blue-collar jobs—south of the border, where Mexican wage rates are about one-tenth of those in the United States. Environmentalists criticize the pact for not doing enough to prevent and clean up pollution in Mexico.

A map of the North American Free Trade Agreement (NAFTA) is shown in Exhibit 39.3.

International Law

Free Trade Area of the Americas (FTAA)

In April 2001, the leaders of 34 of North, Central, and South America nations met at the Summit of the Americas in Quebec City, Canada, to discuss future trade opportunities in the Western Hemisphere. The leaders agreed to a *Plan of Action* to create a regional **Free Trade Area of the Americas (FTAA)**. The FTAA would be an extension of NAFTA, which currently exists between Canada, Mexico, and the United States. The proposed FTAA would include all the countries of North, Central, and South America and would extend from Alaska in the north to Argentina in the south.

The FTAA would eliminate or reduce trade barriers among its member nations and create a trading zone of more than 800 mil-

lion people where trade of over $12 trillion could flourish between seamless economic borders. Negotiations for the creation of the FTAA are conducted, with the United States and Brazil co-chairing the process.

The FTAA is supported by the United States and most large U.S. corporations. The FTAA is not without its critics, however, Labor unions fear loss of jobs, and environmentalists envision more loss of rain forests and further destruction of the environment caused by economic advancement. Brazil and several other nations have also voiced reservations. ■

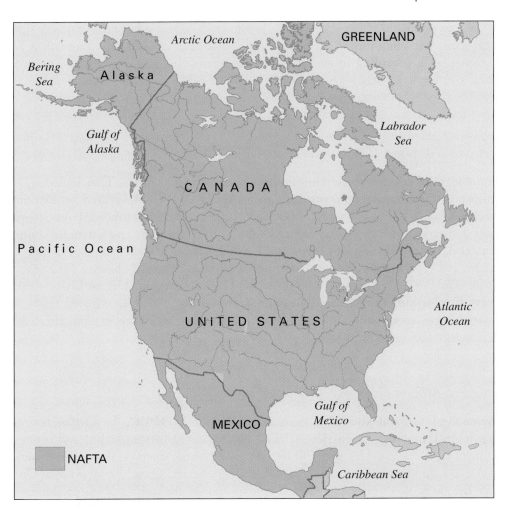

Exhibit 39.3
The North American Free
Trade Agreement (NAFTA)

Latin, Central, and South American Economic Communities

Countries of Latin America and the Caribbean have established several regional organizations to promote economic development and cooperation. These include (1) the **Central American Common Market**, composed of Costa Rica, El Salvador, Guatemala, Honduras, Nicaragua, and Panama; (2) the **MERCOSUR Common Market**, created by Argentina, Brazil, Paraguay, and Uruguay; (3) the **Caribbean Community**, whose member countries are Barbados, Belize, Dominica, Grenada, Jamaica, St. Kitts-Nevis-Anguilla, St. Lucia, St. Vincent, and Trinidad-Tobago; and (4) the **Andean Common Market (ANCOM)**, whose current members are Bolivia, Colombia, Ecuador, and Venezuela.

Mexico, the largest industrialized country in Latin America and the Caribbean, has entered into a free trade agreement with all the countries of Central America as well as Chile, Colombia, and Venezuela.

Business Brief
The importance of regional organizations and their mutual agreements is increasing.

Asian Economic Communities

In 1967, the **Association of South East Asian Nations (ASEAN)** was created. The countries that belong to ASEAN are Brunei Darussalam, Cambodia, Indonesia, Laos, Malaysia, Myanmar, Philippines, Singapore, Thailand, and Vietnam. This is a cooperative association of diverse nations.

My nationalism is intense internationalism. I am sick of the strife between nations or religions.

Gandhi

Two of the world's largest countries, Japan and China, do not belong to any significant economic community. Although not a member of ASEAN, Japan has been instrumental in providing financing for the countries that make up that organization. China also works closely with the countries of ASEAN and is a potential member of ASEAN.

African Economic Communities

Several regional economic communities have been formed in Africa. They include (1) the **Economic Community of West African States (ECOWAS)**, created by Dahomey, Gambia, Ghana, Guinea-Bissau, Ivory Coast, Liberia, Mali, Mauritania, Niger, Nigeria, Senegal, Sierra Leone, Togo, and Upper Volta; (2) the **Economic and Customs Union of Central Africa**, composed of Cameroon, Central African Republic, Chad, Congo, and Gabon; and (3) the **East African Community (EAC)**, created by Kenya, Tanzania, and Uganda. In 1991, 51 African countries of the **Organization of African Unity** signed a **Treaty Establishing the African Economic Community**. This wide-ranging treaty with its large organization of countries is expected to wield more power than the smaller African regional organizations.

Middle Eastern Economic Communities

We need to have the spirit of science in international affairs, to make the conduct of international affairs the effort to find the right solution, the just solution of international problems, not the effort by each nation to get the better of other nations, to do harm to them when it is possible.

Linus Carl Pauling
No More War (1958)

One of the most well-known economic organization is **OPEC**, the **Organization of Petroleum Exporting Countries**. OPEC consists of 11 oil-producing and exporting countries from Africa, Asia, the Middle East, and South America. The member nations are Algeria, Indonesia, Iran, Iraq, Kuwait, Libya, Nigeria, Qatar, Saudi Arabia, United Arab Emirates, and Venezuela. OPEC sets quotas on the output of oil production by member nations. The **Gulf Cooperation Council** was established by Bahrain, Kuwait, Oman, Qatar, Saudi Arabia, and the United Arab Emirates to establish an economic trade area.

Regional Courts

Various treaties have created regional courts to handle disputes among member nations. For example, most regional economic organizations have established courts to enforce provisions of their respective treaties and to solve disputes among member nations. Regional courts, however, usually do not have mechanisms to enforce their judgments.

The World Trade Organization (WTO)

In 1995, the **World Trade Organization (WTO)** was created as part of the Uruguay Round of trade negotiations on the *General Agreement on Tariffs and Trade (GATT)*. GATT is a multilateral treaty that establishes trade agreements and limits tariffs and trade restrictions among its more than 130 member nations.

The WTO is an international organization whose headquarters is located in Geneva, Switzerland. WTO members have entered into many trade agreements among themselves, including international agreements on investments, sale of goods, provision

Mandalay, Myanmar. Many companies in the United States and other countries do not do business in, or with companies from, Myanmar. This is because of alleged human rights violations by the military government of Myanmar. Does this policy help or hurt the people of Myanmar?

of services, intellectual property, licensing, tariffs, subsidies, and the removal of trade barriers.

The WTO, which has been referred to as the "Supreme Court of Trade," has become the world's most important trade organization. The WTO has jurisdiction to enforce the most important and comprehensive trade agreements in the world among its more than 130 member nations. Many herald the WTO as a much-needed world court that can peaceably solve trade disputes among nations.

Business Brief

By enforcing trade agreements among its more than 130 member nations, the WTO has become the world's most important trade organization.

International Law
China Joins the WTO

For the past 50 years, China and the United States have pursued divergent paths. China became the world's largest communist country and the United States the leading democracy. China maintained its agricultural base, while the United States pursued industrialization. Most of China's businesses were state owned, while those in the United States were privately owned under a capitalist system. For over a decade, these two countries engaged in on-again, off-again trade negotiations. Then in November 1999 they formed a landmark trade pact. In exchange for being granted the right to import most goods and services into the United States, China, which had substantially restricted imports into its country, agreed to open its markets to foreign goods and services.

The China–U.S. trade agreement was a prelude to China's trade agreements with other countries. These trade agreements supported China's application to join the WTO. In 2002, China became a member of the WTO. China's entry into the WTO makes it a full partner in the world's trading system.

China's entry into the WTO is not without critics. In the United States, labor unions complain that U.S. manufacturing jobs will be lost to China, while environmentalists complain that little is being done to protect the environment from an industrialized economy the size of China's. In China, workers at state-owned enterprises might lose their jobs to foreign capitalist companies that can produce goods and services more efficiently, and China's already impoverished farmers may be harmed by cheap farm products imported from other countries. ■

WTO Dispute Resolution

One of the primary functions of the WTO is to hear and decide trade disputes between member nations. Before the creation of the WTO, GATT governed trade disputes between signatory nations. This system was inadequate because any member nation that was found to have violated any GATT trade agreement could itself veto any sanctions imposed by GATT's governing body. The WTO solved this problem by adopting a "judicial" mode of dispute resolution to replace GATT's more politically based one.

A member nation that believes that another member nation has breached one of these agreements can initiate a proceeding to have the WTO hear and decide the dispute.

The dispute is first heard by a three-member **panel** of the WTO, which issues a "panel report." The members of the panel are professional judges from member nations. The report is the decision of the panel and contains its findings of fact and law and orders a remedy if a violation has been found. The report is then referred to the **dispute settlement body** of the WTO. This body is required to adopt the panel report unless the body, by consensus, agrees not to adopt it. Because each member nation has a representative on this settlement body, it can be presumed that panel reports will automatically be adopted because the winning nation to the dispute will almost assuredly vote to adopt it. This is a radical change from the former GATT settlement procedure. Under GATT, unanimity was required to enforce a panel report, and the losing party usually voted to "block" the implementation of a panel's findings against it. One of the most important features of the WTO is the elimination of this blocking power of member nations.

The WTO creates an **appellate body** to which a party can appeal a decision of the dispute settlement body. This appeals court is composed of seven professional justices selected from member nations. Appeals are heard by panels composed of three members of the apellate body. Appeals are limited to issues of law, not fact. The entire dispute proceeding is completed within 9 months when a panel report is not appealed and within 12 months when there is an appeal. A shortened period is available if the parties agree or if there is an urgent matter that must be decided quickly.

If a violation of a trade agreement is found, the general report and appellate decision can order the offending nation to cease from engaging in the violating practice and to pay damages to the other party. If the offending nation refuses to abide by the order, the WTO can order retaliatory trade sanctions (e.g., tariffs) by other member nations against the noncomplying nation.

International Law
WTO Audits U.S. Tax Law

The number-one plaintiff in cases brought before the WTO has been the United States. It has initiated and won cases against Japan, Brazil, and the EU to knock down subsidies and other measures instituted by these countries to protect their industries from open trade. But in a recent case, the tables were turned on the United States, which lost an important case brought against it in the WTO by the EU.

This was the situation. The U.S. Tax Code provided that if U.S. companies ran the paperwork concerning the export of goods to Europe through the tax-haven countries in the Caribbean, then the goods would not be subject to U.S. export tax. The goods could be shipped directly from the United States to their destination in

Europe, however, and still qualify for this tax saving, as long as paperwork (which is basically digital) was routed through the Caribbean counties. The EU brought an action before the WTO against the United States, alleging that this tax break was an illegal export subsidy that violated WTO free-trade rules. After a hearing, the WTO ruled that the United States had engaged in a subtle and lucrative export subsidy that violated WTO trade laws. The WTO ordered the United States to dismantle this favorable tax subsidy. This ruling by the WTO is its most significant to date, repealing hundreds of millions of dollars of tax breaks sneakily given by the U.S. government to Microsoft Corporation, Boeing Company, and other large U.S. exporters. [World Trade Organization, 2001] ■

International Law

The International Criminal Court

In the twentieth century, the world witnessed horrible war crimes and crimes against humanity. Most of these crimes were conducted with impunity, and the perpetrators of these crimes went unpunished. To address this problem, at a meeting in 1998, the majority of the countries of the world adopted the **Rome Treaty**, which created the **International Criminal Court (ICC)**. The ICC has authority to prosecute individuals accused of genocide, war crimes, and crimes against humanity. The ICC may prosecute nationals located in the more than 100 countries that have ratified the treaty. The ICC has complementary jurisdiction with the national courts of a country. That is, a nation's courts will have first jurisdiction to criminally prosecute its own national who is suspected of genocide, war crimes, or crimes against humanity. If the nation is unwilling or unable to genuinely prosecute, the ICC can then prosecute the accused national.

The ICC is located in The Hague in the Netherlands. The tribunal came into force on July 1, 2003, and it may prosecute crimes committed after that date. The ICC is comprised of a Pre-Trial Division that investigates alleged crimes and issues indictments, a Trial Division that conduct the criminal trial, and an Appeals Division that hears appeals of decisions of the trial court. The judges of these courts are selected by ICC member nations. ICC rules guarantee the accused substantial rights, including the presumption of innocence and the right to have charges proved beyond a reasonable doubt. The accused also has the rights to counsel, to present evidence, and to remain silent.

The creation and operation of the ICC will assure the world that many perpetrators of the worst crimes against humanity will not go unpunished. However, the ICC does not have complete worldwide jurisdiction because only nationals of countries that have ratified the Rome Treaty are subject to prosecution by the ICC. China, the United States, and Iraq are three countries that have not ratified the Rome Treaty. The United States stated that it did not ratify the treaty because it already had laws in place to punish the crimes subject to prosecution by the ICC. ∎

National Courts Deciding International Disputes

The majority of cases involving international law disputes are heard by **national courts** of individual nations. This is primarily the case for commercial disputes between private litigants that do not qualify to be heard by an international court. Some countries have specialized courts that hear international commercial disputes. Other countries permit such disputes to proceed through their regular court systems. In the United States, commercial disputes between U.S. companies and foreign governments or parties may be brought in federal district court.

Business Brief

The majority of commercial litigation involving international business transactions is heard by national courts.

Judicial Procedure

A party seeking judicial resolution of an international dispute faces several problems, including which nation's courts will hear the case and what law should be applied to the case. Jurisdiction is often a highly contested issue. Absent an agreement providing otherwise, a case involving an international dispute will be brought in the national court of the plaintiff's home country.

Many international contracts contain a **choice of forum** (or **forum-selection**) **clause** that designates which nation's court has jurisdiction to hear a case arising out of contract. In addition, many contracts also include a **choice of law clause** that designates which nation's laws will be applied in deciding the case. Absent these two clauses, and without the parties agreeing to these matters, an international dispute may never be resolved.

Concept Summary — International Contract Clauses Affecting Jurisdiction and Choice of Law

Clause	Description
Forum-selection	A clause that designates the judicial or arbitral forum that will hear and decide a case.
Choice of law	A clause that designates the law to be applied by the court or arbitrator in deciding a case.

The Act of State Doctrine

A general principle of international law is that a country has absolute authority over what transpires *within* its own territory. In furtherance of this principle, the **act of state doctrine** states that judges of one country cannot question the validity of an act committed by another country within that other country's own borders. In *United States v. Belmont*,[2] the U.S. Supreme Court declared, "Every sovereign state must recognize the independence of every other sovereign state; and the courts of one will not sit in judgment upon the acts of the government of another, done within its own territory." This restraint on the judiciary is justified under the doctrine of separation of powers and permits the executive branch of the federal government to arrange affairs with foreign governments.

Consider This Example   Suppose the country of Cuba outlaws the practice of all religions in that country. Paul, a Christian who is a citizen of, and living in, the United States, disagrees with Cuba's law. Paul brings a lawsuit against Cuba in U.S. district court, arguing to the court that the Cuban law should be declared illegal. The U.S. district court will apply the Act of State Doctrine and dismiss Paul's lawsuit. The U.S. court will rule that Cuba's law is an act of that state (country) and that a U.S. court does not have authority to hear and decide Paul's case.

The Doctrine of Sovereign Immunity

One of the oldest principles of international law is the **doctrine of sovereign immunity**. Under this doctrine, *countries* are granted immunity from suits in courts in other countries. For example, if a U.S. citizen wanted to sue the government of China in a U.S. court, he or she could not (subject to certain exceptions).

Originally, the United States granted absolute immunity to foreign governments from suits in U.S. courts. In 1952, the United States switched to the principle of *qualified*, or *restricted, immunity*, which was eventually codified in the **Foreign Sovereign Immunities Act of 1976 (FSIA)**.[3] This act now exclusively governs suits against foreign nations in the United States, whether in federal or state court. Most Western nations have adopted the principle of restricted immunity. Other countries still follow the doctrine of absolute immunity.

Business Brief

A foreign nation may be sued in a court in the United States if that nation has engaged in a *commercial activity* that either (1) is carried on in the United States or (2) is carried on outside the United States but causes a direct effect in the United States.

Exceptions   The FSIA provides that a foreign country is not immune from lawsuits in U.S. courts in the following two situations:

1. The foreign country has waived its immunity, either explicitly or by implication.
2. The action is based on a commercial activity carried on in the United States by the foreign country or carried on outside the United States but causing a direct effect in the United States.

What constitutes "commercial activity" is the most litigated aspect of the FSIA. If it is commercial activity, the foreign sovereign is subject to suit in the United States; if it is not, the foreign sovereign is immune from suit in this country.

In the following case, the U.S. Supreme Court examined the commercial activity exception to the doctrine of sovereign immunity.

U.S. SUPREME COURT CASE
Republic of Argentina v. Weltover, Inc.
504 U.S. 607, 112 S.Ct. 2160, 1992 U.S. Lexis 3542 (1992)
Supreme Court of the United States

Case 39.2
Sovereign Immunity

Background and Facts

In an attempt to stabilize its currency, Argentina and its central bank, Banco Central (collectively Argentina), issued bonds called "Bonods." The bonds, which were sold to investors worldwide, provided for repayment in U.S. dollars through transfers on the New York market, at the bondholder's election. Argentina lacked sufficient foreign exchange to retire the bonds when they matured. Argentina unilaterally extended the time for payment and offered bondholders substitute instruments as a means of rescheduling the debts. Two Panamanian corporations and a Swiss bank refused the rescheduling and insisted that full payment be made in New York. When Argentina did not pay, they brought a breach of contract action against Argentina in U.S. district court in New York. Argentina moved to dismiss, alleging that it was not subject to suit in U.S. courts under the federal FSIA. The plaintiffs asserted that the "commercial activity" exception to the act applied, subjecting Argentina to suit in U.S. court. The district court denied Argentina's motion for dismissal, and the court of appeals affirmed. Argentina appealed to the U.S. Supreme Court.

Issue

Does the commercial exception to the doctrine of sovereign immunity permit the plaintiffs to sue Argentina in a U.S. court?

Court's Reasoning

The U.S. Supreme Court noted that when a foreign government acts, not as regulator of a market, but in the manner of a private player within it, the foreign sovereign's actions are "commercial" within the meaning of the FSIA. The Supreme Court held that the commercial character of the Bonods was confirmed by the fact that they were in almost all respects garden-variety debt instruments: They could be held by private parties, they were negotiable and could be traded on the international market, and they promised a future stream of cash income. The Supreme Court stated, "We conclude that Argentina's issuance of the Bonods was a commercial activity under the FSIA. We have little difficulty concluding that Argentina's unilateral rescheduling of the maturity dates on the Bonods had a direct effect in the United States."

Decision and Remedy

The Supreme Court held that Argentina's issuance of the bonds was a commercial activity that had a direct effect in the United States. Therefore, the commercial activity exception to the FSIA applied, which allowed the plaintiffs to sue Argentina in a U.S. court. The Supreme Court affirmed the decisions of the district court and the court of appeals.

Case Questions

Critical Legal Thinking   Should the United States recognize the doctrine of absolute sovereign immunity or qualified immunity? Explain.

Business Ethics   Did the government of Argentina act ethically in not paying the bonds when due and unilaterally rescheduling the debts?

Contemporary Business   Is there more risk for investors who invest in obligations of foreign countries than in obligations of the U.S. government?

Concept Summary *Act of State and Sovereign Immunity Doctrines Compared*

Doctrine	Description
Act of state	A doctrine that states that an act of a government in its *own country* is not subject to suit in a foreign country's courts.
Sovereign immunity	A doctrine that states that an act of a government in a *foreign country* is not subject to suit in the foreign country. Some countries provide absolute immunity, whereas other countries (such as the United States) provide limited immunity.

International Arbitration

As an alternative to litigation, the parties to an international contract may agree that any dispute that arises between them regarding the transaction will be decided by mandatory arbitration. **Arbitration** is a nonjudicial method of dispute resolution whereby a neutral third party decides the case. The parties agree to be bound by the arbitrator's decision. Generally, arbitration is faster, less expensive, less formal, and more private than litigation.

An **arbitration clause** should specify the arbitrator or the means of selecting the arbitrator. Several organizations conduct international arbitrations, including the American Arbitration Association, the International Chamber of Commerce, the International Center for the Settlement of Investment Disputes, and the United Nations Commission on International Trade Law. International arbitrators are usually businesspeople or lawyers experienced in worldwide commercial transactions. An arbitration clause should also specify the law to be applied by the arbitrator. Arbitration clauses are appearing in an increasing number of international contracts.

An arbitrator issues an *award*, not a judgment. An arbitrator does not have the power to enforce the award it renders. Therefore, if the losing party refuses to pay the award, the winning party must petition a court to enforce the award. More than 50 countries that conduct the bulk of worldwide commercial transactions are signatories to the **United Nations Convention on the Recognition and Enforcement of Foreign Arbitral Awards**.[4] The United States adopted the convention in 1970 and amended the Federal Arbitration Act to reflect this international law.[5] The recipient of an arbitral award subject to the convention can attach property of the loser that is located in any country that is a signatory to the convention.

International Law
Jewish Law and the Torah

Jewish law, which has existed for centuries, is a complex legal system based on ideology and theology of the Torah. The Torah prescribes comprehensive and integrated rules of religious, political, and legal life that together form Jewish thought. Jewish law is decided by rabbis who are scholars of the Torah and other Jewish scriptures. Rabbinic jurisprudence, known as **Halakhah**, is administered by rabbi-judges sitting as the **Beis Din**, Hebrew for the "house of judgment." As a court, the *Beis Din* has roots that go back 3,000 years.

Today, Jews are citizens of countries worldwide. As such, they are subject to the criminal and civil laws of their host countries. But Jews, no matter where they live, abide by the principles of the Torah in many legal matters, such as marriage, divorce, inheritance, and other family matters. Thus, the legal principles embedded in the Torah coexist with the secular laws of Jews' home countries.

The rabbinical judges tend to be actively involved in cases. True to its roots, the *Beis Din* is more a search for the truth than it is an adversarial process. ∎

Israel.

International Law

Islamic Law and the Koran

Approximately 20 percent of the world's population is Muslim. Islam is the principal religion of Afghanistan, Algeria, Bangladesh, Egypt, Indonesia, Iran, Iraq, Jordan, Kuwait, Libya, Malaysia, Mali, Mauritania, Morocco, Niger, North Yemen, Oman, Pakistan, Qatar, Saudi Arabia, Somalia, South Yemen, Sudan, Syria, Tunisia, Turkey, and the United Arab Emirates. *Islamic law* (or *Shari'a*) is the only law in Saudi Arabia. In other Islamic countries, the *Shari'a* forms the basis of family law but coexists with other laws.

The Islamic law system is derived from the Koran, the Sunnah (decisions and sayings of the prophet Muhammad), and reasonings by Islamic scholars. By the tenth century A.D., Islamic scholars decided that no further improvement of the divine law could be made, closed the door of *ijtihad* (independent reasoning), and froze the evolution of Islamic law at that point. Islamic law prohibits *riba*, or the making of unearned or unjustified profit. Making a profit from the sale of goods or the provision of services is permitted. The most notable consequence of *riba* is that the payment of interest on loans is forbidden. To circumvent this result, the party with the money is permitted to purchase the item and resell it to the other party at a profit or to advance the money and become a trading partner who shares in the profits of the enterprise.

Uzbekistan.

Today, Islamic law is primarily used in the areas of marriage, divorce, and inheritance and to a limited degree in criminal law. To resolve the tension between *Shari'a* and the practice of modern commercial law, the *Shari'a* is often ignored in commercial transactions. ■

International Law

Hindu Law—*Dharmasastra*

Over 20 percent of the world's population is Hindu. Most Hindus live in India, where they make up 80 percent of the population. Others live in Burma, Kenya, Malaysia, Pakistan, Singapore, Tanzania, and Uganda. *Hindu law* is a religious law. As such, individual Hindus apply this law to themselves, regardless of their nationality or place of domicile.

Classical Hindu law rests neither on civil codes nor on court decisions, but on the works of private scholars that were passed along for centuries by oral tradition and eventually were recorded in the *smitris* (law books). Hindu law—called *dharmasastra* in Sanskrit, that is, the doctrine of proper behavior—is linked to the divine revelation of Veda (the holy collection of Indian religious songs, prayers, hymns, and sayings written between 2000 and 1000 B.C.). Most Hindu law is concerned with family matters and the law of succession.

After India became a British colony, British judges applied a combination of Hindu law and common law in solving cases. This Anglo-Hindu law, as it was called, was ousted when India gained its independence. In the mid-1950s, India codified Hindu law by enacting the Hindu Marriage Act, the Hindu Minority and

Nepal.

Guardianship Act, the Hindu Succession Act, and the Hindu Adoptions and Maintenance Act. Outside India, Anglo-Hindu law applies in most other countries populated by Hindus. ■

Chapter Summary

The United States and Foreign Affairs, p. 863

The United States and Foreign Affairs

The following two provisions in the U.S. Constitution establish the federal government's authority to regulate international affairs:

1. *Commerce Clause.* This clause vests Congress with the power "to regulate commerce with foreign nations."
2. *Treaty Clause.* This clause gives the president the authority to enter into treaties with foreign nations, subject to a two-thirds vote of the Senate.

Sources of International Law, p. 865

Sources of International Law

1. *Treaties and conventions.* Treaties are agreements between nations that are formally ratified by the supreme power of each signatory nation. Conventions are treaties that are sponsored by international organizations (e.g., the United Nations).
2. *Custom.* A custom is a practice followed by two or more nations over a period of time when dealing with each other.
3. *General principles of law.* General principles of law that are common to the nations of the parties involved in a dispute.
4. *Judicial decisions and teachings.* Judicial decisions of national courts and teachings of the most qualified legal scholars of the nations of the parties involved in a dispute are sources of international law.

The United Nations, p. 866

The United Nations

Governance of the United Nations. The UN is an international organization headquartered in New York City. Most countries of the world are members. Its goals are to maintain peace and security in the world, promote economic and social cooperation, and protect human rights.

Regional International Organizations, p. 869

Regional Economic Organizations

1. European Union (EU) (or Common Market)
2. Central American Common Market
3. MERCOSUR Common Market
4. Caribbean Community
5. Andean Common Market (ANCOM)
6. Economic Community of West African States (ECOWAS)
7. Economic and Customs Union of Central Africa
8. East African Community (EAC)
9. African Economic Community
10. Organization of Petroleum Exporting Countries (OPEC)
11. Gulf Cooperation Council
12. Association of South East Asian Nations (ASEAN)
13. North American Free Trade Agreement (NAFTA)

The World Trade Organization (WTO), p. 872

World Trade Organization

The WTO is an international organization headquartered in Geneva, Switzerland. Many countries of the world are members. Its goals are to limit tariff and trade restrictions and provide a mechanism for resolving trade disputes among its member nations.

National Courts Deciding International Disputes, p. 875

Principles of Judicial Restraint

National courts are limited by the following two principles of judicial restraint:

1. *Act of state doctrine.* The act of state doctrine states that judges of one country cannot question the validity of an act committed by another country *within* that other country's borders.

2. *Doctrine of sovereign immunity.* This doctrine states that countries are granted immunity from suits in courts in other countries. Some countries provide for *absolute immunity*, and other countries (such as the United States) provide *qualified* or *restricted immunity*. *Exceptions:* The United States provides that a foreign country is not immune from lawsuits in U.S. court if:

   a. The foreign country has *waived* its immunity.

   b. The foreign country has engaged in *commercial activity* in the United States or outside the United States that causes a direct effect in the United States.

International Arbitration

1. *Arbitration.* Arbitration is a nonjudicial method of dispute resolution whereby a neutral third party decides the case.

2. *Arbitration clauses.* Arbitration clauses are included in many international contracts that require arbitration of disputes arising from the contract.

 Internet Exercises and Case Questions

Working the Web Internet Exercises

Activities

1. Go to Hieros Gamos, at **www.hg.org**. It is a huge international law site that contains laws from 230 countries in more than 50 languages. Look at the list of countries and review the legal structure of Afghanistan.

2. Go to **travel.state.gov/judicial_assistance.html**. Check on the procedures for enforcement of judgments in foreign countries. Why are there no treaties or conventions that make enforcement of U.S. judgments easier?

3. Survey the alternative dispute resolution (ADR) material at **search.info.usaid.gov**. What are some of the particular advantages to using ADR in other countries?

4. For an outstanding online lecture on many international law topics, visit **www.august1.com/pubs**. It contains outlines and online lectures from Professor Ray August.

Critical Legal Thinking Cases

39.1 Act of State Doctrine   Prior to 1918, the Petrograd Metal Works, a Russian corporation, deposited a large sum of money with August Belmont, a private banker doing business in New York City under the name August Belmont & Co. (Belmont). In 1918, the Soviet government nationalized the corporation and appropriated all its property and assets wherever situated, including the deposit account with Belmont. As a result, the deposit became the property of the Soviet government. In 1933, the Soviet government and the United States entered into an agreement to settle claims and counterclaims between them. As part of the settlement, it was agreed that the Soviet government would take no steps to enforce claims against American nationals (including Belmont) and assigned all such claims to the United States. The United States brought this action against the executors of Belmont's estate to recover the money originally deposited with Belmont by Petrograd Metal Works. Who owns the money? [*United States v. Belmont*, 301 U.S. 324, 57 S.Ct. 758, 1937 U.S. Lexis 293 (1937)]

39.2 Act of State Doctrine   Banco Nacional de Costa Rica is a bank wholly owned by the government of Costa Rica. It is subject to the rules and regulations adopted by the minister of finance and the central bank of Costa Rica. In December 1980, the bank borrowed $40 million from a consortium of private banks located in the United Kingdom and the United States. The bank signed promissory notes agreeing to repay the principal plus interest on the loan in four equal installments due on July 30, August 30, September 30, and October 30, 1981. The money was to be used to provide export financing of sugar and sugar products from Costa Rica. The loan agreements and promissory notes were signed in New York City, and the loan proceeds were tendered to the bank there.

On July 30, 1981, the bank paid the first installment on the loan. The bank did not, however, make the other three installment payments and defaulted on the loan. The lending banks sued the bank in U.S. district court in New York to recover the unpaid principal and interest. The bank alleged in defense that on August 27, 1981, the minister of finance and the central bank of Costa Rica issued a decree forbidding the repayment of loans by the bank to private lenders, including the lending banks in this case. The action was taken because Costa Rica was having trouble servicing debts to foreign creditors. The bank alleged that the act of state doctrine prevented the plaintiffs from recovering on their loans to the bank. Who wins? [*Libra Bank Limited v. Banco Nacional de Costa Rica*, 570 F.Supp. 870, 1983 U.S. Dist. Lexis 14677 (S.D. N.Y. 1983)]

39.3 Forum-Selection Clause   Zapata Off-Shore Company is a Houston, Texas–based American corporation that engages in drilling oil wells throughout the world. Unterweser Reederei, GMBH, is a German corporation that provides ocean shipping and towing services. In November 1967, Zapata requested bids from companies to tow its self-elevating drilling rig *Chaparral* from Louisiana to a point off Ravenna, Italy, in the Adriatic Sea, where Zapata had agreed to drill certain wells. Unterweser submitted the lowest bid and was requested to submit a proposed contract to Zapata, which it did. The contract submitted by Unterweser contained the following provision: "Any dispute arising must be treated before the London Court of Justice." Zapata executed the contract without deleting or modifying this provision.

On January 5, 1968, Unterweser's deep sea tug *Bremen* departed Venice, Louisiana, with the Chaparral in tow, bound for Italy. On January 9, while the flotilla was in international waters in the middle of the Gulf of Mexico, a severe storm arose. The sharp roll of the *Chaparral* in Gulf waters caused portions of it to break off and fall into the sea, seriously damaging the *Chaparral*. Zapata instructed the *Bremen* to tow the *Chaparral*, to Tampa, Florida, the nearest port of refuge, which it did. On January 12, Zapata filed suit against Unterweser and the *Bremen* in U.S. district court in Florida, alleging negligent towing and breach of contract. The defendants assert that suit can be brought only in the London Court of Justice. Who is correct? [*M/S Bremen and Unterweser Reederei, GMBH v. Zapata Off-Shore Company*, 407 U.S. 1, 92 S.Ct. 1907, 1972 U.S. Lexis 114 (1972)]

39.4 International Arbitration   Alberto-Culver Company is an American company that is incorporated in Delaware and has its principal office in Illinois. It manufactures and distributes toiletries and hair care products in the United States and other countries. Fritz Scherk owned three interrelated businesses organized under the laws of Germany and Liechtenstein that were engaged in the manufacture of toiletries. After substantial negotiations, in February 1969, Alberto-Culver entered into a contract with Scherk to purchase his three companies, along with all rights held by these companies to trademarks in cosmetic goods. The contract contained a number of express warranties whereby Scherk guaranteed the sole and unencumbered ownership of these trademarks. The contract also contained a clause that provided that "any controversy or claim that shall arise out of this agreement or breach thereof" was to be referred to arbitration before the International Chamber of Commerce in Paris, France. The transaction closed in June 1969 in Geneva, Switzerland.

Nearly one year later, Alberto-Culver allegedly discovered that the trademark rights purchased under the contract were subject to substantial encumbrances that threatened to give other parties superior rights to the trademarks and to restrict or preclude Alberto-Culver's use of them. Alberto-Culver sued Scherk in U.S. district court in Illinois, alleging fraudulent misrepresentation in violation of Section 10(b) of the federal Securities Exchange Act of 1934. Scherk asserted in defense that the case was subject to mandatory arbitration in Paris. Who is correct? [*Scherk v. Alberto-Culver Co.*, 417 U.S. 506, 94 S.Ct. 2249, 1974 U.S. Lexis 73 (1974)]

Business Ethics Cases

39.5 Business Ethics   Bank of Jamaica is wholly owned by the government of Jamaica. Chisholm & Co. is a Florida corporation that is owned by James Henry Chisholm, a Florida resident. The United States Export-Import Bank (Eximbank) provides financial services and credit insurance to export and import companies. In January 1982, the Bank of Jamaica and Chisholm & Co. agreed that Chisholm & Co. would arrange lines of credit from various banks and procure $50 million of credit insurance from Eximbank to be available to aid Jamaican importers. Chisholm & Co. was to be paid commissions for its services.

Chisholm & Co. negotiated and arranged for $50 million of credit insurance from Eximbank and lines of credit from Florida National Bank, Bankers Trust Company, and Irving Trust Company. Chisholm also arranged meetings between the Bank

of Jamaica and the American banks. Unbeknownst to Chisholm & Co., the Bank of Jamaica went directly to Eximbank to exclude Chisholm & Co. from the Jamaica program and requested that the credit insurance be issued solely in the name of the Bank of Jamaica. As a result, Chisholm & Co.'s Eximbank insurance application was not considered. The Bank of Jamaica also obtained lines of credit from other companies and paid them commissions. Chisholm & Co. sued the Bank of Jamaica in the U.S. district court in Miami, Florida, alleging breach of contract and seeking damages. The Bank of Jamaica filed a motion to dismiss the complaint, alleging that its actions were protected by sovereign immunity. Who wins? Did the Bank of Jamaica act ethically in trying to avoid its contract obligations? [*Chisholm & Co. v. Bank of Jamaica*, 643 F.Supp. 1393, 1986 U.S. Dist. Lexis 20789 (S.D. Fla. 1986)]

39.6 Business Ethics   Nigeria, an African nation, while in the midst of a boom period due to oil exports, entered into $1 billion of contracts with various countries to purchase huge quantities of Portland cement. Nigeria was going to use the cement to build and improve the country's infrastructure. Several of the contracts were with American companies, including Texas Trading & Milling Corporation (Texas Trading). Nigeria substantially overbought cement, and the country's docks and harbors became clogged with ships waiting to unload. Unable to accept delivery of the cement it had bought, Nigeria repudiated many of its contracts, including the one with Texas Trading. When Texas Trading sued Nigeria in a U.S. district court to recover damages for breach of contract, Nigeria asserted in defense that the doctrine of sovereign immunity protected it from liability. Who wins? [*Texas Trading & Milling Corp. v. Federal Republic of Nigeria*, 647 F.2d 300, 1981 U.S. App. Lexis 14231 (2nd Cir. 1981)]

Briefing the Case Writing Assignment

Read Case A.39 in the Case Appendix [*OHG v. Kolodny*]. This case is excerpted from the court's opinion. Review and brief the case. In your brief, be sure to answer the following questions.

1. In the German action, who was the plaintiff? Who was the defendant?

2. Who was the plaintiff in the New York action? Who was the defendant?

3. What was the decision of the German court? Would the decision under New York law have been different? Explain.

4. What was the plaintiff's argument to the New York court? Explain.

5. Did the enforcement of the German judgment violate New York's public policy?

Endnotes

1. The Charter of the United Nations was entered into force on October 24, 1945; it was adopted by the United States on October 24, 1945 [59 Stat. 1031, T.S. 993, 3 Bevans 1153, 1976 Y.B.U.N. 1043].

2. 301 U.S. 324, 57 S.Ct. 758, 1937 U.S. Lexis 293 (1937).
3. 28 U.S.C. §§ 1602–1611.
4. 21 U.S.T. 2517, T.I.A.S. 6997.
5. 9 U.S.C. §§ 201–208.

Appendix A – Case Appendix

Case A.1
Anheuser-Busch, Incorporated vs. Schmoke,

Mayor of Baltimore City, 63 F. 3d 1305 (1995)
United States Court of Appeals, Fourth Circuit
Niemeyer, Circuit Judge

In January 1994, Baltimore exercised the authority granted it by the state and enacted Ordinance 288 prohibiting the outdoor advertising of alcoholic beverages in certain locations in Baltimore City. It also includes an exception permitting such advertising in certain commercially and industrially zoned areas of the City. By its terms, the ordinance was to become effective February 5, 1994. Before enacting the ordinance, the Baltimore City Council conducted public hearings, receiving testimony and previously conducted studies detailing the adverse effects of alcohol consumption on minors and the correlation between underage drinking and the advertising of alcoholic beverages.

The City Council found that alcoholic beverages are the second most heavily advertised products in America (after cigarettes), and that outdoor billboards are a "unique and distinguishable" medium of advertising that subjects the public to involuntary and unavoidable forms of solicitation. The City Council noted that children are exposed to the advertising of alcoholic beverages "simply by walking to school or playing in their neighborhood" and that children's "attitudes favorable to alcohol are significantly related to their exposure to alcohol advertisements." Attempting to tailor its ban, the City Council allowed advertising of alcoholic beverages in commercial and industrial areas, stating that it was "narrowly focus[ing] its efforts on those advertisements which most directly affect minors where they live, attend school, attend church and engage in recreational activities."

On January 14, 1994, several weeks before the ordinance was to become effective, Anheuser-Busch, Inc., filed suit in federal court, facially challenging the constitutionality of the ordinance under the First Amendment. Anheuser-Busch is the nation's largest brewer of beers and malt beverages, producing approximately 15 different brands, including Budweiser, Michelob, and Busch. It advertises in all media, including outdoor billboards and displays. In addition to contending that there is no correlation between alcoholic beverage advertising and underage drinking, Anheuser-Busch asserts that the purpose of its advertising is "to solidify brand loyalty and increase market share by shifting adult beer drinkers from other brands to the advertised brand of beer."

Following a hearing, the district court issued an opinion upholding the constitutionality of the ordinance [(*Anheuser-Busch, Inc. v. Mayor and City Council*, 855 F.Supp. 811 (D.Md.1994)]. The court held the ordinance constitutional after concluding that it "directly advances the City's asserted interest in promoting the welfare and temperance of minors" and is "narrowly tailored" to that end.

On appeal, Anheuser-Busch argues that the ordinance is unconstitutional on its face because (1) it does not directly and materially advance the government's interest in promoting temperance of minors and (2) it is not narrowly tailored to serve that purpose. They also argue that, as applied, the ordinance would impermissibly restrict their noncommercial speech.

We find that it was reasonable for the Baltimore City Council to have concluded that Ordinance 288's regulation of the outdoor advertising of alcoholic beverages directly and materially advances Baltimore's interest in promoting the welfare and temperance of minors. The City Council found that outdoor advertising is a unique and distinct medium which subjects the public to involuntary and unavoidable solicitation, and that children, simply by walking to school or playing in their neighborhood, are exposed daily to this advertising. The City Council pointed to its legislative finding that the majority of research studies show a definite correlation between alcoholic beverage advertising and underage drinking.

We simply do not believe that the liquor industry spends a billion dollars a year on advertising solely to acquire an added market share at the expense of competitors. We hold, as a matter of law, that prohibitions against the advertising of alcoholic beverages are reasonably related to reducing the sale and consumption of those beverages and their attendant problems. The entire economy of the industries that bring these challenges is based on the belief that advertising increases sales.

It is readily acknowledged that limitations on outdoor advertising of alcoholic beverages designed to protect minors also reduce the opportunities for adults to receive advertised information. And adults, who constitute a majority of the population, are the object of the government's legislation. But it also appears that no less restrictive means may be available to advance the government's interest. Anheuser-Busch argues that Baltimore could just as effectively advance its goal of promoting the welfare and temperance of minors by increasing enforcement of existing laws prohibiting sales to, and possession of alcoholic beverages by, minors, or by implementing and encouraging educational programs on the dangers of alcohol. These approaches might indeed prove beneficial in reducing underage drinking, but they do not provide an alternative to the approach selected by the City of curbing the enticement to consume alcoholic beverages. In the face of a problem as significant as that which the City seeks to address, the City must be given some reasonable latitude.

The problem of underage drinking is a most serious one that contributes significantly to a variety of social problems. Baltimore was faced with statistics showing that fully one-half of all deaths of minors were alcohol-related, and 40 to 50 percent of juveniles who drowned or had diving accidents had consumed alcohol immediately prior to the incident. The City Council found that alcohol is overwhelmingly and consistently the most widely used "drug" at all adolescent age levels. It pointed to data which showed that over half of all twelfth graders, 40 percent of tenth graders, and over a quarter eighth graders reported that they consumed alcohol within the past 30 days. Widespread underage drinking was also found to be a major factor in crime. One-third of all juvenile males arrested said they had consumed alcohol within the previous 72 hours, and nearly 40 percent of all youths in adult correctional facilities reported drinking alcohol before committing their crimes.

Through outdoor advertising, children are involuntarily and unavoidably confronted daily with the advertised message. Billboards are "seen without the exercise of choice or volition," and viewers have the message "thrust upon them by all the arts and devices that skill can produce." The City argues that the only means to address this problem is to ban such advertising in locations where children generally walk and play. Such a ban still permits adults to receive advertising messages and information from signs in commercial areas of the City and through the numerous other media to which adults are constantly exposed.

In summary, Baltimore City's regulation of stationary outdoor "advertising that advertises alcoholic beverages" in certain locations directly and materially advances a substantial governmental interest in promoting the welfare and temperance of minors who are involuntarily and unavoidably exposed to such advertisements. While the means selected of limiting the location of such outdoor advertising is not a perfect "fit" with the governmental objective, it nevertheless falls well within the range tolerated by the First Amendment for the regulation of commercial speech.

For the reasons stated, we affirm the judgment of the district court, upholding Baltimore City Ordinance 288 against a facial constitutional challenge under the First Amendment.

AFFIRMED.

Case A.2

Lee v. Weismen, 120 L.Ed. 2d 467,

112 S.Ct. 2649 (1992)
United States Supreme Court
Kennedy, Justice (joined by Blackmun, Stevens, O'Conner, and Souter)

Deborah Weisman graduated from Nathan Bishop Middle School, a public school in Providence, at a formal ceremony in June 1989. She was about 14 years old. For many years it has been the policy of the Providence school committee and the Superintendent of Schools to permit principals to invite members of the clergy to give invocations and benedictions at middle school and high school graduations. Many, but not all, of the principals elected to include prayers as part of the graduation

ceremonies. Acting for himself and his daughter, Deborah's father, Daniel Weisman, objected to any prayers at Deborah's middle school graduation, but to no avail. The school principal, petitioner Robert E. Lee, invited a rabbi to deliver prayers at the graduation exercises for Deborah's class. Rabbi Leslie Gutterman, of the Temple Beth El in Providence, accepted.

It has been the custom of Providence school officials to provide invited clergy with a pamphlet entitled "Guidelines for Civic Occasions," prepared by the National Conference of Christians and Jews. The Guidelines recommended that public prayers at nonsectarian civic ceremonies be composed with "inclusiveness and sensitivity," though they acknowledge that "prayer of any kind may be inappropriate on some civic occasions." The principal gave Rabbi Gutterman the pamphlet before the graduation and advised him the invocation and benediction should be non-sectarian.

Deborah's graduation was held on the premises of Nathan Bishop Middle School on June 29, 1989. Four days before the ceremony, Daniel Weisman, in his individual capacity as a Providence taxpayer and as next friend of Deborah, sought a temporary restraining order in the United States District Court for the District of Rhode Island to prohibit school offices from including an invocation or benediction in the graduation ceremony. The court denied the motion for lack of adequate time to consider it. Deborah and her family attended the graduation, where the prayers were recited. In July 1989, Daniel Weisman filed an amended complaint seeking a permanent injunction barring petitioners, various officials of the Providence public schools, from inviting the clergy to deliver invocations and benedictions at future graduations.

The case was submitted on stipulated facts. The district court held that petitioners' practice of including invocations and benedictions in public school graduations violated the Establishment Clause of the First Amendment, and it enjoined petitioners from continuing the practice. The court applied the three-part Establishment Clause test. Under that test, to satisfy the Establishment Clause a governmental practice must (1) reflect a clearly secular purpose, (2) have a primary effect that neither advances nor inhibits religion, and (3) avoid excessive government entanglement with religion. On appeal, the United States Court of Appeals for the First Circuit affirmed.

These dominant facts mark and control the confines of our decision: State officials direct the performance of a formal religious exercise at promotional and graduation ceremonies for secondary schools. Even for those students who object to the religious exercise, their attendance and participation in the state-sponsored religious activity are in a fair and real sense obligatory, though the school district does not require attendance as a condition for receipt of the diploma.

The controlling precedents as they relate to prayer and religious exercise in primary and secondary public schools compel the holding here that the policy of the city of Providence is an unconstitutional one. It is beyond dispute that, at a minimum, the Constitution guarantees that government may not coerce anyone to support or participate in religion or its exercise, or otherwise act in a way which "establishes a state religion or religious faith, or tends to do so."

We are asked to recognize the existence of a practice of non-sectarian prayer within the embrace of what is known as the Judeo-Christian tradition, prayer which is more acceptable than one which, for example, makes explicit references to the God of Israel, or to Jesus Christ, or to a patron saint. If common ground can be defined which permits once conflicting faiths to express the shared conviction that there is an ethnic and a morality which transcend human invention, the sense of community and purpose sought by all decent societies might be advanced. But though the First Amendment does not allow the government to stifle prayers which aspire to these ends, neither does it permit the government to undertake that task for itself.

The sole question presented is whether a religious exercise may be conducted at a graduation ceremony in circumstances where, as we have found, young graduates who object are induced to conform. No holding by this Court suggests that a school can persuade or compel a student to participate in a religious exercise. That is being done here, and it is forbidden by the Establishment Clause of the First Amendment.

For the reasons we have stated, the judgment of the court of appeals is AFFIRMED.

Scalia, Justice (joined by Rehnquist, White, and Thomas) dissenting, expressed the view that (1) the establishment of religion clause should not have been interpreted so as to invalidate a longstanding American tradition of nonsectarian prayer at public school graduations, (2) graduation invocations and benedictions involve no psychological coercion of students to participate in religious exercises, (3) the only coercion that is forbidden by the establishment of religion clause is that which is backed by a threat of penalty, and (4) the middle school principal did not direct or control the content of the prayers in question, and thus there was no pervasive government involvement with religious activity.

Case A.3

Gnazzo v. G.D. Searle & Co.,

973 F.2d 136 (1992)
U.S. Court of Appeals for the Second Circuit
Pierce, Circuit Judge

On November 11, 1974, Gnazzo had a CU-7 intrauterine device (IUD) inserted in her uterus for contraceptive purposes. The IUD was developed, marketed, and sold by G.D. Searle & Co. (Searle). When Gnazzo's deposition was taken, she stated that her doctor had informed her that "the insertion would hurt, but not for long," and that she "would have uncomfortable and probably painful periods of the first three to four months." On October 11, 1975, Gnazzo found it necessary to return to her physician due to excessive pain and cramping. During this visit she was informed by her doctor that he thought she had Pelvic Inflammatory Disease (PID). She recalled that he stated that the infection was possibly caused by venereal disease or the use of the IUD. The PID was treated with antibiotics and cleared up shortly thereafter. Less than one year later, Gnazzo was again treated for an IUD-associated infection. This infection was also treated with

antibiotics. Gnazzo continued using the IUD until it was finally removed in December of 1977.

Following a laparoscopy in March of 1989, Gnazzo was informed by a fertility specialist that she was infertile because of PID-induced adhesions resulting from her prior IUD use. Subsequent to this determination, and at the request of her then-attorneys, Gnazzo completed a questionnaire dated May 11, 1989. In response to the question, "when and why did you first suspect that your IUD had caused you any harm?", Gnazzo responded "sometime in 1981" and explained: "I was married in April 1981 so I stopped using birth control so I could get pregnant—nothing ever happened (of course) then I started hearing and reading about how damaging IUDs could be. I figured that was the problem, however, my marriage started to crumble so I never pursued the issue."

On May 4, 1990, Gnazzo initiated the underlying action against Searle. In an amended complaint, she alleged that she had suffered injuries as a result of her use of the IUD developed by Searle. Searle moved for summary judgment on the ground that Gnazzo's claim was time-barred by Connecticut's three-year statute of limitations for product liability actions. Searle argued, inter alia, that Gnazzo knew in 1981 that she had suffered harm caused by her IUD. Gnazzo contended that her cause of action against Searle accrued only when she learned from the fertility specialist that the IUD had caused her PID and subsequent infertility.

In a ruling dated September 18, 1991, the district court granted Searle's motion for summary judgment on the ground that Gnazzo's claim was time-barred by the applicable statute of limitations. In reaching this result, the court determined that Connecticut law provided no support for Gnazzo's contention that she should not have been expected to file her action until she was told of her infertility and the IUD's causal connection. This appeal followed.

On appeal, Gnazzo contends that the district court improperly granted Searle's motion for summary judgment because a genuine issue of material fact exists as to when she discovered, or reasonably should have discovered, her injuries and their causal connection to the defendant's alleged wrongful conduct. Summary judgment is appropriate when there is no genuine issue as to any material fact and the moving party is entitled to judgment as a matter of law. We consider the record in the light most favorable to the non-movant. However, the non-movant "may not rest upon the mere allegations of denials of her pleading, but must set forth specific facts showing that there is a genuine issue for trial."

Under Connecticut law, a product liability claim must be brought within "three years from the date when the injury is first sustained or discovered in the exercise of reasonable care should have been discovered." In Connecticut, a cause of action accrues when a plaintiff suffers actionable harm. Actionable harm occurs when the plaintiff discovers or should discover, through the exercise of reasonable care, that he or she has been injured and that the defendant's conduct caused such injury.

Gnazzo contends that "the mere occurrence of a pelvic infection or difficulty in becoming pregnant does not necessarily result in notice to the plaintiff of a cause of action."

Thus, she maintains that her cause of action did not accrue until 1989 when the fertility specialist informed her both that she was infertile and that this condition resulted from her previous use of the IUD.

Under Connecticut law, however, "the statue of limitations begins to run when the plaintiff discovers some form of actionable harm, not the fullest manifestation thereof." Therefore, as Gnazzo's responses to the questionnaire indicate, she suspected "sometime in 1981" that the IUD had caused her harm because she had been experiencing trouble becoming pregnant and had "started hearing and reading about how damaging IUDs could be and had figured that was the problem." Thus, by her own admission, Gnazzo had recognized, or should have recognized, the critical link between her injury and the defendant's causal connection to it. In other words, she had "discovered or should have discovered through the exercise of reasonable care, that she had been injured and that Searle's conduct caused such injury." However, as Gnazzo acknowledged in the questionnaire, she did not pursue the "issue" at the time because of her marital problems. Thus, even when viewed in the light most favorable to Gnazzo, the non-moving party, we are constrained to find that she knew by 1981 that she had "some form of actionable harm." Consequently, by the time she commenced her action in 1990, Gnazzo was time-barred by the Connecticut statute of limitations.

Since we have determined that Gnazzo's cause of action commenced in 1981, we need not address Searle's additional contention that Gnazzo's awareness in 1975 of her PID and her purported knowledge of its causal connection to the IUD commenced the running of the Connecticut statute of limitations at that time.

We are sympathetic to Gnazzo's situation and mindful that the unavoidable result we reach in this case is harsh. Nevertheless, we are equally aware that "it is within the Connecticut General Assembly's constitutional authority to decide when claims for injury are to be brought. Where a plaintiff has failed to comply with this requirement, a court may not entertain the suit." The judgment of the district court is AFFIRMED.

Case A.4
Braun v. Soldier of Fortune Magazine, Inc.

968 F.2nd 1110 (1992)
United States Court of Appeals for the Eleventh Circuit
Anderson, Circuit Judge

In January 1985, Michael Savage submitted a personal service advertisement to Soldier of Fortune (SOF). After several conversations between Savage and SOF's advertising manager, Joan Steel, the following advertisement ran in the June 1985 through March 1986 issues of SOF:

GUN FOR HIRE: 37-year-old professional mercenary desires jobs. Vietnam Veteran. Discrete [*sic*] and very private. Body guard, courier, and other special skills. All jobs considered. Phone (615) 436-9785 (days) or (615) 436-4335

(nights), or write: Rt. 2, Box 682 Village Loop Road, Gatlinburg, TN 37738.

Savage testified that, when he placed the ad, he had no intention of obtaining anything but legitimate jobs. Nonetheless, Savage stated that the overwhelming majority of the 30 to 40 phone calls a week he received in response to his ad sought his participation in criminal activity such as murder, assault, and kidnapping. The ad also generated at least one legitimate job as a bodyguard, which Savage accepted.

In late 1984 or early 1985, Bruce Gastwirth began seeking to murder his business partner, Richard Braun. Gastwirth enlisted the aid of another business associate, John Horton Moore, and together they arranged for at least three attempts on Braun's life, all of which were unsuccessful. Responding to Savage's SOF ad, Gastwirth and Moore contacted him in August 1985 to discuss plans to murder Braun. On August 26, 1985, Savage, Moore, and another individual, Sean Trevor Doutre, went to Braun's suburban Atlanta home. As Braun and his 16-year-old son Michael were driving down the driveway, Doutre stepped in front of Braun's car and fired several shots into the car with a MAC 11 automatic pistol. The shots hit Michael in the thigh and wounded Braun as well. Braun managed to roll out of the car, but Doutre walked over to Braun and killed him by firing two more shots into the back of his head as he lay on the ground.

On March 31, 1988, appellees Michael and Ian Braun filed this diversity against appellants in the United States District Court for the Middle District of Alabama, seeking damages for the wrongful death of their father. Michael Braun also filed a separate action seeking recovery for the personal injuries he received at the time of his father's death. The district court consolidated these related matters.

Trial began on December 3, 1990. Appellees contended that, under Georgia law, SOF was liable for their injuries because SOF negligently published a personal service advertisement that created an unreasonable risk of the solicitation and commission of violent criminal activity, including murder. To show that SOF knew of the likelihood that criminal activity would result from placing an ad like Savage's, appellees introduced evidence of newspaper and magazine articles published prior to Braun's murder which described links between SOF and personal service ads and a number of criminal convictions including murder, kidnapping, assault, extortion, and attempts thereof. Appellees also presented evidence that, prior to SOF's acceptance of Savage's ad, law enforcement officials had contacted SOF staffers on two separate occasions in connection with investigations of crimes.

In his trial testimony, SOF president Robert K. Brown denied having any knowledge of criminal activity associated with SOF's personal service ads at any time prior to Braun's murder in August 1985. Both Jim Graves, a former managing editor of SOF, and Joan Steel, the advertising manager who accepted Savage's advertisement, similarly testified that they were not aware of other crimes connected with SOF ads prior to running Savage's ad. Steel further testified that she had understood the "Gun for Hire" in Savage's ad to refer to a "bodyguard or protection service-type thing," rather than to any illegal activity.

The jury returned a verdict in favor of appellee and awarded compensatory damages on the wrongful death claim in the amount of $2,000,000. The jury also awarded appellee Michael Braun $375,000 in compensatory damages and $10,000,000 in punitive damages for his personal injury claim.

To prevail in an action for negligence in Georgia, a party must establish the following elements:

(1) A legal duty to conform to a standard of conduct raised by the law for the protection of others against unreasonable risks of harm, (2) a breach of this standard, (3) a legally attributable causal connection between the conduct and the resulting injury, and (4) some loss or damage flowing to the plaintiff's legally protected interest as a result of the alleged breach of the legal duty. To the extent that SOF denies that a publisher owes any duty to the public when it publishes personal service ads, its position is clearly inconsistent with Georgia law. We believe, however, that the crux of SOF's argument is not that it had no duty to the public, but that, as a matter of law, there is a risk to the public when a publisher prints an "unreasonable" advertisement if the ad openly solicits criminal activity.

SOF further argues that imposing liability on publishers for the advertisements they print indirectly threatens core, noncommercial speech to which the Constitution accords its full protection. Supreme Court cases discussing the limitations the First Amendment places on state defamation law indicate that there is no constitutional infirmity in Georgia law holding publishers liable under a negligence standard with respect to the commercial advertisements they print. Past Supreme Court decisions indicate, however, that the negligence standard that the First Amendment permits is a "modified" negligence standard. The Court's decisions suggest that Georgia law may impose tort liability on publishers for injury caused by the advertisements they print only if the ad on its face, without the need to investigate, makes it apparent that there is a substantial danger of harm to the public.

We conclude that the First Amendment permits a state to impose upon a publisher liability for compensatory damages for negligently publishing a commercial advertisement where the ad on its face, and without the need for investigation, makes it apparent that there is a substantial danger of harm to the public. The absence of a duty requiring publishers to investigate the advertisements they print and the requirement that the substance of the ad itself must warn the publisher of a substantial danger of harm to the public guarantee that the burden placed on publishers will not impermissibly chill protected commercial speech.

Our review of the language of Savage's ad persuades us that SOF had a legal duty to refrain from publishing it. Savage's advertisement (1) emphasized the term "Gun for Hire," (2) described Savage as a "professional mercenary," (3) stressed Savage's willingness to keep his assignments confidential and "very private," (4) listed legitimate jobs involving the use of a gun-bodyguard and courier-followed by a reference to Savage's "other special skills," and (5) concluded by

stating that Savage would consider "all jobs." The ad's combination of sinister terms makes it apparent that there was a substantial danger of harm to the public. The ad expressly solicits all jobs requiring the use of a gun. When the list of legitimate jobs—i.e., bodyguard and courier—is followed by "other special skills" and "all jobs considered," the implication is clear that the advertiser would consider illegal jobs. We agree with the district court that "the language of this advertisement is such that, even though couched in terms not explicitly offering criminal services, the publisher could recognize the offer of criminal activity as readily as its readers obviously did." We find that the jury had ample grounds for finding that SOF's publication of Savage's ad was the proximate cause of Braun's injuries.

For the foregoing reasons, we AFFIRM the district court's judgment.

Case A.5

Feist Publications, Inc. v. Rural Telephone Service Co., Inc.,

499 U.S. 340, 111 S.Ct. 1282, 113 L.Ed.2d 358 (1991)
United States Supreme Court
O'Connor, Justice

Rural Telephone Service Company is a certified public utility that provides telephone service to several communities in northwest Kansas. It is subject to a state regulation that requires all telephone companies operating in Kansas to issue annually an updated telephone directory. Accordingly, as a condition of its monopoly franchise, Rural publishes a typical telephone directory, consisting of white pages and yellow pages. The white pages list in alphabetical order the names of Rural's subscribers, together with their towns and telephone numbers. The yellow pages list Rural's business subscribers alphabetically by category and feature classified advertisements of various sizes. Rural distributes its directory free of charge to its subscribers, but earns revenue by selling yellow pages advertisements.

Feist Publications, Inc., is a publishing company that specializes in area-wide telephone directories. Unlike a typical directory, which covers only a particular calling area, Feist's area-wide directories cover a much larger geographical range, reducing the need to call directory assistance or consult multiple directories. The Feist directory that is the subject of this litigation covers 11 different telephone service areas in 15 counties and contains 46,878 white pages listings—compared to Rural's approximately 7,700 listings.

Of the 11 telephone companies, only Rural refused to license its listings to Feist. Rural's refusal created a problem for Feist, as omitting these listings would have left a gaping hole in its area-wide directory, rendering it less attractive to potential yellow pages advertisers. Unable to license Rural's white pages listings, Feist used them without Rural's consent.

Rural sued for copyright infringement in the District Court for the District of Kansas, taking the position that Feist, in compiling its own directory, could not use the information contained in Rural's white pages. The district court granted summary judgment to Rural, explaining that "courts have consistently held that telephone directories are copyrightable" and citing a string of lower court decisions. In an unpublished opinion, the Court of Appeals for the Tenth Circuit affirmed "for substantially the reasons given by the district court."

This case concerns the interaction of two well-established propositions. The first is that facts are not copyrightable; the other, that compilations of facts generally are. The key to resolving the tension lies in understanding why facts are not copyrightable. The *sine qua non* of copyright is originality. To qualify for copyright protection, a work must be original to the author. Original, as the term is used in copyright, means only that the work was independently created by the author (as opposed to copied from other works), and that it possesses at least some minimal degree of creativity.

Originality is a constitutional requirement. The source of Congress's power to enact copyright laws is Article 1, §8. C1. 8, of the Constitution, which authorizes Congress to "secure for limited Times to Authors . . . the exclusive Right to their respective Writings." It is this bedrock principle of copyright that mandates the law's seemingly disparate treatment of facts and factual compilations. No one may claim originality as to facts. This is because facts do not owe their origin to an act of authorship. The distinction is one between creation and discovery: the first person to find and report a particular fact has not created the fact; he or she has merely discovered its existence.

If the selection and arrangement of facts are original, these elements of the work are eligible for copyright protection. No matter how original the format, however, the facts themselves do not become original through association.

There is no doubt that Feist took from the white pages of Rural's directory a substantial amount of factual information. At a minimum, Feist copied the names, towns, and telephone numbers of 1,309 of Rural's subscribers. Not all copying, however, is copyright infringement, two elements must be proven: (1) ownership of a valid copyright, and (2) copying of constituent elements of the work that are original. The first element is not at issue here: Feist appears to concede that Rural's directory, considered as a whole, is subject to a valid copyright because it contains some foreword text, as well as original material in its yellow pages advertisements.

The question is whether Rural has proven the second element. In other words, did Feist, by taking 1,309 names, towns, and telephone numbers from Rural's white pages, copy anything that was "original" to Rural? Certainly, the raw data does not satisfy the originality requirement. Rural may have been the first to discover and report the names, towns, and telephone numbers of its subscribers, but this data does not "owe its origin" to Rural. The question that remains is whether Rural selected, coordinated, or arranged these copyrightable facts in an original way. The selection, coordination, and arrangement of Rural's white pages do not satisfy the minimum constitutional standards for copyright protection. Rural's selection of listings could not be more obvious: it publishes the most basic information—name, town, and tele-

phone number—about each person who applies to it for telephone service. This is "selection" of a sort, but it lacks a modicum of creativity necessary to transform mere selection into copyrightable expression. Rural extended sufficient effort to make the white pages directory useful, but insufficient creativity to make it original.

The judgment of the court of appeals is REVERSED.

Case A.6

Schalk v. Texas,

823 S.W.2d 633 (1991)
Court of Criminal Appeals of Texas
Miller, Judge

Appellants Schalk and Leonard are former employees of Texas Instruments (hereafter TI). Both men have doctoral degrees and specialized in the area of speech research at TI. Schalk resigned his position with TI in April 1983 to join a newly developed company, Voice Control Systems (hereafter VCS). In February 1985, Leonard resigned from TI and joined VCS. Several TI employees eventually joined the ranks of VCS. Speech research was the main thrust of the research and development performed by VCS. In fact, VCS was a competitor of TI in this field. In April 1985, Sam Kuzbary, then employed with VCS and a former TI employee, noticed some information which he believed to be proprietary to TI stored in the memory of the computer he was using at VCS. Kuzbary contacted TI and agreed to serve as "informant" for them.

He then searched the premises of VCS and photographed materials which he recognized from his employment with TI. A TI internal investigation revealed that a few hours prior to Schalk's and Leonard's departures from TI, each appellant, utilizing TI computers, copied the entire contents of the directories respectively assigned to them. This information included computer programs which TI claimed to be its trade secrets. Officials of TI then contacted the Dallas District Attorney's office. A search of the premises of VCS resulted in the seizure of computer tapes containing the alleged TI trade secret programs from appellant's offices. Appellants were arrested.

We granted review to consider, first, whether the evidence was sufficient to establish that the computer programs named in the indictments were trade secrets, and second, to determine whether the items listed in the search warrant were sufficiently described so as to preclude a general exploratory search.

Having determined that computer programs are proper subjects for trade secret litigation under Texas civil and criminal law, we now look to the case *sub judice* to determine whether the programs which appellants copied and took with them to VCS are trade secrets as defined by §31.05 of the Penal Code.

§31.05 Theft of trade secrets:
(a) For the purposes of this section:
"Trade secret" means the whole or any part of any scientific or technical information, design, process, procedure, formula, or improvement that has value and that the owner has taken

measures to prevent from becoming available to persons other than those selected by the owner to have access for limited purposes.

Appellants claimed on appeal that the programs did not meet the statutory trade secrets criteria because they alleged their former employer TI failed to take "measures to prevent [the information] from becoming available to persons other than those selected by the owner." We note, as did the court of appeals, that the statute sets no standards for degree of sufficiency of the "measures" taken. Specifically, appellants pointed to considerable disclosure of speech research information, citing the "academic environment" of the laboratory in which they worked as encouraging the sharing of information, rather than maintaining secrecy. Appellants also claimed that TI policy favored protection of its research and development efforts through the patent process, as opposed to trade secret designation. Further, appellants allege that the programs that are the subject of the instant case were not listed in the TI register of trade secrets and that TI was lax in implementing its standard procedures with regard to notifying employees of trade secrets within the company. The precise issue before us in the case *sub judice* is one of the first impression in Texas, to wit: what constitutes requisite "measures" to protect trade secret status?

We now determine whether the information disclosed with TI's permission or encouragement, such as published articles, seminar papers, speeches given at public meetings, information provided to government agencies, etc., was so extensive as to destroy any trade secret status that may have existed regarding the computer software which is the subject of the instant indictments. It is axiomatic that the core element of a trade secret must be that it remain a secret. However, absolute secrecy is not required.

A trade secret can exist in a combination of characteristics and components, each of which, by itself, is in the public domain, but the unified process and operation of which, in unique combination, affords a competitive advantage and is a protectable secret. We find based on the record in this case that the limited disclosure made by TI in regard to the speech research lab activities merely described the application and configuration of the certain elements of the software but did not reveal the actual composition of the programs. The measures used by TI to secure its premises to prevent unauthorized personnel from admission to or exposure to its proprietary research data were reasonable under the circumstances.

We need not decide today whether any one of the preventive measures listed, standing alone, is factually sufficient to support trade secret status. We do find that the combination of employment agreements, strict plant security, restricted computer access, the nonauthorization of disclosure of the subject programs and the general nondisclosure of those programs by TI and its employees served to support trade secret status of the computer programs that are the subject of the instant indictments. Appellants neither requested nor received permission to copy the files containing these programs. The unauthorized copying of the article representing a trade secret constitutes an offense under V.T.C.A. Penal Code §31.05(b)(2).

Therefore we AFFIRM the court of appeals' ruling that the subject programs are trade secrets.

Case A.7
Ramirez v. Plough, Inc.

15 Cal. App. 4th 1110, 12 Cal. Rptr. 2d 423 (1992)
Court of Appeal of California
Thaxter, Judge

Jorge Ramirez, a minor, by his guardian ad litem Rosa Rivera, appeals from a summary judgment in favor of Plough, Inc. Appellant sued Plough alleging negligence, product liability, and fraud. The action sought damages for injuries sustained in March 1986 when Jorge, who was then four months old, contracted Reye's Syndrome after ingesting St. Joseph Aspirin for Children (SJAC). Plough marketed and distributed SJAC.

Reye's syndrome is a serious disease of unknown cause characterized by severe vomiting, lethargy, or irritability which may progress to delirium or coma. The disease generally strikes children or teenagers who are recovering from a mild respiratory tract infection, influenza, chicken pox, or other viral illnesses. The mortality rate of the disease is high, and permanent brain damage occurs in many cases. As a result of contracting Reye's Syndrome, appellant suffered catastrophic injuries including quadriplegia, blindness, and profound mental retardation.

In the early 1980s, there was significant scientific debate concerning the cause of Reye's syndrome. Several state studies suggested a statistical association between the ingestion of aspirin and the disease. In December 1982, the federal government acknowledged the debate. After considering the state studies and their critics, the federal government rejected a proposal which would require a warning label and instead, undertook an independent study. Apparently, Plough participated in efforts to influence government officials and agencies to reject the label proposal which Plough considered premature.

In December 1985, the Food and Drug Administration (FDA) requested that aspirin manufacturers voluntarily place a label on aspirin products warning consumers of the possible association between aspirin and Reye's Syndrome. Plough voluntarily complied and begin including a warning and insert in SJAC packaging. On June 5, 1986, the Reye's Syndrome warning became mandatory.

In March 1986, SJAC labeling bore the following warning: "Warning: Reye's Syndrome is a rare but serious disease which can follow flu or chicken pox in children and teenagers. While the cause of Reye's Syndrome is unknown, some reports claim aspirin may increase the risk of developing this disease. Consult a doctor before use in children or teenagers with flu or chicken pox." In addition, the SJAC package insert included the following statement: "The symptoms of Reye's Syndrome can include persistent vomiting, sleepiness and lethargy, violent headaches, unusual behavior, including disorientation, combativeness, and delirium. If any of these symptoms occur, especially following chicken pox or flu, call your doctor immediately, even if your child has not taken any medication. Reye's Syndrome is Serious, so Early Detection and Treatment are Vital."

Rosa Rivera purchased SJAC on March 12, 1986, and administered it to appellant who was suffering from what appeared to be a cold or upper respiratory infection. She gave appellant the aspirin without reading the directions or warnings appearing on the SJAC packaging. The packaging was in English and Ms. Rivera can speak and understand only Spanish. She did not seek to have the directions or warnings translated from English to Spanish, even though members of her household spoke English.

The trial court granted Plough's motion for summary judgment on the grounds that "there is no duty to warn in a foreign language and there is no causal relationship between plaintiff's injury and defendant's activities."

It is undisputed SJAC was marketed and intended for the treatment of minor aches and pains associated with colds, flu, and minor viral illnesses. The SJAC box promised "fast, effective relief of fever and minor aches and pains of colds." Both parties accept the premise that Plough had a duty to warn consumers that the use of SJAC after a viral infection or chicken pox could lead to Reye's Syndrome, an illness with serious, possibly fatal, consequences. In March 1986, federal regulations requiring a Reye's Syndrome warning had been promulgated and were final, although not yet effective. The FDA had previously solicited voluntary labeling. In response to the request for voluntary labeling, Plough started packaging SJAC with explicit warnings of the risks of Reye's Syndrome. The scientific community had already confirmed and documented the relationship between Reye's Syndrome and the use of aspirin after a viral illness. There is not doubt Plough had a duty to warn of the Reye's Syndrome risk.

The question thus is whether the warning given only in English was adequate under the circumstances. Respondent argues that as a matter of law it has no duty to place foreign-language warnings on products manufactured to be sold in the United States and that holding manufacturers liable for failing to do so would violate public policy.

While the constitutional, statutory, regulatory, and judicial authorities relied on by respondent may reflect a public policy recognizing the status of English as an official language, nothing compels the conclusion that a manufacturer of a dangerous or defective product is immunized from liability when an English-only warning does not adequately inform non-English literate persons likely to use the product.

Plough's evidence showed that over 148 foreign languages are spoken in the United States and over 23 million Americans speak a language other than English in their homes. That evidence plainly does not prove that Plough used reasonable care in giving an English-only warning. Plough, then, resorts to arguing that the burden on manufacturers and society of requiring additional warnings is so "staggering" that the courts should preclude liability as a matter of law. We are not persuaded.

Certainly the burden and costs of giving foreign-language warnings is one factor for consideration in determining whether a manufacturer acted reasonably in using only English. The importance of that factor may vary from case to case depending upon other circumstances, such as the nature of the product, marketing efforts directed to segments of the population unlikely to be English-literate, and the actual and relative size of the consumer market which could reasonably be expected to speak or read only a certain foreign language. Plough presented no evidence from which we can gauge the extent of the burden under the facts of this case.

Ramirez submitted evidence that Plough knew Hispanics were an important part of the market for SJAC and that Hispanics often maintain their first language rather than learn English. SJAC was advertised in the Spanish media, both radio and television. That evidence raises material questions of fact concerning the foreseeability of purchase by a Hispanic not literate in English and the reasonableness of not giving a Spanish-language warning. If Plough has evidence conclusively showing that it would have been unreasonable to give its label warning in Spanish because of the burden, it did not present that evidence below.

Given the triable issues of material fact, if we accepted Plough's arguments in this case in effect we would be holding that failure to warn in a foreign language is not negligence, regardless of the circumstances. Such a sweeping grant of immunity should come from the legislative branch of government, not the judicial. In deciding that Plough did not establish its right to judgment as a matter of law, we do not hold that manufacturers are required to warn in languages other than English simply because it may be foreseeable that non-English literate persons are likely to use their products. Our decision merely recognizes that under some circumstances the standard of due care may require such warning.

Because the evidence shows triable issues of material fact and because Plough did not establish its immunity from liability as a matter of law, its motion for summary judgment should have been denied.

Case A.8

Mark Realty, Inc. v. Rogness,

418 So.2d 373 (1982)
District Court of Appeal of Florida
Cowart, Judge

Tilman A. Rogness, owner, entered into four separate agreements with Mark Realty, Inc., a real estate broker. They were entitled "exclusive right of sale" and gave the broker, for a stated period of time, the exclusive right to sell the property for a certain stated price and on certain terms. The broker sued on the four agreements for brokerage commissions, alleging that during the time provided in the agreements the owner had conveyed the four properties. The owner's answer alleged affirmative defenses to the effect that the owner had "canceled, revoked and terminated" the brokerage agreements before the properties were sold and that the broker had never performed under the agreements.

The trial judge construed the brokerage agreements to constitute mere offers to enter into unilateral contracts under which the broker would be entitled to a commission only if he performed by "finding a purchaser of the above property." If the documents in question are merely offers limited to acceptance by performance only, the trial judge's analysis and conclusion would be correct.

We cannot agree that the documents were only offers for a unilateral contract. The documents illustrate what has been termed "the usual practice" in the making of bargains. One party indicates what he will do and what he requires in exchange and the other then agrees. These documents, when first executed by the owner and tendered to the broker, constituted offers which, when accepted by the broker by his execution, constituted contracts. The contract is bilateral because it contains mutual promises made in exchange for each other by each of the two contracting parties.

The most common recurring brokerage transaction is one in which the owner employs a broker to find a purchaser able and willing to buy, on terms stated in advance by the owner, and in which the owner promises to pay a specific commission for the service. Such a transaction as this is an offer by the owner of a unilateral contract, an offered promise to pay by the owner, creating in the broker a power of accepting the offer by actual rendition of the requested services. The only contemplated contract between the owner and broker is a unilateral contract—a promise to pay a commission for services rendered. Such an offer of a promise to pay a commission for services rendered is revocable by the owner by notice before the broker has rendered any part of the requested service. On the other hand, the transaction between the owner and the broker can be a bilateral contract. An owner who puts his land in the hands of a broker for sale usually clearly promises to pay a commission but the broker rarely promises in return that he will produce a purchaser, although he often promises, expressly or impliedly, that he will make certain efforts to do so. If the parties have thus made mutual promises, the transaction no longer has the status of an unaccepted offer—there is an existing bilateral contract and neither party has a power of revocation. During the term of such a contract the owner may withdraw any power the owner has given the broker to contract with a third party in the owner's name, but this is not a revocation of the contract between the owner and the broker and normally such action constitutes a breach of the brokerage contract.

In this case, the broker promised to inspect the property, to list the property with a multiple listing service, to advertise the property in the local newspaper or other media, to furnish information to inquiring cooperating brokers and prospective purchasers, to show the property, to make efforts to find a purchaser, to "make an earnest and continued effort to sell," and to direct the concentrated efforts of his organization in bringing about a sale.

In the instant case, the contract clearly provided that the brokerage commission would be paid "whether the purchaser be secured by you or me, or by any other person."

Thus the contract granted the broker an exclusive right of sale and the trial court erred in construing the agreement as an offer of a unilateral contract revocable at will at any time prior to performance.

The final judgment is REVERSED.

Case A.9
Traco, Inc. v. Arrow Glass Co., Inc.,

814 S.W.2d 186 (1991)
Court of Appeals of Texas
Chapa, Justice

This is a construction dispute stemming from a quotation given by Traco, Inc., a Three Rivers Aluminum Company, a material supplier of preengineered aluminum and glass sliding doors and windows, to Arrow Glass Company, Inc., a subcontractor, in connection with the USAA Towers project in San Antonio, Texas. Arrow initially brought suit against Traco on the theories of promissory, estoppel and negligence for Traco's failure to supply aluminum and glass sliding doors at the quoted price. After a bench trial, the trial court held for Arrow solely under the theory of promissory estoppel and awarded Arrow judgment against Traco for damages in the amount of $75,843.38, plus attorneys' fees and prejudgment interest.

The facts of this case reflect that on or about October 9, 1986, construction bids were due for the USAA Towers, a $49,000,000 retirement housing project located near Fort Sam Houston, Texas. There were numerous suppliers, subcontractors, and general contractors bidding to obtain work on this project including the appellant, Traco, and the appellee, Arrow.

On bid day, a representative for Arrow received a telephone call from Dale Ferrar of Traco. Mr. Ferrar told Bill Morris, the general manager of Arrow Glass, that Traco was a very large window and sliding glass and aluminum door manufacturer in Pennsylvania. Mr. Ferrar offered its A-2 aluminum and glass sliding doors, as an alternate product substitution, to Arrow, which was bidding that portion of the project. However, after some discussion of the required specifications, the parties realized that Traco's doors would have to be modified in order to comply with the project specifications. Arrow declined to use Traco's bid and, instead, submitted its original bid, using a different supplier of doors. At approximately noon on bid day, Mr. Ferrar phoned Mr. Morris, quoting a new price for the doors which included a modification of the frame depth which, supposedly, enabled the doors to comply with the specifications. At this time, Mr. Morris informed Mr. Ferrar that his bid was low and asked him to recheck his figures. Mr. Ferrar explained that because of Traco's size and the fact that it could manufacture its products under one roof, Traco could sell the project for that amount. Mr. Ferrar also indicated that Traco was seeking a high profile project to represent Traco in the San Antonio area.

After receiving these assurances, Mr. Morris told Mr. Ferrar that he was going to use Traco's bid. Mr. Morris then phoned the contractors to whom he had originally submitted his bid, and deducted $100,000 in reliance upon Traco's bid. Mr. Morris later told Mr. Ferrar that he had received favorable responses from three or four general contractors, and that it appeared Arrow would get the project. Mr. Morris advised Mr. Ferrar that if Arrow obtained the project, then Traco would be awarded the contract on the doors.

The oral quote by Traco was followed with a written bid confirmation on the next day, which reflected the product that would be supplied and the price agreed upon by the parties. The confirmation also included the 1-1/4" frame extended at a cost of $27,860, which, allegedly, brought the doors into compliance with the project specifications.

Sometime in November, long after Mr. Morris had relied upon Mr. Ferrar's representations in submitting his bid, Mr. Morris began hearing rumors that there was a problem with the doors. Mr. Morris contacted Mr. Ferrar, who admitted that there was a problem with the doors meeting the architect's wind load deflection requirement in the specifications. Shortly after learning of this problem, Mr. Morris received a second quote from Traco, wherein Traco offered its A-3 doors, which were a more expensive, heavy grade commercial door that met the deflection requirement, for a price of $304,300. After receiving this bid, Morris objected to the price and demanded that Traco deliver doors meeting the project specifications at the original price quoted. Traco refused and when it became obvious that Arrow would not be able to use Traco's product, Mr. Morris contracted with another supplier who had bid on the project.

The record clearly reflects the following: that it was Traco that initially contacted Arrow and offered to do a certain specific act, i.e., supply the sliding doors required; that Mr. Ferrar phoned Mr. Morris on several occasions and discussed, among other things, the fact that the doors which Traco wished to bid would not comply with the specifications without some modification; and, that Mr. Ferrar assured Mr. Morris that the doors could be modified to comply with the specifications. Thus, under the present facts, Traco's bid gave Arrow "a right to expect or claim the performance of some particular thing"; specifically, Traco's bid constituted a promise to supply sliding doors meeting the project specifications at a specified price.

Appellant initially argues that the trial court erred in rendering judgment for Arrow because Traco's bid was revocable and properly withdrawn 30 days after it was made. Appellant primarily relies upon the argument that its sliding doors are goods as defined by the Texas Business and Commerce Code. Nevertheless, appellant's arguments ignore the appellee's basic contention and legal theory under which this suit was brought. Appellee sought relief under the equitable doctrine of promissory estoppel, on the premise that appellant's promises, by way of its *oral* bid, caused appellee to substantially rely to its detriment. The appellee relied to its detriment when it reduced its bid based on a telephone conversation with the appellant, prior to the time appellant's confirmation letter was sent or received. We must now resolve whether the equitable theory of promissory estoppel applies to bid construction cases and, if so, whether this doctrine applies under

the specific facts of this case. While no Texas case has previously applied the theory of promissory estoppel in a bid construction case, other jurisdictions have consistently applied this doctrine under similar facts, recognizing the necessity for equity in view of the lack of other remedies.

The Texas Supreme Court, in emphasizing that the underlying function of the theory of promissory estoppel is to promote equity, has stated that: "The Vital principal is that he who by his language or conduct leads another to do what he would not otherwise have done, shall not subject such person to loss or injury by disappointing the expectations, upon which he acted. This remedy is always so applied as to promote the ends of justice." Clearly promissory estoppel is "a rule of equity" applied to prevent injustice. As is true in most, if not all, bid construction cases, the present situation does not involve a contract. Therefore, were we to hold that promissory estoppel does not exist in bid construction cases, this would necessarily mean that, notwithstanding any language or conduct by the subcontractor which leads the general contractor to do that which he would not otherwise have done and, thereby, incur loss or injury, the general contractor would be denied all relief. This proposition is untenable and conflicts with the underlying premise of promissory estoppel.

Section 90 of the STATEMENT (SECOND) OF CONTRACTS (1981) states the principle of promissory estoppel as follows: "A promise which the promisor should reasonably expect to induce action or forbearance on the part of the promisee or a third person and which does induce such action or forbearance is binding if injustice can be avoided only by enforcement of the promise." Accordingly, the requirements of promissory estoppel are: "(1) a promise, (2) foreseeability of reliance thereon by the promisor, and (3) substantial reliance by the promisee to his detriment." In order to invoke the doctrine of estoppel, all the necessary elements of estoppel must be present and the failure to establish even one of these elements is fatal to the claimant's cause of action.

Appellant insists, however, that because Traco was not an approved manufacturer and bid its doors as an alternate, that by its nature, Traco's bid was conditional and, therefore, promissory estoppel cannot lie. We fail to see how a bid for a specific door at a specific price, which was submitted in response to solicitations that detailed project specifications, is contingent, or somehow not final, merely because the wrong door was bid upon. The appellant's failure to receive the architect's approval was not due to new specifications but was caused by the appellant's failure to regard those specifications originally required when the appellant offered its doors. Appellant's point is rejected.

Notwithstanding the existence of this promise, the appellant argues that appellee could not have justifiably and reasonably relied upon appellant's bid because: Traco was not an approved manufacturer and bid its A-2 doors as an alternate and, further, Traco's bid was lower than the other suppliers who bid upon the contract.

Because of the withdrawal of Traco's bid, Arrow was compelled to seek another supplier of doors at a much greater cost;

clearly, this constituted an injustice to the appellee. Additionally, appellee's reliance upon appellant's bid was reasonable in view of the appellant's attempts to modify its doors, and Mr. Ferrar's assurances that the doors, as modified, would meet the project specifications.

We hold that the controlling findings of fact support the promissory estoppel theory.

The judgment is AFFIRMED.

Case A.10

Carnival Leisure Industries, Ltd. v. Aubin,

938 F.2d 624 (1991)
United States Court of Appeals, Fifth Circuit
Garwood, Circuit Judge

During a January 1987 visit to the Bahamas, George J. Aubin, a Texas resident, visited Cable Beach Hotel and Casino (the Casino), which was owned and operated by Carnival Leisure Industries, Ltd. (Carnival Leisure). While gambling at the Casino, Aubin received markers or chips from the Casino and the Casino received drafts drawn on Aubin's bank accounts in Texas. Aubin spent all of the markers provided on gambling, although he could also have spent them on food, beverages, souvenirs, or lodging at the Casino. Aubin ultimately gambled and lost $25,000, having given the Casino the same amount in bank drafts.

Carnival Leisure was unable to cash the bank drafts because Aubin had subsequently directed his bank to stop payment. Carnival Leisure sued Aubin in the United States District Court for the Southern District of Texas to enforce the debt. The district court granted Carnival Leisure's motion for summary judgment against Aubin in the amount of $25,000 and attorney's fees and costs. Carnival Leisure claimed that the debt was enforceable under Texas law because public policy had changed and now favored enforcement of gambling debts. The district court agreed. Aubin raises on appeal only the issue of whether public policy in Texas continues to prevent the enforcement of gambling debts.

Carnival Leisure claims, however, that since 1973 the public policy of Texas toward gambling and the legality of gambling debts has changed. Although gambling is generally proscribed in Texas, there has been an exception for the "social" gambler since 1973. The Texas legislature enacted the Bingo Enabling Act in 1981, the Texas Racing Act in 1986, and the Charitable Raffle Enabling Act in 1989. Provisions were added to the Texas Penal Code excepting these three activities from its general proscription against gambling.

The enactment of statutes legalizing some forms of gambling admittedly evidences some dissipation or narrowing of public disapproval of gambling. However, such statutes hardly introduce a judicially cognizable change in public policy with respect to gambling generally. The social gambling permitted is confined to private places where no one receives any benefit other than his personal winnings and all participants are subject to the same risks, a categorically vastly different kind of

activity from the sort involved here. The racing, bingo, and raffling exceptions are narrow, strictly regulated exceptions to a broad public policy in Texas against most forms of gambling. Further, the kind of gambling engaged in here is not of the sort permitted by any of these exceptions.

Even if gambling legislation in Texas were evidence sufficient to warrant judicial notice of a shift in public policy with respect to legalized gambling, such a shift would not be inconsistent with a continued public policy disfavoring gambling on credit. Although Aubin could have used the loaned markers for nongambling purposes at the Casino, it is undisputed that they were in fact used exclusively for gambling. Aubin's gambling debt therefore fits squarely within the terms of the public policy of Texas prohibiting enforcement of gambling debts owed to gambling participants incurred for the purpose of gambling.

We hold that the public policy in Texas against gambling on credit prevents enforcement of a debt incurred for the purpose of gambling and provided by a participant in the gambling activity. The district court's grant of summary judgment in favor of Carnival Leisure is accordingly REVERSED and this case is remanded to the district court for further proceedings consistent with this opinion.

Case A.11

Continental Airlines, Inc. v. McDonnell Douglas Corporation,

216 Cal.App.3d 388, 264 Cal.Rptr. 779 (1990)
Court of Appeals of California
Hoffman, Associate Justice

This action was commenced by plaintiff and respondent Continental Airlines (Continental) in Los Angeles Superior Court on December 3, 1979, and alleged, against defendant and appellant McDonnell Douglas Corporation (Douglas), causes of action for deceit. On January 30, 1986, the jury returned verdicts in favor of Continental for $17 million on its claims for fraud by misrepresentation and fraud by nondisclosure of known facts. The judgment was granted. This appeal is from that judgment. We affirm the judgment as modified.

On March 1, 1978, a Continental DC-10 aircraft, which had been delivered to Continental by Douglas in 1972, was in its takeoff roll at Los Angeles International Airport when two tires burst on the left landing gear. The captain elected to try to stop the plane, but it ran off the end of the runway at 8 miles per hour. The landing gear broke through the tarmac, burrowed into the ground, and was ripped from the wing, making a 3.7 foot hole which allowed fuel to pour from the wing fuel tanks. The plane was severely damaged by the resulting fire and rendered unrepairable.

Douglas had approached Continental in 1968 to sell Continental DC-10 aircraft. Douglas used a series of briefings and sales brochures in its sales campaign. The sales brochure given to Continental consisted of hundreds of pages of technical information drafted by Douglas's engineers, and reviewed by its top management, for the express purpose of explaining the DC-10 design and a "Detail Type Specification" to potential aircraft purchasers. That Specification, as its name implies, described the technical details of the DC-10. The Douglas briefings covered the landing gear and wing design, as did many of its brochures. Continental personnel used the brochures to write portions of Continental's "Tri-Jet Evaluation," a comparison between the DC-10 and Lockheed's L-1011, which became a basis for Continental's decision to purchase the DC-10. When Continental decided to purchase the DC-10 instead of the L-1011 aircraft, it finalized a Purchase Agreement with Douglas which incorporated by reference the Detail Specification for the DC-10.

The brochures contained statements that "the fuel tank will not rupture under crash load conditions"; that the landing gear "are designed for wipe-off without rupturing the wing fuel tank"; that "the support structure is designed to a higher strength than the gear to prevent fuel tank rupture due to an accidental landing gear overload"; that the DC-10 "is designed and tested for crash-worthiness"; that the "landing gear will be tested" to demonstrate the fail safe integrity and wipe-off characteristics of the gear design; and that "good reliability" for the DC-10 landing gear could be predicted with an "unusually high degree of confidence" because of its close similarity to the successful design on the DC-8 and DC-9 aircraft.

Douglas argues that "the Uniform Commercial Code and cases interpreting it have recognized that general promotional observations of this type are merely expressions of opinion that are not actionable as fraudulent statements. The alleged false representations in the subject brochures were not statements of "opinion or mere puffing." They were, in essence, representations that the DC-10 was a safe aircraft. Promises of safety are not statements of opinion—they are representations of fact.

Douglas contends in its opening brief that there was no substantial evidence that its precontract representations were *material* or that Continental reasonably *relied* on them in deciding to purchase the DC-10. The materiality of the representations can hardly be questioned. Any airline shopping for aircraft to service its customers naturally searches for planes that are safe. Where representations have been made in regard to a material matter and action has been taken, in the absence of evidence showing the contrary, reliance on the representations will be presumed. Here, both materiality and reliance are demonstrated by the fact that Continental evaluated the DC-10 breakaway design in its "Tri-Jet Evaluation," which compared the DC-10 with the L-1011 for the purpose of deciding which aircraft to purchase. Douglas was the only possible source for the information; there was no way Continental could independently investigate or analyze the adequacy of that design. The foregoing provides more than substantial evidence that Continental *relied* on Douglas's representations regarding landing gear breakaway in choosing to purchase the DC-10 and that those representations were *material*.

False representations made recklessly and without regard for their truth in order to induce action by another are equivalent of misrepresentations uttered. Therefore, there is substantial evidence of the requisite intent for intentional fraud. For the forgoing reasons we conclude the evidence supports

the jury's findings of liability for fraud. The judgment is modified to reflect an award of prejudgment interest in the amount of $9,549,750. As so modified, the judgment is AFFIRMED.

Case A.12
Chase Precast Corporation v. John J. Paonessa Co., Inc.,

409 Mass. 371, 566 N.E. 2d 603 (1991)
Supreme Judicial Court of Massachusetts
Lynch, Justice

This appeal raises the question whether the doctrine of frustration of purpose may be a defense in a breach of contract action in Massachusetts, and, if so, whether it excuses the defendant John J. Paonessa Company, Inc. (Paonessa), from performance.

The claim of the plaintiff, Chase Precast Corporation (Chase), arises from the cancellation of its contracts with Paonessa to supply median barriers in a highway construction project of the Commonwealth. Chase brought an action to recover its anticipated profit on the amount of the media barriers called for by its supply contracts with Paonessa but not produced. Paonessa brought a cross action against the Commonwealth for indemnification in the event if should be held liable to Chase. After a jury-waived trial, a Superior Court judge ruled for Paonessa on the basis of impossibility of performance. Chase and Paonessa cross-appealed. The appeals court affirmed, noting that the doctrine of frustration of purpose more accurately described the basis of the trial judge's decision than the doctrine of impossibility. We agree. We allowed Chase's application for further appellate review and we now affirm.

The pertinent facts are as follows. In 1982, the Commonwealth, through the Department of Public Works (department), entered into two contracts with Paonessa for resurfacing and improvements to two stretches of Route 128. Part of each contract called for replacing a grass median strip between the north- and southbound lanes with concrete resurfacing and precast concrete median barriers. Paonessa entered into two contracts with Chase under which Chase was to supply, in the aggregate, 25,800 linear feet of concrete median barriers according to the specifications of the department for highway construction. The quantity and type of barriers to be supplied were specified in two purchase orders prepared by Chase.

The highway reconstruction began in the spring of 1983. By late May, the department was receiving protests from angry residents who objected to use of the concrete barriers and removal of the grass median strip. Paonessa and Chase became aware of the protest around June 1. On June 6, a group of about 100 citizens filed an action in the Superior Court to stop installation of the concrete barriers and other aspects of the work. On June 7, anticipating modification by the department, Paonessa notified Chase by letter to stop producing concrete barriers for the projects. Chase did so upon receipt of letter the following day. On June 17, the department and the citizen's group entered into a settlement which provided, in part, that no additional concrete median barriers would be installed. On

June 23, the department deleted the permanent concrete median barriers item from its contract with Paonessa.

Before stopping production on June 8, Chase had produced approximately one-half of the concrete median barriers called for by its contracts with Paonessa, and had delivered most of them to the construction sites. Paonessa paid Chase for all that it had produced, at the contract price. Chase suffered no out-of-pocket expense as a result of cancellation of the remaining portion of barriers.

This court has long recognized and applied the doctrine of impossibility as a defense to an action of breach of contract. Under that doctrine, "where from the nature of the contract it appears that the parties must from the beginning have contemplated the continued existence of some particular specified thing as the foundation of what was to be done, then, in the absence of any warranty that the thing shall exist . . . the parties shall be excused . . . when[cb] performance becomes impossible from the accidental perishing of the thing without the fault of either party."

On the other hand, although we have referred to the doctrine of frustration of purpose in a few decisions, we have never clearly defined it. Other jurisdictions have explained the doctrine as follows: when an event neither anticipated nor caused by either party, the risk of which was not allocated by the contract, destroys the object or purpose of the contract, thus destroying the value of performance, the parties are excused from further performance.

In *Mishara Construction Co.*, we called frustration of purpose a "companion rule" to the doctrine of impossibility. Both doctrines concern the effect of supervening circumstances upon the rights and duties of the parties. The difference lies in the effect of the supervening event. Another definition of frustration of purpose is found in the Restatement (Second) of Contracts §265 (1981). "Where, after a contract is made, a party's principal purpose is substantially frustrated without his fault by the occurrence of an event the nonoccurrence of which was a basic assumption on which the contract was made, his remaining duties to render performance are discharged, unless the language or the circumstances indicate the contrary."

Paonessa bore no responsibility for the department's elimination of the median barriers from the projects. Therefore, whether it can rely on the defense of frustration turns on whether elimination of the barriers was a risk allocated by the contracts to Paonessa. The question is, given the commercial circumstances in which the parties dealt: "Was the contingency which developed one which the parties could reasonably be thought to have foreseen as a real possibility which could affect performance? Was it one of that variety of risks which the parties were tacitly assigning to the promisor by their failure to provide for it explicitly? If it was, performance will be required. If it could not be considered, performance is excused."

The record supports the conclusion that Chase was aware of the department's power to decrease quantities of contract items. The judge found that Chase had been a supplier of median barriers to the department in the past. The provision giving the

department the power to eliminate items or portions thereof was standard in its contracts. The judge's finding that all parties were well aware that lost profits were not an element of damage in either of the public works projects in issue further supports the conclusion that Chase was aware of the department's power to decrease quantities, since the term prohibiting claims for anticipated profit is part of the same sentence in the standard provision as that allowing the engineer to eliminate items or portions of work. In this case, even if the parties were aware generally of the department's power to eliminate contract items, the judge could reasonably have concluded that they did not contemplate the cancellation for a major portion of the project of such a widely used item as concrete median barriers, and did not allocate the risk of such cancellations.

Judgment AFFIRMED.

Case A.13

E.B. Harvey & Company, Inc. v. Protective Systems, Inc.,

1989 Tenn. App. Lexis 105 (1989)
Court of Appeals of Tennessee
Sanders, Presiding Judge

The plaintiff-appellant, E.B. Harvey Company, Inc. (Harvey), is engaged in the manufacture and wholesale of fine jewelry in Chattanooga. It has been engaged in this business for about 10 years. It maintains an inventory in excess of $1 million of gold, silver, precious stones, pearls, and other such materials related to the manufacture of jewelry. A considerable amount of its jewelry is on consignment and, by the very nature of its business, it requires a great deal of insurance. However, the insurance companies will not write the insurance unless it maintains an Underwriters Laboratories (U.L.)–approved AA burglary protection alarm system. The defendant-appellee, Protective Systems, Inc. (Protective), is one of two companies in Hamilton County which furnishes and maintains a U.L.–approved AA burglar protection system. In June 1981, Harvey entered into a three-year contract with Protective to install and maintain a burglar protection system. The contract provided:

It is agreed that Protective is not an insurer and that the payments hereinbefore named are based solely upon the value of the services herein described and it is not the intention of the parties that Protective assume responsibility for any losses occasioned by malfeasance or misfeasance in the performance of the services under this contract or for any loss or damage sustained through burglary, theft, robbery, fire or other cause or any liability on the part of Protective by virtue of this Agreement or because of the relation hereby established.

If there shall at any time be or arise any liability on the part of Protective, by virtue of this Agreement or because of the relation hereby established, whether due to the negligence of Protective or otherwise, such liability is and shall be limited to a sum total in amount to the rental service charge hereunder for a period of service not to exceed six months, which sum shall be paid and received as liquidated damages.

The burglary and hold-up system provided to Harvey operated by means of Grade AA telephone lines between the central monitoring station of Protective and Harvey's premises. Said telephone lines were at all times owned and maintained by the South Central Bell Telephone Company. On July 22, 1984, at 11:14 P.M., an outage condition was indicated on the E.B. Harvey & Company account. For a period of two weeks prior to this date, Protective's computer had been registering an inordinate number of outage signals which had all been traced back to problems in telephone company equipment. For this reason, on July 22, 1984, Protective's president, Pendell Meyers, notified the telephone company of this condition and reported a potential problem to the police department but did not contact a representative of Harvey to notify them of the outage condition.

The phone company was unable to locate the exact nature of the problem despite several telephone conversations with Meyers. The Chattanooga Police Department patrolled the premises surrounding the Harvey's place of business twice that evening but did not note any unusual activity. The following morning, when an employee of Harvey reported to work, it was discovered that a burglary had in fact taken place. Some $200,000 worth of jewelry and inventory was stolen. Harvey sued Protective for damages resulting from the burglary. It alleged that Protective was guilty of negligence for its failure to notify Harvey or its employees of the outage which appeared on the burglary monitoring equipment.

Protective, for answer, denied the allegations of Harvey's complaint and, as an affirmative defense, alleged the contract between the parties with its exculpatory and limitation of liability provisions was enforceable and binding upon Harvey. After hearing testimony, the trial court held the extent of Harvey's recovery against Protective would be 650 percent as liquidated damages. A final judgment was entered and Harvey has appealed.

There is nothing in public policy to render inoperative or nugatory the contractual limitations contained in the agreement. Limitations against liability for negligence or breach of contract have generally been upheld in this state in the absence of fraud or overreaching. Limitations such as those contained in the present contract have generally been deemed reasonable and have been sustained in actions against the providers of burglary and fire alarm systems. Such clauses do not ordinarily protect against liability for fraud or intentional misrepresentation.

We concur with the trial court. The issues are found in favor of the appellees. The judgment of the trial court is AFFIRMED. The cost of this appeal is taxed to the appellant and the case is remanded to the trial court for collection of cost.

Case A.14
Cafazzo v. Central Medical Health Services, Inc.,

668 A.2d 521 (1995)
Supreme Court of Pennsylvania
Montemuro, Justice

In 1986, appellant Albert Cafazzo underwent surgery for implantation of a mandibular prosthesis. In 1992, some time after it was discovered that this device was defective, a com-

plaint was filed against Dr. Norman Stern, the physician who performed the surgery, and the hospital where the operation took place, claiming that "all defendants sell, provide or use certain prosthetic devices," and that they should be held strictly liable as having "provided, sold or otherwise placed in the stream of commerce products manufactured by Vitek, Inc., known as Proplast TMJ Implants." The complaint alleged that the prosthesis was defectively designed, unsafe for its intended use, and lacked any warning necessary in order to ensure safety.

Section 402A of the Restatement (Second) of Torts, provides in relevant part as follows:

(1) One who sells any product in a defective condition unreasonably dangerous to the user or consumer or to his property is subject to liability for physical harm thereby caused to the ultimate user or consumer, or to his property, if:

(a) the seller is engaged in the business of selling such a product, and

(b) it is expected to and does reach the consumer without substantial change in the condition in which it is sold.

The thrust of the inquiry is not on whether a separate consideration is charged for the physical material used in the exercise of medical skill, but what service is performed to restore or maintain the patient's health. The determinative question becomes not what is being charged, but what is being done. The provision of medical services is regarded as qualitatively different from the sale of products.

This distinction is made clearer by the fact that case law also supports the application of 402A where what has been provided is not medical service or products connected with diagnosis and treatment, but rather materials related to mechanical or administrative functions. See *Thomas v. St. Joseph Hospital*, 618 S.W.2d 791 (Tex. Civ. App. 1981) (hospital held strictly liable where hospital gown ignited when lighted match fell on it).

It must be noted that the "seller" need not be engaged solely in the business of selling products such as the defective one to be held strictly liable. An example supporting this proposition appears in comment *f* of the Restatement (Second) of Torts, §402A and concerns the owner of a motion picture theater who offers edibles such as popcorn and candy for sale to movie patrons. The analogue to the instant case is valid in one respect only: both the candy and the TMJ implant are ancillary to the primary activity, viewing a film or undergoing surgery respectively. However, beyond that any comparison is specious. A movie audience is free to purchase or not any food items on offer, and regardless of which option is exercised the primary activity is unaffected. On the other hand, while the implant was incidental to the surgical procedure here, it was a necessary adjunct to the treatment administered, as were the scalpel used to make the incision, and any other material objects involved in performing the operation, all of which fulfill a particular role in provision of medical service, the primary activity.

When one enters the hospital as a patient, he goes there, not to buy medicines or pills, not to purchase bandages or iodine or serum or blood, but to obtain a course of treatment in the hope of being cured of what ails him. We find, consistent with the decisions cited above which distinguish medical services from merchandising, that appellees are not sellers, providers, suppliers or distributors of products such as to activate 402A.

Case A.15
Burnett vs. Purtell,

1992 Ohio App. Lexis 3467 (1992)
Court of Appeals of Ohio
Ford, Presiding Judge

Appellees agreed to purchase a mobile home with shed from appellant. On Saturday, March 3, 1990, appellees paid appellant $6,500 and in return were given the certificate of title to the mobile home as well as a key to the mobile home, but no keys to the shed. At the same time the certificate of title was transferred, the following items remained in the mobile home: the washer and dryer, mattress and box springs, two chairs, items in the refrigerator, and the entire contents of the shed. These items were to be retained by appellant and removed by appellant. To facilitate removal, the estate retained one key to the mobile home and the only keys to the shed.

On Sunday, March 4, 1990, the mobile home was destroyed by fire through the fault of neither party. At the time of the fire, appellant still had a key to the mobile home, as well as the keys to the shed and she had not removed the contents of the mobile home nor the shed. The contents of the shed were not destroyed and have now been removed by appellant. The referee determined that the risk of loss remained with appellant because there was no tender of delivery. Appellant objected to the conclusion of law, but the trial court overruled the objection and entered judgment in favor of appellee. First, the appellant argues that because the certificate of title was transferred, appellees were given a key to the mobile home and the full purchase price was paid by appellees, that the risk of loss had shifted from appellant to appellees. The risk of loss passes to the buyer on his receipt of the goods if the seller is a merchant: otherwise the risk passes to the buyer on tender of delivery.

Analyzing the foregoing elements it is clear that, as the trial court stated, appellant did not tender delivery. The parties agreed that appellees would purchase the mobile home and shed from appellant. The contents of both the shed and the mobile home were to be retained by appellant and removed by appellant. At the time of the fire, appellant had not removed the items that she was required to remove from either the mobile home or the shed. Additionally, all keys to the mobile home were not surrendered and none of the keys to the shed were relinquished. Under this scenario, appellant did not tender conforming goods free of items belonging to her which remained in the trailer, nor did she put the mobile home at appellee's disposition without being fettered with the items previously enumerated. Accordingly, the trial court was correct in determining that appellant did not tender delivery within the meaning of the statute, and consequently the risk of loss remained with her. The trial court was correct in determining that appellant did not tender delivery in a manner suf-ficient to shift the risk of loss to appellees. Therefore, when it ordered appellant to return appellee's purchase money, it effectually mandated that the contract was "avoided."

Based on the foregoing, the judgment of the trial court is AFFIRMED.

Case A.16
LNS Investment Company, Inc. v. Phillips 66 Co.,

731 F. Supp. 1484 (1990)
United States District Court
O'Connor, Chief Judge

Plaintiff is the successor to a company known as CompuBlend Corporation ("CBC"), which blended, labeled, and packaged quart plastic bottles of motor oil for, among others, defendant Phillips 66 Company. On July 29, 1986, W. Peter Buhlinger, defendant's manager of lubricants ("Buhlinger"), wrote a letter to Dan Tutcher, Plaintiff's vice-president of operations ("Tutcher"), which read as follows: This will confirm our verbal agreement wherein Phillips will purchase additional quantities of plastic bottles from CBC during 1986. CBC, in an effort to increase their packaging capacity has committed to purchase several additional molds to blow the Phillips plastic one-quart container. In order to amortize the cost of the additional equipment, Phillips has agreed to take delivery of a maximum of 4,000,000 bottles to be made available by December 31, 1986. This agreement includes the production available now and to be supplemented by the additional equipment. Should CBC not be able to produce the full 4,000,000 quarts by December 31, 1986, this agreement shall be considered satisfied. Phillips's desire is to receive as many bottles packaged with Phillips motor oil in 1986 from CBC as possible.

Plaintiff experienced numerous problems in maintaining even its precontract capacity. Moreover, the quality of goods plaintiff was able to deliver was frequently unacceptable to defendant. Laughlin reiterated defendant's dissatisfaction with plaintiff's products by letter dated October 15, 1986. Discussing bottles tendered by plaintiff, Laughlin stated that "we definitely do not want bottles on the shelf of the quality submitted." On December 16, 1986, Buhlinger wrote that defendant would not renew any commitments to purchase goods from plaintiff after March 31, 1987, due to plaintiff's poor performance under the July 29 agreement. Plaintiff filed this suit on March 12, 1987, alleging, inter alia, that defendant breached the July 29 agreement by failing to purchase plaintiff's full output of plastic bottles through December 31, 1986.

Plaintiff's failure to provide either the quantity or quality of goods contemplated by the July 29 agreement entitled defendant to suspend its performance. Section 84-2-609 of the Code states as follows: Right to adequate assurance of performance. (1) A contract for sale imposes an obligation on each party that the other's expectation of receiving due performance will not be impaired. When reasonable grounds for insecurity arise with respect to the performance of either party the other may in writing demand adequate assurance of due performance and until he receives such assurance may if commercially reasonable suspend any performance for which he has not already received the agreed return.

It was incumbent upon plaintiff to provide adequate assurance of its future performance to defendant. Plaintiff failed to provide defendant with adequate assurance of its future performance. Official UCC Comment 4 states that what constitutes "adequate" assurance of due performance is subject to the same test of factual conditions as what constitutes "reasonable grounds for insecurity." For example, where the buyer can make use of a defective delivery, a mere promise by a seller of good repute that he is giving the matter his attention and that the defect will not be repeated, is normally sufficient. Under the same circumstances, however, a similar statement by a known corner-cutter might well be considered insufficient without the posting of a guaranty or, if so demanded by the buyer, a speedy replacement of the delivery involved. By the same token where a delivery has defects, even though easily curable, which interfere with easy use by the buyer, no verbal assurance can be deemed adequate which is not accomplished by replacement, repair, money-allowance, or other commercially reasonable cure.

Plaintiff's continual excuses for failure to perform, unaccompanied by corresponding remedial action, cannot be deemed adequate assurance under the Code. Accordingly, defendant was entitled to suspend its own performance of the contract by refusing to place orders with plaintiff and/or canceling unfilled orders already placed, thirty days after either or both the September 18, 1986, and October 15, 1986, letters. In view of this conclusion, defendant did not breach the contract by suspending performance in December, 1986, and judgment will be entered in its favor.

Judgment for defendant.

Case A.17

Toys "R" Us, Inc. v. Abir,

1999 WL 61817 (1999)
United States District Court, S.D. New York
Koeltl, Judge

In 1997, plaintiff Toys "R" Us, Inc., filed an action alleging violations of federal law related to trademark dilution against the defendants, Eli Abir and Website Management, who had registered the name *Toysareus.com* as their Internet domain name. The plaintiffs alleged that this domain name diluted the plaintiff's mark TOYS "R" US. In November 1997, this court issued a temporary restraining order enjoining the defendants from "using or inducing others to use the names or marks or any colorable imitation of Plaintiff's TOYS "R" US, KIDS "R" US, BABIES "R" US and/or the family of "R" US marks" pending a decision on the plaintiff's motion for a preliminary injunction.

In December 1997, this court heard argument on the motion for a preliminary injunction. At that time the plaintiffs alleged that the defendants had also registered the domain name *Kidsareus.com*. This court then issued a prelimi-

nary injunction enjoining the defendants from, among other things, using or inducing others to use any colorable imitation of the family of "R" US marks pending final judgment. On August 27, 1998, this court granted the plaintiff's motion for summary judgment on the trademark dilution claims. The following day, the court issued a separate Judgment and Order permanently enjoining the defendants from further infringement of the family of "R" US marks and ordering the transfer of the *Toysareus.com* and *Kidsareus.com* Internet domain names to the plaintiff.

In addition, this court held that because the defendants' conduct in this case was willful, intentional, deliberate, and in bad faith, the plaintiff is entitled to recover attorneys' fees and costs. In order to determine what constitutes "reasonable" attorneys' fees, the starting point is the "lodestar amount," which is the number of hours reasonably expended on the litigation multiplied by a reasonable hourly rate for attorneys and paralegals.

In determining a reasonable hourly rate, courts consider, inter alia, the size and experience of the firm. In this case, Darby & Darby is a well-known New York firm which specializes in intellectual property; the rates charged for its attorneys are comparable to other specialized intellectual property firms in the New York City legal market. The plaintiff's counsel swore in her declaration in support of this application that care was taken to enhance efficiency by assigning, at any one time, only one partner, one mid- to senior-level associate, one to two junior associates, and one to two legal assistants to the prosecution of this case. Having carefully reviewed the itemized request for disbursements, the court finds them neither unnecessary nor excessive for a case of this duration and complexity. The plaintiff is also entitled to costs, as well as those reasonable out-of-pocket expenses incurred by the attorneys and which are normally charged fee-paying clients.

Defendant Eli Abir, who is the owner of defendant Website Management, does not argue that the award requested by the plaintiffs is excessive. Instead, he argues that due to his business and personal circumstances he has limited financial resources and would be unable to pay more than a "symbolic" amount in attorneys' fees. However, nothing in the record in this case justifies a financially based reduction in the award of attorneys' fees and costs. For the reasons stated above, the plaintiff's motion for attorneys' fees and costs is granted in the amount of $55,162.76. SO ORDERED.

Case A.18

Johnson v. Chicago Pneumatic Tool Co.

607 So. 2d 615 (1992)
Court of Appeals of Louisiana
Crain, Judge

This is a products liability action in which William H. Johnson was injured in the course of his employment when a pipejack was accidentally propelled toward Johnson striking him in the back and pinning him between the edge of a large diameter pie which he was grinding and the pipejack. A pipejack is a large mechanical device which is inserted into large pipes which are in the process of being joined together. The pipejack applies pressure forcing the joints into an evenly rounded shape which can then be welded together. The movement of the pipejack was controlled by an air winch manufactured by Chicago Pneumatic Tool Company (Chicago Pneumatic) which had been utilized and incorporated by McDermott, Inc., Johnson's employer, into a system dedicated to the fitting or joining of large-diameter pipe. The accident occurred at the McDermott shipyard when a co-employee either tossed or laid a 50-gallon drum on the ground near the winch in the area where Johnson was working. The drum rolled and toppled over onto the winch throttle pushing the throttle downward which in turn activated the winch and caused the pipejack to move toward Johnson.

Johnson instituted this action against Chicago Pneumatic as manufacturer of the winch, alleging that the winch as designed and manufactured was unreasonably dangerous to normal use. McDermott intervened in this action. After trial on the merits, the jury rendered a special verdict in favor of defendant.

It is uncontroverted that at the time of the accident Johnson was working with his back to the pipejack and the winch; the winch was not being manually operated; and no one was standing at or adjacent to the winch controls. The clutch lever had previously been welded down by McDermott and as a result the clutch remained permanently engaged. Of the other winch controls, the throttle was set in the neutral position and neither the brake nor the safety lock was engaged.

In order to prevail in a products liability action a plaintiff must prove that his damage was a result of a condition of the product which made the product unreasonably dangerous to normal use. The "normal use" of a product encompasses all intended or foreseeable uses and misuses of the product. A manufacturer is obliged to adequately warn the user of any danger inherent in the normal use of the product which is not within the knowledge of or obvious to the normal user. The manufacture is also required to anticipate the environment in which the product will be used and to notify the user of the potential risks arising from foreseeable use or misuse in the foreseeable environment.

The finding of the jury that the winch was not employed in normal use at the time of the accident is a factual determination which should not be set aside unless clearly wrong. A review of the record reveals that McDermott modified the winch by permanently engaging the clutch; that this modification permanently removed one of the safety and control features designed for its safe and proper operation; the disengagement of the clutch without the engagement of the additional safety features would have prevented the accident; the basic safety mechanisms of the winch were not utilized; the winch was installed backwards, thereby requiring the operator to stand away from the controls; and the employees/operators were uninformed regarding familiarity with the controls and proper operation of the winch. After careful review of the record we conclude that the jury's determination in this matter is not manifestly erroneous.

AFFIRMED.

Case A.19

Federal Deposit Insurance Corporation v. Woodside Construction, Inc.,

979 F.2d 172 (1992)
United States Court of Appeals for the Ninth Circuit
Hug, Circuit Judge

This case arose when Donald Galt signed a deed of trust note twice and signed a contract of guaranty twice. The FDIC claims that Galt is liable for $912,000, first because he signed the note as an indorser or, alternatively, because he signed the contract of guaranty as a guarantor. Galt claims that all of his signatures were in a representative capacity and that he did not sign individually as an indorser or as a guarantor. The FDIC maintains that one of the signatures on the note and one of the signatures on the contract of guaranty were signed in Galt's individual capacity, making him liable as an indorser on the note or, alternatively, as a guarantor on the contract of guaranty. The district court granted summary judgment for Galt on both the indorsement issue and the guaranty issue.

Galt obtained a loan from Alaska Mutual Bank for $912,000 on behalf of Woodside Construction of which he was an officer. The loan was evidenced by a promissory note, a deed of trust, a loan agreement, and a contract of guaranty. The signatures appeared on the note as follows:

> *(signature of Galt)*
> *Woodside Construction, Inc.*
> *signature(s)*
> *(signature of Galt)*
> *Donald A. Galt, President*

The contract of guaranty appears on the form as follows:

> *Woodside Construction, Inc.*
> *(signature of Galt)*
> *by Donald A. Galt*
> *Title Vice President*
> *by (signature of Galt)*
> *Title*
> *Guarantors:*
> *Guarantor*
> *Donald A. Galt*

As can be seen, the note bore Galt's signature below the name of the corporation, on the line designating his representative capacity as president. It also bore Galt's signature above the name of the corporation with no representative capacity designated.

The contract of guaranty bore Galt's signature below the name of the corporation, on the line designating his representative capacity, and then bore his signature on a line where no representative capacity was indicated. He did not sign on the line designated for his signature as guarantor.

Alaska National Bank merged with two other banks and became Alliance Bank, which retained this Woodside obligation. The loan was declared to be in default, and Alliance Bank instituted this action in state court. Alliance Bank was closed by the Alaska Department of Commerce and Economic Development, and the FDIC was appointed receiver. This Woodside obligation was sold by FDIC, as receiver, to FDIC in its corporate capacity. The FDIC then removed this case to federal court. The district court entered summary judgment for the FDIC against Woodside Construction on the note but entered summary judgment for Galt against the FDIC. The FDIC appeals the judgment rendered for Galt.

The manner in which Galt signed the promissory note bound him as an indorser in his individual capacity. He signed the note under the corporate name with the designation of his representative capacity. He also signed the note above the corporate name with no designation of any representative capacity. It is this latter signature that creates Galt's liability.

UCC Sec. 3-403(2) provides:

An authorized representative who signs his own name to an instrument:

(a) is personally obligated if the instrument neither names the person represented nor shows that the representative signed in a representative capacity:

(b) except as otherwise established between the immediate parties, is personally obligated if the Instrument names the person represented but does not show that the representative signed in a representative capacity, or if the instrument does not name the person represented but does show that the representative signed in a representative capacity.

Here, the first signature above the principal designation fails to indicate the representative capacity, and the second signature above the representative capacity fails to indicate the principal. Because the FDIC is the holder of the note here, parol evidence of intent is inadmissible, and Galt is personally liable.

The FDIC argues that Galt is liable for attorneys' fees. The note makes the indorser liable for the costs of collection, including attorneys' fees. Because we hold that Galt is the indorser, he is liable for attorneys' fees.

The judgment is REVERSED.

Case A.20
Kedzie & 103rd Currency Exchange, Inc. v. Hodge,

601 N.E.2d 803 (Ill. App. I Dist. [1921])
Appellate Court of Illinois
Linn, Justice

Plaintiff, Kedzie & 103rd Street Currency Exchange, Inc., cashed a check for defendant Fred Fentress (who is not a party to this appeal). Defendant Beula M. Hodge, drawer of the check, notified her bank to stop payment on the check when Fentress, engaged to perform plumbing services, did not appear at her home to begin work. As a holder in due course, plaintiff sought damages from Hodge. The trial court, however, granted Hodge's motion to dismiss based on the defense of illegality.

Plaintiff states the issue as whether a holder in due course of a check takes the check free from the defense of illegality where the drawer of the check issued it as a partial advance payment for plumbing services to be rendered, but the payee was not licensed as a plumber.

Background
Plaintiff, an Illinois corporation doing business as a currency exchange, filed suit after the $500 check it had cashed for Fentress was returned marked "payment stopped." Hodge had made out the check to "Fred Fentress—A-OK Plumbing" as partial payment, in advance for plumbing services at her residence. When he failed to appear on the date work was to begin, Hodge directed her bank to stop payment on the check. Fentress, in the meantime, cashed the check at plaintiff currency exchange, indorsing the back as "Fred Fentress A-OK Plumbing Sole Owner." Plaintiff obtained a default judgment against Fentress.

Hodge filed a motion to dismiss the action as to her, asserting the defense of illegality. She had discovered that Fentress was not a licensed plumber listed with either the state or Chicago. Under An Act in Relation to the Licensing and Regulation of Plumbers (Plumber's Licensing Act), plumbers must obtain a license before practicing their trade. A violation of the act is a Class B misdemeanor for the first offense. According to Hodge, the plumbing contract was illegal and void; therefore, plaintiff took the check subject to the illegality defense. The trial court agreed and entered judgment in favor of Hodge.

Opinion
Under the Uniform Commercial Code (UCC), commercial instruments including checks are meant to be freely negotiable, and to that end a holder in due course will take the instrument free from "all defenses of any party to the instrument with whom the holder has not dealt except such incapacity, or duress, or illegality of the transaction, as renders the obligation of the party a nullity."

Comment 6 to UCC Sec. 3-305 explains that the question of illegality is a matter of state law and if under the law governing the contract the effect of the illegality is to make the obligation entirely null and void, the defense is good.

The dispositive issue before us, therefore, is whether under Illinois law the contract between Hodge and the plumber was null and void. If so, the defense of illegality was properly asserted and applied in this case. If the underlying obligation was merely voidable, however, the defense fails.

The Illinois legislature, by adopting Sec. 3-305 of the UCC, has expressly declared that illegality is an available defense against a holder in due course, as long as the effect of the illegality is to render the obligation sued upon null and void.

Illinois courts should not apply the illegality defense against holders in due course unless the illegal transaction is of the type that wholly nullifies the contract and thereby renders the instrument subject to the illegality defense.

In this state, the legislature has passed extensive legislation relating to the licensing of many trades and professions, recognizing that the regulation of these professions is essential to the public health, safety and welfare. In furtherance of the legislative goals of providing standards and protecting the public health, the Plumber's Licensing Act provides that one who attempts to practice plumbing without a license may suffer substantial penalties, including criminal prosecution and fines. By judicial construction, the unlicensed plumber also forfeits his right to compensation for illegal services rendered. The contract in question is not void unless the Plumber's Licensing Act or other legislation expressly declares it to be.

As a matter of policy, plaintiff argues that it is unfair to expect a currency exchange to police the negotiable instruments it receives to ferret out possible illegalities in the underlying contracts. While the argument is reasonable enough, the same could be made for all of the defenses which defeat the rights of holders in due course. The currency exchange does not have a way to ascertain if a check has been drafted under duress, if it represents a gambling debt, or if it is the check of one without legal capacity to be bound. The so-called "real" defenses are nonetheless valid and cut off the rights of the innocent holder of the instrument to obtain recourse against makers or endorsers of the instrument in question. Currency exchanges are in the business of cashing checks and undertake the attendant risks.

We conclude that the illegality defense asserted in this case is of the type to render the obligation a nullity under Sec. 3-305 of the Code. Therefore, we affirm the trial court's dismissal of the action against Hodge, as maker of the check.

AFFIRMED.

Case A.21

First American Bank and Trust v. Rishoi,

553 So.2d 1387 (Fla. App. 5 Dist. 1990)
District Court of Appeals of Florida
Daniel, Chief Judge

First American Bank and Trust appeals a summary judgment in favor of William M. Rishoi as receiver for Clara Lamstein and the business she operated under the name of Interamerican Business Consultants and Associates, Inc.

In *Crosby v. Lewis*, the Crosbys had purchased $180,000 in cashier's checks, payable to Lamstein, from various banks and financial institutions. The checks were all delivered to Lamstein as investments. Lamstein's business was later closed down by the state on the ground that it was an illegal "ponzi" or pyramiding scheme. The assets of the business were placed in the control of Rishoi as receiver. Eighty thousand dollars of the cashier's checks from the Crosbys had been cashed and deposited by Lamstein prior to the receivership. However, $100,000 in cashier's checks remained uncashed in Lamstein's possession. The Crosby's requested that the banks not pay the cashier's checks. The banks issued stop payment orders on the outstanding cashier's checks and subsequently dishonored the checks when presented by the receiver for payment.

Although the issuing banks were not parties to that action, this court stated:

The banks which issued the cashier's checks are primarily liable to the receiver, and by refusing to honor the checks, they have prima facie violated the duties imposed on them.

Rishoi thereafter instituted suit against First American Bank and Trust claiming that the bank had improperly refused to honor the cashier's checks. The court below concluded that the bank had no right to stop payment on the cashier's checks and entered summary judgment in favor of Rishoi.

On appeal, the bank argues that Rishoi is not a holder in due course and therefore it was justified in refusing to honor the cashier's checks. The bank acknowledges that a cashier's check presented by a holder in due course may not be countermanded after issue. It also acknowledges that cashier's checks are treated as the next best thing to cash in the business community. On public policy grounds, however, the bank urges that it should be able to assist its customers by stopping payment on a cashier's check which has been obtained from a customer by a criminal act.

Warren Finance, Inc. v. Barnett Bank of Jacksonville, N.A., 552 So.2d 194 (Fla. 1989), the Florida Supreme Court recently held that, in accordance with common commercial practice and the use of a cashier's check as a cash substitute, any defenses which a bank may assert to avoid payment must be narrowly limited. The court concluded that, upon presentment for payment by a holder, a bank may only assert its real and personal defenses in order to refuse payment on a cashier's check issued by the bank. The bank may not, however, rely on a third party's defenses to refuse payment. The only inquiry a bank may make on presentment of a cashier's check is whether the payee or indorsee is in fact a legitimate holder, that is, whether the cashier's check is being presented by a thief or one who simply found a lost check, or whether the check has been materially altered. The court concluded that this approach maintains the validity and use of cashier's checks yet acknowledges the valid concerns of banks.

In the present case, the receiver was a legitimate holder and the bank had no real or personal defenses to assert against his claim for payment. Thus, the bank wrongfully dishonored its own obligation and is liable for payment. Accordingly, the trial court properly entered summary judgment in favor of the receiver.

AFFIRMED.

Case A.22

General Motors Acceptance Corporation v. Daniels,

492 A.2d 1306 (1985)
Cole, Judge

In June 1981, John Daniels agreed to purchase a used automobile from Lindsay Cadillac Company (Lindsay Cadillac). Because John had a poor credit rating, his brother, Seymoure, agreed to cosign the installment sales contract. On June 23, 1981, Seymoure accompanied John to Lindsay Cadillac. John signed the contract on the line designated "Buyer." Seymoure signed the contract on the line designated the contract to General Motors Acceptance Corporation (GMAC), a company engaged in the business of financing automobiles. In May 1982, GMAC declared the contract in default. GMAC did not immediately notify Seymoure of the default or that physical damage insurance on the car had lapsed. After attempting to locate the automobile for several months, GMAC brought this action against the Daniel brothers in Maryland court. Because service of process was never effected upon John, the case proceeded to trial against only Seymoure. The trial court held in favor of Seymoure. The appellate court affirmed. GMAC appeals.

Maryland law has consistently maintained a distinction between a contract of suretyship and a contract of guaranty. A review of the distinguishing characteristics of these contracts provides a useful predicate to the resolution to the issue presented in this case.

Suretyship

A contract of suretyship is a tripartite agreement among a principal obligor, his obligee, and a surety. This contract is a direct and original undertaking under which the surety is primarily or jointly liable with the principal obligor, and therefore is responsible at once if the principal obligor fails to perform. A surety is usually bound with his principal by the same instrument, executed at the same time, and on the same consideration. Ultimate liability rests upon the principal obligor rather than the surety, but the obligee has remedy against both. With respect to notice of default, the surety is ordinarily held to know every default of his principal because he is under a duty to make inquiry and ascertain whether the principal obligor is discharging the obligation resting on him. It is generally not necessary for the creditor to notify the surety of the fact that the principal debtor is in default on his promise. It is the duty of surety to the creditor to see that the debt is paid. Consequently, the surety is ordinarily liable without notice.

Guaranty

A contract of guaranty, similar to a contract of suretyship, is an accessory contract. Despite this similarity, a contract of guaranty has several distinguishing characteristics. First, this particular contract is collateral to and independent of the principal contract that is guaranteed and, as a result, the guarantor is not a party to the principal obligation. A guarantor is therefore secondarily liable to the creditor on his contract, and his promise to answer for the debt, default, or miscarriage of another becomes absolute upon default of the principal debtor and the satisfaction of the conditions precedent to liability. Second, the original contract of the principal is not the guarantor's contract, and the guarantor is not bound to take notice of its nonperformance. Rather, the guarantor insures the ability or solvency of the principal. In sum, the guarantor promises to perform if the principal does not. By contrast, a surety promises to do the same thing that the principal undertakes.

Case Sub Justice

With the distinctions between a contract of suretyship and contract of guaranty in mind, we turn to the case sub justice. Our review of the evidence in this case convinces us that the trial court erred in finding that Seymoure was a guarantor rather than a surety with respect to the installment sales contract. In our judgment the indicia for determining whether a contract is one for suretyship or one for guaranty all point to the existence of a suretyship agreement.

Initially, we note that because the contractual language is clear and unambiguous on its face, we confine our review to the contract itself. Seymoure agreed to purchase the subject automobile by affixing his signature to the installment sales contract on the line designated "Co-buyer." The contract clearly stated that all buyers agreed to be jointly and severally liable for the purchase of that vehicle. Therefore, under the objective law of contracts, a reasonable person knew or should have known that he was subjecting himself to primary liability for the purchase of the automobile. In short, although uncompensated sureties are favorites of the law, Seymoure's careless indifference does not insulate him from primary liability on that agreement.

Seymoure executed on the same contract as his brother, thereby making himself a party to the original contract. There is no evidence that Seymoure executed an agreement collateral to and independent of this contract. This fact, standing alone, ordinarily negates the existence of a guaranty. Both Seymoure and John signed the contract at the same time. Although not dispositive, this fact tends to establish the existence of a contract of suretyship rather than a contract of guaranty. Finally, on the facts of this case, it is immaterial that the contract did not expressly designate Seymoure as a "surety." Whether a party has entered into a contract of suretyship or guaranty is to be determined by the substance of the agreement and not by its nomenclature.

We hold that Seymoure signed a contract of suretyship and thus agreed to be primarily and jointly liable with his brother John for the purchase of the automobile. GMAC was therefore not required to notify Seymoure promptly of the default in payments or to proceed against John in the first instance. Accordingly, for the reasons stated earlier, we REVERSE.

Case A.23
Dewsnup v. Timm,

116 L.Ed. 2d 903, 112 S. Ct. 773 (1992)
Supreme Court of the United States
Blackmun, Justice

We are confronted in this case with an issue concerning §506(d) of the Bankruptcy Code. May a debtor "strip down" a creditor's lien on real property to the value of the collateral, as judicially determined, when that value is less than the amount of the claim secured by the lien?

On June 1, 1978, respondents loaned $119,000 to petitioner Aletha Dewsnup and her husband, T. LaMar Dewsnup, since deceased. The loan was accompanied by a Deed of Trust granting a lien on two parcels of Utah farmland owned by the Dewsnups. Petitioner defaulted the following year. Under the terms of the Deed of Trust, respondents at that point could have proceeded against the real property collateral by accelerating the maturity of the loan, issuing a notice of default, and selling the land at a public foreclosure sale to satisfy the debt.

Respondents did issue a notice of default in 1981. Before the foreclosure sale took place, however, petitioner sought reorganization under Chapter 11 of the Bankruptcy Code. That bankruptcy petition was dismissed, as was a subsequent Chapter 11 petition. In June 1984, petitioner filed a petition seeking liquidation under Chapter 7 of the Code. Because of the pendency of these bankruptcy proceedings, respondents were not able to proceed to the foreclosure sale.

Petitioner-debtor takes the position that §506(a) and §506(d) are complementary and to be read together. Because, under §506(a), a claim is secured only to the extent of the judicially determined value of the real property on which the lien is fixed, a debtor can void a lien on the property pursuant to §506(d) to the extent the claim is no longer secured and thus is not "an allowed secured claim." In other words, §506(a) bifurcates classes of claims allowed under §502 into secured claims and unsecured claims; any portion of an allowed claim deemed to be unsecured under §506(a) is not an "allowed secured claim" within the lien-voiding scope of §506(d). Petition argues that there is no exception for unsecured property, abandoned by the trustee.

We conclude that respondents' alternative position, espoused also by the United States, although not without its difficulty, generally is the best of the several approaches. Therefore, we hold that §506(d) does not allow petitioner to "strip down" respondents' lien, because respondents' claim is secured by a lien and has been fully allowed pursuant to §502.

The practical effect of petitioner's argument is to freeze the creditor's secured interest at the judicially determined valuation. By this approach, the creditor would lose the benefit of any increase in the value of the property by the time of the foreclosure sale. The increase would accrue to the benefit of the debtor, a result some of the parties describe as a "windfall."

We think, however, that the creditor's lien stays with the real property until the foreclosure. That is what was bargained for by the mortgagor and the mortgagee. Any increase over the judicially determined valuation during bankruptcy rightly accrues to the benefit of the creditor, not to the benefit of the debtor and not to the benefit of other unsecured creditors whose claims have been allowed and who had nothing to do with the mortgagor–mortgagee bargain.

No provision of the pre-Code statute permitted involuntary reduction of the amount of a creditor's lien for any reason other than payment on the debt.

The judgment of the court of appeals is AFFIRMED.

Case A.24
District of Columbia v. Howell,

607 A.2d 501 (D.C. Pap. 1992)
District of Columbia Court of Appeals
Farrell, Associate Judge

The Murch School Summer Discovery Program was designed to provide hands-on education for gifted and talented eight- and nine-year-old children. The program originated in 1985 when Mrs. Gill, the Murch School principal, attended a reception at Mount Vernon College arranged by Greg Butta, a Ph.D. candidate at The American University, to advertise the success of a summer program he had conducted at Mount Vernon. The program interested Mrs. Gill, and after several discussions, Butta sent her a formal proposal for conducting a similar program at the Murch School. Gill made changes to the proposal, then solicited and received approval for the program from the Assistant Superintendent for the District of Columbia Public Schools.

Butta hired the staff for the summer program, including some of the instructors who had taught in the Mount Vernon program. Mrs. Gill, however, reviewed all of the instructors' resumes, had veto authority over their hiring, and interviewed most of the staff, including A. Louis Jagoe, before the hiring was made final. Jagoe, who was hired to teach chemistry to the eight- and nine-year-olds in the program, held a master's degree in chemistry and was a Ph.D. candidate at The American University. Before the first general staff meeting, he told Butta that as part of the class he would do a luminescence experiment and a "cold-pack" experiment and wanted to make sparklers with the children. Jago and Butta discussed the safety of the sparker experiment only in regard to the location where the children would be allowed to light the sparklers.

On August 1, 1985, a staff meeting was held at which Gill, Butta, and all instructors and counselors were present. Each instructor gave a brief talk about what he or she intended to do in class. Several instructors testified that Jagoe told the group, including Mrs. Gill, that he planned to make sparklers as one of the chemistry experiments. Gill, who was in and out of the meeting, did not remember hearing Jagoe discuss the experiment, although notes she took at the meeting reflect that she heard him discuss the luminescence and cold pack experiments and asked him questions about these. Gill spoke and emphasized the "hands-on" nature of the program and her hopes for its success.

One child attending the program was nine-year-old Dedrick Howell, whose parents enrolled him after receiving the school brochure in the mail. The accident occurred on August 12, 1985. At the beginning of the chemistry class, Jagoe distributed his "recipe" for sparklers to the children and also wrote it on the blackboard. Along with other chemical ingredients, the recipe called for the use of potassium perchlorate as the oxidizing agent. Potassium perchlorate was described at trial as an extremely unstable and highly volatile chemical often used to make rocket fuel. Commercially made sparklers are not made with potassium perchlorate.

The children scooped the chemicals, including the potassium perchlorate, out of jars and, using pestles, ground up the mixture in mortars. While they were combining the chemicals, Jagoe ignited three different chemical mixtures at the front of the room with a butane lighter. Butta was present for one of the ignitions when he entered the room to drop off metal hangers for use in the experiment. Mrs. Gill also entered the room at one point, and saw the children working at tables wearing goggles or glasses. She also saw Jagoe at the front of the room lighting the chemicals with a fire extinguisher on the table next to him.

The children continued to grind the material while a counselor, Rebecca Seashore, distributed pieces of metal hangers to be dipped into the mixture at a later time. Dedrick Howell was specifically told not to dip the hanger into the material until instructed to do so. Moments later the chemicals exploded in front of Dedrick. The chemicals burned at 5000 degrees Fahrenheit, and Dedrick was burned over 25 percent of his body including his hands, arms, chest, and face.

An employer generally is not liable for injuries to third parties caused by an independent contractor over whom (or over whose work) the employer has reserved no control. There are exceptions to the rule, however, one of which is that one who employs an independent contractor to do work involving a special danger to others which the employer knows or has reason to know to be inherent in or normal to the work, or which he contemplates or has reason to contemplate when making the contract, is subject to liability for physical harm caused to such others by the contractor's failure to take reasonable precautions against such danger.

It is sufficient that work of any kind involves a risk, recognizable in advance, of physical harm to others which is inherent in the work itself, or normally to be expected in the ordinary course of the usual or prescribed way of doing it, or that the employer has special reason to contemplate such a risk *under the particular circumstances under which the work is to be done.*

The sparkler experiment combined flammable, combustible chemicals, open flames, and children; for that very reason, presumably, the children had been equipped with goggles. Though sparklers are explosives of a lesser order, conducting controlled explosions is a textbook example of an inherently dangerous activity. It was not unreasonable for the jury to conclude that the manufacture of sparklers by nine-year-old children was an inherently dangerous activity.

Therefore, the jury was well within its authority in finding that Jagoe was an independent contractor performing inherently dangerous work of which the district had actual or constructive knowledge.

The judgment is AFFIRMED as to liability and as to the award of $8 million in damages both for pain and suffering and for past medical expenses.

Case A.25

Catalina Mortgage Co., Inc. v. Monier,

166 Ariz. 71, 800 P.2d 574 (1990)
Supreme Court of Arizona
Feldman, Vice Chief Judge

In 1984, Michael Monier and Talon Financial Corporation (Talon) formed the Coronado Partnership (Coronado). Monier and Talon were general partners; other individuals and entities were limited partners in the venture.

Shortly after its formation, Coronado purchased an office and warehouse complex in Tucson. In 1986, the partnership refinanced this property with a loan from Catalina Mortgage Company (Catalina). Talon's president, Roger Howard, executed a promissory note in the amount of $675,000 on behalf

of Coronado. In mid-1987, Talon withdrew as a general partner, leaving Monier as the sole general partner in Coronado. The promissory note matured and $687,935 plus interest is now due and owing. Coronado filed for protection pursuant to Chapter 11 of the Bankruptcy Code.

In January 1989, Catalina filed a complaint against Monier in United States District Court, seeking judgment for the amount due on the promissory note plus interest, costs, and attorneys' fees. Catalina alleged that Monier was jointly and severally liable with the partnership entity for the debt. Monier answered, contending, among other things, that because the note was an obligation of the partnership, the partnership assets had to be exhausted before the creditor sought recovery from an individual general partner.

Discussion

If a partnership's debt is contractual in nature, common law requires creditors to resort to and exhaust partnership assets before reaching the partners' individual assets. At common law, a partner is only jointly liable for the partnership's contractual debts, though partners are jointly and severally liable for tort obligations.

As adopted in most states, the Uniform Partnership Act (UPA) preserves this common law rule. The Arizona version of the UPA, however, provides that all partners are liable jointly and severally for everything chargeable to the partnership, and for all other debts and obligations of the partnership; but any partner may enter into a separate obligation to perform a partnership contract.

Catalina maintains that because the statute imposes joint and several liability on all partners, it may proceed against Monier without exhausting partnership assets. Catalina distinguishes cases from other jurisdictions that have considered the issue on the grounds that the applicable law imposed only joint liability as opposed to joint and several liability, that some states specifically provide by statute that partnership assets must be exhausted prior to imposing liability on individual partners for contractual obligations, and that the bankruptcy courts in some instances have misconstrued the state law involved.

Several liability is separate and distinct from liability of another to the extent that an independent action may be brought without joinder of others. The individual liability associated with partners that are jointly liable is not separate and distinct from the liability of all the partners jointly. Rather, that individual liability arises only after it has been shown that the partnership assets are inadequate. No direct cause of action may be maintained against the individual partners until the above condition is met. Several liability, on the other hand, imposes no such conditions precedent before one can be held individually liable.

Conclusion

We hold, therefore, that the scheme imposed by Arizona statutes is simply that a general partner is jointly and severally liable for partnership debts. The partner may be sued severally and his assets reached even though the partnership or other partners are not sued and their assets not applied to the debt. Under Arizona law a creditor may obtain a judgment against an individual general partner on a partnership debt and may reach the partner's assets prior to exhausting partnership assets.

Case A.26
Johnson v. Dodgen,

451 N.W.2d. 168 (1990)
Supreme Court of Iowa
Lavorato, Justice

This breach of contract action is the aftermath of a bank failure caused by the embezzlement of $16.7 million by Des Moines stockbroker Gary Lewellyn. In 1967, Joe W. Dodgen agreed to buy controlling interest in the First National Bank of Humboldt under a stock purchase agreement (agreement) calling for monthly payments. Ben P. and Adeline G. St. John, the sellers, died shortly thereafter. Two trusts were then established to receive payments under the agreement.

Dodgen assigned the agreement to his company, Humboldt Realty Insurance Co., Inc. (Humboldt Realty), which was not in existence at the time the agreement was executed, and underwent several name changes until it became known as Iowa Growthland Financial Corporation. After the bank was closed in 1982, Iowa Growthland continued to make payments under the agreement until 1984.

The trusts then sued Dodgen and Iowa Growthland for the payments that were in arrears. Dodgen and Iowa Growthland filed an answer in which they raised failure of consideration as an affirmative defense. Simply put, they were claiming that the consideration for the agreement failed when the bank went out of existence. In addition, Dodgen asserted that he was not personally liable because he signed the agreement as an agent for Humboldt Realty. In its counterclaim, Iowa Growthland sought damages on the theory of unjust enrichment for payments it made after the bank was closed. The case was tried to a jury. By way of answers to special verdict forms, the jury found that the trustees were not entitled to recover for breach of contract, that Dodgen was indeed acting as an agent when he signed the agreement, and that Iowa Growthland was not entitled to damages for its claim of unjust enrichment.

The district court granted new trial on all the issues. Dodgen and Iowa Growthland appealed; the trustees cross-appealed.

We reverse and remand with directions to enter judgment in favor of the trustees pursuant to Iowa Rule of Appellate Procedure 26.

I. Failure of Consideration

Dodgen and Iowa Growthland contend that the continued existence of the bank was the essence or root of the agreement—the thing Dodgen really bargained for. They argue that when the bank was closed the consideration for Dodgen's promise to pay failed. This failure of consideration, they assert, excused any future performance on their part. There is a difference between lack of consideration and failure of consideration. A lack of consideration means no contract is ever formed. In contrast, a failure of consideration means the contract is valid when formed but becomes unenforceable because the performance bargained for has not been rendered. In our view the potential failure of any business that is being sold is always a risk in the contemplation of the parties. If the buyer wants protection against the risk, the simple solution is to hedge against it in the agreement. That was not done here. Consequently, Dodgen assumed that risk.

What Dodgen bargained for was control of the bank through the stock he purchased; he got it and had it for fifteen years. The fact that his investment later turned out worthless does not, in our view, constitute failure of consideration.

A. Essence of the Agreement

Under the agreement here, Dodgen agreed to purchase from St. John 506 shares of capital stock of the bank. The 506 shares represented 50.6 percent of the issued and outstanding stock of the bank. By this purchase, Dodgen was acquiring controlling interest in the bank.

B. The Executory Nature of the Agreement

This issue is inextricable intertwined with the essence of the agreement issue. Dodgen and Iowa Growthland contend that the agreement was still executory when the bank was closed because the trustees had physical possession of the stock. While the trustees are still able to turn over the stock, Dodgen and Iowa Growthland argue such a gesture would be meaningless because the asset that the stock represents is nonexistent. So, they argue, there was a failure of consideration when the bank was closed.

Here we think the parties intended title to the stock to pass to Dodgen once the stock was registered in his name. At this point several things had occurred. Dodgen had made the down payment called for in the agreement and began exercising control of the bank. Likewise, St. John had substantially performed his part of the agreement. Only two promises remained unperformed: Dodgen's full payment of the purchase price and St. John's delivery of physical possession of the stock.

In these circumstances, we think there was a constructive delivery of the stock to Dodgen. Although the collateral provision of the agreement denied Dodgen physical possession of the stock, it did give him the right to such possession upon full payment. The provision also gave him rights of ownership in all other respects. Risk of loss passed with this constructive delivery. The decline in the stock's value gave Dodgen no greater right to avoid his obligation to pay than an enhanced value would have given St. John an excuse for not delivering the stock.

C. Inability to Pledge the Stock as Security

It is true that under the agreement Dodgen could not borrow against the stock. Dodgen and Iowa Growthland assert this constraint as further evidence that consideration for the agreement failed. The short answer to this argument is that Dodgen should not be allowed to take advantage of a provision he agreed to.

II. Unjust Enrichment

We have already determined that there was not, as a matter of law, a failure of consideration. In view of our holding on the failure of consideration issue, we think the district court should have sustained the trustees' motion for directed verdict on the unjust enrichment counterclaim.

III. Agency

The trustees moved for a directed verdict against Dodgen personally because the record showed he signed the agreement. Dodgen resisted the motion, contending there was enough evidence in the record to generate a jury question on his agency defense. The only evidence on this point was Dodgen's testimony. Dodgen testified that when he signed the agreement St. John agreed that Humboldt Realty—Iowa Growthland's precedessor—would be the responsible party. The district court overruled the motion. The jury then determined that Dodgen was acting as an agent for Humboldt Realty when he signed the agreement. For reasons that follow, we think the district court should have sustained the motion for directed verdict.

At the time Dodgen and St. John signed the agreement, Humboldt Realty was not in existence. Ordinarily, in these circumstances Dodgen would be personally liable. The law is clear that an agent who purports to act on behalf of a nonexistent principal is liable as a party to the agreement. The rationale for the rule is simply that in such circumstances there is no agency. This situation frequently happens when a corporate promoter enters into contracts before the corporation is actually incorporated. There is, however, an exception to this rule. If the other contracting party knows that the principal does not exist and looks to the principal alone for responsibility, the promoter is relieved of personal liability.

Here the pivotal question is whether St. John agreed to look to Humboldt Realty alone for payment. We think reasonable minds would conclude from this record that he did not. We have substantial evidence that establishes Dodgen was acting in his personal capacity. First, as the district court ruled, the language of the agreement is unequivocal on this point. For example, the opening paragraph states that "This agreement made and entered into by and between B. P. St. John and Joe W. Dodgen said B. P. St. John being hereafter referred to as the seller and the said Joe W. Dodgen being hereafter referred to as the buyer." Moreover, Dodgen ostensibly signed the agreement in his individual capacity.

Second, St. John and Dodgen were, at the time of the agreement, very knowledgeable in financial and legal matters. It is inconceivable to us that St. John would turn over valuable assets and look solely to a nonexistent corporation for payment. It is also equally inconceivable to us that Dodgen would fail to insist on express language in the agreement that would

relieve him of personal liability. Simply put, we think reasonable minds would conclude that the absence of such language meant that St. John was looking to Dodgen for payment, and Dodgen knew it.

Last, in 1982 Dodgen acknowledged his personal liability. In a letter to one of the trustees—a letter we previously mentioned—Dodgen said:

> You are also correct in that the contract between me and Ben and Adeline St. John is a personal obligation even though it was later assigned to First Investors Services, Inc.

This damaging admission coupled with the other evidence leads us to conclude that the district court should have sustained the motion for directed verdict on the agency issue.

IV. Disposition

We reverse the posttrial ruling of the district court. We remand the case to the district court with directions to enter judgment in favor of the trustees for $160,976—the delinquent amount at the time of the trial—together with interest and costs.

Case A.27
United States v. WRW Corporation,

986 F.2d 138 (1993)
United States Court of Appeals for the Sixth Circuit
Peck, Judge

In 1985, civil penalties totaling $90,350 were assessed against WRW Corporation (WRW), a Kentucky corporation, for serious violations of safety standards under the Federal Mine Safety and Health Act (the Act) which resulted in the deaths of two miners. Following the imposition of civil penalties, WRW liquidated its assets and went out of business.

Three individual defendants, who were the sole shareholders, officers, and directors of WRW, were later indicted and convicted for willful violations of mandatory health and safety standards under the Act. Roger Richardson, Noah Woolum, and William Woolum each served prison sentences and paid criminal fines. After his release from prison, Roger Richardson filed for bankruptcy under Chapter 7 of the Bankruptcy Code.

The United States (the Government) brought this action in May of 1988 against WRW and Roger Richardson, Noah Woolum, and William Woolum to recover the civil penalties previously imposed against WRW. The district court denied the individual defendants' motion to dismiss and granted summary judgment to the Government piercing the corporate veil under state law and holding the individual defendants liable for the civil penalties assessed against WRW. For the reasons discussed herein, we affirm.

Piercing the Corporate Veil

Having determined that the imposition of a $90,350 sanction upon the defendants does not violate principles of double jeopardy, we turn to the defendants' argument that the district court erred in holding the individual defendants liable for the penalty by piercing the corporate veil of WRW under Kentucky law.

The district court held that it was appropriate to pierce WRW's corporate veil under either an equity theory or an alter ego theory, both of which are recognized under Kentucky law. Under either theory, the following factors must be considered when determining whether to pierce the corporate veil: (1) undercapitalization; (2) a failure to observe the formalities of corporate existence; (3) nonpayment or overpayment of dividends; (4) a siphoning off of funds by dominant shareholders; and (5) the majority shareholders having guaranteed corporate liabilities in their individual capacities.

The court first found that WRW was undercapitalized because it was incorporated with only $3,000 of capital, which the record indicates was insufficient to pay normal expenses associated with the operation of a coal mine. The district court next found that WRW failed to observe corporate formalities, noting that no bylaws were produced by the defendants, and all corporate actions taken by the individual defendants were without corporation authorization. Finally, although WRW never distributed any dividends to the individual defendants, and there was no evidence that the individual defendants siphoned off corporate funds, these factors alone do not mitigate against piercing the corporate veil in this case because WRW was never sufficiently capitalized and operated at a loss during its two years of active existence.

In addition to holding that the equities of this case support piercing the corporate veil, the district court held that the corporate veil should be pierced under the "alter ego" theory, because WRW and the defendants did not have separate personalities. In light of the lack of observance of corporate formalities or distinction between the individual defendants and the corporation, we agree with the district court's conclusion that "there was a complete merger of ownership and control of WRW with the individual Defendants."

The specific factual findings made by the district court amply support piercing the corporate veil of WRW and holding the individual defendants liable for the penalty assessed against the corporate entity. For all of the foregoing reasons, judgment of the district court is AFFIRMED.

Case A.28
Neal v. Alabama By-Products Corporation,

No. 8282, 1990. Del. Ch. Lexis 127 (1990)
Court of Chancery of Delaware
Chandler, Vice Chancellor

Alabama By-Products Corporation (ABC) is a Delaware corporation engaged, during the 1970s and 1980s (and for many years before that), primarily in three lines of business. It mined coal on a cost plus basis for Alabama Power Company (a major utility in Alabama); it mined coal for its own account from surface and underground mines that it owned, and it manufactured and sold foundry coke from a plant in Birmingham called the Tarrant plant. To a certain extent ABC was also engaged in the development and sale of timber and forestry products on lands it owned.

ABC's two classes of stock traded in the over-the-counter market and were not listed on an exchange. Trading history in the stock was sporadic, but shows that the average bid price between 1977 and 1984 ranged from $47 to $75 per share. Class A stock had voting rights, while class B did not. At all times relevant to this lawsuit, there were about 757,300 class A shares and 1 million class B shares authorized, issued, and outstanding.

Drummond, an Alabama Corporation, is also engaged in the mining and sale of coal in the state of Alabama. In 1977 it became interested in acquiring ABC. Between September 1977 and February 1978 Drummond acquired, in privately negotiated transactions, about 75,800 class A shares of ABC stock and 188,167 class B shares. Drummond also obtained a controlling interest in Alabama Chemical Products Company (ACPC), a holding company which at the time held 476,420 class A shares of ABC stock (about 63% of those outstanding). Drummond paid the equivalent of $110 per share of ABC stock in these transactions. The book value of ABC's common stock on December 31, 1977, was $55.47 per share. Drummond eventually caused the liquidation of ACPC, with the resulting distribution of the ABC class A stock to Drummond and other ACPC stockholders.

Drummond reconstituted ABC's board of directors in December 1977, replacing five of the nine ABC directors with Drummond designees. At all relevant times for purposes of this litigation, a majority of ABC's directors were also directors or executive officers of Drummond. Around the time that it gained control of ABC's board, Drummond created an executive committee consisting of Gary Neal Drummond, E. A. Drummond and the then current president of ABC. The executive committee had authority to act on behalf of ABC's board of directors. From its controller position, Drummond caused ABC to lease some of its coal reserves to Drummond. Drummond also purchased ABC mined coal and resold it in certain markets.

In late December 1977, Drummond presented a merger proposal to ABC's board, proposing the acquisition of all outstanding shares not owned by Drummond. This proposal was later withdrawn. Three years later, in 1981, Drummond discussed with Goldman, Sachs and Company (Goldman Sachs), its investment banker, the possibility of acquiring the remaining equity in ABC. Goldman Sachs recommended at the time that Drummond propose a cash merger at a minimum price of $85 per share. Nevertheless, Drummond decided not to pursue the acquisition at that time.

On March 17, 1983, Drummond again proposed a merger to ABC's board of directors, a proposal by which each share of ABC not owned by Drummond would have been converted into the right to receive $65 in cash and ABC would have become a wholly owned subsidiary of Drummond. A special committee of ABC's board of directors (consisting of three ABC directors who were not directors or executive officers of Drummond) recommended the retention of the firm of

Kidder, Peabody and Company, Inc. (Kidder Peabody), to evaluate the 1983 merger proposal and to determine whether it was fair to unaffiliated ABC shareholders from a financial point of view. Kidder Peabody's report, submitted in September 1983, concluded that Drummond's $65 cash merger offer was not fair to unaffiliated ABC shareholders from a financial point of view. Drummond's 1983 proposal was later withdrawn.

Drummond acquired additional shares of ABC class A and class B stock in 1984 for $54.40 and $55 per share, respectively. Although it was provided, in connection with the 1984 acquisitions, that additional payments would be made by Drummond if its board of directors formally approved a tender offer for shares or a merger with ABC within stipulated time limits, no tender offer or merger proposal was made during the time limits.

In December 1984, Drummond made a tender offer for any and all outstanding shares of class A and class B common stock of ABC at $75 per share. Neither Drummond nor ABC sought a fairness opinion from an independent investment banker or financial adviser with respect to the tender offer. Nor was a committee of outside ABC directors appointed to review or comment upon the fairness of the proposed transaction. ABC's board decided it would take no position with respect to the fairness of the tender offer price, leaving the ultimate determination to the judgment of the individual shareholder.

As a result of the tender offer, Drummond became the holder of more than 90 percent of ABC's outstanding and issued shares. Then, on August 13, 1985, Drummond effected a short-form merger under Delaware law, pursuant to which the minority shareholders were cashed out at $75.60 per share. This amount was determined by adopting the 1984 tender offer price ($75) and adding a 60-cent quarterly dividend that had been missed in 1985.

Following the August 13, 1985, merger, certain minority shareholders perfected their appraisal rights pursuant to §262 of Title 8 of the Delaware Code. These minority shareholders own approximately 50,000 class A shares and 75,000 class B shares. Neal characterizes this proceeding as a two-pronged action in which separate claims for appraisal and for unfair dealing have been joined. Drummond, as successor to ABC, is the only necessary and appropriate defendant, say petitioners, as to both the unfair dealing claim and the appraisals claim.

Neal argues they have avoided the risk of double recovery by limiting the relief requested for the unfair dealing claim to (1) costs of the proceeding, (2) reasonable attorneys fees and disbursements, and (3) expert witness fees incurred by petitioners as part of the appraisal claim.

Neal also accuses Drummond of postmerger unfair dealing, complaining that Drummond's defense of the $75.60 merger price is based on contrived liabilities and transparent efforts to ascribe negative values to certain ABC assets, all of which were not disclosed to shareholders at the time of the merger. These allegedly manipulative tactics, added to the unfair dealing associated with the notice of merger and merger price, form the basis for petitioners' unfair dealing claim and, they insist, warrant an award of litigation costs.

Neal challenges the fairness of the merger price, noting that it was fixed unilaterally by Drummond without the benefit of independent expert opinion as to its fairness. They also point out that no committee, special or otherwise, was appointed to review the fairness of the merger proposal, that the merger notice to stockholders failed to disclose certain allegedly material financial information, causing stockholders to make decisions with regard to accepting the merger price or seeking appraisal on the basis of very limited information about the assets and prospects of ABC.

Neal contends that ABC's fair value was $193.40 per share on August 13, 1985. That conclusion rests upon the testimony of their valuation expert, Mr. Kenneth McGraw, based on an analysis performed by Benchmark Valuation Consultants, a division of the accounting firm Peat Marwick Maine & Co. (Benchmark), which in turn was based in part on an analysis and valuation of ABC's coal reserves and coal mining operations by Dames & Moore, a firm with expertise in geologic, mining, and natural resource engineering.

McGraw testified that Benchmark valued ABC using three alternative methods: historical earnings, net asset value, and discounted cash flow. By the historical earnings approach, Benchmark arrived at a value of $166 per share of ABC stock. The net asset methodology resulted in a value of $205 per share. The discounted cash flow approach resulted in a valuation of $225 per share. Benchmark then applied a weighted average, assigning the greatest weight (40%) to the historical earnings and net asset value approaches and the lowest weight (20%) to the discounted cash flow methodology, to arrive at a valuation based on all three valuation methodologies of $193.40 per share.

Respondents assert that the merger price was fair. The merger price, in fact, was extremely generous, because respondents contend that ABC's statutory fair value is only $64 per share, more than $11 less than Drummond paid in the merger. Respondents' valuation is based upon the testimony of their expert trial witnesses, Arnold Spangler, a general partner at Lazard Freres & Co. (Lazard), and Robert Wilken of Paul Weir Company (Weir), who estimated the company's coal reserves.

Lazard's valuation appears to have been based on a hybrid discounted cash flow and net asset methodology. The analysis was designed to predict the value of future cash flows from ABC's continuing operations, including ABC-owned mines, power company mines, and the Tarrant coke plant, over a 13-year period from 1985 through 1997. This period corresponded to either the life of a variety of ABC's long-term contracts or to the exhaustion of its coal reserves, leaving only its Tarrant coke operation viable in 1997. Lazard arrived at a net after-tax cash flow that ABC's continuing operations were expected to generate from 1985 to 1997, to which Lazard applied a multiple of five against the 1997 projected net cash flow (the terminal value), arriving at a value for ABC's activities following the terminal year.

The contrasting opinions regarding ABC's value in August 1985 demonstrate how differently petitioners and respondents view the business prospect and asset valuations of ABC. These starkly contrasting views have been presented to the court through expert witnesses who have relied on complex business valuation methodologies. Although Benchmark relied on three different methodologies, there has been remarkably little disagreement over the illegitimacy of the valuation techniques used by the parties in this case. Dispute has been over the assumptions on which the methodologies have been based as well as the underlying information supplied to the experts. With expert opinions arrayed on each side of widely divergent arguments about the worth of certain assets, or the scope of certain liabilities, the court is forced to pick and choose among the competing contentions, in search of a reasonable, and fair, value. That is this court's mandate: determine the fair value of the stock of ABC on August 13, 1985.

Both sides have relied on a discounted future returns model and a net asset model, with petitioners' expert also using a historical earnings analysis. Other valuation approaches, with equivalent theoretical legitimacy, could have been used. But I am satisfied that respondents discounted future cash flow methodology is the appropriate valuation model in this case, especially since it was also used by petitioners' expert.

The more difficult task is to move beyond the analytical framework in order to test the underlying assumptions about ABC that the experts poured into the valuation models. This is the heart of the matter, for, as one commentator has noted, methods of valuation, including a discounted cash flow analysis, are only as good as the inputs to the model. A valuation methodology can produce a correct answer for any type of input. So, the relevant question is not how correct the resulting answer is, but how correct was the input or datum that produced the answer? Accordingly this court must view the assumptions and underlying factual premises for the valuation methodology actually used by both respondents and petitioners. Not every assumption need be scrutinized, however, for the parties have managed to agree, despite their best efforts, on certain assumptions and facts. Serious disputes exist in about eight different areas. The four principal areas of disagreement concern the value of ABC's coal reserves, the value of ABC's investment in the VP-5 mine in Virginia, the amount of ABC's excess working capital and, finally, the EME report on the purported environmental liability at ABC's Tarrant coke plant. The court is satisfied that respondents' discounted future cash flow methodology is the appropriate valuation model in this case, especially since it was also used by petitioners' expert.

The fair value of the petitioners' shares subject to the court's appraisal was $180.67 per share on August 13, 1985. Petitioners shall be entitled to simple interest upon that amount at a rate of 12-1/2 percent, payable from the date of the merger to the date of payment. The costs of this proceeding, other than expert witness costs and attorneys' fees, shall be assessed against the surviving corporation.

An Order consistent with this Memorandum Opinion has been entered.

Case A.29
Water, Waste & Land, Inc., dba Westec v. Lanham,
955 P.2d 997 (1998)
Supreme Court of Colorado
Scott, Justice

Water, Waste, & Land, Inc., the petitioner, is a land development and engineering company doing business under the name "Westec." At the time of the events in this case, Donald Lanham and Larry Clark were managers and also members of Preferred Income Investors, LLC (Company or P.I.I.). The Company is a limited liability company organized under the Colorado Limited Liability Company Act.

In March 1995, Clark contacted Westec about the possibility of hiring Westec to perform engineering work in connection with a development project, which involved the construction of a fast-food restaurant known as Taco Cabana. In the course of preliminary discussions, Clark gave his business card to representatives of Westec. The business card included Lanham's address, which was also the address listed as the Company's principal office and place of business in its articles of organization filed with the secretary of state. While the Company's name was not on the business card, the letters "P.I.I." appeared above the address on the card. However, there was no indication as to what the acronym meant or that P.I.I. was a limited liability company.

After further negotiations, an oral agreement was reached concerning Westec's involvement with the Company's restaurant project.

Although Westec never received a signed contract, in mid-August it did receive verbal authorization from Clark to begin work. Westec completed the engineering work and sent a bill for $9,183 to Lanham. No payments were made on the bill. Westec filed a claim against Clark and Lanham individually as well as against the Company. At trial, the Company admitted liability for the amount claimed by Westec.

Under the common law of agency, an agent is liable on a contract entered on behalf of a principal if the principal is not fully disclosed. In other words, an agent who negotiates a contract with a third party can be sued for any breach of the contract unless the agent discloses both the fact that he or she is acting on behalf of a principal and the identity of the principal. Westec did not know Clark was acting as an agent for the Company or that the letters "P.I.I." stood for "Preferred Income Investors," a limited liability company registered under Colorado law. Clark and Lanham failed to disclose the existence as well as the identity of the limited liability company they represented.

Section 7-80-208 of the Colorado Limited Liability Company Act (1997) states:

> The fact that the articles of organization are on file in the office of the secretary of state is notice that the limited liability company is a limited liability company and is notice of all other facts set forth therein which are required to be set forth in the articles of organization.

In order to relieve Lanham of liability, this provision would have to be read to establish a conclusive presumption that a third party who deals with the agent of a limited liability company always has constructive notice of the existence of the agent's principal. We are not persuaded that the statute can bear such an interpretation.

Such a construction exaggerates the plain meaning of the language in the statute. This broad interpretation would be an invitation to fraud, because it would leave the agent of a limited liability company free to mislead third parties into the belief that the agent would bear personal financial responsibility under any contract, when in fact, recovery would be limited to the assets of a limited liability company not known to the third party at the time the contract was made. This construction would open the door to sharp practices and outright fraud. We may presume that in adopting section 7-80-208, the General Assembly did not intend to create a safe harbor for deceit.

In sum, then, section 7-80-208 places third parties on constructive notice that a fully identified company—that is, identified by a name such as "Preferred Income Investors, LLC," or the like—is a limited liability company provided that its articles of organization have been filed with the secretary of state. Section 7-80-208 is of little force, however, in determining whether a limited liability company's agent is personally liable on the theory that the agent has failed to disclose the identity of the company.

If Clark or Lanham had told Westec's representatives that they were acting on behalf of an entity known as "Preferred Income Investors, LLC," the failure to disclose the fact that the entity was a limited liability company would be irrelevant by virtue of the statute, which provides that the articles of organization operate as constructive notice of the company's limited liability form. Lanham and Clark did not identify Preferred Income Investors, LLC, as the principal in the transaction. The "missing link" between the limited disclosure made by Clark and the protection of the notice statute was the failure to state that "P.I.I.," the Company, stood for "Preferred Income Investors, LLC."

We see no legal basis to excuse the agents of the LLC from liability and therefore we REVERSE the judgment of the district court that found them not liable.

Case A.30
Little v. Howard Johnson Co.,

183 Mich. App. 675
455 N.W. 2d 390 (1990)
Court of Appeals of Michigan
MacKenzie, Judge

Plaintiff Joy Little was injured on January 23, 1982, when she slipped on a walkway which allegedly had not been adequately cleared of ice and snow. The walkway was located on property on which a restaurant business was being operated as a franchise of defendant, Howard Johnson Company. Plaintiff filed suit alleging liability for her injuries. In district court Howard Johnson moved for summary disposition. The circuit court denied defendant's subsequent motion for summary

disposition and the case proceeded to mediation. When it mediated at less than $10,000, the case was removed to district court for lack of circuit court jurisdiction. The district court found no factual dispute and ruled as a matter of law that defendant was neither directly nor vicariously liable for plaintiff's injuries and, accordingly, granted the motion. The circuit court reversed without elaboration.

Little posited three theories under which she claimed Howard Johnson as a franchisor may be held liable for the injuries she sustained at the franchisee's restaurant: (1) direct liability as a possessor of the land, (2) vicarious liability based on agency principles, and (3) liability based on an apparent agency theory.

1. Direct Liability

The general rule in Michigan is that invitors are liable for known dangerous conditions of property and for dangerous conditions which might be discovered with reasonable care. However, an invitor's direct liability requires the presence of both possession and control over the land.

Little contends that defendant should be deemed a "possessor" of the land as a result of the rights of control it retained in its franchise agreement with the restaurant's franchisee. We disagree. The franchise agreement merely provides that the franchisee "at all times will maintain the interior and exterior of the building's and surrounding premises in a clean, orderly, and sanitary condition satisfactory to Howard Johnson." In short, there is no issue of fact that defendant was a possessor of the premises who could be held directly liable for plaintiff's injuries.

2. Vicarious Liability

Generally, a principal is responsible for the negligence of its agent. In Michigan, the test for a principal–agent relationship is whether the principal has the right to control the agent. The threshold question here is what constitutes "control" sufficient to deem a franchisee to be an agent of a franchisor. Howard Johnson argues that a franchisor must have the right to control the day-to-day operations of a franchisee in order to establish an agency relationship. Little, on the other hand, maintains that an agency relationship is created where the franchisor retains the right to set standards regarding the products and services offered by the franchisee, the right to regulate such items as the furnishings and advertising used by the franchisee, and the right to inspect for conformance with the agreement. We agree with defendant.

This court has repeatedly held that in order to establish vicarious liability in such actions, the landowner must have retained some control and direction over the actual day-to-day work. It is not enough that the owner retained mere contractual control, the right to make safety inspections, or general oversight. The franchise agreement in this case primarily insured the uniformity and standardization of products and services offered by a Howard Johnson restaurant. These obligations do not affect the control of daily operations.

3. Apparent Agency

Howard Johnson argues that the district court properly concluded that no genuine issue of fact existed regarding its liability under an agency theory. We agree. Here, Little has failed to offer any documentary evidence that she was harmed as a result of relying on the perceived fact that the franchise was an agent of Howard Johnson. No evidence was presented which indicated that plaintiff justifiably expected that the walkway would be free of ice and snow because she believed that Howard Johnson operated the restaurant. REVERSED.

Case A.31
Lampf, Pleva, Lipkind, Prupis & Petigrow v. Gilbertson,

111 S.CT. 2773, 115 L.ED.2d 321 (1991)
United States Supreme Court
Blackmun, Justice

The controversy arises from the sale of seven Connecticut limited partnerships formed for the purpose of purchasing and leasing computer hardware and software. Petitioner Lampf, Pleva, Lipkind, Prupis & Petigrow is a West Orange, New Jersey, law firm that aided in organizing the partnerships and that provided additional legal services, including the preparation of opinion letters addressing the tax consequences of investing in the partnerships. The several plaintiff-respondents purchased units in one or more of the partnerships during the years 1979 through 1981 with the expectation of realizing federal income tax benefits therefrom.

The partnerships failed, due in part to the technological obsolescence of their wares. In late 1982 and early 1983, Gilbertson et al., received notice that the United States Internal Revenue Service was investigating the partnerships. The IRS subsequently disallowed the claimed tax benefits because of overvaluation of partnership assets and lack of profit motive. On November 3, 1986, and June 4, 1987, Gilbertson et al., filed their respective complaints in the United States District Court for the District of Oregon, naming as defendant's petitioner and others involved in the preparation of offering memoranda for the partnerships. The complaints alleged that plaintiff-respondents were induced to invest in the partnerships by misrepresentations in the offering memoranda, in violation of, among other things, § 10(b) of the 1934 Securities Exchange Act and Rule 10b-5. The claimed misrepresentations were said to include assurances that the investments would entitle the purchasers to substantial tax benefits; that the leasing of the hardware and software packages would generate a profit; that the software was readily marketable; and that certain equipment appraisals were accurate and reasonable. Gilbertson et al., asserted that they became aware of the alleged misrepresentations only in 1985 following the disallowance by the IRS of the tax benefits claimed.

After consolidating the actions for discovery and pretrial proceedings, the district court granted summary judgment for the defendants on the ground that the complaints were not timely filed. The Court of Appeals for the Ninth Circuit reversed and remanded the cases. In view of the divergence of opinion among the circuits regarding the proper limitations period for Rule 10b-5 claims, we granted certiorari to address this important issue.

It is the usual rule that when Congress has failed to provide a statute of limitations for a federal cause of action, a court "borrows" or "absorbs" the local time limitation most analogous to the case at hand. This practice, derived from the Rules of Decision Act, has enjoyed sufficient longevity that we may assume that, in enacting remedial legislation, Congress ordinarily "intends by its silence that we borrow state law." The rule, however, is not without exception.

First, the court must determine whether a uniform statute of limitations is to be selected. Where a federal cause of action tends in practice to "encompass numerous and diverse topics and subtopics," such that a single state limitations period may not be consistently applied within a jurisdiction, we have concluded that the federal interests in predictability and judicial economy counsel the adoption of one source, or class of sources, for borrowing purposes.

Second, assuming a uniform limitations period is appropriate, the court must decide whether this period should be derived from a state or federal source. In making this judgment, the court should accord particular weight to the geographic character of the claim.

Finally, even where geographic considerations counsel federal borrowing, the aforementioned presumption of state borrowing that requires that a court determine that an analogous federal source truly affords a "closer fit" with the cause of action at issue than does any available state-law source. Although considerations pertinent to this determination will necessarily vary depending upon the federal cause of action and the available state and federal analogues, such factors as commonality of purpose and similarity of elements will be relevant.

We conclude that where, as here, the claim asserted is one implied under a statute that also contains an express cause of action with its own time limitation, a court should look first to the statute of origin to ascertain the proper limitations period. In the present litigation, there can be no doubt that the contemporaneously enacted express remedial provisions represent "a federal statute of limitations actually designed to accommodate a balance of interests very similar to that at stake here—a statute that is, in fact, an analogy to the present lawsuit more apt than any of the suggested state-law parallels." The 1934 Act contained a number of express causes of action, each with an explicit limitations period. With only one more restrictive exception, each of these includes some variation of a one-year period after discovery combined with a three-year period of repose. In adopting the 1934 Act, the 73rd Congress also amended the limitations provision of the 1933 Act, adopting the one- and three-year structure for each cause of action contained therein. We therefore conclude that we must reject the Commission's contention that the five-year period contained in § 20A, added to the 1934 Act in 1988, is more appropriate for § 10(b) actions than is the one- and three-year structure in the act's original remedial provisions.

Litigation instituted pursuant to § 10(b) and Rule 10b-5 therefore must be commenced within one year after the discovery of the facts constituting the violation and within three years after such violation. As there is no dispute that the earliest of plaintiff-respondents' complaints was filed more than three years after petitioners' alleged misrepresentations, Gilbertson et al., claims were untimely.

The judgment of the court of appeals is REVERSED.

Case A.32
Texaco, Inc. v. Hasbrouck dba Rick's Texaco,

496 U.S. 543
110 S.Ct. 2535, 110 L.Ed. 2d 492 (1990)
United States Supreme Court
Stevens, Justice

Petitioner (Texaco) sold gasoline directly to respondents and several other retailers in Spokane, Washington, at its retail tank wagon prices (RTW) while it granted substantial discounts to two distributors. During the period between 1972 and 1981, the stations supplied by the two distributors increased their sales volume dramatically, while respondents' sales suffered a corresponding decline. Respondents filed an action against Texaco under the Robinson-Patman Amendment to the Clayton Act (Act), alleging that the distributor discounts violated Section 2(a) of the Act. Respondents recovered treble damages, and the Court of Appeals for the Ninth Circuit affirmed the judgment. We granted certiorari, to consider Texaco's contention that legitimate functional discounts do not violate the act because a seller is not responsible for its customers' independent resale pricing decisions. While we agree with the basic thrust of Texaco's argument, we conclude that in this case it is foreclosed by the facts of record.

Respondents are 12 independent Texaco retailers. They displayed the Texaco trademark, accepted Texaco credit cards, and bought their gasoline products directly from Texaco. Texaco delivered the gasoline to respondents' stations. The retail gasoline market in Spokane was highly competitive throughout the damages period, which ran from 1972 to 1981. Stations marketing the nationally advertised Texaco gasoline competed with other major brands as well as with stations featuring independent brands. Moreover, although discounted prices at a nearby Texaco station would have the most obvious impact on a respondent's trade, the cross-city traffic patterns and relatively small size of Spokane produced a city-wide competitive market. Texaco's throughput sales in the Spokane market declined from a monthly volume of 569,269 gallons in 1970 to 389,557 gallons in 1975. Texaco's independent retailers' share of the market for Texaco gas declined from 76 percent to 49 percent. Seven of the respondents' stations were out of business by the end of 1978.

The respondents tried unsuccessfully to increase their ability to compete with lower priced stations. Some tried converting from full service to self-service stations. Two of the respondents sought to buy their own tank trucks and haul their gasoline from Texaco's supply point, but Texaco vetoed that proposal.

While the independent retailers struggled, two Spokane gasoline distributors supplied by Texaco prospered. Gull Oil Company (Gull) had its headquarters in Seattle and distributed petroleum products in four western states under its own name. In Spokane it purchased its gas from Texaco at prices that ranged from six to four cents below Texaco's RTW price. Gull resold that product under its own name; the fact that it was being supplied by Texaco was not known by either the public or the respondents. In Spokane, Gull supplied about 15 stations; some were "consignment stations" and some were "commission stations." In both situations Gull retained title to the gasoline until it was pumped into a motorist's tank. In the consignment stations, the station operator set the retail prices, but in the commission stations Gull set the prices and paid the operator a commission. Its policy was to price its gasoline at a penny less than the prevailing price for major brands. Gull employed two truck drivers in Spokane who picked up product at Texaco's bulk plant and delivered it to the Gull Stations. It also employed one supervisor in Spokane. Apart from its trucks and investment in retail facilities, Gull apparently owned no assets in that market. At least with respect to the commission stations, Gull is fairly characterized as a retailer of gasoline throughout the relevant period.

The Dompier Oil Company (Dompier) started business in 1954 selling Quaker State Motor Oil. In 1960 it became a full line distributor of Texaco products, and by the mid-1970s its sales of gasoline represented over three-quarters of its business. Dompier purchased Texaco gasoline at prices of 3.95 cents to 3.65 cents below the RTW price. Dompier thus paid a higher price than Gull, but Dompier, unlike Gull, resold its gas under the Texaco brand names. It supplied about eight to ten Spokane retail stations. In the period prior to October 1974, two of those stations were owned by the president of Dompier but the others were independently operated. In the early 1970s, Texaco representatives encouraged Dompier to enter the retail business directly, and in 1974 and 1975 it acquired four stations. Dompier's president estimated at trial that the share of its total gasoline sales made at retail during the middle 1970s was "probably 84 to 90 percent."

Like Gull, Dompier picked up Texaco's product at the Texaco bulk plant and delivered directly to retail outlets. Unlike Gull, Dompier owned a bulk storage facility, but it was seldom used because its capacity was less than that of many retail stations. Again, unlike Gull, Dompier received from Texaco the equivalent of the common carrier rate for delivering the gasoline product to the retail outlets. Thus, in addition to its discount from the RTW price, Dompier made a profit on its hauling function.

The stations supplied by Dompier regularly sold at retail at lower prices than respondents. Even before Dompier directly entered the retail business in 1974, its customers were selling to consumers at prices barely above the RTW price. Dompier's sales volume increased continuously and substantially throughout the relevant period. Between 1970 and 1975 its monthly sales volume increased from 155,152 gallons to 462,956 gallons; this represented an increase from 20.7 percent to almost 50 percent of Texaco's sales in Spokane.

There was ample evidence that Texaco executives were well aware of Dompier's dramatic growth and believed that it was attributable to "the magnitude of the distributor discount and the hauling allowance." In response to complaints from individual respondents about Dompier's aggressive pricing, however, Texaco representatives professed that they couldn't understand it.

Respondents filed suit against Texaco in July 1976. After a four-week trial, the jury awarded damages measured by the difference between the RTW price and the price paid by Dompier. As we subsequently decided in *J. Truett Payne Co. v. Chrysler Motors Corp.*, this measure of damages was improper. Accordingly, although it rejected Texaco's defenses on the issue of liability, the Court of Appeals for the Ninth Circuit remanded the case for a new trial.

At the second trial, Texaco contended that the special prices to Gull and Dompier were justified by cost savings, were the product of a good faith attempt to meet competition, and were lawful "functional discounts." The district court withheld the cost justification defense from the jury because it was not supported by the evidence. It awarded respondents actual damages of $449,900. The jury apparently credited the testimony of respondents' expert witness who had estimated what the respondents' profits would have been if they had paid the same prices as the four stations owned by Dompier.

In Texaco's motion for judgment notwithstanding the verdict, it claimed as a matter of law that its functional discounts did not adversely affect competition within the meaning of the act because any injury to respondents was attributable to decisions made independently by Dompier. The district court denied the motion. In an opinion supplementing its oral ruling denying Texaco's motion for a directed verdict, the court assumed, arguendo, that Dompier was entitled to a functional discount, even on the gas that was sold at retail, but nevertheless concluded that the "presumed legality of functional discounts" had been rebutted by evidence that the amount of the discounts to Gull and Dompier was not reasonably related to the cost of any function that they performed.

The court of appeals affirmed. It reasoned: "As the Supreme Court long ago made clear, and recently affirmed, there may be a Robinson-Patman violation even if the favored and disfavored buyers do not compete, so long as the customers of the favored buyer compete with the disfavored buyer or its customers. Despite the fact that Dompier and Gull, at least in their capacities as wholesalers, did not compete directly with Hasbrouck, a Section 2(a) violation may occur if (1) the discount they received was not cost-based and (2) all or a portion of it was passed on by them to customers of theirs who competed with Hasbrouck. "Hasbrouck presented ample evidence to demonstrate that the services performed by Gull and Dompier were insubstantial and did not justify the functional discount."

The court of appeals concluded its analysis by observing: "To hold that price discrimination between a wholesaler and a retailer could never violate the Robinson-Patman Act would leave immune from antitrust scrutiny a discriminatory pricing procedure that can effectively serve to harm competition. We think such a result would be contrary to the objectives of the Robinson-Patman Act."

In order to establish a violation of the act, respondent had the burden of proving four facts: (1) that Texaco's sales to Gull and Dompier were made in interstate commerce; (2) that the gasoline sold to them was of the same grade and quality as that sold to respondents; (3) that Texaco discriminated in price as between Gull and Dompier on the one hand and respondents on the other; and (4) that the discrimination had a prohibited effect on competition. Moreover, for each respondent to recover damages, he had the burden of proving the extent of his actual injuries.

The first two elements of respondents' case are not disputed in this court, and we do not understand Texaco to be challenging the sufficiency of respondents' proof of damages. Texaco does argue, however, that although it charged different prices, it did not "discriminate in price" within the meaning of the act, and that, at least to the extent that Gull and Dompier acted as wholesalers, the price differentials did not injure competition. We consider the two arguments separately.

A supplier need not satisfy the rigorous requirements of the cost justification defense in order to prove that a particular functional discount is reasonable and accordingly did not cause any substantial lessening of competition between a wholesaler's customers and the suppliers' direct customers. The record in this case, however, adequately supports the finding that Texaco violated the act.

The proof established that Texaco's lower prices to Gull and Dompier were discriminatory throughout the entire nine-year period; that at least Gull, and apparently Dompier as well, was selling at retail during that entire period; that the discounts substantially affected competition throughout the entire market; and that they injured each of the respondents. There is no doubt that respondents proof of a continuing violation of the act throughout the nine year period was sufficient.

The judgment is AFFIRMED.

Case A.33

X-TRA Art, Inc. v. Consumer Product Safety Commission,

1991 W.L. 405183 (N.D. Cal.) (1991)
United States District Court
Patel, District Judge

X-TRA Art, Inc., produces Rainbow Foam Paint (Rainbow) a shaving cream-like paint designed for use by children ages three years and up. In December 1990, Consumers Union, a nonprofit organization, published an article in the children's magazine, "Zillions," which indicated that Rainbow was an unsafe toy because it could catch fire. Plaintiffs demanded a retraction. Irwin Landau, Consumers Union editorial director, initially sent a letter apologizing for the article and indicating that Consumers Union had made a mistake and would publish a retraction. On December 31, 1990, Landau sent plaintiffs another letter indicating that Consumers Union had conducted additional tests on Rainbow, believed the paint to be in violation of the Federal Hazardous Substances Act (FHSA), and had reported it to the Consumer Product Safety Commission (CPSC). Tests conducted by the CPSC indicated that the Rainbow container, when held upright horizontally, and especially upside down, and exposed to a flame at times produced a flame or flashback (a flame extending back to the dispenser).

On January 17, 1991, Lee Baxter of the CPSC sent plaintiffs a Letter of Advice informing plaintiffs that the CPSC had found Rainbow to be a banned hazardous substance under the FHSA because it was flammable. Baxter requested that X-TRA Art cease distribution and sale of the product and reformulate it. The letter provided plaintiffs with an opportunity to submit opposing views and warned plaintiffs of potential criminal liability if X-TRA Art continued to distribute Rainbow. A copy of the letter was sent to the California Department of Health Services, which subsequently recommended to the California Department of Education that Rainbow not be purchased for use in California public schools.

Plaintiffs sent two letters to the CPSC outlining the objections to the Letter of Advice. The CPSC responded in a letter dated March 18, 1991, which addressed plaintiffs' objections and threatened civil penalties if X-TRA Art did not cease distribution of Rainbow.

As a result of the CPSC findings, on April 26, 1991, the United States Attorney for the Connecticut district secured a warrant authorizing the seizure of Rainbow stored at Early Learning Centre, a toy distribution warehouse in Milford, Connecticut. The warrant was executed on April 29 and the Early Learning Centre instructed its outlets to cease sale of the product. The U.S. Attorney issued a press release detailing the seizure action and CPSC findings regarding Rainbow. Plaintiffs have moved for a preliminary injunction to prevent any further government action against Rainbow.

X-TRA Art brought this action to enjoin the CPSC from taking any action to remove Rainbow Foam Paint from the market pursuant to the Federal Hazardous Substances Act. Plaintiffs argue that: (1) the CPSC has failed to follow statutorily mandated procedural requirements in declaring Rainbow a banned hazardous substance pursuant to the FHSA; (2) the CPSC used invalid and improper testing methods in determining that Rainbow is flammable; (3) the CPSC violated provisions of the Consumer Product Safety Act, governing public disclosure of findings concerning safety hazards posed by products; (4) the CPSC cannot establish that substantial injury or illness can be caused as a proximate result of any customary or reasonably foreseeable use of Rainbow, as required by the FHSA; and (5) plaintiffs' rights to due process and equal protection have been violated.

Following an evidentiary hearing on May 7, 1991, the court ordered the government to desist from taking any action against Rainbow for ten days and furthered ordered the parties to file additional briefing on the matter. Having reviewed the parties' papers and held an additional hearing, the court DENIES plaintiffs' motion for a preliminary injunction.

The CPSC argues that under FHSA a product intended for use by children is automatically banned if the CPSC determines said product to be a hazardous substance. Plaintiffs, citing to other provisions of the FSHA, contend that a children's product such as Rainbow may not be banned without notice, comment, and a public hearing. The plain language of the FSHA supports the CPSC's position.

In 1966, Congress amended the FHSLA to authorize the banning of hazardous toys, children's articles and household goods; "Labeling" was deleted from the title of the FHSLA and the Federal Hazardous Substance Act was created. The legislative history of the 1966 amendments makes it clear that, while the banning of hazardous household substances was to occur only after a public hearing, Congress intended that the Secretary (Commission) have the power to ban hazardous toys and children's articles without regulation. There is no question that plaintiffs were provided with notice of the agency action, given the Letter of Advice and the correspondence between plaintiffs and the CPSC which followed. Moreover, in early 1990 the CPSC determined that foam-like string streamers designed for children and dispensed from self-pressurized containers were flammable and therefore were banned hazardous substances. The manufacturer voluntarily recalled its products and reformulated them with a nonflammable propellant. The agency action against the string streamer products appears to have been well publicized. In light of the similarity between the string streamer products and Rainbow Foam Paint, it is surprising to hear plaintiffs argue that they were caught completely off guard by the agency action challenged in this case.

The court concludes that X-TRA Art raised serious legal issues with regard to the procedures utilized by the CPSC in declaring Rainbow Foam Paint a "banned hazardous substance" and that plaintiffs are unlikely to prevail on the merits of the issue. This being the case, plaintiffs' motion for a preliminary injunction is DENIED.

Case A.34

Wiljef Transportation, Inc. v. NLRB,

946 F.2d 1308 (1991)
United States Court of Appeals for the Seventh Circuit
Cudahy, Circuit Judge

This case presents an interesting question concerning the balance between an employer's right of expression and it's employees' right of association. Approximately two months before a vote on unionization, the employer, Wiljef Transportation, Inc. (Wiljef), read to its employees a corporate bylaw which states:

Section 2—Corporate Dissolution. Wiljef Transportation, Inc. hereby expresses as matter of corporate policy that operations will cease and the corporation will be dissolved in the event of unionization of its employees. As hereby authorized by the Board of Directors, this by-law may be announced to the employees of Wiljef Transportation, Inc. at any time deemed appropriate by the Board.

The by-law was adopted in 1979, and the announcement occurred in 1988. In the ensuing union representation election, the employees rejected unionization. The issue in this case is whether the announcement of the by-law constituted a "permitted prediction" of plant closure or a "proscribed threat." The NLRB held that the announcement was a threat in violation of Section 8(a)(1) of the National Labor Relations Act (NLRA), and Wiljef appealed to this court.

An employer's right to communicate its views to its employees is firmly established in the First Amendment and is recognized in Section 8(c) of the NLRA, which provides that "the expressing of any views, argument, or opinion shall not constitute or be evidence of an unfair labor practice if such expression contains no threat of reprisal or force or promise of benefit." On the other hand, the exceptions to the freedom of expression recognized in Section 8(c) reflect the right of employees to associate free of coercion by the employer. Section 8(a)(1) of the NLRA codifies that right by declaring that it is an unfair labor practice to interfere with, restrain or coerce employees exercising their right to organize in unions. The difficulty in cases attempting to relate to these two rights is in determining when speech becomes essentially coercive rather than factually informative or predictive so as to fall outside the protection of the First Amendment and violate the NLRA. The real issue, however, remains credibility and bona fides. A by-law purporting to be a management decision to close a business in the event of unionization is not protected expression unless objective factors demonstrate that it is really controlling on the question of closure. This holding preserves the balance between free expression and the right to organize.

Absent some persuasive evidence of other measures indicating that Wiljef intends to implement the corporate policy described in the by-law, the announcement of the by-law to the employees is coercive and in violation of the NLRA. Objective evidence to lend credibility to the by-law need not be based on economics and need not necessarily indicate circumstances beyond the employer's control.

Analytically the line is clear. To predict a consequence that will occur no matter how well disposed the company is toward unions is not to threaten retaliation; to predict a consequence that will occur because the company wants to punish workers for voting for the union—a consequence desired and freely chosen by a company rather than compelled by economic forces over which it has no control—is.

In light of our conclusion that Wiljef used the by-law in an attempt to coerce its employees and that no objective evidence indicated an intent to implement the by-law, the relief granted by the NLRB is proper. The petition for review is denied, and the order of the NLRB requiring Wiljef to expunge the by-law, cease further coercive activity, and post a notice to employees indicating that it had violated the law and will cease such violations is enforced.

Case A.35
Robinson v. Jacksonville Shipyards, Inc.,

760 F. Supp. 1486 (1991)
United States District Court
Melton, District Judge

Plaintiff Lois Robinson (Robinson) is a female employee of Jacksonville Shipyards, Inc. (JSI). She has been a welder since September 1977. Robinson is one of a very small number of female skilled craftworkers employed by JSI. Between 1977 and the present, Robinson was promoted from third-class welder to second-class welder and from second-class welder to her present position as a first-class welder.

JSI is a Florida corporation that runs several shipyards engaged in the business of ship repair, including the Commercial Yard and the Mayport Yard. As a federal contractor, JSI has affirmative action and nondiscrimination obligations. Defendant Arnold McIlwain (McIlwain) held the office of President from JSI from the time Robinson was hired by the company through the time of the trial of this case.

In addition to a welding department, JSI's other craft departments including shipfitting, sheetmetal, electrical, transportation, shipping, and receiving (including toolroom), carpenter, boilermaker, inside machine, outside machine, rigging, quality assurance, and pipe. Employees in these craft departments may be assigned to work at either the Mayport Yard, situated at the Mayport Naval Station, or the Commercial Yard, situated at a riverfront site in downtown Jacksonville and sometimes referred to as the downtown yard. Robinson's job assignments at JSI have required her to work at both the Commercial Yard and the Mayport yard. Ship repair work is a dangerous profession; JSI acknowledges the need to "provide a working environment that is safe and healthful."

JSI is, in the words of its employees, "a boys club" and "more or less a man's world." Women craftworkers are an extreme rarity. The company's EEO-1 reports from 1980 to 1987 typically show that women form less than 5 percent of the skilled crafts.

Pictures of nude and partially nude women appear throughout the JSI work place in the form of magazines, plaques on the wall, photographs torn from magazines and affixed to the wall or attached to calendars supplied by advertising tool supply companies (vendors' advertising calendars). JSI has never distributed nor tolerated the distribution of a calendar or calendars with pictures of nude or partially nude men. Management employees from the very top down condoned these displays; often they had their own pictures.

Robinson credibly testified to the extensive, pervasive posting of pictures depicting nude women, partially nude women or sexual conduct and to the occurrence of other forms of harassing behavior perpetrated by her male co-workers and supervisors. Her testimony covered the full term of her employment, from 1977 to 1988.

Reported incidents included the following:

(1) pictures in the fab shop area, in January 1985, including one of a woman wearing black tights, the top pulled down to

expose her breasts to view, and one of a nude woman in an outdoor setting apparently playing with a piece of cloth between her legs.

(2) a picture of a nude woman left on the tool box where Robinson returned her tools in the summer of 1986. The photograph depicted the woman's legs spread apart, knees bend up toward her chest, exposing her breasts and genitals. Several men were present and laughed at Robinson when she appeared upset by the picture.

(3) a drawing on a heater control box, approximately one foot square, of a nude woman with fluid coming from her genital area, in 1987, at the Commercial Yard.

(4) a dart board with a drawing of a woman's breast with her nipple as the bull's eye, in 1987 or 1988, at the Commercial Yard.

Robinson also testified about comments of a sexual nature she recalled hearing at JSI from co-workers. In some instances these comments were made while she also was in the presence of the pictures of nude or partially nude women. Among the remarks Robinson recalled are, "Hey pussycat, come here and give me a whiff," "The more you lick it, the harder it gets," "I'd like to get in bed with that," "I'd like to have some of that," "Black women taste like sardines," "It doesn't hurt women to have sex right after childbirth," and so on. Defendants have admitted that pictures of nude or partially nude women have been posted in the shipfitters' trailer at the Mayport Yard during Robinson's employment at JSI.

Based on the foregoing, the court finds that sexually harassing behavior occurred through the JSI working environment with both frequency and intensity over the relevant time period. Robinson did not welcome such behavior.

In April 1987, during the pendency of this lawsuit, JSI adopted a new sexual harassment policy. It was instituted unilaterally, without consulting or bargaining with the union. The official policy statement, signed by Vice-President for Operations Larry Brown, endorses the following policy:

(1) It is illegal and a violation of Jacksonville Shipyards, Inc., Policy for any employee, male or female, to sexually harass another employee by:

a. making unwelcomed sexual advances or request for sexual favors or other verbal or physical conduct of a sexual nature, a condition of an employee's continued employment, or

b. making submission to or rejection of such conduct the basis for employment decisions affecting the employee, or

c. creating an intimidating, hostile, or offensive working environment by such conduct.

(2) Any employee who believes he or she has been the subject of sexual harassment, should report the alleged act immediately to John Stewart Ext. 3716 in our Industrial Relations Department. An investigation of all complaints will be undertaken immediately. Any supervisor, agent or other employee who has been found by the Company to

have sexually harassed another employee will be subject to appropriate sanctions, depending on the circumstances, from a warning in his or her file up to and including termination.

The 1987 policy had little or no impact on the sexually hostile work environment at JSI. Employees and supervisors lacked the knowledge and training in the scope of those acts that might constitute sexual harassment.

The court finds that the policies and procedures at JSI for responding to complaints of sexual harassment are inadequate. The company has done an inadequate job of communicating with employees and supervisors regarding the nature and scope of sexually harassing behavior. This failure is compounded by a pattern of unsympathetic response to complaints by employees who perceive that they are victims of harassment. This pattern includes an unwillingness to believe the accusations, an unwillingness to take prompt and stern remedial action against admitted harassers, and an express condonation of behavior that is and encourages sexually harassing conduct (such as the posting of pictures of nude and partially nude women). In some instances, the process of registering a complaint about sexual harassment became a second episode of harassment.

Ordered and Adjudged

That defendant Jacksonville Shipyards, Inc., is hereby enjoined to cease and desist from the maintenance of a work environment that is hostile to women because of their sex and to remedy the hostile work environment through the implementation, forthwith, of the Sexual Harassment Policy, which consists of the "Statement of Policy," "Statement of Prohibited Conduct," "Schedule of Penalties for Misconduct," "Procedures for Making, Investigating and Resolving Sexual Harassment and Retaliation Complaints," and "Procedures and Rules for Education and Training."

Jacksonville Shipyards, Inc., Sexual Harassment Policy Statement of Policy

Title VII of the Civil Rights Act of 1964 prohibits employment discrimination on the basis of race, color, sex, age, or national origin. Sexual harassment is included among the prohibitions.

Sexual harassment, according to the federal Equal Employment Opportunity Commission (EEOC), consists of unwelcome sexual advances, requests for sexual favors or other verbal or physical acts of a sexual or sex-based nature where (1) submission to such conduct is made either explicitly or implicitly a term or condition of an individual's employment; (2) an employment decision is based on an individual's acceptance or rejection of such conduct; or (3) such conduct interferes with an individual's work performance or creates an intimidating, hostile or offensive working environment.

Case A.36
Michigan Mutual Insurance Co. v. Marriott Corporation,

1992 WL 82498 N.D.Ill. (1992)
United States District Court, N.D. Illinois
Rovner, District Judge

During the period from October 15 through October 22, 1988, Jack Sonneveldt, president of Sonneveldt, Inc., was a paying guest at the O'Hare Marriott Hotel in Chicago, Illinois. He and his party arrived at the hotel in the company's 1984 Probe Prevost 40-foot, customized coach. Sonneveldt unsuccessfully attempted to park the Prevost coach in the hotel's valet parking area. At the request of hotel officials, he moved the Prevost coach to the hotel's general parking lot across the street, in front of the hotel.

Sometime during the evening of October 22, 1988, or the next morning, the Prevost coach was stolen from the Marriott parking lot. Sonneveldt, Inc.'s insurer, Michigan Mutual, paid the company $265,000 in full settlement of the resulting claim. As subrogee of Sonneveldt, Inc., Michigan Mutual brought the instant suit. Michigan Mutual asserts liability under a theory of bailment.

Illinois law requires a plaintiff to establish the following in order to make out a prima facie claim of bailment: (1) an agreement, express or implied, to take possession of the plaintiff's property; (2) delivery and acceptance of the property (in good condition) into the exclusive possession and control of the bailee; and (3) failure to return the property or re-delivery in a damaged state. The bailment claim fails because the complaint does not sufficiently allege that Marriott ever accepted delivery and possession, either actual or constructive, of the Prevost coach.

The Illinois Supreme Court considered delivery and acceptance in the parking lot context in *Wall v. Airport Parking Co. of Chicago*, 41 Ill.2d 506, 244 N.E.2d 190 (1969). The parking lot at issue in *Wall* was lighted, paved, and marked into parking spaces. Motorists entered through an unattended electronic gate where they received a ticket noting the time of their arrival. Motorists also retained the keys to their vehicles and locked them at their own discretion. An attendant was observed only while paying at check-out. Plaintiff's car was stolen while it was parked in this lot, and he sued under a theory of bailment.

Ruling that these facts showed neither delivery nor acceptance, the court affirmed the lower courts' holdings that no bailment had been established.

Michigan Mutual's pleadings do not inferentially suggest that Marriott exercised even the most remote control over the Prevost coach. The complaint indicates that the Sonneveldt driver drove the Prevost coach into the lot and parked the vehicle himself. Nowhere does it suggest that Marriott was left with a set of keys to the coach, or that the hotel otherwise accepted or obtained actual control over the vehicle. Without the keys, Marriott had neither partial nor complete control over the Prevost coach.

Failure to allege some degree of control over the Prevost coach by Marriott necessitates the conclusion that no delivery or acceptance took place. Insofar as Illinois law requires proof of delivery and acceptance in order to establish a prima facie claim of bailment, Michigan Mutual's complaint fails as a matter of law. Consequently, the defendant's motion for judgment on the pleadings is granted.

Case A.37
Walker V. Quillen,

622 A.2d 1097 (1993)
Supreme Court of Delaware
Moore, Justice

Pursuant to Supreme Court Rule 25(a), appellees, Elizabeth Stay Ayres and Clara Louise Quillen, have moved to affirm a judgment of the Court of Chancery granting an implied easement in favor of appellees' servient estate, as against the dominant estate of appellant, Irvin C. Walker (Walker). The appellees content that sufficient evidence supports the findings of the Court of Chancery and that there was no abuse of discretion in granting the implied easement. We agree and affirm.

The appellees own in fee simple absolute a tract of land in Sussex County known as "Bluff Point." The tract is surrounded on three sides by Rehoboth Bay and is landlocked on the fourth side by Walker's land. At one time, the two tracts in question were held by a common owner. In 1878, Bluff Point was sold in fee simple absolute apart from the other holdings, thereby landlocking the parcel. A narrow dirt road, which traverses Walker's land, connects Bluff Point to a public road, and is its only means of access.

Under the doctrine of implied easement or easement by necessity the Court of Chancery found that the appellees were entitled to cross over a portion of Walker's land for access to Bluff Point. The court also found that water access, even if a reasonable substitute for land access, was not feasible because of the shallowness of the water surrounding Bluff Point. There is ample evidence in the record to support the finding that the two tracts originated from the unified holdings of one owner, and that an implied easement was created by the severance which landlocked Bluff Point. The record also sufficiently supports the finding that navigable access to Bluff Point was not feasible. NOW, THEREFORE, IT IS ORDERED that the judgment of the Court of Chancery be, and the same hereby is, AFFIRMED.

Case A.38
Saritejdiam, Inc. v. Excess Insurance Co.,

971 F.2d 910 (1992)
United States Court of Appeals for the Second Circuit
Oakes, Chief Judge

Saritejdiam, Inc. (Saritejdiam) is a New York corporation involved in the wholesaling of diamonds and other precious and semiprecious stones and jewelry. In June 1988, Excess Insurance Company, Ltd. et al. (the Underwriters), a group of London-based insurance companies, issued an insurance policy to Saritejdiam. The policy is called a Jeweler's Block Policy and it insures against all risks of physical loss or damage to insured interests, unless specifically excluded by the policy. This appeal requires us to analyze whether Saritejdiam satisfied a clause in the policy requiring that insured interests remain in the "close personal custody and control" of the insured or its agent while in transit.

On May 13, 1989, Mr. Robert Danilin, an independent contractor/salesman for Saritejdiam, lost a package of loose diamonds valued by Saritejdiam at $267,514. On that day, Danilin, his wife, and stepson, were in Tuxedo, New York visiting a town house they had just purchased there. At approximately 5:50 P.M., the Danilins arrived at the Orange Top Diner on Route 17 in Tuxedo for dinner. Danilin brought a camera bag into the diner containing two stiff, black diamond wallets (one of which held Saritejdiam's diamonds), his checkbook, and credit cards. The three were seated at a table. Robert placed the camera bag on top of an empty chair to his left. During dinner, he touched the camera bag to make sure it was still on the chair. When they finished eating, Danilin paid the check with cash out of his pants pocket. The three then left the diner, got into their car, and headed for a golf driving range. When the Danilins reached their destination, they discovered that the camera bag containing the diamond wallet was not in the car. They sped back to the diner. The camera bag, however, was no longer on the chair where it had been previously placed.

Connie Grievas, the daughter of the proprietors of the Orange Top Diner, apparently witnessed the events that transpired after Danilin paid his bill. Grievas was 11 years old at the time. She told Danilin's stepson and, later on, investigators for the Underwriters, that she went to clear Danilin's table after he paid his check. She noticed that a bag with a handle was left behind. Grievas then went to tell her mother that a customer had left a bag behind. Before she reached her mother, she saw two other customers, a man and a woman, take the bag and walk out. She described the man who picked up the bag as white, approximately 40 years old, with shoulder-length black curly hair, standing 5'7", and wearing dark sunglasses. She described the woman as having blonde, waist-length hair.

On the same day, Saritejdiam reported the loss to the Underwriters. On June 3, 1989, after investigating the claim, the Underwriters refused to cover the lost diamonds. The Underwriters claimed that Saritejdiam had not complied with the Personal Conveyance Clause of the insurance policy. The clause provides: This policy only covers the insured interest in transit when in the close personal custody and control of the Assured and/or Assured's representative and/or agent at all times whilst in transit subject to hotel/motel clause, excluding all losses due to infidelity (emphasis added). The denial letter states that "the results of our investigation have revealed that there is no evidence that the theft took place whilst your property was in the close personal custody and control of your salesman, Robert Danilin."

We must decide whether the loss of the diamonds at the Orange Top Diner occurred while they were in the "close per-

sonal custody and control" of Danilin, Saritejdiam's salesman/independent contractor. If so, Saritejdiam satisfied the requirements of the Personal Conveyance Clause in the policy, and the Underwriters must cover the loss. The issue traditionally arises in disputes over the rights of the finder against those of the owner of the real property on which the disputed personal property was found. The common law generally distinguished between "lost" and "mislaid" property. Property is mislaid when the owner purposely parts with possession of the property, but then unintentionally leaves it behind. We believe that under New York common law the camera bag containing Saritejdiam's diamond wallets would be classified as mislaid property. Saritejdiam's salesman purposely placed the camera bag on the adjacent chair at his table in the Orange Top Diner. He then walked away from the table and forgot to pick up the camera bag. This is a paradigmatic example of mislaid property under New York's common law definition of the term. Accordingly, we believe a New York court would hold that a person simply cannot maintain "close personal custody and control" over mislaid property.

For the foregoing reasons, we REVERSE the order of the district court granting summary judgment for Saritejdiam and enter summary judgment for the Underwriters.

Case A.39
OHG v. Kolodny

NY County, Supreme Court,
1st Jud. Dept., IA Part II (1992)
Baer, Justice

Plaintiff is an auction house dealing in works of art. Defendant is an art dealer. His gallery has purchased fine art from the plaintiff over the years, presumably with happier results than in this case. In 1988, defendant received, in New York, a catalogue sent by plaintiff that described works of art that would be put up for auction by plaintiff. Among these, defendant says, was "a bronze sculpture produced by Hiliare Germain Edgar Degas before 1900," to wit, the "Dancer Gazing." Plaintiff phoned defendant in New York during the auction and solicited a bid for the "Dancer." Without ever having set eyes on the right foot or any other part of the sculpture, plaintiff offered a bid of DM 220,000 and triumphed. Defendant was never told the identity of the consignor of the Degas. Defendant wired to plaintiff the purchase price and a commission.

The "Dancer" arrived shortly thereafter in New York, where she immediately did a pirouette and departed for London. Defendant wished to let no grass grow under either of his feet; he would put the Degas up for resale at Christie's and would, he was confident, earn a great deal of not bronze, but sterling. Eagle eyes at Christie's surveyed the work. Defendant was told, to his horror, that Christie's suspected that the statue was ersatz, in a word, a fake. Defendant contacted Herr Hanstein and advised that his heart was heavy and his wallet, he was afraid, too light. Defendant sought a refund.

Defendant allegedly secured the agreement of plaintiff that the "Dancer" would be given the once or twice over by the world's foremost expert of Degas Bronzes, whose determination would be binding. The statue was brought to New York, where the expert, like many another world's foremost experts, resides. His conclusion unfortunately was that the work was not genuine.

A German court decided in favor of plaintiff, rejected defendant's contention that he was entitled to an offset for the purchase price of the pseudo-Degas. The court held that plaintiff had disclaimed any warranty as to the authenticity of the "Dancer"; that since the job of an auction house is to sell as commission agent many items owned by others, the authenticity of which the auctioneer cannot readily confirm, disclaimers do not violate the law; and that defendant in his letter on the Riopelle had disavowed any offset.

After plaintiff launched its "Blitzkrieg" here in New York, defendant responded with a lawsuit of his own. Defendant seeks to recover the purchase price of the ill-fated Degas. Defendant, relying inter alia upon Article 15 of the New York Arts and Cultural Affairs Law (the "Art Law"), contends that plaintiff is liable for having provided inaccurate information about the Degas and that the German judgment contravenes New York public policy, as a consequence of which its enforcement in favor of plaintiff is *verboten*. The argument, while creative and well presented, must fail.

CPLR Sec. 5304(b)(4) provides that a monetary judgment of a foreign country need not be recognized by New York if the cause of action on which the judgment is based is "repugnant to the public policy of this state." Normally, the judgment of a foreign nation will be given effect. Differences between the laws of New York and those of the many sovereign nations of the world are likely to arise often, but such differences alone cannot constitute a violation of public policy. As Judge Cardozo said, "We are not so provincial as to say that every solution of a problem is wrong because we deal with it otherwise at home." Were we New Yorkers to be overly provincial, we might well inspire foreign nations to reject enforcement of New York judgments, precisely the opposite of the purpose Article 53 was created to achieve and an outcome particularly undesirable as the economy of this country grows every day more intertwined with those of other nations.

The German court applied German law in this case. This is not unreasonable since the auction occurred in Germany and defendant placed his bid during a telephone call with the auction house in Germany. In addition, plaintiff's conditions of sale stated that legal relations between plaintiff and the bidder would be governed by German law. Defendant appeared in the German action, defended, and lost. There is, of course, no claim that German law and procedures are unfair and unworthy of respect here.

The Germans are less Bismarcian than defendant contends. German law, as exemplified by the decision of the Cologne court in this case, is not indifferent to the general sale of fakes by art merchants. The court relied upon the warranty exclusion that formed a condition of sale.

Enforcement of the German judgment would not undermine the public interest, public confidence in the law or security for individual rights, nor violate fundamental notions of what is decent and fair. The German judgment is enforceable.

Appendix B — The Constitution of the United States of America

We the People of the United States, in Order to form a more perfect Union, establish Justice, insure domestic Tranquility, provide for the common defense, promote the general Welfare, and secure the Blessings of Liberty to ourselves and our Posterity, do ordain and establish this Constitution for the United States of America.

Article I

Section 1. All legislative Powers herein granted shall be vested in a Congress of the United States, which shall consist of a Senate and House of Representatives.

Section 2. The House of Representatives shall be composed of Members chosen every second Year by the People of the several states, and the Electors in each State shall have the Qualifications requisite for Electors of the most numerous Branch of the State Legislature.

No Person shall be a Representative who shall not have attained to the Age of twenty five Years, and been seven Years a Citizen of the United States, and who shall not, when elected, be an Inhabitant of that State in which he shall be chosen.

Representatives and direct Taxes shall be apportioned among the several states which may be included within this Union, according to their respective Numbers, which shall be determined by adding to the whole Number of free Persons, including those bound to Service for a Term of Years, and excluding Indians not taxed, three fifths of all other Persons. The actual Enumeration shall be made within three Years after the first Meeting of the Congress of the United States, and within every subsequent Term of ten Years, in such Manner as they shall by Law direct. The number of Representatives shall not exceed one for every thirty Thousand, but each State shall have at Least one Representative; and until such enumeration shall be made, the State of New Hampshire shall be entitled to chuse three, Massachusetts eight, Rhode Island and Providence Plantations one, Connecticut five, New York six, New Jersey four, Pennsylvania eight, Delaware one, Maryland six, Virginia ten, North Carolina five, South Carolina five, and Georgia three.

When vacancies happen in the Representation from any State, the Executive Authority thereof shall issue Writs of Election to fill such vacancies.

The House of Representatives shall chuse their Speaker and other Officers; and shall have the sole Power of Impeachment.

Section 3. The Senate of the United States shall be composed of two Senators from each State, chosen by the Legislature thereof, for six Years; and each Senator shall have one Vote.

Immediately after they shall be assembled in Consequence of the first Election, they shall be divided as equally as may be into three Classes. The Seats of the Senators of the first Class shall be vacated at the Expiration of the second Year, of the second Class at the Expiration of the fourth Year, and the third Class at the Expiration of the sixth Year, so that one third may be chosen every second Year; and if Vacancies happen by Resignation, or otherwise, during the Recess of the Legislature of any State, the Executive thereof may make temporary Appointments until the next meeting of the Legislature, which shall then fill such Vacancies.

No person shall be a Senator who shall not have attained to the Age of thirty Years, and been nine Years a Citizen of the United States, and who shall not, when elected, be an Inhabitant of that State for which he shall be chosen.

The Vice President of the United States shall be President of the Senate, but shall have no Vote, unless they be equally divided.

The Senate shall chuse their other Officers, and also a President pro tempore, in the Absence of the Vice President, or when he shall exercise the Office of President of the United States.

The Senate shall have the sole power to try all Impeachments. When sitting for that Purpose, they shall be an Oath or Affirmation. When the President of the United States is tried, the Chief Justice shall preside: And no Person shall be convicted without the Concurrence of two thirds of the Members present.

Judgment in Cases of Impeachment shall not extend further than to removal from Office, and disqualification to hold and enjoy any Office of honor, Trust or Profit under the United States: but the Party convicted shall nevertheless be liable and subject to Indictment, Trial, Judgment and Punishment, according to Law.

Section 4. The Times, Places and Manner of holding Elections for Senators and Representatives, shall be prescribed in each State by the Legislature thereof: but the Congress may at any time by Law make or alter such Regulations, except as to the Places of choosing Senators.

The Congress shall assemble at least once in every Year, and such Meeting shall be on the first Monday in December, unless they shall by Law appoint a different day.

Section 5. Each House shall be the Judge of the Elections, Returns and Qualifications of its own Members, and a Majority of each shall constitute a Quorum to do Business; but a smaller Number may adjourn from day to day, and may be authorized to compel the Attendance of absent Members, in such Manner, and under such Penalties as each House may provide.

Each House may determine the Rules of its Proceedings, punish its Members for disorderly Behaviour, and, with the Concurrence of two thirds, expel a Member.

Each House shall keep a Journal of its Proceedings, and from time to time publish the same, excepting such Parts as may in their Judgment require Secrecy; and the Yeas and Nays of the Members of either House on any question shall, at the Desire of one fifth of those Present, be entered on the Journal.

Neither House, during the Session of Congress, shall, without the Consent of the other, adjourn for more than three days, nor to any other Place than that in which the two Houses shall be sitting.

Section 6. The Senators and Representatives shall receive a Compensation for their Services, to be ascertained by Law, and paid out of the Treasury of the United States. They shall in all Cases, except Treason, Felony and Breach of the Peace, be privileged from Arrest during their Attendance at the Session of their respective Houses, and in going to and returning from the same; and for any Speech or Debate in either House, they shall not be questioned in any other Place.

No Senator or Representative shall, during the Time for which he was elected, be appointed to any civil Office under the Authority of the United States, which shall have been created, or the Emoluments whereof shall have been encreased during such time; and no Person holding any Office under the United States, shall be a Member of either House during his Continuance in Office.

Section 7. All Bills for raising Revenue shall originate in the House of Representatives; but the Senate may propose or concur with Amendments as on other Bills.

Every Bill which shall have passed the House of Representatives and the Senate, shall, before it become a Law, be presented to the President of the United States; If he approve he shall sign it, but if not he shall return it, with his Objections to that House in which it shall have originated, who shall enter the Objections at large on their Journal, and proceed to reconsider it. If after such Reconsideration two thirds of that House shall agree to pass the Bill, it shall be sent, together with the Objections, to the other House, by which it shall likewise be reconsidered, and if approved by two thirds of that House, it shall become a Law. But in all such Cases the Votes of both Houses shall be determined by Yeas and Nays, and the Names of the Persons voting for and against the Bill shall be entered on the Journal of each House respectively. If any Bill shall not be returned by the President within ten Days (Sundays excepted) after it shall have been presented to him, the Same shall be a Law, in like Manner as if he had signed it, unless the Congress by their Adjournment prevent its Return, in which Case it shall not be a Law.

Every Order, Resolution, or Vote to which the Concurrence of the Senate and House of Representatives may be necessary (except on a question of Adjournment) shall be presented to the President of the United States; and before the Same shall take Effect, shall be approved by him, or being disapproved by him, shall be repassed by two thirds of the Senate and House of Representatives, according to the Rules and Limitations prescribed in the Case of a Bill.

Section 8. The Congress shall have Power to lay and collect Taxes, Duties, Imposts and Excises, to pay the Debts and provide for the common Defence and general Welfare of the United States; but all Duties, Imposts and Excises shall be uniform throughout the United States;

To borrow Money on the credit of the United States;

To regulate Commerce with foreign Nations, and among the several States, and with the Indian Tribes;

To establish an uniform Rule of Naturalization, and uniform Laws on the subject of Bankruptcies throughout the United States;

To coin Money, regulate the Value thereof, and of foreign Coin, and fix the Standard of Weights and Measures;

To provide for the Punishment of counterfeiting the Securities and current Coin of the United States;

To establish Post Offices and post Roads;

To promote the Progress of Science and useful Arts, by securing for limited Times to Authors and Inventors the exclusive Right to their respective Writings and Discoveries;

To constitute Tribunals inferior to the supreme Court;

To define and punish Piracies and Felonies committed on the high Seas, and Offenses against the Law of Nations;

To declare War, grant Letters of Marque and Reprisal, and make Rules concerning Captures on Land and Water;

To raise and support Armies, but no Appropriation of Money to that Use shall be for a longer Term than two Years;

To provide and maintain a Navy;

To make Rules for the Government and Regulation of the land and naval Forces;

To provide for calling forth the Militia to execute the Laws of the Union, suppress Insurrections and repel Invasions;

To provide for organizing, arming, and disciplining, the Militia, and for governing such Part of them as may be employed in the Service of the United States, reserving to the States respectively, the Appointment of the Officers, and the Authority of training the Militia according to the discipline prescribed by Congress;

To exercise exclusive Legislation in all Cases whatsoever, over such District (not exceeding ten Miles square) as may, by Cession of particular States, and the Acceptance of Congress, become the Seat of the Government of the United States, and to exercise like Authority over all Places purchased by the Consent of the Legislature of the State in which the Same shall be, for the Erection of Forts, Magazines, Arsenals, dockYards, and other needful Buildings;—And

To make all Laws which shall be necessary and proper for carrying into Execution the foregoing Powers, and all other Powers vested by this Constitution in the Government of the United States, or in any Department or Officer thereof.

Section 9. The Migration or Importation of such Persons as any of the States now existing shall think proper to admit, shall not be prohibited by the Congress prior to the Year one thousand eight hundred and eight, but a Tax or Duty may be imposed on such Importation, not exceeding ten dollars for each Person.

The Privilege of the Writ of Habeas Corpus shall not be suspended, unless when in Cases of Rebellion or Invasion the public Safety may require it.

No Bill of Attainder or ex post facto Law shall be passed.

No Capitation, or other direct, Tax shall be laid, unless in Proportion to the Census or Enumeration herein before directed to be taken.

No Tax or Duty shall be laid on Articles exported from any State.

No Preference shall be given by any Regulation of Commerce or Revenue to the Ports of one State over those of another; nor shall Vessels bound to, or from, one State, be obliged to enter, clear, or pay Duties in another.

No Money shall be drawn from the Treasury, but in Consequence of Appropriations made by Laws; and a regular Statement and Account of the Receipts and Expenditures of all public Money shall be published from time to time.

No Title of Nobility shall be granted by the United States: And no Person holding any Office of Profit or Trust under them, shall, without the Consent of the Congress, accept of any present, Emolument, Office, or Title, of any kind whatever, from any King, Prince, or foreign State.

Section 10. No State shall enter into any Treaty, Alliance, or Confederation; grant Letters of Marque and Reprisal; coin Money; emit Bills of Credit; make any Thing but gold and silver Coin a Tender in Payment of Debts; pass any Bill of Attainder, ex post facto Law, or Law impairing the Obligation of Contracts, or grant any Title of Nobility.

No State shall, without the Consent of the Congress, lay any Imposts or Duties on Imports or Exports, except what may be absolutely necessary for executing its inspection Laws: and the net Produce of all Duties and Imposts, laid by any State on Imports or Exports, shall be for the Use of the Treasury of the United States; and all such Laws shall be subject to the Revision and Control of the Congress.

No State shall, without the Consent of Congress, lay any Duty of Tonnage, keep Troops, or Ships of War in time of Peace, enter into any Agreement or Compact with another State, or with a foreign Power, or engage in War, unless actually invaded, or in such imminent Danger as will not admit of delay.

Article II

Section 1. The executive Power shall be vested in a President of the United States of America. He shall hold his Office during the Term of four Years, and, together with the Vice President, chosen for the same Term, be elected, as follows:

Each State shall appoint, in such Manner as the Legislature thereof may direct, a Number of Electors, equal to the whole Number of Senators and Representatives to which the State may be entitled in the Congress: but no Senator or Representative, or Person holding an Office of Trust or Profit under the United States, shall be appointed an Elector.

The Electors shall meet in their respective States, and vote by Ballot for two Persons, of whom one at least shall not be an Inhabitant of the same State with themselves. And they shall make a list of all the Persons voted for, and of the Number of Votes for each; which List they shall sign and certify, and transmit sealed to the Seat of the Government of the United States, directed to the President of the Senate. The President of the Senate shall, in the presence of the Senate and House of Representatives, open all the Certificates, and the Votes shall be counted. The Person having the greatest Number of Votes shall be the President, if such Number be a Majority of the whole Number of Electors appointed; and if there be more than one who have such Majority, and have an equal Number of Votes, then the House of Representatives shall immediately choose by Ballot one of them for President; and if no Person have a Majority, then from the five highest on the List the said House shall in like Manner choose the President. But in chusing the President, the Votes shall be taken by States, the Representation from each State having one Vote; A quorum for this Purpose shall consist of a Member or Members from two thirds of the States, and a Majority of all the States shall be necessary to a Choice. In every Case, after the Choice of the President, the Person having the greatest Number of Votes of the Electors shall be the Vice President. But if there should remain two or more who have equal Votes, the Senate shall chuse from them by Ballot the Vice President.

The Congress may determine the Time of Chusing the Electors, and the Day on which they shall give their Votes; which Day shall be the same throughout the United States.

No Person except a natural born Citizen, or a Citizen of the United States, at the time of the Adoption of this Constitution, shall be eligible to the Office of President; neither shall any Person be eligible to that Office who shall not have attained to the Age of thirty five Years, and been fourteen Years a Resident within the United States.

In Case of the Removal of the President from Office, or of his Death, Resignation, or Inability to discharge the Powers and Duties of the said Office, the Same shall devolve on the Vice President, and the Congress may by Law provide for the Case of Removal, Death, Resignation or Inability, both of the President and Vice President, declaring what Officer shall then act as President, and such Officer shall act accordingly, until the Disability be removed, or a President shall be elected.

The President shall, at stated Times, receive for his Services, a Compensation, which shall neither be encreased nor diminished during the Period for which he shall have been elected, and he shall not receive within that Period any other Emolument from the United States, or any of them.

Before he enter on the Execution of his Office, he shall take the following Oath or Affirmation:—"I do solemnly swear (or affirm) that I will faithfully execute the Office of President of the United States, and will to the best of my Ability, preserve, protect and defend the Constitution of the United States."

Section 2. The President shall be Commander in Chief of the Army and Navy of the United States, and of the Militia of the several States, when called into the actual Service of the United States; he may require the Opinion, in writing, of the principal Officer in each of the executive Departments, upon any Subject relating to the Duties of their respective Offices, and he shall have Power to grant Reprieves and Pardons for Offences against the United States, except in Cases of Impeachment.

He shall have Power, by and with the Advice and Consent of the Senate, to make Treaties, provided two thirds of the Senators present concur; and he shall nominate, and by and with the Advice and Consent of the Senate, shall appoint Ambassadors, other public Ministers and Consuls, Judges of the supreme Court, and all other Officers of the United States, whose Appointments are not herein otherwise provided for, and which shall be established by Law: but the Congress may by Law vest the Appointment of such inferior Officers, as they think proper, in the President alone, in the Courts of Law, or in the Heads of Departments.

The President shall have Power to fill up all Vacancies that may happen during the Recess of the Senate, by granting Commissions which shall expire at the End of their next Session.

Section 3. He shall from time to time give to the Congress Information of the State of the Union, and recommend to their Consideration such Measures as he shall judge necessary and expedient; he may, on extraordinary Occasions, convene both Houses, or either of them, and in Case of Disagreement between them, with Respect to the Time of Adjournment, he may adjourn them to such Time as he shall think proper; he shall receive Ambassadors and other public Ministers; he shall take Care that the Laws be faithfully executed, and shall Commission all the Officers of the United States.

Section 4. The President, Vice President and all civil Officers of the United States, shall be removed from Office on Impeachment for, and Conviction of, Treason, Bribery, or other high Crimes and Misdemeanors.

Article III

Section 1. The judicial Power of the United States, shall be vested in one supreme Court, and in such inferior Courts as the Congress may from time to time ordain and establish. The Judges, both of the supreme and inferior Courts, shall hold their Offices during good Behaviour, and shall, at Times, receive for their Services, a Compensation, which shall not be diminished during their Continuance in Office.

Section 2. The judicial Power shall extend to all Cases, in Law and Equity, arising under this Constitution, the Laws of the United States, and Treaties made, or which shall be made, under their Authority;—to all Cases affecting Ambassadors, other public Ministers and Consuls;—to all Cases of admiralty and maritime Jurisdiction;—to Controversies to which the United States shall be a Party;—to controversies between two or more States;—between a State and Citizens of another State;—between Citizens of different States;—between Citizens of the same State claiming Lands under Grants of

different States, and between a State, or the Citizens thereof, and foreign States, Citizens or Subjects.

In all Cases affecting Ambassadors, other public Ministers and Consuls, and those in which a State shall be Party, the supreme Court shall have original Jurisdiction. In all the other Cases before mentioned, the supreme Court shall have appellate Jurisdiction, both as to Law and Fact, with such Exceptions, and under such Regulations as the Congress shall make.

The Trial of all Crimes, except in Cases of Impeachment, shall be by Jury; and such Trial shall be held in the State where the said Crimes shall have been committed; but when not committed within any State, the Trial shall be at such Place or Places as the Congress may by Law have directed.

Section 3. Treason against the United States, shall consist only in levying War against them, or in adhering to their Enemies, giving them Aid and Comfort. No Person shall be convicted of Treason unless on the Testimony of two Witnesses to the same overt Act, or on Confession in open Court.

The Congress shall have Power to declare the Punishment of Treason, but no Attainder of Treason shall work Corruption of Blood, or Forfeiture except during the Life of the Person attainted.

Article IV

Section 1. Full Faith and Credit shall be given in each State to the public Acts, Records, and judicial Proceedings of every other State. And the Congress may by general Laws prescribe the Manner in which such Arts, Records, and Proceedings shall be proved, and the Effect thereof.

Section 2. The Citizens of each State shall be entitled to all Privileges and Immunities of Citizens in the several States.

A person charged in any State with Treason, Felony, or other Crime, who shall flee from Justice, and be found in another State, shall on Demand of the executive Authority of the State from which he fled, be delivered up, to be removed to the State having Jurisdiction of the Crime.

No Person held to Service or Labour in one State, under the Laws thereof, escaping into another, shall, in Consequence of any Law or Regulation therein, be discharged from such Service or Labour, but shall be delivered up on Claim of the Party to whom such Service or Labour may be due.

Section 3. New States may be admitted by the Congress into this Union; but no new state shall be formed or erected within the Jurisdiction of any other State; nor any State be formed by the Junction of two or more States, or Parts of States, without the Consent of the Legislatures of the States concerned as well as of the Congress.

The Congress shall have Power to dispose of and make all needful Rules and Regulations respecting the Territory or other Property belonging to the United States; and nothing in this Constitution shall be so construed as to Prejudice any Claims of the United States, or of any particular State.

Section 4. The United States shall guarantee to every State in this Union a Republican Form of Government, and shall protect each of them against Invasion; and on Application of the Legislature, or of the Executive (when the Legislature cannot be convened) against domestic Violence.

Article V

The Congress, whenever two thirds of both Houses shall deem it necessary, shall propose Amendments to this Constitution, or, on the Application of the Legislatures of two thirds of the several States, shall call a Convention for proposing Amendments, which, in either Case, shall be valid to all Intents and Purposes, as Part of this Constitution, when ratified by the Legislatures of three fourths of the several States, or by Conventions in three fourths thereof, as the one or the other Mode of Ratification may be proposed by the Congress; Provided that no Amendment which may be made prior to the Year One thousand eight hundred and eight shall in any Manner affect the first and fourth Clauses in the Ninth Section of the first Article; and that no State, without its Consent, shall be deprived of its equal Suffrage in the Senate.

Article VI

All Debts contracted and Engagements entered into, before the Adoption of this Constitution, shall be as valid against the United States under this Constitution, as under the Confederation.

This Constitution, and the Laws of the United States which shall be made in Pursuance thereof; and all Treaties made, or which shall be made, under the Authority of the United States, shall be the supreme Law of the Land; and the Judges in every State shall be bound thereby, any Thing in the Constitution or Laws of any State to the Contrary notwithstanding.

The Senators and Representatives before mentioned, and the Members of the several State Legislatures, and all executive and judicial Officers, both of the United States and of the Several States, shall be bound by Oath or Affirmation, to support this Constitution; but no religious Test shall ever be required as a Qualification to any Office or public Trust under the United States.

Article VII

The Ratification of the Conventions of nine States, shall be sufficient for the Establishment of this Constitution between the States so ratifying the Same.

Amendment I [1791]

Congress shall make no law respecting an establishment of religion, or prohibiting the free exercise thereof; or abridging the freedom of speech, or the press; or the right of the people peaceably to assemble, and to petition the Government for a redress of grievances.

Amendment II [1791]

A well regulated Militia, being necessary to the security for a free State, the right of the people to keep and bear Arms, shall not be infringed.

Amendment III [1791]

No Soldier shall, in time of peace be quartered in any house, without the consent of the Owner, nor in time of war, but in a manner to be prescribed by law.

Amendment IV [1791]

The right of the people to be secure in their persons, houses, papers, and effects, against unreasonable searches and seizures, shall not be violated, and no Warrants shall issue, but upon probable cause, supported by Oath or Affirmation, and particularly describing the place to be searched, and the persons or things to be seized.

Amendment V [1791]

No person shall be held to answer for a capital, or otherwise infamous crime, unless on a presentment or indictment of a Grand Jury, except in cases arising in the land or naval forces, or in the Militia, when in actual service in time of War or public danger; nor shall any person be subject for the same offense to be twice put in jeopardy of life or limb; nor shall be compelled in any criminal case to be a witness against himself, nor be deprived of life, liberty, or property, without due process of law; nor shall private property be taken for public use, without just compensation.

Amendment VI [1791]

In all criminal prosecutions, the accused shall enjoy the right to a speedy and public trial, by an impartial jury of the State and district wherein the crime shall have been committed, which district shall have been previously ascertained by law, and to be informed of the nature and cause of the accusation; to be confronted with the Witnesses against him; to have compulsory process for obtaining witnesses in his favor, and to have the Assistance of counsel for his defence.

Amendment VII [1791]

In suits at common law, where the value in controversy shall exceed twenty dollars, the right of trial by jury shall be preserved, and no fact tried by a jury, shall be otherwise reexamined in any Court of the United States, than according to the rules of the common law.

Amendment VIII [1791]

Excessive bail shall not be required, nor excessive fines imposed, nor cruel and unusual punishments inflicted.

Amendment IX [1791]

The enumeration in the Constitution, of certain rights, shall not be construed to deny or disparage others retained by the people.

Amendment X [1791]

The powers not delegated to the United States by the Constitution, nor prohibited by it to the States, are reserved to the States respectively, or to the people.

Amendment XI [1798]

The judicial power of the United States shall not be construed to extend to any suit in law or equity, commenced or prosecuted against one of the United States by Citizens of another State, or by Citizens or Subjects of any Foreign State.

Amendment XII [1804]

The Electors shall meet in their respective states and vote by ballot for President and Vice-President, one of whom, at least, shall not be an inhabitant of the same state with themselves; they shall name in their ballots the person voted for as President, and in distinct ballots the person voted for as Vice-President, and they shall make distinct lists of all persons voted for as President, and of all persons voted for as Vice-President, and of the number of votes for each, which lists they shall sign and certify, and transmit sealed to the seat of the government of the United States, directed to the President of the Senate;—The President of the Senate shall, in the presence of the Senate and House of Representatives, open all the certificates and the votes shall then be counted;—The person having the greatest number of votes for President, shall be the President, if such number be a majority of the whole number of Electors appointed; and if no person have such majority, then from the persons having the highest numbers not exceeding three on the list of those voted for as President, the House of Representatives shall choose immediately, by ballot, the President. But in choosing the President, the votes shall be taken by states, the representation from each state having one vote; a quorum for this purpose shall consist of a member or members from two-thirds of the states, and a majority of all the states shall be necessary to a choice. And if the House of Representatives shall not choose a President whenever the right of choice shall devolve upon them, before the fourth day of March next following, then the Vice-President shall act as President, as in the case of the death or other constitutional disability of the President. The person having the greatest number of votes as Vice-President, shall be the Vice-President, if such number be a majority of the whole number of Electors appointed, and if no person have a majority, then from the two highest numbers on the list, the Senate shall choose the Vice-President; a quorum for the purpose shall consist of two-thirds of the whole number of Senators, and a majority of the whole number shall be necessary to a choice. But no person constitutionally ineligible to the office of President shall be eligible to that of the Vice-President of the United States.

Amendment XIII [1865]

Section 1. Neither slavery nor involuntary servitude, except as a punishment for crime whereof the party shall have been duly convicted, shall exist within the United States, or any place subject to their jurisdiction.

Section 2. Congress shall have power to enforce this article by appropriate legislation.

Amendment XIV [1868]

Section 1. All persons born or naturalized in the United States, and subject to the jurisdiction thereof, are citizens of the United States and of the State wherein they reside. No State shall make or enforce any law which shall abridge the privileges or immunities of citizens of the United States; nor shall any State deprive any person of life, liberty, or property, without due process of law; nor deny to any person within its jurisdiction the equal protection of the laws.

Section 2. Representatives shall be appointed among the several States according to their respective numbers, counting the whole number of persons in each State, excluding Indians not taxed. But when the right to vote at any election for the choice of electors for President and Vice President of the United States, Representatives in Congress, the Executive and Judicial officers of a State, or the members of the Legislature thereof, is denied to any of the male inhabitants of such State, being twenty-one years of age, and citizens of the United States, or in any way abridged, except for participation in rebellion, or other crime, the basis of representation therein shall be reduced in the proportion which the number of such male citizens shall bear to the whole number of male citizens twenty-one years of age in such State.

Section 3. No person shall be a Senator or Representative in Congress, or elector of President and Vice President, or hold any office, civil or military, under the United States, or under any State, who, having previously taken an oath, as a member of Congress, or as an officer of the United States, or as a member of any State legislature, or as an executive or judicial officer of any State, to support the Constitution of the United States, shall have engaged in insurrection or rebellion against the same, or given aid or comfort to the enemies thereof. But Congress may by a vote of two-thirds of each House, remove such disability.

Section 4. The validity of the public debt of the United States, authorized by law, including debts incurred for payment of pensions and bounties for services in suppressing insurrection or rebellion, shall not be questioned. But neither the United States nor any State shall assume or pay any debt or obligation incurred in aid of insurrection of rebellion against the United States, or any claim for the loss or emancipation of any slave; but all such debts, obligations and claims shall be held illegal and void.

Section 5. The Congress shall have power to enforce, by appropriate legislation, the provisions of this article.

Amendment XV [1870]

Section 1. The right of citizens of the United States to vote shall not be denied or abridged by the United States or by any State on account of race, color, or previous condition of servitude.

Section 2. The Congress shall have power to enforce this article by appropriate legislation.

Amendment XVI [1913]

The Congress shall have power to lay and collect taxes on incomes, from whatever source derived, without apportionment among the several States, and without regard to any census or enumeration.

Amendment XVII [1913]

The Senate of the United States shall be composed of two Senators from each State, elected by the people thereof, for six years; and each Senator shall have one vote. The electors in each State shall have the qualifications requisite for electors of the most numerous branch of the State legislatures.

When vacancies happen in the representation of any State in the Senate, the executive authority of each State shall issue writs of election to fill such vacancies; *Provided,* That the legislature of any State may empower the executive thereof to make temporary appointments until the people fill the vacancies by election as the legislature may direct.

This amendment shall not be so construed as to affect the election or term of any Senator chosen before it becomes valid as part of the Constitution.

Amendment XVIII [1919]

Section 1. After one year from the ratification of this article the manufacture, sale, or transportation of intoxicating liquors within, the importation thereof into, or the exportation thereof from the United States and all territory subject to the jurisdiction thereof for beverage purposes is hereby prohibited.

Section 2. The Congress and the several States shall have concurrent power to enforce this article by appropriate legislation.

Section 3. This article shall be inoperative unless it shall have been ratified as an amendment to the Constitution by the legislatures of the several States, as provided in the Constitution, within seven years from the date of the submission hereof to the States by the Congress.

Amendment XIX [1920]

The right of citizens of the United States to vote shall not be denied or abridged by the United States or by any State on account of sex.

Congress shall have power to enforce this article by appropriate legislation.

Amendment XX [1933]

Section 1. The terms of the President and Vice President shall end at noon on the 20th day of January, and the terms of Senators and Representatives at noon on the 3rd day of January, of the years in which such terms would have ended if this article had not been ratified; and the terms of their successors shall then begin.

Section 2. The Congress shall assemble at least once in every year, and such meeting shall begin at noon on the 3rd day of January, unless they shall by law appoint a different day.

Section 3. If, at the time fixed for the beginning of the term of the President, the President elect shall have died, the Vice President elect shall become President. If a President shall not have been chosen before the time fixed for the beginning of his term, or if the President elect shall have failed to qualify, then the Vice President elect shall act as President until a President shall have qualified; and the Congress may by law provide for the case wherein neither a President elect nor a Vice President elect shall have qualified, declaring who shall then act as President, or the manner in which one who is to act shall be selected, and such person shall act accordingly until a President or Vice President shall have qualified.

Section 4. The Congress may by law provide for the case of the death of any of the persons from whom the House of Representatives may choose a President whenever the right of choice shall have devolved upon them, and for the case of the death of any of the persons from whom the Senate may choose a Vice President whenever the right of choice shall have devolved upon them.

Section 5. Sections 1 and 2 shall take effect on the 15th day of October following the ratification of this article.

Section 6. This article shall be inoperative unless it shall have been ratified as an amendment to the Constitution by the legislatures of three-fourths of the several States within seven years from the date of its submission.

Amendment XXI [1933]

Section 1. The eighteenth article of amendment to the Constitution of the United States is hereby repealed.

Section 2. The transportation or importation into any State, Territory, or possession of the United States for delivery or use therein of intoxicating liquors, in violation of the laws thereof, is hereby prohibited.

Section 3. This article shall be inoperative unless it shall have been ratified as an amendment to the Constitution by conventions in the several States, as provided in the Constitution, within seven years from the date of the submission hereof to the States by the Congress.

Amendment XXII [1951]

Section 1. No person shall be elected to the office of the President more than twice, and no person who has held the office of President, or acted as President, for more than two years of a term to which some other person was elected President shall be elected to the office of the President more than once. But this Article shall not apply to any person holding the office of President when this article was proposed by the Congress, and shall not prevent any person who may be holding the office of President, or acting as President, during the term within which this Article becomes operative from holding the office of President, or acting as President during the remainder of such term.

Section 2. This article shall be inoperative unless it shall have been ratified as an amendment to the Constitution by the legislatures of three-fourths of the several States within seven years from the date of its submission to the States by the Congress.

Amendment XXIII [1961]

Section 1. The District constituting the seat of government of the United States shall appoint in such manner as the Congress may direct:

A number of electors of President and Vice President equal to the whole number of Senators and Representatives in Congress to which the District would be entitled if it were a State, but in no event more than the least populous State; they shall be in addition to those appointed by the States, but they shall be considered, for the purposes of the election of President and Vice President, to be electors appointed by a State; and they shall meet in the District and perform such duties as provided by the twelfth article of amendment.

Section 2. The Congress shall have power to enforce this article by appropriate legislation.

Amendment XXIV [1964]

Section 1. The right of citizens of the United States to vote in any primary or other election for President or Vice President, for electors for President or Vice President, or for Senator or Representative in Congress, shall not be denied or abridged by the United States or any State by reason of failure to pay any poll tax or other tax.

Section 2. The Congress shall have power to enforce this article by appropriate legislation.

Amendment XXV [1967]

Section 1. In case of the removal of the President from office or of his death or resignation, the Vice President shall become President.

Section 2. Whenever there is a vacancy in the office of the Vice President, the President shall nominate a Vice President who shall take office upon confirmation by a majority vote of both Houses of Congress.

Section 3. Whenever the President transmits to the President pro tempore of the Senate and the Speaker of the House of Representatives his written declaration that he is unable to discharge the powers and duties of his office, and until he transmits to them a written declaration to the contrary, such powers and duties shall be discharged by the Vice President as Acting President.

Section 4. Whenever the Vice President and a majority of either the principal officers of the executive departments or of such other body as Congress may by law provide, transmit to the President pro tempore of the Senate and the Speaker of the House of Representatives their written declaration that the President is unable to discharge the powers and duties of his office, the Vice President shall immediately assume the powers and duties of the office as Acting President.

Thereafter, when the President transmits to the President pro tempore of the Senate and the Speaker of the House of Representatives his written declaration that no inability exists, he shall resume the powers and duties of his office unless the Vice President and a majority of either the principal officers of the executive department or of such other body as Congress may by law provide, transmit within four days to the President pro tempore of the Senate and the Speaker of the House of Representatives their written declaration that the President is unable to discharge the powers and duties of his office. Thereupon Congress shall decide the issue, assembling within forty-eight hours for that purpose if not in session. If the Congress, within twenty-one days after receipt of the latter written declaration, or, if Congress is not in session, within twenty-one days after Congress is required to assemble, determines by two-thirds vote of both Houses that the President shall continue to discharge the same as Acting President; otherwise, the President shall resume the powers and duties of his office.

Amendment XXVI [1971]

Section 1. The right of citizens of the United States, who are 18 years of age or older, to vote, shall not be denied or abridged by the United States or any State on account of age.

Section 2. The Congress shall have the power to enforce this article by appropriate legislation.

Amendment XXVII [1992]

No law, varying the compensation for the services of the Senators and Representatives, shall take effect, until an election of Representatives shall have intervened.

Appendix C — Uniform Commercial Code (2000 Official Text), Article 2

Article 2 Sales

Part 1. Short Title, General Construction and Subject Matter

§2–101.   Short Title.

This Article shall be known and may be cited as Uniform Commercial Code—Sales.

§2–102.   Scope; Certain Security and Other Transactions Excluded From This Article.

Unless the context otherwise requires, this Article applies to transactions in goods; it does not apply to any transaction which although in the form of an unconditional contract to sell or present sale is intended to operate only as a security transaction nor does this Article impair or repeal any statute regulating sales to consumers, farmers or other specified classes of buyers.

§2–103.   Definitions and Index of Definitions.

(1)   In this Article unless the context otherwise requires

(a)   "Buyer" means a person who buys or contracts to buy goods.

(b)   "Good faith" in the case of a merchant means honesty in fact and the observance of reasonable commercial standards of fair dealing in the trade.

(c)   "Receipt" of goods means taking physical possession of them.

(d)   "Seller" means a person who sells or contracts to sell goods.

(2)   Other definitions applying to this Article or to specified Parts thereof, and the sections in which they appear are:

"Acceptance"	Section 2–606.
"Banker's credit"	Section 2–325.
"Between merchants"	Section 2–104.
"Cancellation"	Section 2–106(4).
"Commercial unit"	Section 2–105.
"Confirmed credit"	Section 2–325.
"Conforming to contract"	Section 2–106.
"Contract for sale"	Section 2–106.
"Cover"	Section 2–712.
"Entrusting"	Section 2–403.
"Financing agency"	Section 2–104.
"Future goods"	Section 2–105.
"Goods"	Section 2–105.
"Identification"	Section 2–501.
"Installment contract"	Section 2–612.
"Letter of Credit"	Section 2–325.
"Lot"	Section 2–105.
"Merchant"	Section 2–104.
"Overseas"	Section 2–323.
"Person in position of seller"	Section 2–707.
"Present sale"	Section 2–106.
"Sale"	Section 2–106.
"Sale on approval"	Section 2–326.
"Sale or return"	Section 2–326.
"Termination"	Section 2–106.

(3)   The following definitions in other Articles apply to this Article:

"Check"	Section 3–104.
"Consignee"	Section 7–102.
"Consignor"	Section 7–102.
"Consumer goods"	Section 9–102.
"Dishonor"	Section 3–502.
"Draft"	Section 3–104.

(4)   In addition Article 1 contains general definitions and principles of construction and interpretation applicable throughout this Article.

§2–104.   Definitions: "Merchant"; "Between Merchants"; "Financing Agency".

(1)   "Merchant" means a person who deals in goods of the kind or otherwise by his occupation holds himself out as having knowledge or skill peculiar to the practices or goods involved in the trans-

action or to whom such knowledge or skill may be attributed by his employment of an agent or broker or other intermediary who by his occupation holds himself out as having such knowledge or skill.

(2)   "Financing agency" means a bank, finance company or other person who in the ordinary course of business makes advances against goods or documents of title or who by arrangement with either the seller or the buyer intervenes in ordinary course to make or collect payment due or claimed under the contract for sale, as by purchasing or paying the seller's draft or making advances against it or by merely taking it for collection whether or not the documents of title accompany the draft. "Financing agency" includes also a bank or other person who similarly intervenes between persons who are in the position of seller and buyer in respect to the goods (Section 2–707).

(3)   "Between merchants" means in any transaction with respect to which both parties are chargeable with the knowledge or skill of merchants.

§2–105. Definitions: Transferability; "Goods"; "Future" Goods; "Lot"; "Commercial Unit".

(1)   "Goods" means all things (including specially manufactured goods) which are movable at the time of identification to the contract for sale other than the money in which the price is to be paid, investment securities (Article 8) and things in action. "Goods" also includes the unborn young of animals and growing crops and other identified things attached to realty as described in the section on goods to be severed from realty (Section 2–107).

(2)   Goods must be both existing and identified before any interest in them can pass. Goods which are not both existing and identified are "future" goods. A purported present sale of future goods or of any interest therein operates as a contract to sell.

(3)   There may be a sale of a part interest in existing identified goods.

(4)   An undivided share in an identified bulk of fungible goods is sufficiently identified to be sold although the quantity of the bulk is not determined. Any agreed proportion of such a bulk or any quantity thereof agreed upon by number, weight or other measure may to the extent of the seller's interest in the bulk be sold to the buyer who then becomes an owner in common.

(5)   "Lot" means a parcel or a single article which is the subject matter of a separate sale or delivery, whether or not it is sufficient to perform the contract.

(6)   "Commercial unit" means such a unit of goods as by commercial usage is a single whole for purposes of sale and division of which materially impairs its character or value on the market or in use. A commercial unit may be a single article (as a machine) or a set of articles (as a suite of furniture or an assortment of sizes) or a quantity (as a bale, gross, or carload) or any other unit treated in use or in the relevant market as a single whole.

§2–106. Definitions: "Contract"; "Agreement"; "Contract for Sale"; "Sale"; "Present Sale"; "Conforming" to Contract; "Termination"; "Cancellation".

(1)   In this Article unless the context otherwise requires "contract" and "agreement" are limited to those relating to the present or future sale of goods. "Contract for sale" includes both a present sale of goods and a contract to sell goods at a future time. A "sale" consists in the passing of title from the seller to the buyer for a price (Section 2–401). A "present sale" means a sale which is accomplished by the making of the contract.

(2)   Goods or conduct including any part of a performance are "conforming" or conform to the contract when they are in accordance with the obligations under the contract.

(3)   "Termination" occurs when either party pursuant to a power created by agreement or law puts an end to the contract otherwise than for its breach. On "termination" all obligations which are still executory on both sides are discharged but any right based on prior breach or performance survives.

(4)   "Cancellation" occurs when either party puts an end to the contract for breach by the other and its effect is the same as that of "termination" except that the cancelling party also retains any remedy for breach of the whole contract or any unperformed balance.

§2–107. Goods to Be Severed from Realty: Recording.

(1)   A contract for the sale of minerals or the like (including oil and gas) or a structure or its materials to be removed from realty is a contract for the sale of goods within this Article if they are to be severed by the seller but until severance a purported present sale thereof which is not effective as a transfer of an interest in land is effective only as a contract to sell.

(2)   A contract for the sale apart from the land of growing crops or other things attached to realty and capable of severance without material harm thereto but not described in subsection (1) or of timber to be cut is a contract for the sale of goods within this Article whether the subject matter is to be severed by the buyer or by the seller even though it forms part of the realty at the time of contracting, and the parties can by identification effect a present sale before severance.

(3)   The provisions of this section are subject to any third party rights provided by the law relating to realty records, and the contract for sale may be executed and recorded as a document transferring an interest in land and shall then constitute notice to third parties of the buyer's right under the contract for sale.

Part 2. Form, Formation and Readjustment of Contra

§2–201. Formal Requirements; Statute of Frauds.

(1)   Except as otherwise provided in this section a contract for the sale of goods for the price of $500 or more is not enforceable by way of action or defense unless there is some writing sufficient to indicate that a contract for sale has been made between the parties and signed by the party against whom enforcement is sought or by his authorized agent or broker. A writing is not insufficient because it omits or incorrectly states a term agreed upon but the contract is not enforceable under this paragraph beyond the quantity of goods shown in such writing.

(2)   Between merchants if within a reasonable time a writing in confirmation of the contract and sufficient against the sender is received and the party receiving it has reason to know its contents, it satisfies the requirements of subsection (1) against such party unless written notice of objection to its contents is given within 10 days after it is received.

(3)   A contract which does not satisfy the requirements of subsection (1) but which is valid in other respects is enforceable

    (a) if the goods are to be specially manufactured for the buyer and are not suitable for sale to others in the ordinary course of the seller's business and the seller, before notice of repudiation is received and under circumstances which reasonably indicate that the goods are for the buyer, has made either a substantial beginning of their manufacture or commitments for their procurement; or

(b) if the party against whom enforcement is sought admits in his pleading, testimony or otherwise in court that a contract for sale was made, but the contract is not enforceable under this provision beyond the quantity of goods admitted; or

(c) with respect to goods for which payment has been made and accepted or which have been received and accepted (Section 2–606).

§2-202. Final Written Expression: Parol or Extrinsic Evidence.

Terms with respect to which the confirmatory memoranda of the parties agree or which are otherwise set forth in a writing intended by the parties as a final expression of their agreement with respect to such terms as are included therein may not be contradicted by evidence of any prior agreement or of a contemporaneous oral agreement but may be explained or supplemented

(a) by course and dealing or usage of trade (Section 1–205) or by course of performance (Section 2–208); and

(b) by evidence of consistent additional terms unless the court finds the writing to have been intended also as a complete and exclusive statement of the terms of the agreement.

§2-203. Seals Inoperative.

The affixing of a seal to a writing evidencing a contract for sale or an offer to buy or sell goods does not constitute the writing a sealed instrument and the law with respect to sealed instruments does not apply to such a contract or offer.

§2-204. Formation in General.

(1) A contract for sale of goods may be made in any manner sufficient to show agreement, including conduct by both parties which recognizes the existence of such a contract.

(2) An agreement sufficient to constitute a contract for sale may be found even though the moment of its making is undetermined.

(3) Even though one or more terms are left open a contract for sale does not fail for indefiniteness if the parties have intended to make a contract and there is a reasonably certain basis for giving an appropriate remedy.

§2-205. Firm Offers.

An offer by a merchant to buy or sell goods in a signed writing which by its terms gives assurance that it will be held open is not revocable, for lack of consideration, during the time stated or if no time is stated for a reasonable time, but in no event may such period of irrevocability exceed three months; but any such term of assurance on a form supplied by the offeree must be separately signed by the offeror.

§2-206. Offer and Acceptance in Formation of Contract.

(1) Unless otherwise unambiguously indicated by the language or circumstances

(a) an offer to make a contract shall be construed as inviting acceptance in any manner and by any medium reasonable in the circumstances;

(b) an order or other offer to buy goods for prompt or current shipment shall be construed as inviting acceptance either by a prompt promise to ship or by the prompt or current shipment of conforming or non-conforming goods, but such a shipment of non-conforming goods does not constitute an acceptance if the seller seasonably notifies the buyer that the shipment is offered only as an accommodation to the buyer.

(2) Where the beginning of a requested performance is a reasonable mode of acceptance an offeror who is not notified of acceptance within a reasonable time may treat the offer as having lapsed before acceptance.

§2-207. Additional Terms in Acceptance or Confirmation.

(1) A definite and seasonable expression of acceptance or a written confirmation which is sent within a reasonable time operates as an acceptance even though it states terms additional to or different from those offered or agreed upon, unless acceptance is expressly made conditional on assent to the additional or different terms.

(2) The additional terms are to be construed as proposals for addition to the contract. Between merchants such terms become part of the contract unless:

(a) the offer expressly limits acceptance to the terms of the offer;

(b) they materially alter it; or

(c) notification of objection to them has already been given or is given within a reasonable time after notice of them is received.

(3) Conduct by both parties which recognizes the existence of a contract is sufficient to establish a contract for sale although the writings of the parties do not otherwise establish a contract. In such case the terms of the particular contract consist of those terms on which the writings of the parties agree, together with any supplementary terms incorporated under any other provisions of this Act.

§2-208. Course of Performance or Practical Construction.

(1) Where the contract for sale involves repeated occasions for performance by either party with knowledge of the nature of the performance and opportunity for objection to it by the other, any course of performance accepted or acquiesced in without objection shall be relevant to determine the meaning of the agreement.

(2) The express terms of the agreement and any such course of performance, as well as any course of dealing and usage of trade, shall be construed whenever reasonable as consistent with each other; but when such construction is unreasonable, express terms shall control course of performance and course of performance shall control both course of dealing and usage of trade (Section 1–205).

(3) Subject to the provisions of the next section on modification and waiver, such course of performance shall be relevant to show a waiver or modification of any term inconsistent with such course of performance.

§2-209. Modification, Rescission and Waiver.

(1) An agreement modifying a contract within this Article needs no consideration to be binding.

(2) A signed agreement which excludes modification or rescission except by a signed writing cannot be otherwise modified or rescinded, but except as between merchants such a requirement on a form supplied by the merchant must be separately signed by the other party.

(3) The requirements of the statute of frauds section of this Article (Section 2–201) must be satisfied if the contract as modified is within its provisions.

(4) Although an attempt at modification or rescission does not satisfy the requirements of subsection (2) or (3) it can operate as a waiver.

(5) A party who has made a waiver affecting an executory portion of the contract may retract the waiver by reasonable notification received by the other party that strict performance will be required of any term waived, unless the retraction would be unjust in view of a material change of position in reliance on the waiver.

§2-210. Delegation of Performance; Assignment of Rights.

(1) A party may perform his duty through a delegate unless otherwise agreed or unless the other party has a substantial interest in having his original promisor perform or control the acts required by the contract. No delegation of performance relieves the party delegating of any duty to perform or any liability for breach.

(2) Except as otherwise provided in Section 9–406, unless otherwise agreed all rights of either seller or buyer can be assigned except where the assignment would materially change the duty of the other party, or increase materially the burden or risk imposed on him by his contract, or impair materially his chance of obtaining return performance. A right to damages for breach of the whole contract or a right arising out of the assignor's due performance of his entire obligation can be assigned despite agreement otherwise.

(3) The creation, attachment, perfection, or enforcement of a security interest in the seller's interest under a contract is not a transfer that materially changes the duty of or increases materially the burden or risk imposed on the buyer or impairs materially the buyer's chance of obtaining return performance within the purview of subsection (2) unless, and then only to the extent that, enforcement actually results in a delegation of material performance of the seller. Even in that event, the creation, attachment, perfection, and enforcement of the security interest remain effective, but (i) the seller is liable to the buyer for damages caused by the delegation to the extent that the damages could not reasonably be prevented by the buyer, and (ii) a court having jurisdiction may grant other appropriate relief, including cancellation of the contract for sale or an injunction against enforcement of the security interest or consummation of the enforcement.

(4) Unless the circumstances indicate the contrary a prohibition of assignment of "the contract" is to be construed as barring only the delegation to the assignee of the assignor's performance.

(5) An assignment of "the contract" or of "all my rights under the contract" or an assignment in similar general terms is an assignment of rights and unless the language or the circumstances (as in an assignment for security) indicate the contrary, it is a delegation of performance of the duties of the assignor and its acceptance by the assignee constitutes a promise by him to perform those duties. This promise is enforceable by either the assignor or the other party to the original contract.

(6) The other party may treat any assignment which delegates performance as creating reasonable grounds for insecurity and may without prejudice to his rights against the assignor demand assurances from the assignee (Section 2–609).

Part 3. General Obligation and Construction of Contract

§2-301. General Obligations of Parties.

The obligation of the seller is to transfer and deliver and that of the buyer is to accept and pay in accordance with the contract.

§2-302. Unconscionable Contract or Clause.

(1) If the court as a matter of law finds the contract or any clause of the contract to have been unconscionable at the time it was made the court may refuse to enforce the contract, or it may enforce the remainder of the contract without the unconscionable clause, or it may so limit the application of any unconscionable clause as to avoid any unconscionable result.

(2) When it is claimed or appears to the court that the contract or any clause thereof may be unconscionable the parties shall be afforded a reasonable opportunity to present evidence as to its commercial setting, purpose and effect to aid the court in making the determination.

§2-303. Allocation or Division of Risks.

Where this Article allocates a risk or a burden as between the parties "unless otherwise agreed", the agreement may not only shift the allocation but may also divide the risk or burden.

§2-304. Price Payable in Money, Goods, Realty, or Otherwise.

(1) The price can be made payable in money or otherwise. If it is payable in whole or in part in goods each party is a seller of the goods which he is to transfer.

(2) Even though all or part of the price is payable in an interest in realty the transfer of the goods and the seller's obligations with reference to them are subject to this Article, but not the transfer of the interest in realty or the transferor's obligations in connection therewith.

§2-305. Open Price Term.

(1) The parties if they so intend can conclude a contract for sale even though the price is not settled. In such a case the price is a reasonable price at the time for delivery if
    (a) nothing is said as to price; or
    (b) the price is left to be agreed by the parties and they fail to agree; or
    (c) the price is to be fixed in terms of some agreed market or other standard as set or recorded by a third person or agency and it is not so set or recorded.

(2) A price to be fixed by the seller or by the buyer means a price for him to fix in good faith.

(3) When a price left to be fixed otherwise than by agreement of the parties fails to be fixed through fault of one party the other may at his option treat the contract as cancelled or himself fix a reasonable price.

(4) Where, however, the parties intend not to be bound unless the price be fixed or agreed and it is not fixed or agreed there is no contract. In such a case the buyer must return any goods already received or if unable so to do must pay their reasonable value at the time of delivery and the seller must return any portion of the price paid on account.

§2-306. Output, Requirements and Exclusive Dealings.

(1) A term which measures the quantity by the output of the seller or the requirements of the buyer means such actual output or requirements as may occur in good faith, except that no quantity unreasonably disproportionate to any stated estimate or in the absence of a stated estimate to any normal or otherwise comparable prior output or requirements may be tendered or demanded.

(2) A lawful agreement by either the seller or the buyer for exclusive dealing in the kind of goods concerned imposes unless

otherwise agreed an obligation by the seller to use best efforts to supply the goods and by the buyer to use best efforts to promote their sale.

§2-307. Delivery in Single Lot or Several Lots.

Unless otherwise agreed all goods called for by a contract for sale must be tendered in a single delivery and payment is due only on such tender but where the circumstances give either party the right to make or demand delivery in lots the price if it can be apportioned may be demanded for each lot.

§2-308. Absence of Specified Place for Delivery.

Unless otherwise agreed
- (a) the place for delivery of goods is the seller's place of business or if he has none, his residence; but
- (b) in a contract for sale of identified goods which to the knowledge of the parties at the time of contracting are in some other place, that place is the place for their delivery; and
- (c) documents of title may be delivered through customary banking channels.

§2-309. Absence of Specific Time Provisions; Notice of Termination.

(1) The time for shipment or delivery or any other action under a contract if not provided in this Article or agreed upon shall be a reasonable time.

(2) Where the contract provides for successive performance but is indefinite in duration it is valid for a reasonable time but unless otherwise agreed may be terminated at any time by either party.

(3) Termination of a contract by one party except on the happening of an agreed event requires that reasonable notification be received by the other party and an agreement dispensing with notification is invalid if its operation would be unconscionable.

§2-310. Open Time for Payment or Running of Credit; Authority to Ship Under Reservation.

Unless otherwise agreed
- (a) payment is due at the time and place at which the buyer is to receive the goods even though the place of shipment is the place of delivery; and
- (b) if the seller is authorized to send the goods he may ship them under reservation, and may tender the documents of title, but the buyer may inspect the goods after their arrival before payment is due unless such inspection is inconsistent with the terms of the contract (Section 2-513); and
- (c) if delivery is authorized and made by way of documents of title otherwise than by subsection (b) then payment is due at the time and place at which the buyer is to receive the documents regardless of where the goods are to be received; and
- (d) where the seller is required or authorized to ship the goods on credit the credit period runs from the time of shipment but post-dating the invoice or delaying its dispatch will correspondingly delay the starting of the credit period.

§2-311. Options and Cooperation Respecting Performance.

(1) An agreement for sale which is otherwise sufficiently definite (subsection (3) of Section 2-204) to be a contract is not made invalid by the fact that it leaves particulars of performance to be specified by one of the parties. Any such specification must be made in good faith and within limits set by commercial reasonableness.

(2) Unless otherwise agreed specifications relating to assortment of the goods are at the buyer's option and except as otherwise provided in subsections (1) (c) and (3) of Section 2-319 specifications or arrangements relating to shipment are at the seller's option.

(3) Where such specification would materially affect the other party's performance but is not seasonably made or where one party's cooperation is necessary to the agreed performance of the other but is not seasonably forthcoming, the other party in addition to all other remedies
- (a) is excused for any resulting delay in his own performance; and
- (b) may also either proceed to perform in any reasonable manner or after the time for a material part of his own performance treat the failure to specify or to cooperate as a breach by failure to deliver or accept the goods.

§2-312. Warranty of Title and Against Infringement; Buyer's Obligation Against Infringement.

(1) Subject to subsection (2) there is in a contract for sale a warranty by the seller that
- (a) the title conveyed shall be good, and its transfer rightful; and
- (b) the goods shall be delivered free from any security interest or other lien or encumbrance of which the buyer at the time of contracting has no knowledge.

(2) A warranty under subsection (1) will be excluded or modified only by specific language or by circumstances which give the buyer reason to know that the person selling does not claim title in himself or that he is purporting to sell only such right or title as he or a third person may have.

(3) Unless otherwise agreed a seller who is a merchant regularly dealing in goods of the kind warrants that the goods shall be delivered free of the rightful claim of any third person by way of infringement or the like but a buyer who furnishes specifications to the seller must hold the seller harmless against any such claim which arises out of compliance with the specifications.

§2-313. Express Warranties by Affirmation, Promise, Description, Sample.

(1) Express warranties by the seller are created as follows:
- (a) Any affirmation of fact or promise made by the seller to the buyer which relates to the goods and becomes part of the basis of the bargain creates an express warranty that the goods shall conform to the affirmation or promise.
- (b) Any description of the goods which is made part of the basis of the bargain creates an express warranty that the goods shall conform to the description.
- (c) Any sample or model which is made part of the basis of the bargain creates an express warranty that the

whole of the goods shall conform to the sample or model.

(2) It is not necessary to the creation of an express warranty that the seller use formal words such as "warrant" or "guarantee" or that he have a specific intention to make a warranty, but an affirmation merely of the value of the goods or a statement purporting to be merely the seller's opinion or commendation of the goods does not create a warranty.

§2–314. Implied Warranty: Merchantability; Usage of Trade.

(1) Unless excluded or modified (Section 2–316), a warranty that the goods shall be merchantable is implied in a contract for their sale if the seller is a merchant with respect to goods of that kind. Under this section the serving for value of food or drink to be consumed either on the premises or elsewhere is a sale.

(2) Goods to be merchantable must be at least such as

(a) pass without objection in the trade under the contract description; and

(b) in the case of fungible goods, are of fair average quality within the description; and

(c) are fit for the ordinary purposes for which such goods are used; and

(d) run, within the variations permitted by the agreement, of even kind, quality and quantity within each unit and among all units involved; and

(e) are adequately contained, packaged, and labeled as the agreement may require; and

(f) conform to the promises or affirmations of fact made on the container or label if any.

(3) Unless excluded or modified (Section 2–316) other implied warranties may arise from course of dealing or usage of trade.

§2–315. Implied Warranty: Fitness for Particular Purpose.

Where the seller at the time of contracting has reason to know any particular purpose for which the goods are required and that the buyer is relying on the seller's skill or judgment to select or furnish suitable goods, there is unless excluded or modified under the next section an implied warranty that the goods shall be fit for such purpose.

§2–316. Exclusion or Modification of Warranties.

(1) Words or conduct relevant to the creation of an express warranty and words or conduct tending to negate or limit warranty shall be construed wherever reasonable as consistent with each other, but subject to the provisions of this Article on parol or extrinsic evidence (Section 2–202) negation or limitation is inoperative to the extent that such construction is unreasonable.

(2) Subject to subsection (3), to exclude or modify the implied warranty of merchantability or any part of it the language must mention merchantability and in case of a writing must be conspicuous, and to exclude or modify any implied warranty of fitness the exclusion must be by a writing and conspicuous. Language to exclude all implied warranties of fitness is sufficient if it states, for example, that "There are no warranties which extend beyond the description on the face hereof."

(3) Notwithstanding subsection (2)

(a) unless the circumstances indicate otherwise, all implied warranties are excluded by expression like "as is", "with all faults" or other language which in com-

mon understanding calls the buyer's attention to the exclusion of warranties and makes plain that there is no implied warranty; and

(b) when the buyer before entering into the contract has examined the goods or the sample or model as fully as he desired or has refused to examine the goods there is no implied warranty with regard to defects which an examination ought in the circumstances to have revealed to him; and

(c) an implied warranty can also be excluded or modified by course of dealing or course of performance or usage of trade.

(4) Remedies for breach of warranty can be limited in accordance with the provisions of this Article on liquidation or limitation of damages and on contractual modification of remedy (Sections 2–718 and 2–719).

§2–317. Cumulation and Conflict of Warranties Express or Implied.

Warranties whether express or implied shall be construed as consistent with each other and as cumulative, but if such construction is unreasonable the intention of the parties shall determine which warranty is dominant. In ascertaining that intention the following rules apply:

(a) Exact or technical specifications displace an inconsistent sample or model or general language of description.

(b) A sample from an existing bulk displaces inconsistent general language of description.

(c) Express warranties displace inconsistent implied warranties other than an implied warranty of fitness for a particular purpose.

§2–318. Third Party Beneficiaries of Warranties Express or Implied.

Note: If this Act is introduced in the Congress of the United States this section should be omitted. (States to select one alternative.)

Alternative A. A seller's warranty whether express or implied extends to any natural person who is in the family or household of his buyer or who is a guest in his home if it is reasonable to expect that such person may use, consume or be affected by the goods and who is injured in person by breach of the warranty. A seller may not exclude or limit the operation of this section.

Alternative B. A seller's warranty whether express or implied extends to any natural person who may reasonably be expected to use, consume or be affected by the goods and who is injured in person by breach of the warranty. A seller may not exclude or limit the operation of this section.

Alternative C. A seller's warranty whether express or implied extends to any person who may reasonably be expected to use, consume or be affected by the goods and who is injured by breach of the warranty. A seller may not exclude or limit the operation of this section with respect to injury to the person of an individual to whom the warranty extends.

§2–319. F.O.B. and F.A.S. Terms.

(1) Unless otherwise agreed the term F.O.B. (which means "free on board") at a named place, even though used only in connection with the stated price, is a delivery term under which

(a) when the term is F.O.B. the place of shipment, the seller must at that place ship the goods in the manner provided in this Article (Section 2–504) and bear the expense and risk of putting them into the possession of the carrier; or

(b) when the term is F.O.B. the place of destination, the seller must at his own expense and risk transport the goods to that place and there tender delivery of them in the manner provided in this Article (Section 2–503);

(c) when under either (a) or (b) the term is also F.O.B. vessel, car or other vehicle, the seller must in addition at his own expense and risk load the goods on board. If the term is F.O.B. vessel the buyer must name the vessel and in an appropriate case the seller must comply with the provisions of this Article on the form of bill of lading (Section 2–323).

(2) Unless otherwise agreed the term F.A.S. vessel (which means "free alongside") at a named port, even though used only in connection with the stated price, is a delivery term under which the seller must

(a) at his own expense and risk deliver the goods alongside the vessel in the manner usual in that port or on a dock designated and provided by the buyer; and

(b) obtain and tender a receipt for the goods in exchange for which the carrier is under a duty to issue a bill of lading.

(3) Unless otherwise agreed in any case falling within subsection (1)(a) or (c) or subsection (2) the buyer must seasonally give any needed instructions for making delivery, including when the term is F.A.S. or F.O.B. the loading berth of the vessel and in an appropriate case its name and sailing date. The seller may treat the failure of needed instructions as a failure of cooperation under this Article (Section 2–311). He may also at his option move the goods in any reasonable manner preparatory to delivery or shipment.

(4) Under the term F.O.B. vessel or F.A.S. unless otherwise agreed the buyer must make payment against tender of the required documents and the seller may not tender nor the buyer demand delivery of the goods in substitution for the documents.

§2–320. C.I.F. and C. & F. Terms.

(1) The term C.I.F. means that the price includes in a lump sum the cost of the goods and the insurance and freight to the named destination. The term C. & F. or C.F. means that the price so includes cost and freight to the named destination.

(2) Unless otherwise agreed and even though used only in connection with the stated price and destination, the term C.I.F. destination or its equivalent requires the seller at his own expense and risk to

(a) put the goods into the possession of a carrier at the port for shipment and obtain a negotiable bill or bills of lading covering the entire transportation to the named destination; and

(b) load the goods and obtain a receipt from the carrier (which may be contained in the bill of lading) showing that the freigt has been paid or provided for; and

(c) obtain a policy or certificate of insurance, including any war risk insurance, of a kind and on terms then current at the port of shipment in the usual amount, in the currency of the contract, shown to cover the same goods covered by the bill of lading and providing for payment of loss to the order of the buyer or for the account of whom it may concern; but the seller may add to the price the amount of the premium for any such war risk insurance; and

(d) prepare an invoice of the goods and procure any other documents required to effect shipment or to comply with the contract; and

(e) forward and tender with commercial promptness all the documents in due form and with any indorsement necessary to perfect the buyer's rights.

(3) Unless otherwise agreed the term C. & F. or its equivalent has the same effect and imposes upon the seller the same obligations and risks as a C.I.F. term except the obligation as to insurance.

(4) Under the term C.I.F. or C. & F. unless otherwise agreed the buyer must make payment against tender of the required documents and the seller may not tender nor the buyer demand delivery of the goods in substitution for the documents.

§2–321. C.I.F. or C. & F.: "Net Landed Weights"; "Payment on Arrival"; Warranty of Condition on Arrival.

Under a contract containing a term C.I.F. or C. & F.

(1) Where the price is based on or is to be adjusted according to "net landed weights", "delivered weights", "out turn" quantity or quality or the like, unless otherwise agreed the seller must reasonably estimate the price. The payment due on tender of the documents called for by the contract is the amount so estimated, but after final adjustment of the price a settlement must be made with commercial promptness.

(2) An agreement described in subsection (1) or any warranty of quality or condition of the goods on arrival places upon the seller the risk of ordinary deterioration, shrinkage and the like in transportation but has no effect on the place or time of identification to the contract for sale or delivery or on the passing of the risk of loss.

(3) Unless otherwise agreed where the contract provides for payment on or after arrival of the goods the seller must before payment allow such preliminary inspection as is feasible; but if the goods are lost delivery of the documents and payment are due when the goods should have arrived.

§2–322. Delivery "Ex-Ship".

(1) Unless otherwise agreed a term for delivery of goods "ex-ship" (which means from the carrying vessel) or in equivalent language is not restricted to a particular ship and requires delivery from a ship which has reached a place at the named port of destination where goods of the kind are usually discharged.

(2) Under such a term unless otherwise agreed

(a) the seller must discharge all liens arising out of the carriage and furnish the buyer with a direction which puts the carrier under a duty to deliver the goods; and

(b) the risk of loss does not pass to the buyer until the goods leave the ship's tackle or are otherwise properly unloaded.

§2–323. Form of Bill of Lading Required in Overseas Shipment; "Overseas".

(1) Where the contract contemplates overseas shipment and contains a term C.I.F. or C. & F. or F.O.B. vessel, the seller unless

otherwise agreed must obtain a negotiable bill of lading stating that the goods have been loaded on board or, in the case of a term C.I.F. or C. & F., received for shipment.

(2) Where in a case within subsection (1) a bill of lading has been issued in a set of parts, unless otherwise agreed if the documents are not to be sent from abroad the buyer may demand tender of the full set; otherwise only one part of the bill of lading need be tendered. Even if the agreement expressly requires a full set

(a) due tender of a single part is acceptable within the provisions of this Article on cure of improper delivery (subsection (1) of Section 2–508); and

(b) even though the full set is demanded, if the documents are sent from abroad the person tendering an incomplete set may nevertheless require payment upon furnishing an indemnity which the buyer in good faith deems adequate.

(3) A shipment by water or by air or a contract contemplating such shipment is "overseas" insofar as by usage of trade or agreement it is subject to the commercial, financing or shipping practices characteristic of international deep water commerce.

§2–324. "No Arrival, No Sale" Term.

Under a term "no arrival, no sale" or terms of like meaning, unless otherwise agreed.

(a) the seller must properly ship conforming goods and if they arrive by any means he must tender them on arrival but he assumes no obligation that the goods will arrive unless he has caused the non-arrival; and

(b) where without fault of the seller the goods are in part lost or have so deteriorated as no longer to conform to the contract or arrive after the contract time, the buyer may proceed as if there had been casualty to identified goods (Section 2–613).

§2–325. "Letter of Credit" Term; "Confirmed Credit".

(1) Failure of the buyer seasonably to furnish an agreed letter of credit is a breach of the contract for sale.

(2) The delivery to seller of a proper letter of credit suspends the buyer's obligation to pay. If the letter of credit is dishonored, the seller may on seasonable notification to the buyer require payment directly from him.

(3) Unless otherwise agreed the term "letter of credit" or "banker's credit" in a contract for sale means an irrevocable credit issued by a financing agency of good repute and, where the shipment is overseas, of good international repute. The term "confirmed credit" means that the credit must also carry the direct obligation of such an agency which does business in the seller's financial market.

§2–326. Sale on Approval and Sale or Return; Rights of Creditors.

(1) Unless otherwise agreed, if delivered goods may be returned by the buyer even though they conform to the contract, the transaction is

(a) a "sale on approval" if the goods are delivered primarily for use, and

(b) a "sale or return" if the goods are delivered primarily for resale.

(2) Goods held on approval are not subject to the claims of the buyer's creditors until acceptance; goods held on sale or return are subject to such claims while in the buyer's possession.

(3) Any "or return" term of a contract for sale is to be treated as a separate contract for sale within the statute of frauds section of this Article (Section 2–201) and as contradicting the sale aspect of the contract within the provisions of this Article on parol or extrinsic evidence (Section 2–202).

§2–327. Special Incidents of Sale on Approval and Sale or Return.

(1) Under a sale on approval unless otherwise agreed

(a) although the goods are identified to the contract the risk of loss and the title do not pass to the buyer until acceptance; and

(b) use of the goods consistent with the purpose of trial is not acceptance but failure seasonably to notify the seller of election to return the goods is acceptance, and if the goods conform to the contract acceptance of any part is acceptance of the whole; and

(c) after due notification of election to return, the return is at the seller's risk and expense but a merchant buyer must follow any reasonable instructions.

(2) Under a sale or return unless otherwise agreed

(a) the option to return extends to the whole or any commercial unit of the goods while in substantially their original condition, but must be exercised seasonably; and

(b) the return is at the buyer's risk and expense.

§2–328. Sale by Auction.

(1) In a sale by auction if goods are put up in lots each lot is the subject of a separate sale.

(2) A sale by auction is complete when the auctioneer so announces by the fall of the hammer or in other customary manner. Where a bid is made while the hammer is falling in acceptance of a prior bid the auctioneer may in his discretion reopen the bidding or declare the goods sold under the bid on which the hammer was falling.

(3) Such a sale is with reserve unless the goods are in explicit terms put up without reserve. In an auction with reserve the auctioneer may withdraw the goods at any time until he announces completion of the sale. In an auction without reserve, after the auctioneer calls for bids on an article or lot, that article or lot cannot be withdrawn unless no bid is made within a reasonable time. In either case a bidder may retract his bid until the auctioneer's announcement of completion of the sale, but a bidder's retraction does not revive any previous bid.

(4) If the auctioneer knowingly receives a bid on the seller's behalf or the seller makes or procures such a bid, and notice has not been given that liberty for such bidding is reserved, the buyer may at his option avoid the sale or take the goods at the price of the last good faith bid prior to the completion of the sale. This subsection shall not apply to any bid at a forced sale.

Part 4. Title, Creditors and Good Faith Purchasers

§2–401. Passing of Title; Reservation for Security; Limited Application of This Section.

Each provision of this Article with regard to the rights, obligations and remedies of the seller, the buyer, purchasers or other third parties applies irrespective of title to the goods except where the provision refers to such title. Insofar as situations are not covered by the other provisions of this Article and matters concerning title become material the following rules apply:

(1) Title to goods cannot pass under a contract for sale prior to their identification to the contract (Section 2–501), and unless otherwise explicitly agreed the buyer acquires by their identification a special property as limited by this Act. Any retention or reservation by the seller of the title (property) in goods shipped or delivered to the buyer is limited in effect to a reservation of a security interest. Subject to these provisions and to the provisions of the Article on Secured Transactions (Article 9), title to goods passes from the seller to the buyer in any manner and on any conditions explicitly agreed on by the parties.

(2) Unless otherwise explicitly agreed title passes to the buyer at the time and place at which the seller completes his performance with reference to the physical delivery of the goods, despite any reservation of a security interest and even though a document of title is to be delivered at a different time or place; and in particular and despite any reservation of a security interest by the bill of lading

  (a) if the contract requires or authorizes the seller to send the goods to the buyer but does not require him to deliver them at destination, title passes to the buyer at the time and place of shipment; but

  (b) if the contract requires delivery at destination, title passes on tender there.

(3) Unless otherwise explicitly agreed where delivery is to be made without moving the goods.

  (a) if the seller is to deliver a document of title, title passes at the time when and the place where he delivers such documents; or

  (b) if the goods are at the time of contracting already identified and no documents are to be delivered, title passes at the time and place of contracting.

(4) A rejection or other refusal by the buyer to receive or retain the goods, whether or not justified, or a justified revocation of acceptance revests title to the goods in the seller. Such revesting occurs by operation of law and is not a "sale".

§2–402. Rights of Seller's Creditors Against Sold Goods.

(1) Except as provided in subsections (2) and (3), rights of unsecured creditors of the seller with respect to goods which have been identified to a contract for sale are subject to the buyer's rights to recover the goods under this Article (Sections 2–502 and 2–716).

(2) A creditor of the seller may treat a sale or an identification of goods to a contract for sale as void if as against him a retention of possession by the seller is fraudulent under any rule of law of the state where the goods are situated, except that retention of possession in good faith and current course of trade by a merchant-seller for a commercially reasonable time after a sale or identification is not fraudulent.

(3) Nothing in this Article shall be deemed to impair the rights of creditors of the seller

  (a) under the provisions of the Article on Secured Transactions (Article 9); or

  (b) where identification to the contract or delivery is made not in current course of trade but in satisfaction of or as security for a pre-existing claim for money, security or the like and is made under circumstances which under any rule of law of the state where the goods are situated would apart from this Article constitute the transaction a fraudulent transfer or voidable preference.

§2–403. Power to Transfer; Good Faith Purchase of Goods; "Entrusting".

(1) A purchaser of goods acquires all title which his transferor had or had power to transfer except that a purchaser of a limited interest acquires rights only to the extent of the interest purchased. A person with voidable title has power to transfer a good title to a good faith purchaser for value. When goods have been delivered under a transaction of purchase the purchaser has such power even though

  (a) the transferor was deceived as to the identity of the purchaser, or

  (b) the delivery was in exchange for a check which is later dishonored, or

  (c) it was agreed that the transaction was to be a "cash sale", or

  (d) the delivery was procured through fraud punishable as larcenous under the criminal law.

(2) Any entrusting of possession of goods to a merchant who deals in goods of that kind gives him power to transfer all rights of the entruster to a buyer in ordinary course of business.

(3) "Entrusting" includes any delivery and any acquiescence in retention of possession regardless of any condition expressed between the parties to the delivery or acquiescence and regardless of whether the procurement of the entrusting or the possessor's disposition of the goods have been such as to be larcenous under the criminal law.

(4) The rights of other purchasers of goods and of lien creditors are governed by the Articles on Secured Transactions (Article 9). [Bulk Transfers/Sales (Article 6)* and Documents of Title (Article 7)].

Part 5. Performance

§2–501. Insurable Interest in Goods; Manner of Identification of Goods.

(1) The buyer obtains a special property and an insurable interest in goods by identification of existing goods as goods to which the contract refers even though the goods so identified are non-conforming and he has an option to return or reject them. Such identification can be made at any time and in any manner explicitly agreed to by the parties. In the absence of explicit agreement identification occurs.

  (a) when the contract is made if it is for the sale of goods already existing and identified;

  (b) if the contract is for the sale of future goods other than those described in paragraph (c), when goods are shipped, marked or otherwise designated by the seller as goods to which the contract refers;

  (c) when the crops are planted or otherwise become growing crops or the young are conceived if the contract is for the sale of unborn young to be born within twelve months after contracting or for the sale of crops to be harvested within twelve months or the next normal harvest season after contracting, whichever is longer.

(2) The seller retains an insurable interest in goods so long as title to or any security interest in the goods remains in him and where the identification is by the seller alone he may until default or insolvency or notification to the buyer that the identification is final substitute other goods for those identified.

(3) Nothing in this section impairs any insurable interest recognized under any other statute or rule of law.

§2-502. Buyer's Right to Goods on Seller's Insolvency.

(1) Subject to subsections (2) and (3) and even though the goods have not been shipped a buyer who has paid a part or all of the price of goods in which he has a special property under the provisions of the immediately preceding section may on making and keeping good a tender of any unpaid portion of their price recover them from the seller if:

    (a) in the case of goods bought for personal, family, or household purposes, the seller repudiates or fails to deliver as required by the contract; or

    (b) in all cases, the seller becomes insolvent within ten days after receipt of the first installment on their price.

(2) The buyer's right to recover the goods under subsection (1)(a) vests upon acquisition of a special property, even if the seller had not then repudiated or failed to deliver.

(3) If the identification creating his special property has been made by the buyer he acquires the right to recover the goods only if they conform to the contract for sale.

§2-503. Manner of Seller's Tender of Delivery.

(1) Tender of delivery requires that the seller put and hold conforming goods at the buyer's disposition and give the buyer any notification reasonably necessary to enable him to take delivery. The manner, time and place for tender are determined by the agreement and this Article, and in particular

    (a) tender must be at a reasonable hour, and if it is of goods they must be kept available for the period reasonably necessary to enable the buyer to take possession; but

    (b) unless otherwise agreed the buyer must furnish facilities reasonably suited to the receipt of the goods.

(2) Where the case is within the next section respecting shipment tender requires that the seller comply with its provisions.

(3) Where the seller is required to deliver at a particular destination tender requires that he comply with subsection (1) and also in any appropriate case tender documents as described in subsections (4) and (5) of this section.

(4) Where goods are in the possession of a bailee and are to be delivered without being moved

    (a) tender requires that the seller either tender a negotiable document of title covering such goods or procure acknowledgment by the bailee of the buyer's right to possession of the goods; but

    (b) tender to the buyer of a non-negotiable document of title or of a written direction to the bailee to deliver is sufficient tender unless the buyer seasonably objects, and receipt by the bailee of notification of the buyer's rights fixes those rights as against the bailee and all third persons; but risk of loss of the goods and of any failure by the bailee to honor the non-negotiable document of title or to obey the direction remains on the seller until the buyer has had a reasonable time to present the document or direction, and a refusal by the bailee to honor the document or to obey the direction defeats the tender.

(5) Where the contract requires the seller to deliver documents

    (a) he must tender all such documents in correct form, except as provided in this Article with respect to bills of lading in a set (subsection (2) of Section 2–323); and

    (b) tender through customary banking channels is sufficient and dishonor of a draft accompanying the documents constitutes non-acceptance or rejection.

§2-504. Shipment by Seller.

Where the seller is required or authorized to send the goods to the buyer and the contract does not require him to deliver them at a particular destination, then unless otherwise agreed he must

    (a) put the goods in the possession of such a carrier and make such a contract for their transportation as may be reasonable having regard to the nature of the goods and other circumstances of the case; and

    (b) obtain and promptly deliver or tender in due form any document necessary to enable the buyer to obtain possession of the goods or otherwise required by the agreement or by usage of trade; and

    (c) promptly notify the buyer of the shipment.

Failure to notify the buyer under paragraph (c) or to make a proper contract under paragraph (a) is a ground for rejection only if material delay or loss ensues.

§2-505. Seller's Shipment Under Reservation.

(1) Where the seller has identified goods to the contract by or before shipment:

    (a) his procurement of a negotiable bill of lading to his own order or otherwise reserves in him a security interest in the goods. His procurement of the bill to the order of a financing agency or of the buyer indicates in addition only the seller's expectation of transferring that interest to the person named.

    (b) a non-negotiable bill of lading to himself or his nominee reserves possession of the goods as security but except in a case of conditional delivery (subsection (2) of Section 2–507) a non-negotiable bill of lading naming the buyer as consignee reserves no security interest even though the seller retains possession of the bill of lading.

(2) When shipment by the seller with reservation of a security interest is in violation of the contract for sale it constitutes an improper contract for transportation within the preceding section but impairs neither the rights given to the buyer by shipment and identification of the goods to the contract nor the seller's powers as a holder of a negotiable document.

§2-506. Rights of Financing Agency.

(1) A financing agency by paying or purchasing for value a draft which relates to a shipment of goods acquires to the extent of the payment or purchase and in addition to its own rights under the draft and any document of title securing it any rights of the shipper in the goods including the right to stop delivery and the shipper's right to have the draft honored by the buyer.

(2) The right to reimbursement of a financing agency which has in good faith honored or purchased the draft under commitment to or authority from the buyer is not impaired by subsequent discovery of defects with reference to any relevant document which was apparently regular on its face.

§2-507. Effect of Seller's Tender; Delivery on Condition.

(1) Tender of delivery is a condition to the buyer's duty to accept the goods and, unless otherwise agreed, to his duty to pay for them. Tender entitles the seller to acceptance of the goods and to payment according to the contract.

(2) Where payment is due and demanded on the delivery to the buyer of goods or documents of title, his right as against the seller to retain or dispose of them is conditional upon his making the payment due.

§2-508. Cure by Seller of Improper Tender or Delivery; Replacement.

(1) Where any tender or delivery by the seller is rejected because non-conforming and the time for performance has not yet expired, the seller may seasonably notify the buyer of his intention to cure and may then within the contract time make a conforming delivery.

(2) Where the buyer rejects a non-conforming tender which the seller had reasonable grounds to believe would be acceptable with or without money allowance the seller may if he seasonably notifies the buyer have a further reasonable time to substitute a conforming tender.

§2-509. Risk of Loss in the Absence of Breach.

(1) Where the contract requires or authorizes the seller to ship the goods by carrier

    (a) if it does not require him to deliver them at a particular destination, the risk of loss passes to the buyer when the goods are duly delivered to the carrier even though the shipment is under reservation (Section 2–505); but

    (b) if it does require him to deliver them at a particular destination and the goods are there duly tendered while in the possession of the carrier, the risk of loss passes to the buyer when the goods are there duly so tendered as to enable the buyer to take delivery.

(2) Where the goods are held by a bailee to be delivered without being moved, the risk of loss passes to the buyer

    (a) on his receipt of a negotiable document of title covering the goods; or

    (b) on acknowledgment by the bailee of the buyer's right to possession of the goods; or

    (c) after his receipt of a non-negotiable document of title or other written direction to deliver, as provided in subsection (4)(b) of Section 2–503.

(3) In any case not within subsection (1) or (2), the risk of loss passes to the buyer on his receipt of the goods if the seller is a merchant; otherwise the risk passes to the buyer on tender of delivery.

(4) The provisions of this section are subject to contrary agreement of the parties and to the provisions of this Article on sale on approval (Section 2–327) and on effect of breach on risk of loss (Section 2–510).

§2-510. Effect of Breach on Risk of Loss.

(1) Where a tender or delivery of goods so fails to conform to the contract as to give a right of rejection the risk of their loss remains on the seller until cure or acceptance.

(2) Where the buyer rightfully revokes acceptance he may to the extent of any deficiency in his effective insurance coverage treat the risk of loss as having rested on the seller from the beginning.

(3) Where the buyer as to conforming goods already identified to the contract for sale repudiates or is otherwise in breach before risk of their loss has passed to him, the seller may to the extent of any deficiency in his effective insurance coverage treat the risk of loss as resting on the buyer for a commercially reasonable time.

§2-511. Tender of Payment by Buyer; Payment by Check.

(1) Unless otherwise agreed tender of payment is a condition to the seller's duty to tender and complete any delivery.

(2) Tender of payment is sufficient when made by any means or in any manner current in the ordinary course of business unless the seller demands payment in legal tender and gives any extension of time reasonably necessary to procure it.

(3) Subject to the provisions of this Act on the effect of an instrument on an obligation (Section 3–310), payment by check is conditional and is defeated as between the parties by dishonor of the check on due presentment.

§2-512. Payment by Buyer Before Inspection.

(1) Where the contract requires payment before inspection nonconformity of the goods does not excuse the buyer from so making payment unless

    (a) the non-conformity appears without inspection; or

    (b) despite tender of the required documents the circumstances would justify injunction against honor under this Act (Section 5–109(b)).

(2) Payment pursuant to subsection (1) does not constitute an acceptance of goods or impair the buyer's right to inspect or any of his remedies.

§2-513. Buyer's Right to Inspection of Goods.

(1) Unless otherwise agreed and subject to subsection (3), where goods are tendered or delivered or identified to the contract for sale, the buyer has a right before payment or acceptance to inspect them at any reasonable place and time and in any reasonable manner. When the seller is required or authorized to send the goods to the buyer, the inspection may be after their arrival.

(2) Expenses of inspection must be borne by the buyer but may be recovered from the seller if the goods do not conform and are rejected.

(3) Unless otherwise agreed and subject to the provisions of this Article on C.I.F. contracts (subsection (3) of Section 2–321), the buyer is not entitled to inspect the goods before payment of the price when the contract provides

    (a) for delivery "C.O.D." or on other like terms; or

    (b) for payment against documents of title, except where such payment is due only after the goods are to become available for inspection.

(4) A place or method of inspection fixed by the parties is presumed to be exclusive but unless otherwise expressly agreed it does not postpone identification or shift the place for delivery or for passing the risk of loss. If compliance becomes impossible, inspection shall be as provided in this section unless the place or method fixed was clearly intended as an indispensable condition failure of which avoids the contract.

§2-514. When Documents Deliverable on Acceptance; When on Payment.

Unless otherwise agreed documents against which a draft is drawn are to be delivered to the drawee on acceptance of the draft if it is payable more than three days after presentment; otherwise, only on payment.

§2-515. Preserving Evidence of Goods in Dispute.

In furtherance of the adjustment of any claim or dispute
- (a) either party on reasonable notification to the other and for the purpose of ascertaining the facts and preserving evidence has the right to inspect, test and sample the goods including such of them as may be in the possession or control of the other; and
- (b) the parties may agree to a third party inspection or survey to determine the conformity or condition of the goods and may agree that the findings shall be binding upon them in any subsequent litigation or adjustment.

Part 6. Breach, Repudiation and Excuse

§2-601. Buyer's Rights on Improper Delivery.

Subject to the provisions of this Article on breach in installment contracts (Section 2–612) and unless otherwise agreed under the sections on contractual limitations of remedy (Sections 2–718 and 2–719), if the goods or the tender of delivery fail in any respect to conform to the contract, the buyer may
- (a) reject the whole; or
- (b) accept the whole; or
- (c) accept any commercial unit or units and reject the rest.

§2-602. Manner and Effect of Rightful Rejection.

(1) Rejection of goods must be within a reasonable time after their delivery or tender. It is ineffective unless the buyer seasonably notifies the seller.

(2) Subject to the provisions of the two following sections on rejected goods (Sections 2–603 and 2–604),
- (a) after rejection any exercise of ownership by the buyer with respect to any commercial unit is wrongful as against the seller; and
- (b) if the buyer has before rejection taken physical possession of goods in which he does not have a security interest under the provisions of this Article (subsection (3) of Section 2–711), he is under a duty after rejection to hold them with reasonable care at the seller's disposition for a time sufficient to permit the seller to remove them; but
- (c) the buyer has no further obligations with regard to goods rightfully rejected.

(3) The seller's rights with respect to goods wrongfully rejected are governed by the provisions of this Article on Seller's remedies in general (Section 2–703).

§2-603. Merchant Buyer's Duties as to Rightfully Rejected Goods.

(1) Subject to any security interest in the buyer (subsection (3) of Section 2–711), when the seller has no agent or place of business at the market of rejection a merchant buyer is under a duty after rejection of goods in his possession or control to follow any reasonable instructions received from the seller with respect to the goods and in the absence of such instructions to make reasonable efforts to sell them for the seller's account if they are perishable or threaten to decline in value speedily. Instructions are not reasonable if on demand indemnity for expenses is not forthcoming.

(2) When the buyer sells goods under subsection (1), he is entitled to reimbursement from the seller or out of the proceeds for reasonable expenses of caring for and selling them, and if the expenses include no selling commission then to such commission as is usual in the trade or if there is none to a reasonable sum not exceeding ten percent on the gross proceeds.

(3) In complying with this section the buyer is held only to good faith and good faith conduct hereunder is neither acceptance nor conversion nor the basis of an action for damages.

§2-604. Buyer's Options as to Salvage of Rightfully Rejected Goods.

Subject to the provisions of the immediately preceding section on perishables if the seller gives no instructions within a reasonable time after notification of rejection the buyer may store the rejected goods for the seller's account or reship them to him or resell them for the seller's account with reimbursement as provided in the preceding section. Such action is not acceptance or conversion.

§2-605. Waiver of Buyer's Objections by Failure to Particularize.

(1) The buyer's failure to state in connection with rejection a particular defect which is ascertainable by reasonable inspection precludes him from relying on the unstated defect to justify rejection or to establish breach
- (a) where the seller could have cured it if stated seasonably; or
- (b) between merchants when the seller has after rejection made a request in writing for a full and final written statement of all defects on which the buyer proposes to rely.

(2) Payment against documents made without reservation of rights precludes recovery of the payment for defects apparent on the face of the documents.

§2-606. What Constitutes Acceptance of Goods.

(1) Acceptance of goods occurs when the buyer
- (a) after a reasonable opportunity to inspect the goods signifies to the seller that the goods are conforming or that he will take or retain them in spite of their non-conformity; or
- (b) fails to make an effective rejection (subsection (1) of Section 2–602), but such acceptance does not occur until the buyer has had a reasonable opportunity to inspect them; or
- (c) does any act inconsistent with the seller's ownership; but if such act is wrongful as against the seller it is an acceptance only if ratified by him.

(2) Acceptance of a part of any commercial unit is acceptance of that entire unit.

§2-607. Effect of Acceptance; Notice of Breach; Burden of Establishing Breach After Acceptance; Notice of Claim or Litigation to Person Answerable Over.

(1) The buyer must pay at the contract rate for any goods accepted.

(2) Acceptance of goods by the buyer precludes rejection of the goods accepted and if made with knowledge of a non-conformity cannot be revoked because of it unless the acceptance was on the reasonable assumption that the non-conformity would be seasonably cured but acceptance does not of itself impair any other remedy provided by this Article for non-conformity.

(3) Where a tender has been accepted

    (a) the buyer must within a reasonable time after he discovers or should have discovered any breach notify the seller of breach or be barred from any remedy; and

    (b) if the claim is one for infringement or the like (subsection (3) of Section 2–312) and the buyer is sued as a result of such a breach he must so notify the seller within a reasonable time after he receives notice of the litigation or be barred from any remedy over for liability established by the litigation.

(4) The burden is on the buyer to establish any breach with respect to the goods accepted.

(5) Where the buyer is sued for breach of a warranty or other obligation for which his seller is answerable over

    (a) he may give his seller written notice of the litigation. If the notice states that the seller may come in and defend and that if the seller does not do so he will be bound in any action against him by his buyer by any determination of fact common to the two litigations, then unless the seller after seasonable receipt of the notice does come in and defend he is so bound.

    (b) if the claim is one for infringement or the like (subsection (3) of Section 2–312) the original seller may demand in writing that his buyer turn over to him control of the litigation including settlement or else be barred from any remedy over and if he also agrees to bear all expense and to satisfy any adverse judgment, then unless the buyer after seasonable receipt of the demand does turn over control the buyer is so barred.

(6) The provisions of subsection (3), (4) and (5) apply to any obligation of a buyer to hold the seller harmless against infringement or the like (subsection (3) of Section 2–312).

§2-608. Revocation of Acceptance in Whole or in Part.

(1) The buyer may revoke his acceptance of a lot or commercial unit whose non-conformity substantially impairs its value to him if he has accepted it

    (a) on the reasonable assumption that its non-conformity would be cured and it has not been seasonably cured; or

    (b) without discovery of such non-conformity if his acceptance was reasonably induced either by the difficulty of discovery before acceptance or by the seller's assurances.

(2) Revocation of acceptance must occur within a reasonable time after the buyer discovers or should have discovered the ground for it and before any substantial change in condition of the goods which is not caused by their own defects. It is not effective until the buyer notifies the seller of it.

(3) A buyer who so revokes has the same rights and duties with regard to the goods involved as if he had rejected them.

§2-609. Right to Adequate Assurance of Performance.

(1) A contract for sale imposes an obligation on each party that the other's expectation of receiving due performance will not be impaired. When reasonable grounds for insecurity arise with respect to the performance of either party the other may in writing demand adequate assurance of due performance and until he receives such assurance may if commercially reasonable suspend any performance for which he has not already received the agreed return.

(2) Between merchants the reasonableness of grounds for insecurity and the adequacy of any assurance offered shall be determined according to commercial standards.

(3) Acceptance of any improper delivery or payment does not prejudice the aggrieved party's right to demand adequate assurance of future performance.

(4) After receipt of a justified demand failure to provide within a reasonable time not exceeding thirty days such assurance of due performance as is adequate under the circumstances of the particular case is a repudiation of the contract.

§2-610. Anticipatory Repudiation.

When either party repudiates the contract with respect to a performance not yet due the loss of which will substantially impair the value of the contract to the other, the aggrieved party may

    (a) for a commercially reasonable time await performance by the repudiating party; or

    (b) resort to any remedy for breach (Section 2–703 or Section 2–711), even though he has notified the repudiating party that he would await the latter's performance and has urged retraction; and

    (c) in either case suspend his own performance or proceed in accordance with the provisions of this Article on the seller's right to identify goods to the contract notwithstanding breach or to salvage unfinished goods (Section 2–704).

§2-611. Retraction of Anticipatory Repudiation.

(1) Until the repudiating party's next performance is due he can retract his repudiation unless the aggrieved party has since the repudiation cancelled or materially changed his position or otherwise indicated that he considers the repudiation final.

(2) Retraction may be by any method which clearly indicates to the aggrieved party that the repudiating party intends to perform, but must include any assurance justifiably demanded under the provisions of this Article (Section 2–609).

(3) Retraction reinstates the repudiating party's rights under the contract with due excuse and allowance to the aggrieved party for any delay occasioned by the repudiation.

§2-612. "Installment Contract"; Breach.

(1) An "installment contract" is one which requires or authorizes the delivery of goods in separate lots to be separately accepted, even though the contract contains a clause "each delivery is a separate contract" or its equivalent.

(2) The buyer may reject any installment which is non-conforming if the non-conformity substantially impairs the value of that installment and cannot be cured or if the non-conformity is a defect in the required documents; but if the non-conformity does not fall within subsection (3) and the seller gives adequate assurance of its cure the buyer must accept that installment.

(3) Whenever non-conformity or default with respect to one or more installments substantially impairs the value of the whole contract there is a breach of the whole. But the aggrieved party reinstates the contract if he accepts a non-conforming installment without seasonably notifying of cancellation or if he brings an action with

respect only to past installments or demands performance as to future installments.

§2-613. Casualty to Identified Goods.

Where the contract requires for its performance goods identified when the contract is made, and the goods suffer casualty without fault of either party before the risk of loss passes to the buyer, or in a proper case under a "no arrival, no sale" term (Section 2–324) then

  (a) if the loss is total the contract is avoided; and
  (b) if the loss is partial or the goods have so deteriorated as no longer to conform to the contract the buyer may nevertheless demand inspection and at his option either treat the contract as avoided or accept the goods with due allowance from the contract price for the deterioration or the deficiency in quantity but without further right against the seller.

§2-614. Substituted Performance.

(1) Where without fault of either party the agreed berthing, loading, or unloading facilities fail or an agreed type of carrier becomes unavailable or the agreed manner of delivery otherwise becomes commercially impracticable but a commercially reasonable substitute is available, such substitute performance must be tendered and accepted.

(2) If the agreed means or manner of payment fails because of domestic or foreign governmental regulation, the seller may withhold or stop delivery unless the buyer provides a means or manner of payment which is commercially a substantial equivalent. If delivery has already been taken, payment by the means or in the manner provided by the regulation discharges the buyers obligation unless the regulation is discriminatory, oppressive or predatory.

§2-615. Excuse by Failure of Presupposed Conditions.

Except so far as a seller may have assumed a greater obligation and subject to the preceding section on substituted performance:

  (a) Delay in delivery or non-delivery in whole or in part by a seller who complies with paragraphs (b) and (c) is not a breach of his duty under a contract for sale if performance as agreed has been made impracticable by the occurrence of a contingency the non-occurrence of which was a basic assumption on which the contract was made or by compliance in good faith with any applicable foreign or domestic governmental regulation or order whether or not it later proves to be invalid.
  (b) Where the causes mentioned in paragraph (a) affect only a part of the seller's capacity to perform, he must allocate production and deliveries among his customers but may at his option include regular customers not then under contract as well as his own requirements for further manufacture. He may so allocate in any manner which is fair and reasonable.
  (c) The seller must notify the buyer seasonably that there will be delay or non-delivery and, when allocation is required under paragraph (b), of the estimated quota thus made available for the buyer.

§2-616. Procedure on Notice Claiming Excuse.

(1) Where the buyer receives notification of a material or indefinite delay or an allocation justified under the preceding section

he may by written notification to the seller as to any delivery concerned, and where the prospective deficiency substantially impairs the value of the whole contract under the provisions of this Article relating to breach of installment contracts (Section 2–612), then also as to the whole,

  (a) terminate and thereby discharge any unexecuted portion of the contract; or
  (b) modify the contract by agreeing to take his available quota in substitution.

(2) If after receipt of such notification from the seller the buyer fails so to modify the contract within a reasonable time not exceeding thirty days the contract lapses with respect to any deliveries affected.

(3) The provisions of this section may not be negated by agreement except in so far as the seller has assumed a greater obligation under the preceding section.

Part 7. Remedies

§2-701. Remedies for Breach of Collateral Contracts Not Impaired.

Remedies for breach of any obligation or promise collateral or ancillary to a contract for sale or not impaired by the provisions of this Article.

§2-702. Seller's Remedies on Discovery of Buyer's Insolvency.

(1) Where the seller discovers the buyer to be insolvent he may refuse delivery except for cash including payment for all goods therefore delivered under the contract, and stop delivery under this Article (Section 2–705).

(2) Where the seller discovers that the buyer has received goods on credit while insolvent he may reclaim the goods upon demand made within ten days after the receipt, but if misrepresentation of solvency has been made to the particular seller in writing within three months before delivery the ten day limitation does not apply. Except as provided in this subsection the seller may not base a right to reclaim goods on the buyer's fraudulent or innocent misrepresentation of solvency or of intent to pay.

(3) The seller's right to reclaim under subsection (2) is subject to the rights of a buyer in ordinary course or other good faith purchaser under this Article (Section 2–403). Successful reclamation of goods excludes all other remedies with respect to them.

§2-703. Seller's Remedies in General.

Where the buyer wrongfully rejects or revokes acceptance of goods or fails to make a payment due on or before delivery or repudiates with respect to a part or the whole, then with respect to any goods directly affected and, if the breach is of the whole contract (Section 2–612), then also with respect to the whole undelivered balance, the aggrieved seller may

  (a) withhold delivery of such goods;
  (b) stop delivery by any bailee as hereafter provided (Section 2–705);
  (c) proceed under the next section respecting goods still unidentified to the contract;
  (d) resell and recover damages as hereafter provided (Section 2–706);
  (e) recover damages for non-acceptance (Section 2–708) or in a proper case the price (Section 2–709);
  (f) cancel.

§2-704. Seller's Right to Identify Goods to the Contract Notwithstanding Breach or to Salvage Unfinished Goods.

(1) An aggrieved seller under the preceding section may

    (a) identify to the contract conforming goods not already identified if at the time he learned of the breach they are in his possession or control;

    (b) treat as the subject of resale goods which have demonstrably been intended for the particular contract even though those goods are unfinished.

(2) Where the goods are unfinished an aggrieved seller may in the exercise of reasonable commercial judgment for the purposes of avoiding loss and of effective realization either complete the manufacture and wholly identify the goods to the contract or cease manufacture and resell for scrap or salvage value or proceed in any other reasonable manner.

§2-705. Seller's Stoppage of Delivery in Transit or Otherwise.

(1) The seller may stop delivery of goods in the possession of a carrier or other bailee when he discovers the buyer to be insolvent (Section 2–702) and may stop delivery of carload, truckload, planeload or larger shipments of express or freight when the buyer repudiates or fails to make a payment due before delivery or if for any other reason the seller has a right to withhold or reclaim the goods.

(2) As against such buyer the seller may stop delivery until

    (a) receipt of the goods by the buyer; or

    (b) acknowledgment to the buyer by any bailee of the goods except a carrier that the bailee holds the goods for the buyer; or

    (c) such acknowledgment to the buyer by a carrier by reshipment or as warehouseman; or

    (d) negotiation to the buyer of any negotiable document of title covering the goods.

(3) (a) To stop delivery the seller must so notify as to enable the bailee by reasonable diligence to prevent delivery of the goods.

    (b) After such notification the bailee must hold and deliver the goods according to the directions of the seller but the seller is liable to the bailee for any ensuing charges or damages.

    (c) If a negotiable document of title has been issued for goods the bailee is not obliged to obey a notification to stop until surrender of the document.

    (d) A carrier who has issued a non-negotiable bill of lading is not obliged to obey a notification to stop received from a person other than the consignor.

§2-706. Seller's Resale Including Contract for Resale.

(1) Under the conditions stated in Section 2–703 on seller's remedies, the seller may resell the goods concerned or the undelivered balance thereof. Where the resale is made in good faith and in a commercially reasonable manner the seller may recover the difference between the resale price and the contract price together with any incidental damages allowed under the provisions of this Article (Section 2–710), but less expenses saved in consequence of the buyer's breach.

(2) Except as otherwise provided in subsection (3) or unless otherwise agreed resale may be at public or private sale including sale by way of one or more contracts to sell or of identification to an existing contract of the seller. Sale may be as a unit or in parcels and at any time and place and on any terms but every aspect of the sale including the method, manner, time, place and terms must be commercially reasonable. The resale must be reasonably identified as referring to the broken contract, but it is not necessary that the goods be in existence or that any or all of them have been identified to the contract before the breach.

(3) Where the resale is at private sale the seller must give the buyer reasonable notification of his intention to resell.

(4) Where the resale is at public sale

    (a) only identified goods can be sold except where there is a recognized market for a public sale of futures in goods of the kind; and

    (b) it must be made at a usual place or market for public sale if one is reasonably available and except in the case of goods which are perishable or threaten to decline in value speedily the seller must give the buyer reasonable notice of the time and place of the resale; and

    (c) if the goods are not to be within the view of those attending the sale the notification of sale must state the place where the goods are located and provide for their reasonable inspection by prospective bidders; and

    (d) the seller may buy.

(5) A purchaser who buys in good faith at a resale takes the goods free of any rights of the original buyer even though the seller fails to comply with one or more of the requirements of this section.

(6) The seller is not accountable to the buyer for any profit made on any resale. A person in the position of a seller (Section 2–707) or a buyer who has rightfully rejected or justifiably revoked acceptance must account for any excess over the amount of his security interest, as hereinafter defined (subsection (3) of Section 2–711).

§2-707. "Person in the Position of a Seller".

(1) A "person in the position of a seller" includes as against a principal an agent who has paid or become responsible for the price of goods on behalf of his principal or anyone who otherwise holds a security interest or other right in goods similar to that of a seller.

(2) A person in the position of a seller may as provided in this Article withhold or stop delivery (Section 2–705) and resell (Section 2–706) and recover incidental damages (Section 2–710).

§2-708. Seller's Damages for Non-Acceptance or Repudiation.

(1) Subject to subsection (2) and to the provisions of this Article with respect to proof of market price (Section 2–723), the measure of damages for non-acceptance or repudiation by the buyer is the difference between the market price at the time and place for tender and the unpaid contract price together with any incidental damages provided in this Article (Section 2–710), but less expenses saved in consequence of the buyer's breach.

(2) If the measure of damages provided in subsection (1) is inadequate to put the seller in as good a position as performance would have done then the measure of damages is the profit (including reasonable overhead) which the seller would have made from full performance by the buyer, together with any incidental damages provided in this Article (Section 2–710), due allowance for costs reasonably incurred and due credit for payments or proceeds of resale.

§2-709. Action for the Price.

(1) When the buyer fails to pay the price as it becomes due the seller may recover, together with any incidental damages under the next section, the price

(a) of goods accepted or of conforming goods lost or damaged within a commercially reasonable time after risk of their loss has passed to the buyer; and

(b) of goods identified to the contract if the seller is unable after reasonable effort to resell them at a reasonable price or the circumstances reasonably indicate that such effort will be unavailing.

(2) Where the seller sues for the price he must hold for the buyer any goods which have been identified to the contract and are still in his control except that if resale becomes possible he may resell them at any time prior to the collection of the judgment. The net proceeds of any such resale must be credited to the buyer and payment of the judgment entitles him to any goods not resold.

(3) After the buyer has wrongfully rejected or revoked acceptance of the goods or has failed to make a payment due or has repudiated (Section 2-610), a seller who is held not entitled to the price under this section shall nevertheless be awarded damages for nonacceptance under the preceding section.

§2-710. Seller's Incidental Damages.

Incidental damages to an aggrieved seller include any commercially reasonable charges, expenses or commissions incurred in stopping delivery, in the transportation, care and custody of goods after the buyer's breach, in connection with return or resale of the goods or otherwise resulting from the breach.

§2-71. Buyer's Remedies in General; Buyer's Security Interest in Rejected Goods.

(1) Where the seller fails to make delivery or repudiates or the buyer rightfully rejects or justifiably revokes acceptance then with respect to any goods involved, and with respect to the whole if the breach goes to the whole contract (Section 2-612), the buyer may cancel and whether or not he has done so may in addition to recovering so much of the price as has been paid

(a) "cover" and have damages under the next section as to all the goods affected whether or not they have been identified to the contract; or

(b) recover damages for non-delivery as provided in this Article (Section 2-713).

(2) Where the seller fails to deliver or repudiates the buyer may also

(a) if the goods have been identified recover them as provided in this Article (Section 2-502); or

(b) in a proper case obtain specific performance or replevy the goods as provided in this Article (Section 2-716).

(3) On rightful rejection of justifiable revocation of acceptance a buyer has a security interest in goods in his possession or control for any payments made on their price and any expenses reasonably incurred in their inspection, receipt, transportation, care and custody and may hold such goods and resell them in like manner as an aggrieved seller (Section 2-706).

§2-712. "Cover"; Buyer's Procurement of Substitute Goods.

(1) After a breach within the preceding section the buyer may "cover" by making in good faith and without unreasonable delay any reasonable purchase of or contract to purchase goods in substitution for those due from the seller.

(2) The buyer may recover from the seller as damages the difference between the cost of cover and the contract price together with any incidental or consequential damages as hereinafter defined (Section 2-715), but less expenses saved in consequence of the seller's breach.

(3) Failure of the buyer to effect cover within this section does not bar him from any other remedy.

§2-713. Buyer's Damages for Non-Delivery or Repudiation.

(1) Subject to the provisions of this Article with respect to proof of market price (Section 2-723), the measure of damages for nondelivery or repudiation by the seller is the difference between the market price at the time when the buyer learned of the breach and the contract price together with any incidental and consequential damages provided in this Article (Section 2-715), but less expenses saved in consequence of the seller's breach.

(2) Market price is to be determined as of the place for tender or, in cases of rejection after arrival or revocation of acceptance, as of the place of arrival.

§2-714. Buyer's Damages for Breach in Regard to Accepted Goods.

(1) Where the buyer has accepted goods and given notification (subsection (3) of Section 2-607) he may recover as damages for any non-conformity of tender the loss resulting in the ordinary course of events from the seller's breach as determined in any manner which is reasonable.

(2) The measure of damages for breach of warranty is the difference at the time and place of acceptance between the value of the goods accepted and the value they would have had if they had been as warranted, unless special circumstances show proximate damages of a different amount.

(3) In a proper case any incidental and consequential damages under the next section may also be recovered.

§2-715. Buyer's Incidental and Consequential Damages.

(1) Incidental damages resulting from the seller's breach include expenses reasonably incurred in inspection, receipt, transportation and care and custody of goods rightfully rejected, any commercially reasonable charges, expenses or commissions in connection with effecting cover and any other reasonable expense incident to the delay or other breach.

(2) Consequential damages resulting from the seller's breach include

(a) any loss resulting from general or particular requirements and needs of which the seller at the time of contracting had reason to know and which could not reasonably be prevented by cover or otherwise; and

(b) injury to person or property proximately resulting from any breach of warranty.

§2-716. Buyer's Right to Specific Performance or Replevin.

(1) Specific performance may be decreed where the goods are unique or in other proper circumstances.

(2) The decree for specific performance may include such terms and conditions as to payment of the price, damages, or other relief as the court may deem just.

(3) The buyer has a right of replevin for goods identified to the contract if after reasonable effort he is unable to effect cover for

such goods or the circumstances reasonably indicate that such effort will be unvailing or if the goods have been shipped under reservation and satisfaction of the security interest in them has been made or tendered. In the case of goods bought for personal, family, or household purposes, the buyer's right of replevin vests upon acquisition of a special property, even if the seller had not then repudiated or failed to deliver.

§2–717. Deduction of Damages From the Price.

The buyer on notifying the seller of his intention to do so may deduct all or any part of the damages resulting from any breach of the contract from any part of the price still due under the same contract.

§2–718. Liquidation or Limitation of Damages; Deposits.

(1) Damages for breach by either party may be liquidated in the agreement but only at an amount which is reasonable in the light of the anticipated or actual harm caused by the breach, the difficulties of proof of loss, and the inconvenience of nonfeasibility of otherwise obtaining an adequate remedy. A team fixing unreasonably large liquidated damages is void as a penalty.

(2) Where the seller justifiably withholds delivery of goods because of the buyer's breach, the buyer is entitled to restitution of any amount by which the sum of his payments exceeds

(a) the amount to which the seller is entitled by virtue of terms liquidating the seller's damages in accordance with subsection (1), or

(b) in the absence of such terms, twenty percent of the value of the total performance for which the buyer is obligated under the contract or $500, whichever is smaller.

(3) The buyer's right to restitution under subsection (2) is subject to offset to the extent that the seller establishes

(a) a right to recover damages under the provisions of this Article other than subsection (1), and

(b) the amount or value of any benefits received by the buyer directly or indirectly by reason of the contract.

(4) Where a seller has received payment in goods their reasonable value or the proceeds of their resale shall be treated as payments for the purposes of subsection (2); but if the seller has notice of the buyer's breach before reselling goods received in part performance, his resale is subject to the conditions laid down in this Article on resale by an aggrieved seller (Section 2–706).

§2–719. Contractual Modification or Limitation of Remedy.

(1) Subject to the provisions of subsections (2) and (3) of this section and of the preceding section on liquidation and limitation of damages,

(a) the agreement may provide for remedies in addition to or in substitution for those provided in this Article and may limit or alter the measure of damages recoverable under this Article, as by limiting the buyer's remedies to return of the goods and repayment of the price or to repair and replacement of non-conforming goods or parts; and

(b) resort to a remedy as provided is optional unless the remedy is expressly agreed to be exclusive, in which case it is the sole remedy.

(2) Where circumstances cause an exclusive or limited remedy to fail of its essential purpose, remedy may be had as provided in this Act.

(3) Consequential damages may be limited or excluded unless the limitation or exclusion is unconscionable. Limitation of consequential damages for injury to the person in the case of consumer goods is prima facie unconscionable but limitation of damages where the loss is commercial is not.

§2–720. Effect of "Cancellation" or "Rescission" on Claims for Antecedent Breach.

Unless the contrary intention clearly appears, expressions of "cancellation" or "rescission" of the contract or the like shall not be construed as a renunciation or discharge of any claim in damages for an antecedent breach.

§2–72. Remedies for Fraud.

Remedies for material misrepresentation or fraud include all remedies available under this Article for non-fraudulent breach. Neither rescission or a claim for rescission of the contract for sale nor rejection or return of the goods shall bar or be deemed inconsistent with a claim for damages or other remedy.

§2–722. Who Can Sue Third Parties for Injury to Goods.

Where a third party so deals with goods which have been identified to a contract for sale as to cause actionable injury to a party to that contract

(a) a right of action against the third party is in either party to the contract for sale who has title to or a security interest or a special property or an insurable interest in the goods; and if the goods have been destroyed or converted a right of action is also in the party who either bore the risk of loss under the contract for sale or has since the injury assumed that risk as against the other,

(b) if at the time of the injury the party plaintiff did not bear the risk of loss as against the other party to the contract for sale and there is no arrangement between them for disposition of the recovery, his suit or settlement is, subject to his own interest, as a fiduciary for the other party to the contract;

(c) either party may with the consent of the other sue for the benefit of whom it may concern.

§2–723. Proof of Market Price: Time and Place.

(1) If an action based on anticipatory repudiation comes to trial before the time for performance with respect to some or all of the goods, any damages based on market price (Section 2–708 or Section 2–713) shall be determined according to the price of such goods prevailing at the time when the aggrieved party learned of the repudiation.

(2) If evidence of a price prevailing at the times or places described in this Article is not readily available the price prevailing within any reasonable time before or after the time described or at any other place which in commercial judgment or under usage of trade would serve as a reasonable substitute for the one described may be used, making any proper allowance for the cost of transporting the goods to or from such other place.

(3) Evidence of a relevant price prevailing at a time or place other than the one described in this Article offered by one party is not admissible unless and until he has given the other party such notice as the court finds sufficient to prevent unfair surprise.

§2-724. Admissibility of Market Quotations.

Whenever the prevailing price or value of any goods regularly bought and sold in any established commodity market is in issue, reports in official publications or trade journals or in newspapers or periodicals of general circulation published as the reports of such market shall be admissible in evidence. The circumstances of the preparation of such a report may be shown to affect its weight but not its admissibility.

§2-725. Statute of Limitations in Contracts for Sale.

(1) An action for breach of any contract for sale must be commenced within four years after the cause of action has accrued. By the original agreement the parties may reduce the period of limitation to not less than one year but may not extend it.

(2) A cause of action accrues when the breach occurs, regardless of the aggrieved party's lack of knowledge of the breach. A breach of warranty occurs when tender of delivery is made, except that where a warranty explicitly extends to future performance of the goods and discovery of the breach must await the time of such performance the cause of action accrues when the breach is or should have been discovered.

(3) Where an action commenced within the time limited by subsection (1) is so terminated as to leave available a remedy by another action for the same breach such other action may be commenced after the expiration of the time limited and within six months after the termination of the first action unless the termination resulted from voluntary discontinuance or from dismissal for failure or neglect to prosecute.

(4) This section does not alter the law on tolling of the statute of limitations nor does it apply to causes of action which have accrued before this Act becomes effective.

Appendix D — Sarbanes-Oxley Act of 2002 (Excerpts)

Title I—Public Company Accounting Oversight Board

Sec. 101 Establishment; Administrative Provisions.

(a) Establishment of Board.—There is established the Public Company Accounting Oversight Board, to oversee the audit of public companies that are subject to the securities laws, and related matters, in order to protect the interests of investors and further the public interest in the preparation of informative, accurate, and independent audit reports for companies the securities of which are sold to, and held by and for, public investors. The Board shall be a body corporate, operate as a nonprofit corporation, and have succession until dissolved by an Act of Congress.

Sec. 102 Registration with the Board.

(a) Mandatory Registration.—It shall be unlawful for any person that is not a registered public accounting firm to prepare or issue, or to participate in the preparation or issuance of, any audit report with respect to any issuer.

(b) Application for Registration.—

    (1) Form of application.—A public accounting firm shall use such form as the Board may prescribe, by rule, to apply for registration under this section.

Sec. 104 Inspections of Registered Public Accounting Firms.

(a) In General.—The Board shall conduct a continuing program of inspections to assess the degree of compliance of each registered public accounting firm and associated persons of that firm with this Act, the rules of the Board, the rules of the Commission, or professional standards, in connection with its performance of audits, issuance of audit reports, and related matters involving issuers.

(b) Inspection Frequency.—

    (1) In general.—Subject to paragraph (2), inspections required by this section shall be conducted—

        (A) annually with respect to each registered public accounting firm that regularly provides audit reports for more than 100 issuers; and

        (B) not less frequently than once every 3 years with respect to each registered public accounting firm that regularly provides audit reports for 100 or fewer issuers.

Sec. 105 Investigations and Disciplinary Proceedings.

(a) In General.—The Board shall establish, by rule, subject to the requirements of this section, fair procedures for the investigation and disciplining of registered public accounting firms and associated persons of such firms.

(c) Disciplinary Procedures.—

    (4) Sanctions.—If the Board finds, based on all of the facts and circumstances, that a registered public accounting firm or associated person thereof has engaged in any act

or practice, or omitted to act, in violation of this Act, the rules of the Board, the provisions of the securities laws relating to the preparation and issuance of audit reports and the obligations and liabilities of accountants with respect thereto, including the rules of the Commission issued under this Act, or professional standards, the Board may impose such disciplinary or remedial sanctions as it determines appropriate, subject to applicable limitations under paragraph (5), including—

        (A) temporary suspension or permanent revocation of registration under this title;

        (B) temporary or permanent suspension or bar of a person from further association with any registered public accounting firm;

        (C) temporary or permanent limitation on the activities, functions, or operations of such firm or person (other than in connection with required additional professional education or training);

        (D) a civil money penalty for each such violation, in an amount equal to—

            (i) not more than $100,000 for a natural person or $2,000,000 for any other person; and

            (ii) in any case to which paragraph (5) applies, not more than $750,000 for a natural person or $15,000,000 for any other person;

        (E) censure;

        (F) required additional professional education or training; or

        (G) any other appropriate sanction provided for in the rules of the Board.

    (5) Intentional or other knowing conduct.—The sanctions and penalties described in subparagraphs (A) through (C) and (D)(ii) of paragraph (4) shall only apply to—

        (A) intentional or knowing conduct, including reckless conduct, that results in violation of the applicable statutory, regulatory, or professional standard; or

        (B) repeated instances of negligent conduct, each resulting in a violation of the applicable statutory, regulatory, or professional standard.

Title II—Auditor Independence

Sec. 201 Services Outside the Scope of Practice of Auditors.

(a) Prohibited Activities.—Section 10A of the Securities Exchange Act of 1934 (15 U.S.C. 78j–1) is amended by adding at the end of the following:

"(g) Prohibited Activities.—Except as provided in subsection (h), it shall be unlawful for a registered public accounting firm (and any associated person of that firm, to the extent determined appropriate by the Commission) that performs for any issuer any audit required by this title or the rules of the Commission under this title or, beginning 180 days after the date of commencement of the operations of the Public Company Accounting Oversight Board established under section 101 of the Sarbanes-Oxley Act of 2002 (in this section referred to as the 'Board'), the rules of the Board, to provide to that issuer, contemporaneously with the audit, any non-audit service, including—

"(1) bookkeeping or other services related to the accounting records or financial statements of the audit client;

"(2) financial information systems design and implementation;

"(3) appraisal or valuation services, fairness opinions, or contribution-in-kind reports;

"(4) actuarial services;

"(5) internal audit outsourcing services;

"(6) management functions or human resources;

"(7) broker or dealer, investment adviser, or investment banking services;

"(8) legal services and expert services unrelated to the audit; and

"(9) any other service that the Board determines, by regulation, is impermissible.

"(h) Preapproval Required for Non-Audit Services.—A registered public accounting firm may engage in any non-audit service, including tax services, that is not described in any of paragraphs (1) through (9) of subsection (g) for an audit client, only if the activity is approved in advance by the audit committee of the issuer, in accordance with subsection (i)."

Sec. 206 Conflicts of Interest.

Section 10A of the Securities Exchange Act of 1934 (15 U.S.C. 78j–1), as amended by this Act, is amended by adding at the end the following:

"(l) Conflicts of Interest.—It shall be unlawful for a registered public accounting firm to perform for an issuer any audit service required by this title, if a chief executive officer, controller, chief financial officer, chief accounting officer, or any person serving in an equivalent position for the issuer, was employed by that registered independent public accounting firm and participated in any capacity in the audit of that issuer during the 1-year period preceding the date of the initiation of the audit."

Title III—Corporate Responsibility

Sec. 301 Public Company Audit Committees.

Section 10A of the Securities Exchange Act of 1934 (15 U.S.C. 78f) is amended by adding at the end the following:

"(m) Standards Relating to Audit Committees.—

"(2) Responsibilities relating to registered public accounting firms.—The audit committee of each issuer, in its capacity as a committee of the board of directors, shall be directly responsible for the appointment, compensation, and oversight of the work of any registered public

accounting firm employed by that issuer (including resolution of disagreements between management and the auditor regarding financial reporting) for the purpose of preparing or issuing an audit report or related work, and each such registered public accounting firm shall report directly to the audit committee.

"(3) Independence.—

"(A) In general.—Each member of the audit committee of the issuer shall be a member of the board of directors of the issuer, and shall otherwise be independent.

"(B) Criteria.—In order to be considered to be independent for purposes of this paragraph, a member of an audit committee of an issuer may not, other than in his or her capacity as a member of the audit committee, the board of directors, or any other board committee—

"(i) accept any consulting, advisory, or other compensatory fee from the issuer; or

"(ii) be an affiliated person of the issuer or any subsidiary thereof.

Sec. 302 Corporate Responsibility for Financial Reports.

(a) Regulations Required.—The Commission shall, by rule, require, for each company filing periodic reports under section 13(a) or 15(d) of the Securities Exchange Act of 1934 (15 U.S.C. 78m, 78o(d)), that the principal executive officer or officers and the principal financial officer or officers, or persons performing similar functions, certify in each annual or quarterly report filed or submitted under either such section of such Act that—

(1) the signing officer has reviewed the report;

(2) based on the officer's knowledge, the report does not contain any untrue statement of a material fact or omit to state a material fact necessary in order to make the statements made, in light of the circumstances under which such statements were made, not misleading;

(3) based on such officer's knowledge, the financial statements, and other financial information included in the report fairly present in all material respects the financial condition and results of operations of the issuer as of, and for, the periods presented in the report;

(4) the signing officers—

(A) are responsible for establishing and maintaining internal controls;

(B) have designed such internal controls to ensure that material information relating to the issuer and its consolidated subsidiaries is made known to such officers by others within those entities, particularly during the period in which the periodic reports are being prepared;

(C) have evaluated the effectiveness of the issuer's internal controls as of a date within 90 days prior to the report; and

(D) have presented in the report their conclusions about the effectiveness of their internal controls based on their evaluation as of that date;

(5) the signing officers have disclosed to the issuer's auditors and the audit committee of the board of directors (or persons fulfilling the equivalent function)—

(A) all significant deficiencies in the design or operation of internal controls which could adversely affect the issuer's ability to record, process, summarize, and report financial data and have identified for the issuer's auditors any material weaknesses in internal controls; and

(B) any fraud, whether or not material, that involves management or other employees who have a significant role in the issuer's internal controls; and

(6) the signing officers have indicated in the report whether or not there were significant changes in internal controls or in other factors that could significantly affect internal controls subsequent to the date of their evaluation, including any corrective actions with regard to significant deficiencies and material weaknesses.

Sec. 303 *Improper Influence on Conduct of Audits.*

(a) Rules to Prohibit.—It shall be unlawful, in contravention of such rules or regulations as the Commission shall prescribe as necessary appropriate in the public interest or for the protection of investors, for any officer or director of an issuer, or any other person acting under the direction thereof, to take any action to fraudulently influence, coerce, manipulate, or mislead any independent public or certified accountant engaged in the performance of an audit of the financial statements of that issuer for the purpose of rendering such financial statements materially misleading.

Title IV—Enhanced Financial Disclosures
Sec. 401 *Disclosures in Periodic Reports.*

(a) Disclosures Required.—Section 13 of the Securities Exchange Act of 1934 (15 U.S.C. 78m) is amended by adding at the end the following:

"(i) Accuracy of Financial Reports.—Each financial report that contains financial statements, and that is required to be prepared in accordance with (or reconciled to) generally accepted accounting principles under this title and filed with the Commission shall reflect all material correcting adjustments that have been identified by a registered public accounting firm in accordance with generally accepted accounting principles and the rules and regulations of the Commission.

"(j) Off–Balance Sheet Transactions.—Not later than 180 days after the date of enactment of the Sarbanes-Oxley Act of 2002, the Commission shall issue final rules providing that each annual and quarterly financial report required to be filed with the Commission shall disclose all material off-balance sheet transactions, arrangements, obligations (including contingent obligations), and other relationships of the issuer with unconsolidated entities or other persons, that may have a material current or future effect on financial condition, changes in financial condition, results of operations, liquidity, capital expenditures, capital resources, or significant components of revenues or expenses."

(b) Commission Rules on Pro Forma Figures.—Not later than 180 days after the date of enactment of the Sarbanes-Oxley

Act of 2002, the Commission shall issue final rules providing that pro forma financial information included in any periodic or other report filed with the Commission pursuant to the securities laws, or in any public disclosure or press or other release, shall be presented in a manner that—

(1) does not contain an untrue statement of a material fact or omit to state a material fact necessary in order to make the pro forma financial information, in light of the circumstances under which it is presented, not misleading; and

(2) reconciles it with the financial condition and results of operations of the issuer under generally accepted accounting principles.

Sec. 402 *Enhanced Conflict of Interest Provisions.*

(a) Prohibition on Personal Loans to Executives.—Section 13 of the Securities Exchange Act of 1934 (15 U.S.C. 78m), as amended by this Act, is amended by adding at the end the following:

"(k) Prohibition on Personal Loans to Executives.—

"(1) In general.—It shall be unlawful for any issuer (as defined in section 2 of the Sarbanes-Oxley Act of 2002), directly or indirectly, including through any subsidiary, to extend or maintain credit, to arrange for the extension of credit, or to renew an extension of credit, in the form of a personal loan to or for any director or executive officer (or equivalent thereof) of that issuer. An extension of credit maintained by the issuer on the date of enactment of this subsection shall not be subject to the provisions of this subsection, provided that there is no material modification to any term of any such extension of credit or any renewal of any such extension of credit on or after that date of enactment.

Sec. 406 *Code of Ethics for Senior Financial Officers.*

(a) Code of Ethics Disclosure.—The Commission shall issue rules to require each issuer, together with periodic reports required pursuant to section 13(a) or 15(d) of the Securities Exchange Act of 1934, to disclose whether or not, and if not, the reason therefor, such issuer has adopted a code of ethics for senior financial officers, applicable to its principal financial officer and comptroller or principal accounting officer, or persons performing similar functions.

(b) Changes in Codes of Ethics.—The Commission shall revise its regulations concerning matters requiring prompt disclosure on Form 8-K (or any successor thereto) to require the immediate disclosure by means of the filing of such form, dissemination by the Internet or by other electronic means, by any issuer of any change in or waiver of the code of ethics for senior financial officers.

(c) Definition.—In this section, the term "code of ethics" means such standards as are reasonably necessary to promote—

(1) honest and ethical conduct, including the ethical handling of actual or apparent conflicts of interest between personal and professional relationships;

(2) full, fair, accurate, timely, and understandable disclosure in the periodic reports required to be filed by the issuer; and

(3) compliance with applicable governmental rules and regulations.

Title V—Analyst Conflicts of Interest

Sec. 501 Treatment of Securities Analysts by Registered Securities Associations and National Securities Exchanges.

(a) Rules Regarding Securities Analysts.—The Securities Exchange Act of 1934 (15 U.S.C. 78a et seq.) is amended by inserting after section 15C the following new section:

"Sec. 15D. Securities Analysts and Research Reports

"(a) Analyst Protections.—The Commission, or upon the authorization and direction of the Commission, a registered securities association or national securities exchange, shall have adopted, not later than 1 year after the date of enactment of this section, rules reasonably designed to address conflicts of interest that can arise when securities analysts recommend equity securities in research reports and public appearances, in order to improve the objectivity of research and provide investors with more useful and reliable information, including rules designed—

"(1) to foster greater public confidence in securities research, and to protect the objectivity and independence of securities analysts, by—

"(A) restricting the prepublication clearance or approval of research reports by persons employed by the broker or dealer who are engaged in investment banking activities, or persons not directly responsible for investment research, other than legal or compliance staff;

"(B) limiting the supervision and compensatory evaluation of securities analysts to officials employed by the broker or dealer who are not engaged in investment banking activities; and

"(C) requiring that a broker or dealer and persons employed by a broker or dealer who are involved with investment banking activities may not, directly or indirectly, retaliate against or threaten to retaliate against any securities analyst employed by that broker or dealer or its affiliates as a result of an adverse, negative, or otherwise unfavorable research report that may adversely affect the present or prospective investment banking relationship of the broker or dealer with the issuer that is the subject of the research report, except that such rules may not limit the authority of a broker or dealer to discipline a securities analyst for causes other than such research report in accordance with the policies and procedures of the firm;

"(2) to define periods during which brokers or dealers who have participated, or are to participate, in a public offering of securities as underwriters or dealers should not publish or otherwise distribute research reports relating to such securities or to the issuer of such securities;

"(3) to establish structural and institutional safeguards within registered brokers or dealers to assure that securities analysts are separated by appropriate informational partitions within the firm from the review, pres-

sure, or oversight of those whose involvement in investment banking activities might potentially bias their judgment or supervision; and

"(4) to address such other issues as the Commission, or such association or exchange, determines appropriate.

"(b) Disclosure.—The Commission, or upon the authorization and direction of the Commission, a registered securities association or national securities exchange, shall have adopted, not later than 1 year after the date of enactment of this section, rules reasonably designed to require each securities analyst to disclose in public appearances, and each registered broker or dealer to disclose in each research report, as applicable, conflicts of interest that are known or should have been known by the securities analyst or the broker or dealer, to exist at the time of the appearance or the date of distribution of the report, including—

"(1) the extent to which the securities analyst has debt or equity investments in the issuer that is the subject of the appearance or research report;

"(2) whether any compensation has been received by the registered broker or dealer, or any affiliate thereof, including the securities analyst, from the issuer that is the subject of the appearance or research report, subject to such exemptions as the Commission may determine appropriate and necessary to prevent disclosure by virtue of this paragraph of material non-public information regarding specific potential future investment banking transactions of such issuer, as is appropriate in the public interest and consistent with the protection of investors;

"(3) whether an issuer, the securities of which are recommended in the appearance or research report, currently is, or during the 1-year period preceding the date of the appearance or date of distribution of the report has been, a client of the registered broker or dealer, and if so, stating the types of services provided to the issuer;

"(4) whether the securities analyst received compensation with respect to a research report, based upon (among any other factors) the investment banking revenues (either generally or specifically earned from the issuer being analyzed) of the registered broker or dealer; and

"(5) such other disclosures of conflicts of interest that are material to investors, research analysts, or the broker or dealer as the Commission, or such association or exchange, determines appropriate.

"(c) Definitions.—In this section—

"(1) the term 'securities analyst' means any associated person of a registered broker or dealer that is principally responsible for, and any associated person who reports directly or indirectly to a securities analyst in connection with, the preparation of the substance of a research report, whether or not any such person has the job title of 'securities analyst'; and

"(2) the term 'research report' means a written or electronic communication that includes an analysis of equity securities of individual companies or industries, and that provides information reasonably sufficient upon which to base an investment decision."

(b) Enforcement.—Section 21B(a) of the Securities Exchange Act of 1934 (15 U.S.C. 78u–2(a)) is amended by inserting "15D," before "15B".

(c) Commission Authority.—The Commission may promulgate and amend its regulations, or direct a registered securities association or national securities exchange to promulgate and amend its rules, to carry out section 15D of the Securities Exchange Act of 1934, as added by this section, as is necessary for the protection of investors and in the public interest.

Title VI—Commission Resources and Authority
Sec. 602 Appearance and Practice Before the Commission.

The Securities Exchange Act of 1934 (15 U.S.C. 78a et seq.) is amended by inserting after section 4B the following:

"Sec 4C. Appearance and Practice Before the Commission

"(a) Authority to Censure.—The Commission may censure any person, or deny, temporarily or permanently, to any person the privilege of appearing or practicing before the Commission in any way, if that person is found by the Commission, after notice and opportunity for hearing in the matter—

"(1) not to possess the requisite qualifications to represent others;

"(2) to be lacking in character or integrity, or to have engaged in unethical or improper professional conduct; or

"(3) to have willfully violated or willfully aided and abetted the violation of, any provision of the securities laws or the rules and regulations issued thereunder.

Title VII—Studies and Reports
Sec. 705 Study of Investment Banks.

(a) GAO Study.—The Comptroller General of the United States shall conduct a study on whether investment banks and financial advisers assisted public companies in manipulating their earnings and obfuscating their true financial condition. The study should address the rule of investment banks and financial advisers—

(1) in the collapse of the Enron Corporation, including with respect to the design and implementation of derivatives transactions, transactions involving special purpose vehicles, and other financial arrangements that may have had the effect of altering the company's reported financial statements in ways that obscured the true financial picture of the company;

(2) in the failure of Global Crossing, including with respect to transactions involving swaps of fiberoptic cable capacity, in the designing transactions that may have had the effect of altering the company's reported financial statements in ways that obscured the true financial picture of the company; and

(3) generally, in creating and marketing transactions which may have been designed solely to enable companies to manipulate revenue streams, obtain loans, or move lia-

bilities off balance sheets without altering the economic and business risks faced by the companies or any other mechanism to obscure a company's financial picture.

Title VIII—Corporate and Criminal Fraud Accountability
Sec. 801 Short Title.

This title may be cited as the "Corporate and Criminal Fraud Accountability Act of 2002".

Sec. 802 Criminal Penalties for Altering Documents.

(a) In General.—Chapter 73 of title 18, United States Code, is amended by adding at the end the following:

§1519. Destruction, alteration, or falsification of records in Federal investigations and bankruptcy

"Whoever knowingly alters, destroys, mutilates, conceals, covers up, falsifies, or makes a false entry in any record, document, or tangible object with the intent to impede, obstruct, or influence the investigation or proper administration of any matter within the jurisdiction of any department or agency of the United States or any case filed under Title 11, or in relation to or contemplation of any such matter or case, shall be fined under this title, imprisoned not more than 20 years, or both.

§1520. Destruction of corporate audit records

"(a)(1) Any accountant who conducts an audit of an issuer of securities to which section 10A(a) of the Securities Exchange Act of 1934 (15 U.S.C. 78j–l(a)) applies, shall maintain all audit or review workpapers for a period of 5 years from the end of the fiscal period in which the audit or review was concluded.

Sec. 807 Criminal Penalties for Defrauding Shareholders of Publicly Traded Companies.

(a) In General.—Chapter 63 of title 18, United States Code, is amended by adding at the end the following:

§1348. Securities fraud

"Whoever knowingly executes, or attempts to execute, a scheme or artifice—

"(1) to defraud any person in connection with any security of an issuer with a class of securities registered under section 12 of the Securities Exchange Act of 1934 (15 U.S.C. 78l) or that is required to file reports under section 15(d) of the Securities Exchange Act of 1934 (15 U.S.C. 78o(d)); or

"(2) to obtain, by means of false or fraudulent pretenses, representations, or promises, any money or property in connection with the purchase or sale of any security of an issuer with a class of securities registered under section 12 of the Securities Exchange Act of 1934 (15 U.S.C. 78l) or that is required to file reports under section 15(d) of the Securities Exchange Act of 1934 (15 U.S.C. 78o(d));

shall be fined under this title, or imprisoned not more than 25 years, or both."

Title IX—White-Collar Crime Penalty Enhancements

Sec. 901 Short Title.

This title may be cited as the "White-Collar Crime Penalty Enhancement Act of 2002".

Sec. 906 Corporate Responsibility for Financial Reports.

(a) In General.—Chapter 63 of title 18, United States Code, is amended by inserting after section 1349, as created by this Act, the following:

§1350. Failure of corporate officers to certify financial reports

(a) Certification of Periodic Financial Reports.—Each periodic report containing financial statements filed by an issuer with the Securities Exchange Commission pursuant to section 13(a) or 15(d) of the Securities Exchange Act of 1934 (15 U.S.C. 78m(a) or 78o(d)) shall be accompanied by a written statement by the chief executive officer and chief financial officer (or equivalent thereof) of the issuer.

"(b) Content.—The statement required under subsection (a) shall certify that the periodic report containing the financial statements fully complies with the requirements of section 13(a) or 15(d) of the Securities Exchange Act of 1934 (15 U.S.C. 78m or 78o(d)) and that information contained in the periodic report fairly presents, in all material respects, the financial condition and results of operations of the issuer.

"(c) Criminal Penalties.—Whoever—

"(1) certifies any statement as set forth in subsections (a) and (b) of this section knowing that the periodic report accompanying the statement does not comport with all the requirements set forth in this section shall be fined not more than $1,000,000 or imprisoned not more than 10 years, or both; or

"(2) willfully certifies any statement as set forth in subsections (a) and (b) of this section knowing that the periodic report accompanying the statement does not comport with all the requirements set forth in this section shall be fined not more than $5,000,000, or imprisoned not more than 20 years, or both."

(b) Clerical Amendment.—The table of sections at the beginning of chapter 63 of title 18, United States Code, is amended by adding at the end the following:
"1350". Failure of corporate officers to certify financial reports."

Title X—Corporate Tax Returns

Sec. 1001 Sense of the Senate Regarding the Signing of Corporate Tax Returns by Chief Executive Officers.

It is the sense of the Senate that the Federal income tax return of a corporation should be signed by the chief executive officer of such corporation.

Title XI—Corporate Fraud Accountability

Sec. 1101 Short Title.

This title may be cited as the "Corporate Fraud Accountability Act of 2002".

Sec. 1102 Tampering with a Record or Otherwise Impeding an Official Proceeding.

Section 1512 of title 18, United States Code, is amended—

(1) by redesignating subsections (c) through (i) as subsections (d) through (j), respectively; and

(2) by inserting after subsection (b) the following new subsection:

"(c) Whoever corruptly—

"(1) alters, destroys, mutilates, or conceals a record, document, or other object, or attempts to do so, with the intent to impair the object's integrity or availability for use in an official proceeding; or

"(2) otherwise obstructs, influences, or impedes any official proceeding, or attempts to do so,
shall be fined under this title or imprisoned not more than 20 years, or both."

Sec. 1105 Authority of the Commission to Prohibit Persons from Serving as Officers or Directors.

(a) Securities Exchange Act of 1934.—Section 21C of the Securities Exchange Act of 1934 (15 U.S.C. 78u–3) is amended by adding at the end the following:

"(f) Authority of the Commission to Prohibit Persons from Serving as Officers or Directors.—In any cease-and-desist proceeding under subsection (a), the Commission may issue an order to prohibit, conditionally or unconditionally, and permanently or for such period of time as it shall determine, any person who has violated section 10(b) or the rules or regulations thereunder, from acting as an officer or director of any issuer that has a class of securities registered pursuant to section 12, or that is required to file reports pursuant to section 15(d), if the conduct of that person demonstrates unfitness to serve as an officer or director of any such issuer."

(b) Securities Act of 1933.—Section 8A of the Securities Act of 1933 (15 U.S.C. 77h–1) is amended by adding at the end of the following:

"(f) Authority of the Commission to Prohibit Persons from Serving as Officers or Directors.—In any cease-and-desist proceeding under subsection (a), the Commission may issue an order to prohibit, conditionally or unconditionally, and permanently or for such period of time as it shall determine, any person who has violated section 17(a)(1) or the rules or regulations thereunder, from acting as an officer or director of any issuer that has a class of securities registered pursuant to section 12 of the Securities Exchange Act of 1934, or that is required to file reports pursuant to section 15(d) of that Act, if the conduct of that person demonstrates unfitness to serve as an officer or director of any such issuer."

Glossary

abandoned property Property that an owner has discarded with the intent to relinquish his or her rights in it and mislaid or lost property that the owner has given up any further attempts to locate. [801]

abatement If the property the testator leaves is not sufficient to satisfy all the beneficiaries named in a will and there are both general and residuary bequests, the residuary bequests are abated first; if a will provides for general bequests, they are reduced proportionately if the residuary bequests are full abated or there are none. [848]

absolute priority rule A rule that says a reorganization plan is fair and equitable to an impaired class of unsecured creditors or equity holders if no class below it receives anything in the plan. [498]

acceptance A manifestation of assent by the offeree to the terms of the offer in a manner invited or required by the offer as measured by the objective theory of contracts. (Section 50 of the Restatement (Second) of Contracts) [192]; Occurs when a buyer or lessee takes any of the following actions after a reasonable opportunity to inspect the goods: (1) signifies the seller or lessor in words or by conduct that the goods are conforming or that the buyer or lessee will take or retain the goods despite their nonconformity or (2) fails to effectively reject the goods within a reasonable time after their delivery or tender by the seller or lessor. Acceptance also occurs if a buyer acts inconsistently with the seller's ownership rights in the goods. [323]

acceptance method The bankruptcy court must approve a plan of reorganization if (1) the plan is *in the best interests* of each class of claims and interests, (2) the plan is *feasible*, (3) at least one class of claims *votes to accept the plan*, and (4) each class of claims and interests is *nonimpaired*. [497]

accession Occurs when the value of personal property increases because it is added to or improved by natural or manufactured means. [798]

accommodation A shipment that is offered to the buyer as a replacement for the original shipment when the original shipment cannot be filled. [293]

accommodation party A party who signs an instrument and lends his or her name (and credit) to another party to the instrument. [422]

accord An agreement whereby the parties agree to accept something different in satisfaction of the original contract. [198]

accord and satisfaction The settlement of a contract dispute. [257]

action for an accounting A formal judicial proceeding in which the court is authorized to (1) review the partnership and the partners' transactions and (2) award each partner his or her share of the partnership assets. [544]

act of monopolizing A required act for there to be a violation of Section 2 of the Sherman Act. Possession of monopoly power without such act does not violate Section 2. [708]

act of state doctrine States that judges of one country cannot question the validity of an act committed by another country within that other country's borders. It is based on the principle that a country has absolute authority over what transpires within its own territory. [876]

actus reus "Guilty act"—the actual performance of the criminal act. [126]

ademption A principle that says if a testator leaves a specific devise of property to a beneficiary, but the property is no longer in the estate when the testator dies, the beneficiary receives nothing. [848]

adequate assurance of performance A party to a sales or lease contract may demand an adequate assurance of performance from the other party if there is an indication that the contract will be breached by that party. [331]

adjudged insane A person who has been adjudged insane by a proper court or administrative agency. A contract entered into by such a person is *void*. [210]

administrative agencies Agencies that the legislative and executive branches of federal and state governments establish. [726]

administrative dissolution Involuntary dissolution of a corporation that is ordered by the secretary of state if the corporation has failed to comply with certain procedures required by law. [576]

administrative law A body of law that governs the operation of administrative agencies. [726]

administrative law judge (ALJ) A judge, presiding over administrative proceedings, who decides questions of law and fact concerning the case. [727]

Administrative Procedure Act (APA) An act that establishes certain administrative procedures that federal administrative agencies must follow in conducting their affairs. [727]

adverse action A denial or revocation of credit or a change in the credit terms offered. [846]

adverse possession When a person who wrongfully possesses someone else's real property obtains title to that property if certain statutory requirements are met. [821]

advertisement A general advertisement is an invitation to make an offer. A specific advertisement is an offer. [187]

affirmative action Policy that provides that certain job preferences will be given to minority or other protected class applicants when an employer makes an employment decision. [787]

affirmative warranty A statement asserting that certain facts are true. [843]

AFL-CIO The 1955 combination of the AFL and the CIO. [752]

after-acquired property Property that the debtor acquires after the security agreement is executed. [466]

Age Discrimination in Employment Act of 1967 A federal act that prohibits age discrimination by employers against employees or prospective employees who are 40 years of age or older. [783]

agency The principal–agent relationship: the fiduciary relationship "which results from the manifestation of consent by one person to another that the other shall act in his behalf and subject to his control, and consent by the other so to act." [509]

agency by ratification An agency that occurs when (1) a person misrepresents him- or herself as another's agent when in fact he or she is not and (2) the purported principal ratifies the unauthorized act. [513]

agency law The large body of common law that governs agency: A mixture of contract law and tort law. [509]

agency shop An establishment where an employee does not have to join the union, but must pay a fee equal to the union dues. [756]

agent A person who has been authorized to sign a negotiable instrument on behalf of another person. [418, 509]

agreement The manifestation by two or more persons of the substance of a contract. [185]

agreement of conversion Document that states the terms for converting an existing business to an LLC. [646]

air pollution Pollution caused by factories, homes, vehicles, and the like that affects the air. [735]

air rights parcel The air space above the surface of the earth of an owner's real property. [814]

alien corporation A corporation that is incorporated in another country. [566]

allonge A separate piece of paper attached to the instrument on which the indorsement is written. [399]

altered check A check that has been altered without authorization that modifies the legal obligation of a party. [445]

alternative dispute resolution (ADR) Methods of resolving disputes other than litigation. [62]

Amendments Besides the Bill of Rights, 17 additions that have been added to the U.S. Constitution. [30]

American Inventory Protection Act A federal statute that permits inventors to file a *provisional application* with the PTO, requires the PTO to issue a patent within three years in most circumstances, and provides for contested reexaminations within the PTO. [5]

Americans with Disabilities Act (ADA) of 1990 Imposes obligations on employers and providers of public transportation, telecommunications, and public accommodations to accommodate individuals with disabilities. [785, 829]

annual financial statement A statement provided to the shareholders that contains a balance sheet, an income statement, and a statement of changes in shareholder equity. [592]

annual shareholders' meeting Meeting of the shareholders of a corporation that must be held annually by the corporation to elect directors and to vote on other matters. [588]

answer The defendant's written response to the plaintiff's complaint that is filed with the court and served on the plaintiff. [55]

anti-assignment clause A clause that prohibits the assignment of rights under the contract. [249]

anticipatory breach A breach that occurs when one contracting party informs the other that he or she will not perform his or her contractual duties when due. [268]

anticipatory repudiation The repudiation of a sales or lease contract by one of the parties prior to the date set for performance. [331]

antideficiency statute A statute that prohibits deficiency judgments regarding certain types of mortgages, such as those on residential property. [462]

anti-delegation clause A clause that prohibits the delegation of duties under the contract. [250]

antitrust laws A series of laws enacted to limit anticompetitive behavior in almost all industries, businesses, and professions operating in the United States. [701]

apparent agency Agency that arises when a principal creates the appearance of an agency that in actuality does not exist. [512]; Agency that arises when a franchisor creates the appearance that a franchisee is its agent when in fact an actual agency does not exist. [667]

appeal The act of asking an appellate court to overturn a decision after the trial court's final judgment has been entered. [61]

appellant The appealing party in an appeal. Also known as petitioner. [61]

appellate body A panel of seven judges selected from WTO member nations that hears and decides appeals from decisions by the dispute settlement body. [874]

appellee The responding party in an appeal. Also known as *respondent*. [61]

appropriate bargaining unit The group that a union seeks to represent. [34]

approval clause A clause that permits the assignment of the contract only upon receipt of an obligor's approval. [249]

arbitration A nonjudicial method of dispute resolution whereby a neutral third party decides the case. [62, 878]

arbitration clause A clause contained in many international contracts that stipulates that any dispute between the parties concerning the performance of the contract will be submitted to an arbitrator or arbitration panel for resolution. [63, 878]

area franchise The franchisor authorizes the franchisee to negotiate and sell franchises on behalf of the franchisor. [659]

arraignment A hearing during which the accused is brought before a court and is (1) informed of the charges against him or her and (2) asked to enter a plea. [129]

arrest warrant A document for a person's detainment based upon a showing of probable cause that the person committed the crime. [128]

arson Willfully or maliciously burning another's building. [132]

Article 2 and Revised Article 2 An article of the UCC that establishes rules that govern the sale of goods. [286]

Article 2A (Leases) Article of the UCC that governs lease of goods. [289]

Article 4 of the UCC Establishes the rules and principles that regulate bank deposit and collection procedures. [437]

Article 7 of the UCC An article of the Uniform Commercial Code that provides a detailed statutory scheme for the creation, perfection, and foreclosure on common carriers' and warehouse operators' liens. [805]

Article 9 of the UCC An article of the Uniform Commercial Code that governs secured transactions in personal property. [464]

articles of incorporation The basic governing documents of the corporation. These documents must be filed with the secretary of state of the state of incorporation. [567]

articles of organization The formal document that must be filed with the Secretary of State to form an LLC. [29]

articles of partnership A written partnership agreement; document that must be filed with the secretary of state to form a limited liability partnership. [543, 552]

articles of termination Document that is filed with the secretary of state that terminates the LLC as of the date of filing or upon a later effective date specified in the document. [652]

assault (1) The threat of immediate harm or offensive contact or (2) any action that arouses reasonable apprehension of imminent harm. Actual physical contact is unnecessary. [73]

assignee The party to whom the right has been transferred. [246]; The transferee in an assignment situation. [397, 827]

assignment The transfer of contractual rights by the obligee to another party. [246]; The transfer of rights under a contract. [397]; A transfer by a tenant of his or her rights under a lease to another. [827]

assignment and delegation Transfer of both rights and duties under the contract. [251]

assignor The obligee who transfers the right. [246]; The transferor in an assignment situation. [397]; The party who transfers the right. [827]

assumption of duties When a delegation of duties contains the term *assumption, I assume the duties,* or other similar language; the delegatee is legally liable to the obligee for nonperformance. [250]

assumption of the risk A defense a defendant can use against a plaintiff who knowingly and voluntarily enters into or participates in a risky activity that results in injury. [89]; A defense in which the defendant must prove that (1) the plaintiff knew and appreciated the risk and (2) the plaintiff voluntarily assumed the risk. [377]

attachment The creditor has an enforceable security interest against the debtor and can satisfy the debt out of the designated collateral. [465]

attestation The action of a will being witnessed by two or three objective and competent people. [845]

attorney–client privilege A rule that says a client can tell his or her lawyer anything about the case without fear that the attorney will be called as a witness against the client. [140]

at-will LLC An LLC that has no specified term of duration. [643]

auction without reserve An auction in which the seller expressly gives up his or her right to withdraw the goods from sale and must accept the highest bid. [189]

auction with reserve Unless expressly stated otherwise, an auction is an auction with reserve; that is, the seller retains the right to refuse the highest bid and withdraw the goods from sale. [189]

authorized shares The number of shares provided for in the articles of incorporation. [574]

automatic stay The result of the filing of a voluntary or involuntary petition; the suspension of certain actions by creditors against the debtor or the debtor's property. [495]

backward vertical merger A vertical merger in which the customer acquires the supplier. [711]

bailee A holder of goods who is not a seller or a buyer (e.g., a warehouse or common carrier). [306, 318, 802]

bailment A transaction where an owner transfers his or her personal property to another to be held, stored, delivered, or for some other purpose. Title to the property does not transfer. [802]

bailment at will A bailment without a fixed term; can be terminated at any time by either party. [805]

bailment for a fixed term A bailment that terminates at the end of the term or sooner by mutual consent of the parties. [805]

bailment for the sole benefit of the bailee A gratuitous bailment that benefits only the bailee. The bailee owes a *duty of utmost care* to protect the bailed property. [804]

bailment for the sole benefit of the bailor A gratuitous bailment that benefits only the bailor. The bailee owes only a *duty of slight care* to protect the bailed property. [804]

bailor The owner of property in a bailment. [802]

bait and switch A type of deceptive advertising that occurs when a seller advertises the availability of a low-cost discounted item but then pressures the buyer into purchasing more expensive merchandise. [733]

bank check A certified check, a cashier's check, or a traveler's check, the payment for which the bank is solely or primarily liable. [439]

Bankruptcy Code A federal statute that establishes rules and procedures for filing bankruptcy and completing bankruptcy. [484]

bankruptcy estate An estate created upon the commencement of a Chapter 7 proceeding that includes all the debtor's legal and equitable interests in real, personal, tangible, and intangible property, wherever located, that exist when the petition is filed, minus exempt property. [487]

bargained-for exchange Exchange that parties engage in that leads to an enforceable contract. [195]

battery Unauthorized and harmful or offensive physical contact with another person. Direct physical contact is not necessary. [73]

bearer paper Bearer paper is negotiated by delivery; indorsement is not necessary. [397]

beneficiary A person or organization who will receive money from the insurer at the time of the insured's death. [839]; A person or organization designated in the will who receives all or a portion of the testator's property at the time of the testator's death. [844] Person for whose benefit a trust is created. [853]

bequest A gift of personal property by will. [848]

Bill of Rights The first 10 amendments to the U.S. Constitution, which were added to the U.S. Constitution in 1791. [30]

bilateral contract A contract entered into by way of exchange of promises of the parties; "a promise for a promise." [175]

bill of lading A document of title that is issued by a common carrier to the bailor when goods are received by the common carrier for transportation. [806]

blank indorsement An indorsement that does not specify a particular indorsee. It creates *bearer paper.* [399]

board of directors A panel of decision makers, the members of which are elected by the shareholders. [594]

bona fide occupational qualification (BFOQ) Employment discrimination based on a protected class (other than race or color) is lawful if it is *job related* and a *business necessity.* This exception is narrowly interpreted by the courts. [781]

bond A long-term debt security that is secured by some form of collateral. [575]

breach Failure of a party to perform an obligation in a sales or lease contract. [318]

breach of contract If a contracting party fails to perform an absolute duty owed under a contract. [266]

breach of the duty of care A failure to exercise care or to act as a reasonable person would act. [80]

bribery When one person gives another person money, property, favors, or anything else of value for a favor in return. Often referred to as a payoff or "kickback." [134]

building codes State and local statutes that impose specific standards on property owners to maintain and repair leased premises. [825]

burglary Taking personal property from another's home, office, commercial, or other type of building. [131]

business judgment rule A rule that protects the decisions of the board of directors, who act on an informed basis, in good faith, and in the honest belief that the action taken was in the best interests of the corporation and its shareholders. [600, 626]

buyer in the ordinary course of business A person who in good faith and without knowledge that the sale violates the ownership or security interests of a third party buys the goods in the ordinary course of business from a person in the business of selling goods of that kind. A buyer in the ordinary course of business takes the goods free of any third-party security interest in the goods. [310]; A person who in good faith and without knowledge of another's ownership or security interest in goods buys the goods in the ordinary course of business from a person in the business of selling goods of that kind [UCC 1-201(9)]. [470]

bylaws A detailed set of rules adopted by the board of directors after the corporation is incorporated that contains provisions for managing the business and the affairs of the corporation. [569]

cancellation The termination of a contract by a contracting party upon the material breach of the contract by the other party. [353]; A seller or lessor may cancel a sales or lease contract if the buyer or lessee rejects or revokes acceptance of the goods, fails to pay for the goods, or repudiates the contract in part or in whole. [326] A buyer or lessee may cancel a sales or lease contract if the seller or lessor fails to deliver conforming goods or repudiates the contract or if the buyer or lessee rightfully rejects the goods or justifiably revokes acceptance of the goods. [329]

case brief A summary of each of the following items of a case: 1. Case name and citation, 2. Key facts, 3. Issue presented, 4. Holding of the court, 5. Court's reasoning. [15]

cashier's check A check issued by a bank where the customer has paid the bank the amount of the check and a fee. The bank guarantees the payment of the check. [440]

causation A person who commits a negligent act is not liable unless his or her act was the cause of the plaintiff's injuries. The two types of causation that must be proven are (1) *causation in fact (actual cause)* and (2) *proximate cause (legal cause)*. [82]

causation in fact or actual cause The actual cause of negligence. A person who commits a negligent act is not liable unless causation in fact can be proven. [82]

certificate of deposit (CD) A two-party negotiable instrument that is a special form of note created when a depositor deposits money at a financial institution in exchange for the institution's promise to pay back the amount of the deposit plus an agreed-upon rate of interest upon the expiration of a set time period agreed upon by the parties. [390]

certificate of interest A document that evidences a member's ownership interest in an LLC. [644]

certificate of limited partnership A document that two or more persons must execute and sign that makes the limited partnership legal and binding. [550]

certified check A type of check where a bank agrees in advance (*certifies*) to accept the check when it is presented for payment. [439]

chain of distribution All manufacturers, distributors, wholesalers, retailers, lessors, and subcomponent manufacturers involved in a transaction. [370]

chain-style franchise The franchisor licenses the franchisee to make and sell its products or distribute services to the public from a retail outlet serving an exclusive territory. [659]

changing conditions defense A price discrimination defense that claims prices were lowered in response to changing conditions in the market for or the marketability of the goods. [714]

Chapter 11 A bankruptcy method that allows reorganization of the debtor's financial affairs under the supervision of the Bankruptcy Court. [494]

Chapter 13 A rehabilitation form of bankruptcy that permits the courts to supervise the debtor's plan for the payment of unpaid debts by installments. [498]

Chapter 7 liquidation bankruptcy The most familiar form of bankruptcy; the debtor's nonexempt property is sold for cash, the cash is distributed to the creditors, and any unpaid debts are discharged. [485]

check A distinct form of draft drawn on a financial institution and payable on demand. [388] An order by the drawer to the drawee bank to pay a specified sum of money from the drawer's checking account to the named payee (or holder). [438]

choice of forum clause Clause in an international contract that designates which nation's court has jurisdiction to hear a case arising out of the contract. Also known as a forum-selection clause. [875]

choice of law clause Clause in an international contract that designates which nation's laws will be applied in deciding a dispute. [875]

Clean Air Act A federal statute enacted to assist states in dealing with air pollution. [735, 737]

Civil Rights Act of 1866 A section of a federal statute that expressly prohibits racial discrimination; it has also been held to forbid discrimination based on national origin. [783]

closely held corporation A corporation owned by one or a few shareholders. [563]

Civil Rights Act A federal statute that prohibits racial discrimination in the transfer of real property. [829]

closing The finalization of a real estate sales transaction that passes title to the property from the seller to the buyer. [819]

codicil A separate document that must be executed to amend a will. It must be executed with the same formalities as a will. [847]

C.O.D. shipment A type of shipment contract where the buyer agrees to pay the shipper cash upon the delivery of the goods. [322]

coinsurance clause A clause that permits an owner who insures his or her property to a certain percent of its value to recover up to the face value of the policy. [841]

collateral Security against repayment of the note that lenders sometimes require; can be a car, a house, or other property. [389]

collateral contract A promise where one person agrees to answer for the debts or duties of another person. [233]

collecting bank The depository bank and other banks in the collection process (other than the payor bank). [446]

collective bargaining The act of negotiating contract terms between an employer and the members of a union. [756]

collective bargaining agreement The resulting contract from a collective bargaining procedure. [756]

"coming and going" rule A rule that says a principal is generally not liable for injuries caused by its agents and employees while they are on their way to or from work. [521]

Commerce Clause A clause of the U.S. Constitution that grants Congress the power "to regulate commerce with foreign nations, and among the several states, and with Indian tribes." [28]

commercial impracticability Nonperformance that is excused if an extreme or unexpected development or expense makes it impractical for the promisor to perform. [258]

commercial speech Speech used by businesses, such as advertising. It is subject to time, place, and manner restrictions. [2]

common carrier A firm that offers transportation services to the general public. The bailee. Owes a *duty of strict liability* to the bailor. [805]

common law Developed by judges who issued their opinions when deciding a case. The principles announced in these cases became precedent for later judges deciding similar cases. [8]

common law of contracts Contract law developed primarily by state courts. [173]

common stock A type of equity security that represents the *residual* value of the corporation. [572]

common stock certificate A document that represents the common shareholder's investment in the corporation. [572]

common stockholder A person who owns common stock. [572]

community property A form of ownership where each spouse owns an equal one-half share of the income of both spouses earned during the marriage and one-half of the assets acquired by this income during the marriage. [817]

comparative negligence A doctrine under which damages are apportioned according to fault. [91]; A doctrine that applies to strict liability actions that says a plaintiff who is contributorily negligent for his or her injuries is responsible for a proportional share of the damages. [378]

compensatory damages An award of money intended to compensate a non-breaching party for the loss of the bargain;

they place the nonbreaching party in the same position as if the contract had been fully performed by restoring the "benefit of the bargain." [270]; Damages that are generally equal to the difference between the value of the goods as warranted and the actual value of the goods accepted at the time and place of acceptance. [366]

competent party's duty of restitution If a minor has transferred money, property, or other valuables to the competent party before disaffirming the contract, that party must place the minor back into status quo. [207]

complaint The document the plaintiff files with the court and serves on the defendant to initiate a lawsuit. [54]

complete performance Occurs when a party to a contract renders performance exactly as required by the contract; discharges that party's obligations under the contract. [267]

conciliation A form of mediation in which the parties choose an interested third party to act as the mediator. [64]

concurrent condition A condition that exists when the parties to a contract must render performance simultaneously; each party's absolute duty to perform is conditioned on the other party's absolute duty to perform. [255]

concurrent jurisdiction Jurisdiction shared by two or more courts. [50]

condition A qualification of a promise that becomes a covenant if it is met. There are three types of conditions: conditions precedent, conditions subsequent, and concurrent conditions. [254]

condition precedent A condition that requires the occurrence of an event before a party is obligated to perform a duty under a contract. [254]

condition precedent based on satisfaction Clause in a contract that reserves the right to a party to pay for the items or services contracted for only if they meet his or her satisfaction. [254]

condition subsequent A condition, if it occurs or doesn't occur, that automatically excuses the performance of an existing contractual duty to perform. [255]

condominium A common form of ownership in a multiple-dwelling building where the purchaser has title to the individual unit and owns the common areas as a tenant in common with the other condominium owners. [818]

confirmation The bankruptcy court's approval of a plan of reorganization. [497]

confusion Occurs if two or more persons commingle fungible goods; title is then acquired by confusion. [799]

conglomerate merger A merger that does not fit into any other category; a merger between firms in totally unrelated businesses. [711]

consequential damages Foreseeable damages that arise from circumstances outside the contract. To be liable for these damages, the breaching party must know or have reason to know that the breach will cause special damages to the other party. [272]

consideration Something of legal value given in exchange for a promise. [194]

consignee The person to whom the bailed goods are to be delivered. [805]

consignment An arrangement where a seller (the consignor) delivers goods to a buyer (the consignee) for sale. [307]

consignor The person shipping the goods. The bailor. [805]

Consolidated Omnibus Budget Reconciliation Act (COBRA) Federal law that permits employees and their beneficiaries to continue their group health insurance after an employee's employment has ended. [763]

consolidation The act of a court to combine two or more separate lawsuits into one lawsuit. [56]; Occurs when two or more corporations combine to form an entirely new corporation. [621]

conspicuous A requirement that warranty disclaimers be noticeable to the average person. [367]

Constitution of the United States of America The supreme law of the United States. [9]

constructive notice Usually written notice to a third party that is put into general circulation, such as in a newspaper. [547]

Consumer Product Safety Act (CPSA) A federal statute that regulates potentially dangerous consumer products and created the Consumer Product Safety Commission. [731]

Consumer Product Safety Commission (CPSC) An independent federal regulatory agency empowered to (1) adopt rules and regulations to interpret and enforce the Consumer Product Safety Act, (2) conduct research on safety, and (3) collect data regarding injuries. [731]

consumer protection laws Federal and state statutes and regulations that promote product safety and prohibit abusive, unfair, and deceptive business practices. [726]

contract in restraint of trade A contract that unreasonably restrains trade. [214]

contracts contrary to public policy Contracts that have a negative impact on society or that interfere with the public's safety and welfare. [213]

contributory negligence A defense that says a person who is injured by a defective product but has been negligent and has contributed to his or her own injuries cannot recover from the defendant. [90, 378]

covenant of good faith and fair dealing Under this implied covenant, the parties to a contract not only held to the express terms of the contract but are also required to act in "good faith" and deal fairly in all respects in obtaining the objective of the contract. [278]

convention Treaty that is sponsored by an international organization. [865]

conversion of personal property A tort that deprives a true owner of the use and enjoyment of his or her personal property by taking over such property and exercising ownership rights over it. [79]

convertible preferred stock Stock that permits the stockholders to convert their shares into common stock. [573]

cooling-off period Requires a union to give an employer at least 60 days' notice before a strike can commence. [758]

cooperative A form of co-ownership of a multiple-dwelling building where a corporation owns the building and the residents own shares in the corporation. [818]

co-ownership When two or more persons own a piece of real property. Also called *concurrent ownership*. [815]

copyright infringement When a party copies a substantial and material part of the plaintiff's copyrighted work without permission. A copyright holder may recover damages and other remedies against the infringer. [109]

Copyright Revision Act of 1976 Federal statute that (1) establishes the requirements for obtaining a copyright and (2) protects copyrighted works from infringement. [108]

corporate citizenship A theory of responsibility that says a business has a responsibility to do good. [164]

corporate seal A design containing the name of the corporation and the date of incorporation that is imprinted by the corporate secretary using a metal stamp on certain legal documents. [570]

corporation A fictitious legal entity that (1) is created according to statutory requirements and (2) is a separate taxpaying entity for federal income tax purposes. [561]

corporations codes State statutes that regulate the formation, operation, and dissolution of corporations. [561]

cost justification defense A defense in Section 2(a) action that provides that a seller's price discrimination is not unlawful if the price differential is due to "differences in the cost of manufacture, sale, or delivery" of the product. [714]

counteroffer A response by an offeree that contains terms and conditions different from or in addition to those of the offer. A counteroffer terminates an offer. [190]

Court of Appeals for the Federal Circuit A court of appeals in Washington, DC, that has special appellate jurisdiction to review the decisions of the Claims Court, the Patent and Trademark Office, and the Court of International Trade. [47]

Court of Chancery Court that granted relief based on fairness. Also called equity court. [8]

covenant An unconditional promise to perform. [254]

covenant of quiet enjoyment A covenant that says that a landlord may not interfere with the tenant's quiet and peaceful possession, use, and enjoyment of the leased premises. [825]

cover The licensee's right to engage in a commercially reasonable substitute transaction after the licensor has breached the contract. [355]; Right of a buyer or lessee to purchase or lease substitute goods if a seller or lessor fails to make delivery of the goods or repudiates the contract or if the buyer or lessee rightfully rejects the goods or justifiably revokes their acceptance. [329]

cram down method A method of confirmation of a plan of reorganization where the court forces an impaired class to participate in the plan of reorganization. [497]

crashworthiness doctrine A doctrine that says automobile manufacturers are under a duty to design automobiles so they take into account the possibility of harm from a person's body striking something inside the

automobile in the case of a car accident. [374]

credit report Information about a person's credit history that can be secured from a credit bureau. [846]

creditor The lender in a credit transaction. [459]

creditor beneficiary Original creditor who becomes a beneficiary under the debtor's new contract with another party. [252]

creditor beneficiary contract A contract that arises in the following situation: (1) a debtor borrows money, (2) the debtor signs an agreement to pay back the money plus interest, (3) the debtor sells the item to a third party before the loan is paid off, and (4) the third party promises the debtor that he or she will pay the remainder of the loan to the creditor. [252]

creditor–debtor relationship Created when a customer deposits money into the bank; the customer is the creditor and the bank is the debtor. [437]

creditor's committee The creditors holding the seven largest unsecured claims are usually appointed to the creditors' committee. Representatives of the committee appear at Bankruptcy Court hearings, participate in the negotiation of a plan of reorganization, assert objections to proposed plans, and so on. [495]

crime A crime is a violation of a statute for which the government imposes a punishment. [125]

criminal fraud Obtaining title to property through deception or trickery. Also known as false pretenses or deceit. [134]

critical legal thinking The process of specifying the issue presented by a case, identifying the key facts in the case and applicable law, and then applying the law to the facts to come to a conclusion that answers the issue presented. [15]

cross-complaint Filed by the defendant against the plaintiff to seek damages or some other remedy. [55]

crossover worker A person who does not honor a strike who either (1) chooses not to strike or (2) returns to work after joining the strikers for a time. [758]

crown jewel A valuable asset of the target corporation's that the tender offeror particularly wants to acquire in the tender offer. [626]

cruel and unusual punishment A clause of the Eighth Amendment that protects criminal defendants from torture or other abusive punishment. [141]

cumulative preferred stock Stock that provides any missed dividend payments must be paid in the future to the preferred shareholders before the common shareholders can receive any dividends. [573]

cumulative voting A shareholder can accumulate all of his or her votes and vote them all for one candidate or split them among several candidates. [589]

cure An opportunity to repair or replace defective or nonconforming goods. [320]

custom The second source of international law, created through consistent, recurring practices between two or more nations over a period of time that have become recognized as binding. [865]

damages A buyer or lessee may recover damages from a seller or lessor who fails to deliver the goods or repudiates the contract; damages are measured as the difference between the contract price (or original rent) and the market price (or rent) at the time the buyer or lessee learned of the breach. [330]

damages for accepted nonconforming goods A buyer or lessee may accept nonconforming goods and recover the damages caused by the breach from the seller or lessor or deduct the damages from any part of the purchase price or rent still due under the contract. [330]

"danger invites rescue" doctrine Doctrine that provides that a rescuer who is injured while going to someone's rescue can sue the person who caused the dangerous situation. [86]

debenture A long-term unsecured debt instrument that is based on the corporation's general credit standing. [575]

debtor The borrower in a credit transaction. [459]

debtor-in-possession A debtor who is left in place to operate the business during the reorganization proceeding. [494]

debt securities Securities that establish a debtor–creditor relationship in which the corporation borrows money from the investor to whom the debt security is issued. [574]

declaration of duties If the delegatee has not assumed the duties under a contract, the delegatee is not legally liable to the obligee for nonperformance. [250]

deductible clause A clause that stipulates that insurance proceeds are payable only

after the insured has paid a certain amount of the damage or loss. [841]

deed A writing that describes a person's ownership interest in a piece of real property. [819]

deed of trust An instrument that gives the creditor a security interest in the debtor's property that is pledged as collateral. [461]

defamation of character False statement(s) made by one person about another. In court, the plaintiff must prove that (1) the defendant made an untrue statement of fact about the plaintiff and (2) the statement was intentionally or accidentally published to a third party. [76]

default Failure to make scheduled payments when due, bankruptcy of the debtor, breach of the warranty of ownership as to the collateral, and other events defined by the parties to constitute default. [471]

defect Something wrong, inadequate, or improper in manufacture, design, packaging, warning, or safety measures of a product. [372]

defect in design A defect that occurs when a product is improperly designed. [372]

defect in manufacture A defect that occurs when the manufacturer fails to (1) properly assemble a product, (2) properly test a product, or (3) adequately check the quality of the product. [372]

defect in packaging A defect that occurs when a product has been placed in packaging that is insufficiently tamperproof. [375]

deferred posting rule A rule that allows banks to fix an afternoon hour of 2:00 p.m. or later as a cutoff hour for the purpose of processing items. [446]

deficiency judgment A judgment that allows a secured creditor to successfully bring a separate legal action to recover a deficiency from the debtor. Entitles the secured creditor to recover the amount of the judgment from the debtor's other property. [460, 472]

delegatee The party to whom the duty has been transferred. [249]

delegation doctrine A doctrine that says when an administrative agency is created, it is delegated certain powers; the agency can only use those legislative, judicial, and executive powers that are delegated to it. [727]

delegation of duties A transfer of contractual duties by the obligor to another party for performance. [249]

delegator The obligor who transferred his or her duty. [249]

demand instrument An instrument payable on demand. [395, 416]

demand note A note payable on demand. [389]

deponent Party who gives his or her deposition. [57]

deposition Oral testimony given by a party or witness prior to trial. The testimony is given under oath and is transcribed. [57]

depository bank The bank where the payee or holder has an account. [446]

derivative lawsuit A lawsuit a shareholder brings against an offending party on behalf of the corporation when the corporation fails to bring the lawsuit. [592]

destination contract A contract that requires the seller to deliver the goods either to the buyer's place of business or to another destination specified in the sales contract. The seller bears the risk of loss during transportation. [303, 319]

devise A gift of real estate by will. [848]

disaffirmance The act of a minor to rescind a contract under the infancy doctrine. Disaffirmance may be done orally, in writing, or by the minor's conduct. [207]

discharge Actions or events that relieve certain parties from liability on negotiable instruments. There are three methods of discharge: (1) payment of the instrument; (2) cancellation; and (3) impairment of the right of recourse. [428]; The termination of the legal duty of a debtor to pay debts that remain unpaid upon the completion of a bankruptcy proceeding. [492]; A discharge is granted to a debtor in a Chapter 13 consumer debt adjustment bankruptcy only after all the payments under the plan are completed by the debtor. [498, 501]

discharge in bankruptcy A real defense against the enforcement of a negotiable instrument; bankruptcy law is intended to relieve debtors of burdensome debts, including negotiable instruments. [425]

disclosure statement A statement that must contain adequate information about the proposed plan of reorganization that is supplied to the creditors and equity holders. [496]

discovery A legal process during which both parties engage in various activities to discover facts of the case from the other party and witnesses prior to trial. [57]

dishonored Occurs when an instrument has been presented for payment and payment has been refused. [417]

disparate impact discrimination Occurs when an employer discriminates against an entire protected class. An example would be where a facially neutral employment practice or rule causes an adverse impact on a protected class. [775]

disparate treatment discrimination Occurs when an employer discriminates against a specific individual because of his or her race, color, national origin, sex, or religion. [775]

disposition of collateral If a secured creditor repossesses collateral upon a debtor's default, he or she may sell, lease, or otherwise dispose of it in a commercially reasonable manner. [472]

disposition of goods A seller or lessor who is in possession of goods at the time the buyer or lessee breaches or repudiates the contract may in good faith resell, release, or otherwise dispose of the goods in a commercially reasonable manner and recover damages, including incidental damages, from the buyer or lessee. [325]

dispute settlement body A board comprised of one representative from each WTO member nation that reviews panel reports. [874]

dissension When an individual director opposes the action taken by the majority of the board of directors. [602]

dissenting shareholder appraisal rights Shareholders who object to a proposed merger, share exchange, or sale or lease of all or substantially all of the property of a corporation have a right to have their shares valued by the court and receive cash payment of this value from the corporation. [623]

distinctive A brand name that is unique and fabricated. [114]

distribution of property *Nonexempt property* of the bankruptcy estate must be distributed to the debtor's secured and unsecured creditors pursuant to the statutory priority established by the Bankruptcy Code. [491]

distributional interest A member's ownership interest in an LLC that entitles the member to receive distributions of money and property from the LLC. [646]

distributional interest The ownership interest that a member has in an LLC. [651]

distributorship franchise The franchisor manufactures a product and licenses a retail franchisee to distribute the product to the public. [658]

diversity of citizenship A case between (1) citizens of different states, (2) a citizen of a state and a citizen or subject of a foreign country, and (3) a citizen of a state and a foreign country where a foreign country is the plaintiff. [50]

dividend preference The right to receive a fixed dividend at stipulated periods during the year (e.g., quarterly). [573]

division of markets When competitors agree that each will serve only a designated portion of the market. [704]

doctrine of sovereign immunity States that countries are granted immunity from suits in courts of other countries. [876]

doctrine of strict liability in tort A tort doctrine that makes manufacturers, distributors, wholesalers, retailers, and others in the chain of distribution of a defective product liable for the damages caused by the defect irrespective of fault. [370]

document of title An actual piece of paper, such as a warehouse receipt or bill of lading, that is required in some transactions of pick up and delivery. [303]

domain name A unique name that identifies an individual's or company's Web site. [346]

domestic corporation A corporation in the state in which it was formed. [566]

donee A person who receives a gift. [797]

donee beneficiary The third party on whom the benefit is to be conferred. [251]

donee beneficiary contract A contract entered into with the intent to confer a benefit or gift on an intended third party. [251]

donor A person who gives a gift. [797]

double jeopardy clause A clause of the Fifth Amendment that protects persons from being tried twice for the same crime. [141]

draft A three-party instrument that is an unconditional written order by one party that orders the second party to pay money to a third party. [387]

Dram Shop Act Statute that makes taverns and bartenders liable for injuries caused to or by patrons who are served too much alcohol. [86]

drawee of a check The financial institution where the drawer has his or her account. [388]; The bank where the drawer has his or her account [438]

drawee of a draft The party who must pay the money stated in the draft. Also called the *acceptor* of a draft. [387]

drawer of a check The checking account holder and writer of the check. [388, 438]

drawer of a draft The party who writes the order for a draft. [387]

Drug Amendment to the FDCA An amendment that gives the FDA broad powers to license new drugs in the United States. [730]

dual-purpose mission An errand or other act that a principal requests of an agent while the agent is on his or her own personal business. [521]

due diligence defense A defense to a Section 11 action that, if proven, makes the defendant not liable. [685]

Due Process Clause A clause that provides that no person shall be deprived of "life, liberty, or property" without due process of the law. [36]

duress Occurs when one party threatens to do a wrongful act unless the other party enters into a contract. [230]

duty not to willfully or wantonly injure The duty an owner owes a trespasser to prevent intentional injury or harm to the trespasser when the trespasser is on his or her premises. [87]

duty of accountability A duty that an agent owes to maintain an accurate accounting of all transactions undertaken on the principal's behalf. [515]

duty of care The obligation we all owe each other not to cause any unreasonable harm or risk of harm. [79]; A duty that corporate directors and officers have to use care and diligence when acting on behalf of the corporation. [600, 649]

duty of loyalty A duty that directors and officers have not to act adversely to the interests of the corporation and to subordinate their personal interests to those of the corporation and its shareholders. [603]

duty of notification An agent's duty to notify the principal of information he or she learns from a third party or other source that is important to the principal. [514]

duty of obedience A duty that directors and officers of a corporation have to act within the authority conferred upon them by the state corporation statute, the articles of incorporation, the corporate bylaws, and the resolutions adopted by the board of directors. [600]

duty of ordinary care The duty an owner owes an invitee or a licensee to prevent injury or harm when the invitee or licensee steps on the owner's premises. [87]; Collecting banks are required to exercise ordinary care in presenting and sending checks for collection. [449]

duty of performance An agent's duty to a principal that includes (1) performing the lawful duties expressed in the contract and (2) meeting the standards of reasonable care, skill, and diligence implicit in all contracts. [514]

duty of reasonable care The duty that a reasonable bailee in like circumstances would owe to protect the bailed property. [804]

duty of slight care A duty not to be grossly negligent in caring for something in one's responsibility. [804]

duty of strict liability A duty that common carriers owe that says if the goods are lost, damaged, destroyed, or stolen, the common carrier is liable even if it was not at fault for the loss. [805]

duty of utmost care A duty of care that goes beyond ordinary care that says common carriers and innkeepers have a responsibility to provide security to their passengers or guests. [88, 804]

duty to compensate A duty that a principal owes to pay an agreed-upon amount to the agent either upon the completion of the agency or at some other mutually agreeable time. [514]

duty to cooperate A duty that a principal owes to cooperate with and assist the agent in the performance of the agent's duties and the accomplishment of the agency. [514]

duty to defend An insurer owes a duty to defend an insured against a lawsuit involving a risk covered by the policy. This duty includes providing a lawyer and paying court costs and deposition fees. [842]

duty to indemnify A duty that a principal owes to protect the agent for losses the agent suffered during the agency because of the principal's misconduct. [514]

duty to reimburse A duty that a principal owes to repay money to the agent if the agent spent his or her own money during the agency on the principal's behalf. [514]

easement A given or required right to make limited use of someone else's land without owning or leasing it. [822]

easement appurtenant A situation created when the owner of one piece of land is given an easement over an adjacent piece of land. [822]

easement in gross An easement that authorizes a person who does not own adjacent land the right to use another's land. [822]

e-commerce The sale of goods and services by computer over the Internet. [341]

electronic mail (e-mail) Electronic written communication between individuals using computers connected to the Internet. [344]

elements of a bailment The following three elements are necessary to create a bailment: (1) personal property, (2) delivery of possession, and (3) a bailment agreement. [802]

emancipation When a minor voluntarily leaves home and lives apart from his or her parents. [209]

embezzlement The fraudulent conversion of property by a person to whom that property was entrusted. [133]

eminent domain The taking of private property by the government for public use, provided just compensation is paid to the private property holder. [830]

Employee Retirement Income Security Act (ERISA) A federal act designed to prevent fraud and other abuses associated with private pension funds. [764]

employer–employee relationship A relationship that results when an employer hires an employee to perform some form of physical service. [510]

employer lockout Act of the employer to prevent employees from entering the work premises when the employer reasonably anticipates a strike. [758]

endorsement An addition to an insurance policy that modifies it. [842]

entrepreneur A person who forms and operates a new business either by him- or herself or with others. [537]

enumerated powers Certain powers delegated to the federal government by the states. [26]

Environmental Impact Statement (EIS) A document that must be prepared for all proposed legislation or major federal action which significantly affects the quality of the human environment. [734]

Environmental Protection Agency (EPA) An administrative agency created by Congress in 1970 to coordinate the implemen-

tation and enforcement of the federal environmental protection laws. [734]

environmental protection laws Federal and state statutes and regulations that limit levels of pollution and require the cleanup of hazardous waste site. [726]

equal dignity rule A rule that says that agent's contracts to sell property covered by the Statute of Frauds must be in writing to be enforceable. [235]

Equal Employment Opportunity Commission (EEOC) The federal administrative agency responsible for enforcing most federal antidiscrimination laws. [774]

equal opportunity in employment The right of all employees and job applicants (1) to be treated without discrimination and (2) to be able to sue employers if they are discriminated against. [774]

Equal Pay Act of 1963 Protects both sexes from pay discrimination based on sex; extends to jobs that require equal skill, equal effort, equal responsibility, and similar working conditions. [783]

Equal Protection Clause A clause that provides that a state cannot "deny to any person within its jurisdiction the equal protection of the laws." [36]

equity A doctrine that permits judges to make decisions based on fairness, equality, moral rights, and natural law. [180]

equity securities Representation of ownership rights to the corporation. Also called *stocks*. [572]

escheats A doctrine that states that if a person dies without a will and has no surviving relatives, his or her property goes to the State. [851]

Establishment Clause A clause to the First Amendment that prohibits the government from either establishing a state religion or promoting one religion over another. [35]

estate Ownership rights in real property; the bundle of legal rights that the owner has to possess, use, and enjoy the property. [814]

estate pour autre vie A life estate measured in the life of a third party. [815]

ethical fundamentalism When a person looks to an outside source for ethical rules or commands. [153]

ethical relativism A moral theory that holds that individuals must decide what is ethical based on their own feelings as to what is right or wrong. [157]

ethics A set of moral principles or values that governs the conduct of an individual or a group. [150]

European Union (Common Market) Comprises many countries of Western Europe; created to promote peace and security plus economic, social, and cultural development. [869]

exclusionary rule A rule that says evidence obtained from an unreasonable search and seizure can generally be prohibited from introduction at a trial or administrative proceeding against the person searched. [138]

exclusive agency contract A contract a principal and agent enter into that says the principal cannot employ any agent other than the exclusive agent. [510]

exclusive jurisdiction Jurisdiction held by only one court. [50]

exclusive license A license that grants the licensee exclusive rights to use informational rights for a specified duration. [350]

exculpatory clause A contractual provision that relieves one (or both) parties to the contract from tort liability for ordinary negligence. [214]

executed contract A contract that has been fully performed on both sides; a completed contract. [179]

executive branch The part of the U.S. government that consists of the President and Vice President. [26]

executive order An order issued by a member of the executive branch of the government. [10]

executory contract A contract that has not been fully performed by either or both sides. [179]; With court approval, executory contracts may be rejected by a debtor in bankruptcy. [496]

exempt property Property that may be retained by a debtor pursuant to federal or state law; debtor's property that does not become part of the bankruptcy estate. [487]

express agency An agency that occurs when a principal and an agent expressly agree to enter into an agency agreement with each other. [510]

express authorization A stipulation in the offer that says the acceptance must be by a specified means of communication. [193]

express contract An agreement that is expressed in written or oral words. [175]

express powers Powers given to a corporation by (1) the U.S. Constitution, (2) state constitutions, (3) federal statutes, (4) state statutes, (5) articles of incorporation, (6) bylaws, and (7) resolutions of the board of directors. [575]

express warranty Any affirmation of fact or promise by the licensor about the quality of its software or information. [351]; A warranty that is created when a seller or lessor makes an affirmation that the goods he or she is selling or leasing meet certain standards of quality, description, performance, or condition. [362]

extortion Threat to expose something about another person unless that other person gives money or property. Often referred to as "blackmail." [132]

extradition Sending a person back to a country for criminal prosecution. [170]

extreme duress Extreme duress, but not ordinary duress, is a real defense against enforcement of a negotiable instrument. [424]

failure to provide adequate instructions A defect that occurs when a manufacturer does not provide detailed directions for safe assembly and use of a product. [375]

failure to warn A defect that occurs when a manufacturer does not place a warning on the packaging of products that could cause injury if the danger is unknown. [375]

Fair Housing Act A federal statute that makes it unlawful for a party to refuse to rent or sell a dwelling to any person because of his or her race, color, national origin, sex, or religion. [829]

Fair Labor Standards Act (FLSA) A federal act enacted in 1938 to protect workers; prohibits child labor and establishes minimum wage and overtime pay requirements. [762]

fair price rule A rule that says any increase in price paid for shares tendered must be offered to all shareholders, even those who have previously tendered their shares. [625]

fair use doctrine A doctrine that permits certain limited use of a copyright by someone other than the copyright holder without the permission of the copyright holder. [109]

false imprisonment The intentional confinement or restraint of another person without authority or justification and without that person's consent. [74]

Family and Medical Leave Act A federal statute that guarantees covered workers unpaid time off from work for the birth or adoption of a child, serious health problems of the workers, and serious health problems of a spouse, child, or parent. [763]

federal administrative agencies Administrative agencies that are part of the executive or legislative branch of government. [727]

Federal Dilution Act of 1995 A federal statute that protects famous marks from dilution. [118]

Federal Insurance Contributions Act (FICA) A federal act that says employees and employers must make contributions into the Social Security fund. [765]

Federal Patent Statute of 1952 Federal statute that establishes the requirements for obtaining a patent and protects patented inventions from infringement. [103]

federal question A case arising under the U.S. Constitution, treaties, or federal statutes and regulations. [50]

Federal Reserve System A system of 12 regional Federal Reserve banks that assist banks in the collection of checks. [446]

Federal Trade Commission (FTC) Federal administrative agency empowered to enforce the Federal Trade Commission Act and other federal consumer protection statutes. [732]

Federal Unemployment Tax Act (FUTA) A federal act that requires employers to pay unemployment taxes; unemployment compensation is paid to workers who are temporarily unemployed. [764]

federalism The U.S. form of government; the federal government and the 50 state governments share powers. [26]

fee simple absolute A type of ownership of real property that grants the owner the fullest bundle of legal rights that a person can hold in real property. [814]

fee simple defeasible A type of ownership of real property that grants the owner all the incidents of a fee simple absolute except that it may be taken away if a specified condition occurs or does not occur. [814]

felony The most serious type of crime; inherently evil crime. Most crimes against the person and some business-related crimes are felonies. [126]

fiduciary duty Duty of loyalty, honesty, integrity, trust, and confidence owed by directors and officers to their corporate employers. [600, 626]

final prospectus A final version of the prospectus that must be delivered by the issuer to the investor prior to or at the time of confirming a sale or sending a security to a purchaser. [680]

final settlement Occurs when the payor bank (1) pays the check in cash, (2) settles for the check without having a right to revoke the settlement, or (3) fails to dishonor the check within certain statutory time periods. [447]

finance lease A three-party transaction consisting of the lessor, the lessee, and the supplier. [289]

financing statement A document filed by a secured creditor with the appropriate government office that constructively notifies the world of his or her security interest in personal property. [467]

fixed amount of money A negotiable instrument must contain a promise or order to pay a fixed amount of money. [393]

fixtures Personal property that is permanently affixed to the real property, such as built-in cabinets in a house. [231]; Goods that are affixed to real estate so as to become a part thereof. [813]

floating lien A security interest in property that was not in the possession of the debtor when the security agreement was executed; includes *after-acquired property*, *future advances*, and *sale proceeds*. [465]

Food and Drug Administration (FDA) Federal administrative agency that administers and enforces the federal Food, Drug, and Cosmetic Act (FDCA) and other federal consumer protection laws. [728]

Food, Drug, and Cosmetic Act (FDCA) A federal statute enacted in 1938 that provides the basis for the regulation of much of the testing, manufacture, distribution, and sale of foods, drugs, cosmetics, and medicinal products. [728]

foreclosure Legal procedure by which a secured creditor causes the judicial sale of the secured real estate to pay a defaulted loan. [462]

Foreign Commerce Clause Clause of the U.S. Constitution that vests Congress with the power "to regulate commerce with foreign nations." [863]

foreign corporation A corporation in any state or jurisdiction other than the one in which it was formed. [566]

Foreign Sovereign Immunities Act Exclusively governs suits against foreign nations that are brought in federal or state courts in the United States; codifies the principle of qualified or restricted immunity. [876]

forged indorsement The forged signature of a payee or holder on a negotiable instrument. [403]

forged instrument A check with a forged drawer's signature on it. [444, 517]

forgery Fraudulently making or altering a written document that affects the legal liability of another person. [133]; A real defense against the enforcement of a negotiable instrument; the unauthorized signature of a maker, drawer, or indorser. [425]

formal contract A contract that requires a special form or method of creation. [178]

formal will A will that meets the requirements of the Statute of Wills. [845]

forum-selection clause Contract provision that designates a certain court to hear any dispute concerning nonperformance of the contract. [53]

forward vertical merger A vertical merger in which the supplier acquires the customer. [711]

four legals Four notices or actions that prevent the payment of a check if they are received by the payor bank before it has finished its process of posting the check for payment. [448]

Fourteenth Amendment Amendment that was added to the U.S. Constitution in 1868. It contains the Due Process, Equal Protection, and Privileges and Immunities clauses. [36]

franchise Established when one party licenses another party to use the franchisor's trade name, trademarks, commercial symbols, patents, copyrights, and other property in the distribution and selling of goods and services. [658]

franchise agreement An agreement that the franchisor and the franchisee enter into that sets forth the terms and conditions of the franchise. [661]

fraud by concealment Occurs when one party takes specific action to conceal a material fact from another party. [228]

fraud in the inception A real defense against the enforcement of a negotiable instrument; a person has been deceived into signing a negotiable instrument thinking that it is something else. [228, 425]

fraud in the inducement A personal defense against the enforcement of a negotiable instrument; a wrongdoer makes a false statement to another person to lead that person to enter into a contract with the wrongdoer. [426]; Occurs when the party knows what he or she is signing out has

been fraudulently induced to enter into the contract. [228]

fraudulent transfer Occurs when (1) a debtor transfers property to a third person within one year before the filing of a petition in bankruptcy and (2) the transfer was made by the debtor with an intent to hinder, delay, or defraud creditors. [490]

Free Exercise Clause A clause to the First Amendment that prohibits the government from interfering with the free exercise of religion in the United States. [35]

freedom of speech The right to engage in oral, written, and symbolic speech, protected by the First Amendment. [31]

freehold estate An estate where the owner has a present possessory interest in the real property. [814]

fresh start The goal of federal bankruptcy law: To discharge the debtor from burdensome debts and allow him or her to begin again. [485]

frolic and detour When an agent does something during the course of his employment to further his own interests rather than the principal's. [521]

FTC franchise rule A rule set out by the FTC that requires franchisors to make full presale disclosures to prospective franchisees. [660]

FTC notice A notice required to be placed on the cover of a franchisor's required disclosure statement to prospect franchisers. [660]

funding a living trust To fund a living trust, the grantor transfers title to his or her property to the trust. [854]

future goods Goods not yet in existence (ungrown crops, unborn stock animals). [303]

future interest The interest that the grantor retains for himself or herself or for a third party. [818]

gambling statutes Statutes that make certain forms of gambling illegal. [211]

gap-filling rule A rule that says an open term can be "read into" a contract. [291]

general duty A duty that an employer has to provide a work environment "free from recognized hazards that are causing or are likely to cause death or serious physical harm to his employees." [761]

general gift Gift that does not identify the specific property from which the gift is to be made. [848]

general government regulation Government regulation that applies to many businesses and industries collectively (e.g., antidiscrimination laws). [726]

general-jurisdiction trial court A court that hears cases of a general nature that are not within the jurisdiction of limited-jurisdiction trial courts. Testimony and evidence at trial are recorded and stored for future reference. [44]

generally known dangers A defense that acknowledges that certain products are inherently dangerous and are known to the general population to be so. [376]

general partners Partners in a limited partnership who invest capital, manage the business, and are personally liable for partnership debts. [549]

general partnership A voluntary association of two or more persons for the carrying on of a business as co-owners for profit. Also called a *partnership*. [541]

general principles of law The third source of international law, consisting of principles of law recognized by civilized nations. These are principles of law that are common to the national law of the parties to the dispute. [865]

general-purpose clause A clause often included in the articles of incorporation that authorizes the corporation to engage in any activity permitted corporations by law. [569]

generic name A term for a mark that has become a common term for a product line or type of service and therefore has lost its trademark protection. [116]

genuineness of assent The requirement that a party's assent to a contract be genuine. [225]

gift A voluntary transfer of title to property without payment of consideration by the donee. To be a valid gift, three elements must be shown: (1) *donative intent*, (2) *delivery*, and (3) *acceptance*. [797]; A transfer of property from one person to another without exchange of money. [820]

gift *causa mortis* A gift that is made in contemplation of death. [797]

gift *inter vivos* A gift made during a person's lifetime that is an irrevocable present transfer of ownership. [797]

gift promise An unenforceable promise because it lacks consideration. [195]

good faith Honesty in fact in the conduct or transaction concerned. The good faith test is subjective. [416]

good faith purchaser for value A person to whom good title can be transferred from a person with voidable title. The real owner cannot reclaim goods from a good faith purchaser for value. [310]

good faith subsequent lessee A person to whom a lease interest can be transferred from a person with voidable title. The real owner cannot reclaim the goods from the subsequent lessee until the lease expires. [310]

Good Samaritan law Statute that relieves medical professionals from liability for ordinary negligence when they stop and render aid to victims in emergency situations. [85]

goods Tangible things that are movable at the time of their identification to the contract. [286]

good title Title that is free from any encumbrances or other defects that are not disclosed but would affect the value of the property. [819]

government contractor defense A defense that says a contractor who was provided specifications by the government is not liable for any defect in the product that occurs as a result of those specifications. [376]

grace period A period of time after the actual expiration date of a payment but during which the insured can still pay an overdue premium without penalty. [963]

grantee The buyer or recipient to whom an interest in real property is transferred. [819]

grantor The seller or donor who transfers an ownership interest in real property. [819]; The person who creates a living trust. [853]

greenmail The purchase by a target corporation of its stock from an actual or perceived tender offeror at a premium. [626]

group boycott When two or more competitors at one level of distribution agree not to deal with others at another level of distribution. [704]

guaranteeing collection A form of accommodation where the accommodation party guarantees *collection* of a negotiable instrument; the accommodation party is *secondarily liable* on the instrument. [422]

guaranteeing payment A form of accommodation where the accommodation party guarantees *payment* of a negotiable instrument; the accommodation party is *primarily liable* on the instrument. [422]

guarantor The person who agrees to pay the debt if the primary debtor does not. [233]; The third person who agrees to be liable in a guaranty arrangement. [474]

guaranty arrangement An arrangement where a third party promises to be *secondarily liable* for the payment of another's debt. [474]

guaranty contract The contract between the guarantor and the original creditor. [233]

guest statute Statute that provides that if a driver of a vehicle voluntarily and without compensation gives a ride to another person, the driver is not liable to the passenger for injuries caused by the driver's ordinary negligence. [86]

hardship discharge A discharge granted if (1) the debtor fails to complete the payments due to unforeseeable circumstances, (2) the unsecured creditors have been paid as much as they would have been paid in a Chapter 7 liquidation proceeding, and (3) it is not practical to modify the plan. [501]

Hart-Scott-Rodino Antitrust Improvement Act Requires certain firms to notify the FTC and the Justice Department in advance of a proposed merger. Unless the government challenges the proposed merger within 30 days, the merger may proceed. [712]

hazardous waste Solid waste that may cause or significantly contribute to an increase in mortality or serious illness or pose a hazard to human health or the environment if improperly managed. [740]

heir A person who has the right to receive property under an intestacy statute. [851]

holder What the transferee becomes if a negotiable instrument has been transferred by negotiation. [397]; A person who is in possession of a negotiable instrument that is drawn, issued, or indorsed to him or his order, or to bearer, or in blank. [414]

holder in due course (HDC) A holder who takes a negotiable instrument for value, in good faith, and without notice that it is defective or is overdue. [414]

holographic will Will that is entirely handwritten and signed by the testator. [850]

honor Payment of a drawer's properly drawn check by the drawee bank. [442]

horizontal merger A merger between two or more companies that compete in the same business and geographical market. [711]

horizontal restraint of trade A restraint of trade that occurs when two or more competitors at the same *level of distribution* enter into a contract, combination, or conspiracy to restrain trade. [703]

hung jury A jury that cannot come to a unanimous decision about the defendant's guilt. The government may choose to retry the case. [130]

identification of goods Distinguishing the goods named in the contract from the seller's or lessor's other goods. [302]

illegal consideration A promise to refrain from doing an illegal act. Such a promise will not support a contract. [197]

illusory promise A contract into which parties enter, but one or both of the parties can choose not to perform their contractual obligations. Thus the contract lacks consideration. [197]

Immigration Reform and Control Act of 1986 (IRCA) A federal statute that makes it unlawful for employers to hire illegal immigrants. [764]

immoral contract A contract whose objective is the commission of an act that is considered immoral by society. [213]

immunity from prosecution The government agrees not to use any evidence given by a person granted immunity against that person. [141]

impairment of right of recourse Certain parties (holders, indorsers, accommodation parties) are discharged from liability on an instrument if the holder (1) releases an obligor from liability or (2) surrenders collateral without the consent of the parties who would benefit by it. [428]

implied agency An agency that occurs when a principal and an agent do not expressly create an agency, but it is inferred from the conduct of the parties. [511]

implied authorization Mode of acceptance that is implied from what is customary in similar transactions, usage of trade, or prior dealings between the parties. [193]

implied exemptions Exemptions from antitrust laws that are implied by the federal courts. [716]

implied powers Powers beyond express powers that allow a corporation to accomplish its corporate purpose. [576]

implied term A term in a contract that can reasonably be supplied by the courts. [186]

implied warranties The law *implies* certain warranties on transferors of negotiable instruments. There are two types of implied warranties: transfer and presentment. [423]

implied warranty of authority An agent who enters into a contract on behalf of another party impliedly warrants that he or she has the authority to do so. [518]

implied warranty of fitness for human consumption A warranty that applies to food or drink consumed on or off the premises of restaurants, grocery stores, fast-food outlets, and vending machines. [364]

implied warranty of habitability A warranty that provides that the leased premises must be fit, safe, and suitable for ordinary residential use. [827]

implied warranty of merchantability Unless properly disclosed, a warranty is implied when sold or leased goods are fit for the ordinary purpose for which they are sold or leased, and other assurances. [363]

implied-in-fact condition A condition that can be implied from the circumstances surrounding a contract and the parties' conduct. [255]

implied-in-fact contract A contract where agreement between parties has been inferred from their conduct. [176]

impossibility of performance Nonperformance that is excused if the contract becomes impossible to perform; must be objective impossibility, not subjective. [257]

imposter A person who impersonates a payee and induces a maker or drawer to issue an instrument in the payee's name and to give it to the imposter. [404]

imposter rule A rule that says if an imposter forges the indorsement of the named payee, the drawer or maker is liable on the instrument and bears the loss. [404]

imputed knowledge Information that is learned by the agent that is attributed to the principal. [515]

inaccessibility exception A rule that permits employees and union officials to engage in union solicitation on company property if the employees are beyond reach of reasonable union efforts to communicate with them. [754]

incidental beneficiary A party who is unintentionally benefited by other people's contracts. [253]

incidental damages When goods are resold or released, incidental damages are

reasonable expenses incurred in stopping delivery, transportation charges, storage charges, sales commissions, and so on. [325]

income beneficiary The person who is entitled to receive income from the living trust. The grantor is usually the income beneficiary. [855]

incontestability clauses A clause that prevents insurers from contesting statements made by insureds in applications for insurance after the passage of a stipulated number of years. [843]

incorporation by reference When integration is made by express reference in one document that refers to and incorporates another document within it. [236]

incorporator The person or persons, partnerships, or corporations that are responsible for incorporation of a corporation. [565]

indenture agreement A contract between the corporation and the holder that contains the terms of a debt security. [575]

independent contractor A person or business who is not an employee who is employed by a principal to perform a certain task on his behalf. [584]; "A person who contracts with another to do something for him who is not controlled by the other nor subject to the other's right to control with respect to his physical conduct in the performance of the undertaking" [Restatement (Second) of Agency]. [527]

indictment The charge of having committed a crime (usually a felony), based on the judgment of a grand jury. [129]

indirect price discrimination A form of price discrimination (e.g., favorable credit terms) that is less readily apparent than direct forms of price discrimination. [714]

indorsee The person to whom a negotiable instrument is indorsed. [398]; A person who is in possession of a negotiable instrument that is drawn, issued, or indorsed to him or his order, or to bearer, or in blank. [438]

indorsement The signature (and other directions) written by or on behalf of the holder somewhere on the instrument. [398]

indorsement for deposit or collection An indorsement that makes the indorsee the indorser's collecting agent (e.g., "for deposit only"). [401]

indorsement of a check Occurs when a payee indorses a check to another party by signing the back of the check. [438]

indorser The person who indorses a negotiable instrument. [398]; The payee who indorses a check to another party. [438]

indorsers' liability *Unqualified indorsers* are secondarily liable on negotiable instruments they indorse; *qualified indorsers* disclaim liability and are not secondarily liable on instruments they indorse. [420]

infancy doctrine A doctrine that allows minors to disaffirm (cancel) most contracts they have entered into with adults. [206]

inferior performance Occurs when a party fails to perform express or implied contractual obligations that impair or destroy the essence of the contract. [268]

informal contract A contract that is not formal. Valid informal contracts are fully enforceable and may be sued upon if breached. [178]

information The charge of having committed a crime (usually a misdemeanor), based on the judgment of a judge (magistrate). [129]

injunction A court order that prohibits a person from doing a certain act. [276]

injury The plaintiff must suffer personal injury or damage to his or her property to recover monetary damages for the defendant's negligence. [81]

innkeepers' statutes State statutes that limit an innkeeper's common law liability. An innkeeper can avoid liability for loss caused to a guest's property if (1) a safe is provided in which the guest's valuable property may be kept and (2) the guest is notified of this fact. [806]

innocent misrepresentation Occurs when a person makes a statement of fact that he or she honestly and reasonably believes to be true, even though it is not. [229]; Occurs when an agent makes an untrue statement that he or she honestly and reasonably believes to be true. [520]

in pari delicto When both parties are equally at fault in an illegal contract. [217]

in personam jurisdiction Jurisdiction over the parties to a lawsuit. [52]

in rem jurisdiction Jurisdiction to hear a case because of jurisdiction over the property of the lawsuit. [52]

insane, but not adjudged insane A person who is insane but has not been adjudged insane by a court or administrative agency. A contract entered into by such person is generally voidable. Some states hold that such a contract is void. [210]

Insecticide, Fungicide, and Rodenticide Act A federal statute that requires pesticides, herbicides, fungicides, and rodenticides to be registered with the EPA; the EPA may deny, suspend, or cancel registration. [739]

INS Form I-9 A form that must be filled out by all U.S. employers for each employee; states that the employer has inspected the employee's legal qualifications to work. [764]

inside director A member of the board of directors who is also an officer of the corporation. [595]

insider trading When an insider makes a profit by personally purchasing shares of the corporation prior to public release of favorable information or by selling shares of the corporation prior to the public disclosure of unfavorable information. [686]

Insider Trading Sanctions Act of 1984 A federal statute that permits the SEC to obtain a civil penalty of up to three times the illegal benefits received from insider trading. [690]

installment contract A contract that requires or authorizes the goods to be delivered and accepted in separate lots. [321]

instrument Term that means *negotiable instrument*. [387]

insurable interest A person who purchases insurance must have a personal interest in the insured item or person. [838]

insurance A means for persons and businesses to protect themselves against the risk of loss. [838]

insured The party who pays a premium to a particular insurance company for insurance coverage. [838]

insurer The insurance company. [838]

intangible property Rights that cannot be reduced to physical form such as stock certificates, certificates of deposit, bonds, and copyrights. [795]

integration The combination of several writings to form a single contract. [236]

intellectual property rights Intellectual property rights, such as patents, copyrights, trademarks, trade secrets, trade names, and domain names are very valuable business assets. Federal and state laws protect intellectual property rights from misappropriation and infringement. [102]

intended beneficiary A third party who is not in privity of contract but who has rights under the contract and can enforce the contract against the obligor. [251]

intentional infliction of emotional distress A tort that says a person whose extreme and outrageous conduct intentionally or recklessly causes severe emotional distress to another person is liable for that emotional distress. Also known as the *tort of outrage*. [76]

intentional interference with contractual relations A tort that arises when a third party induces a contracting party to breach the contract with another party. [277]

intentional misrepresentation Intentionally defrauding another person out of money, property, or something else of value. [92]; Occurs when one person consciously induces another person to rely and act on a misrepresentation. Also called *fraud*. [227]; When a seller or lessor fraudulently misrepresents the quality of a product and a buyer is injured thereby. [368]; Occurs when an agent makes an untrue statement that he or she knows is not true. [520]

intentional tort A category of torts that requires that the defendant possessed the intent to do the act that caused the plaintiff's injuries. [73]; Occurs when a person has intentionally committed a wrong against (1) another person or his or her character, or (2) another person's property. [522]

intermediary bank A bank in the collection process that is not the depository or payor bank. [446]

intermediate appellate court An intermediate court that hears appeals from trial courts. [44]

intermediate scrutiny test Test that is applied to classifications based on protected classes other than race (e.g., sex, age). [36]

International Court of Justice The judicial branch of the United Nations that is located in The Hague, the Netherlands. Also called the *World Court*. [866]

international law Law that governs affairs between nations and that regulates transactions between individuals and businesses of different countries. [863]

Internet A collection of millions of computers that provide a network of electronic connections between computers [341]

interrogatories Written questions submitted by one party to another party. The questions must be answered in writing within a stipulated time. [57]

interstate commerce Commerce that moves between states or that affects commerce between states. [28]

intervention The act of others to join as parties to an existing lawsuit. [56]

intestancy statute A state statute that stipulates how the property of a person who dies without a will is to be distributed to his or her heirs. [851]

intoxicated person A person who is under contractual incapacity because of ingestion of alcohol or drugs to the point of incompetence. [210]

in transit A state in which goods are in the possession of a bailee or carrier and not in the hands of the buyer, seller, lessee, or lessor. [324]

intrastate offering exemption An exemption from registration that permits local businesses to raise capital from local investors to be used in the local economy without the need to register with the SEC. [682]

invasion of the right to privacy A tort that constitutes the violation of a person's right to live his or her life without being subjected to unwarranted and undesired publicity. [75]

investment banker Independent securities companies that assist issuers in selling securities to the public. [678]

involuntary petition A petition filed by creditors of the debtor; alleges that the debtor is not paying his or her debts as they become due. [486]

issued shares Shares that have been sold by the corporation. [574]

issuer The business or party that sells securities to the public. [677]

joint and several liability Partners are *joint* and *severally liable* for tort liability of the partnership. This means that the plaintiff can sue one or more of the partners separately. If successful, the plaintiff can recover the entire amount of the judgment from any or all of the defendant-partners. [544]

joint liability Partners are *jointly liable* for contracts and debts of the partnership. This means that a plaintiff must name the partnership and all of the partners as defendants. If successful, the plaintiff can recover the entire amount of the judgment from any or all of the partners. [545]

joint tenancy A form of co-ownership that includes the right of survivorship. [815]

joint tenant Co-owner in a joint tenancy. [815]

joint venture A voluntary association of two or more parties (natural persons, partnerships, corporations, or other legal entities) to conduct a single or isolated project with a limited duration. [658, 668]

joint will A will that is executed by two or more testators. [850]

judicial branch The part of the government that consists of the Supreme Court and other federal courts. [26]

judicial decision A decision about an individual lawsuit issued by federal and state courts. [11]

judicial decisions and teachings The fourth source of international law, consisting of judicial decisions and writings of the most qualified legal scholars of the various nations involved in the dispute. [865]

judicial dissolution Occurs when a corporation is dissolved by a court proceeding instituted by the state. [577]

jurisdiction The authority of a court to hear a case. [52]

jurisprudence The philosophy or science of law. [5]

Just Compensation Clause A clause of the U.S. Constitution that mandates that the government compensate the property owner and possibly others such as lessees just compensation when the government exercises its power of eminent domains and takes property for government purposes. [830]

Kantian or duty ethics A moral theory that says that people owe moral duties that are based on universal rules, such as the categorical imperative "do unto others as you would have them do unto you." [154]

land The most common form of real property. Includes the land and buildings and other structures permanently attached to the land. [813]

land pollution Pollution of the land that is generally caused by hazardous waste being disposed of in an improper manner. [740]

land use regulation The collective term for the laws that regulate the possession, ownership, and use of real property. [828]

landlord The owner who transfers the leasehold. [824]

landlord–tenant relationship A relationship created when the owner of a freehold estate (landlord) transfers a right to exclu-

sively and temporarily possess the owner's property to another (tenant). [824]

Lanham Trademark Act (as amended) Federal statute that (1) establishes the requirements for obtaining a federal mark and (2) protects marks from infringement. [112]

lapse of time An offer terminates when a stated time period expires. If no time is stated, an offer terminates after a reasonable time. [191]

larceny Taking another's personal property other than from his or her person or building. [131]

law That which must be obeyed and followed by citizens subject to sanctions or legal consequences; a body of rules of action or conduct prescribed by controlling authority, and having binding legal force. [3]

law court A court that developed and administered a uniform set of laws decreed by the kings and queens after William the Conqueror; legal procedure was emphasized over merits at that time. [8]

lease A transfer of the right to the possession and use of the named goods for a set term in return for certain consideration. [289]; A transfer of the right to the possession and use of the real property for a set term in return for certain consideration; the rental agreement between a landlord and a tenant. [824]

leasehold A tenant's interest in the property. [824]

legal entity An LLC is a separate legal entity—an artificial person—that can own property, sue and be sued, enter into and enforce contracts, and such. [638]

legal insanity A state of contractual incapacity as determined by law. [210]

legally enforceable contract If one party fails to perform as promised, the other party can use the court system to enforce the contract and recover damages or other remedy. [171]

legislative branch The part of the U.S. government that consists of Congress (the Senate and the House of Representatives). [26]

lessee The person who acquires the right to possession and use of goods under a lease. [289]

lessor The person who transfers the right of possession and use of goods under the lease. [289]

libel A false statement that appears in a letter, newspaper, magazine, book, photograph, movie, video, and so on. [76]

license A contract that transfers limited rights in intellectual property and informational rights. [349]; Grants a person the right to enter upon another's property for a specified and usually short period of time. [823]

licensee The party who is granted limited rights in or access to intellectual property or informational rights owned by the licensor. [349]

licensing An arrangement where a party that owns trademarks and other intellectual property (the *licensor*) contracts to permit another party (the *licensee*) to use these trademarks and intellectual property in the distribution of goods, services, software, and digital information. [668]

licensing agreement Detailed and comprehensive written agreement between the licensor and licensee that sets forth the express terms of their agreement. [350]

licensing statute Statute that requires a person or business to obtain a license from the government prior to engaging in a specified occupation or activity. [212]

licensor The owner of intellectual property or informational rights who transfers rights in the property or information to the licensee. [349]

licensor's damages If a licensee breaches a contract, the licensor may sue and recover monetary damages from the licensee caused by the breach. [353]

life estate An interest in the land for a person's lifetime; upon that person's death, the interest will be transferred to another party. [815]

limited duty of care A member or manager of an LLC is not liable to the LLC for injuries caused to the LLC by his or her ordinary negligence. The ordinarily negligent member or manager, and the LLC on whose behalf the member or manager was acting when the negligent act occurred, are liable to the injured third party. [650]

limited-jurisdiction trial court A court that hears matters of a specialized or limited nature. [44]

limited liability Members are liable for the LLC's debts, obligations, and liabilities only to the extent of their capital contributions. [639]; Liability that shareholders have only to the extent of their capital contribution. Shareholders are generally not personally liable for debts and obligations of the corporation. [561]

limited liability company (LLC) A hybrid form of business that has the attributes of both partnerships and corporations. [29, 638]

limited liability partnership (LLP) A special form of partnership where all partners are limited partners and there are no general partners. [552]

limited partners Partners in a limited partnership who invest capital but do not participate in management and are not personally liable for partnership debts beyond their capital contribution. [549]

limited partnership A special form of partnership that is formed only if certain formalities are followed. It has both general and limited partners. [548]

limited partnership agreement A document that sets forth the rights and duties of the general and limited parties, the terms and conditions regarding the operation, termination, and dissolution of the partnership, and so on. [550]

line of commerce Includes products or services that consumers use as substitutes. If an increase in the price of one product or service leads consumers to purchase another product or service, the two products are substitutes for each other. [710]

lineal descendants Children, grandchildren, great grandchildren, and so on of the testator. [849]

liquidated damages Damages that are specified in the contract rather than determined by the court. [273, 355]; Damages that will be paid upon a breach of contract and that are established in advance. [332]

liquidation preference The right to be paid a stated dollar amount if the corporation is dissolved and liquidated. [573]

litigation The process of bringing, maintaining, and defending a lawsuit. [54]

living trust A legal entity used for estate planning. [853]

living will A document signed by a person that stipulates his or her wishes to not have his or her life prolonged indefinitely by artificial means. [852]

long-arm statute A statute that extends a state's jurisdiction to nonresidents who were not served a summons within the state. [52]

lost property When a property owner leaves property somewhere because of negligence, carelessness, or inadvertence. [800]

Magnuson–Moss Warranty Act A federal statute that regulates express full and limited warranties made by sellers and lessors. [367]

mail fraud The use of mail to defraud another person. [135]

mailbox rule An acceptance is effective when it is dispatched. [192]

main purpose or leading object exception If the main purpose of a transaction and an oral collateral contract is to provide pecuniary benefit to the guarantor, the collateral contract does not have to be in writing to be enforced. [234]

maker of a CD The bank (borrower). [390]

maker of a note The party who makes the promise to pay (borrower). [389]

manager-managed LLC An LLC that has designated in its articles of organization that it is a manager-managed LLC. [647]

Marine Protection, Research, and Sanctuaries Act A federal statute enacted in 1972 that extends environmental protection to the oceans. [739]

mark The collective name for trademarks, service marks, certification marks, and collective marks that all can be trademarked. [113]

market extension merger A merger between two companies in similar fields whose sales do not overlap. [711]

material alteration A partial defense against enforcement of a negotiable instrument by an HDC. An HDC can enforce an altered instrument in the original amount for which the drawer wrote the check. [425]

material breach A breach that occurs when a party renders inferior performance of his or her contractual duties. [268]

maximizing profits A theory of social responsibility that says a corporation owes a duty to take actions that maximize profits for shareholders. [160]

McCarran-Ferguson Act A federal statute that gave the regulation of insurance to the states. [838]

mediation A form of ADR in which the parties choose a neutral third party to act as the mediator of the dispute. [64]

Medicinal Device Amendment to the FDCA An amendment enacted in 1976 that gives the FDA authority to regulate medicinal devices and equipment. [731]

meeting of the creditors A meeting of the creditors in a bankruptcy case that must occur not less than 10 days nor more than 30 days after the court grants an order for relief. [486]

meeting the competition defense A defense provided in Section 2(b) that says a seller may lawfully engage in price discrimination to meet a competitor's price. [714]

member An owner of an LLC. [639]

member-managed LLC An LLC that has not designated that it is a manager-managed LLC in its articles of organization. [647]

mens rea "Evil intent"—the possession of the requisite state of mind to commit a prohibited act. [126]

merchant A person who (1) deals in the goods of the kind involved in the transaction or (2) by his or her occupation holds himself or herself out as having knowledge or skill peculiar to the goods involved in the transaction. [288]

Merchant Court The separate set of courts established to administer the "law of merchants." [8]

merger Occurs when one corporation is absorbed into another corporation and ceases to exist. [621]

merger clause A clause in a contract that stipulates that it is a complete integration and the exclusive expression of the parties' agreement. [238]

midnight deadline The midnight of the next banking day following the banking day on which the bank received the on them check for collection. [448]

minor A person who has not reached the age of majority. [206]

minor breach A breach that occurs when a party renders substantial performance of his or her contractual duties. [267]

minor's duty of restoration As a general rule, a minor is obligated only to return the goods or property he or she has received from the adult in the condition it is in at the time of disaffirmance. [207]

Miranda rights A warning that must be read to a criminal suspect before he or she is interrogated by the police or other government officials. [140]

mirror image rule States that for an acceptance to exist, the offeree must accept the terms as stated in the offer. [192]

misdemeanor A less serious crime; not inherently evil but prohibited by society.

Many crimes against property are misdemeanors. [126]

mislaid property When an owner voluntarily places property somewhere and then inadvertently forgets it. [800]

misuse A defense that relieves a seller of product liability if the user abnormally misused the product. Products must be designed to protect against foreseeable misuse. [377]

mitigation A nonbreaching party is under a legal duty to avoid or reduce damages caused by a breach of contract. [271]

mixed sale A sale that involves the provision of a service and a good in the same transaction. [287]

mobile sources Sources of air pollution such as automobiles, trucks, buses, motorcycles, and airplanes. [735]

Model Business Corporation Act (MBCA) A model act drafted in 1950 that was intended to provide a uniform law for regulation of corporations. [562]

monetary damages An award of money. [270]

money A "medium of exchange authorized or adopted by a domestic or foreign government." [UCC 1-201(24)] [393]

Money Laundering Control Act A federal statute that makes it a crime to: 1. Knowingly engage in a money transaction through a financial institution involving property worth more than $10,000. 2. Knowingly engage in a financial transaction involving the proceeds of an illegal activity. [135]

monopoly power The power to control prices or exclude competition measured by the market share the defendant possesses in the relevant market. [708]

moral minimum A theory of social responsibility that says a corporation's duty is to make a profit while avoiding harm to others. [162]

mortgage An interest in real property given to a lender as security for the repayment of a loan. [232]; A collateral arrangement where a real property owner borrows money from a creditor who uses a deed as collateral for repayment of the loan. [460]

mortgagee The creditor in a mortgage transaction. [460]

mortgagor The owner-debtor in a mortgage transaction. [460]

motion for judgment on the pleadings Motion that alleges that if all the facts pre-

sented in the pleadings are taken as true, the party making the motion would win the lawsuit when the proper law is applied to these asserted facts. [58]

motion for summary judgment Motion that asserts that there are no factual disputes to be decided by the jury; if so, the judge can apply the proper law to the undisputed facts and decide the case without a jury. These motions are supported by affidavits, documents, and deposition testimony. [58]

motivation test A test to determine the liability of the principal; if the agent's motivation in committing the intentional tort is to promote the principal's business, then the principal is liable for any injury caused by the tort. [522]

mutual benefit bailment A bailment for the mutual benefit of the bailor and bailee. The bailee owes a *duty of ordinary care* to protect the bailed property. [804]

mutual mistake of fact A mistake made by both parties concerning a material fact that is important to the subject matter of the contract. [226]

mutual mistake of value A mistake that occurs if both parties know the object of the contract but are mistaken as to its value. [226]

mutual wills Occurs where two or more testators execute separate wills that leave their property to each other on the condition that the survivor leave the remaining property on his or her death as agreed by the testators. [850]

national ambient air quality standards (NAAQS) Standards for certain pollutants set by the EPA that protect (1) human beings (primary) and (2) vegetation, matter, climate, visibility, and economic values (secondary). [735]

national courts The courts of individual nations. [875]

National Environmental Policy Act (NEPA) A federal statute enacted in 1969 that mandates that the federal government consider the adverse impact a federal government action would have on the environment before the action is implemented. [734]

National Labor Relations Board (NLRB) A federal administrative agency that oversees union elections, prevents employers and unions from engaging in illegal and unfair labor practices, and enforces and interprets certain federal labor laws. [753]

necessaries of life A minor must pay the reasonable value of food, clothing, shelter, medical care, and other items considered necessary to the maintenance of life. [209]

negligence A tort related to defective products where the defendant has breached a duty of due care and caused harm to the plaintiff. [369]; Failure of a corporate director or officer to exercise the duty of care while conducting the corporation's business. [600]

negligence per se Tort where the violation of a statute or ordinance constitutes the breach of the duty of care. [85]

negligent infliction of emotional distress A tort that permits a person to recover for emotional distress caused by the defendant's negligent conduct. [84]

negotiable instrument A special form of contract that satisfies the requirements established by Article 3 of the UCC. Also called commercial paper. [386]; Commercial paper that must meet these requirements: (1) be in writing, (2) be signed by the maker or drawer, (3) be an unconditional promise or order to pay, (4) state a fixed amount of money, (5) not require any undertaking in addition to the payment of money, (6) be payable on demand or at a definite time, and (7) be payable to order or to bearer. [391]

negotiation Transfer of a negotiable instrument by a person other than the issuer to a person who thereby becomes a *holder*. [397]

no evidence of forgery, alteration, or irregularity requirement A holder cannot become an HDC to an instrument that is apparently forged or altered or is so otherwise irregular or incomplete as to call into question its authenticity. [417]

no fault automobile insurance An automobile insurance system where the driver's insurance company pays for any injuries or death the driver and other covered persons suffers in an accident, no matter who caused the accident. [839]

nominal damages Damages awarded when the nonbreaching party sues the breaching party even though no financial loss has resulted from the breach; usually consists of $1 or some other small amount. [274]

nonattainment areas Regions that do not meet air quality standards. [736]

nonconforming uses Uses and buildings that already exist in the zoned area that are permitted to continue even though they do not fit within new zoning ordinances. [829]

nonnegotiable contract Fails to meet the requirements of a negotiable instrument and, therefore, is not subject to the provisions of UCC Article 3. [397]

nonpossessory interest When a person holds an interest in another person's property without actually owning any part of the property. [822]

nonprice vertical restraints Restraints of trade that are unlawful under Section 1 of the Sherman Act if their anticompetitive effects outweigh their procompetitive effects. [706]

nonprofit corporation A corporation that is formed to operate charitable institutions, colleges, universities, and other not-for-profit entities. [563]

nonrestrictive indorsement An indorsement that has no instructions or conditions attached to the payment of the funds. [401]

North American Free Trade Agreement (NAFTA) An international treaty that creates a regional free-trade zone consisting of the United States, Canada, and Mexico. [869]

note An instrument that evidences the borrower's debt to the lender [461]; debt security with a maturity of five years or less. [575]

note and deed of trust An alternative to a mortgage in some states. [532]

notice of dishonor The formal act of letting the party with secondary liability to pay a negotiable instrument know that the instrument has been dishonored. [421]

novation An agreement that substitutes a new party for one of the original contracting parties and relieves the exiting party of liability on the contract. [257]

Nuclear Regulatory Commission (NRC) Federal agency that licenses the construction and opening of commercial nuclear power plants. [741]

Nuclear Waste Policy Act of 1982 A federal statute that says the federal government must select and develop a permanent site for the disposal of nuclear waste. [741]

nuncupative will Oral will that is made before a witness during the testator's last illness. Also called a dying declaration or deathbed will. [850]

Nutrition Labeling and Education Act A federal statute that requires food manufacturers and processors to provide nutritional information on most foods and prohibits them from making scientifically unsubstantiated health claims. [729]

objective theory of contracts A theory that says that the intent to contract is judged by the reasonable person standard and not by the subjective intent of the parties. [174]

obligation An action a party to a sales or lease contract is required by law to carry out. [318]

obscene speech Speech that (1) appeals to the prurient interest, (2) depicts sexual conduct in a patently offensive way, and (3) lacks serious literary, artistic, political, or scientific value. [33]

Occupational Safety and Health Administration (OSHA) A federal administrative agency that is empowered to enforce the Occupational Safety and Health Act. [761]

Occupational Safety and Health Act A federal act enacted in 1970 that promotes safety in the workplace. [761]

offensive speech Speech that is offensive to many members of society. It is subject to time, place, and manner restrictions. [31]

offer The manifestation of willingness to enter into a bargain, so made as to justify another person in understanding that his assent to that bargain is invited and will conclude it. (Section 24 of Restatement (Second) of Contracts) [185]

offeree The party to whom an offer to enter into a contract is made. [172, 185]

offeror The party who makes an offer to enter into a contract. [172, 185]

officers Employees of the corporation who are appointed by the board of directors to manage the day-to-day operations of the corporation. [598]

Older Workers Benefit Protection Act A federal act that prohibits age discrimination in employee benefits. [784]

"on them" item A check presented for payment by the payee or holder where the depository bank and the payor bank are not the same bank. [448]

"on us" item A check that is presented for payment where the depository bank is also the payor bank. That is, the drawer and payee or holder have accounts at the same bank. [447]

one-year "on sale" doctrine A doctrine that says a patent may not be granted if the invention was used by the public for more than one year prior to the filing of the patent application. [106]

one-year rule An executory contract that cannot be performed by its own terms within one year of its formation must be in writing. [233]

operating agreement An agreement entered into among members that governs the affairs and business of the LLC and the relations among members, managers, and the LLC. [644]

order Decision issued by an administrative law judge. [727]

order for relief The filing of either a voluntary petition, an unchallenged involuntary petition, or a grant of an order after a trial of a challenged involuntary petition. [486]

order paper Order paper is negotiated by (1) *delivery* and (2) *indorsement*. [397]

order to pay A drawer's unconditional order to a drawee to pay a payee. [392]

ordinances Laws enacted by local government bodies such as cities and municipalities, counties, school districts, and water districts. [9]

ordinary bailments (1) Bailments for the sole benefit of the bailor, (2) bailments for the sole benefit of the bailee, and (3) bailments for the mutual benefit of the bailor and bailee. [804]

organizational meeting A meeting that must be held by the initial directors of the corporation after the articles of incorporation are filed. [570]

original tenor The original amount for which the drawer wrote the check. [445]

outside director A member of the board of directors who is not an officer of the corporation. [595]

outstanding shares Shares of stock that are in shareholder hands. [574]

overdraft The amount of money a drawer owes a bank after it has paid a check despite insufficient funds in the drawer's account. [444]

pac-man tender offer Occurs when a corporation that is the target of a tender offer makes a *reverse tender offer* for the stock of the tender offeror. [626]

palming off Unfair competition that occurs when a company tries to pass one of its products as that of a rival. [92]

panel A panel of three WTO judges that hears trade disputes between member nations and issues a "panel report." [874]

parol evidence Any oral or written words outside the four corners of the written contract. [238]

parol evidence rule A rule that says if a written contract is a complete and final statement of the parties' agreement, any prior or contemporaneous oral or written statements that alter, contradict, or are in addition to the terms of the written contract are inadmissible in court regarding a dispute over the contract. [238, 295]

participating preferred stock Stock that allows the stockholder to participate in the profits of the corporation along with the common stockholders. [573]

partnership at will A partnership with no fixed duration. [547]

partnership for a term A partnership with a fixed duration. [547]

part performance A doctrine that allows the court to order an oral contract for the sale of land or transfer of another interest in real property to be specifically performed if it has been partially performed and performance is necessary to avoid injustice. [232]

past consideration A prior act or performance. Past consideration (e.g., prior acts) will not support a new contract. New consideration must be given. [198]

patent infringement Unauthorized use of another's patent. A patent holder may recover damages and other remedies against a patent infringer. [105]

Patent and Trademark Office (PTO) A federal administrative agency that reviews patent applications and grants patents. [103]

payable on demand or at a definite time requirement A negotiable instrument must be payable either *on demand or at a definite time*. [394]

payee of a CD The depositor (lender). [390]

payee of a check The party to whom the check is written. [388, 438]

payee of a draft The party who receives the money from a draft. [387]

payee of a note The party to whom the promise to pay is made (lender). [387]

payor bank The bank where the drawer has a checking account and on which the check is drawn. [446]

penal codes A collection of criminal statutes. [125]

per capita A distribution of the estate that makes each grandchild and great grandchild of the deceased inherit equally with the children of the deceased. [849]

perfect tender rule A rule that says if the goods or tender of a delivery fails in any respect to conform to the contract, the buyer may opt either (1) to reject the whole shipment, (2) to accept the whole shipment, or (3) to reject part and accept part of the shipment. [319]

perfection by possession of the collateral If a secured creditor has physical possession of the collateral, no financing statement has to be filed; the creditor's possession is sufficient to put other potential creditors on notice of his or her secured interest in the property. [468]

perfection of a security interest Establishes the right of a secured creditor against other creditors who claim an interest in the collateral. [466]

periodic tenancy A tenancy created when a lease specifies intervals at which payments are due but does not specify how long the lease is for. [824]

permanency requirement A requirement of negotiable instruments that says they must be in a permanent state, such as written on ordinary paper. [391]

permanent trustee A legal representative of the bankruptcy debtor's estate, usually an accountant or lawyer; elected at the first meeting of the creditors. [486]

per se rule A rule that is applicable to those restraints of trade considered inherently anticompetitive. Once this determination is made, the court will not permit any defenses or justifications to save it. [703]

personal defense A defense that can be raised against enforcement of a negotiable instrument by an ordinary holder but not against an HDC. [426]

personal property Property that consists of tangible property such as automobiles, furniture, and jewelry; intangible property such as securities, patents, and copyrights; and instruments, chattel paper, documents of title, and accounts. [465]; Property that consists of tangible property such as automobiles, furniture, and jewelry, and intangible property such as securities, patents, and copyrights. [795]

personal satisfaction test Subjective test that applies to contracts involving personal taste and comfort. [254]

per stirpes   A distribution of the estate that makes grandchildren and great grandchildren of the deceased inherit by representation of their parent. [849]

petition   A document filed with the bankruptcy court that sets the bankruptcy proceedings into motion. [486]

petition for certiorari   A petition asking the Supreme Court to hear one's case. [48]

physical or mental examination   A court may order another party to submit to a physical or mental examination prior to trial. [57]

picketing   The action of strikers walking in front of the employer's premises carrying signs announcing their strike. [757]

piercing the corporate veil   A doctrine that says if a shareholder dominates a corporation and uses it for improper purposes, a court of equity can disregard the corporate entity and hold the shareholder personally liable for the corporation's debts and obligations. [593]

plaintiff   The party who files the complaint. [54]

plan of reorganization   A plan that sets forth a proposed new capital structure for the debtor to have when it emerges from reorganization bankruptcy. The debtor has the exclusive right to file the first plan of reorganization; any party of interest may file a plan thereafter. [496]

plant life and vegetation   Real property that is growing in or on the surface of the land. [813]

pleadings   The paperwork that is filed with the court to initiate and respond to a lawsuit. [54]

plea bargain   When the accused admits to a lesser crime than charged. In return, the government agrees to impose a lesser sentence than might have been obtained had the case gone to trial. [130]

point sources   Sources of water pollution such as paper mills, manufacturing plants, electric utility plants, and sewage plants. [738]

police power   The power of states to regulate private and business activity within their borders. [29]

policy   The insurance contract. [838]

portability requirement   A requirement of negotiable instruments that says they must be able to be easily transported between areas. [391]

possession   A lease grants the tenant *exclusive possession* of the leased premises for the term of the lease or until the tenant defaults on the obligations under the lease. [825]

Postal Reorganization Act   An act that makes the mailing of unsolicited merchandise an unfair trade practice. [733]

posteffective period   The period of time that begins when the registration statement becomes effective and runs until the issuer either sells all of the offered securities or withdraws them from sale. [680]

pour-over will   A will that is necessary to distribute any of the grantor's property not in the living trust at the time of the grantor's death. [855]

power of attorney   An express agency agreement that is often used to give an agent the power to sign legal documents on behalf of the principal. [511]

precedent   A rule of law established in a court decision. Lower courts must follow the precedent established by higher courts. [11]

preemption doctrine   The concept that federal law takes precedence over state or local law. [27]

preemptive rights   Rights that give existing shareholders the option of subscribing to new shares being issued in proportion to their current ownership interest. [591]

preexisting duty   A promise lacks consideration if a person promises to perform an act or do something he or she is already under an obligation to do. [197]

preferential lien   Occurs when (1) a debtor gives an unsecured creditor a secured interest in property within 90 days before the filing of a petition in bankruptcy, (2) the transfer is made for a preexisting debt, and (3) the creditor would receive more because of this lien than it would as an unsecured creditor. [490]

preferential transfer   Occurs when (1) a debtor transfers property to a creditor within 90 days before the filing of a petition in bankruptcy, (2) the transfer is made for a preexisting debt, and (3) the creditor would receive more from the transfer than it would from Chapter 7 liquidation. [489]

preferential transfer to an insider   A transfer of property by an insolvent debtor to an "insider" within one year before the filing of a petition in bankruptcy. [490]

preferred stock   A type of equity security that is given certain preferences and rights over common stock. [573]

preferred stock certificate   A document that represents a shareholder's investment in preferred stock in the corporation. [573]

preferred stockholder   A person who owns preferred stock. [573]

prefiling period   A period of time that begins when the issuer first contemplates issuing the securities and ends when the registration statement is filed. The issuer may not condition the market during this period. [680]

Pregnancy Discrimination Act   Amendment to Title VII that forbids employment discrimination because of "pregnancy, childbirth, or related medical conditions." [777]

premium   The money paid to the insurance company for insurance coverage. [838]

prenuptial agreement   A contract entered into by parties prior to marriage that defines their ownership rights in each other's property; must be in writing. [235]

presentment   A demand for acceptance or payment of an instrument made upon the maker, acceptor, drawee, or other payor by or on behalf of the holder. [421]

presentment across the counter   When a depository physically presents the check for payment at the payor bank instead of depositing an on them check for collection. [448]

presentment warranties   Any person who presents a draft or check for payment or acceptance makes the following three warranties to a drawee or acceptor who pays or accepts the instrument in good faith: (1) The presenter has good title to the instrument or is authorized to obtain payment or acceptance of the person who has good title, (2) the instrument has not been materially altered, and (3) the presenter has no knowledge that the signature of the maker or drawer is unauthorized. [424]

presentment warranty   Each prior transferor warrants that the check has not been altered. [445]

pretrial hearing   A hearing before the trial in order to facilitate the settlement of a case. Also called a settlement conference. [58]

pretrial motion   A motion a party can make to try to dispose of all or part of a lawsuit prior to trial. [58]

price-fixing   Occurs where competitors in the same line of business agree to set the price of the goods or services they sell: raising, depressing, fixing, pegging, or stabilizing the price of a commodity or service. [703]

primary liability Absolute liability to pay a negotiable instrument, subject to certain real defenses. [419]

principal A person who authorizes an agent to sign a negotiable instrument on his or her behalf. [418]; The party who employs another person to act on his or her behalf. [509]

principal–agent relationship An employer hires an employee and gives that employee authority to act and enter into contracts on his or her behalf. [510]

priority The order in which conflicting claims of creditors in the same collateral are solved. [469]

private corporation A corporation formed to conduct privately owned business. [563]

private placement exemption An exemption from registration that permits issuers to raise capital from an unlimited number of accredited investors and no more than 35 nonaccredited investors without having to register the offering with the SEC. [682]

Privileges and Immunities Clause A clause that prohibits states from enacting laws that unduly discriminate in favor of their residents. [38]

privity of contract The state of two specified parties being in contract. [246]

probability of a substantial lessening of competition If there is a probability that a merger will substantially lessen competition or create a monopoly, the court may prevent the merger under Section 7 of the Clayton Act. [710]

procedural due process Requires that the government must give a person proper notice and hearing of the legal action before that person is deprived of his or her life, liberty, or property. [37]

process of certification The accepting bank writes or stamps the word certified on the ordinary check of an account holder and sets aside funds from that account to pay the check. [440]

processing plant franchise The franchisor provides a secret formula or process to the franchisee, and the franchisee manufactures the product and distributes it to retail dealers. [659]

production of documents Request by one party to another party to produce all documents relevant to the case prior to the trial. [57]

products liability The liability of manufacturers, sellers, and others for the injuries caused by defective products. [362]

professional corporation A corporation formed by lawyers, doctors, or other professionals. [563]

professional malpractice The liability of a professional who breaches his or her duty of ordinary care. [84]

profit corporation A corporation created to conduct a business for profit that can distribute profits to shareholders in the form of dividends. [563]

promise to pay A maker's (borrower's) unconditional and affirmative undertaking to repay a debt to a payee (lender). [392]

promissory estoppel An equitable doctrine that prevents the withdrawal of a promise by a promisor if it will adversely affect a promisee who has adjusted his or her position in justifiable reliance on the promise. [199]; An equitable doctrine that permits enforcement of oral contracts that should have been in writing. It is applied to avoid injustice. [235]

promissory note A two-party negotiable instrument that is an unconditional written promise by one party to pay money to another party. [388]

promissory warranty Stipulates that the facts will continue to be true throughout the duration of the policy. [843]

promoter A person or persons who organize and start the corporation, negotiate and enter into contracts in advance of its formation, find the initial investors to finance the corporation, and so forth. [564]

promoter's contracts A collective term for such things as leases, sales contracts, contracts to purchase property, and employment contracts entered into by promoters on behalf of the proposed corporation prior to its actual incorporation. [564]

proof of claim A document required to be filed by unsecured creditors that states the amount of their claim against the debtor. [487]

proper dispatch An acceptance must be properly addressed, packaged, and posted to fall within the mailbox rule. [193]

pro rata rule A rule that says shares must be purchased on a pro rata basis if too many shares are tendered. [625]

prospectus A written disclosure document that must be submitted to the SEC along with the registration statement and

given to prospective purchasers of the securities. [678]

provisional credit Occurs when a collecting bank gives credit to a check in the collection process prior to its final settlement. Provisional credits may be reversed if the check does not "clear." [447]

proximate cause or legal cause A point along a chain of events caused by a negligent party after which this party is no longer legally responsible for the consequences of his or her actions. [82]

proxy The written document that a shareholder signs authorizing another person to vote his or her shares at the shareholders' meetings in the event of the shareholder's absence. [589]

proxy card A written document signed by a shareholder that authorizes another person to vote the shareholder's shares. [617]

proxy contest When opposing factions of shareholders and managers solicit proxies from other shareholders, the side that receives the greatest number of votes wins the proxy contest. [618]

proxy statement A document that fully describes (1) the matter for which the proxy is being solicited, (2) who is soliciting the proxy, and (3) any other pertinent information. [618]

public corporation A corporation formed to meet a specific governmental or political purpose. [563]

publicly held corporation A corporation that has many shareholders and whose securities are often traded on national stock exchanges. [563]

punitive damages Damages that are awarded to punish the defendant, to deter the defendant from similar conduct in the future, and to set an example for others. [277]

purchase money security interest An interest a creditor automatically obtains when it extends credit to a consumer to purchase consumer goods. [468]

purchasing property The most common method of acquiring title to personal property. [796]

qualified individual with a disability A person who (1) has a physical or mental impairment that substantially limits one or more of his or her major life activities, (2) has a record of such impairment, or (3) is regarded as having such impairment. [786]

quasi in rem jurisdiction Jurisdiction allowed a plaintiff who obtains a judgment in one state to try to collect the judgment by attaching property of the defendant located in another state. [52]

quasi- or implied-in-law contract An equitable doctrine whereby a court may award monetary damages to a plaintiff for providing work or services to a defendant even though no actual contract existed. The doctrine is intended to prevent unjust enrichment and unjust detriment. [177]

quiet title action A lawsuit to have a court determine the ownership rights in a parcel of real estate. [819]

quorum The required number of shares that must be represented in person or by proxy to hold a shareholders' meeting. The RMBCA establishes a majority of outstanding shares as a quorum. [589]; The number of directors necessary to hold a board of directors' meeting or transact business of the board. [596]

Racketeer Influenced and Corrupt Organizations Act (RICO) Federal statute that authorizes civil lawsuits against defendants for engaging in a pattern of racketeering activities. [137]

radiation pollution Emissions from radioactive wastes that can cause injury and death to humans and other life and can cause severe damage to the environment. [740]

ratification The act of a minor after the minor has reached the age of majority by which he or she accepts a contract entered into when he or she was a minor. [208]; When a principal accepts an agent's unauthorized contract. [519]

rational basis test Test that is applied to classifications not involving a suspect or protected class. [36]

Rawls's social contract A moral theory that says each person is presumed to have entered into a social contract with all others in society to obey moral rules that are necessary for people to live in peace and harmony. [156]

real defense A defense that can be raised against both holders and HDCs. [424]

real property The land itself as well as buildings, trees, soil, minerals, timber, plants, crops, and other things permanently affixed to the land. [37, 231, 813]

reasonable person test Objective test that applies to commercial contracts and contracts involving mechanical fitness. [255]

receiving stolen property A person (1) knowingly receives stolen property and (2)

intends to deprive the rightful owner of that property. [132]

reclamation The right of a seller or lessor to demand the return of goods from the buyer or lessee under specified situations. [325]

record date A date specified in the corporate bylaws that determines whether a shareholder may vote at a shareholders' meeting. [589]; A date that determines whether a shareholder receives payment of a declared dividend. [592]

recording statute A state statute that requires the mortgage or deed of trust to be recorded in the county recorder's office of the county in which the real property is located. [461, 819]

recovery of damages A seller or lessor may recover damages measured as the difference between the contract price (or rent) and the market price (or rent) at the time and place the goods were to be delivered, plus incidental damages, from a buyer or lessee who repudiates the contract or wrongfully rejects tendered goods. [326]

recovery of goods from an insolvent seller or lessor A buyer or lessee who has wholly or partially paid for goods before they are received may recover the goods from a seller or lessor who becomes insolvent within 10 days after receiving the first payment; the buyer or lessee must tender the remaining purchase price or rent due under the contract. [328]

recovery of lost profits If the recovery of damages would be inadequate to put the seller or lessor in as good a position as if the contract had been fully performed by the buyer or lessee, the seller or lessor may recover lost profits, plus an allowance for overhead and incidental damages, from the buyer or lessee. [326]

recovery of the purchase price or rent A seller or lessor may recover the contracted-for purchase price or rent from the buyer or lessee if the buyer or lessee (1) fails to pay for accepted goods, (2) breaches the contract and the seller or lessor cannot dispose of the goods, or if (3) the goods are damaged or lost after the risk of loss passes to the buyer or lessee. [326]

red light doctrine A doctrine that says a holder cannot qualify as an HDC if he or she has notice of an unauthorized signature or an alteration of the instrument or any adverse claim against or defense to its payment. [417]

redeemable preferred stock Stock that permits the corporation to buy back the preferred stock at some future date. [574]

reformation An equitable doctrine that permits the court to rewrite a contract to express the parties' true intentions. [276]

registered agent A person or corporation that is empowered to accept service of process on behalf of the corporation. [569]

registration statement Document that an issuer of securities files with the SEC that contains required information about the issuer, the securities to be issued, and other relevant information. [678]

regular meeting A meeting held by the board of directors at the time and place established in the bylaws. [596]

Regulation A A regulation that permits the issuer to sell securities pursuant to a simplified registration process. [680]

regulatory statute A licensing statute enacted to protect the public. [212]

rejection Express words or conduct by the offeree that rejects an offer. Rejection terminates the offer. [190]

rejection of nonconforming goods If the goods or the seller's or lessor's tender of delivery fails to conform to the contract, the buyer or lessee may (1) reject the whole, (2) accept the whole, or (3) accept any commercial unit and reject the rest. [328]

relevant geographical market A relevant market that is defined as the area in which the defendant and its competitors sell the product or service. [708]

relevant product or service market A relevant market that includes substitute products or services that are reasonably interchangeable with the defendant's products or services. [708]

relief from stay May be granted in situations involving depreciating assets where the secured property is not adequately protected during the bankruptcy proceedings; asked for by a secured creditor. [495]

religious discrimination Discrimination against a person solely because of his or her religion or religious practices. [780]

remainder If the right of possession returns to a third party upon the expiration of a limited or contingent estate. [818]

rent An agreed upon amount the tenant pays the landlord for the leased premises. [826]

remainder beneficiary The person or persons to whom the assets of the trust are distributed upon the death of the grantor. [855]

replacement workers Workers who are hired to take the place of striking workers.

They can be hired on either a temporary or permanent basis. [758]

replevin An action by a buyer or lessor to recover scarce goods wrongfully withheld by a seller or lessor. [329]

reply Filed by the original plaintiff to answer the defendant's cross-complaint. [56]

repossession A right granted to a secured creditor to take possession of the collateral upon default by the debtor. [471]

res ipsa loquitur Tort where the presumption of negligence arises because (1) the defendant was in exclusive control of the situation and (2) the plaintiff would not have suffered injury but for someone's negligence. The burden switches to the defendant(s) to prove they were not negligent. [85]

resale price maintenance A *per se violation* of Section 1 of the Sherman Act; occurs when a party at one level of distribution enters into an agreement with a party at another level to adhere to a price schedule that either sets or stabilizes prices. [705]

rescission An action to rescind (undo) the contract. Rescission is available if there has been a material breach of contract, fraud, duress, undue influence, or mistake. [225, 274]

residuary gift Gift of the estate left after the debts, taxes, and specific and general gifts have been paid. [848]

Resource Conservation and Recovery Act (RCRA) A federal statute that authorizes the EPA to regulate facilities that generate, treat, store, transport, and dispose of hazardous wastes. [740]

respondeat superior A rule that says an employer is liable for the tortious conduct of its employees or agents while they are acting within the scope of its authority. [521]

Restatement of the Law of Contracts A compilation of model contract law principles drafted by legal scholars. The Restatement is not law. [173]

restitution Returning of goods or property received from the other party to rescind a contract; if the actual goods or property is not available, a cash equivalent must be made. [274]

restricted securities Securities that were issued for investment purposes pursuant to the intrastate, private placement, or small offering exemption. [683]

restrictive indorsement An indorsement that contains some sort of instruction from the indorser. [401]

retention of collateral If a secured creditor repossesses collateral upon a debtor's default, he or she may propose to retain the collateral in satisfaction of the debtor's obligation. [471]

revenue-raising statute A licensing statute with the primary purpose of raising revenue for the government. [213]

reverse discrimination Discrimination against a group that is usually thought of as a majority. [788]

reversion A right of possession that returns to the grantor after the expiration of a limited or contingent estate. [818]

Revised Model Business Corporation Act (RMBCA) A revision of the MBCA in 1984 that arranged the provisions of the act more logically, revised the language to be more consistent, and made substantial changes in the provisions. [562]

Revised Uniform Limited Partnership Act (RULPA) A 1976 revision of the ULPA that provides a more modern, comprehensive law for the formation, operation, and dissolution of limited partnerships. [548]

revocation Withdrawal of an offer by the offeror terminates the offer. [190]; Reversal of acceptance. [324]; Termination of a will. [847]

reward To collect a reward, the offeree must (1) have knowledge of the reward offer prior to completing the requested act and (2) perform the requested act. [188]

rider A separate document that will modify an existing insurance policy. [842]

right of inspection A right that shareholders have to inspect the books and records of the corporation. [592]

right of redemption A right granted to a defaulting debtor or other secured creditor to recover the collateral from a secured creditor before he or she contracts to dispose of it or exercises his or her right to retain the collateral. Requires the redeeming party to pay the full amount of the debt and expenses caused by the debtor's default. [462]

right to cure A licensor has the right to cure a contract under certain conditions. [354]

right to die A personal liberty protected by the U.S. Constitution. [852]

robbery Taking personal property from another person by use of fear or force. [131]

Robinson-Pactman Act Section 2 of the Clayton Act is commonly referred to by this name. [713]

rule of reason A rule that holds that only unreasonable restraints of trade violate Section 1 of the Sherman Act. The court must examine the pro- and anticompetitive effects of the challenged restraint. [702]

rules and regulations Adopted by administrative agencies to interpret the statutes that they are authorized to enforce. [727]

Rule 10b-5 A rule adopted by the SEC to clarify the reach of Section 10(b) against deceptive and fraudulent activities in the purchase and sale of securities. [31]

Sabbath law A law that prohibits or limits the carrying on of certain secular activities on Sundays. [212]

Safe Drinking Water Act A federal statute enacted in 1974 and amended in 1986 that authorizes the EPA to establish national primary drinking water standards. [738]

sale The passing of title from a seller to a buyer for a price. [287]; Also called a *conveyance*. [819]

sale on approval A type of sale in which there is no actual sale unless and until the buyer accepts the goods. [307]

sale or return A contract that says that the seller delivers goods to a buyer with the understanding that the buyer may return them if they are not used or resold within a stated or reasonable period of time. [307]

sale proceeds The resulting assets from the sale, exchange, or disposal of collateral subject to a security agreement. [466]

satisfaction The performance of an accord. [198]

scienter Means international conduct. Scienter is required for there to be a violation of Section 10(b) and Rule 10b-5. [686]

search warrant A warrant issued by a court that authorizes the police to search a designated place for specified contraband, articles, items, or documents. The search warrant must be based on probable cause. [138]

secondary boycott picketing A type of picketing where unions try to bring pressure against an employer by picketing his or her suppliers or customers. [757]

secondary liability Liability on a negotiable instrument that is imposed on a party only when the party primarily liable on the instrument defaults and fails to pay the instrument when due. [420]

"secondary meaning" When an ordinary term has become a brand name. [114]

Section 1 of the Sherman Act Prohibits *contracts*, *combinations*, and *conspiracies* in restraint of trade. [702]; Prohibits tying arrangements involving goods, services, intangible property, and real property. [713]

Section 2 of the Sherman Act Prohibits the act of monopolization and attempts or conspiracies to monopolize trade. [707]

Section 2(a) of the Robinson-Patman Act Prohibits direct and indirect price discrimination by sellers of a commodity of a like grade and quality where the effect of such discrimination may be to substantially lessen competition or to tend to create a monopoly in any line of commerce. [713]

Section 2(b) of the Robinson-Patman Act A defense that provides that a seller may lawfully engage in price discrimination to meet a competitor's price. [896]

Section 3 of the Clayton Act Prohibits tying arrangements involving sales and leases of goods. [713]

Section 5 of the FTC Act Prohibits *unfair and deceptive* practices. [715, 732]

Section 7 of the NLRA A law that gives employees the right to join together and form a union. [753]

Section 8(a) of the NLRA A law that makes it an unfair labor practice for an employer to interfere with, coerce, or restrain employees from exercising their statutory right to form and join unions. [755]

Section 8(b) of the NLRA A law that prohibits unions from engaging in unfair labor practices that interfere with a union election. [755]

Section 10(b) A provision of the Securities Exchange Act of 1934 that prohibits the use of manipulative and deceptive devices in the purchase or sale of securities in contravention of the rules and regulations prescribed by the SEC. [686]

Section 11 A provision of the Securities Act of 1933 that imposes civil liability on persons who intentionally defraud investors by making misrepresentations or omissions of material facts in the registration statement or who are negligent for not discovering the fraud. [685]

Section 12 A provision of the Securities Act of 1933 that imposes civil liability on any person who violates the provisions of Section 5 of the act. [684]

Section 14(a) Provision of the Securities Exchange Act of 1934 that gives the SEC the authority to regulate the solicitation of proxies. [618]

Section 14(e) A provision of the Williams Act that prohibits fraudulent, deceptive, and manipulative practices in connection with a tender offer. [625]

Section 16(a) A section of the Securities Exchange Act of 1934 that defines any person who is an executive officer, a director, or a 10 percent shareholder of an equity security of a reporting company as a *statutory insider* for Section 16 purposes. [690]

Section 16(b) A section of the Securities Exchange Act of 1934 that requires that any profits made by a statutory insider on transactions involving *short-swing profits* belong to the corporation. [690]

Section 24 A provision of the Securities Act of 1933 that imposes criminal liability on any person who willfully violates the 1933 act or the rules or regulations adopted thereunder. [685]

Section 32 A provision of the Securities Exchange Act of 1934 that imposes criminal liability on any person who willfully violates the 1934 act or the rules or regulations adopted thereunder. [690]

section of the country A division of the country that is based on the relevant geographical market; the geographical area that will feel the direct and immediate effects of the merger. [710]

secured credit Credit that requires security (collateral) that secures payment of the loan. [460]

secured transaction A transaction that is created when a creditor makes a loan to a debtor in exchange for the debtor's pledge of personal property as security. [463]

Securities Act of 1933 A federal statute that primarily regulates the issuance of securities by corporations, partnerships, associations, and individuals. [677]

Securities and Exchange Commission (SEC) Federal administrative agency that is empowered to administer federal securities laws. The SEC can adopt rules and regulations to interpret and implement federal securities laws. [676]

Securities Exchange Act of 1934 A federal statute that primarily regulates the trading in securities. [686]

security (1) An interest or instrument that is common stock, preferred stock, a bond, a debenture, or a warrant, (2) an interest or instrument that is expressly mentioned in securities acts, and (3) an investment contract. [676]

security agreement The agreement between the debtor and the secured party that creates or provides for a security interest. [465]

self-dealing If the directors or officers engage in purchasing, selling, or leasing of property with the corporation, the contract must be fair to the corporation; otherwise, it is voidable by the corporation. The contract or transaction is enforceable if it has been fully disclosed and approved. [604]

Self-Employment Contributions Act A federal act that says self-employed persons must pay Social Security taxes equal to the combined employer-employee amount. [765]

self-incrimination The Fifth Amendment states that no person shall be compelled in any criminal case to be a witness against him- or herself. [140]

separate property Property that a spouse owns prior to marriage gifts and inheritances acquired during the marriage, and interest payment dividends, and appreciation of separate property received or accrued during the marriage. [817]

service mark A mark that distinguishes the services of the holder from those of its competitors. [113]

service of process A summons is served on the defendant to obtain personal jurisdiction over him or her. [52]

settlor or trustor Person who creates a trust. [852]

sex discrimination Discrimination against a person solely because of his or her gender. [777]

sexual harassment Lewd remarks, touching, intimidation, posting pinups, and other verbal or physical conduct of a sexual nature that occur on the job. [778]

share exchange When one corporation acquires all the shares of another corporation and both corporations retain their separate legal existence. [621]

Shareholder resolution A resolution submitted by a Shareholder to other shareholders provided he or she meets certain requirements set out in the Securities Exchange Act of 1934 and SEC rules adopted thereunder. The SEC determines if a shareholder proposal qualifies to be submitted to other shareholders for vote. [618]

shareholder voting agreements Agreement between two or more shareholders agreeing on how they will vote their shares. [591]

shipment contract   A contract that requires the seller to ship the goods to the buyer via a common carrier. [303]; The buyer bears the risk of loss during transportation. [303]; A sales contract that requires the seller to send the goods to the buyer, but not a specifically named destination. [319]

short-form merger   A merger between a parent corporation and a subsidiary corporation that does not require the vote of the shareholders of either corporation or the board of directors of the subsidiary corporation. [622]

sight draft   A draft payable on sight. Also called a *demand draft*. [388]

signature   Any name, word, or mark used in lieu of a written signature; any symbol that is (1) handwritten, typed, printed, stamped, or made in almost any other manner and (2) executed or adopted by a party to authenticate a writing. [418]

signature liability   A person cannot be held contractually liable on a negotiable instrument unless his or her signature appears on the instrument. Also called contract *liability*. [417]

signature requirement   A negotiable instrument must be signed by the drawer or maker. Any symbol executed or adopted by a party with a present intent to authenticate a writing qualifies as his or her signature. [391]

signer   A person signing an instrument who acts in the capacity of (1) a maker of notes and certificates of deposit, (2) a drawer of drafts and checks, (3) a drawee who certifies or accepts checks and drafts, (4) an indorser who indorses an instrument, (5) an agent who signs on behalf of others, or (6) an accommodation party. [417]

slander   Oral defamation of character. [76]

small claims court   A court that hears civil cases involving small dollar amounts. [44]

Small Corporate Offering Registration Form (SCOR)   The SCOR form—Form U-7—is a question-and-answer disclosure form that business can complete and file with the SEC if they plan on raising $1 million or less from the public issue of securities. [681]

small offering exemption   For the sale of securities not exceeding $1 million during a 12-month period. [682]

social host liability   Rule that provides that social hosts are liable for injuries caused by guests who become intoxicated at a social function. States vary as to whether they have this rule in effect. [87]

Social Security   Federal system that provides limited retirement and death benefits to covered employees and their dependents. [765]

sole proprietorship   A form of business where the owner is actually the business; the business is not a separate legal entity. [538]

sources of international law   Those things that international tribunals rely on in settling international disputes. [865]

special bailees   Includes common carriers, warehouse companies, and innkeepers. [805]

special federal courts   Federal courts that hear matters of specialized or limited jurisdiction. [47]

special indorsement   An indorsement that contains the signature of the indorser and specifies the person (indorsee) to whom the indorser intends the instrument to be payable. Creates *order paper*. [400]

special meeting   A meeting convened by the board of directors to discuss new shares, merger proposals, hostile takeover attempts, and so forth. [596]

special shareholders' meetings   Meetings of shareholders that may be called to consider and vote on important or emergency issues, such as a proposed merger or amending the articles of incorporation. [588]

specific duty   An OSHA standard that addresses a safety problem of a specific duty nature (e.g., requirement for a safety guard on a particular type of equipment). [761]

specific government regulation   Government regulation that applies to a specific industry (eg. telecommunications laws). [726]

specific gift   Gift of a specifically named piece of property. [848]

specific performance   A remedy that orders the breaching party to perform the acts promised in the contract; usually awarded in cases where the subject matter is unique, such as in contracts involving land, heirlooms, and paintings. [276]; Judgment of the court ordering a licensor to specifically perform the license by making the contracted-for unique information available to the licensee. [355]; A decree of the court that orders a seller or lessor to perform his or her obligations under the contract; usually occurs when the goods in question are unique, such as art or antiques. [329]

stakeholder interest   A theory of social responsibility that says a corporation must consider the effects its actions have on persons other than its stockholders. [163]

stale check   A check that has been outstanding for more than six months. [442]

standing to sue   The plaintiff must have some stake in the outcome of the lawsuit. [52]

stare decisis   Latin: "To stand by the decision." Adherence to precedent. [12]

state action exemptions   Business activities that are mandated by state law are exempt from federal antitrust laws. [716]

state administrative agencies   Administrative agencies that states create to enforce and interpret state law. [727]

state antitakeover statutes   Statutes enacted by state legislatures that protect corporations incorporated in or doing business in the state from hostile takeovers. [628]

state supreme court   The highest court in a state court system; it hears appeals from intermediate state courts and certain trail courts. [45]

statement of disassociation   A document filed with the secretary of state that gives constructive notice that a member has disassociated from an LLC. [651]

stationary sources   Sources of air pollution such as industrial plants, oil refineries, and public utilities. [735]

statute   Written law enacted by the legislative branch of the federal and state governments that establishes certain courses of conduct that must be adhered to by covered parties. [9]

Statute of Frauds   State statute that requires certain types of contracts to be in writing. [231]

statute of limitations   A statute that establishes the period during which a plaintiff must bring a lawsuit against a defendant. [56]; Statute that establishes the time period during which a lawsuit must be brought; if the lawsuit is not brought within this period, the injured party loses the right to sue. [259]; A statute that requires an injured person to bring an action within a certain number of years from the time that he or she was injured by the defective product. [378]

statute of repose   A statute that limits the seller's liability to a certain number of years from the date when the product was first sold. [378]

Statute of Wills   A state statute that establishes the requirements for making a valid will. [844]

statutory exemptions   Exemptions from antitrust laws that are expressly provided in statutes enacted by Congress. [715]

stock dividend   Additional shares of stock paid as a dividend. [592]

stop-payment order   An order by a drawer of a check to the payor bank not to pay or certify a check. [443]

stopping delivery of goods in transit   A seller or lessor may stop delivery of goods in transit if he or she learns of the buyer's or lessee's insolvency or if the buyer or lessee repudiates the contract, fails to make payment when due, or gives the seller or lessor some other right to withhold the goods. [324]

straight voting   Each shareholder votes the number of shares he or she owns on candidates for each of the positions open. [589]

strategic alliance   An arrangement between two or more companies in the same industry whereby they agree to ally themselves to accomplish a designated objective. [669]

strict liability   Liability without fault. [93]

strict liability standard   Common law duty that says innkeepers are liable for lost, damaged, or stolen goods of guests even if they were not at fault for the loss. [806]

strict or absolute liability   Standard for imposing criminal liability without a finding of *mens rea* (intent). [127]

strict scrutiny test   Test that is applied to classifications based on race. [36]

strike   A cessation of work by union members in order to obtain economic benefits or correct an unfair labor practice. [757]

subject matter jurisdiction   Jurisdiction over the subject matter of a lawsuit. [52]

sublease   When a tenant transfers only some of his or her rights under the lease. [827]

sublessee   The new tenant in a sublease situation. [827]

sublessor   The original tenant in a sub-lease situation. [827]

subrogation   If an insurance company pays a claim to an insured for liability or property damage caused by a third party, the insurer succeeds to the right of the insured to recover from the third party. [842]

substantial performance   Performance by a contracting party that deviates only slightly from complete performance. [267]

substantive due process   Requires that government statutes, ordinances, regulations, or other laws be clear on their face and not overly broad in scope. [37]

subsurface rights   Rights to the earth located beneath the surface of the land. [813]

suicide clause   A clause that states that if an insured commits suicide within a time period specified in a life insurance contract, the life insurance company does not have to pay the proceeds of the life insurance policy. [841]

summons   A court order directing the defendant to appear in court and answer the complaint. [55]

superseding event   A defendant is not liable for injuries caused by a superseding or intervening event for which he or she is not responsible. [89]

supervening event   An alteration or modification of a product by a party in the chain of distribution that absolves all prior sellers from strict liability. [376]

supervening illegality   The enactment of a statute, regulation, or court decision that makes the object of an offer illegal. This action terminates the offer. [191]

supramajority voting requirement   A requirement that a greater than majority of shares constitutes a quorum of the vote of the shareholders. [590]

Supremacy Clause   A clause of the U.S. Constitution that establishes that the federal Constitution, treaties, federal laws, and federal regulations are the supreme law of the land. [27]

surety   The third person who agrees to be liable in a surety arrangement. [473]

surety arrangement   An arrangement where a third party promises to be *primarily* liable with the borrower for the payment of the borrower's debt. [473]

taking for value requirement   A holder must *give value* for the negotiable instrument to qualify as an HDC. [415]

taking in good faith requirement   A holder must take the instrument in good faith to qualify as an HDC. [416]

taking possession   A method of acquiring ownership of unowned personal property. [796]

taking without notice of defect requirement   A person cannot qualify as an HDC if he or she has notice that the instrument is defective in certain ways. [416]

tangible property   All real property and physically defined personal property such as buildings, goods, animals, and minerals. [795]

target corporation   The corporation that is proposed to be acquired in a tender offer situation. [624]

tax sale   A method of transferring property ownership that involves a lien on property for unpaid property taxes. If the lien remains unpaid after a certain amount of time, a tax sale is held to satisfy the lien. [820]

tenancy at sufferance   A tenancy created when a tenant retains possession of property after the expiration of another tenancy or a life estate without the owner's consent. [824]

tenancy at will   A lease that may be terminated at any time by either party. [824]

tenancy by the entirety   A form of co-ownership of real property that can be used only by married couples. [816]

tenancy for years   A tenancy created when the landlord and tenant agree on a specific duration for the lease. [824]

tenancy in common   A form of co-ownership where the interest of a surviving tenant-in-common passes to the deceased tenant's estate and not to the cotenants. [816]

tenant   The party to whom the leasehold is transferred. [824]

tender of delivery   The obligation of the seller to transfer and deliver goods to the buyer in accordance with the sales contract. [318]

tender offer   An offer that an acquirer makes directly to a target corporation's shareholders in an effort to acquire the target corporation. [624]

tender offeror   The party that makes a tender offer. [624]

tender of performance   Tender is an unconditional and absolute offer by a contracting party to perform his or her obligations under the contract. [267]

term LLC   An LLC that has a specified term of duration. [643]

termination   The ending of a corporation that occurs only after the winding-up of the corporation's affairs, the liquidation of its assets, and the distribution of the proceeds to the claimants. [577]

termination by acts of the parties An agency may be terminated by the following acts of the parties: (1) mutual agreement, (2) lapse of time, (3) purpose achieved, and (4) occurrence of a specified event. [523]

termination by operation of law An agency is terminated by operation of law, including: (1) death of the principal or agent, (2) insanity of the principal or agent, (3) bankruptcy of the principal, (4) impossibility of performance, (5) changed circumstances, and (6) war between the principal's and agent's countries. [525]

termination statement A document filed by the secured party that ends a secured interest because the debt has been paid. [469]

testator The person who makes a will. [844]

thermal pollution Heated water or material discharged into waterways that upsets the ecological balance and decreases the oxygen content. [738]

time draft A draft payable at a designated future date. [388]

time instrument An instrument payable (1) at a fixed date, (2) on or before a stated date, (3) at a fixed period after sight, or (4) at a time readily ascertainable when the promise or order is issued. [395, 416]

time note A note payable at a specific time. [389]

tippee The person who receives material nonpublic information from a tipper. [689]

tipper A person who discloses material nonpublic information to another person. [689]

title Legal, tangible evidence of ownership of goods. [303]

Title I Title I of the ADA requires an employer to make reasonable accommodations to employees with disabilities that do not cause undue hardship to the employer. [785]

Title I of the Landrum-Griffin Act Referred to as labor's "bill of rights" that gives each union member equal rights and privileges to nominate candidates for union office, vote in elections, and participate in membership meetings. [758]

Title III of the ADA A title of the ADA that prohibits discrimination on the basis of disability in places of public accommodation operated by private entities. [829]

Title VII of the Civil Rights Act of 1964 (Fair Employment Practices Act) Intended to eliminate job discrimination based on five protected classes: *race, color, religion, sex,* or *national origin.* [774]

tort A wrong. There are three categories: (1) intentional torts, (2) unintentional torts (negligence), and (3) strict liability. [73]

tort of misappropriation of the right to publicity An attempt by another person to appropriate a living person's name or identity for commercial purposes. [74]

toxic substances Chemicals used for agricultural, industrial, and mining uses that cause injury to humans, birds, animals, fish, and vegetation. [739]

Toxic Substances Control Act A federal statute enacted in 1976 that requires manufacturers and processors to test new chemicals to determine their effect on human health and the environment before the EPA will allow them to be marketed. [739]

trade acceptance A sight draft that arises when credit is extended (by a seller to a buyer) with the sale of goods. The seller is both the drawer and the payee, and the buyer is the drawee. [388]

trade dress Federal protection of the look and feel of a product a product's packaging, or a service establishment. [115]

trademark A distinctive mark, symbol, name, word, motto, or device that identifies the goods of a particular business. [113]

trademark infringement Unauthorized use of another's mark. The holder may recover damages and other remedies from the infringer. [114]

trademarks and service marks A distinctive mark, symbol, name, word, motto, or device that identifies the goods or services of a particular franchisor. [661]

trade secret A product formula, pattern, design, compilation of data, customer list, or other business secret. [102]; An idea that makes a franchise successful but that does not qualify for trademark, patent, or copyright protection. [661]

transfer Any passage of an instrument other than its issuance and presentment for payment. [423]

transfer warranties Any of the following five implied warranties: (1) The transferor has good title to the instrument or is authorized to obtain payment or acceptance on behalf of one who does have good title; (2) all signatures are genuine or authorized; (3) the instrument has not been materially altered; (4) no defenses of any party are good against the transferor; and (5) the transferor has no knowledge of any insolvency proceeding against the maker, or acceptor, or the drawer of an unaccepted instrument. [423]

traveler's check A form of check sold by banks and other issuers. They are issued without a named payee. The purchaser fills in the payee's name when he or she uses the check to purchase goods or services. [441]

treasury shares Shares of stock repurchased by the company itself. [574]

treaties The first source of international law, consisting of agreements or contracts between two or more nations that are formally signed by an authorized representative and ratified by the supreme power of each nation. [865]

treaty A compact made between two or more nations. [9]

Treaty Clause Clause of the U.S. Constitution that states the president "shall have the power . . . to make treaties, provided two-thirds of the senators present concur." [863]

trespass to land A tort that interferes with an owner's right to exclusive possession of land. [78]

trespass to personal property A tort that occurs whenever one person injures another person's personal property or interferes with that person's enjoyment of his or her personal property. [78]

trial briefs Documents submitted by the parties' attorneys to the judge that contain legal support for their side of the case. [59]

trier of fact The jury in a jury trial; the judge where there is not a jury trial. [59]

trust A legal arrangement established when one person transfers title to property to another person to be held and used for the benefit of a third person. [852]

trust corpus The property held in trust. [853]

trustee Person who holds legal title to the trust corpus and manages the trust for the benefit of the beneficiary or beneficiaries. [852, 854]

tying arrangement A restraint of trade where a seller refuses to sell one product to a customer unless the customer agrees to purchase a second product from the seller. [713]

UCC Statute of Frauds A rule that requires all contracts for the sale of goods costing $500 or more and lease contracts involving payments of $1,000 or more to be in writing. [234, 293]

UCC statute of limitations A rule that provides that an action for breach of any written or oral sales or lease contract must commence within four years after the cause of action accrues. The parties may agree to reduce the limitations period to one year. [332]

ultra vires act An act by a corporation that is beyond its express or implied powers. [576]

unauthorized signature A signature made by a purported agent without authority from the purported principal. [419]

unconditional Promises to pay and orders to pay must be unconditional in order for them to be negotiable. [393]

unconditional promise or order to pay requirement A negotiable instrument must contain either an *unconditional promise to pay* (note or CD) or an *unconditional order to pay* (draft or check). [392]

undue influence Occurs when one person takes advantage of another person's mental, emotional, or physical weakness and unduly persuades that person to enter into a contract; the persuasion by the wrongdoer must overcome the free will of the innocent party or testator. [230, 847]

unenforceable contract A contract where the essential elements to create a valid contract are met, but there is some legal defense to the enforcement of the contract. [179]

unfair advantage theory A theory that holds that a merger may not give the acquiring firm an unfair advantage over its competitors in finance, marketing, or expertise. [712]

unfair competition Competition that violates the law. [92]

Uniform Commercial Code Comprehensive statutory scheme that includes laws that cover aspects of commercial transactions. [173, 286]

Uniform Computer Information Transactions Act (UCITA) Model state law that creates contract law for the licensing of information technology rights. [341, 348]

Uniform Franchise Offering Circular (UFOC) A uniform disclosure document that requires the franchisor to make specific presale disclosures to prospective franchisees. [659]

Uniform Gift to Minors Act and Revised Uniform Gift to Minors Act Acts that establish procedures for adults to make gifts of money and securities to minors. [798]

Uniform Limited Liability Company Act (ULLCA) A model act that provides comprehensive and uniform laws for the formation, operation, and dissolution of LLCs. [638]

Uniform Partnership Act (UPA) Model act that codifies partnership law. Most states have adopted the UPA in whole or part. [541]

Uniform Simultaneous Death Act An act that provides that if people who would inherit property from each other die simultaneously, each person's property is distributed as though he or she survived. [847]

unilateral contract A contract in which the offeror's offer can be accepted only by the performance of an act by the offeree; a "promise for an act." [175]

unilateral mistake When only one party is mistaken about a material fact regarding the subject matter of the contract. [225]

unilateral refusal to deal A unilateral choice by one party not to deal with another party. This does not violate Section 1 of the Sherman Act because there is not concerted action. [706]

unintentional tort or negligence A doctrine that says a person is liable for harm that is the foreseeable consequence of his or her actions. [79]

union shop An establishment where an employee must join the union within a certain number of days after being hired. [756]

United Nations An international organization created by multilateral treaty in 1945 to promote social and economic cooperation among nations and to protect human rights. [866]

United States Copyright Office A federal administrative agency where copyrights may be registered. [108]

unlawful detainer action A legal procedure a landlord can bring to evict a tenant for nonpayment of rent. [826]

unprotected speech Speech that is not protected by the First Amendment and may be forbidden by the government. [32]

unqualified indorsement An indorsement whereby the indorser promises to pay the holder or any subsequent indorser the amount of the instrument if the maker, drawer, or acceptor defaults on it. [400]

unqualified indorser An indorser who signs an *unqualified indorsement* to an instrument. [400]

unreasonable search and seizure Any search and seizure by the government that violates the Fourth Amendment. [138, 831]

unsecured credit Credit that does not require any security (collateral) to protect the payment of the debt. [459]

U.S. Constitution The fundamental law of the United States of America. It was ratified by the states in 1788. [25]

U.S. courts of appeals The federal court system's intermediate appellate courts. [47]

U.S. district courts The federal court system's trial courts of general jurisdiction. [47]

U.S. Supreme Court The Supreme Court was created by Article III of the U.S. Constitution. The Supreme Court is the highest court in the land. It is located in Washington, DC. [47]

usurping a corporate opportunity A director or officer steals a corporate opportunity for him- or herself. [603]

usury law A law that sets an upper limit on the interest rate that can be charged on certain types of loans. [211]

utilitarianism A moral theory that dictates that people must choose the action or follow the rule that provides the greatest good to society. [154]

valid contract A contract that meets all of the essential elements to establish a contract; a contract that is enforceable by at least one of the parties. [178]

variance An exception that permits a type of building or use in an area that would not otherwise be allowed by a zoning ordinance. [829]

venue A concept that requires lawsuits to be heard by the court with jurisdiction that is nearest the location in which the incident occurred or where the parties reside. [53]

vertical merger A merger that integrates the operations of a supplier and a customer. [711]

vertical restraint of trade A restraint of trade that occurs when two or more parties on *different levels of distribution* enter into a contract, combination, or conspiracy to restrain trade. [705]

violation A crime that is neither a felony nor a misdemeanor that is usually punishable by a fine. [126]

voidable contract A contract where one or both parties have the option to avoid their contractual obligations. If a contract is avoided, both parties are released from their contractual obligations. [178]

voidable title Title that a purchase has if the goods were obtained by (1) fraud, (2) a check that is later dishonored, or (3) impersonating another person. [310]

voidable transfer An unusual payment or transfer of property by the debtor on the eve of bankruptcy that would unfairly benefit the debtor or some creditors at the expense of other creditors. Such transfer may be avoided by the bankruptcy court. [489]

void contract A contract that has no legal effect; a nullity. [178]

void title A thief acquires no title to the goods he or she steals. [310]

voluntary dissolution A corporation that has begun business or issued shares can be dissolved upon recommendation of the board of directors and a majority vote of the shares entitled to vote. [576]

voluntary petition A petition filed by the debtor; states that the debtor has debts. [486]

voting trust The shareholders transfer their stock certificates to a trustee who is empowered to vote the shares. [591]

waiting period A period of time that begins when the registration statement is filed with the SEC and continues until the registration statement is declared effective. Only certain activities are permissible during the waiting period. [680]

warehouse company A bailee engaged in the business of storing property for compensation. Owes a *duty of reasonable care* to protect the bailed property. [806]

warehouse receipt A document of title that is issued by a warehouse company to the bailor when goods are received by the warehouse company for storage. [806]

warranties of quality Seller's or lessor's assurance to buyer or lessee that the goods meet certain standards of quality. Warranties may be expressed or implied. [362]

warranty A buyer's or lessee's assurance that the goods meet certain standards. [362]

warranty disclaimer Statements that negate express and implied warranties. [367]

warranty of fitness for a particular purpose A warranty that arises when a seller or lessor warrants that the goods will meet the buyer's or lessee's expressed needs. [365]

waste Occurs when a tenant causes substantial and permanent damage to the leased premises that decreases the value of the property and the landlord's reversionary interest in it. [826]

water pollution Pollution of lakes, rivers, oceans, and other bodies of water. [737]

wetlands Areas that are inundated or saturated by surface water or ground water that support vegetation typically adapted for life in such conditions. [738]

white-collar crimes Crimes usually involving cunning and deceit rather than physical force. [133]

will A declaration of how a person wants his or her property distributed upon death. [838, 844]

will or inheritance A way to acquire title to property that is a result of another's death. [798]; If a person dies with a will, his or her property is distributed to the beneficiaries as designated in the will. If a person dies without a will, his or her property is distributed to the heirs as stipulated in the state's intestacy statute. [820]

Williams Act An amendment to the Securities Exchange Act of 1934 made in 1968 that specifically regulates all tender offers. [624]

winding-up and liquidation The process by which a dissolved corporation's assets are collected, liquidated, and distributed to creditors, shareholders, and other claimants. [577, 651]

wire fraud The use of telephone or telegraph to defraud another person. [135]

withholding delivery The act of the seller or lessor purposefully refusing to deliver goods to the buyer or lessee upon breach of the sales or lease contract by the buyer or lessee or the insolvency of the buyer or lessee. [324]

workers' compensation acts Acts that compensate workers and their families if workers are injured in connection with their jobs. [759]

work-related test A test to determine the liability of a principal; if an agent commits an intentional tort within a work-related time or space, the principal is liable for any injury caused by the agent's intentional tort. [522]

World Trade Organization (WTO) An international organization of more than 130 member nations created to promote and enforce trade agreements among member nations. [872]

World Wide Web An electronic connection of millions of computers that support a standard set of rules for the exchange of information. [343]

writ of certiorari An official notice that the Supreme Court will review one's case. [48]

written order A stop-payment order that is good for six months after the date it is written. [443]

wrongful disassociation Occurs when a member withdraws from (1) a term LLC prior to the expiration of the term or (2) an at-will LLC when the operating agreement eliminates a member's power to withdraw. [650]

wrongful dishonor Occurs when there are sufficient funds in a drawer's account to pay a properly payable check, but the bank does not do so. [444]

wrongful dissolution When a partner withdraws from a partnership without having the right to do so at that time. [25]

wrongful eviction A violation of the covenant of quiet enjoyment. [825]

wrongful termination The termination of an agency contract in violation of the terms of the agency contract. The non-breaching party may recover damages from the breaching party. [526]; Termination of a franchise without just cause. [664]

zoning ordinance Local laws that are adopted by municipalities and local governments to regulate land use within their boundaries. Zoning ordinances are adopted and enforced to protect the health, safety, morals, and general welfare of the community. [828]

Case Index

*Cases cited or discussed are in roman type. Principal cases are in **bold type**.*

Subject Index

Cases